Pension Protection Act of 2006
Key Facts And Figures

The charts below summarize the key provisions in the Pension Protection Act of 2006. See the explanations in CCH's *Pension Protection Act of 2006: Law, Explanation and Analysis* for a complete discussion.

PENSION PROTECTION DEADLINES

100 percent funding — Starts for plan years after 2007, with funding transition rules	
Applicable target funding percentage	*Year*
92 percent	*2008*
94 percent	*2009*
96 percent	*2010*

"At risk" plans — Phase in of less-than-80 percent funding percentage for "at risk" plans	
Funding percentage	*Year*
65 percent	*2008*
70 percent	*2009*
75 percent	*2010*
80 percent	*2011*

Interest rate assumptions	
Provision	*In Effect*
Long-term corporate bond rate	*Through 2007*
Three-segment yield curve for lump-sum distributions	*Plan years beginning after 2007*

- ***Faster vesting of employer nonelective contributions*** – plan years beginning after 2006
- ***Incentives for automatic contribution enrollment*** – plan years beginning after 2007
- ***Combined 401(k)/defined benefit plans for small employers*** – plan years beginning after 2009

Deduction limits — Single-employer plans	
Provision	*In Effect*
150 percent of plan's current liability	*For 2006 and 2007 plan years*
Full funding plus cushion	*After 2007*

Deduction limits — Multi-employer plans	
140 percent of plan's current liability	*After 2007*

RETIREMENT SAVINGS ENHANCEMENTS

Provision	*In Effect*
High three year average compensation for benefit limits	*Years beginning after 2005*
Additional IRA contributions by employees of bankrupt employers	*2006-2009*
Rollover of after-tax contributions from plan to plan or to tax-sheltered annuity	*Tax years beginning after 2006*
Inflation-indexed IRA income ceilings	*Tax years beginning after 2006*
Inflation-indexed income limit for Roth IRA contributions	*Tax years beginning after 2006*
Inflation-indexed saver's credit income ceilings	*Tax years beginning after 2006*
Eligible investment advice arrangements	*Advice provided after 2006*
Deposit of tax refunds into IRAs	*Tax years beginning after 2006*
Special IRA/401(k) withdrawals for military personnel	*Active duty beginning before 12/31/07*
Qualified plan-to Roth IRA rollovers	*Distributions made after 2007*

RETIREMENT SAVINGS – PERMANENT EXTENSIONS

Major retirement provisions enacted pursuant to the Economic Growth and Tax Relief Reconciliation Act of 2001 (EGTRRA) that are made permanent, rather than sunset after 2010:

- Higher IRA contributions: $4,000 in 2006, $5,000 in 2008, adjusted for inflation starting in 2009
- Higher contributions to defined contribution plans: $44,000 in 2006, adjusted for inflation thereafter
- Higher elective deferrals: $15,000 in 2006, adjusted for inflation thereafter
- Higher SIMPLE contributions: $10,000 in 2006, adjusted for inflation thereafter
- Higher annual defined benefit limit: $175,000 in 2006, adjusted for inflation thereafter
- Permanent catch-up contributions: $1,000 for IRAs, no inflation adjustment; $2,500 for SIMPLEs, $5,000 for 401(k)s in 2006, adjusted for inflation thereafter

CHARITABLE DONATION CHANGES

Provision	*In Effect*
Extension of enhanced food donations	*Through 2007*
Direct IRA charitable donations	*Through 2007*
Enhanced conservation easement rules	*For 2006 and 2007*
Tightened rules for donations of clothing and household goods	*Contributions after date of enactment*
Tightened rules for cash donations	*Contributions in tax years starting after date of enactment*
Tighter facade easement rules	*Contributions after date of enactment*
Tighter rules on fractional donations	*Donations after date of enactment*
Recapture of donation benefit for exempt-use property	*After September 1, 2006*
Higher S shareholder basis on contributions	*Through 2007*

LEGISLATION 2006

Pension Protection Act of 2006

(H.R. 4)

As Signed by the President on August 17, 2006

Law, Explanation and Analysis

CCH Editorial Staff Publication

a Wolters Kluwer business

ISBN 13: 978-0-8080-1555-0

ISBN 10: 0-8080-1555-9

4025 W. Peterson Ave.
Chicago, IL 60646-6085
1 800 248 3248
www.onlinestore.cch.com

Printed in the United States of America

Pension Protection Act of 2006:
Strengthening Traditional Pension Plans and More

Anyone who follows federal legislation knows that Congress is anything but predictable. This is particularly true of the 109th Congress. The political process that culminated in the passage of the most comprehensive pension reform package in more than 30 years, the Pension Protection Act of 2006 (Pension Act), is a prime example of just how unpredictable Congress is.

In the wake of Enron and numerous other corporate accounting scandals, the underfunding of traditional pension plans took center stage on Congress's 2005-2006 agenda. The Senate, on November 16, 2005, passed the Pension Security and Transparency Bill of 2005 (Sen. 1783), by a vote of 97-2. A month after the Senate passed its version of a pension reform bill, the House passed, on December 15, 2005, the Pension Protection Bill of 2005 (H.R. 2830), by a vote of 294-132. Although the underlying premise of both bills was the strengthening of the pension system, they differed in many key respects, including the level of required plan contributions and the premiums needed to return the Pension Benefit Guaranty Corporation (PBGC) to solvency. This set the stage for a conference to reconcile the differences between the two bills that would prove to be quite acrimonious.

After more than five months of negotiations, members of the conference committee reportedly worked out such contentious issues as funding, investment advice, and airline relief. They failed to reach an agreement, however, on whether to strip out a number of provisions that would extend expired tax provisions from the pension reform bill and include them in a separate tax measure. In an unprecedented move, the members of the pension conference were dismissed and the House passed the Pension Act, which purported to be the agreement, albeit unsigned, negotiated over five months minus the provisions extending the expiring tax provisions. The Senate followed suit less than one week later. President Bush signed the Pension Act on August 17, 2006.

The Pension Act contains a variety of provisions designed to strengthen the funding rules for single-employer defined benefit pension plans. By tightening the funding rules, the Pension Act seeks to ensure that employers make greater contributions to their pension funds, ensuring their solvency, and avoiding a potential multi-billion dollar taxpayer bailout of the PBGC. The new rules generally apply to plan years beginning after 2007. Additional funding rules apply to multiemployer plans in endangered or critical status. The Pension Act also eliminates the full funding exception to the variable rate PBGC premium. Special PBGC premiums are established for small plans.

The new law includes relief for the airlines in the form of a longer amortization period and a higher amortization interest rate. Somewhat different rules apply for airlines that freeze their plans and those that do not.

The Pension Act creates a prohibited transaction exemption for investment advice provided to plan participants through a computer model that is certified by an independent party. An exemption for advice provided by an adviser whose compensation does not vary with the investments selected is available to both employer-sponsored plans and IRAs.

The more-than-900-page Pension Act, however, not only contains provisions that impact traditional pension plans. The new law also contains a number of provisions impacting charities and charitable donations, a handful of miscellaneous provisions, and technical corrections. Among the provisions included are:

- New recordkeeping requirements for cash donations;
- Federal oversight of charitable organizations;
- Tax-free distributions from IRAs for charitable purposes;
- Stricter rules for donations of used clothing and household goods;
- New treatment of donations of fractional interests;
- Special contribution rules for buildings in registered historical districts; and
- An extension of the rules allowing for Sec. 529 qualified tuition programs.

About This Work and CCH

As always, CCH remains dedicated to responding to the needs of tax professionals and pension plan administrators in helping them quickly understand and work with the new laws as they take effect. CCH's *Pension Protection Act of 2006: Law, Explanation and Analysis* provides readers with a single integrated reference tool covering Titles I through XIII of the Pension Protection Act of 2006.

Along with the relevant Internal Revenue Code provisions, as amended by the Pension Act, as well as Pension Act sections amending ERISA, and supporting committee reports, CCH editors, together with several leading tax practitioners and commentators, have put together the most timely and complete practical analysis of the new law. Tax professionals and pension plan administrators looking for the Joint Committee on Taxation's explanation of the new law, including the related bill text, can find it in a separate CCH publication. Other books and tax services relating to the new legislation can be found at our website www.onlinestore.cch.com.

Mark A. Luscombe

Principal Analyst

CCH Tax and Accounting

Nicholas Kaster

Pension Analyst

Wolters Kluwer Law & Business

August 2006

Contributors

Harold J. Ashner
Keightley & Ashner LLP
Washington, D.C.

Mary Beth Braitman
Ice Miller LLP
Indianapolis, Indiana

Curt Cartolano
Hewitt Associates
Lincolnshire, Illinois

Lisa Erb Harrison
Ice Miller LLP
Indianapolis, Indiana

Robert Keebler
Virchow Krause & Company, LLP
Green Bay, Wisconsin

Elisabeth Kingsley
Harmon, Curran, Spielberg & Eisenberg, LLP
Washington, D.C.

Terry A.M. Mumford
Ice Miller LLP
Indianapolis, Indiana

Vincent O'Brien
Vincent J. O'Brien, CPA, P.C.
Lynbrook, New York

Charles P. Rettig
Hochman, Salkin, Rettig, Toscher & Perez, P.C.
Beverly Hills, California

Dan Schwallie
Hewitt Associates
Cleveland, Ohio

Allen Steinberg
Hewitt Associates
Lincolnshire, Illinois

Conrad Teitell
Cummings & Lockwood
Stamford, Connecticut

Barnaby Zall
Weinberg & Jacobs, LLP
Washington, D.C.

CCH Tax and Accounting Publishing

EDITORIAL STAFF

Explanation and Analysis

¶1 Features of This Publication

This publication is your complete guide to Titles I through XIII of the Pension Protection Act of 2006 (Pension Act), as signed by President Bush on August 17, 2006. The core portion of this publication contains the CCH Explanations and Analysis of the Pension Act. The CCH Explanations outline all of the law changes and what they mean for you and your clients. The explanations feature practical guidance, examples, planning opportunities and strategies, as well as pitfalls to be avoided as a result of the law changes. Insights supplied by expert tax practitioners and pension experts are highlighted throughout our analysis.

The law text and Joint Committee on Taxation (JCT) Technical Explanation are reproduced following the analysis. Any new or amended Internal Revenue Code sections appear here, with changes highlighted in *italics*. The law text for portions of the Pension Act that amended the Employee Retirement Income Security Act (ERISA), or did not otherwise amend the tax code, appear here. The JCT Technical Explanation that provides the legislative history of each provision follows the law text.

The book also contains numerous other features designed to help you locate and understand the changes made by the Pension Act. These features include highlight summaries of important provisions, cross references to related materials, detailed effective dates, and numerous finding tables and indexes. A more detailed description of these features appears below.

HIGHLIGHTS

Highlights are quick summaries of the major provisions of the Pension Protection Act of 2006. The Highlights are arranged by area of interest, such as minimum funding rules, contributions and benefits, and charitable contributions. At the end of each summary is a paragraph reference to the longer CCH Explanation on that topic, giving you an easy way to find the parts of the book that are of most interest to you. *Highlights start at ¶5.*

PARTIES AFFECTED

The first chapter of the book, *Parties Affected*, contains a detailed look at how the new laws affect specific categories of taxpayers and pension plan administrators. This chapter provides a quick reference for readers who want to know the immediate impact that the laws will have on their clients. *Parties Affected starts at ¶101.*

CCH EXPLANATIONS

CCH Explanations are designed to give you a complete, accessible understanding of the new law. Explanations are arranged by subject for ease of use. There are three main finding devices you can use to locate explanations on a given topic. These are:

- A detailed table of contents at the beginning of the publication listing all of the CCH Explanations of the new law;
- A table of contents preceding each chapter; and

- An extensive topical index covering all subjects under the Pension Protection Act of 2006.

Each CCH Explanation contains special features to aid in your complete understanding of the new law. These include:

- A summary at the beginning of each explanation providing a brief overview of the new law;
- A background or prior law discussion that puts the law changes into perspective;
- Practitioner commentary incorporated throughout the explanations, identifying planning opportunities and strategies, as well as pitfalls to avoid;
- Editorial aids, including examples, cautions, planning notes, elections, comments, compliance tips, key rates and figures, and state tax consequences, that highlight the impact of the new laws;
- Charts and examples illustrating the ramifications of specific law changes;
- Captions at the end of each explanation identifying the Code sections added, amended or repealed, as well as the Act sections containing the changes;
- Cross references to the law and JCT Technical Explanation paragraphs related to the explanation;
- A line highlighting the effective date of each law change, marked by an arrow symbol;
- References at the end of the discussion to related information in the Pension Plan Guide, Standard Federal Tax Reporter, Tax Research Consultant, Federal Tax Guide, and the Federal Estate and Gift Tax Reporter.

The CCH Explanations begin at ¶205.

AMENDED CODE PROVISIONS

Changes to the Internal Revenue Code made by the Pension Protection Act of 2006 appear under the heading "Code Sections Added, Amended or Repealed." *Any changed or added law text is set out in italics.* Deleted Code text, or the Code provision prior to amendment, appears in the Amendment Notes following each reconstructed Code provision. An effective date for each Code change is also provided.

The amendment notes contain cross references to the corresponding JCT Technical Explanation and the CCH Explanations that discuss the new law. *The text of the Code begins at ¶5001.*

Sections of the Pension Protection Act that do not amend the Internal Revenue Code, including amendments to ERISA, appear in full text following "Code Sections Added, Amended or Repealed." *The text of these provisions appears in Act Section order beginning at ¶7003.*

COMMITTEE REPORTS

The Joint Committee on Taxation Technical Explanation for H.R. 4, the Pension Protection Act, explains the intent of Congress regarding the provisions of the Pension Act. There was no conference report issued for the Pension Act. The Technical Explanation from the Joint Committee on Taxation is included in this section to aid the reader's understanding, but may not be cited as the official Senate or Conference Committee Report accompanying the Pension Act. At the end of each section, references are provided to the corresponding CCH explanations and the Internal Revenue Code provisions. Subscribers to the electronic version can link from these references to the corresponding material. *The pertinent sections of the Technical Explanation appear in Act Section order beginning at ¶10,010.*

EFFECTIVE DATES

Tables listing the major effective dates provides you with a reference bridge between Code Sections and Act Sections, and between ERISA Sections and Act sections. Both tables also indicate the retroactive or prospective nature of the laws explained. *The IRC Effective Dates Table for the Pension Protection Act begins at ¶20,001. The ERISA Effective Dates Table for the Pension Protection Act begins at ¶20,005.*

SPECIAL FINDING DEVICES

Other special tables and finding devices in this book include:

- A table cross-referencing Code Sections to the CCH Explanations (*see ¶25,001*);
- A table cross-referencing ERISA Sections to the CCH Explanations (*see ¶25,003*);
- A table showing all Code Sections added, amended or repealed (*see ¶25,005*);
- A table showing all ERISA Sections added, amended or repealed (*see ¶25,007*);
- A table showing provisions of other acts that were amended (*see ¶25,010*);
- A table of Act Sections not amending the Internal Revenue Code (*see ¶25,015*); and
- An Act Section amending Code Section table (*see ¶25,020*).
- An Act Section amending ERISA Section table (*see ¶25,025*).

SUNSET PROVISIONS

This book contains charts identifying the Code Sections and ERISA Sections that are no longer subject to the sunset provisions of the Economic Growth and Tax Relief Reconciliation Act of 2001 (P.L. 107-16) (EGTRRA). *The charts are reproduced at ¶29,001 and ¶29,010.* The book also contains a discussion of provisions in the Pension Protection Act that sunset some of the new funding rules for multiemployer plans. *The discussion appears at ¶29,020.*

¶2 Table of Contents

¶3 Detailed Table of Contents

CHAPTER 1. PARTIES AFFECTED

CHAPTER 6. INVESTMENTS OF ASSETS AND FIDUCIARY RULES

CHAPTER 7. CONTRIBUTIONS AND BENEFITS

CHAPTER 10. PLAN QUALIFICATION AND ADMINISTRATION

CHAPTER 11. CHARITABLE CONTRIBUTIONS

CHAPTER 12. EXEMPT ORGANIZATIONS

CHAPTER 13. PERMANENCY OF PENSION PROVISIONS AND OTHER TAX MATTERS

CHAPTER 14. U.S. TAX COURT MODERNIZATION

¶5 Highlights

MINIMUM FUNDING RULES FOR SINGLE-EMPLOYER PLANS

¶205, ¶210, ¶215 **Single-Employer Defined Benefit Plans.** Generally after 2007, employers maintaining single-employer defined benefit plans will have to make a minimum contribution based on the plan's assets, funding target, and target normal cost. The current funding standard account mechanism and two-tiered funding system will be replaced with a single funding method. Plans that fall below specified funding levels will be subject to new limits on the payment of unpredictable contingent event benefits, plan amendments, lump-sum distributions, and benefit accruals.

¶220 **Restrictions on Funding of Nonqualified Deferred Compensation Plans.** Assets that are set aside for the payment of deferred compensation to covered employees under a nonqualified deferred compensation plan, and while a single-employer defined benefit plan is at risk, are treated as property transferred in connection with the performance of services. Covered employees include the chief executive officer, the four highest paid officers for the tax year and individuals subject to Section 16(a) of the Securities Exchange Act of 1934.

¶225 **Interest Rates Applicable to Acquired Plans.** If a fully-funded defined benefit plan is sponsored by a financially-healthy employer that is sold as part of an acquisition or similar transaction, then the interest rate used in determining whether the plan has sufficient assets for purposes of the standard termination rules must be not less than the interest rate used for determining whether the plan is fully funded.

¶235 **Replacement Rate Extended Through 2007.** The use of the replacement interest rate for the funding standard account and for computing a plan's current liability and deficit reduction contribution is extended through 2007.

¶240 **Temporary Relief from Funding Rules.** Certain multiemployer plans maintained by rural cooperatives, PBGC settlement plans, and plans maintained by government defense contractors are granted temporary relief from some of the new funding rules that are generally effective beginning in 2008.

¶245 **Special Funding Rules for Commercial Airline Plans.** Special funding rules are adopted for a defined benefit pension plan sponsored by a commercial passenger airline or by a catering business that principally serves commercial passenger airlines.

MINIMUM FUNDING RULES FOR MULTIEMPLOYER PLANS

¶305 **Minimum Funding Rules for Multiemployer Plans.** The funding rules for multiemployer plans are separated from the single-employer plan funding rules. After 2007, new rules will apply to amortization, reasonable actuarial requirements, alternative minimum funding standards, and deemed approval of changes in the shortfall funding method.

¶310 **Significantly Underfunded Multiemployer Plans.** Underfunded multiemployer plans that are in endangered or critical status must take certain actions to improve their funding status over a multiyear period, or face excise taxes and civil penalties.

¶315 **Testing Insolvency of Multiemployer Plans.** A sponsor of a multiemployer plan in reorganization must forecast the possibility of the plan's future insolvency for five years, rather than for three years.

¶320 **Multiemployer Plans Withdrawal Liability Reforms.** The withdrawal liability rules for multiemployer plans that apply when a contributing employer terminates its participation are modified to provide more protection to the contribution base and ensure the plan's viability.

¶325 **Elections to be Treated as Single-Employer or Multiemployer Plans.** Certain multiemployer plans can revoke their previous elections to be treated as single-employer plans, and certain plans sponsored by tax-exempt employers can irrevocably elect multiemployer status.

¶330 **Retaliation Against Employers.** Retaliation is prohibited against contributing employers to multiemployer plans who exercise their rights under ERISA, testify before Congress or petition for redress of grievances.

FUNDING DISCLOSURES

¶405 **Annual Funding Notices for Defined Benefit Plans.** Defined benefit plan administrators must provide an annual funding notice to the PBGC, each participant and beneficiary, and each labor union representing plan participants. The notice for multiemployer plans must also be provided to each contributing employer.

¶410 **Access to Multiemployer Plan Financial Information.** The ability of participants, beneficiaries, unions, and contributing employers to request and receive plan actuarial and financial information and estimates of potential withdrawal liability from multiemployer plans is expanded, and contributing employers are added to the list of persons entitled to receive ERISA Sec. 204(h) notices.

¶415 **Annual Reporting for Defined Benefit Plans.** The rule requiring defined benefit plans to provide Summary Annual Reports (SARs) is repealed, but they must provide additional information on Form 5500 annual reports.

¶420 **Electronic Annual Report Information.** Plan administrators must file information included in the annual report in an electronic format to accommodate Internet display.

¶425 **Section 4010 filings with the PBGC.** Sponsors of single-employer plans that are less than 80-percent funded must file financial reports with the PBGC that include information about the plans' benefit liabilities, funding targets and funding target attainment percentages.

¶430 **Disclosure of Termination Information.** Upon request from an affected party, the administrator of a terminating plan must provide any information that had to be submitted to the PBGC pursuant to the termination.

PBGC GUARANTEE AND RELATED PROVISIONS

¶505, ¶510 **PBGC Variable Rate Premiums.** New rules govern the interest rate used to determine the unfunded vested benefit for PBGC variable rate premium purposes. The exemption from variable rate premiums for plans that are at the full funding limit is repealed, and the special termination premium for certain underfunded terminating plans is made permanent. For small employer plans, the variable rate premium is capped at $5 per participant.

¶515 **Premium Overpayment Refunds.** The PBGC can pay interest on premium overpayment refunds.

¶520 **Guaranteed Benefits for Shutdown and Contingent Events.** Limits are imposed on PBGC-guaranteed benefits payable due to plant shutdowns and other contingent events.

¶525 **Plan Sponsor's Bankruptcy.** The amount of PBGC-guaranteed benefits is effectively frozen as of the date a contributing plan sponsor enters bankruptcy.

¶530 **Substantial Owner Benefits in Terminated Plans.** The ownership threshold is increased to 50 percent for purposes of the limits on PBGC-guaranteed benefits for business owners who participated in a terminated plan.

¶535 **Benefits Attributable to Recoveries from Employers.** New methods determine a plan participant's share of additional benefits that the PBGC recovers from an employer that sponsored an underfunded terminated plan.

¶540 **Missing Participants.** The PBGC's missing participant program is extended to defined contribution plans, and the PBGC is directed to issue missing-participant regulations for terminated multiemployer plans.

INVESTMENT OF ASSETS AND FIDUCIARY RULES

¶605, ¶610 **Diversification and Divestment Requirements.** Diversification and divestment requirements apply to certain contributions and deferrals in defined contribution plans that are invested in employer securities. The plan administrator must provide eligible participants and beneficiaries with notice of these divestment rights.

¶615 **Periodic Benefit Statements.** Defined contribution plan administrators must provide pension benefit statements to participants and beneficiaries.

¶620 **One-Participant Retirement Plan.** The definition of "one-participant retirement plan" is modified for purposes of the blackout period notice.

¶625 **Investment Advice from Fiduciary Advisors.** A new prohibited transaction exemption applies to eligible investment advice arrangements that allow qualified fiduciary advisers to offer employees personally tailored investment advice about certain retirement plans.

¶630 **Prohibited Transaction Exemptions.** Exemptions to the prohibited transaction rules are allowed for block trading, regulated electronic communications networks, service providers who are not fiduciaries with respect to the assets involved, foreign exchange transactions, and cross trading.

¶635 **Correction Period for Securities and Commodities.** The correction period for prohibited transactions involving securities and commodities is 14 days after the party discovers or should have discovered that the transaction was prohibited.

¶640 **Fiduciary Liability During Blackout Periods.** To ensure that plan fiduciaries do not become subject to liability with respect to certain retirement plans, investment option changes and blackout periods must satisfy new requirements.

¶650 **Criminal Penalties for Interference with ERISA Rights.** The criminal penalties for willfully interfering with the ERISA rights of a participant or beneficiary are increased to a maximum fine of $100,000 or a maximum term of imprisonment of 10 years, or both.

¶655 **Default Investments by Fiduciaries.** Individual account plan participants are deemed to have exercised actual control over account assets if the plan fiduciaries make proper default investments.

CONTRIBUTIONS AND BENEFITS

¶705, ¶710 **Deductible Contributions to Defined Benefit Plans.** Deduction limits are increased for contributions to single-employer and multiemployer defined benefit plans.

¶715 **Deductible Contributions to Combined Plans.** Only contributions that exceed six percent of compensation paid to beneficiaries during the tax year are subject to the overall limit on deductions for contributions to combined plans. Multiemployer plans are exempt from the overall limit, and single-employer plans insured by the PBGC are not taken into account.

¶720 **Vesting of Employer Contributions to Defined Contribution Plans.** The expedited vesting schedule that applies to employer matching contributions is extended to all employer contributions to defined contributions plans.

¶725 **Tax Refunds Deposited to IRAs.** The IRS is to provide forms that let individuals elect to have tax refunds deposited directly into IRAs.

¶730 **IRA Contributions and Bankrupt Employer.** Qualifying individuals who participated in a bankrupt employer's Section 401(k) plan may make additional IRA contributions for 2007 through 2009.

¶735 **Average Compensation for "High Three Years."** For purposes of determining the average compensation for a participant's high three years, the high three years are the three consecutive calendar years during which the participant had the greatest aggregate compensation from the employer.

¶740 **Lump-Sum Adjustments Under Minimum Valuation Rules.** One of three interest rates must be used for the adjustment of a benefit, such as a lump-sum distribution, in a form that is subject to the minimum valuation rules.

¶745 **Permissive Service Credits.** The permissive service credit rules for government employees are expanded, and rules governing nonqualified service credits for school employees are clarified.

HEALTH AND MEDICAL BENEFITS

¶805, ¶810 **Pension Assets Transferred to Health Pans.** Pension plans may transfer excess pension assets to retiree medical accounts to fund future retiree health benefits and collectively bargained retiree health benefit plans. Multiemployer defined benefit plans can also make qualified transfers of excess benefit plan assets to heath plans.

¶820 **Long-Term Health Care Insurance Riders.** Taxable distributions from annuity and life insurance contracts do not include the cost of a qualified long-term care insurance coverage rider that is charged against the cash or cash surrender value of the contract.

¶825 **Excludable Distributions Used for Health Insurance.** Up to $3,000 in annual taxable distributions from a retired public safety officer's government pension plan may be excluded from income if used for health insurance premiums.

PLAN DISTRIBUTIONS AND ROLLOVERS

¶905 **Valuation of Lump Sum Distributions.** The interest rate and the mortality table are changed for calculating the minimum value of a lump-sum distribution and some other forms of optional benefits.

¶910 **Hardship Distributions.** The Treasury Secretary is directed to modify regulations governing hardship distributions from certain defined contribution plans to include events that happen to the participant's beneficiary.

¶915, ¶917 **Early Withdrawal Penalty.** The early withdrawal penalty is waived for certain distributions to qualified public safety employees who separate from service after age 50, and to qualified members of the National Guard or the Reserve who are called to active duty.

¶920 **Distributions During Working Retirement.** A pension plan will not become disqualified solely because it provides for a distribution to an employee who has attained age 62 and who is not separated from employment at the time of the distribution.

¶935 **Direct Rollovers to Roth IRAs.** After 2007, distributions from certain qualified plans and annuities can be rolled over directly into a Roth IRA.

¶940 **Rollover of After-Tax Contributions.** After-tax contributions can be rolled over from a qualified retirement plan to a defined benefit plan or 403(b) annuity.

¶945 **Rollovers for Nonspouses.** Distributions from a decedent's plan can be rolled over into an IRA for a beneficiary who is not the decedent's spouse.

PLAN QUALIFICATION AND ADMINISTRATION

¶1005 **Cash Balance and Pension Equity Plan Conversions.** Hybrid plans that meet new requirements are protected from age discrimination challenges, and lump sum distributions can be based on the participant's hypothetical account balances without violating minimum present value requirements. The wear away approach to the anticutback rule is prohibited when a plan converts to a cash balance or pension equity plan.

¶1015 **Automatic Enrollment in 401(k) Plans.** A 401(k) plan that contains a proper automatic enrollment arrangement satisfies the nondiscrimination rules and the test with respect to matching contributions. The top-heavy rules do not apply to a plan whose only contributions are made under a qualified automatic enrollment feature.

¶1020 **DB/K Plans.** An employer with 500 or fewer employees may establish a combined defined benefit/401(k) plan (a "DB/K" plan).

¶1030, ¶1035 **Railroad Retirement Benefits.** A railroad employee does not have to actually receive railroad retirement benefits in order for a former spouse to be entitled to Tier I or Tier II benefits in a divorce. A former spouse does not lose eligibility for otherwise allowable Tier II benefits upon the employee's death.

¶1040 **Additional Survivor Annuity Option.** Pension plans that must provide benefits in the form of a qualified joint and survivor annuity must offer a qualified optional survivor annuity.

¶1045, ¶1050, ¶1055 **Church Plans.** Annuity payments under qualified church plans may meet the required minimum distribution rules even if the payments are not made under an annuity contract purchased from an insurance company. Income from debt-financed property is not included in the unrelated business taxable income of a church's retirement income account. The 100-percent-of-compensation benefit limit is waived for all but highly compensated employees of qualified church plans.

¶1060 **Governmental Plans.** All governmental retirement plans are exempt from nondiscrimination requirements.

¶1065 **Indian Tribal Government Plans.** Certain retirement plans established and maintained by Indian tribal governments are treated as governmental plans.

¶1070, ¶1075 **Section 457 Plans.** Voluntary early retirement incentive plans and employment retention plans maintained by local education agencies and tax-exempt education associations are subject to special rules and exceptions. Individuals who received certain lump sum distributions under a 457 plan before 1997 may participate in an eligible deferred compensation plan.

¶1080 **Small Retirement Plans.** A one-participant retirement plan with assets of $250,000 or less is exempt from filing an annual report.

¶1090 **Retroactive Plan Amendments.** Certain plan amendments that are made pursuant to changes made by the Pension Protection Act of 2006, or any related regulations, can be given retroactive effect.

CHARITABLE CONTRIBUTIONS

¶1105 **Tax-Free IRA Distributions to Charities.** Individuals at least 70½ years old can distribute up to $100,000 of their IRA balance to charitable organizations in 2006 and in 2007 without recognizing income or claiming a charitable deduction. The distribution counts towards the required minimum distribution.

¶1110 **Contributions of Clothing and Household Items.** Deductions for charitable contributions of clothing or household items are limited to items in good used condition or better, unless the deduction for a single item exceeds $500 and the taxpayer includes a qualified appraisal.

¶1115 **Donations of Fractional Interest in Tangible Personal Property.** New rules determine the amount of the charitable deduction for subsequent contributions of fractional interests in tangible personal property. Any deduction is recaptured and additional tax imposed if the property is not entirely contributed to the donee.

¶1120 **Donations of Taxidermy Property.** Limits apply to the deduction for donations of taxidermy property.

¶1125 **Real Property Contributions for Conservation.** Individual donors deduct up to 50 percent of their contribution base for contributions of qualified conservation real property (or 100 percent for farmers and ranchers).

¶1130 **Contributions of Facade Easements.** Stricter rules apply to the charitable deduction for contributing a facade easement for a building in a registered historic district.

¶1135 **S Corporation's Charitable Contributions.** The amount of a shareholder's basis reduction in the stock of an S corporation by reason of the corporation's charitable contribution equals the shareholder's pro *rata share* of the adjusted basis of the contributed property.

¶1140, ¶1145 **Contributions of Food and Book Inventories.** The enhanced deduction for charitable donations of certain noncorporate taxpayers' food inventories, and certain corporate taxpayer's book inventories, is extended two years until the end of 2007.

¶1150 **Recapture of Tax Benefits.** The deduction for a donation of appreciated personal property is limited to donor's basis if the donee disposes of the property within three years, unless the donee certifies that the property was used or intended to be used in a manner related to the donee's exempt purpose.

¶1155 **Gratuitous Transfers of Employer Securities Clarified.** The annual limitation for transfers of employer securities from a charitable remainder trust to an employee stock ownership plan is determined on the basis of fair market value of securities when allocated to participants, after first allocating all other annual additions for the limitation year.

¶1160, ¶1165 **Distributions from Donor Advised Funds.** Donor advised funds are defined in the Code. A 20-percent tax is imposed on the sponsoring organization for taxable distributions from a donor-advised fund, and a five-percent tax is imposed on fund managers that agreed to the distribution. Excise taxes are imposed on donors, donor advisors and related persons who receive benefits from distributions.

¶1170 **Prohibited Transactions.** For purposes of the excess benefit transaction taxes, disqualified persons include donors to advised funds, advisors to the funds, and investment advisors to the funds.

¶1175 **Excess Business Holdings.** The private foundation excess business holdings rules are extended to donor advised funds.

¶1180 **Charitable Contribution Deductions.** Contributions to donor advised funds generally are fully deductible from income, estate and gift tax, unless the funds are maintained at noncharitable and Type III supporting organizations.

¶1185 **Recordkeeping for Charitable Contributions.** Donors must keep adequate records of charitable contributions of all types of property for any amount.

¶1190 **Split-Interest Trust Reporting.** Changes are made for split-interest trust reporting, including increased failure-to-file penalties, increased confidentiality protection, and elimination of the filing exception for split interest trusts that distribute all their income.

EXEMPT ORGANIZATIONS

¶1205 **Church Conventions and Associations.** Membership in a convention or association of churches may include individuals as well as churches, and the individuals may have voting rights.

¶1210 **Specified Payments from Controlled Entities.** Only excess qualifying specified payments from a controlled entity are included in an exempt organization's UBTI, and they are subject to a valuation misstatement penalty. The organization must report the payments and related information.

¶1215 **Credit Counseling Organizations.** Credit counseling organizations must be organized and operated according to special rules in order to be tax-exempt. Debt management plan services that do not meet these standards are treated as an exempt organization's unrelated trade or business.

¶1220 **Black Lung Disability Trusts.** There is no aggregate limit on the amount of excess black lung benefit trust assets that may be used to pay accident and health benefits or premiums for insurance exclusively covering those benefits for retired coal miners, their spouses and their dependents.

¶1225 **Supporting Organizations.** A supporting organization must hold one of three types of close relationship with a supported organization.

¶1230 **Excess Benefit Transactions Involving Supporting Organizations.** The definitions of "excess benefit," "excess benefit transaction," and "disqualified person" are expanded specifically as those terms relate to supporting organizations.

¶1235 **Excess Business Holdings of Supporting Organizations.** The excess business holding rules have been extended to private foundations that qualify as Type III supporting organizations.

¶1240 **Payments from Supporting Organizations to Private Foundations.** The definition of "qualifying distribution" is modified to prevent payments made by a non-operating private foundation to a supporting organization from constituting a qualifying distribution. Also, the definition of "taxable expenditure" is modified to ensure that any amounts paid to supporting organizations by private foundations is treated as taxable expenditures unless the private foundation exercises expenditure responsibility.

¶1245 **Penalty Excise Taxes on Public Charities, Social Welfare Organizations And Private Foundations.** The initial taxes and dollar limitations for self-dealing and excess benefit transactions are doubled, as are the initial taxes and the dollar limitations on foundation managers with respect to the private foundation excise taxes on the failure to distribute income, excess business holdings, jeopardizing investments, and taxable expenditures.

¶1250 **Excise Tax on Private Foundations.** The base upon which the two-percent excise tax on the net investment income of private foundations is expanded, and the uncertainty regarding regulations promulgated under Code Sec. 4940 is clarified.

¶1255 **Exemption for Blood Collector Organizations.** Qualified blood collector organizations are exempt from the excise taxes on fuel, telecommunications, heavy trucks and trailers, and tires to the extent that the items are used for the exclusive use of the organization for the distribution or collection of blood.

¶1260 **Exempt Entities That Do Not File Returns.** Tax-exempt organizations that do not meet the threshold for filing Form 990 must provide an annual notification to the IRS containing certain contact and financial information.

¶1265 **Sponsoring Organizations.** A sponsoring organization is required to provide additional information on its application for exempt status and on its annual information return.

¶1270 **Returns of Supporting Organizations.** Additional requirements apply to the annual returns of all supporting organizations.

¶1275 **UBTI Returns.** The requirement that charitable organizations make tax materials available for public inspection is extended to returns related to unrelated business taxable income (UBTI).

¶1280 **Disclosure to State Officials.** Information relating to certain proposed IRS actions affecting charitable organizations may be disclosed to state officials, along with return and return information about the charitable organizations that are the subject of the proposed actions.

¶1285 **Acquisitions of Interests in Insurance Contracts.** For the next two years, an applicable exempt organization that acquires an interest in an applicable insurance contract must file an information return.

PERMANENCY OF PENSION PROVISIONS AND OTHER TAX MATTERS

¶1305 **EGTRRA Pension and IRA Provisions.** The 2011 sunset rule of the Economic Growth and Tax Relief Reconciliation Act of 2001 (EGTRRA) is nullified as it applies to the pension and IRA provisions of EGTRRA, making these specific provisions a permanent part of tax and pension law.

¶1310 **Qualified Tuition Programs.** The modifications to the qualified tuition program rules made by EGTRRA are permanently extended and the IRS is granted broad regulatory authority to carry out the purposes and to prevent the abuse of these rules.

¶1315 **Saver's Credit.** The saver's credit, which was initially set to expire after 2006, is made permanent.

¶1320 **Retirement Savings Incentives Indexed for Inflation.** The income limits for contributions to both traditional and Roth IRAs, and for eligibility for the saver's credit, are indexed for inflation beginning in 2007.

¶1325 **Rollover Distributions and Unemployment Compensation.** States are prohibited from reducing unemployment compensation by the amount of retirement or IRA distributions that are rolled over to a similar plan.

¶1330 **Death Benefits from Employer-Owned Life Insurance.** Income from the proceeds of employer-owned life insurance on the lives of officers, directors and highly compensated individuals is excluded from the policyholder's gross income.

¶1335 **Test Room Supervisors and Proctors.** For purposes of the safe haven for treating workers as independent contractors, the consistency requirement does not apply to services performed for a tax-exempt organization by test proctors or room supervisors who assist in the administration of college entrance or placement examinations.

¶1340 **Alaska Hydroelectric Projects and Qualified Bond Requirements.** Bonds used to finance the Lake Dorothy hydroelectric project are qualified private activity bonds with tax-exempt interest, and the interest on the Snettisham hydroelectric project bonds remains tax-exempt.

¶1345 **Penalty Thresholds for Substantial and Gross Valuation Misstatements.** The thresholds for imposing the accuracy-related penalty for underpayment of income, estate and gift taxes due to substantial and gross valuation misstatements are lowered, and the reasonable cause exception is eliminated for gross valuation misstatements regarding charitable deduction property.

¶1350 **Penalty and Disciplinary Action for Appraisers.** A civil penalty is imposed on a person who prepares an appraisal that results in a substantial or gross valuation misstatement, and the appraiser may be disciplined before the penalty is assessed.

¶1355 **Definitions of Qualified Appraisal and Qualified Appraiser.** Definitions for "qualified appraisal" and "qualified appraiser" are codified and revised for purposes of the charitable deduction for donated property.

U.S. TAX COURT MODERNIZATION

¶1405 **Jurisdiction Over CDP Cases.** The U.S. Tax Court's jurisdiction is extended to all appeals of collection due process (CDP) determinations, regardless of the type of tax involved.

¶1415 **Equitable Recoupment.** The Tax Court may apply the doctrine of equitable recoupment to the same extent as federal district courts.

¶1420 **Petition Filing Fees.** The Tax Court may charge a fee of up to $60 for the filing of any petition.

¶1425 **Practitioner Fees for *Pro Se* Taxpayer Services.** The practice fees that the Tax Court may use to employ independent counsel in disciplinary matters may also be used to provide services to *pro se* taxpayers.

Parties Affected

1

BENEFIT PLANS

CHARITABLE ORGANIZATIONS AND DONORS

ENTITIES

BUSINESS

SPECIFIC INDUSTRIES

INDIVIDUALS GENERALLY

PENSION PROTECTION ACT OF 2006

¶101 Overview

As its name implies, the Pension Protection Act of 2006 has its primary impact on the various forms of qualified retirement plans. Since the vast majority of Americans either are sponsors of qualified retirement plans or participants in some form of qualified retirement plan, the Act will have an impact on almost everyone. The primary focus of the legislation is the funding of defined benefit plans and the protection of the Pension Benefit Guaranty Corporation, the government entity that insures defined benefit plans. Some industries, such as airlines and defense contractors, are singled out for favorable treatment. The legislation is not limited to defined benefit plans, however. Among the more than 150 act sections included in the legislation are significant provisions related to investment advice, prohibited transactions and fiduciary rules, portability rules, distribution and contributions rules, health benefits, plan diversification, plan participation, and spousal pension protection. Also included in this law are provisions making permanent the pension provisions of the Economic Growth and Tax Relief Reconciliation Act of 2001, which were generally scheduled to sunset after 2010.

In addition to the pension provisions, other major sections of the legislation relate to new rules for the operation of the Tax Court and a large package of charitable organization provisions related to charitable giving, reforming exempt organizations, and addressing donor advised funds and supporting organizations. There are also a handful of miscellaneous provisions and technical corrections. The more than 900 pages of legislative text spell out the most significant changes to the pension laws in the last 30 years.

RETIREMENT PLANS AND ADMINISTRATORS

¶105 Overall Effect on Retirement Plans

Retirement plans are a focus of this legislation. Most of the changes affect particular types of retirement plans. The legislation does provide, however, that plan changes in general to comply with this legislation may be retroactive to its effective date (¶1090).

¶106 Effect on Retirement Plans Generally

Beyond the primary focus of the Pension Protection Act of 2006 on the funding of defined benefit plans and the financial health of the Pension Benefit Guaranty Corporation (PBGC), there are number of less far ranging, but still important provisions, such as those dealing with prohibited transactions, default investments, and fiduciary rules.

Prohibited transactions.—In connection with prohibited transactions, exemptions from the prohibited transaction rules are provided with respect to block trading, regulated electronic communication networks, service providers who are not fiduciaries, foreign exchange transactions, and cross trading (¶630). Relief is also provided from certain broker-dealer bonding requirements (¶630). The new law also revises the period for correcting certain prohibited transactions involving securities and commodities (¶635).

Asset treatment after failure to exercise investment election.—The Pension Act creates a framework for "default" investments in a case where a participant fails to exercise his or her investment election options under the plan (¶655). The provision requires that a participant receive, within a reasonable time before each plan year, a notice explaining the participant's right to designate the investment of contributions and earnings and, in the absence of an election by the participant, how such funds will be invested. The participant must also be given a reasonable period of time after receipt of the notice and before the beginning of the plan year to make such a designation. The provision is generally effective for plan years beginning after 2006, but final regulations are to be issued within six months of August 17, 2006, the date of enactment.

Clarification of fiduciary rules.—The Pension Act also mandates new rules concerning the application of the prudence standards of ERISA. Within one year of the

August 17, 2006, date of enactment, the Secretary of Labor is to issue final regulations clarifying whether an annuity used as an optional form of benefit to a participant or beneficiary is (1) *not* subject to the "safest available annuity standard" (DOL Interpretative Bulletin 95-1, 29 C.F.R. 2509.95-1), and (2) *is* subject to all other applicable fiduciary standards (¶660).

¶107 Effect on Defined Benefit Plans

A significant portion of the Pension Protection Act of 2006 is devoted to the problems of defined benefit plans, especially underfunding. The new law imposes restrictions on funding deferred compensation when defined pension plans are considered at risk under the law (¶220). The new law also extends the use of long-term corporate bonds rather than 30-year Treasury rates for plan funding (¶235). The law also changes the interest rate assumption and mortality table for calculating lump sum distributions (¶905) and also the interest rate assumption for applying benefit limitations to lump sum distributions (¶740).

As part of the battle against underfunding, the new law increases the funding deduction limits (¶705). The new law also provides that certain excess assets may be transferred to a health account (¶805). The formula for determining compensation limits has been changed to include periods when the employee was not a participant (¶735).

Minimum required contributions for single-employer pension plans.—The Pension Act subjects employers maintaining single-employer defined benefit plans, effective after 2007, to new funding rules that will require them to make a minimum contribution to the plan that is based on the plan's assets (reduced by credit balances), funding target, and target normal cost. Members of an employer's controlled group will also be jointly and severally liable for the required contribution.

The Treasury is authorized, under rules comparable to current law, to provide a temporary waiver of the minimum funding requirements for an employer that is unable to satisfy the minimum funding standard for a plan year without "substantial business hardship." The minimum required contribution for a single employer plan will be reduced by the amount of the waived funding deficiency. However, in the event a plan has a waived funding deficiency for any of the five preceding years, the minimum required contribution for the plan year will be increased by a waiver amortization charge for the plan year.

An employer maintaining a single employer defined benefit plan may be required to provide security to the plan as a condition for a waiver of the minimum funding standards. In addition, no plan amendment that has the effect of increasing plan liabilities may generally be adopted during the waiver period (¶205).

Funding rules for single-employer pension plans repealed for plan years after 2007.—Funding rules applicable to single-employer defined benefit plans are repealed, effective after 2007, by the Pension Act. Current law will apply in 2006 and 2007. However, beginning with the 2008 plan year, the funding standard account mechanism and the current two-tiered funding system will be replaced with a single funding method. An employer maintaining a single-employer defined benefit plan that is not 100-percent funded will not be required to make a deficit reduction contribution, but will be required to make a minimum contribution based on the plan's assets (reduced by credit balances), funding target, and target normal cost and that is sufficient to amortize unfunded plan liabilities over a period of seven years. Unlike current law, under which employers are required to fund up to 90 percent of a plan's total liabilities, the Pension Act increases the funding target to 100 percent of target or current liabilities (¶210).

In addition, the Pension Act radically changes the actuarial assumptions and methods used to determine present value, authorizing a new interest rate and a new mortality table. Specifically, the Act, while retaining the blended rate of corporate bonds, introduces a segmented "yield curve" that would consist of three different interest rates (based on the unweighted average of interest rates on investment grade corporate bonds) applicable to benefits payable in different time periods.

Finally, the Act subjects "at-risk" plans, as determined by the plan's funded status and not by the credit rating of the employer sponsoring the plan, to an at-risk liability assumption that all plan participants eligible for benefits within a 10-year period will elect benefits at the highest present value. The at-risk rules, which are limited to plans with over 500 participants, will increase a plan's target liability.

Benefit limitations implemented under single-employer pension plans.—Single-employer defined benefit plans that fall below specified funding levels will be subject to new limits on the payment of unpredictable contingent event benefits (e.g. shut-down benefits), plan amendments, lump-sum distributions, and benefit accruals. The restrictions, which are based on the plan's ratio of plan assets to target liability (adjusted funding target attainment percentage) and triggered by variant thresholds, will generally be effective beginning in 2008, require benefit accruals to be frozen and prevent underfunded plans that have been in effect for over five years from implementing amendments adding benefits or otherwise increasing plan liabilities or paying the full amount of a lump-sum distribution, without additional contributions by the plan sponsor. Employees must receive written notice of any benefit limitations within 30 days (¶215).

A plan's credit balance may not be used to pay for any required additional contribution. In addition, an employer in bankruptcy may not authorize an increase in benefits or pay lump-sum distributions under a plan that is less than fully funded.

Special valuation rules apply to certain financially-healthy companies involved in acquisitions or other transactions.—For plans that are acquired by another corporate entity as part of an acquisition or similar transaction and that meet certain conditions, the interest rate to be used in determining whether the plan has sufficient assets to meet benefit liabilities for purposes of the standard termination rules (or, in certain circumstances, the rules for termination by the PBGC) must be not less than the interest rate used for determining whether the plan is fully funded. The interest rate rule applies only to a transaction in which the employer maintaining the plan immediately before or after the transaction meets certain criteria with respect to (1) its investment rating and (2) the composition of its domestic workforce (¶225).

Temporary relief from funding rules granted to certain plans.—Temporary relief from the new funding rules, which are generally effective beginning in 2008, is granted to certain defined benefit plans. The new single employer defined benefit plan funding rules will not apply to certain multiple employer plans maintained by rural cooperatives for plan years beginning before January 1, 2017. In addition, the new rules will not apply to certain PBGC settlement plans for plan years beginning before January 1, 2014. Finally, the new rules will generally not apply to plans maintained by certain government defense contractors before plan years beginning before the earlier of (1) the date certain new rules regarding pension costs to be issued by the Cost Accounting Standards Board become effective or (2) January 1, 2011. For plan years beginning after December 31, 2007, and before the first plan year for which the new funding rules apply, all such plans must use a specific interest rate to determine the plan's funding status (¶240).

Plan funding notice rules expanded.—The Pension Act expands funding notice rules for defined benefit plans by requiring plan administrators to provide a plan funding notice for each plan year. This plan funding notice must be provided to the PBGC, each plan participant and beneficiary, each labor organization representing plan participants and beneficiaries, and, for multiemployer plans, to each employer that is obligated to contribute to the plan.

Each defined benefit plan funding notice must contain identifying information, such as (1) the name of the plan, (2) the plan administrator's address and phone number, (3) the address and phone number of the plan's principal administrative officer, (4) each plan sponsor's employer identification number (EIN), and (5) the plan number of the plan. Additional information may also be required depending on whether the plan is a single-employer plan or a multiemployer plan (¶405).

Additional information required for DB plan annual reports.—For defined benefit plans, additional information is to be provided on Form 5500 annual reports. If liabilities to participants or their beneficiaries under the DB plan consist (either in whole or in part) of liabilities under two or more pension plans as of immediately before the plan year, the annual report must include the funded percentage of each of the two or more pension plans as of the last day of the plan year and the funded percentage of the plan with regard to which the annual report is filed as of the last day of the plan year (¶415).

Electronic display of information.—The Pension Act requires that plan administrators file information included in the annual report in an electronic format to accommodate Internet display (in accordance with regulations to be issued by the Secretary of Labor). Within 90 days after the annual report filing date, the Secretary will display such information included in the annual report on an Internet website that the Secretary maintains. The information also must be displayed on any Intranet website that the plan sponsor (or the plan administrator on behalf of the plan sponsor) maintains (¶420).

Change in criteria for persons required to provide information to PBGC.—The Pension Act requires that each contributing sponsor, and each member of a contributing sponsor's controlled group, of a single-employer plan must file annual actuarial and financial information (section 4010 report) with the PBGC if the funding target attainment percentage at the end of the preceding plan year is less than 80 percent. Thus, the $50 million filing threshold for aggregate unfunded vested benefits is eliminated. The information submitted to the PBGC in the section 4010 report must include the amount of benefit liabilities under the plan; the funding target of the plan determined as if the plan has been in at-risk status for at least five plan years; and the funding target attainment percentage of the plan (¶425).

Enhanced disclosure of termination information.—A plan administrator that has filed a notice of intent to terminate must provide to an affected party any information provided to the PBGC. This disclosure must be provided not later than 15 days after receipt of a request from the affected party for the information or the provision of new information to the PBGC relating to a previous request. ERISA regulations define "affected party" as each plan participant, beneficiary of a deceased participant, alternate payees under an applicable qualified domestic relations order, employee organizations that represent any group of participants, and the PBGC. The enhanced disclosure requirements apply to both employer-initiated and involuntary distress terminations. Plan administrators must not disclose the information in a manner that identifies an individual participant or beneficiary (¶430).

New rules for calculating PBGC variable rate premium.—The Pension Act creates new rules for calculating the PBGC variable rate premium beginning in the 2008 plan year. Under these new rules, the determination of "unfunded vested benefits" for purposes of the variable rate premium is modified to conform to the funding rules of the Act (see ¶205 and following). Thus, unfunded vested benefits means, for a plan year, the excess (if any) of (1) the funding target of the plan as determined under ERISA Sec. 303(d) (see ¶210) for the plan year by only taking into account vested benefits and by using a specified interest rate, over (2) the fair market value of plan assets for the plan year which are held by the plan on the valuation date (¶505).

Variable rate premiums capped for plans of very small employers.—The Pension Act encourages small employers to establish defined benefit plans by providing that, for very small plans (those with 25 or fewer employees on the first day of the plan year), the variable rate premium payments for each participant cannot exceed $5.00 multiplied by the number of participants in the plan as of the close of the preceding plan year (¶510).

PBGC authorized to pay interest on premium overpayment refunds.—Under the Pension Act, the PBGC is now authorized to pay interest on overpayments made by payors of PBGC premiums. Interest paid on overpayments is to be calculated at the same rate and in the same manner as interest charged on premium underpayments. Interest on premium underpayments is imposed under Code Sec. 6601(a), which is the same rate as the interest imposed on tax underpayments (¶515).

PBGC guaranteed amount for plant shutdowns and other contingent events phased in over five-year period.—The Pension Act amends ERISA by changing the way the PBGC guarantee for benefits for plant shutdowns and other unpredictable, contingent events will be calculated (¶520). The guarantee will be calculated using the method currently used for benefits associated with plan amendments made within five years of the date of termination. Generally, this means that the guarantee will be phased in over a five-year period at the rate of 20 percent of the guaranteed benefit per year (ERISA Sec. 4022(b)(1) and (7)).

PBGC guarantee frozen as of date contributing plan sponsor enters bankruptcy.—The Pension Act provides that if a plan terminates during the contributing sponsor's bankruptcy, PBGC benefits are guaranteed as of the date of the filing of the bankruptcy petition or similar proceeding (ERISA Sec. 4022(i)). In addition, the priority among participants for purposes of allocating plan assets and employer recoveries to nonguaranteed benefits in the event of plan termination is determined as of the date the sponsor enters bankruptcy or a similar proceeding (ERISA Sec. 4044(e)). Thus, for purposes of determining PBGC guaranteed benefits and the priority status of parties when allocating assets on termination, the date of the bankruptcy filing is substituted for the termination date (¶525).

Guaranteed benefit phase-in rules eased for owner/participants in terminated plans.—The application of the phase-in rule to participants who also own a portion of the business will now vary, depending upon how much of the business they own. For "substantial owners", the same 60-month phase-in rule that applies to nonowner participants applies. For "majority owners", a stricter phase-in rule is applied—the phase-in occurs over a 10-year period and depends on the number of years the plan has been in effect. In addition, the majority owner's guaranteed benefit is limited so that it cannot be more than the amount phased in over 60 months for other participants (¶530).

Definition of "one-participant retirement plan" amended for notice of blackout periods.—For purposes of the blackout notice rules, the definition of the term "one-participant retirement plan" has been amended to mean a retirement plan that, as of the first day of the plan year, only covers one individual (or one individual and the individual's spouse) and the individual owns 100 percent of the plan sponsor whether or not incorporated, or only covers one or more partners (or partners and their spouses) in a plan sponsor (¶620).

Blackout period exception to relief from fiduciary liability.—The Pension Act creates a new exception to the relief from fiduciary liability that ERISA Sec. 404 grants to fiduciaries under circumstances where the plan permits participants and beneficiaries to exercise control over the investment of assets in their accounts. Such relief will not be available under circumstances where a participant or beneficiary is unable to direct the investment of assets due to a suspension of this right by the plan sponsor or fiduciary (a "blackout period,"), which does not meet the requirements of ERISA Sec.101(i)(7) (¶640). Qualified changes in investment options will not cause liability to accrue.

Maximum bond amount increased for plans holding employer securities.—Many employee benefit plans have significant investments in employer securities. While such investments can be beneficial for participants, they can also entail additional risk for participants in a plan sponsored by an employer who is experiencing financial distress. In recognition of the additional risk assumed by plans investing in employer securities, the Pension Act has amended Code Sec. 412(a) by raising the maximum bond amount from $500,000 to $1,000,000 for such plans (¶645).

¶108 Effect on Defined Contribution Plans

Although less of a focus in the Pension Protection Act of 2006 than defined benefit plans, a number of provisions in the new law are designed to further enhance the attractiveness of defined contribution plans. After much debate in Congress, the law includes new rules permitting investment advice to be provided to participants (¶625).

Automatic enrollment.—Companies that offer qualified cash or deferred arrangements (CODAs) (i.e., 401(k) plans) should take note of provisions that are directed at encouraging participation by giving nondiscrimination protection for automatic enrollment and contribution arrangements that meet certain requirements (¶1015). Features such as automatic enrollment and contribution are generally viewed as a way to increase employee participation in retirement plans and to boost the overall savings of Americans for retirement. However, even though provisions of the Economic Retirement Income Security Act of 1974 (ERISA) generally trump state law, controversy has arisen as to whether such arrangements are in conflict with certain state payroll withholding laws. The Pension Act puts any such controversy to rest by preempting state law and by providing nondiscrimination protection for automatic enrollment and contribution arrangements that meet certain requirements. In order to qualify for the automatic enrollment safe harbor, the arrangement must comply with specific rules on automatic deferral, matching or nonelective contributions, and notices.

With respect to automatic deferral, the requirements are met if, under the arrangement, employees that are eligible to participate in the enrollment arrangement are treated as having elected to have the employer make elective contributions equal to a qualified percentage of compensation. The qualified percentage must be at least three percent of compensation, with the minimum rising by one percent for each successive year the deemed election applies to the participant, up to six percent. However, the percentage cannot exceed 10 percent.

In the case of matching contributions, the requirement is satisfied if the employer makes matching contributions on behalf of each employee who is not a highly compensated employee of 100 percent of elective deferrals up to one percent of compensation, plus 50 percent of elective deferral between one percent and up to six percent of compensation An alternative is allowed if the employer is required to make contributions to a defined contribution plan of at least three percent of compensation of behalf of each nonhighly compensated employee.

The Pension Act also provides an exception to the top-heavy rules for these new automatic arrangements. In addition, under a vesting requirement, participants who have completed at least two years of service must be 100 percent vested with respect to matching or other employer contributions to their accounts under these arrangements.

Before the beginning of each plan year, participants must be given a notice explaining their rights under the automatic enrollment arrangement to elect *not* to have elective contributions made on their behalf or to elect to have contributions made in a different amount and how contributions made under the arrangement will be invested in the absence of any investment election by the employee. Employees must be given a reasonable period of time after receipt of such notice and before the first elective contribution is made to make the election with respect to contributions and investments. These changes are effective for plan years beginning after 2007, although the preemption of any conflicting state regulation is effective on August 17, 2006.

Missing participant program extended to multiemployer, defined contribution, and other plans.—The Pension Act directs the Pension Benefit Guaranty Corporations (PBGC) to issue regulations for terminating multiemployer plans similar to the present-law missing participant rules that apply to single-employer defined benefit plans when they terminate (¶540). Therefore, once regulations are issued, the plan administrator of a terminating defined contribution plan generally must purchase annuity contracts from a private insurer to provide the benefits to which participants are entitled and distribute the annuity contracts to the participants. If the plan administrator cannot locate a participant after a diligent search, the plan administrator will have the option to purchase an annuity from an insurer or transfer the participant's designated benefit to the PBGC, which holds the benefit of the missing participant until the PBGC locates the missing participant and distributes the benefit.

Diversification required for qualified trust of defined contribution plan.—A trust that is part of an "applicable defined contribution plan" will not be treated as a qualified trust unless the plan meets certain diversification requirements with regard to investments in employer securities. An "applicable individual account plan" must also meet the diversification requirements. A plan will meet its diversification requirements if it allows an "applicable individual" to direct the plan to divest any employer securities in which a portion of employee contributions and elective deferrals are invested. The individual must then be allowed to direct the reinvestment of an equivalent amount in other investment options that meet certain requirements. The plan must also allow an applicable individual who is a participant in the plan who has completed at least three years of service or is a beneficiary of a participant or of a deceased participant to divest the portion of an account that contains employer contributions, other than elective deferrals, that is invested in employer securities (¶605).

Required notice of diversification rights.—The Pension Act requires a plan administrator to provide a notice to applicable individuals who are eligible to exercise the right to direct the proceeds from the divestment of employer securities with respect to any type of contribution. The notice must be provided not later than 30 days before the first date on which the applicable participant becomes eligible to divest employer securities. The notice must set out the right to direct the divestment of employer securities and must describe the importance of diversifying retirement account assets in investments (¶610).

Required periodic benefit statements.—The Pension Act requires that a plan administrator of a defined contribution plan (other than a one-participant retirement plan) must furnish a pension benefit statement to participants and beneficiaries. The pension benefit statement must be furnished: (1) At least once each calendar quarter to each participant or beneficiary who has the right to direct the investment of assets in his or her account under the plan; (2) At least once each calendar year to a participant or beneficiary who has his or her own account under the plan but does not have the right to direct the investment of the assets of the account; and (3) upon written request to any other plan beneficiary (¶615).

The pension benefit statement must indicate, on the basis of the latest information available, the total benefits accrued and the nonforfeitable benefits, if any, that have accrued or the earliest date on which benefits will become nonforfeitable. The pension benefits statement also needs to include an explanation of any permitted disparity or any floor-offset arrangement that may be applied in determining any accrued benefits.

The statement needs to be written in a manner calculated to be understood by the average plan participant. It may be delivered in written, electronic, or other appropriate form to the extent that the form is reasonably accessible to the participant or beneficiary.

Definition of "one-participant retirement plan" amended for notice of blackout periods.—For purposes of the blackout notice rules, the definition of the term "one-participant retirement plan" has been amended to mean a retirement plan that, as of the first day of the plan year, only covers one individual (or one individual and the individual's spouse) and the individual owns 100 percent of the plan sponsor whether or not incorporated, or only covers one or more partners (or partners and their spouses) in a plan sponsor (¶620).

Electronic display of information.—The Pension Act requires that plan administrators file information included in the annual report in an electronic format to accommodate Internet display (in accordance with regulations to be issued by the Secretary of Labor). Within 90 days after the annual report filing date, the Secretary will display such information included in the annual report on an Internet website that the Secretary maintains. The information also must be displayed on any Intranet website that the plan sponsor (or the plan administrator on behalf of the plan sponsor) maintains (¶420).

New category of prohibited transaction exemption for investment advice added.—The Pension Act adds a new category of prohibited transaction exemption (PTE) under the Code and ERISA in connection with the provision of investment advice through an "eligible investment advice arrangement" to participants and beneficiaries of 401(k) plans and other defined contribution plans who direct the investment of their accounts under the plan and to beneficiaries of IRAs (which includes HSAs, Archer MSAs, and Coverdell education savings accounts (ESAs) for purposes of this provision). Under the Pension Act, qualified "fiduciary advisers" would be able to provide investment advice to 401(k) and other plan participants without running afoul of the prohibited transaction rules under the Code and ERISA, if certain requirements are met.

The exemptions provided under the investment advice provision apply in connection with the provision of investment advice by a fiduciary adviser under an "eligible investment advice arrangement." An eligible investment advice arrangement is an arrangement which either (1) provides that any fees (including any commission or compensation) received by the fiduciary adviser for investment advice or with respect to an investment transaction with respect to plan assets do not vary depending on the basis of any investment option selected, or (2) uses a computer model under an investment advice program in connection with the provision of investment advice to a participant or beneficiary. To qualify as an eligible investment advice arrangement, certain audit, disclosure, record retention and other rules must also be met (¶625).

¶109 Effect on Multiemployer Plans

Changes similar to those for single-employer defined benefit plans have also been made for multiemployer defined benefit plans, with some unique funding provisions for multiemployer plans. The deduction limits for funding multiemployer plans have increased (¶710). The longer amortization periods for multiemployer plans have been reduced and the interest rate assumptions have been modified (¶305). These funding requirements are relaxed for benefits approved through a settlement with the Pension Benefit Guaranty Corporation (PBGC) (¶305). Additional funding rules are imposed on plans in a critical or endangered status (¶310). Multiemployer plans are given an extended period to determine whether they will be insolvent (¶315). The rules for liability for an employer withdrawing from a multiemployer plan are tightened (¶320). The law includes a provision permitting the revocation of an election to be treated as a multiemployer plan (¶325). The PBGC is to undertake a study of multiemployer plans in connection with several of the funding changes scheduled to sunset after 2014 (¶29,020).

Multiemployer financial plan information must be made available upon request.— The Pension Protection Act of 2006 expands the ability of participants, beneficiaries, unions, and contributing employers to request and receive plan actuarial and financial information and estimates of potential withdrawal liability from multiemployer plans. Contributing employers are entitled to receive, upon written request, a notice of the estimated amount of the employer's withdrawal liability if the employer withdrew on the last day of the plan year prior to the date of the request, as well as an explanation of how this estimated liability amount was determined. An ERISA Sec. 204(h) notice of significant reduction in benefit accruals now also must be provided to each employer who has an obligation to contribute to the plan. (¶410).

Additional information required for defined benefit plan annual reports.—For defined benefit plans, additional information is to be provided on Form 5500 annual reports. If liabilities to participants or their beneficiaries under the plan consist (either in whole or in part) of liabilities under two or more pension plans as of immediately before the plan year, the annual report must include the funded percentage of each of the two or more pension plans as of the last day of the plan year and the funded percentage of the plan with regard to which the annual report is filed as of the last day of the plan year. Besides including the funded percentage information described above, annual reports for *multiemployer plans* must also include additional information as of the end of the plan year relating to the notice. (¶415).

Missing participant program extended to multiemployer, defined contribution, and other plans.—The Pension Act directs the PBGC to issue regulations for terminating multiemployer plans similar to the present-law missing participant rules that apply to single-employer defined benefit plans when they terminate (¶540). Therefore, once regulations are issued, the plan administrator of a terminating multiemployer defined benefit pension plan generally must purchase annuity contracts from a private insurer to provide the benefits to which participants are entitled and distribute the annuity contracts to the participants. If the plan administrator cannot locate a participant after a diligent search, the plan administrator will have to purchase an annuity from an insurer or transfer the participant's designated benefit to the PBGC, which holds the benefit of the missing participant until the PBGC locates the missing participant and distributes the benefit.

Retaliation.—The ERISA rules prohibiting retaliation against participants enforcing their ERISA rights is extended to employers in multiemployer plans (¶330).

Excess benefits to health plans.—The new law also provides that certain excess assets may be transferred from a defined benefit plan to a related health plan (¶810).

¶111 Effect on Individual Retirement Accounts (IRAs)

New category of prohibited transaction exemption for investment advice added.—The Pension Protection Act of 2006 adds a new category of prohibited transaction exemption (PTE) under the Code and ERISA in connection with the provision of investment advice through an "eligible investment advice arrangement" to participants and beneficiaries of 401(k) plans and other defined contribution plans who direct the investment of their accounts under the plan and to beneficiaries of IRAs (which includes HSAs, Archer MSAs, and Coverdell education savings accounts (ESAs) for purposes of this provision). Under the Pension Act, qualified "fiduciary advisers" would be able to provide investment advice to 401(k) and other plan participants without running afoul of the prohibited transaction rules under the Code and ERISA, if certain requirements are met.

The exemptions provided under the investment advice provision apply in connection with the provision of investment advice by a fiduciary adviser under an "eligible investment advice arrangement." An eligible investment advice arrangement is an arrangement which either (1) provides that any fees (including any commission or compensation) received by the fiduciary adviser for investment advice or with respect to an investment transaction with respect to plan assets do not vary depending on the basis of any investment option selected, or (2) uses a computer model under an investment advice program in connection with the provision of investment advice to a participant or beneficiary. In the case of an IRA (as opposed to an employer-sponsored plan), the computer model exception will be available only if and when the Labor Department concludes that a viable computer model for this purpose exists. To qualify as an eligible investment advice arrangement, certain audit, disclosure, record retention and other rules must also be met (¶625).

Indexing.—The new law provides for indexing the adjusted gross income levels for IRA and Roth IRA contributions for tax years after 2006 (¶1320).

¶112 Effect on Church Plans

Special rule for church plans that self amortize.—For plan years ending after August 17, 2006, qualified church plans will not fail the Code Sec. 401(a)(9) minimum distribution rules simply because annuity payments pursuant to the plan are not made under an annuity contract purchased from an insurance company so long as the plan complies with the rules under Code Sec. 403(b) (¶1045). To be considered qualified, a church plan must be a money purchase pension plan that is a church plan as defined in Code Sec. 414(e) (without having made an election to have the participation, vesting, and funding rules apply to it) and have been in existence on April 17, 2002.

Exemption for leveraged real estate.—Income from leveraged real estate held by church plans (including those of certain church related organizations) will not be considered unrelated business taxable income for tax years beginning on or after August 17, 2006 (¶1050).

Limit eased for nonhighly compensated individuals.—Beginning in 2007, the Code Sec. 415(b) 100-percent of compensation limitation will not apply to church plans, or those maintained by a convention or association of churches, or a church-controlled elementary or secondary school (¶1055). However, this relaxed rule does not apply to "highly compensated benefits" (i.e., those accrued for a highly compensated employee).

¶113 Effect on Cash Balance and Hybrid Plans

In additions to the provisions enhancing defined contribution plans, the new law also enhances hybrid defined benefit plans by clarifying some of the rules that apply to these plans. Rules are provided for testing these plans for age discrimination (¶1005). The Treasury is also directed to develop regulations to address the treatment of cash balance and other hybrid plans in mergers and acquisitions (¶1010).

¶114 Effect on Government Plans

Several provisions of the new law have a direct impact on government retirement plans. Governmental retirement plans under the new law are permitted to allow public safety officers to exclude some of their retirement income to pay for accident, health or long-term care insurance premiums (¶825). The current moratorium on applying nondiscrimination rules to certain government plans is extended to all government plans (¶1060). Also, certain pension plans of Indian tribal governments are to be treated as government plans (¶1065).

¶115 Effect on Combined Plans

Companies that offer both defined benefit and defined contribution plans also have provisions addressed to them. Contributions to a PBGC-covered defined benefit plan will be deductible without affecting the combined limit on deductible contributions, and, for other plans, only contributions in excess of six percent of compensation will count toward the combined limit (¶715). Multiemployer plans are exempt from the overall limit (¶715). The new law also permits small employers with 500 or fewer employees to set up in one plan document a combined defined benefit-401(k) plan (¶1020).

¶116 Effect on Employee Stock Ownership Plans

Rules are provided to clarify the treatment of transfers from charitable remainder trusts to ESOPs (¶1155). Certain ESOPs are also exempted from the provisions of the new law requiring defined contribution plans to permit diversification (¶605). Provisions from the 2001 Tax Act with respect to prohibited allocations of S corporation stock and dividend reinvestment have been made permanent (¶1305).

RETIREMENT PLAN PARTICIPANTS AND BENEFICIARIES

¶121 Overall Effect on Retirement Plan Participants

Although the primary emphasis of the Pension Protection Act of 2006 was on retirement plans, particularly the funding of defined benefit plans, participants in virtually every type of plan will be the direct and indirect recipients of much good news in the Act. For one thing, the Pension Act makes permanent a number of important provisions originally enacted as part of the Economic Growth and Tax Relief Reconciliation Act of 2001 (EGTRRA), including those that allow greater contribution and benefit limits, as well as special "catch-up" contribution amounts for persons age 50 and older (¶1305). The Act also provides for indexing of the adjusted gross income limits for purposes of the saver's credit and for IRA and Roth IRA contributions (¶1320).

Defined benefit participants should also benefit from provisions that provide greater access to information on plan funding (¶405) and terminations (¶430).

Other provisions that will have a potentially beneficial impact on retirement plan participants include those dealing with greater diversification rights (¶605), benefit statements (¶615), automatic enrollment in 401(k) plans (¶1015), and improved access to investment advice (¶625).

IRA owners will also benefit from a number of provisions, including one that allows charitable contributions made directly from an IRA (¶1105). Participants in lesser known plans, such as 403(b) plans, 457 plans, and SIMPLEs should also note important changes made by the Pension Act. A more detailed analysis of the effect on plan participants of these provisions and others is contained in the following numbered paragraphs.

¶122 Effect on Defined Benefit Plan Participants

PBGC determination of benefits attributable to recoveries from employers accelerated.—The benefit recovery ratio used by the Pension Benefit Guaranty Corporation (PBGC) to determine the amount of the unfunded benefit liabilities of a terminated plan was changed by the Pension Protection Act of 2006. The ratio will now be generally based upon the five-Federal fiscal year period that ends with the third fiscal year immediately prior to the year in which a notice of intent to terminate is dated with respect to a particular plan. As a result, the PBGC will be able to more quickly determine the amount of additional benefits available to share with the participants of a given plan (¶535).

In addition, a recovery ratio for determining amounts recovered for contributions owed to the plan has been created. This recovery ratio will use the same five-year period as the period used for determining the recovery ratio for unfunded benefit liabilities. Thus, the PBGC will determine the recovery amount by multiplying (1) the amount of liability under ERISA Sec. 4062(c) as of the date of plan termination by (2) the ERISA Sec. 4062(c) recovery ratio.

EGTRRA provisions made permanent.—Title IX of the Economic Growth and Tax Relief Reconciliation Act of 2001 (EGTRRA) imposed a sunset date of December 31, 2010, on many provisions of that legislation, including a myriad of provisions relating to IRAs and qualified plans. The Pension Act does away with that sunset provision as it applied to the provisions of subtitles A through F of EGTRRA (the pension and retirement plan provisions).

Accordingly, with respect to defined benefit plan participants, the increase in the Code Sec. 415(b) defined benefit limit (indexed at $175,000 for 2006) will be extended past 2010. Disclosure requirements concerning notification of plan amendments that would reduce the rate of a future benefit accrual are also extended. This and additional provisions of EGTRRA made permanent by the Pension Act are discussed at ¶1305.

Direct rollovers to Roth IRAs.—New rules would allow direct rollovers from an eligible retirement plan to a Roth IRA after December 31, 2007 (¶935). An eligible retirement plan would include a qualified plan, as well as plans governed by Code Sec. 403(b) and Code Sec. 457. For tax years prior to 2010, such rollovers are subject to the $100,000 adjusted gross income limitation.

Rollover by nonspouse beneficiaries.—In what could prove to be a very significant change, new rules effective for distributions after December 31, 2006, would allow a rollover from a qualified retirement plan to an inherited IRA for the benefit of persons other than the surviving spouse (¶945). The rollover must be accomplished via a trustee-to-trustee transfer and the minimum required distribution rules of Code Sec. 401(a)(9)(B) (rather than special rules applicable only to surviving spouses) must be followed. A trust maintained for the benefit of one or more designated beneficiaries shall be treated as a beneficiary.

Rollover of after-tax amounts.—Effective for tax years beginning after 2006, after-tax amounts may be rolled over tax free from a qualified retirement plan to a defined benefit plan (¶940).

Determination of average compensation.—Code Sec. 415(b)(3) is amended to clarify that only compensation earned while an individual is working for the employer, not only when he or she is a participant in a defined benefit plan, is to be used in determining the plan benefit limits (¶735). Accordingly, for purposes of determining the average compensation for a participant's highest three years, the period considered is not more than the three consecutive years in which the participant had the greatest aggregate compensation from the employer.

Plan funding notice.—Defined benefit plan participants and beneficiaries, labor organizations representing them, and in the case of a multiemployer plan, each employer who has an obligation to contribute to the plan, must receive an annual notice describing the funding status of the plan (¶405). Not less than one year after the effective date of the Pension Act, the Secretary of Labor is to publish a model notice for this purpose. This provision is generally effective for plan years beginning after 2007.

Access to multiemployer pension plan information.—Effective for plan years beginning after 2007, participants, beneficiaries, employee representatives, and employers obligated to contribute to a multiemployer plan are entitled to receive, upon request, a copy of any (1) periodic actuarial report that has been in the plan's possession for at least 30 days, (2) quarterly, semi-annual, or annual financial report prepared by plan investment manager, advisor, or other fiduciary, that has been in the plan's possession for at least 30 days, and (3) any application filed under ERISA § 304 (Extension of amortization periods). This information should be supplied within 30 days of receipt of the request and may be provided in written, electronic, or other form (¶ 410).

Disclosure of termination information to participants.—Affected parties, which include plan participants, beneficiaries of a deceased participant, alternate payees under an applicable qualified domestic relations order, employee organizations that represent any group of participants, and the PBGC must, within 15 days after receipt of a request, be provided with information that was required to be given to the PBGC with respect to termination of the plan (¶ 430). The enhanced disclosure requirements apply to both employer-initiated and involuntary distress terminations and are effective for plan years beginning after 2007.

Periodic pension benefit statements.—Under the Pension Act, each participant with a nonforfeitable accrued benefit in a defined benefit plan must receive individual benefit notices at least every three years or upon request (¶ 615). However, alternatively, defined benefit plans may satisfy the requirement by providing participants with notice of the availability of the pension benefit statement and how it may be obtained. The Secretary of Labor is directed to develop a model form of benefit statement within one year after August 17, 2006, the date of enactment. With the exception of collectively bargained plans, the provision is effective for plan years beginning after 2006.

Notice of blackout periods.—In order to exempt one-person and one-partner plans from provisions of the Sarbanes Oxley Act of 2002 (P.L. 107-204) that require notification of blackout periods, the Pension Act amends the definition of a one-participant retirement plan (¶ 620). This provision defines such plans as covering, on the first day of the plan year, one individual (or one individual and his or her spouse) and the individual owns 100 percent of the plan sponsor. It is effective as if included in section 306 of the Sarbanes Oxley Act.

Distributions during working retirement.—Much has been written in recent years concerning the need to provide older workers with incentives to remain in the workforce. The Pension Act contains at least one solution to this problem, by allowing plans to make in-service distribution to employees who are age 62 or older for plan years beginning after 2006 without adversely effecting the plan's qualified status (¶ 920).

¶ 123 Effect on Defined Contribution Plan Participants

EGTRRA provisions made permanent.—Title IX of the Economic Growth and Tax Relief Reconciliation Act of 2001 (EGTRRA) imposed a sunset date of December 31, 2010, on many provisions of that legislation, including a myriad of provisions relating to IRAs and qualified plans. The Pension Protection Act of 2006 does away with that sunset provision as it applied to the provisions of subtitles A through F of EGTRRA (the pension and retirement plan provisions).

Accordingly, with respect to defined contribution plan participants, increases to both the Code Sec. 401(a)(17) considered compensation limit (currently indexed at $220,000) and the Code Sec. 415(c)(1)(A) defined contribution plan increase (indexed at $44,000 for 2006) will be extended past 2010. Also extended are the Code Sec. 402(g)(1) elective deferral limit ($15,000 for 2006) and the 100-percent of compensation limit under Code Secs. 415(c)(1)(B), 403(b), and 457(b)(2). Rules allowing for accelerated vesting of employer matching contributions will also be preserved. In addition, the catch-up rule allowing individuals who are age 50 or above to contribute additional amounts to a 401(k)plan, 403(b), tax-sheltered annuity, SEP, or SIMPLE will remain in place.

Of interest to plan participants contemplating rollovers, rules allowing the IRS some flexibility in waiving the 60-day requirement on rollovers from qualified plans and IRAs are also made permanent. However, it is important to note the IRS's attitude, as evidenced in numerous private letter rulings, not to grant waivers of the 60-day rule to taxpayers who use their retirement plan or IRA as a source of short-term cash for the purchase of real estate or other assets and then do not return the funds within the required time frame.

For retirement plan participants switching jobs, rollovers to and from Code Sec. 401, 403(b), and 457 plans will continue to be allowed.

With respect to retirement plan participants receiving or about to receive required distributions, provisions of EGTRRA required the IRS to revise the life expectancy tables used to compute required minimum distributions (RMDs) from qualified plans and IRAs to conform to more recent life expectancy data. Revision of the tables was done in conjunction with the adoption of revised regulations on RMDs (TD 8987). These rules remain in force. The aforementioned provisions and additional provisions of EGTRRA made permanent by the Pension Act are discussed at ¶1305.

Diversification rights.—In light of cases such as Enron, covered individuals, including participants and their beneficiaries, in certain defined contribution plans should benefit from the fact that the plans will be required to provide greater investment diversity (¶605). The provision governs plans that allow investment in publicly traded employer securities and requires that the plan offer not less than three investment options other than employer securities to which an individual may direct the proceeds from the divestment of employer securities. Except for participants who are 55 or older and have at least three years of service before the first plan year beginning after 2005, the new rules are phased in over a three-year period.

"One-participant retirement plans" and employee stock ownership plans (ESOPs) that do not allow elective deferrals, after-tax employee contributions, or matching contributions, are not covered by this provision. With the exception of certain collectively bargained plans and ESOPs, the new diversification rules are effective for plan years beginning after 2006.

Automatic enrollment.—Employees of companies that offer qualified cash or deferred arrangements (CODAs) (i.e., 401(k) plans) will benefit from provisions that encourage participation by giving nondiscrimination protection for automatic enrollment and contribution arrangements that meet certain requirements (¶1015). Features such as automatic enrollment and contribution are generally viewed as a way to increase employee participation in retirement plans and to boost the overall savings of Americans for retirement. However, even though provisions of the Economic Retirement Income Security Act of 1974 (ERISA) generally trump state law, controversy has arisen as to whether such arrangements are in conflict with certain state payroll withholding laws. The Pension Act puts any such controversy to rest by preempting state law and by providing nondiscrimination protection for automatic enrollment and contribution arrangements that meet certain requirements. In order to qualify for the automatic enrollment safe harbor, the arrangement must comply with specific rules on automatic deferral, matching or nonelective contributions, and notices.

With respect to automatic deferral, the requirements are met if, under the arrangement, employees that are eligible to participate in the enrollment arrangement are treated as having elected to have the employer make elective contributions equal to a qualified percentage of compensation. The qualified percentage must be at least three percent of compensation, with the minimum rising by one percent for each successive year the deemed election applies to the participant, up to six percent. However, the percentage cannot exceed 10 percent.

In the case of matching contributions, the requirement is satisfied if the employer makes matching contributions on behalf of each employee who is not a highly compensated employee of 100 percent of elective deferrals up to one percent of compensation, plus 50 percent of elective deferral between one percent and up to six percent of compensation An alternative is allowed if the employer is required to make contributions to a defined contribution plan of at least three percent of compensation of behalf of each nonhighly compensated employee.

The Pension Act also provides an exception to the top-heavy rules for these new automatic arrangements. In addition, under a vesting requirement, participants who have completed at least two years of service must be 100 percent vested with respect to matching or other employer contributions to their accounts under these arrangements.

Before the beginning of each plan year, participants must be given a notice explaining their rights under the automatic enrollment arrangement to elect *not* to have elective contributions made on their behalf or to elect to have contributions made in a different amount and how contributions made under the arrangement will be invested in the absence of any investment election by the employee. Employees must be given a reasonable period of time after receipt of such notice and before the first elective contribution is made to make the election with respect to contributions and investments. These changes are effective for plan years beginning after 2007, although the preemption of any conflicting state regulation is effective on August 17, 2006.

Faster vesting rules.—Accelerated vesting rules will now apply to all employer contributions (matching and nonelective) to a defined contribution plan effective, generally, for plan years beginning after 2006 (¶720). Delayed effective dates apply to collectively bargained plans and employee stock ownership plans that had loans outstanding on September 26, 2005, for the purpose of acquiring qualified employer securities.

Investment advice.—As a result of the Pension Act's creation of an exemption from the prohibited transaction rules, participants will have greater access to receive investment advice after 2006 (¶625). Under the exemption, a qualified "fiduciary adviser" may provide personally tailored investment advice to plan participants if certain conditions are met. In the case of employer-sponsored plans (as opposed to IRAs), the provision requires that the advice be provided by an adviser whose compensation does not vary with the investment option chosen or through a computer model that is certified by an independent third party.

Direct rollovers to Roth IRAs.—New rules would allow direct rollovers from an eligible retirement plan to a Roth IRA after December 31, 2007 (¶935). An eligible retirement plan would include a qualified plan, as well as plans governed by Code Sec. 403(b) and Code Sec. 457. For tax years prior to 2010, such rollovers are subject to the $100,000 adjusted gross income limitation.

Rollover by nonspouse beneficiaries.—In what could prove to be a very significant change, new rules effective for distributions after December 31, 2006, would allow a rollover from a qualified retirement plan to an inherited IRA for the benefit of persons other than the surviving spouse (¶945). The rollover must be accomplished via a trustee-to-trustee transfer and the minimum required distribution rules of Code Sec. 401(a)(9)(B) (rather than special rules applicable only to surviving spouses) must be followed. A trust maintained for the benefit of one or more designated beneficiaries shall be treated as a beneficiary.

Notice of freedom to divest employer securities.—Participants are entitled to a notice that describes the participant's right to divest employer securities and the importance of diversifying a retirement portfolio (¶610). The notice must be provided not later than 30 days before the first date the participant becomes eligible to divest. Within 180 days of August 17, 2006, the Treasury Secretary is directed to issue a model notice for this purpose. The new requirement is generally effective for plan years beginning after 2006.

Regulations to revise rules on financial hardship.—The Pension Act mandates that new rules be promulgated within 180 days of August 17, 2006, to modify the determination of whether a participant has suffered a hardship for purposes of Code Sec. 401(k)(2)(B)(i)(IV) if certain medical events occur involving the participant's spouse or dependent(s) (¶910).

Periodic pension benefit statements.—Under the Pension Act, participants in defined contribution plans must receive individual benefit notices at least annually (¶615). If the plan includes individual investment direction, these notices must be provided quarterly. The Secretary of Labor is directed to develop a model form of benefit statement within one year after August 17, 2006, the date of enactment. With the exception of collectively bargained plans, the provision is effective for plan years beginning after 2006.

Notice of blackout periods.—In order to exempt one-person and one-partner plans from provisions of the Sarbanes Oxley Act of 2002 (P.L. 107-204) that require notification of blackout periods, the 2006 Pension Act amends the definition of a one-participant retirement plan (¶620). This provision defines such plans as covering, on the first day of the plan year, one individual (or one individual and his or her spouse) and the individual owns 100 percent of the plan sponsor. It is effective as if included in section 306 of the Sarbanes Oxley Act.

¶124 Effect on Code Sec. 403 and 457 Plan Participants

Direct rollovers to Roth IRAs.—New rules would allow direct rollovers from an eligible retirement plan to a Roth IRA after December 31, 2007 (¶935). An eligible retirement plan would include a qualified plan, as well as plans governed by Code Sec. 403(b) and Code Sec. 457. For tax years prior to 2010, such rollovers are subject to the $100,000 adjusted gross income limitation.

Permissive service credits.—In an effort to increase the portability of state and local government retirement plans, the Pension Act clarifies that the definition of the term "permissive service credit" (Code Sec. 415(n)(3)) to allow participants to purchase credit for periods even if no service is performed, subject to limits on nonqualified service (¶745). Effectively, this means that participants can purchase permissive service credit that relates to benefits to which they would not otherwise be entitled under the plan. This provision is effective for contributions to purchase permissive service credits made after 1997. The limitation on nonqualified service credit does not apply to trustee-to-trustee transfers from a 403(b) or 457 plan to a governmental plan to purchase permissive service credit. The latter provision is effective for transfers after 2001.

Rollover of after-tax amounts to TSAs.—Effective for tax years beginning after 2006, after-tax amounts may be rolled over tax free from a qualified retirement plan to a tax-sheltered annuity (¶940).

Regulations to revise rules on financial hardship.—The Pension Act mandates that new rules be promulgated within 180 days of August 17, 2006 to modify the determination of whether a participant has suffered a hardship for purposes of Code Secs. 403(b)(11)(B) and 457(d)(1)(A)(iii) if certain medical events occur involving the participant's spouse or dependent(s) (¶910).

Treasury to issue regs on MRDs for governmental plans.—The Pension Act directs the IRS to develop regulations addressing how Code Sec. 457 governmental plans can meet the requirements of the minimum required distribution rules (Code Sec. 414(d)) through a good-faith interpretation of those rules (¶930).

No preclusion from participating after pre 1997 distribution.—An individual will not be precluded from participating in an eligible deferred compensation plan because he or she received a distribution under Code Sec. 457(e)(9) prior to 1997 (¶1075). The distribution must have been received after separation from service, within 60 days of an election to receive it, and not have exceeded $3,500.

EGTRRA changes made permanent.—Amendments made by the Economic Growth and Tax Relief Reconciliation Act of 2001 (EGTRRA) provided that individuals are no longer required to coordinate the maximum annual deferral amount for Code Sec. 457 plans with contributions made to other types of retirement plans. These amendments will remain in effect. Rules that permit early distributions from a Code Sec. 457 plan pursuant to a qualified domestic relations order (QDRO) will not sunset.

For retirement plan participants switching jobs, rollovers to and from Code Sec. 401, 403(b), and 457 plans will continue to be allowed. The aforementioned provisions and additional provisions of EGTRRA made permanent by the Pension Act are discussed at ¶1305.

¶125 Effect on SIMPLE Participants

EGTRRA changes made permanent.—The increase in the plan employee contribution limit to $10,000 for SIMPLE retirement plans will remain in force beyond 2010. Catch-up amounts for individuals who are age 50 or above will remain at 50 percent of the amounts applicable to other plans. These and additional provisions of the Economic Growth and Tax Relief Reconciliation Act of 2001 made permanent by the Pension Act are discussed at ¶1305.

¶126 Effect on IRA and Roth IRA Participants

EGTRRA provisions made permanent.—Title IX of the Economic Growth and Tax Relief Reconciliation Act of 2001 (EGTRRA) imposed a sunset date of December 31, 2010, on many provisions of that legislation, including a myriad of provisions relating to IRAs and qualified plans. The Pension Protection Act of 2006 does away with that sunset provision as it applied to the provisions of subtitles A through F of EGTRRA (the pension and retirement plan provisions).

Accordingly, with respect to IRA participants in particular, this means that the increased contribution limits, scheduled to rise to $5,000 in 2008 and indexed for inflation in $500 increments after that would remain in effect beyond 2010. What are referred to as "deemed IRAs," which were also introduced by EGTRRA, represent another item that will be preserved under the Pension Act.

In addition, this includes the catch-up rule allowing individuals who are age 50 or above to contribute additional amounts to an IRA ($1,000 in 2006 and thereafter).

In the case of IRA owners contemplating rollovers, rules allowing the IRS some flexibility in waiving the 60-day requirement on rollovers from qualified plans and IRAs would be made permanent. However, it is important to note the IRS's attitude, as evidenced in numerous private letter rulings, not to grant waivers of the 60-day rule to taxpayers who use their retirement plan or IRA as a source of short-term cash for the purchase of real estate or other assets and then do not return the funds within the required time frame.

With respect to IRA owners receiving or about to receive required distributions, provisions of EGTRRA required the IRS to revise the life expectancy tables used to compute required minimum distributions (RMDs) from qualified plans and IRAs to conform to more recent life expectancy data. Revision of the tables was done in conjunction with the adoption of revised regulations on RMDs (TD 8987). These rules remain in force. Revision of the tables was done in conjunction with the adoption of revised regulations on RMDs (TD 8987). These provisions and additional provisions of EGTRRA made permanent by the Pension Act are discussed at ¶1305.

Tax-free distributions from IRAs.—IRA owners who are at least 70½ will be allowed to make tax-free distributions of up to $100,000 per year from their IRAs to public charities under a provision of the Pension Act (¶1105). Such contributions will be treated as a qualified charitable distribution only if a deduction under Code Sec. 170 would otherwise be allowable. This treatment would be available for tax years 2006 and 2007.

This provision may prove to be particularly beneficial to qualifying IRA owners in certain states that do not allow an income tax deduction for charitable gifts. At least six states (Illinois, Indiana, Michigan, New Jersey, Ohio, and Massachusetts) do not allow such a deduction. However, of those states, Illinois does not tax retirement income and both New Jersey and Michigan provide an exclusion for retirement income, but also cap the amount excluded.

Credit for IRA payments in bankruptcy.—The Code Sec. 219(b)(5) deductible amount is increased to three times the normal amount ($3,000 rather than $1,000) for individuals making catch up contributions to compensate for the fact that their employer filed for bankruptcy protection and the employer (or another person) is subject to indictment or conviction from related business transactions (¶730). An eligible individual must have been a participant in the employer's 401(k) plan at least six month's prior to the filing of the bankruptcy case and the employer must have made matching contributions of at least 50 percent of the employee's contributions with the employer's stock.

Taxpayers using this provision are not allowed to also benefit from the otherwise available catch-up rules for persons who are age 50 or older. This provision would apply for tax years beginning in 2007 through 2009, but not after that.

Investment advice.—As a result of the Pension Act's creation of an exemption from the prohibited transaction rules, participants will have greater access to receive investment advice after 2006. (¶625). Under the exemption, a qualified "fiduciary adviser" may provide personally tailored investment advice to plan participants if certain conditions are met. The provision requires that the advice be provided by an advisor whose compensation does not vary with the investment option chosen or through a computer model that is certified by an independent third party. In the case of an IRA (as opposed to an employer-sponsored plan), the computer model exception will be available only if and when the Labor Department concludes that a viable computer model for this purpose exists. For purposes of this provision, references to IRAs include health savings accounts (HSAs), Archer medical savings accounts (MSAs), and Coverdell education savings accounts (ESAs).

Inflation adjustments.—Adjusted gross income limitations applicable to IRAs and Roth IRAs will be adjusted for inflation for tax years beginning after 2006 (¶1320).

¶127 Effect on Roth 401(k) and 403(b) Participants

EGTRRA changes made permanent.—Rules allowing after-tax contributions to Roth 401(k) and 403(b) plans, which just became effective in 2006, will be preserved under the Pension Protection Act of 2006. This treatment also applies to rules governing (1) annual limits on elective deferrals to Roth contribution accounts, (2) qualified (i.e., tax-free) distributions from such accounts, (3) rollovers from a designated Roth account to another designated Roth account or to a Roth IRA, and (4) reporting requirements for designated Roth contributions. Also retained is the modification of the governing safe-harbor regulations reducing from 12 months to six months the period during which an employee is prohibited from making elective and after-tax contributions following a hardship distribution. These provisions and additional provisions of the Economic Growth and Tax Relief Reconciliation Act made permanent by the Pension Act are discussed at ¶1305.

¶128 Effect on Spouses and Former Spouses

Domestic relations orders.—The Pension Protection Act of 2006 mandates that no later than one year after August 17, 2006, regulations are to be issued by the Secretary of Labor clarifying the treatment of domestic relations orders that are issued later than or are revisions to an existing domestic relations order or qualified domestic relations order (¶1025).

Railroad annuities.—A divorced spouse may be entitled to railroad retirement annuities independent of the entitlement of the former spouse employee as a result of the Pension Act's elimination of the requirement that an a railroad employee actually receive railroad retirement benefits (Tier I or Tier II) in order for a divorced spouse to be entitled to such benefits under a divorce decree ¶1030). In addition, railroad retirement annuities payable to a surviving former spouse under a court decree of divorce, annulment, or legal separation will not be terminated upon the death of the employee unless the termination was required by the terms of the decree (¶1035). Both of these provisions would take effect one year after August 17, 2006, the date of enactment.

Survivor annuity option.—The Pension Act creates a new requirement for defined benefit pension plans and money purchase plans to provide a qualified optional survivor annuity (¶1040). The term qualified optional survivor annuity is defined as (1) an annuity for the life of the participant with a survivor annuity for the life of the spouse that is equal to the applicable percentage of the amount of the annuity payable during the joint lives of the participant and the spouse, and (2) that is the actuarial equivalent to a single annuity for the life of the participant. For purposes of this definition, if the survivor annuity under the plan's qualified joint and survivor annuity is less than 75 percent of the annuity payable during the joint lives of the participant and spouse, the applicable percentage is 75 percent. If the survivor annuity under the plan's qualified joint and survivor annuity is greater than or equal to 75 percent of the annuity payable during the joint lives of the participant and spouse, the applicable percentage is 50 percent. This change is generally effective for plan years beginning after 2007, but a delayed effective date applies for collectively bargained plans.

¶129 Effect on Nonspouse Beneficiaries of Retirement Plans

Rollover by nonspouse beneficiary.—The ability to rollover a decedent's interest in a qualified plan, Code Sec. 403(b), or Code Sec. 457 plan, which was previously limited to surviving spouses, will be extended to nonspouse beneficiaries effective for distributions after December 31, 2006 (¶945). The rollover must be accomplished via a trustee-to-trustee transfer and the minimum distribution rules of Code Sec. 401(a)(9) (rather than special rules applicable only to surviving spouses) must be followed.

¶130 Effect on Active Duty Military Reserve Personnel

No 10-percent penalty.—The 10-percent penalty on early retirement withdrawals will not apply to distributions from an IRA, or attributable to elective contributions in a 401(k), 403(b), or similar plan, made to a member of the U.S. military reserves who is called to duty for a period in excess of 179 days during the period after September 11, 2001, and before December 31, 2007 (¶917). The safe harbor period for qualified distributions would extend from the date the individual was called up for active duty until such time as the active duty status ends. Recontributions will be allowed within a two-year period following the close of the active duty period, but in no event can the period end before two years from August 17, 2006, the date of enactment.

¶131 Effect on Public Safety Employees

10-percent penalty waived.—Certain distributions from a governmental plan (Code Sec. 414(d)) to fire, police, or emergency medical personnel would not be subject to the Code Sec. 72(t) 10-percent penalty on early withdrawals (¶915). Effective for distributions made after August 17, 2006, this provision provides relief for distributions from a governmental plan made to a qualified public safety employee who separates from service after age 50.

Funding health insurance premiums.—Public safety officers are allowed to exclude some of their retirement income to pay for accident, health or long-term care insurance premiums (¶825).

BENEFIT PLANS

¶135 Effect on Health Plans

Health plans get a boost from provisions making it easier to transfer excess benefits from defined benefit plans (¶805) and multiemployer plans (¶810). Health plans for associations are also promoted by the new deduction for reserves for health benefits (¶815).

¶136 Effect on 529 Plans

The tax breaks associated with 529 plans enacted as part of the 2001 Tax Act that were scheduled to expire after 2010 have been permanently extended, and the Treasury has been directed to adopt regulations to prevent abuse of 529 plans (¶1310).

¶137 Effect on Long-Term Care Insurance

The new law permits long-term care riders on annuity contracts and provides for special tax treatment for the long-term care component of a life insurance or annuity contract (¶820).

CHARITABLE ORGANIZATIONS AND DONORS

¶141 Overall Effect on Charitable Organizations and Donors

Although titled the Pension Protection Act of 2006, a lot of legislative time and effort was devoted to the treatment of charitable organizations and, to a lesser extent, charitable donors. However, as significant as what made it into the charitable provisions of the Pension Act may be what did not, in particular a provision that would have allowed a charitable deduction for nonitemizers. Touted by a number of prominent legislators, as well as the President's Advisory Panel on Tax Reform, various iterations of this provision have been talked about for several years. In the final analysis, however, the estimated revenue cost of such a measure and the inability to agree on the exact parameters of its allowance apparently doomed its inclusion during the already contentious negotiations surrounding the Pension Act. It may, of course, resurface at a later date in another legislative vehicle.

With respect to the charitable provisions that survived in the Pension Act, there is at least one that will bring a smile to the faces of certain IRA owners with charitable intent. That provisions will allow tax-free donations of up to $100,000 directly from an IRA if the owner is 70½ or older. Donors, particularly farmers and ranchers, of certain qualified conservation real property will benefit from increased limitations for 2006 and 2007 (¶1125). Also good news is that the expansion of the charitable deduction for food and book inventories enacted as part of the response to last year's hurricanes is extended through 2007 (¶1140 and ¶1145). On the other hand, the bulk of the charitable provisions in the Pension Act could most appropriately be dubbed as "loophole closers" or outright revenue raisers.

Among the more egregious of the purported charitable scams targeted by the Pension Act is one involving charitable donations of taxidermy property. No longer will would-be big game hunters be allowed to write off their travel expenses as part of the deductible cost of a charitable donation of a stuffed and mounted animal (¶1120). More subtle are new restrictions on contributions of qualified conservation easements in registered historic districts (¶1130), new rules on gifts of fractional interests in tangible personal property (¶1115), and the required basis adjustment for charitable donations by an S corporation (¶1135).

Additional provisions impose new recordkeeping requirements for cash donations, as well as codifying rules for qualified appraisals and appraisers. A more detailed discussion of these provisions, as well as those effecting specific charitable entities such as donor advised funds, private foundations, and supporting organizations, can be found in the following numbered paragraphs.

¶142 Effect on Donors and Split-Interest Trusts

Tax-free distributions from IRAs.—IRA owners who are at least 70½ will be allowed to make tax-free distributions of up to $100,000 per year from their IRAs to public charities under a provision of the Pension Protection Act of 2006 (¶1105). Such contributions will be treated as a qualified charitable distribution only if a deduction under Code Sec. 170 would otherwise be allowable. This treatment would be available for tax years 2006 and 2007.

This provision may prove to be particularly beneficial to qualifying IRA owners in certain states that do not allow an income tax deduction for charitable gifts. At least six states (Illinois, Indiana, Michigan, New Jersey, Ohio, and Massachusetts) do not allow such a deduction. However, of those states, Illinois does not tax retirement income and both New Jersey and Michigan provide an exclusion for retirement income, but also cap the amount excluded.

New reporting requirements for split-interest trusts.—Effective for tax years beginning after 2006, new rules require that split interest trusts that would otherwise not be required to file a return under Code Sec. 6034(a), but that claim a deduction under Code Sec. 642(c) must furnish information concerning the amount of the deduction taken that year, plus information about amounts paid out and deductions taken in prior years, as well as data on the total income and expenses of the trust and its net worth as of the beginning of the year (¶1190). Increased penalties are also imposed for failure to comply with the filing rules of Code Sec. 6652(c)(2).

Charitable deductions of food inventories.—The expansion of the charitable deduction for contributions of food items by non C corporations, which was made as part of the Katrina Emergency Tax Relief Act of 2005 (P.L. 109-73) and which expired at the end of 2005, is extended through 2007 (¶1140).

Charitable contributions of book inventories.—Similarly, the modification to the provision dealing with charitable donations of books to public schools by corporations (other than S corporations) is also extended through 2007 (¶1145).

Basis adjustment to S corporation stock.—In the case of a charitable contribution of property by an S corporation in tax years 2006 and 2007, the Code Sec. 1367(a) decrease in the basis of a shareholder's S corporation's stock will be equal to the shareholder's pro rata share of the adjusted basis in the donated property (¶1135).

Tax treatment of payments to controlling organizations.—In an effort to curb the purported practice of disguising unrelated business income paid to a tax-exempt organization from a controlled subsidiary as rent, rental payments to controlling organizations will be exempt from tax only if (1) they are reflective of fair market value and (2) made under an arrangement that predates the enactment of the Pension Act (¶1210). Rental payments that exceed fair market value would be subject to a 20-percent penalty over and above the normal tax due. The provision is effective for payments accrued or received during 2006 and 2007.

Conservation contributions of capital gain real property.—Donors of qualified conservation easements will be entitled to new write-off limitations for 2006 and 2007. As opposed to the prior law limit of 30 percent of adjusted gross income (AGI), farmers and ranchers will be allowed to deduct 100 percent of AGI, while all other taxpayers will be limited to 50 percent (¶1125). The amounts may be deducted over a 15-year period.

Contributions of qualified easements clarified.—The Pension Act imposes new restrictions on contributions of qualified conservation easements in registered historic districts. Specifically, the easement must cover the entire exterior of the structure, a written agreement must be entered into, and a qualified appraisal, photos, and a description of all restrictions on development must accompany the taxpayer's return claiming the deduction (¶1130). A $500 filing fee is required for taxpayers seeking a deduction in excess of $10,000 for such contributions. Finally, the combined use of an easement contribution and the rehabilitation credit will result in a reduction in the charitable deduction.

Taxidermy property.—Following press accounts of abusive transactions involving taxidermy property, the Pension Act restricts a charitable deduction for contributions of such property after July 25, 2006, to the taxpayer's direct cost (i.e., the cost of preparing, stuffing, and mounting)(¶1120).

Tax recapture for property not used for exempt purpose.—If tangible personal property is contributed after September 1, 2006, for an exempt use, but that use is not fulfilled, a recapture of the charitable deduction will occur. Revised reporting requirements and a $10,000 fine for fraudulent identification of exempt use property are also added (¶1150).

Deduction for contributions of food and household goods limited.—Under new rules, a charitable deduction for contributions of clothing or household items after August 17, 2006 will not be allowed unless the item is in "good used condition or better." In addition, the IRS may deny a deduction for contributions of clothing or household items having minimal monetary value (¶1110). An exception is provided for a contribution of a single item of clothing or household goods that is not in good used condition, but for which a deduction of more than $500 is claimed and a qualified appraisal accompanies the taxpayer's return.

New recordkeeping requirements for certain contributions.—For any cash gift made in tax years beginning after August 17, 2006, no charitable deduction shall be allowed unless the donor retains a bank record or a written communication from the donee showing the name of the donee organization, the date of the contribution, and the amount (¶1185).

Fractional interests in tangible personal property.—The Pension Act also impacts gifts of fractional interests in tangible personal property made after August 17, 2006 (¶1115). The new rule provides, generally, that no income, or gift tax charitable deduction will be allowed for a contribution of an undivided portion of a taxpayer's entire interest in tangible personal property unless, immediately before the contribution, all interest in the property is held by (1) the taxpayer, or the (2) taxpayer and the donee. Accordingly, the deduction will be denied if a person other than the taxpayer or the donee holds an interest in the property. The IRS is granted the authority to provide regulations governing exceptions for cases in which all the persons who hold an interest in the property make proportionate contributions of an undivided portion of the entire interest such persons hold.

The Pension Act also imposes recapture of the deduction unless the donor completes the transfer of his or her remaining interest in the property within ten years of the date of the initial contribution, or before the donor's death, whichever comes first. In addition, recapture would occur if the donee fails to take substantial physical possession of the property or fails to use the property in a manner related to the donee's exempt purpose within ten years of the date of the initial contribution, or before the donor's death, whichever is earlier.

Finally, the Pension Act imposes a consistent valuation standard on subsequent fractional gifts. Valuation of subsequent gifts would based on the *lesser of* the fair market value of the property at the time of the initial contribution or as of the subsequent contribution.

Tougher rules for overvaluations.—For purposes of the income tax, as well as estate and gift taxes, the thresholds for substantial and gross valuation misstatements are lowered and the reasonable cause exception for gross valuation misstatements involving charitable deduction property is eliminated (¶ 1345). Although generally effective for returns filed after August 17, 2006, the provision also applies to returns filed after July 25, 2006, involving contributions of qualified real property interest restrictions on the exterior of a qualified historic structure.

Appraisals and appraisers subject to scrutiny.—A new provision imposing a penalty on appraisers whose appraisals result in substantial valuation misstatements is added. The penalty can reach as high as 125 percent of the gross income received for the appraisal. (¶ 1350). Definitions of a qualified appraisal and appraisers are also codified (¶ 1355).

¶ 143 Effect on Exempt Organizations Generally

Besides provisions concentrating on donor advised funds and supporting organizations, discussed separately, the following items should be noted by charitable organizations generally.

Reporting requirements on acquisition of interests in insurance policies.—In response to reports of the involvement by tax-exempt organizations in what some commentators have described as tax shelters involving the ownership of life insurance contracts, the Pension Protection Act of 2006 requires that tax-exempt organizations report on such transactions during a two-year period following August 17, 2006 (¶ 1285). The provision is aimed at the direct or indirect acquisition of any applicable insurance contract that is "part of a structured transaction involving a pool of such contracts." The term "applicable life insurance contract" includes any life insurance, annuity, or endowment contract, but does not include those in which all persons holding an interest in the contract have an insurable interest in the insured party independent of that of the exempt organization and the organization's interest is solely as beneficiary. Also excluded from the definition would be a case in which the sole interest in the contract of each person other than the exempt organization is held either (1) as a beneficiary of a trust holding an interest in the contract (but only if the person's designation as beneficiary was on a purely gratuitous basis), or (2) as a trustee who holds an interest in the contract in a fiduciary capacity solely for the benefit of the exempt organization. In addition, the Pension Act creates a new penalty for failure to report on the acquisition of such insurance contracts and mandates that the Treasury prepare a report on the subject for both the House Ways and Means

Committee and the Senate Finance Committee within 30 months of August 17, 2006, the date of enactment.

Excise penalty tax increase.—Excise taxes imposed on self dealing (Code Sec. 4941), excess business holdings (Code Sec. 4943), investments jeopardizing an exempt organization's charitable purpose (Code Sec. 4944), and taxable expenditures (Code Sec. 4945) are doubled for tax years beginning after August 17, 2006 (¶1245).

New standards for credit counseling organizations.—In another example of a provision crafted in response to reports of abusive practices, credit counseling organizations will face tougher rules that are phased in over a four-year period (¶1215). Pursuant to these changes, organizations that are exempt under Code Sec. 501(c)(3) must not receive more than 50 percent of their revenues from debt management plan services, which include services related to the repayment, consolidation, or restructuring of a consumer's debt and the negotiation of lower interest rates and fees. Code Sec. 501(c)(4) organizations must apply to the IRS for exemption. The new rules are generally effective for tax years beginning after August 17, 2006, but an exception for certain existing organizations provides a one-year delay.

Tax base for private foundation net investment income expanded.—Gross investment income will now include capital gains (except for gains from like-kind exchanges), notional principal contracts, annuities, and substantially similar investment income (¶1250).

Convention or association of churches defined.—Under a new definition, any organization that is otherwise a convention or association of churches will not fail to qualify as such merely because the membership of the organization includes individuals as well as churches or because individuals have voting rights in the organization (¶1205).

Notification for entities not required to file.—New rules under Code Sec. 6033 create additional notification requirements for exempt organizations that are not currently required to file returns because its gross receipts fall below the statutory threshold. The notice must include the legal name of the organization and any name under which it operates, the organization's mailing address, taxpayer identification number, the name and address of its principal officer, and evidence of the continuing basis for the organization's exemption from the filing requirements. Loss of exempt status is imposed for failure to file a return or notice (¶1260).

Disclosure to state officials.—In cases in which the IRS has denied or revoked the tax-exempt status of an organization, as well in certain other instances, the IRS may, upon written request, share that information with state officials, such as the state attorney general or tax officer (¶1280). This provision will be effective for requests made on or after August 17, 2006.

Public disclosure of information concerning unrelated business income.—Form 990-T, Exempt Organization Business Income Tax Return, filed by Code Sec. 501(c)(3) organizations will be available publicly with respect to returns filed after August 17, 2006 (¶1275).

Study of donor advised funds and supporting organizations.—The Pension Act directs the Treasury to undertake a study of the organization and operation of donor advised funds and supporting organizations and to report its findings to both the House Ways and Means Committee and the Senate Finance Committee within one year after August 17, 2006, the date of enactment (¶1290). The report is to consider, among other things, the appropriateness of the use of contributed assets, the retention of advisory privileges by a donor, and whether donor advised funds should be required to distribute a specified amount for charitable purposes.

Excise tax exemption for blood collection organizations.—Effective beginning in 2007, qualified blood collector organizations will be exempt from various excise taxes ordinarily imposed on the purchase of items such as fuel, tires, and vaccines, if the items used are for the exclusive use of the organization in the distribution or collection of blood (¶1255).

Revocation of multiemployer status.—Tax exempt employers can revoke the election of multiemployer plan status (¶325).

¶144 Effect on Donor Advised Funds

Definition and taxable distributions.—Donor advised funds are yet another subject of scrutiny in the Pension Protection Act of 2006. The Pension Act defines a donor advised fund as an account or fund that is (1) separately identified by reference to contributions by a donor or donors, (2) owned and controlled by a sponsoring organization, and (3) with respect to which the donor (or persons appointed by the donor) reasonably expects to have advisory privileges as to the distribution of investments of the account because of his or her status as donor. A qualified sponsoring organization would be an organization listed in Code Sec. 170(c), but not a government entity or a private foundation, and that maintains one or more donor advised funds. The term would not include a fund or bank account that makes distributions to a single organizations entity or governmental entity. The Joint Committee on Taxation Technical Explanation of the Pension Protection Act of 2006 (JCX-38-06) cites the example of a donor who contributes to a university in order to establish a fund named after him that exclusively supports the activities of the university as not being a donor advised fund even if he had advisory privileges over the distribution or investment of the fund.

Distributions from donor advised funds that are for noncharitable purposes are taxable as are certain transactions between a donor advised fund and its donors, donor advisors, or related persons (¶1160).

Prohibited benefits.—Any benefits flowing to a donor, donor advisor, or related persons that are more than incidental would be subject to a tax of 125 percent of the benefit (¶1165). With respect to this provision, the Joint Committee on Taxation Technical Explanation of the Pension Protection Act of 2006 (JCX-38-06) cites as an example of an incidental benefit, a situation in which a distribution from a donor's donor advised fund is made to the Girl Scouts of America and the donor's daughter is a member of the local organization. A separate tax (10 percent of the benefit) is imposed on the fund's management for a violation of this provision. Joint and several liability for the tax is imposed.

Excess benefit transactions.—In the case of a donor advised fund, any grant, loan, compensation, or other similar payment from the fund to a disqualified person is considered an excess benefit transaction after August 17, 2006 (¶1170). For purposes of this provision, the term disqualified persons now includes donors, donor advisors, and investment advisors, plus related parties, and entities that such disqualified persons own more than a 35-percent interest in.

Excess business holdings.—For tax years beginning after August 17, 2006, the tax on excess business holdings (Code Sec. 4943) is applied to donor advised funds (¶1175) However, transition rules are available. For purposes of this provision, the term disqualified persons now includes donors, donor advisors, related parties, and entities that such disqualified persons own more than a 35-percent interest in.

Charitable deduction.—Limitations on the income tax deductibility of contributions to donor advised funds are added by the Pension Act (¶1180). Specifically, a contribution to a sponsoring organization for maintenance in a donor advised fund is not deductible for income tax purposes if the sponsoring organization is a veterans organization, a fraternal society, or a cemetery company. In addition, no deduction will be allowed for such contributions if the supporting organization is a Type III supporting organization (other than one that is functionally integrated, Code Sec. 4943(f)(5)(B)). With the exception of the limitation above applicable to cemetery companies, these new rules on deductibility also apply for purposes of federal estate (Code Sec. 2055) and gift taxes (Code Sec. 2522).

The Pension Act also imposes new substantiation rules for contributions to donor advised funds. In addition to satisfying the present-law substantiation requirements, a donor must obtain, with respect to each charitable contribution to a donor advised fund, a contemporaneous written acknowledgment from the sponsoring organization providing that the sponsoring organization has exclusive legal control over the assets contributed. These provisions are effective with respect to contributions made after 180 days following August 17, 2006, the date of enactment.

Returns of sponsoring organizations.—New return requirements are applicable to sponsoring organizations for tax years ending after August 17, 2006 (¶1265). Sponsoring organizations are now required to include (1) the total number of donor advised funds owned by the organization, (2) the aggregate value of assets held in these funds as of the end of the tax year, and (3) the aggregate contribution to and grants from such funds during the tax year.

Study of donor advised funds and supporting organizations.—The Pension Act directs the Treasury to undertake a study of the organization and operation of donor advised funds and supporting organizations and to report its findings to both the House Ways and Means Committee and the Senate Finance Committee within one year after August 17, 2006, the date of enactment (¶1290). The report is to consider, among other things, the appropriateness of the use of contributed assets, the retention of advisory privileges by a donor, and whether donor advised funds should be required to distribute a specified amount for charitable purposes.

¶145 Effect on Supporting Organizations

Requirements.—Several new rules apply to supporting organizations pursuant to provisions of the Pension Protection Act of 2006 (¶1225). For example, after August 17, 2006, a Type III supporting organization (one operated in connection with one or more publicly supported organizations) must inform organizations that it supports as per IRS regulations. A charitable trust that is a Type III supporting organization must also comply with further requirements to establish its responsiveness to the needs of the supported organization, however, existing trusts are given an extended effective date to comply.

In addition, a Type III supporting organization cannot support a foreign organization not organized in the United States, although a transitional rule gives those with existing arrangements until the beginning of the third tax year after August 17, 2006 to comply. Type I (those that are operated, supervised, or controlled by one or more publicly supported organizations) and Type III supporting organizations will be treated as private foundations if they accept gifts from a person (other than a public charity, not a supporting organization) who controls, directly or indirectly, the governing body of a supported organization, or a member of that person's family, or an entity that such disqualified persons own more than a 35-percent interest in.

Payout regulations.—The Pension Act also directs the Secretary of the Treasury to promulgate new regulations governing payments required by Type III supporting organizations that are not functionally integrated (¶1225). The regulations must require these organizations to make distributions of a percentage of income or assets to supported organizations to ensure that a significant amount is paid to those organizations.

Excess benefit transactions.—In the case of a supporting organization, any grant, loan, compensation, or other similar payment from the organization to a disqualified person is considered an excess benefit transaction for transactions occurring after July 25, 2006 (¶1230). For purposes of this provision, the term disqualified persons now includes a substantial contributor to the organization, a member of the substantial contributor's family, and entities that such disqualified persons own more than a 35-percent interest in. A substantial contributor includes any person who contributed or bequeathed an aggregate amount of more than $5,000 to the organization, if that amount is more than two percent of the total contributions and bequests received by the organization before the close of the tax year, and includes, in the case of a trust, the creator of the trust. However, the term does not include organizations described in Code Sec. 509(a) (1), (2), or (4). Finally, in another change that is effective for transactions occurring after August 17, 2006, a disqualified person with respect to a supporting organization is considered to be a disqualified person with respect to the supported organization as well.

Excess business holdings.—For tax years beginning after August 17, 2006, the tax on excess business holdings (Code Sec. 4943) is applied to Type III supporting organizations other than those that are functionally integrated (¶1235). A transition rule exempts holdings of a Type III supporting organization in any business enterprise if, as of November 18, 2005 and thereafter, the assets were held by a state attorney general or other official for the benefit of the community. Another exception allows the IRS to exempt excess business holdings of an organization if it is determined "that such holdings are consistent with the purpose or function constituting the basis for its exemption under section 501." Further transitional rules, similar to those found in Code Sec. 4943(c)(4)—(6), allow for the phased disposal of present holdings.

For purposes of this provision, the term disqualified persons now includes substantial contributors, related parties, and entities that such disqualified persons own more than a 35-percent interest in. Type II supporting organizations are also impacted by this provisions in that the excess business holding rules will apply to them if such organization accepts any gift or contribution from a person (other than a public charity, but not a supporting organization) with direct or indirect control over the governing body of an organization supported by the supporting organization, a member of that person's family, or a 35-percent controlled entity.

Amounts paid by private foundations.—Amounts paid by a nonoperating private foundation to a Type III supporting organization that is not a functionally integrated Type III supporting organization or to any other supporting organization will not be considered a qualifying distribution if a disqualified person directly or indirectly controls the supporting organization or an organization supported by such organization. An amount not considered a qualifying distribution would be deemed a taxable expenditure under Code Sec. 4945. This provision is effective for distributions made after August 17, 2006 (¶1240).

Returns of supporting organizations.—New return requirements apply to supporting organizations for tax years ending after August 17, 2006 (¶1270). A supporting organization must now include information concerning the organizations it provides support to and whether it meets the new definitional requirements of Code Sec. 509(a)(3)(B), as amended by the Pension Act, as well as certifying that it is not controlled directly or indirectly by one or more disqualified persons as per Code Sec. 509(a)(3)(C).

Study of donor advised funds and supporting organizations.—The Pension Act directs the Treasury to undertake a study of the organization and operation of donor advised funds and supporting organizations and to report its findings to both the House Ways and Means Committee and the Senate Finance Committee within one year after August 17, 2006, the date of enactment (¶1290). The report is to consider, among other things, the appropriateness of the use of contributed assets, the retention of advisory privileges by a donor, and whether donor advised funds should be required to distribute a specified amount for charitable purposes.

¶146 Effect on Associations

Associations are permitted a deduction to accumulate reserves for medical benefits (¶815).

ENTITIES

¶147 Overall Effect on Entities

Effect on entities generally.—Like individuals, entities that offer retirement or benefit plans will be generally affected by many of the provisions of this act. The effect of those changes is discussed under the particular type of retirement or benefit plan involved. Many provisions also have an impact on particular types of entities.

¶148 Effect on S Corporations

Charitable contributions of property and allocations of basis.—In the case of a charitable contribution of property by an S corporation in tax years 2006 and 2007, the Code Sec. 1367(a) decrease in the basis of a shareholder's S corporation's stock will be equal to the shareholder's pro rata share of the adjusted basis in the donated property (¶1135).

Plan loans.—The provision in the 2001 Tax Act permitting plan loans for S corporation owners has been made permanent (¶1305).

¶149 Effect on Partnerships

Plan loans.—The provision in the 2001 Tax Act permitting plan loans to partners has been made permanent (¶1305).

¶150 Effect on Cooperatives

Multiemployer plans.—The new single-employer defined benefit plan rules will not apply to certain multiemployer plans maintained by rural cooperatives (¶240).

BUSINESS

¶151 Overall Effect on Business and Employers

Obviously, businesses, both big and small, will be effected by various changes made by the Pension Protection Act of 2006. Most of these changes are discussed elsewhere in the context of specific types of retirement plans. In addition, the Pension Act's impact on specific industries is also discussed separately. The new law also directly targets the following practices.

Corporate owned life insurance.—Under the new law, businesses are required to treat certain proceeds from corporate-owned life insurance (COLI) as income unless specific conditions are met (¶1330).

Criminal penalties increased for interference with ERISA rights.—The Pension Act substantially increases the criminal penalty for coercively interfering with a plan participant's or beneficiary's protected rights under ERISA or under an ERISA plan. A person who improperly interferes with another's protected rights under ERISA is subject to a fine of $100,000 and up to 10 years in prison (¶650).

¶152 Effect on Small Business

Effect on small business generally.—In a continuing effort to make retirement plans more attractive for small business, employers with 500 or fewer employees are permitted to combine a defined benefit and 401(k) plan in one plan document (¶ 1020). Annual reporting is eliminated for a one-participant retirement plan with plan assets of $250,000 or less and is to be simplified for retirement plans with less than 25 participants (¶ 1080). For employers with 25 or fewer employees, there is a new cap on variable rate premiums to fund the PBGC (¶ 510). The credit for plan start-up expenses from the 2001 Tax Act has been permanently extended (¶ 1305).

Combined Defined Benefit and Qualified CODAs.—Under new rules in the Pension Protection Act of 2006, "small employers" will be allowed to create an eligible combined defined benefit and cash or deferred arrangement (CODA) (i.e., 401(k)plans). For purposes of this provision, a small employer is one with 500 or fewer employees. Although such an arrangement would be treated as one plan requiring one Form 5500 and one summary annual report, applicable rules governing defined benefit and defined contribution plans would be applied separately to the components of the plan (¶ 1020). For example, the Code Sec. 415 limits would be applied separately to contributions under the 401(k) plan and to benefits under the defined benefit plan. both of which are part of the combined plan. In addition, all contributions, benefits, and other rights and features provided under a defined contribution or defined benefit plan that is part of a combined plan, must be provided uniformly to all participants. The provision is effective for plan years beginning after 2009.

¶153 Effect on Employers of Domestic Workers

EGTRRA provision made permanent.—EGTRRA removed the 10-percent penalty on nondeductible contributions to qualified retirement plans for domestic workers (although the contributions themselves are still nondeductible). This treatment will remain in effect. This provision and additional provisions of the Economic Growth and Tax Relief Reconciliation Act of 2001 made permanent by the Pension Act are discussed at ¶ 1305).

SPECIFIC INDUSTRIES

¶155 Effect on the Airline Industry

Airlines.—Relaxed defined benefit plan funding rules have been provided for the airline industry, with some companies singled out for special treatment (¶ 245).

Airline caterers.—Relaxed defined benefit plan funding rules have also been provided for airline catering companies (¶ 245)

¶156 Effect on Government Defense Contractors

Relaxed defined benefit plan funding rules have also been included in the legislation for government defense contractors (¶ 240).

¶157 Effect on Interstate Bus Company

Revisions have been made to a special funding rule for an interstate bus company (¶230).

¶158 Effect on the Fishing Industry

A multiemployer plan involved in the fishing industry has been granted a possible exemption from the excise tax on its accumulated funding deficiency if it adopts a rehabilitation plan (¶310).

¶159 Effect on Broker-Dealers

Certain bonding requirements applicable to broker-dealers have been relaxed (¶630).

¶160 Effect on Mining and Miners

The new legislation eliminates the limit on distributions from Black Lung Disease Trusts for retiree health (¶1220).

¶161 Effect on Alaskan Hydroelectric Facilities

Certain bond financing exceptions are provided for a couple of Alaskan hydroelectric facilities (¶1340).

¶162 Effect on Plan Fiduciaries and Parties in Interest

Several provisions in the new law will have an impact on plan fiduciaries and parties in interest. These include the relaxation of rules with respect to investment advice (¶625), the revisions in the prohibited transaction rules (¶630), and the new rules for corrections of prohibited transactions (¶635).

¶163 Effect on Investment Advisers

The new rules with respect to investment advice will also have an impact on investment advisors (¶625).

¶164 Effect on Farmers and Ranchers

Farmers and ranchers will be allowed to deduct qualified conservation easements up to 100 percent of adjusted gross income (¶1125).

INDIVIDUALS GENERALLY

¶171 Overall Effect on Individuals

Effect on individuals generally.—Individuals as participants in and beneficiaries of various forms of retirement and benefit plans are affected by most of the provisions of this new tax law. Such participants and beneficiaries will find a discussion of how these tax law changes have impacted them under the discussion of the particular retirement or benefit plan of which they are a participant or beneficiary. In addition to those changes, the following provisions will have a direct impact on individuals.

Indexing of Saver's Credit.—The adjusted gross income limits to be eligible for the Saver's Credit are adjusted for inflation for tax years after 2006 (¶1320).

Indexing of IRA income limits.—The adjusted gross income limits for IRA and Roth IRA contributions are also adjusted for inflation after 2006 (¶1320).

Limit on exclusion for death benefit for company-owned life insurance.—New limits are placed on the ability of individuals to exclude from tax the payments of company-owned life insurance benefits. There are also various notice, consent and reporting requirements (¶1330).

Exclusion for long-term care charges under life insurance and life annuities.—The new act permits long-term care riders on annuity contracts and allows the cash value of such riders in an annuity contract or a life insurance contract to be paid as a long-term care benefit, allowing a reduction in basis for the long-term care payments, and permitting tax-free transfers between annuity contracts, whether or not they have a long-term care rider (¶820).

Permanent extension of 529 plan tax provisions.—Among the permanent extensions of tax provisions from the 2001 Tax Act are permanent extensions of the tax provisions of Code Sec. 529 that were enacted as part of the 2001 Tax Act, including the provision for tax-free distributions (¶1310). The legislation also provides for regulations to prevent abuse.

Joint and survivor annuities.—The law extends the date by which elections of joint and survivor annuities must be made (¶925).

Investment advice.—The law permits participants to be provided with investment advice under certain conditions (¶625).

SPECIFIC CATEGORIES OF INDIVIDUALS

¶175 Effect on Low and Moderate Income Savers

Saver's credit preserved.—Sometimes referred to as the "saver's credit," the Code Sec. 25B credit for contributions or deferrals to retirement savings accounts is extended beyond the December 31, 2006 termination date set by the Economic Growth and Tax Relief Reconciliation Act of 2001 (EGTRRA). The credit is allowed for joint filers with adjusted gross incomes of $50,000 or less ($25,000 for single individuals). This and other provisions of EGTRRA made permanent by the Pension Protection Act of 2006 are discussed at ¶1305.

Inflation adjustments.—Adjusted gross income limitations applicable to the saver's credit will be adjusted for inflation for tax years beginning after 2006 (¶1320).

¶176 Effect on Highly Compensated Individuals

EGTRRA provisions made permanent.—The amendments made to the top-heavy rules by the Economic Growth and Tax Relief Reconciliation Act of 2001 (EGTRRA) are made permanent. These changes include:

- modification of the definition of a top-heavy plan to include a safe harbor for plans under the Code Sec. 401(k)(12) elective deferral and 401(m)(11) matching contribution requirements;
- modification of the definition of a key employee to include (1) officers with compensation of more than $130,000 (adjusted to $140,000 for 2006), (2) five-percent owners, or (3) one-percent owners with compensation in excess of $150,000;
- inclusion of matching contributions in determining whether the minimum benefit requirements have been met for a defined contribution plan; and
- elimination of the five-year look back period for calculating a participant's accrued benefit or account balance in favor of a one-year period ending on the determination date.

These provisions and other provisions of EGTRRA made permanent by the Pension Protection Act of 2006 are discussed at ¶1305.

¶177 Effect on Older Workers

Status of hybrid plans clarified.—The Pension Protection Act of 2006 clarifies the legal status of so-called hybrid plans, which had been confused because of adverse court decisions against IBM and others alleging that the plans were age discriminatory (¶1005). However, it should be noted that the law change is prospective in nature.

Distributions during working retirement.—In an effort to provide older workers with incentives to remain in the workforce the Pension Act allows plans to make in-service distribution to employees who are age 62 or older for plan years beginning after 2006 without adversely effecting the plan's qualified status (¶ 920).

Tax-free distributions from IRAs.—IRA owners who are at least 70½ will be allowed to make tax-free distributions of up to $100,000 per year from their IRAs to public charities under a provision of the Pension Act (¶ 1105). Such contributions will be treated as a qualified charitable distribution only if a deduction under Code Sec. 170 would otherwise be allowable. This treatment would be available for tax years 2006 and 2007.

Catch-up made permanent.—In addition, the catch-up rule allowing individuals who are age 50 or above to contribute additional amounts to a 401(k)plan, 403(b), tax-sheltered annuity, SEP, or SIMPLE will remain in place (¶ 1305).

¶ 178 Effect on Individuals Receiving Income Tax Refunds

Refunds can be directed to IRA.—A taxpayer will be allowed to direct federal income tax returns to his or her IRA (¶ 725). For tax years beginning after 2006, the IRS will make a form available for this purpose. This provision, however, does not alter the deadline for contributing to and receiving a deduction for a contribution to an IRA.

¶ 179 Effect on Individuals Receiving Unemployment Compensation

No reduction for rollovers.—Effective for unemployment compensation in weeks beginning on or after August 17, 2006, unemployment compensation will not be reduced for any pension or retirement pay that is not includible in gross income because it is part of a rollover distribution (¶ 1325).

¶ 180 Effect on Test Room Supervisors and Proctors

Treated as independent contractors.—Test room supervisors and proctors who assist in the administration of college entrance and placement exams will be treated as independent contractors with respect to payment for services performed after 2006 (¶ 1335).

¶ 181 Effect on Self-Employed Persons

Election out of SECA.—Self employed persons who have elected out of the self-employment system (SECA) because of religious convictions may continue to treat their exempt self-employment income as compensation from a trade or business for purposes of establishing and contributing to a qualified retirement plan or IRA. This and other provisions of the Economic Growth and Tax Relief Reconciliation Act of 2001 are discussed at ¶1305.

THE TAX COURT

¶185 Effect on Tax Court Judges and Persons Dealing With the Court

COLAs for judge's survivor annuities.—The Pension Protection Act of 2006 provides that, annuities paid to the survivors of Tax Court judges will be subject to the same cost of living adjustment accorded to other federal employees under the Civil Service Retirement System (¶1430). This means that future increases will be based on the price index rather than on salaries. The provision applies to increases made under the Civil Service Retirement System that take effect after August 17, 2006.

Cost of life insurance for judges over 65.—Increases in the employee cost of group life insurance for Tax Court judges will be paid by the Tax Court. The provision is effective on August 17, 2006 (¶1435).

Participation in Thrift Savings Plan.—Effective for the next enrollment period beginning after August 17, 2006, Tax Court judges will be allowed to participate in the Thrift Savings Plan (TSP) (¶1440). The TSP is a defined contribution retirement savings plan for civilian employees of the U. S. government and members of the uniformed services. The Federal Retirement Thrift Investment Board administers the TSP.

Surviving spouses and children of special trial judges to get annuities.—A special trial judge of the Tax Court (Code Sec. 7443A) will now be able to elect to have his or her surviving spouse and dependent children receive a survivor's annuity under Code Sec. 7448 (¶1445). Prior to the Pension Act, such annuities were available only to the survivors of regular Tax Court judges.

Tax Court jurisdiction over collection due process cases.—The Pension Act provides that all appeals of collection due process determinations are to be made to the Tax Court (¶1405). Previously, for cases in which the underlying tax liability was related to something other than the income tax or another tax the court had jurisdiction over, appeals would be made a U.S. district court. This provision would be effective for determinations made after 60 days from August 17, 2006.

Provisions for recall of judges.—New rules allow for the recall of a retired special trial judge in order to perform judicial services for up to 90 days per year unless the special trial judge consents to a longer recall period (¶1450).

Authority for special trial judges.—Proceedings to determine employment status that are to be conducted under the small case procedures of Code Sec. 7436(c) may be assigned to a special trial judge (¶1410). This provision applies to proceedings for which a decision has not become final as of August 17, 2006.

Application of equitable recoupment doctrine.—The Pension Act provides statutory clarification that the Tax Court may apply common-law provisions of equitable recoupment, just as federal district courts and the Court of Federal Claims do (¶1415). This provision applies to proceedings for which a decision has not become final as of August 17, 2006.

Tax Court filing fee.—Effective on August 17, 2006, filing fees for the Tax Court are triggered by the filing of a petition (¶1420). Accordingly, in the future, it will not be necessary to amend Code Sec. 7451 each time the court is granted new jurisdiction.

Fee for *pro se* litigants.—Effective on August 17, 2006, practitioners admitted to practice before the Tax Court may be charged a fee of up to $30 per year with the proceeds to be directed to educational and other programs for the benefit of *pro se* litigants (¶1425).

TRUSTS

¶187 Effect on Charitable Remainder Trusts

The rules have been clarified with respect to transfers from CRTs to Employee Stock Option Programs (¶1155).

¶188 Effect on Black Lung Disease Trusts

The limit on distributions from Black Lung Disease Trusts for retiree health expenses and premiums has been eliminated (¶1220).

GOVERNMENT AGENCIES

¶191 Effect on Government Agencies Generally

A number of provisions in the Pension Protection Act of 2006 address Code Sec. 457 plans and their participants. Those provisions are discussed under those plans. Other provisions affecting government entities are discussed below.

¶193 Effect on the PBGC

A significant focus of the new legislation is to improve funding of the Pension Benefit Guaranty Corporation (PBGC). These include provisions for premium rate adjustments (¶505). The PBGC is directed to study multiemployer funding rules (¶29,020). The law provides for the relaxation of funding requirements for PBGC-approved benefits (¶305).

The new law also includes limitations on the PBGC guarantee of benefits due to shutdowns and similar events (¶520).

Senate jurisdiction over confirmation of PBGC Director.—The Pension Protection Act of 2006 establishes that the Director of the PBGC will be appointed by the

President, rather than the Secretary of Labor, and the appointment will be subject to joint confirmation by the Senate Committee on Finance and the Senate Committee on Health, Education, Labor and Pensions (HELP) (¶545).

PIMS parameters must be included in PBGC annual report.—The Pension Act requires that the annual report from the PBGC to Congress, which reports the PBGC's financial status for the prior fiscal year and its expected operations and funds status for the forthcoming five-year period, must include information on the specific simulation parameters used by its Pension Insurance Modeling System (PIMS) in calculating the PBGC's financial statements, including specific initial values, temporal parameters, and policy parameters (¶550).

¶194 Effect on Educational Agencies

Certain voluntary early retirement incentive plans and employee retention plans of educational agencies shall be exempt from immediate taxation as if they were in qualified defined benefit plans but treated as severance plans subject to ERISA's welfare plan rules (¶1070).

¶195 Effect on Plan Administration

The IRS is given the authority to design, modify and waive income or excise taxes with respect to the Employee Plans Compliance Resolution System (¶1085). The law extends the date by which elections of joint and survivor annuities must be made (¶925). Reporting is eliminated or simplified for certain smaller plans (¶1080).

¶196 Effect on State Governments

States are prohibited from reducing unemployment compensation for pension distributions that were rolled over and nontaxable (¶1325).

¶197 Effect on Indian Tribal Governments

Treated as government plans.—Defined benefit and defined contribution plans of Indian tribal governments would be treated as government plans, thus qualifying them for the same exceptions to pension law requirements as state or local government plans (¶1065). Police and fire employees who are participants in a defined benefit plan maintained by an Indian tribal government may receive plan benefits before age 62 without a reduction in the annual dollar limit on such benefits. This provision is effective for plan years beginning on or after August 17, 2006.

Minimum Funding Rules for Single-Employer Plans

2

MINIMUM FUNDING STANDARDS

TRANSITIONAL RELIEF FROM NEW FUNDING STANDARDS

CROSS REFERENCES

Increase in deduction limitation for contributions to single-employer defined benefit plans (*see ¶705*)

Overall limitation on deductions for contributions to combined plans relaxed (*see ¶715*)

MINIMUM FUNDING STANDARDS

¶205 Liability for Minimum Required Contributions

SUMMARY OF NEW LAW

Effective for plan years beginning after 2007, employers maintaining single-employer defined benefit plans are subject to new funding rules that will require them to make a minimum contribution to the plan based on the plan's assets (reduced by credit balances), funding target, and target normal cost. A temporary waiver of the minimum funding requirements may be provided to an employer that is unable to satisfy the minimum funding standard for a plan year without "substantial business hardship." An employer maintaining a single-employer defined benefit plan may be required to provide security to the plan as a condition for a waiver of the minimum funding standards. In addition, no plan amendment may that has the effect of increasing plan liabilities may generally be adopted during the waiver period.

BACKGROUND

An employer maintaining a single-employer pension plan must make an annual minimum funding contribution to ensure that the plan has sufficient assets with which to pay promised retirement benefits. The funding standards generally require an employer to contribute an amount that is sufficient to: (1) pay the normal cost of funding the plan; and (2) amortize unfunded past service liability and changes in past service liability due to plan amendments, assumption changes, and experience gains and losses (ERISA Sec. 302 and Code Sec. 412). The minimum funding rules applicable under current law are detailed at ¶210.

Waiver of minimum funding standards. An employer that is unable to make required funding contributions without incurring temporary substantial business hardship may seek a waiver of the funding standards if meeting the requirements would harm the interests of plan participants (ERISA Sec. 303(a) and Code Sec. 412(d)). Waivers are limited to employers whose financial conditions will improve sufficiently to enable them to eventually pay the waived contributions. Accordingly, waivers will generally not be granted to employers whose financial condition suggests that they will not be able to recover and make plan contributions. In addition, generally no more than three waivers may be granted within any period of 15 consecutive plan years.

An employer may be required to provide security to plans as a condition for the waiver of the minimum funding standard or for an extension of the amortization period (ERISA Sec. 306 and Code Sec. 412(f)). The security requirement may only be imposed if the sum of outstanding balance of the accumulated funding deficiencies, the outstanding balance of the waived funding deficiencies, and the outstanding balance of the decreases in the minimum funding standard equal or exceed $1 million.

BACKGROUND

The amount waived under a single-employer plan must be amortized in no more than five equal annual payments (ERISA Sec. 302(b) and Code Sec. 412(b)(2)). With respect to a multiemployer plan, the amount waived must be amortized in no more than 15 equal annual payments. Amortization payments of a waived funding deficiency may not be waived in a future year.

An employer may amend the plan during the period that a waiver of the funding standards is in effect. However, the amendment may not increase plan benefits, change the accrual of benefits, or change the rate at which benefits become nonforfeitable under the plan, if plan liabilities would be increased as a result. In the event that such an amendment is made during the period that the waiver or extension was in effect, or if a retroactive amendment is made in the preceding 12 months (24 months for a multiemployer plan), the funding relief will not apply in any plan year ending on or after the date on which the amendment was adopted (ERISA Sec. 304(b)(1) and Code Sec. 412(f)(1)).

NEW LAW EXPLAINED

Liability for minimum required contribution and waiver of minimum funding standards.—Effective for plan years beginning after 2007, employers maintaining single-employer defined benefit plans will be required to make a "minimum required contribution" to the plan for a plan year (ERISA Sec. 302(a)(2) and Code Sec. 412(a)(2), as amended by the Pension Protection Act of 2006). The minimum required contribution is based on the plan's assets (reduced by credit balances), funding target, and target normal cost. Specifically, the minimum required contribution applicable for plan years beginning after 2007 to plans in which plan assets (reduced by credit balances) are less than the plan's funding target for the year will be the sum of the target normal cost, shortfall amortization charge, and waiver amortization for the plan year (see the discussion at ¶ 210). Similarly, employers are required to make contributions to or under a multiemployer plan for plan years beginning after 2007 that are sufficient to ensure that the plan does not have an accumulated funding deficiency as of the end of the plan year (see the discussion at ¶ 305).

Joint and several liability for contribution.—The minimum required funding contribution must be paid by the employer sponsor responsible for making contributions to the plan (ERISA Sec. 302(b)(1) and Code Sec. 412(b)(1), as amended by the Pension Act). In the event the employer is a member of a controlled group (as defined under Code Sec. 414(b), (c), (m), or (o)), each member of the group is jointly and severally liable for the payment (ERISA Sec. 302(b)(2) and 302(d)(3), and Code Sec. 412(b)(2) and 412(d)(3), as amended by the Pension Act). Note, joint and several liability also applies in the funding contribution due under a multiemployer plan. Penalties assessed employers for the failure to make minimum required contributions are discussed at ¶ 210.

Waiver of minimum funding requirements: business hardship.—As under current law, the Secretary of the Treasury is authorized to waive the minimum funding requirements applicable to all or any portion of the minimum funding standard for an

NEW LAW EXPLAINED

employer that is unable to satisfy the minimum funding standard for a plan year without "temporary substantial business hardship" (ERISA Sec. 302(c)(1)(A)(i) and Code Sec. 412(c)(1)(A)(i), as amended by the Pension Act). The Secretary of the Treasury is similarly empowered to waive all or any portion of the minimum funding requirements applicable to a multiemployer plan in which 10 percent or more of the participating employers to the participating employer are unable to meet the minimum funding standards for a plan year without "substantial business hardship."

Note, an employer under a single-employer plan or a multiemployer plan will not be able to justify a waiver of the minimum funding standard solely on the basis of business hardship. As under current law, application of the minimum funding standard must also be adverse to the interests of plan participants in the aggregate (ERISA Sec. 302(c)(1)(A)(ii) and Code Sec. 412(c)(1)(A)(ii), as amended by the Pension Act).

> **Comment:** A special rule applies for purposes of determining whether an employer that is a member of a controlled group is experiencing temporary substantial business hardship sufficient to warrant a waiver of the minimum funding requirements for its single-employer plan. Under such circumstances, the temporary substantial business hardship condition must be met by not only the employer, but by the controlled group to which the employer belongs, treating all members of the group as a single employer (ERISA Sec. 302(c)(5)(B) and Code Sec. 412(c)(5)(B), as amended by the Pension Act).

Relief of limited duration. The available funding relief is of a limited duration. As under current law, the Treasury may not waive the minimum funding standards applicable to plan years beginning after 2007 for more than three of any 15 consecutive plan years for a single-employer plan or for more than five of any 15 consecutive plan years for a multiemployer plan (ERISA Sec. 302(c)(1)(A) and Code Sec. 412(c)(1)(A), as amended by the Pension Act).

> **Comment:** The Pension Act also does not change the factors that define temporary substantial business hardship (or substantial business hardship). They include whether: (1) the employer is operating at an economic loss; (2) there is substantial unemployment or underemployment in the employer's industry; (3) sales and profits in the industry are depressed or declining; and (4) it is reasonable to expect that the plan will continue only if the waiver is granted (ERISA Sec. 302(c)(2) and Code Sec. 412(c)(2), as amended by the Pension Act).

Waiver reduces minimum required contribution.—In the event a waiver is granted for a single-employer plan, the minimum required contribution for the plan year will be reduced by the amount of the waived funding deficiency and amortized under ERISA Sec. 303(e) and Code Sec. 430(e) (see the discussion at ¶210) (ERISA Sec. 302(c)(1)(B)(i) and Code Sec. 412(c)(1)(B)(i), as amended by the Pension Act). By contrast, a waiver granted to a multiemployer plan would result in the funding standard account being credited with the amount of the waived funding deficiency and the amount amortized under ERISA Sec. 304(b)(2)(C) and Code Sec. 431(b)(2)(C) (see the discussion at ¶305) (ERISA Sec. 302(c)(1)(B)(ii) and Code Sec. 412(c)(1)(B)(ii), as amended by the Pension Act).

NEW LAW EXPLAINED

Waiver of funding deficiency. A "waived funding deficiency" refers to the portion of the minimum funding standard (determined without regard to the waiver) for a plan year that has been waived by the Secretary of the Treasury and not satisfied by employer contributions (ERISA Sec. 302(c)(3) and Code Sec. 412(c)(3), as amended by the Pension Act). However, no portion of the minimum funding standard for a plan year that is attributable to any waived funding deficiency for any preceding plan year may be waived (ERISA Sec. 302(c)(1)(C) and Code Sec. 412(c)(1)(C), as amended by the Pension Act).

> **Comment:** Under current law, the amount waived for a single-employer plan may be amortized in no more than five equal annual payments. With respect to a multiemployer plan, the amount waived may be amortized in no more than 15 equal annual payments. For plan years beginning after 2007, the waiver amortization charge will be the aggregate total of the waiver amortization installments for the plan year with respect to the waiver amortization base for each of the five preceding plan years (ERISA Sec. 303(e)(1) and Code Sec. 430(e)(1), as added by the Pension Act). The waiver amortization installment is the amount necessary to amortize the waiver amortization base (i.e., the amount of the waived funding deficiency for the plan year) (ERISA Sec. 303(e)(2) and Code Sec. 430(e)(2), as added by the Pension Act). The waiver amortization charge will be included in the determination of the minimum required contribution under the rules discussed at ¶210.

Security for waiver of minimum funding standard.—As under current law, an employer maintaining a single-employer defined benefit plan may be required to provide security to the plan as a condition for a waiver of the minimum funding standards (ERISA Sec. 302(c)(4)(A) and Code Sec. 412(c)(4)(A), as amended by the Pension Act). Any security provided as a condition for a waiver may be perfected and enforced only by the Pension Benefit Guaranty Corporation (PBGC) or, at the direction of the PBGC, by a contributing sponsor or member of the sponsor's controlled group (ERISA Sec. 302(c)(4)(A)(ii) and Code Sec. 412(c)(4)(A)(ii), as amended by the Pension Act).

The Secretary of the Treasury may not grant or modify a waiver without providing the PBGC with notice of the application for a waiver, and opportunity to comment on the application within 30 days after receipt of the notice (ERISA Sec. 302(c)(4)(B) and Code Sec. 412(c)(4)(B), as amended by the Pension Act). The Treasury must consider comments from the PBGC and from employee organizations representing plan participants that are submitted in writing to the Treasury.

> **Comment:** The notice provided to the PBGC is regarded as "tax return information" and subject to the safeguarding and reporting requirements of Code Sec. 6103(p).

Exception to security requirement. The Pension Act authorizes an exception to the security requirement for a waiver involving a plan with respect to which the sum of: (1) the aggregate unpaid minimum required contributions for the plan year (including any increase that would result from a denial of a pending waiver request) and all preceding plan years; and (2) the present value of all waiver amortization installments determined for the plan year and all succeeding plan years, is less than $1

NEW LAW EXPLAINED

million (ERISA Sec. 302(c)(4)(C)(i) and Code Sec. 412(c)(4)(C)(i), as amended by the Pension Act).

An unpaid minimum contribution is a required minimum contribution that is not paid by the specified due date (ERISA Sec. 302(c)(4)(C)(iii)(I), as added by the Pension Act). Under an ordering rule applicable to the calculation of unpaid minimum required contributions, any payment to or under a plan for a plan year is to be allocated first to unpaid minimum required contributions for all preceding plan years on a first- in, first-out basis, and then to the minimum required funding contribution for the plan year (ERISA Sec. 302(c)(4)(C)(iii)(II), as added by the Pension Act).

> **Comment:** The ordering rule is not contained in Code Sec. 412, as amended by the Act. However, the same ordering rule applies to unpaid minimum contributions required under new Code Sec. 430 (see ¶210) (Code Sec. 4971(c)(4), as amended by the Pension Act).

Application and notice of waiver.—A single-employer plan must file an application for a waiver of the minimum funding standard for a plan year no later than the 15th day of the 3rd month beginning after the close of the plan year (ERISA Sec. 302(c)(5)(A) and Code Sec. 412(c)(5)(A), as amended by the Pension Act). This rule does not apply to multiemployer plans. A waiver will not be granted absent satisfactory evidence that the applicant has provided advance notice of the filing of the waiver application to each affected party (as defined under Code Sec. 4001(a)(21)). The notice must describe the extent to which the plan is funded for guaranteed benefits and for benefit liabilities (ERISA Sec. 302(c)(6)(A) and Code Sec. 412(c)(6)(A), as amended by the Pension Act).

Plan amendments during waiver period.—An employer may amend the pension plan during the period that a waiver of the minimum funding requirements is in effect. As under current law, however, no plan amendment may be adopted during the waiver period that increases plan liabilities because of an increase in benefits, change in the accrual of benefits, or change in the rate at which benefits become nonforfeitable. Also, the amendment may not be adopted if a retroactive amendment (see below) has been made in the preceding 12 months (24 months for multiemployer plans) (ERISA Sec. 302(c)(7)(A) and Code Sec. 412(c)(7)(A), as amended by the Pension Act).

As under current law, a plan amendment that increases plan liabilities (and does not comply with a specific exception) will prevent the waiver from applying on or after the date the amendment is adopted. Thus, in the case of a waiver, the amount waived and not yet amortized would become part of the minimum required contribution for the year in which the rule is violated (ERISA Sec. 302(c)(7)(A) and Code Sec. 412(c)(7)(A), as amended by the Pension Act).

Plan amendments authorized. The restriction on plan amendments during the waiver period will not apply to plan amendments that the Secretary of the Treasury determines to be reasonable and which provides for only a de minimis increase in benefits (ERISA Sec. 302(c)(7)(B)(i) and Code Sec. 412(c)(7)(B)(i), as amended by the Pension Act). In addition, the restriction will not apply to amendments required to maintain the tax qualified status of the plan or that repeal retroactive plan amendments adopted within 2½ months after the close of the plan year (two years after the close

NEW LAW EXPLAINED

of the plan year for a multiemployer plan) that do not reduce accrued benefits and that the administrator elects to treat as having been made on the first day of the plan year (see below) (ERISA Sec. 302(c)(7)(B)(ii) and (iii), and Code Sec. 412(c)(7)(B)(ii) and (iii), as amended by the Pension Act).

> **Caution Note:** As under current Code Sec. 412(c)(8), a change in the plan's funding method, valuation date, or plan year may not take effect without approval by the Treasury (ERISA Sec. 302(d)(1) and Code Sec. 412(d)(1), as amended by the Pension Act).

Retroactive plan amendments. As under current law, a plan may retroactively adopt an amendment up to 2½ months after the close of the plan year (two years after the close of the plan year for multiemployer plans). In the event that the amendment does not reduce the accrued benefit of a participant, determined as of the beginning of the first plan year to which the amendment applies and as of the time the amendment is adopted (except to the extent required by circumstances), the plan administrator may elect to treat the amendment as having been made on the first day of the plan year (ERISA Sec. 302(d)(2) and Code Sec. 412(d)(2), as amended by the Pension Act).

However no retroactive amendment reducing a participant's accrued benefits may be adopted unless the plan administrator first notifies the Secretary of the Treasury and the Secretary either approves the amendment or fails to disapprove the amendment within 90 days after the date the notice was filed. In addition, the Secretary may only approve a retroactive amendment reducing accrued benefits if: (1) the amendment is necessary because of the temporary substantial business hardship of a single-employer plan or the substantial business hardship for a multiple employer plan; and (2) a waiver or extension of the amortization period is unavailable or inadequate.

> **Comment:** The Pension Act does not substantively change the retroactive amendment rule from current law.

Exceptions to new rules.—The new rules regarding liability for required contributions for plan years beginning after 2007 are limited to tax qualified plans under Code Sec. 401(a) and annuity plans under Code Sec. 403(a) (Code Sec. 412(e)(1), as amended by the Pension Act). The rules do not apply to: profit-sharing or stock bonus plans; insurance contract plans; governmental plans; church plans; plans which have not provided for employer contributions after September 2, 1974; or plans established by fraternal orders under Code Sec. 501(c)(8) or Voluntary Employees's Beneficiary Associations (VEBAs) under Code Sec. 501(c)(9) if no contributions to the plan are made by employers of plan participants (Code Sec. 412(e)(2), as amended by the Pension Act).

The exemption for insurance contract plans is limited to plans that are funded exclusively by the purchase of individual insurance contracts that provide for level annual premium payments to be paid extending no later than the retirement age for each individual participant. Benefits under the plan must be equal to benefits provided pursuant to each contract at normal retirement age and must be guaranteed by a licensed insurance carrier. In addition, no rights under the contract may have been subject to a security interest during the plan year and no policy loans may be outstanding at any time during the plan year. The Pension Act authorizes an

NEW LAW EXPLAINED

extension of the exception to plans funded exclusively by group insurance contracts that have the same characteristics as individual insurance contracts (Code Sec. 412(e)(3), as amended by the Pension Act).

> **Comment:** The definition of insurance contract plans under Code Sec. 412(e)(3), as amended by the Pension Act, mirrors that contained under current Code Sec. 412(i). Thus, the Act does not effect a substantive change in the law with respect to insurance contract plans.

Terminated multiemployer plans. The new rules regarding liability for required contributions for plan years beginning after 2007 will apply to terminated multiemployer plans until the last day of the plan year in which the plan terminated (Code Sec. 412(e)(4), as amended by the Pension Act).

▶ **Effective date.** The provisions are effective for plan years beginning after 2007 (Act Secs. 101(d) and 111(b) of the Pension Protection Act of 2006).

Law source: Law at ¶5030, ¶5080, ¶5085, ¶5090, ¶5115 and ¶7006. Committee Report at ¶10,010.

- Act Sec. 101 of the Pension Protection Act of 2006, repealing ERISA Secs. 302 through 308 and adding new ERISA Sec. 302;
- Act Sec. 111(a), amending Code Sec. 412;
- Act Sec. 114(a), amending Code Sec. 401(a)(29), (32) and (33);
- Act Sec. 114(b), amending Code Sec. 411;
- Act Sec. 114(c), amending Code Sec. 414(b)(2)(B)(i);
- Act Secs. 101(d) and 111(b), providing effective dates.

Reporter references: For further information, consult the following CCH reporters.

- Pension Plan Guide, ¶3090
- Standard Federal Tax Reporter, 2006FED ¶19,125.01, ¶19,125.035 and ¶19,125.037
- Tax Research Consultant, RETIRE: 30,154, RETIRE: 30,156 and RETIRE: 30,400
- Federal Tax Guide, 2006FTG ¶11,040

¶210 Minimum Funding Standards for Single-Employer Defined Benefit Plans

SUMMARY OF NEW LAW

Effective for plan years beginning after 2007, the current funding standard account mechanism and two-tiered funding system will be replaced with a single funding method. Employers will generally be required to fully fund the present value of all benefits earned or accrued under the plan as of the beginning of the year. Liabilities will be calculated using interest rates derived from a three-segment yield curve based on yields of high grade corporate bonds averaged over two years. A minimum

SUMMARY OF NEW LAW

contribution based on plan assets and accrued liabilities that will be sufficient to amortize a funding shortfall over seven years.

At-risk plans with over 500 participants that are funded below a specified threshold level that reflects the ratio of assets to liabilities will be subject to an increased funding target that will require plan sponsors to make larger minimum funding contributions. At-risk liabilities will be determined pursuant to the assumptions that plan participants within 10 years of retirement will retire at the earliest date and with the most valuable form of benefit allowed under the plan.

Existing credit balances may be retained and future credit balances may be used for funding purposes. Pre-2008 funding standard carryover credit balances will be distinguished from prefunding credit balances accumulated after 2008. Plan sponsors will be provided the option of using a credit balance to reduce the required minimum contribution or waiving the balance. However, an employer's ability to use a credit balance to pay any required minimum contribution will be subject to restrictions, based on the plan's funded status.

BACKGROUND

An employer maintaining a single-employer defined benefit pension plan must make an annual minimum funding contribution to ensure that the plan has sufficient assets with which to pay promised retirement benefits (ERISA Sec. 302 and Code Sec. 412). The funding standards generally require an employer to contribute an amount to the plan that is sufficient to: (1) pay the normal cost of funding the plan; and (2) amortize unfunded past service liability and changes in past service liability due to plan amendments, assumption changes, and experience gains and losses over a period that can exceed 30 years.

Employers are not required to make contributions to a defined benefit plan in excess of the full funding limitation. The full funding limit is the excess, if any, of: (1) the accrued liability under the plan (including normal cost); over (2) the lesser of (a) the market value of plan assets, or (b) the actuarial value of plan assets (ERISA Sec. 302(c)((7)(F) and Code Sec. 412(c)(7)(F). However, the full funding limit may not be less than the excess of 90 percent of the plan's current liability over the actuarial value of plan assets (ERISA Sec. 302(c)(7)(E) and Code Sec. 412(c)(7)(E)). In determining whether a plan is at the 90 percent limit, plan assets are not reduced by credit balances.

Employers may also generally not take a deduction for contributions in a tax year that exceed the full funding limitation. The effect of the full funding limit is to prevent employers from making additional contributions to a fully funded plan even if the accrued liability of the plan is greater than plan assets.

Funding standard account. The administrative mechanism used to implement the funding requirements is the funding standard account. Every plan subject to the minimum funding rules must maintain a funding standard account that is: (1) charged with amounts that must be paid to satisfy the plan's funding obligations; and

BACKGROUND

(2) credited with contributions to the plan, decreases in plan liabilities due to plan or assumption changes, and experience gains (ERISA Sec. 302(b) and Code Sec. 412(b)).

A plan satisfies the minimum funding requirements if an accumulated funding deficiency does not exist at the end of the plan year. The accumulated funding deficiency is the excess of total charges to the funding standard account over total credits to the account. Generally, the minimum contribution for a plan year is the amount by which the charges to funding standard account would exceed credits to the account if no contributions were made to the plan.

Charges to the funding standard account include: (1) normal costs for the plan year; (2) amortization of: unfunded past service liability (generally over a 30-40 year period), the net increase in unfunded past service liability for plan amendments (over a 30-year period), net experience loss (over a five-year period for single-employer plans) and net loss from changes in actuarial assumptions (over a 10-year period for single-employer plans); (3) amounts necessary to amortize each waived funding deficiency (over five plan years for single-employer plans); (4) and the amount necessary to amortize over five plan years the amount credited to the account from an alternative funding standard account that may be adopted in addition the regular funding standard account under a plan sponsor's funding method (ERISA Sec. 302(b)(2) and Code Sec. 412(b)(2)).

The IRS may, at the request of the plan administrator or plan sponsor, extend the amortization periods described above for up to 10 years if necessary to adequately protect the interests of participants and beneficiaries (ERISA Sec. 304(a) and Code Sec. 412(e)). The amortization period may be extended only if the failure to authorize the extension would: (1) be adverse to the interests of plan participants in the aggregate; and (2) cause a substantial risk to the plan's continued operation or substantially curtail retirement benefits or employee compensation.

Credits to the funding standard account include: (1) employer contributions for the plan year; (2) amortization in equal annual installments of the net decrease in unfunded past service liability from plan amendments (over a 30-year period), net experience gain (over a five-year period for single-employer plans), and any net gain resulting from changes in actuarial assumptions (over 10 years for single-employer plans); (3) amount of the waived funding deficiency for the plan year; and (4) the excess of the debit balance in the funding standard account over the debit balance in the alternative funding standard account, if the funding deficiency was determined under the alternative funding standard account for the plan year (ERISA Sec. 302(b)(3) and Code Sec. 412(b)(3)).

Deficit reduction required of underfunded plans. Single-employer defined benefit plans (covering more than 100 participants on each day in the preceding plan year) with unfunded current liability must be funded more rapidly than single-employer plans without unfunded liabilities (ERISA Sec. 302(d) and Code Sec. 412(l)). Plans having a funded current liability percentage of less than 90 percent may be required to make an additional "deficit reduction contribution" (of 18–30 percent of unfunded current liability) over a specified amortization period. The minimum contribution required of such underfunded plans is the greater of: (1) the amount determined under the

BACKGROUND

normal funding rules (discussed above); or (2) the deficit reduction contribution and the amount required to be contributed on account of unpredictable contingent events.

The deficit reduction contribution, for purposes of the additional funding contribution, is the total of the unfunded old liability amount and the unfunded new liability amount (ERISA Sec. 302(d)(2) and Code Sec. 412(l)(2)). The deficit reduction contribution must also include: (1) the expected increase in current liability that is attributable to benefits accruing during the plan year; and (2) the amount needed to amortize increased current liability that is attributable to future changes in required mortality tables (i.e., the unfunded mortality increase amount).

Calculation of the amounts underlying the deficit reduction contribution is based upon the plan's current liability, which generally encompasses all plan obligations to employees and their beneficiaries (ERISA Sec. 302(d)(7) and Code Sec. 412(l)(7)). Current liability is calculated through the use of prescribed mortality tables and specified interest rates.

Interest rates used in calculating current liability. Determining the present value of an underfunded plan's liabilities requires the discounting of future payments at a designated interest rate (ERISA Sec. 302(b)(5) and Code Sec. 412(b)(5)). Thus, the discount rate is not based on the interest the plan is actually earning on its investments. Under the law applicable in 2004 and 2005, the interest rate to be used in determining a plan's current liability could not be above and could not be more than 10 percent below (i.e., between 90 percent to 100 percent) the weighted average of the rate of interest on amounts conservatively invested in long-term corporate bonds for the four-year period ending on the last day before the plan year begins.

Prior to 2002, the permissible range for purposes of determining current liability was based on the weighted average of the rate of interest on 30-year Treasury securities during the four-year period ending on the last day before the beginning of the plan year. The Job Creation and Worker Assistance Act of 2002 (P.L. 107-147) authorized an increase in the maximum interest rate to be used in determining current liability from 105 percent to 120 percent of the weighted average interest rate of 30-year Treasury securities for 2002 and 2003 plan years. The higher interest rate, by effectively decreasing the value of plan liabilities, reduced the plan sponsor's funding obligation.

The Pension Funding Equity Act of 2004 (PFEA) (P.L. 108-218) replaced the previously applicable 30-year Treasury rate used in funding calculations with the four-year weighted average of the long-term corporate bond rate, referenced above. However, the interest rates authorized under the PFEA applied only through 2005. Accordingly, in 2006, current liability is determined pursuant to an interest rate that is 90-105 percent of the average of interest rates on 30-year Treasury securities for the four-year period ending on the last day before the plan year begins.

Mortality table for calculating current liability. The prescribed mortality table for calculating current liability is the 1983 Group Annuity Mortality Table (GAM 83) (ERISA Sec. 302(d)(7)(C) and Code Sec. 412(l)(7)(C)). An employer must use the GAM 83 table and may not adopt a plan-specific mortality table or a table that reflects the increase in average life expectancy since 1983.

BACKGROUND

Note, however, IRS proposed regulations, designed to be effective beginning in 2007, would require use of the RP-2000 Mortality Tables, which reflect improvements in mortality rates (including future improvements) projected to the current year. Separate tables would be provided for annuitants and nonannuitants as well as for disabled participants (Proposed Reg. § 1.412(l)(7)-1).

90-percent funding exemption from additional contribution requirement. The additional funding contribution required of underfunded single-employer defined benefit plans (other than plans with 100 or fewer participants) does not apply to an underfunded plan in a plan year in which the funded current liability percentage is at least 90 percent (ERISA Sec. 302(d)(9) and Code Sec. 412(l)(9)). Thus, an employer is required, under current law, to fund only 90 percent of the plan's current liabilities to preclude the deficit reduction contribution requirement from applying. Moreover, the additional funding contribution will not apply to an underfunded plan in a plan year in which: (1) the funded current liability percentage is at least 80 percent; and (2) the funded current liability percentage for each of the two immediately preceding years (or each of the second and third immediately preceding years) is at least 90 percent (i.e., the "volatility" rule).

> **Comment:** Under current law, the financial health of a plan sponsor, as expressed by the sponsor's credit or bond rating, is not factored into a determination of the plan's funding liability. Thus, an employer's funding contribution is not influenced by whether it is at risk for terminating the plan.

Alternative deficit reduction contribution for airlines and steel industry. The PFEA authorized specified employers maintaining underfunded single-employer defined benefit plans to elect a reduction in the amount of required contributions (ERISA Sec. 302(d)(12) and Code Sec. 412(l)(12)). The alternative deficit reduction contribution relief was available in 2004 and 2005 and was limited to plans maintained by commercial passenger airlines; companies primarily engaged in the production or manufacture of steel mill products or the processing of iron ore pellets; and the Transportation Communications Union. The amount of the alternative deficit reduction contribution that could be elected by an eligible employer was limited to the greater of: (1) 20 percent of the additional contribution that would otherwise be required; or (2) the additional contribution that would be required if the deficit reduction contribution for the plan year was based solely on the expected increase in current liability due to benefits accruing during the plan year.

Plan asset valuation. In determining whether a plan's assets are sufficient to cover liabilities, assets may be valued under any reasonable actuarial method that takes fair market value into account (ERISA Sec. 302(c)(2) and Code Sec. 412(c)(2)). Fair market value is defined as the price at which the property would change hands between a willing buyer and a willing seller.

Alternatively, a plan's valuation method may be based on the average value of plan assets over a period not in excess of the five most recent plan years, including the current year. Average asset valuation (i.e., smoothing) is permitted to the extent actuarial value is between 80 and 120 percent of current fair market value. Note, plan liabilities may be amortized over a four-year period.

BACKGROUND

Employers are generally required to use a current year valuation date. The valuation date must be within the plan year relating to the valuation, or within one month prior to the start of the plan year. Alternatively, employers may elect to value plan assets as of any date within the plan year prior to the plan year to which the valuation refers (ERISA Sec. 302(c)(9) and Code Sec. 412(c)(9)).

Credit balances. In the event a plan's accumulated funding deficiency at the end of a plan year is larger than the full funding limitation, the excess is credited to the funding standard account as a credit balance. A credit balance may result from contributions in excess of minimum required contributions or from large net experience gains. The credit balance may be further enhanced by interest at the rate used by the plan to determine costs. However, the credit balance is also reduced by charges to the funding standard account unless the charge is offset by contributions. The value of a credit balance is that it is automatically applied against charges to the funding standard account and, thus, will reduce required contributions, regardless of the plan's funded status.

In determining whether the plan is required to make a deficit reduction contribution because it has a funded current liability that is under 90 percent, plan assets are not reduced by credit balances in the funding standard account. However, the value of plan assets will be reduced by the credit balance in determining the amount of the deficit reduction contribution.

NEW LAW EXPLAINED

New funding rules to apply in plan years beginning after 2007.—Effective for plan years beginning after 2007, the funding standard account mechanism and the current two-tiered funding system will be replaced with a single funding method. An employer maintaining a single-employer defined benefit plan that is not 100-percent funded will not be required to make a deficit reduction contribution, but will be required to make a minimum contribution based on the plan's assets (reduced by credit balances), funding target, and target normal cost and that is sufficient to amortize unfunded plan liabilities over a period of seven years. Unlike current law, under which employers are required to fund up to 90 percent of a plan's total liabilities, the Pension Act increases the funding target to 100 percent of target or current liabilities.

In addition, the Pension Act radically changes the actuarial assumptions and methods used to determine present value, authorizing a new interest rate and a new mortality table. Specifically, the Pension Act, while retaining the blended rate of corporate bonds, introduces a segmented "yield curve" that would consist of three different interest rates (based on the unweighted average of interest rates on investment grade corporate bonds) applicable to benefits payable in different time periods.

Finally, the Pension Act subjects "at-risk" plans, as determined by the plan's funded status and not by the credit rating of the employer sponsoring the plan, to an at-risk liability assumption that all plan participants eligible for benefits within a 10-year period will elect benefits at the highest present value. The at-risk rules, which are limited to

NEW LAW EXPLAINED

plans with over 500 participants, will increase a plan's target liability. (ERISA Sec. 303 and Code Sec. 430, as added by the Pension Protection Act of 2006.)

Minimum required contribution.—Under the new rules, an employer's contribution to a single-employer defined benefit plan for a plan year may not in the aggregate be less than the "minimum required contribution" (ERISA Sec. 303(a)(2) and Code Sec. 430(a)(2), as added by the Pension Act). The minimum required contribution applicable to plans in which plan assets (reduced by credit balances) are less than the "funding target" of the plan for the year will be the sum of the following factors (ERISA Sec. 303(a)(1) and Code Sec. 430(a)(1), as added by the Pension Act):

(1) Target normal cost: the present value of all benefits expected to accrue or be earned under the plan during the plan year, including benefits attributable to service in a preceding year that are increased because of an increase in compensation during the current plan year (i.e., funding target) (ERISA Sec. 303(b) and Code Sec. 430(b), as added by the Pension Act);

(2) Shortfall amortization charge for the plan year: the total (not less than zero) of the amounts (i.e., the shortfall amortization installments) required to amortize shortfall amortization bases for the plan year and six preceding years (ERISA Sec. 303(c) and Code Sec. 430(c), as added by the Pension Act); and

(3) Waiver amortization charge for the plan year: the aggregate total of the amounts (i.e., the waiver amortization installments) required to amortize the "waiver amortization base" for the plan year over a five-year period (ERISA Sec. 303(e) and Code Sec. 430(e), as added by the Pension Act). The rules governing the waiver of the minimum funding standards are discussed in detail at ¶ 205.

> **Comment:** The waiver amortization installment is determined by application of the certain segment rates dioscussed below (ERISA Sec. 303(e)(3) and Code Sec. 430(e)(3), as added by the Pension Act). The segment rates are also used in determining the shortfall amortization installment base, as discussed below.

If the value of a plan's assets (reduced by any credit balance) equals or exceeds the funding target (i.e., 100 percent of the target liability), the minimum required contribution will be the target normal cost of the plan for the plan year reduced (but not below zero) by the amount by which the plan's assets (reduced by a credit balance) exceed the funding target (ERISA Sec. 303(a)(2) and Code Sec. 430(a)(2), as added by the Pension Act).

Funding target.—The funding target of a plan is the present value of all benefits accrued or earned under the plan as of the beginning of the plan year (ERISA Sec. 303(d) and Code Sec. 430(d), as added by the Pension Act). Benefits that are to be taken into account for purposes of the funding target include early retirement and similar benefits (Joint Committee on Taxation, Technical Explanation of the Pension Protection Act of 2006 (JCX-380-06)). However, benefits that have not accrued during the plan year are not included in a plan's funding target. By contrast, such benefits are taken into account in the determination of normal cost for the plan year.

The funding target attainment percentage (which is particularly relevant in the application of the benefit limits imposed on underfunded plans, discussed at ¶ 215) is

NEW LAW EXPLAINED

the ratio of the value of plan assets for the year (as reduced by credit balances) to the funding target of the plan for the plan year (determined without regard to at-risk status) (ERISA Sec. 303(d)(2) and Code Sec. 430(d)(2), as added by the Pension Act).

Note, the funding target for "at-risk" plans is based on specified actuarial assumptions that are discussed below (ERISA Sec. 303(i) and Code Sec. 430(i), as added by the Pension Act).

> **Comment:** Defined benefit plans are required under ERISA Sec. 103(d) to file an annual report with the Department of Labor, which includes a complete actuarial statement for the plan. The annual report, effective for plan years beginning after 2007, must disclose the percentage by which the current value of plan assets is less than 70 percent of the funding target for single-employer plans under ERISA Sec. 303(d) (or current liability under ERISA Sec. 304(c) for multiemployer plans) (ERISA Sec. 103(d)(11), as amended by the Pension Act).

Shortfall amortization charge.—For purposes of determining the shortfall amortization charge, a plan's "funding shortfall" for a year is the excess of the plan's funding target for the plan year over the value of plan assets (reduced by any credit balance) for the plan year which are held by the plan on the valuation date (ERISA Sec. 303(c)(4) and Code Sec. 430(c)(4), as added by the Pension Act). In the event of a funding shortfall, the plan's minimum required contribution will be increased by the shortfall amortization charge.

Shortfall amortization installments. The amount necessary to amortize the shortfall amortization base in level installments over the seven-year period beginning with the plan year is the shortfall amortization installment (ERISA Sec. 303(c)(2)(A) and Code Sec. 430(c)(2)(A), as added by the Pension Act). The shortfall amortization installment for any plan year in the seven-year period (i.e., the current plan year and the six preceding plan years) with respect to any shortfall amortization base is the annual installment determined for the year for the shortfall amortization base (ERISA Sec. 303(c)(2)(B) and Code Sec. 430(c)(2)(B), as added by the Pension Act.)

> **Comment:** Special amortization rules allow commercial airlines (and catering firms serving airlines) to amortize funding shortfall over 10 years. In addition, commercial airlines that have frozen their plans may elect, prior to 2008, to amortize funding target liability over 17 years at a specified interest rate. The governing rules are discussed at ¶245.

The shortfall amortization base for a plan year is the funding shortfall for the plan year reduced by the present value (determined using the segment rates of ERISA Sec. 303(h)(2)(C) and Code Sec. 430(h)(2)(C)) (discussed below) of the aggregate total of the shortfall amortization installments and waiver amortization installments that have been determined for the plan year and any succeeding plan year with respect to any shortfall amortization bases and waiver amortization bases for preceding plan years (ERISA Sec. 303(c)(3) and Code Sec. 430(c)(3), as added by the Pension Act). Thus, if the value of plan assets (as reduced by credit balances) is equal to or greater than the funding target of the plan, then the shortfall amortization base for the plan year will be zero (ERISA Sec. 303(c)(5)(A) and Code Sec. 430(c)(5)(A), as added by the Pension Act).

NEW LAW EXPLAINED

Shortfall amortization charge may not be less than zero. The amortization schedule will reflect shortfall increases as well as decreases in the funding shortfall, such as those that may be caused by favorable investment experience or an increase in interest rates. Thus, depending on whether the present value of remaining installments with respect to prior year amortization bases is more or less than the plan's funding shortfall, a shortfall amortization base may be positive or negative. However, the shortfall amortization must still be amortized over seven years. In addition, although shortfall amortization installments for a plan year with respect to positive and negative amortization bases are netted in determining the shortfall amortization charge for the plan year, the resulting shortfall amortization charge may not be less than zero (Joint Committee on Taxation, Technical Explanation of the Pension Protection Act of 2006 (JCX-38-06)). Accordingly, negative amortization installments may not offset the waiver amortization installment or normal cost.

> **Comment:** The effect of these changes by the Pension Act will be to deny employers the current option of amortizing past service liabilities over 30 years or losses over 10 years. In addition, the deficit reduction contribution rules, which require amortization of the underfunded amounts over a four to seven year period, will not apply. Furthermore, the IRS is no longer empowered to grant an extension of the amortization period.

Exception to shortfall amortization base for well-funded plans. A plan will not be required to establish a shortfall amortization base for a plan year if the value of plan assets (reduced by a prefunding balance that the employer elects to use to reduce contributions for the year (see below) is equal to or greater than the funding target for the plan year. Under such circumstances, the shortfall amortization base for the plan year will be zero (ERISA Sec. 303(c)(5)(A) and Code Sec. 430(c)(5)(A), as added by the Pension Act).

This exception will be further phased in over four years for plans that are in effect in 2007 and have a current liability percentage of at least 90 percent in 2007, (and, therefore, are not subject to the deficit reduction contribution for 2007) (ERISA Sec. 303(c)(5)(B)(i) and (iv) and Code Sec. 430(c)(5)(B)(i) and (iv), as added by the Pension Act). Under the phase-in rule, a reduced funding target applies for purposes of calculating a funding shortfall and for determining whether a shortfall amortization base must be established. The required funding targets (expressed as the applicable percentage of the funding target) are 92 percent in 2008, 94 percent in 2009, and 96 percent in 2010 (ERISA Sec. 303(c)(5)(B) and Code Sec. 430(c)(5)(B), as added by the Pension Act). Thus, a plan that satisfies the conditions for transition relief will not be required in 2008 to establish a shortfall amortization base if the value of plan assets (reduced by any prefunding balance used to reduce required contributions for the year) is at least equal to 92 percent of the plan's funding target for that year.

> **Comment:** The transition rule will apply only if the shortfall amortization base for each of the preceding years beginning after 2007 was zero (ERISA Sec. 303(c)(5)(B)(iii) and Code Sec. 430(c)(5)(B)(iii), as added by the Pension Act). Accordingly, if a plan's funding target for any year in the transition period is below the applicable percentage, the funding target for the current year and

NEW LAW EXPLAINED

subsequent year will be 100 percent. Under such circumstances, the plan would need to establish a shortfall amortization base.

Deemed amortization upon attainment of funding percentage. In the event that the value of a plan's assets (reduced by any credit balance) is equal to or greater than the plan's funding target for the year (thereby, resulting in a funding shortfall of zero), any shortfall amortization bases for preceding plan years will be eliminated. Specifically, in determining the shortfall amortization charge for the plan year and succeeding plan years, the shortfall amortization bases for all preceding plan years (and all shortfall amortization installments for such bases) will be reduced to zero (ERISA Sec. 303(c)(6) and Code Sec. 430(c)(6), as added by the Pension Act).

Shortfall amortization charge included in termination liability to PBGC trustee. Under current law, in the event a plan terminates in a distress termination or in a termination instituted by the Pension Benefit Guaranty Corporation (PBGC), and the plan is subject to PBGC trusteeship proceedings, each contributing sponsor and each member of its controlled group are liable to the trustee appointed by the PBGC for: (1) the outstanding balance of the accumulated funding deficiencies; (2) the outstanding balance of the amount of funding deficiencies that was waived before the termination date; and (3) the outstanding balance of the amount of decreases in the minimum funding standard allowed before the termination date, plus interest from the termination date (ERISA Sec.4062(c)). The liability is due and payable to the trustee, as of the termination date, in cash or securities acceptable to the trustee.

Effective for plan years beginning after 2007, liability to the PBGC trustee will consist of: (1) the sum of the shortfall amortization charge for the plan year in which the termination date occurs, plus the aggregate total of shortfall amortization installments determined for succeeding plan years (including any increases resulting from the denial of all pending waiver applications); and (2) the sum of the waiver amortization charge under ERISA Sec. 303(e) for the plan year in which the termination date occurs, plus the aggregate total of waiver amortization installments determined for succeeding plan years (ERISA Sec. 4062(c), as amended by the Pension Act).

Waiver amortization charge.—In the event that a plan has a waived funding deficiency for any of the five preceding plan years (pursuant to the rules discussed at ¶205), the minimum required contribution for the plan year will be increased by a waiver amortization charge for the plan year. The waiver amortization charge for a plan year is the aggregate total of waiver amortization installments for the plan year with respect to the waiver amortization base for each of the five preceding plan years (ERISA Sec. 303(e)(1) and Code Sec. 430(e)(1), as added by the Pension Act).

The waiver amortization installment is the amount necessary to amortize the waived amortization base (i.e., the amount of the waived funding deficiency for the plan year) in level annual installments over the five- year period beginning with the succeeding plan year (ERISA Sec. 303(e)(2)(A) and Code Sec. 430(e)(2)(A), as added by the Pension Act). The waiver amortization installment for any plan year in the five-year period with respect to a waiver amortization base is the annual installment determined for the shortfall amortization base (ERISA Sec. 303(e)(2)(B) and Code Sec. 430(e)(2)(B), as added by the Pension Act). The amount of the waiver amortization

NEW LAW EXPLAINED

installment is determined under the segment rates of ERISA Sec. 303(h)(2) and Code Sec. 430(h)(2), discussed below.

In the event that the value of a plan's assets (reduced by any credit balance) is equal to or greater than the plan's funding target for the year (resulting in a funding shortfall for the plan year of zero), the waiver amortization bases for preceding plan years will be eliminated. Specifically, in determining the waiver amortization charge for the plan year and succeeding plan years, the waiver amortization base for all preceding plan years and all the waiver amortization installments for such bases, will be reduced to zero (ERISA Sec. 303(e)(5) and Code Sec. 430(e)(5), as added by the Pension Act).

Credit balances.—Under current law, a credit balance automatically reduces any required contribution, regardless of the plan's funded status. The Pension Act does not eliminate existing credit balances or prevent excess contributions from being maintained as a credit balance after the new funding rules go into effect for plan years beginning after 2007. However, it separates existing credit balances from those that may be accumulated and maintained after the funding rules go into effect. Specifically, the Pension Act divides credit balances into: (1) a funding standard carryover balance, which reflects a balance in the funding standard account at the end of the 2007 plan year; and (2) a prefunding balance, which may be elected by a plan to accumulate excess contributions after application of the new rules for plan years beginning after 2007 (ERISA Sec. 303(f) and Code Sec. 430(f), as added by the Pension Act).

The funding standard carryover balance and the prefunding balance may be credited against the minimum required contribution (if the plan is sufficiently funded), reducing the amount that must be paid for the year. However, credit balances used to offset the required minimum contribution will also reduce the value of plan assets. Accordingly, plan sponsors are allowed the alternative option of electing to reduce or waive the funding standard carryover and the prefunding credit balance so as to prevent the reduction of plan assets.

Funding standard carryover balance. The employer sponsor of a single-employer defined benefit plan that is in effect for a plan year beginning in 2007 and which has a positive credit balance in the funding standard account at the end of such plan year may elect to maintain a funding standard carryover balance until the balance is reduced to zero (ERISA Sec. 303(f) and Code Sec. 430(f), as added by the Pension Act). The balance is adjusted to reflect the plan's investment experience (see below).

The funding standard carryover balance will be reduced (but not below zero), beginning on the first day of each plan year beginning after 2008, by the amount credited towards reducing the minimum required contribution of the plan for the preceding year and by a reduction in the carryover balance elected by the sponsor in order to reduce the amount by which plan assets are reduced in determining the minimum required contribution (see below) (ERISA Sec. 303(f)(7)(C) and Code Sec. 430(f)(7)(C), as added by the Pension Act).

Prefunding balance. The prefunding credit balance consists of a beginning balance of zero and reflects contributions in excess of the minimum funding contribution required for plan years beginning after 2007 (ERISA Sec. 303(f)(6) and Code Sec.

NEW LAW EXPLAINED

430(f)(6), as added by the Pension Act). The prefunding balance will not only reflect excess contributions, but will reflect decreases in the prefunding balance caused by the use of funds to reduce the minimum required contribution of the plan for the preceding plan year and amounts elected as a reduction in the prefunding balance (see below).

Determining increase in prefunding balance. The Pension Act, effective as of the first day of each plan year beginning after 2008, authorizes the prefunding balance to be increased by the amount elected by the plan sponsor for the plan year. The increase may not be greater than the excess of the aggregate total of employer contribution to the plan for the preceding plan year, over the minimum required contributions for the preceding plan year (ERISA Sec. 303(f)(6)(B) and Code Sec. 430(f)(6)(B), as added by the Pension Act).

Excess contributions for the preceding year will be adjusted for interest (at the plan's effective interest rate for the preceding year) accruing during the period between the first day of the current plan year and the date on which the excess contributions were made (ERISA Sec. 303(f)(6)(B)(ii) and Code Sec. 430(f)(6)(B)(ii), as added by the Pension Act). Contributions in a preceding year will be treated as having been first directed to satisfy the minimum required funding contribution.

Excess contributions for a preceding plan year will be reduced (but not below zero) by the contribution the employer would be required to make to avoid the application of benefit limits under ERISA Sec. 206(g) and Code Sec. 436 (see ¶215). Thus, an employer may not retain credit balances that may be used to prevent application of a benefit limit.

Credit balance adjusted for investment experience. The plan sponsor will be required to adjust the prefunding balance and the funding standard carryover balance of the plan, as of the first day of the plan year, to reflect the rate of return (gain or loss) on plan assets from the preceding plan year (ERISA Sec. 303(f)(8) and Code Sec. 430(f)(8), as added by the Pension Act). Specifically, investment return will be determined on the basis of fair market value, taking into account (and in compliance with regulations to be issued by Secretary of the Treasury) all contributions, distributions, and other plan payments made during the period (ERISA Sec. 303(f)(8) and Code Sec. 430(f)(8), as added by the Pension Act). Thus, a plan's credit balance will no longer be determined under the plan's assumed interest rate, irrespective of the plan's investment performance.

Election to apply credit balance against minimum required contribution. Under current law, a credit balance automatically reduces a required contribution in a future year. The Pension Act does not preclude employers from continuing to use credit balances to pay required contributions (and, thus, does not discourage employers from pre-funding their plans). Rather, for plan year beginning in 2008, the sponsor of a plan that is not below a threshold funding level may "elect" to credit all or a portion of the prefunding balance or the funding standard carryover balance plan year against the minimum required contribution for the current plan year (ERISA Sec. 303(f)(3)(A) and Code Sec. 430(f)(3)(A), as added by the Pension Act). The minimum required contribution will be reduced, as of the first day of the plan year, by the credited

NEW LAW EXPLAINED

amount. However, the amount credited may not exceed the minimum required contribution.

> **Comment:** The determination of the amount of the minimum required contribution must take into account any waiver under ERISA Sec. 302(C) and Code Sec. 412(c) (see ¶205).

A plan sponsor who elects to use credit balances to offset the required minimum contribution must first exhaust the funding standard carryover balance before applying any portion of the prefunding balance (ERISA Sec. 303(f)(3)(B) and Code Sec. 430(f)(3)(B), as added by the Pension Act).

In addition, an employer may not use a funding standard carryover or prefunding credit balance to reduce the minimum required contribution if the value of plan assets for the preceding plan year (as reduced by any prefunding balance, but not the funding standard carryover balance) is less than 80 percent of the plan's funding target for the preceding plan year (determined without regard to the plan's at-risk status under ERISA Sec. 303(i)) (ERISA Sec. 303(f)(3)(C) and Code Sec. 430(f)(3)(C), as added by the Pension Act).

> **Comment:** The Pension Act effectively prohibits the use of credit balances to reduce the minimum contribution required of underfunded plans. Thus, contrary to earlier proposals, an underfunded plan may not use a prefunding balance to offset the portion of a required contribution that exceeds the amount exceeding target normal cost or 25 percent of the minimum required contribution.

This is in contrast to current law under which the value of plan assets is not reduced by any credit balance in determining whether the plan's funded current liability percentage is under 90 percent and, thus, whether a deficit reduction contribution is required. The Pension Act does require the value of plan assets to be reduced by the full amount of the prefunding balance in determining the minimum required contribution (ERISA Sec. 303(f)(4)(B) and Code Sec. 430(f)(4)(B), as added by the Pension Act).

> **Comment:** The rule requiring plan assets to be reduced by the full amount of a prefunding credit balance in determining the minimum required contribution is designed to ensure that credit balances are directed towards funding the plan. However, this goal could be undermined if the provision that restricts plans that are less than 80-percent funded from using the credit balance to pay the minimum required contribution discourages employers from prefunding plans.

The Pension Act expands the application of credit balances to reduce plan assets for other funding purposes as well. Under the Act, plan assets will be deemed reduced by the amount of the prefunding balance and the funding standard carryover balance for purposes of determining the plan's funding shortfall and the funding target attainment percentage (ERISA Sec. 303(f)(4)(B)(i) and Code Sec. 430(f)(4)(B)(i), as added by the Pension Act).

Agreement with PBGC may prevent use of credit balance to reduce plan assets. The plan sponsor and the PBGC may negotiate a binding written agreement preventing the use of a credit balance to reduce the minimum required contribution for the plan year.

NEW LAW EXPLAINED

Under such circumstances, plan assets will not be deemed reduced by the plan's funding standard carryover balance or the prefunding balance (ERISA Sec. 303(f)(4)(B)(ii) and Code Sec. 430(f)(4)(B)(ii), as added by the Pension Act).

Election to waive credit balance. Because plan assets are generally reduced by the amount of a credit balance in determining the minimum required contribution, a plan sponsor may alternatively elect to permanently reduce (or waive) a prefunding balance and the funding standard carryover balance for any plan by any amount (but not below zero) (ERISA Sec. 303(f)(5) and Code Sec. 430(f)(5), as added by the Pension Act). The reduction will take effect before the valuation of plan assets for the year and before the application of an election to use the balance to offset the required minimum contribution. Accordingly, by making the election, a plan sponsor may protect plan assets from being reduced by the credit balance in determining the minimum required contribution. However, the funding standard carryover balance must be exhausted before the prefunding balance may be reduced (ERISA Sec. 303(f)(5)(B) and Code Sec. 430(f)(5)(B), as added by the Pension Act).

> **Comment:** The waived amount of a credit balance will be included in plan assets. Thus, a waiver of a credit balance will enhance the plan's funding ratio and may result in a lower minimum required contribution. But if any portion of the prefunding balance is used to reduce a minimum required contribution, the value of plan assets will be deemed reduced by the prefunding balance in determining whether the plan's assets will be less than the applicable funding target, and thus, whether a shortfall amortization base must be established for the plan year (ERISA Sec. 303(f)(4)(A) and Code Sec. 430(f)(4)(A), as added by the Pension Act). The effect of this restriction is to prevent the prefunding balance from being included in plan assets in order to avoid a shortfall amortization base for a plan year (see above) and also being used to reduce the minimum required contribution for the same plan year.

Valuation date.—The valuation date of a plan for any plan year will, generally, be the first day of the plan year (ERISA Sec. 303(g)(2)(A) and Code Sec. 430(g)(2)(A), as added by the Pension Act). Accordingly, plan sponsors will no longer have the discretion to select *any* day during the plan year as the valuation date. An exception applies to small plans. A plan that had 100 or fewer participants on each day during the preceding plan year may designate any day during the plan year as the valuation date for the plan year and succeeding plan years (ERISA Sec. 303(g)(2)(B) and Code Sec. 430(g)(2)(B), as added by the Pension Act). For purposes of the exception, all single-employer defined benefit plans maintained by the same employer or predecessor employer (including members of the employer's controlled group) are treated as one plan (ERISA Sec. 303(g)(2)(C)(ii) and Code Sec. 430(g)(2)(C)(ii), as added by the Pension Act). However, only participants with respect to the employer or controlled group member will be taken into account. A first year plan may fall within the small plan rule if there is a reasonable expectation that it will have 100 or fewer participants during such first plan year (ERISA Sec. 303(g)(2)(C) and Code Sec. 430(g)(2)(C), as added by the Pension Act).

Pre-and post-valuation date contributions. Contributions for a prior year that are made by an employer after the valuation date for the plan year in which the contributions

NEW LAW EXPLAINED

are made will be treated as a plan asset for the current plan year as of the valuation date. However, in the case of any plan year beginning after 2008, only the present value (determined as of the current year valuation date) of the contribution may be taken into account (ERISA Sec. 303(g)(4)(A) and Code Sec. 430(g)(4)(A), as added by the Pension Act). Present value is determined using the effective interest rate for the preceding plan year to which the contribution is allocable. Note, no required contribution for the current plan year is taken into account in valuing plan assets under such circumstances.

In the event contributions are made during the plan year, but before the valuation date for the plan year, the assets of the plan on the valuation date will not include such contributions or interest on the contributions accrued during the period between the date of the contribution and the valuation date (determined pursuant to the plan's effective rate of interest for the current plan year) (ERISA Sec. 303(g)(4)(B) and Code Sec. 403(g)(4)(B), as added by the Pension Act).

Valuation of assets.—The value of plan assets is determined, under current law on the basis of any reasonable actuarial method that takes fair market value into account. Under the Pension Act, the value of plan assets must, generally, be fair market value (ERISA Sec. 303(g)(3)(A) and Code Sec. 403(g)(3)(A), as added by the Pension Act).

A plan may, alternatively, determine the value of plan assets by averaging fair market values (ERISA Sec. 303(g)(3)(B) and Code Sec. 430(g)(3)(B), as added by the Pension Act). The Pension Act , thus, does not eliminate such "smoothing" of asset values. However, the averaging method must: (1) be permitted under regulations to be promulgated by the Secretary of the Treasury; and (2) may not provide for the averaging of fair market value over more than the period beginning on the last day of the 25th month preceding the month in which the valuation date occurs and ending on the valuation date (or a similar period if the valuation date is not the first day of the month) (ERISA Sec. 303(g)(3)(B) and Code Sec. 430(g)(3)(B), as added by the Pension Act).

> **Comment:** Current law allows plan assets to be smoothed over five years and liabilities over four years. The requirement under the Pension Act that plan assets and liabilities be smoothed over two years has raised the specter of volatility in plan contributions that smoothing was designed to neutralize.

Current law allows for smoothing techniques that may produce actuarial values of between 80–120 percent of current fair market value. Under the Pension Act, the smoothing method must result in a plan asset valuation of between 90–110 percent of the fair market value of the assets (ERISA Sec. 303(g)(3)(B)(iii) and Code Sec. 430(g)(3)(B)(iii), as added by the Pension Act).

Interest rate assumptions: segmented yield curve.—The determination of present value and other funding computations will be made on the basis of reasonable actuarial assumptions and methods that take into account the experience of the plan and offer an actuary's best estimate of anticipated experience under the plan (ERISA Sec. 303(h) and Code Sec. 430(h), as added by the Pension Act).

NEW LAW EXPLAINED

Effective for plan years beginning before 2007, the Pension Act extends the use of the corporate bond rate for determining the determination of present value and other funding computations. Thus, through 2007, the applicable interest rate will be based on an interest rate that is not above and not more than 10 percent below the weighted average of rates of interest on amounts conservatively invested in long-term corporate bonds during the 4-year period ending on the last day before the beginning of the plan year (ERISA Sec. 302(b)(5)(B)(ii)(II) and 302(d)(7)(C)(i)(V), and Code Sec. 412(b)(5)(B)(ii)(II) and 412(l)(7)(c)(i)(V), as amended by the Pension Act).

Effective for plan years beginning after 2007, the interest rate used in determining present value will be based on the performance of corporate bonds as reflected in a segmented yield curve that reflects the age of an employer's work force (ERISA Sec. 303(h)(2)(B) and Code Sec. 430(h)(2)(B), as added by the Pension Act). The yield curve will essentially consist of different interest rates applicable to benefits payable in three different time periods (i.e., segments). The applicable interest rate will be determined by the segment in which the expected payment due date falls, ranging from 0–5 years, 5–20 years, or over 20 years. Generally, employers with an older work force will be required to use a short-term corporate bond rate, resulting in higher contributions.

> **Comment:** The yield curve is an acknowledgement that an employer's funding liabilities are, to a large degree, a function of the demographic profile of the plan's population. Accordingly, an employer with an older plan population nearing retirement age will have a larger funding obligation based on its applicable interest rates, as compared to a new company with a younger plan population, because its liabilities would be discounted at short-term interest rates.

Segment rates. The first segment rate applies to benefits that can be reasonably determined to be payable during the five-year period beginning on the first day of the plan year. The applicable interest rate will be based on the corporate bond yield curve for the month taking into account only the portion of the yield curve which is based on bonds maturing during the five-year period beginning in such month (ERISA Sec. 303(h)(2)(B)(i) and (h)(2)(C)(i), and Code Sec. 430(h)(2)(B)(i) and (h)(2)(C)(i), as added by the Pension Act).

The second segment rate applies to benefits that can be reasonably determined to be payable after five years, but within 20 years (ERISA Sec. 303(h)(2)(B)(ii) and Code Sec. 430(h)(2)B)(ii), as added by the Pension Act). The applicable interest rate will be based on the corporate bond yield curve for the month, taking into account only the portion of the yield curve that is based on bonds maturing during the 5–20 year period (ERISA Sec. 303(h)(2)(C)(ii) and Code Sec. 430(h)(2)(C)(ii), as added by the Pension Act).

> **Comment:** Unlike prior proposals, the yield curve adopted by the Pension Act is not based on bonds maturing during "each" of the years in the 15-year period.

The third segment applies to benefits that can be reasonably determined to be payable in over 20 years (ERISA Sec. 303(h)(2)(B)(iii) and Code Sec. 430(h)(2)(B)(iii), as added by the Pension Act). The applicable interest rate will be based on the corporate bond yield curve for the month, taking into account only that portion of the

NEW LAW EXPLAINED

yield curve which is based on bonds maturing during the period beginning after 20 years (ERISA Sec. 303(h)(2)(C)(iii) and Code Sec. 430(h)(2)(C)(iii), as added by the Pension Act).

> **Comment:** The segmented yield curve will be phased in over a three year period, absent a contrary election by the plan sponsor (see below).

Corporate bond yield curve. The yield curve applicable in a month will be prescribed by the Secretary of the Treasury and will reflect the unweighted average, for the 24-month period ending with the month preceding such month, of yields on investment grade corporate bonds with varying maturities that are in the top three quality levels available (ERISA Sec. 303(h)(2)(D) and Code Sec. 430(h)(2)(D), as added by the Pension Act). The interest rate for each segment is based on the average of all rates in the segment.

The Secretary must also provide a description of the methodology used to determine the yield curve and rates that is sufficiently detailed to enable plans to make reasonable projections regarding the yield curve and segment rates for future months based on the plan's projection of future interest rates (ERISA Sec. 303(h)(2)(F) and Code Sec. 430(h)(2)(F), as added by the Pension Act).

The month to which the segment rate applies will generally be the month that includes the valuation date of the plan for the plan year (ERISA Sec. 303(h)(2)(E) and Code Sec. 430(h)(2)(E), as added by the Pension Act). However, at the election of the plan sponsor, the applicable month may be any of the four months preceding the month including the plan's valuation date. Pursuant to this election, the segment rate could be used in any of the four months preceding the month in which the plan year begins. This election will apply in all succeeding plan years, unless revoked with the consent of the Secretary of theTreasury.

As an alternative to the segment rates, a plan sponsor, in determining the minimum required contribution, may elect to use interest rates under the corporate bond yield curve for the month preceding the month in which the plan year begins (ERISA Sec. 303(h)(2)(D)(ii) and Code Sec. 430(h)(2)(D)(ii), as added by the Pension Act). Unlike the segmented yield curve, yields on corporate bonds under the full yield curve are not averaged over 24 months. However, an election to use the full yield curve without averaging may only be revoked with the consent of the Secretary of the Treasury.

Transition rule phases in segmented yield curve. The segmented interest rate will be phased in over a three-year period for plans in existence before 2008 (ERISA Sec. 303(h)(2)(G) and Code Sec. 430(h)(2)(G), as added by the Pension Act.). Under the transition rule, for plan years beginning in 2008 or 2009, the first, second, or third segment rate for a plan with respect to any month will be the sum of:

(1) the product of the segment rate for the month multiplied by the applicable percentage (33⅓ percent for 2008 and 66⅔ percent for 2009); and

(2) the product of the long-term corporate bond rate determined under ERISA Sec. 302(b)(5)(ii)(II) (as in effect for plan years beginning in 2007), multiplied by a percentage equal to 100 percent minus the applicable percentage (33⅓ percent

NEW LAW EXPLAINED

for 2008 and 66⅔ percent for 2009) (ERISA Sec. 303(h)(2)(G) and Code Secs. 412(b)(5)(B)(ii)(II) and 430(h)(2)(G), as added by the Pension Act).

A plan sponsor is not required to phase in the use of the segmented rates. The sponsor may elect to apply the segment rates beginning in 2008. However, plan sponsors should be cautioned that the election may only be revoked with the consent of the Secretary of the Treasury (ERISA Sec. 303(h)(2)(G)(iv) and Code Sec. 430(h)(2)(G)(iv), as added by the Pension Act).

Mortality tables.—The Secretary of the Treasury is required by the Pension Act to prescribe mortality tables to be used in determining present value or making any required funding computation. The tables are to be based on the actual experience of pension plans and projected trends in experience (ERISA Sec. 303(h)(3) and Code Sec. 430(h)(3), as added by the Pension Act). The Secretary of the Treasury will be required to revise the tables at least every 10 years to reflect the actual experience of pension plans and projected trends in experience (ERISA Sec. 303(g)(3)(B) and Code Sec. 430(h)(3)(B), as added by the Pension Act).

Comment: The Pension Act does not require use of the RP-2000 Mortality Table that was introduced in IRS Proposed Reg. § 1.412(l)(7)-1 and designed to be effective in 2007. The RP-2000 Mortality Table reflects improvements in mortality rates, including future improvements, projected to the current year. Accordingly, the Secretary of the Treasury may exercise its discretion under the Act to adopt the Table. However, note that the Pension Act does not allow for the phase in of the prescribed mortality table. Thus, if the RP-2000 Combined Mortality Table is adopted, the Act does not explicitly authorize the Table to be phased in over a specified period of years. Accordingly, differences in assumptions under the RP-2000 Combined Mortality Table and the GAM 83 Table may not be phased in ratably over a specified period.

Plan specific tables. The Pension Act allows a plan sponsor to apply a plan-specific mortality table, but only with approval of the Secretary of the Treasury and under strictly defined conditions (ERISA Sec. 303(h)(3)(C) and Code Sec. 430(h)(3)(C), as added by the Pension Act). The Secretary, however, will not approve a plan-specific table absent credible information, based on the number of participants and the period of time the plan has been maintained, that is sufficient to allow a determination that the proposed table reflects actual plan experience and projected trends in general mortality experience (ERISA Sec. 303(h)(3)(C)(iii) and Code Sec. 430(h)(3)(C)(iii), as added by the Pension Act).

The plan- specific table may only be used in determining present value or making other computations for a period of consecutive plan years specified in the request, but not to exceed 10 years (ERISA Sec. 303(h)(3)(C)(i) and Code Sec. 430(h)(3)(C)(i), as added by the Pension Act). In addition, a plan-specific mortality table may no longer be used (even if the specified period has not elapsed) in the event of significant change in plan participation, caused by a plan spinoff, merger, or other circumstance (ERISA Sec. 303(h)(3)(C)(ii) and Code Sec. 430(h)(3)(C)(ii), as added by the Pension Act). The table will also cease to apply at an earlier date if the table no longer reflects the actual experience of the plan maintained by the sponsor and projected trends in general mortality experience.

NEW LAW EXPLAINED

> **Comment:** The period of years over which the plan-specific mortality table may be used must be consecutive. Thus, a plan sponsor may not apply a plan-specific table to only selected years within a specified period.

In the event an employer sponsors more than one plan, a separate mortality table must be established for each plan. In addition, if the plan sponsor is a member of a controlled group, a separate table must be established for the plan of each member of a controlled group (ERISA Sec. 303(h)((3)(C)(iv) and Code Sec. 430(h)(3(c)(iv), as added by the Pension Act).

The table must satisfy the requirements of ERISA Sec. 303(h)(3)(C)(iii) and Code Sec. 430(h)(3)(C)(iii) separately with respect to each plan in a controlled group. The determination of whether that table reflects the actual experience of the plan and projected trends in general mortality experience will be made by taking into account only the participants of the separate plans and the actual experience of those plans.

> **Comment:** The requirement that employers sponsoring more than one plan apply different plan specific mortality tables to each plan will effectively prevent the situation in which a plan that covers rank and file employees and a plan that covers executive employee use the same mortality table, even where the mortality experience of the plans is substantially different.

Submission for plan-specific mortality table. The plan sponsor must request approval from the Secretary of the Treasury of the proposed plan-specific mortality table. The proposed table must be submitted to the Secretary no later than seven months before the first day of the consecutive period of years during which the table is to apply (ERISA Sec. 303(h)(3)(C)(v)(I) and Code Sec. 430(h)(3)(C)(v)(I), as added by the Pension Act).

The Secretary of the Treasury is allowed 180 days from the date of submission to reject the request and provide a statement of the reasons the proposed plan-specific table fails to comply with the governing requirements. The 180-day period may be extended during the period the Secretary is waiting for further information from the plan sponsor (ERISA Sec. 303(h)(3)(C)(V)(II) and Code Sec. 430(h)(3)(C)(V)(II), as added by the Pension Act). In the event the Secretary does not act on the sponsor's request within the 180-day period (or extended period), the plan-specific table will be treated as effective for the first plan year in the period of consecutive years specified in the request.

Separate mortality table for disabled individuals. The Secretary of the Treasury is required to establish alternative mortality tables for individuals who are entitled to plan benefits because of disability. The separate tables will need to be provided for individuals whose disabilities occurred in plan years beginning before January 1, 1995, and for individuals whose disabilities occurred or occur in plan years beginning on or after that date (ERISA Sec. 303(h)(3)(D)(i) and Code Sec. 430(h)(3)(D)(i), as added by the Pension Act). The Secretary would be required to revise the tables, at least every 10 years, in or order to reflect the actual experience of pension plans and projected trends in such experience (ERISA Sec. 303(h)(3)(D)(iii) and Code Sec. 430(h)(3)(D)(iii), as added by the Pension Act).

NEW LAW EXPLAINED

Accounting for probability of lump-sum benefit payments.—In determining present value or in making other required funding computations, the plan sponsor must account for the probability that future benefit payments will be made in a lump-sum or in another optional form of benefit authorized under the plan. The assumptions used in determining optional forms of benefit under the plan may differ from the assumptions prescribed by the Pension Act for determining present value. However, the plan sponsor must account for any difference in the present value of such future benefit payments resulting from the use of actuarial assumptions in determining benefit payments in the optional form, which are different from those required under the Act (ERISA Sec. 303(h)(4) and Code Sec. 430(h)4), as added by the Pension Act.

Changes in actuarial assumptions require IRS approval.—Actuarial assumptions used in determining the funding target for a single-employer plan with large unfunded vested benefits may not be changed without approval of the IRS (ERISA Sec. 303(h)(5) and Code Sec. 430(h)(5), as added by the Pension Act). The restriction applies to plans with aggregate unfunded vested benefits, as of the close of preceding plan year of the plan and all other plans maintained by contributing sponsors and members of the sponsors' controlled group (other than plans with no unfunded vested benefits) that exceed $50 million (ERISA Sec. 303(h)(5)(B) and Code Sec. 430(h)(5)(B), as added by the Pension Act).

IRS approval is not required, however, if the change in assumptions will not result in a decrease in the funding shortfall of the plan for the current plan year that: (1) exceeds $50 million; or (2) is in excess of $5 million and is five percent or more of the funding target of the plan before the change in assumptions (ERISA Sec. 303(h)(5)(B)(iii) and Code Sec. 430(h)(5)(B)(iii), as added by the Pension Act).

At-risk plans.—Plans with more than 500 participants that have a funded target attainment percentage in the preceding year below designated thresholds will be deemed "at-risk" and subject to increased target liability for plan years beginning after 2007. The funding percentage will be determined by subtracting credit balances from plan assets. The increased at-risk liability payment will be phased in over a five consecutive year period beginning in 2008 (ERISA Sec. 303(i) and Code Sec. 430(i), as added by the Pension Act).

> **Comment:** It is important to clarify that a plan's at-risk funding target and a plan sponsor's attendant funding obligation are not determined by the financial condition of the plan sponsor, as reflected in credit ratings. At-risk status is strictly a function of the plan's funded status and specified participant demographics, discussed below.

"70/80 percent" threshold test for at-risk status. Plans with more than 500 participants during each day of the preceding plan year (aggregating all single-employer defined benefit plans maintained by the employer, predecessor employer or a member of the employer's controlled group) are subject to a two-tiered determination of at-risk status (ERISA Sec. 303(i)(4) and (6)), and Code Sec. 430(i)(4) and (6), as added by the Pension Act). Specifically, a plan is at-risk if:

NEW LAW EXPLAINED

(1) the funding target attainment percentage (i.e., ratio of plan assets (reduced by credit balances) to the funding target for the preceding plan year, determined without regard to at-risk liability) is less than 80 percent; ***and***

(2) the funding target attainment percentage for the preceding plan year, determined by applying the specified at-risk actuarial assumptions, is less than 70 percent (ERISA Sec. 303(i)(4)(A) and Code Sec. 430(i)(4)(A), as added by the Pension Act).

> **Comment:** Both components of the test must apply in order for a plan to be treated as at-risk. Thus, if a plan fails the 70-percent at-risk test, but satisfies the 80-percent ongoing liability test, it will not be subject to at-risk liability.

The 80-percent funding target component of the at-risk test is phased in over a four-year period, beginning in 2008. The applicable percentages will be: 65 percent in 2008, 70 percent in 2009, 75 percent in 2010, and 80 percent in 2011 and thereafter (ERISA Sec. 303(i)(4)(B) and Code Sec. 430(i)(4)(B), as added by the Pension Act). The funding target attainment percentage for the preceding plan year of plan years beginning in 2008 may be estimated, pursuant to regulations to be issued by the Secretary of the Treasury.

> **Comment:** The 70 percent at-risk funding target will apply beginning in 2008. However, the resultant at-risk liability is phased in over five years (see below).

> **Comment:** In applying the 80-percent ongoing liability test and the 70-percent at-risk liability test, funding standard carryover and prefunding credit balances are deducted from plan assets. Thus, the actual value of plan assets will be reduced by credit balances in applying the 80-percent funding target and the 70-percent at-risk funding target.

At-risk actuarial assumptions. The determination of at-risk liability is made by assuming that all employees who will be eligible to elect benefits during the current plan year and in the 10 succeeding plan years will retire at the earliest date authorized under the plan (but not before the end of the plan year for which the at-risk determination is being made) (ERISA Sec. 303(i)(1)(B)(i) and Code Sec. 430(i)(1)(B)(i), as added by the Pension Act). In addition, all employees will be assumed to elect the retirement benefit available under the plan at the assumed retirement age (i.e., earliest retirement date authorized under the plan) that would result in the highest present value of benefits (ERISA Sec. 303(i)(1)((B)(ii) and Code Sec. 430(i)(1))(B)(ii), as added by the Pension Act). A loading factor also applies to certain plans (see below).

An exemption from the at-risk liability assumptions applies to employees of specified automobile and automobile parts manufacturers who rejected early retirement incentive offers made in 2006 that were conditioned on acceptance before 2007 and retirement before 2011 (ERISA Sec. 303(i)(4)(C) and Code Sec. 430(i)(4)(C), as added by the Pension Act). Thus, in determining, for example, whether a plan's funding target attainment percentage was less than 70 percent in the preceding plan year, employees of an automobile manufacturer who rejected an early retirement incentive offer made in 2006 that conditioned substantial amounts of cash and substantially enhanced retirement benefits on retirement before 2011, would be disregarded.

NEW LAW EXPLAINED

Funding target for at-risk plans. At-risk plans are subject to a higher funding target and to a higher target normal cost that will effectively require plan sponsors to make larger minimum funding contributions. The funding target and target normal cost for an at-risk plan for the plan year will be the present value of all benefits accrued or earned under the plan as of the beginning of the plan year, as determined by application of the at-risk actuarial assumptions (ERISA Sec. 303(i)(1)(A) and 303(i)(2)(A) and Code Sec. 430(i)(1)(A) and 430(i)(2)(A), as added by the Pension Act).

However, plans that are at risk for the current year and for two of the four preceding plan years are subject to a "loading factor." The loading factor is designed to reflect the cost of purchasing group annuity contracts in the event that the plan terminates. The funding target will be increased by the sum of $700 per plan participant, plus four percent of the funding target for the plan year determined without regard to the loading factor (ERISA Sec. 303(i)(1)(C) and 303(i)(2)(B) and Code Sec. 430(i)(1)(C) and 430(i)(2)(B), as added by the Pension Act). Target normal cost of such a plan will be increased by four percent of the target normal cost that would be determined without regard to the loading factor. Thus, target normal cost will not be increased by the $700 per participant load factor.

> **Comment:** An at-risk plan will not be required to fund more than 100 percent of its ongoing liability. However, the liability of an at-risk plan, under the additional actuarial assumptions, will be larger than other plans. In addition, the at-risk funding target and at-risk target normal cost of a plan may never be less than the funding target and target normal cost that would result without application of the at-risk rules (ERISA Sec. 303(i)(3) and Code Sec. 430(i)(3), as added by the Pension Act).

Phase-in rules for at-risk liability. At-risk liability will be phased in at 20 percent per year over a period of five consecutive years effective for plan years beginning after 2007. Specifically, if a plan is in at-risk status for a consecutive period of less than five plan years, the amount of the funding target and target normal cost will be: (1) the funding target and normal target cost determined without reference to the at-risk rules; plus (2) an applicable transition percentage for the plan year of the increased funding target or normal cost attributable to the at-risk rules (ERISA Sec. 303(i)(5) and Code Sec. 430(i)(5), as added by the Pension Act).

The applicable transition percentage is based on the consecutive number of years (including the plan year) that the plan is in at-risk status. The transition percentages are 20, 40, 60, and 80 percent for the first, second, third and fourth years, respectively, that the plan is in at-risk status, beginning in 2008 (ERISA Sec. 303(i)(5)(B) and Code Sec. 303(i)(5)(B), as added by the Pension Act). Plan years beginning before 2008 are not considered for purposes of the transition rules (ERISA Sec. 303(i)(5)(C) and Code Sec. 430(i)(5)(C), as added by the Pension Act).

Annual payment of minimum required contribution.—The minimum required contribution for a plan year must be paid within 8½ months after the close of the plan year (ERISA Sec. 303(j)(1) and Code Sec. 430(j)(1), as added by the Pension Act). Payments made on a date other than the valuation date for the plan year must be adjusted for interest accruing for the period from the valuation date to the payment

NEW LAW EXPLAINED

date, at the effective rate of interest for the plan for the year (ERISA Sec. 303(j)(2) and Code Sec. 430(j)(2), as added by the Pension Act).

Under current law, in the event a plan fails to meet the meet the minimum funding requirements, the employer sponsor and all members of a controlled group of which the employer is a member, are subject to two successive nondeductible excise taxes. First, a 10 percent initial tax is imposed on the accumulated funding deficiency of a single-employer plan (five percent for multiemployer plans). In the event a funding deficiency is not corrected within a specified period of time, an additional 100 percent tax is assessed. However, the 100 percent additional tax may be waived by the Secretary of the Treasury if the employer can establish substantial business hardship.

The Pension Act retains the excise tax for employers that fail to make minimum required contributions under the new funding rules and do not obtain a waiver. The sponsor of a single-employer plan is subject to a 10 percent excise tax on the aggregate unpaid minimum required contribution for all plans that remain unpaid as of the end of any plan year ending with or within the tax year (Code Sec. 4971(a), as amended by the Pension Act). An initial tax is assessed on five percent of the accumulated funding deficiency under a multiemployer plan. As under current law, sponsors may be subject to an additional 100 percent tax on the amount of an unpaid minimum contribution for a single-employer plan (or accumulated funding deficiency for a multiemployer plan) remaining unpaid as of the close of the taxable period (Code Sec. 4971(b), as amended by the Pension Act).

An ordering rule governs the payment of outstanding minimum required contributions. Specifically, any payment to a plan for any plan year will be allocated first to the unpaid minimum required contribution for all preceding plan years on a "first-in, first-out" basis, before being directed to the minimum required contribution for the current plan year (Code Sec. 4971(c)(4), as amended by the Pension Act).

Accelerated quarterly contribution for underfunded plans.—Employers maintaining plans that had a funding shortfall for the preceding plan year (i.e., the value of plan assets (reduced by credit balances) was less than the funding target for the preceding year) must make quarterly contributions to the plan (ERISA Sec. 303(j)(3)(A) and Code Sec. 303(j)(3)(A), as added by the Pension Act). In the event the employer fails to pay the full amount of a required quarterly installment, interest will be assessed at the plan's specified rate of interest plus five percentage points. Interest will be assessed on the amount of the underpayment for the due date of the installment until the date on which the remaining portion is contributed to the plan (ERISA Sec. 303(j)(3)(B) and Code Sec. 430(j)((3)(B), as added by the Pension Act). In determining the amount of an underpayment, an ordering rule requires contributions to credited against unpaid required installments in the order in which the installment must be paid (ERISA Sec. 303(j)(3)(B)(iii) and Code Sec. 430(j)(3)(B)(iii), as added by the Pension Act).

Amount of quarterly installment. The quarterly contribution will be 25 percent of the required annual payment. The required annual payment is defined as the lesser of: (1) 90 percent of the minimum required contribution (determined without regard to the accelerated contribution requirement) for the plan year; or (2) 100 percent of the minimum required contribution (determined without regard to the accelerated con-

NEW LAW EXPLAINED

tribution requirement or to any waiver under ERISA Sec. 302(c) or Code Sec. 412(c)) for the preceding plan year (ERISA Sec. 303(j)(3)(D) and Code Sec. 430(j)(3)(D), as added by the Pension Act).

Comment: If the preceding plan year was not a year of 12 months, the required annual payment will be 90 percent of the minimum required contribution (determined without regard to the accelerated contribution requirement).

Comment: Plans with short plan years of under 12 months are not exempt from the accelerated contribution requirement. The Treasury is to prescribe regulations applying the requirements to such plans (ERISA Sec. 303(j)(3)(E) and Code Sec. 430(j)(3)(E), as added by the Pension Act).

The quarterly installments will be due on April 15, July 15, October 15, and January 15 of the following year (ERISA Sec. 303(j)(3)(C)(ii) and Code Sec. 430(j)((3)(C)(ii), as added by the Pension Act).

Liquidity requirement. An employer maintaining a plan that had over 100 participants on each day during the preceding plan year will be treated as failing to pay the full amount of a required quarterly installment if the value of the liquid assets (e.g., cash or marketable securities) paid in the installment is less than the "liquidity shortfall" (ERISA Sec. 303(j)(4)(A) and Code Sec. 430(j)(4)(A), as added by the Pension Act).

Comment: The consequence of the liquidity rule may be an increase in the amount of the required quarterly installment payment. However, the increase may not exceed the amount, which when added to the prior installment for the plan year, is necessary to increase the funding target attainment percentage of the plan for the plan year to 100 percent (ERISA Sec. 303(j)(4)(D) and Code Sec. 430(j)(4)(D), as added by the Pension Act).

A "liquidity shortfall" is defined as the excess (as of the last day of the quarter for which the installment is made) of the "base amount" for the quarter over the value (as of the last day of quarter) of the plan's liquid assets (ERISA Sec. 303(j)(4)(E) and Code Sec. 430(j)(4)(E), as added by the Pension Act). The base amount for any quarter is three times the sum of the adjusted disbursements from the plan for the 12-month period ending on the last day of the quarter. Adjusted disbursements are disbursements from the plan (e.g., purchases of annuities, payment of lump sums and other benefits, and administrative expenses) reduced by the product of the plan's funding target attainment percentage for the plan year and the sum of the annuity purchases, payments of single sums, and other disbursements as specified in Treasury regulations.

Nonrecurring circumstances may cause an increase in the base amount. However, nonrecurring circumstances that have the effect (as certified by an enrolled actuary to the satisfaction of the Secretary of the Treasury) of causing the base amount to exceed two times the sum of the adjusted disbursement from the plan for the 36 months ending on the last day of the quarter, may be disregarded in determining the base amount for the quarter.

Plan lien following employer failure to make required funding contribution.—In the event an employer fails to make a required contribution to a single-employer defined benefit plan before the scheduled date for payment, a lien will be imposed in

NEW LAW EXPLAINED

favor of the plan on the aggregate unpaid balance of the required contribution payments (ERISA Sec. 303(k) and Code Sec. 430(k), as added by the Pension Act). The lien will not be imposed, however, unless: (1) the funding target attainment percentage for the plan is under 100 percent; and (2) the unpaid balance of the missed payment (including interest) when added to the aggregate balance of a preceding payment for which payment was not made before the due date (including interest), exceeds $1 million. The lien will extend to all property and rights to property (real and personal) belonging to the person required to make the payment and other members of the person's controlled group.

Compliance Tip: An employer that fails to make a required funding contribution must notify the PBGC of the failure within 10 days of the contribution due date.

The period of the lien will extend from the due date of the required contribution to the last day of the first plan year in which the aggregate unpaid balance of required contributions is under $1 million. The lien will continue to apply even if the plan's funding target attainment percentage is no longer below 100 percent during the prescribed period of the lien (ERISA Sec. 303(k)(4)(B) and Code Sec. 430(k)(4)(B), as added by the Pension Act).

A plan lien may generally only be perfected and enforced by the PBGC (ERISA Sec. 303(k)(5) and Code Sec. 430(k)(5), as added by the Pension Act). However, the PBGC may allow for the enforcement of the lien by the contributing sponsor or any member of the sponsor's controlled group.

Qualified transfers to retiree health accounts are not plan assets. Employers are authorized under current law (through 2013) to make tax-free transfers of excess defined benefit plan assets (other than those of a multiemployer plan) to a Code Sec. 401(h) retiree health benefits account. A "qualified transfer" of excess assets to a plan that complies with specified vesting and minimum benefit and cost requirements and that is used only to pay qualified retiree health liabilities, will not result in a loss of tax qualified status and will not be taxable or treated as a reversion to the employer. The qualified transfer of excess assets to a retiree health account will also be exempt from treatment under ERISA as a prohibited transaction. However, under the current minimum funding rules, any assets (and allocable income) transferred in a plan year or before the valuation date for the year are to be treated as plan assets as of the valuation date for the year. In addition, the plan is treated as having a net experience loss equal to the amount of the transfer and for which amortization charges begin for the first plan year in which the transfer occurs.

The Pension Act, effective after 2007, excludes qualified transfers to health benefit accounts from treatment as plan assets for purposes of the funding rules (Code Sec. 430(l), as added by the Pension Act). Similarly, transferred assets will not be treated as assets of the plan under the rules of Code Sec. 420 (Code Sec. 420(e)(4), as amended by the Pension Act).

Excess pension assets are defined under the current minimum funding rules by reference to the full funding limits of Code Sec. 412(c). The Pension Act amends the definition of excess pension assets to reflect the modified funding rules, effective for plan years beginning after 2007. Excess pension assets will be (a) the lesser of the fair market value of the plan's assets (reduced by prefunding and funding standard

NEW LAW EXPLAINED

carryover credit balances), or the value of plan assets under Code Sec. 430(g)(3), after reduction for credit balances, over (b) 125 percent of the sum of the funding shortfall and the target normal cost for the plan year (Code Sec. 420(e)(2), as amended by the Pension Act).

▶ **Effective dates.** The provisions apply with respect to plan years beginning after 2007 (Act Secs. 102(c), 107(c) and 112(b) of the Pension Protection Act of 2006).

Law source: Law at ¶5085, ¶5115, ¶5120, ¶5295, ¶5300, ¶5355, ¶7009, ¶7024, and ¶7054. Committee Report at ¶10,010.

— Act Sec. 102(a) of the Pension Protection Act of 2006, adding new ERISA Sec. 303;

— Act Sec. 107(b)(4), amending ERISA Sec. 4026(c);

— Act Sec. 112(a), adding new Code Sec. 430;

— Act Sec. 114(d), amending Code Sec. 420(e)(2) and (4);

— Act Sec. 114(e), amending Code Sec. 4971 and 4972;

— Act Sec. 114(f), amending Code Sec. 6059(b);

— Act Secs. 102(c), 107(e) and 112(b), providing the effective date.

Reporter references: For further information, consult the following CCH reporters.

— Pension Plan Guide, ¶2895

— Standard Federal Tax Reporter, 2006FED ¶19,125.01 and ¶19,125.0215

— Tax Research Consultant, RETIRE: 30,150 and RETIRE: 30,208

— Federal Tax Guide, 2006FTG ¶11,040

¶215 Benefit Limitations Under Single-Employer Pension Plans

SUMMARY OF NEW LAW

Single-employer defined benefit plans that fall below specified funding levels will be subject to new limits on: the payment of unpredictable contingent event benefits (e.g. shutdown benefits), plan amendments, lump-sum distributions, and benefit accruals. The restrictions, which are based on the ratio of the plan assets to target liability and triggered at varying thresholds, will generally be effective beginning in 2008. The limits require benefit accruals to be frozen and prevent underfunded plans that have been in effect for over five years from implementing amendments adding benefits or otherwise increasing plan liabilities or paying the full amount of a lump-sum distribution, without additional contributions by the plan sponsor. Employees must receive written notice of any benefit limitations within 30 days.

BACKGROUND

A single-employer defined benefit plan may entitle participants to an unpredictable contingent event benefit that is payable upon the occurrence during the plan year of specified events, such as the shutdown of an employer's operations. In the event a plan is required to pay a benefit arising from an unpredictable contingent event while its assets are less than its current liabilities, an additional funding contribution must be made (ERISA Sec. 302(d)(1)(B); Code Sec. 412(l)(1)(b)). However, unpredictable contingent event benefits are generally not taken into account for purposes of determining a plan's funding liabilities until the event has occurred.

Plan amendments that increase a plan's current liability (e.g., accelerated lump-sum payments) may not be adopted if the plan's funded current liability percentage is less than 60 percent, unless the employer provides security to the plan. In addition, plan amendments that increase a plan's benefit liabilities because of an increase in benefits, change in the rate of accrual of benefits, or change in the rate at which benefits vest under the plan may not be adopted while the employer is in bankruptcy or during the period of an IRS-approved funding waiver or amortization extension.

Finally, lump-sum distributions may not be made under a plan that has a liquidity shortfall (i.e., fund assets are less than three times the plan disbursements for the year). However, current law does not restrict future benefit accruals in underfunded plans, and employers are allowed under current law to use credit balances to reduce required contributions.

NEW LAW EXPLAINED

New benefit limits imposed on underfunded plans.—A single-employer defined benefit plan may continue to provide unpredictable contingent event benefits. However, an unpredictable contingent event benefit may not be paid if the plan's adjusted funding target attainment percentage for the plan year is less than 60 percent or would be less than 60 percent as a consequence of the occurrence of the event.

An employer also may not adopt an amendment to a single-employer defined benefit plan that is less than 80 percent funded that will have the effect of increasing plan liabilities, unless it makes additional contributions to the plan. The Act continues to authorize accelerated distributions, such as lump-sum payments, but subjects "prohibited payments" under plans that are below specified funding levels to restrictions. Single-employer defined benefit plans must further provide for the cessation of all benefit accruals under the plan in the event that the plan's adjusted funding target attainment percentage is less than 60 percent. The limitations will not, however apply during the first five years that a plan (or a predecessor plan) is in effect.

Finally, the plan administrator of a single-employer defined benefit plan must provide "written" notice to plan participants and beneficiaries within 30 days of the plan becoming subject to the limits on unpredictable contingent event benefits, and prohibited payments.

NEW LAW EXPLAINED

Practical Analysis: Curt Cartolano of Hewitt Associates, Lincolnshire, Illinois, notes that Act Secs. 103 and 113 introduce significant change by creating a direct and broad link between the funded level of a plan and the benefits that can be provided by the plan. This provision imposes new limits on the ability to pay lump sums, grant benefit increases, provide shutdown benefits and even provide ongoing benefit accruals based on the funded status of a qualified defined benefit plan. The new law is effective for plan years beginning after December 31, 2007.

For a plan that becomes subject to one of the restrictions, significant administrative tasks will be involved in communicating with participants, properly administering the plan during the restriction period, and then resuming pre-restriction operation of the plan after the restriction period has ended. Further, plan participants may make decisions around benefit elections or even continued employment based upon the risk of these restrictions applying, particularly the lump sum restriction.

The funding of the plan will also be made more complicated as most sponsors will want to avoid the restrictions. The funded ratio of a plan used for this purpose could be fairly volatile from year to year, though the 24-month averaging of the interest rate used to calculate liabilities and assets will help somewhat in this regard. Also helpful is that the funded ratio is calculated ignoring "at-risk" assumptions, even if the plan is "at-risk." Thus, a plan that becomes "at-risk" will not see its funded ratio decreased for purposes of the benefit restrictions.

Since credit balances are subtracted from assets for purposes of determining the funded ratio (unless the plan's funded ratio exceeds 100 percent without a subtraction of credit balances), plan sponsors will want to perform a multi-year projection of both future contributions and credit balances to determine the best strategy to maintain the funded level of the plan at an appropriate level, preserve credit balances, and anticipate the likelihood of becoming subject to the restrictions.

Adjusted funding target attainment percentage.—The new benefit limits are based on the plan's adjusted funding target attainment percentage (ERISA Sec. 206(g) and Code Sec. 436(b), as added by the Pension Act). A plan's funding target attainment percentage is the ratio of assets (minus funding standard carryover and pre-funding credit balances) to target liability (i.e., funding target) (disregarding the plan's at-risk status (see ¶ 210)) (ERISA Sec. 206(g) (9) (A) and Code Sec. 436(j) (1), as added by the Pension Act). The adjusted funding target attainment percentage reflects plan assets and funding target liabilities as increased by the aggregate amount of annuity purchases made for nonhighly compensated employees by the plan during the preceding two plan years (ERISA Sec. 206(g) (9) (B) and Code Sec. 436(j) (2), as added by the Pension Act).

Note, a special rule applicable to fully funded plans will allow the funding target attainment percentage to be determined without the reduction of plan assets by credit balances (see below).

Estimation of funding target attainment percentage for 2008. In determining the adjusted funding target attainment percentage for plan years beginning in 2008, the funding target attainment percentage for the preceding plan year may be determined under

NEW LAW EXPLAINED

methods of estimation that may be provided by the Treasury (ERISA Sec. 206(g)(10) and Code Sec. 436(k), as added by the Pension Act).

Limits on unpredictable contingent event benefits.—A single-employer defined benefit plan may entitle participants to an unpredictable contingent event benefit that is payable upon the occurrence during the plan year of specified events, such as the shutdown of an employer's operations. The plan must provide that the unpredictable contingent event benefit may not be paid if the plan's adjusted funding target attainment percentage for the plan year is less than 60 percent or would be less than 60 percent as a consequence of the occurrence of the event (ERISA Sec. 206(g)(1)(A) and Code Sec. 436(b)(1), as added by the Pension Act).

> **Comment:** The terms of the plan must incorporate the limit on unpredictable contingent event benefits. Thus, an employer must not only enforce the limit, but must amend its plan to reflect the restriction.

The restriction applies to benefits that are payable as a result of a plant shutdown, or a similar event as determined by the Treasury (ERISA Sec. 206(g)(1)(C)(i) and Code Sec. 436(b)(3)(A), as added by the Pension Act). In addition, the restriction will apply to benefits that are payable solely by reason of an event other than the attainment of any age, performance of any service, receipt or derivation of any compensation, or the occurrence of death or disability (ERISA Sec. 206(g)(1)(C)(ii) and Code Sec. 436(b)(3)(B), as added by the Pension Act).

> **Comment:** An unpredictable contingent event benefit includes, under current law, an event that the Treasury finds to be "reasonably and reliably predictable." Such events have included workforce reductions and sharp declines in the value of employer stock. However, benefits that are contingent on marital status, such as qualified joint and survivor annuities, are not unpredictable contingent event benefits.

Limit applies upon occurrence of event, not upon payment. The determination of whether the limitation on unpredictable contingent event benefits applies is made in the year the event occurs, and not when the benefit payments are actually made (ERISA Sec. 206(g)(1)(A) and Code Sec. 436(b)(1), as added by the Pension Act). Thus, for example, if a plant shutdown occurs in 2008 and the plan's funding target attainment percentage is 50 percent, shutdown benefits may not be paid (absent additional contributions by the employer), even if the benefits will not actually be paid until a later year.

> **Comment:** The limit on plant shutdown and other unpredictable contingent event benefits goes into effect in 2008. The Joint Committee on Taxation notes that benefits being paid as a result of a plant shutdown or other unpredictable contingent event that occurred in the preceding year may continue to be paid without limitation. Thus, benefits being paid because of a plant shutdown in 2006 may continue to be made after 2007 (Joint Committee on Taxation, Technical Explanation of the Pension Protection Act of 2006 (JCX-38-06)).

Contribution equal to increased funding target caused by occurrence of event. An employer may avoid the restrictions applicable to a plan with a funding target attainment percentage under 60 percent by making a contribution (in addition to the minimum

NEW LAW EXPLAINED

required funding contribution for the plan year) equal to the amount of the increase in the funding target of the plan attributable to the occurrence of the unpredictable contingent event (ERISA Sec. 206(g)(1)(B)(i) and Code Sec. 436(b)(2)(A), as added by the Pension Act). Similarly, an employer maintaining a plan with a funding target attainment percentage that would be less than 60 percent as a consequence of the occurrence of an unpredictable contingent event, may avoid the restriction by making a contribution sufficient to raise the funding target attainment percentage to 60 percent (ERISA Sec. 206(g)(1)(B)(ii) and Code Sec. 436(b)(2)(B), as added by the Pension Act).

Limits on amendments increasing benefit liabilities.—An employer may not adopt an amendment to a single-employer defined benefit plan that is less than 80 percent funded that will have the effect of increasing plan liabilities, unless it makes additional contributions to the plan. Specifically, if the "adjusted" funding target attainment percentage as of the evaluation date of the plan for the plan year is less than 80 percent (or would be less than 80 percent as a result of the amendment) the plan may generally not be amended during the year to increase benefits, establish new benefits, change the rate of benefit accrual, or change the rate at which benefits become nonforfeitable (ERISA Sec. 206(g)(2)(A) and Code Sec. 436(c)(1), as added by the Pension Act).

Additional employer contribution may fund benefit increase under amendment. A plan that has an adjusted funding target attainment percentage under 80 percent may be amended to increase benefit liabilities if the employer makes a contribution (in addition to the minimum required contribution for the plan year under ERISA Sec. 303 and Code Sec. 430 (see ¶210)) equal to the amount of the increase in the funding target of the plan that is attributable to the amendment. Similarly, an employer may adopt an amendment that will have the effect of reducing the plan's adjusted funding target attainment percentage below 80 percent, if the employer contributes an additional amount that is sufficient to restore the plan's adjusted funded target attainment percentage to 80 percent (ERISA Sec. 206(g)(2)(B) and Code Sec. 436(c)(2), as added by the Pension Act).

Exemption for compensation-based benefit formulas. A plan amendment that provides for an increase in benefits that is based on a participant's compensation is not subject to the new restrictions. A plan amendment may also provide for an increase in benefits that is not based on a participant's compensation. However, the rate of the benefit increase may not exceed the contemporaneous rate of increase in average wages of participants covered by the amendment (ERISA Sec. 206(g)(2)(C) and Code Sec. 436(c)(3), as added by the Pension Act).

Restrictions on lump-sum distributions and accelerated payments.—Current law prohibits plans with a liquidity shortfall from making lump-sum benefit payments. The Act does not prohibit accelerated distributions, such as lump-sum payments, but subjects "prohibited payments" under plans that are below specified funding levels to restrictions (ERISA Sec. 206(g)(3) and Code Sec. 436(d)(1), as added by the Pension Act).

Prohibited payments. Prohibited payments subject to restriction include payments in excess of the monthly amount paid under a single life annuity (plus Social Security

NEW LAW EXPLAINED

supplements) to a participant or beneficiary whose annuity starting date occurs during a limitation period; any payment for the purchase of an irrevocable commitment from an insurer to pay benefits; and other payments to be specified by Treasury regulations (ERISA Sec. 206(g)(3)(E) and Code Sec. 436(d)(5), as added by the Pension Act).

Suspension of prohibited payments. A plan with an adjusted funding target attainment percentage of under 60 percent may not make a lump-sum distribution or other prohibited payment after the valuation date for the plan year (ERISA Sec. 206(g)(3)(A) and Code Sec. 436(d)(1), as added by the Pension Act). In addition, a defined benefit plan may not make a lump-sum distribution or other prohibited payment during any period in which the plan sponsor is in federal or state bankruptcy proceedings (ERISA Sec. 206(g)(3)(B) and Code Sec. 436(d)(2), as added by the Pension Act).

> **Comment:** A plan that is 100 percent funded (i.e., the plan's adjusted funded target liability percentage is 100 percent) may provide the full amount of a lump-sum benefit, even if the plan sponsor subsequently declares bankruptcy. By contrast, the plan maintained by an employer in bankruptcy may not authorize increased benefits or the payment of lump-sum distributions unless the plan's enrolled actuary certifies that the plan has an adjusted funding target liability percentage of 100 percent (ERISA Sec. 206(g)(3)(B) and Code Sec. 436(d)(2), as added by the Pension Act).

Additional restrictions on lump-sum payments under plans with funding percentage of 60 percent or more. The restrictions on accelerated distributions are not limited to benefits paid under a plan that has an adjusted funding target attainment percentage of less than 60 percent. Lump-sum payments under plans with an adjusted funding target attainment percentage of 60 percent or more, but not greater than 80 percent, are also subject to restriction. Payments under such plans are limited to the lesser of: (1) 50 percent of the lump-sum payment the participant would otherwise receive under the plan, or (2) the present value of the participant's maximum PBGC guaranteed benefit (using the interest rate and mortality table that apply in the determination of minimum lump-sum benefits (under ERISA Sec. 205(g) and Code Sec. 417(e), as amended by the Pension Act (see ¶740)) (ERISA Sec. 206(g)(3)(C) and Code Sec. 436(d)(3)(A), as added by the Pension Act).

In addition to the limit on the amount of the payment, the plan may not make more than one prohibited payment to a participant during any period of consecutive plan years to which the limits on accelerated distributions apply (ERISA Sec. 206(g)(3)(C)(ii)(I) and Code Sec. 436(d)(3)(B)(i), as added by the Pension Act). For purposes of the restriction, a participant and his or her beneficiary (including an alternate payee) are treated as one participant (ERISA Sec. 206(g)(3)(C)(ii)(II) and Code Sec. 436(d)(3)(B)(ii), as added by the Pension Act). If, under the terms of a qualified domestic relations order (QDRO), a participant's accrued benefit is to be allocated to an alternate payee and one or more person, the amount to be distributed will be allocated in the same manner, unless the QDRO provides for different treatment.

NEW LAW EXPLAINED

Exemption for plans that did not provide for benefit accruals during select window period. The prohibited payment restriction will not apply for any plan year if the terms of the plan (as in effect during the period September 1, 2005 to December 31, 2005) did not authorize benefit accruals for any participant (ERISA Sec. 206(g)(3)(D) and Code Sec. 436(d)(4), as added by the Pension Act).

Accruals frozen if plan less than 60 percent funded.—Single-employer defined benefit plans must provide for the cessation of all future benefit accruals under the plan in the event the plan's adjusted funding target attainment percentage is less than 60 percent (ERISA Sec. 206(g)(4)(A), as added by the Pension Act; Code Sec. 436(e)(1), as added by the Pension Act). The benefit accruals will cease as of the valuation date for the plan year.

Service credit not frozen. The limitation on the accrual of benefits under a plan that has an adjusted funding target attainment percentage of less than 60 percent will not prevent service earned during the freeze period from being counted for vesting and other purposes. Similarly, if a plan provides benefits to a participant who terminates employment after attaining age 55 with 25 years of service, a participant who is age 55 and has completed 23 years of service when benefit accruals are frozen will be entitled to benefits upon the attainment of 25 years of service two years later. However, if the freeze on benefit accruals was still in effect when the participant completed 25 years of service, the amount of the benefit would be based on the benefit accrued before the freeze, when the employee had completed only 23 years of service (Joint Committee on Taxation, Technical Explanation of the Pension Protection Act of 2006 (JCX-38-06)).

Employer contributions can prevent freezing of benefit accruals. The limitation on benefit accruals will not apply if the plan sponsor makes a contribution (in addition to its minimum required contribution) sufficient to produce an adjusted funding target attainment percentage of 60 percent (ERISA Sec. 206(g)(4)(B) and Code Sec. 436(e)(2), as added by the Pension Act). Benefit accruals could resume as of the first day of the plan year upon the making of the contribution by the plan sponsor.

Security as alternative to additional contributions.—An employer required to make an additional contribution in order to prevent application of a benefit limitation may, alternatively, provide security to the plan. Security that satisfies specified requirements will be treated as a plan asset for purposes of determining the adjusted funding target attainment percentage (ERISA Sec. 206(g)(5)(A)(i) and Code Sec. 436(f)(1)(A), as added by the Pension Act). The security must be: a corporate surety bond; cash or United States obligation that matures in three years or less, held in escrow by a bank or similar financial institution; or some other form of security that is approved by the parties involved and the Treasury Department (ERISA Sec. 206(g)(5)(A)(ii) and Code Sec. 436(f)(1)(B), as added by the Pension Act).

The security may be perfected and enforced at any time after the earlier of: (1) the date on which the plan terminates; (2) the due date for the payment of a delinquent minimum required contribution; or (3) the valuation date for the last year of a seven consecutive year period during which the plan's adjusted funding target attainment percentage is less than 60 percent (ERISA Sec. 206(g)(5)(A)(iii) and Code Sec. 436(f)(1)(C), as added by the Pension Act).

NEW LAW EXPLAINED

The security may be released, and amounts refunded with accrued interest, at a time to be prescribed by Treasury regulations. The Treasury is directed to provide regulations governing the partial release of a security following an increase in the funding target attainment percentage (ERISA Sec. 206(g)(5)(A)(iv) and Code Sec. 436(f)(1)(D), as added by the Pension Act).

Credit balance may not be used to satisfy additional required contribution.—An employer may not use a prefunding balance or a funding standard carryover balance in satisfaction of an additional contribution that is required to avoid or terminate the application of a limit on the payment of unpredictable contingent event benefits, the adoption of amendments increasing benefit liabilities, or benefit accruals applicable to underfunded plans (ERISA Sec. 206(g)(5)(B) and Code Sec. 436(f)(2), as added by the Pension Act). Note, additional contributions made to avoid the applicable benefit limits will not increase the credit balance (see ¶210) (ERISA Sec. 303(f)(2)(B) and Code Sec. 430(f)(2)(B), as added by the Pension Act.

Special rule exempts fully funded plans from reduction of plan assets. A special rule applies to plans that would be fully funded (*i.e.*, funding target attainment percentage of 100 percent or more) if plan assets were not reduced by a credit balance. Under such circumstances, a plan asset will not be reduced by credit balances in determining whether the benefit limits apply (ERISA Sec. 206(g)(9)(C)(i), as added by the Pension Act; Code Sec. 436(j)(3)(A), as added by the Pension Act).

A transition rule applies during the 2008–2010 period. Pursuant to this rule, a plan may substitute the following applicable percentages for 100 percent for the years 2008 through 2010: 92 percent in 2008, 94 percent in 2009, and 96 percent in 2010 (ERISA Sec. 206(g)(9)(C)(ii) and Code Sec. 436(j)(3)(B), as added by the Pension Act). However, the transition rule will apply to plan years after 2008 only if the funding target attainment percentage of the plan (determined without reducing plan assets by credit balances) for each preceding plan year after 2007 (as well as the current plan year) is not less than the applicable percentage of the preceding year (ERISA Sec. 206(g)(9)(C)(iii) and Code Sec. 436(j)(3)(C), as added by the Pension Act).

Deemed reduction of credit balance under collectively bargained plans. A waiver of a credit balance is allowed in order to improve a plan's funding status and prevent application of a benefit limit. In the event the benefit limits under ERISA Sec. 206(g)(1)–(4) or Code Sec. 436(b)–(e) apply for a plan year, the plan sponsor will generally be treated as having made an election under ERISA Sec. 303(f) or Code Sec. 430(f) (see ¶210) to reduce the prefunding balance or funding standard carryover balance by the amount necessary for the benefit limit not to apply for the plan year (ERISA Sec. 206(g)(5)(C)(i) and Code Sec. 436(f)(3)(A), as added by the Pension Act). Note, however, with respect to benefit limits under ERISA Sec. 206(g)(1), (2), and (4) and Code Sec. 436(b), (c), and (e), the provision will apply only to collectively bargained plans (ERISA Sec. 206(g)(5)(C)(iii) and Code Sec. 436(f)(3)(C), as added by the Pension Act). Thus, under a noncollectively bargained plan, only the prohibited payment limitation is covered by the exemption.

An exception to the deemed reduction of funding balances applies to plans with insufficient funding balances. Specifically, the deemed reduction will not apply if application would not prevent the benefit limit from being in effect for the plan year

NEW LAW EXPLAINED

(ERISA Sec. 206(g)(5)(C)(ii), as added by the Pension Act; Code Sec. 436(f)(3)(B), as added by the Pension Act).

Participant notice of limits on distributions and benefit accruals.—The plan administrator of a single-employer defined benefit plan must provide "written" notice to plan participants and beneficiaries within 30 days of the plan becoming subject to the limits on unpredictable contingent event benefits, and accelerated benefit distributions under ERISA Sec. 206(g)(1)and (3) (ERISA Sec. 101(j)(1), as added by the Pension Act).

In addition, notice must be provided for a plan that is experiencing a severe funding shortfall and subject to the limits on benefit accruals under ERISA Sec. 206(g)(4). The notice must be provided within 30 days after the valuation date for the plan year in which the adjusted funding target attainment percentage for the plan year is less than 60 percent, or, if earlier, the date the percentage is deemed to be less than 60 percent under ERISA Sec. 206(g)(7) (see below) (ERISA Sec. 101(j)(2), as added by the Pension Act). The Treasury is also empowered to require notice to be furnished at an alternative time (ERISA Sec. 101(j) (3), as added by the Pension Act).

> **Comment:** The "written" notice may be provided electronically or in another format that is reasonably accessible to the recipient. Governing ERISA Reg. § 2520.104b-1(c) generally requires a plan administrator to take "appropriate and necessary" measures that are reasonably calculated to ensure that the electronic option for forwarding documents results in the "actual receipt" of transmitted information and documents. Measures reasonably calculated to ensure actual receipt of a document would include use of return-receipts or notice of undelivered electronic mail features, and periodic reviews or surveys. However, note that, if the significance of an electronic document is not reasonably evident as transmitted (e.g., e-mail attachment) a plan participant or beneficiary must receive notice apprising them of the significance of the document. In addition, participants and beneficiaries must, under the Department of Labor rules, be informed at the time a document is furnished electronically of their right to request and obtain a paper version of the document.

Five-year exception for new plans.—The limits on unpredictable contingent event benefits, increased benefits, and benefit accruals under ERISA Sec. 206(g)(1), (2), and (4) and Code Sec. 436(b), (c), and (e) will not apply to a new plan (including a predecessor plan) for the first five plan years (ERISA Sec. 206(g)(6) and Code Sec. 436(g), as added by the Pension Act).

However, the limit on plan amendments that increase benefit liabilities will apply if the employer is in bankruptcy proceedings during the five-year period. In addition, the limit on prohibited payments under ERISA Sec. 206(g)(3) applies to new plans (ERISA Sec. 206(g)(6) and Code Sec. 436(g), as added by the Pension Act).

Presumption of continued underfunding.—Plans subject to a benefit limitation under ERISA Sec. 206(g)(1)–(4) and Code Sec. 436(b)–(e) for the preceding plan year will be presumed to be subject to the limit in the current year until the plan actuary certifies the actual adjusted funding target attainment percentage for the current year. Specifically, the adjusted funding target attainment percentage of the plan as of the valuation date of the plan for the current plan year will be presumed to be equal to

NEW LAW EXPLAINED

the adjusted funding target attainment percentage of the plan as of the valuation date for the preceding plan year (ERISA Sec. 206(g)(7) and Code Sec. 436(h)(1), as added by the Pension Act).

Presumption of underfunding following delayed actuarial certification. In the event the plan's enrolled actuary fails to certify the plan's actual adjusted funding target attainment percentage before the first day of the 10th month of the current year, the plan's adjusted funding target percentage will be conclusively presumed to be less than 60 percent as of the first day of such 10th month (ERISA Sec. 206(g)(7)(B) and Code Sec. 436(h)(2), as added by the Pension Act). The first day of the 10th month will be deemed to be the valuation date of the plan for the current plan year, for purposes of applying the benefit limits.

Presumption of underfunding for "nearly underfunded" plans. A presumption of underfunding also applies to plans that were not subject to benefit limits under ERISA Sec. 206(g) or Code Sec. 436 in the preceding year, but that had an adjusted funding target attainment percentage for the prior plan year that was not more than 10 percentage points greater than the benefit limit threshold (e.g., 60 percent for lump-sum distributions or shut-down benefits). Under the rule, unless the plan's enrolled actuary certifies the actual adjusted funding target attainment percentage of the plan for the current plan year by the first day of the fourth month of the current plan year, the plan's adjusted funding target attainment percentage will be presumed, as of that day, to be 10 percentage points less than the adjusted funding target attainment percentage for the preceding plan year (ERISA Sec. 206(g)(7)(C) and Code Sec. 436(h)(3), as added by the Pension Act). The first day of the fourth month of the current plan year will be deemed to be the valuation date of the plan for the current plan year for purposes of applying the benefit limitation. Thus, the benefit limitation will apply beginning on that date until the plan's actuary certifies the plan's adjusted funding target attainment percentage.

Treatment of plan after end of benefit limitation period.—Following the expiration of the period during which a plan is subject to limits on lump-sum payments and other prohibited payments and the restrictions on benefit accruals under ERISA Sec. 206(g)(3) and (4) and Code Sec. 436(d) and (e), the forms of distribution and benefit accrual authorized under the plan automatically resume, absent a contrary provision in the plan (ERISA Sec. 206(g)(8)(A) and Code Sec. 436(i)(1), as added by the Pension Act). Thus, the plan need not be amended in order to provide for the resumption of lump-sum distributions or benefit accruals. Note, this provision does not apply to limitations on unpredictable contingent event benefits and plan amendments increasing liabilities. In addition, nothing in this provision of the Act is to be construed as affecting the plan's treatment of benefits that would have been paid or accrued but for the limitation (ERISA Sec. 206(g)(8)(B) and Code Sec. 436(i)(2), as added by the Pension Act).

▶ **Effective dates.** The benefit limits under ERISA Sec. 206(g) and Code Sec. 436 generally apply to plan years beginning after December 31, 2007 (Act Secs. 103(c)(1) and 113(b)(1) of the Pension Protection Act of 2006).

Delayed effective date for collectively bargained plans. Plans maintained pursuant to one or more collective bargaining agreements (CBA) that were ratified before January 1, 2008 will

NEW LAW EXPLAINED

not be subject to the benefit limits before the earlier of: (1) the later of the date on which the last CBA relating to the plan terminates (determined without regard to any extension thereof agreed to after August 17, 2006, the date of enactment of the Pension Act), or the first day of the first plan year to which the limits would otherwise apply (i.e., 2008), or (2) January 1, 2010 (Act Secs. 103(c)(2) and 113(b)(2) of the Pension Act). Thus, the limits will apply to collectively bargained plans by 2010 at the latest.

Law source: Law at ¶5135 and ¶7012. Committee Report at ¶10,020.

— Act Sec. 103(a) of the Pension Protection Act of 2006, adding ERISA Sec. 206(g);

— Act Sec. 103(b), redesignating ERISA Sec. 101(j) as (k) and adding new ERISA Sec. 101(j);

— Act Sec. 113(a), adding Code Sec. 436;

— Act Secs. 103(c) and 113(b), providing the effective dates.

Reporter references: For further information, consult the following CCH reporters.

— Pension Plan Guide, ¶2965

— Standard Federal Tax Reporter, 2006FED ¶19,125.052

— Tax Research Consultant, RETIRE: 6,068 and RETIRE: 30,156.20

— Federal Tax Guide, 2006FTG ¶11,087

¶220 Restrictions on Funding of Nonqualified Deferred Compensation Plans by Employers Maintaining Underfunded or Terminated Single-Employer Plans

SUMMARY OF NEW LAW

Assets that are set aside for the payment of deferred compensation to covered employees under a nonqualified deferred compensation plan, and while a single-employer defined benefit plan is at risk, are treated as property transferred in connection with the performance of services. Covered employees include the chief executive officer, the four highest paid officers for the tax year and individuals subject to Section 16(a) of the Securities Exchange Act of 1934.

BACKGROUND

Generally, all qualified employee pension benefit plans are subject to minimum funding standards, unless specifically exempted. The minimum funding standards were enacted to ensure that employers are capable of paying pension benefits that have been promised to employees on retirement. Therefore, defined benefit plans, which provide for specific benefits, are generally subject to the minimum funding standards while defined contribution plans, which do not provide for specific benefits, generally are not. While the Code provisions governing the minimum funding

BACKGROUND

requirements apply only to qualified pension plans, the ERISA provisions apply to both qualified and nonqualified pension plans. As a result, pension plans that are not subject to the qualification requirements of the Code, or do not satisfy those requirements, must still comply with the ERISA requirements.

Amounts deferred under a nonqualified deferred compensation plan and not subject to a substantial risk of forfeiture must be included in the service provider's gross income, unless the plan meets certain requirements (Code Sec. 409A(a)(1)(A)(i)). In the case of assets in a trust (or other arrangement) for purposes of paying nonqualified deferred compensation, such assets are treated as property transferred in connection with the performance of services under Code Sec. 83 at the time set aside, if such assets (or trust or arrangement) are located outside of the United States. A transfer of property in connection with the performance of services also occurs with respect to compensation deferred under a nonqualified deferred compensation plan if the plan provides that, upon a change in the employer's health, assets will be restricted to the payment of nonqualified deferred compensation.

NEW LAW EXPLAINED

Restrictions on funding of nonqualified deferred compensation plans.—During any *restricted period* with respect to a single-employer defined benefit plan, if assets are set aside or reserved (directly or indirectly) in a trust (or other arrangement as determined by the IRS) or transferred to such trust for purposes of paying deferred compensation of an "applicable covered employee" under a nonqualified deferred compensation plan , then such assets will be treated as property transferred in connection with the performance of services for purposes of Code Sec. 83 (whether or not such assets are available to satisfy claims of general creditors) (Code Sec. 409A(b)(3), as added by the Pension Protection Act of 2006).

> **Comment:** This rule does not apply to any assets that are set aside before the restricted period with respect to the defined benefit plan.

A similar rule applies to a nonqualified deferred compensation plan of the plan sponsor or member of a controlled group that includes the plan sponsor. If such nonqualified deferred compensation plan provides that assets will be restricted to the provision of benefits under the plan in connection with a restricted period (or other similar financial measure determined by the IRS) of any defined benefit plan of the employer, or assets are so restricted, then such assets will be treated as property transferred in connection with the performance of services for purposes of Code Sec. 83 (whether or not such assets are available to satisfy claims of general creditors) (Code Sec. 409A(3)(A)(ii), as added by the Pension Act).

> **Comment:** These rules are based on the assessment that it is inappropriate for companies with underfunded defined benefit plans to fund nonqualified deferred compensation plans covering executives while the pension plan is not adequately funded. While rank-file employees have little control over a company's decision to fund its pension plans, executives often have control in determining whether nonqualified deferred compensation will be funded

NEW LAW EXPLAINED

Restricted period. A restricted period with respect to a single-employer defined benefit plan is for purposes of this provision:

(1) any period during which the plan is in at-risk status as defined in new Code Sec. 430(i) (see ¶210),

(2) any period that the plan sponsor is in bankruptcy, and

(3) in the case of a plan that terminates, the 12-month period beginning on the date which is six months before the termination date of the defined benefit pension plan if, as of the termination date, the plan is not sufficient for benefit liabilities.

Special rule for payment of taxes on deferred compensation included in income. If an employer provides directly or indirectly for the payment of any Federal, state or local income taxes with respect to any compensation required to be included in gross income, (1) interest and additional tax under Code Sec. 409A(a)(1)(B)(i)(I) and (II) will be imposed on the amount of such payment in the same manner as if such payment was part of the deferred compensation to which it relates and (2) no deduction will be allowed with respect to such payment.

Applicable covered employee. Covered employees include a corporation's chief executive officer (or an individual acting in such capacity) as of the close of the tax year, the four highest compensated officers for the tax year (other than its chief executive officer), or an individual subject to section 16(a) of the Securities Exchange Act of 1934. An applicable covered employee means any (1) covered employee of the plan sponsor, (2) covered employee of a member of a controlled group which includes the plan sponsor, and (3) former employee who was a covered employee at the time of termination of employment with the plan sponsor or a member of the controlled group which includes the plan sponsor (Code Sec. 409A(b)(3)(D), as added by the Pension Act).

▶ **Effective date.** The provision applies to transfers or other reservation of assets after August 17, 2006 (Act Sec. 116(c) of the Pension Protection Act of 2006).

Law source: Law at ¶5070. Committee Report at ¶10,070.

— Act Sec. 116(a) of the Pension Protection Act of 2006, redesignating Code Sec. 409A(b)(3) and (4) as (4) and (5), respectively, and adding new Code Sec. 409A(b)(3);

— Act Sec. 116(b), amending Code Sec. 409A(b)(4) and (5) as redesignated;

— Act Sec. 116(c), providing the effective date.

Reporter references: For further information, consult the following CCH reporters.

— Pension Plan Guide, ¶9530

— Standard Federal Tax Reporter, 2006FED ¶18,960.037

— Tax Research Consultant, RETIRE: 3,000 and RETIRE: 6,000

— Federal Tax Guide, 2006FTG ¶11,720

¶225 Special Rules for Certain Plans for Cessation or Change in Membership of Controlled Group

SUMMARY OF NEW LAW

If a fully-funded defined benefit plan is sponsored by a financially-healthy employer that is sold as part of an acquisition or similar transaction (or a series of such transactions), then the interest rate to be used in determining whether the plan has sufficient assets to meet benefit liabilities for purposes of the standard termination rules (or, in certain circumstances, the rules for termination by the PBGC) must be not less than the interest rate used for determining whether the plan is fully funded.

BACKGROUND

An employer may choose to utilize the Pension Benefit Guaranty Corporation's (PBGC's) standard termination process in order to terminate a defined benefit plan, if, as of the termination date, the assets in the plan are sufficient to satisfy all benefit liabilities (ERISA Sec. 4041(b)(1)(D)). Benefit liabilities are defined generally as the present value of all benefits due under the plan (this amount is referred to as "termination liability") (Joint Committee on Taxation, Technical Explanation of the Pension Protection Act of 2006 (JCX-38-06), August 3, 2006). As part of determining present value, certain interest rate and mortality assumptions prescribed by the PBGC must be used.

NEW LAW EXPLAINED

Special valuation rules apply to certain financially-healthy companies involved in acquisitions or other transactions.—For plans that are acquired by another corporate entity as part of an acquisition or similar transaction (or series of transactions) and that meet certain conditions, the interest rate to be used in determining whether the plan has sufficient assets to meet benefit liabilities for purposes of the standard termination rules (or, in certain circumstances, the rules for termination by the PBGC) must be not less than the interest rate used for determining whether the plan is fully funded (ERISA Sec. 4041(b)(5), as added by the Pension Protection Act of 2006).

In order to qualify for this treatment, certain criteria must be met:

- The employer maintaining the plan after the acquisition or other transaction (or series of transactions) may not be a member of the same controlled group as the employer that maintained the plan prior to the transaction (or series of transactions); and
- The plan must be "fully funded" (ERISA Sec. 4041(b)(5)(A), as added by the Pension Act).

NEW LAW EXPLAINED

Definition of "fully funded". For this purpose, "fully funded" means that:

- For transactions (or series of transactions) occurring in a plan year beginning before January 1, 2008, the funded current liability percentage determined under the deficit reduction contribution rules under ERISA Sec. 302(d) must be at least 100 percent;
- For transactions (or series of transactions) occurring in a plan year beginning on or after January 1, 2008, the funding target attainment percentage under the rules for receiving a variance from the minimum funding standards under ERISA Sec. 303 (see ¶ 210) must be at least 100 percent as of the valuation date for that plan year (ERISA Sec. 4041(b)(5)(C), as added by the Pension Act).

Limited application. The interest rate rule applies only to a transaction (or series of transactions) in which the employer maintaining the plan immediately before or after the transaction meets certain criteria with respect to (1) its investment rating and (2) the composition of its domestic workforce (ERISA Sec. 4041(b)(5)(B), as added by the Pension Act).

First, such an employer must either:

- possess an outstanding senior unsecured debt instrument which is rated investment grade by each of the nationally recognized statistical rating organizations for corporate bonds that has issued a credit rating for such instrument, or
- if no such debt instrument of such employer has been rated by such an organization, but one or more rating organization has provided the employer with an issuer credit rating, then all of the rating organizations that have provided the employer with an issuer credit rating must have rated it investment grade (ERISA Sec. 4041(b)(5)(B)(i), as added by the Pension Act).

In addition, the employer maintaining the plan after the transaction (or series of transactions) must employ at least 20 percent of the employees located in the United States who were employed by the employer immediately before the transaction took place (ERISA Sec. 4041(b)(5)(B)(ii), as added by the Pension Act).

Finally, the special treatment will not apply to the transaction (or series of transactions) if the plan undergoes a distress termination or a termination by the PBGC after the close of the two-year period which begins on the date on which the first such transaction occurs (ERISA Sec. 4041(b)(5)(D), as added by the Pension Act).

▶ **Effective date.** The provision applies to any transaction (or series of transactions) occurring on and after August 17, 2006 (Act Sec. 409(b) of the Pension Protection Act of 2006).

Law source: Law at ¶7084. Committee Report at ¶10,300.

— Act Sec. 409(a) of the Pension Protection Act of 2006, adding ERISA Sec. 4041(b)(5);

— Act Sec. 409(b), providing the effective date.

Reporter references: For further information, consult the following CCH reporters.

— Pension Plan Guide, ¶6591

— Standard Federal Tax Reporter, 2006FED ¶19,071.075

— Tax Research Consultant, RETIRE: 45,050 and RETIRE: 45,104

TRANSITIONAL RELIEF FROM NEW FUNDING STANDARDS

¶230 Modification of Pension Funding Requirements for Plans Subject to Current Transition Rule for Interstate Bus Company

SUMMARY OF NEW LAW

The special rule that treats certain bus company plans as having a funded current liability percentage of at least 90 percent for determining the amount of required contributions (100 percent for purposes of determining whether quarterly contributions are required) has been expanded to plan years beginning in 2006 and in 2007. For plan years beginning after 2007, rules relating to determining minimum required contributions and variable rate premiums have been modified.

BACKGROUND

Defined benefit pension plans are required to meet certain minimum funding requirements. In some cases, additional contributions are required if a single-employer plan is underfunded. Additional contributions are not required from a plan with a funded current liability percentage of at least 90 percent. A plan with a funded current liability percentage of less than 100 percent for the preceding plan year must make estimated contributions for the current plan year. The PBGC insures benefits under most single-employer defined benefit pension plans in the event the plan is terminated with insufficient assets to pay for plan benefits. The PBGC is funded in part by a flat-rate premium per plan participant and a variable rate premium based on the amount of unfunded vested benefits under the plan.

A special rule modifies the minimum funding requirements in the case of plans that: (1) were not required to pay a variable rate PBGC premium for the plan year beginning in 1996, (2) do not, in plan years beginning after 1995 and before 2009, merge with another plan, and (3) are sponsored by a company that is engaged primarily in interurban or interstate passenger bus service. This special rule generally treats a plan as having a funded current liability percentage of at least 90 percent for plan years beginning after 1996 and before 2004 if for such plan year the funded current liability percentage is at least 85 percent. If the funded current liability of the plan is less than 85 percent for any plan year beginning after 1996 and before 2004, the relief from the minimum funding requirements generally applies only if certain specified contributions are made. For plan years beginning in 2004 and 2005, the funded current liability percentage of the plan is treated as at least 90 percent for determining the amount of required contributions (100 percent for purposes of determining whether quarterly contributions are required). Thus, for these years, additional contributions and quarterly contributions are not required. The mortality table used under the plan is used in determining the amount of unfunded vested

BACKGROUND

benefits under the plan for purposes of calculating PBGC variable rate premiums. For plan years beginning after 2005 and before 2010, the funded current liability percentage generally will be deemed to be at least 90 percent if the actual funded current liability percentage is at least at certain specified levels. The relief from the minimum funding requirement generally applies for a plan year beginning in 2006, 2007, or 2008 only if contributions to the plan for the plan year equal at least the expected increase in current liability due to benefits accruing during the plan year.

NEW LAW EXPLAINED

Modified pension funding requirements for certain bus companies.—The special rule that treats certain bus company plans as having a funded current liability percentage of at least 90 percent for determining the amount of required contributions (Code Sec. 412(I)(9)(A) and ERISA Sec. 302(d)(9)(A)) and 100 percent for purposes of determining whether quarterly contributions are required (Code Sec. 412(m)) and ERISA Sec. 302(e)), has been expanded to plan years beginning in 2006 and 2007. This means that the plan will be treated as not having a shortfall for any plan year and that, additional contributions and quarterly contributions are not required with the respect to the plan. Also, for purposes of determining unfunded vested benefits under ERISA Sec. 4006(a)(3)(E)(iii), the mortality table used is the one used by the plan (Act Sec. 115(d) of the Pension Protection Act of 2006). The modified funding rules that otherwise apply to these companies, for plan years beginning after 1996 and before 2010, are eliminated for years beginning after December 31, 2007 (Act Sec. 115(e) of the Pension Act).

For any plan year beginning after December 31, 2007, the new rules relating to determining minimum required contributions (see ¶ 210) and variable rate premiums (see ¶ 505) have been modified for plans that: (1) are sponsored by a company engaged primarily in the interurban or interstate bus service; (2) were not required to pay a variable rate PBGC premium for the plan year beginning in 1996; and (3) have not, in any plan years beginning after 1995, merged with another plan (other than a plan sponsored by an employer that was in 1996 within the controlled group of the plan sponsor). For purposes of the required quarterly contribution requirement under Code Sec. 430(j)(3)and ERISA Sec. 303(j)(3), the plan is treated as not having a funding shortfall for any plan year (Act Sec. 115(a) and (b) of the Pension Act).

Also for plan years beginning after 2007, the mortality table used by the plan is also used in determining any present value or making any computation under the minimum funding rules under Code Sec. 412 and ERISA Sec. 302 (see ¶ 205) and determining unfunded vested benefits under ERISA Sec. 4006(a)(3)(E)(iii)(see ¶ 235). Under a special phase-in for purposes of determining whether a shortfall amortization base is required for plan years beginning after 2007 and before 2012, the applicable percentage of the plan's shortfall is: 90 percent for 2008, 92 percent for 2009, 94 percent for 2010 and 96 percent for 2011. For purposes of the quarterly contributions requirement, the plan is treated as not having a funding shortfall for any plan year (Act Sec. 115(b) of the Pension Act).

NEW LAW EXPLAINED

Comment: This phase-in is in lieu of the phase-in otherwise applicable under Code Sec. 430(c)(5)(B) and ERISA Sec. 303(c)(5)(b) relating to new funding rules for single-employer plans.

▶ **Effective date.** The transitional funding rules for 2006 and 2007 under the Retirement Protection Act of 1994 apply to plan years beginning after December 31, 2005 (Act Sec. 115(d)(2) of the Pension Protection Act of 2006). The repeal of the modified funding rules under Sec. 769(c) of the Retirement Protection Act is effective on December 31, 2007, and applies to plan years beginning after that date (Act Sec. 115(e)(2) of the Pension Act). The provision modifying the Pension Act rules applies to plan years beginning after December 31, 2007 (Act Sec. 115(a) of the Pension Act).

Law source: Law at ¶7027. Committee Report at ¶10,060.

— Act Sec. 115(a)-(b), modifying rules in Code Secs. 412 and 430 and ERISA Secs. 302, 303 and 4006;

— Act Sec. 115(d)(1) and (e)(1), amending Section 769(c) of the Retirement Protection Act of 1994;

— Act Sec. 115 (a), (d)(2) and (e)(2), providing the effective dates.

Reporter references: For further information, consult the following CCH reporters.

— Pension Plan Guide, ¶2895

— Standard Federal Tax Reporter, 2006FED ¶19,125.032

— Tax Research Consultant, RETIRE: 30,164.05

— Federal Tax Guide, 2006FTG ¶11,040

¶235 Replacement Interest Rate Extended Through 2007

SUMMARY OF NEW LAW

The use of the replacement interest rate for the funding standard account and for computing a plan's current liability and deficit reduction contribution is extended through 2007.

BACKGROUND

Charges and credits to the funding standard account (Code Sec. 412(b)(1)) are made using an interest rate that is within a permissible range of the weighted average of the interest rates on 30-year Treasury securities for a four-year period ending on the last day before the plan year begins (Code Sec. 412(b)(5)). In computing the deficit reduction contribution (Code Sec. 412(l)(1)), the current liability of a plan is determined using this same rate (Code Sec. 412(l)(7)(C)(i)). Due to changes in the bond market, the 30-year Treasury rate became an inappropriate benchmark. A replacement rate was specified for plan years beginning after December 31, 2003 and before

BACKGROUND

January 1, 2006. The replacement interest rate is a weighted average of long-term investment grade corporate bonds.

NEW LAW EXPLAINED

Replacement interest rate for the funding standard account and deficit reduction contribution applies to 2006 and 2007.—The replacement interest rate will apply to plan years beginning after December 31, 2003 and before January 1, 2008 (Act Sec. 301 of the Pension Protection Act of 2006).

> **Comment:** The IRS publishes a notice each month containing information about the replacement interest rate. The notice specifies the composite corporate bond rate, the corporate weighted average interest rate and the permissible range. The IRS uses two or more bond rate indices maintained by financial service firms. Each index tracks bond rates in the top three quality levels available, meaning investment grade. The composite rate is based on the average of daily values for yield to maturity for bonds included in the index. The IRS then applies a weighting methodology to the composite rates for the preceding 48 months to arrive at a weighted average rate.

▶ **Effective date.** No specific effective date is provided by the Act. The provision is, therefore, considered effective on August 17, 2006, the date of enactment.

Law source: Law at ¶5085A and ¶7054. Committee Report at ¶10,190.

— Act Sec. 301(a) of the Pension Protection Act of 2006, amending ERISA Secs. 302(b)(5)(B)(ii)(II), 302(d)(7)(C)(i)(IV)and 4006(a)(3)(E)(iii)(V);

— Act Sec. 301(b), amending Code Sec. 412(b)(5)(B)(ii)(II) and 412(l)(7)(C)(i)(IV);

— Act Sec. 301(c), amending Sec. 101(c)(2)(A)(ii) of the Pension Funding Equity Act of 2004.

Reporter references: For further information, consult the following CCH reporters.

— Pension Plan Guide, ¶2975

— Standard Federal Tax Reporter, 2006FED ¶19,125.032

— Tax Research Consultant, RETIRE: 30,164.05 and RETIRE: 30,170

— Federal Tax Guide, 2006FTG ¶11,040

¶240 Temporary Relief from Funding Rules for Certain Defined Benefit Plans

SUMMARY OF NEW LAW

Temporary relief from the new funding rules, which are generally effective beginning in 2008, is granted to certain defined benefit plans. The new single-employer defined benefit plan funding rules will not apply to certain multiple employer plans maintained by rural cooperatives for plan years beginning before January 1, 2017. In addition, the new rules will not apply to certain Pension Benefit Guaranty Corpora-

SUMMARY OF NEW LAW

tion (PBGC) settlement plans for plan years beginning before January 1, 2014. Finally, the new rules will generally not apply to plans maintained by certain government defense contractors before plan years beginning before the earlier of (1) the date certain new rules regarding pension costs to be issued by the Cost Accounting Standards Board become effective or (2) January 1, 2011. For plan years beginning after December 31, 2007, and before the first plan year for which the new funding rules apply, all such plans must use a specific interest rate to determine the plan's funding status.

BACKGROUND

Employers that maintain defined benefit plans must adhere to funding standards stipulated in ERISA and in the Internal Revenue Code. The minimum funding rules applicable to single-employer plans also apply to plans that are maintained by multiple employers, but not pursuant to collective bargaining agreements. Significant changes to the current funding rules governing single-employer defined benefit plans are contained in the Pension Protection Act of 2006 (see ¶210). These changes are generally effective for plan years beginning after 2007 (Act Sec. 102(c) of the Pension Act).

NEW LAW EXPLAINED

Temporary relief from funding rules granted to certain plans.—Temporary relief from the new funding rules is granted to multiple employer plans maintained by rural cooperatives, PBGC settlement plans, and plans maintained by government defense contractors. In addition, during the period in which the new funding rules will not apply, such plans must use a special interest rate for purposes of determining the plan's current funding liability that assumes benefits will be payable in 20 years.

Multiple employer plans of rural cooperatives. In the case of multiple employer plans maintained by rural cooperatives that offer electrical, telephone or certain agricultural services, the new funding rules do not apply to plan years beginning before the earlier of: (1) the first plan year for which the plan ceases to be an eligible cooperative plan or (2) January 1, 2017 (Act Sec. 104(a) of the Pension Protection Act of 2006).

In order to be eligible for the special treatment, a defined benefit plan must meet three requirements. First, it must have been in existence on July 26, 2005 (Act Sec. 104(a) of the Pension Act). Second, it must be maintained by more than one employer—that is, it must be a multiple employer plan. Third, at least 85 percent of the employers maintaining the plan must be:

- Rural cooperatives—tax-exempt organizations under Code Sec. 401(k)(7)(B) that provide electricity on a mutual or cooperative basis to the public in rural areas and cooperative telephone companies; or
- An agricultural cooperative—a tax-exempt organization under Code Sec. 1381(a) that provides marketing and other services to farmers for the purpose of selling their

NEW LAW EXPLAINED

crops and other agricultural products and that is more than 50-percent owned by agricultural producers or cooperatives owned by agricultural producers, or an organization that is more than 50-percent owned or controlled by such a cooperative organization (Act Sec. 104(c) of the Pension Act).

In addition, plans maintained by more than one employer and maintained by a rural telephone cooperative association, as defined under ERISA Sec. 3(40)(B)(v), may be treated as cooperative plans eligible for the transition relief from the funding rules (Act Sec. 104(c) of the Pension Act).

> **Comment:** According to Senator Pat Roberts (R-KS), more than 1,700 rural cooperatives across the United States participate in a multiple-employer plan. These plans provide benefits for over 109,000 workers and retirees (Congressional Record, November 16, 2005, p. S12911).

Pension Benefit Guaranty Corporation (PBGC) settlement plans. In the case of certain "PBGC settlement plans" in existence on July 26, 2005, the new funding rules do not apply with respect to such a plan for plan years beginning before January 1, 2014 (Act Sec. 105(a) of the Pension Act).

A PBGC settlement plan is a single-employer defined benefit plan subject to the funding rules which meets a specific set of requirements. The plan must have been originally sponsored by a bankrupt employer, giving rise to a PBGC claim against the plan for not greater than $150 million. Another employer, from a different controlled group, must have assumed sponsorship of the plan, such that the PBGC claim against the plan was either settled or withdrawn. Finally, the plan must have been spun off from a plan that was subsequently terminated by the PBGC (Act Sec. 105(c) of the Pension Act).

> **Comment:** This relief is apparently intended primarily to benefit Smithfield Farms, which took over the pension plan of a bankrupt meat provider that Smithfield had purchased in 2003 (Mary Williams Walsh, "Major Changes Raise Concerns on Pension Bill", New York Times, March 19, 2006).

Plans maintained by certain government defense contractors. In the case of certain government defense contractor plans, the new rules will not apply to plan years beginning before the earliest of:

(1) the first plan year for which the plan ceases to be an eligible government contractor plan;

(2) the effective date of the Cost Accounting Standards Pension Harmonization Rule, or

(3) January 1, 2011 (Act Sec. 106(a) of the Pension Act).

In order to be eligible for special treatment under this section, a defined benefit plan must meet the following requirements:

- The plan must be maintained by a corporation (or a member of the same affiliated group) whose primary source of revenue is derived from defense contracts with the U.S. government;

NEW LAW EXPLAINED

- Revenue from such defense contracts must have exceeded five billion dollars in the previous fiscal year; and
- Pension plan costs that are assignable under those government contracts are governed by provisions of the Cost Accounting Standards (Act 106(c) of the Pension Act).

Cost Accounting Standards Pension Harmonization Rule. The Cost Accounting Standards Board, which regulates costs (including pension costs) associated with government contracts, is required, not later than January 1, 2010, to issue revised rules that harmonize its provisions governing government-reimbursable pension plan costs with the minimum required contribution rules under ERISA. Any such final rule adopted by the Cost Accounting Standards Board must be called the Cost Accounting Standards Pension Harmonization Rule (Act Sec. 106(d) of the Pension Act).

> **Comment:** Defense contractor relief may benefit firms such as Raytheon Company, Lockheed Martin Corporation and Northrop Grumman Corporation ("Defense Contractors May See Delay in New U.S. Pension Rules," Dow Jones, July 25, 2006).

Third segment interest rate. In applying the present law funding rules to multiple employer plans maintained by rural cooperatives, PBGC settlement plans, and plans of government defense contractors, for plan years beginning after December 31, 2007, and before the first plan year for which the new funding rules apply, a specific interest rate must be used (Act Secs. 104(b), 105(b) and 106(b) of the Pension Act). The plans must use the third segment rate of the segmented yield curve adopted under the Pension Act (see ¶210). The yield curve consists of different interest rates applicable to benefits payable in three different time periods. The third segment normally applies to benefits that can be reasonably determined to be payable in 20 years (ERISA Sec. 303(h)(2)(B)(iii), as added by the Pension Act). The applicable interest rate, which will be determined by the Treasury, will be based on the corporate bond yield curve for the month, taking into account only that portion of the yield curve which is based on bonds maturing during periods beginning after the 20-year period beginning on the first day of the plan year (ERISA Sec. 303(h)(2)(C)(iii), as added by the Pension Act).

> **Comment:** Use of the third segment rate to determine funding liabilities, rather than the entire segmented yield curve, will allow affected employers to use a higher discount rate assumption when calculating the present value of plan liabilities. Thus the present value of plan liabilities may be smaller than it would be if the entire yield curve approach required by the new law were used. A decrease in plan liabilities under a higher discount rate reduces the plan sponsor's funding obligation.

▶ **Effective date.** No specific effective dates are provided by the Act. The provisions are, therefore, considered effective on August 17, 2006, the date of enactment.

Law source: Law at ¶7015, ¶7018, and ¶7021. Committee Report at ¶10,030, ¶10,040, and ¶10,050.

— Act Sec. 104(a) and (c) of the Pension Protection Act of 2006, affecting application of the new minimum funding standards to eligible cooperative plans;

NEW LAW EXPLAINED

- — Act Sec. 105(a) and (c), affecting application of new minimum funding standards to certain PBGC settlement plans;
- — Act Sec. 106(a) and (c), affecting application of new minimum funding standards to certain government contractors;
- — Act Sec. 104(b), affecting application of Code Sec. 412(b)(5)(B) and ERISA Sec. 302(b)(5)(B), as in effect before amendments made by the Pension Act, to eligible cooperative plans;
- — Act Sec. 105(b), affecting application of Code Sec. 412(b)(5)(B) and ERISA Sec. 302(b)(5)(B), as in effect before amendments made by the Pension Act, to certain PBGC settlement plans;
- — Act Sec. 106(b), affecting application of Code Sec. 412(b)(5)(B) and ERISA Sec. 302(b)(5)(B), as in effect before amendments made by the Pension Act, to certain government contractors;
- — Act Sec. 106(d).

Reporter references: For further information, consult the following CCH reporters.

- — Pension Plan Guide, ¶2895
- — Standard Federal Tax Reporter, 2006FED ¶19,125.01
- — Federal Tax Guide, 2006FTG ¶11,040

¶245 Special Funding Rules for Plans Maintained by Commercial Airlines

SUMMARY OF NEW LAW

Special funding rules are adopted for a defined benefit pension plan sponsored by a commercial passenger airline or by a catering business that principally serves commercial passenger airlines. The plan sponsor may elect to amortize the unfunded liability of the plan over a period of 17 years. In the alternative, the plan sponsor may elect to amortize the shortfall amortization base over a period of 10 years.

BACKGROUND

A defined benefit pension plan sponsored by a single employer is required to meet the minimum funding standard. In general, the minimum contribution is the amount which will prevent an accumulated funding deficiency. A funding standard account is established in order to track the charges and credits made for the plan year. If charges exceed credits as of the end of the plan year, an accumulated funding deficiency exists. The charges include the normal cost of the plan with adjustments for other items including past service costs. The funding standard account is credited for contributions, experience gains, and other items. Costs are determined using an approved actuarial method. The degree to which a plan is considered funded is

BACKGROUND

determined by comparing the actuarial value of plan assets to the current liability of the plan. The current liability is the present value of the plan's accrued liabilities. An additional contribution is required for a plan that is less than 90 percent funded. For plan years beginning after December 27, 2003 and before December 28, 2005, the additional contribution could be reduced in certain cases (the alternative deficit reduction contribution). In addition, a waiver of the minimum funding standard could be granted where the sponsor is undergoing temporary business hardship and the full contribution would be adverse to the interests of the plan participants.

NEW LAW EXPLAINED

Amortization of unfunded liability of a commercial passenger airline defined benefit pension plan that freezes benefits.—*Election.* An eligible defined benefit pension plan may elect to compute the minimum contribution as an amount that will amortize the unfunded plan liability. So long as the contributions to the plan are not less than the amount determined under the elected formula, the plan will not be treated as having an accumulated funding deficiency. The election is made by the plan sponsor in accordance with IRS guidance. The plan sponsor may select the plan year to which the election applies; however, it must be a plan year that begins in 2006 or a plan year that begins in 2007. The election for a plan year beginning in 2006 must be made not later than December 31, 2006. The election for a plan year beginning in 2007 must be made not later than December 31, 2007. A new plan year can be designated in the election and the plan year change will not require IRS approval. Once made, the election remains in effect for subsequent plan years. The election may be revoked with IRS consent (Act Sec. 402(d) of the Pension Act). For plans that can not meet the eligibility requirements, there is an alternative election to amortize the shortfall amortization base which is explained below. The alternative election must be made not later than December 31, 2007 (Act Sec. 402(d)(1)(B) of the Pension Protection Act of 2006).

> **Comment:** Troubled financial circumstances in the passenger airline industry have caused some companies to file for bankruptcy. In this event, plan participants lose benefits and the burden on the Pension Benefit Guaranty Corporation (PBGC) increases. Congress is concerned that the minimum funding requirements could consume cash that is needed to keep the business in operation. By allowing the airlines more time to fund the plan, more bankruptcies and plan terminations might be avoided.

Eligibility. To be eligible, the plan must be sponsored by a single employer that is either a commercial passenger airline or a business principally engaged in providing catering services to a commercial passenger airline. The plan must restrict the accrual and increase of benefits. Pension, death or disability, and social security supplement (Code Sec. 411(a)(9)) benefits must be frozen at the level existing immediately before the first day of the plan year of election. All other plan benefits, if there are any, must be eliminated. The benefit restriction, however, would not be necessary for eligibility to the extent that the freeze or elimination would interfere with vesting standards compliance (Code Sec. 411(d)(6)). If an accrued benefit would increase as a result of an increase in the general limit on contributions and benefits (Code Sec. 415), the

NEW LAW EXPLAINED

eligible plan must be changed so that the accrued benefit does not increase while the election is in effect. This type of plan amendment will not be treated as a violation of the vesting standards.

There is an additional eligibility requirement for the period prior to commencement of the plan year of election. The period begins on July 26, 2005 and ends on the day before the first day of the plan year of election. During this period no applicable benefit increase can take effect. An applicable benefit increase is an increase in plan liabilities due to a plan amendment or other cause specified by IRS regulations. The increase in liability would be on account of benefit increases, changes in benefit accruals, or changes in the rate of benefit vesting.

The restriction on benefit accruals and increases does not apply to a plan participant with a disability status. If the participant was receiving disability benefits as of the date the plan was amended to restrict accruals and increases, the participant may still be credited with imputed service for the period of disability on or after the amendment date. A participant who was receiving sick pay on the amendment date and was later determined disabled would also be permitted credit for imputed service (Act Sec. 402(b) of the Pension Act).

Minimum required contribution. For any plan year when the election is in effect, the minimum required contribution is the amount necessary to amortize the unfunded plan liability in equal annual installments over the remainder of the amortization period. The amortization period is a 17-plan year period commencing with the plan year of election. The minimum required contribution is computed separately for each plan year as of the first day of the plan year. The unfunded liability is the unfunded accrued liability of the plan determined by the unit credit funding method. For the purpose of computing this amount, the value of plan assets is the fair market value of the assets. The interest rate used is 8.85 percent. Any actuarial assumptions must be reasonable (Code Sec. 412(c)(3)). When the amortization period is over, the minimum funding standards will once again apply to the plan except that the prefunding balance and the funding standard carryover balance as of the first day of the first post-amortization plan year shall be zero (Act Sec. 402(e) of the Pension Act).

Example: Once the election is made, the amortization period is fixed. As each year elapses, the relative benefit of amortization lessens. If at the beginning of plan year 2 the unfunded plan liability is $40 million, the minimum contribution for plan year 2 is $40 million divided by 16 (the remaining years in the amortization period) or about $2.5 million. At the beginning of plan year 3, the minimum contribution for plan year 3 would be determined using a 15-year period for amortization.

Transition rule for plan spinoff. An allocation must be made in the event of a plan spinoff from an eligible plan that occurs during the plan year that includes August 17, 2006, the enactment date of the Pension Act, if the spinoff occurs before the enactment date. The minimum required contribution is determined as if the plans were a single plan, based on the full 12-month plan year prior to the spin-off. The employer designates the

NEW LAW EXPLAINED

allocation of minimum required contribution between the plans (Act Sec. 402(e)(5) of the Pension Act).

Effect on funding standard account. Any charge or credit in the funding standard account and any prefunding balance (Code Sec. 430, as added by the Pension Act) is reduced to zero as of the day before the first day of the first plan year of election (Act Sec. 402(f)(1) of the Pension Act).

Waived funding deficiencies. Any waived funding deficiency determined under rules in effect prior to August 17, 2006, the enactment date (Sections 302 and 303 of the Employee Retirement Income Security Act of 1974 (ERISA) and Code Sec. 412), are deemed satisfied as of the first day of the first plan year of election. The waived amount is taken into account in determining the plan's unfunded liability. A plan amendment adopted in order to satisfy the accrual restrictions is not treated as a violation of the waiver restrictions (Code Sec. 412(f)). Similarly, an increase in benefits under a separate defined contribution plan or multiemployer plan is not treated as a violation (Act Sec. 402(f)(2) of the Pension Act).

Successor plans. The IRS has the authority to disqualify certain successor plans unless all benefit obligations of the electing plan have been satisfied. The authority to disqualify applies where a plan has made the election to amortize the unfunded liability or the alternative election to amortize the shortfall amortization base and the employer establishes or maintains one or more other defined benefit plans (that are not multi-employer plans) that provide, in combination, benefit accruals to a substantial number of successor employees. A successor employee is an employee who is or was covered by the electing plan. An employee who performs substantially the same type of work in the same business operation as an employee covered by the electing plan is also a successor employee (Act Sec. 402(g)(1) of the Pension Act).

Plan terminations. There is a special rule for a plan electing to amortize the unfunded liability if it is terminated within the ten-year period beginning on the first day of the first plan year of election. The plan will be treated as terminated on the first day of the first plan year of election and guaranteed benefits will be computed as of that date. If guaranteed benefits computed as of the actual termination date exceed the amount computed as of the deemed termination date, plan assets are allocated first to pay the excess amount (Act Sec. 402(g)(2)(A) of the Pension Act).

Termination premium. If a plan that has elected to amortize the unfunded liability is terminated within the five-year period beginning on the first day of the first plan year of election, the termination premium is $2,500 per participant. There is no exception for a termination in connection with a bankruptcy filed before October 18, 2005 (Act Sec. 402(g)(2)(B) of the Pension Act).

Deduction limit. The overall deduction limit applies to a plan eligible for these elections notwithstanding the exception for PBGC-insured defined benefit plans (Act Sec. 402(g)(3) of the Pension Act).

NEW LAW EXPLAINED

Notice. Notice of a plan amendment (if required to comply with these special funding rules) must be furnished within 15 days if the plan is maintained in connection with a collective bargaining agreement (Act Sec. 402(g)(4) of the Pension Act).

Modified minimum coverage requirements. In measuring the minimum coverage requirements, the category of excluded employees is modified so that certain management pilots are treated as covered by a collective bargaining agreement. This change applies to management pilots who manage the flight operations of air pilots who are represented in accordance with title II of the Railway Labor Act. In addition, the management pilots must be in the group of employees who benefit from the benefit trust under analysis (Code Sec. 410(b)(3), as amended by the Pension Act). This modification is effective for years beginning before, on, or after August 17, 2006 (Act Sec. 402(h)(2) of the Pension Act).

Alternative deficit reduction contribution. The alternative deficit reduction contribution procedure is extended to plan years beginning before December 28, 2007 (Act Sec. 402(i) of the Pension Act).

Election to amortize the shortfall amortization base. If the plan sponsor does not elect to amortize the unfunded plan liability, an alternative election is available to amortize the shortfall amortization base. The alternative election permits the plan sponsor to apply the general minimum funding standard (Code Sec. 430(a), as added by the Pension Act) using a 10-year amortization period instead of a 7-year period. See ¶ 210.

▶ **Effective date.** The provisions apply to plan years ending after August 17, 2006 (Act Sec. 402(j) of the Pension Protection Act of 2006). However, the modifications to the minimum coverage rules apply to years beginning before, on, or after August 17, 2006 (Act Sec. 402(h)(2) of the Pension Act).

Law source: Law at ¶5075 and ¶7063. Committee Report at ¶10,230.

— Act Sec. 402 of the Pension Protection Act of 2006

— Act Sec. 402(g)(2)(A), adding ERISA Sec. 4022(h);

— Act Sec. 402(h), amending Code Sec. 410(b)(3);

— Act Sec. 402(i), affecting application of Code Sec. 412(l)(12) and ERISA Sec. 302(d)(12);

— Act Sec. 402(j), providing the effective date.

Reporter references: For further information, consult the following CCH reporters.

— Pension Plan Guide, ¶2970

— Standard Federal Tax Reporter, 2006FED ¶18,997.047, ¶19,125.0215 and ¶19,125.032

— Tax Research Consultant, RETIRE: 30,000

— Federal Tax Guide, 2006FTG ¶11,040

Minimum Funding Rules for Multiemployer Plans

CROSS REFERENCES

Deduction limits for multiemployer plans (*see ¶710*)

Deduction limits for combination of plans (*see ¶715*)

¶305 Changes in Minimum Funding Rules for Multiemployer Plans

SUMMARY OF NEW LAW

The funding rules for multiemployer plans have been set out separately from the single-employer plan funding rules. The same general framework remains, but changes have been made for plan years beginning after 2007 that will: (1) reduce the amortization periods for certain supplemental costs to 15 years, (2) change the amortization extension and funding waiver interest rate to the plan rate, (3) tighten the reasonableness requirement for actuarial assumptions, (4) eliminate the alternative minimum funding standard, (5) make available an automatic five-year amortization extension with an additional five-year extension, and (6) provide a route for deemed approval of changes in the use of the shortfall funding method.

BACKGROUND

A multiemployer plan is a plan to which more than one unrelated employer contributes, that is established pursuant to one or more collective bargaining agreements,

BACKGROUND

and that satisfies such other requirements as the Secretary of Labor may prescribe by regulation (Code Sec. 414(f)(1); ERISA Sec. 3(37). In general, the required level of contributions to a multiemployer plan is specified in the applicable collective bargaining agreements, and the level of plan benefits is established by the plan trustees.

Minimum funding standard. A multiemployer plan satisfies the minimum funding standard for a plan year if, as of the end of that plan year, the plan does not have an accumulated funding deficiency. An accumulated funding deficiency exists for any plan year if the total charges to the plan's funding standard account for all plan years (see below) exceed the total credits to the account for all plan years (Code Sec. 412(a); ERISA Sec. 302(a)). Certain plans are eligible to use an alternative minimum funding standard, which measures the deficiency as the excess of the total charges to the alternative minimum funding standard account for all plan years over the total credits to the account for those years. Since charges to the alternative minimum funding standard account are computed differently from charges to the standard funding account, the accumulated funding deficiency may be lower when the alternative method is used (Code Sec. 412(g); ERISA Sec. 305).

Funding standard account. A multiemployer plan must have a funding standard account. For each plan year, the funding standard account is charged with the normal cost of the plan and credited with employer contributions (Code Sec. 412(b); ERISA Sec. 302(b)). The normal cost is the cost of future benefits allocated to the year by the funding method used by the plan for current employees and (under some funding methods) for separated employees.

Amortization of supplemental costs. Changes in supplemental costs are also either charged or credited to the funding standard account. A supplemental cost for a plan year is the cost of future benefits that would not be met by future contributions or plan assets. For example, an unfunded past service liability existing on the date that the plan is first effective or an increase or decrease in unfunded past service liabilities caused by plan amendments is amortized in equal payments generally over 30 years and charged or credited to the funding standard account. Any gain or loss resulting from changes in actuarial assumptions is amortized in equal payments generally over 30 years and charged or credited to the funding standard account. Any increase or decrease resulting from changes in the plan's net experience gain or loss are amortized in equal payments over 15 years and charged or credited to the funding standard account. Amortization takes place in equal installments until the amount is fully amortized (Code Sec. 412(b)(2), (3); ERISA Sec. 302(b)(2), (3)).

Extension of amortization periods. The period of years required to amortize an unfunded liability may be extended upon application to the IRS. A plan can request an extension for a period not in excess of 10 years. The IRS has authority to grant the extension if the employer shows that the extension would provide adequate protection for participants and their beneficiaries, and denial of the extension would (1) substantially risk the voluntary continuation of the plan or might cause a substantial curtailment of retirement benefits or employee compensation, and (2) be adverse to the interests of the participants. Note that the approval function over extension requests was statutorily placed with the Department of Labor (DOL), but was later

BACKGROUND

transferred to the IRS (Rev. Proc. 2004-44, I.R.B. 2004-31, 134; Code Sec. 412(e); ERISA Sec. 304).

Special interest rates for funding waivers and extensions. For multiemployer plans, the interest rate used with respect to determining the amortization on the waived amount of a funding deficiency and extensions of amortization periods is the federal short term rate (Code Secs. 412(d)(1)(B), (e), 6621(b); ERISA Sec. 304(a)).

Shortfall funding method. A multiemployer plan may use the shortfall funding method for determining charges to the funding standard account. This method adapts the plan's otherwise applicable funding method by computing charges on the basis of estimated units of service or production, such as hours worked under a collective bargaining agreement. Except in a plan's initial year, a plan's adoption of the shortfall method or its ceasing to use the shortfall method is subject to IRS approval (Reg. § 1.412(c)(1)-2(i)).

Reasonableness of actuarial assumptions. All costs, liabilities, rates of interest, and other factors under the plan must be determined on the basis of actuarial assumptions and methods which, *in the aggregate*, are reasonable, taking into account the experiences of the plan and reasonable expectations. Also, the actuarial assumptions and methods must, in combination, offer the actuary's best estimate of anticipated experience under the plan (Code Sec. 412(c)(3); ERISA Sec. 302(c)(3)).

Special exemption from withdrawal liability rules. The construction and entertainment industries are afforded a partial exemption from the employer withdrawal liability rules. Generally, a firm in either of these fields will be allowed to withdraw from a plan without incurring any liability, unless it continues to perform work in the covered area of the sort performed by the covered employees (ERISA Sec. 4203(b), (c)). Multiemployer plans covering employees in other industries may request Pension Benefit Guaranty Corporation (PBGC) approval of plan amendments establishing similar special withdrawal liability rules (ERISA Sec. 4203(f)).

NEW LAW EXPLAINED

Multiemployer plan funding rules modified.—The funding rules for multiemployer plans that were primarily found in Code Sec. 412 have been set out separately in new Code Sec. 431 and ERISA Sec. 304. The rules have been left largely intact, except for changes that will: (1) reduce the amortization periods for certain supplemental costs to 15 years, (2) change the amortization extension period and funding waiver interest rate to the plan rate, (3) tighten the reasonableness requirement for actuarial assumptions, (4) eliminate the alternative minimum funding standard, (5) make available an automatic five-year amortization extension with an additional five-year extension, and (6) provide a route for deemed approval of changes in the use of the shortfall funding method.

Amortization periods set at uniform 15 years, subject to extensions. The Pension Protection Act of 2006 reduces the 30-year amortization periods for various supplemental costs charged or credited to a multiemployer plan's standard funding account down to a uniform 15 years. These changes apply to certain supplemental costs charged or

NEW LAW EXPLAINED

credited to the standard funding account for amounts first amortized in plan years beginning in 2008 and thereafter. The amortization periods may be extended for up to 10 years (see below). Under the new law, the amortization period is 15 years rather than 30 years for the following charges to the standard funding account:

- unfunded past service liabilities under the plan on the first day of the first plan year for plans that come into existence on or after January 1, 2008,
- net increases in unfunded past service liabilities arising from plan amendments, and
- net losses resulting from changes in actuarial assumptions (Code Sec. 431(b)(2) and ERISA Sec. 304(b)(2), as added by the Pension Act).

Under the new law, the amortization period is 15 years rather than 30 years for the following credits to the standard funding account:

- net decreases in unfunded past service liabilities arising from plan amendments, and
- net gains resulting from changes in actuarial assumptions (Code Sec. 431(b)(3) and ERISA Sec. 304(b)(3), as added by the Pension Act).

The amortization period for experience gains and losses remains the same at 15 years (Code Sec. 431(b)(2), (3) and ERISA Sec. 304(b)(2), (3), as added by the Pension Act). To the extent that a plan amendment increases the unfunded past service liability by reason of a short-term increase in benefits payable under the plan for a period that does not exceed 14 years from the effective date of the amendment, the 15-year amortization period is changed to the number of years of the period of increased benefits (Code Sec. 431(b)(7)(G) and ERISA Sec. 304(b)(7)(G), as added by the Pension Act).

> **Comment:** The change brings the multiemployer plan amortization periods in line with the single-employer plan amortization periods. Shortening the amortization periods results in quicker reflection of funding liability changes to the standard funding account. It also increases the volatility of pension funding obligations. Plan sponsors will have to fund increased costs by making larger yearly outlays because the payments will be spread over fewer years.

Grandfather provision. The old amortization rules will continue to apply for amounts first amortized in plan years beginning before 2008 (Code Sec. 431(b)(4) and ERISA Sec. 304(b)(4), as added by the Pension Act). No recalculation of amortization periods already in effect is required (Joint Committee on Taxation, Technical Explanation of the Pension Protection Act of 2006 (JCX-38-06)).

> **Example:** In 2007, a multiemployer plan starts amortizing a net increase in funding liability of $300,000 caused by a plan amendment. The plan can amortize this amount over 30 years at $10,000 a year (disregarding interest). If, however, the plan has to start amortizing the amount in the 2008 plan year, the amortization period is only 15 years and the installment amount is $20,000 a year (disregarding interest).

Alternative minimum funding standard. The alternative minimum funding standard account is eliminated under the new law. Thus, for plan years beginning after 2007, the

NEW LAW EXPLAINED

accumulated funding deficiency of a multiemployer plan will be determined by examining the charges and credits to the funding standard account (ERISA Sec. 304(a), as added by the Pension Act).

Automatic extension of amortization period. The amortization extension procedure is changed for plan years beginning after 2007. The sponsor of a multiemployer plan can apply to the IRS for an automatic extension of the period required to amortize any unfunded past service liability, investment loss, or experience loss. The IRS must extend the amortization period for a period of up to five years. The plan's actuary must certify that: (1) absent the extension, the plan would have an accumulated funding deficiency in the current plan year or any of the nine succeeding plan years, (2) the plan sponsor has adopted a plan to improve the plan's funding status, (3) taking into account the extension, the plan is projected to have sufficient assets to pay its expected benefit liabilities and other anticipated expenditures in a timely manner, and (4) required advance notice has been provided to affected parties. The automatic extension will not apply with respect to applications submitted after December 31, 2014 (Code Sec. 431(d)(1) and ERISA Sec. 304(d)(1), as added by the Pension Act).

Additional five-year amortization period extension. The plan sponsor can apply for an additional extension of the amorization period of up to five years over and above the automatic five-year extension. As under present law, the plan must show that the additional extension would provide adequate protection for participants and their beneficiaries, and denial of the extension would (1) substantially risk the continuation of the pension plan or might cause a substantial curtailment of retirement benefits or employee compensation, and (2) be adverse to the interests of the participants. The IRS must act on the application within 180 days after submission. If the IRS rejects the application, it must notify the plan of the specific reason for the rejection (Code Sec. 431(d)(2) and ERISA Sec. 304(d)(2), as added by the Pension Act).

> **Comment:** Extending an amortization period reduces each year's pension outlay by spreading out the cost of funding benefits over a greater number of years.

> **Comment:** The maximum possible amortization extension period remains 10 years, the major difference being that the initial five years is automatically granted if the plan meets the requirements. This change is a significant benefit because amortization requests can be time-consuming and the results uncertain. The automatic procedure allows plan sponsors to act quickly to gain a measure of funding relief.

Advance notice requirement for amortization period extension requests. The plan must provide advance notice of its filing of an application for an extended amortization period to all affected parties. Affected parties include participants, beneficiaries of deceased participants, alternate payees under an applicable qualified domestic relations order (QDRO), employee organizations representing participants, and the Pension Benefit Guaranty Corporation (PBGC) (ERISA Sec. 4001(a)(21)). The notice must include a description of the extent to which the plan is funded for guaranteed benefits and for benefit limitations. The IRS must take into consideration any comments an affected party might have (Code Sec. 431(d)(3) and ERISA Sec. 304(d)(3), as added by the Pension Act).

NEW LAW EXPLAINED

Interest rates for funding waivers and amortization extension periods. The new law eliminates the special rate of interest based on the short-term federal rate for funding waivers and amortization period extensions for plan years beginning after 2007. A plan must charge or credit the funding standard account with interest consistent with the rate or rates that the plan uses to determine costs (Code Sec. 431(b)(6) and ERISA Sec. 304(b)(6), as added by the Pension Act).

Extensions of amortization periods that are granted pursuant to applications filed on or before June 30, 2005, can continue to be applied by using the old special rate, which was based on the federal short-term rate (Act Secs. 201(d), 211(b) of the Pension Act). As under the old law, the plan's general funding interest rate, which it uses to calculate its costs for purposes of determining its current liabilities, has to be within a permissible range. The permissible range is not more than 5 percent above, and not more than 10 percent below, the weighted average of the rates of interest on 30-year Treasury securities during the 4-year period ending on the last day before the beginning of the plan year (Code Sec. 431(c)(6)(E)(ii) and ERISA Sec. 304(c)(6)(E)(ii), as added by the Pension Act). Previously, the permissible range was not more than 10 percent above and 10 percent below the weighted average of the 30-year Treasury bond rates.

> **Comment:** The Treasury suspended issuance of new 30-year bonds back when the federal deficit looked like less of a problem than it does today. Congress initially responded so that in the case of plan years beginning after December 31, 2003, and before January 1, 2006, the benchmark interest rate for the permissible range is based on long-term investment grade corporate bonds during the four-year period ending on the last day before the beginning of the plan year. With the deficit looming large again, the Treasury has resumed issuing its 30-year bonds. The 30-year Treasury bond typically has among the lowest long-range rates available, usually significantly lower than the lowest corporate bond rates. The new law on interest rates for funding waivers and amortization extension periods for multiemployer plans uses the 30-year Treasury bond as the benchmark. However, for other funding purposes, use of the corporate bond rate has been extended for two years to plan years beginning before 2008 (see ¶235).

> **Comment:** The signature of the shift from short-term to long-term federal rules is that over time, long-term rates tend to be significantly higher than short-term rates. Indeed, the spread in much of the early to mid-2000's was in the one- to two-percent range (sometimes more), which is consistent with long-term trends. The rate convergence (indeed, on some days rate inversion) we are currently experiencing is thought to be caused by short-term inflationary expectations that should subside as the business cycle progresses.

Reasonableness of actuarial assumptions. The reasonableness requirement is changed for actuarial assumptions and methods used to determine costs, liabilities, interest rates and other factors with respect to multiemployer plans is modified for plan years beginning after 2007. Rather than requiring reasonable actuarial assumptions and methods *in the aggregate, each* actuarial assumption and method used must be reasonable, taking into account the plan's experience and reasonable expectations. Also, as under prior law, the actuarial assumptions and methods must, in combina-

NEW LAW EXPLAINED

tion, offer the actuary's best estimate of anticipated experience under the plan (Code Sec. 431(c)(3) and ERISA Sec. 304(c)(3), as added by the Pension Act).

Deemed approval of shortfall funding method. The shortfall funding method adapts the plan's otherwise applicable funding method for determining charges to the funding standard account. Under the shortfall method, the net shortfall charge to the funding standard account is computed on the basis of estimated units of service or production for which a certain amount per unit is charged. For example, charges can be computed based on hours worked under a collective bargaining agreement. Except for the first plan year, for which the plan can elect to use the shortfall method without IRS approval, a plan has to obtain IRS approval to adopt or discontinue use of the shortfall method (Reg. § 1.412(c)(1)-2(i)). Under the Pension Act, a multiemployer plan is deemed to have the IRS's approval to adopt, use, or cease to use the shortfall funding method for plan years beginning after 2007, and beginning before 2015, if:

(1) the plan has not used the shortfall funding method during the preceding five-year period and

(2) no extension of an amortization period with respect to the plan is in effect or has been in effect for such five-year period (Act Sec. 201(b)(2) of the Pension Act).

Plan amendments increasing benefits generally cannot be adopted while the shortfall funding method is in use (Act Sec. 201(b)(4) of the Pension Act). The provision should not be construed as affecting a plan's ability to adopt the shortfall funding method with IRS approval or its right to change funding methods as otherwise permitted (Act Sec. 201(b)(5) of the Pension Act). Deemed approval of the shortfall method will not apply to plan years beginning after December 31, 2014 (Act Sec. 221(c)(1) of the Pension Act).

Grandfather rule for benefits funded under an agreement. The changes discussed here do not apply to benefit increases funded under an agreement to which a multiemployer plan is a party if certain conditions are met. The agreement must have been approved by the PBGC prior to June 30, 2005. The agreement must provide for benefit increases, and provide special withdrawal liability rules similar to those available in the entertainment and construction industries (ERISA Sec. 4203(f)). A firm in either of these fields is allowed to withdraw from a plan without incurring any liability, unless it continues to perform work in the covered area of the sort performed by the covered employees (ERISA Sec. 4203(b), (c)). In addition, the benefit increases must occur under a plan amendment adopted prior to June 30, 2005, and the plan must be funded in compliance with the agreement and any amendments to it (Act Sec. 206 of the Pension Act).

> **Comment:** The Pension Act makes members of a controlled group liable for a member's obligation to a multiemployer plan (Code Sec. 412(b)(2), ERISA Sec. 302(b)(2), as amended by the Pension Act). This change is discussed at ¶ 205.

▶ **Effective date.** The amendments made to the multiemployer plan minimum funding rules apply to plan years beginning after 2007 (Act Secs. 201(d)(1), 211(b)(1) of the Pension Protection Act of 2006). In the case of an amortization extension granted under ERISA Sec. 304 and Code Sec. 412(e) (prior to amendment by the Pension Act), with respect to any application filed with the Secretary of the Treasury on or before June 30, 2005, the

NEW LAW EXPLAINED

extension (and any modification thereof) will be applied and administered under the rules of such sections as in effect before August 17, 2006, the date of enactment of the Pension Act, including the use of the rate of interest under Code Sec. 6621(b) (Act Secs. 201(d)(2), 211(b)(2) of the Pension Act).

Sunset provision. The provisions of, and amendments relating to, the use of the shortfall funding method by multiemployer plans that are collectively bargained plans will not apply to plan years beginning after December 31, 2014 (Act Sec. 221(c)(1) of the Pension Protection Act of 2006). See ¶29,020 for the CCH explanation of the sunset provision, ¶7051 for the law, and ¶10,180 for the related committee report.

Law source: Law at ¶5090, ¶5125, ¶5295, ¶5355, ¶7030 and ¶7045. Committee Report at ¶10,010, ¶10,080 and ¶10,160.

— Act Sec. 114(c), (e) and (f) of the Pension Protection act of 2006, amending Code Secs. 414(1)(2)(B)(i), 4971, 4972 and 6059(b), respectively;

— Act Sec. 201(a) adding ERISA Sec. 304 and striking ERISA Sec. 301(d)

— Act Sec. 206;

— Act Sec. 211(a), adding Code Sec. 431;

— Act Secs. 201(d) and 211(b), providing the effective dates.

Reporter references: For further information, consult the following CCH reporters.

— Pension Plan Guide, ¶260, ¶2885 and ¶2890

— Standard Federal Tax Reporter, 2006FED ¶19,125.01

— Tax Research Consultant, RETIRE: 57,200

— Federal Tax Guide, 2006FTG ¶11,040

¶310 Additional Funding Rules for Significantly Underfunded Multiemployer Plans

SUMMARY OF NEW LAW

Multiemployer plans that are so underfunded as to be in "endangered" or "critical" status are required to adopt funding improvement and rehabilitation plans and take certain actions to improve their funding status over a multiyear period. Excise taxes and civil penalties may apply if a plan does not adopt or comply with a required funding improvement or rehabilitation plan.

BACKGROUND

Multiemployer plans are retirement plans established under one or more collective bargaining agreements to which multiple unrelated employers contribute. Such plans may also cover employees who are not covered by a collective bargaining agreement. There are approximately 1,600 multiemployer plans, covering 9.9 million employees,

BACKGROUND

insured by the Pension Benefit Guaranty Corporation (PBGC), mainly in the trucking, retail food, construction, mining, and garment industries.

A multiemployer plan is governed by a board of trustees consisting of an equal number of employer and employee representatives. The board of trustees (or if there is no board of trustees, the plan administrator) is considered the sponsor of a multiemployer plan.

Generally, the contributions made by employers to a multiemployer plan are based on the number of hours worked by active participants and are set in the relevant collective bargaining agreements. The level of benefits is set by the trustees. If hours worked decline while the number of participants receiving benefits holds steady or increases, a plan is likely to become underfunded.

Funding standards apply to defined benefit retirement plans (and to certain defined contribution retirement plans). Multiemployer plans are generally subject to the same funding requirements that apply to single employer plans, though some adjustments to the rules are made. The funding standards generally require that the employer (or employers) sponsoring a plan make quarterly contributions to the plan in an amount that is sufficient to fund both the normal cost of the plan (the cost of benefits allocable to the current year) and an allocated portion of unfunded past service liabilities, increases or decreases in past service liabilities, and experience gains and losses. Various amortization schedules are prescribed to determine the portions of unfunded past service liabilities and experience gains and losses allocated to each year. All costs, liabilities, rates of interest, and other relevant factors must be determined on the basis of actuarial assumptions and methods that are reasonable, taking into account the experience of the plan and reasonable expectations.

An accumulated funding deficiency exists for any plan year if the total charges to the plan's funding standard account for all plan years exceed the total credits to the account for all plan years (Code Sec. 412(a)). Accumulated funding deficiencies of a multiemployer plan are subject to a five-percent initial and 100-percent additional excise tax (Code Sec. 4971).

Special rules apply to any multiemployer plan that is in "reorganization status." Typically this situation will arise if the plan's funding level is low and current accruals are small relative to the vested accrued liabilities. A plan is in reorganization status for a year if the required funding contribution exceeds the plan's vested benefits charge. The vested benefits charge is generally the amount needed to amortize, in equal annual installments, unfunded vested benefits under the plan over: (1) 10 years, in the case of vested benefits payable to individuals who are already receiving benefit payments; and (2) 25 years, in the case of benefits payable to other individuals.

When a plan is in reorganization status:

(1) benefits derived from employer contributions that exceed a de minimis amount must be paid in the form of a life annuity;

(2) the plan is eligible for a special funding credit;

(3) year-to-year increases in contributions are capped; and

BACKGROUND

(4) the plan may be amended to reduce or eliminate accrued benefits in excess of those guaranteed by the PBGC.

Also, in any plan year in which a multiemployer plan is in reorganization, the accumulated funding deficiency of the plan is based on the plan's vested benefits charge, reduced by an overburden credit (Code Sec. 418B) instead of on the normal cost of the year's benefits and allocable amortized costs (Code Sec. 412(a)).

If a multiemployer plan is insolvent, that is, it does not have assets sufficient to pay benefits when due during the current or next plan year, the plan is required to reduce benefits to the level that can be funded by the plan's assets. If the plan's assets are not sufficient to fund the minimum benefits guaranteed by the PBGC, the PBGC will provide loans to the plan. These loans are typically not repaid. In fiscal 2005, the PBGC paid out $13.8 million to 29 insolvent plans. As of September 2005, the PBGC estimated that multiemployer plans were underfunded by $200 billion, and may require future financial assistance of $418 million.

For discussion of new funding rules for single employer plans, see ¶205. For discussion of changes to the basic funding rules for multiemployer plans, see ¶305.

NEW LAW EXPLAINED

Additional funding rules for significantly underfunded multiemployer plans.—All multiemployer plans are now required to obtain an annual actuarial certification regarding their funding status. Special funding and operational requirements apply for plans that are certified to be in "endangered" or "critical" status (Code Sec. 432 and ERISA Sec. 305, as added by the Pension Protection Act of 2006). The new requirements generally apply to plan years beginning after 2007 for multiemployer plans in effect on July 16, 2006 (Act Secs. 202(f) and 212(e) of the Pension Act). The requirements are subject to a sunset provision, so that for plan years beginning after 2014 there will be no new certifications of endangered or critical status. The requirements will continue to apply to plans that are already in endangered or critical status at the end of 2014 (Act Sec. 221(c) of the Pension Act). See ¶ 29,020.

Actuarial certification of funded status. Not later than the 90th day of each plan year, the actuary for every multiemployer plan must certify to the IRS and to the plan sponsor whether or not the plan is in endangered status and whether or not it is or will be in critical status for the year. If a plan has previously been certified as endangered or critical and is currently in a funding improvement or rehabilitation period, the actuary must certify whether or not the plan is making the scheduled progress in meeting the requirements of its funding improvement or rehabilitation plan (Code Sec. 432(b)(3)(A) and ERISA Sec. 305(b)(3)(A), as added by the Pension Act). If the actuary fails to provide the required certification in time, the Secretary may assess a penalty of up to $1,100 per day against the plan administrator (Code Sec. 432(b)(3)(C) and ERISA Sec. 305(b)(3)(C), as added by the Pension Act).

In determining a plan's status or its progress, the actuary must use reasonable actuarial estimates, assumptions and methods that offer the actuary's best estimate of anticipated

NEW LAW EXPLAINED

experience under the plan in making projections of the current value of the assets of the plan and the present value of the plan's liabilities. Those projections are made for each plan year as of the beginning of the year. The projected present value of plan liabilities for any plan year must be calculated based on the most recent of (1) the actuarial statement required under ERISA with respect to the most recently filed annual report or (2) the actuarial valuation for the previous plan year. Projections of plan assets must assume either (1) reasonably anticipated employer contributions for the current and succeeding plan years assuming that one or more collective bargaining agreements under which contributions are required will continue in effect, or (2) if the actuary determines that no material demographic changes have occurred, that employer contributions for the most recent plan year will continue indefinitely. The actuary may take into account information provided by the sponsor with regard to the future of the employers' industry in making projections of future experience (Code Sec. 432(b)(3)(B) and ERISA Sec. 305(b)(3)(B), as added by the Pension Act).

The actuary's calculations with respect to a plan's normal cost, actuarial accrued liability, and improvements in a plan's funded percentage for purposes of these funding requirements must be made using the unit credit funding method, whether or not that method is used for the plan's actuarial valuation (Code Sec. 432(i)(8) and ERISA Sec. 305(i)(8), as added by the Pension Act).

Notice of certification. If the plan actuary certifies that a plan is or will be in endangered or critical status for a plan year, the plan sponsor must, within thirty days after the date of the certification, provide notification of the plan's status to the participants and beneficiaries, the bargaining parties, the PBGC, and the Secretary of Labor (Code Sec. 432(b)(3)(D)(i) and ERISA Sec. 305(b)(3)(D)(i), as added by the Pension Act). The bargaining parties include any employer who has an obligation to contribute under the plan and any union which represents the employees of such an employer (Code Sec. 432(i)(1) and ERISA Sec. 305(i)(1), as added by the Pension Act).

If it is certified that the plan is or will be in critical status, the notice must include an explanation of the possibility that adjustable benefits may be reduced for participants and beneficiaries who begin receiving benefits after the notice is provided (Code Sec. 432(b)(3)(D)(ii) and ERISA Sec. 305(b)(3)(D)(ii), as added by the Pension Act). The Department of Labor is to develop a model notice for this purpose (Code Sec. 432(b)(3)(D)(iii) and ERISA Sec. 305(b)(3)(D)(iii), as added by the Pension Act).

Critical status. A multiemployer plan is in critical status for a plan year if the plan actuary determines that it meets any one of four tests as of the beginning of the plan year (Code Sec. 432(b)(2) and ERISA Sec. 305(b)(2), as added by the Pension Act).

> **Comment:** Generally speaking, the result of these four tests is that a plan that is less than 65% funded will be in critical status if it is projected that:
>
> (1) it will have an accumulated funding deficiency within five years; or
>
> (2) it will not have sufficient assets to pay the promised benefits within seven years.

NEW LAW EXPLAINED

Any plan, regardless of its funded percentage, will be in critical status if it is projected that:

(1) it will have an accumulated funding deficiency within four years;

(2) it will not have sufficient assets to pay promised benefits within five years; or

(3) all of the following are true:

(a) the present value of benefits for inactive participants is greater than the present value of benefits for active participants;

(b) expected contributions are less than the sum of the plan's normal cost and the interest on its unfunded liabilities; and

(c) the plan will have an accumulated funding deficiency within five years.

Under the first of the four tests, a plan is in critical status if it is significantly underfunded and not projected to improve its funded percentage over the next seven years. Specifically, a plan is in critical status under this test if its funded percentage is less than 65 percent and the sum of (1) the fair market value of the plan assets, and (2) the present value of the reasonably anticipated employer contributions for the current plan year and each of the next six plan years (assuming the terms of all current collective bargaining agreements continue in effect) is less than the sum of the present value of (1) all nonforfeitable benefits projected to be payable under the plan during the current year and the next six plan years, and (2) administrative expenses for those years.

Under the second test, a plan is in critical status if it is expected that credits to its funding standard account will not exceed charges to the account for the current plan year or for any of the next three or four plan years. Specifically, a plan is in critical status if it has an accumulated funding deficiency for the current plan year, not taking into account any extension of amortization periods (under Code Sec. 431(d) and ERISA Sec. 304(d), as added by the Pension Act), or the plan is projected to have an accumulated funding deficiency for any of the next three plan years (the next four plan years if the plan's funded percentage is 65 percent or less), not taking into account any extension of amortization periods.

Under the third test, plans in shrinking industries are likely to be in critical status. Specifically, a plan is in critical status if:

(1) the plan's normal cost for the current plan year, plus interest for the year on the amount of unfunded benefit liabilities under the plan as of the last day of the preceding plan year, exceeds the present value of the reasonably anticipated employer contributions for the current plan year;

(2) the present value, as of the beginning of the plan year, of the nonforfeitable benefits of inactive participants (those who are no longer working in covered service) is greater than the present value of the nonforfeitable benefits of active participants; and

NEW LAW EXPLAINED

(3) the plan has an accumulated funding deficiency for the current plan year, not taking into account any extension of amortization periods (under Code Sec. 431(d) and ERISA Sec. 304(d), as added by the Pension Act), or the plan is projected to have an accumulated funding deficiency for any of the next four plan years, not taking into account any extension of amortization periods.

Under the fourth test, a plan is in critical status if the current assets and expected contributions over the next five years are not sufficient to satisfy the plan's expected obligations over that period. Specifically, a plan is in critical status if the sum of (1) the fair market value of the current plan assets, and (2) the present value of the reasonably anticipated employer contributions for the current year and each of the next four plan years (assuming the terms of all current collective bargaining agreements continue in effect), is less than the sum of the present value of (1) all benefits projected to be payable under the plan during the current year and the next four plan years, and (2) administrative expenses for those years.

Endangered status. A multiemployer plan is in endangered status if the plan actuary determines that it is not in critical status for the plan year but that it meets either of two tests at the beginning of the plan year. Under the first test, a plan is in endangered status if its funded percentage is less than 80 percent. Under the second test, a plan is in endangered status if it has an accumulated funding deficiency for the current plan year or is projected to have an accumulated funding deficiency for any of the next six plan years, taking into account any extension of amortization periods (under Code Sec. 431(d) and ERISA Sec. 304(d), as added by the Pension Act). A plan that satisfies both of these tests is in "seriously endangered" status (Code Sec. 432(b)(1) and ERISA Sec. 305(b)(1), as added by the Pension Act).

Funded percentage. A plan's funded percentage is the value of its assets divided by its accrued liability (Code Sec. 432(i)(2) and ERISA Sec. 305(i)(2), as added by the Pension Act).

Requirements for endangered plans. An endangered plan must adopt and implement a funding improvement plan (FIP) designed to allow the plan to meet applicable funding improvement benchmarks during a funding improvement period, and must satisfy certain special operational requirements after the date of the certification and throughout the funding improvement period (Code Sec. 432(a)(1) and ERISA Sec. 305(a)(1), as added by the Pension Act).

Funding improvement plan. The sponsor of an endangered plan must adopt a FIP not later than the 330th day of the plan year for which the plan is first certified as endangered (the initial determination year) (Code Sec. 432(c)(1)(A) and ERISA Sec. 305(c)(1)(A), as added by the Pension Act). A FIP is a plan consisting of the actions, including options or a range of options to be proposed to the bargaining parties, which based on reasonably anticipated experience and under reasonable actuarial assumptions will result in the plan meeting certain funding improvement benchmarks (Code Sec. 432(c)(3)(A) and ERISA Sec. 305(c)(3)(A), as added by the Pension Act).

The FIP must be designed to allow an endangered plan to achieve two benchmarks. If the plan is not in seriously endangered status, the adoption of the measures contained in the FIP must be projected to result in the plan (1) reducing its unfunded

NEW LAW EXPLAINED

percentage, by the end of a ten-year funding improvement period, by at least 33 percent; and (2) not having an accumulated funding deficiency for any plan year during the funding improvement period (Code Sec. 432(c)(3)(A), (4)(A) and ERISA Sec. 305(c)(3)(A), (4)(A), as added by the Pension Act).

If a seriously endangered plan has a funded percentage of 70 percent or less at the beginning of the initial determination year, a less rigorous version of the first benchmark applies. Adoption of the FIP must be projected to result in such a plan reducing its unfunded percentage, by the end of a 15-year funding improvement period, by at least 20 percent (Code Sec. 432(c)(3)(B), (4)(B) and ERISA Sec. 305(c)(3)(B), (4)(B), as added by the Pension Act). This less rigorous benchmark also applies for seriously endangered plans that have a funded percentage higher than 70 percent if the actuary certifies, within 30 days of its initial certification of the plan's seriously endangered status, that based on the terms of the plan and the collective bargaining agreements then in place the plan is not projected to meet the stricter version of the benchmarks (Code Sec. 432(c)(5)(A)(i) and ERISA Sec. 305(c)(5)(A)(i), as added by the Pension Act). The 20-percent improvement and 15-year period benchmark is available for those plans only for years beginning on or before the date that collective bargaining agreements covering 75 percent or more of the plan's active participants will have expired. For subsequent years the FIP generally must be formulated based on the 33-percent and 10-year period benchmark (Code Sec. 432(c)(5)(A)(ii) and ERISA Sec. 305(c)(5)(A)(ii), as added by the Pension Act).

However, if the actuary certifies in its annual certification for a subsequent year that such a plan is still not projected to satisfy the 33-percent improvement benchmark by the end of the 10-year period, based on the terms of the plan and the collective bargaining agreements then in effect, the plan may continue to formulate its FIP to target the 20-percent benchmark over a 15-year funding improvement period (Code Sec. 432(c)(5)(B) and ERISA Sec. 305(c)(5)(B), as added by the Pension Act).

Example: An endangered plan has a funded percentage of 76 percent at the beginning of the initial determination year, and so has an unfunded percentage of 24 percent. The plan must adopt a FIP projected to reduce its unfunded percentage to no more than 16.08 percent by the end of a ten-year funding improvement period.

Example: Another plan is seriously endangered and has a funded percentage at the beginning of its initial determination year of 65 percent, so that its unfunded percentage is 35 percent. The plan must adopt a FIP projected to reduce its unfunded percentage to no more than 28 percent by the end of a 15-year funding improvement period.

Example: A third plan is seriously endangered and has a funded percentage at the beginning of its initial determination year of 75 percent, so that its un-

NEW LAW EXPLAINED

funded percentage is 25 percent. The plan actuary certifies, within 30 days of its initial certification of the plan's seriously endangered status, that based on the terms of the plan and the collective bargaining agreements then in place the plan is not projected to improve its funded percentage above 83.25 percent (75 percent + (33 percent × 25 percent)) by the end of a ten-year funding improvement period. The initial FIP must be projected to reduce the plan's unfunded percentage to no more than 20 percent by the end of a 15-year funding improvement period.

For plan years beginning after the date on which collective bargaining agreements in effect on the due date of the initial certification and covering 75 percent of the participants in the plan have expired, the plan's FIP must be projected to reduce the plan's unfunded percentage by 33 percent by the end of a ten-year funding improvement period, unless the actuary again certifies that the plan is not projected to meet those goals.

If there are fewer than 60 days remaining before the FIP is required to be adopted and the board or group that constitutes the plan sponsor is not able to agree on a plan, any member of the board or group may require that the sponsor enter into an expedited dispute resolution procedure for the development and adoption of the plan (Code Sec. 432(g) and ERISA Sec. 305(g), as added by the Pension Act). The statute does not provide any guidance or restrictions as to the nature of the dispute resolution procedure.

Once the deadline for adoption of a FIP has passed, an employer required to contribute to the plan or an employee organization representing active participants in the plan can file in federal court for an order compelling the sponsor to adopt one (ERISA Sec. 502(a)(10), as added by the Pension Act).

Within 30 days after the adoption of the FIP, the sponsor of an endangered plan must provide to the bargaining parties a schedule or schedules showing revised benefit and/or contribution structures which, if adopted, might reasonably be expected to allow the plan to achieve the applicable funding benchmarks (Code Sec. 432(c)(1)(B) and ERISA Sec. 305(c)(1)(B), as added by the Pension Act). The schedules must include:

(1) one proposal showing how the benchmarks can be achieved by reductions in future benefit accruals (and if the maximum allowable reductions will not be sufficient to achieve the applicable benchmarks, by increasing contributions) (the default schedule); and

(2) one proposal showing how the benchmarks can be achieved by increasing contributions, without reducing future benefit accruals.

In addition to schedules showing these extreme methods of achieving the benchmarks, the sponsor of an endangered plan may choose to prepare and provide to the bargaining parties additional relevant information (Code Sec. 432(c)(1)(B)(ii) and ERISA Sec. 305(c)(1)(B)(ii), as added by the Pension Act).

NEW LAW EXPLAINED

If, upon the expiration of a collective bargaining agreement in effect at the time the plan entered into endangered status, an employer and its employees' union are unable to reach a new agreement that includes contribution or benefit schedules necessary to meet the applicable benchmarks, the plan sponsor must implement the default schedule. This default schedule must be implemented as of the earlier of (1) the date the Secretary of Labor certifies that the parties are at an impasse or (2) the date 180 days after the expiration of the old collective bargaining agreement (Code Sec. 432(c)(7) and ERISA Sec. 305(c)(7), as added by the Pension Act).

When the funding improvement period begins. The funding improvement period for a FIP is generally the 10-year (or 15-year) period beginning on the first day of the first plan year beginning after the second anniversary of the adoption of the FIP. However, the period will begin earlier if the collective bargaining agreements covering 75 percent of the plan's participants expire before that time. Specifically, if the collective bargaining agreements in effect on the due date of the initial actuarial certification of endangered status and covering at that time at least 75 percent of the active participants in the plan expire before the second anniversary of the adoption of the FIP, the funding improvement period will begin on the first day of the first plan year beginning after the expiration date of the last of those collective bargaining agreements (Code Sec. 432(c)(4)(A) and ERISA Sec. 305(c)(4)(A), as added by the Pension Act).

Funding plan adoption period. The funding plan adoption period is the period beginning on the day of the actuary's initial certification of the plan's endangered status and ending on the day before the first day of the funding improvement period (Code Sec. 432(c)(8) and ERISA Sec. 305(c)(8), as added by the Pension Act).

Transitions from endangered status. A funding plan adoption period or funding improvement period will end early if the plan's actuary certifies that the plan is no longer in endangered status (and is not in critical status). The truncated period will end as of the end of the plan year before the new certification (Code Sec. 432(c)(4)(C)(i) and ERISA Sec. 305(c)(4)(C)(i), as added by the Pension Act).

If a plan that has been in endangered status is for a later year certified to be in critical status, the then current funding plan adoption period or funding improvement period will end as of the close of the plan year preceding the first plan year in the plan's rehabilitation period (Code Sec. 432(c)(4)(C)(ii) and ERISA Sec. 305(c)(4)(C)(i), as added by the Pension Act).

If the actuary certifies that the plan is still endangered for the first year after the end of a funding improvement period, the plan will begin a new round of funding improvements without regard to the prior FIP, except that the plan may not be amended in a way that is inconsistent with the prior FIP until a new FIP is adopted (Code Sec. 432(c)(4)(D) and ERISA Sec. 305(c)(4)(D), as added by the Pension Act).

Updating the funding improvement plan and schedules. The sponsor of an endangered plan must update the FIP each year and file the update with the plan's annual Form 5500 filing. Any schedule of contribution rates provided by the sponsor must be updated annually to reflect actual plan experience. A schedule of contribution rates provided by the sponsor and relied upon by bargaining parties in reaching a collective bargaining

NEW LAW EXPLAINED

agreement must remain in effect for the duration of that agreement (Code Sec. 432(c)(6) and ERISA Sec. 305(c)(6), as added by the Pension Act).

> **Comment:** The law requires that updated funding improvement plans be filed with the plan's annual report, but, in what seems to be an oversight, does not require that funding improvement plans be filed upon their adoption.

Operational requirements for endangered plans. Special operational requirements apply to endangered plans (Code Sec. 432(d) and ERISA Sec. 305(d), as added by the Pension Act). At no time during the funding plan adoption period or the funding improvement period may the plan sponsor accept any collective bargaining agreement or participation agreement that provides for (1) lower contributions for any participants, (2) a suspension of contributions with respect to any period of service, or (3) any new direct or indirect exclusion of younger or newly hired employees from plan participation (Code Sec. 432(d)(1)(A), (2)(B) and ERISA Sec. 305(d)(1)(A), (2)(B), as added by the Pension Act).

During the plan adoption period, the sponsor cannot amend an endangered plan in any way that increases plan liabilities by reason of an increase in benefits, change in accruals, or change in the vesting rate, unless the amendment is necessary to maintain the plan's qualified status or required by law (Code Sec. 432(d)(1)(B) and ERISA Sec. 305(d)(1)(B), as added by the Pension Act). The sponsor of a seriously endangered plan is required during the plan adoption period to take all reasonable steps that are consistent with the plan and the law and which are expected, based on reasonable assumptions, to increase the plan's funded percentage and postpone the occurrence of an accumulated funding deficiency for at least one year. These reasonable steps may include applying for extensions of amortization periods (under Code Sec. 431(d) and ERISA Sec. 304(d)), using the shortfall funding method in making funding standard account computations, amending the plan's benefits structure, and reducing future benefit accruals (Code Sec. 432(d)(1)(C) and ERISA Sec. 305(d)(1)(C), as added by the Pension Act).

Once a FIP has been adopted, the multiemployer plan may not be amended in a way inconsistent with the FIP, and amendments increasing benefits, including future benefit accruals, are further restricted. A plan may be amended to increase benefits only if the actuary certifies that the benefit increase is consistent with the funding improvement plan and is paid for out of contributions not required by the FIP to meet the applicable benchmarks in accordance with the schedule contemplated in the FIP (Code Sec. 432(d)(2)(A), (C) and ERISA Sec. 305(d)(2)(A), (C), as added by the Pension Act).

> **Compliance Pointer:** It may be prudent to include language in a FIP to specify that benefit increases are not necessarily inconsistent with the FIP.

Excise taxes and enforcement with respect to endangered plans. Several excise tax liabilities may arise with respect to an endangered plan. An employer that fails to timely make a contribution required under an endangered plan's FIP is subject to an excise tax in the amount of 100 percent of the contribution (Code Sec. 4971(g)(2), as added by the Pension Act). If a seriously endangered plan fails to satisfy the applicable benchmarks by the end of the funding improvement period, the plan is treated as having an accumulated funding deficiency (subject to the excise tax under Code Sec.

NEW LAW EXPLAINED

4971) for the last year of the funding improvement period (and each succeeding year until the applicable benchmarks are met) equal to the greater of the amount of contributions necessary to meet the applicable benchmarks or the amount of the plan's accumulated funding deficiency as calculated under the general rules (Code Sec. 4971(g)(3), as added by the Pension Act). For endangered plans, these excise taxes are in addition to the usual excise tax on accumulated funding deficiencies under Code Sec. 4971 (Code Sec. 4971(g)(1)(B), as added by the Pension Act). (Plans in critical status are exempt from the general excise tax. See *Excise taxes and enforcement with regard to critical plans,* below). If the failure to make the required contributions in a timely manner or to meet the applicable funding improvement benchmarks was due to reasonable cause and not to willful neglect, all or part of these taxes may be waived. Reasonable cause includes unanticipated and material market fluctuations, the loss of a significant contributing employer, or other factors that make collection of the tax excessive or otherwise inequitable relative to the failure involved (Code Sec. 4971(g)(5), as added by the Pension Act).

The Secretary of Labor may assess a penalty of up to $1,100 per day against a plan sponsor if (ERISA Sec. 502(c)(8), as amended by the Pension Act):

(1) the sponsor fails to timely adopt a required funding improvement plan; or

(2) in the case of a plan that is not seriously endangered, the plan fails to meet the applicable benchmarks by the end of the funding period.

If the sponsor fails to update or comply with the terms of the funding improvement plan it has adopted, any participating employer or union can file a civil action for an order compelling the sponsor to update or comply with the plan (ERISA Sec. 502(a)(10), as added by the Pension Act).

Requirements for critical plans. A plan in critical status must adopt and implement a rehabilitation plan designed to enable the plan to emerge from critical status, and must satisfy certain special operational requirements throughout the rehabilitation plan adoption and rehabilitation periods (Code Sec. 432(a)(2) and ERISA Sec. 305(a)(2), as added by the Pension Act). A plan in critical status is not subject to the general funding requirements if it has adopted and is in compliance with the requirements of a rehabilitation plan (Code Sec. 412(b)(3) and ERISA Sec. 302(b)(3), as added by the Pension Act).

Rehabilitation plan. The sponsor of a critical plan must adopt a rehabilitation plan not later than the 330th day of the plan year for which the plan is first certified as critical (the initial critical year) (Code Sec. 432(e)(1)(A) and ERISA Sec. 305(e)(1)(A), as added by the Pension Act). A rehabilitation plan is a plan consisting of the actions, including options or a range of options to be presented to the bargaining parties and which, under reasonable actuarial assumptions, will allow the plan to emerge from critical status by the end of the rehabilitation period. Those actions may include reductions in plan expenditures, reductions in future benefit accruals, and increases in contributions, if agreed to by the bargaining parties (Code Sec. 432(e)(3)(A)(i) and ERISA Sec. 305(e)(3)(A)(i), as added by the Pension Act). The plan must provide annual standards for determining whether its requirements are being met (Code Sec.

NEW LAW EXPLAINED

432(e)(3)(A), flush language and ERISA Sec. 305(e)(3)(A), flush language, as added by the Pension Act).

A rehabilitation plan must include one or more schedules showing revised benefit and/or contribution structures which, if adopted, may reasonably be expected to allow the plan to emerge from critical status. The schedules must reflect reductions in future benefit accruals and adjustable benefits and increases in contributions that the sponsor determines are reasonably necessary to emerge from critical status. One such schedule, the default schedule, must assume that there are no increases in contributions under the plan other than those necessary to emerge from critical status after future benefit accruals and other benefits have been reduced as much as the law allows (Code Sec. 432(e)(3)(A), flush language and ERISA Sec. 305(e)(3)(A), flush language, as added by the Pension Act). The schedules must include an allowance for funding the benefits of participants for whom contributions are not currently required (Code Sec. 432(e)(8)(A)(iii), and ERISA Sec. 305(e)(8)(A)(iii), as added by the Pension Act).

The plan sponsor must provide copies of the schedules to the bargaining parties within 30 days after the adoption of the rehabilitation plan (Code Sec. 432(e)(1)(B)(i), and ERISA Sec. 305(e)(1)(B)(i), as added by the Pension Act). The sponsor may prepare additional relevant information for the bargaining parties as well (Code Sec. 432(e)(1)(B)(ii) and ERISA Sec. 305(e)(1)(B)(ii), as added by the Pension Act).

If, upon the expiration of a collective bargaining agreement in effect at the time the plan entered into critical status, an employer and its employees' union are unable to agree on a new contract that includes contribution or benefit schedules necessary to allow the plan to emerge from critical status, the plan sponsor must implement the default schedule described above that reduces future benefit accruals as necessary and to the extent allowed, and thereafter increases contributions. This proposal must be implemented as of the earlier of the date the Secretary of Labor certifies that the parties are at an impasse or the date 180 days after the expiration of the old collective bargaining agreement (Code Sec. 432(e)(3)(C) and ERISA Sec. 305(e)(3)(C), as added by the Pension Act).

A plan has emerged from critical status when the plan actuary certifies, in its annual certification, that the plan is not projected to have an accumulated funding deficiency for the current year or any of the next nine plan years, without use of the shortfall method or any extension of amortization periods (under Code Sec. 431(d) and ERISA Sec. 304(d)) (Code Sec. 432(e)(4)(B) and ERISA Sec. 305(e)(4)(B), as added by the Pension Act).

If the plan sponsor determines that despite all reasonable measures the plan cannot be expected to emerge from critical status by the end of the rehabilitation period, the rehabilitation plan must include reasonable measures that will allow the plan to emerge from critical status at a later time or to at least delay the plan's becoming insolvent (Code Sec. 432(e)(3)(A)(ii) and ERISA Sec. 305(e)(3)(A)(ii), as added by the Pension Act). In such a case the rehabilitation plan must set forth the alternatives considered, explain why the plan cannot reasonably be expected to emerge from critical status by the end of the rehabilitation period, and specify when, if ever, the plan is expected to emerge from critical status under the rehabilitation plan (Code

NEW LAW EXPLAINED

Sec. 432(e)(3)(A), flush language and ERISA Sec. 305(e)(3)(A), flush language, as added by the Pension Act).

The default schedule in a rehabilitation plan generally cannot entirely eliminate future accruals. The minimum rate of future accruals under a default schedule cannot be less than the lower of (1) the accrual rate under the plan as of the first day of the initial critical year, or (2) a monthly benefit (payable as a single life annuity at the participant's normal retirement age) equal to one percent of the contributions required to be made with respect to a participant, or the equivalent standard accrual rate for a participant or group of participants under the collective bargaining agreements in effect as of the first day of the initial critical year. The plan sponsor has broad discretion in choosing an equivalent standard accrual rate. The equivalent standard accrual rate is determined by the plan sponsor based on the standard or average contribution base units that the sponsor determines to be representative for active participants and such other factors as the sponsor determines to be relevant (Code Sec. 432(e)(6) and ERISA Sec. 305(e)(6), as added by the Pension Act).

If there are fewer than 60 days remaining before the rehabilitation plan is required to be adopted and the board or group that constitutes the plan sponsor is not able to agree on a plan, any member of the board or group may require that the sponsor enter into an expedited dispute resolution procedure for the development and adoption of the plan (Code Sec. 432(g) and ERISA Sec. 305(g), as added by the Pension Act). The statute does not provide any guidance or restrictions as to the nature of the dispute resolution procedure.

Once the deadline for adoption of a plan has passed, an employer required to contribute to the plan or a union representing active participants in the plan can file in federal court for an order compelling the sponsor to adopt a plan (ERISA Sec. 502(a)(10), as added by the Pension Act).

Cutbacks of adjustable benefits. Although ERISA Sec. 204(g)generally prohibits reductions in benefits that have already been earned, certain cutbacks are allowed when a plan is in critical status. The sponsor of a critical plan must make cutbacks in "adjustable benefits" if it decides they are appropriate. No cutback can be made in the benefits of any participant or beneficiary who has already begun receiving benefits, except that an increase in benefits that was adopted or took effect within 60 months of the first day of the initial critical year can be reduced or eliminated (Code Sec. 432(e)(8)(A) and ERISA Sec. 305(e)(8)(A), as added by the Pension Act).

Adjustable benefits generally include nearly every aspect of a plan apart from normal retirement benefits in the form of a joint-and-survivor annuity (Code Sec. 432(e)(8)(A)(iv) and ERISA Sec. 305(e)(8)(A)(iv), as added by the Pension Act). They include:

(1) other benefits, rights and features under the plan, including post-retirement death benefits, 60-month guarantees, disability benefits not yet in pay status, and similar benefits;

(2) any early retirement benefits or retirement-type subsidies;

(3) any benefit payment option other than the qualified joint-and-survivor annuity; and

NEW LAW EXPLAINED

(4) benefit increases that were adopted or took effect less than 60 months before the first day of the initial critical year.

Before implementing a reduction in adjustable benefits the sponsor must give 30 days notice of the change to all participants and beneficiaries, each employer who contributes to the plan, and each union representing participants employed by any employer. The notice must contain information enabling the participants and beneficiaries to understand the effect of the reductions on their benefits, including an estimate of any affected benefit that the individual would otherwise have been eligible for as of the effective date of the change, and information as to the individual's rights and remedies and how to contact the Department of Labor for more information and assistance. The notice must be written so as to be understandable by the average plan participant. It may be provided on paper, electronically or in any other form, so long as it is reasonably accessible to the recipients. The Department of Labor is required to promulgate regulations including a model notice and prescribing the form and manner in which the notice is to be given (Code Sec. 432(e)(8)(C) and ERISA Sec. 305(e)(8)(C), as added by the Pension Act).

Reductions in benefits under a rehabilitation plan are disregarded in determining a plan's unfunded vested benefits for purposes of determining an employer's withdrawal liability (Code Sec. 432(e)(9)(A) and ERISA Sec. 305(e)(9)(A), as added by the Pension Act).

Rehabilitation period. The rehabilitation period for a critical plan is generally the 10-year period beginning on the first day of the first plan year beginning after the second anniversary of the adoption of the rehabilitation plan. However, the period will begin earlier if collective bargaining agreements covering 75 percent of the plan's participants expire before that time. Specifically, if the collective bargaining agreements in effect on the due date of the initial actuarial certification of critical status and covering at that time at least 75 percent of the active participants in the plan expire before the second anniversary of the adoption of the rehabilitation plan, the rehabilitation period will begin on the first day of the first plan year beginning after the expiration date of the last of those collective bargaining agreements (Code Sec. 432(e)(4)(A) and ERISA Sec. 305(e)(4)(A), as added by the Pension Act).

A plan's rehabilitation period will end early if the plan's actuary later certifies that the plan is not projected to have an accumulated funding deficiency for the plan year or any of the next nine plan years, without regard to the use of the shortfall method and taking into account any extension of amortization periods (under Code Sec. 431(d) and ERISA Sec. 304(d)). The truncated period will end as of the end of the plan year before the new certification (Code Sec. 432(e)(4) and ERISA Sec. 305(e)(4), as added by the Pension Act).

Rehabilitation plan adoption period. The rehabilitation plan adoption period is the period beginning on the day of the actuary's initial certification of the plan's critical status and ending on the day before the first day of the rehabilitation period (Code Sec. 432(e)(5) and ERISA Sec. 305(e)(5), as added by the Pension Act).

Updating the rehabilitation plan and schedules. The sponsor of a critical plan must update the rehabilitation plan each year and file the update with the plan's annual Form 5500 filing. Any schedule of contribution rates provided by the sponsor must

NEW LAW EXPLAINED

be updated annually to reflect actual plan experience. Any schedule of contribution rates provided by the sponsor and relied upon by bargaining parties in reaching a collective bargaining agreement must remain in effect for the duration of that agreement (Code Sec. 432(e)(3)(B) and ERISA Sec. 305(e)(3)(B), as added by the Pension Act).

> **Comment:** The law requires that updated rehabilitation plans be filed with the plan's annual report, but, in what seems to be an oversight, does not require that rehabilitation plans be filed upon their adoption.

Operational requirements for critical plans. Special operational requirements apply to critical plans (Code Sec. 432(f) and ERISA Sec. 305(f), as added by the Pension Act). After notice of the plan's critical status has been sent to the bargaining parties and participants, the plan generally is not allowed to pay out large lump-sum benefits. Specifically, the plan may not pay:

(1) any amount greater than the monthly amount paid under a single life annuity;

(2) any payment for an irrevocable commitment from an insurer to pay benefits; or

(3) any other payments prohibited by regulations.

This prohibition does not apply to involuntary cash-outs of benefits up to $5,000 or to any retroactive payment with respect to a prior period (Code Sec. 432(f)(2) and ERISA Sec. 305(f)(2), as added by the Pension Act).

Benefit reductions under this provision are not taken into account in determining the plan's unfunded vested benefits for purposes of determining the withdrawal liability of an employer withdrawing from the plan (Code Sec. 432(f)(3) and ERISA Sec. 305(f)(3), as added by the Pension Act).

During the rehabilitation plan adoption period, the plan sponsor may not accept any collective bargaining agreement or participation agreement that provides for reduced contributions by reason of (1) lower contributions for any participants, (2) a suspension of contributions with respect to any period of service, or (3) any new direct or indirect exclusion of younger or newly hired employees from plan participation (Code Sec. 432(f)(4)(A) and ERISA Sec. 305(f)(4)(A), as added by the Pension Act). A critical plan cannot be amended during the adoption period in any way that increases plan liabilities by reason of an increase in benefits, change in accruals or change in the vesting rate, unless the amendment is required to maintain the plan's qualified status or required by law (Code Sec. 432(f)(4)(B) and ERISA Sec. 305(f)(4)(B), as added by the Pension Act).

Once a rehabilitation plan has been adopted, the multiemployer plan may not be amended in a way inconsistent with the rehabilitation plan, and amendments increasing benefits, including future benefit accruals, are restricted. A critical plan can be amended to increase benefits only if the plan actuary certifies that the increase is paid for out of increased contributions not contemplated by the rehabilitation plan, and that after taking into account the increased benefits the plan is still reasonably projected to emerge from critical status by the end of the rehabilitation period on the schedule contemplated in the rehabilitation period (Code Sec. 432(f)(1) and ERISA Sec. 305(f)(1), as added by the Pension Act).

NEW LAW EXPLAINED

Employer surcharges. Employers contributing to critical plans are encouraged to renegotiate their collective bargaining agreements to adopt a schedule of contributions and benefits consistent with the rehabilitation plan sooner rather than later by the imposition of a surcharge on contributions. A temporary surcharge in the amount of five percent of the required contribution is imposed on all contributing employers for the first year a plan is in critical status. In later years, for as long as the plan remains in critical status, the surcharge is ten percent of the required contribution. The surcharge amounts themselves cannot be the basis for any benefit accruals under the plan. The surcharge takes effect 30 days after the employer has been notified by the sponsor that the plan is in critical status and that the surcharge is in effect. The surcharges are due and payable on the same schedule as the contributions on which they are based, and any failure to make the required payment is treated as a delinquent contribution under ERISA. However, the surcharge does not apply with respect to employees who are covered by a collective bargaining agreement that includes terms consistent with a schedule provided by the sponsor under the rehabilitation plan (Code Sec. 432(e)(7) and ERISA Sec. 305(e)(7), as added by the Pension Act).

Surcharges are not taken into account in determining an employer's withdrawal liability except for purposes of determining the unfunded vested benefits attributable to the employer. The Pension Benefit Guaranty Corporation is required to prescribe simplified methods for calculating withdrawal liability in these situations (Code Sec. 432(e)(9)(B), (C) and ERISA Sec. 305(e)(9)(B), (C), as added by the Pension Act).

Excise taxes and enforcement with regard to critical plans. Several excise tax liabilities may arise with respect to a plan in critical status. First, an employer that fails to timely make a contribution required under a critical plan's rehabilitation plan is subject to an excise tax in the amount of 100 percent of the contribution (Code Sec. 4971(g)(2), as added by the Pension Act). Second, if a plan in critical status fails to satisfy the applicable requirements by the end of the rehabilitation period, or is certified for three consecutive plan years as having failed to make the scheduled progress under its rehabilitation plan, the plan is treated as having an accumulated funding deficiency (subject to the excise tax under Code Sec. 4971) for the last year of the rehabilitation period or 3-consecutive-year period (and each succeeding year until the applicable requirements are met) equal to the greater of (1) the amount of contributions necessary to meet the applicable requirements or (2) the amount of the plan's accumulated funding deficiency as calculated under the general rules (Code Sec. 4971(g)(3), as added by the Pension Act). Unlike endangered plans, a multiemployer plan that is in critical status for a plan year is not subject to the general excise tax on accumulated funding deficiencies (Code Sec. 4971(g)(1)(A), as added by the Pension Act). However, if the sponsor of a plan in critical status fails to adopt a rehabilitation plan before the 331st day of the first critical year, an excise tax is imposed on the sponsor. This tax is in the amount of the greater of (1) the general excise tax on accumulated funding deficiencies that would be imposed on the plan if it were not excluded from the tax because of its critical status, or (2) $1,100 per day for the period beginning the day after the required date of the actuarial certification of critical status and ending on the day on which the rehabilitation plan is adopted (Code Sec. 4971(g)(4), as added by the Pension Act).

NEW LAW EXPLAINED

If a taxable failure to make required contributions in a timely manner or to meet the applicable requirements or make scheduled progress for three years was due to reasonable cause and not to willful neglect, the IRS may waive all or part of these taxes. Reasonable cause includes unanticipated and material market fluctuations, the loss of a significant contributing employer, or other factors to the extent that collection of the tax would be excessive or otherwise inequitable relative to the failure involved (Code Sec. 4971(g)(5), as added by the Pension Act). Note that the tax on a failure to adopt a rehabilitation plan cannot be waived.

In addition, the Secretary of Labor may assess a penalty of up to $1,100 per day against a plan sponsor that fails to timely adopt a required rehabilitation plan (ERISA Sec. 502(c)(8), as amended by the Pension Act).

> **Comment:** Under existing law all members of a controlled group are jointly and severally liable for any excise tax imposed under Code Sec. 4971 with respect to a single employer plan, but this joint and several liability rule does not apply if the plan is a multiemployer plan (Code Sec. 4971(e)(2)(A)). It appears that the Pension Act was intended to change the rule for multiemployer plans to match the general rule. However, the language of the Act refers to Code Sec. 4971(c)(2), instead of to Code Sec. 4971(e)(2)(A) (Act Sec. 212(b)(2) of the Pension Act). A technical correction will likely be forthcoming.

If the sponsor fails to update or comply with the terms of the rehabilitation plan it has adopted, any participating employer or union can file a civil action for an order compelling the sponsor to update or comply with the rehabilitation plan (ERISA Sec. 502(a)(10), as added by the Pension Act).

> **Caution Note:** A special rule in the Pension Act applies only in the case of a multiemployer pension plan:
>
> (1) with fewer than 100 participants;
>
> (2) with respect to which the contributing employers participated in a federal fishery capacity reduction program;
>
> (3) with respect to which the employers participated in the Northeast Fisheries Assistance Program;
>
> (4) with respect to which the annual normal cost is less than $100,000; and
>
> (5) which is experiencing a funding deficiency on August 17, 2006, the date of enactment of the Act.
>
> Such a plan is exempt from the excise tax on its accumulated funding deficiency for any tax year beginning before the earlier of the tax year in which the sponsor adopts a rehabilitation plan or the tax year that contains January 1, 2009 (Act Sec. 214 of the Pension Act).

Nonbargained participants. If an employer contributes to a multiemployer plan that is in endangered or critical status on behalf of both employees who are covered by a collective bargaining agreement and employees who are not so covered, benefits and contributions (including surcharges on contributions) for the nonbargained employees are to be determined as if those employees were covered under the first to expire of the employer's collective bargaining agreements in force when the plan entered

NEW LAW EXPLAINED

endangered or critical status (Code Sec. 432(h)(1) and ERISA Sec. 305(h)(1), as added by the Pension Act). If an employer contributes to an endangered or critical plan only on behalf of nonbargained employees, the employer will be treated as the bargaining party, and its participation agreement with the plan as a collective bargaining agreement that expires on the first day of the first plan year that begins after the employer is provided with the schedules of contributions and benefits that the sponsor is required to provide (Code Sec. 432(h)(2) and ERISA Sec. 305(h)(2), as added by the Pension Act).

> **Comment:** Another special rule in the Pension Act provides that the new funding requirements do not apply to benefit increases that occur under a plan amendment adopted prior to June 30, 2005, in compliance with an agreement providing for increased benefits and special withdrawal liability rules that was approved by the PBGC before that date. The benefits must be funded pursuant to the agreement, and the entire plan must be funded in compliance with the agreement. The agreement must provide for special withdrawal liability rules similar to those available in the entertainment and construction industries, which allow employers to withdraw from plans without any withdrawal liability if they cease doing business in the covered area (ERISA Sec. 4203(b), (c), (f); Act Sec. 206 of the Pension Act).

▶ **Effective date.** The provisions imposing additional funding rules on multiemployer plans in endangered or critical status apply with respect to plan years beginning after 2007. For a multiemployer plan under which benefits were reduced pursuant to a plan amendment adopted on or after January 1, 2002, and before June 30, 2005, and which, pursuant to the plan document, trust agreement, or a formal written communication from the sponsor to the participants provided before June 30, 2005, provided for the restoration of the reduced benefits, the provision will not apply to restrict those benefit restorations (Act Secs. 202(f) and 212(e) of the Pension Protection Act of 2006).

With regard to the provisions relating to certain benefits funded under an agreement approved by the PBGC and to the plan maintained by employers who participated in the Northeast Fisheries Assistance Program, no specific effective date is provided by the Act. The provisions are, therefore, considered effective on August 17, 2006 (Act Secs. 206 and 214 of the Pension Act).

Sunset provision. The provisions of, and amendments relating to, the additional funding rules for multiemployer plans in endangered or critical status contained in Act Secs. 202 and 212 will not apply to plan years beginning after December 31, 2014 (Act Sec. 221(c)(1) of the Pension Act). See ¶29,020 for the explanation of the sunset provision, ¶7051 for the law, and ¶10,180 for the related committee report.

Law source: Law at ¶5085A, ¶5130, ¶5295, ¶7033, ¶7045, and ¶7048. Committee Reports at ¶10,090, ¶10,160, and ¶10,170.

— Act Sec. 202(a), (b), (c), (d), and (e) of the Pension Protection Act of 2006, adding new ERISA Secs. 302(b)(3), 305, 502(a)(10), and 502(c)(8);

— Act Sec. 202(f), providing the effective date;

— Act Sec. 206;

— Act Sec. 212(a), adding new Code Sec. 432;

NEW LAW EXPLAINED

— Act Sec. 212(b), amending Code Sec. 4971 and adding Code Sec. 4971(g);

— Act Sec. 212(c), adding Code Sec. 412(b)(3);

— Act Sec. 212(d);

— Act Sec. 212(e), providing the effective date;

— Act Sec. 214.

Reporter references: For further information, consult the following CCH reporters.

— Pension Plan Guide, ¶2800, ¶2925 and ¶2955

— Standard Federal Tax Reporter, 2006FED ¶34,324.01

— Tax Research Consultant, RETIRE: 30,152, RETIRE: 57,210 and RETIRE: 57,510

— Federal Tax Guide, 2006FTG ¶11,040

¶315 Testing Insolvency of Multiemployer Plans

SUMMARY OF NEW LAW

Sponsors of multiemployer plans in reorganization will need to perform a test at the end of the first plan year in reorganization, and every three years thereafter as long as the plan is in reorganization, to determine whether the plan will become insolvent during any of the next five plan years. If the sponsor determines that insolvency is possible in any of the next five plan years, the solvency determination will need to be made annually, instead of every three years, until the plan potentially will not be insolvent for at least the next five plan years.

BACKGROUND

A multiemployer plan is a plan that requires more than one employer to contribute, and is maintained under a collective bargaining agreement between an employee organization and more than one employer (Code Sec. 414(f)(1); ERISA Sec. 4001(a)(3)). Multiemployer plans that are in financial difficulty may be subject to special rules regarding funding, adjustments in accrued benefits and changes in benefit payments.

The Pension Benefit Guaranty Corporation (PBGC) insures multiemployer plans against insolvency. When a multiemployer plan enters into a reorganization due to severe financial stress, the plan sponsor is required to make a solvency determination at the end of the first plan year in reorganization, and every three years thereafter while in reorganization. Generally, the solvency determination is based on whether the value of plan assets exceeds three times the total amount of benefit payments for the plan year. If the value of plan assets is not more than three times the total benefit payments, the sponsor must forecast whether the plan will become insolvent in any of the next three plan years (Code Sec. 418E(d)(1); ERISA Sec. 4245(d)(1)). If the sponsor determines that insolvency is probable in the three-year time frame, it must

BACKGROUND

give notice of the plan's potential future insolvency to the Secretary of the Treasury, the PBGC, the contributing companies, and the plan participants and beneficiaries (Code Sec. 418E(e); ERISA Sec. 4245(e)). The sponsor also must take appropriate steps to return the plan to solvency, including, but not limited to, obtaining financial assistance from the PBGC (Code Sec. 418E(f); ERISA Sec. 4245(f)).

NEW LAW EXPLAINED

Measures to forestall insolvency of multiemployer plans.—The number of years that a sponsor of a multiemployer plan in reorganization must forecast the possibility of the plan's future insolvency will be increased from three plan years to five plan years, for solvency determinations made in plan years beginning after 2007 (Code Sec. 418E(d)(1) and ERISA Sec. 4245(d)(1), as amended by the Pension Protection Act of 2006). Thus, if the sponsor makes the solvency determination and finds that the value of plan assets does not exceed three times the total benefit payments for the plan year, the sponsor will need to determine whether the plan has the potential to become insolvent for any of the next five plan years, rather than the next three plan years.

> **Comment:** Extending the length of the forecast period is intended to help the PBGC anticipate the insolvency of multiemployer plans and the potential need to provide such plans with financial assistance.

This change still requires the sponsor of a multiemployer plan that enters into a reorganization to make the solvency determination at the end of the first plan year and every three years thereafter while in reorganization. However, for plan years beginning after 2007, if the sponsor determines that the plan has the potential to become insolvent in any of the next five plan years, the sponsor will have to complete the solvency determination annually, rather than every three years. The solvency determination will have to be conducted on an annual basis until the sponsor can make the determination that the plan will not be insolvent in any of the next five plan years (Code Sec. 418E(d)(1) and ERISA Sec. 4245(d)(1), as amended by the Pension Act). This new obligation of the plan sponsor is in addition to meeting the notification requirements and taking the necessary steps to insure solvency of the plan.

▶ **Effective date.** The provision applies to determinations made in plan years beginning after 2007 (Act Secs. 203(b) and 213(b) of the Pension Protection Act of 2006).

Law source: Law at ¶5110 and ¶7036. Committee Report at ¶10,100.

— Act Sec. 203(a) of the Pension Protection Act of 2006, amending ERISA Sec. 4245(d)(1);

— Act Sec. 213(a), amending Code Sec. 418E(d)(1);

— Act Secs. 203(b) and 213(b), providing the effective date.

Reporter references: For further information, consult the following CCH reporters.

— Pension Plan Guide, ¶6994, ¶7248 and ¶7250

— Standard Federal Tax Reporter, 2006FED ¶19,291.01 and ¶19,291.026

— Tax Research Consultant, RETIRE: 57,510

¶320 Multiemployer Plans Withdrawal Liability Rules

SUMMARY OF NEW LAW

The withdrawal liability rules for a multiemployer plan that apply when a contributing employer completely or partially terminates its participation are reformed to afford more protection to the plan's contribution base and ensure the plan's viability. The reforms impact how the withdrawal liability is calculated, when a withdrawal has occurred and when withdrawal liability payments must be made.

BACKGROUND

A multiemployer plan is a plan in which more than one employer is required to contribute and which is maintained under a collective bargaining agreement between an employee organization and more than one employer (Code Sec. 414(f)(1); ERISA Sec. 4001(a)(3)). Multiemployer plans that are in financial difficulty may be subject to special rules regarding funding, adjustments in accrued benefits and changes in benefit payments.

In the late 1970's, concerns were raised that the withdrawal of large contributing employers from multiemployer plans could unduly increase the financial burden on the remaining contributing employers. To allay these fears and promote the fiscal health of multiemployer plans, the Multiemployer Pension Plan Amendments Act of 1980 (MPPAA) (P.L. 96-364) was enacted. This legislation created a withdrawal liability for contributing employers that completely or partially terminated their participation in these plans. Such employers must continue funding a proportional share of the plan's unfunded vested benefits by making annual withdrawal liability payments to the plan.

The withdrawal liability of a contributing employer generally equals a portion of the unfunded vested benefits accrued by its employees at the time of the employer's complete or partial withdrawal from the plan (ERISA Secs. 4201 and 4211). A complete withdrawal generally occurs when the contributing employer permanently ceases operations or permanently ceases to have the obligation to contribute to the plan (ERISA Sec. 4203(a)). A partial withdrawal generally occurs when the employer's contribution obligation decreases by at least 70 percent at the end of the plan year or there is a partial cessation of the employer's contribution obligation (ERISA Sec. 4205(a)). A number of limitations and exceptions cap the amount of the withdrawal liability and provide a method to contest a plan sponsor's finding of partial or compete withdrawal or the amount of the withdrawal liability.

Asset sale limitation. One limitation on withdrawal liability applies to contributing employers that sell all or substantially all of their assets in an arm's-length transaction to a third party (ERISA Sec. 4225(a)(1)). In that situation, the withdrawal liability is limited to the greater of: (1) a portion of the liquidation or dissolution value of the employer after the sale, or (2) the unfunded vested benefits attributable to the employees of the employer (ERISA Sec. 4225(a)(1)). Where the employer withdraws

BACKGROUND

from several multiemployer plans, the limitation must be apportioned among the plans (ERISA Sec. 4225(e)).

Partial withdrawal limitation. There is a partial cessation of an employer's contribution obligation to a multiemployer plan and, thus, a partial withdrawal from the plan, when contributions under a collective bargaining agreement cease, but the employer continues to perform the same type of work within the agreement's jurisdiction or the employer transfers the same work to another location. An employer with an obligation to contribute to a multiemployer plan under multiple collective bargaining agreements incurs a withdrawal liability if the employer permanently ceases to have an obligation to contribute under at least one but not all of the agreements, and continues to do work in the jurisdiction for which a contribution was required or transfers the work to another location (ERISA Sec. 4205(a) and (b)). An employer that permanently ceases covered work under one of the collective bargaining agreements but contracts the work to a third party is not considered to have transferred the work to another location (PBGC Opinion Letter 86-17).

Forgiveness or "free look" rule. Under the "free look" rule, an employer first entering a multiemployer plan may withdraw from the plan without incurring a withdrawal liability if certain requirements are met (ERISA Sec. 4210). These requirements are related to the length of time the employer had an obligation to the plan and to the amount of contributions made during the obligation period. Plans that primarily cover employees in the construction and building industries, however, are not eligible for the free look rule and, thus, employers that withdraw from such plans are not exempt from withdrawal liability (ERISA Sec. 4210(b)(1)).

Computing withdrawal liability. In computing withdrawal liability, most multiemployer plans can be amended to provide that the amount of unfunded benefits allocable to an employer that withdraws from the plan is determined under an alternative method, such as the modified presumptive method. Plans that primarily cover employees in the building and construction industry, however, may not be amended to permit use of an alternative method (ERISA Sec. 4211(c)).

Dispute resolution. Plan sponsors decide when a withdrawal liability is incurred and the amount of the withdrawal liability (ERISA Sec. 4219). The sponsor's assessment of withdrawal liability is presumed correct unless the employer shows by a preponderance of the evidence that the determination was unreasonable or clearly erroneous. Disputes between an employer and the plan sponsor can arise over withdrawal liability. These disputes begin with arbitration of the issues and, if either party is unhappy with the result, proceed to court (ERISA Sec. 4221).

Plan sponsors may disregard any transaction that they believe was undertaken to evade or avoid a withdrawal penalty. A special rule may apply if a plan sponsor disregards a transaction and the employer receives a notification of withdrawal liability and a demand for payment after October 31, 2003. If the sponsor's determination was based on its disregard of a transaction that occurred before January 1, 1999, and at least five years before the date of the withdrawal, and the employer contests the sponsor's determination, then the employer has no obligation to make withdrawal liability payments until a final decision by the arbitrator or a court upholds the plan sponsor's determination (ERISA Sec. 4221(f)).

NEW LAW EXPLAINED

Withdrawal liability reforms.—The recent bankruptcies of several large employers, the consolidation of companies within several industries and the increase in outsourcing of contract work have caused some employers to terminate their participation in multiemployer plans. Although these employers generally remain liable for a portion of the plan's unfunded vested benefits, there are limits on their withdrawal liability. To try to ensure the fiscal health of these plans and relieve the stress on the resources of the Pension Benefit Guaranty Corporation (PBGC), several of the withdrawal liability rules and limitations are amended or repealed entirely.

Asset sale limitations updated. The withdrawal liability limitation rules for the sale of all or substantially all of the assets of a contributing employer to an unrelated third party or parties are updated and clarified (ERISA Sec. 4225, as amended by the Pension Protection Act of 2006). Employers that sell all or substantially all of their assets to an unrelated third party or parties in an arm's-length transaction are responsible to the PBGC for a portion of the unfunded vested benefits accrued by their employees. The amount of the withdrawal liability limitation cannot exceed the greater of:

(1) a portion of the liquidation or dissolution value of the employer determined after the sale or exchange, as determined according to an updated table in ERISA Sec. 4225(a)(2) (as amended by the Pension Protection Act of 2006), or

(2) in the case of a plan using the attributable method of allocating withdrawal liability, the unfunded vested benefits attributable to employees of the employer (ERISA Sec. 4225(a)(2), as amended by the Pension Act).

The table in ERISA Sec. 4225(a)(2) is updated to reflect more accurately the increased liquidation or dissolution valuation of employers (ERISA Sec. 4225(a)(2), as amended by the Pension Act). The revised table widens the brackets and increases the minimum liquidation or dissolution value from $2 million to $5 million:

If the liquidation or distribution value of the employer after the sale or exchange is—	*The portion is—*
Not more than $5,000,000	30 percent of the amount
More than $5,000,000, but not more than $10,000,000	$1,500,000, plus 35 percent of the amount in excess of $5,000,000
More than $10,000,000, but not more than $15,000,000	$3,250,000, plus 40 percent of the amount in excess of $10,000,000
More than $15,000,000, but not more than $17,500,000	$5,250,000, plus 45 percent of the amount in excess of $15,000,000
More than $17,500,000, but not more than $20,000,000	$6,375,000, plus 50 percent of the amount in excess of $17,500,000
More than $20,000,000, but not more than $22,500,000	$7,625,000, plus 60 percent of the amount in excess of $20,000,000

NEW LAW EXPLAINED

If the liquidation or distribution value of the employer after the sale or exchange is—	*The portion is—*
More than $22,500,000, but not more than $25,000,000	$9,125,000, plus 70 percent of the amount in excess of $22,500,000
More than $25,000,000	$10,875,000, plus 80 percent of the amount in excess of $25,000,000

However, if a plan calculating withdrawal liability under the attributable method, the withdrawal liability is simply the unfunded vested benefits attributable to employees of the employer (ERISA Sec. 4225(a)(1)(B), as amended by the Pension Act).

> **Comment:** ERISA Sec. 4225(b), dealing with determining the limitation on the withdrawal liability of employers that are in liquidation or dissolution, was not amended.

Partial withdrawal limitation expanded. The definition of partial withdrawal is amended to include the transfer of work to another party or parties owned or controlled by the employer (ERISA Sec. 4205(b)(2)(A)(i), as amended by the Pension Act). This change is effective for work transferred on or after August 17, 2006, the date of enactment of the Pension Act. Contributing employers to multiemployer plans that permanently cease to have an obligation to contribute under one or more but not all collective bargaining agreements, and that simply outsource the work to another party owned or controlled by them, are considered to have partially withdrawn from the plan. Thus, they incur a withdrawal liability for the unfunded vested benefits.

Extension of "free look" rule to construction industry plans. Multiemployer plans that primarily cover employees in the building and construction industries will be allowed to adopt the current "free look" rule that permits an employer to withdraw completely or partially from the plan without incurring a withdrawal liability if certain requirements are met (ERISA Sec. 4210(b)(1), as repealed by the Pension Act). Effective for plan withdrawals occurring on or after January 1, 2007, construction and building industry employers can completely or partially withdraw from a multiemployer plan without incurring a withdrawal liability if the employer:

(1) was first obligated to contribute to the plan after September 26, 1980,

(2) was required to contribute to the plan for no more than the lesser of (a) six consecutive plan years preceding the date on which the employer withdraws, or (b) the number of years required for vesting under the plan,

(3) was required to make contributions to the plan for each plan year that were less than two percent of all employer contributions to the plan for each plan year, and

(4) has never avoided withdrawal liability based on the free look rule (ERISA Sec. 4210(a)).

As under current law, other conditions that must be met in order to apply the free look rule involve amendments to the plan to provide for the free look rule, provisions governing nonpayment of benefits based on service performed for the employer before it was required to contribute to the plan, and a required ratio of plan assets to benefit payments for the plan year preceding the first plan year for which the

NEW LAW EXPLAINED

employer was required to contribute of at least 8 to 1 (ERISA Sec. 4210(b), as amended by the Pension Act).

New "fresh start" option for construction industry plans. A "fresh start" option will allow a plan to make amendments regarding the application of the presumptive method of computing withdrawal liability (ERISA Sec. 4211(c)(5)(E), as added by the Pension Act). For plan withdrawals occurring on or after January 1, 2007, this option allows a multiemployer plan, including plans that primarily cover the building and construction industries, to be amended to provide that the presumptive method of computing withdrawal liability prescribed in ERISA Sec. 4211(b) shall be applied by using a plan year specified in the amendment and for which there was no unfunded vested benefits, instead of the plan year ended before September 26, 1980.

Dispute resolution. Employers can use a new election to contest a withdrawal liability finding by a plan sponsor. This new procedure applies if: (1) the plan sponsor finds that a complete or partial withdrawal occurred or that the employer is liable for withdrawal liability payments, and (2) the sponsor's finding of withdrawal liability is due to a transaction that occurred on or after December 31, 1998, and at least five years (two years for a small employer) prior to the withdrawal, and the transaction's purpose was to evade or avoid a withdrawal liability (ERISA Sec. 4221(g), as added by the Pension Act). The person liable for the withdrawal liability imposed by the plan sponsor may contest the plan sponsor's determination through an arbitration proceeding or in a court of competent jurisdiction. The new rule relieves the contesting employer of the obligation to pay the withdrawal liability until a final decision is reached by an arbitrator or court (ERISA Sec. 4221(g)(2), as added by the Pension Act).

In order to avoid the obligation of making withdrawal liability payments until a final arbitration or court decision upholds the plan sponsor's withdrawal liability determination, the electing person:

(1) must provide notice to the plan sponsor of the election within 90 days after the plan sponsor notifies the electing person of its withdrawal liability, and

(2) may need to provide a surety bond or deposit amounts in escrow in the amount of the withdrawal liability payments that would otherwise be due (ERISA Sec. 4221(g)(2), as added by the Pension Act).

The surety bond or escrow deposit is required if a final arbitration or court decision of the withdrawal liability dispute has not been rendered within 12 months from the date of the notice of liability. On the first day after the 12-month period the electing person must provide the plan with a bond from an acceptable corporate surety company or proof of an amount held in escrow by a bank or financial institution in an amount equal to the withdrawal liability payments that would otherwise be due for the 12-month period beginning with the first anniversary of such notice. The bond or escrow must remain in effect until there is a final decision in the arbitration proceeding or in court of the withdrawal liability dispute. If the plan sponsor's determination is upheld, the bond or escrow is paid over to the plan (ERISA Sec. 4221(g)(2)(B), as added by the Pension Act).

If the withdrawal liability dispute is not resolved after 12 months from the posting of the bond or escrow, the electing person shall, at the start of each succeeding

NEW LAW EXPLAINED

12-month period, provide an additional bond or amount in escrow that equals the withdrawal liability payments that would otherwise be payable to the plan during that period (ERISA Sec. 4221(g)(4), as added by the Pension Act). The furnishing of the bond or the escrow reduces the withdrawal liability payment obligation of the electing person (ERISA Sec. 4221(g)(5), as added by the Pension Act).

A small employer, for purposes of the two-year rule, is defined as any employer that, for the calendar year in which the disregarded transaction occurred and for each of the three preceding years on average:

(1) employs not more than 500 employees, and

(2) is required to make contributions to the plan for not more than 250 employees (ERISA Sec. 4221(g)(3)(A), as added by the Pension Act).

A controlled group that is treated as a single employer under ERISA Sec. 4001(b)(1), without taking into consideration the transaction that was the basis of the withdrawal liability finding under ERISA Sec. 4212, is treated as a single employer for purposes of this new election (ERISA Sec. 4221(g)(3)(B), as added by the Pension Act).

▶ **Effective dates.** The following are the effective dates for the reforms to the withdrawal liability rules:

— The amendments to the asset sale limitation in ERISA Sec. 4225 apply to sales occurring on or after January 1, 2007 (Act Sec. 204(a)(3) of the Pension Protection Act of 2006).

— The amendment to the partial withdrawal limitation in ERISA Sec. 4205(b)(2)(A)(i) applies with respect to work transferred on or after August 17, 2006 (Act Sec. 204(b)(2) of the Pension Act).

— The repeal of the free look rule in ERISA Sec. 4210(b)and the addition of a fresh start option in ERISA Sec. 4211(c)(5) apply with respect to plan withdrawals occurring on or after January 1, 2007 (Act Sec. 204(c)(3) of the Pension Act).

— The addition of a dispute resolution election in ERISA Sec. 4221(g) applies to any person that receives a notification under ERISA Sec. 4219(b)(1) on or after August 17, 2006, the date of enactment of the Pension Act, with respect to a transaction that occurred after December 31, 1998 (Act Sec. 204(d)(2) of the Pension Act).

Law source: Law at ¶7039. Committee Report at ¶10,110, ¶10,120, ¶10,130 and ¶10,140.

— Act Sec. 204(a) of the Pension Protection Act of 2006, amending ERISA Sec. 4225(a);

— Act Sec. 204(b)(1), amending ERISA Sec. 4205(b)(2)(A)(i);

— Act Sec. 204(c)(1), striking ERISA Sec. 4210(b)(1);

— Act Sec. 204(c)(2), adding ERISA Sec. 4211(c)(5)(E);

— Act Sec. 204(d)(1), adding ERISA Sec. 4221(g);

— Act Sec. 204(a)(3), (b)(2), (c)(3) and (d)(2), providing the effective date.

Reporter references: For further information, consult the following CCH reporters.

— Pension Plan Guide, ¶6900

— Standard Federal Tax Reporter, 2006FED ¶19,158A.01

— Tax Research Consultant, RETIRE: 39,210, RETIRE: 57,250 and RETIRE: 57,300

— Federal Tax Guide, 2006FTG ¶11,035

¶325 Revocation of Election to be Treated as Single-Employer Plan; Election to be Treated as Multiemployer Plan

SUMMARY OF NEW LAW

Certain plans that irrevocably elected multiemployer status after enactment of the Multiemployer Pension Plan Amendments Act of 1980 can revoke that election. Certain plans sponsored by tax-exempt employers can irrevocably elect multiemployer status. Plans must make the revocation or election within one year after August 17, 2006, the date of enactment of the Pension Protection Act of 2006.

BACKGROUND

A multiemployer plan is a plan to which more than one unrelated employer contributes, that is established pursuant to one or more collective bargaining agreements, and that satisfies such other requirements as the Secretary of Labor may prescribe (Code Sec. 414(f); ERISA Sec. 3(36)). In the Multiemployer Pension Plan Amendments Act of 1980 (P.L. 96-364), Congress increased multiemployer pension plan premiums and effectively shifted the primary risk of underfunding from the Pension Benefit Guaranty Corporation (PBGC) to contributing employers. The 1980 legislation also broadened the definition of multiemployer plans. The 1980 legislation added Code Sec. 414(f)(5) and ERISA Sec. 3(37)(E), under which a plan had up to one year after August 17, 2006 to irrevocably elect to continue to be treated as a single-employer plan. A plan was allowed to make this election if it was a single-employer plan under prior law and had paid PBGC premiums for the three plan years preceding August 17, 2006 as a single-employer plan.

NEW LAW EXPLAINED

Plans can revoke single-employer election.—The Pension Protection of Act of 2006 allows multiemployer plans to revoke an election made under Code Sec. 414(f)(5) and ERISA Sec. 3(37)(E), to be treated as a single-employer plan. To qualify, the plan must satisfy the requirements of a multiemployer plan for each of the three plan years before enactment of the Pension Act. Plans have up to one year after August 17, 2006, the date of enactment of the Pension Act, to make the revocation (Code Sec. 414(f)(6)(A) and ERISA Sec. 3(37)(G)(i), as added by the Pension Act). The revocation must be made under procedures prescribed by the PBGC.

Election to be treated as multiemployer plans. Under the Pension Act, certain plans are eligible to elect to be treated as multiemployer plans. The election must be made within one year of August 17, 2006, the date of enactment of the Pension Act. A plan is eligible to make this election if more than one employer is required to contribute to the plan, and the plan is maintained pursuant to one or more collective bargaining agreements between one or more employee organizations. In addition, a plan that was established in Chicago, Illinois, on August 12, 1881, and is sponsored by a Code Sec. 501(c)(5) organization that is exempt from tax under Code Sec. 501(a) is eligible to elect

NEW LAW EXPLAINED

multiemployer status. An eligible plan must meet the following requirements before it can make the election:

- the plan must have met its eligibility criteria for each of the three plan years immediately before August 17, 2006, the date of enactment of the Pension Act;
- substantially all of the plan's employer contributions for each of those plan years were made or required to be made by organizations that were exempt from tax under Code Sec. 501; and
- the plan was established prior to September 2, 1974 (Code Sec. 414(f)(6)(A)(ii) and ERISA Sec. 3(37)(G)(i)(II), as added by the Pension Act).

> **Comment:** The plan adopted on August 12, 1881, in Chicago apparently refers to a staff pension plan for a construction trade union.

The election to revoke is effective for all purposes under ERISA and the tax code, starting with the first plan year ending after August 17, 2006, the date of the enactment of the Pension Act (Code Sec. 414(f)(6)(B) and ERISA Sec. 3(37)(G)(ii), as added by the Pension Act). Once made, the election to revoke is irrevocable. However, a plan that elects to be treated as a multiemployer plan will cease to be a multiemployer plan as of the plan year beginning immediately after the first plan year for which the majority of its employer contributions were made (or required to be made) by organizations that were not exempt from tax under Code Sec. 501 (Code Sec. 414(f)(6)(C) and ERISA Sec. 3(37)(G)(iii), as added by the Pension Act). Just because the plan makes this election does not imply that the plan was not a multiemployer plan prior to the date of the election or would not be a multiemployer plan without regard to the election (Code Sec. 414(f)(6)(D) and ERISA Sec. 3(37)(G)(iv), as added by the Pension Act).

A plan must provide notice of the impending election no later than 30 days before the election to each plan participant and beneficiary, each labor organization representing such participants or beneficiaries, and each employer obligated to contribute to the plan. The notice must describe the principal differences between the guarantee programs and benefit restriction for single employer and multiemployer plans. The Secretary of Labor is directed to prescribe a model notice within 180 days after the date the Pension Act is enacted. Failure to provide the notice is treated as a failure to file an annual report, and subject to an ERISA penalty of $1,100 per day (ERISA Sec. 3(37)(G)(v), as added by the Pension Act; Joint Committee on Taxation, Technical Explanation of the Pension Protection Act of 2006 (JCX-38-06)).

► **Effective date.** No specific effective date is provided by the Act. The provision is, therefore, considered effective on August 17, 2006, the date of enactment.

Law source: Law at ¶5090 and ¶7222. Committee Report at ¶11,090.

— Act Sec. 1106(a) of the Pension Protection Act of 2006, adding ERISA Sec. 3(37)(G);

— Act Sec. 1106(b), adding Code Sec. 414(f)(6).

Reporter references: For further information, consult the following CCH reporters.

— Pension Plan Guide, ¶1558 and ¶6905

— Standard Federal Tax Reporter, 2006FED ¶19,158A.01

¶330 Retaliation Against Employers Prohibited

SUMMARY OF NEW LAW

Retaliation against contributing employers to multiemployer plans who exercise their rights under ERISA, testify before Congress or petition for redress of grievances, is prohibited.

BACKGROUND

ERISA contains various safeguards to protect the rights of plan participants and beneficiaries. Specifically, ERISA Sec. 510 protects plan participants and beneficiaries against retaliation for exercising any right under a plan or ERISA or interference with the attainment of any protected rights. It is unlawful for any person to discharge, fire, suspend, expel, discipline, or discriminate against a participant or beneficiary either for exercising any right to which he is entitled under the provisions of an employee benefit plan or ERISA or for the purpose of interfering with the attainment of such a right. It is also unlawful for any person to discharge, fine, suspend, expel or discriminate against any person because he has given information or has testified or is about to testify in any inquiry or proceeding relating to ERISA or the Welfare and Pension Plans Disclosure Act. A civil action to enforce these protections may be brought under ERISA Sec. 502 (ERISA Sec. 510).

NEW LAW EXPLAINED

Prohibition on retaliation against employers exercising their rights to petition the federal government.—ERISA's prohibition against retaliation is extended to provide protection to employers who contribute to multiemployer plans. Under the new law, a plan sponsor or any other person may not discriminate against a contributing employer for exercising rights under ERISA or for giving information or testifying in any inquiry or proceeding relating to ERISA before Congress (ERISA Sec. 510, as amended by the Pension Protection Act of 2006).

> **Comment:** This provision is intended to close a loophole in the existing whistleblower protections. In June 2005, a witness testified before a Senate subcommittee on behalf of several small employers regarding proposed multiemployer plan reforms. Subsequent to that testimony, it was alleged that all or most of the companies on whose behalf the witness appeared were targeted for possible audits by a large multiemployer fund. This provision is intended to protect employers who exercise their rights under ERISA, testify before Congress or petition for redress of grievances, from retaliation by the plans to which they have an obligation to contribute (Joint Committee on Taxation, Technical Explanation of the Pension Protection Act of 2006 (JCX-38-06); *A Pension Double Header: Reforming Hybrid and Multi-Employer Pension Plans*, hearing before the Retirement Security & Aging Subcommittee of the Senate Health, Education, Labor & Pensions Committee, 109th Cong. (June 7, 2005)).

NEW LAW EXPLAINED

▶ **Effective date.** No specific effective date is provided by the Act. The provision is, therefore, considered effective on August 17, 2006, the date of enactment.

Law source: Law at ¶7042. Committee Report at ¶10,150.

— Act Sec. 205 of the Pension Protection Act of 2006, amending ERISA Sec. 510.

Reporter references: For further information, consult the following CCH reporter.

— Pension Plan Guide, ¶5705

Funding Disclosures

4

¶405 Annual Funding Notices for Defined Benefit Plans

SUMMARY OF NEW LAW

Defined benefit plan administrators, of both single-employer and multiemployer plans, are required to provide an annual funding notice for each plan year. This notice must be provided to the Pension Benefit Guaranty Corporation (PBGC), to each participant and beneficiary, and to each labor union representing plan participants. For multiemployer plans, this plan funding notice must also be provided to each contributing employer. Except for small plans, the annual funding notice for defined benefit plans must be provided within 120 days after the end of the plan year. The Labor Department has been directed to issue a model notice within one year after August 17, 2006, the date of enactment of the Pension Protection Act of 2006.

BACKGROUND

Defined benefit plans generally must meet certain minimum funding requirements that are designed to help ensure that these plans are adequately funded. Certain notices must be provided to participants in single-employer defined benefit plans relating to the plan's funding status. For instance, employers in a single-employer defined benefit plan are required to notify plan participants if the employer fails to make required contributions (unless a funding waiver request is pending) (ERISA Sec. 101(d)). Further, for underfunded single-employer plans for which PBGC varia-

BACKGROUND

ble rate premiums are required, the plan administrator must notify participants of the plan's funding status and the limits on the PBGC's benefit guarantee if the plan terminates while it is underfunded (ERISA Sec. 4011).

Plan administrators of multiemployer defined benefit plans must provide an annual funding notice to (1) each participant and beneficiary, (2) each labor union representing plan participants, (3) each employer that is obligated to contribute to the plan, and (4) to the PBGC (ERISA Reg. §2520.101-4(f)). The notice must include (1) identifying information, including the name of the plan, the address and phone number of the plan administrator and the plan's principal administrative officer, each plan sponsor's employer identification number (EIN), and the plan identification number; (2) a statement as to whether the plan's funded current liability percentage for the plan year to which the notice relates is at least 100 percent (and if not, a statement of the percentage); (3) a statement of the value of the plan's assets, the amount of benefit payments, and the ratio of the assets to the payments for the plan year to which the notice relates; (4) a summary of the rules governing insolvent multiemployer plans, including the limitations on benefit payments and any potential benefit reductions and suspensions (and the potential effects of such limitations, reductions, and suspensions on the plan); (5) a general description of the benefits under the plan that are eligible to be guaranteed by the PBGC and the limitations of the guarantee and circumstances in which such limitations apply; and (6) any additional information the plan administrator elects to include to the extent it is not inconsistent with regulations prescribed by the Secretary of Labor (ERISA Sec. 101(f)(2)). No similar requirement applies for single-employer defined benefit plans.

The annual funding notice for multiemployer plans must be provided no later than two months after the deadline (including extensions) for filing the plan's annual report (i.e., nine months after the end of the plan year unless the annual report's due date has been extended) (ERISA Sec. 101(f)(3); ERISA Reg. §2520.101-4(d)).

NEW LAW EXPLAINED

Plan funding notice rules expanded.—Defined benefit plan administrators, for both single-employer and multiemployer defined benefit plans, are required to provide an annual funding notice for each plan year. This annual funding notice must be provided to:

1. the PBGC;
2. each plan participant and beneficiary;
3. each labor organization representing plan participants and beneficiaries; and
4. for multiemployer plans, to each contributing employer (ERISA Sec. 101(f)(1), as amended by the Pension Protection Act of 2006).

> **Comment:** The Pension Act expands the annual funding notice rules that previously applied only to multiemployer plans so that they also apply to single-employer plans. The information that must be provided in the notice has been changed and the timing of the notice has been accelerated.

NEW LAW EXPLAINED

Contents of notice. Each defined benefit plan annual funding notice must contain identifying information, such as (1) the name of the plan, (2) the plan administrator's address and phone number, (3) the address and phone number of the plan's principal administrative officer, (4) each plan sponsor's employer identification number (EIN), and (5) the plan number of the plan (ERISA Sec. 101(f)(2)(A), as amended by the Pension Act).

Besides the identifying information described above, each plan annual funding notice must include specific information. This information varies depending on whether the plan is a single-employer plan or a multiemployer plan (ERISA Sec. 101(f)(2)(B), as amended by the Pension Act).

For single-employer plans, the following specific information is required in the defined benefit plan annual funding notice:

1. a statement as to whether the plan's funding target attainment percentage (as defined under the ERISA Sec. 303(d)(2) minimum funding rules for single-employer plans) for the plan year relating to the notice as well as for the two prior plan years is at least 100 percent or, if not, the actual percentage;
2. a statement of (a) the total assets (separately stating the prefunding balance and the funding standard carryover balance) and liabilities of the plan (determined in the same manner as under ERISA Sec. 303) for the plan year for which the latest annual report was filed and for the two preceding plan years, and (b) the value of the plan's assets and liabilities for the plan year to which the notice relates as of the last day of the plan year determined using fair market value and the interest rate used in determining variable rate premiums;
3. a summary of the rules governing termination of single-employer plans; and
4. if applicable, a statement that each contributing sponsor (and each member of the contributing sponsor's controlled group) of the single-employer plan was required to provide the information under ERISA Sec. 4010 (see ¶425) for the plan year to which the notice relates.

For multiemployer plans, the following specific information is required in the defined benefit plan annual funding notice:

1. a statement as to whether the plan's funded percentage (as defined under the ERISA Sec. 305(i) minimum funding rules for multiemployer plans) for the plan year relating to the notice as well as for the two prior plan years is at least 100 percent or, if not, the actual percentage;
2. a statement of the value of the plan's assets and liabilities for the plan year to which the notice relates as of the last day of the plan year and the two prior plan years;
3. whether the plan was in critical or endangered status under ERISA Sec. 305 for the plan year (see ¶310) and, if so (a) a summary of any funding improvement plan, rehabilitation plan, or modification adopted under ERISA Sec. 305 during the plan year to which the notice relates, and (b) a statement describing how a person may get a copy of the plan's funding improvement or rehabilitation plan

NEW LAW EXPLAINED

adopted under ERISA Sec. 305, as well as the actuarial and financial data that demonstrate any action taken by the plan towards fiscal improvement; and

4. a summary of the rules governing reorganization or insolvency, including the limits on benefit payments.

Multiemployer plans are also required to provide a statement that the plan administrator will provide a copy of the annual Form 5500 filed under ERISA Sec. 104(a), on written request. A copy of the annual Form 5500 must be provided, upon written request, to any labor organization representing plan participants and beneficiaries as well as to any contributing employer (ERISA Sec. 101(f)(2)(C), as amended by the Pension Act).

The following is also required, for both single-employer and multiemployer plans (ERISA Sec. 101(f)(2)(B), as amended by the Pension Act):

- a statement of the number of participants who are (a) retired or separated from service and receiving benefits; (b) retired or separated from service and entitled to future benefits; and (c) active participants under the plan;
- a statement setting forth the plan's funding policy and the plan's asset allocation of investments (expressed as percentages of total assets) as of the end of the plan year to which the notice relates;
- for any plan amendments, scheduled benefit increases or reductions, or other known event taking effect in the current plan year and having a material effect on plan liabilities or assets for the year, an explanation of the amendment, scheduled increase or reduction, or event, and a projection to the end of the plan year as to the effect of the amendment, scheduled increase or reduction, or event on plan liabilities;
- a general description of the benefits under the plan that are eligible to be guaranteed by the PBGC, along with an explanation of the limits on the guarantee and the circumstances under which such limits apply; and
- a statement that a person may obtain a copy of the plan's annual report upon request, through the Labor Department's Internet website, or through an intranet website maintained by the applicable plan sponsor (or plan administrator on behalf of the plan sponsor).

Each plan's annual funding notice may also include any additional information that the plan administrator chooses to include, to the extent that this information is not inconsistent with Labor Department regulations (ERISA Sec. 101(f)(2)(C), as amended by the Pension Act).

Comment: The purpose of these expanded funding notice requirements is to provide greater awareness of, and transparency to, retirement security. The annual funding notice will give participants, beneficiaries, unions, and, for multiemployer plans, contributing employers, a timely look at the true financial state of the plan for the most recent and two preceding years. Additional notices are required when benefits limitations are triggered or the company files for bankruptcy.

NEW LAW EXPLAINED

Timing of notice. The defined benefit plan annual funding notice must be provided no later than 120 days after the end of the plan year relating to the notice (ERISA Sec. 101(f)(3)(A), as amended by the Pension Act).

For small plans, instead of adhering to the 120-day rule, the required defined benefit plan annual funding notice should be provided with the annual Form 5500. This is typically due seven months after the end of the plan year. This small employer exception applies if, on each day during the preceding plan year, a plan had 100 or fewer participants (ERISA Sec. 101(f)(3)(B), as amended by the Pension Act).

> **Comment:** Congress believes that funding information should be provided on a more timely basis than under prior law.

Format of notice. The Secretary of Labor will issue regulations describing the form of and manner for providing the defined benefit plan annual funding notice. The annual funding notice must be written in a manner that can be understood by the average plan participant.

Further, the defined benefit plan annual funding notice may be provided in written, electronic, or other appropriate form as long as it is reasonably accessible to those persons to whom it must be provided (ERISA Sec. 101(f)(4), as amended by the Pension Act).

> **Planning Note:** The Secretary of Labor has been directed to publish a model notice in conjunction with this provision within one year after August 17, 2006, the date of enactment of the Pension Act. The Labor Secretary may issue any interim final rules that she determines appropriate to carry out this provision (Act Sec. 501(c) of the Pension Act).

Repeal of notice to participants of funding status. The ERISA Sec. 4011 notice to participants, which describes the plan's current liability funding percentage, is no longer required (ERISA Sec. 4011 as repealed by the Pension Act). This information has been folded into the new annual funding notice.

► **Effective date.** This provision generally applies to plan years beginning after December 31, 2007. However, the repeal of the ERISA Sec. 4011 notice to participants of funding status applies to plan years beginning after December 31, 2006 (Act Sec. 501(d)(1) of the Pension Protection Act of 2006). A special transition rule applies to the ERISA Sec. 101(f) requirements to report a plan's funding target attainment percentage or funded percentage. For any plan year beginning before January 1, 2008, this reporting requirement will be treated as met if the plan reports (1) for plan years beginning in 2006, the plan's funded current liability percentage for that plan year, and (2) for plan years beginning in 2007, the funding target attainment percentage or funded percentage determined using methods of estimation provided by the Secretary of the Treasury (Act Sec. 501(d)(2) of the Pension Act).

Law source: Law at ¶7096. Committee Report at ¶10,340.

— Act Sec. 501(a) of the Pension Protection Act of 2006, amending ERISA Sec. 101(f);

— Act Sec. 501(b), striking ERISA Sec. 4011 and amending ERISA Sec. 1;

— Act Sec. 501(c);

— Act Sec. 501(d), providing the effective date.

NEW LAW EXPLAINED

Reporter references: For further information, consult the following CCH reporters.

— Pension Plan Guide, ¶4085, ¶4100, ¶4267, ¶4295 and ¶6973

— Tax Research Consultant, RETIRE: 51,352 and RETIRE: 51,356.15

— Federal Tax Guide, 2006FTG ¶11,060 and ¶11,095

¶410 Access to Multiemployer Plan Financial Information

SUMMARY OF NEW LAW

The ability of participants, beneficiaries, unions, and contributing employers to request and receive plan actuarial and financial information and estimates of potential withdrawal liability from multiemployer plans has been expanded. Contributing employers also are entitled to receive, upon written request, a notice of what the estimated amount of the employer's withdrawal liability would be if the employer withdrew on the last day of the plan year prior to the date of the request, as well as an explanation of how this estimated liability amount was determined. Contributing employers have been added to the list of persons who are entitled to receive ERISA Sec. 204(h) notices.

BACKGROUND

Pension plan administrators are required to file information about the plan every year with the Labor Department, the Treasury Department, and the Pension Benefit Guaranty Corporation (PBGC). A plan administrator meets its filing obligation with all three agencies by filing a Form 5500 with the Labor Department. The annual Form 5500 is due by the last day of the seventh month after the end of the plan year but may be extended by up to two and a half months.

For defined benefit plans, the annual report must include an actuarial statement, covering such information as the value of the plan's assets, the plan's accrued and current liabilities, the plan's actuarial cost method and actuarial assumptions, and plan contributions. This report must be signed by an actuary enrolled to practice before all three agencies (Code Sec. 6059(b); Reg. § 301.6059-1(c) and (d)).

Notice of significant reduction in benefit accruals. A defined benefit plan may not be amended to provide for a "significant" reduction in the rate of future benefit accruals unless the plan administrator furnishes sufficient written notice (i.e., an ERISA Sec. 204(h) notice) of the amendment. Notice may also be required if a plan amendment eliminates or reduces an early retirement benefit or retirement-type subsidy (ERISA Sec. 204(h)).

The plan administrator is required to provide the 204(h) notice to any participant or alternate payee whose rate of future benefit accrual may reasonably be expected to be significantly reduced by the plan amendment (and to any employee organization

BACKGROUND

representing affected participants). The notice must be written in a manner that can be understood by the average plan participant and must provide sufficient information to allow recipients to understand the effect of the amendment. The plan administrator is generally required to provide the notice at least 45 days before the effective date of the plan amendment (Reg. § 54.4980F-1, Q&A-9(a)).

If adequate notice is not provided, an excise tax of $100 per day in the noncompliance period will apply, for each participant and beneficiary, with respect to which a failure to meet the notice requirements occurs (Code Sec. 4980F). In addition, ERISA Sec. 204(h) specifies special rules for "egregious" failures to provide notice, under which participants are generally entitled to the greater of the benefit provided under the plan prior to amendment or the benefit under the amended plan (ERISA Sec. 204(h)(6)).

NEW LAW EXPLAINED

Multiemployer financial plan information provided upon request.—Upon written request, each multiemployer plan administrator must furnish specified financial information for the plan to any plan participant or beneficiary, employee representative, or any contributing employer. The information that must be made available includes (ERISA Sec. 101(k)(1), as added by the Pension Protection Act of 2006):

- a copy of any periodic actuarial report (including any sensitivity testing) received by the plan for any plan year that has been in the plan's possession for at least 30 days;
- a copy of any quarterly, semiannual, or annual financial report prepared for the plan by any plan investment manager, advisor, or other fiduciary that has been in the plan's possession for at least 30 days; and
- a copy of any application requesting an extension of amortization periods (filed with the Secretary of the Treasury under Code Sec. 431(d) or ERISA Sec. 304 (as added by the Pension Act) (see ¶ 305), as well as any determination made upon this application by the Treasury Secretary.

> **Caution Note:** Any actuarial or financial report required to be provided under this provision is subject to confidentiality limits. These required reports may not (a) include any individually identifiable information regarding any plan participant, beneficiary, employee, fiduciary, or contributing employer; or (b) reveal any proprietary information about the plan, any contributing employer, or entity providing services to the plan (ERISA Sec. 101(k)(2)(C), as added by the Pension Act).

Timing of actuarial and financial reports. Multiemployer financial plan information must be provided to the participant, beneficiary, or contributing employer requesting it within 30 days after the request (ERISA Sec. 101(k)(2)(A), as added by the Pension Act).

NEW LAW EXPLAINED

> **Comment:** The Labor Department has been directed to issue regulations describing the form and manner in which these actuarial and financial reports must be delivered. These regulations are to be issued not later than one year after August 17, 2006, the date of enactment (Act Sec. 502(a)(3) of the Pension Act).

Notice of potential withdrawal liability. Upon written request, a multiemployer plan sponsor or administrator must provide, to any employer who has an obligation to contribute to the plan, a notice of:

- the estimated amount of what the employer's withdrawal liability would be if the employer withdrew on the last day of the plan year preceding the date of the request; and
- an explanation of how this estimated withdrawal liability amount was determined, including (a) the actuarial assumptions and methods used to determine the value of plan liabilities and assets; (b) the data regarding employer contributions, unfunded vested benefits, and annual changes in the plan's unfunded vested benefits, and (c) the application of any relevant limits on the estimated withdrawal liability (ERISA Sec. 101(l)(1), as added by the Pension Act).

In connection with a participant, the term "employer contribution" means a contribution made by an employer as an employer of the participant (ERISA Sec. 101(l)(1), as added by the Pension Act).

Timing of notice of potential withdrawal liability. Any required notice of potential withdrawal liability must be provided to the requesting employer within 180 days after the request is made and in a form and manner to be prescribed in Labor Department regulations. Subject to Labor Department regulations, a period longer than 180 days may be allowed for plans that determine withdrawal liability under ERISA Secs. 4211(c)(4) and (5) (ERISA Sec. 101(l)(2), as added by the Pension Act).

Format and limits of notices and reports. The actuarial or other financial reports and the notice of potential withdrawal liability may be provided in a written, electronic, or other appropriate form to the extent that the form is reasonably accessible to persons and to employers requesting a copy of the form (ERISA Sec. 101(k)(2)(B) and 101(l)(2)(B), as added by the Pension Act).

Anyone entitled to a copy of any actuarial or financial report or to the notice of potential withdrawal liability is not entitled to receive more than one copy of any report or notice during any 12-month period. The person required to provide the notice may impose a reasonable charge to cover the cost of copying, mailing, and other expenses involved in furnishing copies of these notices. The Secretary of Labor is authorized to impose a limit, in regulations, on what constitutes a reasonable charge (ERISA Sec. 101(k)(3) and 101(l)(3), as added by the Pension Act).

Penalties. The Secretary of Labor may impose a penalty of up to $1,000 per day for each violation of the requirement to provide, upon request, actuarial or other financial information to any plan participant or beneficiary, employee representative, or contributing employer. A $1,000 per day penalty also may be imposed for any failure to provide the notice of potential withdrawal liability (ERISA Sec. 502(c)(4), as amended by the Pension Act).

NEW LAW EXPLAINED

Notice of amendment reducing future accruals. Contributing employers have been added to the list of persons who are entitled to receive ERISA Sec. 204(h) notices. As a result, an applicable pension plan may not be amended to provide for a significant reduction in the rate of future benefit accruals unless the plan administrator gives the required 204(h) notice to each participant and alternate payee, to each employee organization representing applicable individuals, and to each contributing employer (Code Sec. 4980F(e)(1) and ERISA Sec. 204(h)(1), as amended by the Pension Act).

▶ **Effective date.** This provision is effective for plan years beginning after December 31, 2007 (Act Sec. 502(d) of the Pension Protection Act of 2006).

Law source: Law at ¶5320 and ¶7099. Committee Report at ¶10,350.

— Act Sec. 502(a)(1) of the Pension Protection Act of 2006, redesignating ERISA Sec. 101(k) as ERISA Sec. 101(l) and adding new ERISA Sec. 101(k);

— Act Sec. 502(a)(2), amending ERISA Sec. 502(c)(4);

— Act Sec. 502(a)(3);

— Act Sec. 502(b)(1), redesignating ERISA Sec. 101(l) (as amended by Act Sec. 502(a)(1)) as ERISA Sec. 101(m) and adding new ERISA Sec. 101(l);

— Act Sec. 502(b)(2), amending ERISA Sec. 502(c)(4) (as amended by Act Sec. 502(a)(2));

— Act Sec. 502(c)(1), amending ERISA Sec. 204(h)(1);

— Act Sec. 502(c)(2), amending Code Sec. 4980F(e)(1);

— Act Sec. 502(d), providing the effective date.

Reporter references: For further information, consult the following CCH reporters.

— Pension Plan Guide, ¶2687, ¶2688, ¶4085, ¶4205 and ¶7243

— Standard Federal Tax Reporter, 2006FED ¶34,619.01, ¶34,619.021 and ¶34,619.024

— Tax Research Consultant, RETIRE: 15,404.05, RETIRE: 51,356.10 and RETIRE: 78,052

¶415 Additional Annual Reporting Requirements for Defined Benefit Plans

SUMMARY OF NEW LAW

The Pension Protection Act of 2006 requires filing of extensive additional information by multiemployer defined benefit plans (and some additional information by single-employer defined benefit plans). The additional information is required to be filed with the Form 5500 annual reports. The rule requiring defined benefit plans to provide Summary Annual Reports (SARs) has been repealed.

BACKGROUND

Pension plan administrators are required to file information about the plan every year with the Labor Department, the Treasury Department, and the Pension Benefit

BACKGROUND

Guaranty Corporation (PBGC). A plan administrator meets its filing obligation with all three agencies by filing a Form 5500 with the Labor Department. The annual Form 5500 is due by the last day of the seventh month after the end of the plan year but this deadline may be extended by up to two and a half months.

For defined benefit plans, the annual report must include an actuarial statement covering such information as the value of the plan's assets, the plan's accrued and current liabilities, the plan's actuarial cost method and actuarial assumptions, and plan contributions. This report must be signed by an actuary enrolled to practice before all three agencies (Code Sec. 6059(b); Reg. § 301.6059-1(c) and (d).

Summary annual reports (SARs). A participant must be provided with a copy of the full annual report on written request. In addition, the plan administrator must automatically provide participants with a summary of the annual report within two months after the due date of the annual report (i.e., by the end of the ninth month after the end of the plan year unless an extension applies) (ERISA Sec. 104(b)(3); ERISA Reg. § 2520.104b-10). The summary annual report (SAR) must include a statement indicating whether contributions were made to keep the plan funded in accordance with minimum funding requirements, or whether contributions were not made and the amount of the deficit. The current value of plan assets is also required to be disclosed (ERISA Reg. § 2520.104b-10(d)(3) and (4)). If an extension applies for the Form 5500, the SAR must be provided within two months after the extended due date (ERISA Sec. 104(b)(3); ERISA Reg. § 2520.104b-10(c)). A plan administrator who fails to provide a SAR to a participant within 30 days of the participant making a request for the report may be liable to the participant for a civil penalty of up to $110 a day from the date of the failure (ERISA Sec. 502(c)(1); ERISA Reg. § 2575.502c-1).

NEW LAW EXPLAINED

Additional information required for defined benefit plans.—For defined benefit plans, additional information must be provided on Form 5500 annual reports for plan years beginning after 2007. If liabilities to participants or their beneficiaries under the defined benefit (DB) plan consist (either in whole or in part) of liabilities under two or more pension plans as of immediately before the plan year, the annual report must include (1) the funded percentage of each of the two or more pension plans as of the last day of the plan year, and (2) the funded percentage of the plan with regard to which the annual report is filed as of the last day of the plan year (ERISA Sec. 103(f)(1)(A), as added by the Pension Protection Act of 2006).

> **Comment:** For single-employer plans, "funded percentage" is defined as the funding target attainment percentage under the single-employer minimum funding rules under ERISA Sec. 303(d)(2) (see ¶ 210). For multiemployer plans, the term is defined under the multiemployer plan funding rules under ERISA Sec. 305(i)(2) (see ¶ 310) (ERISA Sec. 103(f)(1)(B), as added by the Pension Act).

Additional information for multiemployer plans. Besides including the funded percentage information described above, annual reports for multiemployer plans must also include, as of the end of the plan year relating to the notice, the following information (ERISA Sec. 101(f)(2), as added by the Pension Act):

NEW LAW EXPLAINED

- the number of employers required to contribute to the plan;
- a list of employers that contribute more than five percent of the total contributions to the plan during the plan year;
- the number of participants for whom no employer contributions were made for the plan year and for each of the two prior plan years;
- the ratio of (a) the number of participants for whom no employer had an obligation to make an employer contribution during the plan year to (b) the number of participants for whom no employer had an obligation to make an employer contribution during each of the two prior plan years;
- whether the plan received an amortization extension for the plan year (under Code Sec. 431(d) or ERISA Sec. 304(d), as added by the Pension Act) (see ¶305) and, if so, the amount of the difference between the minimum required contribution for the year and the minimum required contribution that would have been required without regard to the extension, as well as the period of this amortization extension;
- whether the plan used the shortfall funding method (under ERISA Sec. 305) (see ¶310) for the plan year and, if so, the amount of the difference between the minimum required contribution for the year and the minimum required contribution that would have been required without regard to the use of the shortfall funding method, as well as the period for which the shortfall funding method was used;
- whether the plan was in critical or endangered status (under ERISA Sec. 305) (see ¶310) for the plan year and, if so, a summary of any funding improvement or rehabilitation plan (or modification) adopted during the plan year, and the funded percentage of the plan;
- the number of employers that withdrew from the plan during the prior plan year and the total amount of withdrawal liability assessed (or estimated to be assessed) against these withdrawn employers; and
- for multiemployer plans that have merged with another plan or to which a transfer of assets and liabilities has been made, the actuarial valuation of the assets and liabilities of each affected plan during the year prior to the effective date of the merger or transfer (based on the most recent data available as of the day before the first day of the plan year) or other valuation method performed under standards and procedures adopted by Labor Department regulations.

> **Comment:** The Labor Department has been directed to issue regulations, within one year after August 17, 2006, the date of enactment of the Pension Act. These regulations are needed to help multiemployer defined benefit plans (1) identify and list plan participants for whom there is no employer with an obligation to make an employer contribution under the plan, and (2) report information required under new ERISA Sec. 103(f)(2)(D) (Act Sec. 503(a)(2) of the Pension Act). According to the Joint Committee on Taxation, the Labor Secretary may provide guidance as needed to apply this rule to contributions made on a basis other than hours worked, such as on the basis of units of production (Joint Committee on Taxation, Technical Explanation of the Pension Protection Act of 2006 (JCX-38-06)).

NEW LAW EXPLAINED

Plan retirement projections. An annual report under ERISA Sec. 103(d) for a plan year includes a complete actuarial statement applicable to the plan year. Under the Pension Act, this actuarial statement should explain the actuarial assumptions and methods used in projecting future retirements and forms of the benefit distributions under the plan (ERISA Sec. 103(d)(12), as added by the Pension Act).

Repeal of SAR requirements for DB plans. The requirement that defined benefit plans provide summary annual reports (SARs) under ERISA Sec. 104(b)(3) has been repealed for defined benefit plans subject to new ERISA Sec. 103(f), as added by the Pension Act, for plan years beginning after 2007. An annual funding notice requirement for defined benefit plans (see ¶405) has been added under the Act (ERISA Sec. 104(b)(3), as amended by the Pension Act).

Furnishing summary plan information to contributing employers and employee representatives. Within 30 days after the due date of the annual report, multiemployer plan administrators are required to provide to each employee organization and to contributing employers a report that contains the following information (ERISA Sec. 104(d)(1), as added by the Pension Act):

- a description of the plan's contribution schedules and benefit formulas, as well as any modification to these schedules and formulas during the plan year;
- the number of employers obligated to contribute to the plan;
- a list of the employers that contributed more than five percent of the total plan contributions during the plan year;
- the number of plan participants for whom no employer contributions were made for the plan year and for the two prior plan years;
- whether the plan was in critical or endangered status (under ERISA Sec. 305) (see ¶310) for the plan year and, if so, include (1) a list of the actions taken by the plan to improve its funding status and (2) a statement describing how a person may obtain a copy of the plan's improvement or rehabilitation plan under ERISA Sec. 305, as well as the actuarial and financial data that demonstrates any action taken by the plan towards fiscal improvement;
- the number of employers that withdrew from the plan during the prior plan year and the total amount of withdrawal liability assessed (or estimated to be assessed) against these withdrawn employers, as reported on the annual report for the plan year;
- for multiemployer plans that have merged with another plan or to which a transfer of assets and liabilities has been made, the actuarial valuation of the assets and liabilities of each affected plan during the year prior to the effective date of the merger or transfer (based on the most recent data available as of the day before the first day of the plan year) or other valuation method performed under standards and procedures that the Labor Department may adopt;
- a description as to whether the plan (1) has sought or received an amortization extension for the plan year (under Code Sec. 431(d) or ERISA Sec. 304(d), as added by the Pension Act) (see ¶305), or (2) used the shortfall funding method (under ERISA Sec. 305) (see ¶310) for the plan year; and

NEW LAW EXPLAINED

- notification of the recipient's right to a copy of the annual report filed with the Labor Department under ERISA Sec. 103(f), a summary plan description (SPD), and a summary of any material modification (SMM) of the plan, upon written request.

Comment: A recipient is not entitled to receive more than one copy of any of these reports during a 12-month period. In addition, a plan administrator may impose a reasonable charge on the recipient to cover the costs of copying, mailing, and other expenses involved in furnishing copies (ERISA Sec. 104(d)(1)(I), as added by the Pension Act).

Caution Note: The Pension Act makes it clear that no language that has been added waives any other provision requiring plan administrators to provide information , upon request, to contributing employers (ERISA Sec. 104(d)(2), as added by the Pension Act).

Model form to be adopted. Within one year after August 17, 2006, the date of enactment of the Pension Act, the Secretary of Labor has been directed to issue a model form for providing the statements, schedules, and other material required to be provided under ERISA Sec. 101(f). The Secretary of Labor may issue any interim final regulations as deemed appropriate to carry out the provisions of this subsection (Act Sec. 503(e)).

▶ **Effective date.** This provision applies to plan years beginning after December 31, 2007 (Act Sec. 503(f) of the Pension Protection Act of 2006).

Law source: Law at ¶7102. Committee Report at ¶10,360.

— Act Sec. 503(a)(1) of the Pension Protection Act of 2006, amending ERISA Sec. 103(a)(1)(B) and adding new ERISA Sec. 103(f);

— Act Sec. 503(a)(2);

— Act Sec. 503(b), redesignating ERISA Secs. 103(d)(12) and (13) as 103(d)(13) and (14) and adding new ERISA Sec. 103(d)(12);

— Act Sec. 503(c), amending ERISA Sec. 104(b)(3) and ERISA Sec. 101(a)(2);

— Act Sec. 503(d), amending ERISA Sec. 104, redesignating ERISA Sec. 104(d) as 104(e)and adding new ERISA Sec. 104(d);

— Act Sec. 503(e);

— Act Sec. 503(f), providing the effective date.

Reporter references: For further information, consult the following CCH reporters.

— Pension Plan Guide, ¶4085, ¶4100, ¶4205 and ¶4265

— Standard Federal Tax Reporter, 2006FED ¶17,507.075, ¶17,507.0751, ¶36,502.01 and ¶36,522.01

— Tax Research Consultant, RETIRE: 51,352 and RETIRE: 78,052

— Federal Tax Guide, 2006FTG ¶11,095, ¶22,163 and ¶22,165

¶420 Electronic Display of Annual Report Information

SUMMARY OF NEW LAW

Plan administrators must file information included in the annual report in an electronic format to accommodate Internet display.

BACKGROUND

ERISA requires plan administrators to file a comprehensive annual report, disclosing information relating to the plan's qualified status, financial condition and operation. Annual reports are filed on the Form 5500 series. The Form 5500 series consolidates the annual report forms required by the Internal Revenue Service (IRS), the Department of Labor (DOL), and the Pension Benefit Guaranty Corporation (PBGC). The Form 5500 (Annual Return/Report of Employee Benefit Plan) is filed with the DOL's Employee Benefits Security Administration (EBSA), which forwards relevant information to the IRS and the PBGC.

The annual report must be filed with the EBSA on or before the last day of the seventh month following the close of the plan year. Generally, this is July 31 for calendar-year plans. An extension of up to two and one-half months (i.e., through October 15 for calendar-year plans) may be requested by filing a Form 5558 (Application for Extension of Time To File Certain Employee Plan Returns).

Sixty days after the annual report is filed, the plan administrator must provide to each participant and beneficiary a copy of a summary annual report (SAR), which contains summary financial data taken from the Form 5500.

NEW LAW EXPLAINED

Electronic display of information.—Identification, basic plan information and actuarial information included in the annual report for any plan year must be filed with the Secretary of Labor in an electronic format that accommodates Internet display (in accordance with regulations to be issued by the Secretary). Within 90 days after the annual report filing date, the Secretary will display such information included in the annual report on an Internet website that the Secretary maintains. The information also must be displayed on any intranet website that the plan sponsor (or the plan administrator on behalf of the plan sponsor) maintains (ERISA Sec. 104(b)(5), as added by the Pension Protection Act of 2006).

▶ **Effective date.** The provision applies to plan years beginning after December 31, 2007 (Act Sec. 504(b) of the Pension Protection Act of 2006).

Law source: Law at ¶7105. Committee Report at ¶10,360.

— Act Sec. 504(a) of the Pension Protection Act of 2006, adding new ERISA Sec. 104(b)(5);

— Act Sec. 504(b), providing the effective date.

NEW LAW EXPLAINED

Reporter references: For further information, consult the following CCH reporters.

— Pension Plan Guide, ¶4085 and ¶4265

— Standard Federal Tax Reporter, 2006FED ¶17,507.075, ¶17,507.0751, ¶36,502.01 and ¶36,522.01

— Tax Research Consultant, RETIRE: 51,356.10

— Federal Tax Guide, 2006FTG ¶11,095, ¶22,163 and ¶22,165

¶425 Section 4010 filings with the PBGC

SUMMARY OF NEW LAW

Sponsors of single-employer plans must file financial reports with the Pension Benefit Guaranty Corporation (PBGC) if their plans are less than 80 percent funded. These reports must include information about the plans' benefit liabilities, funding targets and funding target attainment percentages.

BACKGROUND

Contributing sponsors, and each member of a contributing sponsor's controlled group, that maintain substantially underfunded plans must submit annual financial and actuarial reports to the PBGC (ERISA Sec. 4010). A contributing plan sponsor and each member of the contributing sponsor's controlled group must file the required information if:

1. the aggregate unfunded vested benefits of all underfunded plans maintained by members of the controlled group exceed $50 million (disregarding plans with no unfunded vested benefits) at the end of the preceding plan year;
2. any member of the controlled group fails to make a required installment or other required payment to a plan, resulting in aggregate unpaid contributions in excess of $1 million, and the missed contributions are not paid within 10 days after the due date; or
3. any plan maintained by a member of a controlled group has been granted one or more minimum funding waivers that are in excess of $1 million and that, at the end of the plan year ending with the information year, remain unpaid (ERISA Sec. 4010(b)).

Required information. Filers must provide identifying information, plan actuarial information, and financial information for each member of the filer's controlled group and for each plan maintained by any member of the controlled group. The PBGC may require a filer to submit actuarial or financial information deemed necessary to determine plan assets and liability or the financial status of the filer (ERISA Sec. 4010(b); ERISA Reg. § 4010.6(b)).

NEW LAW EXPLAINED

Change in criteria for persons required to provide information to PBGC.—Each contributing sponsor for a single-employer plan, and each member of the contributing sponsor's controlled group, must file annual actuarial and financial information (section 4010 report) with the Pension Benefit Guaranty Corporation (PBGC) if the funding target attainment percentage at the end of the preceding plan year is less than 80 percent (ERISA Sec. 4010(b)(1), as amended by the Pension Protection Act of 2006). Thus, the $50 million aggregate unfunded vested benefits filing threshold for section 4010 reports is eliminated.

> **Comment:** The term "funding target attainment percentage" has the meaning provided under ERISA Sec. 302(d)(2) (see ¶210).

Additional information required in section 4010 report. The information submitted to the PBGC in the section 4010 report must include:

- the amount of benefit liabilities under the plan;
- the funding target of the plan, determined as if the plan has been in at-risk status for at least five plan years; and
- the funding target attainment percentage of the plan.

The amount of benefit liabilities under the plan is determined using the assumptions used by the PBGC in determining liabilities (ERISA Sec. 4010(d), as added by the Pension Act).

Definitions. For purposes of the additional information that must be included in the section 4010 report, the term "funding target" has the meaning provided under ERISA Sec. 303(d)(1) (see ¶210).

The term "funding target attainment percentage" has the meaning provided under ERISA Sec. 302(d)(2) (see ¶210).

The term "at risk status" has the meaning provided in ERISA Sec. 303(i)(4) (see ¶210) (ERISA Sec. 4010(d), as added by the Pension Act).

Notice to Congress. On an annual basis, the PBGC must provide the Senate Committees on Health, Education, Labor, and Pensions and Finance and the House Committees on Education and the Workforce and Ways and Means with a summary report in the aggregate of the section 4010 report information submitted to the PBGC (ERISA Sec. 4010(e), as added by the Pension Act).

> **Practical Analysis:** Harold J. Ashner of Keightley & Ashner LLP, Washington, D.C., notes that the change in the primary reporting threshold under ERISA Sec. 4010—from more than $50 million in total underfunding for *all* controlled group plans on a premium basis to less than an 80 percent funding level for *any* controlled group plan on the basis of the new funding rules—may serve both to include and exclude particular controlled groups. Several controlled groups that were previously subject to reporting because of their size (*e.g.*, where a very large plan is 99 percent funded with $51 million in underfunding on a premium basis) will now be exempt. On the

NEW LAW EXPLAINED

other hand, except to the extent the PBGC provides reporting relief, the new threshold will sweep in even the smallest controlled groups, if they maintain a plan that is less than 80 percent funded on the new basis. Significantly, the new threshold (absent PBGC reporting relief) subjects an entire controlled group to the requirement to submit financial and actuarial information based on its maintenance of any *one* plan that fails the 80 percent test, even if that is a very small plan and all of the group's larger plans are far better funded or even overfunded. Also of significance is that the Act did not adopt the Administration's proposal to make the content of an ERISA Sec. 4010 report available to the public.

▶ **Effective date.** The provision applies to years beginning after 2007 (Act Sec. 505(c) of the Pension Protection Act of 2006).

Law source: Law at ¶7108. Committee Report at ¶10,370.

— Act Sec. 505(a) of the Pension Protection Act of 2006, amending ERISA Sec. 4010(b) by striking paragraph (1) and inserting new ERISA Sec. 4010(b)(1);

— Act Sec. 505(b), adding new ERISA Sec. 4010(d);

— Act Sec. 505(c), providing the effective date.

Reporter references: For further information, consult the following CCH reporters.

— Pension Plan Guide, ¶6518

— Tax Research Consultant, RETIRE: 51,356.15

¶430 Disclosure of Termination Information to Plan Participants

SUMMARY OF NEW LAW

Not later than 15 days after receipt of a request from an affected party, the plan administrator of a terminating plan must provide the affected party with any information that was required to be submitted to the Pension Benefit Guaranty Corporation (PBGC) pursuant to the termination. The enhanced disclosure requirements apply to both employer-initiated and involuntary distress terminations. Plan administrators must not disclose the information in a manner that identifies an individual participant or beneficiary.

BACKGROUND

Generally, single-employer defined benefit plans may be terminated voluntarily by the employer or involuntarily by the PBGC. Plan administrators of single-employer defined benefit plans that are terminating through a distress termination are required to provide notice to various parties as well as to file numerous forms with the IRS and the PBGC (ERISA Sec. 4041(c)). The notice and reporting requirements imposed

BACKGROUND

by ERISA are numerous. To begin the termination process, a notice of intent to terminate a defined benefit plan in a distress termination must be given to plan participants at least 60 days (and no more than 90 days) prior to the proposed termination date. The notice that must be provided to all affected parties other than the PBGC must be issued at or before the time the administrator files the notice with the PBGC.

The notice to the PBGC is to be filed on Form 600 (Distress Termination, Notice of Intent to Terminate). However, there is no prescribed form for the notice of intent to terminate that must be issued to other affected parties. Although the plan administrator must include certain specific information in the notice given to each affected party, only a general and brief description of the facts surrounding the plan's status is provided. On the contrary, the information provided to the PBGC is much more specific regarding the status of the plan (ERISA Sec. 4041(c)(2)(A)).

NEW LAW EXPLAINED

Enhanced disclosure of termination information.—A plan administrator that has filed a notice of intent to terminate must provide to an affected party any information provided to the Pension Benefit Guaranty Corporation (PBGC). This disclosure must be provided not later than 15 days after receipt of a request from the affected party for the information or the provision of new information to the PBGC relating to a previous request (ERISA Sec. 4041(c)(2)(D), as added by the Pension Protection Act of 2006).

> **Comment:** An "affected party" is defined as each plan participant, beneficiary of a deceased participant, alternate payees under an applicable qualified domestic relations order (QDRO), employee organizations that represent any group of participants, and the PBGC (ERISA Sec. 4001(a)(21); ERISA Reg. §4001.2).

Involuntary terminations. A plan administrator of a single-employer plan that has received a notice from the PBGC of a determination that the plan should be terminated must provide to an affected party any information provided to the PBGC in connection with the plan termination. Such information must be provided to the affected party not later than 15 days after receipt of a request from the affected party for such information or the provision of any new information to the PBGC relating to a previous request by an affected party. In addition, the PBGC is required to provide a copy of the administrative record, including the trusteeship decision record in connection with a plan termination (ERISA Sec. 4042(c)(3), as added by the Pension Act).

Form and manner of information. The PBGC may prescribe the form and manner of the provision of information. Specifically, the form must include delivery in written, electronic, or other appropriate form provided that the information is reasonably accessible to the requesting party. A plan administrator may charge a reasonable fee for any information that is provided in other than electronic form (ERISA Sec. 4041(c)(2)(D) and ERISA Sec. 4042(c)(3), as added by the Pension Act).

Confidentiality. The plan administrator must not provide information pursuant to a request from an affected party in a form that includes any information that may

NEW LAW EXPLAINED

directly or indirectly be associated with, or otherwise identify, an individual participant or beneficiary. In addition, a court may limit disclosure of confidential information (as described under the Freedom of Information Act) to any authorized representative of the participants or beneficiaries that agrees to ensure the confidentiality of such information. For this purpose, an authorized representative means any employee organization representing participants in the pension plan (ERISA Sec. 4041(c)(2)(D) and ERISA Sec. 4042(c)(3), as added by the Pension Act).

▶ **Effective date.** The provision is effective for any plan termination under Title IV of the Employee Retirement Income Security Act of 1974 (ERISA) with respect to which the notice of intent to terminate, or, in the case of a termination by the PBGC, a notice of determination under ERISA Sec. 4042, occurs after August 17, 2006 (Act Sec. 506(c)(1) of the Pension Protection Act of 2006). If notice under ERISA Sec. 4041(c)(2)(D) or ERISA Sec. 4042(c)(3) (as added by Act Sec. 506 of the Pension Act) would otherwise be required to be provided before the 90th day after August 17, 2006, the date of enactment, such notice shall not be required to be provided until such 90th day (Act Sec. 506(c)(2) of the Pension Act).

Law source: Law at ¶7111. Committee Report at ¶10,380.

— Act Sec. 506(a)(1) of the Pension Protection Act of 2006, adding new ERISA Sec. 4041(c)(2)(D);

— Act Sec. 506(a)(2), amending ERISA Sec. 4041(c)(1);

— Act Sec. 506(b), amending ERISA Sec. 4042(c), redesignating ERISA Sec. 4042(c)(3) as (2) and adding new ERISA Sec. 4042(c)(3);

— Act Sec. 506(c), providing the effective date.

Reporter references: For further information, consult the following CCH reporters.

— Pension Plan Guide, ¶6564, ¶6597 and ¶6798

— Standard Federal Tax Reporter, 2006FED ¶19,071.075

— Tax Research Consultant, RETIRE: 45,112.10

PBGC Guarantee and Related Provisions

PBGC PREMIUMS

¶505 PBGC Variable Rate Premium

SUMMARY OF NEW LAW

For 2006 and 2007 plan years, the interest rate used to determine the unfunded vested benefit for PBGC variable rate premium purposes is 85 percent of the corporate bond rate. For post-2007 plan years, the variable rate premium will be based on a plan's unfunded vested benefits valued using a three segmented yield curve of investment-grade corporate bonds with varying maturities and in the top three quality levels. The exemption from paying variable rate premiums for plans that are at the full

SUMMARY OF NEW LAW

funding limit will be repealed. In addition, the special termination premium for certain underfunded terminating plans, which was scheduled to sunset in 2011, is made permanent.

BACKGROUND

The Pension Benefit Guaranty Corporation (PBGC) is funded in part by premiums paid annually by covered plans. All covered single-employer defined benefit plans are required to pay a flat per-participant premium. In addition, underfunded plans are subject to a variable rate premium based on the level of underfunding. The variable rate premium is paid in addition to the flat-rate premium. No variable rate premium is imposed for a year if contributions to the plan for the prior year were at least equal to the full funding limit for that year. The full funding limit, under Code Sec. 412(c)(7), is not less than the excess, if any, of 90 percent of the plan's current liability over the actuarial value of the plan's assets (ERISA Sec. 4006(a)(3)(E)(iv)).

The flat-rate premium is $30 per participant per year (ERISA Sec. 4006(a)(3)(A)(i)). The flat-rate premium amount was increased from $19 to $30 by the Deficit Reduction Act of 2005 (P.L. 109-171), effective for plan years beginning on or after January 1, 2006. In addition, single-employer plans that are terminated under ERISA Sec. 4041(c)(2)(B)(ii) or (iii) or ERISA Sec. 4042 (distress terminations where the PBGC takes over as trustee of the terminated plan) are subject to a termination premium of $1,250 multiplied by the number of participants in the plan immediately before the termination date (ERISA Sec. 4006(a)(7)). If the employer is in bankruptcy reorganization under Chapter 11 of the U.S. Code (or under any similar law of a state or political subdivision of a state), the additional premium will not apply until the conclusion of the bankruptcy proceeding. The additional premium is due 30 days after any "applicable 12-month period" and the designated payor is the person who is the contributing sponsor as of immediately before the termination date. An applicable 12-month period is the 12-month period beginning with the first month following the month in which the termination date occurs and each of the first two successive 12-month periods. This additional premium is generally effective for plan years beginning after December 31, 2005. However, the premium will not apply to a single-employer plan that is terminated during the pendency of any bankruptcy reorganization under Chapter 11 of the U.S. Code (or under any similar law of a state or political subdivision of a state), if the proceeding is pursuant to a bankruptcy filing occurring before October 18, 2005. In addition, the bankruptcy premiums will not apply to plans terminated after December 31, 2010 (ERISA Sec. 4006(a)(7)(E)).

The variable rate premium is based on the amount of potential liability that the plan creates for the PBGC. The variable rate premium is equal to $9.00 per $1,000 of unfunded vested benefits as of the end of the preceding plan year. The amount of a plan's unfunded vested benefits is the excess of the plan's vested benefits (current liability) over the value of the plan's assets. Thus, unfunded vested benefits generally represent the amount that would be the unfunded current liability (within the meaning of ERISA Sec. 302(d)(8)(A)) if only vested benefits were taken into account. In determining the amount of unfunded vested benefits, the interest rate used is

BACKGROUND

generally 85 percent of the interest rate on 30-year Treasury securities for the month preceding the month in which the plan year begins (ERISA Sec. 4006(a)(3)(E)(iii)(II)). In the case of plan years beginning after December 31, 2003, and before January 1, 2006, the interest rate used is 85 percent of the annual rate of interest determined by the Treasury Secretary on amounts invested conservatively in long-term investment grade corporate bonds for the month preceding the month in which the plan year begins (ERISA Sec. 4006(a)(3)(E)(iii)(V)).

NEW LAW EXPLAINED

New rules for calculating PBGC variable rate premium.—New rules for calculating the Pension Benefit Guaranty Corporation (PBGC) variable rate premium are provided beginning in the 2008 plan year. Under these new rules, the determination of "unfunded vested benefits" for purposes of the variable rate premium is modified to conform to the funding rules of the Act (see ¶ 205 and following). Thus, unfunded vested benefits means, for a plan year, the excess (if any) of (1) the funding target of the plan (including at-risk assumptions), as determined under ERISA Sec. 303(d) (see ¶ 210) for the plan year, by only taking into account vested benefits and by using the interest rate specified below, over (2) the fair market value of plan assets for the plan year which are held by the plan on the valuation date (ERISA Sec. 4006(a)(3)(E)(iii), as added by the Pension Protection Act of 2006).

> **Comment:** While the rules calculating the variable rate premium are changed, the variable rate premium rate remains at $9.00 per $1,000 of unfunded vested benefits.

> **Practical Analysis:** Harold J. Ashner of Keightley & Ashner LLP, Washington, D.C., notes that many employers will see their PBGC variable-rate premiums increase dramatically. This is particularly so for those employers sponsoring plans that have been able to take advantage of the full-funding limit exemption, which is set to disappear beginning with premiums due for the 2008 plan year. Aside from the loss of the exemption, the measure of underfunding on which the variable-rate premium is based will go up for many employers (also starting in 2008), depending on how they fare under the new funding rules (particularly the "at-risk" rules). And the variable-rate premium will be more volatile and unpredictable than the funding obligation from year to year, given the absence from the variable-rate premium calculation of even the limited smoothing of asset values and interest rates that applies for funding purposes. For all these reasons, and taking into account as well the recent significant increase in the PBGC flat-rate premium, employers may want to review with their legal counsel and the plan's actuary the various strategies that may be used to keep the PBGC premium to a minimum.

Interest rate. The interest rate to be used in calculating the funding target in (1) above is the first, second, and third segment rates which would be determined under the new funding rules (see ¶ 210) if the segment rates were applied by using the monthly yields for the month preceding the month the plan year begins on investment grade corporate

NEW LAW EXPLAINED

bonds with varying maturities, and in the top three quality levels, rather than on the average of such yields for a 24-month period (ERISA Sec. 4006(a)(3)(E)(iv), as added by the Pension Act).

Temporary rules allowing use of corporate bond rate are extended. The new variable rate rules described above apply for plan years beginning in 2008. For 2006 and 2007 plan years, the temporary rules for determining unfunded vested benefits set out in ERISA Sec. 4006(a)(3)(E)(iii)(V) are extended (ERISA Sec. 4006(a)(3)(E)(iii)(V), as amended by the Pension Act) (see ¶ 301). Thus, for those years, the interest rate used in determining the amount of unfunded vested benefits for variable rate premium purposes is 85 percent of the annual rate of interest determined by the Treasury Secretary on amounts invested conservatively in long-term investment grade corporate bonds for the month preceding the month in which the plan year begins.

Full funding limit repealed. The rule providing that no variable rate premium is required if contributions for the prior plan year were at least equal to the full funding limit no longer applies.

> **Comment:** The new provisions are designed to address two fundamental problems with the PBGC premium structure. First, the premium structure did not adequately reflect the different levels of risk posed by plans of strong and weak companies. Second, the premium structure failed to raise sufficient revenue to eliminate the PBGC's deficit (which was reported to be nearly $23 billion in fiscal year 2005) or to cover expected future losses.
>
> The first step in shoring up the PBGC's financial condition was taken by Congress with the enactment of the Deficit Reduction Act of 2005 (P.L. 109-171) on February 8, 2006. The Deficit Reduction Act raised the flat-rate premium from $19 to $30 for 2006 plan years and made the flat-rate premium subject to inflation adjustments starting in the 2007 plan year. The Deficit Reduction Act, however, did not make any changes with respect to the variable rate premium.
>
> In testimony before the Senate Budget Committee, former PBGC executive director Bradley Belt said that the variable rate premium failed to raise sufficient revenue for the Agency for two reasons. First, the full funding limit exemption generally relieves plans that are funded for 90 percent of current liability from paying the variable rate premium. "As a result," he said, "less than 20 percent of participants" are in plans that pay a variable rate premium. In addition, he said, variable rate premium revenue is artificially low because current liability "understates liabilities at plan termination, often dramatically so." By eliminating the full funding limit, all underfunded plans would pay the variable rate premium. "Charging underfunded plans more gives employers an additional incentive to fully fund their pension promises," Belt said (Testimony before the Committee on Budget, U.S. Senate, June 15, 2005).

Termination premiums. The additional termination premium enacted under the Deficit Reduction Act of 2005 (P.L. 109-171) is made permanent (ERISA Sec. 4006(a)(7)(E), repealed by the Pension Act). This special rule generally imposes a charge of $1,250 per participant per year for three years after plan termination for certain un-

NEW LAW EXPLAINED

derfunded terminating plans. As originally enacted, this special premium did not apply with respect to any plan terminated after December 31, 2010.

> **Practical Analysis:** Harold J. Ashner of Keightley & Ashner LLP, Washington, D.C., observes that the now-permanent "exit fee" of $1,250 per participant, per year, for three years, can add up quickly to a significant amount (*e.g.*, $30 million for an 8,000-participant plan). Assuming this provision is ultimately upheld by the courts, it may interfere with the feasibility of many reorganizations and thus lead instead to asset sales followed by liquidation.

▶ **Effective date.** The new PBGC variable rate provisions are effective for plans terminated after December 31, 2005 (Act Sec. 401(a)(2) of the Pension Protection Act of 2006).

The provision making the termination premiums permanent is effective as if included in the provision of the Deficit Reduction Act of 2005 to which it relates (Act Sec. 401(b)(2)(B) of the Pension Protection Act of 2006).

Law source: Law at ¶7060. Committee Report at ¶10,220.

— Act Sec. 301(a)(3) of the Pension Protection Act of 2006, amending ERISA Sec. 4006(a)(3)(E)(iii)(V).

— Act Sec. 401(a)(1), striking ERISA Sec. 4006(a)(3)(E)(iii) and (iv), and adding new (iii) and (iv).

— Act Sec. 401(b)(1), repealing ERISA Sec. 4006(a)(7)(E).

— Act Sec. 401(b)(2), amending ERISA Sec. 4006(a)(7)(C)(ii).

— Act Sec. 401(a)(2) and 401(b)(2)(B), providing the effective dates.

Reporter references: For further information, consult the following CCH reporters.

— Pension Plan Guide, ¶6465

— Standard Federal Tax Reporter, 2006FED ¶19,125.021 and ¶19,125.0277

— Tax Research Consultant, RETIRE: 57,510.30

¶510 Variable Rate Premiums for Plans of Small Employers

SUMMARY OF NEW LAW

For plans of small employers (i.e., those with 25 or fewer employees), the PBGC per participant variable rate premium is capped at $5 multiplied by the number of plan participants.

BACKGROUND

The Pension Benefit Guaranty Corporation (PBGC) is funded in part by premiums paid by covered plans. All covered single-employer plans are required to pay a flat per-participant premium of $30 (ERISA Sec. 4006(a)(3)(A)(i)). In addition, underfunded plans are subject to a variable rate premium equal to $9.00 for each $1,000 of unfunded vested benefits as of the close of the preceding plan year (ERISA Sec. 4006(a)(3)(E)(ii)). There is no special exception to the variable rate premium for small plans.

NEW LAW EXPLAINED

Variable rate premiums capped for plans of small employers.—For small plans, the PBGC variable rate premium payments for each participant cannot exceed $5.00 multiplied by the number of participants in the plan as of the close of the preceding plan year (ERISA Sec. 4006(a) (3) (H) (i), as added by the Pension Protection Act of 2006).

> **Comment:** The variable rate premium is viewed as one impediment to the establishment of defined benefit plans. The trend in recent years has been for employers, especially smaller employers, to shift away from defined benefit plans. The variable rate premium cap is intended to encourage small employers to establish defined benefit plans.

> **Practical Analysis:** Harold J. Ashner of Keightley & Ashner LLP, Washington, D.C., observes that this provision will provide sorely needed relief for many small plans for which the PBGC variable-rate premium, which is calculated as a percentage of underfunding for *vested* benefits, has been excessive in relation to underfunding for *guaranteed* benefits. There has often been a large gap between vested and guaranteed benefits for small plans due to the special limitations on the guarantee for substantial owners. Although Act Sec. 407 applies special limitations on the guarantee only to those substantial owners who are *majority* (50 percent *or* more) owners, large gaps between vested and guaranteed benefits are likely to continue for many small plans. This new cap on the variable-rate premium is available only where, as of the first day of the plan year, on an aggregated basis counting all contributing sponsors and all controlled group members, there are 25 or fewer employees. If this test is met, the cap is available regardless of whether the plan covers substantial or majority owners and regardless of the number of participants in the plan. Note that adding a 26th employee on December 30 rather than on January 2 could prove to be very costly.

"Small employers" defined. Small employers that are subject to the variable rate premium cap are those with 25 or fewer employees on the first day of the plan year. All employees of the contributing sponsor's controlled group members are to be taken into account. In the case of a plan to which more than one unrelated contributing sponsor contributed, employees of all contributing sponsors (and their controlled group members) are to be taken into account in determining whether the "25 or fewer" limit has been met (ERISA Sec. 4006(a)(3)(H)(ii), as added by the Pension Act).

NEW LAW EXPLAINED

> **Example:** ABC Company has a defined benefit plan with 20 participants at the close of the preceding plan year. The per participant variable rate premium will be $100 (20 participants multiplied by $5.00). The total variable rate premium owed by the plan will be $2,000 ($100 per participant multiplied by 20 participants).

▶ **Effective date.** This provision is effective for plan years beginning after December 31, 2006 (Act Sec. 405(b) of the Pension Protection Act of 2006).

Law source: Law at ¶7072. Committee Report at ¶10,260.

— Act Sec. 405(a) of the Pension Protection Act of 2006, amending ERISA Sec. 4006(a)(3)(E)(i) and adding ERISA Sec. 4006(a)(3)(H);

— Act Sec. 405(b), providing the effective date.

Reporter references: For further information, consult the following CCH reporters.

— Pension Plan Guide, ¶6465

— Standard Federal Tax Reporter, 2006FED ¶17,508.01 and ¶17,513.01

¶515 Premium Overpayment Refunds

SUMMARY OF NEW LAW

The PBGC is authorized to pay interest on premium overpayment refunds. Interest paid on overpayments is to be calculated at the same rate and in the same manner as interest charged on premium underpayments.

BACKGROUND

Single-employer and multiemployer defined benefit plans are generally required to make annual premium payments to the Pension Benefit Guaranty Corporation (PBGC). If any premium payment is not paid by the last day prescribed for a payment, late payment penalty and interest charges will be imposed on the unpaid amount. For late premium payments, interest will generally accrue on the unpaid amount from the date payment is due until payment is made. The interest rate imposed is the quarterly rate determined under Code Sec. 6601(a) for underpayments (ERISA Sec. 4007(b)). However, while the PBGC charges interest on premium underpayments, it is not authorized to pay interest on premium overpayments.

NEW LAW EXPLAINED

PBGC authorized to pay interest on premium overpayment refunds.—The Pension Benefit Guaranty Corporation (PBGC) is authorized to pay interest on the amount of any overpayments refunded to payors of PBGC premiums (ERISA Sec. 4007(b)(2), as

NEW LAW EXPLAINED

added by the Pension Protection Act of 2006). This authority is subject to regulations prescribed by the PBGC.

Interest paid on overpayments is to be calculated at the same rate and in the same manner as interest charged on premium underpayments. Interest on premium underpayments is imposed under Code Sec. 6601(a), which is the same rate as the interest imposed on tax underpayments.

▶ **Effective date.** The provision applies to interest accruing for periods beginning not earlier than August 17, 2006 (Act Sec. 406(b) of the Pension Protection Act of 2006).

Law source: Law at ¶7075. Committee Report at ¶10,270.

— Act Sec. 406(a) of the Pension Protection Act of 2006, adding ERISA Sec. 4007(b)(2);

— Act Sec. 406(b), providing the effective date.

Reporter references: For further information, consult the following CCH reporters.

— Pension Plan Guide, ¶5520 and ¶6927

— Standard Federal Tax Reporter, 2006FED ¶39,415.01

PBGC BENEFITS

¶520 Limitation on Reduction in PBGC Guarantee for Shutdown and Other Benefits

SUMMARY OF NEW LAW

Limits will be imposed on the extent to which the Pension Benefit Guaranty Corporation (PBGC) will guarantee benefits that become payable due to plant shutdowns and other contingent events. The PBGC plan termination guarantee for benefits in the event of plant shutdowns and other unpredictable, contingent events will be phased in over a five-year period, generally at a rate of 20 percent of the guaranteed benefit per year.

BACKGROUND

A defined benefit plan may provide for certain benefits that become payable upon the occurrence of an unpredictable, contingent event, such as a plant shutdown. For purposes of the funding rules, such benefits are not pre-funded; that is, plans need not take them into account for funding purposes until the event on which the benefit is contingent occurs (ERISA Sec. 302(d)(7)(B)). Thus, employers do not pay PBGC premiums that reflect the potential cost of the benefits.

> **Comment:** Generally, shutdown benefits provide an incentive to employees who are at or near normal retirement age to retire at the time of the plant shutdown. Note that shutdown benefits that are in the form of a layoff benefit may not be

BACKGROUND

provided in a defined benefit plan (Reg. § 1.401-1(b)(1)(i)). Shutdown benefits are found primarily in the plans of large unionized companies, including those in the automobile and steel industries.

The PBGC guarantees the payment of a certain portion of vested benefits to participants when a covered plan terminates (ERISA Sec. 4022). Some limits apply. For example, with respect to increases in plan benefits as a result of plan amendments adopted within five years of the date of termination, a phase-in approach applies. This means that the guarantee for the increased amounts will be phased in over a five-year period (ERISA Sec. 4022(b)(1) and (7)). Shutdown and other contingent benefits are currently guaranteed by the PBGC if the triggering event occurs before plan termination.

Comment: Exposure to liability from shutdown benefits has grown. For example, in 2003 there was a potential exposure of over $15 billion (Letter from Steven Kandarian, former PBGC Executive Director, to Senators Charles Grassley, Chairman, and Max Baucus, Ranking Member, of the Senate Finance Committee, April 1, 2003).

NEW LAW EXPLAINED

PBGC guaranteed amount for plant shutdowns and other contingent events phased in over five-year period.—The PBGC guarantee for benefits for plant shutdowns and other unpredictable, contingent events will be calculated using the method currently used for benefits associated with plan amendments made within five years of the date of termination (ERISA Sec. 4022(b)(8), as added by the Pension Protection Act of 2006). Generally, this means that the guarantee will be phased in over a five-year period at the rate of 20 percent of the guaranteed benefit per year (ERISA Sec. 4022(b)(1) and (7)).

The PBGC guarantee will be phased in under the following formula: (1) the number of years since the date the shutdown or other event occurred (not to exceed five) multiplied by (2) the greater of (a) 20 percent of the guaranteed benefit or (b) $20 per month (ERISA Sec. 4022(b)(7)).

For purposes of the PBGC guarantee, an “unpredictable contingent event benefit” refers to a benefit payable solely by reason of a plant shutdown or a similar event. Note that the phase-in rule will not apply to benefits payable due to the following events:

- The attainment of any age;
- Performance of any service;
- Receipt of compensation; or
- Death or disability (ERISA Sec. 206(g)(1)(C), as added by the Pension Act) (see ¶ 215).

► **Effective date.** The provision applies to benefits that become payable as a result of an event that occurs after July 26, 2005 (Act Sec. 403(b) of the Pension Protection Act of 2006).

NEW LAW EXPLAINED

Law source: Law at ¶7066. Committee Report at ¶10,240.

— Act Sec. 403(a) of the Pension Protection Act of 2006, amending ERISA Sec. 4022(b);

— Act Sec. 403(b), providing the effective date.

Reporter references: For further information, consult the following CCH reporters.

— Pension Plan Guide, ¶6522

— Standard Federal Tax Reporter, 2006FED ¶17,507.029

¶525 Guaranteed Benefits and Asset Allocations When Plan Sponsor Enters Bankruptcy

SUMMARY OF NEW LAW

If a plan terminates after an employer enters bankruptcy, the date of the bankruptcy filing is substituted for the termination date for purposes of determining the maximum PBGC benefit guarantee and for purposes of determining the asset allocation for retirees or those who could have retired three years prior to the termination date. Thus, the amount of PBGC-guaranteed benefits is frozen when a contributing sponsor enters bankruptcy.

BACKGROUND

As part of its responsibilities under ERISA's termination insurance provisions, the Pension Benefit Guaranty Corporation (PBGC) must guarantee a certain amount of benefits for participants of terminating plans that are underfunded. Generally, the PBGC will guarantee the amount, as of the termination date of a single-employer plan, of a benefit provided under the plan to the extent that the benefit does not exceed the maximum limits specified below, if:

(1) the benefit is nonforfeitable;

(2) the benefit qualifies as a pension benefit; and

(3) the participant is entitled to the benefit (ERISA Sec. 4022; ERISA Reg. § 4022.3).

The maximum amount of benefits guaranteed by the PBGC per participant upon plan termination is determined under formulas contained in PBGC regulations. For plans terminating in 2006, the monthly benefit guarantee is $3,971.59 ($47,659.08 per year) (ERISA Reg. § 4011.11).

Upon the termination of a single-employer plan, the plan administrator allocates the plan assets "available to pay for benefits" under the plan in order among six priority categories (ERISA Sec. 4044). Thus, if a plan has sufficient assets to pay all benefits in a particular priority category, remaining assets are then allocated to the next lower priority category (ERISA Reg. § 4044.10(d)).

NEW LAW EXPLAINED

Bankruptcy filing date is termination date for PBGC benefit guarantees and asset allocations.—If a plan terminates during the contributing sponsor's bankruptcy, Pension Benefit Guaranty Corporation (PBGC) benefits are guaranteed as of the date of the filing of the bankruptcy petition under Title 11 of the United States Code or similar proceeding (ERISA Sec. 4022(g), as added by the Pension Protection Act of 2006).

In addition, if a plan terminates during the contributing sponsor's bankruptcy, the determination of who and what benefit is in the third asset allocation priority category as set out in ERISA Sec. 4044(a)(3) is made as of the date of the filing of the bankruptcy petition under Title 11 of the United States Code or similar proceeding (ERISA Sec. 4044(e), as added by the Pension Act). Under ERISA Sec. 4044(a)(3), priority class 3 benefits include benefits payable as an annuity to retired participants who began receiving benefits as of the three-year period ending on the termination date of the plan, including those benefits which could have been received for at least three years if the employee had so retired, based on plan provisions in effect five years prior to termination under which such benefits would be the least.

Thus, under the Act, for purposes of determining PBGC guaranteed benefits and the priority status of parties in asset allocation category 3, when allocating assets on termination, the date of the bankruptcy filing is substituted for the termination date.

> **Comment:** In testimony before the Senate Budget Committee, former PBGC executive director Bradley Belt noted that the PBGC and plan participants "may suffer greater losses if an underfunded plan later terminates while the plan sponsor or members of its controlled group are in a bankruptcy proceeding" (Testimony before the Committee on Budget, U.S. Senate, June 15, 2005).
>
> The PBGC reports that many plan sponsors continue to operate their plans until late in the bankruptcy process and then terminate the plan just prior to emerging from bankruptcy or prior to liquidation. During the time the sponsor is in bankruptcy, payment of lump-sums and annuity purchases may drain plan assets, which may reduce assets available for payment of non-guaranteed benefits to other participants. Benefits may also continue to accrue during bankruptcy and the PBGC limits on guarantees may continue to increase as a result of inflation adjustments, which may further increase unfunded benefits and the liability of the pension insurance system (S. Rep. No. 109-174). The provisions freezing the PBGC limit when a company enters bankruptcy is intended to stem financial losses for both the PBGC and plan participants.

Practical Analysis: Harold J. Ashner of Keightley & Ashner LLP, Washington, D.C., notes that the requirement to treat the date of the bankruptcy petition as the termination date applies only for two purposes: (1) determining guaranteed benefits, and the extent to which the PBGC will share its employer liability recoveries to pay unfunded *nonguaranteed* benefits, under ERISA Sec. 4022; and (2) determining benefits entitled to "Priority Category 3" protection under ERISA Sec. 4044. Significantly, the requirement does not apply in determining employer liability under ERISA

NEW LAW EXPLAINED

Sec. 4062, nor does it apply in allocating assets to the various Priority Categories under ERISA Sec. 4044 (except to the extent it affects the benefits that are guaranteed or entitled to Priority Category 3 protection).

▶ **Effective date.** This provision applies with respect to proceedings initiated under Title 11 of the United States Code, or under any other similar Federal law or law of a state or political subdivision, on or after the date that is 30 days after August 17, 2006 (Act Sec. 404(c) of the Pension Protection Act of 2006).

Law source: Law at ¶7069. Committee Report at ¶10,250.

— Act Sec. 404(a) of the Pension Protection Act of 2006, adding ERISA Sec. 4022(g);

— Act Sec. 404(b), adding ERISA Sec. 4044(e);

— Act Sec. 404(c), providing the effective date.

Reporter references: For further information, consult the following CCH reporters.

— Pension Plan Guide, ¶5720

— Standard Federal Tax Reporter, 2006FED ¶17,508.021

— Tax Research Consultant, RETIRE: 45,104.10

¶530 Rules for Substantial Owner Benefits in Terminated Plans

SUMMARY OF NEW LAW

Rules that limit the amount of phased-in benefit the PBGC will guarantee for business owners who participate in a terminated plan will apply only to owners of 50 percent or more of the business, rather than to owners of more than 10 percent of the business.

BACKGROUND

When a defined benefit plan covered by the Pension Benefit Guaranty Corporation (PBGC) terminates without sufficient assets to pay promised benefits, the PBGC guarantees the payment of benefits to participants. Generally, the PBGC will guarantee all basic benefits that are payable in periodic installments for the life (or lives) of the participant and his or her beneficiaries. These benefits must be nonforfeitable at the time of termination (ERISA Sec. 4022(a)).

Certain limits apply to the amount of guaranteed benefits. One limit relates to situations in which either a new plan has been created, or an existing plan has been amended to increase benefits, during the 60-month period just prior to the date the plan terminates. With respect to those benefits—i.e., all benefits under the new plan or the increased benefits associated with the plan amendment—the PBGC guarantee

BACKGROUND

is phased in over a set period of time. For non-owner participants, this generally means that the guarantee will be phased in over a 60-month period at the rate of 20 percent of the guaranteed benefit per year (ERISA Sec. 4022(b)(1) and (7)). For owners with a more than 10 percent ownership interest in a corporation or partnership (currently called "substantial owners"), however, benefits are generally phased in over a 30-year period (ERISA Sec. 4022(b)(5)). The effect of these rules can be to leave the business owner with a smaller PBGC guaranteed benefit than a similarly-situated non-owner.

> **Comment:** Some industry experts argue that this lack of comparable PBGC insurance, coupled with the perceived high administrative costs associated with a defined benefit plan, have discouraged small business owners from establishing and maintaining such plans.

Asset allocation rules. Similarly, special asset allocation rules (under which the PBGC prioritizes the order in which each participant receives his or her benefits from a terminated plan) apply to owners with a more than 10 percent ownership interest in the business (ERISA Sec. 4044(a)(4)).

NEW LAW EXPLAINED

Guaranteed benefit phase-in rules eased for owner/participants in terminated plans.—The application of the phase-in rule to participants who also own a portion of the business will now vary, depending upon how much of the business they own. For "substantial owners", the same 60-month phase-in rule that applies to non-owner participants applies (ERISA Sec. 4021(d), as added by the Pension Protection Act of 2006 and ERISA Sec. 4022(b)(5), as amended by the Pension Act). For "majority owners", a stricter phase-in rule is applied. Under that rule, the amount of benefits guaranteed is determined by multiplying:

- A fraction (which may not exceed one), where the numerator is the number of years from (1) the later of the effective date of the amendment or the plan adoption date and (2) the termination date, and the denominator is 10; by the
- Amount of benefits that would be guaranteed under the phase-in rules for participants who are not majority owners (ERISA Sec. 4022(b)(5)(B), as amended by the Pension Act).

Thus, in effect, for majority owners the phase-in occurs over a 10-year period and depends on the number of years the plan has been in effect. In addition, the majority owner's guaranteed benefit is limited so that it cannot be more than the amount phased in over 60 months for other participants.

Substantial owners. A person is a "substantial owner" if he or she, during the 60-month period ending on the date the plan termination occurs, owns:

- The entire interest in an *unincorporated trade or business*;
- More than 10 percent of either the capital interest or the profits of a *partnership*; or

NEW LAW EXPLAINED

- More than 10 percent in value of either the voting stock or all the stock of a *corporation.*

Note that in the case of a corporation, the constructive ownership rules of Code Sec. 1563 will generally apply, as will the common control rules of Code Sec. 414(c) (ERISA Sec. 4021(d), as added by the Pension Act).

Majority owners. A person is a "majority owner" if he or she, during the 60-month period ending on the date the plan termination occurs, owns:

- The entire interest in an *unincorporated trade or business*;
- 50 percent or more of either the capital interest or the profits of a *partnership*; or
- 50 percent or more in value of either the voting stock or all the stock of a *corporation.*

Note that in the case of a corporation, the constructive ownership rules of Code Sec. 1563 will generally apply, as will the common control rules of Code Sec. 414(c) (ERISA Sec. 4022(b)(5)(A), as amended by the Pension Act).

Asset allocation rules. The asset allocation rules will apply to "substantial owners" in the same manner that they do to other participants (ERISA Sec. 4044(a)(4), as amended by the Pension Act and ERISA Sec. 4044(b)(3), as added by the Pension Act).

▶ **Effective date.** The provisions that amend ERISA Sec. 4021(b)(9) and ERISA Sec. 4043(c)(7) take effect on January 1, 2006 (Act Sec. 407(d)(2) of the Pension Protection Act of 2006). All other provisions apply to plan terminations for which notices of intent to terminate are provided, or for which the PBGC provides notices of determination with respect to involuntary terminations, after December 31, 2005 (Act Sec. 407(d)(1) of the Pension Protection Act of 2006).

Law source: Law at ¶7078. Committee Report at ¶10,280.

— Act Sec. 407(a) of the Pension Protection Act of 2006, amending ERISA Sec. 4022(b)(5);

— Act Sec. 407(b), amending ERISA Sec. 4044(a) and (b);

— Act Sec. 407(c)(1), amending ERISA Sec. 4021(b)(9)and adding new ERISA Sec. 4021(d);

— Act Sec. 402(c)(2), amending ERISA Sec. 4043(c)(7);

— Act Sec. 407(d), providing the effective dates.

Reporter references: For further information, consult the following CCH reporters.

— Pension Plan Guide, ¶6534

— Standard Federal Tax Reporter, 2006FED ¶19,160A.025 and ¶19,160A.032

— Tax Research Consultant, RETIRE: 39,354 and RETIRE: 60,456

¶535 PBGC Computation of Benefits Attributable to Recoveries from Employers

SUMMARY OF NEW LAW

Methods used by the PBGC to determine a plan participant's share of additional benefits recovered by the PBGC from an employer that sponsored an underfunded terminated plan are modified. With respect to the benefit recovery ratio for unfunded benefit liabilities, the five-year period the PBGC uses to compute the ratio will begin two years earlier. With respect to the recovery of unpaid employer contributions for purposes of computing additional benefits, a new recovery ratio is created.

BACKGROUND

When a defined benefit plan covered by the Pension Benefit Guaranty Corporation (PBGC) terminates without sufficient assets to pay promised benefits, the PBGC guarantees payment of those benefits to participants, within certain limits. In general, the PBGC guarantees all basic, nonforfeitable benefits that are payable in periodic installments over the life (or lives) of the participant and his or her beneficiaries, up to a certain annual limit. For plans terminating in 2006, the maximum guaranteed monthly benefit for an individual who retires at age 65 is $3,971.59 per month or $47,659.08 annually (ERISA Reg. § 4011.11).

As part of the plan termination process for underfunded plans, the PBGC will seek to recover additional benefits from the plan sponsor employer that exceed the benefit amounts subject to the guarantee limits. These additional benefits fall into two categories: (1) unfunded benefit liabilities and (2) unpaid employer contributions owed to the plan. The employer (including members of its controlled group) is liable under ERISA for these amounts (ERISA Sec. 4062(a)).

Unfunded benefit liabilities. Any additional amounts recovered for unfunded benefit liabilities will be shared between the PBGC and the plan participants. The amounts are allocated to plan participants in accordance with ERISA's asset allocation rules (ERISA Sec. 4044).

> **Comment:** The additional amounts recovered that the PBGC retains are used by the agency to help cover its losses for paying unfunded guaranteed benefits.

Except in the case of large plans, the formula used to determine the participants' share of these additional amounts is a ratio calculated using the PBGC's past recovery experience with terminated plans, rather than the actual amount recovered from a specific plan. The benefit recovery ratio is (1) the value of the PBGC recoveries from terminated plans during a specified period to (2) the total amount of unfunded benefit liabilities of those terminated plans during the same specified period (ERISA Sec. 4022(c)(3)(A)).

The specified period used in the benefit recovery ratio is the five-Federal fiscal year period that ends with the fiscal year immediately prior to the fiscal year in which a

BACKGROUND

notice of intent to terminate is dated with respect to a particular plan (ERISA Sec. 4022(c)(3)(B)).

Note that for large plans, the benefit recovery ratio that takes PBGC prior experience into account is not used. Instead, actual recovery amounts with respect to the specific plan are used to determine the portion of the amounts recovered that will be allocated to participants (ERISA Sec. 4022(c)(3)(C)).

> **Comment:** For this purpose, a "large" plan is a terminated plan in which the amount of outstanding benefit liabilities exceeds $20 million.

Unpaid employer contributions. Amounts recovered from terminated plans attributable to unpaid employer contributions are determined based upon the specific plan, rather than upon prior PBGC experience (ERISA Sec. 4062(c)).

NEW LAW EXPLAINED

PBGC computation of benefits attributable to recoveries from employers modified.—Methods used by the Pension Benefit Guaranty Corporation (PBGC) to determine a plan participant's share of additional benefits (benefits that exceed PBGC guarantee limits) recovered by the PBGC from an employer that sponsored an underfunded terminated plan are modified.

Treatment of unfunded benefit liabilities. The benefit recovery ratio used by the PBGC to determine the amount of the unfunded benefit liabilities of a terminated plan will now generally be based upon the five-Federal fiscal year period that ends with the third fiscal year preceding the fiscal year in which occurs the date of a notice of intent to terminate (or, in the case of an involuntary termination by the PBGC, a notice of determination) with respect to a particular plan (ERISA Sec. 4022(c)(3)(B)(ii), as amended by the Pension Protection Act of 2006).

> **Comment:** A "notice of intent to terminate" (NOIT) must be provided to the PBGC, to participants and to other affected parties at least 60 days, but not more than 90 days, before the proposed termination date (ERISA Reg. §4041.23). Among other things, the NOIT must contain representations as to whether the plan has assets sufficient to meet benefit liabilities.

Treatment of unpaid employer contributions. In addition, a recovery ratio for determining amounts recovered for unpaid employer contributions owed to the plan is created. This recovery ratio will use the same five-year period as the new period used for determining the recovery ratio for unfunded benefit liabilities (see, above). Thus, the PBGC will determine the recovery amount by multiplying (1) the amount of liability under ERISA Sec. 4062(c) as of the date of plan termination by (2) the ERISA Sec. 4062(c) recovery ratio (ERISA Sec. 4044(e)(1), as added by the Pension Act).

The ERISA Sec. 4062(c) recovery ratio is the ratio which (1) the sum of all PBGC recoveries of unpaid employer contributions in connection with plan terminations during the applicable five-year period bears to (2) the sum of all the liabilities associated with unpaid employer contributions during the same five-year period (ERISA Sec. 4044(e)(2), as added by the Pension Act).

NEW LAW EXPLAINED

Treatment of large plans remains unchanged. As under current law, the recovery ratio based on PBGC prior experience will not be used for large plans, either with respect to unfunded benefit liabilities or unpaid employer contributions. Instead, the actual experience of the terminated plan is used (ERISA Sec. 4044(e)(3), as added by the Pension Act).

Determinations made by PBGC. The PBGC will make determinations regarding the amount of recovered benefits available for participants (ERISA Sec. 4044(e)(4)).

▶ **Effective date.** The provision applies to any plan termination for which a notice of intent to terminate is provided (or, in the case of a termination by the PBGC, for which a notice of determination under ERISA Sec. 4042 is issued) on or after the date which is 30 days after August 17, 2006 (Act Sec. 408(c) of the Pension Protection Act of 2006).

Law source: Law at ¶7081. Committee Report at ¶10,290.

— Act Sec. 408(a) of the Pension Protection Act of 2006, amending ERISA Sec. 4022(c)(3)(B)(ii);

— Act Sec. 408(b)(1), amending ERISA Sec. 4022(c)(3)(A);

— Act Sec. 408(b)(2), adding ERISA Sec. 4044(e);

— Act Sec. 408(c), providing the effective date.

Reporter references: For further information, consult the following CCH reporters.

— Pension Plan Guide, ¶6534

— Standard Federal Tax Reporter, 2006FED ¶18,347.033, ¶18,364.01 and ¶19,125.032

¶540 Missing Participants

SUMMARY OF NEW LAW

The PBGC must issue missing participant distribution regulations for multiemployer plans that terminate similar to the missing participant regulations that apply to single-employer defined benefit plans. The PBGC's missing participant program is extended to defined contributions plans and other plans that are not subject to the PBGC termination insurance program.

BACKGROUND

When a single-employer defined benefit pension plan terminates under a standard termination, the plan administrator generally must purchase annuity contracts from a private insurer to provide the benefits to which participants are entitled and distribute the annuity contracts to the participants. If the plan administrator cannot locate a participant after a diligent search, the plan administrator must purchase an annuity from an insurer or transfer the participant's designated benefit to the PBGC, which holds the benefit of the missing participant until the PBGC locates the missing participant and distributes the benefit.

BACKGROUND

Currently, the PBGC missing participant program is not available to multiemployer plans, defined contribution plans, and other plans not covered by Title IV of ERISA.

NEW LAW EXPLAINED

Missing participant program extended to multiemployer, defined contribution, and other plans.—The law directs the PBGC to issue regulations for terminating multiemployer plans similar to the present-law missing participant rules that apply to single-employer defined benefit plans when they terminate (ERISA Sec. 4050(c), as added by the Pension Protection Act of 2006).

> **Comment:** In the Senate Finance Committee Report that accompanied an earlier version of the bill, the Committee recognized that no statutory provision or formal regulatory guidance exists concerning an appropriate method of handling the benefits of missing participants in terminated multiemployer plans, defined contribution plans, and other plans not subject to the PBGC termination insurance program. Therefore, sponsors of these plans faced uncertainty with respect to the benefits of missing participants. The Committee believed that it is appropriate to extend the established PBGC missing participant program to these plans in order to reduce uncertainty for plan sponsors and increase the likelihood that missing participants will receive their retirement benefits (S. Rep. No. 109-174).

> **Comment:** Defined benefit plan administrators are required to either buy an annuity or transfer a missing participant's designated benefit to the PBGC. This requirement will also apply to multiemployer plan administrators when final regulations are implemented. However, the expansion of the missing participant program to other pension plans (see below) will be voluntary.

Other plans. Plan administrators of pension plans not subject to the PBGC missing participant program and not subject to the termination insurance program under present law will be permitted, but not required, to elect to transfer missing participant benefits to the PBGC upon plan termination (ERISA Sec. 4050(d)(1) and (4), as added by the Pension Act). Plan administrators will be required to provide benefit information to the PBGC (ERISA Sec. 4050(d)(2), as added by the Pension Act). The PBGC will pay the participant, when located, either a single sum or any other form specified by PBGC regulations (ERISA Sec. 4050(d)(3), as added by the Pension Act).

The missing participants program is specifically extended to defined contribution plans, defined benefit pension plans that have no more than 25 active participants and are maintained by professional service employers, and the portion of defined benefit pension plans that provide benefits based upon the separate accounts of participants and therefore are treated as defined contribution plans under ERISA (ERISA Sec. 4050(d)(4)(A)(ii), as added by the Pension Act).

▶ **Effective date.** The provisions are effective for distributions made after final regulations implementing ERISA Sec. 4050(c) and (d) are prescribed (Act Sec. 410(c) of the Pension Protection Act of 2006).

NEW LAW EXPLAINED

Law source: Law at ¶7087. Committee Report at ¶10,310.

— Act Sec. 410(a) of the Pension Protection Act of 2006, amending ERISA Sec. 4050;

— Act Sec. 410(b), amending ERISA Sec. 206(f);

— Act Sec. 410(c), providing the effective date.

Reporter references: For further information, consult the following CCH reporters.

— Pension Plan Guide, ¶6800

— Standard Federal Tax Reporter, 2006FED ¶17,925E.01 and ¶19,071.021

— Tax Research Consultant, RETIRE: 45,262

PBGC ADMINISTRATION

¶545 Appointment of PBGC Director

SUMMARY OF NEW LAW

The Director of the Pension Benefit Guaranty Corporation (PBGC) is appointed by the President, by and with the advice and consent of the Senate.

BACKGROUND

The Pension Benefit Guaranty Corporation (PBGC), a corporation within the Department of Labor (DOL), has been administered by a board of directors consisting of the Secretary of Labor, the Secretary of Commerce and the Secretary of the Treasury. The Secretary of Labor, in his role as chairman of the board of directors, appointed the PBGC Director. The appointment was not subject to Senate confirmation.

NEW LAW EXPLAINED

Senate jurisdiction over confirmation of PBGC Director.—The Director of the Pension Benefit Guaranty Corporation (PBGC) is appointed by the President, rather than the Secretary of Labor, and the appointment is subject to joint confirmation by the Senate Committee on Finance and the Senate Committee on Health, Education, Labor and Pensions (HELP) (ERISA Sec. 4002(a), as amended by the Pension Protection Act of 2006). If one committee votes to order reported a nomination, the other must report within 30 calendar days or be automatically discharged (5 U.S.C. Sec. 5314, as amended by the Pension Act).

> **Comment:** This provision results from the PBGC Confirmation Act of 2006, introduced by Senator Baucus (D-MT) and Senator Grassley (R-IA). The Senators indicated surprise that the position was not already subject to Senate approval,

NEW LAW EXPLAINED

> and indicated that the position of PBGC Director was too important a position not to be subject to Senate oversight (Introduction to PBGC Confirmation Act of 2006, S. 2919, May 24, 2006).

The PBGC Director, members of the PBGC board of directors, and those appointed by either the PBGC Director or the board, are authorized to make any investigation the PBGC deems necessary, including administering oaths and subpoenaing witnesses, in order to enforce any ERISA provision (ERISA Sec. 4003, as amended by the Pension Act).

Transition period. The term of the individual serving as Executive Director of the PBGC on August 17, 2006, the date of enactment of the Pension Act, will expire on that date. The individual, or any other individual, may serve as interim Director until an individual is appointed as Director by the President (Act Sec. 411(d) of the Pension Protection Act of 2006).

▶ **Effective date.** No specific effective date is provided. The provision is, therefore, considered effective on August 17, 2006, the date of enactment.

Law source: Law at ¶7090. Committee Report at ¶10,320.

— Act Sec. 411(a)(1) of the Pension Protection Act of 2006, amending ERISA Sec. 4002(a);

— Act Sec. 411(a)(2), amending ERISA Sec. 4003(b);

— Act Sec. 411(b), amending 5 U.S.C. Sec. 5314;

— Act Sec. 411(d).

Reporter references: For further information, consult the following CCH reporter.

— Pension Plan Guide, ¶10,650

¶550 Information Required in PBGC Annual Report

SUMMARY OF NEW LAW

The annual Pension Benefit Guaranty Corporation (PBGC) report to Congress on its financial performance during the prior fiscal year must include information on the parameters used in its financial modeling, as well as a comparison of its average return on investments as contrasted with standard securities investment indices.

BACKGROUND

Under ERISA Sec. 4008, as soon as practicable after the close of the fiscal year, the Pension Benefit Guaranty Corporation (PBGC) is required to submit a report to the President and Congress setting forth the state of its finances for the past fiscal year, with an actuarial projection of expected operations for the upcoming five-year period.

NEW LAW EXPLAINED

PIMS parameters.—The required annual report from the Pension Benefit Guaranty Corporation (PBGC) to Congress, on the PBGC's financial status for the prior fiscal year and its expected operations and funds status for the forthcoming five-year period, must include information on the specific simulation parameters used by its Pension Insurance Modeling System (PIMS) in calculating the PBGC's financial statements, including specific initial values, temporal parameters, and policy parameters (ERISA Sec. 4008(b) (1), as added by the Pension Protection Act of 2006).

Comment: The PBGC's Pension Insurance Modeling System (PIMS) has a database with detailed information on about 400 actual pension plans, sponsored by nearly 300 firms. These plans represent about 50 percent of the liabilities and underfunding in the defined benefit system. PIMS extrapolates the results of various simulations to the universe of single-employer plans (PBGC publication "Impact on Contributions, Funded Ratios, and Claims Against the Pension Insurance Program of the Administration's Pension Reform Proposal", April 6, 2005).

Caution Note: The PBGC cautions that the PIMS model is not predictive; that is, it is not intended to provide a single best estimate of future events. For instance, it does not take into account the effects of incentives within the legislation, nor the possible effects of economic conditions or competitive factors in employers' determinations to continue or terminate the plans they sponsor.

Comparison with investment indices. The annual report must set forth the PBGC's average annual return on its investments for the year of the report, comparing this return with an amount equal to:

- 60% of the average annual return of the Standard and Poor's 500 Index (S&P 500) for the year, and
- 40% of the average annual return of a fixed-income index such as the Lehman Aggregate Bond Index for the year (ERISA Sec. 4008(b)(2), as added by the Pension Act).

Statement of deficit or surplus. The annual report must state the amount the PBGC's deficit or surplus would have been for the year had it earned a return on its investments equivalent to the standard securities investment indices as set forth above (ERISA Sec. 4008(b)(3), as added by the Pension Act).

▶ **Effective date.** No specific effective date is provided by the Act. The provision is, therefore, considered effective on August 17, 2006, the date of enactment.

Law source: Law at ¶7093. Committee Report at ¶10,330.

— Act Sec. 412(2) of the Pension Protection Act of 2006, adding ERISA Sec. 4008(b).

Reporter references: For further information, consult the following CCH reporter.

— Pension Plan Guide, ¶10,650

Investment of Assets and Fiduciary Rules

6

INVESTMENT OF ASSETS

¶605 Diversification Requirements for Defined Contribution Plans

SUMMARY OF NEW LAW

Defined contribution plans must meet diversification requirements with regard to any portion of employee contributions, elective deferrals and employer contributions invested in employer securities. With regard to employee contributions and elective deferrals invested in employer securities, an individual must be allowed to elect to direct the plan to divest employer securities into other investment options. An individual who is a participant in the plan with at least 3 years of service or is a beneficiary of such a participant must be able to elect to divest the portion of the account invested in employer securities that is attributable to employer contributions in other investment options.

BACKGROUND

Retirement plan assets may not be invested in employer securities unless the investment is in "qualified" employer securities (ERISA Sec. 407(a)(1)). Defined benefit plans and money purchase plans are prohibited from acquiring "qualified" employer securities if, after the acquisition, more than 10-percent of the assets of the plan are invested in employer securities (ERISA Sec. 407(a)(2)). With the exception of elective deferrals discussed below, this 10-percent limitation does not apply to defined contribution plans except for money purchase plans (ERISA Sec. 407(b)(1)).

If a plan with elective deferral provisions requires that a portion of the elective deferrals be used to acquire "qualified" employer securities, then the 10-percent limitation on the acquisition applies with regard to that portion of the elective deferrals (ERISA Sec. 407(b)(2)(B)). Further, if a person other than the participant directs that any portion of the elective deferrals be used to acquire employer securities, the 10-percent limitation also applies. The 10-percent limitation does not apply if:

(1) the amount required to be invested in employer securities does not exceed more than one percent of any employee's compensation;

(2) the fair market value of all defined contribution plans maintained by the employer is no more than 10 percent of the fair market value of all retirements plans of the employer; or

(3) the plan is an ESOP.

"Qualified" employer stock is any stock issued by the employer or an affiliate of the employer (ERISA Sec. 407(d)(1)).

NEW LAW EXPLAINED

Diversification required for qualified trust of defined contribution plan.—A trust that is part of an "applicable defined contribution plan" will not be treated as a qualified trust unless the plan meets certain diversification requirements with regard to investments in employer securities (Code Sec. 401(a)(35), as added by the Pension Protection Act of 2006). An "applicable individual account plan" must also meet the diversification requirements (ERISA Sec. 204(j)(1), as added by the Pension Act).

> **Comment:** The new law was enacted in response to recent events that have focused public attention on the investment of retirement plan assets in employer securities. The bankruptcies of several large publicly traded companies, such as Enron Corporation, were accompanied with the loss of employees' retirement savings because defined contribution plan assets were invested in employer securities.

Employee contributions and elective deferrals. A plan will meet its diversification requirements if it allows an "applicable individual" to direct the plan to divest any employer securities in which a portion of employee contributions and elective deferrals are invested (Code Sec. 401(a)(35)(B) and ERISA Sec. 204(j)(2), as added by the Pension Act). The individual must then be allowed to direct the reinvestment of an equivalent amount in other investment options that meet requirements discussed below.

An "applicable individual" is any participant in the plan and any beneficiary who has an account under the plan with respect to which the beneficiary is entitled to exercise the rights of a participant (Code Sec. 401(a)(35)(G)(i) and ERISA Sec. 204(j)(6)(A), as added by the Pension Act).

> **Example:** Lori Lindt is a participant in the ABC Corporation 401(k) Plan. Lindt was required under the plan to invest a portion of her elective deferrals to the plan into employer securities. Lindt now has the option to divest up to one hundred percent of elective deferrals invested in employer securities and to reinvest the amount in other investment options.

Employer contributions. The plan will meet its diversification requirements if an applicable individual who is a participant in the plan and has completed at least 3 years of service or is a beneficiary of a participant or of a deceased participant is allowed to divest that portion of an account that contains employer contributions, other than elective deferrals, that is invested in employer securities or employer property (Code Sec. 401(a)(35)(C) and ERISA Sec. 204(j)(3), as added by the Pension Act). The applicable individual must be able to reinvest an equivalent amount in other investment options that meet the requirements discussed below.

The rules on divesting that portion of employer contributions invested in employer securities will be phased in over a three year period (Code Sec. 401(a)(35)(H) and ERISA Sec. 204(j)(7), as added by the Pension Act). For that portion of the account attributable to employer contributions invested in employer securities and that were acquired in a plan year beginning before January 1, 2007, the applicable individual may only divest an applicable percentage. The applicable percentage will be determined as follows:

NEW LAW EXPLAINED

- 33-percent in the first plan year;
- 66-percent in the second plan year; and
- 100 percent in the third and following plan years.

Example: David Smythe is a participant in the XYZ Corporation 401(k) Plan. Smythe has completed 3 years of service in the plan year before January 1, 2007. In February of 2004, 2005, 2006 and 2007, the XYZ Corporation made an employer contribution into Smythe's account and required the contributions to be invested in the company's publicly traded securities. Since Smythe is a participant in the plan and had completed 3 years of service, he is an applicable individual eligible to divest that portion of his employer contributions invested in employer securities. As of January 1, 2007, Smythe may elect to divest 33 percent of that portion of his account attributable to the company's contributions made in 2004, 2005 and 2006. Smythe may elect to divest 100 percent of the employer contribution invested in employer securities in 2007 because the securities were acquired after January 1, 2007.

Example: Jenny Davison has in her 401(k) account 120 shares of employer common stock contributed as matching contributions before January 1, 2007. As of January 1, 2007, Jenny may elect to divest up to 40 shares (33 percent of 120 shares) of the stock. As of January 1, 2008, Jenny may elect to divest up to a total of 79 shares or an additional 39 shares (66 percent of 120 shares). As of January 1, 2009, Jenny my elect to divest 100 percent of stock or 120 shares (Joint Committee on Taxation, Technical Explanation of the Pension Protection Act of 2006 (JCX-38-06)).

Each class of securities will be treated separately. The three year phase in rules do not apply to an applicable individual participant who has attained age 55 and who has completed at least 3 years of service before the first plan year beginning after December 31, 2005.

Investment options. Not less than three investment options other than employer securities must be offered in which an applicable individual may direct the proceeds from the divestment of employer securities. Each of the investment options must be diversified and have materially different risk and return characteristics (Code Sec. 401(a)(35)(D)(i) and ERISA Sec. 204(j)(4), as added by the Pension Act).

Example: Danielle Goddard is a participant in the WXY Corporation Retirement Plan and has a portion of her employee contributions invested in employer securities. WXY Corporate Retirement Plan provides participants with the opportunity to divest employer securities and to invest in a choice of three

NEW LAW EXPLAINED

> funds. All three funds have similar risk and return characteristics. These investment options do not meet the diversification requirements.

A plan may limit the time for divestment and reinvestment of employer securities to periodic, reasonable opportunities occurring no less frequently than quarterly (Code Sec. 401(a)(35)(D)(ii)(I) and ERISA Sec. 204(j)(4)(B)(i), as added by the Pension Act). Such a limit will not cause the plan to fail to meet the diversification requirements. However, the plan will fail to meet the diversification requirements if the plan imposes restrictions or conditions with respect to the investment of employer securities that are not imposed on the investment of other assets (Code Sec. 401(a)(35)(D)(ii)(II) and ERISA Sec. 204(j)(4)(B)(ii), as added by the Pension Act). This requirement will not apply to any restrictions or conditions required by securities laws.

Applicable defined contribution or individual account plan. The term "applicable defined contribution plan" means any defined contribution plan that holds any publicly traded employer securities (Code Sec. 401(a)(35)(E)(i), as added by the Pension Act). An "applicable individual account plan" means any individual account plan as defined by ERISA Sec. 3(34) that holds any publicly traded employer securities (ERISA Sec. 204(j)(5)(A), as added by the Pension Act).

An employee stock ownership plan (ESOP) will not be considered an applicable defined contribution or individual account plan if:

(1) there are no contributions to the plan (or earnings) that are held within the plan and are subject to Code Sec. 401(k) and Code Sec. 401(m); and

(2) the plan is a separate plan for purposes of Code Sec. 414(l) with respect to any other defined benefit plan or defined contribution plan maintained by the same employer or employers (Code Sec. 401(a)(35)(E)(ii) and ERISA Sec. 204(j)(5)(B), as added by the Pension Act).

One-Participant Plans. A "one-participant retirement plan" will not be considered an applicable defined contribution or individual account plan (Code Sec. 401(a)(35)(E)(iv) and ERISA Sec. 204(j)(5)(C), as added by the Pension Act).

A retirement plan will only be considered a "one-participant retirement plan" if certain requirements are met. As of the first day of the plan year, the plan must only cover one individual (or one individual and the individual's spouse) and the individual must own 100 percent of the plan sponsor whether or not incorporated, or must only cover one or more partners (or partners and their spouses) in the plan sponsor. The plan must meet the minimum coverage requirements of Code Sec. 410(b) without being combined with any other plan of the business that covers the employees of the business. The plan may not provide benefits to anyone except the individual (and the individual's spouse) or the partners (and their spouses). The plan must not cover a business that is a member of an affiliated service group, a controlled group of corporations, or a group of businesses under common control. Finally, the plan must not cover a business that uses the services of leased employees (within the meaning of Code Sec. 414(n)). A two-percent shareholder of an S corporation is included in the term partner.

NEW LAW EXPLAINED

Plans treated as holding publicly traded employer securities. In certain instances, a plan holding employer securities that are not publicly traded will be treated as holding publicly traded employer securities for purpose of the diversification requirements. A plan will be treated as holding publicly traded securities if any employer corporation, or any member of a controlled group of corporations that includes such employer corporation, has issued a class of stock that is publicly traded employer securities (Code Sec. 401(a)(35)(F)(i) and ERISA Sec. 204(j)(D)(i), as added by the Pension Act).

There is an exception to treating a plan as holding publicly traded securities (Code Sec. 401(a)(35)(F)(ii) and ERISA Sec. 204(j)(D)(ii), as added by the Pension Act). A plan holding securities that are not publicly traded will not be treated as holding publicly traded securities if:

(1) no employer corporation, or no parent corporation of an employer corporation, has issued any publicly traded employer securities; and

(2) no employer corporation, or parent corporation, has issued any special class of stock that grants particular rights to, or bears particular risks for, the holder or issuer with respect to any employer corporation or to any member of a controlled group of corporation that includes the employer corporation that has issued any publicly traded employer securities.

▶ **Effective date.** This provision generally applies to plan years beginning after December 31, 2006 (Act Sec. 901(c)(1) of the Pension Protection Act of 2006).

In the case of a plan maintained pursuant to one or more collective bargaining agreements between employee representatives and one or more employers ratified on or before August 17, 2006, the date of enactment of the Pension Act, the provision is effective the earlier of:

(1) the later of December 31, 2007, or the date on which the last of such collective bargaining agreements terminates, which is determined without regard to any extension after August 17, 2006; or

(2) December 31, 2008 (Act Sec. 901(c)(2) of the Pension Protection Act of 2006).

The provision which applies to employer securities is effective for plan years beginning after the earlier of December 31, 2007, or the first date on which the fair market value of the securities exceeds the guaranteed minimum value specified by the employee stock ownership plan in which the securities are held, for employer securities that: (1) are attributable to employer contributions other than elective deferrals and (2) as of September 17, 2003, consist of preferred stock and are within an employee stock ownership plan, the terms of which provide that the value of the securities cannot be less than the guaranteed minimum value specified by the plan on that date (Act Sec. 901(c)(3) of the Pension Protection Act of 2006).

Law source: Law at ¶5030, ¶5065, ¶5315 and ¶7180. Committee Report at ¶10,950.

— Act Sec. 901(a)(1) of the Pension Protection Act of 2006, adding Code Sec. 401(a)(35);

— Act Sec. 901(a)(2)(A), adding Code Sec. 401(a)(28)(B)(v);

— Act Sec. 901(a)(2)(B), amending Code Sec. 409(h)(7);

— Act Sec. 901(a)(2)(C), amending Code Sec. 4980(c)(3)(A);

— Act Sec. 901(b), redesignating ERISA Sec. 204(j) as (k) and adding new (j);

NEW LAW EXPLAINED

— Act Sec. 901(b)(2), adding ERISA Sec. 407(b)(3)(D);

— Act Sec. 901(c), providing the effective date.

Reporter references: For further information, consult the following CCH reporters.

— Pension Plan Guide, ¶4470 and ¶4595

— Standard Federal Tax Reporter, 2006FED ¶17,507.028 and ¶17,507.03

— Tax Research Consultant, RETIRE: 3,214.40

¶610 Notice of Right to Divest Employer Securities

SUMMARY OF NEW LAW

A notice must be provided by the plan administrator to an applicable individual not later than 30 days before the first day that the individual is eligible to divest employer securities with respect to any type of contribution. The Secretary of the Treasury is authorized to issue a model notice to satisfy this requirement.

BACKGROUND

A plan administrator is required to furnish a number of notices and information under ERISA with regard to plans (ERISA Sec. 101). For example, a summary plan description must be provided that includes administrative information about the plan, the plan's requirements as to eligibility for participation and benefits, the plan's vesting provisions, and the procedures for claiming benefits under the plan. In addition, if a plan administrator fails or refuses to provide required notices and information to a participant within 30 days of the participant's written request, the participant may bring a civil action to recover $100 a day from the plan administrator or other relief the court deems proper.

NEW LAW EXPLAINED

Required notice of diversification rights.—A plan administrator must provide a notice to applicable individuals who are eligible to exercise the right to direct the proceeds from the divestment of employer securities with respect to any type of contribution. The new rules giving individuals the right to divest employer securities are discussed at ¶ 605. The notice must be provided not later than 30 days before the first date on which the applicable participant becomes eligible to divest employer securities. The notice must set out the right to direct the divestment of employer securities and must describe the importance of diversifying retirement account assets in investments (ERISA Sec. 101(m), as added by the Pension Protection Act of 2006).

NEW LAW EXPLAINED

> **Example:** Rhys Davidson is hired in January, 2007 and is eligible to participate in his company's 401(k) plan as of his date of hire. The portion of Davidson's account attributable to employer contributions under the plan are automatically invested in employer securities. Davidson will not be eligible to divest and direct the proceeds of this portion of his account until he has completed three years of service in January, 2010. The administrator of the 401(k) plan must provide Davidson with notice of his right to direct the proceeds of divesting the employer securities in his account 30 days before he becomes eligible to divest employer securities.

The notices must be written in a manner calculated to be understood by the average plan participant. It may be delivered in written, electronic, or other appropriate form to the extent that the form used is reasonably accessible to the recipient of the notice (ERISA Sec. 101(m), as added by the Pension Act).

Penalties. Plan administrators that fail to comply with the requirement to provide the diversification rights notice may be assessed a penalty of up to $100 a day from the date of noncompliance. Plan administrators are subject to a separate penalty for each individual participant or beneficiary to whom notice has not been provided (ERISA Sec. 502(c)(7), as amended by the Pension Act).

Model notice. Within 180 days after August 17, 2006, the date of enactment, the Secretary of the Treasury must issue a model notice that will satisfy the notice requirements (Act Sec. 507(c) of the Pension Act).

▶ **Effective date.** This provision is effective for plan years beginning after December 31, 2006 (Act Sec. 507(d)(1) of the Pension Protection Act of 2006). If the notice would otherwise be required to be provided before the 90th day after August 17, 2006, the date of enactment of the Pension Act, the notice will not be required to be provided until the 90th day (Act Sec. 507(d)(2) of the Pension Protection Act of 2006).

Law source: Law at ¶7114. Committee Report at ¶10,390.

— Act Sec. 507(a) of the Pension Protection Act of 2006, redesignating ERISA Sec. 101(m) as (n) and adding new (m);

— Act Sec. 507(b), amending ERISA Sec. 502(c)(7);

— Act Sec. 507(c);

— Act Sec. 507(d), providing the effective date.

Reporter references: For further information, consult the following CCH reporters.

— Pension Plan Guide, ¶7526B and ¶4485

— Standard Federal Tax Reporter, 2006FED ¶17,512.01

— Tax Research Consultant, RETIRE: 51,352

¶615 Periodic Benefit Statement for Participants and Beneficiaries in Defined Contribution Plans

SUMMARY OF NEW LAW

A plan administrator of a defined contribution plan (other than a one-participant retirement plan) must provide a pension benefit statement to participants and beneficiaries. The statement must be furnished at least once each calendar quarter to participants and beneficiaries who have the right to direct the investment of the assets of their accounts; once each calendar year to participants and beneficiaries who have accounts but do not have the right to direct the investment of the account assets; and upon written request to a plan beneficiary not described above. A plan administrator of a defined benefit plan must provide a pension benefit statement at least once every three years to each participant with a nonforfeitable accrued benefit and who is employed by the employer at the time the statement is furnished and to a participant or beneficiary of the plan upon written request.

BACKGROUND

A plan administrator of an employee pension benefit plan must furnish a statement of benefit rights to any plan participant or beneficiary who requests it in writing. On the basis of the latest information available, the plan administrator must provide a statement that shows the total benefits accrued and the nonforfeitable pension benefits, if any, that have accrued, or the earliest date on which the benefits will become nonforfeitable (ERISA Sec. 105(a)). No more than one statement need be provided to a participant or beneficiary during any 12-month period (ERISA Sec 105(b)).

NEW LAW EXPLAINED

Required periodic benefit statements.—A plan administrator of a defined contribution plan (other than a one-participant retirement plan) must furnish a pension benefit statement to participants and beneficiaries (ERISA Sec. 105(a)(1)(A), as amended by the Pension Protection Act of 2006). The pension benefit statement must be furnished:

(1) at least once each calendar quarter to each participant or beneficiary who has the right to direct the investment of assets in his or her account under the plan;

(2) at least once each calendar year to a participant or beneficiary who has his or her own account under the plan but does not have the right to direct the investment of the assets of the account; and

(3) upon written request to a plan beneficiary not described in (1) or (2) above.

Comment: The Senate Finance Committee believes that regular information concerning the value of retirement benefits, especially benefits that accumulate in a defined contribution plan account, is necessary to increase employee awareness and appreciation of the importance of retirement savings (Report on Na-

NEW LAW EXPLAINED

tional Employee Savings and Trust Equity Guarantee Act (S. 1953), Senate Finance Committee, November 2, 2005.)

Content of pension benefit statement. A pension benefit statement must indicate, on the basis of the latest information available, the total benefits accrued and the nonforfeitable benefits, if any, that have accrued or the earliest date on which benefits will become nonforfeitable (ERISA Sec. 105(a)(2)(A)(i), as amended by the Pension Act). The statement must also include an explanation of any permitted disparity or any floor-offset arrangement that may be applied in determining any accrued benefits (ERISA Sec. 105(a)(2)(A)(ii), as amended by the Pension Act).

The statement must be written in a manner calculated to be understood by the average plan participant (ERISA Sec. 105(a)(2)(A)(iii), as amended by the Pension Act). It may be delivered in written, electronic, or other appropriate form to the extent that the form is reasonably accessible to the participant or beneficiary (ERISA Sec. 105(a)(2)(A)(iv), as amended by the Pension Act).

A pension benefit statement for a defined contribution plan must include the value of each investment to which assets in a participant's or beneficiary's account have been allocated, determined as of the most recent valuation date under the plan. The value must include any assets held in the form of employer securities, without regard to whether the securities were contributed by the plan sponsor or acquired at the direction of the plan or the participant or beneficiary (ERISA Sec. 105(a)(2)(B)(i), as amended by the Pension Act).

Requirements for quarterly statements for participants with the right to direct investment of account assets. For a pension benefit statement covering a defined contribution plan that must be provided at least once each calendar quarter to participants or beneficiaries who have the right to direct the investment of their account assets, the statement must include an explanation of any limitations or restrictions on any right of the participant or beneficiary to direct the investment. The notice must include an explanation, written in a manner calculated to be understood by the average plan participant, regarding the importance of a well-balanced and diversified investment portfolio for the long-term retirement security of the participants and beneficiaries, as well as include a statement of the risk that holding more than 20 percent of a portfolio in the securities of one entity (including employer securities) may not be adequately diversified. Further, the notice must direct the participant or beneficiary to the Internet website of the Department of Labor for information sources on individual investing and diversification (ERISA Sec. 105(a)(2)(B)(ii), as amended by the Pension Act).

Alternative annual statements for participants without the right to direct investment of account assets. The requirements that a notice be provided annually to a participant or beneficiary who has a defined contribution plan account will be met if, at least annually, the plan updates the information that is required to be provided in the pension benefit statement, or provides in a separate statement, information that will enable a participant or beneficiary to determine their nonforfeitable vested benefits (ERISA Sec. 105(a)(2)(C), as amended by the Pension Act).

Pension benefit statements for participants in a defined benefit plan. A plan administrator of a defined benefit plan (other than a one-participant retirement plan) must furnish a

NEW LAW EXPLAINED

pension benefit statement to participants and beneficiaries (ERISA Sec. 105(a)(1)(B), as amended by the Pension Act). The pension benefit statement must be furnished:

(1) at least once every three years to each participant with a nonforfeitable accrued benefit and who is employed by the employer maintaining the plan at the time the statement is to be furnished; and

(2) to a participant or beneficiary of the plan upon written request.

The information furnished under item (1) above may be based on reasonable estimates determined under regulations prescribed by the Secretary of Labor, in consultation with the Pension Benefit Guaranty Corporation.

The Secretary of Labor may provide that the years during which no employee or former employee receives any benefits under the plan need not be taken into account when determining the three-year period for when to provide the pension benefit statement (ERISA Sec. 105(a)(3)(B), as amended by the Pension Act).

Alternative notice for participants of defined benefit plans. For a defined benefit plan, the annual benefit statement requirements will be treated as met if at least once a year the plan administrator provides to participants notice of availability of the pension benefit statement and the ways in which the participant may be obtain the statement. The notice may be delivered in written, electronic or other appropriate form to the extent the form used is reasonably accessible to the participants (ERISA Sec. 105(a)(3)(A), as amended by the Pension Act).

One statement in a 12-month period. No more than one statement need be provided to a participant or beneficiary in a defined contribution plan or defined benefit plan who requests a pension benefit statement in writing during any 12-month period (ERISA Sec. 105(b), as amended by the Pension Act).

Model statements. The Secretary of Labor must within one year after August 17, 2006, the date of enactment, develop one or more model benefit statements that are written in a manner calculated to be understood by the average plan participant and that may be used by plan administrators in complying with the requirement to provide pension benefit statements to participants and beneficiaries. The Secretary of Labor is authorized to issue any interim final rules necessary to develop the required model benefit statements (Act Sec. 508(b) of the Pension Act).

▶ **Effective date.** The provisions are effective for plan years beginning after December 31, 2006 (Act Sec. 508(c)(1) of the Pension Protection Act of 2006).

In the case of a plan maintained pursuant to one or more collective bargaining agreements between employee representatives and one or more employers ratified on or before August 17, 2006, the date of the enactment of the Pension Act, the provision is effective the earlier of:

(1) The later of December 31, 2007, or the date on which the last of such collective bargaining agreements terminates, which is determined without regard to any extension after August 17, 2006; or

(2) December 31, 2008 (Act Sec. 508(c)(2) of the Pension Protection Act of 2006).

NEW LAW EXPLAINED

Law source: Law at ¶7117. Committee Report at ¶10,400.

— Act Sec. 508(a)(1) of the Pension Protection Act of 2006, amending ERISA Sec. 105(a);

— Act Sec. 508(a)(2)(A), striking ERISA Sec. 105(d);

— Act Sec. 508(a)(2)(B), amending ERISA Sec.105(b);

— Act Sec. 508(a)(2)(C), amending ERISA Sec. 502(c)(1);

— Act Sec. 508(b);

— Act Sec. 508(c), providing the effective date.

Reporter references: For further information, consult the following CCH reporters.

— Pension Plan Guide, ¶4270, ¶4310, ¶5775 and ¶5955

— Tax Research Consultant, RETIRE: 51,352

— Federal Tax Guide, 2006FTG ¶11,095

¶620 Notice to Participants and Beneficiaries of Blackout Periods

SUMMARY OF NEW LAW

The definition of a "one-participant retirement plan" for purposes of the blackout period notice has been amended to provide that the plan on the first day of the plan year may only cover one individual (and the individual's spouse) who owns 100 percent of the plan sponsor or one or more partners (and their spouses) in the plan sponsor.

BACKGROUND

The Senate Finance Committee as part of its consideration of the National Employee Savings and Trust Equity Guarantee Act (S.B. 1953) requested the Joint Committee staff to undertake a study of Enron and related entities and their compensation arrangements including qualified retirement plans. The Joint Committee staff found that Enron provided a variety of advanced notices to participants of the proposed blackout period; however, not all participants received the same notices. Certain active participants received additional reminders of the blackout that were not provided to other participants. This finding supports the Senate Finance Committee's view of the need to provide participants with a blackout notice with sufficient information for them to make appropriate decisions with regard to the investments in their accounts (National Employee Savings and Trust Equity Guarantee Act, Senate Finance Committee Report, November 2, 2005).

The Sarbanes-Oxley Act of 2002 (P.L. 107-204) amended ERISA to require plan administrators to provide advance notice of a blackout period to participants and beneficiaries who would be impacted by the period. A blackout period is any period

BACKGROUND

during which the ability of a participant or beneficiary to direct or diversify assets in his or her plan account is temporarily suspended, limited, or restricted if that suspension, limitation, or restriction is for more than three consecutive business days (ERISA Sec. 101(i)(7)(A); ERISA Reg. § 2520.101-3(d)(1)(i)).

The notice requirement does not apply to one-participant retirement plans (ERISA Sec. 101(i)(8)(A), as added by P.L. 107-204 (Sarbanes-Oxley Act of 2002), Act Sec. 306(b)(1); ERISA Reg. § 2520.101-3(d)(3)). Thus, the blackout notice is not required of a plan that on the first day of the plan year: (1) covers only the owner-employer (and the employer's spouse) or covers only one or more partners (and their spouses), (2) satisfies the minimum coverage requirements of Code Sec. 410(b), without being combined with any other plan of the business, (3) provides benefits only to the employer or partners (and their spouses), (4) does not cover members of an affiliated service group, controlled group, or business under common control, and (5) does not cover a business that leases employees (ERISA Sec. 101(i)(8)(B), as added by P.L. 107-204 (Sarbanes-Oxley Act of 2002), Act Sec. 306(b)(1)).

NEW LAW EXPLAINED

One-participant retirement plan for notice of blackout periods.—For purposes of the blackout notice rules, the term "one-participant retirement plan" means a retirement plan that as of the first day of the plan year only covers one individual (or one individual and the individual's spouse) and the individual owns 100 percent of the plan sponsor whether or not incorporated, or only covers one or more partners (or partners and their spouses) in a plan sponsor (ERISA Sec. 101(i)(8)(B), as amended by the Pension Protection Act of 2006). For a discussion on the fiduciary rules for blackouts, see ¶ 640.

> **Comment:** This provision clarifies the definition of a one-participant retirement plan that is not subject to the blackout period notice requirements by changing "employer" who owns the entire business to "one individual" who owns 100 percent of the plan sponsor. Further, it conforms the definition to the definition applied for purposes of the diversification requirements (see ¶ 605).

► **Effective date.** This provision is effective as if included in the provisions of section 306 of the Sarbanes-Oxley Act of 2002 (P.L. 107-204) (Act Sec. 509(a)(2) of the Pension Protection Act of 2006). The provisions of Section 306 of the Sarbanes-Oxley Act took effect 180 days after the date of the enactment of the Act (Sec. 306(c) of the Sarbanes-Oxley Act). The President signed the Sarbanes-Oxley Act into law on July 30, 2002.

Law source: Law at ¶ 7120. Committee Report at ¶ 10,410.

— Act Sec. 509(a)(1) of the Pension Protection Act of 2006, amending ERISA Sec. 101(i)(8)(B);

— Act Sec. 509(a)(2), providing the effective date.

Reporter references: For further information, consult the following CCH reporters.

— Pension Plan Guide, ¶ 4325 and ¶ 7526B

— Tax Research Consultant, RETIRE: 51,352

INVESTMENT ADVICE AND PROHIBITED TRANSACTION EXEMPTIONS

¶625 Investment Advice Provided to Participants by Fiduciary Advisers

SUMMARY OF NEW LAW

Under a new prohibited transaction exemption, qualified "fiduciary advisers" can offer personally tailored professional investment advice to help employees manage their 401(k) and other plans. For 401(k) plans, fiduciary advisers may provide investment advice pursuant to "eligible investment advice arrangement" under which (1) portfolio recommendations are generated for a participant based on an unbiased computer model that has been certified and audited by an independent third party, or (2) fiduciary advisers provide their investment advice services by charging a flat fee that does not vary depending on the investment option chosen by the participant. The Secretary of Labor has been directed to determine whether investment advice provided through a computer model is feasible for IRAs and other tax-favored savings accounts.

BACKGROUND

ERISA requires employee benefit plans, including 401(k) and other employer-sponsored plans, to name one or more fiduciaries that are responsible for maintaining and administering the plan. In addition to the fiduciaries named in the plan, investment advisers are also considered to be fiduciaries. Fiduciaries and some other parties are prohibited from engaging in specified transactions involving plan assets, and fiduciaries may not knowingly permit a plan to engage in these prohibited transactions. Fiduciaries that violate the prohibited transaction rules, or otherwise fail to act prudently and in the exclusive interest of plan participants and beneficiaries, are personally liable to, among other things, make good any losses to the plan resulting from a breach of their fiduciary duties (Code Sec. 4975 and ERISA Sec. 404(a)).

Who is affected. A transaction is prohibited only if it involves a disqualified person (Code Sec. 4975(c)). Disqualified persons include a fiduciary of the plan, a person providing services to the plan, and an employer with employees covered by the plan. For this purpose, a fiduciary includes any person who: (1) exercises any authority or control respecting management or disposition of the plan's assets, (2) renders investment advice for a fee or other compensation with respect to any plan moneys or property, or has the authority or responsibility to do so, or (3) has any discretionary authority or responsibility in the administration of the plan (Code Sec. 4975(e)(2) and ERISA Sec. 3(14)).

> **Comment:** Under ERISA, the prohibited transaction rules affect a "party in interest." Under the Code, the prohibited transaction rules affect a "disqualified person." The two terms are substantially the same in most respects, but the

BACKGROUND

ERISA term "party in interest" includes a somewhat broader range of persons than does the Code-defined disqualified person.

Exemptions from the prohibited transaction rules are available. A number of exemptions are provided by statute (Code Sec. 4975(d)(1) and ERISA Sec. 408). There are also two types of administrative exemptions: class exemptions, which furnish relief to any qualified parties that engage in transactions of the type covered by the class exemption, and individual exemptions, which offer relief only to the specific parties requesting an exemption (Code Sec. 4975(c) and ERISA Sec. 408(a)).

Prohibited transactions. Prohibited transactions include: (1) the sale, exchange or leasing of property, (2) the lending of money or other extension of credit, (3) the furnishing of goods, services or facilities, (4) the transfer to, or use by or for the benefit of, the income or assets of the plan, (5) in the case of a fiduciary, any act that deals with the plan's income or assets for the fiduciary's own interest or account, and (6) the receipt by a fiduciary of any consideration for the fiduciary's own personal account from any party dealing with the plan in connection with a transaction involving the income or assets of the plan (Code Sec. 4975(c) and ERISA Sec. 406). Transactions between a retirement plan and a party-in-interest or disqualified person are prohibited unless there is a statutory, class, or individual exemption. For example, certain loans to plan participants are exempt from the prohibited transaction rules (Code Sec. 4975(d)(1) and ERISA Sec. 406(a)).

Penalties for violations. Under the Code, a disqualified person who participates in a prohibited transaction is subject to a two-tier excise tax. The first level tax is 15 percent of the amount involved in the transaction (Code Sec. 4975(a)). The second level tax is imposed if the prohibited transaction is not corrected within a certain period, and is 100 percent of the amount involved (Code Sec. 4975(b)).

Under ERISA Sec. 502(i), the Secretary of Labor is authorized to assess civil penalties against parties in interest who engage in prohibited transactions with plans that are not subject to the excise tax imposed by Code Sec. 4975. The amount of the civil penalty may not exceed five percent of the amount involved in the transaction, except that, if a prohibited transaction is not corrected within 90 days, the penalty may be up to 100 percent of the amount involved.

Comment: Although ERISA calls for the coordinated action of the IRS and the Labor Department in the administration of the prohibited transaction rules, duplicate efforts have resulted in delays, especially in the granting of prohibited transaction exemptions. As a result, under the ERISA Reorganization Plan, the Secretary of the Treasury has transferred to the Secretary of Labor the general authority to issue regulations, rulings, opinions, and exceptions under Code Sec. 4975, concerning the tax on prohibited transactions. However, an exception to this transfer of authority was made for rules involving the correction or undoing of a prohibited transaction. Thus, the correction of a prohibited transaction may involve the coordinated efforts of the IRS and the Department of Labor.

ERISA also subjects a fiduciary to civil or criminal penalties for the breach of fiduciary duty (ERISA Secs. 501 and 502(i)). A plan fiduciary who breaches any of the fiduciary responsibilities, obligations, or duties imposed by ERISA is personally liable to the plan for any losses suffered by the plan because of the breach. The

BACKGROUND

fiduciary must also restore to the plan any profits that he or she has made through the use of plan assets. In addition, a fiduciary is subject to other appropriate relief, including removal as ordered by a court (ERISA Sec. 409). In some instances, an ERISA fiduciary may be liable for breaches committed by a co-fiduciary (ERISA Sec. 405).

> **Comment:** The party in interest or disqualified person participating in the prohibited transaction is personally liable for the excise tax. A plan may not pay the excise tax imposed on the party in interest or the disqualified person.

Participant-directed accounts. A retirement plan may provide for individual accounts and permit a participant or beneficiary to exercise control over assets in his or her account, which is referred to as a "participant-directed plan" or "ERISA Sec. 404(c) plan." Under this type of plan, a participant or beneficiary who exercises such control is not deemed to be a fiduciary. Moreover, no person who is otherwise a fiduciary is liable under the fiduciary responsibility rules for any loss or for any breach that results from the participant's or beneficiary's exercise of control over his or her account.

In order to qualify as a participant-directed account under ERISA Sec. 404(c), a plan must give participants the opportunity to choose from a broad range of investment alternatives, receive investment instruction with appropriate frequency, diversify investments, and obtain sufficient information to make informed investment decisions. Fiduciaries are not relieved of their duty to consider the prudence of the investment alternatives made available to participants under the plan and to maintain oversight over the investment options.

Employers may choose, but are not required, to provide investment education to employees maintaining participant-directed accounts. Certain types of investment information may be provided by employers without incurring liability as investment advisers (DOL Reg. § 2509.96-1, also known as DOL Interpretive Bulletin 96-1). These include:

- plan information;
- general financial and investment information;
- asset allocation models; and
- interactive investment materials.

Many sponsoring employers currently offer investment education materials to participants in 401(k) plans. For example, ninety-one percent of large companies provided investment education to 401(k) plan participants in 2005, according to a recent survey conducted by Hewitt Associates, a benefits administration and consulting firm. In contrast, 37 percent offered participants access to outside investment advisory services. Although providing investment education materials has become very widespread, many employers have been more reluctant to offer specific investment advice to participants for fear of running afoul of ERISA's fiduciary liability rules.

NEW LAW EXPLAINED

Requirements for prohibited transaction exemption for investment advice.— *Summary.* The Pension Protection Act of 2006 adds a new category of prohibited transaction exemption (PTE) under the Code and ERISA in connection with providing investment advice through an "eligible investment advice arrangement" to participants and beneficiaries of 401(k) plans and other defined contribution plans who direct the investment of their accounts under the plan, and to beneficiaries of IRAs.

> **Comment:** The investment advice provisions relating to IRAs also apply to health savings accounts (HSAs), Archer medical savings accounts (MSAs), and Coverdell education savings accounts (ESAs). References to IRAs include these other arrangements as well.

Under the new PTE, qualified "fiduciary advisers" can offer personally tailored professional investment advice to help employees manage their 401(k) plans, individual retirement accounts (IRAs), and other individual account plans. The fiduciary adviser may be affiliated with the investment funds offered in a 401(k) plan, but the advisor must meet disclosure, qualification, and other self-dealing safeguards. Employers or plan sponsors are not obligated to monitor the specific advice given to any particular participant or beneficiary, though they retain the responsibility to prudently select and monitor advice providers. Fiduciary advisers are personally liable for the investment advice that they provide.

Individualized investment advice may be provided to 401(k) plan participants without running afoul of the prohibited transaction rules, if fiduciary advisers provide investment advice under an "eligible investment advice arrangement." Such an arrangement requires that investment advice is provided (1) through an unbiased computer model that has been certified and audited by an independent third party, or (2) by fiduciary advisers whose investment advice service fees and commissions do not vary depending on the investment option chosen by the participant.

The Secretary of Labor, in consultation with the Secretary of the Treasury, is directed to determine by December 31, 2007, whether investment advice provided through a computer model is feasible for IRAs.

General rules for investment advice exemption. Under the Pension Act, qualified "fiduciary advisers" can provide investment advice to 401(k) and other plan participants without running afoul of the prohibited transaction rules under the Code and ERISA. Thus, if the applicable requirements are satisfied, the following are exempt from prohibited transaction treatment:

- providing investment advice to a participant or beneficiary regarding any security or property available as a plan investment;
- an investment transaction (i.e., a sale, acquisition, or holding of a security or other property) pursuant to the investment advice; and
- the direct or indirect receipt of fees or other compensation by a fiduciary adviser or its affiliates (or any employee, agent, or registered representative of the fiduciary or adviser or its affiliates) in connection with the providing investment advice or

NEW LAW EXPLAINED

an investment transaction pursuant to the investment advice (Code Sec. 4975(d)(17) and ERISA Sec. 408(b)(14), as added by the Pension Act).

A number of stringent safeguards must be met (see below) in order to be eligible for the prohibited transaction exemption for investment advice.

> **Comment:** The prohibited transaction exemption provided for investment advice does not alter, in any way, any existing individual or class prohibited transaction exemption provided by statute or by administrative action (Act Sec. 601(c) of the Pension Act).

Eligible investment advice arrangements. The exemptions provided under the investment advice provision apply in connection with a fiduciary adviser providing investment advice under an "eligible investment advice arrangement." An eligible investment advice arrangement is an arrangement that either (1) provides that any fees (including any commission or compensation) received by the fiduciary adviser for investment advice or with respect to an investment transaction with respect to plan assets do not vary depending on the basis of any investment option selected, or (2) uses a computer model under an investment advice program as described below in connection with the provision of investment advice to a participant or beneficiary (Code Sec. 4975(f)(8)(B) and ERISA Sec. 408(g)(3), as added by the Pension Act). To qualify as an eligible investment advice arrangement, certain audit, disclosure, record retention and other rules (see below) must also be met.

In the case of an eligible investment advice arrangement with respect to a defined contribution plan, the arrangement must be expressly authorized by a plan fiduciary other than (1) the person offering the investment advice program, (2) any person providing investment options under the plan, or (3) any affiliate of (1) or (2) (Joint Committee on Taxation, Technical Explanation of the Pension Protection Act of 2006 (JCX-38-06)).

Fiduciary advisers. For purposes of the provision, "fiduciary adviser" is defined as a person who is a fiduciary of the plan by reason of the provision of investment advice to a participant or beneficiary and who is also:

(1) registered as an investment adviser under the Investment Advisers Act of 1940 or under laws of the state in which the fiduciary maintains its principal office and place of business;

(2) a bank, a similar financial institution supervised by the United States or a state, or a savings association (as defined under the Federal Deposit Insurance Act), but only if the advice is provided through a trust department that is subject to periodic examination and review by federal or state banking authorities;

(3) an insurance company qualified to do business under state law;

(4) registered as a broker or dealer under the Securities Exchange Act of 1934;

(5) an affiliate of any of the preceding; or

(6) an employee, agent or registered representative of any of the preceding who satisfies the requirements of applicable insurance, banking and securities laws relating to the provision of advice (Code Sec. 4975(f)(8)(J) and ERISA Sec. 408(g)(11), as added by the Pension Act).

NEW LAW EXPLAINED

> **Comment:** A person who develops the computer model or markets the investment advice program or computer model is treated as a person who is a plan fiduciary by reason of the provision of investment advice and is treated as a fiduciary adviser. However, the Secretary of Labor may prescribe rules under which only one fiduciary adviser may elect to be treated as a plan fiduciary (Code Sec. 4975(f)(8)(J) and ERISA Sec. 408(g)(11)(A), as added by the Pension Act).

"Affiliate" means an affiliated person as defined under section 2(a)(3) of the Investment Company Act of 1940. "Registered representative" means a person described in section 3(a)(18) of the Securities Exchange Act of 1934 or a person described in section 202(a)(17) of the Investment Advisers Act of 1940.

Computer model for investment advice. As mentioned above, an eligible investment advice arrangement can be an arrangement that uses a qualified computer model under an "investment advice program" (Code Sec. 4975(f)(8)(C)(i) and ERISA Sec. 408(g)(3)(A), as added by the Pension Act). The computer model must:

(1) apply generally accepted investment theories that take into account the historic returns of different asset classes over defined periods of time,

(2) use relevant information about the participant, which may include age, life expectancy, retirement age, risk tolerance, other assets or sources of income, and preferences as to certain types of investments,

(3) use prescribed objective criteria to provide asset allocation portfolios comprised of investment options available under the plan,

(4) operate in a manner that is not biased in favor of investments offered by the fiduciary adviser or a person with a material affiliation or contractual relationship with the fiduciary adviser, and

(5) take into account all investment options under the plan in specifying how a participant's account balance should be invested, and not be inappropriately weighted with respect to any investment option (Code Sec. 4975(f)(8)(C)(ii) and ERISA Sec. 408(g)(3)(B), as added by the Pension Act).

The computer model must be certified by an "eligible investment expert" before it is used. The expert must certify, in accordance with any regulations issued by the Secretary of Labor, that the computer model meets the requirements of the law. If, under the regulations, there are material changes to the computer model, a new certification must be obtained for the modified model. An eligible investment expert is any person who meets the requirements of the Secretary of Labor, and who does not bear any material affiliation or contractual relationship with any investment adviser or a related person (or any employee, agent, or registered representative of the investment adviser or related person) (Code Sec. 4975(f)(8)(C)(iii) and ERISA Sec. 408(g)(3)(C), as added by the Pension Act).

The advice provided by any investment advice program must be exclusive. In other words, it must be the only advice generated by the computer model under the program, and it must occur solely at the direction of the participant or beneficiary. A participant or beneficiary may request other investment advice, but only if the request has not been solicited by any person connected with carrying out the eligible investment advice arrangement (Code Sec. 4975(f)(8)(C)(iv) and ERISA Sec. 408(g)(3)(D), as added by the Pension Act).

NEW LAW EXPLAINED

Feasibility of using computer models for IRAs and similar plans. The Secretary of Labor, in consultation with the Secretary of the Treasury, is directed to gather information to determine whether investment advice provided through a computer model would be feasible for individual retirement accounts and individual retirement annuities (IRAs), Archer medical savings accounts (MSAs), health savings accounts (HSAs), or Coverdell education savings accounts (ESAs). Information is to be gathered, at a minimum, from the top 50 trustees (based on total assets) of these types of plans and from others who offer computer model investment advice programs based on non-proprietary products. The collected information must include information for the current and previous year on the computer modeling capabilities of those who offer such programs. In addition, the collected information on modeling capabilities must include such capability for investment accounts (Act Sec. 601(b)(3)(A) of the Pension Act).

Thus, the Secretary of Labor, in consultation with the Secretary of the Treasury, must determine if there is any computer model investment advice program that (1) utilizes relevant information about the account beneficiary, which may include age, life expectancy, retirement age, risk tolerance, other assets or sources of income, and preferences as to certain types of investments, (2) takes into account the full range of investments, including equities and bonds, in determining the options for the investment portfolio of the account beneficiary, and (3) allows the account beneficiary, in directing the investment of assets, sufficient flexibility in obtaining advice to evaluate and select investment options (Act Sec. 601(b)(3)(B) of the Pension Act).

> **Planning Note:** The Secretary of Labor must report the results of the feasibility study on the use of the computer model for IRA investment advice to Congress no later than December 31, 2007 (Act Sec. 603(b)(3)(B) of the Pension Act).

Certifying computer models for IRAs. The computer model program certification requirements that apply to employer sponsored retirement plans will not apply to IRAs and similar plans until the date the Secretary of Labor certifies that there is a computer model investment advice program that meets the feasibility requirements for those plans, as discussed above (Act Sec. 601(b)(3)(C)(i) of the Pension Act).

If the Secretary of Labor determines that an appropriate model is not available for these plans, the Secretary is directed to grant a class exemption from the prohibited transaction rules that protects account holders from biased advice without requiring fee-leveling or a computer model. The exemption will not be available to any person that fails to respond within 60 days to the Secretary's request for information about the feasibility of computer models for these plans, unless the failure was due to reasonable cause and not willful neglect (Act Sec. 601(b)(3)(C)(ii) of the Pension Act). If the Secretary grants the class exemption, and subsequently certifies a computer model program, the exemptions will cease to apply after the later of (1) two years after that certification, or (2) three years after the first day the exemption took effect (Act Sec. 601(b)(3)(D)(i) of the Pension Act).

Anyone may request a certification for a computer model investment advice program. The Secretary must make a decision about certifying the computer model investment advice program within 90 days of the request. If the certification is denied, the Secretary must provide notice of, and reasons for, the denial within 10

NEW LAW EXPLAINED

days to the House Committees on Ways and Means and on Education and the Workforce, and the Senate Committees on Finance and on Health, Education, Labor, and Pensions (Act Sec. 601(b)(3)(D)(ii) of the Pension Act).

Annual audits. A qualified independent auditor must conduct an annual audit of the investment advice arrangement to ensure that it meets the requirements of the new law (Code Sec. 4975(f)(8)(E)(i) and ERISA Sec. 408(g)(5), as added by the Pension Act). The specific findings of the audit must be provided in a written report to the fiduciary that authorized use of the arrangement (Code Sec. 4975(f)(8)(E)(i)(II) and ERISA Sec. 408(g)(5), as added by the Pension Act).

An auditor is deemed "independent" if it is not related to (1) the person offering the arrangement to the plan and (2) any person providing investment options under the plan (Code Sec. 4975(f)(8)(E)(iii) and ERISA Sec. 408(g)(5), as added by the Pension Act). An independent auditor is qualified to conduct an audit if written assurance is provided that he or she has the proper technical training or experience and proficiency (Code Sec. 4975(f)(8)(E)(i) and ERISA Sec. 408(g)(5), as added by the Pension Act).

For Code purposes only, in the case of IRAs, Archer MSAs, HSAs and Coverdell education savings accounts, in lieu of annual audits conducted by independent auditors, audits must be conducted at such times and in such manner as the Secretary of Labor may determine (Code Sec. 4975(f)(8)(E)(ii), as added by the Pension Act).

Notice and disclosure. Before investment advice is given about securities or other property offered as an investment option, the fiduciary adviser is required to provide to a participant or beneficiary written notification (which may be in electronic form), including information related to:

(1) the role of any related party (i.e., any party having a material affiliation or contractual relationship to the financial adviser) with respect to the development of the investment advice program and the selection of available investment options under the plan;

(2) the past performance and historical rates of return for each available investment option offered under the plan;

(3) any fees or other compensation to be received by the financial adviser or its affiliates (including any compensation provided by a third party) (a) with respect to the provision of the advice or (b) in connection with the sale, acquisition or holding of the security or other property (investment transactions);

> **Comment:** The Secretary of Labor is directed to issue a model form for the disclosure of fees or other compensation (Code Sec. 4975(f)(8)(H)(ii) and ERISA Sec. 408(g)(8)(B), as added by the Pension Act).

(4) any material affiliation or contractual relationship of the financial adviser or its affiliate in the security or other property involved in the investment transaction;

(5) the manner and circumstances under which any participant or beneficiary information will be used or disclosed;

NEW LAW EXPLAINED

(6) the kinds of services provided by the fiduciary adviser with respect to the advice given;

(7) the adviser's status as a fiduciary of the plan; and

(8) the ability of the recipient of the advice to enter into a separate arrangement with another adviser that has no material affiliation with, and receives no compensation with respect to, the security or other property (Code Sec. 4975(f)(8)(F)(i) and ERISA Sec. 408(g)(6)(A), as added by the Pension Act).

The information described above must be maintained in accurate form by the fiduciary adviser at all times while the advisory services are being provided to the participant or beneficiary. Further, the information must be provided to the advice recipient, without charge, at least annually or upon request, as well as at a time reasonably contemporaneous to any material change to the information provided. The notification must be conspicuous and clearly written, designed so as to be understood by the average plan participant, and sufficiently accurate and comprehensive so as to reasonably inform participants and beneficiaries of the required information (Code Sec. 4975(f)(8)(F)(ii) and (H)(i) and ERISA Sec. 408(g)(6)(B) and (8)(A), as added by the Pension Act).

Investment transactions. Rules are provided with respect to the sale, acquisition or holding of the security or other property (investment transactions) (Code Sec. 4975(f)(8)(G) and ERISA Sec. 408(g)(7), as added by the Pension Act). As noted above, the financial adviser is required to disclose any fees or other compensation the adviser or its affiliates are to receive in connection with an investment transaction. In addition, the adviser must provide the necessary disclosure in accordance with all relevant securities laws. Further, any compensation received by the adviser (or its affiliate) in connection with an investment transaction must be reasonable. Finally, the terms of the investment transaction must be no less favorable to the plan than an arm's length transaction would be.

Maintaining evidence of compliance. A record retention rule applies to fiduciary advisers under both the Code and ERISA. The fiduciary adviser must maintain any records necessary for determining whether the prohibited transaction exemption requirements were met for at least six years after providing the investment advice (Code Sec. 4975(f)(8)(I) and ERISA Sec. 409(g)(9), as added by the Pension Act).

> **Comment:** Under the record retention requirements, a prohibited transaction is not considered to have occurred solely because required records were lost or destroyed before the end of the six-year period due to circumstances beyond the fiduciary adviser's control (Code Sec. 4975(f)(8)(I) and ERISA Sec. 409(g)(9), as added by the Pension Act).

Fiduciary rules and investment advice. Subject to certain requirements, an employer or other person who is a plan fiduciary, other than a fiduciary adviser, is not treated as failing to meet the fiduciary requirements of ERISA solely by reason of providing investment advice as permitted under the provision or by contracting for or otherwise arranging for the advice. This rule applies if: (1) the advice is provided under an arrangement between the employer or plan fiduciary and the fiduciary adviser for the fiduciary adviser to provide investment advice as permitted under the provision;

NEW LAW EXPLAINED

(2) the terms of the arrangement require compliance by the fiduciary adviser with the requirements of the provision; and (3) the terms of the arrangement include a written acknowledgement by the fiduciary adviser that the fiduciary adviser is a plan fiduciary with regard to providing the advice (ERISA Sec. 408(g)(1), as added by the Pension Act; Joint Committee on Taxation, Technical Explanation of the Pension Protection Act of 2006 (JCX-38-06)).

The provision does not exempt the employer or a plan fiduciary from fiduciary responsibility under ERISA for the prudent selection and periodic review of a fiduciary adviser who provides investment advice pursuant to an arrangement with the employer or plan fiduciary. The employer or plan fiduciary does not have the duty to monitor the specific investment advice given by a fiduciary adviser. The provision also makes it clear that nothing in the fiduciary responsibility provisions of ERISA is to be construed to preclude using plan assets to pay for reasonable expenses in providing investment advice (Joint Committee on Taxation, Technical Explanation of the Pension Protection Act of 2006 (JCX-38-06)).

Interaction with existing PTEs. Any prohibited transaction exemption under Code Sec. 4975(d) and ERISA Sec. 408(g)(7) provided by the Pension Act does not in any way change any current individual or class exemptions provided by statute or administrative action (Act Sec. 601(c) of the Pension Act).

▶ **Effective date.** This provision is generally effective with respect to investment advice provided after December 31, 2006 (Act Sec. 601(a)(3) and 601(b)(4) of the Pension Protection Act of 2006). The provision relating to the Secretary of Labor's feasibility study for using computer models for IRAs is effective on August 17, 2006 (Act Sec. 601(b)(3)(E) of the Pension Act).

Law source: Law at ¶5305 and ¶7123. Committee Report at ¶10,420.

— Act Sec. 601(a)(1) of the Pension Protection Act of 2006, adding ERISA Sec. 408(b)(14);

— Act Sec. 601(a)(2), adding ERISA Sec. 408(g);

— Act Sec. 601(a)(3), providing the effective date;

— Act Sec. 601(b)(1), amending Code Sec. 4975(d)(15) and (16), and adding Code Sec. 4975(d)(17);

— Act Sec. 601(b)(2), adding Code Sec. 4975(f)(8);

— Act Sec. 601(b)(3);

— Act Sec. 601(b)(4), providing the effective date;

— Act Sec. 601(c).

Reporter references: For further information, consult the following CCH reporters.

— Pension Plan Guide, ¶4415, ¶4420, ¶4485 and ¶4605

— Standard Federal Tax Reporter, 2006FED ¶34,410.03

— Tax Research Consultant, RETIRE: 60,252.05

— Federal Tax Guide, 2006FTG ¶11,045 and ¶21,245

¶630 Amendments Relating to Prohibited Transactions

SUMMARY OF NEW LAW

Exemptions to the prohibited transaction rules are allowed for block trading, regulated electronic communications networks, service providers who are not fiduciaries with respect to the assets involved, foreign exchange transactions, and cross trading.

BACKGROUND

Transactions between a "disqualified person" and a qualified plan may be subject to a two-tiered excise tax on prohibited transactions. The excise tax is imposed on the disqualified person who participated in the prohibited transaction for each year in a tax period (Code Sec. 4975(a)). The Internal Revenue Code and the Employee Retirement Income Security Act of 1974 (P.L. 93-406) (ERISA) specifically exempt certain transactions from the excise tax (Code Sec. 4975(c)(3); Code Sec. 4975(d); ERISA Sec. 404(c)). Additionally, with certain exceptions, administrative exemptions may be granted by the Department of Labor (DOL) (Code Sec. 4975(c)(2)). The statutory exemptions allowed under Code Sec. 4975 are, in most cases, subject to certain qualifications. Parallel exemptions exist under Sec. 408 of ERISA.

Coordination of Departments of Treasury and Labor. After the enactment of ERISA, both the Department of the Treasury and the Department of Labor (DOL) had regulatory authority over many of the same substantive provisions. In 1978, the IRS and the DOL signed an agreement (Reorganization Plan No. 4 of 1978 (43 FR 47713); Executive Order No. 12108, December 28, 1978 (44 FR 1065)). Under the agreement, with certain exceptions, the DOL has the authority to issue all regulations, rulings, opinions and exemptions under Code Sec. 4975 (Sec. 102, ERISA Reorganization Plan).

NEW LAW EXPLAINED

Exemption for block trading.—To achieve better execution, reduce costs and provide for more efficient plan asset transactions, pension assets may be included in block trades (Code Sec. 4975(d)(18) and ERISA Sec. 408(b)(15), as added by the Pension Protection Act of 2006). This exemption from the prohibited transaction rules includes any transaction involving the purchase or sale of securities between a plan and a party in interest (other than a fiduciary with respect to the plan) if:

(1) the transaction involves a block trade;

(2) at the time of the transaction, the interest of the plan (together with the interests of any other plans maintained by the same plan sponsor) does not exceed 10 percent of the aggregate size of the block trade;

(3) the terms of the transaction, including the price, are at least as favorable to the plan as an arm's-length transaction; and

NEW LAW EXPLAINED

(4) the compensation associated with the purchase and sale is not greater than an arm's-length transaction.

A "block trade" is any trade of at least 10,000 shares or with a market value of at least $200,000 that will be allocated across two or more unrelated client accounts of a fiduciary (Code Sec. 4975(f)(9) and ERISA Sec. 408(b)(15)(B), as added by the Pension Act).

Electronic communication network. There is also an exemption from the prohibited transaction rules for any transaction involving the purchase and sale of securities between a plan and a party in interest if:

(1) the transaction is executed through an electronic communication network, alternative trading system, or similar execution system or trading venue subject to the applicable federal or foreign regulating entity;

(2) either:

   (a) the transaction is made under rules designed to match purchases and sales at the best price available through the execution system in accordance with the applicable rules of the Securities and Exchange Commission or other related governmental authority, or

   (b) neither the execution system nor the parties to the transaction take into account the identity of the parties in the execution of trades;

(3) the price and compensation associated with the purchase and sale is at least as favorable as an arm's-length transaction;

(4) if the party in interest has an ownership interest in the system or venue, the system or venue has been authorized by the plan sponsor or other independent fiduciary; and

(5) not less than 30 days prior to the initial transaction executed through any system or venue, a plan fiduciary is provided written or electronic notice of the execution (Code Sec. 4975(d)(19) and ERISA Sec. 408(b)(16), as added by the Pension Act).

Service providers. An exemption is added for service providers who are not fiduciaries with respect to the assets involved (Code Sec. 4975(d)(20) and ERISA Sec. 408(b)(17), as added by the Pension Act). The exemption applies only if, in connection with a sale or exchange, lease, extension of credit, or transfer of plan income or assets transaction, the plan receives no less, nor pays no more, than adequation consideration.

"Adequate consideration" means:

(1) For a security where there is a generally recognized market, the price of the security on a national securities exchange. If the security is not traded on such an exchange, a price not less favorable to the plan than the offering price for the security as established by the current bid and asked prices quoted by persons independent of the issuer and of the party in interest. Factors such as the size of the transaction and marketability of the security must be taken into account for all securities.

NEW LAW EXPLAINED

(2) For an asset other than a security where there is a generally recognized market, the fair market value of the asset as determined in good faith by a fiduciary (Code Sec. 4975(f)(10) and ERISA Sec. 408(b)(17)(B), as added by the Pension Act).

Foreign exchange transactions. An exemption from the prohibited transaction rules has been added for certain foreign exchange transactions (Code Sec. 4975(d)(21) and ERISA Sec. 408(b)(18), as added by the Pension Act). The exemption applies to any foreign exchange transaction between a bank or broker-dealer (or affiliate of either), and a plan, where the bank or broker-dealer is a trustee, custodian, fiduciary, or other party in interest, if:

(1) the transaction is in connection with the purchase, holding, or sale of securities or other investment assets;

(2) at the time the foreign exchange transaction is entered into, the terms of the transaction are not less favorable to the plan than the terms generally available in comparable arm's-length foreign exchange transactions, or the terms provided by the bank or broker-dealer in comparable foreign exchange transactions;

(3) the exchange rate used by the bank or broker-dealer for an exchange does not deviate by more or less than three percent from the inter-bank bid and asked rates at the time of the transaction as displayed on an independent service that reports rates of exchange in the foreign currency market for the currency; and

(4) the bank or broker-dealer does not have investment discretion, or provide investment advice, with respect to the transaction.

Definition of plan asset. The term "plan assets" means plan assets as defined by any prescribed regulations (ERISA Sec. 3(42), as added by the Pension Act). However, under the regulations, the assets of any entity will not be treated as plan assets if, immediately after the most recent acquisition of any equity interest in the entity, less than 25 percent of the total value of each class of equity interest in the entity is held by benefit plan investors.

The value of any equity interest held by a person, other than a benefit plan investor, who has discretionary authority or control with respect to the assets of the entity or any person who provides investment advice for a fee with respect to the assets, or any affiliate of the person, will be disregarded for purposes of the 25-percent threshold.

Cross trading. There is an exemption from the prohibited transaction rules for any transaction involving the purchase and sale of a security between a plan and any other account managed by the same investment manager if:

(1) the transaction is a purchase or sale, for no consideration other than cash payment against prompt delivery of a security for which market quotations are readily available;

(2) the transaction is made at the independent current market price of the security;

(3) no brokerage commission, fee, or other remuneration is paid in connection with the transaction;

NEW LAW EXPLAINED

(4) a fiduciary for each plan participating in the transaction authorizes in advance of any cross trades the investment manager to engage in cross trades at the investment manager's discretion;

(5) each plan participating in the transaction has assets of at least $100,000,000, except that if the assets of a plan are invested in a master trust containing the assets of plans maintained by employers in the same controlled group the master trust has assets of at least $100,000,000;

(6) the investment manager provides to the plan fiduciary who authorized cross trading a quarterly report detailing all cross trades executed by the investment manager in which the plan participated during the quarter;

(7) the investment manager does not base its fee schedule on the plan's consent to cross trading, and no other service is conditioned on the plan's consent to cross trading;

(8) the investment manager has adopted, and cross trades are made in accordance with, written cross-trading policies and procedures;

(9) the investment manager has designated an individual responsible for periodically reviewing these purchases and sales to ensure compliance with the written policies and procedures (Code Sec. 4975(d)(22) and ERISA Sec. 408(b)(19), as added by the Pension Act).

> **Comment:** Following the review, the individual must issue an annual written report, signed under penalty of perjury, describing the steps performed during the review, the level of compliance, and any specific instances of non-compliance. In addition, the report must notify the plan fiduciary of the plan's right to terminate participation in the cross-trading program at any time.

Bonding relief. ERISA's bonding rules are amended to reflect the regulation of broker-dealers and investment advisers under securities law (Act Sec. 611(b) of the Pension Act). No bond is required of any entity that is registered as a broker or a dealer under section 15(b) of the Securities Exchange Act of 1934 if the broker or dealer is subject to the fidelity bond requirements of a self-regulatory organization as defined under that act (ERISA Sec. 412(a), as amended by the Pension Act).

▶ **Effective date.** The provision applies to transactions occuring after August 17, 2006 (Act Sec. 611(h)(1) of the Pension Protection Act of 2006). The bonding relief provisions apply to plan years beginning after August 17, 2006 (Act Sec. 611(h)(2) of the Pension Act).

Law source: Law at ¶5305 and ¶7126. Committee Report at ¶10,430, ¶10,440, ¶10,450, ¶10,460, ¶10,470, ¶10,480 and ¶10,490.

— Act Sec. 611(a) of the Pension Protection Act of 2006, adding ERISA Sec. 408(b)(15) and Code Sec. 4975(d)(18);

— Act Sec. 611(b), amending ERISA Sec. 412(a);

— Act Sec. 611(c), adding ERISA Sec. 408(b)(16) and Code Sec. 4975(d)(19);

— Act Sec. 611(d), adding ERISA Sec. 408(b)(17) and Code Sec. 4975(d)(20);

— Act Sec. 611(e), adding ERISA Sec. 408(b)(18) and amending Code Sec. 4975(d)(21);

— Act Sec. 611(f), adding ERISA Sec. 3(42);

NEW LAW EXPLAINED

— Act Sec. 611(g), adding ERISA Sec. 408(b)(19) and Code Sec. 4975(d)(22);

— Act Sec. 611(h), providing the effective date.

Reporter references: For further information, consult the following CCH reporters.

— Pension Plan Guide, ¶4435, ¶4540, ¶4620 and ¶5945

— Standard Federal Tax Reporter, 2006FED ¶34,410.03

— Tax Research Consultant, RETIRE: 60,252.05

— Federal Tax Guide, 2006FTG ¶11,045 and ¶21,245

¶635 Correction Period for Securities and Commodities

SUMMARY OF NEW LAW

The correction period for prohibited transactions involving securities and commodities is 14 days after the party discovers or should have discovered that the transaction was prohibited.

BACKGROUND

Transactions between a "disqualified person" and a qualified plan may be subject to a two-tiered excise tax on prohibited transactions. The excise tax is imposed on the disqualified person who participated in the prohibited transaction for each year in a tax period (Code Sec. 4975(a)). The Internal Revenue Code and the Employee Retirement Income Security Act of 1974 (P.L. 93-406) (ERISA) specifically exempt certain transactions from the excise tax (Code Sec. 4975(c)(3) and (d); ERISA Sec. 404(c)). Additionally, with certain exceptions, administrative exemptions may be granted by the Department of Labor (Code Sec. 4975(c)(2)).

An additional second-tier excise tax is equal to 100 percent of the "amount involved" and is imposed if the transaction is not corrected within the tax period (Code Sec. 4975(a) and (b); Reg. § 54.4975-1). The payment of the tax does not relieve disqualified persons of their duty to the plan or of their obligation to correct the transaction.

NEW LAW EXPLAINED

Correction period amended.—A 14-day correction period has been added for certain transactions that occur by mistake between a plan and a party in interest. The transaction must be in connection with the acquisition, holding, or disposition of a security or commodity (Code Sec. 4975(d)(23) and ERISA Sec. 408(b)(20), as added by the Pension Protection Act of 2006).

NEW LAW EXPLAINED

The correction period is the 14-day period beginning on the date on which the disqualified person, fiduciary or party in interest discovers, or reasonably should have discovered, that the transaction would constitute a prohibited transaction (Code Sec. 4975(f)(11) and ERISA Sec. 408(b)(20)(D), as added by the Pension Act).

However, a correction does not apply:

(1) to any transaction between a plan and a plan sponsor or its affiliates that involves the acquisition or sale of an employer security or the acquisition, sale, or lease of employer real property, or

(2) to prohibited transactions if, at the time the transaction occurs, the disqualified person, fiduciary or party in interest knew, or reasonably should have known, that the transaction would constitute a violation.

If the prohibited transaction has been corrected, then no tax should be assessed on the transaction. If tax has been assessed, then the assessment should be abated. If the tax has been collected, it should be credited or refunded as an overpayment.

To "correct" a transaction means:

(1) to undo the transaction to the extent possible and to make good to the plan or affected account any losses resulting from the transaction, and

(2) to restore to the plan or affected account any profits made through the use of assets of the plan (Code Sec. 4975(f)(11)(D)(iii) and ERISA Sec. 408(b)(20)(E)(iii), as added by the Pension Act).

▶ **Effective date.** The provision applies to any transaction which the fiduciary or disqualified person discovers, or reasonably should have discovered, after August 17, 2006, constitutes a prohibited transaction (Act Sec. 612(c) of the Pension Protection Act of 2006).

Law source: Law at ¶5305 and ¶7129. Committee Report at ¶10,500.

— Act Sec. 612(a) of the Pension Protection Act of 2006, adding ERISA Sec. 408(b)(20)(A)–(E);

— Act Sec. 612(b), adding Code Sec. 4975(d)(23) and Code Sec. 4975(f)(11);

— Act Sec. 612(c), providing the effective date.

Reporter references: For further information, consult the following CCH reporters.

— Pension Plan Guide, ¶4565

— Standard Federal Tax Reporter, 2006FED ¶34,410.01

— Tax Research Consultant, RETIRE: 48,254

— Federal Tax Guide, 2006FTG ¶11,045 and ¶21,245

FIDUCIARY LIABILITY

¶640 Fiduciary Liability During Blackout Periods

SUMMARY OF NEW LAW

For plans that give participants and beneficiaries control over the investment of assets in their accounts, plan fiduciaries may become subject to liability during periods when participants' rights to direct investments under the plan are suspended, unless the suspension, or "blackout period," meets the requirements of this provision. Plan fiduciaries will have relief from potential liability if they make qualified changes in investment options in accordance with the requirements of this provision.

BACKGROUND

A pension plan may provide for individual accounts and permit a participant or beneficiary to exercise control over assets in his or her account. Under these participant-directed plans, a participant or beneficiary who exercises such control is not deemed to be a fiduciary. Moreover, no person who is otherwise a fiduciary is liable under the fiduciary responsibility rules for any loss or for any breach that results from the participant's or beneficiary's exercise of control over his or her account.

NEW LAW EXPLAINED

Blackout period exception to relief from fiduciary liability.—The provision creates a new exception to the relief from fiduciary liability that ERISA Sec. 404(c) grants to fiduciaries under circumstances where the plan permits participants and beneficiaries to exercise control over the investment of assets in their accounts. Such relief will not be available under circumstances where a participant or beneficiary is unable to direct the investment of assets due to a suspension of this right by the plan sponsor or fiduciary (a "blackout period"), which does not meet ERISA Sec. 101(i)(7) requirements (ERISA Sec. 404(c)(1), as amended by the Pension Protection Act of 2006).

Comment: The ERISA Sec. 101(i)(7) definition of "blackout period":

- includes a period of more than three consecutive business days during which the ability of plan participants or beneficiaries to direct their plan account investments or obtain loans or distributions to which they are otherwise entitled is temporarily suspended or restricted; and
- excludes certain permissible suspensions, limitations or restrictions on the right to direct account investments pursuant to, for instance, qualified domestic relations orders (QDROs) or regularly scheduled suspensions under previously disclosed plan terms.

NEW LAW EXPLAINED

Qualified changes in investment options will not cause liability to accrue.—If a "qualified change in investment options" is made to a self-directed plan, fiduciary liability will not accrue to plan administrators or other fiduciaries as long as:

- at least thirty and not more than sixty days prior to the effective date of the change, the administrator furnishes written notice of the change to the participants and beneficiaries containing a comparison of the existing and new investment options and a description of the default investments that will be made absent contrary instructions from the participant or beneficiary;
- the participant or beneficiary has not provided the plan, prior to the effective date of the change, investment instructions that are contrary to the proposed reallocation of investments in their account; and
- the investment of the participant or beneficiary's account immediately before the effective date of the proposed reallocation of investments was the result of the participant or beneficiary exercising control over the investment of assets in the account (ERISA Sec. 404(c)(4)(C), as amended by the Pension Act).

Comment: The term "qualified change in investment options" means a change in the investment options, offered to individual account plan participants or beneficiaries, under which account assets are reallocated among new investment options that are reasonably similar in risk and rate of return characteristics to the options offered prior to the change (ERISA Sec. 404(c)(4)(B), as amended by the Pension Act).

Planning Note: Not later than one year after August 17, 2006, the date of enactment, the Secretary of Labor is to issue interim final regulations providing guidance, including safe harbors, on how plan sponsors or other affected fiduciaries can satisfy their fiduciary responsibilities during any blackout period (Joint Committee on Taxation, Technical Explanation of the Pension Protection Act of 2006 (JCX-38-06)).

▶ **Effective date.**

(1) *In general.*—The amendments made by this section shall apply to plan years beginning after December 31, 2007 (Act Sec. 621(b)(1) of the Pension Protection Act of 2006).

(2) *Special rule for collectively bargained agreements.*—In the case of a plan maintained pursuant to one or more collective bargaining agreements between employee representatives and one or more employers ratified on or before August 17, 2006, the date of the enactment of this Act, paragraph (1) shall be applied to benefits pursuant to, and individuals covered by, any such agreement by substituting for "December 31, 2007" the earlier of—

(A) the later of—

(i) December 31, 2008, or

(ii) the date on which the last of such collective bargaining agreements terminates (determined without regard to any extension thereof after August 17, 2006), or

(B) December 31, 2009 (Act Sec. 621(b)(2) of the Pension Protection Act of 2006).

NEW LAW EXPLAINED

Law source: Law at ¶7132. Committee Report at ¶10,510.

— Act Sec. 621(a)(1)(A) of the Pension Protection Act of 2006, amending ERISA Sec. 404(c)(1);

— Act Sec. 621(a)(1)(B), amending ERISA Sec. 404(c)(1)(A)(ii);

— Act Sec. 621(a)(1)(C), adding ERISA Sec. 404(c)(1)(B) and (C);

— Act Sec. 621(a)(2), adding ERISA Sec. 404(c)(4); and

— Act Sec. 621(b), providing the effective date.

Reporter references: For further information, consult the following CCH reporters.

— Pension Plan Guide, ¶4325, ¶4485, ¶7526B and ¶7526C

— Standard Federal Tax Reporter, 2006FED ¶17,515.032

¶645 Increased Maximum Bond Amount for Plans Holding Employer Securities

SUMMARY OF NEW LAW

The maximum bond amount required of fiduciaries of employee benefit plans holding employer securities is raised from $500,000 to $1,000,000.

BACKGROUND

ERISA requires every fiduciary and plan official of an employee benefit plan, with certain exceptions, to be bonded. The bonding requirement is intended to protect employee benefit plan participants against losses resulting from fraud or dishonesty on the part of plan officials who handle plan assets. Absent a qualifying bond, a plan official is prohibited from receiving, handling, or otherwise exercising control of any funds or property of an employee benefit plan. Qualifying bonds must have a corporate surety which is an acceptable surety on federal bonds and meet certain other requirements. The amount of the bond required is fixed annually based upon the amount of funds handled by the plan.

NEW LAW EXPLAINED

Maximum bond amount raised.—For the bonds required of fiduciaries of employee benefit plans with investments in employer securities, the maximum bond amount is raised from $500,000 to $1,000,000 (ERISA Sec. 412(a), as amended by the Pension Protection Act of 2006).

NEW LAW EXPLAINED

> **Comment:** Prior to the enactment of this provision, the maximum bond amount for all employee benefit plans had remained unchanged since 1962, when it was enacted under a predecessor law to ERISA (Senate Finance Committee report 107-242 on the National Employee Savings and Trust Equity Guarantee Act (NESTEG)).

While investments in employer securities can be beneficial for participants, they can also entail additional risk for participants in a plan sponsored by an employer who is experiencing financial distress. Under the revised provision, in recognition of the additional risk assumed by plans investing in employer securities, the bond amount for such plans must be:

- not less than 10 percent of the funds handled, but at least $1,000, and
- not more than $1,000,000, unless the Secretary of Labor prescribes a larger amount after notice and an opportunity for interested parties to be heard (ERISA Sec. 412(a), as amended by the Pension Act).

> **Caution Note:** The $1,000,000 maximum bond amount only apples to plans holding employer securities, as defined in Code Sec. 407(d)(1). For benefit plans that do not hold employer securities, the $500,000 maximum bond amount remains unchanged.

> **Comment:** A plan would not be considered to hold employer securities where the only such securities held by the plan are part of a broadly-diversified fund of assets, such as mutual funds or index funds (Joint Committee on Taxation, Technical Explanation of the Pension Protection Act of 2006 (JCX-38-06).

▶ **Effective date.** The amendment made by this section shall apply to plan years beginning after December 31, 2007 (Act Sec. 622(b) of the Pension Protection Act of 2006).

Law source: Law at ¶7135. Committee Report at ¶10,520.

— Act Sec. 622(a) of the Pension Protection Act of 2006, amending ERISA Sec. 412(a);

— Act Sec. 622(b), providing the effective date.

Reporter references: For further information, consult the following CCH reporters.

— Pension Plan Guide, ¶4435 and ¶4525

— Tax Research Consultant, RETIRE: 48,110

¶650 Criminal Penalties for Coercive Interference with Protected Rights

SUMMARY OF NEW LAW

The criminal penalties for willfully interfering with a participant's or beneficiary's ERISA rights have been increased to a maximum fine of $100,000 or a maximum term of imprisonment of 10 years, or both.

BACKGROUND

It is a crime for anyone to use fraud, force, or violence or to restrain, coerce, or intimidate any plan participant or beneficiary in order to interfere with or prevent them from exercising any ERISA or ERISA plan right. Willfully violating this provision is a criminal offense subject to a fine of $10,000 or imprisonment for up to one year, or both (ERISA Sec. 511, as amended by the Pension Protection Act of 2006). Civil remedies for interfering with ERISA-protected rights are also available (ERISA Sec. 510).

NEW LAW EXPLAINED

Enhanced penalties for interfering with ERISA rights.—The Pension Protection Act of 2006 substantially increases the criminal penalty for coercively interfering with a plan participant's or beneficiary's protected rights under ERISA or under an ERISA plan (ERISA Sec. 511), as amended by the Pension Protection Act of 2006. A person who improperly interferes with another's protected rights under ERISA is subject to a fine of $100,000 or up to 10 years in prison, or both.

> **Comment:** Until the Pension Act, the criminal penalties for interfering with ERISA protected rights had not been increased since ERISA was enacted in 1974.

As a result of this increase, criminal penalties for interfering with ERISA-protected rights are more in line with criminal penalties for willful violations of ERISA's reporting and disclosure requirements. The reporting and disclosure rule penalties were substantially increased by the Sarbanes-Oxley Act of 2002 (P.L. 107-204) (ERISA Sec. 501).

> **Comment:** The Pension Act increases the criminal penalty for interfering with ERISA-protected rights. However, the civil remedies under ERISA were not addressed by this provision of the Pension Act (ERISA Sec. 510).

▶ **Effective date.** This provision is effective for violations occurring on and after August 17, 2006 (Act Sec. 623(b) of the Pension Protection Act of 2006).

Law source: Law at ¶7138. Committee Report at ¶10,530.

— Act Sec. 623(a) of the Pension Protection Act of 2006, amending ERISA Sec. 511;

— Act Sec. 623(b), providing the effective date.

Reporter references: For further information, consult the following CCH reporter.

— Pension Plan Guide, ¶5700 and ¶5965

¶655 Treatment of Investment of Assets Where Participant Fails to Exercise Investment Election

SUMMARY OF NEW LAW

A participant in an individual account plan will be deemed to have exercised actual control over assets in his or her account if the plan's fiduciaries make default investments for the participant in accordance with guidance provided by the Department of Labor.

BACKGROUND

A pension plan may provide for individual accounts and permit a participant or beneficiary to exercise control over assets in his or her account (ERISA Sec. 404(c)). Under this type of plan, a participant or beneficiary who exercises such control is not deemed to be a fiduciary. Moreover, no person who is otherwise a fiduciary of the plan will be liable under the fiduciary responsibility rules for any loss or breach that results from the participant's or beneficiary's exercise of actual control over his or her account assets. For this purpose, a plan qualifies as an individual account plan, if the plan:

- offers a broad range of investment options;
- provides the participants with the opportunity to give investment instructions; and
- provides enough information for plan participants to make informed investment choices.

To provide a broad range of investment alternatives, the plan must offer participants the opportunity to exercise control over investments that materially affect the potential return on assets. In addition, it must also allow participants to choose from at least three investment alternatives, each of which is diversified and has materially different risk and return characteristics. Finally, a plan must give participants the opportunity to diversify investments so as to minimize the risk of large losses.

> **Comment:** A participant's right to choose an investment option from a broad range of investment alternatives and to allocate assets does not empower the participant to control the selection of investment funds by the plan sponsor.

In the event a plan participant does not exercise control and submit investment instructions, the plan fiduciaries make default investments for the benefit of the participant. Under such circumstances, the plan's fiduciaries will *not* be relieved of liability for investing the assets in a participant's account. In other words, it is the participant's *actual exercise of control* and not the opportunity to exercise control that protects the plan's fiduciaries from liability for investment decisions. Thus, the plan fiduciaries need to continuously monitor the default funds to make sure they are prudent choices.

NEW LAW EXPLAINED

No fiduciary liability in default investment arrangements.—Effective for plan years beginning after December 31, 2006, a participant in an individual account plan who does not submit investment instructions to the plan administrator will be treated as exercising actual control over the assets in his or her account if the plan's fiduciaries default investments are made in accordance with regulations prescribed by the Department of Labor. Such regulations will provide plan fiduciaries with guidance on the appropriateness of designating default investments that include a mix of asset classes consistent with capital preservation, long-term capital appreciation, or a blend of both (ERISA Sec. 404(c) (5) (A), as added by the Pension Protection Act of 2006).

> **Comment:** The Pension Act directs the Secretary of Labor to issue the regulations under this provision within six months of August 17, 2006, the date of enactment (Act Sec. 624(b)(2) of the Pension Act).

In order for participants to be deemed to exercise actual control over assets in their individual account when the plan makes default investments on their behalf, the plan must provide a notice to the participants of their rights and obligations. Specifically, within a reasonable time before each plan year, each participant must be provided a notice explaining his or her rights under the plan to designate how contributions and earnings will be invested. In addition, the notice must explain how, in the absence of any investment election by the participant, the contributions and earnings will be invested. The notice must also inform each participant that they will have a reasonable period of time after receipt of the notice and before the beginning of the plan year to make a designation of how contributions and earning should be invested (ERISA Sec. 404(c)(5)(B), as added by the Pension Act).

> **Comment:** The form of the notice must be accurate and comprehensive and written in a manner calculated to be understood by the average employee eligible to participate.

▶ **Effective date.** The provision applies to plan years beginning after December 31, 2006 (Act Sec. 624(b)(1) of the Pension Protection Act of 2006). Regulations must be issued no later than six months after August 17, 2006, the date of enactment (Act Sec. 624(b)(2) of the Pension Act).

Law source: Law at ¶7141. Committee Report at ¶10,540.

— Act Sec. 624(a) of the Pension Protection Act of 2006, adding ERISA Sec. 404(c)(5);

— Act Sec. 624(b), providing the effective date.

Reporter references: For further information, consult the following CCH reporters.

— Pension Plan Guide, ¶4485 and ¶7526B

— Standard Federal Tax Reporter, 2006FED ¶17,515.032

¶660 Fiduciary Standards Clarified for Buying Annuities Used for Defined Contribution Plan Distributions

SUMMARY OF NEW LAW

The Secretary of Labor is directed to issue regulations clarifying the fiduciary standards applicable to the selection of an annuity contract as an optional form of distribution from an individual account plan to a participant or beneficiary.

BACKGROUND

There are two types of qualified retirement plans: defined contribution plans (also known as individual account plans), and defined benefit plans (such as traditional pension plans). In a defined contribution plan, such as a 401(k) plan or a profit-sharing plan, the sponsor's contributions are either discretionary in amount or based on a formula, and no specific benefits are promised to participants. In contrast, a sponsor's contributions to a defined benefit plan vary, based on the amount necessary to maintain specific, defined benefits that are promised to participants.

The Employee Retirement Income Security Act of 1974 (ERISA) governs *fiduciary standards* applicable to most qualified retirement plans (ERISA Secs. 404 through 414). Fiduciaries must:

- discharge their duties with respect to the plan solely in the interest of the participants and beneficiaries,
- act for the exclusive purpose of providing benefits to the participants and beneficiaries and defraying reasonable plan administration expenses, and
- act with the care, skill, prudence and diligence under the prevailing circumstances that a prudent person acting in a like capacity and familiar with such matters would use (ERISA Sec. 404(a)(1)).

These fiduciary standards also apply to the selection of annuity providers for the purpose of distributions from qualified retirement plans, where the plan intends to transfer liability for benefits to the annuity provider (29 CFR 2509.95-1(b)). Regulations issued by the Department of Labor effectively presume that when a pension plan purchases an annuity from an insurer as a distribution of benefits, it intends to transfer the plan's liability for the benefits to the annuity provider (29 CFR 2510.3-3(d)(2)(ii)). Fiduciary standards that apply to the selection of an annuity provider are established in the Department of Labor's Interpretive Bulletin 95-1 (also known as ERISA Interpretive Bulletin 95-1) (29 CFR 2509.95-1).

The selection of an annuity provider for purposes of a plan benefit distribution, whether upon separation or retirement of a participant or upon the termination of a plan, is a fiduciary decision. Fiduciaries choosing an annuity provider for the purpose of making a benefit distribution must take steps calculated to obtain the *safest annuity available* unless, under the circumstances, it would be in the interests of

BACKGROUND

participants and beneficiaries to do otherwise. At a minimum, the fiduciary obligation of prudence also requires plan fiduciaries to conduct an objective, thorough and analytical search that identifies and selects annuity providers based on their creditworthiness and ability to pay claims. Factors that a fiduciary should consider include:

(1) the quality and diversification of the annuity provider's investment portfolio,

(2) the size of the insurer relative to the proposed contract,

(3) the level of the insurer's capital and surplus,

(4) the lines of business of the annuity provider and other indications of an insurer's exposure to liability,

(5) the structure of the annuity contract and guarantees supporting the annuities, such as the use of separate accounts, and

(6) the availability of additional protection through state guaranty associations and the extent of their guarantees (29 CFR 2509.95-1(c)).

Unless they possess the necessary expertise to evaluate these factors, fiduciaries must obtain the advice of a qualified, independent expert (29 CFR 2509.95-1(c)).

While plan benefits should never be put at risk by the purchase of an unsafe annuity, there are situations where it may be in the interest of the participants and beneficiaries to purchase other than the safest available annuity. For instance, the safest available annuity may be only marginally safer, but disproportionately more expensive than competing annuities; or the provider offering the safest available annuity may lack the ability to administer the benefits. In contrast, a fiduciary may not purchase a riskier annuity solely because a defined benefit plan has insufficient assets to purchase a safer annuity. Instead, the fiduciary may have to condition the purchase of annuities on additional employer contributions. Similarly, a fiduciary's decision to purchase more risky, lower-priced annuities in order to ensure or maximize a reversion of excess assets to the employer-sponsor in connection with the termination of an over-funded pension plan violates the fiduciary's duties, because the interests of the plan participants and beneficiaries lies in receiving the safest annuity available, and other participants and beneficiaries have no countervailing interests (29 CFR 2509.95-1(d)). Fiduciaries with an interest in the sponsoring employer have a potential conflict of interest when selecting annuities and, therefore, must obtain and follow independent expert advice calculated to identify annuity providers with the highest claims-paying ability that are willing to write the business (29 CFR 2509.95-1(e)).

NEW LAW EXPLAINED

Fiduciary rules clarified.—The Secretary of Labor is directed to issue final regulations clarifying that the selection of an annuity contract as an optional form of distribution from a defined contribution plan to a participant or beneficiary:

NEW LAW EXPLAINED

(1) is not subject to the safest available annuity standard under the Department of Labor's Interpretive Bulletin 95–1 (29 CFR 2509.95–1), and

(2) is subject to all otherwise applicable fiduciary standards (Act Sec. 625(a) of the Pension Protection Act of 2006).

The regulations must be issued no later than one year after August 17, 2006, the date of enactment (Act Sec. 625(a) of the Pension Act).

> **Comment:** According to the Joint Committee on Taxation, the regulations are intended to clarify that the plan sponsor or other plan fiduciary must act in accordance with the prudence standards of ERISA Sec. 404(a), which are codified at 29 U.S.C. 1104(a). It is not intended that there be a single safest available annuity contract, since the plan fiduciary must select the most prudent option specific to its plan and its participants and beneficiaries. It also is not intended that the regulations restate all of the factors contained in the interpretive bulletin (Joint Committee on Taxation, Technical Explanation of the Pension Protection Act of 2006 (JCX-38-06)).

▶ **Effective date.** This section shall take effect on August 17, 2006 (Act Sec. 625(b) of the Pension Protection Act of 2006).

Law source: Law at ¶7144. Committee Report at ¶10,550.

— Act Sec. 625(a) of the Pension Protection Act of 2006.

— Act Sec. 625(b), providing the effective date.

Reporter references: For further information, consult the following CCH reporters.

— Pension Plan Guide, ¶3617 and ¶4473

— Tax Research Consultant, RETIRE: 48,100

Contributions and Benefits

7

EMPLOYER CONTRIBUTIONS

INDIVIDUAL RETIREMENT PLANS

BENEFIT LIMITATIONS

CROSS REFERENCES

EMPLOYER CONTRIBUTIONS

¶705 Increase in Deduction Limitation for Contributions to Single-Employer Defined Benefit Plans

SUMMARY OF NEW LAW

Larger deduction limits are provided for contributions to single-employer defined benefit plans, particularly for plans that are determined to be at-risk plans.

BACKGROUND

An employer's contributions to a qualified retirement plan are generally deductible, but the amount that qualifies for the deduction is limited. The amount of the limitation is based on the type of plan involved. In some cases, contributions in excess of the limitation (the non-deductible contribution) may be subject to an excise tax in the amount of ten percent of the amount of the non-deductible contribution.

A defined contribution plan is a plan that provides for an individual account for each participant and for benefits based solely on contributions made to the account, gains and losses arising out of investments made with the contributions and forfeitures of accounts of other participants that may be allocated to the participant's account (Code Sec. 414(i)). A defined benefit plan is any plan that is not a defined contribution plan (Code Sec. 414(j)). These include pension and annuity plans that offer a specific retirement benefit to employees, typically in the form of a monthly pension based on the employee's wages and years of service. The employer's annual contributions to defined benefit plans are based on actuarial assumptions and are not allocated to employees' individual accounts. An employer may use either the level funding method or the normal cost method to determine the amount of the limitation on the contribution deduction.

Under the level funding method, the limitation on the amount of deductible contributions is the amount necessary to provide the remaining unfunded cost of the participants' past and current service credits distributed as a level amount of the remaining future service of each participant (Code Sec. 404(a)(1)(A)(ii)).

Under the normal cost method, the limitation on the amount of deductible contributions is the amount equal to the normal cost of the plan, plus, if past service or other supplementary pension or annuity credits are provided by the plan, an amount necessary to amortize the unfunded costs attributable to such credits in equal annual payments over ten years (Code Sec. 404(a)(1)(A)(iii)).

Regardless of the type of defined benefit plan, the maximum limitation for contribution deductions cannot be any less than the unfunded current liability (Code Sec. 404(a)(1)(D)(i)). The unfunded current liability is the excess of the current liability of the plan over the value of the plan's assets, as determined by any reasonable actuarial method taking into account fair market value (Code Sec. 412(l)(8)(A)). For a plan that

BACKGROUND

is covered by the Pension Benefit Guaranty Corporation (PBGC) and terminates during the plan year, the unfunded current liability is replaced by the amount necessary to make the plan sufficient for benefit liabilities (Code Sec. 404(a)(1)(D)(iv)). A plan is sufficient for benefit liabilities if there is no amount of unfunded guaranteed benefits under the plan (ERISA Sec. 4041(d)).

In the case of a plan that has 100 or fewer participants, unfunded current liability does not include liability attributable to benefit increases for highly compensated individuals (Code Sec. 404(a)(1)(D)(ii)). Generally, a highly compensated individual is either a five-percent owner for either the current or prior year or an individual who received compensation in excess of an inflation adjusted amount for the previous year. For 2005, that amount was $95,000 and for 2006, that amount is $100,000 (Code Sec. 414(q)). In determining the number of participants in the plan, all defined benefit plans maintained by the employer are to be considered as one plan, but only the participants in the plan that are employees of the employer will be counted (Code Sec. 404(a)(1)(D)(iii)).

If an employer sponsors one or more defined benefit plans in addition to one or more defined contribution plans, the contribution deduction is limited to the greater of (1) 25 percent of the compensation paid or accrued for that year to the participants in all such plans or (2) the amount necessary to meet the minimum funding requirements of the defined benefit plan for the year, but not less than the amount of the plan's unfunded current liability (Code Sec. 404(a)(7)(A)). This limitation is subject to two exceptions. First, this limitation cannot have the effect or reducing the deductibility of a contribution otherwise allowed if no employee is a beneficiary under more than one trust or under a trust and an annuity plan (Code Sec. 404(a)(7)(C)(i). Also, if the only amounts contributed to the defined contribution plan are elective deferrals, as defined in Code Sec. 402(g)(3), then the limitation does not apply.

Generally, the deduction limitation rules apply equally regardless of whether the plans are sponsored by a single employer or multiple employers.

There is concern that the limitation on the amount of deductible contributions made to a defined benefit plan hinders the ability of the employer to adequately fund the plan. This is especially true in times of overall economic prosperity, when employers may have the ability to make up for years in which an economic downturn limited the amount of available cash to fully fund the plans as needed. This situation puts pressure upon the assets of the PBGC, which subsequently limits that entity's ability to insure the plans of other employers.

NEW LAW EXPLAINED

Deduction limits increased.—The Internal Revenue Code is amended to provide increases in deduction limits for contributions to defined benefit plans, with different limits placed upon single-employer plans, multiemployer plans (see ¶ 710) and combined plans (consisting of both defined benefit and defined contribution plans) (see ¶ 715). A multiemployer plan is any plan to which more than one employer is required to contribute (Code Sec. 414(f)(1)). A single-employer plan is generally defined as any

NEW LAW EXPLAINED

plan that is not a multiemployer plan. All trades and businesses which are under common control will be regarded as a single employer (Code Secs. 414(c) and (f)(2)).

For years beginning in 2006 and 2007, the maximum deduction limitation for contributions to single-employer defined benefit plans cannot be any less than the unfunded current liability determined under Code Sec. 412(l)(8)(A), as in effect in 2006 and 2007. However, when calculating unfunded current liability under Code Sec. 412(l)(8)(A), a single-employer plan subtracts the value of the plan's assets from 150 percent of the current liability of the plan (Code Sec. 404(a)(1)(D)(i), as amended by the Pension Protection Act of 2006).

In years beginning after December 31, 2007, the annual deduction limitation for contributions to a single-employer defined benefit plan is the *greater* of (1) the minimum contribution required under new Code Sec. 430, as added by the Pension Act (see ¶ 210) or (2) an alternative amount computed under new Code Sec. 404(o)(1)(A) and discussed in this paragraph.

For plans that are "at-risk" under Code Sec. 430(i), the alternative amount is the excess of the sum of:

- the funding target for the plan year,
- the target normal cost for the plan year, and
- the "cushion amount" for the plan year, over

the value of the assets held by the plan as of the valuation date for the plan year (Code Sec. 404(o)(2)(A), as added by the Pension Act).

However, if the plan is not an "at-risk" plan as defined in Code Sec. 430(i), as added by the Pension Act, the alternative amount may not be less than the sum of the funding target and the target normal cost for the plan year (both determined as if it were an "at-risk" plan) less the value of the plan assets. The computation for plans that are not at risk essentially removes the cushion amount from the limitation alternative. For further discussion of "at-risk" plans, see ¶ 210. In determining the value of the assets, the valuation date is the date determined under Code Sec. 430(g)(2), as added by the Pension Act.

Cushion amount defined. The "cushion amount" is generally the sum of 50 percent of the funding target for the plan year and the amount by which the funding target would increase for the year if the plan took into account expected future increases in compensation or, if the plan does not base benefits for past services on compensation, expected increases in benefits in succeeding plan years (Code Sec. 404(o)(3), as added by the Pension Act). The determination of expected increases in benefits must be based on the average annual increase in benefits over of the previous six plan years.

In computing the cushion amount, the plan's actuary must assume that the annual compensation limitation under Code Sec. 404(l) and the annual benefit limitation under Code Sec. 415(b) apply (Code Sec. 404(o)(3)(B)(i), as added by the Pension Act). In the case of a plan covered by the PBGC, the plan's actuary may take into account cost-of-living compensation limitation increases expected to occur in succeeding plan years

NEW LAW EXPLAINED

under Code Sec. 401(a)(17) notwithstanding Code Sec. 404(l) (Code Sec. 404(o)(3)(B)(ii), as added by the Pension Act).

Cushion amount for plans with 100 or fewer participants. In determining the cushion amount, the funding target of a plan with 100 or fewer participants does not include benefit increases for highly compensated individuals, as defined in Code Sec. 414(q), resulting from a plan amendment made or effective (whichever is later) within the previous two years (Code Sec. 404(o)(4)(A), as added by the Pension Act). For purposes of determining the number of plan participants, all defined benefit plans maintained by the same employer (or any member of the employer's controlled group) are treated as one plan. However, only participants of the employer (or controlled group member) are taken into account (Code Sec. 404(o)(4)(B), as added by the Pension Act).

Terminating plans. As under current law, the deduction limit for a single-employer plan covered by the PBGC which terminates during the plan year may not be less than the amount required to make the plan sufficient for benefit liabilities (as defined in ERISA Sec. 4041(d)) (Code Sec. 404(o)(5), as added by the Pension Act).

Coordination of actuarial assumptions and definitions with Code Sec. 430. Any actuarial assumptions made with regard to the deduction limitations for single-employer plans under new Code Sec. 404(o) will be made in the same manner as the actuarial assumptions under new Code Sec. 430, as added by the Pension Act (Code Sec. 404(o)(6), as added by the Pension Act). In addition, any term used in new Code Sec. 404(o) that is also used in new Code Sec. 430 share the same meaning (Code Sec. 404(o)(7), as added by the Pension Act).

Application of overall deduction limit. In applying the overall deduction limitation on contributions to combinations of defined benefit plans and defined contribution plans (Code Sec. 404(a)(7)), single-employer defined benefit pension plans covered by the PBGC insurance program are not taken into account (Code Sec. 404(a)(7)(C)(iv), as added by the Pension Act). In addition, in applying the overall deduction limit, the amount necessary to meet the minimum funding requirement with respect to a single-employer defined benefit pension plan that is not insured by the PBGC is treated as not less than the plan's funding shortfall as determined under the minimum funding rules of Code Sec. 430 (Code Sec. 404(a)(7)(A)), as amended by the Pension Act). For a discussion of the changes to deduction limitations for contributions to combination plans, see ¶ 715.

▶ **Effective date.** The provision regarding the maximum deduction amount for contributions to a single-employer defined benefit plan in 2006 and 2007 applies to years beginning after December 31, 2005 (Act Sec. 801(e)(2) of the Pension Protection Act of 2006). The provision regarding the deduction limitation on contributions to single-employer defined benefit plans after 2007 applies to years beginning after December 31, 2007 (Act Sec. 801(e)(1) of the Pension Act).

Law source: Law at ¶5045 and ¶5050. Committee Report at ¶10,570.

— Act Secs. 801(a)(1) and 801(c)(1) of the Pension Protection Act of 2006, amending Code Sec. 404(a)(1)(A);

— Act Sec. 801(a)(2), adding Code Sec. 404(o);

NEW LAW EXPLAINED

— Act Sec. 801(b), adding Code Sec. 404(a)(7)(C)(iv);

— Act Sec. 801(c), amending Code Sec. 404(a)(1)(B), 404(a)(7) and 404A(g)(3)(A);

— Act Sec. 801(d), amending Code Sec. 404(a)(1)(D) and striking Code Sec. 404(a)(1)(F); and

— Act Sec. 801(e), providing effective dates.

Reporter references: For further information, consult the following CCH reporters.

— Pension Plan Guide, ¶2835

— Standard Federal Tax Reporter, 2006FED ¶18,348.025

— Tax Research Consultant, RETIRE: 33,252, RETIRE: 33,306 and RETIRE: 36,050

— Federal Tax Guide, 2006FTG ¶11,035

¶710 Increase in Deduction Limitation for Contributions to Multiemployer Defined Benefit Plans

SUMMARY OF NEW LAW

Larger deduction limits are provided for contributions to multiemployer defined benefit plans.

BACKGROUND

An employer's contributions to a qualified retirement plan are generally deductible, but the amount that qualifies for the deduction is limited. The amount of the limitation is based on the type of plan involved. In some cases, contributions in excess of the limitation (the nondeductible contribution) may be subject to an excise tax in the amount of ten percent of the amount of the nondeductible contribution.

A defined contribution plan is a plan that provides for an individual account for each participant and for benefits based solely on contributions made to the account, gains and losses arising out of investments made with the contributions and forfeitures of accounts of other participants that may be allocated to the participant's account (Code Sec. 414(i)). A defined benefit plan is any plan that is not a defined contribution plan (Code Sec. 414(j)). These include pension and annuity plans that offer a specific retirement benefit to employees, typically in the form of a monthly pension based on the employee's wages and years of service. The employer's annual contributions are based on actuarial assumptions and are not allocated to employees' individual accounts. An employer may use either the level funding method or the normal cost method to determine the amount of the limitation on the contribution deduction.

Regardless of the type of defined benefit plan, the maximum limitation for contribution deductions cannot be any less than the unfunded current liability (Code Sec. 404(a)(1)(D)(i)). The unfunded current liability is the excess of the current liability of

BACKGROUND

the plan over the value of the plan's assets, as determined by any reasonable actuarial method taking into account fair market value (Code Sec. 412(l)(8)(A)). For a plan that is covered by the Pension Benefit Guaranty Corporation (PBGC) and terminates during the plan year, the unfunded current liability is replaced by the amount necessary to make the plan sufficient for benefit liabilities (Code Sec. 404(a)(1)(D)(iv)). A plan is sufficient for benefit liabilities if there is no amount of unfunded guaranteed benefits under the plan (ERISA Sec. 4041(d)).

In the case of a plan that has 100 or fewer participants, unfunded current liability does not include liability attributable to benefit increases for highly compensated individuals (Code Sec. 404(a)(1)(D)(ii)). Generally, a highly compensated individual is either a five-percent owner for either the current or prior year or an individual who received compensation in excess of an inflation adjusted amount for the previous year. For 2005, that amount was $95,000 and for 2006, that amount is $100,000 (Code Sec. 414(q)). In determining the number of participants in the plan, all defined benefit plans maintained by the employer are to be considered as one plan, but only the participants in the plan that are employees of the employer will be counted (Code Sec. 404(a)(1)(D)(iii)).

Generally, the deduction limitation rules apply equally regardless of whether the plans are sponsored by a single employer or multiple employers.

There is concern that the limitation on the amount of deductible contributions made to a defined benefit plan hinders the ability of the employer to adequately fund the plan. This is especially true in times of overall economic prosperity, when employers may have the ability to make up for years in which an economic downturn limited the amount of available cash to fully fund the plans as needed. This situation puts pressure upon the assets of the PBGC, which subsequently limits that entity's ability to insure the plans of other employers.

NEW LAW EXPLAINED

Deduction limits increased.—The Internal Revenue Code is amended to provide increases in deduction limits for contributions to defined benefit plans, with different limits placed upon single-employer plans (see ¶ 705), multiemployer plans and combined plans (consisting of both defined benefit and defined contribution plans) (see ¶ 715). A multiemployer plan is any plan maintained pursuant to a collective bargaining agreement and to which more than one employer is required to contribute (Code Sec. 414(f)(1)).

For years beginning in 2006 and 2007, the maximum amount of the deduction limitation for contributions to multiemployer plans cannot be less than 140 percent of the current liability of the plan minus the value of the plan's assets (Code Sec. 404(a)(1)(D)(i), as amended by the Pension Protection Act of 2006). This is the same formula that was used prior to amendment by the Pension Act, except that the current liability component is increased by 40 percent (i.e., from 100 percent of current liability for 140 percent of currently liability). This same provision increases the deduction limitation for contributions to single-employer plans, but with a different applicable percentage. For the

NEW LAW EXPLAINED

limitations of deductions to single-employer plans, see ¶ 705. For these years, the special rules that apply to plans with 100 or fewer participants and to terminating plans with PBGC coverage will continue to apply to multiemployer plans (Code Secs. 404(a)(1)(D)(iii) and (iv)).

For years beginning after December 31, 2007, the maximum amount of the deduction limitation for contributions to multiemployer plans also cannot be less than 140 percent of the current liability of the plan minus the value of the plan's assets (Code Sec. 404(a)(1)(D), as amended by the Pension Act). The determination of the value of the plan's assets is made in the same manner as before under Code Sec. 412(l)(8), prior to amendment by the Pension Act, using any reasonable actuarial method taking fair market value into account (Code Sec. 431(c)(2), as added by the Pension Act). However, in computing the current liability of the plan, benefits that are not nonforfeitable under the plan after termination of the plan should not be taken into account (Code Sec. 431(c)(6)(C), as added by the Pension Act).

> **Comment:** These two calculations of unfunded current liability are essentially the same. Code Sec. 404(a)(1)(D) is first amended to provide for a higher computation for both single-employer and multiemployer plans in 2006 and 2007, and then is amended again so the higher amount only applies to multiemployer plans after 2007.

Finally, in years beginning after December 31, 2007, the special rules that apply to plans with 100 or fewer participants and in the case of terminating plans with PBGC coverage no longer apply to multiemployer plans (Code Sec. 404(a)(1)(D), as amended by the Pension Act).

▶ **Effective date.** The provision that provides an increased limit in the current funding liability for multiemployer and single-employer plans in 2006 and 2007 applies to multiemployer plans in years beginning after December 31, 2005 (Act Sec. 801(e)(2) of the Pension Protection Act of 2006). The provision that continues the increased current funding liability limit for multiemployer plans only applies to multiemployer plans in years beginning after December 31, 2007 (Act Sec. 802(b) of the Pension Act).

Law source: Law at ¶5045. Committee Report at ¶10,570.

— Act Sec. 801(d)(1) of the Pension Protection Act of 2006, amending Code Sec. 404(a)(1)(D)(i);

— Act Sec. 802(a), amending Code Sec. 404(a)(1)(D); and

— Act Secs. 801(e)(2) and 802(b) providing effective dates.

Reporter references: For further information, consult the following CCH reporters.

— Pension Plan Guide, ¶2835 and ¶5440

— Standard Federal Tax Reporter, 2006FED ¶18,348.025

— Tax Research Consultant, RETIRE: 33,252 and RETIRE: 36,050

— Federal Tax Guide, 2006FTG ¶11,035

¶715 Overall Limitation on Deductions for Contributions to Combined Plans Relaxed

SUMMARY OF NEW LAW

The overall limitation on deductions to combined plans only applies to contributions to defined contribution plans only to the extent the contributions exceed six percent of compensation paid during the tax year to the beneficiaries. Multiemployer plans are exempted from the overall limit. A single-employer plan insured by the Pension Benefit Guaranty Corporation (PBGC) is also not taken into account in applying the limit.

BACKGROUND

An employer's contributions to a qualified retirement plan are generally deductible, but the amount that qualifies for the deduction is limited. The amount of the limitation is based on the type of plan involved. In some cases, contributions in excess of the limitation (the nondeductible contribution) may be subject to an excise tax in the amount of ten percent of the amount of the nondeductible contribution.

A defined contribution plan is a plan that provides for an individual account for each participant and for benefits based solely on contributions made to the account, gains and losses arising out of investments made with the contributions and forfeitures of accounts of other participants that may be allocated to the participant's account (Code Sec. 414(i)). A defined benefit plan is any plan that is not a defined contribution plan (Code Sec. 414(j)).

If an employer sponsors one or more defined benefit plans in addition to one or more defined contribution plans, the contribution deduction is limited to the greater of (1) 25 percent of the compensation paid or accrued for that year to the participants in all such plans or (2) the amount necessary to meet the minimum funding requirements of the defined benefit plan for the year, but not less than the amount of the plan's unfunded current liability (Code Sec. 404(a)(7)(A)). This limitation is subject to two exceptions. First, this limitation cannot have the effect of reducing the deductibility of a contribution otherwise allowed if no employee is a beneficiary under more than one trust or under a trust and an annuity plan (Code Sec. 404(a)(7)(C)(i). Also, if the only amounts contributed to the defined contribution plan are elective deferrals, as defined in Code Sec. 402(g)(3), then the limitation does not apply.

There is concern that the limitation on the amount of deductible contributions made to a defined benefit plan hinders the ability of the employer to adequately fund the plan. This is especially true in times of overall economic prosperity, when employers may have the ability to make up for years in which an economic downturn limited the amount of available cash to fully fund the plans as needed. This situation puts pressure upon the assets of the PBGC, which subsequently limits that entity's ability to insure the plans of other employers.

NEW LAW EXPLAINED

Applicability of overall combination plan deduction limit relaxed.—The new law amends the overall deduction limitation on contributions to combinations of defined benefit plans and defined contribution plans contained in Code Sec. 404(a)(7). These changes generally have the effect of allowing contributions to be subject to a higher limitation amount.

First, the overall deduction limitation for contributions to combination plans applies to contributions to one or more defined contribution plans only to the extent that the contributions exceed six percent of the compensation otherwise paid or accrued to the beneficiaries under the plans for the tax year. Furthermore, if amounts are carried over from preceding tax years under the operation of Code Sec. 404(a)(7)(B), providing for a carryover of amounts contributed in excess of the overall limitation, those carried over amounts are treated as employer contributions to a defined contribution plan to the extent attributable to employer contributions to the plans in the preceding tax years (Code Sec. 404(a)(7)(C)(iii), as added by the Pension Protection Act of 2006.

Next, this overall limitation is not applicable to multiemployer plans (Code Sec. 404(a)(7)(C)(v), as added by the Pension Act). A multiemployer plan is any plan maintained pursuant to a bargaining agreement to which more than one employer is required to contribute (Code Sec. 414(f)(1)).

Finally, for years beginning after December 31, 2007, if a single-employer plan is insured by the Pension Benefit Guaranty Corporation (PBGC), then the plan is not taken into account in applying the overall limitation on deductions (Code Sec. 404(a)(7)(C)(iv), as added by the Pension Act. A single-employer plan is any plan which is not a multiemployer plan.

The combined effect of these three changes means that the limitation on deductions to combined plans only applies to single employer plans, not insured by the PBGC, making contributions in excess of six percent of amounts otherwise paid to beneficiaries, where contributions to the defined contribution plans are in a form other than elective deferrals.

For a discussion of the limits on contributions to single-employer plans, see ¶ 705 and for a discussion of the limits on contributions to multiemployer plans, see ¶ 710.

▶ **Effective date.** The provision regarding the restrictions upon the applicability of the deduction limits to single-employer plans applies to years beginning after December 31, 2007 (Act Sec. 801(e)(1) of the Pension Protection Act. The other two provisions apply to contributions for tax years beginning after December 31, 2005 (Act Sec. 803(d) of the Pension Act).

Law source: Law at ¶5045 and ¶5300. Committee Reports at ¶10,570 and ¶10,580.

— Act Sec. 801(b) of the Pension Protection Act of 2006, adding Code Sec. 404(a)(7)(C)(iv);

— Act Sec. 803(a) adding Code Sec. 404(a)(7)(C)(iii);

— Act Sec. 803(b) adding Code Sec. 404(a)(7)(C)(v);

— Act Sec. 803(c) amending Code Sec. 4972(c)(6)(A); and

— Act Secs. 801(e)(1) and 803(d), providing effective dates.

NEW LAW EXPLAINED

Reporter references: For further information, consult the following CCH reporters.

— Pension Plan Guide, ¶7527A

— Standard Federal Tax Reporter, 2006FED ¶18,350.01

— Tax Research Consultant, RETIRE: 33,306

— Federal Tax Guide, 2006FTG ¶11,035

¶720 Vesting Schedule Expedited for Employer Contributions to Defined Contribution Plans

SUMMARY OF NEW LAW

The expedited vesting schedule that applies to employer matching contributions is extended to all employer contributions to defined contribution plans.

BACKGROUND

In most qualified defined contribution retirement plans, employer contributions that match contributions made by employees must vest under one of these vesting schedules:

- cliff vesting, under which a participant must acquire a nonforfeitable right to 100 percent of the participant's accrued benefit derived from employer matching contributions upon the completion of three years of service; or
- graded vesting (also known as graduated vesting or two-to-six-year vesting), under which a participant must have a nonforfeitable right to 20 percent of the participant's accrued benefit derived from employer matching contributions for each year of service, beginning with the participant's second year of service and ending with 100 percent after six years of service (Code Sec. 411(a)(12)).

A slower vesting schedule applies to all employer contributions to defined benefit plans, and to non-matching employer contributions to defined contributions plans. For these contributions, cliff vesting can occur upon the completion of five years of service. Graduated vesting, also known as three-to-seven-year vesting, can occur at the rate of 20 percent per year, beginning with the participant's third year of service and ending with 100 percent after seven years of service (Code Sec. 411(a)(2)).

A *collectively bargained plan* is a single plan that is maintained under one or more collective bargaining agreements between employee representatives and one or more employers (a collectively bargained plan that includes more than one employer is a multiemployer plan) (Code Sec. 413). Collectively bargained plans are subject to the same vesting rules for employer contributions, but all employers that are parties to the collective bargaining agreement are treated as a single employer (Code Sec. 413(b)(4)).

BACKGROUND

An *employee stock ownership plan* (ESOP) is a defined contribution plan that is designed to invest primarily in qualifying employer securities (Code Sec. 4975(e)(7)). Qualifying employer securities generally are common stock of the employer or an affiliate that (i) is readily tradable on an established securities market, or (ii) has a combination of voting power and dividend rights at least equal to the classes of stock of the employer or affiliate with the greatest voting power and dividend rights (Code Sec. 4975(e)(8)). An ESOP can borrow funds to purchase employer securities without violating the prohibited transaction rules (Code Sec. 4975(d)(3)).

NEW LAW EXPLAINED

Faster vesting for employer matching contributions to defined contribution plans.—A defined contribution plan (such as profit-sharing and 401(k) plans) must vest all employer contributions according to the schedule that currently applies only to employer matching contributions. Thus, if a defined contribution plan uses cliff vesting, accrued benefits derived from all employer contributions must vest with the participant after three years of service. If a defined contribution plan uses graduated vesting, accrued benefits derived from all employer contributions must vest with the participant at the rate of 20 percent per year, beginning with the second year of service (Code Sec. 411(a)(2)(B), as amended by the Pension Protection Act of 2006; ERISA Sec. 203(a), as amended by the Pension Act).

This chart summarizes these new vesting schedules for employer matching contributions to defined contribution plans:

VESTING PERCENTAGE

Year	*3-Year Cliff*	*6-Year Graduated*
1	0%	0%
2	0%	20%
3	100%	40%
4	100%	60%
5	100%	80%
6	100%	100%

> **Comment:** The faster vesting schedules may increase an employer's cost of maintaining a defined contribution plan because they may decrease forfeitures that could otherwise be used to pay administrative expenses or reduce future employer contributions.

The faster vesting schedule generally applies to plan years beginning after December 31, 2006, but it does not apply to any employee before the date the employee has one hour of service under the plan in any plan year to which the amendments apply (Act Sec. 904(c)(3) of the Pension Act).

For plans maintained under one or more *collective bargaining agreements* ratified before August 17, 2006, the date of enactment, the expedited vesting schedule does not apply to contributions made on behalf of employees covered by the agreement for plan years beginning before the earlier of:

NEW LAW EXPLAINED

- January 1, 2009, or
- the later of (i) January 1, 2007, or (ii) the date on which the last of the collective bargaining agreements terminates, determined without regard to any extension of the agreement on or after August 17, 2006 (Sec. 904(c)(2) of the Pension Act).

If an *ESOP* incurred a loan for the purpose of acquiring qualifying employer securities, and that loan is still outstanding on September 26, 2005, the expedited vesting schedule does not apply to any plan year beginning before the earlier of (1) the date the loan is fully repaid, or (2) the date on which the loan was scheduled to be fully repaid as of September 26, 2005. This effective date controls over the special effective date for collectively bargained plans (Section 904(c)(4) of the Pension Act).

Defined benefit plans are not affected. Thus, all employer contributions to defined benefit plans can continue to vest under the five-year cliff vesting schedule, or the three-to-seven-year graduated vesting schedule (Code Sec. 411(a)(2)(A), as amended by the Pension Act).

> **Comment:** In defined contribution plans, also known as individual account plans, contributions are based on a specified formula, or on the plan sponsor's discretion, and no specific benefits are promised to the participants. In contrast, a defined benefit plan, such as a traditional pension plan, provides benefits to participants according to a formula set out in the plan. Employers can make matching contributions only to defined contribution plans, and not to defined benefit plans (Code Sec. 401(m)(4)).

▶ **Effective date.** The provision generally applies to plan years beginning after December 31, 2006. However, for plans maintained under one or more collective bargaining agreements ratified before August 17, 2006, the date of enactment, the provision applies to contributions made on behalf of employees covered by the agreement for plan years beginning on the earlier of (i) January 1, 2007 or, if later, the date on which the last of the collective bargaining agreements terminates (determined without regard to any extension of the agreement on or after August 17, 2006), or (ii) January 1, 2009. For employee stock ownership plans that had outstanding on September 26, 2005, a loan incurred for the purpose of acquiring qualifying employer securities, the provision does not apply to any plan year beginning before the earlier of the date the loan is fully repaid, or the date on which the loan was, as of September 26, 2005, scheduled to be fully repaid (Act Sec. 904(c) of the Pension Protection Act of 2006).

Law source: Law at ¶5080 and ¶7189. Committee Report at ¶10,980.

— Act Sec. 904(a) of the Pension Protection Act of 2006, amending Code Sec. 411(a)(2) and removing Code Sec. 411(a)(12);

— Act Sec. 904(b), amending ERISA Sec. 203(a).

— Act Sec. 904(c), providing the effective date.

Reporter references: For further information, consult the following CCH reporters.

— Pension Plan Guide, ¶2530 and ¶7467

— Standard Federal Tax Reporter, 2006FED ¶19,076.026

— Tax Research Consultant, RETIRE: 18,102

— Federal Tax Guide, 2006FTG ¶11,020

INDIVIDUAL RETIREMENT PLANS

¶725 Direct Payment of Tax Refunds to Individual Retirement Accounts

SUMMARY OF NEW LAW

The IRS has been instructed to provide forms on which individuals may elect to have a portion of their tax refund deposited directly into an individual retirement account.

BACKGROUND

Generally, the IRS is required to refund any overpayment of tax to a taxpayer (Code Sec. 6402). Under current IRS procedures, a taxpayer may elect to have the IRS deposit his or her refund directly into a checking or savings account, rather than have the refund issued by check. The direct deposit option is available whether a taxpayer files a return electronically or by mail (IRS Publication 1345, Handbook for Authorized IRS e-file Providers; IRS Form 1040, U.S. Individual Income Tax Return (2005)). Taxpayers who use direct deposit currently do not have the option to divide a refund into more than one account (IRS Form 1040).

The IRS touts several advantages to receiving refunds by direct deposit rather than by check. According to the IRS, taxpayers who file their returns electronically and elect direct deposit receive their refunds in half the time as those who file paper returns and receive their refunds by check. Taxpayers who file paper returns and elect direct deposit receive their refunds a week sooner than those who receive refunds by check (IRS News Release IR-2006-44, March 15, 2006). Direct deposit refunds are also more secure, convenient and less costly to the government (IRS Form 1040, U.S. Individual Income Tax Return, Instructions, p. 59 (2005)).

The number of taxpayers electing to receive their refunds by direct deposit has increased steadily since the IRS began offering the service. In 2001, more than 31 million taxpayers selected direct deposit refunds (IRS News Release IR-2001-49, April 26, 2001). During the 2006 filing season, the IRS issued more than 53 million direct deposit refunds, a 7 percent increase from the previous year (IRS News Release IR-2006-68, April 26, 2006).

NEW LAW EXPLAINED

Direct deposit of tax refunds to individual retirement plans.—The IRS has been instructed to make available forms on which individuals may elect to have a portion of their tax refund deposited directly into an individual retirement account (Act Sec. 830(a) of the Pension Protection Act of 2006). Beginning with the 2007 tax year, the IRS must make available a form or modify existing forms so that a taxpayer can direct that all or a portion of his or her refund can be deposited into an individual retirement plan, as defined in Code Sec. 7701(a)(37).

NEW LAW EXPLAINED

Comment: A House Ways and Means Committee report noted that this provision will provide further opportunities for retirement savings. According to the Committee Report, "taxpayers should be encouraged to use their tax refunds to enhance their retirement savings by being able to have such refunds deposited directly into an IRA" (House Committee Report on the Pension Protection Act of 2005 (H.R. Rep. No. 109-232, pt. 2)).

Comment: IRS recently announced a new program that will allow taxpayers who use direct deposit to divide their refunds in up to three financial accounts, such as checking, savings and retirement accounts. New Form 8888, to be created by the IRS, will give all individual filers the ability to split their refunds. Taxpayers will attach the new form to their returns indicating amounts of each allocation and providing account information. Refunds may be deposited with any U.S. financial institution so long as taxpayers provide valid routing and account numbers. Taxpayers who want their entire refund deposited directly into one account can still use the appropriate line on the Form 1040 series. The program will take effect in January 2007 (IRS News Release IR-2006-85, May 31, 2006).

Caution Note: Generally, the deadline for contributing to an IRA and receiving a tax deduction is the date on which the contributing taxpayer's tax return is due, not including extensions, for the tax year for which a deduction is claimed (Code Sec. 219(f)(3)). This deadline is usually April 15 of the year after the year for which the contribution is made. This provision does not modify the rules relating to IRAs, including the rules relating to timing and deductibility of contributions (Joint Committee on Taxation, Technical Explanation of the Pension Protection Act of 2006 (JCX-38-06)). Therefore, taxpayers who want their IRA contribution to relate back to the prior year should allow sufficient time for their refund to be directly deposited by April 15. Taxpayers who file their return close to the filing deadline may risk losing the deduction for their contribution by having their refund deposited to their IRA after April 15.

▶ **Effective date.** The form required by the provision is to be made available for tax years beginning after December 31, 2006 (Act Sec. 830(b) of the Pension Protection Act of 2006).

Law source: Law at ¶7165. Committee Report at ¶10,710.

— Act Sec. 830(a) of the Pension Protection Act of 2006;

— Act Sec. 830(b), providing the effective date.

Reporter references: For further information, consult the following CCH reporters.

— Pension Plan Guide, ¶8500 and ¶8546

— Standard Federal Tax Reporter, 2006FED ¶18,922.01 and ¶38,519.026

— Tax Research Consultant, FILEBUS: 12,308.25 and RETIRE: 66,202

— Federal Tax Guide, 2006FTG ¶11,425 and ¶22,415

¶730 Additional IRA Contributions for Individuals Affected by an Employer's Bankruptcy

SUMMARY OF NEW LAW

Qualifying individuals who participated in a bankrupt employer's qualified 401(k) plan and received at least 50 percent matching contributions made in the employer's stock are permitted to make additional contributions to an IRA for 2007, 2008 and 2009.

BACKGROUND

An individual may establish an individual retirement account (IRA) as a means of accumulating retirement savings on a tax-favored basis. In general, there are two kinds of IRAs: the traditional IRA and the Roth IRA. Both are subject to annual contribution limits. For 2006 and 2007, the annual limit on IRA contributions is $4,000. For 2008, the annual limit increases to $5,000. However, an individual taxpayer who has reached age 50 is also permitted to make additional catch-up contributions to an IRA. The annual catch-up contribution limit for 2006 and thereafter is $1,000 (Code Secs. 219(b)(5) and 408A(c)(2)).

Contributions to a traditional IRA are deductible if certain conditions are met. However, contributions to a Roth IRA are never deductible. A contribution to a traditional IRA may not be fully deductible if the taxpayer or the taxpayer's spouse is an active participant in an employer-sponsored retirement plan (Code Sec. 219(g)). Eligibility to make nondeductible contributions to a traditional IRA is not limited by income, while eligibility to make contributions to a Roth IRA is subject to modified adjusted gross income limits. The maximum Roth IRA contribution is phased out between $150,000 to $160,000 in the case of married taxpayers filing jointly; between $0 and $10,000 for married taxpayers filing separate returns; and between $95,000 to $110,000 for all other taxpayers (Code Sec. 408A(c)(3)(A))

An individual whose employer sponsors a qualified cash or deferred arrangement (a 401(k) plan) can elect to contribute a portion of his or her current compensation to a retirement account on a pre-tax basis. These contributions are commonly referred to as elective contributions or elective deferrals. An individual may also be permitted to make after-tax contributions to a plan. Depending on the specific plan, these contributions may be matched by the employer in whole or in part, up to a percentage of the employee's base salary. Matching contributions are often made in the form of shares of the employer's stock.

NEW LAW EXPLAINED

Additional IRA contributions in certain bankruptcy cases.—Eligible individuals who are affected by an employer's bankruptcy can elect to make additional contributions to an IRA of up to $3,000 in 2007 through 2009 (Code Sec. 219(b)(5)(C), as added by the Pension Protection Act of 2006).

NEW LAW EXPLAINED

To be eligible to make additional contributions to an IRA:

1. An individual must have been a participant in an employer's 401(k) plan under which the employer matched at least 50 percent of the employee's contributions with the employer's stock;
2. The employer must have been a debtor in bankruptcy in a preceding tax year;
3. The employer or any other person must have been subject to an indictment or conviction in a preceding tax year resulting from business transactions related to the bankruptcy case; and
4. The individual must have been a participant in the employer's 401(k) plan on the date six months before the bankruptcy case was filed (Code Sec. 219(b)(5)(C), as added by the Pension Act).

> **Comment:** According to a Senate Finance Committee Report that addressed this issue in an earlier bill, Congress believes that if employer matching contributions are made in the form of employer stock and the employer's bankruptcy causes employees to lose a substantial portion of their retirement savings, the employees should be permitted to make up for the losses by making additional IRA contributions (Senate Finance Committee Report (S. Rep. No. 109-174)). However, because the provision requires both that an employer be in bankruptcy and that the employer or another individual was subject to an indictment or conviction stemming from related business transactions, only a limited number of taxpayers are likely to be affected by the change.

> **Comment:** This provision is apparently a response to the losses of pension savings incurred by employees of Enron following the company's bankruptcy. However, some former Enron employees have pointed out that many of the people who are eligible to make additional IRA contributions under this provision may not have the resources to do so.

Taxpayers who elect to make additional contributions to an IRA under this provision are precluded from making catch-up contributions to an IRA that may otherwise be allowed for taxpayers aged 50 and older (Code Sec. 219(b)(5)(C)(i), as added by the Pension Act).

▶ **Effective date.** The provision applies to tax years beginning after December 31, 2006 (Act Sec. 831(b) of the Pension Protection Act of 2006).

Law source: Law at ¶5025. Committee Report at ¶10,720.

— Act Sec. 831(a) of the Pension Protection Act of 2006, redesignating Code Sec. 219(b)(5)(C) as 219(b)(5)(D) and adding new Code Sec. 219(b)(5)(C);

— Act Sec. 831(b), providing the effective date.

Reporter references: For further information, consult the following CCH reporters.

— Pension Plan Guide, ¶8543 and ¶9275

— Standard Federal Tax Reporter, 2006FED ¶18,922.0229

— Tax Research Consultant, RETIRE: 66,202

— Federal Tax Guide, 2006FTG ¶6450, ¶11,425 and ¶11,460

BENEFIT LIMITATIONS

¶735 Determination of Average Compensation for Benefit Limitation Purposes

SUMMARY OF NEW LAW

For purposes of determining the average compensation for a participant's high three years, the high three years are the period of three consecutive calendar years during which the participant had the greatest aggregate compensation from the employer.

BACKGROUND

Annual benefits payable to a participant under a defined benefit plan generally may not exceed the lesser of: (1) 100 percent of the average compensation for the employee's high three years, or (2) $175,000 (for 2006) (Code Sec. 415(b)(1)). The dollar limit is reduced proportionately for individuals with less than ten years of plan participation and the compensation limit is reduced proportionately for individuals with less than ten years of service (Code Sec. 415(b)(5)).

In determining the average compensation for a participant's high three years, the high three years are the period of three consecutive calendar years during which the participant was both an active participant in the plan and had the greatest aggregate compensation from the employer. The plan may use any 12-month period instead of the calendar year, provided it does so uniformly and consistently. If a participant has less than three years of service, the limit is the average compensation for the actual period of service (Code Sec. 415(b)(3); Reg. § 1.415-3(a)(3)).

Proposed regulations issued in 2005 clarify that an employee must be an active participant in the plan in each of the high three years (Proposed Reg. § 1.415(b)-1(a)(5)). Thus, only compensation earned in periods during which an individual is an active participant would count towards the annual defined benefit limitation.

NEW LAW EXPLAINED

Determination of high-three years' average compensation for benefit limitation purposes.—For purposes of determining the average compensation for a participant's high three years, the high three years are the period of not more than three consecutive calendar years during which the participant had the greatest aggregate compensation from the employer (Code Sec. 415(b)(3), as amended by the Pension Protection Act of 2006).

▶ **Effective date.** The provision applies to years beginning after December 31, 2005 (Act Sec. 832(b) of the Pension Protection Act of 2006).

NEW LAW EXPLAINED

Law source: Law at ¶5095. Committee Report at ¶10,730.

— Act Sec. 832(a) of the Pension Protection Act of 2006, amending Code Sec. 415(b)(3);

— Act Sec. 832(b), providing the effective date.

Reporter references: For further information, consult the following CCH reporters.

— Pension Plan Guide, ¶1561

— Standard Federal Tax Reporter, 2006FED ¶19,218.023

— Tax Research Consultant, RETIRE: 36,150

— Federal Tax Guide, 2006FTG ¶11,035

¶740 Lump-Sum Calculation for Minimum Valuation Rules

SUMMARY OF NEW LAW

The adjustment of a benefit, such as a lump-sum distribution, in a form that is subject to the minimum valuation rules must be made using an interest rate that is not less than the greatest of: (1) 5.5 percent; (2) the rate that provides a benefit of not more than 105 percent of the benefit that would be provided if the applicable interest rate for determining minimum lump sums were the interest rate assumption; or (3) the interest rate specified in the plan.

BACKGROUND

An annual benefit paid by a defined benefit plan in the form of a straight-life annuity generally may not exceed the lesser of: (1) 100 percent of the participant's highest average compensation during a consecutive three-year period of plan participation or (2) $175,000 (the inflation-adjusted limit for 2006) (Code Sec. 415(b)(1)). Certain forms of benefit, such as a lump-sum benefit, are adjusted to an equivalent straight-life annuity for purposes of applying this limitation. The adjustment is made under a minimum valuation rule that uses an interest rate assumption that is not less than the greater of: (1) the applicable interest rate described in Code Sec. 417(e)(3) (i.e., the interest rate on 30-year Treasury securities in the month prior to the distribution which is used to determine a minimum lump-sum distribution) or (2) the interest rate specified in the plan (Code Sec. 415(b)(2)(B), Code Sec. 415(b)(2)(E)(i), and Code Sec. 415(b)(2)(E)(ii), prior to amendment by the Pension Funding Equity Act of 2004 (P.L. 108-218)). However, under a temporary provision that applies to plan years beginning in 2004 and 2005, the interest rate may not be less than the greater of (1) 5.5 percent or (2) the interest rate specified in the plan (Code Sec. 415(b)(2)(E)(ii), as amended by P.L. 108-218).

NEW LAW EXPLAINED

Interest rate assumption for applying benefit limitations to lump-sum distributions.—Effective for distributions made in years beginning after December 31, 2005, for purposes of adjusting a benefit from a defined benefit plan in a form that is subject to the minimum value rules (e.g., a lump-sum distribution), the interest rate assumption may not be less than the greatest of:

(1) 5.5 percent;

(2) the rate that provides a benefit of not more than 105 percent of the benefit that would be provided if the applicable interest rate (as defined in Code Sec. 417(e)(3)) were the interest rate assumption; or

(3) the interest rate specified in the plan (Code Sec. 415(b)(2)(E)(ii), as amended by the Pension Protection Act of 2006).

Caution Note: As noted in the "Background" section above, the Code Sec. 417(e)(3) applicable interest rate is currently based on the rate for 30-year Treasury notes for the month before the date of the distribution. However, the new law has also amended the definition of the applicable interest rate in Code Sec. 417(e)(3), effective for plan years beginning after December 31, 2007. The new definition of applicable interest rate will be based on rates provided by investment grade corporate bonds. These rates should be higher than 30-year Treasury yields. See ¶905.

Comment: There are now three possible interest rate assumptions rather than two. The temporary 5.5 percent rate for 2004 and 2005 plan years is made permanent. The applicable interest rate previously defined solely by reference to the 30-year Treasury rate is changed to a rate that provides a minimum lump-sum benefit of 105 percent of the benefit provided by the 30-year Treasury rate. As noted above, however, this interest rate assumption ends in plan years beginning after December 31, 2007 and is replaced with a presumably higher interest rate assumption based on corporate yields.

Planning Note: Anticutback rules (Code Sec. 411(d)(6) and ERISA Sec. 204(g)) prohibit amendments to a qualified retirement plan that decrease the accrued benefits of a plan participant. If certain requirements are met, however, a plan amendment to implement the change made by this provision may be made retroactively without violating the anticutback rule. See ¶1090.

▶ **Effective date.** The provision applies to distributions made in years beginning after December 31, 2005 (Act Sec. 303(b) of the Pension Protection Act of 2006).

Law source: Law at ¶5095. Committee Report at ¶10,210.

— Act Sec. 303(a) of the Pension Protection Act of 2006, amending Code Sec. 415(b)(2)(E)(ii);

— Act Sec. 303(b), providing the effective date.

Reporter references: For further information, consult the following CCH reporters.

— Pension Plan Guide, ¶1561 and ¶1607

— Standard Federal Tax Reporter, 2006FED ¶19,218.025

— Tax Research Consultant, RETIRE: 36,154.20

¶745 Purchase of Permissive Service Credit

SUMMARY OF NEW LAW

Government employees can purchase permissive service credit that relates to benefits to which they are not otherwise entitled under a governmental plan. Service as an elementary or secondary school employee is determined under the law of the jurisdiction in which the service was performed. The limitation on nonqualified service credit does not apply to trustee-to-trustee transfers from a 403(b) or 457 plan to a governmental plan to purchase permissive service credit.

BACKGROUND

Many state and local governmental retirement plans ease the portability of pension benefits by permitting their employees to voluntarily purchase permissive service credit for their service with another governmental employer, or for other service as provided in the plan. A "permissive service credit" is credit for a period of service, recognized by the plan for purposes of calculating the employee's plan benefit, which the employee has *not* received under the plan, but can receive only if he or she voluntarily contributes an amount (actuarially determined under the plan) that does not exceed the amount necessary to fund the benefit attributable to the service credit (Code Sec. 415(n)(3)(A)). The contribution is in addition to regular contributions made by, or on behalf of, the employee to the plan.

In a private letter ruling, the IRS has held permissive service credit treatment did not apply to inactive participants of a state defined benefit plan, who were fully vested in the plan, and who sought to make voluntary plan contributions to purchase certain enhancements under an alternative benefit program. The plan and the enhancement program constituted two benefit structures in a single plan, the IRS ruled, so the enhanced benefit is treated as credit for service already received (IRS Letter Ruling 200229051).

Contributions to a governmental plan to purchase permissive service credit will be taken into account by: (1) treating the accrued benefit derived from the contributions as an annual benefit, for purposes of the defined benefit plan limit; or (2) treating the contributions as annual additions, for purposes of the defined contribution plan limit (Code Sec. 415(n)(1)). If an employee repays contributions and earnings to a governmental plan that were previously refunded due to a service credit forfeiture under the plan (or under another plan maintained by a governmental employer within the same state), then the repayment is not taken into account for purposes of the limitations on contributions and benefits (Code Sec. 415(k)(3)). Service credit obtained as a result of such repayment will also not be considered permissive service credit for purposes of the limitations on contributions and benefits.

Nonqualified service. A governmental plan will fail to meet the requirements of the permissive service credit rules if more than five years of permissive service credit is

BACKGROUND

purchased by an employee for nonqualified service, or if any nonqualified service is taken into account for an employee with less than five years of participation in the plan (Code Sec. 415(n)(3)(B)). "Nonqualified service" is service *other than:*

- service as a federal, state or local government employee, except for military service or service for credit obtained due to a service credit forfeiture repayment;
- service as an employee of a government employees association;
- service as an employee of an elementary or secondary school (through grade 12), as determined under state law; or
- military service recognized by the plan, but not if the individual is entitled to reemployment rights.

Service is nonqualified, however, if a plan participant can receive a retirement benefit for the same service under more than one plan; this restriction does not apply to military service (Code Sec. 415(n)(3)(C)).

> **Comment:** For this purpose, "service" as a government employee or as a school employee includes parental, medical, sabbatical and similar leave.

Transfers from 403(b) and 457 plans. An individual taxpayer can exclude from gross income a direct trustee-to-trustee transfer of funds from a Code Sec. 403(b) annuity or Code Sec. 457 plan to a defined benefit governmental plan if the transfer's purpose is to: (1) purchase permissive service credit under the plan; or (2) repay contributions and earnings with respect to a previous forfeiture of service credit (Code Secs. 403(b)(13) and 457(e)(17)).

NEW LAW EXPLAINED

Permissive service credit treatment expanded.—The permissive service credit rules are expanded to include service credit relating to benefits to which the plan participant *is not otherwise entitled* under the governmental plan, rather than service credit which the participant *has not received* under the plan (Joint Committee on Taxation, Technical Explanation of the Pension Protection Act of 2006 (JCX-38-06)). Specifically, permissive service credit may include service credit for periods for which there is no performance of service, subject to the limits on nonqualified service. In addition, permissive service credit may include service credited to an employee to provide an increased benefit for service credit that a participant is already receiving under the plan (Code Sec. 415(n)(3)(A), as amended by the Pension Protection Act of 2006).

> **Practical Analysis:** Mary Beth Braitman, Terry A.M. Mumford and Lisa Erb Harrison, of Ice Miller LLP, Indianapolis, Indiana, note that the Act provides significant relief concerning the definition of "permissive service credit" as interpreted by the IRS in several recent private letter rulings. First, it clarifies that participants (as opposed to just current employees) are eligible for this provision. Second, this section provides that permissive service may include periods for which there is no performance

NEW LAW EXPLAINED

of service and also may include service already credited where an increased (or enhanced) benefit is being purchased.

In other words, the Act makes it clear that a defined benefit governmental plan may allow so-called air time purchases or buy-ups (*e.g.*, to a higher benefit tier or formula) to be purchased under the special limits of Code Sec. 415(n) or *via* an in-service, trustee-to-trustee transfer from a 457(b) deferred compensation plan or 403(b) tax-sheltered annuity plan. As the JCT's Technical Explanation (JCX-38-06) provides, the definition now relates to *benefits* to which the participant is not otherwise entitled to under the plan, rather than service credit which the participant has not received under the plan. It also clarifies and expands the elementary and secondary education service definition.

Please note that these changes do not mandate that a qualified governmental defined benefit plan allow any particular service purchases, nor that participants who are no longer employed must be eligible for purchases.

In addition, a 457(b) deferred compensation plan and 403(b) tax-sheltered annuity plan is not required to allow in-service transfers for this purpose. Whether or not such transfers are permitted is still up to the individual plan terms. The Act also clarifies that once such a transfer is made, the defined benefit plan's distribution rules apply to the transferred amounts.

Example: Purchasing permissive service credit to provide an increased benefit for a period of service already credited under the plan can occur where a lower benefit level is converted to a higher benefit level otherwise offered under the same plan (Joint Committee on Taxation, Technical Explanation of the Pension Protection Act of 2006 (JCX-38-06)). Thus, the amendment appears to effectively nullify the impact of IRS Letter Ruling 200229051.

Nonqualified service credit limitation. In determining the limitation on nonqualified service credit, service as an elementary or secondary school employee is determined under the law of the jurisdiction in which the service was performed, rather than simply under "state law" (Code Sec. 415(n)(3)(C)(ii), as amended by the Pension Act).

Example: Permissive service credit can be granted for time spent teaching outside of the United States without being considered nonqualified service credit (Joint Committee on Taxation, Technical Explanation of the Pension Protection Act of 2006 (JCX-38-06)).

Transfers from 403(b) and 457 plans. The limitations on nonqualified service credit will not apply to trustee-to-trustee transfers from a Code Sec. 403(b) annuity or Code Sec. 457 plan to a governmental defined benefit plan to purchase permissive service credit. Thus, failure of the transferee plan to satisfy the five years of nonqualified service credit or five-year participation rules will not cause the transferred amounts to be included in a plan participant's gross income. Such transferred amounts, however, will be subject to

NEW LAW EXPLAINED

the distribution rules that apply to the governmental plan. These special rules apply regardless of whether the transfer is made between plans maintained by the same employer (Code Sec. 415(n)(3)(D), as added by the Pension Act).

▶ **Effective date.** The amendments relating to changes in the definition of a permissive service credit and nonqualified service are effective for contributions to purchase permissive service credits made in years beginning after December 31, 1997 (Act Sec. 821(d)(1) of the Pension Protection Act of 2006; Act Sec. 1526(a) of the Taxpayer Relief Act of 1997 (P.L. 105-34)). The amendments relating to transfers from a Code Sec. 403(b) annuity or Code Sec. 457 plan apply to trustee-to-trustee transfers after December 31, 2001 (Act Sec. 821(d)(2) of the Pension Act; Act Sec. 647(c) of the Economic Growth and Tax Relief Reconciliation Act of 2001 (P.L. 107-16)).

Law source: Law at ¶5095. Committee Report at ¶10,620.

— Act Sec. 821(a) of the Pension Protection Act of 2006, amending Code Sec. 415(n)(1) and (3)(A);

— Act Sec. 821(b), adding Code Sec. 415(n)(3)(D);

— Act Sec. 821(c), amending Code Sec. 415(n)(3)(B) and (C);

— Act Sec. 821(d), providing the effective dates.

Reporter references: For further information, consult the following CCH reporters.

— Pension Plan Guide, ¶8017A

— Standard Federal Tax Reporter, 2006FED ¶19,218.026

— Tax Research Consultant, RETIRE: 36,212

— Federal Tax Guide, 2006FTG ¶11,660

Health and Medical Benefits

¶805 Funding Future Retiree and Collectively Bargained Health Benefit Plans

SUMMARY OF NEW LAW

Pension plans may now transfer excess pension assets to retiree medical accounts to fund *future* retiree health benefit and collectively bargained retiree health benefit plans.

BACKGROUND

Since 1962 pension plans have been able to maintain separate accounts providing health benefits for retired employees. The separate account requirement was put in place to keep assets accumulated for payment of post-retirement health benefits strictly separated from assets accumulated for payment of pension benefits. Before changes were made by the Revenue Reconciliation Act of 1990 (P.L. 101-508) (1990 Act), it was not possible to transfer excess pension assets to a retiree medical account without adverse tax consequences. In this regard, Congress came to recognize two facts: (1) the continuing cost escalations of medical care made it difficult for many employers to fund retiree medical accounts by way of current contributions; and (2) excess assets currently earmarked for plan benefits presented a possible funding source for retiree health benefits.

BACKGROUND

Subject to restrictions, the 1990 Act made it possible for pension plans (other than multiemployer plans) to transfer retirement plan assets to retiree medical accounts, generally effective for "qualified transfers" after 1990 and before 2014. If made within this time frame, a transfer is a qualified transfer if it contravenes no law and satisfies specified requirements regarding the use of the transferred assets, the vesting of the accrued retirement benefits, and the health benefit coverage for retirees (Code Sec. 420(b) and (c)).

Assets transferred in a qualified transfer (and any income derived from those assets) can only be used to pay current retiree health benefits for the tax year of the transfer. Amounts not so expended must be returned at the end of the tax year to the pension plan's general retirement account (Code Sec. 420(c)(1)). Only one qualified transfer can be made in any tax year of the employer, and the transfer is not allowed to fund either future health benefits of retirees or collectively bargained retiree health benefits (Code Sec. 420(b)(2) and (3)).

For purposes of determining whether a pension plan has excess benefits that may be transferred to a retiree medical account, the term "excess pension assets" means the value of the plan's assets (as calculated for purposes of the full funding limitation under Code Sec. 412(c)), over the greater of: (1) the accrued liability under the plan (including normal cost); or (2) 125 percent of the plan's current liability (Code Sec. 420(e)(2)).

NEW LAW EXPLAINED

Transfers to cover future retiree health and collectively bargained health benefits.—For transfers made after August 17, 2006, the date of enactment of the Pension Protection Act of 2006, an employer will have two additional means of funding retiree health benefits: the "qualified future transfer" and the "collectively bargained transfer." With several exceptions discussed below, the rules that apply to these two new transfer elections generally follow the qualified transfer rules enacted by the Revenue Reconciliation Act of 1990 (P.L. 101-508) (1990 Act). Like the qualified transfer rules of the 1990 Act, qualified future transfers and collectively bargained transfers are funded from excess pension plan assets. Also, a transfer that meets all of the requirements for being a qualified future transfer or a collectively bargained transfer will avoid the otherwise applicable negative tax consequences that typically follow a withdrawal of excess plan benefits. Thus, as a qualified transfer or collectively bargained transfer:

(1) neither the qualified status of the retirement benefit portion of the plan nor that of the health benefits account will be affected by the transfer;

(2) no amount will be included in the gross income of the employer because of the transfer;

(3) the transfer will not be treated as a reversion subject to the excise tax imposed by Code Sec. 4980; and

(4) the transfer will not be treated as a prohibited transaction subject to the excise tax imposed by Code Sec. 4975.

NEW LAW EXPLAINED

Like the 1990 Act rules, the new rules relating to qualified future transfers and collectively bargained transfers do not apply to transfers from a multiemployer plan, see ¶ 810 (Code Sec. 420(f)(1), as added by the Pension Protection Act of 2006).

> **Comment:** The new rules relating to qualified future transfers and collectively bargained transfers will not apply to transfers made after December 31, 2013 (Joint Committee on Taxation, Technical Explanation of the Pension Protection Act of 2006 (JCX-38-06)).

> **Practical Analysis:** Mary Beth Braitman, Terry A.M. Mumford and Lisa Erb Harrison of Ice Miller LLP, Indianapolis, Indiana, note that governmental plans need to realize that Code Sec. 420, as amended in this provision, creates the only mechanism whereby assets may be transferred between pension plan reserves and retiree medical reserves. Unless the plan can meet the requirements of Code Sec. 420, no such transfer may be made.

Qualified future and collectively bargained transfers. With respect to qualified future transfers and collectively bargained transfers, the term "transfer period" means a period of consecutive tax years (not less than two) which begins and ends during the 10-tax-year period beginning with the tax year in which the transfer is made (Code Sec. 420(f)(5), as added by the Pension Act). To be a qualified future transfer or a collectively bargained transfer, a transfer generally must meet the requirements for a qualified transfer. In addition, specific rules apply for determining excess pension assets, limitations on amounts transferred, and minimum cost requirements (Code Sec. 420(f)(2)(A), as added by the Pension Act). Collectively bargained transfers also have additional rules. For example, there are specific minimum cost requirements for collectively bargained transfers.

Special definitions applicable to collectively bargained transfers. A "collectively bargained health plan" is defined as a group health plan or arrangement for retired employees and their spouses and dependents that is maintained pursuant to one or more collective bargaining agreements (Code Sec. 420(f)(6)(D), as added by the Pension Act). "Collectively bargained health benefits" means health benefits or coverage provided to:

(1) retired employees (who, immediately before the collectively bargained transfer, are entitled to receive such benefits upon retirement and are entitled to pension benefits under the plan);

(2) spouses and dependents of such retired employees; and

(3) if specified by the collective bargaining agreement governing the transfer, active employees who, following their retirement, are entitled to receive such benefits and are entitled to pension benefits under the plan. Such coverage may also be provided to the spouses and dependents of these employees (Code Sec. 420(f)(6)(C), as added by the Pension Act).

The "collectively bargained cost maintenance period" means, with respect to each covered retiree and his or her covered spouse and dependents, the shorter of the

NEW LAW EXPLAINED

remaining lifetime of the covered retiree and the covered spouse or dependents, or the period of coverage provided by the collectively bargained health plan (determined as of the date of the collectively bargained transfer) for these covered individuals (Code Sec. 420(f)(6)(A), as added by the Pension Act).

The term "collectively bargained retiree health liabilities" means the present value, as of the beginning of a tax year and determined in accordance with the applicable collective bargaining agreement, of all collectively bargained health benefits (including administrative expenses) for such tax year and all later tax years during the collectively bargained cost maintenance period (Code Sec. 420(f)(6)(B)(i), as added by the Pension Act). These health liabilities must be reduced by the value (as of the close of the plan year preceding the year of the collectively bargained transfer) of the assets in all health benefits accounts or welfare benefit funds (as defined in Code Sec. 419(e)(1)) set aside to pay for the collectively bargained retiree health liabilities (Code Sec. 420(f)(6)(B)(ii), as added by the Pension Act). If an employee is a key employee (within the meaning of Code Sec. 416(I)(1)), with respect to any plan year ending in a tax year, that employee is not to be taken into account in computing collectively bargained retiree health liabilities for such tax year, or in calculating collectively bargained employer cost under Code Sec. 420(c)(3)(C) (Code Sec. 420(f)(6)(B)(iii), as added by the Pension Act).

Definition of collectively bargained transfer. If a transfer of excess pension assets meets the definition of a "collectively bargained transfer," the transfer is a qualified transfer under Code Sec. 420. In addition to the qualified transfer requirements, the following rules must also be met with respect to a collectively bargained transfer:

(1) the transfer must be made in accordance with a collective bargaining agreement (Code Sec. 420(f)(2)(E)(i)(I), as added by the Pension Act);

(2) the employer, before the transfer, must deliver a written notice designating the transfer as a collectively bargained transfer to each employee organization that is a party to the collective bargaining agreement (Code Sec. 420(f)(2)(E)(i)(II), as added by the Pension Act); and

(3) the transfer must be made with respect to an employer plan which, in its tax year ending in 2005, provided health benefits or coverage to retirees and their spouses and dependents under all benefit plans maintained by the employer, but only if the aggregate costs (including administrative expenses) of these benefits meet a five-percent-of-gross receipts test. This test is satisfied if the aggregate costs of such benefits or coverage that would have been allowable as a deduction to the employer (if such benefits or coverage had been paid directly by the employer and the employer used the cash method or accounting) is at least five percent of the employer's gross receipts (determined in accordance with the last sentence of Code Sec. 420(c)(2)(E)(ii)(II)) for such tax year. A plan that is maintained by a successor to the employer may also satisfy the above requirements (Code Sec. 420(f)(2)(E)(i)(III), as added by the Pension Act).

Any assets that are transferred to a health benefit account in a collectively bargained transfer (including income allocable thereto) must only be used to pay collectively bargained retiree health liabilities (other than liabilities of key employees not taken

NEW LAW EXPLAINED

into account under the rules of Code Sec. 420(f)(6)(B)(iii), as added by the Pension Act), for the tax year of the transfer, or for any subsequent tax year during the collectively bargained cost maintenance period (Code Sec. 420(f)(2)(E)(ii), as added by the Pension Act).

Excess pensions assets. Qualified future transfers and collectively bargained transfers can be made to the extent that the plan assets exceed the greater of the plan's accrued liability or 120 percent of the plan's current liability (Code Sec. 420(f)(2)(B)(i), as added by the Pension Act).

> **Comment:** The above rule is identical to the rule for determining excess pension assets when transferring assets to fund qualified *current* retiree health benefits, except that a 125 percent, rather than a 120 percent, requirement applies to the plan's current liabilities (Code Sec. 420(e)(2), as amended by the Pension Act).

After transferring excess pension assets to fund future retiree or collectively bargained health benefits, an employer is required to maintain the pension plan's funded status at the minimum level during the transfer period.

If, on the valuation date of any plan year in the transfer period, the retirement plan's liabilities (as determined under Code Sec. 420(e)(2)(B)), exceed the value of its assets (as determined under Code Sec. 420(e)(2)(A)), the employer maintaining the plan must take either of two actions. First, the employer may choose to make an additional contribution to the pension plan in an amount that will reduce the excess of liabilities over assets to zero. Failing that, the employer would have to transfer that same amount from the health benefits account back to the pension retirement account (Code Sec. 420(f)(2)(B)(ii), as added by the Pension Act).

Limits on amounts transferred. With regard to the transfer of excess pension assets to fund *current* retiree health benefits, the transfer is limited to the amount which is reasonably estimated to be the amount that the employer will pay (whether directly or through reimbursement) out of the account during the tax year of the transfer (Code Sec. 420(b)(3)). A qualified transfer to cover *future* retiree health costs is not limited to the amount computed under Code Sec. 420(b)(3). Rather, the maximum for future retiree health costs is equal to the sum of:

(1) the amount determined under Code Sec. 420(b)(3) for the tax year of the transfer; plus

(2) the sum of the yearly qualified current retiree health liabilities that the plan reasonably estimates will be incurred for each of the remaining years in the transfer period, in accordance with guidance to be issued by the IRS (Code Sec. 420(f)(2)(C)(i), as added by the Pension Act).

The amount of excess pension assets transferred in a *collectively bargained transfer* cannot exceed the amount that is reasonably estimated to be the amount the employer will pay (whether directly or through reimbursement) out of the account during the collectively bargained cost maintenance period for collectively bargained retiree health liabilities. The above determination is to be made in accordance with the collective bargaining agreement and generally accepted accounting principles (Code Sec. 420(f)(2)(C)(ii), as added by the Pension Act).

NEW LAW EXPLAINED

In applying the amount-of-transfer limitations of Code Sec. 420(b)(3) to any subsequent transfer during a tax year in a transfer period or collectively bargained cost maintenance period, qualified current retiree health liabilities must be reduced by any such liabilities that had been taken into account with respect to the qualified future transfer or collectively bargained transfer to which such period relates (Code Sec. 420(f)(3), as added by the Pension Act).

Minimum cost requirements—Qualified future transfers. The minimum cost requirements of Code Sec. 420(c)(3) will be satisfied if the annual average cost of the future retiree health benefits provided during the period beginning with the first year of the transfer period and ending with the last day of the fourth year following the transfer period is not less than the employer's cost determined under Code Sec. 420(c)(3)(A) with respect to the transfer (Code Sec. 420(f)(2)(D)(i)(I), as added by the Pension Act). Under Code Sec. 420(c)(3), the employer's cost for each tax year in the "health maintenance period" (the five tax years beginning with the tax year of the transfer) must not be less than the higher of the employer's cost for each of the two tax years immediately before the tax year of the transfer.

Instead of meeting the minimum cost requirement determined under Code Sec. 420(f)(2)(D)(i)(I), as added by the Pension Act, an employer may elect to meet the requirements under Code Sec. 420(c)(3), as they existed prior to the amendments made by section 535 of the Tax Relief Extension Act of 1999 (P.L. 106-170) (Code Sec. 420(f)(2)(D)(ii), as added by the Pension Act). Under pre-1999 Act Code Sec. 420(c)(3), the employer cost during the health maintenance period must be substantially the same as the cost of health benefits provided by the employer during the taxable year immediately before the taxable year of the transfer.

Minimum cost requirements—Collectively bargained transfers. The minimum cost requirements of Code Sec. 420(c)(3) will be met if the collectively bargained employer cost for each tax year during the collectively bargained cost maintenance period is not less than the amount specified by the collective bargaining agreement (Code Sec. 420(f)(2)(D)(i)(II), as added by the Pension Act). For purposes of this rule, "collectively bargained employer cost" is defined as the average cost per covered individual of providing collectively bargained retiree health benefits, as determined in accordance with the applicable collective bargaining agreement. Such an agreement may provide for a reduction in the collectively bargained employer cost to the extent that any portion of the collectively bargained retiree health benefits are provided or financed by a government program, or other source (Code Sec. 420(f)(2)(D)(iii), as added by the Pension Act).

Deduction limitation—Collectively bargained plans. An employer may contribute an amount to a health benefits account or a welfare benefit fund (as defined in Code Sec. 419(e)(1)) with respect to collectively bargained health liabilities, provided the transferred assets are required to be used exclusively to pay collectively bargained retiree health liabilities under the rules of Code Sec. 420(c)(1)(B). The deductibility of such a contribution will be governed by the limits applicable to the deductibility of contributions to a welfare benefit plan funded under a collective bargaining agreement (as determined under Code Sec. 419A(f)(5)(A)) without regard to whether the contributions are made to a health benefits account or welfare benefit fund, and without

NEW LAW EXPLAINED

regard to the contribution deduction rules of Code Sec. 404 or other provisions of Code Sec. 420. The IRS is directed to provide rules to ensure that the application of Code Sec. 420 within this context does not result in a double deduction for the same contribution or for two or more contributions relating to the same collectively bargained retiree health liabilities (Code Sec. 420(f)(4), as added by the Pension Act).

▶ **Effective date.** The amendments made by this section shall apply to transfers after August 17, 2006 (Act Sec. 841(b) of the Pension Protection Act of 2006).

Law source: Law at ¶5115. Committee Report at ¶10,750.

— Act Sec. 114(d)(1) of the Pension Protection Act of 2006, amending Code Sec. 420(e)(2);

— Act Sec. 841(a) adding Code Sec. 420(f);

— Act Sec. 841(b), providing the effective date.

Reporter references: For further information, consult the following CCH reporters.

— Pension Plan Guide, ¶908 and ¶9291

— Standard Federal Tax Reporter, 2006FED ¶19,303.01, ¶19,303.021, ¶19,303.022 and ¶19,303.025

— Tax Research Consultant, RETIRE: 48,158.10

— Federal Tax Guide, 2006FTG ¶11,050

¶810 Transfer of Excess Pension Assets to Multiemployer Health Plans

SUMMARY OF NEW LAW

Multiemployer defined benefit plans are permitted to make qualified transfers of excess benefit plan assets to heath plans.

BACKGROUND

Defined benefit plan assets generally may not revert to an employer prior to termination of the plan and satisfaction of all plan liabilities. A reversion prior to plan termination may constitute a prohibited transaction and may result in plan disqualification. A pension plan may provide medical benefits to retired employees through a separate account that is part of such plan. A qualified transfer of excess assets of a defined benefit plan to such a separate account within the plan may be made in order to fund retiree health benefits.

Excess assets generally means the excess, if any, of the value of the plan's assets over the greater of the accrued liability under the plan or 125 percent of the plan's current liability. Subject to rules and restrictions, a qualified transfer does not generally result in plan disqualification, is not a prohibited transaction, and is not treated as a reversion. However, qualified transfer may not be made from a multiemployer plan.

BACKGROUND

Special deduction rules apply to a multiemployer defined benefit plan established before January 1, 1954, under an agreement between the federal government and employee representatives in a certain industry.

NEW LAW EXPLAINED

Multiemployer defined benefit plans permitted to make qualified transfers of excess benefit plan assets to a heath plan.—Multiemployer defined benefit plans are now allowed to make qualified transfers of excess defined benefit plan assets to retiree health plans. This change is accomplished by treating all references to "an employer" in Code Sec. 420 relating to transfers of excess pension assets to retiree health accounts as a reference to all employers maintaining the plan, or if appropriate, to the plan sponsor (Code Sec. 420(e)(5)(A), as added by the Pension Protection Act of 2006). The IRS will make necessary adjustments to reflect the fact that the plan is not maintained by a single employer (Code Sec. 420(e)(5)(B) as added by the Pension Act).

Comment: Multiemployer benefit plans enable tens of thousands of mostly small employers to provide retirement, medical and other benefits to millions of their employees. The benefits provided are of a significantly better quality than these employers would ever have been able or willing to provide individually. Employers who participate in multiemployer plans face competition day-in and day-out from employers who provide either no benefits or minuscule benefits to their employees. The intent of this provision is to make employers who contribute to plans more efficient, better organized and more sophisticated in order to survive and to stay competitive.

Comment: The expanded funding permitted for single employers under Code Sec. 420(f) of the Pension Act is not applicable to multiemployer plans, see ¶805.

Caution Note: A qualified transfer still may not be made from a multiemployer plan that does not satisfy the Code Sec. 420 rules. For example, no more than one qualified transfer may be made in any tax year.

▶ **Effective date.** The provision applies to transfers made in tax years beginning after December 31, 2006 (Act Sec. 842(b) of the Pension Protection Act of 2006).

Law source: Law at ¶5115. Committee Report at ¶10,010 and ¶10,760.

— Act Sec. 842(a)(1) of the Pension Protection Act of 2006, amending Code Sec. 420(a);

— Act Sec. 842(a)(2), adding Code Sec. 420(e)(5);

— Act Sec. 842(b), providing the effective date.

Reporter references: For further information, consult the following CCH reporters.

— Pension Plan Guide, ¶908, ¶6786 and ¶9291

— Standard Federal Tax Reporter, 2006FED ¶19,303.01

— Tax Research Consultant, RETIRE: 48,156.30 and RETIRE: 48,158.10

¶815 Allowance of Reserve for Medical Benefits of Bona Fide Association Plans

SUMMARY OF NEW LAW

The account limit applicable to funded welfare benefit plans may include a reserve of up to 35 percent of the plan's annual costs for medical benefits (other than retiree medical benefits) provided through a plan sponsored by a bona fide association.

BACKGROUND

A welfare benefit fund is any fund that is part of a plan of an employer through which the employer provides welfare benefits to employees or their beneficiaries (Code Sec. 419(e)(1)). Contributions to a welfare benefit fund that meet the usual deductibility requirements (e.g., Code Secs. 162 and 212) are deductible for the tax year in which paid to the extent they do not exceed the qualified cost of the plan for that year (Code Sec. 419(a) and (b)). The qualified cost is generally the sum of: (1) the qualified direct cost of the plan for the tax year; and (2) the permissible additions to a qualified asset account (Code Sec. 419(c)(1)). The qualified cost is reduced by the after-tax income of the fund for the year (Code Sec. 419(c)(2)).

The qualified direct cost generally represents the expenses of the welfare benefit fund attributable to the cost of providing the current benefits. The qualified direct cost is the aggregate amount (including administrative expenses) that would have been allowed as a deduction to the employer with respect to the benefits provided during the tax year if the benefits were provided directly by the employer and the employer used the cash method of accounting (Code Sec. 419(c)(3)(A)).

A qualified asset account may be established for the payment of disability benefits, medical benefits, supplemental unemployment or severance pay benefits, and life insurance or death benefits (Code Sec. 419A(a)). Additions to a qualified asset account are taken into account in computing the deductible qualified cost only to the extent they do not result in the account exceeding the account limit (Code Sec. 419A(b)). The account limit is the amount estimated to be reasonably and actuarially necessary to fund the liabilities of the plan for the amount of claims incurred but unpaid (as of the close of the tax year) and the administrative costs of such claims (Code Sec. 419A(c)). The account limit may include a reserve for post-retirement medical or life insurance benefits funded over the working lives of the covered employees (Code Sec. 419A(c)(2)). For this purpose, medical benefits consist of the providing of medical care either directly or through insurance (Code Sec. 419A(f)(2)).

The account limits do not apply to a welfare benefit fund that is part of a ten-or-more-employer plan. A ten-or-more-employer plan is a plan to which more than one employer contributes and no employer normally contributes more than ten percent of the total contributions. A ten-or-more-employer plan may not maintain experience-rating arrangements with respect to individual employers (Code Sec. 419A(f)(6)).

NEW LAW EXPLAINED

Additional reserve allowed for medical benefits of plans sponsored by bona fide associations.—The Pension Protection Act of 2006 allows an applicable account limit to include a reserve for medical benefits (other than post-retirement medical benefits) of bona fide association plans. The reserve amount for any tax year may not exceed 35 percent of the sum of the qualified direct costs and the change in incurred, but unpaid, claims for that year (Code Sec. 419A(c)(6)(A), as added by the Pension Act). For this purpose, an applicable account limit is an account limit for a qualified asset account with respect to medical benefits provided through a plan maintained by a bona fide association (Code Sec. 419A(c)(6)(B), as added by the Pension Act).

> **Comment:** The amendment allows employers to deduct the amounts contributed to fund the additional reserve for medical benefits provided through a bona fide association.

The definition of a bona fide association is set forth in section 2791(d)(3) of the Public Health Service Act and includes an association that has been actively in existence for at least five years and has been formed and maintained in good faith for purposes other than obtaining insurance. A bona fide association must not condition membership on any health status-related factor relating to an individual (including an employee or a dependent of an employee) and must make health insurance coverage available to all members regardless of any health status-related factors. In addition, the association must not make the offered health insurance coverage available other than in connection with a member of the association and must meet any other additional requirements imposed by state law (42 U.S.C. 300gg-91(d)(3)).

▶ **Effective date.** The provision applies to tax years beginning after December 31, 2006 (Act Sec. 843(b) of the Pension Protection Act of 2006).

Law source: Law at ¶5112. Committee Report at ¶10,770.

— Act Sec. 843(a) of the Pension Protection Act of 2006, adding Code Sec. 419A(c)(6);

— Act Sec. 843(b), providing the effective date.

Reporter references: For further information, consult the following CCH reporters.

— Pension Plan Guide, ¶9140

— Standard Federal Tax Reporter, 2006FED ¶19,301.01, ¶19,301.025 and ¶19,301.028

— Tax Research Consultant, COMPEN: 42,156

¶820 Long-Term Health Care Insurance Riders on Annuity and Life Insurance Contracts

SUMMARY OF NEW LAW

The cost of a qualified long-term care insurance coverage rider that is charged against the cash value of an annuity contract or the cash surrender value of a life insurance contract will not be treated as a taxable distribution under the contract. Modifications

SUMMARY OF NEW LAW

are made to the existing rules when long-term care coverage is provided as a rider on a life insurance contract.

BACKGROUND

A qualified long-term care insurance contract is treated as an accident and health insurance contract (Code Sec. 7702B(a)(1)). In 2006, benefits on per diem contracts are excludable from income subject to a $250 per day dollar cap or an annual cap of $91,250. Actual long-term care costs in excess of the caps, however, are also excludable from income. Amounts in excess of the caps that are not used to pay for long-term care services are fully includible in income without regard to the rules allowing a tax-free return of basis under Code Sec. 72.

A qualified long-term care contract is not permitted to provide for cash surrender value or other money that can be paid, assigned, or pledged as collateral for a loan. In addition, all premium refunds must be used to reduce future premiums or increase future benefits (Code Sec. 7702B(b)(1)).

If long-term care insurance coverage is provided as a rider on a life insurance contract, the requirements applicable to long-term care insurance contracts apply as if the portion of the contract providing the coverage were a separate contract (Code Sec. 7702B(e)). As a result, if the applicable requirements are met by the long-term care portion of the contract, health care benefits received under the contract are treated in the same manner as long-term care insurance benefits whether or not the benefit payments cause a reduction in the contract's death benefit or cash surrender value.

Certain tax-free exchanges of insurance and annuity contracts are allowed (Code Sec. 1035). Specifically, no gain or loss is recognized on the exchange of:

(1) a life insurance contract for another life insurance contract or for an endowment or annuity contract or an ltcc;

(2) an endowment contract for an annuity contract or for another endowment contract providing for regular payments beginning at a date not later than the beginning date under the old contract; or

(3) one annuity contract for another annuity contract.

Gain realized on the exchange of an endowment contract or annuity contract for a life insurance contract or an exchange of an annuity contract for an endowment contract must be recognized.

NEW LAW EXPLAINED

Treatment of annuity and life insurance contracts with a long-term care insurance feature.—New rules provide favorable tax treatment for a long-term care insurance contract that is provided by a rider on or as part of an annuity or life insurance contract. Modifications are also made to the existing rules applicable when such a contract is provided as a rider on or part of a life insurance contract. The provisions are

NEW LAW EXPLAINED

generally effective for tax years beginning after December 31, 2009, except as noted below.

> **Comment:** An annuity or life insurance contract that provides qualified long-term care insurance as a rider or part of the contract is referred to as a "combination contract."

Changes made by the Pension Protection Act of 2006 include the following:

- Charges against the cash value of a combination contract for qualified long-term care insurance coverage are not included in income but reduce the investment in the contract.
- The portion of a combination contract providing long-term care insurance coverage (whether or not qualified) is treated as a separate contract and amounts received are treated in the same manner as long-term care insurance benefits whether or not the payment causes a reduction in the death benefit or cash surrender value of the life insurance contract or the cash value of an annuity contract.
- No medical expense deduction is allowed for charges attributable to the provision of qualified long-term care coverage under a combination contract.
- Certain retirement-related arrangements are not treated as annuity contracts for purposes of the provision.
- Noncombination contracts and combination contracts may be exchanged in a Code Sec. 1035 nonrecognition transaction.
- Annual information reports must show cash value reductions and income exclusions.
- For purposes of the definition of a life insurance contract:
  - — specified policy acquisition expenses that must be capitalized are determined using 7.7 percent of the net premiums for the tax year on the long-term care contract; and
  - — charges against the contract's cash surrender value for coverage under a long-term care insurance rider reduce premiums paid for purposes of computing the guideline premium limitation.

Exclusion from gross income. Charges against the cash value of an annuity contract or the cash surrender value of a life insurance contract for coverage under a qualified long-term care insurance contract which is part of or a rider on the annuity or life insurance contract reduce the investment in the contract (but not below zero) and are not includible in gross income (Code Sec. 72(e)(11), as added by the Pension Protection Act of 2006).

Tax-free exchanges. As noted above, present law allows the tax-free exchange of certain insurance and annuity contracts (Code Sec. 1035). The new law expands this provision to also allow the tax-free exchange of:

(1) a life insurance contract for a qualified long-term care insurance contract;

(2) a contract of endowment insurance for a qualified long-term care insurance contract;

NEW LAW EXPLAINED

(3) an annuity contract for a qualified long-term care insurance contract; and

(4) a qualified long-term care insurance contract for a qualified long-term care insurance contract (Code Sec. 1035(a), as amended by the Pension Act).

For purposes of the nonrecognition rules, an annuity or life insurance contract will not fail to be treated as an annuity or life insurance contract solely because a qualified long-term care insurance contract is a part of or a rider on the annuity or insurance contract (Code Sec. 1035(b)(2) and (3), as amended by the Pension Act).

> **Comment:** The new law does not amend Code Sec. 1035(b)(1) to provide that an endowment contract will not fail to be treated as an endowment contract if a qualified long-term care insurance contract is part of or a rider on the endowment contract.

> **Caution Note:** The changes to the nonrecognition rules apply to exchanges occurring after December 31, 2009 (Act Sec. 844(g)(2) of the Pension Act).

> **Comment:** Under the new law, a taxpayer will be able to receive a qualified long-term care insurance contract in exchange for an annuity, endowment, or life insurance contract without recognizing gain or loss. One long-term care insurance contract may also be exchanged tax-free for another such contract. A life insurance contract can be exchanged tax-free for an annuity contract whether or not the contracts (one or both contracts) are combination contracts. Similarly, an annuity contract can be exchanged tax-free for an annuity contract whether or not one or both are combination contracts. The current rule which prevents the tax-free exchange of an annuity or endowment contract for a life insurance contract (or an annuity contract for an endowment contract) continues to apply (whether or not the contracts are combination contracts).

Treatment of long-term health insurance coverage provided under a combination contract. Except as provided in regulations, when long-term health care coverage (whether or not qualified) is provided by a rider on or as part of a life-insurance or annuity contract, the portion of the contract that provides the coverage is treated as a separate long-term health insurance contract for all purposes of the Code (Code Sec. 7702B(e)(1), as amended by the Pension Act). The portion that provides long-term health care coverage refers to only the terms and benefits under the life insurance contract or annuity contract that are in addition to the terms and benefits under the contract without regard to long-term care coverage (Code Sec. 7702B(e)(3), as amended by the Pension Act).

> **Comment:** Previously, the separate contract rule only applied to long-term care coverage provided under an insurance contract (Code Sec. 7702B(e)(1), prior to amendment by the Pension Act). Now it also applies to long-term care coverage provided under an annuity contract. The Pension Act also makes a retroactive technical correction with respect to combination insurance contracts that clarifies that separate contract treatment applies not only for purposes of Code Sec. 7702B but for purposes of all other Code provisions (Code Sec. 7702B(e)(3), as amended by the Pension Act).

None of the following retirement related arrangements may be treated as an annuity contract for purposes of the rule that treats long-term health care insurance coverage

NEW LAW EXPLAINED

provided with an annuity contract as a separate contract (Code Sec. 7702B(e)(4), as amended by the Pension Act):

(1) A tax-exempt trust forming part of a stock bonus, pension, or profit-sharing plan (i.e., a qualified plan) (Code Sec. 401(a)).

(2) A contract—

- purchased by a tax-exempt Code Sec. 401(a) trust,
- purchased as part of a qualified annuity plan described in Code Sec. 403(a),
- purchased by a section 501(c)(3) organization or public school (i.e., a contract described in Code Sec. 403(b)),
- provided for employees of a life insurance company under a pension plan contract described in Code Sec. 818(a)(3), or
- from an individual retirement account or an individual retirement annuity.

(3) A contract purchased by an employer for the benefit of the employee or the employee's spouse.

An applicable dividend paid in cash by a C corporation with respect to applicable employer securities to a participant or beneficiary (i.e., a dividend described in Code Sec. 404(k)) is treated as paid under a separate contract that was purchased by a tax-exempt Code Sec. 401(a) trust.

No itemized medical expense deduction may be claimed for any payment made for coverage under a qualified long-term care insurance contract if the payment is made as a charge against the cash surrender value of a life insurance contract or the cash value of an annuity contract (Code Sec. 7701B(e)(2), as amended by the Pension Act).

> **Comment:** Under prior law, a medical expense deduction for charges against a life insurance contract's cash surrender value that were attributable to a qualifed long-term care rider were deductible as medical expenses (i.e., deductible as insurance premiums subject to the generally applicable 7.5 percent adjusted gross income limitation) if the charges were includible in income because the life insurance contract was treated as a modified endowment contract under Code Secs. 72(e)(10) and 7702B(e)(3) (Code Sec. 7702B(e)(3), prior to amendment by the Pension Act).

Information reporting. The person who makes a charge against the cash value of a combination annuity contract or a charge against the cash surrender value of a combination life insurance contract that is not includible in income under this provision must file an annual information return with the IRS that shows the charges against the contract for the calendar year, the amount of the reduction in the investment in the contract resulting from the charges, and the name, address, and taxpayer identification number of the contract holder (Code Sec. 6050U(a), as added by the Pension Act).

The filer must also provide the contract holder with a written statement that shows the information shown on the information return and provides the name, address, and phone number of the information contract of the person making the payments. This statement is due on or before January 31 of the year following the calendar year

NEW LAW EXPLAINED

for which the information return is filed (Code Sec. 6050U(b), as added by the Pension Act).

The penalty imposed by Code Sec. 6721 for failure to file a timely and correct information return with the IRS by the due date applies (Code Sec. 6724(d)(1)(B)(xix), as added by the Pension Act). Generally, this penalty is $50 per return up to a maximum penalty of $250,000 per calendar year. The Code Sec. 6722 penalty for failure to file a timely and correct payee statement also applies (Code Sec. 6724(d)(2)(CC), as added by the Pension Act). This penalty is generally $50 per statement up to a maximum of $100,000.

Treatment of policy acquisition expenses. A combination annuity or life insurance contract is treated as a specified insurance contract not described in Code Secs. 848(c)(1)(A) (i.e., a specified insurance contract that is an annuity contract) or 848(c)(1)(B) (i.e., a specified insurance contract that is a group life insurance contract) (Code Sec. 848(e)(6), as added by the Pension Act). Consequently, the specified policy acquisition expenses that must be capitalized is determined using 7.7 percent of the net premiums for the tax year as prescribed by Code Sec. 848(c)(1)(C) for specified insurance contracts that are not annuity contract or group life insurance contracts.

> **Comment:** Rates of 1.75 percent and 2.05 percent respectively apply to specified insurance contracts that are annuity contracts and group life insurance contracts.

Guideline premium limitation. A life insurance contract is required to meet the guideline premium limitation described in Code Sec. 7702(c) if it does not meet the alternative cash value accumulation test described in Code Sec. 7702(b). Under present law, the guideline premium limitation is increased by the charges (but not premium payments) against the life insurance contract's cash surrender value for long-term health care coverage (whether or not qualified) less charges the imposition of which reduces the premiums paid for the contract (Code Sec. 7702B(e)(2), prior to repeal by the Pension Act).

For tax years beginning after December 21, 2009, the guideline premium limitation is not directly increased by charges against a life insurance contract's cash surrender value for coverage under the long-term care insurance portion of the contract. Because these charges will be excluded from the holder's income, they reduce premiums paid under Code Sec. 7702(f)(1) for purposes of the guideline premium limitation. The reduction in premiums paid is intended to be equal to the sum of any charges other than premium payments against the life insurance contract's cash surrender value for long-term care coverage made to that date under the contract.

> **Comment:** Code Sec. 7702B(e)(2), the so-called "pay-as-you-go rule," is repealed effective for tax years beginning after December 31, 2009. However, the new law effectively recreates the results of the rule by requiring a reduction in premiums paid rather than an increase in the guideline premium limitation.

▶ **Effective date.** Generally, the provision applies to contracts issued after December 31, 1996, but only with respect to tax years beginning after December 31, 2009 (Act Sec. 844(g)(1) of the Pension Protection Act of 2006). The amendments relating to nonrecognition transactions apply to exchanges occurring after December 31, 2009 (Act Sec. 844(g)(2)). The amendments relating to information returns and penalties, apply to charges against a contract made after December 31, 2009 (Act Sec. 844(g)(3)). The amendments

NEW LAW EXPLAINED

relating to specified policy acquisition costs, applies to specified policy acquisition expenses determined for tax years beginning after December 31, 2009 (Act Sec. 844(g)(4)). The technical correction relating to separate contract treatment generally applies to contracts issued after December 31, 1996 (Act Sec. 844(g)(5) of the Pension Act and Act Sec. 321(f) of the Health Insurance Portability and Accountability Act of 1996 (P.L. 104-191)).

Law source: Law at ¶5010, ¶5190, ¶5195, ¶5345, ¶5425, and ¶5490. Committee Report at ¶10,780.

— Act Sec. 844(a) of the Pension Protection Act of 2006, redesignating Code Sec. 72(e)(11) as (12) and adding new Code Sec. 72(e)(11);

— Act Sec. 844(b), amending Code Sec. 1035(a) and (b);

— Act Sec. 844(c), amending Code Sec. 7702B(e);

— Act Sec. 844(d), adding Code Sec. 6050U and amending Code Sec. 6724(d)(1) and (2);

— Act Sec. 844(e), adding Code Sec. 848(e)(6);

— Act Sec. 844(f), amending Code Sec. 7702B(e), as in effect before amendment by Act Sec. 844(c);

— Act Sec. 844(g), providing the effective date.

Reporter references: For further information, consult the following CCH reporters.

— Pension Plan Guide, ¶9102 and ¶9444

— Standard Federal Tax Reporter, 2006FED ¶6114.01, ¶6114.021, ¶6114.09, ¶26,367.021, ¶29,682.01, ¶40,285.025, ¶40,285.03, ¶43,168.01 and ¶43,168.034

— Tax Research Consultant, INDIV: 30,404.05, INDIV: 30,422, INDIV: 30,502, COMPEN: 45,066.20 and FILEBUS: 9,350

¶825 Plan Distributions for Health Insurance Premiums of Retired Public Safety Officers

SUMMARY OF NEW LAW

Up to $3,000 of otherwise taxable distributions from a government pension plan may be excluded from income annually if used to pay for qualified health insurance premiums of retired public safety officers.

BACKGROUND

Distributions from a qualified retirement plan under Code Sec. 401(a), a qualified annuity plan under Code Sec. 403(a), a tax-sheltered annuity under Code Sec. 403(b), an eligible deferred compensation plan maintained by a state or local government under Code Sec. 457, or an individual retirement arrangement under Code Sec. 408 are generally included in income in the year of the distribution except to the extent

BACKGROUND

attributable to after-tax contributions. A 10-percent penalty tax may apply to early withdrawals (Code Sec. 72(t)).

NEW LAW EXPLAINED

Income exclusion for distributions from government retirement plans used to pay health insurance premiums for public safety officers.—The new law provides that gross income does not include any distributions from an eligible retirement plan of an electing retired public safety officer to the extent that the distributions do not exceed the amount paid for qualified health insurance premiums of the officer, his or her spouse, or dependents for the tax year (Code Sec. 402(l), as added by the Pension Protection Act of 2006). The maximum annual exclusion, however, is capped at $3,000 (Code Sec. 402(l)(2), as added by the Pension Act).

The provision applies to distributions made in tax years beginning after December 31, 2006 (Act Sec. 845(c) of the Pension Act).

Practical Analysis: Mary Beth Braitman, Terry A.M. Mumford and Lisa Erb Harrison of Ice Miller LLP, Indianapolis, Indiana call the income tax exclusion in this provision one of the most dramatic changes in the Act for governmental plans. This section allows "eligible retired public safety officers" to make an election to exclude from federal taxable gross income up to $3,000 of their retirement plan benefits. Governmental plans need to begin immediately reviewing their membership to see who qualifies for this election. This section (unlike other sections that use different definitions of public safety officers) uses the definition in Act Sec. 1204(8)(A) of the Omnibus Crime Control and Safe Streets Act of 1986 (42 U.S.C. § 3796b(9)(A)). That definition includes the following individuals serving a public agency in an official capacity:

- an individual involved in crime and juvenile delinquency control or reduction, or enforcement of the criminal laws (including juvenile delinquency), including, but not limited to police, corrections, probation, parole, and judicial officers;
- professional firefighters;
- officially recognized or designated public employee members of a rescue squad or ambulance crew;
- officially recognized or designated members of a legally organized volunteer fire department; and
- officially recognized or designated chaplains of volunteer fire departments, fire departments, and police departments.

The member must be separated from service by reason of disability or attainment of normal retirement age to be eligible for this exclusion.

This exclusion pertains to distributions from governmental defined benefit plans, governmental defined contribution plans, governmental 403(b) tax-sheltered annuity plans and governmental 457(b) eligible deferred compensation plans.

NEW LAW EXPLAINED

In some plans, all members will be eligible because all members are public safety officers and all payments to members are made only by reason of disability or normal retirement. In other plans, all members will meet the threshold definition but will not qualify for the exclusion because they are receiving a termination or retirement benefit before normal retirement age. In other plans, only some members will qualify as public safety officers, and in still other plans there will be no eligible members.

The next step is to consider what qualifies for the exclusion. The Act permits the exclusion solely for premiums for health insurance coverage or long-term care insurance for the retired public safety officer, spouse and dependents. The coverage must be in an "accident or health insurance" plan or a qualified long-term care insurance contract.

The income exclusion is only available if the governmental plan agrees to deduct and then remit premiums directly to the provider of the accident or health insurance plan or qualified long-term care insurance contract. In order to implement this, a governmental plan needs to develop appropriate election forms for its eligible public safety members prior to January 1, 2007. This applies to the plan's existing retiree and disabilitant population, as well as new retirees. Consequently, the plan may want to focus first on getting its existing eligible payees' elections processed in November and December 2006. For some plans, this may be a fairly easy process. For others, where their retired members are in different insurance plans (*e.g.,* employer based with many employers) this may include consideration of a structure for direct payment to many different insurance carriers (for example, if retirees remain on the cities' health insurance programs).

The other important implementation issue arises with respect to the coordination that may be required. All eligible retirement plans of an employer must be treated as a single plan, *i.e.,* retirees only get one $3,000 exclusion, even if they are receiving benefits from several plans, *e.g.* a defined benefit plan and a 457 deferred compensation plan.

Eligible retirement plan. The distribution must be made from an "eligible retirement plan." An eligible retirement plan is a governmental plan (as defined in Code Sec. 414(d)) (Code Sec. 402(l)(4)(A), as added by the Pension Act). This includes:

(1) a tax-exempt employees' trust forming part of a qualified pension, profit sharing, or stock bonus plan (Code Sec. 402(c)(8)(B)(iii));

(2) a qualified employee annuity plan described in Code Sec. 403(a) (Code Sec. 402(c)(8)(B)(iv));

(3) a Code Sec. 457(b) deferred compensation plan of a state or local government (Code Sec. 402(c)(8)(B)(v)); and

(4) an annuity purchased by a section 501(c)(3) organization or a public school (Code Sec. 402(c)(8)(B)(vi)).

Related plans treated as single plan. All eligible retirement plans of an employer are treated as a single plan for purposes of the exclusion provision (Code Sec. 402(l)(5)(B), as added by the Pension Act).

NEW LAW EXPLAINED

Exclusion applies to otherwise taxable distributions only. An amount is treated as a distribution for purposes of the election only to the extent it would be taxable if the exclusion did not apply (Code Sec. 402(l)(3)(A), as added by the Pension Act).

Application of Code Sec. 72. Code Sec. 72 is applied in a special way for purposes of determining the amount that is treated as an otherwise taxable distribution. Specifically, in determining the extent to which a distribution would be taxable without regard to the exclusion, the aggregate amount distributed from an eligible retirement plan during the tax year up to the maximum eligible amount (i.e., the lesser of $3,000 or the actual premiums paid) is treated as includible in gross income to the extent the amount does not exceed the aggregate amount that would have been included in income if all amounts distributed from all eligible retirement plans were treated as one contract for purposes of determining the inclusion of the distribution under Code Sec. 72. Proper adjustments are required in applying Code Sec. 72 to other distributions during the tax year and subsequent tax years (Code Sec. 402(l)(3)(B), as added by the Pension Act).

Retired public safety officers. The exclusion is only available to an "eligible retired public safety officer." This is an individual who, by reason of disability or attainment of normal retirement age, has separated from service as a public safety officer with the employer who maintains the eligible government retirement plan from which the distribution is made (Code Sec. 402(l)(4)(B), as added by the Pension Act). The provision only applies to retired public safety officers who were employees.

In general, public safety officers include law enforcement officers, firefighters, chaplains, ambulance crews, and rescue squads. A law enforcement officer is an individual involved in crime and juvenile delinquency control or reduction, or enforcement of the laws, including, but not limited to, police, corrections, probation, parole, and judicial officers. These terms are defined in section 1204(9)(A) of the Omnibus Crime Control and Safe Streets Act of 1968 which is codified in 42 U.S.C. 3796b(8)(A) (Code Sec. 402(l)(4)(C), as added by the Pension Act).

Premiums must be used to pay for insurance. The exclusion only applies to distributions used to pay for "qualified health insurance premiums." These are premiums paid for coverage by an accident or health insurance plan or a qualified long-term care insurance contract (described in Code Sec. 7702B(b)) for the eligible retired public safety officer, his or her spouse, and dependents (Code Sec. 402(l)(4)(D), as added by the Pension Act). The payment of the insurance premiums must be made directly to the provider of the health insurance plan or qualified long-term care contract by deduction from a distribution from the eligible retirement plan (Code Sec. 402(l)(5), as added by the Pension Act).

> **Caution Note:** The exclusion will not apply if the premiums are paid by the retired officer and reimbursed with pension distributions (Joint Committee on Taxation, Technical Explanation of the Pension Protection Act of 2006 (JCX-38-06)).

Annual election required. An annual election must be made by the eligible retired public safety officer for the exclusion to apply. The election applies to the officer's tax year (Code Sec. 401(l)(1), as added by the Pension Act).

NEW LAW EXPLAINED

The election must be made after separation from service with respect to amounts not previously distributed from the plan. The election must require that the distribution be used to pay for the qualified premiums (Code Sec. 401(l)(6)(A), as added by the Pension Act). As noted above, the distribution must be in the form of a deduction made directly from the plan distribution to the insurance provider.

Neither the inclusion of an election provision in a plan nor a distribution pursuant to an election will negate a plan's qualified status under Code Sec. 401. The plan will also not be considered to have engaged in a Code Sec. 503(b) prohibited transaction (Code Secs. 401(l)(6)(B) and 403(a)(2), as added by the Pension Act).

No deduction for excluded amounts. Distributed amounts that qualify for exclusion from a public safety officer's gross income under this provision may not be taken into account in computing the itemized medical expense deduction under Code Sec. 213 (Code Sec. 401(l)(7), as added by the Pension Act). In addition, retirement plan distributions that are excluded under this provision may not be taken into account when computing the deduction against gross income allowed by Code Sec. 162(l) for self-employed health insurance costs (Code Sec. 401(l)(8), as added by the Pension Act).

> **Comment:** Thus, a public safety officer who is self-employed after retirement from government service cannot claim a deduction for self-employed health insurance premiums that are paid with excluded distributions.

Conforming amendments. Code Sec. 403(a), which requires application of the Code Sec. 72 annuity rules to determine the taxable portion of an employee annuity, is amended to provide that distributions that are excludable from gross income under the new provision are not subject to tax under Code Sec. 72 (Code Sec. 403(a)(2), as added by the Pension Act). A similar rule applies to annuities purchased by Code Sec. 501(c)(3) organizations and public schools (Code Sec. 403(b)(2), as added by the Pension Act). Code Sec. 457 is also amended to clarify that distributions from a deferred compensation plan of a governmental entity that are excluded from income under the new provision are not includible in income (Code Sec. 457(a)(3), as added by the Pension Act).

▶ **Effective date.** The amendments apply to distributions in tax years beginning after December 31, 2006 (Act Sec. 845(c) of the Pension Protection Act of 2006).

Law source: Law at ¶5035, ¶5040, and ¶5140. Committee Report at ¶10,790.

— Act Sec. 845(a) of the Pension Protection Act of 2006, adding Code Sec. 402(l);

— Act Sec. 845(b), adding Code Sec. 403(a)(2), Code Sec. 403(b)(2), and Code Sec. 457(a)(3);

— Act Sec. 845(c), providing the effective date.

Reporter references: For further information, consult the following CCH reporters.

— Pension Plan Guide, ¶3643

— Standard Federal Tax Reporter, 2006FED ¶6140.01, ¶6140.0682 and ¶18,207.01

— Tax Research Consultant, RETIRE: 42,054, RETIRE: 42,554.20 and RETIRE: 69,350

— Federal Tax Guide, 2006FTG ¶11,660

Plan Distributions and Rollovers

DISTRIBUTION OF BENEFITS

¶905 Valuation of Lump-Sum Distributions

SUMMARY OF NEW LAW

The interest rate and mortality table used to calculate the minimum value of a lump-sum distribution, and certain other forms of optional benefits, are changed with respect to plan years beginning after 2007.

BACKGROUND

Defined benefit plans generally allow a retiring participant to elect to receive a lump-sum distribution in lieu of lifetime annuity payments. The lump-sum payment must have a present value that is at least equivalent to the value of the life annuity. The minimum present value is determined using statutory assumptions set forth in Code Sec. 417(e)(3) and ERISA Sec. 205(g)(3).

Under present law, these statutory assumptions consist of an applicable mortality table (published by the IRS) and an applicable interest rate. The applicable interest rate is the annual interest rate of 30-year Treasury securities for the month before the date of distribution or at such other time specified in IRS regulations. The regulations provide various options for determining the interest rate, such as the period for which the interest rate will remain constant and the use of averaging.

NEW LAW EXPLAINED

Interest rate and mortality table updated.—The new law changes the applicable mortality table and interest rate used to calculate the new minimum value of a lump-sum distribution paid from a defined benefit plan (Code Sec. 417(e)(3) and ERISA Sec. 205(g)(3), as amended by the Pension Protection Act of 2006). Generally, the new rules will reduce the lump sum that would otherwise be payable under present law by increasing the applicable interest rate. The provision is effective for plan years beginning after December 31, 2007.

Mortality table. The mortality table to be used for calculating lump-sum distributions is based on the mortality table specified for the plan year under the new minimum funding standard rules for single-employer defined benefit plans, see ¶210 (Code Sec. 417(e)(3)(B) and ERISA Sec. 205(g)(3)(B)(i), as amended by the Pension Act). The IRS is directed to prescribe gender-neutral tables for use in determining minimum lump sums. (Joint Committee on Taxation, Technical Explanation of the Pension Protection Act of 2006 (JCX-38-06)).

> **Comment:** The minimum funding rules allow the use of substitute tables based on a plan's particular experience (Code Sec. 430(h)(3)(C) and ERISA Sec. 303(h)(3)(C)) and separate mortality tables for the disabled (Code Sec. 430(h)(3)(D) and ERISA Sec. 303(h)(3)(D)). These tables may not be used for

NEW LAW EXPLAINED

> purposes of computing lump-sum distributions and other forms of benefits (Code Sec. 417(e)(3)(B) and ERISA Sec. 205(g)(3)(B)(i), as amended by the Pension Act).

Applicable interest rate. The applicable interest rate is the adjusted first, second, and third segment rates applied under the minimum funding rules of new Code Sec. 430(h)(2)(C) and ERISA Sec. 303(h)(2)(C) (see ¶210), with certain modifications, for the month before the date of distribution or such other time as prescribed by the IRS (Code Sec. 417(e)(3)(C) and ERISA Sec. 205(g)(3)(B)(ii), as amended by the Pension Act).

For purposes of determining the amount of a lump-sum distribution, the first segment rate, with respect to a particular month, is a rate of interest determined on the basis of the "corporate bond yield curve" for the month, taking into account only that portion of the yield curve based on bonds maturing during the five-year period commencing with that month. The second segment is similarly defined except that the interest rate is determined on the basis of the corporate bond yield curve for the month, taking into account only the portion of the yield curve based on bonds maturing during the 15-year period that begins at the end of the five-year first-segment period. The third segment rate only takes into account the portion of the yield curve based on bonds maturing during periods beginning after the end of the 15-year second segment period (Code Secs. 417(e)(3)(D) and 430(h)(2)(C), and ERISA Secs. 205(g)(3)(B)(iii) and 303(h)(2)(C), as amended and added by the Pension Act).

Adjustments. For purposes of the minimum funding rules, the corporate bond yield curve for a particular month reflects a 24-month weighted average of yields on investment grade corporate bonds with varying maturities in the top three quality levels available (Code Sec. 430(h)(2)(D)(i) and ERISA Sec. 303(h)(2)(D), as added by the Pension Act). However, for purposes of the lump-sum valuation rules, the yield curve is based on yields on investment grade bonds with varying maturities (i.e., a monthly interest rate), rather than a 24-month weighted average (Code Sec. 417(e)(3)(D)(i) and ERISA Sec. 205(g)(3)(B)(iii)(I), as amended by the Pension Act).

> **Comment:** The adjusted first, second, and third segment rates for purposes of a lump-sum valuation are derived from a corporate bond yield curve prescribed by the IRS which reflects the yields on investment grade corporate bonds with varying maturities. Thus, the applicable interest rate for purposes of a lump-sum distribution calculation depends upon how many years in the future a participant's annuity payment would be made. A higher interest rate usually applies the longer that the annuity will be paid.

The IRS is required to publish for each month the corporate bond yield curve used for purposes of calculating the amount of a lump-sum distribution. The IRS must describe the method used to determine the yield curves so as to enable plans to make reasonable projections regarding the yield curve (Code Sec. 430(h)(2)(F) and ERISA Sec. 303(h)(2)(F), as added by the Pension Act).

Transition rule for distributions in 2008, 2009, 2010, and 2011 plan years. For plan years beginning in 2008 through 2011, the first, second, and third segment rate for any month is equal to the sum of: (1) the product of the segment rate determined under

NEW LAW EXPLAINED

the general rule above, multiplied by the applicable percentage (i.e., the transitional percentage for the plan year listed below); and (2) the product of the rate determined under the rules in effect for plan years beginning prior to 2008 (i.e., the rate determined under the rules which are being replaced), multiplied by a percentage equal to 100 percent minus the applicable percentage (Code Sec. 417(e)(3)(D) and ERISA Sec. 205(g)(3)(B)(iii), as amended by the Pension Act). The applicable percentages for plan years beginning in the year specified are:

2008	20%
2009	40%
2010	60%
2011	80%

Comment: Under the transitional rule, lump-sum values are determined as a weighted average of two values: (1) the value of the lump sum determined under the methodology of present law; and (2) the value of the lump sum determined using the methodology of the new law. For example, in the case of a distribution in a 2008 plan year, the weighting factor is 80 percent for the lump-sum value determined under present law and 20 percent of the lump-sum value determined under the new law.

Planning Note: Anticutback rules (Code Sec. 411(d)(6) and ERISA Sec. 204(g)) prohibit amendments to a qualified retirement plan that decrease the accrued benefits of a plan participant. If certain requirements are met, however, a plan amendment to implement the change made by this provision may be made retroactively without violating the anticutback rule. See ¶ 1090.

▶ **Effective date.** The provision applies with respect to plan years beginning after December 31, 2007 (Act Sec. 302(c) of the Pension Protection Act of 2006).

Law source: Law at ¶5105 and ¶7057. Committee Report at ¶10,200.

— Act Sec. 302(a) of the Pension Protect Act of 2006, amending ERISA Sec. 205(g);

— Act Sec. 302(b), amending Code Sec. 417(e)(3);

— Act Sec. 302(c), providing the effective date.

Reporter references: For further information, consult the following CCH reporters.

— Pension Plan Guide, ¶2667, ¶3716 and ¶6714

— Standard Federal Tax Reporter, 2006FED ¶19,262.01

— Tax Research Consultant, RETIRE: 15,300 and RETIRE: 15,352

— Federal Tax Guide, 2006FTG ¶11,070

¶910 Modification of Rules Regarding Hardships and Unforeseen Financial Emergencies

SUMMARY OF NEW LAW

The Secretary of the Treasury is directed to modify the regulations for determining whether a participant in certain qualified plans has had a hardship or unforeseen financial emergency to permit such distributions if such an event occurs to a person who is the participant's beneficiary under the plan.

BACKGROUND

Distributions from 401(k) plans, tax sheltered annuities, 457 plans or nonqualified deferred compensation plans subject to Code Sec. 409A may not be made prior to the occurrence of one or more specified events. In the case of a 401(k) plan or a tax-sheltered annuity, a hardship is one of the events upon which a distribution is permitted (Code Sec. 401(k)(2)(B)(i)(IV)). Distributions from 457 plans and nonqualified deferred compensation plans subject to Code Sec. 409A may be made in the case of an unforeseeable emergency (Code Sec. 457(d)(1)(A)(iii)). Under regulations, a hardship or unforeseeable emergency includes a hardship or unforeseeable emergency of a participant's spouse or dependent (Reg. § 1.457-6(c)(2)(i)).

NEW LAW EXPLAINED

Rules determining whether a hardship has occurred to be modified to include beneficiaries.—The Pension Protection Act of 2006 provides that, within 180 days of August 17, 2006, the date of enactment, the Secretary of the Treasury must modify the regulations for determining whether a participant has had a hardship for purposes of receiving a distribution from a 401(k) plan. The modification must provide that if an event (including the occurrence of a medical expense) would constitute a hardship under the plan if it occurred with respect to the participant's spouse or dependent (as defined in Code Sec. 152), then the event will, to the extent permitted under the plan, constitute a hardship if it occurs with respect to any beneficiary of the participant under the plan as well (Act Sec. 826 of the Pension Act).

Practical Analysis: Mary Beth Braitman, Terry A.M. Mumford and Lisa Erb Harrison of Ice Miller LLP, Indianapolis, Indiana, note that this amendment directs the Treasury to issue regulations within six months to provide greater flexibility for purposes of hardship or unforeseeable financial emergency distributions from 401(k), 403(b) and 457(b) plans, as well as nonqualified deferred compensation plans under Code Sec. 409A. Under current regulations, a hardship or unforeseeable financial emergency includes a hardship or unforeseeable financial emergency of a participant's spouse or dependent. The Treasury is directed to modify the hardship regulations to permit a hardship or unforeseeable financial emergency distribution with respect to

NEW LAW EXPLAINED

any beneficiary of a participant designated under the plan, who experiences a hardship or unforeseen financial emergency.

Governmental 403(b) and 457(b) plans (and governmental grandfathered 401(k) plans) will need to evaluate their hardship and unforeseen financial emergency distribution provisions in order to determine whether to permit this additional flexibility.

The Secretary must also issue similar regulations for determining whether a participant has had a hardship for purposes of receiving a distribution from a tax-sheltered annuity or an unforeseen financial emergency for purposes of receiving a distribution from a nonqualified deferred compensation plan and a deferred compensation plan of state and local governments and tax-exempt organizations (Act Sec. 826 of the Pension Act).

▶ **Effective date.** No specific effective date is provided by the Act. The provision is, therefore, considered effective on August 17, 2006, the date of enactment.

Law source: Law at ¶7162. Committee Report at ¶10,670.

— Act Sec. 826 of the Pension Protection Act of 2006.

Reporter references: For further information, consult the following CCH reporters.

— Pension Plan Guide, ¶7470, ¶7660, ¶7665 and ¶8017

— Standard Federal Tax Reporter, 2006FED ¶18,112.05, ¶18,112.051, ¶18,282.0403, ¶18,960.021 and ¶21,536.045

— Tax Research Consultant, RETIRE: 3,202

— Federal Tax Guide, 2006FTG ¶11,240

¶915 Treatment of Certain Distributions to Public Safety Employees

SUMMARY OF NEW LAW

Qualified public safety employees, who separate from service, may take distributions from government pension plans without being subject to the 10-percent early withdrawal penalty tax after age 50.

BACKGROUND

A taxpayer who receives a distribution from a qualified retirement plan prior to age 59½, death, or disability is generally subject to a 10-percent early withdrawal penalty tax on the amount includible in income, unless an exception to the tax applies (Code Sec. 72(t)). Among the exceptions, the early distribution tax does not apply to distributions made to an employee who separates from service after age 55, or to distributions that are part of a series of substantially equal periodic payments made

BACKGROUND

for the life (or life expectancy) of the employee or the joint lives (or life expectancies) of the employee and his or her beneficiary (Code Sec. 72(t)(2)).

NEW LAW EXPLAINED

Waiver of penalty tax for public safety employees after age 50.—The 10-percent early withdrawal penalty tax does not apply to distributions from a government plan made to qualified public safety employees who separate from service after age 50 (Code Sec. 72(t)(10)(A), as added by the Pension Protection Act of 2006). A "qualified public safety employee" means any employee of a State or political subdivision of a State who provides police protection, fire-fighting services, or emergency medical services for any area within the jurisdiction of the State or political subdivision (Code Sec. 72(t)(10)(B), as added by the Pension Act).

> **Practical Analysis:** Mary Beth Braitman, Terry A.M. Mumford and Lisa Erb Harrison of Ice Miller LLP, Indianapolis, Indiana, observe that this section contains important relief for public safety employees in governmental plans with some type of a partial lump sum option, a deferred retirement option feature ("DROP"), or other non–substantially equal periodic payments. It creates an exception from the 10-percent premature distribution penalty for payments made to a qualified member who separates from service (*e.g.,* retires) after age 50 (rather than age 55). Governmental plans need to immediately begin considering whether their operating system or plan structure clearly identifies who is a "qualified public safety employee" under this section. The definition of qualified public safety employee includes any employee who provides police protection, firefighting services or emergency medical services for any area within the jurisdiction of the employing state or political subdivision. For some plans, this will include all plan members. For other plans that cover such employees, along with other general employees, special programming may be necessary yet this year to ensure correct coding on 2006 Form 1099-Rs, for distributions made after enactment.

▶ **Effective date.** This provision applies to distributions after August 17, 2006 (Act Sec. 828(b) of the Pension Protection Act of 2006).

Law source: Law at ¶5010. Committee Report at ¶10,690.

— Act Sec. 828(a) of the Pension Protection Act of 2006, adding Code Sec. 72(t)(10);

— Act Sec. 828(b), providing the effective date.

Reporter references: For further information, consult the following CCH reporters.

— Pension Plan Guide, ¶5470 and ¶8017

— Standard Federal Tax Reporter, 2006FED ¶6140.0682

— Tax Research Consultant, RETIRE: 42,554.20 and RETIRE: 69,350

— Federal Tax Guide, 2006FTG ¶11,086 and ¶11,087

¶917 Treatment of Distributions to Individuals Called to Active Duty in Excess of 179 Days

SUMMARY OF NEW LAW

Generally, a qualified reservist distribution from an IRA or attributable to elective deferrals under a 401(k) plan, 403(b) annuity, or certain similar arrangements are not subject to the 10-percent early withdrawal tax if the qualified reservist was ordered or called to active duty for a period in excess of 179 days.

BACKGROUND

A taxpayer who receives a distribution from a qualified retirement plan prior to age 59½, death, or disability is generally subject to a 10-percent early withdrawal penalty tax on the amount includible in income, unless an exception to the tax applies (Code Sec. 72(t)). Among the exceptions, the early distribution tax does not apply to distributions made to an employee who separates from service after age 55, or to distributions that are part of a series of substantially equal periodic payments made for the life (or life expectancy) of the employee or the joint lives (or life expectancies) of the employee and his or her beneficiary (Code Sec. 72(t)(2)). In the case of certain amounts held in a qualified cash or deferred arrangement (a 401(k) plan) or in a tax-sheltered annuity (a 403(b) annuity), assets may not be distributed before severance from employment, age 59-1/2, death, disability, or financial hardship of the employee.

NEW LAW EXPLAINED

Penalty-free withdrawals from retirement plans for individuals called to active duty for a period in excess of 179 days.—The 10-percent early withdrawal penalty tax will not apply to a qualified reservist distribution:

(1) from an IRA or attributable to elective deferrals under a 401(k) plan, 403(b) annuity, or certain similar arrangements;

(2) made to an individual who is a reservist or national guardsman (as defined in 37 U.S.C. 101(24)), and who was ordered or called to active duty for a period *in excess* of 179 days or for an indefinite period; and

(3) that is made during the period beginning on the date of the order or call to duty and ending at the close of the active duty period.

(Code Sec. 72(t)(2)(G)(iii), as added by the Pension Protection Act of 2006).

> **Comment:** A 401(k) plan or 403(b) annuity does not violate the distribution requirements that apply to those plans by making a qualified reservist distribution (Joint Committee on Taxation, Technical Explanation of the Pension Protection Act of 2006 (JCX-38-06)).

NEW LAW EXPLAINED

Caution Note: The title of Act Sec. 827 of the Pension Act reads "Penalty-free Withdrawals from Retirement Plans for Individuals Called to Active Duty for at Least 179 Days" and press statements from many sources, including Sen. Orrin Hatch (R-Utah) and the National Council on Teacher Retirement, state that this provision would apply to reservists called to active duty for "at least" 179 days. However, the text of new Code Sec. 72(t)(2)(G)(iii)(II) states that it applies to an individual called to active duty *in excess* of 179 days or for an indefinite period.

Comment: It appears that Congress' decision to limit this provision to individuals called to active duty in excess of 179 days was based upon military guidelines for "short tour opportunities." There are three general categories of short tour opportunities: (1) Active Duty for Special Work; (2) Temporary Tour of Active Duty; and (3) Contingency Operation Temporary Tour of Active Duty.

All three of these tours are normally limited to 179 days or less in one fiscal year.

An individual who receives a qualified reservist distribution may repay (in one or more contributions) the amount of the distribution at any time during the two-year period after the end of the active duty period. To permit repayment, the dollar limitations that would otherwise apply to IRA contributions do not apply to repayment contributions during the applicable two-year period. However, no deduction is allowed for any contribution made under this provision (Code Sec. 72(t)(2)(G)(ii), as added by the Pension Act).

This provision applies to individuals ordered or called to active duty after September 11, 2001, and before December 31, 2007. The two-year period for making recontributions of qualified reservist distributions does not end before the date that is two years after August 17, 2006 (Code Sec. 72(t)(2)(G)(iv), as added by the Pension Act).

Practical Analysis: Mary Beth Braitman, Terry A.M. Mumford and Lisa Erb Harrison, of Ice Miller LLP, Indianapolis, Indiana, observe that governmental 401(k) plans, governmental plans with deemed IRAs, and governmental 403(b) plans may be particularly interested in the provisions of this section, given the number of plan members in the reserves in some states.

▶ **Effective date.** This provision applies to distributions made after September 11, 2001. If a refund or credit of any overpayment of tax resulting from this provision would be prevented before the close of the one-year period beginning on August 17, 2006 by operation of any law or rule of (including *res judicata*), a refund or credit may still be made or allowed if the claim is filed before the close of the one-year period (Act Sec. 827(c) of the Pension Protection Act of 2006).

Law source: Law at ¶5010, ¶5030 and ¶5040. Committee Report at ¶10,680.

— Act Sec. 827(a) of the Pension Protection Act of 2006, adding Code Sec. 72(t)(2)(G);

— Act Sec. 827(b), amending Code Secs. 401(k)(2)(B)(i), 403(b)(7)(A)(ii) and 403(b)(11);

— Act Sec. 827(c)(2);

— Act Sec. 827(c)(1), providing the effective date.

NEW LAW EXPLAINED

Reporter references: For further information, consult the following CCH reporters.

— Pension Plan Guide, ¶5470, ¶7720 and ¶8577D

— Standard Federal Tax Reporter, 2006FED ¶6140.0682, ¶18,112.05 and ¶18,282.0403

— Tax Research Consultant, RETIRE: 42,554.20

— Federal Tax Guide, 2006FTG ¶11,086 and ¶11,087

¶920 Distributions During Working or Phased Retirement

SUMMARY OF NEW LAW

A pension plan will not fail to meet the ERISA definition of a pension plan or the Code Sec. 401 qualification requirements solely because it provides for a distribution to an employee who has attained age 62 and who is not separated from employment at the time of the distribution.

BACKGROUND

Under the Employee Retirement Income Security Act of 1974 (ERISA), a pension plan is any plan, fund, or program established or maintained by an employer or by an employee organization, or by both, to the extent that the plan, fund or program provides retirement income to employees, or results in a deferral of income by employees for periods extending to the termination of covered employment or beyond, regardless of the method of calculating the contributions made to the plan, or the method of calculating or distributing the benefits under the plan (ERISA Sec. 3(2)(A)).

For purposes of the Code Sec. 401 qualification requirements applicable to pension, profit-sharing and stock bonus plans, a pension plan is a plan established and maintained by an employer primarily to provide definitely determinable benefits to employees over a period of years, usually for life, after retirement. Neither the contributions nor the benefits are dependent on the employer's profits. The retirement benefits are generally based on the years of service and compensation (Reg. §§1.401-1(b)(1)(i) and 1.401(a)-1(b)).

In general, a pension plan may not provide for distributions before the attainment of normal retirement age (usually age 65) to participants who have not separated from employment (see Rev. Rul. 74-254, 1974-1 CB 91). Proposed regulations, however, allow a pension plan to pay a portion of a participant's benefits before attainment of normal retirement age in the case of a phased retirement program. Under a phased retirement program, employees who are at least age 59½ and are eligible for retirement may reduce the number of hours they customarily work by at least 20 percent, and receive a pro rata portion of their accrued retirement benefits. The pro rata

BACKGROUND

portion is based on the reduction in the employee's work schedule during the phased retirement period (Proposed Reg. § § 1.401(a)-1(b)(1)(iv) and 1.401(a)-3).

NEW LAW EXPLAINED

Pension plans can make distributions during working or phased retirement.— For purposes of the ERISA definition of a pension plan, a distribution from a plan, fund, or program will not be treated as made in a form other than retirement income or as a distribution prior to termination of covered employment solely because the distribution is made to an employee who has attained age 62 and who is not separated from employment at the time of the distribution but instead is in a phased retirement program (ERISA Sec. 3(2)(A), as amended by the Pension Protection Act of 2006).

Similarly, a pension plan will not fail to meet the Code Sec. 401 qualification requirements solely because it provides for a distribution to an employee who has attained age 62 and who is not separated from employment at the time of the distribution but instead is in a phased retirement program (Code Sec. 401(a)(36), as added by the Pension Act).

> **Practical Analysis:** Mary Beth Braitman, Terry A.M. Mumford and Lisa Erb Harrison of Ice Miller LLP, Indianapolis, Indiana warn that governmental plans should be particularly aware of Act Sec. 905, as the concept of working in retirement has frequently been controversial (or challenging) for those plans. This section allows (but does not mandate) a qualified plan to provide that a distribution may be made to an employee who reaches age 62 even though the employee has not separated from service. Previously, the prohibition on in-service distributions had been generally interpreted as not preventing benefit commencement to an employee who had reached normal retirement (or eligibility for an unreduced benefit). This gives a "bright line" rule on what is a permissible plan design, although not necessarily precluding other designs.

▶ **Effective date.** The provision applies to distributions in plan years beginning after December 31, 2006 (Act Sec. 905(c) of the Pension Protection Act of 2006).

Law source: Law at ¶5030 and ¶7192. Committee Report at ¶10,990.

— Act Sec. 905(a) of the Pension Protection Act of 2006, amending ERISA Sec. 3(2)(A);

— Act Sec. 905(b), adding Code Sec. 401(a)(36);

— Act Sec. 905(c), providing the effective date.

Reporter references: For further information, consult the following CCH reporters.

— Pension Plan Guide, ¶465 and ¶5470

— Standard Federal Tax Reporter, 2006FED ¶17,507.01 and ¶17,507.03

— Tax Research Consultant, RETIRE: 9,050 and RETIRE: 42,102

— Federal Tax Guide, 2006FTG ¶11,086

¶925 Notice and Consent Period Regarding Distributions

SUMMARY OF NEW LAW

The notice and consent period for certain distributions from qualified plans is expanded from 90 to 180 days.

BACKGROUND

Certain distributions from qualified retirement plans are subject to notice and consent requirements. For example, if the present value of a participant's vested accrued benefit exceeds $5,000, the plan is prohibited from distributing the participant's benefit without the consent of the participant (i.e., "cash-out" distributions) (Code Sec. 411(a)(11)). In order for the consent to be effective, the participant must receive a general description of the material features of the optional forms of benefit available under the plan. In addition, so long as a benefit is immediately distributable, a participant must be informed of the right (if any) to defer receipt of the distribution. The plan must provide notice to the participant no less than 30 days and no more than 90 days before the date that the distribution commences (Reg. § 1.411(a)-11(c)(2)(iii)). Both the notice and consent must be provided in either a written paper document or "through an electronic medium reasonably accessible to the participant" (e.g., e-mail) (Reg. § 1.411(a)-11(f)).

> **Comment:** The participant's consent is required for any distribution only while it is immediately distributable (i.e., prior to the later of the time that a participant has attained normal retirement age or age 62).

Certain plans may also be subject to requirements relating to survivor annuities (see Code Sec. 401(a)(11)(B) and ERISA Sec. 205(b)(1)). With regard to such plans, where a vested participant does not die before the annuity starting date, the accrued benefit is to be provided in the form of a qualified joint and survivor annuity ("QJSA") (Code Sec. 401(a)(11) and ERISA Sec. 205(a)(1)). A QJSA is an annuity for the life of the participant with a survivor annuity for the life of the spouse that meets certain valuation and actuarial requirements (Code Sec. 417(b) and ERISA Sec. 205(d)). The plan must provide that a participant may elect, at any time during the applicable election period, to waive the QJSA form of benefit. A participant is permitted to revoke such election to waive at any time during the applicable election period. A participant's election to waive the QJSA is not effective unless the spouse of the participant consents in writing to such election (Code Sec. 417(a)(1) and (2), and ERISA Sec. 205(c)(1) and (2)).

> **Comment:** In the case of an election to waive the QJSA, the "applicable election period" means the 90-day period ending on the annuity starting date (Code Sec. 417(a)(6)(A) and ERISA Sec. 205(c)(7)).

BACKGROUND

The plan is required to provide the participant with a written explanation of the following:

- the terms and conditions of the QJSA;
- the participant's right to make (and the effect of) an election to waive the joint and survivor annuity form of benefit;
- the rights of the participant's spouse with respect to the participant's waiver of the QJSA; and
- the right to make (and the effect of) a revocation of a waiver of the QJSA (Code Sec. 417(a)(3)(A) and ERISA Sec. 205(c)(3)(A)).

The written explanation must provide certain information with respect to each of the optional forms of benefit presently available to the participant, such as a description of the financial effect of electing the optional form of benefit (see Reg. § 1.417(a)(3)-1(b), (c)). In general, a plan must provide the written explanation of the QJSA to the participant no less than 30 days and no more than 90 days before the annuity starting date. The consent to the distribution must be made not more than 90 days before the annuity starting date and, in general, no later than the annuity starting date (Reg. § 1.417(e)-1(b)(3)(i)).

> **Comment:** No consent is needed for distribution of a QJSA after the benefit is no longer immediately distributable. In addition, no consent of the spouse is needed for distribution of a QJSA at any time.

Finally, many distributions by a qualified plan may be received by an employee (or an employee's surviving spouse) free of tax if, within 60 days of the distribution, they are transferred to an IRA or to another eligible retirement plan. Generally, all distributions from a qualified retirement plan, a tax-sheltered annuity and governmental section 457 plan are eligible to be rolled over to a similar plan or arrangement except for: (1) distributions that are part of a series of substantially equal periodic distributions; (2) distributions that are required under the minimum distribution rules; or (3) hardship distributions (Code Sec. 402(c)(4)).

Plan administrators are required to provide recipients of eligible rollover distributions with a written explanation detailing the direct rollover rules, the mandatory income tax withholding on distributions not directly rolled over, and the tax treatment of distributions not rolled over, including the special tax treatment available for certain lump-sum distributions (Code Sec. 402(f)). The explanation must also include a discussion of the potential restrictions and tax consequences that may apply to distributions from the new plan that are different from those applicable to the distributing plan.

A plan administrator is deemed to have complied with the explanation requirement if the explanation is furnished to the recipient no less than 30 days and no more than 90 days before the plan makes the distribution. However, if a participant, after receiving the notice, affirmatively elects to make or not make a direct rollover, the reasonable time period requirement will not be violated merely because the election is implemented less than 30 days after the explanation was furnished, provided that the following requirement is met. The plan administrator must provide information to the participant clearly indicating that the participant has a right to consider the decision of whether or not to elect a direct rollover for at least 30 days after the notice

BACKGROUND

is provided. Any method may be used to inform the participant of the relevant time period, provided that it is reasonably designed to attract the participant's attention.

NEW LAW EXPLAINED

Period for notice and consent expanded from 90 to 180 days.—The Secretary of the Treasury is directed to modify the regulations under the Code that apply to mandatory "cash-out" distributions, distributions of survivor annuities, and eligible rollover distributions in order to double the length of the notice and consent period (Act Sec. 1102(a)(1)(B) of the Pension Protection Act of 2006). The regulations under ERISA that apply to same distributions are also to be modified to double the length of the notice and consent period (Act Sec. 1102(a)(2)(B)).

Following the modification of the regulations, a plan must provide a participant with notice of his or her rights no less than 30 days and no more than 180 days before the date that the distribution commences. The participant's consent to the distribution may not be made more than 180 days before the date that the distribution commences. In regard to QJSAs, a plan must generally provide the written explanation mandated by Code Sec. 417(a)(3) to participants no less than 30 days and no more than 180 days before the annuity starting date. The written consent of the participant and the participant's spouse to the QJSA distribution must be made not more than 180 days before the annuity starting date and, in general, no later than the annuity starting date.

> **Comment:** The modification of Reg. § 1.402(f)-1 involves the written explanation that must be provided to a distributee relating to distributions that are eligible for rollover treatment (see Code Sec. 402(f)).

> **Comment:** According to a report of the Senate Finance Committee that accompanied a bill that was a precursor to the Pension Act, the 90-day period did not always provide an employee with enough time to evaluate the available distribution alternatives, make the appropriate selection, and notify the plan of his or her decision. In addition, the Committee found it to be administratively burdensome for a plan to send multiple distribution notices to an employee who did not make a distribution election within 90 days. Extending the period to 180 days is designed to alleviate these perceived problems (Report to accompany S. 1953, the National Employee Savings and Trust Equity Guarantee Act of 2005, Senate Rept. 109-174, November 2, 2005).

The Pension Act also expands the application election period for a participant to waive the QJSA form of benefit (Code Sec. 417(a)(6)(A) and ERISA Sec. 205(c)(7)(A), as amended by the Pension Act). As a result, a participant may elect to waive a QJSA during the 180-day period ending on the annuity starting date.

Modification of regulations regarding right to defer. The Secretary of Treasury is also directed to modify the regulations that apply to mandatory "cash-out" distributions to provide that the description of a participant's right (if any) to defer receipt of a distribution must also describe the consequences of failing to defer such receipt (Act Sec. 1102(b)(1) of the Pension Act). A plan will not be treated as failing to meet the requirements with respect to any description of consequences made within 90 days

NEW LAW EXPLAINED

after the modifications to the regulations are issued if the plan administrator makes a "reasonable attempt" to comply with such requirements (Act Sec. 1102(b)(2)(B) of the Pension Act).

> **Comment:** According to the Senate Finance Committee, participants who are entitled to defer distributions should be informed of the impact that a decision not to defer will have on the taxation and accumulation of their retirement benefits (Senate Rept. 109-174).

▶ **Effective date.** The amendments and modifications made or required to be made by these provisions apply to years beginning after December 31, 2006 (Act Secs. 1102(a)(3) of the Pension Protection Act of 2006). Modifications regarding a participant's right to defer apply to years beginning after December 31, 2006 (Act Sec. 1102(b)(2)(B) of the Pension Act).

Law source: Law at ¶5105 and ¶7213. Committee Report at ¶11,050.

— Act Sec. 1102(a)(1) of the Pension Protection Act of 2006, amending Code Sec. 417(a)(6)(A);

— Act Sec. 1102(a)(2), amending ERISA Sec. 205(c)(7)(A);

— Act Secs. 1102(a)(3) and (b)(2), providing the effective dates.

Reporter references: For further information, consult the following CCH reporters.

— Pension Plan Guide, ¶1516, ¶1543 and ¶7643

— Standard Federal Tax Reporter, 2006FED ¶17,730.0455, ¶18,219A.075 and ¶19,071.075

— Tax Research Consultant, RETIRE: 42,212

— Federal Tax Guide, 2006FTG ¶11,060

¶930 Application of Required Minimum Distribution Rules to Governmental Plans

SUMMARY OF NEW LAW

The Secretary of the Treasury is directed to issue regulations under which a governmental plan is treated as satisfying the required minimum distribution (RMD) rules if it complies with a good faith interpretation of those rules.

BACKGROUND

Generally, a "governmental plan" is a type of retirement plan established and maintained for its employees by the U.S. government, the government of any state or political subdivision thereof, or any agency or instrumentality of a governmental unit (Code Sec. 414). These plans resemble other qualified retirement plans in their treatment of participants, but they do not offer the same tax benefits to employers (and those tax benefits would be largely irrelevant to governmental units and exempt entities). Governmental plans can be more difficult to amend than other qualified

BACKGROUND

plans, because they are subject to a greater degree of public oversight, and they may be constrained by state statutes or constitutions.

For distributions made after 2001, governmental plans are subject to the same required minimum distribution (RMD) rules that Code Sec. 401(a)(9) imposes on most other qualified retirement plans (Code Sec. 457(d)(2)). The RMD rules direct the plan to begin the distribution of minimum benefits by the required beginning date, and complete the distribution of plan benefits over a specified time period (Code Sec. 401(a)(9)(A)). These starting dates and distribution periods vary depending on whether the plan participant was alive when the distributions began, and whether a deceased participant's beneficiary is a surviving spouse (Code Sec. 401(a)(9)(B)). For distributions made before 2002, governmental plans had to satisfy a special set of RMD rules (Code Sec. 457(d)(2), prior to amendment by the Economic Growth and Tax Reconciliation Act of 2001, P.L. 107-16, Act §649(a) (June 7, 2001)).

When a plan fails to satisfy the minimum distribution rules, the participant is subject to an excise tax equal to 50 percent of the required minimum distributions that were not distributed for the year (Code Sec. 4974(a)). The IRS can waive the tax if the participant establishes that the shortfall was due to reasonable error, and reasonable remedial steps are being taken (Code Sec. 4974(d)). Since qualified plans must comply with the RMD rules, a plan that demonstrates a pattern of violating the RMD rules can become disqualified.

NEW LAW EXPLAINED

RMD standards may apply to governmental plans.—The Secretary of the Treasury is directed to issue regulations under which a governmental plan is treated as satisfying the required minimum distribution (RMD) requirements imposed by Code Sec. 401(a)(9), if the plan satisfies a reasonable, good faith interpretation of those requirements. The regulations will apply to years in which the RMD rules apply to the plan (Act Sec. 823 of the Pension Protection Act of 2006). Although this provision is effective on August 17, 2006, the date of enactment, the Report of the Joint Committee on Taxation states that the regulations should apply to periods before that date (Joint Committee on Taxation, Technical Explanation of the Pension Protection Act of 2006 (JCX-38-06)).

> **Comment:** This provision is apparently intended to provide greater flexibility in complying with RMD requirements to accommodate plan designs commonly used by governmental plans.

> **Practical Analysis:** Mary Beth Braitman, Terry A.M. Mumford and Lisa Erb Harrison of Ice Miller LLP, Indianapolis, Indiana, note that the Act contains long-sought relief for governmental plans with respect to the minimum distribution rules of Code Sec. 401(a)(9). It allows governmental plans to comply with "a reasonable good faith interpretation" of these rules. This should allow plans to devise a compliance strategy that addresses the intent of these rules, while being sensitive to state laws permitting certain distribution options, as well as administrative issues associated with these

NEW LAW EXPLAINED

rules. The Act does not exempt governmental plans from the minimum distribution rules, it simply gives them more flexibility in satisfying the rules. The JCT's Technical Explanation (JCX-38-06) comments that the Secretary of Treasury is to issue regulations under which a governmental plan will be treated as complying with these rules if the plan complies with a reasonable good faith interpretation of the statutory requirements.

▶ **Effective date.** No specific effective date is provided by the Act. The provision is, therefore, considered effective on August 17, 2006, the date of enactment.

Law source: Law at ¶7156. JCT Report at ¶10,640.

— Act Sec. 823 of the Pension Protection Act of 2006.

Reporter references: For further information, consult the following CCH reporters.

— Pension Plan Guide, ¶3617 and ¶8255

— Standard Federal Tax Reporter, 2006FED ¶21,536.045

— Tax Research Consultant, COMPEN: 15,152.45 and RETIRE: 42,150

ROLLOVERS

¶935 Direct Rollovers From Eligible Retirement Plans to Roth IRAs

SUMMARY OF NEW LAW

Beginning January 1, 2008, distributions from tax-qualified retirement plans, tax-sheltered annuities and section 457 plans can be rolled over directly into a Roth IRA, subject to the restrictions that currently apply to rollovers from a traditional IRA into a Roth IRA.

BACKGROUND

In general, there are two types of individual retirement accounts (IRAs): traditional IRAs and Roth IRAs. Traditional and Roth IRAs are both subject to annual contribution limits equal to the lesser of a statutory dollar amount or 100 percent of taxable compensation. For 2006 and 2007, the annual limit on contributions to a traditional IRA or Roth IRA is $4,000. For 2008, the annual limit increases to $5,000 (Code Sec. 219(b)(5)(A)). However, an individual taxpayer who has reached age 50 is also permitted to make additional catch-up contributions to an IRA. The catch-up contribution limit is $1,000 (Code Sec. 219(b)(5)(B)).

Contributions to a traditional IRA are deductible if certain conditions are met, while contributions to a Roth IRA are never deductible. A contribution to a traditional IRA

BACKGROUND

may not be fully deductible if the taxpayer or the taxpayer's spouse is an active participant in an employer-sponsored retirement plan (Code Sec. 219(g)). Taxpayers who cannot make deductible (or fully deductible) contributions to a traditional IRA may make nondeductible contributions up to the maximum annual contribution limit. A taxpayer may also elect to treat deductible contributions as nondeductible contributions (Code Sec. 408(o)).

Distributions from traditional IRAs (unless they are returns of nondeductible contributions) are taxable (Code Sec. 408(d)(1)), while qualified distributions from a Roth IRA are not. A qualified Roth IRA distribution is one made on or after the date on which the individual attains age 59½, on account of the individual's death or disability or for qualified first-time homebuyer expenses (Code Sec. 408A(d)(2)(A)). Additionally, a Roth IRA distribution is not qualified unless it is made more than five years after the first tax year for which the taxpayer or the taxpayer's spouse made a contribution to the Roth IRA (Code Sec. 408A(d)(2)(B)). Distributions from traditional IRAs made prior to the individual's attainment of age 59½ and nonqualified distributions from Roth IRAs are both subject to an additional 10-percent tax (Code Sec. 72(t)).

Rollover contributions. Subject to certain requirements, distributions from a tax-qualified retirement plan, tax-sheltered annuity or section 457 plan can be rolled over tax free into a traditional IRA. However, distributions from a tax-qualified retirement plan, tax-sheltered annuity or section 457 plan cannot be directly rolled over into a Roth IRA.

Under present law, only an individual whose adjusted gross income does not exceed $100,000 can roll over amounts from a traditional IRA to a Roth IRA (Code Sec. 408A(c)(3)(B), prior to repeal by the Tax Increase Prevention and Reconciliation Act of 2005 (P.L. 109-222)). For married individuals filing a joint return, amounts from a traditional IRA can be rolled over into a Roth IRA only if the couple's adjusted gross income does not exceed $100,000 (Code Sec. 408A(c)(3)(B), prior to repeal by P.L. 109-222)). Married individuals filing separate returns may *not* rollover amounts from a traditional IRA to a Roth IRA regardless of the individual's adjusted gross income. However, for tax years beginning after December 31, 2009, the $100,000 AGI limit and filing status requirement to convert a traditional IRA to a Roth IRA is eliminated (Code Sec. 408A(c), as amended by P.L. 109-222). In such cases, the amount rolled over will be included in the individual's income as a distribution, but the 10 percent additional tax for early withdrawals will not apply (Code Sec. 408A(d)(3)(A)(ii)). Individuals who convert from a traditional IRA to a Roth IRA in 2010 will recognize the conversion in income ratably in 2011 and 2012 unless they elect to recognize the income in full in 2010 (Code Sec. 408A(d)(3)(A)(iii), as amended by P.L. 109-222)).

NEW LAW EXPLAINED

Rollover of Distributions Directly Into a Roth IRA.—Distributions from eligible retirement plans made after December 31, 2007, can be rolled over directly into a Roth IRA (Code Sec. 408A(e), as amended by the Pension Protection Act of 2006). In addition to traditional IRAs, eligible retirement plans include qualified trusts, tax-sheltered

NEW LAW EXPLAINED

annuities and governmental 457 plans (Code Sec. 402(c)(8)(B)). However, the rollover contribution must meet the rollover requirements applicable to the specific type of retirement plan.

For tax years beginning prior to January 1, 2010, the restrictions that previously applied to rollovers from a traditional IRA into a Roth IRA will apply to any rollover from an eligible retirement plan directly into a Roth IRA. Thus, a rollover to a Roth IRA will be allowed only if, for the tax year of the distribution to which the contribution relates, the taxpayer's adjusted gross income does not exceed $100,000 and the taxpayer is not a married individual filing a separate return (Code Sec. 408A(c)(3)(b), as amended by the Pension Act of 2006).

Practical Analysis: Robert S. Keebler of Virchow Krause & Company LLP, Green Bay, Wisconsin, notes that the direct rollover (*i.e.* trustee-to-trustee transfer) of qualified retirement plan assets to a Roth IRA will eliminate the logistical problems for those who want to do Roth IRA conversions and provides the following example.

One of my clients, Dr. Z, had a $2,000,000 401(k) plan balance, and wanted to convert $200,000 to a Roth IRA in 2004. Instead of doing a direct rollover from his 401(k) to a Roth IRA, he had to set up a temporary traditional IRA account first. Because of procedural issues on the financial institution's part in setting up the two types of IRAs and making transfers between the two accounts, the Roth IRA conversion could not be completed before the end of 2004. However, had we been able to roll the 401(k) directly into the Roth IRA, the transfer could have been accomplished before year end. Thus, this new provision in the tax law will allow for a streamlining of Roth IRA conversions and reduce the possibility of procedural errors.

Caution Note: A rollover into a Roth IRA is not tax free. Except to the extent it represents a return of after-tax contributions, any amount that is rolled over to a Roth IRA is includible in gross income as a distribution since qualified distributions from a Roth IRA are not taxed. However, the 10 percent tax on early distributions will not apply to the rollover.

Planning Note: For rollovers in 2010, the taxpayer will recognize the distribution amount in income ratably in 2011 and 2012 unless the taxpayer elects to recognize it all in 2010 (Code Sec. 408A(d)(3)(A)(iii), as amended by the Tax Increase Prevention and Reconciliation Act of 2005 (P.L. 109-222)). No special provision is made for years after 2010, so taxpayers making rollovers in 2011 and thereafter will have to recognize the entire amount of the distribution as income in the tax year the distribution takes place.

Practical Analysis: Mary Beth Braitman, Terry A.M. Mumford and Lisa Erb Harrison of Ice Miller LLP, Indianapolis, Indiana, observe that this amendment provides for governmental retirement plans (including qualified defined benefit and defined contribution plans, 403(b) tax-sheltered annuity plans, and 457(b) eligible deferred compensation plans) to make direct rollovers of eligible rollover distributions from such

NEW LAW EXPLAINED

plans to Roth IRAs, subject to the rules that apply to rollovers from a traditional IRA to a Roth IRA. Thus, for example, a rollover from a tax-qualified retirement plan into a Roth IRA is includible in gross income (except to the extent it represents a return of after-tax contributions), and the 10-percent early distribution tax does not apply. Also, such rollovers are subject to the limitations on rollovers to Roth IRAs based on modified adjusted gross income under Code Sec. 408A(c)(3)(B).

Because many governmental employees are in income tax brackets which permit Roth IRAs rollovers, the expansion of these rollover rules will be particularly helpful to them. Governmental plans may need to amend their distribution forms to cover this provision.

Comment: This change will make it easier for an individual to convert a traditional IRA to a Roth IRA after 2007. Prior to the change, taxpayers will continue to have to go through a two-step process to reach the same result: roll over an interest in a qualified plan to a traditional IRA, and then convert the traditional IRA to a Roth IRA.

▶ **Effective date.** This provision applies to distributions after December 31, 2007 (Act Sec. 824(c) of the Pension Protection Act of 2006).

Law source: Law at ¶5060. Committee Report at ¶10,650.

— Act Sec. 824(a) of the Pension Protection Act of 2006, amending Code Sec. 408A(e);

— Act Sec. 824(b), amending Code Sec. 408A(c)(3)(B) as in effect before the Tax Increase Prevention and Reconciliation Act of 2005 (P.L. 109-222) and (d)(3);

— Act Sec. 824(c), providing the effective date.

Reporter references: For further information, consult the following CCH reporters.

— Pension Plan Guide, ¶3766, ¶3798 and ¶7710

— Standard Federal Tax Reporter, 2006FED ¶18,207.022, ¶18,922.0356, ¶18,930.032, ¶18,930.033, ¶18,930.035, ¶18,930.036 and ¶21,536.048

— Tax Research Consultant, RETIRE: 42,212.05 and RETIRE: 42,450

— Federal Tax Guide, 2006FTG ¶11,087

¶940 Rollover of After-Tax Contributions to Defined Benefit Plans and Annuity Contracts

SUMMARY OF NEW LAW

After-tax contributions can be rolled over in a trustee-to-trustee transfer from a qualified retirement plan to a defined benefit plan or a tax-sheltered annuity (403(b) plan).

BACKGROUND

Employee after-tax contributions to a qualified retirement plan may be rolled over into another qualified retirement plan, but only if the rollover distribution is transferred either: (1) in a direct trustee-to-trustee transfer to a defined contribution plan which separately accounts for the pre-tax and after-tax portions; or (2) to an individual retirement account or individual retirement annuity, other than an endowment contract (collectively "IRA") (Code Sec. 402(c)(2)). Defined benefit plans and tax-sheltered annuities for public school or Code Sec. 501(c)(3) tax-exempt organization employees (i.e., "403(b) plans") cannot receive rollovers of after-tax contributions from qualified retirement plans.

NEW LAW EXPLAINED

Rollover of after-tax contributions to defined benefit plan or tax-sheltered annuity.—After-tax contributions from qualified retirement plans can be rolled over not only to a defined contribution plan or an IRA, but also to a defined benefit plan or a 403(b) tax-sheltered annuity (Code Sec. 402(c)(2)(A), as amended by the Pension Protection Act of 2006). A rollover to a defined benefit plan or tax-sheltered annuity must be a direct trustee-to-trustee rollover, and the transferee plan must separately account for after-tax contributions and earnings thereon.

> **Comment:** This amendment expands the opportunities for rollover of after-tax contributions.

> **Practical Analysis:** Mary Beth Braitman, Terry A.M. Mumford and Lisa Erb Harrison of Ice Miller LLP, Indianapolis, Indiana, observe that this amendment will provide greater flexibility for governmental defined benefit plans that wish to accept eligible rollover distributions. It will permit qualified plans (whether defined benefit or defined contribution) and 403(b) tax-sheltered annuity plans to accept after-tax direct rollover amounts from a qualified retirement plan, so long as the plan separately accounts for such after-tax amounts (previously only qualified defined contribution plans could accept such after-tax rollover amounts).
>
> The expansion of the rollover rules is particularly helpful for governmental defined benefit plans, many of which permit members to purchase additional service credit under the plan for prior service with other public employers, thereby increasing the years of service used to determine their benefit under the governmental defined benefit plan. Rollovers are often a critical source of funds for governmental plan members to use in purchasing additional service credit. Governmental plans may need to amend the plan terms in order to implement this permissive feature if current rollover language governing the plan is not broad enough.

▶ **Effective date.** The provision applies to tax years beginning after December 31, 2006 (Act Sec. 822(b) of the Pension Protection Act of 2006).

NEW LAW EXPLAINED

Law source: Law at ¶5035. Committee Report at ¶10,630.

— Act Sec. 822(a) of the Pension Protection Act of 2006, amending Code Sec. 402(c)(2)(A);

— Act Sec. 822(b), providing the effective date.

Reporter references: For further information, consult the following CCH reporters.

— Pension Plan Guide, ¶3771, ¶3798 and ¶8275

— Standard Federal Tax Reporter, 2006FED ¶18,207.022, ¶18,282.0435 and ¶18,922.0356

— Tax Research Consultant, RETIRE: 42,500

— Federal Tax Guide, 2006FTG ¶11,087

¶945 Rollovers by Nonspouse Beneficiaries

SUMMARY OF NEW LAW

Distributions from a deceased person's eligible retirement plan to a nonspouse beneficiary may be rolled over tax-free into an IRA via trustee-to-trustee transfer. Payouts from the transferee IRA must follow the minimum distribution rules that apply to nonspouse beneficiaries.

BACKGROUND

Distributions from a qualified retirement plan, a 403(a) employee annuity plan, a tax-sheltered annuity for public school or 501(c)(3) exempt organization employees ("403(b) plan"), a deferred compensation plan for state or local government or tax-exempt organization employees ("457 plan"), or an individual retirement account or an individual retirement annuity that is not an endowment contract (collectively "IRA") generally are subject to tax in the year distributed (Code Secs. 402(a), 403(a)(1) and (b)(1), 408(d)(1), and 457(a)). However, eligible rollover distributions may be rolled over tax free within 60 days into an eligible retirement plan (Code Secs. 402(c), 403(a)(4) and (b)(8), 408(d)(3), and 457(e)(16)). Generally, an eligible rollover distribution is any distribution to the plan participant or IRA owner, but does not include certain periodic distributions, the minimum required distributions or hardship distributions (Code Sec. 402(c)(4)).

If a participant/owner dies, distributions from the plan or IRA to his or her surviving spouse can be similarly rolled over as if the spouse were the participant/owner (Code Secs. 402(c)(9) and 408(d)(3)(C)(ii)(II)). Such rollovers are not available for distributions to a beneficiary who is not the surviving spouse. In fact, an IRA acquired by an nonspouse beneficiary due to an IRA owner's death is considered an "inherited" account, which may not be rolled over (Code Sec. 408(d)(3)(C)).

Minimum distribution rules. Prior to a participant/owner's death, distributions from the plan or IRA generally must begin by April 1 of the calendar year following the later of the calendar year in which he or she attains age 70½ or retires (Code Secs. 401(a)(9)(A) and (C), 403(b)(10), 408(a)(6) and (b)(3), and 457(d)(2); Reg. § 1.401(a)(9)-1, Q&A-1). If minimum distributions have begun before his or her death, the remaining interest generally must be distributed to the beneficiary at least as

BACKGROUND

rapidly as under the minimum distribution method used before the date of death. If the participant/owner dies before minimum distributions have begun, then either: (1) the entire remaining interest must be distributed within five years after his or her death; or (2) distributions must begin within one year after the participant/owner's death and be paid out over the life or life expectancy of the beneficiary (Code Sec. 401(a)(9)(B)).

If the beneficiary is the participant/owner's surviving spouse, distributions do not need to begin until the date the deceased participant/owner would have attained age 70½ (Code Sec. 401(a)(9)(B)(iv)). If the surviving spouse makes an eligible rollover distribution into his or her own plan or IRA, minimum distributions do not need to begin until the surviving spouse turns age 70½. This special treatment is not available to nonspouse beneficiaries.

NEW LAW EXPLAINED

Rollover by nonspouse beneficiaries.—The Pension Protection Act of 2006 allows distributions from an eligible retirement plan (as defined under Code Sec. 402(c)(8)(B)) of a deceased participant/owner to be rolled over by a nonspouse beneficiary. If a direct trustee-to-trustee transfer is made to an IRA that has been established to receive the distribution on behalf of a beneficiary who is not the participant/owner's surviving spouse, the following treatment applies:

- the transfer is treated as an eligible rollover distribution;
- the transferee IRA is treated as an inherited account; and
- the required minimum distribution rules applicable where the participant/owner dies before the entire interest is distributed apply to the transferee IRA; the special rules for surviving spouse beneficiaries do not apply (Code Sec. 402(c)(11)(A), as added by the Pension Act).

Practical Analysis: Mary Beth Braitman, Terry A.M. Mumford and Lisa Erb Harrison of Ice Miller LLP, Indianapolis, Indiana, observe that this amendment provides an additional option for non-spouse beneficiaries of distributions from qualified retirement plans, 403(b) tax-sheltered annuity plans and 457(b) deferred compensation plans, who previously were not permitted to rollover distributions from such plans. Now, if a distribution would otherwise be an eligible rollover distribution, a non-spouse beneficiary may rollover the distribution to an individual retirement account or individual retirement annuity established for the purpose of receiving such distribution and the account or annuity will be treated as an inherited individual retirement account or annuity. Thus, for example, distributions from the inherited IRA would be subject to the minimum distribution rules applicable to beneficiaries.

Governmental plans will need to begin immediately examining their distribution forms and options for this change.

NEW LAW EXPLAINED

The rollover rules for distributions from 403(a) employee annuity plans, 403(b) plans and 457 plans specifically provide that the nonspouse beneficiary rollover rule applies (Code Secs. 403(a)(4)(B), 403(b)(8)(B) and 457(e)(16)(B), as amended by the Pension Act).

> **Comment:** The new rollover rule does not permit a nonspouse beneficiary to roll over distributions from a qualified employer plan like a 401(k) the same as a surviving spouse. As noted above, the rollover is permitted only if the transferee IRA is treated as an inherited IRA of the nonspouse beneficiary. Thus, the nonspouse beneficiary will not be treated as the owner of the rolled over assets and those assets once transferred to the inherited IRA may not be further rolled over.
>
> According to the Senate Finance Committee Report that accompanied an earlier version of the Pension bill, retirement plans often pay out distributions to nonspouse beneficiaries in a lump sum soon after a plan participant's death, even though the minimum distribution rules permit a longer payout period (S. Rep. No. 109-174). The amendment gives nonspouse beneficiaries more flexibility to extend the payout period, in accordance with the minimum distribution rules. Thus, the interest rolled into the transferee IRA must be distributed to the designated nonspouse beneficiary at least as rapidly as under the distribution method used before the participant died. If the participant dies before minimum distributions have begun, the entire rolled-over interest must be distributed within five years after the participant's death, or must begin within one year after the participant's death and be paid out over the beneficiary's life or life expectancy.
>
> The change made by the Pension Act essentially duplicates the existing planning technique of having a plan participant roll over their account in their employer's retirement plan into an IRA before he or she dies. However, under the new rule, this can now all be done straight out of the 401(k) or other employer plan at the employee's death without having to roll over the assets to an IRA during the employee's life. The change does not affect the ability of the nonspouse beneficiary to name a successor beneficiary as permitted by the IRA trust (i.e., "stretch IRAs"), so long as the distribution continues to meet the required minimum distribution rules applicable to the original nonspouse beneficiary.

Trusts. Except as otherwise provided by the IRS, a trust that is maintained for the benefit of one or more designated beneficiaries must be treated as a trust designated beneficiary for purposes of the rollover available to nonspouse beneficiaries (Code Sec. 402(c)(11)(B), as added by the Pension Act).

> **Practical Analysis:** Robert S. Keebler of Virchow Krause & Company LLP, Green Bay, Wisconsin, observes that from a malpractice management perspective, the most important aspect of the new IRA provisions is the ability to transfer qualified retirement plan assets from a deceased person's qualified plan to an inherited IRA for the benefit of a beneficiary. In my 20 years of practice, I have seen countless families and tax advisors who would have benefited from this provision. In most

NEW LAW EXPLAINED

cases, a parent died leaving a large pension plan to a child whereby the child was forced, under the qualified plan's rules, to take funds out of the qualified retirement plan within five years (and in some cases immediately). Under the Act, the child can now transfer the funds via a trustee-to-trustee transfer to an IRA in the parent's name, allowing the child to take funds out over his or her life expectancy. Furthermore, under the provisions of the new law, trustees of trusts that are named as beneficiaries of qualified retirement plans are allowed to perform these rollovers to inherited IRAs. At the present time, we are representing a lady whose deceased brother left her a large pension plan. Under present law, she would be forced withdraw the entire pension plan balance within five years. However, it appears that our client, the beneficiary, will now be allowed to move funds from the plan to an inherited IRA even though she inherited the pension plan prior to the enactment of the Act. Thus, our client will be able to take IRA distributions over her life expectancy instead of over a five-year period.

▶ **Effective date.** The provision applies to distributions after December 31, 2006 (Act Sec. 829(b) of the Pension Protection Act of 2006).

Law source: Law at ¶5035, ¶5040 and ¶5140. Committee Report at ¶10,700.

— Act Sec. 829(a)(1) of the Pension Protection Act of 2006, adding Code Sec. 402(c)(11);

— Act Sec. 829(a)(2), amending Code Sec. 403(a)(4)(B);

— Act Sec. 829(a)(3), amending Code Sec. 403(b)(8)(B);

— Act Sec. 829(a)(4), amending Code Sec. 457(e)(16)(B);

— Act Sec. 829(b), providing the effective date.

Reporter references: For further information, consult the following CCH reporters.

— Pension Plan Guide, ¶8255 and ¶8604

— Standard Federal Tax Reporter, 2006FED ¶18,207.022, ¶18,217A.01, ¶18,282.0435, ¶18,922.0322 and ¶21,536.048

— Tax Research Consultant, RETIRE: 42,460.05 and RETIRE: 66,456

— Federal Tax Guide, 2006FTG ¶11,084, ¶11,435 and ¶11,450

Plan Qualification and Administration

CASH BALANCE/HYBRID PLANS

¶1005 Cash balance and pension equity plan conversions

¶1010 Application of cash balance and pension equity plan rules in mergers and acquisitions

CASH OR DEFERRED ARRANGEMENTS

¶1015 Automatic enrollment in 401(k) plans

¶1020 Combined defined benefit and 401(k) plans

SPOUSAL PROTECTIONS

¶1025 Regulations on time and order of issuance of DROs

¶1030 Entitlement of divorced spouses to railroad retirement annuities

¶1035 Surviving former spouses' entitlement to tier II railroad retirement benefits

¶1040 Additional survivor annuity option

CHURCH AND GOVERNMENT PLANS

¶1045 Church plans that self-annuitize

¶1050 Income from leveraged real estate held by church plans

¶1055 Church plan rule for benefit limitations

¶1060 Nondiscrimination exemption extended to all governmental plans

¶1065 Treatment of Indian tribal government plans

¶1070 Code Sec. 457 exceptions extended to voluntary early retirement incentive and employee retention plans

¶1075 Participation in Code Sec. 457 plans after cash-outs

PLAN ADMINISTRATION

¶1080 Reporting simplification for small retirement plans

¶1085 Employee plans compliance resolution system (EPCRS)

¶1090 Provisions related to plan amendments

CROSS REFERENCE

Vesting schedule expedited for employer contributions to defined contribution plans (*see* ¶720)

CASH BALANCE/HYBRID PLANS

¶1005 Cash Balance and Pension Equity Plan Conversions

SUMMARY OF NEW LAW

The new law protects a hybrid plan from age discrimination challenges if the plan meets certain requirements. Lump sum distributions from a hybrid plan can be based on the participant's hypothetical account balances without violating minimum present value requirements. The wearaway approach to the anti-cutback rule is prohibited.

BACKGROUND

Hybrid plans are defined benefit plans that combine elements of traditional defined benefit plans with elements of defined contribution plans. The main difference between a hybrid and a traditional defined benefit plan is that retirement benefits are more evenly accrued throughout an employee's career instead of being backloaded near the end of the employee's career. With a traditional defined benefit plan the benefit accrual entitles the employee to a stream of payments at normal retirement age. Accruals throughout an employee's career are based on the present value of this stream of income. The present value of such payments is much lower in an employee's early years than it is in his or her later years. That is why accruals are said to be backloaded for traditional plans.

In contrast, accruals for hybrid plans are not based on the present value of retirement income. Instead, they are based on the value of the amount credited in any particular year. Since these amounts are also credited with interest, there is no analogous present value issue. Accruals tend to be far more steady throughout an employee's career. This feature makes the plan more attractive to younger employees, especially those who do not anticipate staying in the same plan until retirement. Hybrid plans are also attractive to employers because their funding obligations are less volatile, and plan benefits are easier to explain to employees. Cash balance plans and pension equity plans are common types of hybrid plans.

Cash balance plans. A cash balance pension plan is a hybrid defined benefit plan that provides guaranteed benefits for employees. Generally, cash balance plans result from the conversion of traditional defined benefit plans. Cash balance plans establish a separate hypothetical account for each employee. They do not provide a benefit based on a combination of the employee's length of service and salary. Since the benefits are not based solely on actual contributions and forfeitures, nor on invest-

BACKGROUND

ment experiences and plan expenses allocated to the account, the arrangement is treated as a defined benefit plan rather than as a defined contribution plan.

The amount of an employee's hypothetical account balance in a cash balance plan is determined by hypothetical annual allocations, known as pay credits, and hypothetical earnings, known as interest credits. For example, the employer hypothetically credits a specified percentage of compensation (pay credits) to each employee's account and hypothetically credits each account with interest earned (interest credits) according to the terms of the plan. Generally, cash balance plans are designed to include the right to future interest on the pay credit when a participant's account receives the hypothetical pay credit for the year of service. The right to future interest is known as front-loaded interest credit. The right to future interest is not contingent on the participant remaining in the employ of the employer. The amounts to be contributed are actuarially determined to ensure sufficient funds to provide the promised benefit.

Pension equity plans. A pension equity plan (PEP) is another type of hybrid defined benefit pension plan. Generally, benefits are described as a percentage of final average pay. The percentage is determined on the basis of points received for each year of service and the points are often weighted for older or longer service employees. Interest credits are usually provided for the period between the participant's termination of employment and the commencement of benefits.

Age discrimination prohibition. Benefit accruals under a defined benefit pension plan are subject to the prohibition on age discrimination under Code Sec. 411(b)(1)(H) and ERISA Sec. 204(b)(1)(H). The rate of an employee's benefit accrual may not be reduced and the accrual may not cease because of the attainment of any age. The age discrimination prohibition, however, is not violated solely because the plan imposes a limit on the amount of benefits that the plan provides, or a limit on the number of years of service or years of participation that are taken into account, for purposes of determining benefit accrual under the plan, as long as these limits are determined without regard to age. The subsidized portion of any early retirement benefit may be disregarded in determining benefit accruals.

Courts have been split on whether hybrid plans cause age discrimination problems. The problematic feature of hybrid plans for age discrimination purposes is that a dollar of accrued benefits for a younger employee has a higher present value than a dollar of accrued benefits for an older employee. For example, suppose Sam age 50 and Sara age 30 are in the same cash balance plan, and each is credited with $2,000 in pay credits in the current plan year. If they both start retirement benefits at normal retirement age, Sara's $2,000 is worth more in retirement benefits than Sam's because Sara's has 20 more years to grow before she retires. Although many courts have upheld hybrid plans against age discrimination challenges, employers have been wary about jumping on the hybrid plan bandwagon pending a clear statement from the IRS or Congress that hybrid plans are bulletproof against litigation.

BACKGROUND

Minimum present value rules and the whipsaw effect. Defined benefit pension plans, including hybrid plans, must provide benefits in the form of a life annuity that begins at normal retirement age, or a lump-sum that is subject to the minimum present value rules and cannot be less than the present value of the life annuity payable at normal retirement age. The lump-sum distribution is determined by projecting the hypothetical account balance to normal retirement age using the plan's interest rate, converting it to an actuarially equivalent annuity using the interest rate and mortality assumptions specified in the plan, and then discounting back to the date of distribution using certain statutorily prescribed interest and mortality assumptions for converting accrued benefits to a lump-sum. A discrepancy can occur if the interest rate under the plan is different than the statutorily prescribed interest rate. If the plan rate is higher than the statutory rate, the lump-sum benefit will be larger than the hypothetical account balance. This is commonly referred to as the whipsaw effect and raises the question of which amount, lump-sum or hypothetical account balance, must be distributed.

Conversions to cash balance plans and the wearaway approach to the anticutback rule. When a qualified retirement plan is amended, the anti-cutback rule precludes a resulting reduction in benefits that have already accrued. In the event of a conversion, a plan has several options on how to handle the anti-cutback rule. There is no violation of the anti-cutback rule if any of the following provisions are included in the amended plan.

(1) The participant's accrued benefit is determined as the greater of:

  (a) the pre-amendment accrued benefit, and

  (b) the benefit determined by applying the new benefit formula to all of the participant's years of service before and after amendment.

(2) The participant's benefit is determined as the sum of the pre-amendment accrued benefit and the immediately generating additional accrued benefits computed by application of the new formula to the years of service after amendment (commonly known as the no-wearway approach since there is no break in benefit accruals).

(3) The amended plan provides a grandfather provision that allows:

  (a) application of the pre-amendment benefit formula where it provides a greater benefit than the new formula, or

  (b) pre-amendment participant choice between the old and new formulas.

Note that under the first approach, if a participant's pre-amendment accrued benefit is greater than the benefit provided under the new formula, there may be a period during which the participant does not accrue any additional benefits. This period is known as the wearaway period. The wearaway period has been the target of much criticism on behalf of adversely affected employees.

Hybrid plans on hold. Cash balance and pension equity plans exhibit both defined contribution (individual employee account) and defined benefit (investment risk and reward with employer) plan characteristics, but are subject to regulation as defined benefit plans, hence the applicability of the age discrimination prohibition and the

BACKGROUND

minimum present value and anti-cutback rules. The application of these rules to hybrid plans, however, is not always clear as evidenced by the disparity in result in age discrimination court decisions. In addition, the IRS has not issued determination letters on hybrid plans since 1999. Although over nine million American workers are currently covered by these plans, employers have become wary due to the lack of guidance. Some plans have been frozen and the number of conversions has been significantly reduced. Employees can benefit from clarification of the applicable rules since employers who find the rules clear and not overly burdensome are more likely to convert to and maintain these plans.

NEW LAW EXPLAINED

Cash balance and pension equity plans do not violate age discrimination or minimum present value rules.—The Pension Protection Act of 2006 made several changes related to cash balance and pension equity hybrid defined benefit plans. These changes include clarification of the age discrimination and minimum present value rules applicable to defined benefit plans, including cash balance and pension equity plans. In addition, the requirements for conversion to cash balance and pension equity plans have been clarified.

> **Practical Analysis:** Dan Schwallie of Hewitt Associates, Cleveland, Ohio, notes that Congress approved significant legislation affecting cash balance and other "hybrid" defined benefit plans (*e.g.*, pension equity plans) as part of the Pension Protection Act of 2006. The Act provides prospective relief from age discrimination claims for hybrid plans that comply with the Act. It also permits compliant hybrid plans, after August 17, 2006, the date of enactment, to pay a lump sum distribution equal to the participant's account balance (or accumulated percentage of final average pay, in the case of a pension equity plan), thereby prospectively eliminating the so-called whipsaw issue. The Act also bans the use of "wear away" for any conversion of a defined benefit plan to a hybrid plan after June 29, 2005; instead requiring a participant's benefit to be no less than the sum of the participant's old-formula benefit at conversion plus the participant's benefit earned for post conversion service under the new hybrid formula. The Act states that no inference is to be drawn from its provisions with respect to age discrimination or whipsaw issues prior to June 29, 2005. The intent of the "no inference" language is to indicate that the provisions of the Act do not apply prior to June 29, 2005 in evaluating age discrimination or whipsaw claims.

Age discrimination rules. A defined benefit pension plan, including a hybrid cash balance plan or pension equity plan (PEP), does not violate the age discrimination prohibition in Code Sec. 411(b)(1)(H)(i) if a participant's entire accrued benefit (as determined as of any date under the terms of the plan) is equal to or greater than that of any similarly situated, younger individual who is or could be a participant (Code Sec. 411(b)(5)(A)(i), ERISA Sec. 204(b)(5)(A)(i), and Age Discrimination in Employment Act of 1967 (ADEA) Sec. 4(i)(10)(A)(i), as added by the Pension Protection Act of 2006). A

NEW LAW EXPLAINED

participant is *similarly situated* to any other individual if such participant is identical to such other individual in every respect, including period of service, compensation, position, date of hire, work history, and any other respect, except for age (Code Sec. 411(b)(5)(A)(ii), ERISA Sec. 204(b)(5)(A)(ii), and ADEA Sec. 4(i)(10)(A)(ii), as added by the Pension Act).

> **Comment:** The effect of this language is to clarify that reflecting in the plan that older workers have less time until retirement age does not constitute age discrimination if everything else is equal. The clarification will be welcomed by employers. As Judge Easterbrook put it in a recent decision, reversing a controversial district court decision and upholding IBM's hybrid plan under the old law: "Treating the time value of money as a form of discrimination is not sensible." (*Cooper v. IBM Personal Pension Plan*, CA7, 2006-2 USTC ¶50,448).

Accrued benefit for purposes of the antidiscrimination rule. Accrued benefit for these purposes means the benefit accrued to date (Code Sec. 411(b)(5)(G), ERISA Sec. 204(b)(5)(G), and ADEA Sec. 4(i)(10)(G), as amended by the Pension Act). The subsidized portion of any early retirement benefit or retirement-type subsidy is disregarded in determining the accrued benefit as of any date, except for applicable plan amendments adopted after June 29, 2005 (Code Sec. 411(b)(5)(A)(iii), ERISA Sec. 204(b)(5)(A)(iii), and ADEA Sec. 4(i)(10)(A)(iii), as added by the Pension Act). See *conversion to cash balance plan or PEP*, below. Pursuant to the terms of the plan, the accrued benefit may be expressed as an annuity payable at normal retirement age (traditional defined benefit plan), the balance of a hypothetical account (cash balance hybrid plan), or the current value of the accumulated percentage of the employee's final average compensation (pension equity hybrid plan) (Code Sec. 411(b)(5)(A)(iv), ERISA Sec. 204(b)(5)(A)(iv), and ADEA Sec. 4(i)(10)(A)(iv), as added by the Pension Act).

A defined benefit plan, including a hybrid plan, providing offsets against benefits under the plan is not age discriminatory to the extent that the offsets are permitted in applying the qualified plan requirements of Code Sec. 401(a) (Code Sec. 411(b)(5)(C), ERISA Sec. 204(b)(5)(C), and ADEA Sec. 4(i)(10)(C), as added by the Pension Act). Furthermore, plan provisions allowing disparity in contributions or benefits are not age discriminatory as long as the defined benefit plan disparity requirements of Code Sec. 401(l) are satisfied (Code Sec. 411(b)(5)(D), ERISA Sec. 204(b)(5)(D), and ADEA Sec. 4(i)(10)(D), as added by the Pension Act).

In computing an accrued benefit, indexing is the periodic adjustment of the accrued benefit by using a recognized investment index or methodology (Code Sec. 411(b)(5)(E)(iii), ERISA Sec. 204(b)(5)(E)(iii), and ADEA Sec. 4(i)(10)(E)(iii), as added by the Pension Act). A defined benefit plan providing for indexing of accrued benefits under the plan is not age discriminatory. However, the indexing cannot result in an accrued benefit being less than the accrued benefit determined without regard to the indexing except in the case of benefits provided in the form of a variable annuity (Code Sec. 411(b)(5)(E)(i) and (ii), ERISA Sec. 204(b)(5)(E)(i) and (ii), and ADEA Secs. 4(i)(10)(E)(i) and (ii), as added by the Pension Act).

Applicable defined benefit plans. A defined benefit plan to which the amended age discrimination rules are applicable is a defined benefit plan in which the accrued

NEW LAW EXPLAINED

benefit is calculated as the balance of a hypothetical account maintained for the participant or as an accumulated percentage of the participant's final average compensation (Code Sec. 411(a)(13)(C)(i), ERISA Sec. 203(f)(3)(A), and ADEA Sec. 4(i)(10)(B)(v)(IV), as added by the Pension Act). The term "applicable defined benefit plan" includes both cash balance and pension equity plans.

The Secretary of the Treasury is directed to issue regulations that include in the definition of an applicable defined benefit plan any defined benefit plan that has an effect similar to an applicable defined benefit plan (Code Sec. 411(a)(13)(C)(ii) and ERISA Sec. 203(f)(3)(B), as added by the Pension Act).

An applicable defined benefit plan does not violate the age discrimination prohibition if it provides that:

(1) an employee who has completed three years of service is 100 percent vested in the plan;

(2) the interest rate applicable to interest credits is equal to or less than the market rate of return; and

(3) in the case of a plan amendment after June 29, 2005 that converts a defined benefit plan to a cash balance plan or PEP, each pre-amendment participant's accrued benefit after the amendment is not less than the sum of the participant's accrued benefit for years of service before and after the effective date of the amendment.

Three-year vesting. An applicable defined benefit plan must provide that an employee who has completed at least three years of service has a non-forfeitable right to 100 percent of the employee's accrued benefit derived from employer contributions to avoid violation of the age discrimination prohibition (Code Sec. 411(a)(13)(B) and ERISA Sec. 203(f)(2), as added by the Pension Act).

Interest credits. An applicable defined benefit plan violates the age discrimination prohibition unless the plan provides that the interest credit for any plan year shall be calculated at a rate that is not greater than the market rate of return (Code Sec. 411(b)(5)(B)(i)(I), ERISA Sec. 204(b)(5)(B)(i)(I), and ADEA Sec. 4(i)(10)(B)(i)(I), as added by the Pension Act). The plan may provide for a reasonable minimum guaranteed rate of return, or for a rate of return equal to the greater of a fixed or variable rate of return as long as the rate is not greater than the market rate of return. If an interest credit is less than zero, it cannot reduce the account balance to less than the aggregate amount of contributions credited to the account (Code Sec. 411(b)(5)(B)(i)(II), ERISA Sec. 204(b)(5)(B)(i)(II), and ADEA Sec. 4(i)(10)(B)(i)(II), as added by the Pension Act). The Secretary of the Treasury may provide regulations governing the calculation of a market rate of return and permissible methods of crediting interest to the account (Code Sec. 411(b)(5)(B)(i)(III), ERISA Sec. 204(b)(5)(B)(i)(III), and ADEA Sec. 4(i)(10)(B)(i)(III), as added by the Pension Act).

Practical Analysis: Dan Schwallie of Hewitt Associates, Cleveland, Ohio, observes that employers currently sponsoring, or considering sponsoring, a hybrid plan will want to ensure that interest crediting rates under the plan do not exceed a market

NEW LAW EXPLAINED

rate of return (to be defined by the Treasury) and provide full vesting within three years of service, in order to take advantage of the Act's relief from age discrimination claims and eliminate potential whipsaw issues when paying lump sums. Interest crediting must never reduce the acount balance (or similar plan amount) below the total contributions credited a participant under the plan. The vesting and interest crediting requirements generally apply to periods beginning on or after June 29, 2005. However, the vesting and interest crediting requirements apply to years beginning after December 31, 2007 for a hybrid plan in existence on June 29, 2005, unless the plan sponsor elects to apply them to an earlier period after June 29, 2005. Employers with existing hybrid plans may want to consider whether they need to elect an earlier period to take advantage of the Act's relief from whipsaw claims for periods prior to 2008. Different effective dates apply to collectively bargained hybrid plans. Hybrid plan sponsors will also need to ensure that the value of any old-formula early retirement subsidies are added to a participant's account balance (or similar plan amount) if, at the time of retirement, the participant meets the requirements for such subsidies.

In order to meet the interest credit requirements, an applicable defined benefit plan must provide that upon termination of the plan:

(1) the rate of interest used to determine accrued benefits under the plan must be equal to the average of the rates of interest used under the plan during the five-year period ending on the termination date, if the interest credit rate under the plan is a variable rate; and

(2) the interest rate and mortality table used to determine the amount of any benefit under the plan payable in the form of an annuity payable at normal retirement age must be the rate and table specified under the plan for such purpose as of the termination date, unless the interest credit rate is a variable rate and then the average of the interest rates over the five-year period ending on the termination date is used (Code Sec. 411(b)(5)(B)(vi), ERISA Sec. 204(b)(5)(B)(vi), and ADEA Sec. 4(i)(10)(B)(vi), as added by the Pension Act).

Conversion to cash balance plan or PEP. An applicable plan amendment is an amendment to a defined benefit plan that has the effect of converting the plan to an applicable defined benefit plan, *i.e.,* a cash balance or pension equity plan (Code Sec. 411(b)(5)(B)(v)(I), ERISA Sec. 204(b)(5)(B)(v)(I), and ADEA Sec. 4(i)(10)(B)(v)(I), as added by the Pension Act). If an applicable plan amendment is adopted after June 29, 2005, each pre-amendment participant's accrued benefit after the amendment cannot be less than the sum of:

(1) the participant's accrued benefit for years of service before the effective date of the amendment, determined pursuant to the pre-amendment plan terms, plus

(2) the participant's accrued benefit for years of service after the effective date of the amendment, determined pursuant to the post-amendment plan terms (Code Sec. 411(b)(5)(B)(ii) and (iii), ERISA Sec. 204(b)(5)(B)(ii) and (iii), and ADEA Sec. 4(i)(10)(B)(ii) and (iii), as added by the Pension Act).

NEW LAW EXPLAINED

Comment: The wearaway effect (that is, the freezing of benefits after a conversion to a cash balance pension plan, a practice especially hard on older workers) is removed, since there is no period after conversion when additional benefits do not accrue. Compliance with the anti-cutback rules is achieved because the participant's pre-amendment accrued benefit is not reduced as a result of the conversion.

Practical Analysis: Dan Schwallie of Hewitt Associates, Cleveland, Ohio, notes that employers considering converting a defined benefit plan to a hybrid plan, and those employers who converted to a hybrid plan after June 29, 2005, will also want to ensure that each participant's benefit after the conversion is no less than the sum of the participant's old-formula benefit at the time of conversion plus the participant's benefit earned for post-conversion service under the new hybrid formula. A participant's hybrid plan benefit can be larger, but not less than this sum, even if the participant is allowed to choose a full-service old-formula benefit instead. The Act does not incorporate various conversion strategies historically adopted by employers and included in some prior hybrid plan proposals, such as participant choice. Freezing an existing defined benefit plan and establishing a new hybrid plan would be treated as converting the existing plan to a hybrid plan under the Act.

For purposes of determining a retired participant's accrued benefit before the effective date of the amendment, the plan must credit the accumulation account or similar account with the amount of any early retirement benefit or retirement-type subsidy for the plan year in which the participant retires if, as of such time, the participant has met the age, years of service, and other requirements under the plan for entitlement to such benefit or subsidy (Code Sec. 411(b)(5)(B)(iv), ERISA Sec. 204(b)(5)(B)(iv), and ADEA Sec. 4(i)(10)(B)(iv), as added by the Pension Act).

If the benefits of two or more defined benefit plans established or maintained by an employer are coordinated in such a manner as to have the effect of the adoption of an applicable plan amendment, the sponsor of the defined benefit plan or plans providing for such coordination is treated as having adopted an applicable plan amendment as of the date such coordination begins (Code Sec. 411(b)(5)(B)(v)(II), ERISA Sec. 204(b)(5)(B)(v)(II), and ADEA Sec. 4(i)(10)(B)(v)(II), as added by the Pension Act). The Secretary of the Treasury will issue regulations to prevent avoidance of the applicable plan amendment rules through the use of two or more plan amendments rather than a single amendment (Code Sec. 411(b)(5)(B)(v)(III), ERISA Sec. 204(b)(5)(B)(v)(III), and ADEA Sec. 4(i)(10)(B)(v)(III), as added by the Pension Act).

Minimum present value of accrued benefit. A cash balance plan or PEP making a lump-sum distribution complies with the minimum present value rules of Code Sec. 417(e) if the present value of the accrued benefit of any participant is equal to the amount expressed as the balance of a plan participant's hypothetical account or as an accumulated percentage of the participant's final average compensation (Code Sec. 411(a)(13)(A) and ERISA Sec. 203(f)(1), as added by the Pension Act). Similarly, there is no violation of the employer contribution vesting rules of Code Sec. 411(a)(2), nor the

NEW LAW EXPLAINED

accrued benefit determination rules of Code Sec. 411(c) (applicable in the case of plans that do not allow employee contributions). The plan, however, must provide that employees who have completed three years of service are 100 percent vested and that the interest credit rate is not more than the market rate of return.

> **Comment:** The benefit entitlement of a participant in a hybrid plan who elects a lump-sum distribution is his hypothetical account balance. Employers should be pleased that there is no longer any whipsaw effect because the hybrid plan cannot provide interest credits to accounts at a rate higher than a market rate of return, as determined by the Treasury.

Status of prior conversions. No inference is to be drawn regarding the application of the age discrimination rules, as effective prior to these amendments, to cash balance plans or PEPs, or to conversions to those plans. Furthermore, no inference should be drawn regarding application of the minimum present value rules to cash balance plans or PEPs prior to the effective date of these amendments (Act Sec. 701(d) of the Pension Act).

> **Comment:** Employer groups have been worried about the legal status of past conversions in the event Congress goes on record prospectively authorizing conversions. This language is intended to make it clear that Congress is expressing no opinion on conversions that occurred prior to the effective date of the amendments made by the Pension Act.

▶ **Effective date.** Generally, the amendments made by this section apply to periods beginning on or after June 29, 2005 (Act Sec. 701(e)(1) of the Pension Protection Act of 2006). The minimum present value amendments apply to distributions made after August 17, 2006 (Act Sec. 701(e)(2) of the Pension Act). In the case of a plan in existence on June 29, 2005, the interest credit and three year vesting requirements apply to years beginning after December 31, 2007, unless the plan sponsor elects the application of such requirements for any period after June 29, 2005, and before the first year beginning after December 31, 2007 (Act Sec. 701(e)(3) of the Pension Act). In the case of a plan maintained pursuant to one or more collective bargaining agreements between employee representatives and one or more employers ratified on or before August 17, 2006, the interest credit and three year vesting requirements do not apply, for purposes of applying the age discrimination and minimum present value provisions, to plan years beginning before the earlier of: (a) the date on which the last of such collective bargaining agreements terminates (without extensions), or January 1, 2008; or (b) January 1, 2010 (Act Sec. 701(e)(4) of the Pension Act). The conversion amendments apply to plan amendments adopted after, and taking effect after, June 29, 2005, except that the plan sponsor may elect to have such amendments apply to plan amendments adopted before, and taking effect after, such date (Act Sec. 701(e)(5) of the Pension Act).

Law source: Law at ¶5080 and ¶7147. Committee Report at ¶10,560.

— Act Sec. 701(a)(1) of the Pension Protection Act of 2006, adding ERISA Sec. 204(b)(5);

— Act Sec. 701(a)(2), adding ERISA Sec. 203(f);

— Act Sec. 701(b)(1), adding Code Sec. 411(b)(5);

— Act Sec. 701(b)(2), adding Code Sec. 411(a)(13);

— Act Sec. 701(c), adding Sec. 4(i)(10) of the Age Discrimination in Employment Act of 1967;

NEW LAW EXPLAINED

— Act Sec. 701(d);

— Act Sec. 701(e), providing the effective date.

Reporter references: For further information, consult the following CCH reporters.

— Pension Plan Guide, ¶135 and ¶2555

— Standard Federal Tax Reporter, 2006FED ¶19,076.34

— Tax Research Consultant, RETIRE: 39,058

— Federal Tax Guide, 2006FTG ¶11,020 and ¶11,610

¶1010 Application of Cash Balance and Pension Equity Plan Rules in Mergers and Acquisitions

SUMMARY OF NEW LAW

The Secretary of the Treasury is directed to issue regulations regarding the application of the cash balance and pension equity hybrid defined benefit plan rules in merger and acquisition transactions.

BACKGROUND

Although cash balance and pension equity plans exhibit characteristics of both defined contribution and defined benefit plans, they are subject to regulation as defined benefit plans. These hybrid plans are subject to the defined benefit plan age discrimination prohibition and the minimum present value and anti-cutback rules. The application of these rules to the hybrid plans is not always clear, however. The waters become even murkier when a merger, acquisition, or similar transaction is involved.

NEW LAW EXPLAINED

Regulations to issue on the application of cash balance and pension equity plan rules to mergers and acquisitions.—The Secretary of the Treasury or his delegate must prescribe regulations for the application of the age discrimination, minimum present value and conversion rules discussed at ¶ 1005 in cases when the conversion of a defined benefit pension plan to a cash balance or pension equity plan is made with respect to a group of employees who become employees of the plan sponsor by reason of a merger, acquisition, or similar transaction. The regulations must be available no later than 12 months after August 17, 2006, the date of enactment of the Pension Protection Act of 2006 (Act Sec. 702 of the Pension Act).

NEW LAW EXPLAINED

> **Practical Analysis:** Dan Schwallie of Hewitt Associates, Cleveland, Ohio, observes that a number of questions will need to be answered through regulations or other guidance before employers feel confident in deciding their next steps. The Treasury is to issue regulations to include plans similar to cash balance and pension equity plans as hybrid plans; to describe how the requirements of the Act apply to hybrid plan conversions in the context of mergers and acquisitions; to prevent avoidance of the Act's conversion requirements through the use of two or more amendments; as well as to calculate a market rate of return to cap interest crediting. Nevertheless, employers should begin reviewing whether a hybrid plan continues to be, or could be, the right choice in their particular situation. This review should take into consideration the prospective relief from age discrimination claims offered by the Act, as well as the potential protection for prior periods offered by the August 7, 2006, decision of the U.S. Seventh Circuit Court of Appeals in *Cooper v. IBM Personal Pension Plan* (CA-7, 2006-2 USTC ¶50,448).

▶ **Effective date.** No specific effective date is provided by the Act. The provision is, therefore, considered effective on August 17, 2006, the date of enactment.

Law source: Law at ¶7150. Committee Report at ¶10,560.

— Act Sec. 702 of the Pension Protection Act of 2006.

Reporter references: For further information, consult the following CCH reporters.

— Pension Plan Guide, ¶135

— Standard Federal Tax Reporter, 2006FED ¶19,076.034

— Tax Research Consultant, RETIRE: 39,058

CASH OR DEFERRED ARRANGEMENTS

¶1015 Automatic Enrollment in 401(k) Plans

SUMMARY OF NEW LAW

A 401(k) plan that contains an automatic enrollment arrangement that meets certain requirements is treated as satisfying the nondiscrimination rules for 401(k) plans and the test with respect to matching contributions. A plan whose only contributions are made pursuant to a qualified automatic enrollment feature is not subject to the top-heavy rules.

BACKGROUND

Most defined contribution plans may include a qualified cash or deferred arrangement (a 401(k) plan), under which employees may elect to receive cash or to have contributions made to the plan. The contributions are referred to as "elective defer-

BACKGROUND

rals" or "elective contributions." A 401(k) plan may be designed so that the employee will receive compensation as cash unless the employee makes an affirmative election to make contributions or salary deferrals to the plan. Alternatively, a plan may provide that elective contributions are made at a specified percentage of salary unless the employee elects otherwise. These types of arrangements are sometimes referred to as "automatic enrollment" or "negative election" plans. The IRS has approved automatic election features, but requires employees to have an effective opportunity to elect to receive cash instead of contributions.

A similar nondiscrimination test applies to elective deferrals under a 401(k) plan that is designed to ensure that the rate of elective deferrals by highly compensated employees does not exceed that of rank and file employees by more than a specified percentage. Under a safe harbor, a 401(k) plan is deemed to satisfy the special nondiscrimination test if the plan satisfies one of two contribution requirements and satisfies a notice requirement. A similar nondiscrimination test applies to employer matching contributions. A safe harbor section 401(k) plan that provides for matching contributions is deemed to satisfy the test if it satisfies the safe harbor contribution and notice requirements under Code Sec. 401(k) and three rules pertaining to the rate of matching. Special rules also apply in the case of a top-heavy plan that provides more than 60 percent of its benefits to key employees. A plan that consists solely of contributions that satisfy the safe harbor plan rules for elective and matching contributions is not considered a top-heavy plan.

Tax-sheltered annuities (section 403(b) annuities) may provide for contributions on a salary reduction basis, similar to section 401(k) plans. Matching contributions under a section 403(b) annuity are subject to the same nondiscrimination rules as matching contributions under a section 401(k) plan.

Special rules provide for distributions of elective contributions that exceed the amount permitted under the nondiscrimination rules or the dollar limit on such contributions.

The Employee Retirement Income Security Act (ERISA) imposes standards on the conduct of plan fiduciaries, including persons who make investment decisions with respect to plan assets. ERISA fiduciary liability does not apply to investment decisions made by plan participants if participants exercise control over the investment of their individual accounts and the plan complies with numerous requirements under ERISA Sec. 404(c). ERISA also generally preempts all State laws relating to employee benefit plans, other than applicable criminal laws and laws relating to insurance, banking, or securities.

A ten percent excise tax is imposed on an employer making excess contributions or excess aggregate contributions to a qualified retirement plan. The tax does not apply to any excess contributions or excess aggregate contributions that, together with income allocable to the contributions, are distributed or forfeited (if forfeitable) within 2½ months after the close of the plan year. In addition, if certain requirements are met, excess contributions may be recharacterized as after-tax employee contributions, no later than 2½ months after the close of the plan year to which the excess contributions relate.

NEW LAW EXPLAINED

Increasing participation through automatic contribution arrangements.—There is some evidence that an automatic enrollment arrangement can improve retirement savings rates for low- and middle-income participants. The Pension Protection Act of 2006 encourages employers to adopt such a feature by providing nondiscrimination safe harbors for elective deferrals and matching contributions under plans that include an automatic enrollment feature, as well as allowing erroneous contributions to be distributed.

> **Comment:** The Pension Act uses the term "automatic contribution arrangements" to refer to the commonly used terms "automatic enrollment arrangement" and "automatic enrollment feature." This explanation will use the more commonly used terms, enrollment arrangement or enrollment feature when referring to this type of arrangement.

Practical Analysis: Allen Steinberg of Hewitt Associates, Lincolnshire, Illinois, notes that the new safe harbor for automatic enrollment plans provides employers with a promising new plan design alternative.

In recent years, many employers have considered either safe harbor designs and/or automatic enrollment under current law; a substantial number of employers have adopted these designs—but many others have shied away from these approaches for a variety of reasons. The structure of the new alternative under the Act—combining a new form of safe harbor status with automatic enrollment—should render this approach more accessible to an even wider group of employers. Here are some of the key factors that may contribute to the popularity of this new approach:

- "Traditional" safe harbor rules (enacted as part of the Small Business Job Protection Act of 1996) required either (1) a minimum employer matching contribution of 100 percent of the first three percent of compensation deferred plus 50 percent of the next two percent of compensation deferred (for a maximum potential employer cost of four percent of compensation for employees saving five percent of compensation); or (2) a nonelective employer contribution of three percent of compensation. The Act safe harbor may seem more affordable to some employers, requiring a maximum employer match equal to 3.5 percent of compensation for those employees saving six percent of compensation (or a three-percent nonelective contribution).
- Traditional safe harbor plans required full and immediate vesting on the employer contributions used to satisfy the safe harbor. The Act safe harbor allows plans to use two-year cliff vesting for employer contributions. This too may seem more acceptable to employers than the full and immediate vesting required by traditional safe harbor rules. This is especially true in light of the fact that under Act all employer contributions to a defined contribution plan must now use three-year "cliff" vesting (or six-year graded vesting).
- The new safe harbor offers immediate relief from ADP/ACP testing when the new provisions take effect at the beginning of the 2008 plan year. This is true even though an employer can choose to offer automatic enrollment only to newly hired employees (if additional procedural requirements are met). By contrast, in a typical

NEW LAW EXPLAINED

automatic enrollment plan (if offered only to new hires), it may take several years for the ADP/ACP test results to show the full impact of automatic enrollees.

Of course, employers need to look beyond the provisions of the Act—and consider their own workforce characteristics—in determining which design alternative will work best for them. For example, some employers with many lower-paid employees and high turnover have found that automatic enrollment creates a high number of small account balances that impose an unacceptable administrative burden.

This safe harbor alternative is further enhanced by other provisions of the Act that will provide employers more comfort with automatic enrollment designs (even those that do not meet the safe harbor requirements). These other provisions supporting the adoption of automatic enrollment include the expanded fiduciary protection under ERISA Sec. 404(c) (Act Sec. 624), clarified application of ERISA preemption rules for automatic enrollment plans (Act Sec. 902(f)), and expanded provisions allowing plan corrections and repayments for automatic enrollment plans (Act Sec. 902(d) and (e)).

Nondiscrimination requirements for automatic enrollment arrangements.—The Pension Act provides that a 401(k) plan that contains an automatic enrollment feature that satisfies certain requirements is treated as satisfying the nondiscrimination rules for deferrals and matching contributions for 401(k) plans and is not subject to the top heavy rules (Code Sec. 401(k)(13)(A), as added by the Pension Act). For purposes of the nondiscrimination requirements, a qualified automatic enrollment arrangement is defined as any cash or deferred arrangement which satisfies certain requirements with respect to automatic deferral, matching or nonelective contributions and notice to employees (Code Sec. 401(k)(13)(B), as added by the Pension Act).

Automatic deferral. The automatic deferral requirements are met if, under the arrangement, employees that are eligible to participate in the enrollment arrangement are treated as having elected to have the employer make elective contributions equal to a qualified percentage of compensation. (Code Sec. 401(k)(13)(C)(i), as added by the Pension Act). The qualified percentage cannot be more that 10 percent and must be equal to at least three percent of compensation for the first year the deemed election applies to the participant, four percent for the second plan year, five percent during the third year and six percent for the fourth and subsequent years. The qualified percentage must be applied uniformly to all eligible employees. (Code Sec. 401(k)(13)(C)(iii), as added by the Pension Act). A lower specified percentage applies to automatic contribution arrangements under DB/K plans (see ¶ 1020).

An employee may affirmatively elect not to have such elective contributions made or to make the elective contributions at a different level (Code Sec. 401(k)(13)(C)(ii), as added by the Pension Act). Employees eligible to participate in the automatic enrollment arrangement (or a predecessor arrangement) immediately before the date on which the arrangement became a qualified automatic enrollment arrangement and who had an election in effect to either participate at a certain percentage or not to participate, are not included in the meaning of eligible employees for purposes of applying the automatic deferral provision (Code Sec. 401(k)(13)(C)(iv), as added by the Pension Act).

NEW LAW EXPLAINED

Matching or nonelective contribution requirement. The Pension Act provides that the matching contributions requirement (for purposes of the nondiscrimination rules) is satisfied if, under the arrangement, the employer makes matching contributions on behalf of each employee who is not a highly compensated employee, equal to the sum of 100 percent of the elective contributions of the employee to the extent that such contributions do not exceed one percent of compensation plus 50 percent of so much of such compensation that exceeds one percent (Code Sec. 401(k)(13)(D)(i)(I), as added by the Pension Act). For purposes of this provision, the following requirements must also be satisfied:

(1) matching contributions are not provided with respect to elective deferrals in excess of six percent of compensation;

(2) the rate of matching contribution does not increase as the rate of an employee's elective deferrals increases; and

(3) the rate of matching contribution with respect to any rate of elective deferral of a highly compensated employee is no greater than the rate of matching contribution with respect to the same rate of deferral of a nonhighly compensated employee (Code Sec. 401(k)(13)(D)(ii), as added by the Pension Act).

Alternatively, the matching contributions requirements are met if the employer is required to make a contribution to a defined contribution plan of at least three percent of an employee's compensation on behalf of each nonhighly compensated employee who is eligible to participate in the automatic enrollment arrangement (Code Sec. 401(k)(13)(D)(i)(II), as added by the Pension Act).

Both of the matching tests are subject to the rules regarding contributions not taken into account and other plans (Code Sec. 401(k)(13)(D)(iv), as added by the Pension Act).

> **Comment:** New safe harbor rules for automatic contribution plans apply with respect to matching contributions under a section 403(b) annuity through the operation of Code Sec. 403(b)(12) (Joint Committee on Taxation, Technical Explanation of the Pension Protection Act of 2006 (JCX-38-06)).

In determining whether a qualified automatic enrollment arrangement satisfies the nondiscrimination requirements under Code Sec. 401(k)(13)(D)(i) with respect to employer contributions, including matching contributions, any employee who has completed at least two years of service must have a nonforfeitable right to 100 percent of the employee's accrued benefit from the employer contributions. In addition, matching or other employer contributions are subject to the withdrawal rules applicable to elective contributions (Code Sec. 401(k)(13)(D)(iii), as added by the Pension Act).

Notice requirement. Within a reasonable period before each plan year, each employee covered by the arrangement must receive a notice explaining the employee's rights and obligations under the arrangement and the notice must be sufficiently accurate and comprehensive to inform the employee of such rights and obligations by being written in a manner that is understandable by the average employee to whom the arrangement applies (Code Sec. 401(k)(13)(E)(i), as added by the Pension Act). The

NEW LAW EXPLAINED

notice must explain the employee's right under the arrangement to elect not to have elective contributions made on the employee's behalf or to elect to have contributions made in a different amount and how contributions made under the automatic enrollment arrangement will be invested in the absence of any investment election by the employee (Code Sec. 401(k)(13)(E)(ii), as added by the Pension Act). The employee must be given a reasonable period of time after receipt of such notice and before the first elective contribution is made to make the election with respect to contributions and investments (Code Sec. 401(k)(13)(E)(ii)(III), as added by the Pension Act).

Nondiscrimination test for matching contributions. A defined contribution plan is treated as meeting the requirements of Code Sec. 401(m)(2) with respect to matching contributions if the plan is a qualified automatic enrollment arrangement as defined in Code Sec. 401(k)(13) and meets the limitation on matching contributions requirements of Code Sec. 401(k)(11)(B) (Code Sec. 401(m)(12) as added by the Pension Act).

Exclusion from definition of top-heavy plan. The Pension Act amends Code Sec. 416(g)(4)(H) so that the term "top-heavy plan" does not include a plan which consists solely of: (1) a cash or deferred arrangement that meets the requirements of Code Sec. 401(k)(13) and (2) matching contributions with respect to which the requirements of Code Sec. 401(m)(12) are satisfied (Code Sec. 416(s)(4)(H), as amended by the Pension Act).

Special rules for certain withdrawals from eligible automatic enrollment arrangements.—If an arrangement allows an employee to elect to make "permissible withdrawals" of erroneous contributions, the amount withdrawn is included in the employee's gross income in the year of the distribution. The ten-percent early withdrawal tax under Code Sec. 72(t) is not imposed with respect to the distribution and the arrangement is not treated as violating any restriction on distributions by allowing the withdrawal. With respect to distributions to an employee as a result of this election, employer matching contributions are forfeited or subject to other treatment that the IRS may prescribe (Code Sec. 414(w)(1) as added by the Pension Act).

> **Comment:** The amount treated as an erroneous contribution is limited to the amount of automatic contributions made during the 90-day period that the employee elects to treat as an erroneous contribution (Joint Committee on Taxation, Technical Explanation of the Pension Protection Act of 2006 (JCX-38-06)).

Permissible withdrawals. The Pension Act defines "permissible withdrawal" as any withdrawal from an eligible automatic contribution arrangement which is made pursuant to an employee election and consists of elective contributions and earnings attributable to those contributions (Code Sec. 414(w)(2)(A), as added by the Pension Act). The election must be made within 90 days of the first elective contribution with respect to the employee under the arrangement (Code Sec. 414(w)(2)(B) as added by the Pension Act). The amount of any distributions under this election must be equal to the amount of elective contributions made with respect to the first payroll period to which the eligible automatic contribution arrangement applies to the employee and any succeeding payroll period beginning before the effective date of the election

NEW LAW EXPLAINED

(and earnings attributable to those contributions) (Code Sec. 414(w)(2)(C) as added by the Pension Act).

Eligible automatic enrollment (contribution) arrangement. An eligible automatic enrollment arrangement for purposes of the special rules for withdrawals is defined as an arrangement:

(1) under which a participant may elect to have the employer make payments as contributions under the plan or to the participant directly in cash;

(2) under which the participant is treated as having elected to have the employer make contributions in an amount equal to a uniform percentage of compensation provided under the plan until the participant elects not to have the contributions made or changes the percentage at which the contributions are made;

(3) under which, in the absence of a participant's investment election, contributions are invested in accordance with regulations issued by the Secretary of Labor; and

(4) which satisfies certain notice requirements described below (Code Sec. 414(w)(3) as added by the Pension Act).

Notice requirements. Before the beginning of each plan year, the administrator of the plan must give to each employee who is a participant in an automatic contribution arrangement for such plan year a notice of the employee's rights and obligations under the arrangement. The notice must be sufficiently accurate and comprehensive to inform employees of their rights and obligations and must be written in a manner that is understandable by the average employee to whom the arrangement applies. The notice must contain a notice explaining the employee's right to elect not to have elective contributions made on the employee's behalf or to elect to change the contribution percentage. The employee must be given a reasonable amount of time to make the election before the first elective contribution is made. Finally, the notice must explain how the contributions will be invested in the absence of any investment election by the employee (Code Sec. 414(w)(4) and ERISA Sec. 514(e), as added by the Pension Act).

Applicable employer plan. The term "applicable employer plan," for purposes of the special rules for withdrawals under Code Sec. 414(w), means:

(1) qualified pension plans under Code Sec. 401(a) which are exempt from tax under Code Sec. 501(a);

(2) plans under which amounts are contributed by an individual's employer for a Code Sec. 403(b)annuity contract; and

(3) governmental eligible deferred compensation plans under Code Sec. 457(b) (Code Sec. 414(w)(5), as added by the Pension Act).

A withdrawal under Code Sec. 414(w)(1) (subject to the limitation of Code Sec. 414(w)(2)(C)) is not taken into account for purposes of applying the participation and discrimination standards for cash or deferred arrangements under Code Sec. 401(k)(3) (Code Sec. 414(w)(6), as added by the Pension Act).

NEW LAW EXPLAINED

Forfeiture of erroneous automatic contributions. The Pension Act adds erroneous automatic contributions as a permitted forfeiture with respect to the treatment of forfeited matching contributions for purposes of the minimum vesting standards (Code Sec. 411(a)(3)(G), as amended by the Pension Act) and for purposes of exempting cash or deferred arrangements from disqualification due to the distribution of excess contributions (Code Sec. 401(k)(8)(E) as amended by the Pension Act). ERISA Sec. 203(a)(3)(F) is also amended to provide that a matching contribution is not treated as forfeitable merely because such contribution is forfeitable, if the contribution to which the matching contribution relates is treated as an erroneous automatic contribution (Act Sec. 902(d)(2)(E) of the Pension Act).

Expansion of corrective distribution period for automatic enrollment arrangement excess contributions.—With respect to an eligible automatic enrollment arrangement, the excise tax on excess contributions does not apply if the distribution (or forfeiture) of the excess contributions or aggregate excess contributions together with related earnings occurs within six months after the end of the plan year (Code Sec. 4979(f), as amended by the Pension Act). Any excess contributions or excess aggregate contributions (and allocable income) that are distributed within the required time frame are treated as earned and received by the recipient in the tax year in which the distribution was made (Code Sec. 4979(f)(2) as amended by the Pension Act). Only the earnings attributable to the excess contributions or excess aggregate contributions through the end of the related plan year for which the contributions were made must be distributed (Code Sec. 401(k)(8)(A)(i) and (m)(6)(A), as amended by the Pension Act; Joint Committee on Taxation, Technical Explanation of the Pension Protection Act of 2006 (JCX-38-06)).

Preemption of conflicting state regulation.—Any State law that would directly or indirectly prohibit or restrict the inclusion of an automatic contribution arrangement in a plan is pre-empted (ERISA Sec. 514(e)(1), as added by the Pension Act). The Labor Secretary is authorized to issue regulations that establish minimum standards that these arrangements would be required to satisfy in order for preemption to apply.

> **Comment:** The provision may be designed to prevent state garnishment laws from blocking the implementation of automatic contribution arrangements.

▶ **Effective date.** These provisions apply to plan years beginning after December 31, 2007, except that the amendments made by Act Sec. 902(f), regarding the preemption of conflicting state regulation, take effect on August 17, 2006 (Act Sec. 902(g) of the Pension Protection Act of 2006).

Law source: Law at ¶5030, ¶5080, ¶5090, ¶5100, ¶5310 and ¶7183. Committee Report at ¶10,960.

— Act Sec. 902(a) of the Pension Protection Act of 2006, adding Code Sec. 401(k)(13);

— Act Sec. 902(b), redesignating Code Sec. 401(m)(12) as (m)(13) and adding new Code Sec. 401(m)(12);

— Act Sec.902(c), amending Code Sec. 416(g)(4)(H)(i) and (ii);

— Act Sec. 902(d), adding Code Sec. 414(w), and amending Code Secs. 411(a)(3)(G), 401(k)(8)(E) and ERISA Sec. 203(a)(3)(F);

NEW LAW EXPLAINED

— Act Sec. 902(e), amending Code Secs. 4979(f), 401(k)(8)(A)(i) and 401(m)(6)(A);

— Act Sec. 902(f), adding ERISA Sec. 514(e) and amending ERISA Sec. 502(c)(4);

— Act Sec. 902(g), providing the effective date.

Reporter references: For further information, consult the following CCH reporters.

— Pension Plan Guide, ¶7407

— Standard Federal Tax Reporter, 2006FED ¶18,112.01

— Tax Research Consultant, RETIRE: 3,210, RETIRE: 21,050 and RETIRE: 27,150

— Federal Tax Guide, 2006FTG ¶11,200

¶1020 Combined Defined Benefit and 401(k) Plans

SUMMARY OF NEW LAW

Employers with 500 or fewer employees may establish a combined defined benefit/401(k) plan (a "DB/K" plan). The relevant Code and ERISA provisions are applied separately to the defined benefit and 401(k) plans that are part of a DB/K plan, subject to certain exceptions. The DB/K plan must meet certain benefit, contribution, vesting and nondiscrimination requirements.

BACKGROUND

Qualified retirement plans can be broadly classified into two categories: (1) defined contribution plans, and (2) defined benefit plans. Some plans have the features of both defined contribution and defined benefit plans and are called "hybrid plans."

Defined contribution plans. A defined contribution plan provides for an individual account for each participant. The benefits are based solely on the amount contributed to the participant's account and any income, expenses, gains and losses, and forfeitures of accounts of other participants that may be allocated to the participant's account (Code Sec. 414(i) and ERISA Sec. 3(34)). Because the accounts rise or fall based on the trust fund's investment performance, a defined contribution plan does not guarantee a fixed level of benefits upon retirement.

A defined contribution plan may include a qualified cash or deferred arrangement, under which employees may elect to receive cash or to have contributions made to the plan by the employer on behalf of the employee in lieu of receiving cash (i.e., 401(k) plans) (Code Sec. 401(k)). Such contributions are referred to as elective deferrals or elective contributions and are limited in amount (Code Sec. 402(g)(3)). A 401(k) plan may provide that elective deferrals are made for an employee at a specified rate unless the employee elects otherwise, provided that the employee has an effective opportunity to elect to receive cash in lieu of the default contributions

BACKGROUND

(i.e., automatic enrollment). Besides elective deferrals, a 401(k) plan may provide for: (1) matching contributions, which are employer contributions that are made only if an employee makes elective deferrals; and (2) nonelective contributions, which are employer contributions that are made without regard to whether an employee makes elective deferrals (Code Sec. 401(k)). No benefit other than the matching contributions may be contingent on whether the employee makes elective deferrals.

Defined benefit plans. A defined benefit plan is any plan that is not a defined contribution plan (Code Sec. 414(j)). ERISA defines it generally as a pension plan other than an individual account plan (ERISA Sec. 3(35)). Upon retirement, a defined benefit plan provides fixed or determinable benefits, which are insured by the Pension Benefit Guaranty Corporation (PBGC). Employer contributions necessary to provide such benefits are determined on an actuarial basis.

Hybrid plans. One type of a hybrid plan is the cash balance plan. The cash balance plan is a defined benefit plan that provides guaranteed benefits insured by the PBGC. Unlike traditional defined benefit plans, however, cash balance plans establish a separate hypothetical account for each employee. The employer credits a specified percentage of compensation (i.e., pay credits) to each account and credits each account with interest earned (i.e., interest credits). The amounts to be contributed are actuarially determined to ensure sufficient funds to provide the promised benefit. Participants may elect to receive their benefit in a lump-sum or as an annuity (Reg. § 1.401(a)(4)-8(c)(3)). Floor offset plans, target benefit plans, and pension equity plans are other types of hybrid plans (see ¶ 1005).

Funding. The assets of both defined contribution and defined benefit plans must be held in trust for the exclusive benefit of participants and beneficiaries (Code Sec. 401(a)). Defined benefit pension plans are subject to funding rules, which require employers to make contributions at specified minimum levels. Investment of defined benefit pension plan assets in employer securities or real property is generally limited. The minimum funding rules and investment limitations generally do not apply to defined contribution plans (Code Sec. 412; see also ERISA Secs. 302-307).

Nondiscrimination requirements. The contributions or benefits provided under a qualified retirement plan generally must not discriminate in favor of highly compensated employees (Code Sec. 401(a)(4)). The regulations under Code Sec. 401(a)(4) provide detailed rules for determining whether this requirement is satisfied and for testing the amount of contributions or benefits provided under the plan and the benefits, rights and features offered under the plan.

A special nondiscrimination test compares the actual deferral percentages (ADPs) of highly compensated and nonhighly compensated employee groups under a 401(k) plan (the ADP test). The ADP for each group generally is the average of the deferral percentages separately calculated for the employees in the group who are eligible to make elective deferrals for all or a portion of the plan year. The plan generally satisfies the ADP test if the ADP of the highly compensated employee group for the current plan year is either: (1) not more than 125 percent of the ADP of the nonhighly compensated employee group for the prior plan year; or (2) not more than 200 percent of the ADP of the nonhighly compensated employee group for the prior plan

BACKGROUND

year and not more than two percentage points greater than the ADP of the nonhighly compensated employee group for the prior plan year.

Under a safe harbor, a 401(k) plan is deemed to satisfy the special nondiscrimination test if the plan satisfies a contribution requirement and a notice requirement. The contribution requirement is satisfied if the employer either satisfies the matching contribution requirement under Code Sec. 401(k)(12)(B) or makes a nonelective contribution of at least three percent of an employee's compensation on behalf of each nonhighly compensated employee eligible to participate in the arrangement (Code Sec. 401(k)(3)).

Employer matching contributions are also subject to a special nondiscrimination test, which compares the average actual contribution percentages (ACPs) of matching contributions for the highly compensated and nonhighly compensated employee groups (the ACP test). The plan generally satisfies the ACP test if the ACP of the highly compensated employee group for the current plan year is either: (1) not more than 125 percent of the ACP of the nonhighly compensated employee group for the prior plan year, or (2) not more than 200 percent of the ACP of the nonhighly compensated employee group for the prior plan year and not more than two percentage points greater than the ACP of the nonhighly compensated employee group for the prior plan year. A plan may also satisfy the ACP test if it satisfies a special matching contribution safe harbor (Code Sec. 401(m)).

Vesting requirements. A qualified retirement plan generally must satisfy one of two alternative minimum vesting requirements. A plan satisfies the first requirement if a participant acquires a nonforfeitable right to 100 percent of the participant's accrued benefit derived from employer contributions upon the completion of five years of service. The second requirement is satisfied if a participant has a nonforfeitable right to at least 20 percent of the participant's accrued benefit derived from employer contributions after three years of service, 40 percent after four years of service, 60 percent after five years of service, 80 percent after six years of service, and 100 percent after seven years of service. Special vesting rules apply to elective deferrals and matching contributions (Code Sec. 411; see also ERISA Secs. 202 and 203). Elective deferrals must be immediately vested, while matching contributions must vest under one of the alternative minimum vesting schedules (see ¶720).

Top-heavy plans. A top-heavy plan provides cumulative benefits primarily to key employees. An employee is a key employee if, during the prior year, the employee was (1) an officer with compensation in excess of a certain amount ($140,000 for 2006), (2) a five-percent owner, or (3) a one-percent owner with compensation in excess of $150,000. A top-heavy plan must provide minimum employer contributions (in the case of a defined contribution plan) or minimum benefits (in the case of a defined benefit plan) to participants who are not key employees. In addition, a top-heavy plan must provide more rapid vesting for participants who are not key employees under two alternative minimum vesting schedules (Code Sec. 416).

Other requirements. Qualified retirement plans are subject to various other requirements, including limits on contributions and benefits and spousal protections. In the case of a defined contribution plan, annual additions with respect to each plan participant cannot exceed the lesser of 100 percent of the participant's compensation

BACKGROUND

or $44,000 (for 2006). Annual additions are the sum of employer contributions, employee contributions, and forfeitures with respect to an individual under all defined contribution plans of the same employer. In the case of a defined benefit pension, annual benefits payable under the plan generally may not exceed the lesser of 100 percent of average compensation or $175,000 (for 2006) (Code Sec. 415).

Defined benefit pension plans are required to provide benefits in the form of annuity unless the participant (and her spouse, if married) consents to another form of benefit. In addition, in the case of a married participant, benefits generally must be paid in the form of a qualified joint and survivor annuity (QJSA) unless the participant and her spouse consent to another form of distribution. These spousal protection requirements generally do not apply to a defined contribution plan that does not offer annuity distributions (Code Secs. 401(a)(11) and 417).

Annual reporting. Qualified retirement plans are subject to annual reporting. The plan administrator generally must file an annual return with the Secretary of the Treasury and an annual report with the Secretary of Labor. In the case of a defined benefit pension plan, certain information is also required to be filed with the PBGC. The reporting requirement with respect to each agency may be satisfied by filing Form 5500 with the Department of Labor. A plan administrator must provide participants with a summary of the annual report within two months after the due date of the annual report. In addition, a copy of the full annual report must be provided to participants on written request (Code Sec. 6058 and ERISA Secs. 101 through 106 and 4065).

NEW LAW EXPLAINED

Combined defined benefit/401(k) plans may be established by small employers.—A defined benefit plan and an applicable defined contribution plan may be combined in a single eligible combined plan (a "DB/K" plan). The assets of the DB/K plan must be held in a single trust and must be clearly identified and allocated to the defined benefit plan and the applicable defined contribution plan to the extent necessary for the separate application of the Code and ERISA. In addition, the DB/K plan must be maintained by a small employer and must meet certain benefit, contribution, vesting and nondiscrimination requirements. For this purpose, a small employer is an employer who employed an average of at least two but not more than 500 employees on business days during the preceding calendar year and who employs at least two employees on the first day of the plan year (Code Sec. 414(x)(2)(A) and ERISA Sec. 210(e)(2)(A), as added by the Pension Protection Act of 2006). An applicable defined contribution plan is a defined contribution plan that includes a qualified cash or deferred arrangement (i.e., a 401(k) plan) (Code Sec. 414(x)(7), as added by the Pension Act). The corresponding ERISA provision refers to the applicable defined contribution plan as the "applicable individual account plan," which also includes a qualified cash or deferred arrangement (ERISA Sec. 210(e)(6), as added by the Pension Act).

NEW LAW EXPLAINED

Comment: According to a Senate Committee Report to an earlier version of the Pension Act (S.109-174), the creation of a DB/K plan is in response to the decline in coverage under defined benefit plans and a corresponding increase in coverage under defined contribution plans, particularly 401(k) plans. The growth in 401(k) plans generally reflects a reaction to the cost of maintaining and difficulty of administering defined benefit plans. However, defined benefit plans guarantee a fixed level of benefits for retired employees and, thus, provide greater retirement income security. Defined benefit plan coverage in combination with a 401(k) plan may provide enhanced retirement savings, but maintaining multiple plans may result in burdensome administrative costs, especially for smaller employers. The DB/K plan addresses these concerns by providing meaningful benefits to employees at reduced administrative costs to employers.

Subject to certain exceptions discussed below, the provisions of the Code and ERISA are applied to any defined benefit plan and 401(k) plan that are part of a DB/K plan as if each were not part of the DB/K plan (Code Sec. 414(x)(1) and ERISA Sec. 210(e)(1), as added by the Pension Act).

Comment: Thus, for example, the Code Sec. 415 limitations apply separately to contributions under the 401(k) plan and to benefits under the defined benefit plan, both of which are part of the DB/K plan. Similarly, the spousal protection rules apply to the defined benefit plan but not to the 401(k) plan.

Defined benefit plan requirements. A defined benefit plan that is part of a DB/K plan must provide each participant with a benefit of not less than the applicable percentage of the participant's final average pay. For this purpose, final average pay is determined using the consecutive-year period (not exceeding five years) during which the participant has the greatest aggregate compensation. The applicable percentage is the lesser of (1) one percent multiplied by the participant's years of service, or (2) 20 percent (Code Sec. 414(x)(2)(B)(i), (ii) and ERISA Sec. 210(e)(2)(B)(i), (ii), as added by the Pension Act).

Any benefits provided under a defined benefit plan that is part of a DB/K plan (including any benefits provided in addition to required benefits) must be fully vested after three years of service (Code Sec. 414(x)(2)(D)(i) and ERISA Sec. 210(e)(2)(B), as added by the Pension Act).

Cash balance plan. A special rule applies to a Code Sec. 411(a)(13)(B) applicable defined benefit plan, under which the accrued benefit is calculated as the balance of a hypothetical account or as an accumulated percentage of the participant's final average compensation, and which meets the interest credit requirements of Code Sec. 411(b)(5)(B)(i) (see ¶1005). Such a plan is treated as meeting the benefit requirement if each participant receives a pay credit for each plan year of not less than a certain percentage of compensation that is determined based on the participant's age. If the participant's age as of the beginning of the year is 30 or less, the percentage is two percent; if the age is over 30 but less than 40, the percentage is four percent; if the age is 40 or over but less than 50, the percentage is six percent; and if the age is 50 or over, the percentage is eight percent. A defined benefit plan that is part of a DB/K plan must provide the required benefit to each participant, regardless of whether the

NEW LAW EXPLAINED

participant makes elective deferrals to the applicable defined contribution plan that is part of the DB/K plan (Code Sec. 414(x)(2)(B)(iii), (iv) and ERISA Sec. 210(e)(2)(B)(iii), (iv), as added by the Pension Act).

Applicable defined contribution plan requirements. Certain automatic enrollment and matching contribution requirements must be met with respect to a 401(k) plan that is part of a DB/K plan. First, the qualified cash or deferred arrangement under the plan must constitute an automatic contribution arrangement (see ¶1015) (Code Sec. 414(x)(2)(C)(i)(I) and ERISA Sec. 210(e)(2)(C)(i)(I), as added by the Pension Act). An automatic contribution arrangement must generally provide that each employee eligible to participate in the arrangement is treated as having elected to make elective contributions in an amount of four percent of the employee's compensation. The employee, however, may elect not to make such contributions or to make contributions at a different rate. The automatic contribution arrangement must also meet certain notice requirements. Participants must generally be given notice of their right to elect not to make contributions or to make contributions at a different rate, and must be given a reasonable period of time after receiving the notice to make the election. In addition, participants must be given notice of their rights and obligations within a reasonable period before each year (Code Sec. 414(x)(5) and ERISA Sec. 210(e)(4), as added by the Pension Act).

Second, the employer must make matching contributions on behalf of each employee eligible to participate in the arrangement in an amount equal to 50 percent of the employee's elective deferrals, but no more than four percent of the compensation. The rate of matching contributions with respect to any elective deferrals for highly compensated employees must not be greater than the matching contribution rate for nonhighly compensated employees. Matching contributions in addition to the required matching contributions can also be made (Code Sec. 414(x)(2)(C)(i)(II) and ERISA Sec. 210(e)(2)(C)(i), as added by the Pension Act).

The employer can also make nonelective contributions under the 401(k) plan. These contributions, however, are not taken into account in determining whether the matching contribution requirement is met (Code Sec. 414(x)(2)(C)(ii) and ERISA Sec. 210(e)(2)(C)(ii), as added by the Pension Act).

Matching contributions under the 401(k) plan (including contributions in excess of the required matching contributions) are fully vested when made, while nonelective contributions are fully vested after three years of service (Code Sec. 414(x)(2)(D)(ii) and ERISA Sec. 210(e)(2)(D)(ii), as added by the Pension Act).

> **Comment:** Because, under the DB/K plan, the employer-paid guaranteed retirement benefits can be supplemented by the employees' own tax-deferred contributions, the employees may be able to significantly increase their retirement savings.

Uniform provision, nondiscrimination and other requirements. All contributions, benefits, and other rights and features that are provided under a defined benefit plan or an applicable defined contribution plan that is part of a DB/K plan must be provided uniformly to all participants (Code Sec. 414(x)(2)(E) and ERISA Sec. 210(e)(2)(E), as added by the Pension Act).

NEW LAW EXPLAINED

> **Comment:** This requirement applies regardless of whether nonuniform contributions, benefits, or other rights or features could be provided without violating the nondiscrimination rules. However, it is intended that a plan will not violate the uniformity requirement merely because benefits accrued for periods before a defined benefit or defined contribution plan became part of a DB/K plan are protected (Joint Committee on Taxation, Technical Explanation of the Pension Protection Act of 2006 (JCX-38-06)).

A 401(k) plan that is part of a DB/K plan satisfies the actual deferral percentage (ADP) test under Code Sec. 401(k)(3) on a safe-harbor basis. Matching contributions under an applicable defined contribution plan must satisfy the actual contribution percentage (ACP) test or may satisfy the matching contribution safe harbor under Code Sec. 401(m). Nonelective contributions under a 401(k) plan and benefits under a defined benefit plan, which are part of a DB/K plan, are generally subject to the nondiscrimination rules applicable to such plans (Code Sec. 414(x)(3) and ERISA Sec. 210(e)(3), as added by the Pension Act). However, none of those plans can be combined with another plan in determining whether the nondiscrimination requirements are met (Code Sec. 414(x)(2)(F)(iii) and ERISA Sec. 210(e)(2)(F)(iii), as added by the Pension Act).

In addition, the permitted disparity rules under Code Sec. 401(l) do not apply in determining whether an applicable defined contribution plan or a defined benefit plan that is part of a DB/K plan satisfies the contribution or benefit requirements, or the nondiscrimination requirements (Code Sec. 414(x)(2)(F) and ERISA Sec. 210(e)(2)(F), as added by the Pension Act).

Further, a 401(k) plan and a defined benefit plan that are part of a DB/K plan are treated as meeting the top-heavy requirements of Code Sec. 416 (Code Sec. 414(x)(4), as added by the Pension Act).

Annual reporting. A DB/K plan is treated as a single plan for purposes of annual reporting (Code Sec. 414(x)(6)(B) and ERISA Sec. 210(e)(5)(B), as added by the Pension Act).

> **Comment:** The DB/K plan will be simpler to administer because all the information required with respect to the defined benefit plan and the 401(k) plan that are part of the DB/K plan must be provided in a single Form 5500. In addition, only a single summary annual report must be provided to the participants.

► **Effective date.** The provision applies to plan years beginning after December 31, 2009 (Act Sec. 903(c) of the Pension Protection Act of 2006).

Law source: Law at ¶5090 and ¶7186. Committee Report at ¶10,970.

— Act Sec. 903(a) of the Pension Protection Act of 2006, adding Code Sec. 414(x);

— Act Sec. 903(b), adding ERISA Sec. 210(e);

— Act Sec. 903(c), providing the effective date.

Reporter references: For further information, consult the following CCH reporters.

— Pension Plan Guide, ¶135

— Standard Federal Tax Reporter, 2006FED ¶19,159M.01

— Tax Research Consultant, RETIRE: 3,056 and RETIRE: 6,052

— Federal Tax Guide, 2006FTG ¶11,015

SPOUSAL PROTECTIONS

¶1025 Regulations on Time and Order of Issuance of DROs

SUMMARY OF NEW LAW

Within one year of August 17, 2006, the date of enactment of the Pension Protection Act of 2006, the Secretary of Labor is to issue regulations that clarify the status of certain domestic relations orders in terms of whether they are qualified domestic relations orders (QDROs).

BACKGROUND

In general, benefits that are provided under a qualified retirement plan cannot be assigned or alienated. An exception to this prohibition on assignment is a qualified domestic relations order ("QDRO") (Code Sec. 401(a)(13)(B) and ERISA Sec. 206(d)(3)(A)). A QDRO is a domestic relations order that creates or recognizes a right of an alternate payee (including a former spouse) to receive all or a portion of the benefits payable with respect to a plan participant (Code Sec. 414(p)(1)(A) and ERISA Sec. 206(d)(3)(B)).

> **Comment:** A domestic relations order is defined as any judgment, decree, or order that: (1) relates to the provision of child support, alimony payments, or marital property rights to a spouse, former spouse, child, or other dependent; and (2) is made pursuant to a State domestic relations law, including a community property law (Code Sec. 414(p)(1)(B) and ERISA Sec. 206(d)(3)(B)(ii)).

A QDRO must meet certain procedural requirements (see Code Sec. 414(p)(2) and ERISA Sec. 206(d)(3)(C)). In addition, a QDRO cannot require the plan to provide any type or form of benefit (or any option) that is not otherwise provided under the plan, or to provide increased benefits (Code Sec. 414(p)(3) and ERISA Sec. 206(d)(3)(D)).

A QDRO may not require the payment of benefits to an alternate payee that are required to be paid to another alternate payee under a domestic relations order that was previously determined to be a QDRO (Code Sec. 414(p)(3)(C) and ERISA Sec. 206(d)(3)(D)(iii)). There are no specific rules regarding the treatment of a domestic relations order as a QDRO if the order is issued after another domestic relations order or a QDRO, or revises another domestic relations order or a QDRO.

There are, however, specific rules that apply during any period in which a determination is being made as to whether a domestic relations order is a QDRO, whether by the plan administrator, a court, or otherwise. During such a determination period, the plan administrator is required to separately account for the amounts (referred to as the "segregated amounts") that would have been payable to the alternate payee during the period if the order had been determined to be a QDRO (Code Sec. 414(p)(7) and ERISA Sec. 206(d)(3)(H)).

NEW LAW EXPLAINED

Secretary of Labor to issue regulations clarifying status of certain domestic relations orders.—No later than one year after August 17, 2006, the date of the enactment of the Pension Protection Act of 2006, the Secretary of Labor is directed to issue regulations under Code Sec. 414(p) and ERISA Sec. 206(d)(3) that clarify the status of certain domestic relations orders (Act Sec. 1001 of the Pension Act). Specifically, the regulations are to clarify that a domestic relations order that otherwise satisfies the requirements to be a QDRO will not fail to be treated as a QDRO solely because (1) the order is issued after, or revises, another domestic relations order or QDRO; or (2) of the time at which it is issued (Act Sec. 1001(1) of the Pension Act). In addition, the regulations are to clarify that such a domestic relations order is subject to the same requirements and protections that apply to QDROs, including the provisions of Code Sec. 414(p)(7) and ERISA Sec. 206(d)(3)(H) (relating to procedures for the period during which it is being determined whether a domestic relations order is a QDRO) (Act Sec. 1001(2) of the Pension Act).

Comment: A Senate Finance Committee report that accompanied a bill that was a precursor to the Pension Act found that there was uncertainty about the treatment of domestic relations orders that are issued subsequent to divorce or that revise a previous domestic relations order or QDRO, even in cases involving the same former spouse. The Committee believed that clarification of the treatment of such domestic relations orders was warranted (Report to accompany S. 1953, the National Employee Savings and Trust Equity Guarantee Act of 2005, Senate Rept. 109-174, November 2, 2005).

▶ **Effective date.** No specific effective date is provided by the Act. The provision is, therefore, considered effective on August 17, 2006, the date of enactment.

Law source: Law at ¶7198. Committee Report at ¶11,010.

— Act Sec. 1001 of the Pension Protection Act of 2006.

Reporter references: For further information, consult the following CCH reporters.

— Pension Plan Guide, ¶1351

— Standard Federal Tax Reporter, 2006FED ¶17,733.031

— Tax Research Consultant, RETIRE: 9,308

— Federal Tax Guide, 2006FTG ¶11,085

¶1030 Entitlement of Divorced Spouses to Railroad Retirement Annuities

SUMMARY OF NEW LAW

The requirement that a railroad employee actually receive railroad retirement benefits in order for their former spouse to be entitled to any of the Tier I or Tier II benefits awarded under a state court divorce decision has been eliminated.

BACKGROUND

Benefits under the Railroad Retirement Act are classified into two tiers. Tier I is financed by taxes on employers and employees equal to the Social Security payroll tax and provides qualified railroad retirees, along with their qualified dependents, spouses, widows or widowers, with benefits roughly equal to Social Security benefits. Covered workers and their employers pay Tier I tax, instead of Social Security payroll tax. Most railroad retirees collect Tier I benefits. Tier II of the system replicates a private pension plan with employers and employees contributing a certain percentage of pay toward the system to finance defined benefits to eligible railroad retirees and their qualified spouses, dependents, widows or widowers, upon retirement. However, the Federal Government collects the Tier II payroll contributions and pays out the benefits.

Former spouses of living railroad employees were not eligible to receive benefits under Tier I or Tier II until the railroad employee actually receives railroad retirement benefits, regardless of whether a state divorce court has awarded the retirement benefits to the former spouse.

NEW LAW EXPLAINED

Former spouse entitled to Railroad Retirement Act benefits independent of employee's receipt of benefits.—A former spouse of a railroad employee is now able to receive benefits paid under the Railroad Retirement Act awarded by a State divorce court, independent of whether the railroad employee is entitled to receive such benefits (45 U.S.C. Sec. 231a(c)(4)(i), as amended by the Pension Protection Act of 2006).

> **Comment:** With this amendment, Congress intended to provide more equitable treatment of former spouses of railroad employees (Senate Finance Committee, Report on the National Employee Savings and Trust Equity Guarantee Act (S. Rpt. 109-174)).

▶ **Effective date.** The provision is effective one year after August 17, 2006 (Act Sec. 1002(b) of the Pension Protection Act of 2006).

Law source: Law at ¶7201. Committee Report at ¶11,020.

— Act Sec. 1002(a)(1) of the Pension Protection Act of 2006, amending 45 U.S.C. Sec. 231a(c)(4)(i);

— Act Sec. 1002(a)(2), amending 45 U.S.C. Sec. 231a(e)(5);

— Act Sec. 1002(b), providing the effective date.

Reporter references: For further information, consult the following CCH reporters.

— Pension Plan Guide, ¶1351

— Standard Federal Tax Reporter, 2006FED ¶19,156D.021

¶1035 Surviving Former Spouses' Entitlement to Tier II Railroad Retirement Benefits

SUMMARY OF NEW LAW

A former spouse of a railroad employee does not lose eligibility for otherwise allowable Tier II benefits under the Railroad Retirement Act upon the death of the railroad employee.

BACKGROUND

Benefits under the Railroad Retirement Act are classified into two tiers. Tier I is financed by taxes on employers and employees equal to the Social Security payroll tax and provides qualified railroad retirees, along with their qualified dependents, spouses, widows or widowers, with benefits roughly equal to Social Security benefits. Covered workers and their employers pay Tier I tax, instead of Social Security payroll tax. Most railroad retirees collect Tier I benefits, rather than Social Security. Tier II of the system replicates a private pension plan with employers and employees contributing a certain percentage of pay toward the system to finance defined benefits to eligible railroad retirees and their qualified spouses, dependents, widows or widowers, upon retirement.

The former spouse of a railroad employee may qualify for Tier I benefits. Tier II benefits paid to a former spouse terminate, however, upon the death of the railroad employee.

NEW LAW EXPLAINED

Extension of Tier II Railroad Retirement Act benefits to surviving former spouses pursuant to divorce agreements.—A former spouse of a railroad employee does not lose eligibility for otherwise allowable Tier II benefits under the Railroad Retirement Act upon the death of the railroad employee (45 U.S.C. Sec. 231d(d), as added by the Pension Protection Act of 2006).

> **Comment:** With this amendment, Congress intends to provide more equitable treatment of former spouses of railroad employees (Senate Finance Committee, Report on the National Employee Savings and Trust Equity Guarantee Act (S. Rpt. 109-174)).

▶ **Effective date.** The provision is effective one year from August 17, 2006 (Act Sec. 1003(b)) of the Pension Protection Act of 2006).

Law source: Law at ¶7204. Committee Report at ¶11,020.

— Act Sec. 1003(a) of the Pension Protection Act of 2006, adding 45 U.S.C. Sec. 231d(d);

— Act Sec. 1003(b), providing the effective date.

Reporter references: For further information, consult the following CCH reporters.

— Pension Plan Guide, ¶9980

— Standard Federal Tax Reporter, 2006FED ¶19,156D.01

¶1040 Additional Survivor Annuity Option

SUMMARY OF NEW LAW

Pension plans that are required to provide benefits in the form of a qualified joint and survivor annuity are required to offer as an option a qualified optional survivor annuity.

BACKGROUND

A defined benefit pension plan or money purchase pension plan is required to provide a qualified joint and survivor annuity (QJSA) unless the participant and their spouse consent to another form of benefit. A QJSA is an annuity for the life of the participant with a survivor annuity for the life of the participant's spouse that is not less than 50 percent (and not greater than 100 percent) of the amount of the annuity that is payable during the joint lives of the participant and spouse. A QJSA must be the actuarial equivalent of the normal form of life annuity or, if greater, of any optional form of life annuity offered under the plan.

In the case of a married participant who dies before the commencement of retirement benefits, the plan must provide the surviving spouse with a qualified preretirement survivor annuity (QPSA). A QPSA must provide the surviving spouse with a benefit that is not less than the benefit that would have been provided under the survivor portion of a QJSA. In the case of a defined benefit plan or money purchase plan, a QPSA is an annuity for the life of the surviving spouse of the participant that satisfies whichever of the following is relevant.

(1) *Death after earliest retirement age.* In the case of a participant who dies after attaining the earliest retirement age under the plan, the amount of payments under the QPSA may not be less than the payments that would have been made under a QJSA if the participant had retired with an immediate joint and survivor annuity on the day before the participant's death. The amount of the QPSA is calculated as of the date of death.

(2) *Death before earliest retirement age.* In the case of a participant who dies on or before the earliest retirement age under the plan, the amount of payments under the QPSA may not be less than the payments that would have been made under a QJSA if the participant had separated from service on the date of death, survived until the earliest retirement age, retired with a QJSA upon reaching that age, and died on the following day.

Notice. A written explanation is required to be provided to a participant, with respect to either a QJSA or a QPSA (Code Sec. 417(a)(3)(A); Reg. § 1.417(a)(3)-1). The explanation must include the terms and conditions of the qualified joint and survivor annuity.

NEW LAW EXPLAINED

Requirement for additional survivor annuity option.—The provision revises the minimum survivor annuity requirements to require that, at the election of a participant, benefits will be paid in the form of a "qualified optional survivor annuity" (Code Sec. 417(g), as added, and ERISA Sec. 205(d), as amended, by the Pension Protection Act of 2006). A qualified optional survivor annuity is:

(1) an annuity for the life of the participant with a survivor annuity for the life of the spouse that is equal to the applicable percentage of the amount of the annuity that is payable during the joint lives of the participant and the spouse; and

(2) the actuarial equivalent to a single annuity for the live of the participant.

If the survivor annuity under the plan's qualified joint and survivor annuity is less than 75 percent of the annuity payable during the joint lives of the participant and spouse, the applicable percentage is 75 percent. If the survivor annuity under the plan's qualified joint and survivor annuity is greater than or equal to 75 percent of the annuity payable during the joint lives of the participant and spouse, the applicable percentage is 50 percent.

Example: The survivor annuity under a plan's qualified joint and survivor annuity is 50 percent. Then the survivor annuity under the qualified optional survivor annuity must be 75 percent.

Notice. The written explanation required to be provided to participants explaining the terms and conditions of the qualified joint and survivor annuity must also include the terms and conditions of the qualified optional survivor annuity (Code Sec. 417(a)(3)(A)(i) and ERISA Sec. 205(c)(3)(A)(i), as amended by the Pension Act).

Comment: The provision will allow participants greater choice in selecting their form of benefit, so they can choose the form of benefit most appropriate to their situation. For example, some couples may prefer an option that pays a smaller benefit to the couple while they are alive with a larger benefit to the surviving spouse.

▶ **Effective date.** The provision is effective for plan years beginning after December 31, 2007 (Act Sec. 1004(c)(1) of the Pension Protection Act of 2006). In the case of a plan maintained pursuant to any collective bargaining agreement ratified on or before August 17, 2006, the amendments made by this section apply to the first plan year beginning on or after the earlier of: (1) the later of (a) January 1, 2008, or (b) the date on which the last of such collective bargaining agreements terminates (determined without regard to any extension after August 17, 2006, the date of enactment of the Pension Act), or (2) January 1, 2009 (Act Sec. 1004(c)(2) of the Pension Act).

Law source: Law at ¶5105. Committee Report at ¶11,030.

— Act Sec. 1004(a) of the Pension Protection Act of 2006, amending Code Sec. 417(a)(1)(A), 417(a)(3)(A)(i) and adding Code Sec. 417(g);

— Act Sec. 1004(b), amending ERISA Sec. 205(c)(1)(A), 205(c)(3)(A)(i) and 205(d);

— Act Sec. 1004(c), providing the effective date.

NEW LAW EXPLAINED

Reporter references: For further information, consult the following CCH reporters.

— Pension Plan Guide, ¶1480 and ¶1486

— Standard Federal Tax Reporter, 2006FED ¶17,730.03

— Tax Research Consultant, RETIRE: 42,200

— Federal Tax Guide, 2006FTG ¶11,020 and ¶11,087

CHURCH AND GOVERNMENT PLANS

¶1045 Church Plans that Self-Annuitize

SUMMARY OF NEW LAW

Annuity payments under qualified church plans may meet the minimum distribution rules of Code Sec. 401(a)(9) even if the payments are not made under an annuity contract purchased from an insurance company. The payments must otherwise meet the requirements under Code Sec. 403(b)(9).

BACKGROUND

Qualified retirement plans are subject to minimum distribution rules under Code Sec. 401(a)(9). Special rules apply to payments under an annuity contract that a plan purchased from an insurance company using the employee's benefit (Reg. § 1.401(a)(9)-6, Q&A-4). In certain cases, Treasury regulations provide that these rules apply to annuity payments from a retirement income account maintained by a church, even though the payments are not made under an annuity purchased from an insurance company (Reg. § 1.403(b)-3, Q&A-1(c)(3)). Such church accounts include those maintained by an association or convention of churches, including an organization providing benefits to church employees (as described in Code Sec. 414(e)(3)(A)) (Code Sec. 403(b)(9)).

NEW LAW EXPLAINED

Grandfather rule for church plans that self-annuitize.—Under a grandfather rule, annuity payments provided under a qualified church plan will not fail to meet the minimum distribution rules of Code Sec. 401(a)(9) merely because the payments are self-annuitized, that is, not made under an annuity contract purchased from an insurance company. The payments must otherwise fulfill the minimum distribution rules with respect to retirement income accounts provided by churches described in Code Sec. 403(b)(9).

NEW LAW EXPLAINED

A qualified church plan is any money purchase pension plan described in Code Sec. 401(a) that is a church plan (as defined in Code Sec. 414(e)), with respect to which a Code Sec. 410(d) election (to have coverage and certain other normally inapplicable qualification requirements apply) has not been made. To qualify, the plan must also have been in existence on April 17, 2002.

> **Comment:** No inference should be drawn as to the proper application of the minimum distribution rules to church plans prior to the effective date of this provision (Joint Committee on Taxation, Technical Explanation of the Pension Protection Act of 2006 (JCX-38-06)).

▶ **Effective date.** The provision is effective for plan years ending after August 17, 2006 (Act Sec. 865(a) of the Pension Protection Act of 2006).

Law source: Law at ¶7177. Committee Report at ¶10,910.

— Act Sec. 865 of the Pension Protection Act of 2006.

Reporter references: For further information, consult the following CCH reporters.

— Pension Plan Guide, ¶8051

— Standard Federal Tax Reporter, 2006FED ¶19,157A.01

— Tax Research Consultant, RETIRE: 69,300

¶1050 Income from Leveraged Real Estate Held by Church Plans

SUMMARY OF NEW LAW

A retirement income account of a church (or certain other church-related organizations) qualifies for exemption from the unrelated business income tax (UBIT) on income from debt-financed property.

BACKGROUND

Debt-financed income of a tax-exempt entity is subject to unrelated business income tax (UBIT) under Code Sec. 514. Debt-financed property generally is property that is held to produce income and with respect to which there is acquisition indebtedness. Code Sec. 514(c)(9) provides an exception to the UBIT rules for debt-financed property held by qualifying organizations, including qualified retirement plans.

NEW LAW EXPLAINED

Exemption for income from leveraged real estate held by church plans.—A retirement income account of a church or other church-related organizations defined in Code Sec. 403(b)(9) is a qualified organization for purposes of the exemption from the

NEW LAW EXPLAINED

UBIT debt-financed property rules. Other church-related organizations such as an association or convention of churches (see ¶ 1205) and organizations that provide benefits to church employees also qualify for the exemption. Thus, debt-financed income of such organizations will not be subject to unrelated business income tax (UBIT) under Code Sec. 514.

▶ **Effective date.** The provision is effective for tax years beginning on or after August 17, 2006 (Act Sec. 866(b) of the Pension Protection Act of 2006).

Law source: Law at ¶5170. Committee Report at ¶10,920.

— Act Sec. 866(a) of the Pension Protection Act of 2006, amending Code Sec. 514(c)(9)(C);

— Act Sec. 866(b), providing the effective date.

Reporter references: For further information, consult the following CCH reporters.

— Pension Plan Guide, ¶8000

— Standard Federal Tax Reporter, 2006FED ¶22,859.021

— Tax Research Consultant, EXEMPT: 18,252 and RETIRE: 69,300

— Federal Tax Guide, 2006FTG ¶16,370

¶1055 Church Plan Rule for Benefit Limitations

SUMMARY OF NEW LAW

The 100 percent of compensation benefit limit under Code Sec. 415(b)(1)(B) will be waived for all but highly compensated employees of qualified church plans.

BACKGROUND

Code Sec. 415(b) limits the amount of benefits and contributions that may be provided under a tax-qualified retirement plan. In the case of a defined benefit plan, the limit on annual benefits payable under the plan is the lesser of: (1) a dollar amount that is adjusted for inflation ($175,000 for 2006); and (2) 100 percent of the participant's average compensation for the three highest years. The 100 percent compensation limit is waived for government and multiemployer plans, but not for church plans.

NEW LAW EXPLAINED

Church plan rule for benefit limitations.—Beginning in 2007, the 100 percent of compensation limit will not apply to a plan maintained by a church, a convention or association of churches (see ¶ 1205), or a qualified church-controlled elementary or secondary school as defined in Code Sec. 3121(w)(3)(A), except with respect to "highly compensated benefits." Highly compensated benefits are defined as any benefits ac-

NEW LAW EXPLAINED

crued for an employee in any year on or after the first year in which the employee is a highly compensated employee of the organization. A highly compensated employee is one who: (1) is a more than five-percent owner at any time during the determination year or the preceding year or (2) received compensation in excess of $80,000, adjusted for inflation ($100,000 for 2006), during the preceding year and, if the employer so elects, was in the top-paid group (i.e., top 20 percent of employees by compensation) of employees for that year (Code Sec. 414(q)).

For purposes of applying the 100 percent of compensation limit to highly compensated benefits, all the benefits of the employee that would otherwise be taken into account in applying the limit will be taken into account. In other words, the limit does not apply only to those benefits accrued on or after the first year in which the employee is a highly compensated employee.

▶ **Effective date.** The provision is effective for years beginning after December 31, 2006 (Act Sec. 867(b) of the Pension Protection Act of 2006).

Law source: Law at ¶5095. Committee Report at ¶10,930.

— Act Sec. 867(a) of the Pension Protection Act of 2006, amending Code Sec. 415(b)(11);

— Act Sec. 867(b), providing the effective date.

Reporter references: For further information, consult the following CCH reporters.

— Pension Plan Guide, ¶1561 and ¶8054

— Standard Federal Tax Reporter, 2006FED ¶19,218.022

— Tax Research Consultant, RETIRE: 36,150 and RETIRE: 69,300

— Federal Tax Guide, 2006FTG ¶11,035

¶1060 Nondiscrimination Exemption Extended to All Governmental Plans

SUMMARY OF NEW LAW

All governmental retirement plans are exempt from nondiscrimination requirements.

BACKGROUND

A qualified retirement plan is subject to numerous requirements under the Code and Titles I and IV of the Employee Retirement Income Security Act of 1974 (ERISA) relating to various aspects of qualification and enforcement, such as plan participation, coverage, vesting, funding, fiduciary conduct, and reports that must be provided to plan participants and government agencies.

Qualified plans are also subject to nondiscrimination rules whose intent is to ensure that plans do not impermissively favor higher-paid employees. Specifically, a qualified pension plan cannot provide greater benefits or contributions for highly compen-

BACKGROUND

sated employees (HCEs) than the benefits or contributions that are provided for nonhighly compensated employees (Code Secs. 401(a)(4) and 414(q)).

All qualified plans maintained by private employers are subject to the nondiscrimination requirements. Although classified as qualified plans, not all governmental plans are subject to ERISA or Code regulations. A "governmental plan" is one established and maintained for government employees by the following entities: (1) the federal government; (2) a state government; (3) a political subdivision of a state; or (4) any agency or instrumentality of the federal government or any state government. A plan that has been established and maintained by the *federal* government for its employees is *nonexempt* from ERISA and must satisfy nondiscrimination and minimum participation rules. Additionally, any cash or deferral arrangement plan (CODA) maintained by the federal government is subject to an "actual deferral percentage" (ADP) test, which is a special nondiscrimination test that is applied to all elective deferral plans (Code Sec. 401(k)(3)).

> **Comment:** The Code and ERISA vary in the definition of a governmental plan. Under Code Sec. 414(d) a governmental plan is defined as "a plan established *and* maintained for its employees by the Government of the United States, by the government of any State or political subdivision thereof, or by any agency or instrumentality of any of the foregoing." However, ERISA defines a governmental plan as one "established *or* maintained" for government employees (ERISA Sec. 3(32)).

However, pursuant to the Taxpayer Relief Act of 1997 (TRA '97), plans established by *state or local* government entities are *exempt* from the nondiscrimination rules, minimum participation requirements and ADP testing (Code Sec. 401(a)(5)(G), as amended by Secs. 1505 (a)(1) and 1505(d)(2) of TRA '97. State and local government retirement plans are also exempt from virtually all of ERISA's qualification and enforcement provisions (ERISA Sec. 3(32)).

NEW LAW EXPLAINED

Moratorium on nondiscrimination requirements extended to all governmental plans.—The moratorium on the nondiscrimination and minimum participation requirements that was previously applicable only to state or local governmental plans has been extended to all governmental plans (Code Sec. 401(a)(5)(G) and 401(a)(26)(G), as amended by the Pension Protection Act of 2006). The moratorium on the nondiscrimination and participation rules includes an exemption from the actual deferral percentage (ADP) test for all governmental cash or deferred arrangements plans (Code Sec. 401(k)(3)(G), as amended by the Pension Act.)

► **Effective date.** The provision is effective for any year beginning after August 17, 2006 (Act Sec. 861(c) of the Pension Protection Act 2006).

Law source: Law at ¶5030 and ¶7171. Committee Report at ¶10,870.

— Act Sec. 861(a)(1) of the Pension Protection Act of 2006, amending Code Sec. 401(a)(5)(G) and 401(a)(26)(G);

NEW LAW EXPLAINED

— Act Sec. 861(a)(2), amending Code Sec. 401(k)(3)(G) and section 1505(d) of the Taxpayer Relief Act of 1997 (P.L. 105-34);

— Act Sec. 861(c), providing the effective date.

Reporter references: For further information, consult the following CCH reporters.

— Pension Plan Guide, ¶8240

— Standard Federal Tax Reporter, 2006FED ¶17,717.0255, ¶17,921.01 and ¶18,112.036

— Tax Research Consultant, RETIRE: 3,210, RETIRE: 39,050 and RETIRE: 69,350

— Federal Tax Guide, 2006FTG ¶11,020, ¶11,610 and ¶11,660

¶1065 Treatment of Indian Tribal Government Plans

SUMMARY OF NEW LAW

Certain retirement plans established and maintained by Indian tribal governments are included in the definition of "governmental plan," and are subject to some provisions applicable to state and local government plans.

BACKGROUND

The Internal Revenue Code and the Employee Retirement Income Security Act (ERISA) treat "governmental plans" differently than other qualified retirement plans. The statutory definition of a governmental plan includes a plan established or maintained for its employees by the U.S. Government, the government of a State or a political subdivision of a State, or any agency or instrumentality of any of the foregoing (Code Sec. 414(d) and ERISA Sec. 3(32)). These governmental plans are exempt from ERISA's participation, minimum coverage, vesting, and funding provisions, and from the Pension Benefit Guaranty Corporation (PBGC) provisions in Title IV of ERISA (ERISA Secs. 4(b)(1) and 4021(b)(2)). In addition, although employee contributions to defined benefit plans are generally subject to tax, pickup contributions to State (including political subdivisions and instrumentalities) governmental plans can be made on a pretax basis (Code Sec. 414(h)(2)).

The maximum annual benefit under a defined benefit plan generally may not exceed the lesser of a "dollar limit" ($175,000 for 2006, as adjusted for inflation) or a "compensation limit" (100 percent of average compensation for the participant's highest-paid three consecutive years during which he or she was an active plan participant) (Code Sec. 415(b)). The dollar limit amount generally must be reduced if benefits are paid before the participant reaches age 62 (Code Sec. 415(b)(2)(C)). However, governmental plans are not subject to the compensation limit (Code Sec. 415(b)(11)), and the early retirement reduction of the dollar limit does not apply to certain police or fire department employees who are participants in a defined benefit plan maintained by a State or its political subdivision (Code Sec. 415(b)(2)(G) and (H)). A special "accrued benefit" provision can also apply to some participants in a

BACKGROUND

plan maintained for its employees by a State or its political subdivision (or an agency or instrumentality of thereof) if (i) the participant first became a participant before January 1, 1990, and (ii) before the close of the first plan year beginning after December 31, 1989, the employer elected to have the provision apply. In that case, the annual benefit limitation is not less than the participant's accrued benefit, determined without regard to plan amendments made after October 14, 1987 (Code Sec. 415(b)(10)).

NEW LAW EXPLAINED

Certain Indian tribal government plans are governmental plans, and are subject to some rules governing state plans.—The statutory definition of "governmental plan" is amended to include certain plans established and maintained by an Indian tribal government, a subdivision of an Indian tribal government, or an agency or instrumentality of either (Code Sec. 414(d) and ERISA Secs. 3(32) and 4021(b)(2), as amended by the Pension Protection Act of 2006). To meet the statutory definition, (i) all of the plan participants must be tribal government employees, and (ii) substantially all of these employees' services must be in the performance of noncommercial, essential government functions. A plan that meets these requirements does not have to comply with the Pension Benefit Guaranty Corporation (PBGC) provisions in Title IV of ERISA (ERISA Sec. 4021(b)(2), as amended by the Pension Act).

Comment: According to the Joint Committee on Taxation, a plan established and maintained by an Indian tribal government for teachers in tribal schools could be a governmental plan. However, a plan covering tribal employees of a casino, hotel, marina, service station, or convenience store operated by the tribal government is not considered a governmental plan (Joint Committee on Taxation, Technical Explanation of the Pension Protection Act of 2006 (JCX-38-06)).

Practical Analysis: Mary Beth Braitman, Terry A.M. Mumford and Lisa Erb Harrison of Ice Miller LLP, Indianapolis, Indiana, find that this section creates exciting possibilities for governmental plans. A few governmental plans had been very innovative in exploring ways to allow Indian tribal governments to participate in the governmental plan. A few private letter rulings had been issued as to when a tribal government situation involved a governmental plan under ERISA or the Internal Revenue Code. This provision of the Act gives greater clarity to the issue. It allows an Indian tribal government and its subdivisions, agencies or instrumentalities to establish and maintain a governmental plan, and it affords such plans the same treatment as other governmental plans under ERISA and the Code.

However, that plan may only cover employees substantially all of whose services are in the performance of essentially governmental functions, but that are not commercial activities. The JCT's Technical Explanation (JCX-38-06) provides examples of this distinction—a governmental plan could include the teachers in tribal schools, but could not include a plan covering tribal employees who are employed by a hotel,

NEW LAW EXPLAINED

casino, service station, convenience store or marina operated by a tribal government.

Indian tribal governments and subdivisions. An "Indian tribal government" for these purposes includes the governing body of a tribe, band, community, village, or group of Indians that exercises governmental functions, as determined by the Secretary of the Treasury after consultation with the Secretary of the Interior (Code Sec. 414(d), as amended by the Pension Act; see also Code Sec. 7701(a)(40)). A subdivision of an Indian tribal government is determined in accordance with Code Sec. 7871(d), which requires a determination by the Secretary of the Treasury, after consultation with the Secretary of the Interior, that the subdivision has been delegated the right to exercise one or more of the substantial governmental functions of the Indian tribal government (Code Sec. 414(d), as amended by the Pension Act).

Rules governing state plans. Certain provisions applicable to a plan established by the government of a State or political subdivision thereof, or any agency or instrumentality of the foregoing, also apply to Indian tribal plans that are governmental plans. Pretax pickup contributions may be made by Indian tribal governmental plans (Code Sec. 414(h)(2), as amended by the Pension Act). The accrued-benefit exception to a defined benefit plan's maximum annual benefit limitation for plans maintained by a State (or its political subdivision or their agencies and instrumentalities) also applies to Indian tribal plans that are governmental plans (Code Sec. 415(b)(10), as amended by the Pension Act).

Police and fire department employees. With regard to plan benefit limitations, the exception from the early retirement reduction for qualifying police and fire department employees who are participants in a plan maintained by a State (or its political subdivision) is extended to qualifying police and fire employees who are participants in a defined benefit plan maintained by an Indian tribal government (or political subdivision) (Code Sec. 415(b)(2)(H), as amended by the Pension Act). Thus, these tribal employees may currently receive plan benefits before they reach the age of 62 without a reduction in the annual dollar limit on plan benefits.

> **Planning Note:** To qualify for this exception, the period of service taken into account in determining the amount of the participant's plan benefit must include at least 15 years of qualifying service (Code Sec. 415(b)(2)(H), as amended by the Pension Act).

▶ **Effective date.** The provision applies to any year beginning on or after August 17, 2006 (Act Sec. 906(c) of the Pension Protection Act of 2006).

Law source: Law at ¶5090, ¶5095 and ¶7195. Committee Report at ¶11,000.

— Act Sec. 906(a) of the Pension Protection Act of 2006, amending Code Sec. 414(d) and ERISA Secs. 3(32) and 4021(b)(2);

— Act Sec. 906(b)(1)(A), amending Code Sec. 415(b)(2)(H);

— Act Sec. 906(b)(1)(B), amending Code Sec. 415(b)(10);

— Act Sec. 906(b)(1)(C), amending Code Sec. 414(h)(2);

NEW LAW EXPLAINED

— Act Sec. 906(b)(2), amending ERISA Sec. 4021(b);

— Act Sec. 906(c), providing the effective date.

Reporter references: For further information, consult the following CCH reporters.

— Pension Plan Guide, ¶8100 and ¶8137

— Standard Federal Tax Reporter, 2006FED ¶19,156D.021 and ¶19,218.031

— Tax Research Consultant, RETIRE: 69,352 and SALES: 51,056.15

¶1070 Code Sec. 457 Exceptions Extended to Voluntary Early Retirement Incentive and Employee Retention Plans

SUMMARY OF NEW LAW

Voluntary early retirement incentive plans maintained by local education agencies and tax-exempt education associations are treated as bona fide severance plans under Code Sec. 457. Employment retention plans maintained by such agencies and associations are afforded special tax treatment for the portion of the plans that do not exceed a certain limit ($30,000 in 2006).

BACKGROUND

State and local governments (including their political subdivisions and agencies) as well as certain tax-exempt entities may maintain deferred compensation plans for their employees ("457 Plans"). Code Sec. 457 provides for two types of plans—eligible plans and ineligible plans. A plan is eligible if it meets certain requirements with regard to participation, deferral limits, payout, access to plan assets and income, and termination. Contributions made to eligible governmental plans must be held in trust for the exclusive benefit of the participants (Code Sec. 457(g)) and are not taxable to the employee until they are actually paid. In the case of tax-exempt entities, contributions made to an eligible plan must remain the property of the employer subject to claims by its general creditors (Code Sec. 457(b)(6)) and are not taxable until paid or otherwise made available to the employee. The contributions that can be deferred are subject to a maximum annual limit, which is $15,000 for 2006 (Code Sec. 457(e)(15)). Employees who have reached the annual contribution limit and who will reach at least the age of 50 before the end of the tax year may elect to have "catch-up" contributions made to the plan of up to $5,000 for 2006 (Code Sec. 457(e)(18)).

Plans that do not meet one or more of the eligibility requirements are considered ineligible plans, and contributions made to these plans are included in the employee's gross income, unless those amounts are subject to a substantial risk of forfeiture. That is, the contributions are not included in the employee's gross income if the employee's right to receive compensation is conditioned upon the future

BACKGROUND

performance of substantial services by any individual (Code Sec. 457(f)). However, once the risk of forfeiture is no longer substantial, those amounts are includible in the employee's gross income.

Arrangements with regard to bona fide vacation leave, sick leave, compensatory time, severance pay, disability pay, or death benefits are not considered deferred compensation plans for purposes of Code Sec. 457 (Code Sec. 457(e)(11)(A)(i)). Plans may, however, allow employees to defer accumulated vacation, sick, or back pay if such an agreement is entered into prior to the beginning of the month in which the amounts are paid or made available to the employee (Reg. § 1.457-4(d)). In addition, Code Sec. 457 does not apply to:

- qualified plans as described in Code Sec. 401(a) (Code Sec. 457(f)(2)(A));
- annuity plans or contracts described in Code Sec. 403 (Code Sec. 457(f)(2)(B));
- portions of any plan that consists of a property transfer under Code Sec. 83 (third-party option arrangements) (Code Sec. 457(f)(2)(C));
- portions of any plan that consists of a trust to which Code Sec. 402(b) applies (Code Sec. 457(f)(2)(D));
- plans maintained by churches and church-controlled organizations (Code Sec. 457(e)(13));
- length-of-service awards to emergency service volunteers (Code Sec. 457(e)(11)(A)(ii));
- nonelective deferred compensation attributed to services performed as an independent contractor (Code Sec. 457(e)(12)); and
- any Code Sec. 415(m) qualified government excess benefit plan (Code Sec. 457(f)(2)(E)).

Governmental and church 457 plans are exempt from the participation, vesting, funding, trust documentation, and fiduciary responsibility rules of the Employee Retirement Income Security Act of 1974 (ERISA) (P.L. 93-406). However, nongovernmental, tax-exempt plans are not exempt unless the plan fits within one of the other exemptions under ERISA. Such exemptions include top-hat, excess benefit, and severance and welfare plans. Thus, if a plan is structured as an employee benefit welfare plan providing for such benefits as medical, disability, death, unemployment, vacation, sick or severance, the plan is not subject to ERISA.

Both ERISA and the Age Discrimination in Employment Act of 1967 (ADEA) prohibit the exclusion of employees from participation in retirement plans based on an employee's age. For example, a plan may not permit the involuntary retirement of any employee. However, voluntary early retirement incentive plans may be offered provided they are consistent with the purposes of the ADEA.

NEW LAW EXPLAINED

Code Sec. 457 exceptions extended to voluntary early retirement incentive plans and employee retention plans.—The new law provides special rules in applying Code Sec. 457 to "voluntary early retirement incentive plans" and to "employee retention

NEW LAW EXPLAINED

plans" of local educational agencies and tax-exempt educational associations that principally represent employees of one or more agencies. A voluntary early retirement incentive plan makes payments or supplements as an early retirement benefit, a retirement-type subsidy, or a social security supplement in coordination with a defined benefit pension plan maintained by a State or local government or by an association (Code Sec. 457(e)(11)(D), as added by the Pension Protection Act of 2006). An employee retention plan provides compensation, upon termination of employment, to an employee for purposes of retaining the services of the employee or rewarding the employee for service with the educational agency or association (Code Sec. 457(f)(4)(D), as added by the Pension Act).

Voluntary early retirement incentive plans. A voluntary early retirement incentive plan maintained by local educational agency or tax-exempt education association in coordination with a defined benefit plan is treated as a bona fide severance plan under Code Sec. 457 (Code Sec. 457(e)(11)(D), as added by the Pension Act). Payments or supplements made by the plan as early retirement benefits, retirement-type subsidies, or Social Security supplements are not subject to the requirements or limits of Code Sec. 457 to the extent that such payments or supplements could otherwise have been provided under the agency's or association's defined benefit plan. To determine the extent such payments or supplements could have been be made under the defined benefit plan, the accrual and vesting rules of the defined benefit plan must be applied.

Voluntary retirement incentive plans maintained by local educational agencies or tax-exempt educational associations are treated as employee welfare benefit plans and, thus, they are exempt from the participation, vesting, funding, trust, and fiduciary requirements of ERISA (ERISA Sec. 3(2)(B), as amended by the Pension Act).

In addition, voluntary retirement incentive plans maintained by local educational agencies or tax-exempt educational associations are treated as a part of the defined benefit plan maintained by the agencies and associations, and payments made under the plans do not constitute severance pay under ADEA (ADEA Sec. 4(l)(1), as amended by the Pension Act).

Employee retention plans. The portion of an employee retention plan maintained by a local educational agency or tax-exempt educational association that provides benefits payable to the employee in an amount not exceeding twice the maximum annual limit ($30,000 in 2006 ($15,000 annual limit × 2)) are not subject to Code Sec. 457 (Code Sec. 457(f)(2)(F) and (f)(4), as added by the Pension Act). However, this exception only applies to years preceding the year in which the benefits are paid or otherwise made available to the employee (Code Sec. 457(f)(4)(B)(i), as added by the Pension Act). In addition, the amount of an employment retention plan (up to $30,000 in 2006) is not treated as providing for the deferral of compensation for tax purposes (Code Sec. 457(f)(4)(B)(ii), as added by the Pension Act).

Employee retention plans maintained by local educational agencies or tax-exempt educational associations are treated as employee welfare benefit plans and, thus, they are exempt from the participation, vesting, funding, trust, and fiduciary requirements of ERISA (ERISA Sec. 3(2)(B), as amended by the Pension Act).

NEW LAW EXPLAINED

- **Effective date.** The treatment of voluntary early retirement incentive and employee retention plans apply to tax years and plan years ending after August 17, 2006 (Act Sec. 1104(d) of the Pension Protection Act of 2006).

Law source: Law at ¶5140 and ¶7219. Committee Report at ¶11,070.

— Act Sec. 1104(a) of the Pension Protection Act of 2006, adding Code Sec. 457(e)(11)(D) and section 4(l)(1) of the Age Discrimination in Employment Act of 1967;

— Act Sec. 1104(b), adding Code Sec. 457(f)(2)(F) and (f)(4);

— Act Sec. 1104(c), amending ERISA Sec. 3(2)(B);

— Act Sec. 1104(d), providing the effective date.

Reporter references: For further information, consult the following CCH reporters.

— Pension Plan Guide, ¶1621

— Standard Federal Tax Reporter, 2006FED ¶21,536.01

— Tax Research Consultant, COMPEN: 15,150

¶1075 Participation in Code Sec. 457 Plans After Cash-Outs

SUMMARY OF NEW LAW

Individuals who elected to receive lump sum distributions under an eligible deferred compensation plan of a State or local government or a tax-exempt organization on or before December 31, 1996, may still participate in an eligible deferred compensation plan. The cash-out distribution must have been received after separation from service, within 60 days of making the election and cannot have exceeded $3,500.

BACKGROUND

A section 457 plan is an eligible deferred compensation plan of a State or local government or tax-exempt employer that meets certain requirements (Code Sec. 457(b)). Generally, amounts deferred under a Code Sec. 457 plan sponsored by a State or local government are includible in income only when the amounts are paid, and not when otherwise made available to the taxpayer (Code Sec. 457(a)(1)(A)). On the other hand, amounts deferred under tax-exempt nongovernmental plans are includible in gross income when the amounts are paid or "otherwise made available" to the participant or other beneficiary (Code Sec. 457(a)(1)(B)).

Benefits are not treated as "made available" under an eligible tax-exempt organization plan merely because an employee may elect to receive the total amount payable under the plan or because the plan may distribute such amount without the participant's consent. However, in order for this rule to apply, the total amount payable: (1) cannot exceed $5,000, and (2) can only be distributed if no amount has been deferred

BACKGROUND

under the plan for such participant during the two-year period ending on the date of the distribution, and if there has been no prior distribution under the plan to such participant (Code Secs. 457(e)(9)(A) and 411(a)(11)(A)). Thus, each participant is limited to one such in-service distribution from the plan. Further, benefits are also not treated as made available under an eligible tax-exempt entity plan merely because an employee may elect to defer the start of distributions from the plan (Code Sec. 457(e)(9)(B)).

Prior to the enactment of the Small Business Job Protection Act of 1996 (P.L. 104-188), a section 457 plan could allow participants with accounts of $3,500 or less to elect a cash-out distribution from their accounts without causing the total account to be treated as constructively received, thereby subjecting it to tax. Thus, for tax years beginning before 1997, benefits were not treated as "made available" (that is, constructively received) under a section 457 plan merely because an employee could elect to receive a small lump-sum payment after separation from service and within 60 days of election. However, this rule applied only if the total deferred benefit of the employee did not exceed $3,500 and no additional amounts could be deferred under the plan with respect to the employee (Code Sec. 457(e)(9), prior to amendment by P.L. 104-188).

NEW LAW EXPLAINED

Distributions under deferred compensation plans of state and local governments.—Individuals who elected to receive lump sum distributions under a deferred compensation plan of a State or local government or a tax-exempt organization on or before December 31, 1996 (under Code Sec. 457(e)(9), prior to the enactment of Small Business Job Protection Act of 1996 (P.L. 104-188)) may still participate in an eligible deferred compensation plan (Act Sec. 825, Pension Protection Act of 2006).

> **Comment:** The Pension Act allows an employee who otherwise may be deemed ineligible to defer any amount under a section 457 plan to participate in any eligible deferred compensation plan. However, this provision applies only to individuals who made the election on or before December 31, 1996, and the amount distributed did not exceed $3,500. Further, the employee must have received the a lump-sum distribution after separation from service and within 60 days from making the election. The lump-sum payment will not be deemed as "made available" or constructively received by reason of the employee's subsequent deferrals or participation in another eligible deferred compensation plan.

> **Practical Analysis:** Mary Beth Braitman, Terry A.M. Mumford and Lisa Erb Harrison of Ice Miller LLP, Indianapolis, Indiana, note that this amendment provides relief for individuals who received distributions from an eligible deferred compensation plan prior to the amendments of the Small Business Job Protection Act of 1996 by permitting such individuals to participate in eligible deferred compensation plans without a waiting (or hold-out) period.

NEW LAW EXPLAINED

▶ **Effective date.** No specific effective date is provided by the Act. The provision is, therefore, considered effective on August 17, 2006, the date of enactment.

Law source: Law at ¶7159. Committee Report at ¶10,660.

— Act Sec. 825 of the Pension Protection Act of 2006.

Reporter references: For further information, consult the following CCH reporters.

— Pension Plan Guide, ¶8020

— Standard Federal Tax Reporter, 2006FED ¶21,536.047

— Tax Research Consultant, COMPEN: 15,152 and COMPEN: 15,156

PLAN ADMINISTRATION

¶1080 Reporting Simplification for Small Retirement Plans

SUMMARY OF NEW LAW

A one-participant retirement plan is exempt from filing an annual report (Form 5500) if the plan's assets are $250,000 or less. In addition, the Secretary of Treasury and Secretary of Labor are directed to develop a simplified annual return for any retirement plan with less than 25 participants.

BACKGROUND

Employers who maintain tax-qualified retirement plans, or the plan administrators, are required to file an annual return with the IRS stating information with respect to the qualification, financial condition, and operation of the plan (Code Sec. 6058). A similar annual report is required to be filed with the Department of Labor (DOL) and certain other information may be required to be filed by defined benefits plans with the Pension Benefit Guaranty Corporation (PBGC). The employer or plan administrator may fulfill these reporting requirements by filing Form 5500, and any accompanying schedules, with the DOL.

There are two versions of Form 5500 that may be filed. Form 5500-EZ is a simpler form that can be used in the case of a one-participant retirement plan. A qualified retirement plan is considered a one-participant plan if:

- the only participant of the plan on the first day of the plan year is: (1) the sole owner of the business (whether incorporated or not) that maintains the plan (and his or her spouse); or (2) partners in a partnership (and their spouses) that maintain the plan;

BACKGROUND

- the plan is not aggregated with any other plan the owner may have that covers other employees of the business to meet the minimum coverage requirements of Code Sec. 410(b);
- the plan does not provide benefits for anyone except the owner and his or her spouse, or in the case of a partnership, one or more partners and their spouses;
- the business that maintains the plan is not a member of a related group of employers; and
- that plan does not cover individuals of a business that uses leased employees.

Generally, the plan sponsor or plan administrator does not have to file Form 5500-EZ (or Form 5500) for a one participant retirement plan if the plan does not have an accumulated funding deficiency for the plan year and: (1) its total assets at the end of every plan year beginning after 1993 is $100,000 or less; or (2) the employer has two or more one-participant plans that together had total plan assets of $100,000 or less at the end of every plan year beginning after 1993. However, Form 5500-EZ must be filed for the final plan year even if the total plan assets have always been less than $100,000.

If a plan does not meet the requirements for filing Form 5500-EZ, then the long version of Form 5500, and related schedules, must be filed to meet the annual reporting requirements. The amount of detailed financial information that must be provided on the long version of Form 5500 will vary depending on the characteristics and size of the plan in question. Generally, however, if the plan has more than 100 plan participants at the beginning of the plan year, more information must be provided.

NEW LAW EXPLAINED

Reporting simplification.—The Pension Protection Act of 2006 directs the Secretary of the Treasury to modify the dollar threshold with respect to the annual reporting requirements for one-participant retirement plans to insure that plans with $250,000 or less in assets at the close of the plan year need not file a Form 5500 return (Act Sec. 1103(a) of the Pension Act). The term "partner" is also modified to include an individual who owns more than two percent of an S corporation. The changes will apply to plan years of one-participant retirement plans beginning after 2006.

> **Comment:** For purposes of including a partner who owns more than two percent of an S corporation, the Code Sec. 1372(b) definition of a partnership for fringe benefit purposes is applied.

The Secretary of the Treasury and the Secretary of Labor are also directed to provide, for plan years beginning after 2006, a simplified annual return for any retirement plan that covers less than 25 participants on the first day of a plan year (Act Sec. 1103(b) of the Pension Act). However, to qualify for the simplified annual return, the plan must meet the same qualification requirements of a one-participant retirement plan except that the plan may provide benefits to participants other than the owner (or his or her spouse) or the partners (and their spouses).

NEW LAW EXPLAINED

▶ **Effective date.** The provision relating to the dollar threshold for filing Form 5500-EZ (or Form 5500) is effective for plan years beginning on or after January 1, 2007 (Act Sec. 1103(a)(4) of the Pension Protection Act of 2006).

Law source: Law at ¶7216. Committee Report at ¶11,060.

— Act Sec. 1103(a) and (b) of the Pension Protection Act of 2006;

— Act Sec. 1103(a)(4), providing the effective date.

Reporter references: For further information, consult the following CCH reporters.

— Pension Plan Guide, ¶4085 and ¶4170

— Standard Federal Tax Reporter, 2006FED ¶17,507.0751 and ¶36,502.01

— Tax Research Consultant, RETIRE: 51,356.05 and RETIRE: 78,052

¶1085 Employee Plans Compliance Resolution System (EPCRS)

SUMMARY OF NEW LAW

The Secretary of the Treasury is authorized to update and improve the Employee Plans Compliance Resolution System (EPCRS), the IRS's voluntary compliance and administrative enforcement program for tax-sheltered annuities (TSAs), qualified plans, SIMPLE IRAs, and simplified employee pensions (SEPs), so that employers can correct plan compliance failures without risking plan disqualification, and continue to provide their employees with tax-favored retirement benefits.

BACKGROUND

The IRS provides a variety of correction programs permitting sponsors of retirement plans to correct plan qualification failures and continue to provide their employees with tax-favored retirement benefits. These correction programs are designed for retirement plans that are intended to satisfy the requirements of qualified plans, qualified annuities, tax sheltered annuities, SEPs or SIMPLE plans. This collection of programs, called the Employee Plans Compliance Resolution System (EPCRS), was recently revised in Rev. Proc. 2006-27, I.R.B. 2006-22, 945, which modified and superseded Rev. Proc. 2003-44, 2003-1 CB 1051, the prior consolidated statement of programs under EPCRS. Although the procedure is generally effective September 1, 2006, certain sections are effective on or after May 30, 2006, and plan sponsors are permitted, at their option, to apply these provisions on or after May 30, 2006.

Under EPCRS, plan sponsors and other plan professionals can correct certain errors in employee retirement plans, in some cases without even having to notify the IRS. Correcting plans in this way allows participants to continue receiving tax-favored retirement benefits and protects the retirement benefits of employees and retirees. However, plan sponsors who fail to take advantage of EPCRS will not receive the

BACKGROUND

favorable tax treatment available in EPCRS programs if the problems are discovered upon examination. In addition, the procedure makes it clear that EPCRS remains unavailable in cases where either the plan or the plan sponsor has been a party to an abusive tax avoidance transaction and the plan failure is directly or indirectly related to that transaction.

> **Comment:** According to Carol Gold, Director of IRS's Employee Plans Division, "EPCRS is a valuable program for plan sponsors who need to make corrections that result from inadvertent errors. It is definitely not available to those who deliberately engage in abusive tax transactions that jeopardize the integrity of the plan and take advantage of the participants" (IRS News Release IR-2006-75, May 5, 2006).

EPCRS consists of the following three main components that allow plan administrators to correct technical and administrative plan problems.

(1) *Self-Correction Program (SCP).* Under the Self-Correction Program (SCP), administrators that have established compliance practices and procedures may generally correct insignificant operational failures under a qualified plan, a 403(b) plan, a SEP, or a SIMPLE IRA, at any time without paying any fee or sanction, provided the SEP or SIMPLE IRA is established and maintained on an IRS-approved document. In addition, in the case of a qualified plan that is the subject of a favorable IRS determination letter, or in the case of a 403(b) plan, administrators may generally correct significant (within a two-year period) and insignificant operational failures without payment of any fee or sanction.

(2) *Voluntary Correction Program (VCP).* Under the Voluntary Correction Program (VCP), administrators may at any time before an audit, pay a limited fee and receive the IRS's approval for a correction of operational, plan document, demographic and employer eligibility qualification failures. VCP is available to a qualified plan, a 403(b) plan, SEP or SIMPLE IRA. In addition, under VCP, there are special procedures for anonymous and group submissions.

(3) *Audit Closing Agreement Program (Audit CAP).* Under the Audit Closing Agreement Program (Audit CAP), administrators may make corrections while the plan is under audit and pay a sanction based on the nature, extent and severity of the failure being corrected, as well as to the extent to which correction occurred before audit. If the IRS and the plan sponsor cannot reach an agreement regarding the correction, the failure, or the amount of the sanction, the plan will be disqualified, or, in the case of a 403(b) plan, SEP, or SIMPLE IRA, the plan cannot rely on this procedure.

According to Rev. Proc. 2006-27, EPCRS is based on the following general principles:

- Administrators should be encouraged to establish practices and procedures that ensure the plans are operated according to applicable Code requirements.
- Administrators should satisfy applicable plan document requirements.
- Administrators should make voluntary and timely correction of any plan failures, whether involving discrimination in favor of highly compensated employees, plan operations, the terms of the plan document, or adoption of a plan by an ineligible

BACKGROUND

employer. Timely and efficient correction protects participating employees by providing them with their expected retirement benefits, including favorable tax treatment.

- Limited fees for voluntary corrections have been approved by the IRS, thereby promoting voluntary compliance and reducing uncertainty with regard to employers' and participants' potential tax liability.
- Incentives to make corrections promptly should be ensured by providing fees and sanctions graduated in a series of steps.
- Sanctions for plan failures identified on audit should be reasonable in light of the nature, extent, and severity of the violation.
- EPCRS administration should be consistent and uniform.
- Administrators should be able to rely on the availability of EPCRS in taking corrective actions to maintain the tax-favored status of their plans.

In addition, all of the programs comprising EPCRS are governed by a uniform set of correction principles. Generally, a qualification failure is not considered corrected unless full correction is made with respect to all participants and beneficiaries, for all tax years, regardless of whether the tax year is closed, considering the terms of the plan at the time of the failure. The correction method should restore the plan to the position in which it would have been had the failure not occurred. Current and former participants and beneficiaries should be restored to the benefits and rights they would have had if the failure had not occurred.

Corrections are to be reasonable and appropriate. Depending on the nature of the failure, more than one reasonable and appropriate correction may exist. Any standardized correction method permitted is deemed to be reasonable and appropriate. Whether any other particular correction method is reasonable and appropriate is determined according to the facts and circumstances and the following principles:

- The method should resemble one already provided for in the Code and regulations.
- The method for qualification failures relating to nondiscrimination should provide benefits for non-highly compensated employees.
- The method should keep plan assets in the plan, except to the extent the Code, regulations or other publications already provide for distribution.
- The method should not violate another qualified plan requirement.

Generally, where more than one correction method is available to correct an operational failure for a plan year, the correction method should be applied consistently in correcting operational failures of the same type for that plan year. Similarly, earnings adjustment methods generally should be applied consistently with respect to corrective contributions or allocations for a particular type of operational failure for a plan year.

NEW LAW EXPLAINED

Secretary authorized to establish and implement the Employee Plans Compliance Resolution System (EPCRS).—The provision clarifies that the Secretary of the Treasury has full authority to establish and implement the Employee Plans Compliance Resolution System (EPCRS) and any other employee plans correction policies. Accordingly, the Secretary is authorized to waive income, excise or other taxes to ensure that any tax, penalty or sanction is not excessive. The Secretary is also required to ensure that a reasonable relationship connects the tax, penalty or sanction with the nature, extent and severity of the failure (Act Sec. 1101(a) of the Pension Protection Act of 2006).

> **Comment:** This provision represents formal legislative approval of EPCRS, which has evolved from a series of IRS revenue procedures beginning in 1992. In a report addressing an earlier version of this provision, the Senate Finance Committee commended the IRS for the establishment of EPCRS. The Committee noted that future improvements should facilitate use by small employers of the compliance and correction programs, and that the flexibility of the programs should be expanded (S. Rep. No. 109-174).

Improvements. The Secretary is directed to continue updating and improving the EPCRS, with special attention given to: (1) educating small employers as to the availability and use of the program; (2) accounting for the special concerns and circumstances faced by small employers in compliance and correction of compliance failures; (3) extending the duration of the SCP's self-correction period for significant compliance failures; (4) expanding the availability to correct insignificant compliance failures under the SCP during audit; and (5) assuring that any tax, penalty, or sanction imposed due to a compliance failure is not excessive and bears a reasonable relationship to the nature, extent and severity of the failure (Act Sec. 1101(b) of the Pension Act).

▶ **Effective date.** No specific effective date is provided by the Act. The provision is, therefore, considered effective on August 17, 2006, the date of enactment.

Law source: Law at ¶7210. Committee Report at ¶11,040.

— Act Sec. 1101 of the Pension Protection Act of 2006.

Reporter references: For further information, consult the following CCH reporters.

— Pension Plan Guide, ¶6200

— Standard Federal Tax Reporter, 2006FED ¶17,507.043, ¶17,507.0432, ¶17,507.0434 and 17,507.0437

— Tax Research Consultant, RETIRE: 51,450

¶1090 Provisions Related to Plan Amendments

SUMMARY OF NEW LAW

Plan amendments made pursuant to changes made the Pension Protection Act of 2006 may be given retroactive effect.

BACKGROUND

Under certain circumstances, a remedial amendment period is provided during which a plan may be amended retroactively in order to comply with the plan qualification requirements. Plan amendments reflecting changes in the law generally must be made by the due date for filing the employer's income tax return for the tax year in which the change to the law is effective. The Secretary of the Treasury can extend the time by which the plan amendments are required to be made (Code Sec. 401(b)).

In general, a participant's accrued benefit is not permitted to be decreased by a plan amendment (Code Sec. 411(d)(6)(A) and ERISA Sec. 204(g)(1)). The prohibition on the reduction of accrued benefits is often referred to as the "anti-cutback rule."

NEW LAW EXPLAINED

Certain plan amendments can be retroactively effective.—Certain plan amendments that are made pursuant to changes made by the Pension Protection Act of 2006, or any regulations issued under the Pension Act, can be retroactively effective (Act Sec. 1107(a) of the Pension Protection Act of 2006). The provision applies to any pension plan or annuity contract amendment that is: (1) made pursuant to any amendment made by the Pension Act or pursuant to any regulation issued under the Pension Act, and (2) made on or before the last day of the first plan year beginning on or after January 1, 2009 (referred to hereafter as "the cut-off date") (Act Sec. 1107(b)(1) of the Pension Act).

> **Comment:** The cut-off date for governmental plans (as defined in Code Sec. 414(d)) is January 1, 2011 (Act Sec. 1107(b)(1) of the Pension Act).

For the provision to apply to a plan amendment, the plan must be operated as if such amendment was in effect during the period:

(1) beginning on the date that the legislative or regulatory amendment related to the Pension Act takes effect (or, in the case of an amendment not required by such legislative or regulatory change, the effective date specified by the plan); and

(2) ending on the cut-off date (or, if earlier, the date that the plan amendment was adopted) (Act Sec. 1107(b)(2)(A) of the Pension Act).

In addition, the plan amendment must apply retroactively for such period (Act Sec. 1107(b)(2)(B) of the Pension Act).

Effect of provision. If the plan or contract amendment meets the requirements of the provision, then the plan will be treated as being operated in accordance with the terms of the plan during the period described in the preceding paragraph (Act Sec. 1107(a)(1) of the Pension Act). In addition (except as provided by the Secretary of the Treasury), the plan will not violate the anti-cutback rule by reason of the amendment (Act Sec. 1107(a)(2) of the Pension Act).

> **Comment:** Noting that the Secretary of the Treasury is empowered to provide exceptions to the relief from the anti-cutback rule, the technical explanation of the Pension Act states that it is intended that the Secretary will not permit "inappropriate reductions" in contributions or benefits that are not directly

NEW LAW EXPLAINED

related to the provisions under the Pension Act (Joint Committee on Taxation, Technical Explanation of the Pension Protection Act of 2006 (JCX-38-06)).

▶ **Effective date.** No specific date is provided by the Act. The provision is, therefore, considered effective on August 17, 2006, the date of enactment.

Law source: Law at ¶7225. Committee Report at ¶11,100.

— Act Sec. 1107 of the Pension Protection Act of 2006.

Reporter references: For further information, consult the following CCH reporters.

— Pension Plan Guide, ¶869

— Standard Federal Tax Reporter, 2006FED ¶17,929.01

— Tax Research Consultant, RETIRE: 51,052.20

Charitable Contributions

CONTRIBUTIONS AND DEDUCTIONS

DONOR ADVISED FUNDS

REPORTING REQUIREMENTS

CROSS REFERENCES

Penalty thresholds lowered for substantial and gross valuation misstatements (*see ¶1345*)

Penalty and disciplinary action imposed on appraisers (*see ¶1350*)

Definitions of qualified appraisal and qualified appraiser clarified (*see ¶1355*)

Study on Donor Advised Funds and Supporting Organizations (*see ¶1290*)

CONTRIBUTIONS AND DEDUCTIONS

¶1105 Tax-Free IRA Distributions to Charities

SUMMARY OF NEW LAW

Individuals aged 70 1/2 or older can distribute up to $100,000 of their IRA balance to charitable organizations in 2006 and in 2007 without recognizing income and without taking a charitable deduction. The distribution counts towards the required minimum distribution.

BACKGROUND

It can make good tax sense to donate an unneeded but required taxable IRA distribution to a charity and shelter the income with a charitable deduction. Under the present rules, however, donating an IRA distribution to a charity can be expensive. Although income from the distribution is theoretically counterbalanced by the charitable deduction, in practice the extra tax is likely to be more than the extra deduction. The taxpayer must first take a taxable distribution of the funds. This distribution is subject to the normal limits placed on IRA distributions (Code Sec. 408(d)). The subsequent donation is subject to the itemized deduction phase-out limits for high income earners (Code Sec. 68), and the deduction limits applicable to charitable contributions (Code Sec. 170).

Taxation of traditional IRA distributions. For traditional IRAs, contributions are generally deductible in the tax year made (Code Sec. 219), and distributions are included in income in the tax year of withdrawal (Code 408(d)). Individuals can designate contributions as nondeductible, in which case distributions of the nondeductible contributions are not taxable (Code Sec. 408(o), Form 8606, Nondeductible IRAs). For Roth IRAs, contributions are not deductible (Code Sec. 408A(c)), and qualified distributions are not taxable (Code Sec. 408A(d)).

Distributions of nondeductible traditional IRA contributions. Special rules apply to withdrawals from a traditional IRA for an individual who has made both deductible and nondeductible contributions. The portion of the distribution representing nondeduct-

BACKGROUND

ible contributions (and hence not taxable when withdrawn) is determined by multiplying the amount of the distribution by the ratio for the remaining nondeductible contributions to the account balance (Pub. 590, Individual Retirement Arrangements). In making this determination, all of an individual's traditional IRAs are treated as a single IRA, all distributions during any tax year are treated as a single distribution, and the value of the contract, income on the contract, and investment in the contract are computed as of the close of the calendar year (Code Sec. 408(d)(2)).

Roth IRA distributions. Contributions to a Roth IRA are nondeductible. Qualified distributions (which satisfy a five-year holding period requirement, and are made after the original owner turns 59½, dies, becomes disabled, or is used for a first-time home purchase) are not taxable. Nonqualified distributions from Roth IRAs are included in income under the annuity rules. Most distributions from a Roth IRA are treated first as a return of contributions followed by a distribution of earnings (Code Sec. 408A(d)(4)(B)). In making the distribution determination, all of an individual's Roth IRAs are treated as a single IRA, all distributions during any tax year are treated as a single distribution, and the value of the contract, income on the contract, and investment in the contract are computed as of the close of the calendar year (Code Sec. 408A(d)(4)(A)).

Charitable deduction. An individual who itemizes deductions rather than taking the standard deduction can deduct the amount of cash or the fair market value of property contributed to a Code Sec. 170(b)(1)(A) organization, up to 50 percent of the taxpayer's contribution base (adjusted gross income computed without reference to net operating loss carrybacks) in the tax year of the contribution. These institutions are sometimes called 50-percent organizations, and they include educational institutions, hospitals, medical research organizations, organizations supporting government schools, governmental units, publicly supported organizations, supporting organizations of churches, educational institutions, hospitals, medical research organizations, organizations supporting government schools and publicly supported organizations, common fund foundations, private operating foundations, and conduit foundations.

NEW LAW EXPLAINED

Qualified charitable distributions from IRAs.—An exclusion from gross income is provided for otherwise taxable IRA distributions of up to $100,000 in qualified charitable distributions from either a traditional IRA or Roth IRA (Code Sec. 408(d)(8)(A), as added by the Pension Protection Act of 2006). Such distributions are not to be taken into account for charitable deduction purposes (Code Sec. 408(d)(8)(E), as added by the Pension Act). This rule applies to distributions made in tax years beginning after December 31, 2005, and sunsets for distributions made in tax years beginning after December 31, 2007 (Act Sec. 1201(c)(1) of the Pension Protection Act and Code Sec. 408(d)(8)(F), as added by the Pension Act).

> **Planning Note:** As a result of the new rule, up to $100,000 of an individual's IRA balances can be donated in tax year 2006 and again in tax year 2007 with no reportable income and no deduction to muddy the waters. This change is helpful

NEW LAW EXPLAINED

for those who do not need to take distributions from their IRA, and who would prefer to avoid tax on the minimum required distributions that must be made with respect to a traditional IRA after the owner reaches age 70½. It's a limited time offer, so an IRA owner whose required minimum distribution in 2006 and 2007 is less than $100,000 may want to top-off the distribution to take full advantage of the $200,000 maximum donation over the course of the two tax years.

Practical Analysis: Barnaby Zall, of Weinberg & Jacobs, LLP, Rockville, Maryland, refers to Act Sec. 1201 as the "save the whales from your IRA" provision. This provision permits tax-free charitable contributions from retirement savings, likely boosting charitable giving from middle-class retirees who believe they have sufficient other funds to cover their needs. The net effect of these distributions, however, will be to transfer funds intended as long-term and emergency reserves into present usage by charities; how this will affect federal pension, Medicare and other social welfare obligations is unknown. In addition, major financial institutions holding these funds may promote these transfers as painless. Professionals assisting in financial planning, however, should carefully explain the possible effects of such contributions on financial reserves, and not simply promote the transfers. In short, these transfers are not for every person, but only for those for whom the contingencies are understood.

Qualified charitable distribution. A qualified charitable distribution is any distribution from an individual retirement plan (other than a Simplified Employee Pension plan, or a Simple Retirement Account), which the trustee makes directly to a 50-percent organization described in Code Sec. 170(b)(1)(A). The distribution can be made on or after the date the person for whose benefit the plan is maintained attains 70½. The distribution is treated as a qualified charitable distribution only to the extent that the IRA distribution would be otherwise includible in gross income (Code Sec. 408(d)(8)(B), as added by the Pension Act).

Practical Analysis: Robert S. Keebler of Virchow Krause & Company LLP, Green Bay, Wisconsin, observes that the charitable IRA distribution provision is interesting and certainly well intended, but very limited in scope. This provision is only valid for the 2006 and 2007 tax years and the annual contribution is capped at $100,000. In addition, the distribution must be made by a person who is at least age 70 and the distribution must be one that would have been included in income if not for this provision. Because of these restrictive conditions, the provision will have little or no impact on most taxpayers. Nevertheless, for some older clients who have charitable intentions this will provide an excellent way to contribute retirement plan assets to charity without having to recognize income.

Take for example my client, Mrs. D. Mrs. D is 71 and a widow who does not need the funds in her $1,500,000 IRA. At Mrs. D's death, her IRA will pass to charity. Because Mrs. D is very healthy, she could easily live for another 15 to 20 years. However, it is

NEW LAW EXPLAINED

very likely that she will withdraw the greater share of her IRA before she dies, thus negating any income tax benefit of leaving the IRA to charity. When I talked with Mrs. D to discuss this new provision in the tax law, she was eager to take advantage of this strategy in 2007 because she could give a portion of her IRA to charity during her lifetime without creating adverse income tax consequences.

Comment: Note that a qualified charitable distribution can be made only by individual old enough to be subject to minimum distribution requirements (Reg. § 1.408-8).

Comment: Qualified charitable distributions are taken into account for purposes of minimum distribution rules applicable to traditional IRAs to the same extent the distribution would have been taken into account if the distribution not been directly distributed as a qualified distribution (Joint Committee on Taxation, Technical Explanation of the Pension Protection Act of 2006 (JCX-38-06)). Thus a qualified distribution does double duty: it provides for tax-free distributions and, at the same time, helps to reduce the need to make subsequent required minimum distributions. This is another reason to top-off a distribution and take full advantage of the $100,000 limit in each year.

Comment: Making charitable distributions out of a Roth IRA may have fewer tax advantages than making charitable distributions out of a traditional IRA since qualified distributions from Roth IRAs are not taxed, and Roth IRAs are not subject to required minimum distributions during the original owner's lifetime. However, even with Roth IRAs, a qualified distribution does have the advantage of avoiding the limits normally imposed on charitable deductions.

Charities that qualify. The taxpayer can take advantage of this provision by distributing IRA funds to a 50-percent organization described in Code Sec. 170(b)(1)(A) (so named because they can be deducted up to 50 percent of the taxpayer's contributions base in the contribution year). These organizations include educational institutions, hospitals, medical research organizations, organizations supporting government schools, governmental units, publicly supported organizations, common fund foundations, private operating foundations, and conduit foundations. Note that not all 50-percent organizations qualify. Distributions to supporting organizations described in Code Sec. 509(a)(3) (i.e., organizations that support churches, educational institutions, hospitals, medical research organizations, organizations supporting government schools and publicly supported organizations) are not qualified distributions (Code Sec. 408(d)(8)(B)(i), as added by the Pension Act).

Comment: The Pension Act also provides that distributions to donor advised funds, described in newly added Code Sec. 4966(d)(2) (as added by Act Sec. 1231 of the Pension Act), are not qualified distributions. For discussion of donor advised funds, see ¶ 1160.

Contributions must be otherwise deductible. For direct distributions to a Code Sec. 170(b)(1)(A) organization to be a qualified charitable distribution, the entire amount must be allowable as a charitable deduction under Code Sec. 170 (disregarding the percentage limitations). Accordingly, if the deductible contribution is reduced for any

NEW LAW EXPLAINED

reason (e.g., a benefit received in exchange or subtantiation problems), the exclusion is not available for any part of the IRA distribution.

> **Example:** Beth has a traditional IRA with a balance of $100,000, consisting only of deductible contributions and earnings. She has no other IRA. She distributes the entire $100,000 directly to a charity. Ordinarily, the entire amount would be included in Beth's income in the year of distribution. Accordingly, the entire amount is eligible for qualified charitable distribution treatment. Beth will not report the distribution as income, nor will she take the amount into account for charitable deduction purposes.

IRAs with nondeductible contributions. Distributions of nondeductible contributions from a traditional IRA are not includible in income and, therefore, are not eligible for qualified charitable distribution treatment. Ordinarily, if a taxpayer has nondeductible contributions in any of his or her IRAs, a proportionate amount of the IRA distribution is treated as nontaxable. However, a special ordering rule applies to separate taxable distributions from nontaxable IRA distributions for charitable distribution purposes. Under that rule, a distribution is treated first as income up to the aggregate amount that would otherwise be includible in gross income if the aggregate balance of all IRAs having the same owners were distributed during the same year. Proper adjustments are to be made respecting subsequent distributions to reflect the qualified charitable distribution (Code Sec. 408(d)(8)(D), as added by the Pension Act).

> **Example:** Jose has a traditional IRA with a balance of $100,000. He has no other IRA. Of that amount, $80,000 represents deductible contributions and earnings, and $20,000 represents nondeductible contributions. Suppose Jose distributes $80,000 from the IRA directly to a charity. Ordinarily, 20 percent ($20,000 / $100,000) of the $80,000 distribution (i.e., $16,000) would be treated as a nontaxable return of nondeductible contributions. However, under operation of the special rule, all $80,000 is treated as includible in income. For purposes of subsequent distributions, $20,000 of IRA will be treated as nondeductible contributions.

> **Practical Analysis:** Conrad Teitell of Cummings & Lockwood, Stamford, Connecticut, observes that the new income-tax-free rollover from an IRA to most public charities is a boon for generous individuals and the charities. Using an IRA rollover to make a charitable gift can often be more advantageous than traditional methods of making charitable gifts. And, of course, it will be a Brobdingnagian—huge—source of additional funds for charities.
>
> Quickly stated, for 2006 and 2007 an individual age 70 or older can make direct charitable gifts from an IRA of up to $100,000 per year to qualified charities (specified soon) and not have to report the IRA distribution as taxable income on his

NEW LAW EXPLAINED

or her federal income tax return. However, there is no charitable deduction for the distribution (that would be biting the apple twice).

Here are some tax windfalls followed by some pitfalls.

Some windfalls:

- Donors can make charitable gifts from IRAs to satisfy the annual minimum distribution requirement (according to the JCT's Technical Explanation (JCX-38-06)).
- The approximately two thirds of taxpayers who take the standard deduction — and thus can't deduct their charitable gifts — can now get the equivalent of a deduction by making gifts directly from their IRAs to qualified charities. Not being taxed on income is the equivalent of a deduction.
- Itemizers who bump into the adjusted gross income ceilings on deductibility of charitable gifts can use distributions from IRAs to make additional gifts. And since they aren't taxable on the distributions, they have the equivalent of additional charitable deductions.
- The two percent in 2006 and 2007 "haircut" rule (formerly three percent) is avoided. Thus donors with adjusted gross income above $150,500 ($75,250 if married filing separately) won't have the tax benefit of their gifts whittled down if the gifts are made from the donors' IRAs to qualified charities (rather than making a "traditional" gift directly to a charity).

  If a donor's state income tax law doesn't allow charitable deductions, making the gift from the donor's IRA to the charity will be the equivalent of a state income tax charitable deduction if the distribution from the IRA to the charity isn't subject to state income tax. Caution. State laws differ so check out all the ramifications in your state.

Some pitfalls:

- To be qualified, donee charities must be public charities described in Code Sec. 170(b)(1)(A). This rules out distributions to private foundations. Query. Would a distribution from a conduit (passthrough) foundation be deemed a distribution to a charity described in Code Sec. 170(b)(1)(A)?
- Important exception. IRA distributions to supporting organizations and donor advised funds are ineligible donees even though they are public charities.
- The entire IRA distribution must go to the charity with no *quid pro quo* for the donor — *e.g.*, a rubber chicken dinner.
- Unlike earlier bills passed by the House and Senate, but not enacted, a distribution from an IRA to fund a charitable remainder trust or gift annuity is not tax-free to the donor.
- To avoid the donor's being taxable on the distribution, it should be directly from the IRA to the charity — not from the IRA to the donor and then to the charity.
- The rollover must be from an IRA and not other type of retirement plan. However, a two step in often possible: roll over tax free from the other type of pension plan into an IRA; and then the IRA makes the distribution directly to the charity.

NEW LAW EXPLAINED

Reminder. The current and continuing laws allow tax-free (no-income-in-respect-of-a-decedent) distributions to charities at death for both outright and life-income gifts. There is no ceiling, nor limitation on the types of charitable donees. Thus distributions to private foundations and public charities (including supporting organizations and donor advised funds) qualify. To avoid IRD concerns, the gift must be properly structured.

Conclusion. This IRA/charitable rollover legislation has been sought by charities for over two decades. It isn't the whole loaf (no rollover for life-income gifts, a $100,000 cap, limitation on qualified donee charities and a two-year sunset). Yet, it's a great start and millions upon millions of additional funds will, I believe, flow to our nation's charities. And, I'll bet you a copy of the Code and the Regs that you and your clients will soon be receiving communications from myriad charities heralding the new IRA/ charitable rollover.

▶ **Effective date.** The provision applies to distributions made in tax years beginning after December 31, 2005 (Act Sec. 1201(c)(1) of the Pension Protection Act of 2006).

Law source: Law at ¶5055. Committee Report at ¶11,110.

— Act Sec. 1201(a) of the Pension Protection Act of 2006, adding Code Sec. 408(d);

— Act Sec. 1201(c)(1), providing the effective date.

Reporter references: For further information, consult the following CCH reporters.

— Standard Federal Tax Reporter, 2006FED ¶11,620.01, ¶18,922.03 and ¶18,922.0326

— Tax Research Consultant, INDIV: 51,250, RETIRE: 66,502 and RETIRE: 66,758

— Federal Tax Guide, 2006FTG ¶6575, ¶11,445 and ¶11,460

¶1110 Charitable Contributions of Clothing and Household Items

SUMMARY OF NEW LAW

Deductions for charitable contributions of clothing or household items are limited to items in good used condition or better. Also, the IRS by regulation may deny charitable deductions for clothing or household items of minimal value. An exception exists for single items if the claimed deduction exceeds $500 in value and a qualified appraisal is included with the tax return.

BACKGROUND

Taxpayers who itemize deductions generally may claim a deduction for qualifying charitable contributions (Code Sec. 170). Although the amount of the deduction allowable with respect to contributions of property may vary depending on the type of contributed property, the type of donee, and the taxpayer's income, the amount of

BACKGROUND

the charitable deduction associated with charitable contributions of noncash property is generally the property's fair market value on the date of contribution. The amount of a deduction for a contribution of tangible personal property that is used by the donee in a manner unrelated to the donee's exempt purpose is the fair market value of the item, reduced by the amount of gain, which generally results in a deduction equal to the donor's basis in the item. Clothing and household items are included in this category. However, since the value of clothing and household items is generally lower at the time of the contribution than the donor's basis, donors usually deduct the fair market value of the items, regardless of whether the property is used for exempt purposes by the donee.

A donor claiming a charitable contribution deduction must maintain reliable written records regarding the contribution. For contributions of property, the donor must obtain a receipt from the donee. The receipt should include information such as the name of the donee organization, the date and location of the contribution, and a detailed description of the property contributed (Reg. § 1.170A-13(a)). If obtaining a receipt is impracticable, a donor must maintain reliable written information regarding the contribution, such as the type and value of the property (Reg. § 1.170A-13(b)). Charitable contributions of property of $250 or more must be substantiated by obtaining a contemporaneous written acknowledgment from the donee which contains a description of the property contributed, whether the donor received any goods or services in consideration for the contribution, and the good faith estimate of value of any such goods or services (Code Sec. 170(f)(8)). If the deduction claimed for noncash contributions exceeds $500, the taxpayer must generally attach a completed Form 8283, Noncash Charitable Contributions, to the tax return for the year in which the deduction is claimed (Code Sec. 170(f)(11)). Donors who claim a deduction of more than $5,000 must obtain a qualified appraisal and attach an appraisal summary to the tax return. For deductions exceeding $500,000, a qualified appraisal must be attached to the return.

NEW LAW EXPLAINED

Limitations on deductions for charitable contributions of clothing or household items.—A deduction under Code Sec. 170 for the charitable contribution of a clothing or household item by an individual, partnership or corporation will only be permitted if the item is in good used condition or better (Code Sec. 170(f)(16)(A), as added by the Pension Protection Act of 2006). By regulation, the IRS can deny a deduction for the contribution of a clothing or household item that has minimal monetary value (Code Sec. 170(f)(16)(B), as added by the Pension Act). However, these restrictions do not apply if:

(1) a deduction of more than $500 is claimed for the single clothing or household item, and

(2) the taxpayer includes a qualified appraisal with respect to the item with the tax return on which the deduction is claimed (Code Sec. 170(f)(16)(C), as added by the Pension Act).

NEW LAW EXPLAINED

Comment: According to the Joint Committee on Taxation (JCT), the IRS statistics for the amount claimed as deductions for clothing and household items in 2003 exceeded $9 billion. The JCT expects the IRS, consistent with the goals of improving tax administration, to assiduously exercise its authority to disallow a deduction for some items of low value and ensure that donated clothing and households items are of meaningful use to charitable organizations (Joint Committee on Taxation, Technical Explanation of the Pension Protection Act of 2006 (JCX-38-06), citing Internal Revenue Service, Statistics of Income Division, *Individual Noncash Charitable Contributions*, 2003, Figure A (Spring 2006)).

In the case of a partnership or S corporation making such contributions, these restrictions apply at the entity level, and the deduction is denied at the partner or shareholder level (Code Sec. 170(f)(16)(E), as added by the Pension Act).

"Household items" include furniture, furnishings, electronics, appliances, linens, and other similar items (Code Sec. 170(f)(16)(D)(i), as added by the Pension Act). The term does not include food, paintings, antiques, other objects of art, jewelry, gems, or collections (Code Sec. 170(f)(16)(D)(ii), as added by the Pension Act).

Practical Analysis: Barnaby Zall, of Weinberg & Jacobs, LLP, Rockville, Maryland, points out that this provision reflects the IRS's and Congress's concern that persons are abusing the clothing and household deduction provisions, which total $9 billion a year. One interesting development which may influence this concern is the proliferation of personal deduction software programs, such as those which compare descriptions of donated items to values captured from major online auction houses, such as E-Bay. This provision implicitly permits continued use of such software, but requires the Treasury and the IRS to review the situation in future years.

► **Effective date.** The provision applies to contributions made after August 17, 2006 (Act Sec. 1216(b) of the Pension Protection Act of 2006).

Law source: Law at ¶5020. Committee Report at ¶11,240.

— Act Sec. 1216(a) of the Pension Protection Act of 2006, adding Code Sec. 170(f)(16);

— Act Sec. 1216(b), providing the effective date.

Reporter references: For further information, consult the following CCH reporters.

— Standard Federal Tax Reporter, 2006FED ¶11,620.01 and ¶11,660.024

— Tax Research Consultant, INDIV: 51,152

— Federal Tax Guide, 2006FTG ¶6587 and ¶6597

¶1115 Value of Fractional Interest in Tangible Personal Property Determined for Charitable Deduction

SUMMARY OF NEW LAW

The amount of the charitable deduction for additional contributions of fractional interests in tangible personal property is the value of the initial fractional contribution or the value on the additional contribution date, whichever is less. Any deduction will be recaptured and an additional tax imposed if the property is not entirely contributed to the donee, substantial physical possession is not taken by the donee, or the property is not used by the donee for exempt purposes, within a certain timeframe.

BACKGROUND

Generally, a contribution of a partial interest in property to a qualified charitable organization, that is, a contribution of less than the donor's entire interest, does not qualify for the income (Code Sec. 170(f)(3)(A)), estate (Code Sec. 2055(e)(2)), or gift (Code Sec. 2522(c)(2)) tax charitable deductions. A contribution of a partial interest in trust does qualify for the charitable deduction provided that the trust is either a charitable remainder trust in which the charity receives the remainder of the property after the payment of an annuity or unitrust amount to a noncharitable beneficiary, a charitable lead trust in which the charity receives the right to receive the payment of an annuity or unitrust amount for a certain term, or a pooled income fund. In addition, if a donor transfers an undivided portion of his or her entire interest in property, a deduction is allowable. For purposes of the charitable deduction, an undivided portion is a fraction or percentage of each and every substantial interest and right that the donor owns in the property for the entire time that the donor owns the property. A gift of the right, as a tenant in common along with the donor, to the possession, dominion, and control of the property to a qualified charity for a portion of each year appropriate to its interest in the property is treated as a gift of an undivided portion and a deduction is allowable (Reg. § 1.170A-7(b)(1)).

Example: Lorraine Larson, owner of an apartment complex, transfers the right to receive income from the property for a term of 10 years to a qualified charity. Larson will not receive a charitable deduction. However, if Larson only owns an income interest in the property for a term of 10 years, a contribution of that interest will qualify for the deduction because the gift consists of her entire interest. Also, if Larson transfers 20 percent of her income interest for a 10-year period, a deduction is allowable because the gift is of a percentage of her entire interest that extends over the term of her interest. But what if Larson transfers a 20-percent tenancy-in-common interest to the charity that entitles the charity to the possession, dominion and control of her income interest for 20 percent of the year? Under Reg. § 1.170A-7(b)(1), Larson may claim a charitable deduction.

BACKGROUND

As a general rule, a gift of tangible personal property, such as a work of art, will not qualify for the income, estate, or gift tax charitable deduction if the charity's possession, use, or enjoyment of the property begins at a future time. Such a future interest occurs when a donor reserves or retains for himself or herself or a close family relative the right to use, possess, or enjoy the property resulting in the charity's interest taking effect on a future date. A deduction may only be allowable after the intervening interests have terminated or the intervening interest is held by a party other than the donor or close family relative (Reg. § 1.170A-5(a)(1)). However, the donor of an undivided present interest in property may claim a deduction when the gift is made even though the donee's initial possession may not begin immediately (Reg. § 1.170A-5(a)(2)). For example, if a donor makes a gift of an undivided fractional one-quarter interest in a painting that entitles the charitable donee to possession during three months of each year, the donor may claim a deduction upon the donee's receipt of the deed of gift provided that the donee's initial possession is not deferred for longer than one year. An undivided interest will be treated as a present rather than a future interest for purposes of the charitable deduction if the donee has the *right* to possession, not necessarily actual, physical possession, of the property during each year following the donation. In addition, a deduction is allowable in each subsequent year that an additional gift is made of an undivided interest in the same property (*J. Winokur*, 90 TC 733, Dec. 44,712, Acq. 1989-1 CB 1).

NEW LAW EXPLAINED

Consistent valuation required for contributions of fractional interests made in the same property.—The amount of the income, estate, or gift tax charitable deduction for additional contributions of tangible personal property in which the donor has previously made a contribution of an undivided fractional interest (an initial fractional contribution) is equal to the lesser of (1) the value of the property used to determine the charitable deduction for the initial fractional contribution; or (2) the fair market value of the property at the time of the additional contribution (Code Secs. 170(o)(2), 2055(g)(1), and 2522(e)(2), as added by the Pension Protection Act of 2006).

> **Example 1:** Julie Downer contributed a 25-percent interest in a sculpture to the local art museum in June 2007 that entitles the museum to possession of the sculpture for three months of each year. A charitable deduction of up to $250,000 is allowable based on the sculpture's fair market value of $1,000,000 at the time of contribution. Downer makes similar contributions of a 25-percent interest in both June of 2008 and June of 2009, giving the museum an undivided 75% interest in the sculpture. If at the time of the additional gifts, the value of the property has risen to $1,125,000 in 2008 and $1,150,000 in 2009, the charitable deduction for both 2008 and 2009 will be determined using the lower value at the time of the initial fractional contribution.

NEW LAW EXPLAINED

Compliance Pointer: Contributions made before August 17, 2006, the date of enactment of the Pension Act, will not be treated as initial fractional contributions; rather, the first contribution after August 17, 2006, is considered the initial fractional contribution, regardless of whether the donor made earlier contributions in the same item of tangible personal property (Joint Committee on Taxation, Technical Explanation of the Pension Protection Act of 2006 (JCX-38-06)).

Recapture of deduction for income and gift tax purposes and addition to tax. Any income tax or gift tax charitable deduction allowed for contributions of undivided interests in tangible personal property will be recaptured (with interest) if:

(1) the donor fails to contribute all of the remaining interests in the property to the donee (or another charitable organization if the donee is no longer in existence) before the earlier of the tenth anniversary of the initial fractional contribution or the donor's date of death; or

(2) the donee fails to take substantial physical possession of the property or fails to use the property in a manner related to the donee's exempt purpose during the period beginning after the initial fractional contribution and ending on the earlier of the tenth anniversary of the initial contribution or the donor's date of death (Code Secs. 170(o)(3) and 2522(e)(3), as added by the Pension Act).

Example 2: If, for the three-month period in Example 1, the museum included the sculpture in an art exhibit it sponsored in 2010, Downer would still be entitled to a charitable deduction because the related-use requirement would be satisfied.

Further, if an income tax or a gift tax charitable deduction is recaptured, as described above, an additional tax will be imposed in an amount equal to 10 percent of the amount recaptured (Code Sec. 170(o)(3)(B) and Code Sec. 2522(e)(3)(B), as added by the Pension Act).

Example 3: If, however, in Example 1, the museum fails to take possession of the sculpture for the three-month period by 2009, then Downer must repay the charitable deductions she claimed in 2006, 2007 and 2008, plus interest and an additional tax equal to 10% of the recaptured amount.

Comment: In a prior version of this provision (S. 2020), the IRS was granted authority to issue regulations preventing circumvention of the recapture rule in cases where a fractional interest is first transferred to a third party controlled by the donor and then to the charity (Joint Committee on Taxation, Description of the Chairman's Modification to the Provisions of the "Tax Relief Act of 2005" (JCX-77-05)). However, the provision, as enacted, did not address this potential for abuse.

NEW LAW EXPLAINED

Denial of income and gift tax deduction in certain cases. Both the income tax and gift tax charitable deduction will be allowed for the contribution of a fractional interest in tangible personal property only if the taxpayer, or the taxpayer and the donee, hold all interests in the property immediately before the contribution (Code Secs. 170(o)(1)(A) and 2522(e)(1)(A), as added by the Pension Act). Thus, if a person other than the taxpayer or donee holds an interest in the property, the deduction will be denied. However, the Secretary of Treasury may provide exceptions to this rule if each such holder makes a proportional contribution of his or her interest in the property (Code Secs. 170(o)(1)(B) and 2522(e)(1)(B), as added by the Pension Act).

▶ **Effective date.** These provisions apply to contributions, bequests, and gifts made after August 17, 2006 (Act Sec. 1218(d) of the Pension Protection Act of 2006).

Law source: Law at ¶5020, ¶5205, and ¶5210. Committee Report at ¶11,260.

— Act Sec. 1218(a) of the Pension Protection Act of 2006, redesignating Code Sec. 170(o) as (p) and adding new Code Sec. 170(o);

— Act Sec. 1218(b), redesignating Code Sec. 2055(g) as (h) and adding new Code Sec. 2055(g);

— Act Sec. 1218(c), redesignating Code Sec. 2522(e) as (f) and adding new Code Sec. 2522(e);

— Act Sec. 1218(d), providing the effective date.

Reporter references: For further information, consult the following CCH reporters.

— Standard Federal Tax Reporter, 2006FED ¶11.660.01, ¶11.660.03 and ¶11.660.021

— Tax Research Consultant, INDIV: 51,354

— Federal Tax Guide, 2006FTG ¶6629

— Federal Estate and Gift Tax Reporter, ¶6380.03 and ¶11,513.01

¶1120 Charitable Contributions of Taxidermy Property

SUMMARY OF NEW LAW

For the charitable contribution of taxidermy property, long-term capital gains that would have been realized if the property had been sold by the taxpayer at its fair market value are excluded from charitable contribution deductions. A donor's basis in taxidermy property is limited to direct costs paid or incurred by the donor for preparing, stuffing, or mounting the property.

BACKGROUND

As a general rule, taxpayers may deduct the amount of cash and the fair market value of property contributed to an organization described in Code Sec. 501(c)(3) or to a federal, state, or local governmental entity. As an added incentive, such deductions

BACKGROUND

may also be taken for federal estate and gift tax purposes within certain limitations. Within the realm of 501(c)(3) organizations, more generous deduction rules generally apply to charitable contributions made to public charities than those made to private foundations. On the other hand, contributions to nongovernmental, non-charitable tax-exempt organizations are generally not deductible, although such organizations may claim a federal income tax exemption with respect to such donations.

The amount of the deduction allowable for a tax year with respect to a charitable contribution of property is determined based on the type of property contributed, the type of charitable organization to which the property is contributed, and the income of the taxpayer. A deduction for charitable contributions of capital gain property is generally allowed in the amount of the fair market value of the contributed property on the date of contribution. A taxpayer may deduct the fair market value of taxidermy property if the property is used to further the donee's exempt purpose. However, if the property is not used to further the donee's exempt or governmental purpose, the deductible amount is the fair market value *reduced by the amount of any gain*. This generally results in a deduction equal to the taxpayer's basis (Code Sec. 170(e)(1)(B)).

NEW LAW EXPLAINED

Charitable deductions for contributed taxidermy property limited.—For taxidermy property that is contributed by the person who prepared, stuffed, or mounted the property or by a person who paid or incurred the cost of preparation, stuffing, or mounting, the amount of the claimed charitable contribution must be reduced by the amount of gain that would have been long-term capital gain if the property had been sold by the taxpayer at its fair market value. Fair market value is determined at the time the contribution is made (Code Sec. 170(e)(1)(B)(iv), as added by the Pension Protection Act of 2006). Thus, the amount that will be allowed as a deduction for a charitable contribution of taxidermy property is the lesser of the donor's basis in the property or the fair market value of the property.

Basis determination. If taxidermy property is contributed and a charitable contribution deduction is claimed by the person who prepared, stuffed, or mounted the property, or by any person who paid or incurred the cost of such preparation, stuffing, or mounting, only the cost of preparing, stuffing, or mounting the taxidermy property may be included in calculating the basis of the property (Code Sec. 170(f)(15)(A), as added by the Pension Act).

> **Comment:** This special rule for determining the donor's basis in taxidermy property is intended to include only the *direct* costs of preparing, stuffing or mounting that are paid or incurred by the donor claiming the charitable contribution deduction. Indirect costs, such as transportation, equipment or other costs related to hunting or killing the animal may not be included in the donor's basis, and are, therefore, not deductible (Joint Committee on Taxation, Technical Explanation of the Pension Protection Act of 2006 (JCX-38-06)).

NEW LAW EXPLAINED

Comment: Reducing the abuse of the lenient deduction rules for such charitable contributions was a primary motivation for amending the rules. According to the Humane Society of the United States, the charitable contribution deduction rules for taxidermy property were being exploited by trophy hunters; the rules allowed them to unfairly deduct the costs of their hunting excursions. The modified rules do not allow the donor to claim a deduction for such expenses and also eliminate the deduction for value based on the rarity of the animal.

"Taxidermy property" defined. The term "taxidermy property" means any work of art which—

(1) is the reproduction or preservation of an animal, in whole or in part,

(2) is prepared, stuffed, or mounted for purposes of recreating one or more characteristics of such animal, and

(3) contains a part of the body of the dead animal (Code Sec. 170(f)(15)(B), as added by the Pension Act).

▶ **Effective date.** The provision applies to contributions made after July 25, 2006 (Act Sec. 1214(c) of the Pension Protection Act of 2006).

Law source: Law at ¶5020. Committee Report at ¶11,220.

— Act Sec. 1214(a) of the Pension Protection Act of 2006, adding Code Sec. 170(e)(1)(B)(iv);

— Act Sec. 1214(b), adding Code Sec. 170(f)(15);

— Act Sec. 1214(c), providing the effective date.

Reporter references: For further information, consult the following CCH reporters.

— Standard Federal Tax Reporter, 2006FED ¶11,660.01 and ¶11,660.021

— Tax Research Consultant, IRS: 51,152

¶1125 Charitable Contributions of Real Property for Conservation Purposes

SUMMARY OF NEW LAW

Individual donors are allowed to take charitable deductions of up to 50 percent of their contribution base for contributions of qualified conservation real property; this limit is raised to 100 percent of the contribution base for farmers and ranchers. Corporate donors that qualify as farmers or ranchers may also be able to claim a conservation charitable deduction of up to 100 percent of taxable income, subject to special rules for determining taxable income for this purpose.

BACKGROUND

An individual's deduction for charitable contributions made in the tax year is limited to a percentage of the individual donor's contribution base. This contribution base is

BACKGROUND

equal to the donor's adjusted taxable income, computed without regard to the charitable deduction or to any net operating loss (NOL) carryback under Code Sec. 172. For donations of cash to public charities and organizations described in Code Sec. 170(b)(1)(A), a donor's contribution base is 50 percent, the maximum allowed for charitable contributions by an individual.

An individual's contribution base for cash donations to private foundations and certain organizations not qualifying under Code Sec. 170(b)(1)(A) is generally 30 percent (Code Sec. 170(b)(1)(B)(i)). An individual may carry forward contributions that exceed the percentage limitations of his or her adjusted gross income for a tax year. The excess may be deducted in each of the five succeeding years until it is used up (Code Sec. 170(d)(1)).

Capital gain property. A deduction for charitable donations of capital gain appreciated real property to a "maximum deduction" charitable organization under Code Sec. 170(b)(1)(A) is generally limited to 30 percent of the donor's contribution base, if the donor uses the property's fair market value to compute the deduction. If, however, the taxpayer elects to limit the charitable deduction to the basis in the appreciated property, contributions of capital gain property to a "maximum deduction" organization are deductible up to 50 percent of the donor's contribution base (Code Sec. 170(b)(1)(C)(iii)). No such election is available for capital gain property contributed to organizations other than "maximum deduction" organizations. Deductions for contributions of capital gain property to semi-public or private charities are limited to 20 percent of the donor's contribution base (Code Sec. 170(b)(1)(D)(i)(I)).

> **Comment:** So-called "maximum deduction" charitable organizations include: public charities, private operating foundations, private nonoperating foundations that distribute contributions within two and one-half months of year's end, and private nonoperating foundations that maintain a common fund.

Corporations. No matter how large its charitable contributions, a corporation's charitable contribution deduction for the tax year generally may not exceed 10 percent of its taxable income, computed without regard to the charitable contributions deduction, the dividends received deduction, the public utility dividends paid deduction, the manufacturing deduction, and without deducting any NOL or capital loss carrybacks (Code Sec. 170(b)(2)). If a corporation contributes more than it is allowed to deduct in a given year, it can carry over the excess contributions to the five succeeding tax years. In the succeeding years, the deduction allowed for new contributions plus carryovers from earlier years is limited to 10 percent of taxable income (as described above), with new contributions deducted first. If carryovers from two years are deductible in any year, the oldest is deducted first. Any contributions that have not been deducted by the end of the five-year period are lost (Code Sec. 170(d)(2)).

Qualified conservation contributions. Although a charitable deduction is not usually allowed for a contribution of a partial interest in property, an exception is made for a qualified conservation contribution (Code Sec. 170(f)(3)(B)(iii)). A qualified conservation contribution is a contribution of a qualified real property interest, to a qualified organization, exclusively for conservation purposes (Code Sec. 170(h)(1)(C)). The contribution may consist of all of the owner's interest in the property, except for certain mineral interests, or it may be limited to an easement or restrictive covenant

BACKGROUND

that prevents the development of land, safeguarding its natural character (Code Sec. 170(h)(2)(A)-(C)). A qualified organization includes certain governmental units, public charities that meet certain public support tests, and certain supporting organizations (Code Sec. 170(h)(3)). A qualified conservation purpose includes the preservation of land areas for outdoor recreation, the protection of a natural habitat, the preservation of open space, including farmland and forest land for the scenic enjoyment of the general public, or the preservation of an historic structure (Code Sec. 170(h)(4)(i)-(iv)).

NEW LAW EXPLAINED

Donations of real property for conservation purposes encouraged.—The rules for deducting charitable contributions are modified to encourage taxpayers to make donations of capital gain real property to qualified charities for conservation purposes. In addition to these new rules, which apply to individual taxpayers generally, other provisions seek to encourage both corporate and individual farmers and ranchers to make charitable donations of real property for conservation purposes.

Provisions applying to individual taxpayers generally. An individual donor's qualified conservation contribution to a "maximum deduction" organization (under Code Sec. 170(b)(1)(A)) will be allowed to the extent that the aggregate of such contributions does not exceed the excess of 50 percent of the donor's contribution base over the amount of all other charitable contributions allowable under Code Sec. 170(b)(1) (Code Sec. 170(b)(1)(E)(i), as added by the Pension Protection Act of 2006). Thus, the donor making a conservation contribution will have a contribution base of 50 percent, rather than a base of 20 or 30 percent (which would otherwise generally be applicable to donations of capital gain appreciated property). If the value of the donor's contribution exceeds the 50-percent contribution base, the excess may be carried forward for 15 years (Code Sec. 170(b)(1)(E)(ii), as added by the Pension Act). The contribution base and the carry forward rules for donations of appreciated capital gain real property are to be applied separately from those that apply to other donations under Code Sec. 170(b)(1)(A), (B), (C) or (D) (Code Sec. 170(b)(1)(E)(iii), as added by the Pension Act). The Joint Committee Report clarifies that the 50-percent contribution base limitation applies first to contributions other than qualified conservation contributions and then to qualified conservation contributions (Joint Committee on Taxation, Technical Explanation of the Pension Protection Act of 2006 (JCX-38-06)).

Example: John Walker has a contribution base of $100,000 for 2006, and makes a qualified conservation contribution of property having a fair market value of $80,000. Walker also makes $60,000 worth of other charitable contributions subject to the 50 percent limitation. He is allowed a deduction of $50,000 for 2006 for the other contributions (50 percent of the $100,000 contribution base), and is allowed a carryforward of the excess $10,000 for up to five years. No current deduction for 2006 is allowed for the qualified conservation contribu-

NEW LAW EXPLAINED

> tion, but the full \$80,000 qualified conservation contribution may be carried forward up to 15 years.

The above provisions are effective for charitable contributions of individuals made in tax years beginning after December 31, 2005, and before January 1, 2008 (Code Sec. 170(b)(1)(E)(vi), as added by the Pension Act).

Contributions of property used in agriculture or livestock production. If an individual is a "qualified farmer or rancher" (defined below) for the tax year in which a charitable contribution of capital gain real estate is made, the individual's contribution base for that year is raised from 50 percent to 100 percent (Code Sec. 170(b)(1)(E)(iv)(I), as added by the Pension Act). For the 100 percent limitation to apply, the qualified real property interest must include a restriction that the property remain generally available for agriculture or livestock production. The Joint Committee Explanation clarifies that there is no requirement that the property be used in agriculture or livestock production, only that the property remain available for such purposes (Joint Committee on Taxation, Technical Explanation of the Pension Protection Act of 2006 (JCX-38-06)). Furthermore, this additional condition only applies to contributions made after August 17, 2006, the date of enactment (Code Sec. 170(b)(1)(E)(iv)(II), as added by the Pension Act).

A "qualified farmer or rancher" is an individual whose gross income from the trade or business of farming is greater than 50 percent of the taxpayer's gross income for the tax year. The term "farming" includes: cultivation of the soil, raising agricultural or horticultural commodities and preparing those commodities for market, as well as the planting, cultivating, caring for, cutting down and preparing trees for market (Code Sec. 2032A(e)(5)). The 100 percent contribution base limitation applies first to contributions other than qualified conservation contributions (to the extent allowable under other percentage limitations), and then to qualified conservation contributions (Code Sec. 170(b)(1)(E)(iv)(II), as added by the Pension Act).

> **Practical Analysis:** Barnaby Zall, of Weinberg & Jacobs, LLP, Rockville, Maryland, states that because conservation easements are not subject to the "partial interest" rule, this provision offers expanded deductions and carry-forward benefits for a variety of contributions of interests or easements for conservation purposes. The expanded benefits are available only to farmers and ranchers, including non–publicly traded corporations. A key restriction is that the land "be available" for continued agricultural use, but there is no requirement that the land actually be used for that purpose. Thus, the land could be used for recreation or public education, so long as it might also be used for ranching, for example. For certain farmers and ranchers, the availability of these deductions and carry-forwards could provide an alternative to developing agricultural land.

Provisions benefiting corporate farmers and ranchers. A corporation that during the contribution year is a "qualified farmer or rancher" is allowed to deduct charitable contributions of conservation property to "maximum deduction" charitable organiza-

NEW LAW EXPLAINED

tions described in Code Sec. 170(b)(1)(A), to the extent that the aggregate of such contributions is not more than the excess of the corporation's taxable income over the amount of allowable charitable deductions (which cannot exceed 10 percent of its taxable income) (Code Sec. 170(b)(2)(A) and (B), as added by the Pension Act). In order for a corporation to be a qualified farmer or rancher, it must meet the same requirements that an individual is subject to, *plus,* the corporation's stock must not be readily tradable on an established securities market at any time during the contribution year, *and,* in the case of contributions made after August 17, 2006, the date of enactment, the contributed property that is used in agriculture or livestock production (or available for such production) must be subject to a restriction that it remain available for such production (Code Sec. 170(b)(2)(B)(i)(I) and (II), as added by the Pension Act).

Like the deduction for charitable contributions for conservation purposes made by individual farmers and ranchers, corporate farmers and ranchers may carry forward any excess charitable conservation contributions for up to 15 years, subject to the 100-percent limitation. Also, the special provisions for corporate conservation contributions are effective for charitable contributions of capital gain real estate made in tax years beginning after December 31, 2005, and before January 1, 2008 (Code Sec. 170(b)(2)(B)(iii), as added by the Pension Act).

Taxable income. For purposes of the charitable deduction of a corporate farmer or rancher donating capital gain real estate for conservation purposes, "taxable income" is computed without regard to: the charitable contributions deduction, the dividends received deduction, the public utility dividends paid deduction, the manufacturing deduction, and without deducting any NOL or capital loss carrybacks (Code Sec. 170(b)(2)(C), as added by the Pension Act).

Facade easement contributions. The Pension Act also places new restrictions on facade easement contributions; see ¶ 1130.

▶ **Effective date.** The provision applies to contributions made in tax years beginning after December 31, 2005 (Act Sec. 1206(c) of the Pension Protection Act of 2006).

Law source: Law at ¶5020 and ¶5180. Committee Report at ¶11,160.

— Act Sec. 1206(a)(1) of the Pension Protection Act of 2006, redesignating Code Sec. 170(b)(1)(E) and (F) as (F) and (G), respectively, and adding new Code Sec. 170(b)(1)(E);

— Act Sec. 1206(a)(2), amending Code Sec. 170(b)(2);

— Act Sec. 1206(b)(1), amending Code Sec. 170(d)(2);

— Act Sec. 1206(b)(2), amending Code Sec. 545(b)(2);

— Act Sec. 1206(c), providing the effective date.

Reporter references: For further information, consult the following CCH reporters.

— Standard Federal Tax Reporter, 2006FED ¶11,660.022, ¶11,660.045 and ¶11,710.01

— Tax Research Consultant, INDIV: 51,256 and INDIV: 51,364

— Federal Tax Guide, 2006FTG ¶6595 and ¶6631

¶1130 Charitable Contributions of Facade Easements on Certified Historic Structures

SUMMARY OF NEW LAW

The requirements for claiming a charitable deduction for the contribution of a facade easement for a building in a registered historic district are tightened. Deductions are disallowed completely for personal residences, unless the residence is listed individually in the National Register of Historic Places. The deduction is reduced to take account of the rehabilitation credit.

BACKGROUND

A contribution of a partial interest in property is generally not eligible for a charitable deduction. There are exceptions, and one of them is for qualified conservation contributions (Code Sec. 170(f)(3)(B)(iii)). A qualified conservation contribution is a contribution of a qualified real property interest, to a qualified organization, exclusively for conservation purposes (Code Sec. 170(h)(1)). Qualified real property includes a restriction granted in perpetuity on the use of real property (Code Sec. 170(h)(2)(C)). A facade easement may qualify as a qualified conservation contribution (e.g., IRS Letter Ruling 199933029 (May 24, 1999)). A qualified organization includes certain governmental units, public charities that meet certain public support tests, and certain supporting organizations (Code Sec. 170(h)(3)). A qualified conservation purpose includes preservation of a certified historic structure (Code Sec. 170(h)(4)(A)(iv)).

Facade easements. A facade easement is a legal agreement that can be used to preserve the architectural, historic and cultural features of the facade of a building or structure. Under the agreement, the historic property owner transfers the right to change the facade to a qualified organization. The terms of the easement might permit subsequent property owners to make alterations to the facade if the owner obtains consent from the qualified organization that holds the easement.

Valuation. If the value of the donated property is $5,000 or more, a donor must attach a qualified appraisal of the property to qualify for the charitable deduction (Code Sec. 170(f)(11)(C)).

Certified historic structures. There are two ways buildings, structures, and land can qualify for certified historic structure status. First, they can be individually listed with the National Register of Historic Places (National Register). Second, they can be located in a registered historic district and be certified by the National Park Service (operating out of the Interior Department) as being of historic significance to the district (Code Sec. 170(h)(4)(B)). A structure for these purposes means any structure, whether or not it is depreciable (Reg. § 1.170A-14(d)(5)(iii)), which means that certified historic structures can include personal residences. A registered historic district means (1) any district listed in the National Register, or (2) a district designated under a statute of the appropriate state or local government certified by the Secretary of the Interior as containing the appropriate criteria, and Secretary of the Interior

BACKGROUND

certification that the district meets substantially all of the requirements for listing a district in the National Register (Code Secs. 47(c)(3)(B), 170(h)(4)(B)).

NEW LAW EXPLAINED

New restrictions on facade easement contributions.—For contributions made after July 25, 2006, a donated easement for buildings located in registered historic districts must contain certain new restrictions in order for the taxpayer to qualify for a deduction. The easement must preserve the entire exterior of the building including the front, sides, rear, and height of the building. It must also prohibit any change to the exterior of the building that is inconsistent with the historical character of the exterior (Code Sec. 170(h) (4) (B) (i), as added by the Pension Protection Act of 2006).

> **Comment:** Note that the new stricter requirements do not apply to all historic structures. Structures that are certified historic structures because they are listed in the National Register of Historic Places (National Register) are not subject to the new requirements. The stricter requirements apply to historic structures that are certified historic structures because they are in a registered historic district and are certified by the National Park Service as being of historic significance to the district.

> **Comment:** The less stringent standard for structures listed in the National Register may reflect the fact that a government official must nominate a structure to the National Register. In contrast, the owner initiates the procedure for certification that a structure is of historic significance to the registered historic district in which it is located. To get listed on the National Register, the structure must be nominated by the state historic preservation officer of the state in which the property is located, by the federal preservation officer for properties under federal ownership or control, or by the tribal preservation officer if the property is on tribal lands. To get certification from the National Park Service that a structure is of historic significance to the registered historic district in which it is located, the owner applies to the National Park Service.

Written agreement. Under the new rules for buildings in registered historic districts, the donor and donee must enter into a written agreement certifying that:

(1) the donee is a qualified organization with a purpose of environmental protection, land conservation, open space preservation, or historic preservation; and

(2) the donee has the resources to manage and enforce the restriction and a commitment to do so (Code Sec. 170(h)(4)(B)(ii), as added by the Pension Act).

> **Comment:** Congress is trying to address the problem of donee organizations that are too flexible in allowing facade modifications.

Documentation to be included with taxpayer's return. The taxpayer's return for the tax year of the contribution (if made in a tax year beginning after August 17, 2006, the date of enactment of the Pension Act) must include:

(1) a qualified appraisal of the qualified property interest,

(2) photographs of the entire exterior of the building, and

NEW LAW EXPLAINED

(3) a description of all restrictions on the development of the building (Code Sec. 170(h)(4)(B)(iii), as added by the Pension Act).

Comment: An appraisal is ordinarily required only if the value of the donated property is $5,000 or more (Code Sec. 170(f)(11)(C)). The change here eliminates the $5,000 threshold amount for valuation of facade easements.

Disallowance of deduction for structures (including personal residences) and land in historic districts. For contributions made after August 17, 2006, the date of enactment of the Pension Act, the new law narrows the definition of certified historic structures. Under the old law, buildings, structures (including nondepreciable structures such as personal residences), and land areas could be certified historic structures if they were either in the National Register, or located in a registered historic district. Now, certified historic structures are defined more narrowly to include:

(1) buildings if located in a registered historic district; and

(2) structures, buildings, or land areas if in the National Register (Code Sec. 170(h)(4)(C), as redesignated and amended by the Pension Act).

Comment: The key change here is the elimination of structures and land from the items eligible for the deduction if eligibility turns on location in a registered historic district as opposed to inclusion in the National Register. A structure for these purposes had been viewed broadly to include any structure, whether or not depreciable (Reg. § 1.170A-14(d)(5)(iii)), which would include personal residences.

$500 filing fee. To obtain a deduction for contributions of facade easements for buildings located in registered historic districts, the taxpayer must submit a $500 fee with the taxpayer's return, for the tax year of the contribution, if the deduction is in excess of $10,000. The fee is to be used for the enforcement of the qualified conservation contribution rule (Code Sec. 170(f)(13), added by the Pension Act). The fee requirement applies to contributions made 180 days after August 17, 2006, the date of enactment (Act Sec. 1231(e)(3) of the Pension Act).

Reduced deduction for portion of the qualified conservation contribution attributable to the rehabilitation credit. The amount of a qualified conservation contribution is reduced by an amount that bears the same ratio to the fair market value of the contribution as the sum of the rehabilitation credits allowed to the taxpayer under Code Sec. 47 for the five preceding tax years with respect to any building which is part of such contribution, bears to the fair market value of the building on the date of the contribution (Code Sec. 170(f)(14), as added by the Pension Act). This reduced deduction provision applies to contributions made after August 17, 2006, the date of enactment of the Pension Act (Act Sec. 1231(e)(2) of the Pension Act).

Example: Marge owns a building at 123 Main St. that has a fair market value of $200,000 at the time she makes a qualified conservation contribution. The qualified conservation contribution has a fair market value of $50,000. Marge has claimed $20,000 in rehabilitation credits under Code Sec. 47 on the building over the last five years. The amount of her qualified contribution deduction is

NEW LAW EXPLAINED

reduced by $5,000, the amount which, when divided by the value of the contribution ($50,000), results in the same ratio (1 to 10) as the sum of the rehabilitation credits ($20,000) does when it is divided by the fair market value of the building ($200,000).

Practical Analysis: Barnaby Zall, of Weinberg & Jacobs, LLP, Rockville, Maryland, observes that in Act Secs. 1213 through 1219, as in Act Secs. 1204, 1205 and 1206, Congress is generally limiting deductions to the value of a contribution as useable or used by the recipient organization. These limitations are the result of specific media coverage of abuses, and represent an attempt to restrict regulation to abuses. Compare that precision with the *stale potato chip* enhanced deduction under Act Sec. 1202, the organizational micro-management of Act Sec. 1220's new crackdown on credit counseling organizations, or the elaborate definitional and taxation requirements for donor-advised funds and supporting organizations in Act Secs. 1226 through 1241.

▶ **Effective date.** The rules for buildings in registered historic districts apply to contributions made after July 25, 2006 (Act Sec. 1213(e)(1) of the Pension Protection Act of 2006). The disallowance of the deduction for structures and land, and the reduction for the rehabilitation credit, apply to contributions made after August 17, 2006 (Act Sec. 1213(e)(2) of the Pension Act). The filing fee shall apply to contributions made 180 days after August 17, 2006, the date of enactment (Act Sec. 1213(e)(3) of the Pension Act).

Law source: Law at ¶5020. Committee Report at ¶11,210.

— Act Sec. 1213(a) of the Pension Protection Act of 2006), redesignating Code Sec. 170(h)(4)(B) as (C), and adding new Code Sec. 170(h)(4)(B);

— Act Sec. 1213(b), amending redesignated Code Sec. 170(h)(4)(C);

— Act Sec. 1213(c), adding Code Sec. 170(f)(13);

— Act Sec. 1213(d), adding Code Sec. 170(f)(14);

— Act Sec. 1213(e), providing the effective date.

Reporter references: For further information, consult the following CCH reporters.

— Standard Federal Tax Reporter, 2006FED ¶11,710.01 and ¶11,710.025

— Tax Research Consultant, INDIV: 51,364

— Federal Tax Guide, 2006FTG ¶6631

¶1135 Basis Adjustment to Stock of S Corporation Making Charitable Contribution

SUMMARY OF NEW LAW

The amount of a shareholder's basis reduction in the stock of an S corporation by reason of a charitable contribution made by the corporation equals the shareholder's pro rata share of the adjusted basis of the contributed property.

BACKGROUND

If an S corporation contributes money or other property to a charity, each shareholder takes into account the shareholder's pro rata share of the contribution in determining its own income tax liability (Code Sec. 1366(a)(1)(A)). The shareholder's basis in the stock of the S corporation is reduced by the amount of the charitable contribution, which is generally the fair market value of the contributed property, that flows through to the shareholder (Code Sec. 1367(a)(2)(B)).

NEW LAW EXPLAINED

Modified rule for basis reduction in stock of S corporation making charitable contribution of property.—The amount of a shareholder's basis reduction in the stock of an S corporation by reason of a charitable contribution made by the corporation equals the shareholder's pro rata share of the adjusted basis of the contributed property (Code Sec. 1367(a)(2), as amended by the Pension Protection Act of 2006).

> **Caution Note:** This amendment **does not apply** to contributions made in tax years beginning after December 31, 2007 (Code Sec. 1367(a)(2), as amended by the Pension Act). The prior rule requiring reduction in the stock basis by the fair market value of the contributed property will, therefore, apply to such contributions.
>
> **Comment:** This provision has the effect of preserving the intended benefit of the fair market value deduction for the contributed appreciated property without causing the shareholders to recognize gain or a reduced loss that is attributable to the appreciation upon a subsequent sale of the stock.

Example: An S corporation with one individual shareholder makes a charitable contribution of stock with a basis of $4,000 and a fair market value of $10,000. The shareholder will be treated as having made a $10,000 charitable contribution (or a lesser amount if the special rules of Code Sec. 170(e) apply), and will reduce the basis of the S corporation stock by $4,000 (provided that his basis in the S corporation stock prior to the reduction is at least $4,000) (see Joint Committee on Taxation, Technical Explanation of the Pension Protection Act of 2006 (JCX-38-06)).

NEW LAW EXPLAINED

Comment: The IRS has reached a similar result in the case of charitable contributions made by a partnership (see Rev. Rul. 96-11, 1996-1 C.B. 140).

▶ **Effective date.** The provision applies to contributions made in tax years beginning after December 31, 2005 (Act Sec. 1203(b) of the Pension Protection Act of 2006).

Law source: Law at ¶5200. Committee Report at ¶11,130.

— Act Sec. 1203(a) of the Pension Protection Act of 2006, amending Code Sec. 1367(a)(2);

— Act Sec. 1203(b), providing the effective date.

Reporter references: For further information, consult the following CCH reporters.

— Standard Federal Tax Reporter, 2006FED ¶11,660.01, ¶31,084.028 and ¶32,101.01

— Tax Research Consultant, SCORP: 402.05

— Federal Tax Guide, 2006FTG ¶13,210

¶1140 Charitable Contributions of Food Inventory

SUMMARY OF NEW LAW

The enhanced deduction for charitable donations of food inventory by noncorporate taxpayers that are engaged in a trade or business is extended two years and is set to expire for contributions made after December 31, 2007.

BACKGROUND

Generally, the amount of the deduction for gifts of property to charity is measured by the fair market value of the property on the date of contribution. However, for both individuals and corporations, the amount of the deduction for a charitable contribution of ordinary income property, such as inventory, is usually limited to the donor's basis in the donated property (Code Sec. 170(e)). Under an exception to this general rule, many C corporations can claim an enhanced deduction for inventory that is contributed to a qualified charity or private operating foundation for use in the care of the ill, the needy or infants. The amount of the enhanced deduction equals the lesser of (1) the donated item's basis plus one-half of the item's unrealized appreciation, or (2) two times the donated item's basis.

A corporation's charitable contribution deduction for a year is limited to 10 percent of the corporation's taxable income, computed with certain adjustments (Code Sec. 170(b)(2)). A corporation can carry over charitable contributions that exceed 10 percent of its taxable income for a five-year period (Code Sec. 170(d)(2)).

In response to the hurricane disasters along the Gulf coast in 2005, Congress, under the Katrina Emergency Tax Relief Act of 2005 (P.L. 109-73), temporarily modified the

BACKGROUND

rules relating to charitable contributions in several ways. Under one provision, noncorporate, as well as corporate, taxpayers could claim an enhanced deduction for donations of food inventory during a temporary period (Code Sec. 170(e)(3)(C)). The food inventory had to consist of items fit for human consumption and had to be contributed to a qualified charity or private operating foundation for use in the care of the ill, the needy or infants.

Any taxpayer engaged in one or more trades or businesses that made qualified donations of food inventories on or after August 28, 2005, and before January 1, 2006, was eligible to claim the enhanced deduction for such donations (Code Sec. 170(e)(3)(C)(i) and (iv)). It did not matter whether the trade or business was conducted in corporate form. Thus, partnerships, S corporations and sole proprietorships could claim the enhanced deduction for donations of food inventory during the temporary period.

The amount of the enhanced deduction for donated food inventory equaled the lesser of (1) the donated item's basis plus one-half of the item's appreciation, or (2) two times the donated item's basis. For food items, the amount of appreciation was the amount of gain that would be realized if the donated food item was sold at fair market value on the date of the gift (Announcement 2005-84, I.R.B. 2005-48, 1064).

For a taxpayer other than a C corporation, the total deduction for donations of food inventory during the tax year was limited to a maximum of 10 percent of the taxpayer's net income from those trades or businesses making such donations (Code Sec. 170(e)(3)(C)(ii)). Therefore, if a taxpayer owned three businesses and only one made a qualified contribution of food inventory, the taxpayer's deduction for such donation was limited to a maximum of 10 percent of his or her income from the business making the donation, not 10 percent of his or her total income (Joint Committee on Taxation, Technical Explanation of the Katrina Emergency Tax Relief Act of 2005 (JCX-69-05).

Donated food inventories had to consist of "apparently wholesome food" (Code Sec. 170(e)(3)(C)(i)(II). "Apparently wholesome food" was defined as food intended for human consumption that meets all quality and labeling standards imposed by federal, state, and local laws and regulations even though the food may not be readily marketable due to appearance, age, freshness, grade, size, surplus, or other conditions (Section 22(b)(2) of the Bill Emerson Good Samaritan Food Donation Act (42 U.S.C. 1791(b)(2)); Code Sec. 170(e)(3)(C)(iii)).

NEW LAW EXPLAINED

Enhanced charitable deduction for food donations extended.—The enhanced deduction for charitable donations of food inventory by any taxpayer, whether or not a C corporation, engaged in a trade or business is extended for another two years. Thus, taxpayers may claim the enhanced deduction for food inventory donations contributed on or after August 28, 2005, and on or before December 31, 2007 (Code Sec. 170(e)(3)(C)(iv), as amended by the Pension Protection Act of 2006).

NEW LAW EXPLAINED

Practical Analysis: Barnaby Zall, of Weinberg & Jacobs, LLP, Rockville, Maryland, calls Act Sec. 1202 the "stale potato chip" deduction. This provision extends for two years a provision in the Hurricane Katrina relief legislation to encourage the contribution of "wholesome" food to charities. This prevision presents a valuable planning opportunity for businesses, since there is no requirement that the donor actually be in the food business to obtain the enhanced deduction. There is no limitation on where the food may be used, and the food may be outdated if it is otherwise "wholesome." Though possibly helpful to some social service charities, the influential Panel on the Nonprofit Sector didn't recommend it as a necessary reform or incentive. It limits the use of the enhanced deduction by businesses other than C corporations, probably to limit the provision's use as a tax shelter. This is part of a trend in incentives to boost certain contributions. One may expect more in-kind donations of food as sponsorship for charitable events.

Comment: The Joint Committee on Taxation, Technical Explanation of the Pension Protection Act of 2006 (JCX-38-06) emphasized that, as under the Katrina Relief Act, for taxpayers other than C corporations, the total deduction for contributions of food inventory is limited to a maximum of 10 percent of the taxpayer's net income from all sole proprietorships, S corporations, partnerships or other non-C corporations making such donations.

Example: Ann Kelsey is the sole proprietor of a grocery store and also is a partner in a real estate business. The grocery store business makes a qualified charitable contribution of food inventory. Kelsey's deduction for the food donation is limited to 10 percent of the net income from the grocery store business. Since the real estate business did not make a qualified contribution of food inventory, her share of income from the real estate business is not taken into account in computing the limit on the charitable deduction.

Comment: The Joint Committee pointed out that the 10-percent limitation has no effect on the operation of otherwise applicable percentage limitations. Thus, if 10 percent of a sole proprietor's net income from the business exceeded 50 percent of the proprietor's contribution base (adjusted gross income computed without regard to charitable contributions and net operating loss carrybacks), the available deduction for the tax year, with respect to contributions of food inventory to public charities, would be 50 percent of the proprietor's contribution base. Under the law, such contributions may be carried over if they exceed the 50-percent limitation. However, contributions of food inventory by the sole proprietor that exceed the 10-percent limitation but not the 50-percent limitation could not be carried over.

▶ **Effective date.** This provision is effective for contributions made after December 31, 2005 (Act Sec. 1202(b)(2) of the Pension Protection Act of 2006). However, the provision is set to terminate so that it will not apply to contributions made after December 31, 2007 (Act Sec. 1202(b)(1) of the Pension Act).

NEW LAW EXPLAINED

Law source: Law at ¶5020. Committee Report at ¶11,120.

- Act Sec. 1202(a) of the Pension Protection Act of 2006, amending Code Sec. 170(e)(3)(C)(iv);
- Act Sec. 1202(b), providing the effective date.

Reporter references: For further information, consult the following CCH reporters.

- Standard Federal Tax Reporter, 2006FED ¶11,620.059, ¶11,660.027 and ¶11,680.031
- Tax Research Consultant, CCORP: 9,354
- Federal Tax Guide, 2006FTG ¶6589

¶1145 Charitable Contributions of Book Inventory

SUMMARY OF NEW LAW

The enhanced deduction for corporate donations of book inventory is extended for another two years and is set to expire for contributions made after December 31, 2007.

BACKGROUND

Generally, the amount of the deduction for gifts of property to charity is measured by the fair market value of the property on the date of contribution. However, for both individuals and corporations, the amount of the deduction for a charitable contribution of ordinary income property, such as inventory, is usually limited to the donor's basis in the donated property (Code Sec. 170(e)). Under an exception to this general rule, many C corporations can claim an enhanced deduction for inventory that is contributed to a qualified charity or private operating foundation for use in the care of the ill, the needy or infants. The amount of the enhanced deduction equals the lesser of (1) the donated item's basis plus one-half of the item's appreciation, or (2) two times the donated item's basis. A second exception allows a C corporation to claim a similar enhanced deduction for certain ordinary income property that is donated to a college, university, or tax-exempt scientific organization for use in research (Code Sec. 170(e)(4)).

In response to the hurricane disasters along the Gulf coast in 2005, Congress, under the Katrina Emergency Tax Relief Act of 2005 (P.L. 109-73), temporarily modified the rules relating to charitable contributions in several ways. One provision essentially took the present-law enhanced deduction for donations of inventory to a qualified charity or private operating foundation and extended it to qualified donations of book inventory to public schools (Code Sec. 170(e)(3)(D)). The enhanced deduction generally increased the deductible amount from the donated inventory item's basis to the lesser of (1) the donated inventory item's basis plus one-half of the item's appreciation, or (2) two times the donated inventory item's basis.

BACKGROUND

Any corporation (other than an S corporation) that made a qualified book contribution on or after August 28, 2005, and before January 1, 2006, was eligible for the enhanced deduction for such donation (Code Sec. 170(e)(3)(D)(iv)). A qualified book contribution meant a charitable contribution of books to a public school that provided elementary or secondary education (kindergarten through grade 12) and maintained a regular faculty and curriculum with a regularly enrolled student body (Code Sec. 170(e)(3)(D)(ii)). In addition, the donee educational institution was required to certify in writing that:

(1) the books were suitable in terms of currency, content and quality for use in the school's educational programs, and

(2) the school would actually use the books in its educational programs (Code Sec. 170(e)(3)(D)(iii)).

NEW LAW EXPLAINED

Enhanced charitable deduction for book donations extended.—The enhanced deduction for corporate donations of book inventory (i.e., qualified book contributions) is extended for another two years. Thus, C corporations may claim a charitable deduction for book inventory donations contributed on or after August 28, 2005, and on or before December 31, 2007 (Code Sec. 170(e)(3)(D)(iv), as amended by the Pension Protection Act of 2006).

Practical Analysis: Barnaby Zall, of Weinberg & Jacobs, LLP, Rockville, Maryland, points out that, in contrast to the "stale potato chip" enhanced deduction, this extension of another Katrina deduction booster requires the donee organization to certify that the donation is suitable for its needs and will be used in its programs. Note that this provision also does not include the planning opportunities for non–C corporation business entities that are contained in the stale potato chip enhanced deduction.

▶ **Effective date.** This provision is effective for contributions made after December 31, 2005 (Act Sec. 1204(b)(2) of the Pension Protection Act of 2006). However, the provision is set to terminate so that it will not apply to contributions made after December 31, 2007 (Act Sec. 1204(b)(1) of the Pension Act).

Law source: Law at ¶5020. Committee Report at ¶11,140.

— Act Sec. 1204(a) of the Pension Protection Act of 2006, amending Code Sec. 170(e)(3)(D)(iv);

— Act Sec. 1204(b), providing the effective date.

Reporter references: For further information, consult the following CCH reporters.

— Standard Federal Tax Reporter, 2006FED ¶11,620.059 and ¶11,680.031

— Tax Research Consultant, CCORP: 9,354

— Federal Tax Guide, 2006FTG ¶6589

¶1150 Recapture of Tax Benefit on Donated Property Not Used for Exempt Purpose

SUMMARY OF NEW LAW

If a charitable organization receives appreciated tangible personal property as a charitable contribution and disposes of the property within three years of receiving it, the donor may not derive any tax benefit beyond a deduction in the amount of the property's basis. This rule will not apply if the donee provides a certification that the property was intended to be used or was put to a use related to the donee's exempt purpose.

BACKGROUND

Generally, if appreciated property whose sale would have resulted in long-term capital gain (capital gain property) is contributed to a charitable organization, the amount of the charitable deduction allowed is its fair market value on the date of contribution (Code Sec. 170(e)(1)(A)). An exception is made for certain contributions of property, including tangible personal property if its use by the donee is unrelated to the purpose or function that earned the donee a Code Sec. 501 exemption (Code Sec. 170(e)(1)(B)(i)). In that case, the charitable deduction for the contributed property is reduced by the amount of any long-term capital gain that would have been realized if the property had been sold (Code Sec. 170(e)(1)(B)). Essentially, the deduction is limited in that case to the taxpayer's basis in the donated capital gain property.

If the donee organization sells, exchanges or otherwise disposes of donated property with a claimed value of more than $5,000 (other than publicly traded securities) within two years of receiving the contribution, the donee must file Form 8282, Donee Information Return (Sale, Exchange or Other Disposition of Donated Property) with the IRS. In addition, the donee must provide the donor with a copy of that information return (Code Sec. 6050L(a)(1)).

NEW LAW EXPLAINED

Recapture of charitable deduction absent certification of exempt use if property is disposed of within three years.—If a donee organization disposes of "applicable property" within three years of when the property was contributed and the donee hasn't made a "certification," then the donor's tax benefit is subject to adjustment. Thus, the tax benefit of contributing appreciated capital gain property, rather than being a deduction equal to its fair market value at the time of contribution, may be limited to the taxpayer's basis in the donated property (Code Sec. 170(e)(7)(C), as added by the Pension Protection Act of 2006).

"Applicable property" is charitable deduction property (as defined in Code Sec. 6050L(a)(2)(A)) that is appreciated tangible personal property identified by the donee

NEW LAW EXPLAINED

organization as related to the purpose or function constituting the donee's basis for tax exemption and for which a deduction in excess of the donor's basis is claimed. Charitable deduction property means any contributed property (other than publicly traded securities) for which a deduction was claimed if the claimed value of the donated property exceeds $5,000.

Where there is no "certification" and a donee organization sells, exchanges, or otherwise disposes of the applicable property in the donor's tax year in which the contribution was made, the donor's deduction is limited to basis and not fair market value. If the donated property is disposed of in a subsequent year within three years of the contribution, the donor must include as ordinary income for the year in which the disposition occurs an amount equal to the excess (if any) of (i) the amount of the deduction previously claimed by the donor as a charitable contribution with respect to such property, over (ii) the donor's basis in such property at the time of the contribution (Code Sec. 170(e)(1)(B)(i), as amended by the Pension Act, and Code Sec. 170(e)(7), as added by the Pension Act).

The limitation on the deduction in the first tax year or the recapture of the tax benefit in a subsequent year does not apply if the donee organization makes a certification to the IRS. A certification is a written statement signed under penalty of perjury by an officer of the donee organization which either—

(1) certifies that the property's use was related to the donee's exempt purpose or function and describes how the property was used and how such use furthered the exempt purpose or function; or

(2) states the intended use of the property by the donee at the time of the contribution and certifies that such intended use became impossible or infeasible to implement.

(Code Sec. 170(e)(7)(D), as added by the Pension Act).

> **Comment:** In essence, the claim that donated property was put to an exempt use now triggers much more scrutiny if the donee does not retain that property at least until the end of the third year after the property was donated.

> **Comment:** These new rules do not apply to any contribution of exempt use property with a claimed value of $5,000 or less.

Reporting requirements. The information return requirements that apply to a disposition of contributed property by a charitable organization are extended to dispositions made within three years after receipt (increased from two years) (Code Sec. 6050L(a)(1), as amended by the Pension Act). Also, the information that must be reported now includes a description of the donee's use of the property and a statement indicating whether its use was related to its exempt purpose or function (Code Sec. 6050L(a)(1)(F) and (G), as added by the Pension Act). Finally, if the donee does indicate such a related use, it must include with the return the certification discussed above.

Penalty. Also in conjunction with the new recapture rules discussed above, Congress has added a penalty for the fraudulent identification of exempt use property (Code Sec. 6720B, as added by the Pension Act). In addition to any criminal penalty, any person who identifies applicable property (as defined in Code Sec. 170(e)(7)(C)) as

NEW LAW EXPLAINED

having a use that is related to the donee's exempt purpose or function and who knows that the contributed property is not intended for such a use is subject to a $10,000 penalty.

> **Comment:** Other penalties may apply, such as the penalty for aiding and abetting the understatement of tax liability.

▶ **Effective date.** The provisions providing for the recapture of charitable deductions under Code Sec. 170(e) apply to contributions after September 1, 2006 (Act Sec. 1215(d)(1) of the Pension Protection Act of 2006). The amendments to the reporting provisions of Code Sec. 6050L(a) apply to returns filed after September 1, 2006 (Act Sec. 1215(d)(2) of the Pension Act). The addition of the penalty provision under Code Sec. 6720B applies to identifications made after August 17, 2006 (Act Sec. 1215(d)(3) of the Pension Act).

Law source: Law at ¶5020, ¶5340 and ¶5415. Committee Report at ¶11,230.

— Act Sec. 1215(a)(1) of the Pension Protection Act of 2006, amending Code Sec. 170(e)(1)(B)(i);

— Act Sec. 1215(a)(2), adding Code Sec. 170(e)(7);

— Act Sec. 1215(b), amending Code Sec. 6050L(a)(1);

— Act Sec. 1215(c), adding Code Sec. 6720B;

— Act Sec. 1215(d), providing the effective date.

Reporter references: For further information, consult the following CCH reporters.

— Standard Federal Tax Reporter, 2006FED ¶11,660.045 and ¶36,262.01

— Tax Research Consultant, INDIV: 51,150 and INDIV: 51,206

— Federal Tax Guide, 2006FTG ¶6587

¶1155 Allocation Rules for Qualified Gratuitous Transfers of Employer Securities

SUMMARY OF NEW LAW

The annual limitation for allocating transfers of employer securities from a charitable remainder trust to an employee stock ownership plan is determined on the basis of fair market value of securities when allocated to participants, after first allocating all other annual additions for the limitation year.

BACKGROUND

If a charitable remainder trust holds qualified employer securities transferred from a decedent dying before January 1, 1999, the securities transferred to an employee stock ownership plan (ESOP) in a "qualified gratuitous transfer" will qualify for the estate tax charitable deduction. The deduction is limited to the extent of the present value of the remainder interest in the trust. A transfer of qualified securities is treated as a

BACKGROUND

"qualified gratuitous transfer" if (1) the securities are transferred to the trust by a decedent dying before January 1, 1999, (2) the decedent and his or her family members owned no more than 10 percent of the value of the outstanding stock at the time of the transfer to the ESOP, (3) the ESOP owns at least 60 percent of the value of the stock after the transfer, (4) the ESOP was in existence on August 1, 1996, (5) the employer agrees to pay an excise tax on certain prohibited distributions and allocations of the securities, and (6) no income tax deduction is allowable for the transfer.

In addition to the requirements listed above, an ESOP must meet certain antidiscrimination, administrative and distribution and allocation requirements. The ESOP is required to first allocate annual additions for the limitation year (i.e., employer contributions, employee contributions and forfeitures) up to the limitation under Code Sec. 415(c), which limits the annual contribution and benefit amounts that may be provided under a qualified plan. The transferred employer securities are held in a suspense account and then allocated each year up to a special limit. For tax years after December 31, 2001, a qualified gratuitous transfer is generally limited to the lesser of $30,000 or 25 percent of the employee's compensation (Code Sec. 664(g)(7)). The $30,000 amount is also adjusted for inflation with a base period of October 1, 1993, and quarterly adjustments.

NEW LAW EXPLAINED

Method clarified for allocating employer securities in qualified gratuitous transfer.—The method for allocating qualified employer securities to an ESOP in a qualified gratuitous transfer is clarified. The fair market value of the qualified employer securities at the time the securities are allocated to participants is used to allocate the securities up to the participant's Code Sec. 664(g)(7) limitation (i.e., the lesser of $30,000 or 25 percent of compensation) (Code Sec. 664(g)(3)(E), as amended by the Pension Act).

▶ **Effective date.** The provision is effective on August 17, 2006 (Act Sec. 868(b) of the Pension Protection Act of 2006).

Law source: Law at ¶5185. Committee Report at ¶10,940.

— Act Sec. 868(a) of the Pension Protection Act of 2006, amending Code Sec. 664(g)(3)(E);

— Act Sec. 868(b), providing the effective date.

Reporter references: For further information, consult the following CCH reporters.

— Standard Federal Tax Reporter, 2006FED ¶24,468.053 and ¶24,468.07

— Tax Research Consultant, RETIRE: 75,650

— Federal Tax Guide, 2006FTG ¶19,045

— Federal Estate and Gift Tax Reporter, ¶17,075.05

DONOR ADVISED FUNDS

¶1160 Taxes on Sponsoring Organizations of Donor Advised Funds on Taxable Distributions

SUMMARY OF NEW LAW

Donor advised funds are now defined in the Code. A 20-percent tax is imposed on sponsoring organizations on taxable distributions from donor advised funds. A five-percent tax is imposed on fund management agreeing to the taxable distribution.

BACKGROUND

Some charitable organizations (including community foundations) establish accounts to which donors may contribute and thereafter provide nonbinding advice or recommendations with regard to distributions from the fund or the investment of assets in the fund. The accounts are commonly referred to as "donor advised funds." Donors who make contributions to charities for maintenance in a donor advised fund generally claim a charitable contribution deduction at the time of the contribution. Although sponsoring charities frequently permit donors (or other persons appointed by donors) to provide nonbinding recommendations concerning the distribution or investment of assets in a donor advised fund, sponsoring charities generally must have legal ownership and control of the assets following the contribution.

In recent years, a number of financial institutions have formed charitable corporations for the principal purpose of offering donor advised funds, sometimes referred to as "commercial" donor advised funds. In addition, some established charities have begun operating donor advised funds in addition to their primary activities. The IRS has recognized several organizations that sponsor donor advised funds, including "commercial" donor advised funds, as Code Sec. 501(c)(3) public charities. The term "donor advised fund" is not defined by statute or in regulations.

Donor advised funds have become an important means of stimulating charitable contributions from a broad range of donors who wish to make significant philanthropic gifts, either for immediate benefit to a charity or charities, or for long-term support of ongoing or emergent community needs (Panel on the Nonprofit Sector's *Report to Congress and the Nonprofit Sector on Governance, Transparency, and Accountability* (June 2005)).

The maximum itemized deduction (50 percent of a taxpayer's contribution base) is allowable if it consists of contributions to entities such as churches, publicly supported charitable, religious, educational, scientific, or literary organizations, private operating foundations, and Code Sec. 509(a)(3) supporting organizations. Type I supporting organizations are "operated, supervised, or controlled by" the supported organization. Type II supporting organizations are "supervised or controlled in connection with" the supported organization. Type III supporting organizations are "operated in connection with" the supported organization.

BACKGROUND

Generally, an excise tax is imposed on any undistributed income of a private foundation (Code Sec. 4942). An additional excise tax will be imposed on any income remaining undistributed at the end of the tax period. The income of the foundation must be distributed as qualifying distributions. Private foundations must make qualifying distributions to the extent of their minimum investment return for the year. However, a foundation may set aside funds for periods up to 60 months for certain major projects (Code Sec. 4942(g)(2)). Excess qualifying distributions may be carried forward for a period of five tax years immediately following the tax year in which the excess was created.

"Expenditure responsibility" means that a foundation exerts all reasonable efforts and establishes adequate procedures: (1) to see that the grant is spent only for the purpose for which it is made; (2) to obtain full and complete reports from the grantee organization on how the funds are spent; and (3) to make full and detailed reports on the expenditures to the IRS (Code Sec. 4945(h)).

NEW LAW EXPLAINED

Tax imposed on sponsoring organizations of donor advised funds for taxable distributions.—A 20-percent tax is imposed on any sponsoring organization for taxable distributions (Code Sec. 4966(a), as added by the Pension Protection Act of 2006). A five-percent tax is imposed on the agreement of any fund manager to the making of a distribution if the manager knows it is a taxable distribution. For any taxable distribution, there is a $10,000 limit on the amount of tax imposed on management.

Practical Analysis: Barnaby Zall, of Weinberg & Jacobs, LLP, Rockville, Maryland, notes that beginning in the 1980s, the amount of assets held in these types of organizations skyrocketed into the billions. These organizations are not private foundations and thus are not subject to the more stringent private foundation management rules, but in many ways, they are similar to private foundations, holding funds and distributing them to other charitable organizations. These new rules are designed to encourage the immediate re-granting of such funds, rather than the long-term warehousing of funds, and to reduce the ability of individual donors to achieve a personal benefit (as opposed to charitable benefit). For example, the intermediate sanctions rules of Code Sec. 4958are applied to certain distributions from donor-advised funds, even though the donor must affirm in writing that the fund has absolute legal control over the funds; this is an extension of the traditional Code Sec. 4958concept of "indirect" benefit. The language of these sections, however, is sweeping in scope, so that professionals who advise donors to use donor-advised funds, for example, should also explain the new reporting and donation rules. As a planning matter, although the provision does not say so, by referencing Code Sec. 4958concepts, the provision may provide the same type of "safe harbor" protection for donors through professional opinions of counsel, as are available to organizations under existing rules.

NEW LAW EXPLAINED

"Taxable distribution" defined. A taxable distribution is any distribution from a donor advised fund:

(1) to any natural person, or

(2) to any other person if:

- the distribution is for any purpose other than one specified in Code Sec. 170(c)(2)(B) (religious, charitable, scientific, literary, education, etc.), or
- the sponsoring organization does not exercise Code Sec. 4945(h) expenditure responsibility (Code Sec. 4966(c), as added by the Pension Act).

Taxable distributions do not include distributions from a donor advised fund to:

(1) any Code Sec. 170(b)(1)(A) organization (churches, educational organizations, medical or health-care organizations, etc.), other than a disqualified supporting organization,

(2) the sponsoring organization of the donor advised fund, or

(3) any other donor advised fund.

"Donor advised fund" defined. A donor advised fund is a fund or account :

(1) that is separately identified by reference to contributions of a donor or donors;

(2) that is owned and controlled by a sponsoring organization; and

(3) with respect to which a donor (or any person appointed or designated by the donor (a "donor advisor") has, or reasonably expects to have, advisory privileges with respect to the distribution or investment of amounts held in the fund or account by reason of the donor's status as a donor (Code Sec. 4966(d)(2), as added by the Pension Act).

A distinct fund or account of a sponsoring organization does not meet the first prong of the definition unless the fund or account refers to contributions of a donor or donors, such as by naming the fund after a donor, or by treating a fund on the books of the sponsoring organization as attributable to funds contributed by a specific donor or donors. Although a sponsoring organization's general fund is a "fund or account," the fund will not, as a general matter, be treated as a donor advised fund because the general funds of an organization typically are not separately identified by reference to contributions of a specific donor or donors; rather, contributions are pooled anonymously within the general fund. Similarly, a fund or account of a sponsoring organization that is distinct from the organization's general fund and that pools contributions of multiple donors generally will not meet the first prong of the definition unless the contributions of specific donors are in some manner tracked and accounted for within the fund. Accordingly, if a sponsoring organization establishes a fund dedicated to the relief of poverty within a specific community, or a scholarship fund, and the fund attracts contributions from several donors but does not separately identify or refer to contributions of a donor or donors, the fund is not a donor advised fund even if a donor has advisory privileges with respect to the fund. However, a fund or account may not avoid treatment as a donor advised fund even though there is no formal recognition of

NEW LAW EXPLAINED

such separate contributions on the books of the sponsoring organization if the fund or account operates as if contributions of a donor or donors are separately identified (Joint Committee on Taxation, Technical Explanation of the Pension Protection Act of 2006 (JCX-38-06)).

The second prong of the definition provides that the fund be owned and controlled by a sponsoring organization. To the extent that a donor or person other than the sponsoring organization owns or controls amounts deposited to a sponsoring organization, a fund or account is not a donor advised fund. In cases where a donor retains control of an amount provided to a sponsoring organization, there may not be a completed gift for purposes of the charitable contribution deduction.

The third prong of the definition provides that with respect to a fund or account of a sponsoring organization, a donor or donor advisor has or reasonably expects to have advisory privileges with respect to the distribution or investment of amounts held in the fund or account by reason of a donor's status as a donor. Advisory privileges are distinct from a legal right or obligation. For example, if a donor executes a gift agreement with a sponsoring organization that specifies certain enforceable rights of the donor with respect to a gift, the donor will not be treated as having "advisory privileges" due to such enforceable rights for purposes of the donor advised fund definition.

The term "donor advised fund" does not include a fund or account:

(1) which makes distributions only to a single identified organizations or governmental entity, or

(2) where a donor's or donor advisor's advisory privileges are with respect to which individuals receive grants for travel, study or other similar purposes. These grants should meet the requirements of Code Sec. 4945(g).

The IRS may exempt a fund or account from treatment as a donor advised fund if the fund:

(1) is advised by a committee and not directly or indirectly controlled by the donor or advisor (or any related parties), or

(2) will benefit a single identified charitable purpose (Code Sec. 4966(d)(2)(C), as added by the Pension Act).

A "sponsoring organization" is an organization that:

(1) is described in Code Sec. 170(c) (other than Code Sec. 170(c)(1), and without regard to Code Sec. 170(c)(2)(A));

(2) is not a private foundation as defined in Code Sec. 509(a); and

(3) maintains one or more donor advised funds (Code Sec. 4966(d)(1), as added by the Pension Act).

"Fund manager" defined. A fund manager means, with respect to any sponsoring organization of a donor advised fund:

(1) an officer, director, or trustee of the sponsoring organization (or an individual having similar powers or responsibilities), and

NEW LAW EXPLAINED

(2) with respect to any act (or failure to act), the employees of the sponsoring organization having authority or responsibility with respect to such act (or failure to act) (Code Sec. 4966(d)(3), as added by the Pension Act).

"Disqualified supporting organization" defined. A disqualifying organization means, with respect to any distributions:

(1) any Type III supporting organization (defined in Code Sec. 4943(f)(5)(A)) that is not a functionally integrated Type III supporting organization, and

(2) any Type I and Type II supporting organization or functionally integrated Type III supporting organization if the donor or any person designated by the donor controls a supported organization of the organization or the IRS determines that a distribution to such organization in inappropriate (Code Sec. 4966(d)(4), as added by the Pension Act).

Joint and several liability. If more than one person is liable for the five-percent tax on fund management, all such persons are jointly and severally liable for the entire amount of the tax (Code Sec. 4966(b)(1), as added by the Pension Act).

Abatement. The excise taxes are subject to abatement if it is established that the taxable event was due to reasonable cause and not willful neglect (Code Sec. 4963, as amended by the Pension Act).

▶ **Effective date.** The provision applies to tax years beginning after August 17, 2006 (Act Sec. 1231(c) of the Pension Protection Act of 2006).

Law source: Law at ¶5280 and ¶5285. Committee Report at ¶11,350.

— Act Sec. 1231(a) of the Pension Protection Act of 2006, adding Code Sec. 4966;

— Act Sec. 1231(b), amending Code Sec. 4963;

— Act Sec. 1231(c), providing the effective date.

Reporter references: For further information, consult the following CCH reporter.

— Standard Federal Tax Reporter, 2006FED ¶22,609.01 and ¶22,812.023

¶1165 Taxes on Prohibited Benefits

SUMMARY OF NEW LAW

Excise taxes are imposed on donors, donor advisors and related persons who receive a benefit from a distribution from a donor advised fund.

BACKGROUND

Excise taxes are imposed on excess benefit transactions between disqualified persons and public charities (Code Sec. 4958). An excess benefit transaction generally is a transaction in which an economic benefit is provided by a public charity, directly or

BACKGROUND

indirectly, to or for the use of a disqualified person, if the value of the economic benefit provided exceeds the value of the consideration (including the performance of services) received for providing a benefit.

An excess benefit transaction tax is imposed on the disqualified person and, in certain cases, on the organization managers, but is not imposed on the public charity. An initial tax of 25 percent of the excess benefit amount is imposed on the disqualified person that receives the excess benefit. An additional tax on the disqualified person of 200 percent of the excess benefit applies if the violation is not corrected within a specified period. A tax of 10 percent of the excess benefit is imposed on an organization manager who knowingly participated in the excess benefit transaction, if the manager's participation was willful and not due to reasonable cause, and if the initial tax was imposed on the disqualified person.

Some charitable organizations establish accounts to which donors may contribute and thereafter provide nonbinding advice or recommendations with regard to distributions from the fund or the investment of assets in the fund. These accounts are commonly referred to as "donor advised funds." Donors who make contributions to charities for maintenance in a donor advised fund generally claim a charitable contribution deduction at the time of the contribution. Although sponsoring charities frequently permit donors (or other persons appointed by donors) to provide nonbinding recommendations concerning the distribution or investment of assets in a donor advised fund, sponsoring charities generally must have legal ownership and control of such assets following the contribution. If the sponsoring charity does not have this control (or permits a donor to exercise control over amounts contributed), the donor's contributions may not qualify for a charitable deduction and, in the case of a community foundation, the contribution may be treated as being subject to a material restriction or condition by the donor.

> **Comment:** The Panel on the Nonprofit Sector's *Report to Congress and the Nonprofit Sector on Governance, Transparency, and Accountability* states that "Because the donor retains the right to advise the charity regarding distributions of funds held in a donor advised fund, policymakers have expressed concern that some donors will recommend distributions intended to benefit themselves and their families."

NEW LAW EXPLAINED

Excise taxes imposed on prohibited benefits.—An excise tax is imposed on the advice of certain persons that have a sponsoring organization make a distribution from a donor advised fund that results in the person receiving, directly or indirectly, more than an incidental benefit from the distribution (Code Sec. 4967(a), as added by the Pension Protection Act of 2006). The tax is imposed on any person who recommended the distribution and on the recipient of the benefit. However it is not imposed on investment advisors (see ¶ 1170).

NEW LAW EXPLAINED

Amount of tax. The tax imposed is:

(1) 125 percent of the amount of the benefit on the person who *advised* the distribution or received the benefit as a result of the distribution (Code Sec. 4967(a)(1), as added by the Pension Act)

(2) 10 percent of the benefit on the agreement of any *fund manager* to the making of a distribution, knowing that the distribution would confer an improper benefit, unless the agreement is not willful and is due to reasonable cause (Code Sec. 4967(a)(2), as added by the Pension Act). The tax imposed on fund managers is limited to $10,000.

> **Practical Analysis:** Elizabeth Kingsley of Harmon, Curran, Spielberg & Eisenberg LLP, Washington, D.C., notes that Act Secs. 1231 and 1232 (creating new Code Secs. 4966and 4967to impose taxes on the taxable distributions and excess benefit transactions of donor advised funds ("DAFs")) strike an odd balance. DAFs have been used to avoid the restrictions that accompany private foundation status, so one would expect that an attempt to curb their perceived abuses would bring the treatment of DAFs more in line with that of foundations. In a number of ways this provision disadvantages DAFs significantly more than private foundations: Grants to individuals are *per se* taxable, rather than restricted; grants to Code Sec. 509(a)(2) and (a)(3)public charities require expenditure responsibility, which is not true for foundations; and compensation paid to disqualified persons is considered *per se* an excess benefit. This dichotomy adds another dimension to consider in making plans for charitable giving and adds another layer of complexity to this area of the law.

No additional tax is imposed on any distribution if a tax has already been imposed with respect to the distribution under the excess benefit transaction rules of Code Sec. 4958.

Joint and several liability. If more than one person is liable for the tax, all such persons are jointly and severally liable for the entire amount of the tax (Code Sec. 4967(c)(1), as added by the Pension Act).

Abatement. The excise taxes are subject to abatement if it is established that the taxable event was due to reasonable cause and not to willful neglect (Code Sec. 4963, as amended by the Pension Act).

▶ **Effective date.** The provision applies to tax years beginning after August 17, 2006 (Act Sec. 1231(c) of the Pension Protection Act of 2006).

Law source: Law at ¶5280 and ¶5290. Committee Report at ¶11,350.

— Act Sec. 1231(a) of the Pension Protection Act of 2006, adding Code Sec. 4967;

— Act Sec. 1231(b), amending Code Sec. 4963;

— Act Sec. 1231(c), providing the effective date.

Reporter references: For further information, consult the following CCH reporter.

— Standard Federal Tax Reporter, 2006FED ¶22,609.01 and ¶22,812.023

¶1170 Prohibited Transactions

SUMMARY OF NEW LAW

Disqualified persons, for purposes of the excess benefit transaction taxes, have been extended to include donors to advised funds, advisors to the funds and investment advisors to the funds.

BACKGROUND

An excise tax is imposed on excess benefit transactions between disqualified persons and public charities (Code Sec. 4958). An *excess benefit transaction* generally is a transaction in which an economic benefit is provided by a public charity, directly or indirectly, to or for the use of a disqualified person, if the value of the economic benefit provided exceeds the value of the consideration (including the performance of services) received for providing the benefit.

For purposes of the excess benefit transaction rules, a *disqualified person* is any person in a position to exercise substantial influence over the affairs of the public charity at any time in the five-year period ending on the date of the transaction at issue. Persons holding certain powers, responsibilities, or interests (e.g., officers, directors, or trustees) are considered to be in a position to exercise substantial influence over the affairs of the public charity. A disqualified person also includes certain family members of such a person, and certain entities that satisfy a 35-percent control test with respect to the persons.

An excess benefit transaction tax is imposed on the disqualified person and, in certain cases, on the organization managers, but is not imposed on the public charity.

NEW LAW EXPLAINED

Donors, donor advisors, investment advisors treated as disqualified persons.— Donors, donor advisors, and investment advisors to donor advised funds (and persons related to them) automatically are treated as disqualified persons with respect to the sponsoring organization under the excess benefit transaction rules of Code Sec. 4958 and (Code Sec. 4958(f)(1), as amended by the Pension Protection Act of 2006).

Investment advisor. The term "investment advisor" means, with respect to any Code Sec. 4966(d)(1) sponsoring organization, any person (other than an employee of the sponsoring organization) compensated by the sponsoring organization for managing the investment of, or providing investment advice with respect to, assets maintained in donor advised funds owned by the sponsoring organization (Code Sec. 4958(f)(8), as added by the Pension Act).

Excess benefit transactions. Distributions from a Code Sec. 4966(d)(2) donor advised fund (see ¶ 1160) to a person that, with respect to the fund, is a donor, donor adviser, or a person related to a donor or donor adviser (though not an investment advisor) automatically will be treated as an excess benefit transaction under Code Sec. 4958, with

NEW LAW EXPLAINED

the entire amount paid to the disqualified person being deemed the amount of the excess benefit (Code Sec. 4958(c)(2), as amended by the Pension Act).

An excess benefit transaction includes any distribution to a donor, donor advisor, or a related person, whether in the form of a grant, loan, compensation arrangement, expense reimbursement, or other payment.

Correction. Any amount repaid as a result of correcting an excess benefit transaction will not be held in or credited to any donor advised fund (Code Sec. 4958(f)(6), as amended by the Pension Act).

▶ **Effective date.** The provision applies to transactions occurring after August 17, 2006 (Act Sec. 1232(c) of the Pension Protection Act of 2006).

Law source: Law at ¶5275. Committee Report at ¶11,350.

— Act Sec. 1232(a) of the Pension Protection Act of 2006, adding Code Sec. 4958(f)(1)(D) and (E)and adding Code Sec. 4858(f)(7) and (8);

— Act Sec. 1232(b), redesignating Code Sec. 4958(c)(2) as (3) and adding new Code Sec. 4958(c)(2) and amending Code Sec. 4958(f)(6);

— Act Sec. 1232(c), providing the effective date.

Reporter references: For further information, consult the following CCH reporters.

— Standard Federal Tax Reporter, 2006FED ¶22,604.025 and ¶22,812.021

— Tax Research Consultant, EXEMPT: 6,056.10

— Federal Tax Guide, 2006FTG ¶21,360

¶1175 Excess Business Holdings of Donor Advised Funds

SUMMARY OF NEW LAW

The private foundation excess business holdings rules are now imposed on donor advised funds.

BACKGROUND

The excess business holdings of a foundation are the amount of stock or other interest in a business enterprise that exceeds the permitted holdings. A private foundation is generally permitted to hold up to 20 percent of the voting stock of a corporation, reduced by the percentage of voting stock actually or constructively owned by disqualified persons. There are two exceptions to this rule. First, if one or more third persons, who are not disqualified persons, have effective control of a corporation, the private foundation and all disqualified persons together may own up to 35 percent of the corporation's voting stock. Second, a private foundation is not treated as having excess business holdings in any corporation in which it (together with certain other

BACKGROUND

related private foundations) owns not more than two percent of the voting stock and not more than two percent of the value of all outstanding shares of all classes of stock.

A private foundation is not permitted any holdings in sole proprietorships that are business enterprises unless they were held before May 26, 1969, or acquired by gift or bequest thereafter. For determining the holdings in a business enterprise of either a private foundation or a disqualified person, any stock or other interest owned directly or indirectly by or for a corporation, partnership, estate, or trust is considered owned proportionately by or for its shareholders, partners, or beneficiaries.

NEW LAW EXPLAINED

Excess business holdings rules apply to donor advised funds.—The excess business holdings rules have been extended to apply to donor advised funds (see ¶ 1160) (Code Sec. 4943(e), as added by the Pension Protection Act of 2006). In applying the rules, donor advised funds will be considered private foundations.

A disqualified person, with respect to a donor advised fund and the excess business holding rules, is any person who is:

(1) described in Code Sec. 4966(d)(2)(A)(iii) (a donor, or any person appointed or designated by the donor, who has advisory privileges with respect to distribution or investment amounts held in a fund by reason of the donor's status as a donor);

(2) a member of the family of the individual described in (1); or

(3) a 35-percent controlled entity (Code Sec. 4966(e)(2), as added by the Pension Act).

Present holdings. Transition rules apply to the present holdings of donor advised funds. A reduction of a fund's excess interest in holdings apply similar to those of Code Sec. 4943(c)(4)—(6) (Code Sec. 4966(e)(3), as added by the Pension Act).

Under the transition rules, in general, where the existing holdings of a supporting organization and disqualified persons are in excess of 50 percent (of a voting stock interest, profits interest, or beneficial interest), and not 20 percent or 35 percent as under the general rule, but are not in excess of 75 percent, a 10-year period is available before the holdings must be reduced to 50 percent. If such holdings are more than 75 percent, the reduction to 50 percent need not occur for a 15-year period. The 15-year period is expanded to 20 years if the holdings are more than 95 percent. After the expiration of the 10-, 15-, or 20-year period, if disqualified persons have holdings in a business enterprise in excess of two percent of the enterprise, the supporting organization has 15 additional years to dispose of any of its own holdings that are above 25 percent of the holdings in the enterprise. If disqualified persons do not have such holdings, then the supporting organization has 15 additional years to dispose of any of its own holdings that are above 35 percent of the holdings in the enterprise (Joint Committee on Taxation, Technical Explanation of the Pension Protection Act of 2006 (JCX-38-06)).

▶ **Effective date.** The provision is effective for tax years beginning after August 17, 2006 (Act Sec. 1233(b) of the Pension Protection Act of 2006).

NEW LAW EXPLAINED

Law source: Law at ¶5260. Committee Report at ¶11,350.

— Act Sec. 1233(a) of the Pension Protection Act of 2006, adding Code Sec. 4943(e);

— Act Sec. 1233(b), providing the effective date.

Reporter references: For further information, consult the following CCH reporters.

— Tax Research Consultant, EXEMPT: 21,456, EXEMPT: 24,500 and EXEMPT: 24,506

— Federal Tax Guide, 2006FTG ¶21,235

¶1180 Charitable Contributions to Donor Advised Funds

SUMMARY OF NEW LAW

Contributions to donor advised funds generally will be fully deductible from income, estate and gift tax. However, there are exceptions for contributions made to donor advised funds maintained at noncharitable and Type III supporting organizations.

BACKGROUND

Contributions to Code Sec. 501(c)(3) organizations are deductible, subject to certain limitations, as an itemized deduction from federal income taxes. These contributions also generally are deductible for estate and gift tax purposes. However, if the taxpayer retains control over the assets transferred to charity, the transfer may not qualify as a completed gift for purposes of claiming an income, estate, or gift tax deduction.

An individual can deduct contributions only if they are made to a qualified organization (Code Sec. 170(c)). No deduction is allowed for certain contributions to a post or organization of war veterans (Code Sec. 170(c)(3)), a domestic fraternal organization operating under the lodge system (Code Sec. 170(c)(4)), or a cemetery company (Code Sec. 170(c)(5)). Deductible gifts for gift tax purposes can include gifts to a post or organization of war veterans and to a domestic fraternal organization operating under the lodge system (Code Sec. 2522(a)(3) and (4)). A similar deduction is allowed for estate tax purposes (Code Sec. 2055(a)(3) and (4)).

Code Sec. 509(a)(3) supporting organizations are public charities that carry out their exempt purposes by supporting one or more other exempt organizations, usually other public charities. Like all charitable organizations, a supporting organization must be organized and operated exclusively for purposes described in Code Sec. 501(c)(3). A supporting organization must also be organized and operated exclusively to support specified supported organizations. Moreover, a supporting organization must have one of three relationships with the supported organizations, all of which are intended to ensure that the supporting organization is responsive to the needs or demands of the supported organization and intimately involved in its operations and

BACKGROUND

that the public charity is motivated to be attentive to the operations of the supporting organization. Type III supporting organizations are "operated in connection with" the supported organization.

NEW LAW EXPLAINED

Limitations on deduction for donations to advised funds.—Contributions to a donor advised fund (see ¶ 1106) will not be eligible for a charitable deduction for:

(1) *income* tax purposes if the fund's Code Sec. 4966(d)(1) sponsoring organization is an organization described in Code Sec. 170(c)(3), (4), (5) (i.e., a war veterans organization, lodge or cemetery corporation), or a Code Sec. 4943(f)(5) Type III supporting organization that is not a functionally integrated Type III supporting organization (see ¶ 1225);

(2) *gift* tax purposes if the fund's Code Sec. 4966(d)(1) sponsoring organization is an organization described in Code Sec. 2522(a)(3) or (4) (i.e., a war veterans organization or lodge) or a Code Sec. 4943(f)(5) Type III supporting organization that is not a functionally integrated Type III supporting organization (see ¶ 1225); or

(3) *estate* tax purposes if the fund's Code Sec. 4966(d)(1) sponsoring organization is an organization described in Code Sec. 2055(a)(3) or (4) (i.e., a war veterans organization or lodge) or a Code Sec. 4943(f)(5) Type III supporting organization that is not a functionally integrated Type III supporting organization (see ¶ 1225) (Code Secs. 170(f)(18), 2055(e)(5) and 2522(c)(5), as added by the Pension Protection Act of 2006).

Substantiation. An otherwise allowable contribution to a donor advised fund will be allowed only if the taxpayer obtains written acknowledgment of the fund's control of the assets. Specifically a donor must obtain a contemporaneous written acknowledgment from the sponsoring organization providing that the sponsoring organization has exclusive legal control over the assets contributed. The contemporaneous written acknowledgment is similar to the acknowledgment needed to substantiate gifts of $250 or more under Code Sec. 170(f)(8)(C) (Code Secs. 170(f)(18)(B), 2055(e)(5)(B) and 2522(c)(5)(B), as added by the Pension Act).

> **Comment:** Because donors may receive conflicting information about donor advised funds and their rights and responsibilities with respect to such funds, the Panel on the Nonprofit Sector suggested that the IRS should require sponsoring charities to have written agreements with every donor affirming that the charity holding the funds has exclusive legal control over the fund.

> **Caution Note:** Denial of a deduction where the donor fails to receive the required written acknowledgment of exclusive control is "very questionable," the American Bar Association's Section of Taxation has written in comments to a similar provision S.2020, an earlier version of the Pension Act. "Although such a requirement is consistent with the Panel on the Nonprofit Sector's recommendations, the broad definition of donor-advised fund... could reach unintended restricted gifts where the donor has some voice in the use, or even the invest-

NEW LAW EXPLAINED

ment, of a contribution. It is one more trap for the unwary. To be safe, charities are likely to include the written acknowledgement of exclusive control in every gift receipt they issue, regardless of whether it involves a donor-advised fund, which may defeat the purpose of the provision."

▶ **Effective date.** The provision applies to contributions made after the date which is 180 days after August 17, 2006 (Act Sec. 1234(d) of the Pension Protection Act of 2006).

Law source: Law at ¶5020, ¶5205 and ¶5210. Committee Report at ¶11,350.

— Act Sec. 1234(a) of the Pension Protection Act of 2006, adding Code Sec. 170(f)(18);

— Act Sec. 1234(b), adding Code Sec. 2055(e)(5);

— Act Sec. 1234(c), adding Code Sec. 2522(c)(5);

— Act Sec. 1234(d), providing the effective date.

Reporter references: For further information, consult the following CCH reporters.

— Standard Federal Tax Reporter, 2006FED ¶11,620.032, ¶11,620.038, ¶22,604.025 and ¶22,812.03

— Tax Research Consultant, INDIV: 51,100

— Federal Tax Guide, 2006FTG ¶6577

— Federal Estate and Gift Tax Reporter, ¶6420.01 and ¶11,621.01

REPORTING REQUIREMENTS

¶1185 Recordkeeping Requirements for Charitable Contributions

SUMMARY OF NEW LAW

Charitable donations of cash must be substantiated either with a bank record or written communication from the donee, regardless of the amount of the donation.

BACKGROUND

Donors need to maintain reliable written records regarding the contribution when a donor claims a deduction for a charitable contribution. If a donor makes a contribution of money to the charitable organization, the donor must maintain one of the following:

(1) a cancelled check;

(2) a receipt (or a letter or other written communication) from the donee showing the name of the donee organization, the date the contribution was made, and the amount of the contribution; or

BACKGROUND

(3) if the first two are not available, then other reliable written records showing the name of the donee organization, the date the contribution was made, and the amount of the contribution (Reg. § 1.170A-13(a)).

If the donated property is other than money, the donor must generally maintain a receipt from the donee organization indicating the name of the donee, the date and location of the donation, and a detailed description (but not the value) of the donated property. A receipt for the donated property need not be obtained if it would be impracticable to do so, but the donor must maintain reliable written records regarding the contribution (Reg. § 1.170A-13(b)).

The substantiation requirements apply to charitable donations of $250 or more. The taxpayer is not allowed a charitable deduction without substantiation of the contribution by a contemporaneous written acknowledgement of the contribution by the donee organization (Code Sec. 170(f)(8)). The written acknowledgement must include:

(1) the amount of the cash contribution; and

(2) a description (but not value) of any property other than cash contributed to the donee organization;

(3) whether the donee provided any goods or services in consideration for the contribution; and

(4) a good faith estimate of the value of any such goods and services.

If the total charitable deduction claimed for non-cash property is more than $500, the donor must attach a completed Form 8283, Noncash Charitable Contributions, to the donee's income tax return for the year in which the deduction is claimed. If the donor fails to attach Form 8283, the deduction will not be allowed. (Code Sec. 170(f)(11)). For donated property with a value of more than $5,000, donors are required to obtain a qualified appraisal for the donated property.

An exception to this substantiation was made if the donee filed a return with the IRS reporting the information that would be included in the written acknowledgement. If the contributions were made by payroll deduction, the written acknowledgement could be substantiated by an employer-provided document, such as a paystub or W-2, showing the amount deducted under Reg. § 1.170A-13(c). For the substantiation to be contemporaneous, the donor must obtain it no later than the date he or she actually files a return for the year that the gift was made, or by the due date or extended due date if the return is filed after either of those dates (Code Sec. 170(f)(8)(C); Reg. § 1.170A-13(f)(3)).

NEW LAW EXPLAINED

Charitable contributions recordkeeping requirements modified.—Donors of charitable contributions of cash, checks or other monetary gifts must retain certain records of the gift, regardless of the amount. Specifically, the donor must maintain either:

NEW LAW EXPLAINED

(1) a bank record; or

(2) a receipt, letter, or other written communication from the donee indicating the name of the donee organization, the date the contribution was made, and the amount of the contribution.

If these records are not kept for each donation made, then no deduction is allowed for the charitable contribution (Code Sec. 170(f)(17), as added by the Pension Act). The provision more closely aligns the substantiation rules for cash contributions with the substantiation rules for contributing other property to charitable organizations.

Comment: According to the Joint Committee on Taxation, Technical Explanation of the Pension Protection Act of 2006 (JCX-38-06), the provision is intended to provide more clarity, both to taxpayers and the IRS, regarding the written records needed a charitable contribution to be allowed. Note that the rules are codified, making the former rules in Reg. § 1.170A-13(a) inapplicable for contributions made in tax years beginning after August 17, 2006.

▶ **Effective date.** The provision applies to contributions made in tax years beginning after August 17, 2006 (Act Sec. 1217(b) of the Pension Protection Act of 2006).

Law source: Law at ¶5020. Committee Report at ¶11,250.

— Act Sec. 1217(a) of the Pension Protection Act of 2006, adding Code Sec. 170(f)(17);

— Act Sec. 1217(b), providing the effective date.

Reporter references: For further information, consult the following CCH reporters.

— Standard Federal Tax Reporter, 2006FED ¶11,700.01 and ¶11,700.022

— Tax Research Consultant, INDIV: 51,454 and INDIV: 51,456

— Federal Tax Guide, 2006FTG ¶6577

¶1190 Split-Interest Trust Reporting

SUMMARY OF NEW LAW

Changes are made for split-interest trust reporting, including increased failure to file penalties, increased confidentiality protection, and elimination of filing exception for split-interest trusts that distribute all their income.

BACKGROUND

Charitable remainder trusts (both charitable annuity trusts and charitable remainder unity trusts, Code Sec. 664), pooled income funds (Code Sec. 642(c)), and charitable gift annuities (Code Sec. 501(m)(5)), are split-interest entities. Split-interest entities are used to pass on remainder interests to a charitable organization, and provide current income to a beneficiary for life. Unlike most transfers of a future interest to a charity, the transfer qualifies for a current charitable deduction. Income from trust assets is taxed to the beneficiary. The character of the income for the beneficiary (that is,

BACKGROUND

whether the income is ordinary, capital gain, or other income) in the case of remainder trusts is the same as it would be if it were taxed at the trust level (Code Sec. 664).

Split-interest filing requirements. Split-interest entities must file an annual information return, Form 1041A, U.S. Information Return Trust Accumulation of Charitable Amounts (Code Sec. 6034), which requires disclosure of information regarding the trust's noncharitable beneficiaries. An exception is made for split-interest trusts that are required to currently distribute in a tax year all net income to beneficiaries (Code Sec. 6034(b)). Failure to file the return may result in a penalty on the trust and the trustee of $10 a day for as long as the failure continues, up to a maximum of $5,000 per return (Code Sec. 6652(c)(2)(A)). These returns must be made publicly available (Code Sec. 6104(b)). Spit-interest trusts must also file Form 5227, Split-Interest Trust Information Return, which requires disclosure of information regarding a trust's noncharitable beneficiaries (Code Sec. 6011, Reg. § 53.6011-1(d)), though there is no requirement that the form be made publicly available. The penalty for failure to file Form 5227 is based on the amount of tax imposed, and since split-interest entities are generally not taxed, no penalty applies.

NEW LAW EXPLAINED

Form 1041A penalties increased.—Increased penalties apply for failure to file or failure to provide required information on Form 1041A, U.S. Information Return Trust Accumulation of Charitable Amounts. Penalties are increased from $10 to $20 per day, up to $10,000 for any one return. For split-interest trusts with gross income in excess of $250,000, the penalty is $100 per day, up to a maximum of $50,000. An additional penalty may be assessed against the person required to file the return if that person knowingly fails to file the return, (Code Sec. 6652(c)(2)(C), as added by the Pension Act).

Confidentiality of noncharitable beneficiaries. Information regarding beneficiaries of split-interest trusts, other than charitable organizations, no longer must be made available to the public (Code Sec. 6104(b), as amended by the Pension Act).

Filing exception repealed. The filing exception for split-interest trusts that distribute all current income to the beneficiaries is repealed (Code Sec. 6034, as amended by the Pension Act).

▶ **Effective date.** The provision applies to returns for tax years beginning after December 31, 2006 (Act Sec. 1201(c)(2) of the Pension Protection Act of 2006).

Law source: Law at ¶5330, ¶5365 and ¶5390. Committee Report at ¶11,110.

— Act Sec. 1201(b)(1) of the Pension Protection Act of 2006, amending Code Sec. 6034;

— Act Sec. 1201(b)(2), amending Code Sec. 6652(c);

— Act Sec. 1201(b)(3), amending Code Sec. 6104(b);

— Act Sec. 1201(c)(2), providing the effective date.

Reporter references: For further information, consult the following CCH reporters.

— Standard Federal Tax Reporter, 2006FED ¶24,308.03 and ¶24,468.043

— Tax Research Consultant, ESTTRST: 15,360 and PENALTY: 3,208.15

— Federal Tax Guide, 2006FTG ¶22,041

Exempt Organizations

12

EXEMPT STATUS

¶1205 Definition of a Convention or Association of Churches

SUMMARY OF NEW LAW

Membership in a convention or association of churches may include church organizations as well as individuals who have voting rights in those organizations.

BACKGROUND

Churches and religious organizations are generally exempt from income tax and receive other favorable treatment under tax law. Congress has enacted special tax laws applicable to churches, religious organizations and ministers in recognition of their unique status in American society and of their rights guaranteed by the First Amendment of the Constitution of the United States (IRS Publication 1828, Tax Guide for Churches and Religious Organizations).

A convention or association of churches is a cooperative undertaking by churches of the same or differing denominations (Rev. Rul. 74-224, 1974-1 CB 61). Generally, an association or convention of churches has churches as members. However, membership in some conventions is extended to individual members of a member church that is in good and regular standing with the convention. Voting privileges for elections and during conventions are usually restricted to representatives designated by member churches.

An organization, whether a civil law corporation or otherwise, is associated with a church or a convention or association of churches if it shares common religious bonds and convictions with that church or convention or association of churches (Code Sec. 414(e)(3)(D)). A church or a convention or association of churches is excluded from the definition of a private foundation as an activity-based public charity (Code Sec. 170(b)(1)(A)(i)). A religious organization may be classified as a church if it serves a religious purpose. A religious purpose may be established by the existence of an established congregation served by an organized ministry, the provision of regular religious purposes and religious education for the young and the dissemination of a doctrinal code, as well as other appropriate factual circumstances.

Applicable tax provisions that refer to a church or a convention or association of churches include those on retirement plans (Code Secs. 403(b)(9), 410(d) and 414(e)), tax-exemption (Code Secs. 501(c)(3) and 509(a)), and deductibility of charitable contributions (Code Sec. 170(b)(1)(A)).

NEW LAW EXPLAINED

Convention or association of churches defined.—Any organization that is otherwise a convention or association of churches shall not fail to qualify as such merely because

NEW LAW EXPLAINED

the membership of such organizations includes individuals as well as churches or because individuals have voting rights in such organization (Code Sec. 7701(o), as added by the Pension Protection Act of 2006). In other words, the tax-exempt status and the applicability of other tax provisions affecting conventions or associations of churches are not affected by the fact that these organizations have individuals as members and these individuals have voting rights.

> **Comment:** Although the term "convention or association of churches" has a historical meaning generally referring to a cooperative undertaking by churches of the same denomination, nothing in the legislative or religious history of the term prevents its application to a cooperative undertaking by churches of differing denominations, assuming such convention or association otherwise qualifies for recognition of exemption as an organization described in Code Sec. 501(c)(3). The term is not limited in its application to a group of churches of the same denomination (Rev. Rul. 74-224, 1974-1 CB 61).

▶ **Effective date.** No specific effective date is provided by the Act. The provision is, therefore, considered effective on August 17, 2006, the date of enactment.

Law source: Law at ¶5485. Committee Report at ¶11,300.

— Act Sec. 1222 of the Pension Protection Act of 2006, redesignating Code Sec. 7701(o) as 7701(p) and adding new Code Sec. 7701(o).

Reporter references: For further information, consult the following CCH reporters.

— Standard Federal Tax Reporter, 2006FED ¶11,620.03 and ¶22,609.01

— Tax Research Consultant, EXEMPT: 21,052

— Federal Tax Guide, 2006FTG ¶16,060

¶1210 Qualifying Specified Payments from Controlled Entities

SUMMARY OF NEW LAW

Only excess qualifying specified payments from a controlled entity are included in an exempt organization's UBTI, and they are subject to a valuation misstatement penalty. The organization must report the payments and related information.

BACKGROUND

If an exempt organization receives or accrues a specified payment from an entity that it controls, the payment is taxable as unrelated business taxable income (UBTI) to the extent it either reduces the controlled entity's net unrelated income or increases its net unrelated loss. Specified payments are interest, annuities, royalties or rents, but not dividends (Code Sec. 512(b)(13)(A) and (C)).

BACKGROUND

For a controlled entity that is also tax-exempt, net unrelated income is the entity's UBTI. For a taxable controlled entity, net unrelated income is the portion of the entity's taxable income that would be UBTI if the entity were a tax-exempt organization with the same exempt purposes as the controlling organization. Net unrelated loss is determined under similar rules (Code Sec. 513(b)(13)(B)).

Control. An exempt organization is considered to "control" another entity if it owns:

- more than 50 percent of a corporation's stock (by vote or by value),
- more than 50 percent of a partnership's profits interests or capital interests, or
- more than 50 percent of the beneficial interests in any other entity (Code Sec. 513(b)(13)(D)).

These control rules replace earlier rules that defined "control" as ownership of at least 80 percent of voting stock, determined without regard to constructive ownership. The current control rules generally are effective for tax years beginning after August 8, 1997, but they do not apply to certain payments made during the two tax years beginning on or after that date (Act Sec. 1041 of the Taxpayer Relief Act of 1997 (P.L. 105-34)).

Anti-abuse rules. The IRS may distribute, apportion or allocate gross income, deductions, credits or allowances between or among two or more organizations, trades or businesses that are owned or controlled, directly or indirectly, by the same interests. The IRS must first determine that its distribution, apportionment or allocation is necessary to prevent the evasion of taxes or to reflect clearly the income of the entities (Code Sec. 482). The purpose of these rules is to place a controlled taxpayer on a tax parity with an uncontrolled taxpayer, by determining the true taxable income from the controlled entity's property and business. Generally, the IRS does not reallocate if a transaction meets an arms' length standard; that is, if the results of the transaction are consistent with results that would have been realized if uncontrolled taxpayers had engaged in the same transaction under the same circumstances (Reg. § 1.482-1A(b)(1)). The IRS most commonly exercises its reallocation authority in the international context, when commonly controlled entities use transfer pricing arrangements to try to minimize their U.S. tax liability.

Returns. Most exempt organizations must file annual information returns on Form 990, Return of Organization Exempt from Tax (Code Sec. 6033(a)). Some exempt organizations can file Form 990-EZ, Short Form Return of Organization Exempt From Income Tax). An exempt organization that has annual UBTI of at least $1,000 must also file a tax return on Form 990-T, Exempt Organization Business Income Tax Return (Reg. § 1.6012-2(e)).

NEW LAW EXPLAINED

UBTI includes only excess qualifying specified payments.—Qualifying specified payments received or accrued from a controlled entity after 2005 and before 2008 are included in an exempt organization's unrelated business taxable income (UBTI) only to the extent they are excess payments.

NEW LAW EXPLAINED

> **Comment:** According to the Joint Committee on Taxation, it is intended that there be further study of these arrangements in light of these new rules, before any determination is made to extend or expand them (Joint Committee on Taxation, Technical Explanation of the Pension Protection Act of 2006 (JCX-38-06)).

A *qualifying specified payment* is a specified payment made under a binding written contract in effect on August 17, 2006, including renewals of such contracts under substantially similar terms (Code Sec. 512(b)(13)(E)(iii), as amended by the Pension Protection Act of 2006). *Excess payments* are the portion of the qualifying specified payments received or accrued by the organization that exceeds the amount that would have been paid or accrued if the payment met the requirements prescribed by the anti-abuse reallocation rules of Code Sec. 482 (Code Sec. 512(b)(13)(E)(i), as amended by the Pension Act).

> **Example:** An exempt entity receives rent payments from its controlled subsidiary that exceed fair market value, as determined in accordance with Code Sec. 482. This excess is included in the parent organization's unrelated business income, to the extent that it reduces the controlled entity's net unrelated income or increases its net unrelated loss.

> **Practical Analysis:** Barnaby Zall, of Weinberg & Jacobs, LLP, Rockville, Maryland, finds that Act Sec. 1205 may cause a huge change in the way revenue-generating activities are structured. The provision provides more incentives for multi-layer exempt organization corporate structures, with revenue-generating activities placed in separate subsidiaries. Because only the excess payments to the parent organization (over fair market value) are taxed, careful structuring of contracts and relationships could both boost organizational resources (by reducing unrelated business tax liability) and reduce legal exposure (through isolation of riskier activities in subsidiaries). As a planning measure, any relationship must be carefully documented as "arm's-length," and any calculation of fair market value should be amply substantiated.

Penalty. A valuation misstatement penalty applies to excess qualifying specified payments that are included in UBTI. Any Federal income tax imposed on the controlling organization (including tax on UBTI) is increased by an amount equal to 20 percent of the excess payment, determined with (or, if larger, without) regard to return amendments or supplements (Code Sec. 512(b)(13)(E)(ii), as amended by the Pension Act).

> **Comment:** The Pension Act also lowers the threshold for imposing the penalty for income tax underpayments attributable to substantial or gross valuation misstatements. See ¶1345.

Returns. A controlling organization that must include qualifying specified payments in UBTI must also include on its annual tax return (a) any interest, annuities, royalties or rents received from each controlled entity; (b) any loans made to each controlled

NEW LAW EXPLAINED

entity; and (c) any transfers of funds between the controlling organization and each controlled entity (Code Sec. 6033(h), as amended by the Pension Act).

> **Compliance Pointer:** Most exempt organizations file annual information returns on Form 990, Return of Organization Exempt from Tax, and report UBTI on Form 990-T, Exempt Organization Business Income Tax Return.

Treasury Report. No later than January 1, 2009, the Secretary of the Treasury must submit to the Senate Finance Committee and the House Ways and Means Committee a report of IRS effectiveness in administering the changes to the rules governing inclusion of specified payments in UBTI, and the related valuation misstatement penalty. The report must also address the extent to which payments by controlled entities to controlling organizations meet the anti-abuse requirements of Code Sec. 482. The report must include the results of any audits of controlling organizations or controlled entities, along with recommendations relating to the tax treatment of payments from controlled entities to controlling organizations (Act Sec. 1205(b)(2) of the Pension Act).

▶ **Effective date.** The rules relating to the inclusion of qualifying specified payments in UBTI and the imposition of the valuation misstatement penalty apply to payments received or accrued after December 31, 2005 (Act Sec. 1025(c)(1) of the Pension Protection Act of 2006). The rules relating to the controlling organization's tax return apply to returns due (without extensions) after August 17, 2006 (Act Sec. 1205(c)(2) of the Pension Protection Act of 2006).

Law source: Law at ¶5160, ¶5325 and ¶7228. Committee Report at ¶11,150.

— Act Sec. 1205(a) of the Pension Protection Act of 2006, redesignating Code Sec. 512(b)(13)(E) as (F), and adding new Code Sec. 512(b)(13)(E);

— Act Sec. 1205(b), redesignating Code Sec. 6033(h) as (i), and adding new Code Sec. 6033(h);

— Act Sec. 1205(c), providing the effective date.

Reporter references: For further information, consult the following CCH reporters.

— Standard Federal Tax Reporter, 2006FED ¶22,837.01 and ¶35,425.021

— Tax Research Consultant, ACCTNG: 30,054, EXEMPT: 15,204 and EXEMPT: 15,304

— Federal Tax Guide, 2006FTG ¶16,320

¶1215 Additional Standards for Credit Counseling Organizations

SUMMARY OF NEW LAW

Credit counseling organizations must be organized and operated according to special rules in order to be exempt from federal income taxation. Debt management plan services provided by exempt organizations that do not meet these standards are treated as an unrelated trade or business.

BACKGROUND

Credit counseling organizations that meet certain requirements can be treated as Code Sec. 501(c) tax-exempt organizations. Hundreds of active tax-exempt credit counseling agencies currently operate in the United States (Joint Committee on Taxation, Technical Explanation of the Pension Protection Act of 2006 (JCX-38-06)).

The "models" for credit counseling organizations seeking exempt status to follow have been set forth in revenue rulings. The IRS has determined that a nonprofit organization formed to advise, counsel and assist individuals in solving their financial difficulties, by budgeting their income and expenses and effecting an orderly debt payment program, is a Code Sec. 501(c)(4) social welfare organization (Rev. Rul. 65-299, 1965-2 CB 165). Similarly, the IRS has ruled that a nonprofit organization formed to help reduce personal bankruptcy by informing the public on personal money management and aiding low-income individuals and families with financial problems is a Code Sec. 501(c)(3) charitable or educational organization (Rev. Rul. 69-441, 1969-2 CB 115).

Credit counseling industry under scrutiny. The tax-exempt credit counseling industry has come under increased scrutiny in recent years. Some people believe that many credit counseling organizations seek 501(c)(3) status primarily to become exempt from federal and state consumer protection laws. In response Congress has conducted hearings investigating the activities of credit counseling organizations under such laws. In addition as part of a broad examination and compliance program, the IRS has audited several tax-exempt credit counseling firms, and found that many are primarily profit-motivated sellers of debt-reduction plans, who offer little or no counseling or educational services, and serve the private interests of related for-profit businesses, officers and directors. The IRS Chief Counsel's Office has also come to a similar conclusion (IRS Chief Counsel Advice 200431023, July 13, 2004). As a result, the IRS has announced steps to ensure that these agencies comply with the law (IRS News Release IR-2006-80, May 15, 2006; Joint Committee on Taxation, Technical Explanation of the Pension Protection Act of 2006 (JCX-38-06)).

> **Comment:** According to the Chief Counsel, the critical inquiry for determining exempt status is whether the organization conducts its counseling program to improve an individual's understanding of and ability to address his or her financial problems. This inquiry involves assessing the organization's methodology for conducting its counseling activities (IRS Chief Counsel Advice 200620001, May 9, 2006; Joint Committee on Taxation, Technical Explanation of the Pension Protection Act of 2006 (JCX-38-06)).

Persons filing bankruptcy must get credit counseling. The increased scrutiny of the credit counseling industry comes at a time when amendments to the federal bankruptcy law now require persons seeking bankruptcy protection to consult with credit counseling organizations. Under the Bankruptcy Abuse Prevention and Consumer Protection Act of 2005 (P.L. 109-8), an individual cannot be a bankruptcy debtor without first receiving, from a nonprofit budget and credit counseling agency that has been approved by the U.S. Trustee or bankruptcy administrator, a briefing that outlines credit counseling opportunities and assists the person in performing a budget analysis. That act provides minimum qualifications for a counseling agency to be approved, but does not require the agency to be a 501(c)(3) organization (Joint

BACKGROUND

Committee on Taxation, Technical Explanation of the Pension Protection Act of 2006 (JCX-38-06)).

Unrelated business income. With limited exceptions, tax-exempt organizations may be subject to tax on income from an unrelated trade or business. An unrelated trade or business is any trade or business that is not substantially related to the organization's exempt purposes. The Code sets forth several activities which either are or are not "unrelated trade or business" activities (Code Sec. 513).

NEW LAW EXPLAINED

Requirements for exempt status of credit counseling organizations expanded.— The Pension Protection Act of 2006 sets forth the standards that a credit counseling organization must meet to be tax-exempt (Code Sec. 501(q), as added by the Pension Act). According to the Joint Committee on Taxation, Technical Explanation of the Pension Protection Act of 2006 (JCX-38-06), the standards build upon and are consistent with the requirements in IRS Chief Counsel Advice 200431023 and 200620001 for determining exempt status, and are not intended to affect the approval process for credit counseling agencies under the Bankruptcy Abuse Prevention and Consumer Protection Act of 2005 (P.L. 109-8).

Under the new law, an organization for which the provision of credit counseling services is a substantial purpose cannot be tax-exempt unless it qualifies as a Code Sec. 501(c)(3) charitable or educational organization or a Code Sec. 501(c)(4) social welfare organization. In addition, the organization must be organized and operated according to the following requirements (Code Sec. 501(q)(1), as added by the Pension Act).

(1) *Tailored credit counseling services.* The organization must provide credit counseling services tailored to consumers' specific needs and circumstances (Code Sec. 501(q)(1)(A)(i), as added by the Pension Act).

(2) *No loans.* The organization must make no loans to debtors (other than loans with no fees or interest), and must not negotiate loans on behalf of debtors (Code Sec. 501(q)(1)(A)(ii), as added by the Pension Act).

(3) *Incidental credit improvement services.* The organization can provide services that improve a consumer's credit record, history or rating, but only if those services are incidental to providing credit counseling services. The organization cannot charge a separately-stated fee for credit record, history or rating improvement services (Code Sec. 501(q)(1)(A)(iii) and (iv), as added by the Pension Act).

(4) *No refusal to provide services.* The organization must not refuse to provide credit counseling services due to a consumer's inability to pay, ineligibility for debt management plan enrollment, or unwillingness to enroll in a debt management plan (Code Sec. 501(q)(1)(B), as added by the Pension Act).

(5) *Reasonable fee policy.* The organization must establish and implement a fee policy which: (i) requires that any fee charged to a consumer is reasonable; (ii) allows waiver of fees if the consumer is unable to pay; and (iii) except as allowed by state

NEW LAW EXPLAINED

law, prohibits charging a fee based on a percentage of the consumer's debt, the consumer's payments to be made under a debt management plan, or the consumer's projected or actual savings resulting from debt management plan enrollment (Code Sec. 501(q)(1)(C), as added by the Pension Act).

(6) *Independent board members with public interest.* The organization must at all times have a board of directors or other governing body ("board") that is controlled by persons who represent the broad interests of the public (*e.g.*, public officials, persons having special knowledge or expertise in credit or financial education, community leaders). Not more than 20 percent of the board's voting power may be vested in persons who are employed by the organization or will benefit financially, directly or indirectly, from its activities (other than through the receipt of reasonable directors' fees, or the repayment of consumer debt to creditors other than the organization or its affiliates). In addition not more than 49 percent of the board's voting power maybe vested in persons employed by the organization or who will benefit financially, directly or indirectly, from its activities (other than through the receipt of reasonable directors' fees) (Code Sec. 501(q)(1)(D), as added by the Pension Act).

(7) *Limited ownership of related service providers.* The organization must not own more than 35 percent of the total combined voting power of a corporation, the profits interest of a partnership, or the beneficial interest of an estate or trust, any of which are in the trade or business of lending money, repairing credit, or providing debt management plan services, payment processing or similar services. This does not apply if the corporation, partnership or trust is a 501(c)(3) organization (Code Sec. 501(q)(1)(E), as added by the Pension Act).

(8) *Referral fees.* The organization must receive no amount for providing referrals to others for debt management services, and must pay no amount to others for obtaining consumer referrals (Code Sec. 501(q)(1)(F), as added by the Pension Act). For example, if an organization pays or receives a fee for using or maintaining a locator service for consumers to find a credit counseling organization, the fee is not considered a referral (Joint Committee on Taxation, Technical Explanation of the Pension Protection Act of 2006 (JCX-38-06)).

Comment: Requirements (4), (5) and (6) above address core issues related to tax-exempt status that have been problematic in the credit counseling industry: the provision of services and waiver of fees without regard to ability to pay, the establishment of a reasonable fee policy, and the presence of independent board members. In providing these specific requirements, it was not intended that similar or more stringent requirements should not be adhered to by other exempt organizations providing fees for services (Joint Committee on Taxation, Technical Explanation of the Pension Protection Act of 2006 (JCX-38-06)).

For these purposes "credit counseling services" means: (i) providing educational information to the general public on budgeting, personal finance, financial literacy, saving and spending practices, and the sound use of consumer credit; (ii) assisting individuals and families with financial problems by providing them with counseling; or (iii) a combination of these activities (Code Sec. 501(q)(4)(A), as added by the

NEW LAW EXPLAINED

Pension Act). "Debt management plan services" are services related to the repayment, consolidation or restructuring of a consumer's debt, and include the negotiation with creditors of lower interest rates, the waiver or reduction of fees, and the marketing and processing of debt management plans (Code Sec. 501(q)(4)(B), as added by the Pension Act).

Practical Analysis: Barnaby Zall, of Weinberg & Jacobs, LLP, Rockville, Maryland, observes that more than a million Americans worked with credit counseling organizations in 2003, reducing high credit card debt and recovering from major medical expenses. Following highly publicized reports of abuses, these new requirements for credit counseling organizations will likely eliminate most such organizations, even those which have not been abusive. Virtually every credit counseling organization relies on contributions from consumers and creditors—the two forms of income which will be limited by this provision—and the transition period in this provision may simply be used by existing organizations to close operations. Equally important, the new Code Sec. 501(q) requires specific organizational structure and operations at a detailed level. It is unclear if this provision is a harbinger of congressional micro-management (infringing on traditional federalism concepts) or an isolated reaction. Note, however, that footnote 435 of the JCT's Technical Explanation (JCX-38-06) suggests all exempt organizations will be evaluated under certain criteria at play in this provision, whether or not they are credit counseling organizations or even charities.

Additional requirements for charitable or educational organizations. In addition to meeting the general requirements listed above, a 501(c)(3) credit counseling organization is not tax-exempt unless it is also organized and operated according to several other requirements. The organization must not solicit contributions from consumers during the initial counseling process, or while the consumer is receiving the organization's services (Code Sec. 501(q)(2)(A)(i), as added by the Pension Act). Also, the organization's aggregate revenues which are from payments of consumers' creditors and are attributable to debt management plan services cannot exceed an applicable percentage of the organization's total revenues (Code Sec. 501(q)(2)(A)(ii), as added by the Pension Act). The applicable percentage is 50 percent of the organization's total revenues; for 501(c)(3) credit counseling organizations that exist on August 17, 2006, the Pension Act's enactment date, the applicable percentage is 80 percent for the first tax year after August 17, 2006, 70 percent for the second tax year, 60 percent for the third tax year, and 50 percent thereafter (Code Sec. 501(q)(2)(B), as added by the Pension Act).

Comment: According to the Joint Committee on Taxation, Technical Explanation of the Pension Protection Act of 2006 (JCX-38-06), satisfying the aggregate revenues requirement—both in an exemption application, and on an ongoing operational basis—is not a safe harbor. It provides no affirmative evidence that an organization's primary purpose is an exempt purpose, or that its debt management plan services revenues are related to exempt purposes.

NEW LAW EXPLAINED

Additional requirements for social welfare organizations. In addition to the general requirements listed above, a 501(c)(4) credit counseling organization is not exempt unless it also notifies the Secretary of the Treasury (as set forth in the Regulations) that it is applying for recognition as a credit counseling organization (Code Sec. 501(q)(3), as added by the Pension Act).

Debt management plan services as unrelated trade or business. Debt management plan services are treated as an "unrelated trade or business," for purposes of the tax on unrelated business income of charitable organizations, if the services are provided by any organization that is not a Code Sec. 501(q) credit counseling organization (Code Sec. 513(j), as added by the Pension Act).

Comment: The Joint Committee on Taxation, Technical Explanation of the Pension Protection Act of 2006 (JCX-38-06) states that in order for income not to be unrelated trade or business income, the debt management plan service must contribute importantly to the accomplishment of credit counseling services, and not be conducted on a scale larger than is reasonably necessary to accomplish such services.

Example: Providing debt management plan services would not be substantially related to accomplishing exempt purposes if the organization recommended and enrolled an individual consumer in a debt management plan only after determining whether the individual satisfied the financial criteria established by the creditors for the plan, *without*: (1) considering whether it was an appropriate action in light of the consumer's particular needs and objectives; (2) discussing the disadvantages of a debt management plan with the consumer; and (3) presenting other possible options to the consumer.

▶ **Effective date.** These provisions generally apply to tax years beginning after August 17, 2006 (Act Sec. 1220(c)(1) of the Pension Protection Act of 2006). However, in the case of any Code Sec. 501(c)(3) or (4) organization with respect to which the provision of credit counseling services is a substantial purpose on August 17, 2006, the provisions apply to tax years beginning after the date which is one year after August 17, 2006 (Act Sec. 1220(c)(2) of the Pension Act).

Law source: Law at ¶5145 and ¶5165. Committee Report at ¶11,280.

— Act Sec. 1220(a) of the Pension Protection Act of 2006, redesignating Code Sec. 501(q) as (r), and adding new Code Sec. 501(q);

— Act Sec. 1220(b), adding new Code Sec. 513(j);

— Act Sec. 1220(c), providing the effective dates.

Reporter references: For further information, consult the following CCH reporters.

— Standard Federal Tax Reporter, 2006FED ¶22,609.035 and ¶22,846.01

— Tax Research Consultant, EXEMPT: 3,100 and EXEMPT: 3,300

— Federal Tax Guide, 2006FTG ¶16,065

¶1220 Transfers of Excess Funds from Black Lung Disability Trusts

SUMMARY OF NEW LAW

The aggregate limit on the amount of excess black lung benefit trust assets that may be used to pay accident and health benefits or premiums for insurance exclusively covering such benefits for retired coal miners and their spouses and dependents is eliminated.

BACKGROUND

A qualified black lung benefit trust is exempt from Federal income taxation. Contributions to a qualified black lung benefit trust generally are deductible to the extent such contributions are necessary to fund the trust. However, no assets of a qualified black lung benefit trust may be used for, or diverted to, any purpose other than:

(1) to satisfy liabilities, or pay insurance premiums to cover liabilities, arising under the Black Lung Acts;

(2) to pay administrative costs of operating the trust;

(3) to pay accident and health benefits or premiums for insurance exclusively covering such benefits (including administrative and other incidental expenses relating to such benefits) for retired coal miners and their spouses and dependents (within certain limits); or

(4) investment in Federal, State, or local securities and obligations, or in time demand deposits in a bank or insured credit union (Code Sec. 501(c)(21)).

Additionally, trust assets may be paid into the national Black Lung Disability Trust Fund, or into the general fund of the U.S. Treasury.

The amount of assets in qualified black lung benefit trusts available to pay accident and health benefits or premiums for insurance exclusively covering such benefits (including administrative and other incidental expenses relating to such benefits) for retired coal miners and their spouses and dependents may not exceed a yearly limit or an aggregate limit, whichever is less. The yearly limit is the amount of trust assets in excess of 110 percent of the present value of the liability for black lung benefits determined as of the close of the preceding tax year of the trust. The aggregate limit is the excess of the sum of the yearly limit as of the close of the last tax year ending before October 24, 1992, plus earnings thereon as of the close of the tax year preceding the tax year involved over the aggregate payments for accident of health benefits for retired coal miners and their spouses and dependents made from the trust since October 24, 1992 (Code Sec. 501(c)(21)(C)). Each of these determinations is required to be made by an independent actuary. In general, amounts used to pay retiree accident or health benefits are not includible in the income of the company, nor is a deduction allowed for those amounts.

NEW LAW EXPLAINED

Transfer of excess funds from black lung disability trusts.—The aggregate limit on the amount of excess black lung benefit trust assets that may be used to pay accident and health benefits or premiums for insurance exclusively covering such benefits for retired coal miners and their spouses and dependents is eliminated (Code Sec. 501(c)(21)(C), as amended by the Pension Protection Act of 2006). The annual limit under prior law continues to be applicable. Health benefits for this purpose includes administrative and other incidental expenses relating to covered benefits.

> **Comment:** The reason for this change is that better than expected market performance of black lung trust assets and fewer black lung claims have resulted in a situation where some coal companies have significant unanticipated excess assets in their black lung trusts. Removing the aggregate limit on the amount of black lung benefit trusts available to pay accident and health benefits or premiums for insurance exclusively covering such benefits for retired coal miners will allow coal companies to use greater amounts of their excess black lung trust assets to fund such benefits.

> **Comment:** Earlier versions of the Pension Act included the requirement that each fiscal year the Secretary of the Treasury would transfer certain amounts to the United Mine Workers of America (UMWA) Combined Benefit Fund. This provision was not included in the final version.

► **Effective date.** This provision is effective for tax years beginning after December 31, 2006 (Act Sec. 862(b) of the Pension Protection Act of 2006).

Law source: Law at ¶5145. JCT Report at ¶10,880.

— Act Sec. 862(a) of the Pension Protection Act of 2006, amending Code Sec. 501(c)(21)(C);

— Act Sec. 862(b), providing the effective date.

Reporter references: For further information, consult the following CCH reporters.

— Standard Federal Tax Reporter, 2006FED ¶22,655.01

— Tax Research Consultant, EXEMPT: 30,058

— Federal Tax Guide, 2006FTG ¶16,025

SUPPORTING ORGANIZATIONS

¶1225 Requirements for Supporting Organizations

SUMMARY OF NEW LAW

A definition for "supported organization" had been created, the three alternative types of supporting organization has been statutorily described, and new requirements for supporting organizations have been added.

BACKGROUND

Code Sec. 501(c)(3) organizations are classified as either public charities or private foundations. Private foundations are those 501(c)(3) organizations that are not granted the status of public charities. Because private foundations receive their support from a relatively small number of supporters who frequently also have some control over their operations, private foundations are subject to anti-abuse provisions and excise taxes not applicable to public charities.

Private foundations may be either private operating foundations or private non-operating foundations. Private operating foundations operate their own charitable programs, but most private foundations are private non-operating foundations which generally are grant-making organizations.

However, Code Sec. 509(a)(3) provides that 501(c)(3) organizations that provide support to other 501(c)(3) public charities will themselves be considered to be public charities rather than private foundations. This "supporting organization" status allows organizations that otherwise would be considered to be non-operating private foundations to avoid the anti-abuse provisions and excise taxes otherwise applicable to private foundations.

To qualify as a supporting organization, the 501(c)(3) organization must meet three tests:

(1) it must be organized and operated at all times exclusively for the benefit of, to perform the functions of, or to carry out the purposes of one or more publicly supported charities ("organizational and operational test");

(2) it must be operated, supervised or controlled by (or in connection with) one or more publicly supported charities ("relationship test"); *and*

(3) it must not be controlled, directly or indirectly, by disqualified persons (as defined by Code Sec. 4946) other than foundation managers, and publicly supported charities (this is the "lack of control test" (Code Sec. 509(a)(3)).

To satisfy the relationship test, a supporting organization must hold one of three statutorily described close relationships with the supported organization. Supporting organizations are generally described in Code Sec. 509(a)(3)(B), but the three types of support relationships are more fully described in Reg. § 1.509(a)-4(f)(2). Based on these relationships, the supporting organizations have commonly been referred to as Type I, Type II and Type III supporting organizations. In a Type I support relationship, one or more of the supported organizations must exercise a substantial degree of control over the programs, activities and policies of the supporting organization (Reg. § 1.509(a)-4(g)(1)). In a Type II relationship, there must be common control or supervision by persons controlling or supervising both the supporting organization and the publicly supported charity (Reg. § 1.509(a)-4(h)(1)). Type III supporting organizations are operated in connection with one or more publicly supported organizations, and are required to demonstrate that they are responsive to the needs and demands of those supported organizations, and that both (1) the Type III organization is significantly involved in the operations of that/those organization(s), and (2) that those supported organizations are dependent upon the supporting organization for the type of support it provides (Reg. § 1.509(a)-4(i)(1)).

NEW LAW EXPLAINED

New requirements for supporting organizations.—To satisfy the relationship test of Code Sec. 509(a)(3)(B), a supporting organization must hold one of three statutorily described close relationships (referred to as Type I, Type II, or Type III) with a supported organization. Code Sec. 509(a)(3)(B) has been amended to include language similar to that contained in Reg.§ 1.509(a)-4(f)(2), which describes the three alternatives by which supporting organizations can qualify for purposes of the relationship test (Code Sec. 509(a)(3)(B), as amended by the Pension Protection Act of 2006). In addition, a definition of supported organization has been created and several new requirements must now be fulfilled to be a valid Type III supporting organization.

Supported organizations. The Pension Act creates a definition of "supported organization," which is defined as an organization described in either Code Sec. 509(a)(1) or (2) and to which a supporting organization either: (1) is organized and operated for the benefit of such supported organization, or (2) performs the functions of or carries out the purposes of the supported organization (Code Sec. 509(a)(f)(3), as added by the Pension Act).

Information reporting. In each tax year, the Type III organization must provide each supported organization with any information that may be required by the IRS by way of regulation or otherwise, designed to ensure that the supporting organization remains responsive to the needs and demands of the supported organization (Code Sec. 509(f)(1)(A), as added by the Pension Act). According to the Joint Committee Report, this could be satisfied by the supporting organization's submitting documentation such as a copy of the supporting organization's governing documents, the organization's annual information return filed with the IRS (Form 990 series), any tax return filed (Form 990-T series), and an annual report (including a description of all of the support provided by the supporting organization, how such support was calculated, and a projection of the next year's support) (Joint Committee on Taxation, Technical Explanation of the Pension Protection Act of 2006 (JCX-38-06)).

Foreign supporting organizations. Type III supporting organizations may not be operated in connection with any supported organization that is not organized in the United States (Code Sec. 509(f)(1)(B)(i), as added by the Pension Act). However, for Type III supporting organizations that supports a foreign organization on August 17, 2006, this general rule does not apply until the first day of the organization's third tax year beginning after August 17, 2006 (Code Sec. 509(f)(1)(B)(ii), as added by the Pension Act).

Organizations controlled by donors. If a Type I or Type III supporting organization supports an organization that is controlled by a donor (with certain exceptions), then the supporting organization is treated as a private foundation (rather than as a public charity) for purposes of the relationship test (Code Sec. 509(f)(2)(A), as added by the Pension Act). Specifically, Type I and Type III organizations will not satisfy the relationship test if they accept any gifts or contributions from:

NEW LAW EXPLAINED

(1) any person (other than an organization described in Code Sec. 509(a)(1), (2) or (4)) who controls, directly or indirectly, either alone or together with persons listed in (2) and (3) below, the governing body of a supported organization;

(2) any family member (as described in Code Sec. 4958(f)(4)) of a person described in (1), above; or

(3) a 35-percent controlled entity which is defined as:

  (a) a corporation in which persons described in clause (i) or (ii) of Code Sec. 509(f)(2)(B) own more than 35 percent of the total combined voting power,

  (b) a partnership in which such persons own more than 35 percent of the profits interest, or

  (c) a trust or estate in which such persons own more than 35 percent of the beneficial interest (Code Sec. 509(f)(2)(B), as added by the Pension Act).

Charitable trusts as Type III supporting organizations. A trust will not be considered to be a Type III supporting organization (operated in connection with any organization described in Code Sec. 509(a)(1) or (2)) *solely* based on the facts that: (1) it is a charitable trust under state law, (2) the supported organization is beneficiary of the trust; *and* (3) the supported organization has the power of enforce the trust and compel an accounting (Act Sec. 1241(c) of the Pension Act).

Payout requirements for Type III supporting organizations. The terms "Type III supporting organization" and "functionally integrated Type III supporting organization" are defined in Code Sec. 4943(f)(5)(A) and (B) (as added by the Pension Act). The IRS is authorized to promulgate new regulations specifying the payout requirements of Type III supporting organizations that are not functionally integrated Type III supporting organizations. To ensure that significant amounts are paid out to the supported organizations, the regulations will require distributions of a specified percentage of either income or assets by the supporting organizations (Act Sec. 1241(d) of the Pension Act).

For rules to the application of, and returns of, supporting organizations, see the discussion at ¶1270.

▶ **Effective date.** This provision is generally effective on August 17, 2006 (Act Sec. 1241(e)(1) of the Pension Protection Act of 2006). However, for charitable trusts that are considered to be Type III supporting organizations, the provision is effective on the date that is one year after August 17, 2006 (Act Sec. 1241(e)(2) of the Pension Act).

Law source: Law at ¶5155 and ¶7243. Committee Report at ¶11,360.

— Act Sec. 1241(a) of the Pension Protection Act of 2006, amending Code Sec. 509(a)(3)(B);

— Act Sec. 1241(b), adding Code Sec. 509(f);

— Act Sec. 1241(c) affecting application of Code Sec. 509(a)(3)(B)(iii);

— Act Sec. 1241(d);

— Act Sec. 1241(e), providing the effective date.

NEW LAW EXPLAINED

Reporter references: For further information, consult the following CCH reporters.

— Standard Federal Tax Reporter, 2006FED ¶22,812.01 and ¶22,812.021

— Tax Research Consultant, EXEMPT: 21,200

— Federal Tax Guide, 2006FTG ¶16,130

¶1230 Excess Benefit Transactions Involving Supporting Organizations

SUMMARY OF NEW LAW

The definitions of "excess benefit," "excess benefit transaction," and "disqualified person" have been expanded specifically as those terms relate to Code Sec. 509(a)(3) supporting organizations.

BACKGROUND

Intermediate sanctions in the form of excise taxes may be imposed under Code Sec. 4958 against the managers and "disqualified persons" of tax-exempt organizations who engage in "excess benefit transactions" (see the discussion at ¶1245). An excess benefit transaction is any transaction in which:

- an economic benefit is provided by a tax-exempt organization, directly or indirectly, to or for the use of any disqualified person; *and*
- the value of the economic benefit provided exceeds the value of the consideration (including the performance of services) received for providing the benefit.

All benefits and consideration exchanged between a disqualified person and the organization (including all entities controlled by the organization) are taken into account, except certain specifically disregarded benefits.

For this purpose, a disqualified person is any individual who is in a position to exercise substantial authority over an organization's affairs. Any person who has substantial powers, responsibilities, or interests, in an organization, regardless of the individual's official title, is in a position to exercise substantial influence over the affairs of the tax-exempt organization and, therefore, is considered to be a disqualified person. This includes: voting members of the governing body; presidents, chief executive officers, or chief operating officers; treasurers and chief financial officers; and persons with a material financial interest in a provider-sponsored organization.

In addition, disqualified persons include certain family members of an individual in a position to exercise substantial influence, and certain 35-percent controlled entities. Family members include a spouse, brothers or sisters (by whole or half blood), spouses of brothers or sisters (by whole or half blood), ancestors, children, grandchildren, great grandchildren, and spouses of children, grandchildren, and great grandchildren. A 35-percent entity includes: a corporation in which a disqualified person owns more than 35-percent of the combined voting power; a partnership in which a disqualified person owns more than 35-percent of the profits interest; or a

BACKGROUND

trust or estate in which a disqualified person owns more than 35-percent of the beneficial interest.

A disqualified person includes anyone who has met the definition at any time during the five year lookback period immediately preceding a transaction at issue.

NEW LAW EXPLAINED

Excess benefit transactions involving supporting organizations.—The rules relating to excess benefit transactions have been expanded to include transactions involving supporting organizations that are organized and operated exclusively for the benefit of, to perform the functions of, or to carry out the purposes of a tax-exempt organization. Specifically, the definition of a disqualified person now includes any person who with respect to a Code Sec. 509(a)(3) supporting organization: (1) was in a position to exercise substantial influence over the affairs of the organization at any time during the five-year period preceding the transaction in question; (2) was a member of the family of such an individual; or (3) was a 35-percent controlled entity (Code Sec. 4958(f)(1)(D), as added by the Pension Protection Act of 2006).

The definitions of "excess benefit" and "excess benefit transaction" have also been clarified to apply to supporting organizations as defined by Code Sec. 509(a)(3). Any grant, loan, compensation or similar payment made by a supporting organization to a substantial contributor, a family member of a substantial contributor (under Code Sec. 4958(f)(4)), or a 35-percent controlled entity constitutes an excess benefit transaction. Also, any loan a supporting organization provides to a disqualified person (excluding for this purpose any organizations described in Code Sec. 509(a)(1), (2) or (4)) also constitutes an excess benefit transaction. The "excess benefit" is defined as the amount of any such grants, loans, compensation or similar payments (Code Sec. 4958(c)(3)(A), as added by the Pension Act).

A "substantial contributor" is a person who contributed or bequeathed in excess of $5,000 to the supporting organization if such aggregate contributions constitute in excess of two percent of the total contributions and bequests received by the supporting organization in the tax year in which the funds are received. In the case of contributions by a trust, contributions by the trust and by the creator of the trust will be aggregated for purposes of applying this rule. Rules similar to the rules of Code Sec. 507(d)(2)(B) and (C) (which relate to substantial contributors, and when a person ceases to be a substantial contributor) are to be applied for these purposes. However, any organizations described in Code Sec. 509(a)(1), (2) or (4) will not be considered to be substantial contributors under this rule (Code Sec. 4958(c)(3)(C), as added by the Pension Act).

A 35-percent controlled entity is, for this purpose, defined as one of the following:

(1) a corporation in which a substantial contributor to a supporting organization or a family member (under Code Sec. 4958(f)(4)) of such an individual owns more than 35 percent of the total combined voting power;

NEW LAW EXPLAINED

(2) a partnership in which such persons own more than 35 percent of the profits interest; or

(3) a trust or estate in which such persons own more than 35 percent of the beneficial interest (Code Sec. 4958(c)(3)(B), as added by the Pension Act).

For rules relating to the application of, and returns of, supporting organizations, see the discussion at ¶ 1270.

► **Effective date.** The provision modifying the definition of disqualified person is effective for transactions occurring after August 17, 2006 (Act Sec. 1242(c)(1) of the Pension Protection Act of 2006). The provision modifying the definitions of excess benefit and excess benefit transaction is effective for transactions occurring after July 25, 2006 (Act Sec. 1242(c)(2) of the Pension Act).

Law source: Law at ¶5275. Committee Report at ¶11,360.

— Act Sec. 1242(a) of the Pension Protection Act of 2006, redesignating Code Sec. 4958(f)(1)(D) and (E) as Code Sec. 4958(f)(1)(E) and (F), respectively, and adding new Code Sec. 4958(f)(1)(D);

— Act Sec. 1242(b), redesignating Code Sec. 4958(c)(3) as Code Sec. 4958(c)(4) and adding new Code Sec. 4958(c)(3);

— Act Sec. 1242(c), providing the effective date.

Reporter references: For further information, consult the following CCH reporters.

— Standard Federal Tax Reporter, 2006FED ¶22,812.023 and ¶34,255.01

— Tax Research Consultant, EXEMPT: 6,056 and EXEMPT: 21,200

— Federal Tax Guide, 2006FTG ¶16,130 and ¶21,360

¶1235 Excess Business Holdings of Supporting Organizations

SUMMARY OF NEW LAW

The excess business holding rules have been extended to private foundations that qualify as Type III supporting organizations.

BACKGROUND

The excess business holdings of a private foundation are the amount of stock or other interest in a business enterprise that exceeds its permitted holdings. A private foundation is generally permitted to hold up to 20 percent of the voting stock of a corporation, reduced by the percentage of voting stock actually or constructively owned by disqualified persons. There are two exceptions to this rule. First, if one or more persons who are not disqualified persons have effective control of a corporation, the private foundation and all disqualified persons together may own up to 35

BACKGROUND

percent of the corporation's voting stock. Second, a private foundation is not treated as having excess business holdings in any corporation in which it (together with certain other related private foundations) owns not more than two percent of the voting stock and not more than two percent of the value of all outstanding shares of all classes of stock. A private foundation may own nonvoting stock only if all of the disqualified persons own in aggregate 20 percent or less of the voting stock.

A private foundation is not permitted any holdings in sole proprietorships that are business enterprises unless they were held before May 26, 1969, or acquired by gift or bequest thereafter. For determining the holdings in a business enterprise of either a private foundation or a disqualified person, any stock or other interest owned directly or indirectly by or for a corporation, partnership, estate, or trust is considered owned proportionately by or for its shareholders, partners, or beneficiaries.

Generally, a private foundation has 90 days in which to dispose of excess business holdings from the date on which it knows or should have known that such acquisition constituted excess business holdings. However, if the excess business holdings are acquired by gift or bequest, the foundation has five years in which to dispose of them.

An initial tax of five percent is imposed on excess business holdings that are not disposed of within the applicable grace period (Code Sec. 4943(a)). If this initial tax has been imposed and the private foundation still retains excess business holdings at the close of its tax year, an additional tax equal to 200 percent of any remaining excess business holdings is imposed (see the discussion at ¶1245).

NEW LAW EXPLAINED

Excess business holding of supporting organizations.—The excess business holding rules have been extended to certain private foundations that qualify as supporting organizations. A supporting organization will be covered by the new excess holdings rules if it is:

(1) a Type III supporting organization (that is, a supporting organization that demonstrates that it is responsive to the needs and demands of the supported organization), other than a functionally integrated Type III supporting organization (as defined below); *or*

(2) an organization that meets the requirements of Code Sec. 509(a)(3)(A) (the organizational and operational test) and Code Sec. 509(a)(3)(C) (the lack of control test) (see the discussion at ¶ 1225), *and*

  (a) is supervised or controlled in connection with one or more organizations described in Code Sec. 509(a), *but only if*

  (b) such organization accepts any gift or contribution from a person described in Code Sec. 509(f)(2)(B) (Code Sec. 4943(f)(3), as added by the Pension Act).

Exceptions. Functionally integrated Type III supporting organizations are Type III supporting organizations that are excepted by regulation from the requirement to make payments to supported organizations because the organization's activities are related to

NEW LAW EXPLAINED

performing the functions of, or carrying out the purposes of, those supported organizations (Code Sec. 4943(f)(5)(B), as added by the Pension Act).

In addition, the IRS has the authority to exempt the excess business holdings of any organization from application of these rules if the organization establishes to the IRS's satisfaction that the excess holdings are consistent with the exempt purposes constituting the basis for the organization's tax-exempt status under Code Sec. 501(a) (Code Sec. 4943(f)(2), as added by the Pension Act).

The term excess business holdings does not include any holdings of a Type III supporting organization if, as of November 18, 2005, and at all time thereafter, such business holdings are held for the benefit of the community pursuant to a directive or similar order made by the Attorney General of a State, or other appropriate State official, with jurisdiction over the organization (Code Sec. 4943(f)(6), as added by the Pension Act).

Disqualified persons. A disqualified person, with respect to a supporting organizations and the excess business holding rules, is any person who is:

(1) at any time during the five year period preceding the transaction in question, was in position to exercise substantial influence over the affairs of the organization,

(2) was a member of the family of such an individual,

(3) a 35-percent controlled entity,

(4) any person described in Code Sec. 4958(c)(3)(B), as added by the Pension Act (see the discussion at ¶ 1225), *or*

(5) an organization that is effectively controlled (directly or indirectly) by the same person(s) controlling the organization, and to which substantially all of its contributions were made by substantial contributors or other persons in position to exercise substantial influence over the affairs of the organization (directly or indirectly), or members of that persons family, as defined by Code Sec. 4846(d).

Persons "in position to exercise substantial influence over the affairs of the organization" includes substantial contributors, as defined by Code Sec. 4958(c)(3)(C) (see the discussion at ¶ 1230) (Code Sec. 4958(c)(3)(B), as added by the Pension Act).

> **Comment:** Specifically, the definition of substantial contributor contained in Code Sec. 4958(c)(3)(C), as added by the Pension Act, states that rules "similar to the rules of" Code Sec. 507(d)(2)(B) and (C) apply for purposes of defining substantial contributor as applied to Code Sec. 4958(c), as amended by the Pension Act.

A substantial contributor is a person who contributed or bequeathed in excess of $5,000 to the supporting organization if such aggregate contributions constitute in excess of two percent of the total contributions and bequests received by the supporting organization in the tax year in which the funds are received. In the case of contributions by a trust, contributions by the trust and by the creator of the trust will be aggregated for purposes of applying this rule.

Other persons in a position to exercise substantial influence include any officer, director or trustee of the organization (or person holding the powers or responsibilities normally attributable to such positions), or the owner of more than 20 percent of

NEW LAW EXPLAINED

the total combined voting power of a corporation, the profits interest of a partnership, or the beneficial interest of a trust or unincorporated enterprise that qualifies as a substantial contributor (Code Sec. 4943(f)(4)(B), as added by the Pension Act).

Present holdings. Transition rules apply to the present holdings of Type III supporting organizations. A reduction of an organization's excess interest in holdings apply under application of a modified version of Code Sec. 4943(c)(4), (5), and (6) (Code Sec. 4943(f)(7), as added by the Pension Act).

For rules relating to the application of, and returns of, supporting organizations, see the discussion at ¶ 1270.

▶ **Effective date.** The provision is effective for tax years beginning after August 17, 2006 (Act Sec. 1243(b) of the Pension Protection Act of 2006).

Law source: Law at ¶5260. Committee Report at ¶11,360.

— Act Sec. 1243(a) of the Pension Protection Act of 2006, adding Code Sec. 4943(f);

— Act Sec. 1243(b), providing the effective date.

Reporter references: For further information, consult the following CCH reporters.

— Standard Federal Tax Reporter, 2006FED ¶34,072.01, ¶34,072.028 and ¶34,072.075

— Tax Research Consultant, EXEMPT: 21,200 and EXEMPT: 24,500

— Federal Tax Guide, 2006FTG ¶16,130 and ¶21,235

¶1240 Payments from Private Foundations to Supporting Organizations

SUMMARY OF NEW LAW

The definition of a "qualifying distribution" has been modified to prevent payments made by a non-operating private foundation to a supporting organization from constituting a qualifying distribution. Also, the definition of taxable expenditure has been modified to ensure that any amounts paid to supporting organizations by private foundations will be treated as taxable expenditures unless the private foundation exercises expenditure responsibility.

BACKGROUND

Private non-operating foundations are subject to an excise tax for failure to distribute accumulated income. (Non-operating private foundations generally are grant-making organizations that do not operate their own charitable programs.) Private foundations that fail to make current distributions are subject to a two-level tax—an initial and an additional tax—which is imposed if the remaining taxable income is not distributed within a specified period. A third-level tax accompanying involuntary termination of a foundation's exempt status also exists for repeated, flagrant violations.

BACKGROUND

Non-operating foundations are required to annually distribute their minimum investment return, as adjusted downward for certain taxes and adjusted upward for certain loan repayments, proceeds from asset dispositions and unused set-asides. The minimum investment return generally equals five percent of a foundation's net investment assets.

The initial tax imposed for failure to distribute accumulated income equals 15 percent of the amount that should have been distributed. This initial tax is imposed each year until the private foundation is notified of its obligation to pay out or until the foundation actually makes the required payouts (Code Sec. 4942(a)). A second-tier tax, equal to 100 percent of the undistributed income, is imposed if the foundation fails to make the necessary charitable distributions within a "taxable period" that begins on the first day of the tax year and ends on the earlier of the date on which the deficiency notice for the initial tax is mailed, or the date on which the initial tax is assessed (see the discussion at ¶1245) (Code Sec. 4942(b)).

Qualifying distributions by the non-operating foundation reduce the amount required to be distributed ("the distributable amount"). By reducing the distributable amount, the qualifying distributions are reflected in the reduced undistributed income against which the various levels of tax sanctions are taken. Distributions that may be chalked up against the minimum payout include:

(1) distributions to public charities and to private operating foundations;

(2) direct expenditures (including administrative expenses) for charitable purposes; and

(3) expenditures for assets to be used for charitable purposes (Code Sec. 4942(g)).

An initial tax of 10 percent is imposed by Code Sec. 4945 on private foundation "taxable expenditures," which are expenses involving lobbying, electioneering (including voter registration drives), grants to individuals (unless made under objective standards), grants to other organizations (unless the foundation accepts responsibility for proper use of the funds), and for any purpose other than an exempt purpose described in Code Sec. 170(c)(2)(B) (religious, charitable, scientific, literary, educational, to foster national or international amateur sports competition, or for prevention of cruelty to children and/or animals).

NEW LAW EXPLAINED

Treatment of amounts paid from private foundations to supporting organizations.—The definition of qualifying distribution contained in Code Sec. 4942(g) has been modified to generally prevent payments made by a non-operating private foundation to a supporting organization from constituting a qualifying distribution (Code Sec. 4942(g)(4), as amended by the Pension Protection Act of 2006). Specifically, no payments made to a Type III supporting organization that is not a functionally integrated Type III supporting organization may be counted as qualifying distributions (see the discussion at ¶1225) (Code Sec. 4942(g)(4)(A)(i), as amended by the Pension Act). In addition, no payments made to Type I or Type II supporting organizations, or to organizations the are supervised or controlled in connection with such organization(s),

NEW LAW EXPLAINED

or to functionally integrated Type III supporting organizations, may be considered to be qualifying distributions if:

(1) a disqualified person of the private foundation controls, directly or indirectly, either that organization or a supported organization, *or*

(2) such a distribution is declared inappropriate by regulation issued by the IRS (Code Sec. 4942(g)(4)(A)(ii), as amended by the Pension Act).

Also, the definition of taxable expenditure has been modified to reflect the changes the Pension Act has made to Code Secs. 509(a)(3) and 4942(g)(4) and ensure that any amounts paid to supporting organizations by private foundations will be treated as taxable expenditures unless the private foundation exercises expenditure responsibility under Code Sec. 4945(h) with respect to the grant (Code Sec. 4945(d)(4)(A), as amended by the Pension Act).

For rules relating to the application of, and returns of, supporting organizations, see the discussion at ¶ 1270.

▶ **Effective date.** The provision is effective for distributions and expenditures occurring after August 17, 2006 (Act Sec. 1244(c) of the Pension Protection Act of 2006).

Law source: Law at ¶5255 and ¶5270. Committee Report at ¶11,360.

— Act Sec. 1244(a) of the Pension Protection Act of 2006, amending Code Sec. 4942(g)(4);

— Act Sec. 1244(b), amending Code Sec. 4945(d)(4)(A);

— Act Sec. 1244(c), providing the effective date.

Reporter references: For further information, consult the following CCH reporters.

— Standard Federal Tax Reporter, 2006FED ¶34,047.034, ¶34,047.068 and ¶34,107.021

— Tax Research Consultant, EXEMPT: 21,200 and EXEMPT: 24,400

— Federal Tax Guide, 2006FTG ¶16,130 and ¶21,230

EXCISE TAXES

¶1245 Increase in Penalty Excise Taxes on Public Charities, Social Welfare Organizations and Private Foundations

SUMMARY OF NEW LAW

The initial taxes and dollar limitations for self-dealing and excess benefit transactions are doubled. The initial taxes and the dollar limitations on foundation managers with respect to the private foundation excise taxes on the failure to distribute income, excess business holdings, jeopardizing investments, and taxable expenditures are also doubled.

BACKGROUND

Excess benefit transaction. Excise taxes are imposed on excess benefit transactions between disqualified persons (see the discussion at ¶1230) and charitable organizations (other than private foundations) or social welfare organizations. The excess benefit tax is imposed on the disqualified person and, in certain cases, on the organization manager, but is not imposed on the exempt organization. An initial tax of 25 percent of the excess benefit amount is imposed on the disqualified person that receives the excess benefit. An additional tax on the disqualified person of 200 percent of the excess benefit applies if the violation is not corrected. A tax of 10 percent of the excess benefit (not to exceed $10,000 with respect to any excess benefit transaction) is imposed on an organization manager that knowingly participated in the excess benefit transaction, but only if the manager's participation was willful and not due to reasonable cause, and if the initial tax was imposed on the disqualified person.

Self-dealing by private foundations. Excise taxes are imposed on acts of self-dealing between a disqualified person and a private foundation. An initial tax of five percent of the amount involved with respect to an act of self-dealing is imposed on any disqualified person (other than a foundation manager acting only as such) who participates in the act of self-dealing. If such a tax is imposed, a 2.5-percent tax of the amount involved, up to $10,000 per act, is imposed on a foundation manager who participated in the act of self-dealing knowing it was such an act, unless such participation was not willful and was due to reasonable cause. These initial taxes may not be abated.

If the act of self-dealing is not corrected, a tax of 200 percent of the amount involved is imposed on the disqualified person and a tax of 50 percent of the amount involved is imposed on a foundation manager who refused to agree to correcting the act of self-dealing. This tax is limited to $10,000 per act.

Tax on failure to distribute income. Private nonoperating foundations are required to pay out a minimum amount each year as qualifying distributions. Failure to pay out the minimum results in an initial excise tax on the foundation of 15 percent of the undistributed amount. An additional tax of 100 percent of the undistributed amount applies if an initial tax is imposed and the required distributions have not been made by the end of the applicable tax period.

Tax on excess business holdings. Private foundations are subject to tax on excess business holdings. The initial tax is equal to five percent of the value of the excess business holdings held during the foundation's applicable tax year. An additional tax is imposed if an initial tax is imposed and at the close of the applicable taxable period the foundation continues to hold excess business holdings. The amount of the additional tax is equal to 200 percent of such holdings.

Tax on jeopardizing investments. Private foundations and foundation managers are subject to tax on investments that jeopardize the foundation's charitable purpose. In general, an initial tax of five percent of the amount of the investment applies to the foundation and to foundation managers who participated in the making of the investment knowing that it jeopardized the carrying out of the foundation's exempt purposes. The initial tax on foundation managers may not exceed $5,000 per invest-

BACKGROUND

ment. If the investment is not removed from jeopardy (e.g., sold or otherwise disposed of), an additional tax of 25 percent of the amount of the investment is imposed on the foundation and five percent of the amount of the investment on a foundation manager who refused to agree to removing the investment from jeopardy. The additional tax on foundation managers may not exceed $10,000 per investment.

Tax on taxable expenditures. Certain expenditures of private foundations are subject to tax. For each taxable expenditure, a tax is imposed on the foundation of 10 percent of the amount of the expenditure, and an additional tax of 100 percent is imposed on the foundation if the expenditure is not corrected. Also, a tax of 2.5 percent of the expenditure (up to $5,000) is imposed on a foundation manager who agrees to making a taxable expenditure knowing that it is a taxable expenditure. An additional tax of 50 percent of the amount of the expenditure (up to $10,000) is imposed on a foundation manager who refuses to agree to correct the expenditure.

NEW LAW EXPLAINED

Penalty excise taxes on public charities, social welfare organizations, and private foundations increased.—The penalty excise taxes on public charities, social welfare organizations, and private foundations for self-dealing, excess benefit transactions, failure to distribute income, excess business holdings, jeopardizing investments, and taxable expenditures are increased.

The initial taxes and dollar limitations for self-dealing and excess benefit transactions are doubled:

(1) For acts of self-dealing other than the payment of compensation by a private foundation to a disqualified person, the initial tax on the self-dealer is doubled to 10 percent of the amount involved (Code Sec. 4941(a)(1), as amended by the Pension Protection Act of 2006).

(2) The initial tax on foundation managers is doubled to five percent of the amount involved (Code Sec. 4941(a)(2), as amended by the Pension Act).

(3) The dollar limitation on the amount of the initial and additional taxes on foundation managers per act of self-dealing is doubled to $20,000 per act (Code Sec. 4941(c)(2), as amended by the Pension Act).

(4) The dollar limitation on organization managers of public charities and social welfare organizations for participation in excess benefit transactions is doubled to $20,000 per transaction (Code Sec. 4958(d)(2), as amended by the Pension Act).

The new provisions also double the amounts of the initial taxes and the dollar limitations on foundation managers with respect to the private foundation excise taxes on the failure to distribute income, excess business holdings, jeopardizing investments, and taxable expenditures:

(1) For a *failure to distribute income*, the initial tax on a nonoperating foundation is doubled to 30 percent of the undistributed amount (Code Sec. 4942(a), as amended by the Pension Act).

NEW LAW EXPLAINED

(2) For *excess business holdings*, the initial tax on excess business holdings is doubled to 10 percent of the value of such holdings (Code Sec. 4943(a)(1), as amended by the Pension Act).

(3) For *jeopardizing investments*:

- the initial tax is doubled to 10 percent of the amount of the investment that is imposed on the foundation and on foundation managers (Code Sec. 4944(a), as amended by the Pension Act);
- the dollar limitation on the initial tax on foundation managers is doubled to $10,000 per investment (Code Sec. 4944(d)(2), as amended by the Pension Act); and
- the dollar limitation on the additional tax on foundation managers is doubled to $20,000 per investment (Code Sec. 4944(d)(2), as amended by the Pension Act).

(4) For *taxable expenditures*:

- the initial tax on the foundation is doubled to 20 percent of the amount of the expenditure (Code Sec. 4945(a)(1), as amended by the Pension Act);
- the initial tax on the foundation manager is doubled to five percent of the amount of the expenditure (Code Sec. 4945(a)(2), as amended by the Pension Act);
- the dollar limitation on the initial tax on foundation managers is doubled to $10,000 (Code Sec. 4945(c)(2), as amended by the Pension Act); and
- the dollar limitation on the additional tax on foundation managers is doubled to $20,000 (Code Sec. 4945(c)(2), as amended by the Pension Act).

Excess benefit transaction. An excess benefit transaction generally is a transaction in which an economic benefit is provided by a charitable or social welfare organization directly or indirectly to or for the use of a disqualified person, if the value of the economic benefit provided exceeds the value of the consideration (including the performance of services) received by the organization in exchange for the benefit.

Comment: The excess benefit transaction tax is commonly referred to as "intermediate sanctions" because it imposes penalties generally considered to be less punitive than revocation of the organization's exempt status.

Practical Analysis: Barnaby Zall, of Weinberg & Jacobs, LLP, Rockville, Maryland, observes that when Code Sec. 4958, or "intermediate sanctions," was first passed, it was touted as applying only to major transgressions and not to "foot faults." Since then it has morphed into a generally applicable rule used not only for conflict of interest violations but also for paperwork and judgment infractions. This provision, doubling these penalties and those for private foundation infractions, may have several effects. Careful organization managers and directors will likely increase their reliance on outside counsel, increasing costs. An unintended consequence, highlighted in the recent decision of the U.S. Court of Appeals for the Fifth Circuit in *M.T.*

NEW LAW EXPLAINED

Caracci (CA-5, 2006-2 USTC ¶50,395) may be that courts will be even more exacting and unforgiving in reviewing the IRS's decisions to impose these substantial taxes.

> **Comment:** A foundation may include as a qualifying distribution the salaries, occupancy expenses, travel costs, and other reasonable and necessary administrative expenses that the foundation incurs in operating a grant program. A qualifying distribution also includes any amount paid to acquire an asset used (or held for use) directly in carrying out one or more of the organization's exempt purposes and certain amounts set-aside for exempt purposes.

In general, an organization is permitted to adjust the distributable amount in those cases where distributions during the five preceding years have exceeded the payout requirements.

Tax on excess business holdings. In general, a private foundation is permitted to hold 20 percent of the voting stock in a corporation, reduced by the amount of voting stock held by all disqualified persons. If it is established that no disqualified person has effective control of the corporation, a private foundation and disqualified persons together may own up to 35 percent of the voting stock of a corporation. A private foundation is not treated as having excess business holdings in any corporation if it owns (together with certain other related private foundations) not more than two percent of the voting stock and not more than two percent in value of all outstanding shares of all classes of stock in that corporation. Similar rules apply with respect to holdings in a partnership ("profits interest" is substituted for "voting stock" and "capital interest" for "nonvoting stock") and to other unincorporated enterprises (by substituting "beneficial interest" for "voting stock").

Private foundations are not permitted to have holdings in a proprietorship. Foundations generally have a five-year period to dispose of excess business holdings (acquired other than by purchase) without being subject to tax. This five-year period may be extended an additional five years in limited circumstances.

Jeopardizing investments. Generally jeopardizing investments are those that show a lack of reasonable business care and prudence in providing for the long- and short-term financial needs of the foundation for it to carry out its exempt function. No single factor determines a jeopardizing investment. No category of investments is treated as an intrinsic violation, but careful scrutiny is applied to:

(1) trading in securities on margin,

(2) trading in commodity futures,

(3) investing in working interests in oil and gas wells,

(4) buying "puts," "calls," and "straddles,"

(5) buying warrants, and

(6) selling short (Reg. § 53.4944-1(a)(2)(i)).

An investment is considered removed from jeopardy when the foundation sells or otherwise disposes of the investment and the proceeds are not investments that jeopardize the foundation's exempt purpose (Reg. § 53.4944-5(b)).

NEW LAW EXPLAINED

Tax on taxable expenditures. In general, taxable expenditures are expenses:

(1) for lobbying;

(2) to influence the outcome of a public election or carry on a voter registration drive (unless certain requirements are met);

(3) as a grant to an individual for travel, study, or similar purposes unless made pursuant to procedures approved by the IRS;

(4) as a grant to an organization that is not a public charity or exempt operating foundation unless the foundation exercises expenditure responsibility with respect to the grant; or

(5) for any non-charitable purpose.

> **Planning Note:** In general, expenditure responsibility requires that a foundation make all reasonable efforts and establish reasonable procedures to ensure that the grant is spent solely for the purpose for which it was made, to obtain reports from the grantee on the expenditure of the grant, and to make reports to the IRS regarding such expenditures (Code Sec. 4945(h)).

Abatement in certain cases. Any violation of the private foundation rules (i.e., rules regarding self-dealing, failure to distribute income, excess business holdings, investments that jeopardize charitable purpose, taxable expenditures, excess benefit transactions) currently results in imposition of an initial excise tax on the foundation or, in the case of self-dealing, on the disqualified person who entered into the prohibited transaction with the foundation. The IRS has discretionary authority to not assess or, if assessed, to abate, credit or refund these first-tier excise taxes, if it is established that:

(1) the violation was due to reasonable cause and not willful neglect and

(2) the event was corrected within the applicable correction period (Code Sec. 4962).

▶ **Effective date.** The amendments apply to tax years beginning after August 17, 2006 (Act Sec. 1212(f) of the Pension Protection Act of 2006).

Law source: Law at ¶5250, ¶5255, ¶5260, ¶5265, ¶5270 and ¶5275. Committee Report at ¶11,200.

— Act Sec. 1212(a) of the Pension Protection Act of 2006, amending Code Secs. 4941(a), (c)(2), and 4958(d)(2);

— Act Sec. 1212(b), amending Code Sec. 4942(a);

— Act Sec. 1212(c), amending Code Sec. 4943(a)(1);

— Act Sec. 1212(d), amending Code Sec. 4944(a) and (d)(2);

— Act Sec. 1212(e), amending Code Sec. 4945(a) and (c)(2);

— Act Sec. 1212(f), providing the effective date.

NEW LAW EXPLAINED

Reporter references: For further information, consult the following CCH reporters.

— Standard Federal Tax Reporter, 2006FED ¶34,031.01, ¶34,031.03, ¶34,047.068, ¶34,072.027, ¶34,087.01, ¶34,107.01, ¶34,107.068 and ¶34,255.01

— Tax Research Consultant, EXEMPT: 6,056, EXEMPT: 24,150, EXEMPT: 24,300, EXEMPT: 24,502, EXEMPT: 24,602 and EXEMPT: 24,652

— Federal Tax Guide, 2006FTG ¶21,200 et seq.

¶1250 Expansion of Base of Excise Tax on Private Foundations

SUMMARY OF NEW LAW

The base upon which the two-percent excise tax on the net investment income of private foundations is expanded, and the uncertainty regarding regulations promulgated under Code Sec. 4940 is clarified.

BACKGROUND

Under Code Sec. 4940(a), private foundations are subject to a two-percent excise tax on their net investment income for a particular tax year. Net investment income is generally defined as the sum of the foundation's gross investment income and capital gain net income less the ordinary and necessary business expenses incurred for the production of that income (Code Sec. 4940(c)(1)). Items specifically included in gross investment income are interest, dividends, rents, payments with respect to securities loans, and royalties (Code Sec. 4940(c)(2)). No other items are specifically included in this definition. In calculating capital gain net income, the gains and losses from the disposition of property used for the production of interest, dividends, rents and royalties are to be taken into account (Code Sec. 4940(c)(4)(A)). Furthermore, capital loss carryovers are not included in this calculation (Code Sec. 4940(c)(4)(C)).

With Reg. § 53.4940, an attempt was made to expand the base used to determine the excise tax. Gross investment income was expanded to include items described in the unrelated business income tax regulations (Reg. § 1.512(b)-1) such as annuities, income from notional principal contracts and other substantially similar income from ordinary and routine investments. Further, the definition of capital gains net income was changed in the regulations to provide that only gains and losses from property held for investment purposes will be included in the calculation. And while this would appear to narrow the tax base, the regulation provided that property will be deemed held for investment purposes even if it is immediately disposed of upon its receipt if it is a type of property *that generally produces* interest, dividends, rents, royalties or capital gains through appreciation. Thus, the regulation actually broadened the definition of capital gains net income to include significantly more property than would be included under Code Sec. 4940(c) standing alone.

BACKGROUND

Predictably, the regulation was challenged by a taxpayer. In *Zemurray Foundation v US*, CA-5, 82-2 USTC ¶9609, the Fifth Circuit did not find error with the regulation treating property as held for investment purposes if it is a type of property that generally produces the taxed types of income, as opposed to property that is actually used for the production of this income. However, on remand, the district court found that the property in question in the case was not susceptible for use in the production of income. Furthermore, the district court found that including capital gains through appreciation in net investment income went beyond the limits of Code Sec. 4940(c)(4)(A).

The IRS conceded this issue in General Counsel Memorandum 39538 (July 23, 1986), stating that only gains and losses from the sale or other disposition of property of the type that generally produces interest, dividends, rents, and royalties, and other property used for the production of income are taken into account when calculating the excise tax on net investment income, as opposed to including sale proceeds from property that only produces capital gains through appreciation. While this position still appears to go beyond the bounds of Code Sec. 4940, it is much narrower than the definition of net investment income found in the regulation by excluding capital gains through appretiation.

Furthermore, while the Code bars only the use of capital loss carryovers in calculating capital gain net income (Code Sec. 4940(c)(4)(C)), the regulation excludes the use of both carryovers and carrybacks (Reg. § 53.4940-1(f)(3)).

While the principal effect of this regulation was to expand the base for the excise tax, it did limit the base in one way. The capital gain net income was not to include the gains and losses from the sale or disposition of property used for the exempt purpose of the private foundation (Reg. § 53.4940-1(f)(1)).

As a result, whether the regulations apply is unclear in light of *Zemurray* and the General Counsel Memorandum.

NEW LAW EXPLAINED

Tax base expanded and application of regulations clarified.—The definition of gross investment income is expanded to include income from sources similar to interest, dividends, rents, payments with respect to securities loans, and royalties (Code Sec. 4940(c)(2), as amended by the Pension Protection Act of 2006). This broader definition most likely includes income from annuities, notional principal contracts and other substantially similar income from ordinary and routine investments.

Amendments also change the definition of capital gain net income. Now, gain or loss from a sale or disposition of property is included if the property is used for the production of gross investment income (Code Sec. 4940(c)(4)(A), as amended by the Pension Act).

> **Comment:** Though not readily apparent from the text of the Pension Act, the Joint Committee on Taxation explains that this amendment will include Reg § 53.4940's "capital gains through appreciation." This is because income produced through appreciation is similar to capital gains on property held for the

NEW LAW EXPLAINED

production of dividends, given that both types of property are held for investment purposes (Joint Committee on Taxation, Technical Explanation of the Pension Protection Act of 2006 (JCX-38-06)).

The definition of capital gain net income is also amended to incorporate the regulation's ban on the carryback of losses. This is in addition to the existing prohibition on including loss carryovers (Code Sec. 4940(c)(4)(C), as amended by the Pension Act).

Finally, the regulation's exclusion from capital gain net income of gain and loss on the sale of property used in the foundation's exempt purpose is not picked up by the Pension Act. Moreover, the Joint Committee on Taxation (JCX-38-06) specifically states that the provision does not apply. However, under rules similar to those under Code Sec. 1031 (governing like-kind exchanges), gain and loss on property used for a period not less than one year for a function that constitutes the foundation's exempt purpose will not be included in calculating capital gain net income if the property is immediately exchanged after the period of use for like-kind property to be used primarily for the foundation's exempt purpose (Code Sec. 4940(c)(4)(D), as added by the Pension Act).

Caution Note: One such rule that the amendment specifies is the Code Sec. 1031(a)(2) exception of securities (stocks, bonds, etc.) and inventory from the like-kind exchange rules. The Joint Committee on Taxation also gives the example of the Code Sec. 1031(a)(3) requirement that the exchange be completed within 180 days after the transfer of the property. Both the amended Code and the Joint Committee report make clear that the list of applicable rules is not exhaustive. Presumably, then, other rules of Code Sec. 1031 exchanges apply here as well (e.g., identification of exchange property within 45 days, related party rules, etc.).

Practical Analysis: Barnaby Zall, of Weinberg & Jacobs, LLP, Rockville, Maryland, notes that this provision reverses a 1982 court decision (*Zemurray Foundation,* CA-5, 82-2 USTC ¶9609)), which limited this tax to items specifically enumerated in the Internal Revenue Code. This provision expands the Code to cover items similar to those enumerated, thus adopting the losing IRS position.

▶ **Effective date.** The provision applies to tax years beginning after August 17, 2006 (Act Sec. 1221(c) of the Pension Protection Act of 2006).

Law source: Law at ¶5155 and ¶5245. Committee Report at ¶11,290.

— Act Sec. 1221(a)(1) of the Pension Protection Act of 2006, amending Code Secs. 4940(c)(2) and 509(e);

— Act Sec. 1221(b), amending Code Sec. 4940(c)(4);

— Act Sec. 1221(c), providing the effective date.

Reporter references: For further information, consult the following CCH reporters.

— Standard Federal Tax Reporter, 2006FED ¶34,002.01, ¶34,002.021, ¶34,002.075 and ¶34,002.08

— Tax Research Consultant, EXEMPT: 24,602 and EXEMPT: 24,104

— Federal Tax Guide, 2006FTG ¶21,200

¶1255 Exemption for Blood Collector Organizations

SUMMARY OF NEW LAW

Qualified blood collector organizations are exempt from the excise taxes on fuel, telecommunications, heavy trucks and trailers, and tires to the extent that the items are used for the exclusive use of the organization for the distribution or collection of blood.

BACKGROUND

The American Red Cross is a Congressionally chartered corporation. It is responsible for giving aid to members of the U.S. Armed Forces, to disaster victims in the United States and abroad to help people prevent, prepare for, and respond to emergencies. According to its website, http://www.redcross.org, the Red Cross is responsible for collecting almost half of the nation's blood supply.

The Red Cross has been given an exemption from certain excise taxes generally because the full benefit of the exemption accrues to the United States. Specifically, on April 18, 1979, the IRS exempted the Red Cross from certain retail and manufacturers level excise taxes with respect to articles sold to the Red Cross for its exclusive use (Notice, 1979-1 CB 478). In addition, the IRS ruled that the Red Cross is exempt from the heavy vehicle use tax imposed by Code Sec. 4481 (Rev. Rul. 76-510). Finally, the Red Cross is exempt from the communications excise taxes imposed by Code Sec. 4251 (Code Sec. 4253(c)).

No exemption, however, was provided from the gas guzzler tax (Code Sec. 4064), and the manufacturers level taxes imposed on fuel (Code Sec. 4081), on fuel used on inland waterways (Code Sec. 4042), and on coal (Code Sec. 4121). Although the tax on fuel was not explicitly exempted, the Red Cross can obtain a refund of fuel taxes paid pursuant to Code Secs. 6416(b)(2) and 6427(l).

NEW LAW EXPLAINED

Blood collector organizations.—In addition to the American Red Cross, other "qualified blood collector organizations" are now exempt from certain retail and manufacturers level excise taxes. A "qualified blood collector organization" is a Code Sec. 501(c)(3) organization that is:

(1) primarily engaged in the collection of human blood;

(2) registered with the IRS for the exemption; and

(3) registered by the Food and Drug Administration to collect blood (Code Sec. 7701(a)(49), as added by the Pension Protection Act of 2006).

The new excise tax exemptions only apply if the items are for the exclusive use of the Code Sec. 501(c)(3) organization in the collection, storage or transportation of blood. The specific exemptions are:

NEW LAW EXPLAINED

- the special fuels/alternative fuels tax under Code Sec. 4041 (Code Sec. 4041(g)(5), as added by the Pension Act);
- the retail tax on heavy trucks and trailers imposed by Code Sec. 4051 (Code Sec. 4221(a)(6), as added by the Pension Act);
- the excise tax on tires imposed by Code Sec. 4071 (Code Sec. 4221(a)(6), as added by the Pension Act);
- the communications tax imposed by Code Sec. 4251 (Code Sec. 4253(k), as added by the Pension Act); and
- the heavy vehicle use tax imposed by Code Sec. 4481 (Code Sec. 4483(h)(1), as added by the Pension Act).

In the case of the heavy vehicle use tax, only "qualified blood collector vehicles" will qualify for the tax exemption. A qualified blood collector vehicle is one in which at least 80 percent of the vehicle's use in the prior taxable period is devoted to the collection, storage or transportation of blood (Code Sec. 4483(h)(2), as added by the Pension Act). For new vehicles, a vehicle will be treated as a qualified blood collector vehicle (and thus exempt from the heavy vehicle use tax) if the collector organization certifies to the IRS that the organization reasonably expects at least 80 percent of the vehicle's use will be in the collection, storage or transportation of blood (Code Sec. 4483(h)(3), as added by the Pension Act).

Communication taxes. Similar to other exemptions from the Code Sec. 4251 communications tax, in order for the exemption to apply, the blood collector organization must provide an exemption certificate to the communications service provider (Code Sec. 4253(l), as amended by the Pension Act). The organization can provide an exemption certificate for each item separately paid or may provide a blanket certificate that can cover a period of up to one year (Reg. § 49.4253-11).

Refunds and credits. The Pension Act also makes conforming amendments to allow for the credit or refund of these taxes and any tax paid on gasoline for the exclusive use of the blood collector organization (Code Secs. 6416(b)(2) and 6421(c), as amended by the Pension Act). The Pension Act also permits a refund of tax for diesel fuel, kerosene or aviation fuel used by a qualified blood collector organization (Code Sec. 4041(g)(5), as added by the Pension Act, and Code Sec. 6427(l)).

> **Comment:** It is expected that the Red Cross excise tax exemptions will be reexamined in conjunction with a review of its charter (Joint Committee on Taxation, Technical Explanation of the Pension Protection Act of 2006 (JCX-38-06)).

▶ **Effective date.** All of the new exemptions are effective on January 1, 2007, except for the heavy vehicle highway use tax exemption (Act. Sec. 1207(g)(1) of the Pension Protection Act of 2006). Since the heavy vehicle use tax applies an annual basis from July 1 through June 30, the exemption from that tax applies to tax periods beginning on or after July 1, 2007 (Act Sec. 1207(g)(2) of the Pension Act).

NEW LAW EXPLAINED

Law source: Law at ¶5225, ¶5230, ¶5235, ¶5240, ¶5380, ¶5385 and ¶5485. Committee Report at ¶11,170.

— Act Sec. 1207(a) of the Pension Protection Act of 2006, adding Code Sec. 4041(g)(5);

— Act Sec. 1207(b), adding Code Sec. 4221(a)(6) and amending Code Secs. 4221(a) and 6421(c);

— Act Sec. 1207(c), redesignating Code Sec. 4253(k) as 4253(l) and adding new Code Sec. 4253(k);

— Act Sec. 1207(d), redesignating Code Sec. 4483(h) as (i), and adding new Code Sec. 4483(h);

— Act Sec. 1207(e), amending Code Sec. 6416(b)(2) and (b)(4);

— Act Sec. 1207(f), adding Code Sec. 7701(a)(49);

— Act Sec. 1207(g), providing the effective date.

Reporter references: For further information, consult the following CCH reporters.

— Federal Excise Tax Reporter, ¶5700.07, ¶15,515.01, ¶18,715.01, ¶29,975.01, ¶48,215.035 and ¶48,885.02.

— Tax Research Consultant, EXCISE: 3,106.10, EXCISE: 3,160, EXCISE: 6,112.30, EXCISE: 9,064 and EXCISE: 18,000

— Federal Tax Guide, 2006FTG ¶21,200 et. seq.

REPORTING REQUIREMENTS

¶1260 Notification Requirements for Tax-Exempt Entities Not Currently Required to File

SUMMARY OF NEW LAW

Tax-exempt organizations that need not file the Form 990 information return annually because they have gross receipts in each tax year that are normally not more than $25,000 must now provide an annual notification to the IRS containing certain contact and financial information. Failing to provide this notification can result in the loss of their exempt status.

BACKGROUND

Generally, under Code Sec. 6033(a)(1), all tax-exempt organizations must file an annual information return on Form 990, Return of Organization Exempt from Income Tax (see Rev. Proc. 96-10, 1996-1 CB 577). The return serves as the primary source of information about the organization's finances, governance, operations, and programs.

BACKGROUND

The penalty for failure to file Form 990 or for failure to include all required information is $20 for each day the failure continues. The maximum penalty per return is $10,000 or five percent of the organization's gross receipts, whichever is less. However, organizations with annual gross receipts exceeding $1 million are subject to an increased penalty of $100 per day, with a maximum penalty of $50,000. No penalty is imposed if failure to file a completed return is due to reasonable cause (Code Sec. 6652(c)(1)(A)).

The Tax Code provides certain mandatory exceptions to this filing requirement (Code Sec. 6033(a)(3)(A)). Among these is an exception for several categories of organizations (but excluding private foundations) whose gross receipts in each tax year are normally not more than $5,000 (Code Sec. 6033(a)(3)(A)(ii)). Besides these exceptions, the IRS can create discretionary exceptions to the Code Sec. 6033(a)(1) requirement to file an annual information return. The IRS has the latitude to create such an exception if it determines that the filing of certain returns is not necessary to efficiently administer the internal revenue laws (Rev. Proc. 96-10, 1996-1 CB 577).

The IRS exercised this discretionary authority by expanding the filing exception to include Code Sec. 501(c) exempt organizations (other than private foundations) whose gross receipts in each tax year are not normally more than $25,000 (thus expanding the $5,000 limit in the statutory exception) (Announcement 82-88, 1982-25 I.R.B. 23).

In its recommendations to Congress, the Panel on the Nonprofit Sector discussed the IRS's list of organizations qualified to receive tax-deductible contributions under Code Sec. 501(c)(3). The Panel commented that the list contains outdated information for the many organizations that are not required to file annual information returns, and may include organizations that have ceased operations or no longer qualify for tax-exemption (Panel on the Nonprofit Sector, Strengthening Transparency Governance Accountability of Charitable Organizations: A Final Report to Congress and the Nonprofit Sector (June 2005)). The panel recommended amending the law to require all Code Sec. 501(c)(3) organizations that are currently excused from filing an annual information return because their annual gross receipts fall below $25,000 to file an annual notice with basic contact and financial information.

Code Sec. 6104 contains the rules that provide for the public disclosure and inspection of materials relating to tax-exempt organizations and pension plans. The rules are intended to facilitate the public's scrutiny of tax-exempt organization activities. Among other things, Code Sec. 6104 allows for the disclosure and public inspection of annual information returns that must be filed by these organizations (Code Sec. 6104(b) and (d)).

NEW LAW EXPLAINED

Tax-Exempt Organizations with Low Gross Receipts Must Now Provide Annual Notification.—Under the Pension Protection Act of 2006, tax-exempt organizations that formerly had no obligation to file an annual information return because their gross receipts are normally not more than $25,000 must annually provide, in electronic form, certain information to the IRS in a manner that the IRS will prescribe by regulations

NEW LAW EXPLAINED

(Code Sec. 6033(i), as added by the Pension Act). That information includes the organization's legal name, any name under which it operates and does business, its mailing address and Internet web site address (if any), its taxpayer identification number, the name and address of a principal officer, and evidence of the continuing basis for the organization's exemption from the filing requirements under Code Sec. 6033(a)(1) (Code Sec. 6033(i)(1) as added by the Pension Act). Also, the organization must furnish notice to the IRS when the organization's existence is terminated (Code Sec. 6033(i)(2) as added by the Pension Act).

Practical Analysis: Barnaby Zall, of Weinberg & Jacobs, LLP, Rockville, Maryland, notes that previously, smaller organizations, churches and some other organizations did not have to file annual information returns (Form 990). This provision, building on the IRS's successful electronic filings by political organizations, requires all such organizations to electronically provide certain information annually, including name of an officer and "evidence of its continued exemption" from filing the annual return. An organization that repeatedly fails to file this information loses its tax exemption. It is unclear how this will affect state government organizations and some other organizations. Also, this information will be subject to the regular exempt organization disclosure requirements, so that all such organizations will have to make this information publicly available upon request; the disclosure rules, however, could be interpreted to permit the organization to direct inquiries to the IRS electronic database if it is made publicly available.

Loss of Tax-Exempt Status. No monetary penalty is associated with the failure of a tax-exempt organization to provide information under Code Sec. 6033(i) (Code Sec. 6652(c)(1)(E), as added by the Pension Act). However, tax-exempt organizations that must file annual information returns and notices can lose their exempt status for failing to file as required. Code Sec. 6033(a)(1) describes organizations required to file annual information returns (Form 990). And as discussed above, Code Sec. 6033(i) describes tax-exempt organizations whose gross receipts are normally not more than $25,000—organizations that under the Pension Act must now provide annual notification of basic contact and financial information. If either kind of organization fails to file the required annual return or notice for three consecutive years, the organization's tax-exempt status under Code Sec. 501(a) is revoked as of the date that the third annual return or notice was due, and the organization must apply to have that status reinstated. If, however, the organization can show reasonable cause for failing to file, the IRS in its discretion may reinstate the organization's exempt status effective from the date of the revocation (Code Sec. 6033(j)(3), as added by the Pension Act).

Comment: Whether or not an organization was originally required to apply for tax-exempt status, any organization that has its tax-exempt status revoked must apply to be reinstated (Code Sec. 6033(j)(2), as added by the Pension Act).

NEW LAW EXPLAINED

Caution Note: A revocation of tax-exempt status for failure to file is not subject to an action for declaratory judgment relief (Code Sec. 7428(b)(4), as added by the Pension Act).

Under the Pension Act, the IRS must notify every organization that must provide notification under Code Sec. 6033(i) of that requirement and of the penalty under Code Sec. 6033(j) for failing to provide the notification. In addition, the IRS must publicize the Code Sec. 6033(j) penalty for failure to file a return under Code Sec. 6033(a)(1) or (i).

Comment: Regarding inspection and disclosure requirements, in an early version of the Pension bill, the information provided annually by tax-exempt organizations was not subject to the disclosure rules under Code Sec. 6104(d)(1), nor was it subject to the public inspection rules under Code Sec. 6104(b). The bill sections that caused the annual notification to be exempt from these rules were dropped, however, from the final version of the Pension Act. This reflects Congress's specific intention to subject the annual notice required by Code Sec. 6033(i) to the disclosure and public inspection rules under Code Sec. 6104, which are generally applicable to exempt organizations (see Joint Committee on Taxation, Technical Explanation of the Pension Protection Act of 2006 (JCX-38-06)).

▶ **Effective date.** The provisions apply to notices and returns with respect to annual periods beginning after 2006.

Law source: Law at ¶5325, ¶5390, ¶5440 and ¶7237. Committee Report at ¶11,310.

— Act Sec. 1223(a) of the Pension Protection Act of 2006, redesignating Code Sec. 6033(i) as (j) and adding new Code Sec. 6033(i);

— Act Sec. 1223(b), redesignating Code Sec. 6033(j), as redesignated by Act Sec. 1233(a), as Code Sec. 6033(k) and adding new Code Sec. 6033(j);

— Act Sec. 1223(c), adding Code Sec. 7428(b)(4);

— Act Sec. 1223(d), adding Code Sec. 6652(c)(1)(E);

— Act Sec. 1223(f), providing the effective date.

Reporter references: For further information, consult the following CCH reporters.

— Standard Federal Tax Reporter, 2006FED ¶35,425.01, ¶39,490.0218 and ¶41,723.01

— Tax Research Consultant, EXEMPT: 12,252

— Federal Tax Guide, 2006FTG ¶16,010 and ¶22,085

¶1265 Applications and Returns of Sponsoring Organizations

SUMMARY OF NEW LAW

A sponsoring organization is required to provide additional information on its application for tax-exempt status and on its annual information return.

BACKGROUND

Organizations wishing to apply for tax-exempt status generally must file either a Form 1023, Application for Recognition of Exemption Under Section 501(c)(3) of the Internal Revenue Code, or a Form 1024, Application for Recognition of Exemption Under Section 501(a), with the IRS. Applications should include a copy of an organization's articles of incorporation, by-laws, balance sheet, statement of receipts and expenditures, and a description of its proposed activities.

Tax-exempt organizations that are required to file an annual return must file Form 990, Return of Organization Exempt From Income Tax or Form 990-EZ. This information return provides information on an organization's programs and activities and is not used to report and pay taxes. The return must set forth the organization's gross income, expenses, disbursements for exempt purposes, fund balances, balance sheet, total contributions, the names and addresses of persons contributing $5,000 or more during the tax year (or substantial contributors, in the case of private foundations) and the names, addresses and compensation of its officers, directors, trustees and foundation managers (Code Sec. 6033(b); Reg. § 1.6033-2(a)(2)). In addition to the Code Sec. 6033(b) requirements, Code Sec. 501(c)(3) organizations must report the following additional information: information regarding direct or indirect transfers and other direct or indirect transactions and relationships with other Code Sec. 501(c) organizations (other than Code Sec. 501(c)(3) organizations) and political organizations described in Code Sec. 527, including political campaign committees and political action committees (Code Sec. 6033(b)(9)). Organizations with gross receipts less than $25,000 are not required to file Form 990 (however, see the discussion at ¶ 1260).

NEW LAW EXPLAINED

Additional return requirements for sponsoring organizations.—On its annual Form 990, Return of Organization Exempt From Tax, a Code Sec. 4966(d)(1) sponsoring organization must:

(1) list the total number of donor advised funds it owns at the end of the tax year;

(2) indicate the aggregate value of assets held by its donor advised funds at the end of the tax year; and

(3) indicate the aggregate contributions to and grants made from the funds during the tax year (Code Sec. 6033(k), as added by the Pension Protection Act of 2006).

Exempt status application. On its Form 1023, Application for Recognition of Exemption Under Section 501(c)(3) of the Internal Revenue Code, a sponsoring organization must give notice:

(1) whether the organization maintains or intends to maintain donor advised funds, and

(2) the manner in which the organization plans to operate the funds.

For rules relating to donor adviced funds and charitable contributions, see the discussion at ¶ 1160 and following.

NEW LAW EXPLAINED

▶ **Effective date.** The provisions relating to annual returns of sponsoring organizations apply to returns filed for tax years ending after August 17, 2006 (Act Sec. 1235(a)(2) of the Pension Protection Act of 2006). Provisions relating to matters included on exempt status application apply to organizations applying for tax-exempt status after August 17, 2006 (Act Sec. 1235(b)(2)).

Law source: Law at ¶5150 and ¶5325. Committee Report at ¶11,350.

— Act Sec. 1235(a)(1) of the Pension Protection Act of 2006, amending Code Sec. 6033 by redesignating Code Sec. 6033(k) as (l) (prior to redesignation by Act Sec. 1245, see ¶1270) and adding new Code Sec. 6033(k);

— Act Sec. 1235(b)(1), adding Code Sec. 508(f);

— Act Sec. 1235(a)(2) and 1235(b)(2), providing the effective dates.

Reporter references: For further information, consult the following CCH reporters.

— Standard Federal Tax Reporter, 2006FED ¶22,795.01 and ¶34,425.021

— Federal Tax Guide, 2006FTG ¶16,010 and ¶22,085

¶1270 Returns of Supporting Organizations

SUMMARY OF NEW LAW

Additional requirements have been added for the annual returns of all supporting organizations.

BACKGROUND

Organizations exempt from federal income tax under Code Sec. 501(a) are required to file an annual information return with the IRS (Code Sec. 6033(a)(1)). The return includes information on the organization's finances and operations. The information return requirement does not apply to several categories of exempt organizations. Organizations exempt from the filing requirement include organizations, other than private foundations, where the gross receipts in each tax year normally are not more than $25,000 (however, see the discussion at ¶1260). The IRS has the discretionary authority to relieve *any* organization from the annual filing if it determines that such a filing is not necessary for the efficient administration of the internal revenue laws.

Supporting organizations are public charities that carry out their exempt purposes by supporting one or more other exempt organizations, usually other public charities. Type I supporting organizations are "operated, supervised, or controlled by" the supported organization. Type II supporting organizations are "supervised or controlled in connection with" the supported organization. Type III supporting organizations are "operated in connection with" the supported organization.

NEW LAW EXPLAINED

Additional return information required for supporting organizations.—All Code Sec. 509(a)(3) supporting organizations are required to file an annual information return (Form 990 series) with the IRS, regardless of the organization's gross receipts (Code Sec. 6033(a)(3)(B), as amended by the Pension Protection Act of 2006). The IRS will not have the discretionary authority to relieve any supporting organization from the annual filing requirement.

On its annual information return, a supporting organization must:

(1) list the Code Sec. 509(f)(3) organizations with respect to which it provides support;

(2) indicate whether it is a Type I, Type II or Type III supporting organization; and

(3) certify that the organization is not controlled directly or indirectly by disqualified persons (other than by foundation managers and other than one or more publicly supported organizations) (Code Sec. 6033(l), as added by the Pension Act).

> **Comment:** It is intended that supporting organizations be able to certify that the majority of the organization's governing body is comprised of individuals who were selected based on their special knowledge or expertise in the particular field or discipline in which the supporting organization is operating, or because they represent the particular community that is served by the supported public charities (Joint Committee on Taxation, Technical Explanation of the Pension Protection Act of 2006 (JCX-38-06)).

> **Comment:** The organization's Form 1023 application for exemption should include which type of organization it is.

For rules relating to supporting organizations, see the discussion at ¶1225 and following.

▶ **Effective date.** The amendments apply to returns filed for tax years ending after August 17, 2006 (Act Sec. 1245(c) of the Pension Protection Act of 2006).

Law source: Law at ¶5325. Committee Report at ¶11,360.

— Act Sec. 1245(a) of the Pension Protection Act of 2006, amending Code Sec. 6033(a)(3)(B);

— Act Sec. 1245(b), amending Code Sec. 6033 by redesignating Code Sec. 6033(l) as (m) (after redesignation by Act Sec. 1235, see ¶1265) and adding new Code Sec. 6033(l);

— Act Sec. 1245(c), providing the effective date.

Reporter references: For further information, consult the following CCH reporters.

— Standard Federal Tax Reporter, 2006FED ¶35,425.01 and ¶35,425.021

— Tax Research Consultant, EXEMPT: 21,552

— Federal Tax Guide, 2006FTG ¶16,010 and ¶22,085

¶1275 Disclosure of UBTI Returns by Charitable Organizations

SUMMARY OF NEW LAW

The requirement that charitable organizations make tax materials available for public inspection is extended to returns related to unrelated business taxable income (UBTI).

BACKGROUND

Charitable organizations (also known as a Code Sec. 501(c)(3) organizations or public charities), nonexempt private foundations and nonexempt charitable trusts must make available for public inspection: (1) their three most recent tax returns, and (2) their exemption application materials (Code Sec. 6104(d)).

Returns. To satisfy the disclosure requirements, the exempt entity generally must provide a copy of its actual return, any amended return, and any accompanying schedules and attachments. The annual return for most exempt organizations is some version of Form 990, Return of Organization Exempt From Income Tax. Annual returns do not include: Schedule A of Form 990-BL; Form 990-T, Exempt Organization Business Income Tax Return; Schedule K-1 of Form 1065; or Form 1120-POL, U.S. Income Tax Return For Certain Political Organizations. For exempt organizations other than private foundations, annual returns also do not include the name and address of any contributor (Reg. § 301.6104(d)-1(B)(4)).

Application materials. An entity's exempt status application materials include its application for recognition of exemption, any papers submitted in support of the application, and any letter or other document issued by the IRS with respect to the application (Code Sec. 6104(d)(5)). These materials do not include applications filed by groups that have not yet been recognized as exempt, or materials that are exempt from the return disclosure requirements (Reg. § 301.6104(d)-1(b)(3)(iii)). The IRS withholds information in application materials if its public disclosure would adversely affect the national defense. Upon the organization's written request, the IRS may also withhold information related to any trade secret, patent, process, style of work, or apparatus of the organization (Reg. § 301.6104(a)-5(a)). Applications for exempt status are usually made on: Form 1023, Application for Recognition of Exemption Under Section 501(c)(3); Form 1024, Application for Recognition of Exemption Under Section 501(a); or Form 1028, Application for Recognition of Exemption.

Disclosure procedures. An exempt entity satisfies the disclosure requirements by making its returns and application materials available for public inspection during regular business hours at its principal office, and at each of its regional or district offices with at least three employees. A copy of the materials must also be provided to any individual who makes a personal or written request for them at the entity's principal, regional or district office, although the entity can charge a reasonable fee for reproduction and mailing costs. The entity generally must fulfill personal requests immediately, and written requests within 30 days (Code Sec. 6104(d)(1)).

BACKGROUND

Penalties. Any person who fails to make an organization's annual returns available for public inspection is subject to a penalty of $20 for each day the failure occurs. The maximum penalty for any single annual return is $10,000 (Code Sec. 6652(c)(1)(C)). The same penalty applies to any person who fails to make exemption application materials available for public inspection, except there is no maximum penalty (Code Sec. 6652(c)(1)(D)). If more than one person fails to comply with the disclosure requirements, each person is jointly and severally liable for the full amount of the penalty (Code Sec. 6652(c)(5)(B)). Any person who willfully fails to comply with the public inspection requirements is subject to an additional penalty of $5,000 (Code Sec. 6685).

NEW LAW EXPLAINED

Charitable organizations must make UBTI returns available for public inspection.—The requirement that charitable organizations make their returns and exemption application materials available for public inspection is extended to any returns related to the organization's unrelated business taxable income (UBTI). This new disclosure requirement is limited to Code Sec. 501(c)(3) organizations; it does not apply to nonexempt private foundations and nonexempt charitable trusts (Code Sec. 6104(d)(1)(A)(ii), as amended by the Pension Protection Act of 2006).

Compliance Pointer: Most organizations with UBTI file Form 990-T, Exempt Organization Business Income Tax Return. The new disclosure requirement effectively nullifies the regulation that exempts this form from the public disclosure requirements (Reg. § 301.6104(d)-1(B)(4)(ii)).

The new public disclosure requirement is subject to the existing exceptions to the disclosure requirements provided by Code Sec. 6104 (d)(3), as well as the existing penalties for failing to satisfy the disclosure requirements provided by Code Secs. 6152(c)(1)(C), 6152(c)(1)(D) and 6685.

Practical Analysis: Barnaby Zall, of Weinberg & Jacobs, LLP, Rockville, Maryland, observes that under prior law, although annual information returns (Form 990) had to be disclosed, returns showing unrelated business income (Form 990-T) could remain confidential, on the theory that business competitors could obtain an advantage from public disclosures. This provision makes the UBI returns publicly discloseable on the same terms as the annual information returns. As a planning strategy, organizations which do not wish to disclose proprietary information which might harm their revenue-generating businesses can ask the IRS to permit them to withhold disclosure. The IRS does not have any significant guidance or track record on whether it will grant this type of request.

Comment: A draft report by the Independent Sector's Panel on the Nonprofit Sector recognized a concern that the public does not adequately understand and cannot adequately monitor the taxable activities of exempt organizations, or the relationships between an organization's taxable affiliates and its directors and

NEW LAW EXPLAINED

officers. However, the Panel concluded that disclosure of UBTI returns could jeopardize an exempt organization's ability to recruit partners for joint ventures, limit its investment opportunities, cause the market to undervalue its taxable subsidiaries, and give for-profit competitors an unfair advantage. Rather than requiring disclosure of UBTI returns, the Panel recommended that the IRS amend Form 990 to increase the disclosure of information about unrelated business activities, and make public charities subject to reporting requirements currently applicable to certain managers and directors of private foundations.

▶ **Effective date.** The amendments apply to returns filed after August 17, 2006 (Act Sec. 1225(b) of the Pension Protection Act of 2006).

Law source: Law at ¶5365. Committee Report at ¶11,330.

— Act Sec. 1225(a) of the Pension Protection Act of 2006, amending Code Sec. 6104(d)(1)(A);

— Act Sec. 1225(b), providing the effective date.

Reporter references: For further information, consult the following CCH reporters.

— Standard Federal Tax Reporter, 2006FED ¶36,911.01, ¶36,911.0216 and ¶36,911.022

— Tax Research Consultant, EXEMPT: 12,254 and EXEMPT: 12,258.05

¶1280 Disclosure to State Officials of Proposed Actions Relating to Exempt Organizations

SUMMARY OF NEW LAW

Information relating to certain *proposed* IRS actions affecting charitable organizations may now be disclosed to State officials along with return and return information about the charitable organizations that are the subject of the proposed actions.

BACKGROUND

In order to help states enforce their laws that apply to tax-exempt organizations, the IRS is obligated to notify the appropriate State officer (the State attorney general, State tax officer, or other State official charged with overseeing charitable organizations) of the following information regarding any organization exempt from tax under Code Sec. 501(a):

(1) a refusal of the IRS to recognize the organization's exemption;

(2) the operation of the organization in a manner that no longer meets the requirements of its exemption; and

(3) the mailing of a notice of deficiency for any tax imposed under Code Sec. 507, chapter 41, or chapter 42. These taxes include various taxes imposed on private foundations, the tax on termination of private foundation status, taxes on public charities for certain excess lobbying expenses, taxes on the political expenditures

BACKGROUND

> and excess benefit transactions of Code Sec. 501(c)(3) organizations, and certain taxes on black lung benefit trusts and foreign organizations (Joint Committee on Taxation, Technical Explanation of the Pension Protection Act of 2006 (JCX-38-06)).

The IRS must also make any information about the above disclosures available for inspection and copying by an appropriate State officer if the information is relevant to any determination under state law (Code Sec. 6104(c); Reg. § 301.6104(c)-1). Willful unauthorized disclosure or inspection of returns or return information is subject to a fine or imprisonment, or both (Code Secs. 7213 and 7213A).

NEW LAW EXPLAINED

Information regarding proposed IRS actions may now be disclosed to state officials.—Under the Pension Protection Act of 2006, the information disclosed to State officials now includes *proposed* actions relating to charitable organizations. Specifically, for Code Sec. 501(c)(3) organizations exempt from tax under Code Sec. 501(a), or organizations that have applied under Code Sec. 508(a) to become Code Sec. 501(c)(3) organizations, the IRS may disclose the following to the appropriate State officer:

(1) a notice of proposed refusal to recognize the organization as a Code Sec. 501(c)(3) organization or a notice of proposed revocation of an organization's recognition as a tax-exempt organization;

(2) the issuance of a letter of proposed deficiency of tax under Code Sec. 507 or chapter 41 or 42 (see background); and

(3) the names, addresses, and taxpayer identification numbers of organizations that have applied to become Code Sec. 501(c)(3) organizations (Code Sec. 6104(c)(2)(A), as amended by the Pension Act).

Returns and return information of the organizations that are the subject of such disclosures may also be made available for inspection by or disclosed to an appropriate State officer (Code Sec. 6104(c)(2)(B), as amended by the Pension Act).

Practical Analysis: Barnaby Zall, of Weinberg & Jacobs, LLP, Rockville, Maryland, observes that for years, IRS and state government officials have complained that statutory privacy protections have prevented their cooperation in the investigation and prosecution of persons abusing charitable organizations. Administration of this privacy protection was simple, because all disclosure was forbidden. This provision breaks down that wall and permits any government official claiming to need the information for the investigation of state law violations, including the catch-all term of "fraud," to obtain confidential tax return information. Similarly, the IRS can provide return information to state officials if the IRS believes that the information in its possession indicates noncompliance with state law. The provision preserves both the penalties and civil liability exposure for federal employees who wrongfully dis-

NEW LAW EXPLAINED

close return information, so this provision will likely generate years of litigation ironing out the scope of what can be disclosed.

Procedures. The IRS may disclose the information upon written request by an appropriate State officer if it is needed to administer State laws regulating the relevant organizations (Code Sec. 6104(c)(2)(C), as added by the Pension Act). Even without a request, the IRS may disclose the information to an appropriate State officer if the return or return information may constitute evidence of noncompliance under the laws within the jurisdiction of that officer (Code Sec. 6104(c)(2)(D), as added by the Pension Act).

To facilitate the administration of state laws regulating the charitable funds or charitable assets of Code Sec. 501(c) exempt organizations other than those described in Code Sec. 501(c)(1) or (3), the IRS may make returns and return information of those organizations available to the appropriate State officer or an officer or employee of the State designated by the State officer to receive this information (Code Sec. 6104(c)(3), as added by the Pension Act).

The definition of an appropriate State officer has expanded in conjunction with the new provision allowing for the disclosure of return and return information of organizations described in Code Sec. 501(c) other than organizations described in Code Sec. 501(c)(1) or (3). Specifically, with respect to such organizations, an appropriate State official is defined as the head of an agency designated as having primary responsibility for overseeing the solicitation of funds for charitable purposes (Code Sec. 6104(c)(6)(B)(iv), as added by the Pension Act).

The return and return information disclosed under amended Code Sec. 6104(c) may be disclosed in civil administrative and civil judicial proceedings to enforce State laws regulating those organizations producing the disclosed returns (Code Sec. 6104(c)(4), as added by the Pension Act). This information will not be disclosed, however, if the IRS determines that the disclosure would seriously impair federal tax administration (Code Sec. 6104(c)(5), as added by the Pension Act).

Disclosure of returns and return information under Code Sec. 6104(c) are subject to the disclosure, recordkeeping, and safeguard provisions in Code Sec. 6103, including the requirement that the IRS maintain a permanent system of records of requests for disclosure and that the appropriate State officer maintains various safeguards that protect against unauthorized disclosure (Code Sec. 6103(p)(3) and (4), as amended by the Pension Act).

Penalties. The willful unauthorized *disclosure* of returns or return information described in Code Sec. 6104(c) is a felony subject to a possible $5,000 fine or five years of imprisonment, or both (Code Sec. 7213(a)(2), as amended by the Pension Act). The willful unauthorized *inspection* of such returns or return information carries up to a $1,000 fine or one year of imprisonment, or both (Code Sec. 7213A, as amended by the Pension Act).

NEW LAW EXPLAINED

Finally, for the knowing or negligent unauthorized disclosure or inspection of this information, a taxpayer can bring a civil action for damages (Code Sec. 7431(a)(2), as amended by the Pension Act).

▶ **Effective date.** The provisions take effect on August 17, 2006 but do not apply to requests made before that date (Act Sec. 1224(c) of the Pension Protection Act of 2006).

Law source: Law at ¶5360, ¶5365, ¶5430, ¶5435 and ¶5445. Committee Report at ¶11,320.

— Act Sec. 1224(a) of the Pension Protection Act of 2006, amending Code Sec. 6104(c);

— Act Sec. 1224(c), providing the effective date.

Reporter references: For further information, consult the following CCH reporters.

— Standard Federal Tax Reporter, 2006FED ¶36,911.026

— Tax Research Consultant, IRS: 30,206 and EXEMPT: 12,260.25

¶1285 Acquisitions of Interests in Insurance Contracts

SUMMARY OF NEW LAW

An applicable exempt organization which acquires a direct or indirect interest in an applicable insurance contract must file an information return. The reporting requirement is temporary and will not apply to reportable acquisitions occurring after two years from August 17, 2006, the date of enactment.

BACKGROUND

There has been a recent increase in transactions involving the acquisition of life insurance contracts using arrangements in which both exempt organizations (primarily charities) and private investors have an interest in the contract. The exempt organization has an insurable interest in the insured individuals, either because they are donors, and they consent or otherwise under applicable State insurable interest rules. Private investors provide capital used to fund the purchase of the life insurance contracts, sometimes together with annuity contracts. Both the private investors and the charity have an interest in the contracts, directly or indirectly, through the use of trust, partnerships, or other arrangements for sharing the rights to the contracts. Both the charity and the private investors receive cash amounts in connection with the investment in the contracts while the life insurance is in force or as the insured individuals die.

NEW LAW EXPLAINED

Reporting on certain acquisitions of interests in insurance contracts.—An applicable exempt organization which acquires a direct or indirect interest in any applicable insurance contract in any case in which such acquisition is a part of a structural

NEW LAW EXPLAINED

transaction involving a pool of such contracts, must file an information return. The return must contain the name, address and taxpayer identification number of the applicable exempt organization and of the issuer of the applicable insurance contract. It must also contain any other information prescribed by the IRS (Code Sec. 6050V, as added by the Pension Protection Act of 2006).

> **Comment:** The reporting requirements are temporary and will not apply to reportable acquisitions occurring after two years from August 17, 2006.

An *applicable exempt organization* is one that is exempt from Federal income tax by reason of being described in Code Sec. 501(c) (including one organized outside the United States), a government or political subdivision of a government, and an Indian tribal government. An *applicable insurance contract* is any life insurance, annuity or endowment contract in which both an exempt organization and any person that is not an exempt organization have directly or indirectly held an interest in the contract (whether or not the interests are held at the same time). The term, applicable insurance contract does not apply if:

(1) each person (other than an applicable exempt organization) with a direct or indirect interest in the contract has an insurable interest in the insured independent of any interest of an applicable exempt organization in the contract;

(2) the sole interest in the contract of an applicable exempt organization or each person other than an applicable exempt organization is a named beneficiary; or

(3) the sole interest in the contract of each person other than the applicable exempt organization is either (a) as a beneficiary of a trust holding an interest in the contract, but only if the person's designation as such a beneficiary was made without consideration and solely on a purely gratuitous basis, or (b) as a trustee who holds an interest in the contract in a fiduciary capacity solely for the benefit of applicable exempt organizations or of persons otherwise meeting one of the first two exceptions.

Penalties. The return required by this provision is treated as an information return that is subject to the penalty imposed by Code Sec. 6721(a) for failure to timely file or failure to provide correct or required information (Code Sec. 6724(d), as amended by the Pension Act). In the case of intentional disregard of the return filing requirements, a penalty equal to 10 percent of the value of the benefit of any contract with respect to which information is required to be included on the return (Code Sec. 6721(e) , as amended by the Pension Act).

> **Comment:** The Code Sec. 6721(a) penalty is only $50 per return. Thus, the real incentive for complying with the reporting requirement is the potential 10 percent penalty.

Study. The Secretary of the Treasury is required to issue a report within 30 months after August 17, 2006, on the use by tax exempt organizations of applicable insurance contracts for the purpose of sharing the benefits of the organization's insurance interest in individuals insured under such contracts with investors. The study will also examine whether such activities are consistent with the tax exempt status of such organizations (Act Sec. 1211(c) of the Pension Act).

NEW LAW EXPLAINED

> **Comment:** The study may consider whether these insurance arrangements may be used to improperly shelter income from tax and whether they should be considered listed transactions under Reg. § 1.6011-4(b)(2) (Joint Committee on Taxation, Technical Explanation of the Pension Protection Act of 2006 (JCX-38-06)).

▶ **Effective date.** The provision applies to acquisitions of contracts after August 17, 2006 (Act Sec. 1211(d) of the Pension Protection Act of 2006).

Law source: Law at ¶5350, ¶5420 and ¶5425 and ¶7231. Committee Report at ¶11,190.

— Act Sec. 1211(a) of the Pension Protection Act of 2006, adding Code Sec. 6050V;

— Act Sec. 1211(b)(1) redsignating Code Sec. 6724(d)(1)(B)(xiv) through (xix) as Code Sec. 6724(d)(1)(B)(xv) through (xx), respectively, and adding new Code Sec. 6724(d)(1)(B)(xiv);

— Act Sec. 1211(b)(2), adding Code Sec. 6721(e)(2)(D);

— Act Sec.1211(c);

— Act Sec. 1211(d), providing the effective date.

Reporter references: For further information, consult the following CCH reporters.

— Standard Federal Tax Reporter, 2006FED ¶35,425.01, ¶40,220.021, ¶40,220.029 and ¶40,285.025

— Tax Research Consultant, EXEMPT: 12,252

STUDIES

¶1290 Study on Donor Advised Funds and Supporting Organizations

SUMMARY OF NEW LAW

The Secretary of the Treasury must conduct a study and submit a report on the organization and operation of donor advised funds and supporting organizations.

BACKGROUND

"Donor-advised funds" are a type of planned giving instrument. A donor creates an account with a donor-advised fund by contributing cash, bonds, stocks or other assets. A charity or foundation administers and manages the fund. The fund invests the donor's contributions and generates income for the account. In addition to securing a tax deduction, the donor can recommend how and when to distribute the contribution in the form of grants to qualified non-profit organizations. Many donor-advised funds require a minimum contribution of $100,000, but some charities have lowered that to $10,000.

BACKGROUND

For a contribution to qualify as a completed gift to the charity, the charity must have ultimate authority over how the assets in each account are invested and distributed in furtherance of its exempt purposes. While the donor may recommend charitable distributions from the account, the charity must be free to accept or reject the donor's recommendations. Payments to a charity are deductible as "charitable contributions" only if they meet all the requirements of Code Sec. 170. A payment to a charitable organization that is intended to benefit a taxpayer is not a "charitable contribution" within the meaning of Code Sec. 170(c). Thus, payments to a charitable organization to establish a separate fund are not deductible charitable contributions if a taxpayer expects that the taxpayer, the taxpayer's family, or related parties will receive personal benefits (such as the payment of tuition or other personal expenses) from the fund.

A "donor advised fund" is a fund or account that is:

(1) separately identified by reference to contributions of a donor or donors;

(2) owned and controlled by a sponsoring organization; and

(3) with respect to which a donor (or any person appointed or designated by the donor) has, or reasonably expects to have, advisory privileges with respect to the distribution or investment of amounts held in the separately identified fund or account by reason of the donor's status as a donor (see the discussion at ¶1160) (Code Sec. 4966(d)(2)(A), as added by the Pension Protection Act of 2006).

However, the term "donor advised fund" does not include a fund or account from which are made grants to individuals for travel, study, or other similar purposes, provided that:

(1) a donor's or donor advisor's advisory privileges are performed exclusively by the donor or donor advisor in his or her capacity as a member of a committee appointed by the sponsoring organization;

(2) no combination of a donor and persons related to or appointed by the donor, control, directly or indirectly, the committee; and

(3) all grants from the fund or account satisfy requirements similar to those described in Code Sec. 4945(g) (concerning grants to individuals by private foundations) (Code Sec. 4966(d)(2)(B), as added by the Pension Act of 2006).

Donor advised funds have become an important means of stimulating charitable contributions from a broad range of donors who wish to make significant philanthropic gifts, either for immediate benefit to a charity or charities, or for long-term support of ongoing or emergent community needs (Panel on the Nonprofit Sector's *Report to Congress and the Nonprofit Sector on Governance, Transparency, and Accountability* (June 2005)).

> **Comment:** The IRS's Exempt Organizations Division has placed donor-advised funds under its tax-exempt monitoring priorities after it had identified some abusive "donor advised fund" arrangements. The IRS has learned that these funds have been abused by insiders who use them to make noncharitable payments because the funds are not effectively controlled by a charity or charities.

BACKGROUND

"Supporting organizations" are public charities that carry out their exempt purposes by supporting one or more other exempt organizations, usually other public charities. The key feature of a supporting organization is a strong relationship with an organization it supports. The strong relationship enables the supported organization to oversee the operations of the supporting organization. Therefore, the supporting organization is classified as a public charity, even though it may be funded by a small number of persons in a manner that is similar to a private foundation. To qualify as a "supporting organization", three tests must be met:

(1) the organization must be formed for the benefit, or to carry out the purposes, of one or more specified publicly supported charities;

(2) the activities of the organization must support or benefit the supported public charity; and

(3) the organization must maintain a significant involvement in the charity's operations, and the charity must be dependent on the organization for its support (Code Sec. 509(a)(3)).

> **Comment:** Some promoters have encouraged individuals to establish and operate supporting organizations described in Code Sec. 509(a)(3) for their own benefit. There are a variety of methods of abuse, but a common theme is a "charitable" donation of an amount to the supporting organization, and a return of the donated amounts to the donor, often in the form of a loan. To disguise the abuse, the transaction may be routed through one or more intermediary organizations controlled by the promoter (Section 509(a)(3) Supporting Organizations, IRS website at http://www.irs.ustreas.gov/charities).

For rules relating to supporting organizations, see the discussion at ¶1225 and following.

NEW LAW EXPLAINED

Study and report on organization and operation of donor advised funds and supporting organizations.—The Secretary of the Treasury shall undertake a study on the organization and operation of "donor advised funds" and of certain "supporting organizations" (Act Sec. 1226(a), Pension Protection Act of 2006). The study will monitor the effectiveness of the new rules governing the activities of these organizations and how the issues affecting them are addressed. Specifically, the study shall determine:

(1) whether the deductions allowed for the income, gift or estate taxes for charitable contributions to sponsoring organizations of donor advised funds or to "supporting organizations" described in Code Sec. 509(a)(3) are appropriate in consideration of the use of contributed assets or the use of the assets of such organizations (see ¶1180);

(2) whether donor advised funds should be required to be distributed for charitable purposes a specified amount in order to ensure that the sponsoring organization is

NEW LAW EXPLAINED

operating consistent with the purpose or functions constituting the basis for its exemption;

(3) whether the retention by donors to organizations of rights or privileges with respect to amounts transferred to such organizations is consistent with the treatment of such transfers as completed gifts qualify for a deduction for income, gift or estate taxes; and

(4) whether the three issues raised above are also issues with respect to other forms of charities or charitable donations.

Report. Not later than one year after August 17, 2006, the date of the enactment of the Pension Act, the Secretary of the Treasury must submit a report on the study and recommendations to the Committee on Finance of the Senate and the Committee on Ways and Means of the House of Representatives (Act Sec. 1226(b), Pension Act of 2006). The Committees also expect the Secretary to comment on any actions, such as audits, guidance or regulations, taken to address the issues discussed in the study (Joint Committee on Taxation, Technical Explanation of the Pension Protection Act of 2006 (JCX-38-06)).

Comment: Certain promoters, or organizations that claim Code Sec. 501(c)(3) status, may encourage individuals to establish purported "donor advised fund" arrangements that can be used for the taxpayer's personal benefit. The promoter may even refer to the separate fund or account as the "taxpayer's foundation" or the "taxpayer's family public charity." The IRS is actively examining these types of arrangements and may in appropriate cases disallow deductions under Code Sec. 170 for payments in connection with these arrangements. In addition, taxpayers may be taxed on investment income earned on, or benefits received from, the separate funds or accounts. Moreover, an organization that participates in these arrangements may fail to qualify for, or jeopardize, its tax-exempt status under Code Sec. 501(c)(3) (Abusive "Donor Advised Fund" Arrangements, IRS Headliner Volume 88 (June 25, 2004)).

▶ **Effective date.** No specific effective date is provided by the Act. The provision is, therefore, considered effective on August 17, 2006, the date of enactment.

Law source: Law at ¶7240. Committee Report at ¶11,340.

— Act Sec. 1226 of the Pension Protection Act of 2006.

Reporter references: For further information, consult the following CCH reporter.

— Standard Federal Tax Reporter, 2006FED ¶22,609.01

Permanency of Pension Provisions and Other Tax Matters

BENEFIT PLANS

¶1305 Permanency of EGTRRA Pension and IRA Provisions

SUMMARY OF NEW LAW

Many of the changes made by the Economic Growth and Tax Relief Reconciliation Act of 2001 (EGTRRA) (P.L. 107-16) are set to expire in 2011. The Pension Protection Act of 2006 nullifies the sunset rule as it applies to the pension and IRA provisions of EGTRRA, making these specific provisions a permanent part of tax and pension law.

BACKGROUND

EGTRRA made numerous changes to the tax law including, but not limited to, reducing income tax rates, increasing benefits under certain pension plans and eliminating the unified gift and estate tax. In order to comply with section 313 of the Congressional Budget Act of 1974 (2 USCG. 644), Congress had to include the EGTRRA sunset provision. Section 313 of the Congressional Budget Act was permanently incorporated into the Budget Act of 1990. Act Sec. 313, commonly referred to as the "Byrd rule", permits Senators to raise a point of order on the Senate floor against "extraneous" provisions contained in a reconciliation bill. If the point of order is sustained by the presiding officer (and not overturned if the ruling is appealed by any Senator), the offending provision is stricken unless three- fifths of the Senate membership vote to waive the rule with respect to that provision. One type of extraneous provision is a provision that would increase net outlays or decrease revenues for a fiscal year beyond the years covered by the reconciliation act in question. EGTRRA included the sunset provision to prevent any of the law's provisions from becoming subject to a point of order. Under the sunset provision, the provisions of EGTRRA generally expired after 2010.

NEW LAW EXPLAINED

EGTRRA pension and IRA provisions made permanent.—The pension and individual retirement arrangement provisions of EGTRRA are no longer subject to the EGTRRA sunset provision (Act Sec. 811 of the Pension Protection Act of 2006, see also ¶ 29,000 and ¶ 29,010). Therefore, these provisions will not expire in 2011. The provisions are as follows:

Limits on Contributions and Benefits

- *Increase in benefit and contribution limits - defined benefit plans.* The permissible maximum annual benefit of a qualified defined benefit plan is the lesser of $160,000, subject to a cost-of-living adjustment ($175,000 for 2006), or 100 percent of compensation for the employee's highest three consecutive years of service. This maximum is lowered to half of the maximum annual benefit ($87,500 for 2006) for participants in

NEW LAW EXPLAINED

certain union-negotiated plans. If a participant retires before age 62 (with certain exceptions for commercial airline pilots) or after age 65, the maximum annual benefit will be increased or decreased, respectively (Code Sec. 415(b) and (d)).

- *Benefit limits for governmental and multiemployer defined benefit plans.* The rule limiting defined benefit plan distributions to 100 percent of a participant's average compensation for the participant's high three years is inapplicable to governmental plans and multiemployer plans. Thus, the benefits are limited to the annual dollar limit that is adjusted annually for cost-of-living increases ($175,000 for 2006) (see ¶ 1055 for explanation of related provision) (Code Sec. 415(b)(11)). Multiemployer plans cannot be combined or aggregated with nonmultiemployer plans for purposes of applying the 100 percent of compensation limit to the non-multiemployer plan, or with any other multiemployer plan for purpose of applying other limits under Code Sec. 415.

- *Increase in benefit and contribution limits - defined contribution plans.* The permissible maximum contribution on behalf of a participant in a qualified defined contribution plan is $40,000, subject to a cost-of-living adjustment ($44,000 for 2006) (Code Secs. 415(c) and 451(d)).

- *Increase in benefit and contribution limits - qualified trusts.* The maximum compensation that may be taken into account in determining a plan participant's account and benefits under qualified plans is $200,000, subject to a cost-of-living adjustment ($220,000 for 2006). The limit is also taken into account in applying the employer deduction rules, for nondiscrimination testing purposes for salary reduction simplified employee pension plans (SEPs) and for nondiscrimination testing purposes for voluntary benefit associations (VEBAs) and supplemental unemployment compensation benefit trusts (SUBs) (Code Secs. 401(a)(17), 404(l), 408(k) and 505(b)(7)).

- *Increase in benefit and contribution limits - elective deferrals.* The maximum amount of compensation a plan participant can elect to defer with respect to 401(k) plans, Code Sec. 403(b) annuities and Code Sec. 408(k) salary reduction SEPs in 2006 and after is $15,000, subject to a cost-of-living adjustment (Code Sec. 402(g)(1)).

- *Increase in benefit and contribution limits - deferred compensation plans of state and local governments and tax-exempt entities.* The maximum amount of compensation a plan participant can elect to defer with respect to Code Sec. 457 plans in 2006 and after is $15,000, subject to a cost-of-living adjustment (Code Sec. 457(b)(2)).

- *Increase in benefit and contribution limits - Simple Retirement Accounts.* The maximum amount of compensation a plan participant can elect to defer with respect to a SIMPLE retirement account in 2006 and after is $10,000, subject to a cost-of-living adjustment (Code Sec. 408(p)(2)).

- *Increase in benefit and contribution limits - compensation limits for self-employed individuals.* For purposes of defining earnings of self-employed individuals, the term "earned income" includes income earned from services performed by individuals exempt from the self-employment tax for religious reasons. The rules apply when

NEW LAW EXPLAINED

determining compensation for purposes of all qualified retirement plans, IRAs and SIMPLE plans (Code Secs. 401(c)(2) and 408(p)(6)(A)(ii)).

- *Increase in benefit and contribution limits - rounding rule relating to defined benefit plans and defined contribution plans.* Any cost-of-living increase to the maximum benefits available under a defined benefit plan which is not a multiple of $5,000 is rounded to the next lowest multiple of $5,000. Any cost-of-living increase to the maximum benefits available under a defined contribution plan which is not a multiple of $1,000 is rounded to the next lowest multiple of $1,000 (Code Sec. 415(d)).
- *Catch-up contributions for individuals age 50 or over.* Increased dollar amounts on elective deferrals for employees age 50 or older are allowed for contributions made to 401(k) plans, Code Sec. 403(b) annuities, SEPs, SIMPLEs and deferrals under Code Sec. 457 plans. For plans other than SIMPLE plans, the applicable dollar amount is $5,000 for tax years beginning in 2006 and after. For SIMPLE plans, the applicable dollar amount is $2,500 for tax years beginning in 2006 and after. The amounts are adjusted for inflation, beginning in 2007 and after (Code Sec. 414(v)).
- *Equitable treatment for contributions of employees to defined contribution plans.* The percentage-of-compensation limitation for contributions to defined contribution plans, tax-sheltered annuities and Code Sec. 457 plans is 100 percent of includible compensation (Code Secs. 403(b), 415(c)(1),(k)(4) and 457(b)(2)).
- *Faster vesting of certain employer matching contributions.* Vesting requirements for a qualified plan participant's nonforfeitable right to employer matching contributions is either three years for 100 percent vesting or vesting in 20 percent increments from year two to year six and more years of service (see ¶ 720 for a related explanation) (Code Sec. 411(a)(2) and (12) and ERISA Sec. 203(a)).
- *Repeal of coordination of requirements for deferred compensation plans of state and local governments and tax-exempt organizations - general.* Individuals are not required to coordinate the maximum annual deferral amount for a Code Sec. 457 plan with contributions to other plans (Code Sec. 457(c)).
- *Repeal of the multiple-use test.* The multiple-use test, which is applied to determine whether a Code Sec. 401(k) plan meets nondiscrimination requirements, is permanently repealed (Code Sec. 401(m)(9)).

Practical Analysis: Mary Beth Braitman, Terry A.M. Mumford and Lisa Erb Harrison of Ice Miller LLP, Indianapolis, Indiana, find that Act Sec. 811 repeals the sunset provisions of the Economic Growth and Tax Relief Reconciliation Act of 2001 (EGTRRA) with respect to the provisions relating to pensions and IRAs. Under EGTRRA, the provisions relating to pensions and IRAs did not apply for taxable, plan or limitation years beginning after December 31, 2010. In addition to benefiting participants in governmental plans by making permanent the increased limits on contributions, benefits and compensation, increased portability, *etc.*, the removal of the sunset provisions is particularly helpful to governmental plans who often face a

NEW LAW EXPLAINED

much more challenging task in amending plan documents, which often must go through the legislative process or rules-making process.

Practical Analysis: Vincent O'Brien, President of Vincent J. O'Brien, CPA, PC, Lynbrook, New York, observes that, now that the increases in the employer limits on contributions to defined contribution plans have been made permanent, the money purchase pension plan appears to be extinct, and the one-person 401(k) plan appears to be here to stay.

MPPPs: A money purchase pension plan ("MPPP") is a defined contribution plan that requires annual contributions to be made, pursuant to the formula contained in the plan document, even if the employer does not earn a profit during a given year. On the other hand, profit-sharing plans do not require employer contributions when an employer does not earn a profit for that year.

Prior to 2002, the limit on an employer's contributions to a profit-sharing plan was 15 percent of an employee's compensation, while the limit on employer contributions to an MPPP was 25 percent of compensation. As a result, to utilize the higher limit offered by an MPPP, many employers adopted both types of plans: an MPPP requiring contributions of 10 percent of compensation, and a profit-sharing plan (allowing an additional 15 percent of compensation to be contributed).

Beginning in 2002, the limit for employer contributions to profit-sharing plans was increased to 25 percent, substantially reducing the usefulness of MPPPs and inducing many employers to freeze or terminate their MPPPs or merge them into a profit-sharing plan. (Rev. Rul. 2002-42 discusses the consequences of merging or converting MPPPs into profit-sharing plans.) Now that this provision has been made permanent, it would appear that MPPPs will become extinct.

One-Person 401(k)s: The one-person 401(k) plan became popular beginning in 2002, due to the change in the rule for employee elective deferrals. Prior to 2002, if an employee elected to defer a portion of his or her compensation to a 401(k) plan, the elective deferral reduced the amount that the employer could contribute to the employee's account. (Such employer contributions were generally limited to 15 percent of the employee's compensation, and the elective deferral was counted as part of this amount, even though it was from the employee, not the employer.)

Beginning in 2002, the limit on employer contributions was increased to 25 percent for profit-sharing plans, and such plans that offer a 401(k) elective deferral feature are no longer required to count employee elective deferrals against the 25 percent-of-compensation limit on employer contributions. Thus, plans covering one person (*e.g.*, for the self-employed or for S corporations with only one employee who also owns 100 percent of the stock), are able to receive larger contributions.

Now that this rule has been made permanent, the one-person 401(k) will continue to be a useful tool when selecting a retirement plan.

Example: Jane, who is 45 years old, is the 100 percent shareholder and the only employee of an S corporation. She has $100,000 of W-2 wages for 2006, before considering elective deferrals. If the company adopts a profit-sharing plan or a

NEW LAW EXPLAINED

simplified employee pension ("SEP"), it will be able to make an employer contribution of up to $25,000 for Jane (25 percent x $100,000).

Alternatively, if the company adopts a 401(k) plan with a profit-sharing feature, Jane will be permitted to make an elective deferral of up to $15,000 (assuming that she has made no elective deferrals to any other plan during the year). Even if she makes the elective deferral, the company will still be permitted to make an employer contribution of up to $25,000. Thus, with the 401(k) plan, the total contribution to her account can be as high as $40,000 ($25,000 + $15,000), instead of the $25,000 available with a plain profit-sharing plan or SEP.

Deduction of Qualified Plan Contributions

- *Deduction limits - modification of limits.* The limit on employer's deductible contributions to defined contribution plans, stock bonus or profit sharing plans, and SEP plans is 25 percent of compensation (Code Sec. 404(a)(3)(A) and (h)(1)(C)).
- *Deduction limits - compensation.* The definition of compensation for purposes of determining an employer's deduction limit includes certain wages paid to a participant who is totally and permanently disabled and numerous types of elective deferrals (Code Secs. 404(a)(12) and 415(c)(3)).
- *Elective deferrals not taken into account for purposes of deduction limits.* Certain elective deferrals are excluded for purposes of determining certain deduction limitations of the plan sponsor (Code Sec. 404(n)).
- *Waiver of tax on nondeductible contributions for domestic or similar workers.* The 10-percent excise tax on nondeductible contributions will not apply when the sole reason that a contribution to a SIMPLE plan is nondeductible is that it was not made in connection with the employer's trade or business. This allows employers to make contributions to a plan for a household worker (Code Sec. 4972(c)(6)(B)).
- *Contributions to multiemployer plans not a method of accounting.* An employer's determination concerning whether a contribution to a multiemployer pension plan is on account of a prior year is not a method of accounting. Thus, the employer's decision to deduct contributions in the prior plan year under Code Sec. 404(a)(6), is not a change of accounting method under Code Sec. 446, and, therefore, is not subject to adjustment under Code Sec. 481 (Act Sec. 658 of EGTRRA).

IRAs

- *Modification of IRA contribution limits.* The maximum deductible contribution to an IRA for 2006 and 2007 is $4,000 and will increase to $5,000 for 2008 and years thereafter. The deductible amount is increased by $1,000 for individuals 50 years of age and older, for 2006 and thereafter. In addition, a cost-of-living increase to the maximum deductible IRA contribution begins after 2008 (see ¶ 730 for a related provision) (Code Secs. 219(b), 408 and 408A).
- *Deemed IRAs under employer plans.* Qualified plans may offer participants the option of making contributions to deemed IRAs (Code Sec. 408(q)). The deemed IRAs are subject to ERISA's exclusive benefit, fiduciary responsibility and administration and

NEW LAW EXPLAINED

enforcement rules. ERISA reporting, disclosure, participation, vesting and funding rules do not apply (ERISA Sec. 4(c)).

- *Option to treat elective deferrals as after-tax Roth contributions.* Employers that maintain plans under Code Sec. 401(k) or Code Sec. 403(b) may offer a "qualified Roth contribution program" under either type of plan. The annual limit on elective deferrals to Roth contribution accounts is the total of all the employee's pre-tax elective deferrals (including contributions to a SEP and elective employer contributions to SIMPLE plans) and after-tax Roth contributions. Distributions from a Roth contribution account can be rolled over into another Roth contribution account or Roth IRA. Roth account contributions must be reported on the participant's Form W-2 (Code Secs. 402(c)(8)(B) and (g), 402A and 6051(a)(8)).

Pension Funding Rules

- *Repeal of 160 percent of current liability funding limit.* The full funding limit for 2004 and years after is repealed (Code Sec. 412(c)(7) and ERISA Sec. 302(c)(7)).
- *Exception from excise tax on nondeductible contributions.* In determining the amount of nondeductible contributions made in a given year, an employer can elect not to take into account any contributions to a defined benefit pension plan except to the extent the contributions exceed the accrued liability full funding limitation. Therefore, contributions in excess of the current liability full funding limit are not subject to the excise tax on non-deductible contributions (Code Sec. 4972(c)(7)).
- *Asset valuation.* Under an exception to the asset valuation timing rule, the asset valuation date can be in the prior plan year. For the exception to apply, the value of the plan assets cannot be less than 100 percent of the plan's current liability on the prior plan year valuation date. The 100-percent threshold is increased to 125 percent in the case of a change in funding method made to take advantage of a prior plan year valuation (Code Sec. 412(c)(9) and ERISA Sec. 302(c)(9)(B)).
- *Diversification of 401(k) plan assets.* The Taxpayer Relief Act of 1997 mandated the diversification of 401(k) plan investments. In general, the provision prohibits the acquisition of securities or real property of a sponsoring employer if the property exceeds 10-percent of the fair market value of the assets of all pension plans maintained by the employer. For this purpose, the portion of a Code Sec. 401(k) plan that consists of elective deferrals is treated as a separate plan. The provision does not apply to elective deferrals invested in assets consisting of qualifying employer securities, qualifying employer real property or both, when assets are acquired before January 1, 1999 (Section 1524(b) of the Taxpayer Relief Act of 1997).
- *Disclosure of plan amendments that reduce the rate of future benefit accruals.* Disclosure is required of plan amendments that reduce the rate of future benefit accruals to affected plan participants (e.g., conversion of a defined benefit plan to a cash balance plan) (Code Sec. 4980F). An excise tax may be imposed for failure to meet the disclosure requirements. Under ERISA, written notice must be given if a defined benefit plan or individual account plan, which is subject to funding standards, is

NEW LAW EXPLAINED

amended to provide a significant reduction in the rate of future benefits (see ¶ 410 for a related explanation) (ERISA Sec. 204(h)).

Distributions from Qualified Plans

- *Modification of minimum distribution rules.* The IRS was authorized to, and did issue life expectancy tables used for the purpose of determining minimum distributions (see Reg. § 1.401(a)(9)-9) (Act Sec. 634 of EGTRRA).
- *Tax treatment of Code Sec. 457 plan benefits upon divorce.* Code Sec. 457 plans allow for early distributions under a valid qualified domestic relations order (QDRO) (Code Sec. 414(p)(11) and (p)(12)).
- *Provisions relating to hardship distributions.* A participant in a Code Sec. 401(k) plan can take an early hardship withdrawal if, among other things, the provisions of the plan do not allow the participant to make any contributions to any other of the plan's sponsor plans for six months following the distribution (see Reg. § 1.401(k)-1(d)(3)(E)(2)). In addition, hardship distributions are ineligible for rollover treatment (Code Sec. 402(c)(4)(C)).
- *Elimination of "same desk" rule.* If the sponsor of Code Sec. 401(k) plan, Code Sec. 457 plan, or Code Sec. 403(b) annuity is liquidated, acquired or merged with or by another employer, the participants of the plan may receive a distribution from the plan even if they continue on the same job for the different employer (Code Secs. 401(k)(2)(b)(i), 403(b)(7)(A)(ii) and(11)(A), and 457(d)(1)(A)(ii)).
- *Purchase of service credit in governmental defined benefit plans.* A taxpayer is not required to include in gross income the amount of a trustee-to-trustee transfer from either a Code Sec. 403(b) annuity or Code Sec. 457 plan to a defined benefit governmental plan where the transfer is used for: (1) the purchase of permissive service credits under the government plan; or (2) repaying contributions and earnings with respect to a previous forfeiture of service credit (Code Secs. 403(b)(13) and 457(e)(17)).
- *Employers may disregard rollovers for purposes of cash-out amounts.* A qualified retirement plan does not need to take a participant's rollovers into account when determining whether the plan may involuntarily cash out the participant. A similar rule applies for Code Sec. 457 plans maintained by tax-exempt entities and state or local governments (Code Sec. 411(a)(11)(D) and ERISA Sec. 203(a)(4)).
- *Minimum distribution and inclusion requirements for Code Sec. 457 plans.* Code Sec. 457 plans are subject to the minimum distribution rules found under Code Sec. 401(a)(9). Amounts deferred under a government Code Sec. 457 plan are includable in income only when the amounts are paid, while participants in Code Sec. 457 plans sponsored by tax-exempt employers have to include deferred amounts when the amounts are paid or "otherwise made available." Distributions from any type of Code Sec. 457 plan attributable to a rollover amount may be subject to the penalties under Code Sec. 72(t) (Code Sec. 457(a) and (d)(2)).
- *Plan loans for Subchapter S owners, partners, and sole proprietors.* Qualified plans can make loans to owner-employees who are subchapter S shareholders, partners in a

NEW LAW EXPLAINED

partnership and sole proprietors, without triggering the excise taxes imposed on prohibited transactions (Code Sec. 4975(f)(6) and ERISA Sec. 408(d)(2)(C)).

- *Treatment of forms of distribution.* A defined contribution plan to which benefits are transferred is not necessarily treated as reducing a participant's or beneficiary's accrued benefit even if the transferee plan does not provide all forms of distribution that had been offered by the initial plan if certain requirements are met. See Reg. § 1.411(d)-3 (Code Sec. 411(d)(6) and ERISA Sec. 204(g)).

Rollovers

- *Rollovers allowed among various types of plans.* Eligible rollover distributions from a qualified retirement plan, a Code Sec. 403(b) annuity or a Code Sec. 457 government plan can be rolled over to any similar plan or arrangement (Code Secs. 402(c)(8)(B), 403(b)(8)(A) and 457(e)(16)). In addition, the surviving spouse of a deceased participant in qualified retirement plan is entitled to make a tax-free rollover of an eligible distribution from her deceased spouse's plan to another qualified plan, a Code Sec. 457 government plan, a Code Sec. 403(b) annuity, as well as into an IRA (see ¶ 945 for a related explanation) (Code Sec. 402(c)(9)).
- *Rollovers of IRAs into workplace retirement plan.* An eligible rollover distribution from an individual retirement account may be rolled over into a qualified employer plan, a Code Sec. 457 deferred compensation plan, or a Code Sec. 403(b) annuity (Code Sec. 408(d)(3)(A)).
- *Rollovers of after-tax contributions.* An employee may roll over after-tax contributions from a qualified plan to certain other qualified plans through a direct trustee-to-trustee transfer (see ¶ 940 for a related explanation) (Code Secs. 401(a)(31)(B) and 402(c)(2)).
- *Automatic rollover of involuntary distributions.* A direct rollover is the default option for involuntary distributions that exceed $1,000 when the qualified retirement plan provides that the nonforfeitable accrued benefits which do not exceed $5,000 must be distributed immediately. The distribution must be rolled over automatically to a designated IRA, unless the participant elects to have the distribution transferred to a different IRA or a qualified plan or to receive it directly (Code Sec. 401(a)(31)(B)). The written explanation that the plan administrator is required to give must explain that an automatic distribution by direct transfer applies to the distribution (Code Sec. 402(f)(1)(A)). If the automatic rollover occurs, the participant or beneficiary is treated as exercising control over the assets in the account or annuity upon the earlier of (1) a rollover of all or part of the amount to another account or annuity or (2) one year after the transfer is made, or in accordance with the regulations provided by the Secretary of Labor (ERISA Sec. 404(c)(3)).
- *Hardship exception to 60-day rule.* The IRS is permitted to waive the 60-day rollover period if failure to make a waiver would be against equity or good conscience (Code Secs. 402(c)(3) and 408(d)(3)(I)).

NEW LAW EXPLAINED

ESOPs

- *Prohibited allocation of S corporation stock.* Employee stock ownership plans (ESOPs) are prohibited from benefitting persons who own above a certain threshold of S corporation stock. An ESOP has a "nonallocation" year in a plan year in which at least 50 percent of the S corporation's stock is owned or attributable to a disqualified person. The prohibited allocation is treated as a deemed distribution of income to the disqualified person and is taxed accordingly (Code Secs. 409(p) and 4975(e)(7)). The ESOP is subject to a 50-percent tax on the prohibited allocation (Code Sec. 4979A).
- *ESOP dividends reinvestment.* An expanded deduction is allowed for dividends paid to an ESOP that are voluntarily reinvested back into the ESOP for more employer stock (Code Sec. 404(k)(2)(A)(ii), (iii), and (iv)). The IRS may disallow the deduction for ESOP dividends if the dividends are paid for the purpose of avoiding or evading tax (Code Sec. 404(k)(5)(A)).

Nondiscrimination and Top Heavy Rules

- *Modification of top heavy rules - simplification of definition of key employee.* Determination of key employee status only takes place during the plan year including the plan's determination date. In addition, the definition of an officer who is a key employee is an officer with annual compensation exceeding $130,000, adjusted for inflation ($140,000 for 2006) (Code Sec. 416(i)(1)(A)).
- *Modification of top heavy rules - matching contributions taken into account for minimum contribution requirements.* Employer matching contributions to defined contribution plans are taken into account in determining whether a plan has met the minimum benefit requirements (Code Sec. 416(c)(2)(A)).
- *Modification of top heavy rules - distributions during last year before determination date taken into account.* In determining whether a plan is top heavy, distributions made in the year ending on the determination date are taken into account in determining that participant's accrued benefit (in the case of a defined benefit plan) or account balance (in the case of a defined contribution plan). However, a participant's distributions for the five years preceding the determination date are taken into account if the distributions were not triggered by severance from employment, death, or disability. Furthermore, in determining top heavy status, plans do not include the accrued benefit and the account balance of plan participants who have not performed for the plan sponsor during the year ending on the determination date (Code Sec. 416(g)(3) and (g)(4)).
- *Modification of top heavy rules - definition of top heavy plans.* 401(k) plans that meet the ADP nondiscrimination test under Code Sec. 401(k)(12) and the matching contribution requirements of Code Sec. 401(m)(11) are exempt from top heavy status. If a 401(k) plan is a member of an top heavy aggregation group, contributions to the plan are taken into account to determine if another plan in the group meets the minimum distribution requirements for defined contribution plans (see ¶ 1015 for a related explanation) (Code Sec. 416(g)(4)(H)).
- *Modification of top heavy rules - exception if key employees or former key employees do not benefit under the plan.* In determining whether a defined benefit plan meets the

NEW LAW EXPLAINED

minimum benefit requirement, any year in which the plan does not benefit key employees or former key employees is not considered a year of service for purposes of determining an employee's years of service (Code Sec. 416(c)(1)(C)(iii)).

- *Treatment of nonresident aliens engaged in international transportation services.* Compensation for services performed by nonresident aliens in connection with the individual's temporary presence in the United States as a regular crew member of a foreign vessel engaged in transportation between the United States and a foreign country or U.S. possession is not U.S. source income. This rule applies for all purposes of the tax law including qualified retirement plans, employer provided group term life insurance and employer provided accident and health plans and allows employers to disregard such foreign employees when applying the nondiscrimination minimum coverage requirements (Code Sec. 861(a)(3)).
- *Coverage rules for tax-exempt employees.* The IRS is directed to amend the regulations under Reg. § 1.410(b)-6(g) in light of changes made by the Small Business Job Protection Act of 1997 (P.L. 104-188), which allowed nongovernmental tax-exempt organizations to maintain Code Sec. 401(k) plans. The regulations will provide that employees of a tax-exempt organization who are eligible to make salary reduction contributions under a Code Sec. 403(b) annuity plan may be treated as excludable employees when testing whether a 401(k) plan, or similarly arranged 401(m) plan, meets the minimum coverage requirements of Code Sec. 410(b). For the exclusion to apply, no employee must be eligible to participate in the 401(k) plan or the 401(m) plan and at least 95 percent of the employees of the employer who are not employees of the organization are eligible to participate in the 401(k) or the 401(m) plan (Act Sec. 664 of EGTRRA).
- *Repeal of special definition of highly compensated employees.* The 1986 special transitional rule for determining highly compensated employees is permanently repealed. Under the special rule, in the case of an employer incorporated on December 15, 1924, if more than half of the employer's employees in the top paid group earn less than $25,000 (indexed for inflation), then the members of the top-paid group are considered highly compensated with regard to their level of compensation (Act Sec. 1114(c)(4) of the Tax Reform Act of 1986 (P.L. 99-514)).

Other Retirement Saving Incentives

- *Credit for pension plan start-up costs of small employers.* Certain employers with no more than 100 employees can take a credit of up to $500 for qualified pension plan start-up costs (Code Sec. 45E).
- *Saver's credit.* The saver's credit allows low- and middle-income taxpayers a nonrefundable credit for contributions made to qualified plans (see ¶ 1315 and ¶ 1320 for related explanations) (Code Sec. 25B).
- *Qualified retirement planning services.* Employee-provided qualified retirement planning services are excludable from employee's gross wages. The exclusion applies to qualified retirement planning services offered to employees and their spouses by sponsoring qualified retirement plans (Code Sec. 132(a)(7) and (m)).

NEW LAW EXPLAINED

▶ **Effective date.** No specific effective date is provided by the Act. The provision is, therefore, considered effective on August 17, 2006, the date of enactment.

Law source: Law at ¶7153. Committee Report at ¶10,600.

— Act Sec. 811 of the Pension Protection Act of 2006.

Reporter references: For further information, consult the following CCH reporters.

— Standard Federal Tax Reporter, 2006FED ¶3270.06

— Tax Research Consultant, RETIRE: 75,050

— Federal Tax Guide, 2006FTG ¶11,001 et seq.

¶1310 Modifications to Qualified Tuition Programs Made Permanent

SUMMARY OF NEW LAW

The modifications to the Code Sec. 529 qualified tuition program rules made by the Economic Growth and Tax Relief Reconciliation Act of 2001 (P.L. 107-16) are permanently extended and the IRS is granted broad regulatory authority to carry out the purposes and to prevent the abuse of these rules.

BACKGROUND

Code Sec. 529 provides tax-exempt status to qualified tuition programs (QTPs). QTPs include pre-paid tuition plans established by a State or by one or more eligible educational institutions, and higher education savings account plans established by a State. Under the pre-paid tuition plans, participants purchase tuition credits or certificates on behalf of a designated beneficiary entitling the beneficiary to a waiver or payment of qualified higher education expenses (QHEEs). Savings account plans generally allow participants to contribute to an account established for the sole purpose of meeting the QHEEs of the designated account beneficiary (Code Sec. 529(b)(1).

Contributions to a QTP are not deductible by the contributor or includible in income by the designated beneficiary (Code Sec. 529(c)(1)). Distributions made to pay QHEEs are generally not subject to income tax (Code Sec. 529(c)(3)(B)). In addition, a change in the designated beneficiary is not treated as a distribution if the new beneficiary is a member of the old beneficiary's family (Code Sec. 529(c)(3)(C)(ii)).

For purposes of the QTP rules, QHEEs include tuition, fees, books, supplies, and equipment required for the designated beneficiary's enrollment or attendance at an eligible educational institution. QHEEs also include expenses for special needs services for a special needs beneficiary incurred in connection with such enrollment or attendance, and room and board for students who are enrolled at least half-time (Code Sec. 529(e)(3)).

BACKGROUND

Amendments by the Economic Growth and Tax Relief Reconciliation Act of 2001. The Economic Growth and Tax Relief Reconciliation Act of 2001 (EGTRRA) (P.L. 107-16) made a number of changes to the QTP rules in order to bring greater clarity and certainty in the application of these rules and to encourage savings and college attendance. EGTRRA allowed eligible private educational institutions to establish their own pre-paid tuition plans. A QTP maintained by a private institution must provide that the amounts are held in a qualified trust and that the program has received a ruling or determination from the IRS that it satisfies the applicable QTP requirements. For this purpose, a qualified trust is a trust that is created or organized in the United States for the exclusive benefit of the designated beneficiaries and meets the Code Sec. 408(a)(2) and (5) requirements (Code Sec. 529(b)(1)).

In addition, EGTRRA excluded from gross income both in-kind and cash distributions from QTPs to the extent that the distributions are used to pay QHEEs for tax years beginning after December 31, 2001. In the case of QTPs established by a private institution, the exclusion applies to distributions made in tax years beginning on or after January 1, 2004 (Code Sec. 529(c)(3)(B)). EGTRRA also repealed the more than de minimis penalty imposed on distributions not used for QHEEs and provided for the imposition of a 10-percent additional tax, subject to exceptions for death, disability or the receipt of a scholarship. The additional tax penalty does not apply to any payment or distribution made before January 1, 2004, that is includible in gross income but used for QHEEs of the designated beneficiary (Code Sec. 529(c)(6)). Special rules coordinating the QTP provision with the Hope and lifetime learning credit provisions were also enacted (Code Sec. 529(c)(3)(B)).

EGTRRA further permitted tax-free rollovers of credits (or other amounts) from one QTP to another QTP for the benefit of the same beneficiary. The rollover treatment does not apply to more than one transfer within any 12-month period with respect to the same beneficiary (Code Sec. 529(c)(3)(C)). For purposes of tax-free rollovers and changes of designated beneficiaries, the definition of members of the family was extended to include first cousins of the original beneficiary (Code Sec. 529(e)(2)(D)).

The definition of QHEEs was also expanded to include expenses for special needs services of a special needs beneficiary that are incurred in connection with the beneficiary's enrollment or attendance at an eligible educational institution (Code Sec. 529(e)(3)(A)). Finally, EGTRRA revised the limitation on the room and board expenses that are part of the QHEEs to include the greater of (1): the board and room allowance determined under Section 472 of the Higher Education Act of 1965 (20 U.S.C. § 1087ll), as in effect on June 7, 2001; or (2) the actual room and board expenses charged by an eligible institution (Code Sec. 529(e)(3)(B)(ii)).

The EGTRRA amendments apply to tax years beginning after December 31, 2001, except that the exclusion from gross income for distributions from QTPs established and maintained by an entity other than a state applies to distributions made in tax years beginning after December 31, 2003 (Act Sec. 402(h) and (b)(1) of EGTRRA). However, in order to comply with reconciliation procedures under the Congressional Budget of 1974, EGTRRA included a sunset provision pursuant to which all EGTRRA provisions expire at the end of 2010. Specifically, EGTRRA provisions will not apply to tax, plan or limitation years beginning after December 31, 2010 (Act Sec. 901(a)(1)

BACKGROUND

of EGTRRA). The Code and ERISA will thereafter be applied as if EGTRRA had never been enacted (Act Sec. 901(b) of EGTRRA).

Gift tax, generation-skipping transfer tax and estate tax treatment. Contributions to QTPs are treated as a gift to the beneficiary and qualify for the per-donee annual gift tax exclusion ($12,000 for 2006). To the extent of such exclusions, contributions also are exempt from the generation-skipping transfer (GST) tax. A contributor may contribute in a single year up to five times the per-donee annual gift tax exclusion amount to a QTP and treat the contribution, for gift tax and GST tax purposes, as having been made ratably over the five-year period beginning with the calendar year in which the contribution is made (Code Sec. 529(c)(2)).

In addition, a distribution from a QTP generally is not subject to gift or GST tax. An exception applies in the case of a change of the designated beneficiary if the new beneficiary is in a generation below that of the old beneficiary or if the new beneficiary is not a member of the old beneficiary's family (Code Sec. 529(c)(5)).

QTP account balances or prepaid tuition benefits are also generally excluded from the gross estate of any individual. However, accounts distributed on account of the death of the designated beneficiary are includible in the beneficiary's gross estate. If the contributor has elected the special five-year allocation rule for gift tax annual exclusion purposes, any amounts contributed that are allocable to the years within the five-year period remaining after the year of the contributor's death are includible in the contributor's gross estate (Code Sec. 529(c)(4)).

NEW LAW EXPLAINED

EGTRRA modifications permanently extended.—The Pension Protection Act of 2006 repeals the sunset provisions of Act Sec. 901 of the Economic Growth and Tax Relief Reconciliation Act of 2001 (EGTRRA) (P.L. 107-16) to the extent that they apply to the modifications to the qualified tuition program (QTP) rules made by Act Sec. 402 of EGTRRA (Act Sec. 1304(a) of the Pension Act). Thus, all EGTRRA amendments to Code Sec. 529 are permanently extended.

In addition, the IRS is authorized to issue regulations, including regulations under the estate tax, gift tax and generation-skipping transfer (GST) tax provisions, that are necessary or appropriate to carry out the purposes and to prevent the abuse of the QTP rules (Code Sec. 529(f), as added by the Pension Act).

> **Comment:** The grant of such a broad regulatory power is in response to the concern that the current rules present opportunities for abuse of QTPs and that the current transfer tax treatment of QTPs is unclear and, in some cases, inconsistent with the general transfer tax provisions. Taxpayers, for example, may use QTPs to avoid gift and GST taxes by establishing and contributing to multiple QTP accounts with different designated beneficiaries with the intention of subsequently changing those beneficiary to a single, common beneficiary and distributing the entire amount to that beneficiary without further transfer tax consequences. QTPs may also be used to avoid the restrictions of qualified retirement accounts.

NEW LAW EXPLAINED

The purpose of the regulations issued pursuant to this regulatory authority is to clarify the tax treatment of certain transfers and to ensure that QTPs are used for the intended purpose of saving for higher education expenses for the designated beneficiary. The regulations may impose recordkeeping and reporting requirements, limit the persons who may be contributors to a QTP, and determine any special rules for the operation and federal tax consequences of QTPs if the contributors are not individuals (Joint Committee on Taxation, Technical Explanation of the Pension Protection Act of 2006 (JCX-38-06)).

Practical Analysis: Vincent O'Brien, President of Vincent J. O'Brien, CPA, PC, Lynbrook, New York, observes that, since saving for future college expenses is a long-term project, the scheduled expiration of federal tax-free treatment of qualified distributions from 529 plans created an uncertainty that was at odds with the purpose of these accounts. Nevertheless, the use of 529 plans has skyrocketed since the tax-free provision became effective in 2002. Now that tax-free treatment has been made permanent, individuals and their advisors can be more comfortable when considering the usefulness of these accounts. Whether or not an advisor recommends a 529 plan, it is important to address the need to save for future college expenses, since the cost of higher education continues to grow rapidly.

When comparing the after-tax returns of taxable investments to the returns of 529 plans, clearly, the tax-free treatment of 529 plans gives them a huge advantage. However, it is important to look at the specific details of a plan before concluding that it is the right fit for a given client or situation.

Every state now offers a 529 plan, as do many private institutions, and each plan has its own history of investment returns and management fees. It is essential to review these returns and fees before selecting a plan, because, even tax-free treatment on earnings may not offset poor returns and/or very high fees.

State tax consequences are also an important consideration when selecting a plan. More than half of the states now offer a personal income tax deduction or other incentive for contributions made to their own state's plan. Typically, these incentives are not applicable for contributions made to the plans of other states or to private institutions, so an account owner needs to contribute to his or her home state's plan to obtain the deduction.

As a result, if an account owner (such as a grandparent) and the beneficiary live in different states, the account owner should determine whether his or her home state's plan will accept accounts for nonresident beneficiaries. If so, opening an account with that plan may prove more beneficial than opening it in the state where the beneficiary lives.

▶ **Effective date.** No specific effective date is provided by the Act. The provision is, therefore, considered effective on August 17, 2006, the date of enactment.

Law source: Law at ¶5175 and ¶7255. Committee Report at ¶11,400.

— Act Sec. 1304(a) of the Pension Protection Act of 2006;

— Act Sec. 1304(b), adding Code Sec. 529(f).

NEW LAW EXPLAINED

Reporter references: For further information, consult the following CCH reporters.

— Standard Federal Tax Reporter, 2006FED ¶3270.06 and ¶22,945.01

— Tax Research Consultant, INDIV: 60,204

— Federal Tax Guide, 2006FTG ¶16,230

— Federal Estate and Gift Tax Reporter, ¶16,665.01

¶1315 Saver's Credit Made Permanent

SUMMARY OF NEW LAW

The saver's credit, which was initially set to expire after 2006, is now a permanent credit.

BACKGROUND

To encourage low- and middle income taxpayers to establish or maintain private savings accounts to ensure adequate savings for retirement, Congress established a temporary nonrefundable credit for contributions or deferrals to retirement savings plans under the Economic Growth and Tax Relief Reconciliation Act of 2001 (P.L. 107-16) (Code Sec. 25B). This temporary credit was initially scheduled to expire for tax years beginning after December 31, 2006 (Code Sec. 25B(h)). The amount of the credit for a tax year is equal to the applicable percentage times the amount of qualified retirement savings contributions (not to exceed $2,000) made by an eligible individual in the tax year to certain specified retirement plans. The applicable percentage is determined by the taxpayer's filing status and adjusted gross income (AGI). The contribution amount is to be reduced by any distributions received from the specified qualified retirement plans during the testing period. The credit may be used against both a taxpayer's regular and alternative minimum tax liability.

NEW LAW EXPLAINED

Saver's credit now permanent.—The saver's credit, which was initially set to expire for tax years beginning after December 31, 2006, is now a permanent credit (Code Sec. 25B, as amended by the Pension Protection Act of 2006). For tax years beginning after 2006, the income limitations used to determine the credit are also indexed for inflation (see ¶ 1320).

▶ **Effective date.** No specific date is provided by the Act. The provision is, therefore, considered effective on August 17, 2006, the date of enactment.

Law source: Law at ¶5005. Committee Report at ¶10,610.

— Act Sec. 812 of the Pension Protection Act of 2006, striking Code Sec. 25B(h).

NEW LAW EXPLAINED

Reporter references: For further information, consult the following CCH reporters.

— Pension Plan Guide, ¶3357, ¶7413, ¶7500 and ¶8190

— Standard Federal Tax Reporter, 2006FED ¶3838.01 and ¶3838.06

— Tax Research Consultant, INDIV: 57,550

— Federal Tax Guide, 2006FTG ¶2230

¶1320 Income Limits on Certain Retirement Savings Incentives Indexed for Inflation

SUMMARY OF NEW LAW

The income limits for contributions to both traditional and Roth IRAs are indexed for inflation beginning in 2007. In addition, the income limits applicable to the saver's credit are indexed for inflation beginning in 2007.

BACKGROUND

There are limits on the amount of contributions that may be made annually to traditional and Roth IRAs maintained by an individual. For purposes of this limit, all IRAs of an individual must be aggregated. Thus, the limitations do not apply with respect to contributions made to each IRA maintained by an individual. Rather, they apply to the contributions made to all IRAs maintained by an individual.

The maximum annual contribution that can be made to an individual's IRAs is the lesser of the individual's compensation for the year or $4,000 for tax years beginning in 2006 and 2007, and $5,000 for tax years beginning in 2008 (Code Secs. 219(b) and 408(o)). Thereafter, the contribution limit will be adjusted for inflation. Individuals age 50 and over may make additional annual catch-up contributions to an IRA of $1,000 for tax years 2006 and thereafter. The individual must have reached age 50 before the end of the tax year to be eligible to make the catch-up contribution. The limit on catch-up contributions is not indexed for inflation.

An individual's contributions to a traditional IRA may be deductible up to the contribution limit. However, active participation in an employer-sponsored retirement plan by the individual (or his or her spouse) may eliminate or reduce the amount of the deduction as it is phased out depending the taxpayer's modified adjusted gross income (AGI) and filing status (Code Sec. 219(g)). For unmarried individuals, the phaseout occurs when modified AGI is between $50,000 and $60,000. For married individuals filing a joint return, the phase out occurs when modified AGI is between $75,000 and $85,000 for 2006, and $80,000 and $100,000 for 2007 and thereafter. However, if a married individual filing a joint return is not an active participant in an employer-sponsored plan, but his or her spouse is, then the deduction phase out occurs when modified AGI is between $150,000 and $160,000. For married individuals who file separate returns, the phase out occurs when

BACKGROUND

modified AGI is between $0 and $10,000. These AGI limitations are statutorily set and not indexed for inflation.

Individuals who cannot make deductible contributions, may still make nondeductible contributions both to a traditional and Roth IRA subject to the contributions limits. However, the amount of contributions that can be made to a Roth IRA may be eliminated or reduced depending on the individual's modified AGI and regardless of whether the individual is an active participant in an employer-sponsored retirement plan (Code Sec. 408A(c)). For unmarried individuals, the phase out of contributions to a Roth IRA occurs when modified AGI is between $95,000 and $110,000. For married individuals filing a joint return, the phaseout occurs when modified AGI is between $150,000 and $160,000. For married individuals who file separate returns, the phase out occurs when modified AGI is between $0 and $10,000. These AGI limitations are statutorily set and not indexed for inflation.

Saver's credit. To encourage low- and middle-income taxpayers to establish or maintain private savings accounts to ensure adequate savings for retirement, a temporary nonrefundable credit for contributions or deferrals to retirement savings plans was established (Code Sec. 25B, as added by the Economic Growth and Tax Relief Reconciliation Act of 2001 (P.L. 107-16)). The amount of the credit is equal to the applicable percentage times the amount of qualified retirement savings contributions (not to exceed $2,000) made by an eligible individual in the tax year to certain specified retirement plans (Code Sec. 25B(a)). The applicable percentage is determined by the taxpayer's filing status and adjusted gross income (AGI) (Code Sec. 25B(b)). The contribution amount is to be reduced by any distributions received from the specified qualified retirement plans during the testing period. The credit may be used against both a taxpayer's regular and alternative minimum tax liability. Under present law, the maximum credit rate is 50 percent, which is completely phased out at $50,000 for joint return filers, $37,500 for head of household filers, and at $25,000 for single and married filing separately filers.

NEW LAW EXPLAINED

Income limits on certain retirement savings incentives indexed.—The income limits for IRA contributions are also indexed for inflation beginning in 2007. The indexed amount will be rounded to the nearest multiple of $1,000. The indexing applies to: (1) the income limits for deductible contributions to a traditional for active participants in an employer-sponsored retirement plan; (2) the income limits if the individual is not an active participant in an employer-sponsored plan, but the individual's spouse is; and (3) the income limits for Roth IRA contributions (Code Secs. 219(g)(8) and 408A(c)(3)(C), as added by the Pension Act).

> **Comment:** According to the Joint Committee on Taxation, Technical Explanation of the Pension Protection Act of 2006 (JCX-38-06), the provision does not affect the phase-out ranges under present law. For example, in the case of an active participant in an employer-sponsored plan, the phase-out range is $20,000 for married taxpayers filing a joint return and $10,000 for an individual taxpayer.

NEW LAW EXPLAINED

Practical Analysis: Mary Beth Braitman, Terry A.M. Mumford and Lisa Erb Harrison of Ice Miller LLP, Indianapolis, Indiana, observe that the Economic Growth and Tax Relief Reconciliation Act of 2001 (EGTRRA) established a nonrefundable tax credit for eligible taxpayers for qualified retirement savings contributions up to $2,000, subject to a phase-out based on the adjusted gross income of the taxpayer (with a maximum tax credit of the lesser of $1,000 or the individual's tax liability without the credit). This amendment provides for inflation adjustments to the income limitations applicable to the ability to claim the tax saver's credit. Further, Act Sec. 812 makes permanent the tax saver's credit, which was set to expire after December 31, 2006.

The tax saver's credit is an important incentive for eligible individuals to make elective deferrals to an eligible deferred compensation plan, a 403(b) tax-sheltered annuity plan or a voluntary after-tax contributions to a tax-sheltered annuity or qualified retirement plan. The indexing of these income limitations should provide further savings opportunities for such individuals. Governmental plans can play an important role in encouraging retirement savings for their participants by educating members on this tax credit.

The Act also provides for inflation adjustments (in $1,000 increments) to the income limits applicable to determining eligibility for Roth IRA contributions and deductible IRA contributions.

Saver's credit. The adjusted gross income amounts used to figure the amount of the saver's credit will also be indexed for inflation beginning in 2007. The indexed amount will be rounded to the nearest multiple of $500. Under the indexed income limits, the income limits for single taxpayers is one-half of the amount for married taxpayers filing a joint return and the limit for heads of household is three-fourths of the amount for joint returns (Code Sec. 25B(b), as amended by the Pension Protection Act of 2006).

Comment: The $2,000 maximum credit amount is not indexed for inflation.

▶ **Effective date.** The amendments made by these provisions apply to tax years beginning after 2006 (Act Sec. 833(d) of the Pension Protection Act of 2006).

Law source: Law at ¶5005, ¶5025, and ¶5060. Committee Report at ¶10,740.

— Act Sec. 833(a) of the Pension Protection Act of 2006, amending Code Sec. 25B(b);

— Act Sec. 833(b), adding Code Sec. 219(g)(8);

— Act Sec. 833(c), adding Code Sec. 408A(c)(3)(C);

— Act Sec. 833(d), providing the effective date.

Reporter references: For further information, consult the following CCH reporters.

— Pension Plan Guide, ¶8564 and ¶8577

— Standard Federal Tax Reporter, 2006FED ¶3838.03, ¶12,662.01 and ¶18,930.024

— Tax Research Consultant, INDIV: 57,552

— Federal Tax Guide, 2006FTG ¶2230 and ¶11,425

INCOME AND EMPLOYMENT TAXES

¶1325 Effect of Rollover Distributions on Unemployment Compensation

SUMMARY OF NEW LAW

In order to meet certification requirements, states are prohibited from reducing unemployment compensation for retirement or IRA distributions that are rolled over to a similar plan by an individual.

BACKGROUND

The Federal Unemployment Tax Act (FUTA) imposes an annual excise tax on employers based on each employee's taxable wages up to a certain amount ($7,000) to fund the joint federal-state program that provides benefits to workers during temporary periods of unemployment. An employer may subtract a credit for the amount of state unemployment contributions actually paid to a state unemployment compensation plan in order to compute its net annual FUTA tax liability (Code Sec. 3302). However, the credit may only be claimed if the state law that establishes the state unemployment compensation plan is approved by the U.S. Department of Labor (Code Sec. 3304). By October 31 of each calendar year, the Secretary of Labor submits its certification of approval of each state's law that meets a variety of certification requirements to the Secretary of Treasury (Code Secs. 3303 and 3304). Among the requirements that must be met, a state unemployment law must provide that unemployment benefits payable to an individual must be reduced by the amount of retirement benefits received by that individual. (Code Sec. 3304(a)(15)).

> **Comment:** Some states take this further by reducing unemployment compensation by the amount of rollover distributions from one retirement plan or individual retirement account (IRA) to a similar plan or IRA. Such a provision, according to the Senate Finance Committee, defeats the main purpose of permitting rollover distributions, that is, to ensure that contributions made to retirement plans and IRAs are used for retirement, not to meet an individual's cost of living expenses due to unemployment (S. Rep. No. 109-174).

NEW LAW EXPLAINED

Rollover distributions does not reduce unemployment compensation.—The certification requirement that a state unemployment law must provide for the reduction of an individual's unemployment compensation by any retirement benefits received does not apply to distributions made from a retirement plan or an IRA which is not included in gross income because it is on eligible rollover distribution (Code Sec. 3304(a), as amended by the Pension Protection Act of 2006). Thus, in order for a state to meet the

NEW LAW EXPLAINED

certification requirements, rollover distributions cannot offset the amount of unemployment compensation payable to an individual.

▶ **Effective date.** This provision applies to weeks beginning on or after August 17, 2006 (Act Sec. 1105(b) of the Pension Protection Act of 2006).

Law source: Law at ¶5220. Committee Report at ¶11,080.

— Act Sec. 1105(a) of the Pension Protection Act of 2006, amending Code Sec. 3304(a);

— Act Sec. 1105(b), providing the effective date.

Reporter references: For further information, consult the following CCH reporters.

— Pension Plan Guide, ¶3766

— Standard Federal Tax Reporter, 2006FED ¶33,384.01 and ¶33,506.01

— Tax Research Consultant, COMPEN: 6,064 and RETIRE: 42,450

¶1330 Death Benefits from Employer-Owned Life Insurance

SUMMARY OF NEW LAW

Income from the proceeds of employer-owned life insurance on the lives of officers, directors and highly compensated individuals is excluded from gross income of the policyholder. The amount excluded is equal to the sum of premiums and other payments made by the policyholder for the contract.

BACKGROUND

Proceeds received from a life insurance policy paid out because of the death of the insured are excluded from gross income under Code Sec. 101(a). Generally, all amounts payable on the death of the insured are excluded, whether these amounts represent the return of premiums paid, the increased value of the policy due to investment, or the death benefit feature (i.e., the policy proceeds exceeding the value of the contract immediately prior to the death of the insured).

An exclusion is not allowed for any premiums paid on any life insurance, annuity, or endowment contract if the taxpayer is either directly or indirectly a beneficiary of the policy. (Code Sec. 264(a)(1)). Interest paid on any debt with respect to a life insurance, annuity, or endowment contract owned by the taxpayer covering the life of any individual, excepting a key person, is also includable in the gross income of the taxpayer. Interest may be deductible under the key person exception to the extent that the aggregate amount of the debt does not exceed $50,000 per insured individual. For this purpose, a key person is an individual who is an officer or a 20-percent owner of the taxpayer. However, the total number of key persons may not exceed the greater of five individuals or the lesser of 20 individuals of five percent of the total officers and employees of the taxpayer.

BACKGROUND

Under Code Sec. 264(f), the pro rata portion of interest expense of a taxpayer (who is not a natural person) that can be allocated to the unborrowed policy cash value of a policy is generally included in gross income. For purposes of company-owned life insurance policies, an exception is made for policies of those persons who are 20 percent owners, officers, directors, or employees of the company.

NEW LAW EXPLAINED

Treatment of death benefits from employer-owned life insurance.—The new law provides that the amount excluded from gross income of an applicable policyholder with respect to an employer-owned life insurance contract is not to exceed the premiums and other amounts paid by the policyholder for the life insurance policy (Code Sec. 101(j)(1), as added by the Pension Protection Act of 2006). Thus, the excess death benefit is included in income. For this purpose, an applicable policyholder is the person (including related persons under Code Secs. 267(b) and 707(b)(1) or persons engaged in commonly-controlled trades or businesses within the meaning of Code Sec. 52) that owns the contract, if the person is engaged in a trade or business, and if the person (or a related person) is directly or indirectly a beneficiary of the contract (Code Sec. 101(j)(2)(B), as added by the Pension Act).

An employer-owned life insurance contract is defined as a life insurance contract that: (1) is owned by a person engaged in a trade or business and that person (or a related person) is a beneficiary under the contract; and (2) covers the life of the individual who is an employee of the trade or business of the applicable policyholder on the date the contract was issued (Code Sec. 101(j)(3), as added by the Pension Act). If coverage for each insured under a master contract is treated as a separate contract for purposes of Code Sec. 817(h), Code Sec. 7702, and Code Sec. 7702A, coverage for each insured will also be treated as a separate contract.

Exceptions. The income inclusion rule does not apply to an amount received by reason of the death of an insured individual who, with respect to the applicable policyholder, was an employee at any time during the 12-month period before the insured's death, or who, at the time the contract was issued, was:

- a director;
- a highly compensated employee under Code Sec. 414(q) (determined without regard to the election regarding the top-paid 20 percent of employees), or
- a highly compensated individual as defined by the rules relating to self-insured medical reimbursement plans, under Code Sec. 105(h)(5), who is in a group of the highest paid 35 percent of employees (Code Sec. 101(j)(2)).

All notice and consent requirements must be met in order for the exception to the income inclusion rule to apply (Code Sec. 101(j)(2)(A) and (4), as added by the Pension Act).

> **Comment:** The provision generally applies to all contracts issued after August 17, 2006, except for contracts issued after such date pursuant to an exchange

NEW LAW EXPLAINED

made under Code Sec. 1035. Additionally, certain material increases in the death benefit or other material changes for contracts issued prior to August 17, 2006 will generally cause the life insurance contract to be treated as a new contract (Act Sec. 863(d) of the Pension Act). This may cause the new life insurance contract to fall under this provision, except for existing lives under a master contract.

Comment: Material increases to the death benefit that will not cause a contract to be treated as a new contract include where the death benefits increase due to normal operation of the contract or, in the case of variable contracts and universal life contracts, where the death benefit increases due to market performance or contract design. Administrative changes, changes from general to separate account, or changes as a result of the exercise of an option or right granted under the contract as originally issued are not considered material changes so as to cause the contract to be treated as a new contract. Further, changes to the contract required under Code Sec. 7702 will not cause the contract to be treated as a new contract.

The income inclusion rule does not apply to proceeds that are paid to a member of the insured's family under Code Sec. 267(c)(4), to any individual who is the designated beneficiary of the insured under the contract (other than an applicable policyholder), to a trust established for the benefit of the insured's family or a designated beneficiary, or to the estate of the insured. Further, the rule does not apply to proceeds that are used to purchase an equity (or capital or profits) interest in the policyholder from any person who is the insured's heir (Code Sec. 101(j)(2)(B), as added by the Pension Act).

Comment: According to the Joint Committee on Taxation, Technical Explanation of the Pension Protection Act of 2006 (JCX-38-06), the proceeds from such a contract are intended to be paid or used by the due date of the tax year of the applicable policyholder in which they are received as a death benefit. The purpose is to make the payment or use of these proceeds known in the tax year for which the exception from the income inclusion rule is claimed.

There are notice and consent requirements that must be met with regard to a policyholder taking out a life insurance policy on a valued employee and intending to claim exemption from gross income (Code Sec. 101(j)(4), as added by the Pension Act). The notice and consent requirements are met if, before the issuance of the contract, the employee:

(1) is notified in writing that the policyholder intends to ensure the life of the employee and of the maximum face amount of the policy for which the employee can be insured;

(2) provides written consent to being insured under the contract and that such coverage may continue after the insured terminates employment; and

(3) is informed in writing that an applicable policyholder will be a beneficiary of any proceeds payable upon the death of the employee.

An employee is defined as an officer, director, or highly compensated employee (within the meaning of Code Sec. 414(q)). An insured, with respect to an employer-

NEW LAW EXPLAINED

owned life insurance contract, is defined as an individual covered by the contract who is a United States citizen or resident (Code Sec. 101(j)(5), as added by the Pension Act).

Information returns. Applicable policyholders are required to report to the IRS on an annual basis:

(1) the number of employees of the applicable policyholder at the end of the year;

(2) the number of employees insured under employer-owned life insurance contracts at the end of the year;

(3) the total amount of insurance in force at the end of the year under such contracts;

(4) the name, address, and taxpayer identification number of the applicable policyholder and the type of business in which it is engaged; and

(5) a statement that the applicable policyholder has a valid consent for each insured employee or, if not all consents were obtained, the total number of insured employees who did not provide a valid consent (Code Sec. 6039I, as added by the Pension Act).

Further, the applicable policyholder is required to keep all records necessary to determine whether the requirements of the reporting rule and the income inclusion rule are met.

▶ **Effective date.** The amendments made by this section shall apply to life insurance contracts issued after August 17, 2006, except for a contract issued after such date pursuant to Code Sec. 1035 for a contract issued on or prior to that date (Act Sec. 863(d) of the Pension Protection Act of 2006).

Law source: Law at ¶5015 and ¶5335. Committee Report at ¶10,890.

— Act Sec. 863(a) of the Pension Protection Act of 2006, adding Code Sec. 101(j);

— Act Sec. 863(b), adding Code Sec. 6039I;

— Act Sec. 863(c), amending Code Sec. 101(a);

— Act Sec. 863(d), providing the effective date.

Reporter references: For further information, consult the following CCH reporters.

— Pension Plan Guide, ¶9630

— Standard Federal Tax Reporter, 2006FED ¶6504.01

— Tax Research Consultant, INDIV: 30,302 and INDIV: 30,304

— Federal Tax Guide, 2006FTG ¶4028

¶1335 Consistency Requirement Does Not Apply to Test Room Supervisors and Proctors

SUMMARY OF NEW LAW

The consistency requirement in section 530 of the Revenue Reconciliation Act of 1978 (P.L. 95-600) does not apply with respect to services performed after December 31, 2006 by test proctor or room supervisors who assist in the administration of college entrance or placement examinations if the services are being performed for a tax-exempt organization.

BACKGROUND

Section 530 of the Revenue Act of 1978 (P.L. 95-600) protects taxpayers who have consistently treated workers as independent contractors rather than employees. The rule covers workers who are common law employees, but it does not cover certain technical service workers. Section 530 prohibits the IRS from challenging a taxpayer's treatment of an individual as an independent contractor for employment tax purposes if: (1) the taxpayer had a reasonable basis for not treating the individual as an employee; (2) the taxpayer did not treat the worker or any worker in a similar position as an employee for payroll tax purposes; and (3) the taxpayer has filed all required federal tax returns, including information returns, in a manner consistent with the worker not being an employee. This rule governs employee status only with respect to employment taxes and not for other purposes. Section 530 safe haven relief is for employers, not workers, and, therefore, it does not convert a worker from the status of an employee to the status of an independent contractor.

NEW LAW EXPLAINED

Treatment of test room supervisors and proctors who assist in the administration of college entrance and placement exams.—Section 530 of the Revenue Act of 1978 (P.L. 95-600) is amended to provide that with respect to an individual providing services as a test room supervisor or proctor by assisting in the administration of college entrance or placement examinations, the consistency requirement does not apply with respect to services performed after December 31, 2006, and remuneration paid with respect to such services (Act Sec. 530(f)(1) of P.L. 95-600, as added by the Pension Protection Act of 2006). The amendment applies if the individual is: (1) performing the services for a Code Sec. 501(c) organization that is exempt from tax under Code Sec. 501(a); and (2) not otherwise treated as an employee of such organization for purposes of employment taxes (Act Sec. 530(f)(2) of P.L. 95-600, as added by the Pension Act).

Therefore, if the above requirements are satisfied, the IRS is prohibited from challenging the treatment of such individuals as independent contractors for employment tax purposes, even if the organization previously treated such individuals as employees

NEW LAW EXPLAINED

(Joint Committee on Taxation, Technical Explanation of the Pension Protection Act of 2006 (JCX-38-06)).

▶ **Effective date.** This provision shall apply to remuneration for services performed after December 31, 2006 (Act Sec. 864(b) of the Pension Protection Act of 2006).

Law source: Law at ¶7174. Committee Report at ¶10,900.

— Act Sec. 864(a) of the Pension Protection Act of 2006, adding Act. Sec. 530(f) to the Revenue Reconciliation Act of 1978 (P.L. 95-600);

— Act Sec. 864(b), providing the effective date.

Reporter references: For further information, consult the following CCH reporters.

— Standard Federal Tax Reporter, 2006FED ¶33,538.026

— Tax Research Consultant, COMPEN: 3,110

¶1340 Alaska Hydroelectric Projects Excepted from Certain Qualified Bond Requirements

SUMMARY OF NEW LAW

Bonds used to finance the Lake Dorothy hydroelectric project are qualified private activity bonds with tax-exempt interest although the current service area was not serviced on January 1, 1997, and electricity is furnished beyond the local area. In addition, the interest on the Snettisham hydroelectric project bonds remains tax-exempt even though electricity is furnished beyond the local area.

BACKGROUND

Interest on bonds issued by State and local governments to finance government activities is generally excluded from gross income. Interest on State and local government bonds issued to finance activities of private persons, however, is taxable unless an exception applies. Private activity bond interest may be exempt from federal income tax if the bonds are issued for certain purposes permitted by the Code. For example, interest on bonds issued to finance private facilities for the local furnishing of electricity or gas is tax-exempt as qualified private activity bond interest if certain criteria are satisfied (Code Sec. 142(f)).

First, the furnishing of electricity or gas *locally* is generally satisfied by the two county rule requiring that the private facility not serve an area exceeding two contiguous counties, or a city and a contiguous county (Code Sec. 142(f)(1)). Second, the local furnishing of electricity or gas exception is generally limited to bonds for facilities:

(1) of persons who were engaged in the local furnishing of electricity or gas on January 1, 1997, or a successor in interest to such person; and

BACKGROUND

(2) that serve areas served by those persons on such date (service area limitation) (Code Sec. 142(f)(3)).

Legislation may modify the criteria applicable to qualified private activity bonds. Pursuant to the Small Business Job Protection Act of 1996 (P.L. 104-188), bonds issued to finance the acquisition of the Snettisham hydroelectric project from the Alaska Power Administration were excepted from the limitations of Code Sec. 142(f)(3). The bonds for this acquisition were subject to the State of Alaska's private activity bond volume limit.

NEW LAW EXPLAINED

Bonds for Alaska hydroelectric projects excepted from service area limitation and local requirement.—Bonds issued prior to May 31, 2006, to finance the Lake Dorothy hydroelectric project are not subject to the service area limitation of Code Sec. 142(f)(3)(A)(ii) (Act Sec. 1303(b) of the Pension Protection Act of 2006). Furthermore, for purposes of applying the two county rule to bonds issued before May 31, 2006, to finance the Lake Dorothy hydroelectric project or to finance the acquisition of the Snettisham hydroelectric project, the furnishing of electric service to the City of Hoonah, Alaska is disregarded (Act Sec. 1303(a) and (b) of the Pension Act).

> **Comment:** Exceptions to the criteria generally applicable to bonds used to provide facilities for the local furnishing of electricity under Code Sec. 142(a)(8) have been provided. The exceptions apply for purposes of determining whether any private activity bond issued before May 31, 2006, and used to finance the acquisition of the Snettisham hydroelectric facility or to finance the Lake Dorothy hydroelectric project is a qualified private activity bond under Code Sec. 142(a)(8).

The Lake Dorothy hydroelectric facility is the hydroelectric facility located approximately ten miles south of Juneau, Alaska, and commonly referred to as the Lake Dorothy project (Act Sec. 1303 (c)(1) of the Pension Act). The Snettisham hydroelectric facility is the hydroelectric project acquired from the Alaska Power Administration pursuant to legislation enacted by Congress in 1996 (Act Sec. 1303(c)(2) of the Pension Act).

> **Comment:** The city of Hoonah, Alaska, is outside the local two county rule area for both the Lake Dorothy and Snettisham hydroelectric projects.

▶ **Effective date.** No specific effective date is provided by the Act. The provision is, therefore, considered effective on August 17, 2006, the date of enactment.

Law source: Law at ¶7252. Committee Report at ¶11,390.

— Act Sec. 1303 of the Pension Protection Act of 2006.

Reporter references: For further information, consult the following CCH reporters.

— Standard Federal Tax Reporter, 2006FED ¶7752.035

— Tax Research Consultant, SALES: 51,208.15

VALUATIONS

¶1345 Penalty Thresholds Lowered for Substantial and Gross Valuation Misstatements

SUMMARY OF NEW LAW

The thresholds for imposing the accuracy-related penalty for underpayment of income, estate and gift taxes due to substantial and gross valuation misstatements have been lowered. The reasonable cause exception has also eliminated for gross valuation misstatements regarding charitable deduction property.

BACKGROUND

A 20-percent accuracy-related penalty is imposed on an underpayment of income tax caused by a substantial valuation misstatement (Code Sec. 6662(a) and (b)(3)). A substantial valuation misstatement occurs where: (1) the value or adjusted basis of any property claimed on any federal income tax return is 200 percent or more of the amount determined to be the correct valuation or adjusted basis; (2) the claimed price for any service, property or use of property in connection with any transaction between controlled taxpayers described in Code Sec. 482 is 200 percent or more, or 50 percent or less, of the correct Code Sec. 482 price; or (3) the net Code Sec. 482 transfer price adjustment for the tax year exceeds the lesser of $5 million or 10 percent of the taxpayer's gross receipts (Code Sec. 6662(e)(1)). However, no penalty is imposed unless the underpayment portion attributable to a substantial valuation misstatement exceeds $5,000 or $10,000 for corporations other than S corporations or personal holding companies (Code Sec. 6662(e)(2)).

Gross valuation misstatements. The penalty doubles to 40 percent for a gross valuation misstatement, which occurs where the property value or adjusted basis claimed on the return is 400 percent or more of the correct amount. For controlled taxpayer transactions, gross valuation misstatement occurs if the claimed price is 400 percent or more, or 25 percent or less, of the correct Code Sec. 482 price, or the net Code Sec. 482 transfer price adjustment for the tax year exceeds the lesser of $20 million or 20 percent of the taxpayer's gross receipts (Code Sec. 6662(h)(1), (2)(A)).

Estate and gift taxes. The 20-percent penalty is also imposed on a tax underpayment resulting from a substantial estate or gift tax valuation understatement, which occurs where the value of any property claimed on any federal estate or gift tax return is 50 percent or less of the correct valuation (Code Sec. 6662(b)(5) and (g)(1)). The penalty doubles to 40 percent for a gross valuation misstatement, which occurs where the property value claimed on the return is 25 percent or less of the correct amount (Code Sec. 6662(h)(2)(C)). No penalty is imposed unless the underpayment portion due to substantial estate or gift tax valuation understatement exceeds $5,000 (Code Sec. 6662(g)(2)).

BACKGROUND

Reasonable cause exception. The 20-percent accuracy-related penalty for underpayment will not be imposed if there was reasonable cause for the underpayment and the taxpayer acted in good faith (Code Sec. 6664(c)(1)). For any underpayment due to a substantial or gross valuation overstatement of charitable deduction property, the reasonable cause exception applies only if the claimed property value was based on a qualified appraisal made by a qualified appraiser, and the taxpayer made a good faith investigation of the contributed property's value in addition to obtaining the appraisal (Code Sec. 6664(c)(2)).

NEW LAW EXPLAINED

Lower penalty thresholds for substantial and gross valuation misstatements imposed.—The thresholds for imposing the accuracy-related penalty for substantial and gross valuation misstatements have been lowered, potentially exposing more returns to underpayment penalties. The 20-percent penalty is imposed on an income tax underpayment resulting from a substantial valuation misstatement if the value or adjusted basis of any property claimed on any federal income tax return is 150 percent (instead of 200 percent) or more of the correct valuation or adjusted basis (Code Sec. 6662(e)(1)(A), as amended by the Pension Protection Act of 2006). The 40-percent penalty for gross valuation misstatements is imposed where the property value or adjusted basis claimed on the return is 200 percent (instead of 400 percent) or more of the correct amount (Code Sec. 6662(h)(2)(A)(i), as amended by the Pension Act).

Controlled taxpayer transactions. The rules involving property or services used in connection with a controlled taxpayer transaction described in Code Sec. 482 remain the same. In such situations, a substantial valuation misstatement occurs where the price claimed on the return for any services, property or use of property in connection with any transaction between controlled taxpayers is 200 percent or more, or 50 percent or less, of the correct Code Sec. 482 amount, or where the net Code Sec. 482 transfer price adjustment for the tax year exceeds the lesser of $5 million or 10 percent of the taxpayer's gross receipts (Code Sec. 6662(e)(1)(B)). A gross valuation misstatement occurs where the net Code Sec. 482 transfer price adjustment for the tax year exceeds the lesser of $20 million or 20 percent of the taxpayer's gross receipts (Code Sec. 6662(h)(2)(A)(iii)), or the claimed price is 400 percent or more, or 25 percent or less, of the correct Code Sec. 482 price (Code Sec. 6662(h)(2)(A)(ii), as amended by the Pension Act).

Estate and gift taxes. The 20-percent underpayment penalty on a substantial estate or gift tax valuation understatement is imposed if the value of any property claimed on any federal estate or gift tax return is 65 percent (instead of 50 percent) or less of the correct valuation amount (Code Sec. 6662(g)(1), as amended by the Pension Act). The 40-percent penalty for gross valuation misstatements is imposed where the property value claimed on the return is 40 percent (instead of 25 percent) or less of the correct amount (Code Sec. 6662(h)(2)(C), as amended by the Pension Act).

Reasonable cause exception. The reasonable cause exception for underpayments due to gross valuation misstatements on charitable deduction property is eliminated (Code

NEW LAW EXPLAINED

Sec. 6664(c)(2), as amended by the Pension Act). However, the exception still exists for substantial valuation misstatements on charitable deduction property, and for gross valuation misstatements on property for which a charitable deduction is not being claimed.

> **Comment:** The definitions of "qualified appraisal" and "qualified appraiser" have been amended (see ¶1355).

▶ **Effective date.** The provisions apply to returns filed after August 17, 2006 (Act Sec. 1219(e)(1) of the Pension Protection Act of 2006). However, in the case of a contribution of a qualified real property interest which is a restriction with respect to the exterior of a building that is a certified historic structure described in Code Sec. 170(h)(4)(C)(ii), and an appraisal with respect to the contribution, the provisions apply to returns filed after July 25, 2006 (Act Sec. 1219(e)(3) of the Pension Act).

Law source: Law at ¶5395 and ¶5400. Committee Report at ¶11,270.

— Act Sec. 1219(a)(1) of the Pension Protection Act of 2006, amending Code Sec. 6662(e)(1)(A) and (g)(1);

— Act Sec. 1219(a)(2), amending Code Sec. 6662(h)(2)(A) and (C);

— Act Sec. 1219(a)(3), amending Code Sec. 6664(c)(2);

— Act Sec. 1219(e)(1) and (3), providing the effective dates.

Reporter references: For further information, consult the following CCH reporters.

— Pension Plan Guide, ¶3030 and ¶5455

— Standard Federal Tax Reporter, 2006FED ¶39,654.01 and ¶39,661.026

— Tax Research Consultant, PENALTY: 3,110 and PENALTY: 3,114

— Federal Tax Guide, 2006FTG ¶6597 and ¶22,527

— Federal Estate and Gift Tax Reporter, ¶21,790.09 and ¶21,840.05

¶1350 Penalty and Disciplinary Action Imposed on Appraisers

SUMMARY OF NEW LAW

A civil penalty is imposed on a person who prepares an appraisal that results in a substantial or gross valuation misstatement. The Secretary of the Treasury may discipline an appraiser without first assessing the civil penalty for aiding and abetting in an understatement of another person's tax liability.

BACKGROUND

A penalty is imposed on any person who: (1) aids, assists in or advises with respect to a tax return, claim or other document; (2) knows or has reason to believe that the document will be used in connection with a material federal tax matter; and (3) knows that this would result in an understatement of another person's tax liability

BACKGROUND

(Code Sec. 6701(a)). The penalty is $1,000, or $10,000 if the document relates to a corporation's tax liability (Code Sec. 6701(b)(1) and (2)).

> **Comment:** Although the penalty is typically assessed against return preparers, Congress specifically authorized the IRS to assess the penalty against appraisers who violate the provision (IRS Chief Counsel Advice 200512016, Feb. 8, 2004).

If the penalty has been assessed against an appraiser, then after notice and an opportunity for hearing, the Secretary of the Treasury may provide that appraisals by the appraiser will have no probative effect in any administrative proceeding before the Treasury or the IRS and bar the appraiser from presenting evidence or testimony in such a proceeding (31 U.S.C. Sec. 330(c); Treasury Dept. Circular 230, 31 C.F.R. Sec. 10.50(b)).

NEW LAW EXPLAINED

Penalty and disciplinary action imposed on appraisers for substantial or gross valuation misstatements.—The Pension Protection Act of 2006 adds a civil penalty to be assessed against appraisers for certain types of valuation misstatements. A person who prepares an appraisal of property value must pay a penalty if: (1) he or she knows, or reasonably should have known, that the appraisal would be used in connection with a federal tax return or refund claim; and (2) the claimed value of the appraised property results in a substantial valuation misstatement related to income tax under Code Sec. 6662(e) or a gross valuation misstatement under Code Sec. 6662(h) (Code Sec. 6695A(a), as added by the Pension Act).

> **Comment:** The penalty thresholds for an income tax understatement due to a substantial or gross valuation misstatement have been lowered (see ¶1345).

The penalty amount is the *lesser* of: (1) the greater of $1,000 or 10 percent of the tax underpayment amount attributable to the misstatement; or (2) 125 percent of the gross income received by the appraiser for preparing the appraisal (Code Sec. 6695A(b), as added by the Pension Act). However, no penalty is imposed if the appraiser establishes that the appraised value was more likely than not the proper value (Code Sec. 6695A(c), as added by the Pension Act).

> **Comment:** Unlike the Code Sec. 6701 penalty for aiding and abetting a tax understatement, the Code Sec. 6695A penalty does not require that the appraiser have knowledge of any resulting understatement. This should make the elements of the Code Sec. 6695A penalty easier for the government to prove.

Rules applicable to appraiser penalty. The Code Sec. 6695A appraiser penalty is in addition to any other penalties provided by law. Deficiency procedures for income, estate, gift and certain excise taxes do not apply to the assessment or collection of the appraiser penalty. Any credit or refund claim for a paid appraiser penalty must be filed according to Treasury Regulations, and any refund claim for an overpayment of the appraiser penalty assessed must be filed within three years from the time the penalty was paid. For purposes of the appraiser penalty, a "return" means any federal income tax return, and a "claim for refund" means a claim for refund of, or credit against, any federal income tax (Code Sec. 6696, as amended by the Pension Act).

NEW LAW EXPLAINED

> **Comment:** Code Sec. 6696 as amended does not provide a limitation period for assessment of the Code Sec. 6695A appraiser penalty. This may have been an oversight that may be corrected in a future technical amendment.

Disciplinary actions against appraisers. The Pension Act also gives the Secretary of the Treasury wider latitude to discipline appraisers. The requirement that the Code Sec. 6701 civil penalty for aiding and abetting a tax understatement must be assessed *before* the Secretary may discipline an appraiser has been stricken (31 U.S.C. §330(c), as amended by the Pension Act).

> **Comment:** Removal of the Code Sec. 6701 penalty language from the 31 U.S.C. Sec. 330(c) discipline provision was most likely intended to allow the Secretary to discipline appraisers against whom the Code Sec. 6695A appraiser penalty is aimed without having to first impose the penalty for aiding and abetting in tax understatement. However, 31 U.S.C. Sec. 330(c) as amended could be read as empowering the Secretary to discipline an appraiser *regardless* of whether or not the appraiser has committed an act that is subject to penalty.

▶ **Effective date.** The provisions apply to appraisals prepared with respect to returns or submissions filed after August 17, 2006 (Act Sec. 1219(e)(2) of the Pension Protection Act of 2006). However, in the case of a contribution of a qualified real property interest which is a restriction with respect to the exterior of a building that is a certified historic structure described in Code Sec. 170(h)(4)(C)(ii), and an appraisal with respect to the contribution, the provisions regarding the penalty on appraisers whose appraisals result in substantial or gross valuation misstatements apply to returns filed after July 25, 2006 (Act Sec. 1219(e)(3) of the Pension Act).

Law source: Law at ¶5405, ¶5410 and ¶7234. Committee Report at ¶11,270.

— Act Sec. 1219(b) of the Pension Protection Act of 2006, adding Code Sec. 6695A and amending Code Sec. 6696;

— Act Sec. 1219(d), amending 31 U.S.C. Sec. 330(c);

— Act Sec. 1219(e)(2) and (3), providing the effective dates.

Reporter references: For further information, consult the following CCH reporters.

— Pension Plan Guide, ¶480 and ¶3020

— Standard Federal Tax Reporter, 2006FED ¶39,980.01, ¶40,035.01 and ¶40,035.03

— Tax Research Consultant, PENALTY: 3,258 and PENALTY: 3,110.10

— Federal Tax Guide, 2006FTG ¶6597 and ¶22,527

¶1355 Definitions of Qualified Appraisal and Qualified Appraiser Clarified

SUMMARY OF NEW LAW

Definitions for "qualified appraisal" and "qualified appraiser" are codified and revised for purposes of the charitable deduction for donated property.

BACKGROUND

If a taxpayer claims a charitable deduction greater than $5,000 for donated property, he or she generally must obtain a qualified appraisal of the property and attach an appraisal summary to the federal tax return for the tax year of the donation (Code Sec. 170(f)(11)(C); Reg. § 1.170A-13(c)(2)(i)). For contributions greater than $500,000, the qualified appraisal itself must be attached to the return (Code Sec. 170(f)(11)(D)). These requirements do not apply to donations of: (1) cash; (2) patents and other intellectual property; (3) publicly-traded securities for which market quotations are readily available on an established securities market; (4) inventory or property held by the taxpayer primarily for sale to customers in the ordinary course of his or her trade or business; and (5) a qualified vehicle sold by the donee organization without any significant intervening use or material improvement and for which an acknowledgment is provided (Code Sec. 170(f)(11)(A)(ii)(I)).

A "qualified appraisal" is an appraisal document that:

(1) relates to an appraisal made not earlier than 60 days before the appraised property's donation date, and not later than the due date (including extensions) of the tax return on which the charitable deduction is first claimed;

(2) is prepared, signed, and dated by a qualified appraiser;

(3) does not involve an appraisal fee based on a percentage of the property's appraised value, unless the fee was paid to certain not-for-profit organizations; and

(4) includes: (i) a detailed description of the property; (ii) the property's physical condition; (iii) the donation date; (iv) the terms of any agreement relating to the property's use, sale or other disposition; (v) the appraiser's name, address and taxpayer identification number, and that of the appraiser's employer or partnership; (vi) the appraiser's qualifications; (vii) a statement that the appraisal was prepared for income tax purposes; (viii) the date on which the property was valued; (ix) the property's appraised fair market value on the donation date; (x) the valuation method used; and (xi) the specific basis for valuation, if any (Code Sec. 170(f)(11)(E); Reg.§ 1.170A-13(c)(3)).

A "qualified appraiser" is an individual who:

(1) holds himself or herself out to the public as an appraiser, or regularly performs appraisals;

(2) is qualified to make appraisals of the property type being valued;

BACKGROUND

(3) is not a person specifically prohibited from being a qualified appraiser of particular property (such as the donor, the donee, or others with a connection to the donor or donee); and

(4) understands that he or she can be subject to civil penalties for aiding and abetting a tax understatement due to an intentionally false or fraudulent value overstatement (Reg.§ 1.170A-13(c)(5)(i)).

An individual is not a qualified appraiser with respect to a particular donation if the donor had knowledge of facts that would cause a reasonable person to expect the appraiser to falsely overstate the value of the donated property (Reg.§ 1.170A-13(c)(5)(ii)).

Substantial or gross valuation misstatements of charitable property. A 20-percent accuracy-related penalty is imposed on an underpayment of income tax caused by a substantial valuation misstatement (Code Sec. 6662(a) and (b)(3)). The penalty doubles to 40 percent for a gross valuation misstatement, which occurs where the property value or adjusted basis claimed on the return is 400 percent or more of the correct amount (Code Sec. 6662(h)(1), (2)(A)). The penalties will not be imposed if there was reasonable cause for the underpayment and the taxpayer acted in good faith (Code Sec. 6664(c)(1)). For any underpayment due to a substantial or gross valuation overstatement of charitable deduction property, the reasonable cause exception applies only if the claimed property value was based on a qualified appraisal made by a qualified appraiser, and the taxpayer obtained the appraisal and made a good faith investigation of the contributed property's value (Code Sec. 6664(c)(2)). The definitions listed above for qualified appraisal and qualified appraiser also apply to the reasonable cause exception for valuation misstatements of charitable deduction property (Code Sec. 6664(c)(3)(B) and (C)).

NEW LAW EXPLAINED

Revised definitions of "qualified appraisal" and "qualified appraiser."— The Pension Protection Act of 2006 revises the definitions of qualified appraisal and qualified appraiser for purposes of the substantiation and documentation requirements for charitable contributions of property valued at more than $5,000. As amended, a "qualified appraisal" is an appraisal of property which is:

(1) treated as a qualified appraisal under the Regulations or other guidance prescribed by the Secretary of the Treasury; and

(2) conducted by a qualified appraiser in accordance with generally-accepted appraisal standards and any Regulations or other guidance prescribed by the Secretary (Code Sec. 170(f)(11)(E)(i), as amended by the Pension Act).

The definition of qualified appraiser is now codified. A "qualified appraiser" is an individual who:

(1) has earned an appraisal designation from a recognized professional appraiser organization, or has otherwise met minimum education and experience requirements set forth in the Regulations;

NEW LAW EXPLAINED

(2) regularly performs appraisals for pay; and

(3) meets other requirements the Secretary may prescribe in Regulations or other guidance (Code Sec. 170(f)(11)(E)(ii), as amended by the Pension Act).

However, an individual cannot be a qualified appraiser with respect to any *specific* appraisal unless he or she:

(1) demonstrates verifiable education and experience in valuing the property type being appraised; and

(2) has not been prohibited from practicing before the IRS under 31 U.S.C. Sec. 330(c) at any time during the three-year period ending on the appraisal date (Code Sec. 170(f)(11)(E)(iii), as amended by the Pension Act).

Comment: Reg.§ 1.170A-13(c)(3) and (5) continue to provide detailed guidance on the requirements for a qualified appraisal and a qualified appraiser.

Comment: For additional discussion of the disciplinary sanctions under 31 U.S.C. Sec. 330(c), see ¶ 1350.

Reasonable cause exception for tax underpayment penalty. The amended definitions of qualified appraisal and qualified appraiser apply to the reasonable cause exception for substantial valuation misstatements of charitable deduction property (Code Sec. 6664(c)(3)(B) and (C), as amended by the Pension Act).

Comment: The reasonable cause exception has been amended, and no longer applies to gross valuation misstatements of charitable deduction property. For further discussion, see ¶ 1345.

▶ **Effective date.** The provisions apply to appraisals prepared with respect to returns or submissions filed after August 17, 2006 (Act Sec. 1219(e)(2) of the Pension Protection Act of 2006).

Law source: Law at ¶5020 and ¶5400. Committee Report at ¶11,270.

— Act Sec. 1219(c)(1) of the Pension Protection Act of 2006, amending Code Sec. 170(f)(11)(E);

— Act Sec. 1219(c)(2), amending Code Sec. 6664(c)(3)(B) and (C);

— Act Sec. 1219(e)(2), providing the effective date.

Reporter references: For further information, consult the following CCH reporters.

— Standard Federal Tax Reporter, 2006FED ¶11,700.04, ¶11,700.041 and ¶39,661.026

— Tax Research Consultant, INDIV: 51,458 and PENALTY: 3,110.20

— Federal Tax Guide, 2006FTG ¶6597 and ¶22,527

U.S. Tax Court Modernization 14

JURISDICTION AND FILINGS

¶1405 Jurisdiction of Tax Court Over Collection Due Process Cases

SUMMARY OF NEW LAW

The provision modifies the jurisdiction of the U.S. Tax Court by providing that all appeals of collection due process (CDP) determinations should be made to the Tax Court.

BACKGROUND

Taxpayers are entitled to a written notice, at least 30 days prior to a proposed levy, that explains their right to request a hearing to challenge the levy action (Code Sec.

BACKGROUND

6330(a)). Similar rules apply with regard to liens (Code Sec. 6320). The hearing is conducted by the IRS Office of Appeals and is referred to as a collection due process (CDP) hearing. The CDP determination made by the IRS hearing officer is issued in a written Notice of Determination.

Taxpayers have 30 days after the date the Notice of Determination is issued within which to seek judicial review from a court (Code Sec. 6330(d)(1)). Typically, this is the U.S. Tax Court unless the Tax Court lacks jurisdiction over the underlying tax liability; in that case, the appeal must be brought in the U.S. District Court. If the appeal is filed with the wrong court, the taxpayer has an additional 30 days after that court's determination to file with the proper court.

The Tax Court was established under Article 1 of the United States Constitution (Code Sec. 7441) and is a court of limited jurisdiction (Code Sec. 7442). Its primary function is to review deficiencies asserted against taxpayers by the IRS for additional income, estate, and gift taxes but, in general, it has no jurisdiction over other types of taxes or nontax matters as it only has the jurisdiction that is expressly conferred on it by statute (Code Sec. 7442). Therefore, the Tax Court may not have jurisdiction over the underlying tax liability with respect to an appeal of a due process hearing relating to a collections matter. Further, an appeal of a due process hearing, whether this falls within the jurisdiction of the Tax Court or of a U.S. District Court, may not even involve the underlying tax liability.

NEW LAW EXPLAINED

Consolidation of review of collection due process cases.—The provision modifies the jurisdiction of the Tax Court by providing that all appeals of collection due process (CDP) determinations are to be made to the Tax Court. Within 30 days of a CDP determination, a person may appeal that determination to the Tax Court (Code Sec. 6330(d)(1), as amended by the Pension Protection Act of 2006). Thus, the Tax Court will have jurisdiction over all appeals of CDP determinations regardless of the type of tax specified in the Notice of Determination. This extension of the Tax Court's jurisdiction is effective for CDP determinations made after the date which is 60 days after August 17, 2006, the date of enactment of the Pension Act (Act Sec. 855(b) of the Pension Act).

> **Comment:** The Tax Court, thus, becomes a court of unlimited jurisdiction for purposes of reviewing CDP determinations. This jurisdictional change improves the efficiency of the CDP appeal process by eliminating any possibility of filing an appeal in the wrong court, with its attendant time delay. This is a major improvement in pre-levy situations where time is usually of the essence for both parties.

Practical Analysis: Charles P. Rettig, Esq., of Hochman, Salkin, Rettig & Perez, PC, Beverly Hills, California, observes that Act Sec. 855 amends Code Sec. 6330(d)(1)by providing that all adverse CDP appeal determinations must proceed to

NEW LAW EXPLAINED

the U.S. Tax Court, regardless of whether the Tax Court would have jurisdiction over the underlying tax liability. Taxpayers have a right to a CDP hearing by the IRS Office of Appeals if they timely file a Request for a CDP Hearing (Form 12153) regarding a specific tax period within 30 days following (i) the first Notice of a Federal Tax Lien Filing; (ii) before the IRS sends the first Final Notice—Notice of Intent to Levy; (iii) Notice of Levy on Your State Tax Refund; or (iv) when IRS issues a Notice of Jeopardy Levy. If the taxpayer does not agree with the CDP determination by Appeals, they can request judicial review in the Tax Court (by filing a Petition for Redetermination within 30 days following the Appeals determination) only if they have timely filed Form 12153. The Tax Court decision is final and binding on both the taxpayer and the IRS. The Tax Court has developed an expertise in handling collection appeals and this amendment to Code Sec. 6330(d)(1) resolves prior confusion that has existed regarding the proper judicial forum for resolving CDP appeals. As an alternative to CDP, a taxpayer can file a Collection Appeal (CAP) Request (IRS Form 9423), which provides an expedited procedure but does not afford an opportunity for judicial review of the determination by the IRS Office of Appeals.

▶ **Effective date.** This amendment applies to determinations made after the date which is 60 days after August 17, 2006 (Act Sec. 855(b) of the Pension Protection Act of 2006).

Law source: Law at ¶5375. Committee Report at ¶10,820.

— Act Sec. 855(a) of the Pension Protection Act of 2006, amending Code Sec. 6330(d)(1);

— Act Sec. 855(b), providing the effective date.

Reporter references: For further information, consult the following CCH reporters.

— Standard Federal Tax Reporter, 2006FED ¶38,134.025, ¶38,134.028, ¶38,184.025, ¶38,184.027 and ¶42,058.055

— Tax Research Consultant, IRS: 48,056.25, IRS: 51,056.25, LITIG: 6,136.25 and LITIG: 9,252.05

— Federal Tax Guide, 2006FTG ¶28,859

¶1410 Assignment of Employment Status Cases

SUMMARY OF NEW LAW

The chief judge of the U.S. Tax Court may assign employment tax cases that are subject to the small case procedures to special trial judges and may authorize special trial judges to decide these small tax cases.

BACKGROUND

In the context of an audit of any person, if there is an actual controversy involving a determination by the IRS as part of the examination that (1) one or more individuals

BACKGROUND

performing services for that person are employees of that person or (2) that person is not entitled to relief under section 530 of the Revenue Act of 1978, then the U.S. Tax Court has jurisdiction to determine whether the IRS is correct and the proper amount of employment tax under that determination (Code Sec. 7436(a)). Further, any redetermination by the Tax Court has the force and effect of a decision of the Tax Court and is reviewable as such. If the amount of employment taxes in dispute is $50,000 or less for each calendar quarter involved, the taxpayer may elect small case procedures (Code Sec. 7436(c)). However, the decision resulting from a small case procedure is not reviewable in any other court nor does it constitute authority for any other case not involving the same person and the same determinations.

The chief judge of the Tax Court may assign certain types of proceedings to be heard and decided by a special trial judge (Code Sec. 7443A). Further, the chief judge may designate any other proceeding as one to be presided over by a special trial judge.

NEW LAW EXPLAINED

Authority to hear and decide certain employment status cases.—The provision clarifies that the chief judge of the U.S. Tax Court may assign employment tax cases that are subject to the small case procedure under Code Sec. 7436(c) to special trial judges (Code Sec. 7443A(b), as amended by the Pension Protection Act of 2006); and may authorize special trial judges to decide these small tax cases (Code Sec. 7443A(c), as amended by the Pension Act). This provision is intended to improve the workflow of the Tax Court. It applies to any proceeding under Code Sec. 7436(c) with respect to which a decision has not become final prior to August 17, 2006, the date of enactment (Act Sec. 857(c) of the Pension Act).

Practical Analysis: Charles P. Rettig, Esq., of Hochman, Salkin, Rettig & Perez, PC, Beverly Hills, California, states that Act Sec. 857 provides specific authority allowing determinations under Code Sec. 7436 regarding (i) the status of workers as employees or (ii) availability of relief under Section 530 of the Revenue Act of 1978, to be made by Special Trial Judges. Taxpayers may elect to have their matter heard by a Special Trial Judge if the amount of employment taxes in dispute is $50,000 or less for each calendar quarter involved. Decisions by the Special Trial Judges are not reviewable by any other court and are not precedent for other cases. These matters are typically heard on an expedited basis and would allow for a prompt determination, which is often desirable for future planning in the context of an ongoing business operation.

▶ **Effective date.** The provision is effective for any proceeding under Code Sec. 7436(c) with respect to which a decision has not become final prior to August 17, 2006 (Act Sec. 857(c) of the Pension Protection Act of 2006).

Law source: Law at ¶5450. Committee Report at ¶10,830.

— Act Sec. 857(a) of the Pension Protection Act of 2006, redesignating Code Sec. 7443A(b)(5) as (6) and adding new Code Sec. 7433A(b)(5);

NEW LAW EXPLAINED

— Act Sec. 857(b), amending Code Sec. 7443A(c);

— Act Sec. 857(c), providing the effective date.

Reporter references: For further information, consult the following CCH reporters.

— Standard Federal Tax Reporter, 2006FED ¶41,788G.05 and ¶42,061.01

— Tax Research Consultant, LITIG: 6,808 and LITIG: 7,060

— Federal Tax Guide, 2006FTG ¶28,538

¶1415 Application of Doctrine of Equitable Recoupment in Tax Court

SUMMARY OF NEW LAW

The U.S. Tax Court may apply the doctrine of equitable recoupment to the same extent as it may be applied in federal civil tax cases by the U.S. District Courts or the U.S. Court of Claims.

BACKGROUND

The common law principle of equitable recoupment permits the defensive use of an otherwise time-barred claim to defeat or reduce an opponent's claim if both claims arose from the same transaction. Within the context of federal tax law, a taxpayer may, therefore, defeat or reduce an IRS tax claim by offsetting it with an otherwise time-barred taxpayer claim against the IRS, provided both claims arose from the same transaction. Both the U.S. District Courts and the U.S. Court of Federal Claims may apply equitable recoupment when deciding tax refund cases (*Stone v. White*, 37-1 USTC ¶9303; *Bull v. United States*, 35-1 USTC ¶9346. However, there has been a split of authority regarding a taxpayer's right to invoke the equitable recoupment doctrine in a U.S. Tax Court proceeding. The U.S. Court of Appeals for the Sixth Circuit held that the Tax Court may not apply the doctrine (*Estate of Mueller v. Commissioner*, 98-2 USTC ¶60,325, *cert. den.*, 525 U.S. 1140 (1999)); the U.S. Court of Appeals for the Ninth Circuit reached the opposite conclusion, however, in *Branson v. Commissioner*, 2001-2 USTC ¶60,419, *cert. den.*, (Mar. 18, 2002).

NEW LAW EXPLAINED

Confirmation of authority.—The provision clarifies the applicability of the doctrine of equitable recoupment and confirms that the Tax Court may apply the doctrine to the same extent as it may be applied in federal civil tax cases by the U.S. District Courts or the U.S. Court of Claims (Code Sec. 6214(b), as amended by the Pension Protection Act of 2006). In its technical explanation, the Joint Committee on Taxation states that no implication is intended as to whether the Tax Court has the authority to continue to

NEW LAW EXPLAINED

apply other equitable principles in deciding matters over which it has jurisdiction (Joint Committee on Taxation, Technical Explanation of the Pension Protection Act of 2006 (JCX-38-06)).

> **Comment:** The provision is intended to simplify matters for both the taxpayer and the IRS by eliminating uncertainty or confusion from differing results for similarly situated taxpayers in differing circuits.

> **Practical Analysis:** Charles P. Rettig, Esq., of Hochman, Salkin, Rettig & Perez, PC, Beverly Hills, California, observes that the amendment to Code Sec. 6214(b) permits the Tax Court to allow an offset of time-barred claims to reduce or defeat claims arising from the same transaction. Equitable recoupment arises when a single "transaction, item or taxable event" is subject to two inconsistent taxes. The doctrine permits a party to a tax dispute to raise a time-barred claim in order to reduce or eliminate the money owed on the timely claim. Equitable recoupment cannot be used offensively to seek a money payment, only defensively to offset an adjudicated deficiency. Because equitable recoupment has the potential to completely override the statute of limitations, the party raising an equitable recoupment claim must satisfy several criteria. First, the same "transaction, item or taxable event" must be subject to two taxes. Second, the taxes must be inconsistent in that the Tax Code authorizes only a single tax. Third, the tax sought to be recouped must be time barred. Fourth, there must be an "identity of interest" between the parties paying the duplicative tax. Finally, the court in which the recoupment claim is brought must independently have jurisdiction to adjudicate the claim. Equitable recoupment cannot be the sole basis of jurisdiction.

▶ **Effective date.** The provision applies to any action or proceeding in the United States Tax Court with respect to which a decision has not become final (as determined under Code Sec. 7481) as of August 17, 2006 (Act Sec. 858(b) of the Pension Protection Act of 2006).

Law source: Law at ¶5370. Committee Report at ¶10,840.

— Act Sec. 858(a) of the Pension Protection Act of 2006, amending Code Sec. 6214(b);

— Act Sec. 858(b), providing the effective date.

Reporter references: For further information, consult the following CCH reporters.

— Standard Federal Tax Reporter, 2006FED ¶37,554.021, ¶39,080.04 and ¶39,080.051

— Tax Research Consultant, IRS: 30,352.10 and LITIG: 6,134.05

— Federal Tax Guide, 2006FTG ¶28,668

— Federal Estate and Gift Tax Reporter, ¶20,780.06

¶1420 Types of Petitions Subject to Filing Fees

SUMMARY OF NEW LAW

The U.S. Tax Court may charge a fee of up to $60 for the filing of any petition. This filing fee may be charged in any type of case commenced by the filing of a petition.

BACKGROUND

The U.S. Tax Court is authorized under Code Sec. 7451 to impose a filing fee of up to $60 for the filing of certain types of petitions. Although some types of petitions are not specifically mentioned in Code Sec. 7451, the practice of the Tax Court has been to impose a filing fee in all cases commenced by petition (Tax Court Rule 20).

The types of petitions explicitly mentioned in Code Sec. 7451 include those for the redetermination of a deficiency, as well as petitions for declaratory judgment under Code Sec. 7476 (certain retirement plan qualifications), Code Sec. 7477 (gift tax valuations), Code Sec. 7478 (tax status of a proposed issue of municipal bonds), Code Sec. 7479 (installment payment of estate taxes attributable to a closely held business interest), and Code Sec. 7428 (qualification or classification of a Code Sec. 501(c)(3) organization, charitable contribution donee, private foundation, private operating foundation, or farmers' cooperative). The statutory list also includes petitions for judicial review under Code Sec. 6226 (final partnership administrative adjustments) and under Code Sec. 6228(a) (administrative adjustment request not allowed in full). Types of petitions which are not explicitly mentioned in Code Sec. 7451 include petitions with respect to an award of reasonable administrative costs and the review of an IRS failure to abate interest (Tax Court Rule 20).

NEW LAW EXPLAINED

Filing fees.—The U.S. Tax Court is authorized to impose a fee of up to $60 for the filing of *any* petition (Code Sec. 7451, as amended by the Pension Protection Act of 2006). Code Sec. 7451 no longer specifies types of petitions that may be subjected to a fee.

According to the Joint Committee on Taxation (JCT), this change means that the Tax Court may charge a filing fee in all cases commenced by the filing of a petition. The JCT points out that no negative inference should be drawn from this change as to whether the Tax Court already had this authority under pre-Pension Act law (Joint Committee on Taxation, Technical Explanation of the Pension Protection Act of 2006 (JCX-38-06)).

> **Comment:** With respect to the commencement of a case, Tax Court Rule 20(b) sets the filing fee at $60 for cases commenced by the filing of a petition. The rule also allows for a waiver of the fee for petitioners who establish their inability to pay.

▶ **Effective date.** The provision is effective on August 17, 2006 (Act Sec. 859(b) of the Pension Protection Act of 2006).

NEW LAW EXPLAINED

Law source: Law at ¶5470. Committee Report at ¶10,850.

— Act Sec. 859(a) of the Pension Protection Act of 2006, amending Code Sec. 7451;

— Act Sec. 859(b), providing the effective date.

Reporter references: For further information, consult the following CCH reporters.

— Standard Federal Tax Reporter, 2006FED ¶38,580.048, ¶42,080.05, ¶42,080.023, ¶42,119.03 and ¶42,073.01

— Tax Research Consultant, LITIG: 6,218

— Federal Tax Guide, 2006FTG ¶28,668

¶1425 Practitioner Fees May Be Used for *Pro Se* Taxpayer Services

SUMMARY OF NEW LAW

The practice fees that may be used by the U.S. Tax Court to employ independent counsel in disciplinary matters may also be used to provide services to *pro se* taxpayers.

BACKGROUND

The U.S. Tax Court may impose a registration fee of up to $30 per year on practitioners admitted to practice before the Court (Code Sec. 7475). These practice fees may be used by the Tax Court to employ independent counsel in disciplinary matters.

NEW LAW EXPLAINED

Fees to benefit *pro se* taxpayers.—In addition to using practitioner fees to employ independent counsel in disciplinary matters, the U.S. Tax Court may now use the fees to provide services to *pro se* taxpayers (Code Sec. 7475(b), as amended by the Pension Protection Act of 2006).

> **Comment:** Many *pro se* taxpayers who represent themselves are not familiar with Tax Court procedures and applicable legal requirements. Prior to August 17, 2006, the date of enactment of the Pension Act, a taxpayer who represented himself or herself before the Tax Court risked losing, on technical grounds, a case he or she may have otherwise won on the merits. Although the effect of making practice fees available to provide services to these taxpayers remains to be seen, those with strong cases on the merits may see more positive results.

According to the Joint Committee on Taxation, permitted uses of the fees include providing programs to educate taxpayers representing themselves on procedural

NEW LAW EXPLAINED

requirements for contesting a tax deficiency before the Tax Court (Joint Committee on Taxation, Technical Explanation of the Pension Protection Act of 2006 (JCX-38-06)).

▶ **Effective date.** The provision is effective on August 17, 2006 (Act Sec. 860(b) of the Pension Protection Act of 2006).

Law source: Law at ¶5480. Committee Report at ¶10,860.

— Act Sec. 860(a) of the Pension Protection Act of 2006, amending Code Sec. 7475(b);

— Act Sec. 860(b), providing the effective date.

Reporter references: For further information, consult the following CCH reporters.

— Standard Federal Tax Reporter, 2006FED ¶42,132.01

— Tax Research Consultant, LITIG: 6,062.05 and LITIG: 6,062.15

— Federal Tax Guide, 2006FTG ¶28,668

TAX COURT JUDGES

¶1430 Cost-of-Living Adjustments for Tax Court Judicial Survivor Annuities

SUMMARY OF NEW LAW

Cost-of-living increases to benefits paid to the surviving spouse and dependants of Tax Court judges under the survivors' annuity plan are based on the price index, rather than salary increases.

BACKGROUND

A Tax Court judge may elect to participate in a survivors' annuity plan, which provides annuity benefits to the judge's surviving spouse and dependent children. An increase in the salary of a Tax Court judge, pursuant to Code Sec. 7443(c), will also result in an increase in each annuity payable from the survivors' annuity fund. The amount of increase in the annuity amount is determined by multiplying the amount of the annuity on the date that the salary increase becomes effective, by three percent for each full five percent increase in the judge's salary.

On the other hand, federal judges that fall within the scope of section 8340 of Title 5 of the United States Code receive a cost-of-living adjustment for annuities based on the price index at the time that the annuity is payable. Such adjustment is independent of any increase, or lack thereof, in the salaries of federal judges.

NEW LAW EXPLAINED

Cost-of-living increases for Tax Court judicial survivor annuities based on price index.—The provision revises the method of calculating the cost-of-living increases for annuity payments made from the survivors' annuity fund to the surviving spouse and dependant children of a Tax Court judge. Under the modified provision, the amount of the annuity is increased at the same time, and by the same amount, as an increase in the annuity amount under 5 U.S.C. Sec. 8340, which provides for cost-of-living increases for annuities for the survivors of federal judges under the Civil Service Retirement and Disability Fund (Code Sec. 7448(s), as amended by the Pension Protection Act of 2006).

The cost-of-living adjustment for annuities is based on the percent change in the price index for the base quarter of such year, over the price index for the base quarter of the preceding year in which an adjustment under this subsection was made. This amount is then adjusted to the nearest 1/10 of 1 percent. The term "base quarter" is defined as the calendar quarter ending on September 30 of such year.

> **Comment:** Rather than basing cost-of-living adjustments for benefits on increases in pay for active Tax Court judges, as was the case prior to the amendment, the rate of adjustment for cost-of-living will be based on the price index and will be equal to the adjustment made for other federal judges. This provision, along with several other benefit modifications are aimed at eliminating the disparity in compensation and benefits between Tax Court judges and other federal judges.

► **Effective date.** The provision is effective with respect to increases made under section 8340(b) of Title 5, United States Code, in annuities payable under subchapter III of chapter 83 of that title, taking effect after August 17, 2006 (Act Sec. 851(b) of the Pension Protection Act of 2006).

Law source: Law at ¶5465. Committee Report at ¶10,800.

— Act Sec. 851(a), amending Code Sec. 7448(s);

— Act Sec. 851(b), providing the effective date.

Reporter references: For further information, consult the following CCH reporter.

— Standard Federal Tax Reporter, 2006FED ¶42,071.01

¶1435 Life Insurance Coverage for Tax Court Judges

SUMMARY OF NEW LAW

The Tax Court is authorized to pay, on behalf of U.S. Tax Court Judges, age 65 or over, any increase in the cost of Federal Employees' Group Life Insurance including any expenses generated by such payments, as authorized by the chief judge in a manner consistent with such payments authorized by the Judicial Conference of the United States.

BACKGROUND

U.S. Tax Court judges receive the same salary as U.S. District Court judges (Code Sec. 7443(c)). Tax Court judges also have some benefits, including specific retirement and survivor benefit programs, that are similar to benefits enjoyed by District Court judges. However, changes in benefits for the District Court judges and other federal courts have not applied to Tax Court judges, requiring an update of benefits provided to the Tax Court judges in order to maintain equivalence of benefits for them. For example, Tax Court judges participate in the Federal Employees Group Life Insurance program (FEGLI). Retired Tax Court judges are eligible to participate in the FEGLI program as the result of an administrative determination of their eligibility, rather than a specific statutory provision.

NEW LAW EXPLAINED

Cost of life insurance for Tax Court judges age 65 or over.—In order to address the disparity between the benefits provided to U.S. District Court judges and other federal judges, the Tax Court is authorized to pay on behalf of Tax Court judges, age 65 or over, any increase in the cost of Federal Employees' Group Life Insurance (FEGLI) (Code Sec. 7472, as amended by the Pension Protection Act of 2006). This includes any expenses generated by such payment, as authorized by the chief judge of the Tax Court.

Comment: Authorizations by the chief judge must be made in a manner consistent with payments authorized by the Judicial Conference of the United States, which is the body with policy-making authority over the administration of the courts of the federal judiciary (28 U.S.C. Sec. 604(a)(5)).

▶ **Effective date.** No specific effective date is provided by the Act. The provision is, therefore, considered effective on August 17, 2006, the date of enactment.

Law source: Law at ¶5475. Committee Report at ¶10,800.

— Act Sec. 852 of the Pension Protection Act of 2006, amending Code Sec. 7472.

Reporter references: For further information, consult the following CCH reporter.

— Standard Federal Tax Reporter, 2006FED ¶42,059.01 and ¶42,126.01

¶1440 Participation of Tax Court Judges in Thrift Savings Plan

SUMMARY OF NEW LAW

Tax Court judges are permitted to participate in the Thrift Savings Plan for Federal employees, beginning when the next administrative enrollment period begins.

BACKGROUND

The Thrift Savings Plan (TSP) provides federal employees and members of the uniformed services with a way to save for retirement. The TSP is a tax-deferred defined contribution plan similar to a 401(k) plan. The TSP is part of the Federal Employees' Retirement System (FERS). Regulations under this program are issued by the Executive Director of the Federal Retirement Thrift Investment Board. The assets of the TSP are maintained in the Thrift Savings Fund. Federal employees who are participants of FERS, the Civil Service Retirement System (CSRS) or equivalent retirement plans, as well as uniformed service members, can join the TSP once hired. There is no provision specifically authorizing participation in the Thrift Savings Plan by judges of the U.S. Tax Court.

NEW LAW EXPLAINED

Participation of Tax Court judges in Thrift Savings Plan.—Tax Court judges will now be permitted to elect to contribute to the Thrift Savings Fund and participate in the Thrift Savings Plan (TSP) (Code Sec. 7447(j), as added by the Pension Protection Act of 2006). The maximum allowable percentage of "basic pay" that may be contributed to the Thrift Savings Fund has increased to 100 percent for years 2006 and after (5 U.S.C. Sec. 8440f). In addition, additional contributions are permitted, and such contributions are controlled by Code Sec. 414(v). Contribution elections may only be made during administratively-established enrollment periods (Code Sec. 7447(j)(1)(B), as added by the Pension Act; 5 U.S.C. Sec. 8432(b)).

> **Comment:** Since both regular and additional contributions are withheld from wages, the provision for additional contributions is probably moot for years 2006 and after. In years prior to 2006, the maximum contributions limitation ranged from 6 to 10 percent.

Basic pay does not include any retired pay received by Tax Court judges under Code Sec. 7447(d) (Code Sec. 7447(j)(3)(A), as added by the Pension Act). Also, no employer contributions may be made for the benefit of any Tax Court judge (Code Sec. 7447(j)(3)(B), as added by the Pension Act; 5 U.S.C. Sec. 8432(c)).

Any Tax Court judge who has elected to participate in the Thrift Savings Plan and subsequently ceases to serve as a Tax Court judge, whether by retirement under Code Sec. 7447(b) or for any other reason, is entitled and may elect to withdraw the balance of his/her account in one of the following ways (Code Sec. 7447(j)(3)(C), as added by the Pension Act; 5 U.S.C. Sec. 8433(b)):

(1) as an annuity;

(2) in a single payment;

(3) in two or more substantially equal payments made not less frequently than annually; or

(4) by any combination of the payments, above, as prescribed by regulation.

However, if any Tax Court judge retires or resigns without having met the age and service requirements described in Code Sec. 7447(b)(2) and the balance in that judge's Thrift Savings Plan account is less than an amount that may be prescribed in

NEW LAW EXPLAINED

regulations by the Executive Director of the Federal Retirement Thrift Investment Board, any nonforfeitable account balance will be paid to the participant in a single payment (Code Sec. 7447(j)(3)(E), as added by the Pension Act).

Tax Court judges who make the election to participate in the Thrift Savings Plan are subject to 5 U.S.C. Sec. 8351(b)(5), which requires certain disclosures to the spouses of participants. While a spouse will not have the right to consent or waive consent with respect to contributions or earnings, any election or change of election regarding the account by the participant will not be effective until the spouse has been notified that the election or change of election has been made. Likewise, any approved withdrawal from the account or authorized loan taken against the account balance will not be effective until the spouse has been notified that an application for such withdrawal or loan has been made. These notification requirements do not apply if the nonforfeitable balance in the account is $3,500 or less. They can also be waived if the participant establishes that the whereabouts of the spouse cannot be determined (Code Sec. 7447(j)(3)(D), as added by the Pension Act).

▶ **Effective date.** The provision is effective on August 17, 2006; however, Tax Court judges may only elect to participate in the plan when the next administrative enrollment period following August 17, 2006, begins (Act Sec. 853(b) of the Pension Protection Act of 2006).

Law source: Law at ¶5460. Committee Report at ¶10,800.

— Act Sec. 853(a) of the Pension Protection Act of 2006, adding Code Sec. 7447(j);

— Act Sec. 853(b), providing the effective date.

Reporter references: For further information, consult the following CCH reporters.

— Standard Federal Tax Reporter, 2006FED ¶42,070.01

— Tax Research Consultant, RETIRE: 69,354.05

¶1445 Special Trial Judges Eligible for Survivor Annuity Plan

SUMMARY OF NEW LAW

Special trial judges of the U.S. Tax Court may elect to participate in the survivors' annuity plan available to Tax Court judges.

BACKGROUND

The chief judge of the Tax Court is granted the authority to appoint special trial judges to handle certain cases, including:

- any declaratory judgment proceeding;
- any proceeding where neither the amount of the deficiency placed in dispute nor the amount of any claimed overpayment exceeds $50,000 (Code Sec. 7463);

BACKGROUND

- innocent spouse relief redeterminations involving $50,000 or less (Code Sec. 6015(e));
- any redetermination of employment status;
- any proceeding regarding notice and opportunity for a collection due process (CDP) hearing upon filing of a tax lien (Code Sec. 6320) or before levy (Code Sec. 6330); and
- any other proceeding which the chief judge may designate (Code Sec. 7443A(b)).

Special trial judges of the Tax Court essentially serve the same purpose as magistrate judges of U.S. District Courts established under Article III of the United States Constitution. Magistrate judges may preside over misdemeanor trials and trials when both parties agree to have the case heard by the magistrate judge instead of a District Court judge. Despite such similarities, several disparities exist in the compensation and benefits between the two types of judges. Magistrate judges receive a salary of an annual rate up to 92 percent of the salary of a District Court judge, are appointed for a specific term, are subject to removal only in limited circumstances, and are eligible for coverage under special retirement and survivor benefit programs. Special trial judges of the Tax Court receive 90 percent of the salary of a Tax Court judge and are appointed for indefinite terms. Additionally, special trial judges are eligible for the benefit programs available to Federal executive branch employees, including the Civil Service Retirement System and the Federal Employees' Retirement System.

NEW LAW EXPLAINED

Special trial judges of the Tax Court eligible for survivor annuities.—Several changes are made to Code Sec. 7448, allowing special trial judges of the Tax Court to elect to participate in the survivors' annuity plan for Tax Court judges (Code Sec. 7448(b)(2), as added by the Pension Protection Act of 2006). The election must be made no later than the latest of:

(1) twelve months after August 17, 2006, the date of enactment of this provision;

(2) six months after the date the judge takes office; or

(3) six months after the date the judge marries.

> **Comment:** The objective of this provision is to reduce the disparities between special trial judges of the Tax Court and magistrate judges of District Courts in terms of the status of the position, salary and benefits. This will better enable the Tax Court to attract and retain qualified persons to serve in the position of special trial judge.

For this purpose, a special trial judge is defined as a judicial officer appointed by the chief judge of the Tax Court pursuant to Code Sec. 7443A, including any individual receiving a retirement annuity under the Federal Civil Service Retirement System or the Federal Employees' Retirement System (Chapters 83 or 84 of Title 5 of the United States Code) and regardless of whether the individual was recalled to perform judicial duties as a special trial judge (Code Sec. 7448(a)(5), as added by the Pension Act).

NEW LAW EXPLAINED

> **Comment:** A retired special trial judge of the Tax Court may generally be recalled to perform judicial duties up to 90 days a year (see ¶1450 for more information).

For purposes of calculating the amount of the annuity to be received under the survivor's annuity plan, a special trial judge's salary includes the salary received as a special trial judge under Code Sec. 7443A(d), any amount received as a retirement annuity under the Federal Civil Service Retirement System or Federal Employees' Retirement System (Chapters 83 or 84 of Title 5 of the United States Code), and any compensation received after being recalled to perform judicial duties (Code Sec. 7448(a)(6), as added by the Pension Act). Years of service performed as a special trial judge are also included in the basis for calculating the amount of the annuity to be received (Code Sec. 7448(n), as amended by the Pension Act).

> **Comment:** Service as a special trial judge of the Tax Court will not be considered "employment" for purposes of calculating Social Security and Medicare taxes, thus affording special trial judges the same beneficial treatment afforded to other Federal judges, including Tax Court judges (Code Sec. 3121(b)(5)(E) and section 210(a)(5)(E) of the Social Security Act, as amended by the Pension Act).

▶ **Effective date.** No specific effective date is provided by the Act. The provision is, therefore, considered effective on August 17, 2006, the date of enactment.

Law source: Law at ¶5215, ¶5465 and ¶7168. Committee Report at ¶10,810.

— Act Sec. 854 of the Pension Protection Act of 2006, amends Code Sec. 7448 by redesignating Code Sec. 7448(a)(5), (6), (7), and (8) as (7), (8), (9) and (10) respectively, and adding new Code Sec. 7448(a)(5) and (a)(6);

— Act Sec. 854(b), amending Code Sec. 7448(b);

— Act Sec. 854(c), amending Code Sec. 7448(c)(1), (d), (f), (g), (h),(j), (m)(1), (n), (u), Code Sec. 3121(b)(5)(E), and Sec. 210(a)(5)(E) of the Social Security Act;

Reporter references: For further information, consult the following CCH reporter.

— Standard Federal Tax Reporter, 2006FED ¶42,071.01

¶1450 Recall of Retired Tax Court Special Trial Judges

SUMMARY OF NEW LAW

A retired special trial judge of the Tax Court may generally be recalled to perform judicial duties up to 90 days a year.

BACKGROUND

Judges of the U.S. Tax Court are required to retire by the age of 70 (Code Sec. 7447). Any judge, however, may retire beginning at age 65 if certain service requirements are met. At or after retirement, any individual who was a Tax Court judge who has

BACKGROUND

elected to receive retirement pay under Code Sec. 7447(d) may be recalled by the chief judge of the Tax Court to perform judicial duties upon request. The individual, however, may not be recalled for a period of more than 90 days in any calendar year without his or her consent. In addition, a recalled Tax Court judge is relieved from recall duties in case of illness or disability. For purposes of determining retirement pay, time served by a judge in recalled status is counted.

The chief judge of the Tax Court is granted authority to appoint several special trial judges to handle certain cases (see ¶1445). However, there is no specific provision for the Tax Court to recall special trial judges to perform judicial duties when needed.

NEW LAW EXPLAINED

Recall of retired special trial judges provided.—Any retired special trial judge may now be recalled by the chief judge of the Tax Court to perform judicial duties upon request (Code Sec. 7443B, as added by the Pension Protection Act of 2006). A special trial judge may not, however, be recalled for more than 90 days in any one year without his or her consent, and is relieved of recall duties in case of illness or disability. For the year in which a retired special trial judge serves a period of recall, he or she receives, in addition to any annuity provided, an amount equal to the difference between that annuity and the current salary of the office to which the special trial judge is recalled.

▶ **Effective date.** No specific effective date is provided by the Act. The provision is, therefore, considered effective on August 17, 2006, the date of enactment.

Law source: Law at ¶5455. Committee Report at ¶10,810.

— Act Sec. 856(a) of the Pension Protection Act of 2006, adding Code Sec. 7443B.

Reporter references: For further information, consult the following CCH reporter.

— Standard Federal Tax Reporter, 2006FED ¶42,059D.01

Code Sections Added, Amended or Repealed

[¶ 5001]

INTRODUCTION.

The Internal Revenue Code provisions amended by the Pension Protection Act of 2006 (H.R. 4) are shown in the following paragraphs. Deleted Code material or the text of the Code Section prior to amendment appears in the amendment notes following each amended Code provision. *Any changed or added material is set out in italics.*

[¶ 5005] CODE SEC. 25B. ELECTIVE DEFERRALS AND IRA CONTRIBUTIONS BY CERTAIN INDIVIDUALS.

* * *

»»→ Caution: Code Sec. 25B(b), below, as amended by H.R. 4, applies to tax years beginning after 2006.

(b) APPLICABLE PERCENTAGE.—For purposes of this section—

(1) JOINT RETURNS.—In the case of a joint return, the applicable percentage is—

(A) if the adjusted gross income of the taxpayer is not over $30,000, 50 percent,

(B) if the adjusted gross income of the taxpayer is over $30,000 but not over $32,500, 20 percent,

(C) if the adjusted gross income of the taxpayer is over $32,500 but not over $50,000, 10 percent, and

(D) if the adjusted gross income of the taxpayer is over $50,000, zero percent.

(2) OTHER RETURNS.—In the case of—

(A) a head of household, the applicable percentage shall be determined under paragraph (1) except that such paragraph shall be applied by substituting for each dollar amount therein (as adjusted under paragraph (3)) a dollar amount equal to 75 percent of such dollar amount, and

(B) any taxpayer not described in paragraph (1) or subparagraph (A), the applicable percentage shall be determined under paragraph (1) except that such paragraph shall be applied by substituting for each dollar amount therein (as adjusted under paragraph (3)) a dollar amount equal to 50 percent of such dollar amount.

(3) INFLATION ADJUSTMENT.—In the case of any taxable year beginning in a calendar year after 2006, each of the dollar amount[s] in paragraph (1) shall be increased by an amount equal to—

(A) such dollar amount, multiplied by

(B) the cost-of-living adjustment determined under section 1(f)(3) for the calendar year in which the taxable year begins, determined by substituting "calendar year 2005" for "calendar year 1992" in subparagraph (B) thereof.

Any increase determined under the preceding sentence shall be rounded to the nearest multiple of $500.

* * *

[CCH Explanation at ¶ 1320. Committee Reports at ¶ 10,740.]

Amendments

• 2006, Pension Protection Act of 2006 (H.R. 4)

H.R. 4, § 833(a):

Amended Code Sec. 25B(b). **Effective** for tax years beginning after 2006. Prior to amendment, Code Sec. 25B(b) read as follows:

(b) APPLICABLE PERCENTAGE.—For purposes of this section, the applicable percentage is the percentage determined in accordance with the following table:

Adjusted Gross Income						
Joint return		*Head of a household*		*All other cases*		*Applicable*
Over	*Not over*	*Over*	*Not over*	*Over*	*Not over*	*percentage*
	$30,000		$22,500		$15,000	50
30,000	32,500	22,500	24,375	15,000	16,250	20
32,500	50,000	24,375	37,500	16,250	25,000	10
50,000		37,500		25,000		0

(h) [*Stricken.*]

[CCH Explanation at ¶ 1315. Committee Reports at ¶ 10,610.]

Amendments

• 2006, Pension Protection Act of 2006 (H.R. 4)

H.R. 4, § 812:

Amended Code Sec. 25B by striking subsection (h). **Effective** 8-17-2006. Prior to being stricken, Code Sec. 25B(h) read as follows:

(h) TERMINATION.—This section shall not apply to taxable years beginning after December 31, 2006.

[¶ 5010] CODE SEC. 72. ANNUITIES; CERTAIN PROCEEDS OF ENDOWMENT AND LIFE INSURANCE CONTRACTS.

* * *

(e) AMOUNTS NOT RECEIVED AS ANNUITIES.—

* * *

»»→ Caution: Code Sec. 72(e)(11), below, as added by H.R. 4, applies to contracts issued after December 31, 1996, but only with respect to tax years beginning after December 31, 2009.

(11) SPECIAL RULES FOR CERTAIN COMBINATION CONTRACTS PROVIDING LONG-TERM CARE INSURANCE.—Notwithstanding paragraphs (2), (5)(C), and (10), in the case of any charge against the cash value of an annuity contract or the cash surrender value of a life insurance contract made as payment for coverage under a qualified long-term care insurance contract which is part of or a rider on such annuity or life insurance contract—

(A) the investment in the contract shall be reduced (but not below zero) by such charge, and

(B) such charge shall not be includible in gross income.

»»→ Caution: Former Code Sec. 72(e)(11) was redesignated as Code Sec. 72(e)(12), below, by H.R. 4, applicable to contracts issued after December 31, 1996, but only with respect to tax years beginning after December 31, 2009.

(12) ANTI-ABUSE RULES.—

(A) IN GENERAL.—For purposes of determining the amount includible in gross income under this subsection—

(i) all modified endowment contracts issued by the same company to the same policyholder during any calendar year shall be treated as 1 modified endowment contract, and

(ii) all annuity contracts issued by the same company to the same policyholder during any calendar year shall be treated as 1 annuity contract.

The preceding sentence shall not apply to any contract described in paragraph (5)(D).

(B) REGULATORY AUTHORITY.—The Secretary may by regulations prescribe such additional rules as may be necessary or appropriate to prevent avoidance of the purposes of this subsection through serial purchases of contracts or otherwise.

* * *

[CCH Explanation at ¶ 820. Committee Reports at ¶ 10,780.]

Amendments

• 2006, Pension Protection Act of 2006 (H.R. 4)

H.R. 4, § 844(a):

Amended Code Sec. 72(e) by redesignating paragraph (11) as paragraph (12) and by inserting after paragraph (10) a new paragraph (11). **Effective** for contracts issued after 12-31-1996, but only with respect to tax years beginning after 12-31-2009.

(t) 10-PERCENT ADDITIONAL TAX ON EARLY DISTRIBUTIONS FROM QUALIFIED RETIREMENT PLANS.—

* * *

(2) SUBSECTION NOT TO APPLY TO CERTAIN DISTRIBUTIONS.—Except as provided in paragraphs (3) and (4), paragraph (1) shall not apply to any of the following distributions:

* * *

(G) DISTRIBUTIONS FROM RETIREMENT PLANS TO INDIVIDUALS CALLED TO ACTIVE DUTY.—

(i) IN GENERAL.—Any qualified reservist distribution.

(ii) AMOUNT DISTRIBUTED MAY BE REPAID.—Any individual who receives a qualified reservist distribution may, at any time during the 2-year period beginning on the day after the end of the active duty period, make one or more contributions to an individual retirement plan of such individual in an aggregate amount not to exceed the amount of such distribution. The dollar limitations otherwise applicable to contributions to individual retirement plans shall not apply to any contribution made pursuant to the preceding sentence. No deduction shall be allowed for any contribution pursuant to this clause.

(iii) QUALIFIED RESERVIST DISTRIBUTION.—For purposes of this subparagraph, the term "qualified reservist distribution" means any distribution to an individual if—

(I) such distribution is from an individual retirement plan, or from amounts attributable to employer contributions made pursuant to elective deferrals described in subparagraph (A) or (C) of section 402(g)(3) or section 501(c)(18)(D)(iii),

(II) such individual was (by reason of being a member of a reserve component (as defined in section 101 of title 37, United States Code)) ordered or called to active duty for a period in excess of 179 days or for an indefinite period, and

(III) such distribution is made during the period beginning on the date of such order or call and ending at the close of the active duty period.

(iv) APPLICATION OF SUBPARAGRAPH.—This subparagraph applies to individuals ordered or called to active duty after September 11, 2001, and before December 31, 2007. In no event shall the 2-year period referred to in clause (ii) end before the date which is 2 years after the date of the enactment of this subparagraph.

* * *

(10) DISTRIBUTIONS TO QUALIFIED PUBLIC SAFETY EMPLOYEES IN GOVERNMENTAL PLANS.—

(A) IN GENERAL.—In the case of a distribution to a qualified public safety employee from a governmental plan (within the meaning of section 414(d)) which is a defined benefit plan, paragraph (2)(A)(v) shall be applied by substituting "age 50" for "age 55".

(B) QUALIFIED PUBLIC SAFETY EMPLOYEE.—For purposes of this paragraph, the term "qualified public safety employee" means any employee of a State or political subdivision of a State who provides police protection, firefighting services, or emergency medical services for any area within the jurisdiction of such State or political subdivision.

* * *

[CCH Explanation at ¶ 915 and ¶ 917. Committee Reports at ¶ 10,680 and ¶ 10,690.]

Amendments

• 2006, Pension Protection Act of 2006 (H.R. 4)

H.R. 4, § 827(a):

Amended Code Sec. 72(t)(2) by adding at the end a new subparagraph (G). **Effective** for distributions after 9-11-2001. For a waiver of limitations, see Act Sec. 827(c)(2), below.

H.R. 4, § 827(c)(2), provides:

(2) WAIVER OF LIMITATIONS.—If refund or credit of any overpayment of tax resulting from the amendments made by this section is prevented at any time before the close of the 1-year period beginning on the date of the enactment of this Act by the operation of any law or rule of law (including res judicata), such refund or credit may nevertheless be made or allowed if claim therefor is filed before the close of such period.

H.R. 4, § 828(a):

Amended Code Sec. 72(t) by adding at the end a new paragraph (10). **Effective** for distributions after 8-17-2006.

[¶ 5015] CODE SEC. 101. CERTAIN DEATH BENEFITS.

(a) PROCEEDS OF LIFE INSURANCE CONTRACTS PAYABLE BY REASON OF DEATH.—

(1) GENERAL RULE.—Except as otherwise provided in paragraph (2), subsection (d), *subsection (f), and subsection (j)*, gross income does not include amounts received (whether in a single sum or otherwise) under a life insurance contract, if such amounts are paid by reason of the death of the insured.

* * *

[CCH Explanation at ¶ 1330. Committee Reports at ¶ 10,890.]

Amendments

• 2006, Pension Protection Act of 2006 (H.R. 4)

H.R. 4, § 863(c)(1):

Amended Code Sec. 101(a)(1) by striking "and subsection (f)" and inserting "subsection (f), and subsection (j)". **Effective** for life insurance contracts issued after 8-17-2006, except for a contract issued after such date pursuant to an exchange described in Code Sec. 1035 for a contract issued on or prior to that date. For purposes of the preceding sentence, any material increase in the death benefit or other material change shall cause the contract to be treated as a new contract except that, in the case of a master contract (within the meaning of Code Sec. 264(f)(4)(E)), the addition of covered lives shall be treated as a new contract only with respect to such additional covered lives.

(j) TREATMENT OF CERTAIN EMPLOYER-OWNED LIFE INSURANCE CONTRACTS.—

(1) GENERAL RULE.—In the case of an employer-owned life insurance contract, the amount excluded from gross income of an applicable policyholder by reason of paragraph (1) of subsection (a) shall not exceed an amount equal to the sum of the premiums and other amounts paid by the policyholder for the contract.

(2) EXCEPTIONS.—In the case of an employer-owned life insurance contract with respect to which the notice and consent requirements of paragraph (4) are met, paragraph (1) shall not apply to any of the following:

(A) EXCEPTIONS BASED ON INSURED'S STATUS.—Any amount received by reason of the death of an insured who, with respect to an applicable policyholder—

(i) was an employee at any time during the 12-month period before the insured's death, or

(ii) is, at the time the contract is issued—

(I) a director,

(II) a highly compensated employee within the meaning of section 414(q) (without regard to paragraph (1)(B)(ii) thereof), or

(III) a highly compensated individual within the meaning of section 105(h)(5), except that "35 percent" shall be substituted for "25 percent" in subparagraph (C) thereof.

(B) EXCEPTION FOR AMOUNTS PAID TO INSURED'S HEIRS.—Any amount received by reason of the death of an insured to the extent—

(i) the amount is paid to a member of the family (within the meaning of section 267(c)(4)) of the insured, any individual who is the designated beneficiary of the insured under the contract (other than the applicable policyholder), a trust established for the benefit of any such member of the family or designated beneficiary, or the estate of the insured, or

(ii) the amount is used to purchase an equity (or capital or profits) interest in the applicable policyholder from any person described in clause (i).

(3) EMPLOYER-OWNED LIFE INSURANCE CONTRACT.—

(A) IN GENERAL.—For purposes of this subsection, the term "employer-owned life insurance contract" means a life insurance contract which—

(i) is owned by a person engaged in a trade or business and under which such person (or a related person described in subparagraph (B)(ii)) is directly or indirectly a beneficiary under the contract, and

(ii) covers the life of an insured who is an employee with respect to the trade or business of the applicable policyholder on the date the contract is issued.

For purposes of the preceding sentence, if coverage for each insured under a master contract is treated as a separate contract for purposes of sections 817(h), 7702, and 7702A, coverage for each such insured shall be treated as a separate contract.

(B) APPLICABLE POLICYHOLDER.—For purposes of this subsection—

(i) IN GENERAL.—The term "applicable policyholder" means, with respect to any employer-owned life insurance contract, the person described in subparagraph (A)(i) which owns the contract.

(ii) RELATED PERSONS.—The term "applicable policyholder" includes any person which—

(I) bears a relationship to the person described in clause (i) which is specified in section 267(b) or 707(b)(1), or

(II) is engaged in trades or businesses with such person which are under common control (within the meaning of subsection (a) or (b) of section 52).

(4) NOTICE AND CONSENT REQUIREMENTS.—The notice and consent requirements of this paragraph are met if, before the issuance of the contract, the employee—

(A) is notified in writing that the applicable policyholder intends to insure the employee's life and the maximum face amount for which the employee could be insured at the time the contract was issued,

(B) provides written consent to being insured under the contract and that such coverage may continue after the insured terminates employment, and

(C) is informed in writing that an applicable policyholder will be a beneficiary of any proceeds payable upon the death of the employee.

(5) DEFINITIONS.—For purposes of this subsection—

(A) EMPLOYEE.—The term "employee" includes an officer, director, and highly compensated employee (within the meaning of section 414(q)).

(B) INSURED.—The term "insured" means, with respect to an employer-owned life insurance contract, an individual covered by the contract who is a United States citizen or resident. In the case of a contract covering the joint lives of 2 individuals, references to an insured include both of the individuals.

[CCH Explanation at ¶ 1330. Committee Reports at ¶ 10,890.]

Amendments

• 2006, Pension Protection Act of 2006 (H.R. 4)

H.R. 4, § 863(a):

Amended Code Sec. 101 by adding at the end a new subsection (j). **Effective** for life insurance contracts issued after 8-17-2006, except for a contract issued after such date pursuant to an exchange described in Code Sec. 1035 for a contract issued on or prior to that date. For purposes of the preceding sentence, any material increase in the death benefit or other material change shall cause the contract to be treated as a new contract except that, in the case of a master contract (within the meaning of Code Sec. 264(f)(4)(E)), the addition of covered lives shall be treated as a new contract only with respect to such additional covered lives.

[¶ 5020] CODE SEC. 170. CHARITABLE, ETC., CONTRIBUTIONS AND GIFTS.

* * *

(b) PERCENTAGE LIMITATIONS.—

(1) INDIVIDUALS.—In the case of an individual, the deduction provided in subsection (a) shall be limited as provided in the succeeding subparagraphs.

* * *

(E) CONTRIBUTIONS OF QUALIFIED CONSERVATION CONTRIBUTIONS.—

(i) IN GENERAL.—Any qualified conservation contribution (as defined in subsection (h)(1)) shall be allowed to the extent the aggregate of such contributions does not exceed the excess of 50 percent of the taxpayer's contribution base over the amount of all other charitable contributions allowable under this paragraph.

(ii) CARRYOVER.—If the aggregate amount of contributions described in clause (i) exceeds the limitation of clause (i), such excess shall be treated (in a manner consistent with the rules of subsection (d)(1)) as a charitable contribution to which clause (i) applies in each of the 15 succeeding years in order of time.

(iii) COORDINATION WITH OTHER SUBPARAGRAPHS.—For purposes of applying this subsection and subsection (d)(1), contributions described in clause (i) shall not be treated as described in subparagraph (A), (B), (C), or (D) and such subparagraphs shall apply without regard to such contributions.

(iv) SPECIAL RULE FOR CONTRIBUTION OF PROPERTY USED IN AGRICULTURE OR LIVESTOCK PRODUCTION.—

(I) IN GENERAL.—If the individual is a qualified farmer or rancher for the taxable year for which the contribution is made, clause (i) shall be applied by substituting "100 percent" for "50 percent".

(II) EXCEPTION.—Subclause (I) shall not apply to any contribution of property made after the date of the enactment of this subparagraph which is used in agriculture or livestock production (or available for such production) unless such contribution is subject to a restriction that such property remain available for such production. This subparagraph shall be applied separately with respect to property to which subclause (I) does not apply by reason of the preceding sentence prior to its application to property to which subclause (I) does apply.

(v) DEFINITION.—For purposes of clause (iv), the term "qualified farmer or rancher" means a taxpayer whose gross income from the trade or business of farming (within the meaning of section 2032A(e)(5)) is greater than 50 percent of the taxpayer's gross income for the taxable year.

(vi) TERMINATION.—This subparagraph shall not apply to any contribution made in taxable years beginning after December 31, 2007.

(F) CERTAIN PRIVATE FOUNDATIONS.—The private foundations referred to in subparagraph (A)(vii) and subsection (e)(1)(B) are—

(i) a private operating foundation (as defined in section 4942(j)(3)),

(ii) any other private foundation (as defined in section 509(a)) which, not later than the 15th day of the third month after the close of the foundation's taxable year in which contributions are received, makes qualifying distributions (as defined in section 4942(g), without regard to paragraph (3) thereof), which are treated, after the application of section 4942(g)(3), as distributions out of corpus (in accordance with section 4942(h)) in an amount equal to 100 percent of such contributions, and with respect to which the taxpayer obtains adequate records or other sufficient evidence from the foundation showing that the foundation made such qualifying distributions, and

(iii) a private foundation all of the contributions to which are pooled in a common fund and which would be described in section 509(a)(3) but for the right of any substantial contributor (hereafter in this clause called "donor") or his spouse to designate annually the recipients, from among organizations described in paragraph (1) of section 509(a), of the income attributable to the donor's contribution to the fund and to direct (by deed or by will) the payment, to an organization described in such paragraph (1), of the corpus in the common fund attributable to the donor's contribution; but this clause shall apply only if all of the income of the common fund is required to be (and is) distributed to one or more organizations described in such paragraph (1) not later than the 15th day of the third month after the close of the taxable year in which the income is realized by the fund and only if all of the corpus attributable to any donor's contribution to the fund is required to be (and is) distributed to one or more of such organizations not later than one year after his death or after the death of his surviving spouse if she has the right to designate the recipients of such corpus.

(G) CONTRIBUTION BASE DEFINED.—For purposes of this section, the term "contribution base" means adjusted gross income (computed without regard to any net operating loss carryback to the taxable year under section 172).

(2) CORPORATIONS.—In the case of a corporation—

(A) IN GENERAL.—The total deductions under subsection (a) for any taxable year (other than for contributions to which subparagraph (B) applies) shall not exceed 10 percent of the taxpayer's taxable income.

(B) QUALIFIED CONSERVATION CONTRIBUTIONS BY CERTAIN CORPORATE FARMERS AND RANCHERS.—

(i) IN GENERAL.—Any qualified conservation contribution (as defined in subsection (h)(1))—

(I) which is made by a corporation which, for the taxable year during which the contribution is made, is a qualified farmer or rancher (as defined in paragraph (1)(E)(v)) and the stock of which is not readily tradable on an established securities market at any time during such year, and

(II) which, in the case of contributions made after the date of the enactment of this subparagraph, is a contribution of property which is used in agriculture or livestock production (or available for such production) and which is subject to a restriction that such property remain available for such production,

shall be allowed to the extent the aggregate of such contributions does not exceed the excess of the taxpayer's taxable income over the amount of charitable contributions allowable under subparagraph (A).

(ii) CARRYOVER.—If the aggregate amount of contributions described in clause (i) exceeds the limitation of clause (i), such excess shall be treated (in a manner consistent with the rules of subsection (d)(2)) as a charitable contribution to which clause (i) applies in each of the 15 succeeding years in order of time.

(iii) TERMINATION.—This subparagraph shall not apply to any contribution made in taxable years beginning after December 31, 2007.

(C) TAXABLE INCOME.—For purposes of this paragraph, taxable income shall be computed without regard to—

(i) this section,

(ii) part VIII (except section 248),

(iii) any net operating loss carryback to the taxable year under section 172,

(iv) section 199, and

(v) any capital loss carryback to the taxable year under section 1212(a)(1).

* * *

[CCH Explanation at ¶1125. Committee Reports at ¶11,160.]

Amendments

• 2006, Pension Protection Act of 2006 (H.R. 4)

H.R. 4, §1206(a)(1):

Amended Code Sec. 170(b)(1) by redesignating subparagraphs (E) and (F) as subparagraphs (F) and (G), respectively, and by inserting after subparagraph (D) a new subparagraph (E). **Effective** for contributions made in tax years beginning after 12-31-2005.

H.R. 4, §1206(a)(2):

Amended Code Sec. 170(b)(2). **Effective** for contributions made in tax years beginning after 12-31-2005. Prior to amendment, Code Sec. 170(b)(2) read as follows:

(2) CORPORATIONS.—In the case of a corporation, the total deductions under subsection (a) for any taxable year shall not exceed 10 percent of the taxpayer's taxable income computed without regard to—

(A) this section,

(B) part VIII (except section 248),

(C) section 199,

(D) any net operating loss carryback to the taxable year under section 172, and

(E) any capital loss carryback to the taxable year under section 1212(a)(1).

(d) CARRYOVERS OF EXCESS CONTRIBUTIONS.—

* * *

(2) CORPORATIONS.—

(A) IN GENERAL.—Any contribution made by a corporation in a taxable year (hereinafter in this paragraph referred to as the "contribution year") in excess of the amount deductible for such year under *subsection (b)(2)(A)* shall be deductible for each of the 5 succeeding taxable years in order of time, but only to the extent of the lesser of the two following amounts: (i) the excess of the maximum amount deductible for such succeeding taxable year under *subsection (b)(2)(A)* over the sum of the contributions made in such year plus the aggregate of the excess contributions which were made in taxable years before the contribution year and which are deductible under this subparagraph for such succeeding taxable year; or (ii) in the case of the first succeeding taxable year, the amount of such excess contribution, and in the case of the second, third, fourth, or fifth succeeding taxable year, the portion of such excess contribution not deductible under this subparagraph for any taxable year intervening between the contribution year and such succeeding taxable year.

(B) SPECIAL RULE FOR NET OPERATING LOSS CARRYOVERS.—For purposes of subparagraph (A), the excess of—

(i) the contributions made by a corporation in a taxable year to which this section applies, over

(ii) the amount deductible in such year under the limitation in *subsection (b)(2)(A)*,

shall be reduced to the extent that such excess reduces taxable income (as computed for purposes of the second sentence of section 172(b)(2)) and increases a net operating loss carryover under section 172 to a succeeding taxable year.

[CCH Explanation at ¶1125. Committee Reports at ¶11,160.]

Amendments

• 2006, Pension Protection Act of 2006 (H.R. 4)

H.R. 4, §1206(b)(1):

Amended Code Sec. 170(d)(2) by striking "subsection (b)(2)" each place it appears and inserting "subsection (b)(2)(A)". **Effective** for contributions made in tax years beginning after 12-31-2005.

(e) CERTAIN CONTRIBUTIONS OF ORDINARY INCOME AND CAPITAL GAIN PROPERTY.—

* * *

(1) GENERAL RULE.—The amount of any charitable contribution of property otherwise taken into account under this section shall be reduced by the sum of—

* * *

(B) in the case of a charitable contribution—

(i) of tangible personal property—

(I) if the use by the donee is unrelated to the purpose or function constituting the basis for its exemption under section 501 (or, in the case of a governmental unit, to any purpose or function described in subsection (c)), or

(II) which is applicable property (as defined in paragraph (7)(C)) which is sold, exchanged, or otherwise disposed of by the donee before the last day of the taxable year in which the contribution was made and with respect to which the donee has not made a certification in accordance with paragraph (7)(D),

(ii) to or for the use of a private foundation (as defined in section 509(a)), other than a private foundation described in subsection (b)(1)(E),

(iii) of any patent, copyright (other than a copyright described in section 1221(a)(3) or 1231(b)(1)(C)), trademark, trade name, trade secret, know-how, software (other than software described in section 197(e)(3)(A)(i)), or similar property, or applications or registrations of such property, *or*

(iv) of any taxidermy property which is contributed by the person who prepared, stuffed, or mounted the property or by any person who paid or incurred the cost of such preparation, stuffing, or mounting,

* * *

(3) SPECIAL RULE FOR CERTAIN CONTRIBUTIONS OF INVENTORY AND OTHER PROPERTY.—

* * *

(C) SPECIAL RULE FOR CONTRIBUTIONS OF FOOD INVENTORY.—

* * *

(iv) TERMINATION.—This subparagraph shall not apply to contributions made after December 31, *2007*.

(D) SPECIAL RULE FOR CONTRIBUTIONS OF BOOK INVENTORY TO PUBLIC SCHOOLS.—

* * *

(iv) TERMINATION.—This subparagraph shall not apply to contributions made after December 31, *2007*.

* * *

(7) RECAPTURE OF DEDUCTION ON CERTAIN DISPOSITIONS OF EXEMPT USE PROPERTY.—

(A) IN GENERAL.—In the case of an applicable disposition of applicable property, there shall be included in the income of the donor of such property for the taxable year of such donor in which the applicable disposition occurs an amount equal to the excess (if any) of—

(i) the amount of the deduction allowed to the donor under this section with respect to such property, over

(ii) the donor's basis in such property at the time such property was contributed.

(B) APPLICABLE DISPOSITION.—For purposes of this paragraph, the term "applicable disposition" means any sale, exchange, or other disposition by the donee of applicable property—

(i) after the last day of the taxable year of the donor in which such property was contributed, and

(ii) before the last day of the 3-year period beginning on the date of the contribution of such property,

unless the donee makes a certification in accordance with subparagraph (D).

(C) APPLICABLE PROPERTY.—For purposes of this paragraph, the term "applicable property" means charitable deduction property (as defined in section 6050L(a)(2)(A))—

(i) which is tangible personal property the use of which is identified by the donee as related to the purpose or function constituting the basis of the donee's exemption under section 501, and

(ii) for which a deduction in excess of the donor's basis is allowed.

(D) CERTIFICATION.—A certification meets the requirements of this subparagraph if it is a written statement which is signed under penalty of perjury by an officer of the donee organization and—

(i) which—

(I) certifies that the use of the property by the donee was related to the purpose or function constituting the basis for the donee's exemption under section 501, and

(II) describes how the property was used and how such use furthered such purpose or function, or

(ii) which—

(I) states the intended use of the property by the donee at the time of the contribution, and

(II) certifies that such intended use has become impossible or infeasible to implement.

[CCH Explanation at ¶1120, ¶1140, ¶1145 and ¶1150. Committee Reports at ¶11,120, ¶11,140, ¶11,220 and ¶11,230.]

Amendments

• 2006, Pension Protection Act of 2006 (H.R. 4)

H.R. 4, §1202(a):

Amended Code Sec. 170(e)(3)(C)(iv) by striking "2005" and inserting "2007". **Effective** for contributions made after 12-31-2005.

H.R. 4, §1204(a):

Amended Code Sec. 170(e)(3)(D)(iv) by striking "2005" and inserting "2007". **Effective** for contributions made after 12-31-2005.

H.R. 4, §1214(a):

Amended Code Sec. 170(e)(1)(B) by striking "or" at the end of clause (ii), by inserting "or" at the end of clause (iii), and by inserting after clause (iii) a new clause (iv). **Effective** for contributions made after 7-25-2006.

H.R. 4, §1215(a)(1):

Amended Code Sec. 170(e)(1)(B)(i). **Effective** for contributions after 9-1-2006. Prior to amendment, Code Sec. 170(e)(1)(B)(i) read as follows:

(i) of tangible personal property, if the use by the donee is unrelated to the purpose or function constituting the basis for its exemption under section 501 (or, in the case of a governmental unit, to any purpose or function described in subsection (c)),

H.R. 4, §1215(a)(2):

Amended Code Sec. 170(e) by adding at the end a new paragraph (7). **Effective** for contributions after 9-1-2006.

(f) DISALLOWANCE OF DEDUCTION IN CERTAIN CASES AND SPECIAL RULES.—

* * *

(11) QUALIFIED APPRAISAL AND OTHER DOCUMENTATION FOR CERTAIN CONTRIBUTIONS.—

* * *

(E) QUALIFIED APPRAISAL AND APPRAISER.—For purposes of this paragraph—

(i) QUALIFIED APPRAISAL.—The term "qualified appraisal" means, with respect to any property, an appraisal of such property which—

(I) is treated for purposes of this paragraph as a qualified appraisal under regulations or other guidance prescribed by the Secretary, and

(II) is conducted by a qualified appraiser in accordance with generally accepted appraisal standards and any regulations or other guidance prescribed under subclause (I).

(ii) QUALIFIED APPRAISER.—Except as provided in clause (iii), the term "qualified appraiser" means an individual who—

(I) has earned an appraisal designation from a recognized professional appraiser organization or has otherwise met minimum education and experience requirements set forth in regulations prescribed by the Secretary,

(II) regularly performs appraisals for which the individual receives compensation, and

(III) meets such other requirements as may be prescribed by the Secretary in regulations or other guidance.

(iii) SPECIFIC APPRAISALS.—An individual shall not be treated as a qualified appraiser with respect to any specific appraisal unless—

(I) the individual demonstrates verifiable education and experience in valuing the type of property subject to the appraisal, and

(II) the individual has not been prohibited from practicing before the Internal Revenue Service by the Secretary under section 330(c) of title 31, United States Code, at any time during the 3-year period ending on the date of the appraisal.

* * *

»»→ *Caution: Code Sec. 170(f)(13), below, as added by H.R. 4, applies to contributions made 180 days after August 17, 2006.*

(13) CONTRIBUTIONS OF CERTAIN INTERESTS IN BUILDINGS LOCATED IN REGISTERED HISTORIC DISTRICTS.—

(A) IN GENERAL.—No deduction shall be allowed with respect to any contribution described in subparagraph (B) unless the taxpayer includes with the return for the taxable year of the contribution a $500 filing fee.

(B) CONTRIBUTION DESCRIBED.—A contribution is described in this subparagraph if such contribution is a qualified conservation contribution (as defined in subsection (h)) which is a restriction with respect to the exterior of a building described in subsection (h)(4)(C)(ii) and for which a deduction is claimed in excess of $10,000.

(C) DEDICATION OF FEE.—Any fee collected under this paragraph shall be used for the enforcement of the provisions of subsection (h).

(14) REDUCTION FOR AMOUNTS ATTRIBUTABLE TO REHABILITATION CREDIT.—In the case of any qualified conservation contribution (as defined in subsection (h)), the amount of the deduction allowed under this section shall be reduced by an amount which bears the same ratio to the fair market value of the contribution as—

(A) the sum of the credits allowed to the taxpayer under section 47 for the 5 preceding taxable years with respect to any building which is a part of such contribution, bears to

(B) the fair market value of the building on the date of the contribution.

(15) SPECIAL RULE FOR TAXIDERMY PROPERTY.—

(A) BASIS.—For purposes of this section and notwithstanding section 1012, in the case of a charitable contribution of taxidermy property which is made by the person who prepared, stuffed, or mounted the property or by any person who paid or incurred the cost of such preparation, stuffing, or mounting, only the cost of the preparing, stuffing, or mounting shall be included in the basis of such property.

(B) TAXIDERMY PROPERTY.—For purposes of this section, the term "taxidermy property" means any work of art which—

(i) is the reproduction or preservation of an animal, in whole or in part,

(ii) is prepared, stuffed, or mounted for purposes of recreating one or more characteristics of such animal, and

(iii) contains a part of the body of the dead animal.

(16) CONTRIBUTIONS OF CLOTHING AND HOUSEHOLD ITEMS.—

(A) IN GENERAL.—In the case of an individual, partnership, or corporation, no deduction shall be allowed under subsection (a) for any contribution of clothing or a household item unless such clothing or household item is in good used condition or better.

(B) ITEMS OF MINIMAL VALUE.—Notwithstanding subparagraph (A), the Secretary may by regulation deny a deduction under subsection (a) for any contribution of clothing or a household item which has minimal monetary value.

(C) EXCEPTION FOR CERTAIN PROPERTY.—Subparagraphs (A) and (B) shall not apply to any contribution of a single item of clothing or a household item for which a deduction of more than $500 is claimed if the taxpayer includes with the taxpayer's return a qualified appraisal with respect to the property.

(D) HOUSEHOLD ITEMS.—For purposes of this paragraph—

(i) IN GENERAL.—The term "household items" includes furniture, furnishings, electronics, appliances, linens, and other similar items.

(ii) EXCLUDED ITEMS.—Such term does not include—

(I) food,

(II) paintings, antiques, and other objects of art,

(III) jewelry and gems, and

(IV) collections.

(E) SPECIAL RULE FOR PASS-THRU ENTITIES.—In the case of a partnership or S corporation, this paragraph shall be applied at the entity level, except that the deduction shall be denied at the partner or shareholder level.

(17) RECORDKEEPING.—No deduction shall be allowed under subsection (a) for any contribution of a cash, check, or other monetary gift unless the donor maintains as a record of such contribution a bank record or a written communication from the donee showing the name of the donee organization, the date of the contribution, and the amount of the contribution.

»»→ Caution: Code Sec. 170(f)(18), below, as added by H.R. 4, applies to contributions made after the date which is 180 days after August 17, 2006.

(18) CONTRIBUTIONS TO DONOR ADVISED FUNDS.—A deduction otherwise allowed under subsection (a) for any contribution to a donor advised fund (as defined in section 4966(d)(2)) shall only be allowed if—

(A) the sponsoring organization (as defined in section 4966(d)(1)) with respect to such donor advised fund is not—

(i) described in paragraph (3), (4), or (5) of subsection (c), or

(ii) a type III supporting organization (as defined in section 4943(f)(5)(A)) which is not a functionally integrated type III supporting organization (as defined in section 4943(f)(5)(B)), and

(B) the taxpayer obtains a contemporaneous written acknowledgment (determined under rules similar to the rules of paragraph (8)(C)) from the sponsoring organization (as so defined) of such donor advised fund that such organization has exclusive legal control over the assets contributed.

* * *

[CCH Explanation at ¶1110, ¶1120, ¶1130, ¶1180, ¶1185 and ¶1355. Committee Reports at ¶11,210, ¶11,220, ¶11,240, ¶11,250,¶11,270 and ¶11,350.]

Amendments

• 2006, Pension Protection Act of 2006 (H.R. 4)

H.R. 4, §1213(c):

Amended Code Sec. 170(f) by adding at the end a new paragraph (13). **Effective** for contributions made 180 days after 8-17-2006.

H.R. 4, §1213(d):

Amended Code Sec. 170(f), as amended by Act Sec. 1213(c), by adding at the end a new paragraph (14). **Effective** for contributions made after 8-17-2006.

H.R. 4, §1214(b):

Amended Code Sec. 170(f), as amended by this Act, by adding at the end a new paragraph (15). **Effective** for contributions made after 7-25-2006.

H.R. 4, §1216(a):

Amended Code Sec. 170(f), as amended by this Act, by adding at the end a new paragraph (16). **Effective** for contributions made after 8-17-2006.

H.R. 4, §1217(a):

Amended Code Sec. 170(f), as amended by this Act, by adding at the end a new paragraph (17). **Effective** for contributions made in tax years beginning after 8-17-2006.

H.R. 4, §1219(c)(1):

Amended Code Sec. 170(f)(11)(E). **Effective** generally for appraisals prepared with respect to returns or submissions filed after 8-17-2006. Prior to amendment, Code Sec. 170(f)(11)(E) read as follows:

(E) QUALIFIED APPRAISAL.—For purposes of this paragraph, the term "qualified appraisal" means, with respect to any property, an appraisal of such property which is treated for purposes of this paragraph as a qualified appraisal under regulations or other guidance prescribed by the Secretary.

H.R. 4, §1234(a):

Amended Code Sec. 170(f), as amended by this Act, by adding at the end a new paragraph (18). **Effective** for contributions made after the date which is 180 days after 8-17-2006.

(h) QUALIFIED CONSERVATION CONTRIBUTION.—

* * *

(4) CONSERVATION PURPOSE DEFINED.—

* * *

(B) SPECIAL RULES WITH RESPECT TO BUILDINGS IN REGISTERED HISTORIC DISTRICTS.—In the case of any contribution of a qualified real property interest which is a restriction with respect to the exterior of a building described in subparagraph (C)(ii), such contribution shall not be considered to be exclusively for conservation purposes unless—

(i) such interest—

(I) includes a restriction which preserves the entire exterior of the building (including the front, sides, rear, and height of the building), and

(II) prohibits any change in the exterior of the building which is inconsistent with the historical character of such exterior,

(ii) the donor and donee enter into a written agreement certifying, under penalty of perjury, that the donee—

(I) is a qualified organization (as defined in paragraph (3)) with a purpose of environmental protection, land conservation, open space preservation, or historic preservation, and

(II) has the resources to manage and enforce the restriction and a commitment to do so, and

(iii) in the case of any contribution made in a taxable year beginning after the date of the enactment of this subparagraph, the taxpayer includes with the taxpayer's return for the taxable year of the contribution—

(I) a qualified appraisal (within the meaning of subsection (f)(11)(E)) of the qualified property interest,

(II) photographs of the entire exterior of the building, and

(III) a description of all restrictions on the development of the building.

(C) CERTIFIED HISTORIC STRUCTURE.—For purposes of subparagraph (A)(iv), the term "certified historic structure" means—

(i) *any building, structure, or land area which* is listed in the National Register, or

(ii) *any building which* is located in a registered historic district (as defined in section 47(c)(3)(B)) and is certified by the Secretary of the Interior to the Secretary as being of historic significance to the district.

A building, structure, or land area satisfies the preceding sentence if it satisfies such sentence either at the time of the transfer or on the due date (including extensions) for filing the transferor's return under this chapter for the taxable year in which the transfer is made.

* * *

[CCH Explanation at ¶1130. Committee Reports at ¶11,210.]

Amendments

• 2006, Pension Protection Act of 2006 (H.R. 4)

H.R. 4, §1213(a)(1):

Amended Code Sec. 170(h)(4) by redesignating subparagraph (B) as subparagraph (C) and by inserting after subparagraph (A) a new subparagraph (B). **Effective** for contributions made after 7-25-2006.

H.R. 4, §1213(b)(1)-(3):

Amended Code Sec. 170(h)(4)(C), as redesignated by Act Sec. 1213(a), by striking "any building, structure, or land area which", by inserting "any building, structure, or land area which" before "is listed" in clause (i), and by inserting "any building which" before "is located" in clause (ii). **Effective** for contributions made after 8-17-2006.

(o) SPECIAL RULES FOR FRACTIONAL GIFTS.—

(1) DENIAL OF DEDUCTION IN CERTAIN CASES.—

(A) IN GENERAL.—No deduction shall be allowed for a contribution of an undivided portion of a taxpayer's entire interest in tangible personal property unless all interest in the property is held immediately before such contribution by—

(i) the taxpayer, or

(ii) the taxpayer and the donee.

(B) EXCEPTIONS.—The Secretary may, by regulation, provide for exceptions to subparagraph (A) in cases where all persons who hold an interest in the property make proportional contributions of an undivided portion of the entire interest held by such persons.

(2) VALUATION OF SUBSEQUENT GIFTS.—In the case of any additional contribution, the fair market value of such contribution shall be determined by using the lesser of—

(A) the fair market value of the property at the time of the initial fractional contribution, or

(B) the fair market value of the property at the time of the additional contribution.

(3) RECAPTURE OF DEDUCTION IN CERTAIN CASES; ADDITION TO TAX.—

(A) RECAPTURE.—The Secretary shall provide for the recapture of the amount of any deduction allowed under this section (plus interest) with respect to any contribution of an undivided portion of a taxpayer's entire interest in tangible personal property—

(i) in any case in which the donor does not contribute all of the remaining interest in such property to the donee (or, if such donee is no longer in existence, to any person described in section 170(c)) before the earlier of—

(I) the date that is 10 years after the date of the initial fractional contribution, or

(II) the date of the death of the donor, and

(ii) in any case in which the donee has not, during the period beginning on the date of the initial fractional contribution and ending on the date described in clause (i)—

(I) had substantial physical possession of the property, and

(II) used the property in a use which is related to a purpose or function constituting the basis for the organizations' exemption under section 501.

(B) ADDITION TO TAX.—The tax imposed under this chapter for any taxable year for which there is a recapture under subparagraph (A) shall be increased by 10 percent of the amount so recaptured.

(4) DEFINITIONS.—For purposes of this subsection—

(A) ADDITIONAL CONTRIBUTION.—The term "additional contribution" means any charitable contribution by the taxpayer of any interest in property with respect to which the taxpayer has previously made an initial fractional contribution.

(B) INITIAL FRACTIONAL CONTRIBUTION.—The term "initial fractional contribution" means, with respect to any taxpayer, the first charitable contribution of an undivided portion of the taxpayer's entire interest in any tangible personal property.

[CCH Explanation at ¶1115. Committee Reports at ¶11,260.]

• 2006, Pension Protection Act of 2006 (H.R. 4)

H.R. 4, §1218(a):

Amended Code Sec. 170 by redesignating subsection (o) as subsection (p) and by inserting after subsection (n) a new subsection (o). **Effective** for contributions, bequests, and gifts made after 8-17-2006.

(p) OTHER CROSS REFERENCES.—

(1) For treatment of certain organizations providing child care, see section 501(k).

(2) For charitable contributions of estates and trusts, see section 642(c).

(3) For nondeductibility of contributions by common trust funds, see section 584.

(4) For charitable contributions of partners, see section 702.

(5) For charitable contributions of nonresident aliens, see section 873.

(6) For treatment of gifts for benefit of or use in connection with the Naval Academy as gifts to or for the use of the United States, see section 6973 of title 10, United States Code.

(7) For treatment of gifts accepted by the Secretary of State, the Director of the International Communication Agency, or the Director of the United States International Development Cooperation Agency, as gifts to or for the use of the United States, see section 25 of the State Department Basic Authorities Act of 1956.

(8) For treatment of gifts of money accepted by the Attorney General for credit to the "Commissary Funds, Federal Prisons" as gifts to or for the use of the United States, see section 4043 of title 18, United States Code.

(9) For charitable contributions to or for the use of Indian tribal governments (or their subdivisions), see section 7871.

[CCH Explanation at ¶ 1115. Committee Reports at ¶ 11,260.]

Amendments

• **2006, Pension Protection Act of 2006 (H.R. 4)**

H.R. 4, § 1218(a):

Amended Code Sec. 170 by redesignating subsection (o) as subsection (p). **Effective** for contributions, bequests, and gifts made after 8-17-2006.

[¶ 5025] CODE SEC. 219. RETIREMENT SAVINGS.

* * *

(b) MAXIMUM AMOUNT OF DEDUCTION—

* * *

(5) DEDUCTIBLE AMOUNT.—For purposes of paragraph (1)(A)—

* * *

»»→ Caution: Code Sec. 219(b)(5)(C), below, as added by H.R. 4, applies to tax years beginning after December 31, 2006.

(C) CATCHUP CONTRIBUTIONS FOR CERTAIN INDIVIDUALS.—

(i) IN GENERAL.—In the case of an applicable individual who elects to make a qualified retirement contribution in addition to the deductible amount determined under subparagraph (A)—

(I) the deductible amount for any taxable year shall be increased by an amount equal to 3 times the applicable amount determined under subparagraph (B) for such taxable year, and

(II) subparagraph (B) shall not apply.

(ii) APPLICABLE INDIVIDUAL.—For purposes of this subparagraph, the term "applicable individual" means, with respect to any taxable year, any individual who was a qualified participant in a qualified cash or deferred arrangement (as defined in section 401(k)) of an employer described in clause (iii) under which the employer matched at least 50 percent of the employee's contributions to such arrangement with stock of such employer.

(iii) EMPLOYER DESCRIBED.—An employer is described in this clause if, in any taxable year preceding the taxable year described in clause (ii)—

(I) such employer (or any controlling corporation of such employer) was a debtor in a case under title 11 of the United States Code, or similar Federal or State law, and

(II) such employer (or any other person) was subject to an indictment or conviction resulting from business transactions related to such case.

(iv) QUALIFIED PARTICIPANT.—For purposes of clause (ii), the term "qualified participant" means any applicable individual who was a participant in the cash or deferred arrangement described in such clause on the date that is 6 months before the filing of the case described in clause (iii).

(v) TERMINATION.—This subparagraph shall not apply to taxable years beginning after December 31, 2009.

»»→ Caution: Former Code Sec. 219(b)(5)(C) was redesignated as Code Sec. 219(b)(5)(D), below, by H.R. 4, applicable to tax years beginning after December 31, 2006.

(D) COST-OF-LIVING ADJUSTMENT.—

(i) IN GENERAL.—In the case of any taxable year beginning in a calendar year after 2008, the $5,000 amount under subparagraph (A) shall be increased by an amount equal to—

(I) such dollar amount, multiplied by

(II) the cost-of-living adjustment determined under section 1(f)(3) for the calendar year in which the taxable year begins, determined by substituting "calendar year 2007" for "calendar year 1992" in subparagraph (B) thereof.

(ii) ROUNDING RULES.—If any amount after adjustment under clause (i) is not a multiple of $500, such amount shall be rounded to the next lower multiple of $500.

* * *

[CCH Explanation at ¶ 730. Committee Reports at ¶ 10,720.]

Amendments

• **2006, Pension Protection Act of 2006 (H.R. 4)**

H.R. 4, §831(a):

Amended Code Sec. 219(b)(5) by redesignating subparagraph (C) as subparagraph (D) and by inserting after subparagraph (B) a new subparagraph (C). **Effective** for tax years beginning after 12-31-2006.

(g) LIMITATION ON DEDUCTION FOR ACTIVE PARTICIPANTS IN CERTAIN PENSION PLANS.—

* * *

»»→ Caution: Code Sec. 219(g)(8), below, as added by H.R. 4, applies to tax years beginning after 2006.

(8) INFLATION ADJUSTMENT.—In the case of any taxable year beginning in a calendar year after 2006, the dollar amount in the last row of the table contained in paragraph (3)(B)(i), the dollar amount in the last row of the table contained in paragraph (3)(B)(ii), and the dollar amount contained in paragraph (7)(A), shall each be increased by an amount equal to—

(A) such dollar amount, multiplied by

(B) the cost-of-living adjustment determined under section 1(f)(3) for the calendar year in which the taxable year begins, determined by substituting "calendar year 2005" for "calendar year 1992" in subparagraph (B) thereof.

Any increase determined under the preceding sentence shall be rounded to the nearest multiple of $1,000.

* * *

[CCH Explanation at ¶ 1320. Committee Reports at ¶ 10,740.]

Amendments

• **2006, Pension Protection Act of 2006 (H.R. 4)**

H.R. 4, §833(b):

Amended Code Sec. 219(g) by adding at the end a new paragraph (8). **Effective** for tax years beginning after 2006.

[¶5030] CODE SEC. 401. QUALIFIED PENSION, PROFIT-SHARING, AND STOCK BONUS PLANS.

(a) REQUIREMENTS FOR QUALIFICATION.—A trust created or organized in the United States and forming part of a stock bonus, pension, or profit-sharing plan of an employer for the exclusive benefit of his employees or their beneficiaries shall constitute a qualified trust under this section—

* * *

(5) SPECIAL RULES RELATING TO NONDISCRIMINATION REQUIREMENTS.—

* * *

(G) *GOVERNMENTAL* PLANS.—Paragraphs (3) and (4) shall not apply to a governmental plan (within the meaning of *section 414(d)).*

* * *

(26) ADDITIONAL PARTICIPATION REQUIREMENTS.—

* * *

(G) *EXCEPTION FOR* GOVERNMENTAL PLANS.—This paragraph shall not apply to a governmental plan (within the meaning of *section 414(d)).*

* * *

(28) ADDITIONAL REQUIREMENTS RELATING TO EMPLOYEE STOCK OWNERSHIP PLANS.—

* * *

(B) DIVERSIFICATION OF INVESTMENTS.—

* * *

Caution: Code Sec. 401(a)(28)(B)(v), below, as added by H.R. 4, applies generally to plan years beginning after December 31, 2006.

(v) EXCEPTION.—This subparagraph shall not apply to an applicable defined contribution plan (as defined in paragraph (35)(E)).

(29) BENEFIT LIMITATIONS ON PLANS IN AT-RISK STATUS.—In the case of a defined benefit plan (other than a multiemployer plan) to which the requirements of section 412 apply, the trust of which the plan is a part shall not constitute a qualified trust under this subsection unless the plan meets the requirements of section 436.

* * *

(32) TREATMENT OF FAILURE TO MAKE CERTAIN PAYMENTS IF PLAN HAS LIQUIDITY SHORTFALL.—

(A) IN GENERAL.—A trust forming part of a pension plan to which *section 430(j)(4)* applies shall not be treated as failing to constitute a qualified trust under this section merely because such plan ceases to make any payment described in subparagraph (B) during any period that such plan has a liquidity shortfall (as defined in *section 430(j)(4)*).

* * *

(C) PERIOD OF SHORTFALL.—For purposes of this paragraph, a plan has a liquidity shortfall during the period that there is an underpayment of an installment under *section 430(j)* by reason of paragraph (5)(A) thereof.

(33) PROHIBITION ON BENEFIT INCREASES WHILE SPONSOR IS IN BANKRUPTCY.—

* * *

(B) EXCEPTIONS.—This paragraph shall not apply to any plan amendment if—

(i) the plan, were such amendment to take effect, would have a *funding target attainment percentage (as defined in section 430(d)(2))* of 100 percent or more,

(ii) the Secretary determines that such amendment is reasonable and provides for only de minimis increases in the liabilities of the plan with respect to employees of the debtor,

(iii) such amendment only repeals an amendment described in *section 412(c)(2)*, or

(iv) such amendment is required as a condition of qualification under this part.

* * *

(D) EMPLOYER.—For purposes of this paragraph, the term "employer" means the employer referred to in *section 412(b)(2) (without regard to subparagraph (B) thereof)*.

* * *

→ *Caution: Code Sec. 401(a)(35), below, as added by H.R. 4, applies generally to plan years beginning after December 31, 2006.*

(35) DIVERSIFICATION REQUIREMENTS FOR CERTAIN DEFINED CONTRIBUTION PLANS.—

(A) IN GENERAL.—A trust which is part of an applicable defined contribution plan shall not be treated as a qualified trust unless the plan meets the diversification requirements of subparagraphs (B), (C), and (D).

(B) EMPLOYEE CONTRIBUTIONS AND ELECTIVE DEFERRALS INVESTED IN EMPLOYER SECURITIES.—In the case of the portion of an applicable individual's account attributable to employee contributions and elective deferrals which is invested in employer securities, a plan meets the requirements of this subparagraph if the applicable individual may elect to direct the plan to divest any such securities and to reinvest an equivalent amount in other investment options meeting the requirements of subparagraph (D).

(C) EMPLOYER CONTRIBUTIONS INVESTED IN EMPLOYER SECURITIES.—In the case of the portion of the account attributable to employer contributions other than elective deferrals which is invested in employer securities, a plan meets the requirements of this subparagraph if each applicable individual who—

(i) is a participant who has completed at least 3 years of service, or

(ii) is a beneficiary of a participant described in clause (i) or of a deceased participant,

may elect to direct the plan to divest any such securities and to reinvest an equivalent amount in other investment options meeting the requirements of subparagraph (D).

(D) INVESTMENT OPTIONS.—

(i) IN GENERAL.—The requirements of this subparagraph are met if the plan offers not less than 3 investment options, other than employer securities, to which an applicable individual may direct the proceeds from the divestment of employer securities pursuant to this paragraph, each of which is diversified and has materially different risk and return characteristics.

(ii) TREATMENT OF CERTAIN RESTRICTIONS AND CONDITIONS.—

(I) TIME FOR MAKING INVESTMENT CHOICES.—A plan shall not be treated as failing to meet the requirements of this subparagraph merely because the plan limits the time for divestment and reinvestment to periodic, reasonable opportunities occurring no less frequently than quarterly.

(II) CERTAIN RESTRICTIONS AND CONDITIONS NOT ALLOWED.—Except as provided in regulations, a plan shall not meet the requirements of this subparagraph if the plan imposes restrictions or conditions with respect to the investment of employer securities which are not imposed on the investment of other assets of the plan. This subclause shall not apply to any restrictions or conditions imposed by reason of the application of securities laws.

(E) APPLICABLE DEFINED CONTRIBUTION PLAN.—For purposes of this paragraph—

(i) IN GENERAL.—The term "applicable defined contribution plan" means any defined contribution plan which holds any publicly traded employer securities.

(ii) EXCEPTION FOR CERTAIN ESOPS.—*Such term does not include an employee stock ownership plan if—*

(I) there are no contributions to such plan (or earnings thereunder) which are held within such plan and are subject to subsection (k) or (m), and

(II) such plan is a separate plan for purposes of section 414(l) with respect to any other defined benefit plan or defined contribution plan maintained by the same employer or employers.

(iii) EXCEPTION FOR ONE PARTICIPANT PLANS.—*Such term does not include a one-participant retirement plan.*

(iv) ONE-PARTICIPANT RETIREMENT PLAN.—*For purposes of clause (iii), the term "one-participant retirement plan" means a retirement plan that—*

(I) on the first day of the plan year covered only one individual (or the individual and the individual's spouse) and the individual owned 100 percent of the plan sponsor (whether or not incorporated), or covered only one or more partners (or partners and their spouses) in the plan sponsor,

(II) meets the minimum coverage requirements of section 410(b) without being combined with any other plan of the business that covers the employees of the business,

(III) does not provide benefits to anyone except the individual (and the individual's spouse) or the partners (and their spouses),

(IV) does not cover a business that is a member of an affiliated service group, a controlled group of corporations, or a group of businesses under common control, and

(V) does not cover a business that uses the services of leased employees (within the meaning of section 414(n)).

For purposes of this clause, the term "partner" includes a 2-percent shareholder (as defined in section 1372(b)) of an S corporation.

(F) CERTAIN PLANS TREATED AS HOLDING PUBLICLY TRADED EMPLOYER SECURITIES.—

(i) IN GENERAL.—*Except as provided in regulations or in clause (ii), a plan holding employer securities which are not publicly traded employer securities shall be treated as holding publicly traded employer securities if any employer corporation, or any member of a controlled group of corporations which includes such employer corporation, has issued a class of stock which is a publicly traded employer security.*

(ii) EXCEPTION FOR CERTAIN CONTROLLED GROUPS WITH PUBLICLY TRADED SECURITIES.—*Clause (i) shall not apply to a plan if—*

(I) no employer corporation, or parent corporation of an employer corporation, has issued any publicly traded employer security, and

(II) no employer corporation, or parent corporation of an employer corporation, has issued any special class of stock which grants particular rights to, or bears particular risks for, the holder or issuer with respect to any corporation described in clause (i) which has issued any publicly traded employer security.

(iii) DEFINITIONS.—*For purposes of this subparagraph, the term—*

(I) "controlled group of corporations" has the meaning given such term by section 1563(a), except that "50 percent" shall be substituted for "80 percent" each place it appears,

(II) "employer corporation" means a corporation which is an employer maintaining the plan, and

(III) "parent corporation" has the meaning given such term by section 424(e).

(G) OTHER DEFINITIONS.—*For purposes of this paragraph—*

(i) APPLICABLE INDIVIDUAL.—*The term "applicable individual" means—*

(I) any participant in the plan, and

(II) any beneficiary who has an account under the plan with respect to which the beneficiary is entitled to exercise the rights of a participant.

(ii) ELECTIVE DEFERRAL.—The term "elective deferral" means an employer contribution described in section 402(g)(3)(A).

(iii) EMPLOYER SECURITY.—The term "employer security" has the meaning given such term by section 407(d)(1) of the Employee Retirement Income Security Act of 1974.

(iv) EMPLOYEE STOCK OWNERSHIP PLAN.—The term "employee stock ownership plan" has the meaning given such term by section 4975(e)(7).

(v) PUBLICLY TRADED EMPLOYER SECURITIES.—The term "publicly traded employer securities" means employer securities which are readily tradable on an established securities market.

(vi) YEAR OF SERVICE.—The term "year of service" has the meaning given such term by section 411(a)(5).

(H) TRANSITION RULE FOR SECURITIES ATTRIBUTABLE TO EMPLOYER CONTRIBUTIONS.—

(i) RULES PHASED IN OVER 3 YEARS.—

(I) IN GENERAL.—In the case of the portion of an account to which subparagraph (C) applies and which consists of employer securities acquired in a plan year beginning before January 1, 2007, subparagraph (C) shall only apply to the applicable percentage of such securities. This subparagraph shall be applied separately with respect to each class of securities.

(II) EXCEPTION FOR CERTAIN PARTICIPANTS AGED 55 OR OVER.—Subclause (I) shall not apply to an applicable individual who is a participant who has attained age 55 and completed at least 3 years of service before the first plan year beginning after December 31, 2005.

(ii) APPLICABLE PERCENTAGE.—For purposes of clause (i), the applicable percentage shall be determined as follows:

Plan year to which subparagraph (C) applies:	*The applicable percentage is:*
1st	*33*
2d	*66*
3d and following	*100.*

Caution: Code Sec. 401(a)(36), below, as added by H.R. 4, applies to distributions in plan years beginning after December 31, 2006.

(36) DISTRIBUTIONS DURING WORKING RETIREMENT.—A trust forming part of a pension plan shall not be treated as failing to constitute a qualified trust under this section solely because the plan provides that a distribution may be made from such trust to an employee who has attained age 62 and who is not separated from employment at the time of such distribution.

Paragraphs (11), (12), (13), (14), (15), (19), and (20) shall apply only in the case of a plan to which section 411 (relating to minimum vesting standards) applies without regard to subsection (e)(2) of such section.

* * *

[CCH Explanation at ¶ 205, ¶ 305, ¶ 605, ¶ 920 and ¶ 1060. Committee Reports at ¶ 10,010, ¶ 10,950 and ¶ 10,990.]

Amendments

- **2006, Pension Protection Act of 2006 (H.R. 4)**

H.R. 4, § 114(a)(1):

Amended Code Sec. 401(a)(29). **Effective** 8-17-2006. Prior to amendment, Code Sec. 401(a)(29) read as follows:

(29) SECURITY REQUIRED UPON ADOPTION OF PLAN AMENDMENT RESULTING IN SIGNIFICANT UNDERFUNDING.—

(A) IN GENERAL.—If—

(i) a defined benefit plan (other than a multiemployer plan) to which the requirements of section 412 apply adopts an amendment an effect of which is to increase current liability under the plan for a plan year, and

(ii) the funded current liability percentage of the plan for the plan year in which the amendment takes effect is less than 60 percent, including the amount of the unfunded current liability under the plan attributable to the plan amendment,

the trust of which such plan is a part shall not constitute a qualified trust under this subsection unless such amendment does not take effect until the contributing sponsor (or any member of the controlled group of the contributing sponsor) provides security to the plan.

(B) FORM OF SECURITY.—The security required under subparagraph (A) shall consist of—

(i) a bond issued by a corporate surety company that is an acceptable surety for purposes of section 412 of the Employee Retirement Income Security Act of 1974,

(ii) cash, or United States obligations which mature in 3 years or less, held in escrow by a bank or similar financial institution, or

(iii) such other form of security as is satisfactory to the Secretary and the parties involved.

(C) AMOUNT OF SECURITY.—The security shall be in an amount equal to the excess of—

(i) the lesser of—

(I) the amount of additional plan assets which would be necessary to increase the funded current liability percentage under the plan to 60 percent, including the amount of the unfunded current liability under the plan attributable to the plan amendment, or

(II) The amount of the increase in current liability under the plan attributable to the plan amendment and any other plan amendments adopted after December 22, 1987, and before such plan amendment, over

(ii) $10,000,000.

(D) RELEASE OF SECURITY.—The security shall be released (and any amounts thereunder shall be refunded together with any interest accrued thereon) at the end of the first plan year which ends after the provision of the security and for which the funded current liability percentage under the plan is not less than 60 percent. The Secretary may prescribe regulations for partial releases of the security by reason of increases in the funded current liability percentage.

(E) DEFINITIONS.—For purposes of this paragraph, the terms "current liability", "funded current liability percentage", and "unfunded current liability" shall have the meanings given such terms by section 412(l), except that in computing unfunded current liability there shall not be taken into account any unamortized portion of the unfunded old liability amount as of the close of the plan year.

H.R. 4, §114(a)(2)(A)-(B):

Amended Code Sec. 401(a)(32) by striking "[section] 412(m)(5)" each place it appears and inserting "section 430(j)(4)" in subparagraph (A), and by striking "section 412(m)" and inserting "section 430(j)" in subparagraph (C). **Effective** 8-17-2006.

H.R. 4, §114(a)(3)(A)-(C):

Amended Code Sec. 401(a)(33) by striking "funded current liability percentage (within the meaning of [as defined in] section 412(l)(8))" and inserting "funding target attainment percentage (as defined in section 430(d)(2))" in subparagraph (B)(i), by striking "subsection 412(c)(8)" and inserting "section 412(c)(2)" in subparagraph (B)(iii), and by striking "section 412(c)(11) (without regard to subparagraph (B) thereof)" and inserting "section 412(b)(2) (without regard to subparagraph (B) thereof)" in subparagraph (D). **Effective** 8-17-2006.

H.R. 4, §861(a)(1):

Amended Code Sec. 401(a)(5)(G) by striking "section 414(d))" and all that follows and inserting "section 414(d)).". **Effective** for any year beginning after 8-17-2006. Prior to amendment, Code Sec. 401(a)(5)(G) read as follows:

(G) STATE AND LOCAL GOVERNMENTAL PLANS.—Paragraphs (3) and (4) shall not apply to a governmental plan (within the meaning of section 414(d)) maintained by a State or local government or political subdivision thereof (or agency or instrumentality thereof).

H.R. 4, §861(a)(1):

Amended Code Sec. 401(a)(26)(G) by striking "section 414(d))" and all that follows and inserting "section 414(d)).". **Effective** for any year beginning after 8-17-2006. Prior to amendment, Code Sec. 401(a)(26)(G) read as follows:

(G) EXCEPTION FOR STATE AND LOCAL GOVERNMENTAL PLANS.—This paragraph shall not apply to a governmental plan (within the meaning of section 414(d)) maintained by a State or local government or political subdivision thereof (or agency or instrumentality thereof).

H.R. 4, §861(b)(1):

Amended the heading of Code Sec. 401(a)(5)(G) by striking "STATE AND LOCAL GOVERNMENTAL" and inserting "GOVERNMENTAL". **Effective** for any year beginning after 8-17-2006.

H.R. 4, §861(b)(2):

Amended the heading of Code Sec. 401(a)(26)(G) by striking "EXCEPTION FOR STATE AND LOCAL" and inserting "EXCEPTION FOR". **Effective** for any year beginning after 8-17-2006.

H.R. 4, §901(a)(1):

Amended Code Sec. 401(a) by inserting after paragraph (34) a new paragraph (35). For the **effective** date, see Act Sec. 901(c), below.

H.R. 4, §901(a)(2)(A):

Amended Code Sec. 401(a)(28)(B) by adding at the end a new clause (v). For the **effective** date, see Act Sec. 901(c), below.

H.R. 4, §901(c), provides:

(c) EFFECTIVE DATES.—

(1) IN GENERAL.—Except as provided in paragraphs (2) and (3), the amendments made by this section shall apply to plan years beginning after December 31, 2006.

(2) SPECIAL RULE FOR COLLECTIVELY BARGAINED AGREEMENTS.—In the case of a plan maintained pursuant to 1 or more collective bargaining agreements between employee representatives and 1 or more employers ratified on or before the date of the enactment of this Act, paragraph (1) shall be applied to benefits pursuant to, and individuals covered by, any such agreement by substituting for "December 31, 2006" the earlier of—

(A) the later of—

(i) December 31, 2007, or

(ii) the date on which the last of such collective bargaining agreements terminates (determined without regard to any extension thereof after such date of enactment), or

(B) December 31, 2008.

(3) SPECIAL RULE FOR CERTAIN EMPLOYER SECURITIES HELD IN AN ESOP.—

(A) IN GENERAL.—In the case of employer securities to which this paragraph applies, the amendments made by this section shall apply to plan years beginning after the earlier of—

(i) December 31, 2007, or

(ii) the first date on which the fair market value of such securities exceeds the guaranteed minimum value described in subparagraph (B)(ii).

(B) APPLICABLE SECURITIES.—This paragraph shall apply to employer securities which are attributable to employer contributions other than elective deferrals, and which, on September 17, 2003—

(i) consist of preferred stock, and

(ii) are within an employee stock ownership plan (as defined in section 4975(e)(7) of the Internal Revenue Code of 1986), the terms of which provide that the value of the securities cannot be less than the guaranteed minimum value specified by the plan on such date.

(C) COORDINATION WITH TRANSITION RULE.—In applying section 401(a)(35)(H) of the Internal Revenue Code of 1986 and section 204(j)(7) of the Employee Retirement Income Security Act of 1974 (as added by this section) to employer securities to which this paragraph applies, the applicable percentage shall be determined without regard to this paragraph.

H.R. 4, § 905(b):

Amended Code Sec. 401(a), as amended by this Act, by inserting after paragraph (35) a new paragraph (36). **Effective** for distributions in plan years beginning after 12-31-2006.

(k) CASH OR DEFERRED ARRANGEMENTS.—

* * *

(2) QUALIFIED CASH OR DEFERRED ARRANGEMENT.—A qualified cash or deferred arrangement is any arrangement which is part of a profit-sharing or stock bonus plan, a pre-ERISA money purchase plan, or a rural cooperative plan which meets the requirements of subsection (a)—

(A) under which a covered employee may elect to have the employer make payments as contributions to a trust under the plan on behalf of the employee, or to the employee directly in cash;

(B) under which amounts held by the trust which are attributable to employer contributions made pursuant to the employee's election—

(i) may not be distributable to participants or other beneficiaries earlier than—

(I) severance from employment, death, or disability,

(II) an event described in paragraph (10),

(III) in the case of a profit-sharing or stock bonus plan, the attainment of age 59½,

(IV) in the case of contributions to a profit-sharing or stock bonus plan to which section 402(e)(3) applies, upon hardship of the employee, *or*

(V) in the case of a qualified reservist distribution (as defined in section 72(t)(2)(G)(iii)), the date on which a period referred to in subclause (III) of such section begins, and

(ii) will not be distributable merely by reason of the completion of a stated period of participation or the lapse of a fixed number of years;

(C) which provides that an employee's right to his accrued benefit derived from employer contributions made to the trust pursuant to his election is nonforfeitable, and

(D) which does not require, as a condition of participation in the arrangement, that an employee complete a period of service with the employer (or employers) maintaining the plan extending beyond the period permitted under section 410(a)(1) (determined without regard to subparagraph (B)(i) thereof).

(3) APPLICATION OF PARTICIPATION AND DISCRIMINATION STANDARDS.—

* * *

(G) *GOVERNMENTAL PLAN*.—A governmental plan (within the meaning of section 414(d)) shall be treated as meeting the requirements of this paragraph.

* * *

(8) ARRANGEMENT NOT DISQUALIFIED IF EXCESS CONTRIBUTIONS DISTRIBUTED.—

(A) IN GENERAL.—A cash or deferred arrangement shall not be treated as failing to meet the requirements of clause (ii) of paragraph (3)(A) for any plan year if, before the close of the following plan year—

»»→ ***Caution:*** ***Code Sec. 401(k)(8)(A)(i), below, as amended by H.R. 4, applies to plan years beginning after December 31, 2007.***

(i) the amount of excess contributions for such plan year (and any income allocable to such contributions *through the end of such year*) is distributed, or

(ii) to the extent provided in regulations, the employee elects to treat the amount of the excess contributions as an amount distributed to the employee and then contributed by the employee to the plan.

Any distribution of excess contributions (and income) may be made without regard to any other provision of law.

* * *

»»→ ***Caution:*** ***Code Sec. 401(k)(8)(E), below, as amended by H.R. 4, applies to plan years beginning after December 31, 2007.***

(E) TREATMENT OF MATCHING CONTRIBUTIONS FORFEITED BY REASON OF EXCESS DEFERRAL OR CONTRIBUTION *OR ERRONEOUS AUTOMATIC CONTRIBUTION*.—For purposes of paragraph (2)(C), a matching contribution (within the meaning of subsection (m)) shall not be treated as forfeitable merely because such contribution is forfeitable if the contribution to which the matching contribution relates is treated as an excess contribution under subparagraph (B), an excess deferral under section 402(g)(2)(A), *an erroneous automatic contribution under section 414(w)*, or an excess aggregate contribution under section 401(m)(6)(B).

* * *

»»→ ***Caution:*** ***Code Sec. 401(k)(13), below, as added by H.R. 4, applies to plan years beginning after December 31, 2007.***

(13) ALTERNATIVE METHOD FOR AUTOMATIC CONTRIBUTION ARRANGEMENTS TO MEET NON-DISCRIMINATION REQUIREMENTS.—

(A) IN GENERAL.—A qualified automatic contribution arrangement shall be treated as meeting the requirements of paragraph (3)(A)(ii).

(B) QUALIFIED AUTOMATIC CONTRIBUTION ARRANGEMENT.—For purposes of this paragraph, the term "qualified automatic contribution arrangement" means any cash or deferred arrangement which meets the requirements of subparagraphs (C) through (E).

(C) AUTOMATIC DEFERRAL.—

(i) IN GENERAL.—The requirements of this subparagraph are met if, under the arrangement, each employee eligible to participate in the arrangement is treated as having elected to have the employer make elective contributions in an amount equal to a qualified percentage of compensation.

(ii) ELECTION OUT.—The election treated as having been made under clause (i) shall cease to apply with respect to any employee if such employee makes an affirmative election—

(I) to not have such contributions made, or

(II) to make elective contributions at a level specified in such affirmative election.

(iii) QUALIFIED PERCENTAGE.—For purposes of this subparagraph, the term "qualified percentage" means, with respect to any employee, any percentage determined under the arrangement if such percentage is applied uniformly, does not exceed 10 percent, and is at least—

(I) 3 percent during the period ending on the last day of the first plan year which begins after the date on which the first elective contribution described in clause (i) is made with respect to such employee,

(II) 4 percent during the first plan year following the plan year described in subclause (I),

(III) 5 percent during the second plan year following the plan year described in subclause (I), and

(IV) 6 percent during any subsequent plan year.

(iv) AUTOMATIC DEFERRAL FOR CURRENT EMPLOYEES NOT REQUIRED.—Clause (i) may be applied without taking into account any employee who—

(I) was eligible to participate in the arrangement (or a predecessor arrangement) immediately before the date on which such arrangement becomes a qualified automatic contribution arrangement (determined after application of this clause), and

(II) had an election in effect on such date either to participate in the arrangement or to not participate in the arrangement.

(D) MATCHING OR NONELECTIVE CONTRIBUTIONS.—

(i) IN GENERAL.—The requirements of this subparagraph are met if, under the arrangement, the employer—

(I) makes matching contributions on behalf of each employee who is not a highly compensated employee in an amount equal to the sum of 100 percent of the elective contributions of the employee to the extent that such contributions do not exceed 1 percent of compensation plus 50 percent of so much of such compensation as exceeds 1 percent but does not exceed 6 percent of compensation, or

(II) is required, without regard to whether the employee makes an elective contribution or employee contribution, to make a contribution to a defined contribution plan on behalf of each employee who is not a highly compensated employee and who is eligible to participate in the arrangement in an amount equal to at least 3 percent of the employee's compensation.

(ii) APPLICATION OF RULES FOR MATCHING CONTRIBUTIONS.—The rules of clauses (ii) and (iii) of paragraph (12)(B) shall apply for purposes of clause (i)(I).

(iii) WITHDRAWAL AND VESTING RESTRICTIONS.—An arrangement shall not be treated as meeting the requirements of clause (i) unless, with respect to employer contributions (including matching contributions) taken into account in determining whether the requirements of clause (i) are met—

(I) any employee who has completed at least 2 years of service (within the meaning of section 411(a)) has a nonforfeitable right to 100 percent of the employee's accrued benefit derived from such employer contributions, and

(II) the requirements of subparagraph (B) of paragraph (2) are met with respect to all such employer contributions.

(iv) APPLICATION OF CERTAIN OTHER RULES.—The rules of subparagraphs (E)(ii) and (F) of paragraph (12) shall apply for purposes of subclauses (I) and (II) of clause (i).

(E) NOTICE REQUIREMENTS.—

(i) IN GENERAL.—The requirements of this subparagraph are met if, within a reasonable period before each plan year, each employee eligible to participate in the arrangement for such year receives written notice of the employee's rights and obligations under the arrangement which—

(I) is sufficiently accurate and comprehensive to apprise the employee of such rights and obligations, and

(II) is written in a manner calculated to be understood by the average employee to whom the arrangement applies.

(ii) TIMING AND CONTENT REQUIREMENTS.—A notice shall not be treated as meeting the requirements of clause (i) with respect to an employee unless—

(I) the notice explains the employee's right under the arrangement to elect not to have elective contributions made on the employee's behalf (or to elect to have such contributions made at a different percentage),

(II) in the case of an arrangement under which the employee may elect among 2 or more investment options, the notice explains how contributions made under the arrangement will be invested in the absence of any investment election by the employee, and

(III) the employee has a reasonable period of time after receipt of the notice described in subclauses (I) and (II) and before the first elective contribution is made to make either such election.

* * *

[CCH Explanation at ¶ 917, ¶ 1015 and ¶ 1060. Committee Reports at ¶ 10,680, ¶ 10,870 and ¶ 10,960.]

Amendments

• 2006, Pension Protection Act of 2006 (H.R. 4)

H.R. 4, § 827(b)(1):

Amended Code Sec. 401(k)(2)(B)(i) by striking "or" at the end of subclause (III), by striking "and" at the end of subclause (IV) and inserting "or", and by inserting after subclause (IV) a new subclause (V). **Effective** for distributions after 9-11-2001. For a waiver of limitations, see Act Sec. 827(c)(2), below.

H.R. 4, § 827(c)(2), provides:

(2) WAIVER OF LIMITATIONS.—If refund or credit of any overpayment of tax resulting from the amendments made by this section is prevented at any time before the close of the 1-year period beginning on the date of the enactment of this Act by the operation of any law or rule of law (including res judicata), such refund or credit may nevertheless be made or allowed if claim therefor is filed before the close of such period.

H.R. 4, § 861(a)(2):

Amended Code Sec. 401(k)(3)(G) by striking "maintained by a State or local government or political subdivision thereof (or agency or instrumentality thereof)" after "section 414(d))". **Effective** for any year beginning after 8-17-2006.

H.R. 4, § 861(b)(3):

Amended Code Sec. 401(k)(3)(G) by inserting "GOVERNMENTAL PLAN.—"after "(G)". **Effective** for any year beginning after 8-17-2006.

H.R. 4, § 902(a):

Amended Code Sec. 401(k) by adding at the end a new paragraph (13). **Effective** for plan years beginning after 12-31-2007.

H.R. 4, § 902(d)(2)(C):

Amended Code Sec. 401(k)(8)(E) by inserting "an erroneous automatic contribution under section 414(w)," after "402(g)(2)(A),". **Effective** for plan years beginning after 12-31-2007.

H.R. 4, § 902(d)(2)(D):

Amended the heading of Code Sec. 401(k)(8)(E) by inserting "OR ERRONEOUS AUTOMATIC CONTRIBUTION" before the period. **Effective** for plan years beginning after 12-31-2007.

H.R. 4, § 902(e)(3)(B)(i):

Amended Code Sec. 401(k)(8)(A)(i) by adding "through the end of such year" after "such contributions". **Effective** for plan years beginning after 12-31-2007.

(m) NONDISCRIMINATION TEST FOR MATCHING CONTRIBUTIONS AND EMPLOYEE CONTRIBUTIONS.—

* * *

(6) PLAN NOT DISQUALIFIED IF EXCESS AGGREGATE CONTRIBUTIONS DISTRIBUTED BEFORE END OF FOLLOWING PLAN YEAR.—

→ Caution: Code Sec. 401(m)(6)(A), below, as amended by H.R. 4, applies to plan years beginning after December 31, 2007.

(A) IN GENERAL.—A plan shall not be treated as failing to meet the requirements of paragraph (1) for any plan year if, before the close of the following plan year, the amount of the excess aggregate contributions for such plan year (and any income allocable to such contributions *through the end of such year*) is distributed (or, if forfeitable, is forfeited). Such contributions (and such income) may be distributed without regard to any other provision of law.

* * *

→ Caution: Code Sec. 401(m)(12), below, as added by H.R. 4, applies to plan years beginning after December 31, 2007.

(12) ALTERNATIVE METHOD FOR AUTOMATIC CONTRIBUTION ARRANGEMENTS.—A defined contribution plan shall be treated as meeting the requirements of paragraph (2) with respect to matching contributions if the plan—

(A) is a qualified automatic contribution arrangement (as defined in subsection (k)(13)), and

(B) meets the requirements of paragraph (11)(B).

»»→ *Caution: Former Code Sec. 401(m)(12) was redesignated as Code Sec. 401(m)(13), below, by H.R. 4, applicable to plan years beginning after December 31, 2007.*

(13) CROSS REFERENCE.—

For excise tax on certain excess contributions, see section 4979.

* * *

[CCH Explanation at ¶ 1015. Committee Reports at ¶ 10,960.]

Amendments

• **2006, Pension Protection Act of 2006 (H.R. 4)**

H.R. 4, § 902(b):

Amended Code Sec. 401(m) by redesignating paragraph (12) as paragraph (13) and by inserting after paragraph (11) a new paragraph (12). **Effective** for plan years beginning after 12-31-2007.

H.R. 4, § 902(e)(3)(B)(ii):

Amended Code Sec. 401(m)(6)(A) by adding "through the end of such year" after "to such contributions". **Effective** for plan years beginning after 12-31-2007.

[¶ 5035] CODE SEC. 402. TAXABILITY OF BENEFICIARY OF EMPLOYEES' TRUST.

* * *

(c) RULES APPLICABLE TO ROLLOVERS FROM EXEMPT TRUSTS.—

* * *

(2) MAXIMUM AMOUNT WHICH MAY BE ROLLED OVER.—In the case of any eligible rollover distribution, the maximum amount transferred to which paragraph (1) applies shall not exceed the portion of such distribution which is includible in gross income (determined without regard to paragraph (1)). The preceding sentence shall not apply to such distribution to the extent—

»»→ *Caution: Code Sec. 402(c)(2)(A), below, as amended by H.R. 4, applies to tax years beginning after December 31, 2006.*

(A) such portion is transferred in a direct trustee-to-trustee transfer to a qualified trust *or to an annuity contract described in section 403(b) and such trust or contract provides for separate accounting* for amounts so transferred *(and earnings thereon)*, including separately accounting for the portion of such distribution which is includible in gross income and the portion of such distribution which is not so includible, or

(B) such portion is transferred to an eligible retirement plan described in clause (i) or (ii) of paragraph (8)(B).

* * *

»»→ *Caution: Code Sec. 402(c)(11), below, as added by H.R. 4, applies to distributions after December 31, 2006.*

(11) DISTRIBUTIONS TO INHERITED INDIVIDUAL RETIREMENT PLAN OF NONSPOUSE BENEFICIARY.—

(A) IN GENERAL.—*If, with respect to any portion of a distribution from an eligible retirement plan of a deceased employee, a direct trustee-to-trustee transfer is made to an individual retirement plan described in clause (i) or (ii) of paragraph (8)(B) established for the purposes of receiving the distribution on behalf of an individual who is a designated beneficiary (as defined by section 401(a)(9)(E)) of the employee and who is not the surviving spouse of the employee—*

(i) the transfer shall be treated as an eligible rollover distribution for purposes of this subsection,

(ii) the individual retirement plan shall be treated as an inherited individual retirement account or individual retirement annuity (within the meaning of section 408(d)(3)(C)) for purposes of this title, and

(iii) section 401(a)(9)(B) (other than clause (iv) thereof) shall apply to such plan.

(B) CERTAIN TRUSTS TREATED AS BENEFICIARIES.—*For purposes of this paragraph, to the extent provided in rules prescribed by the Secretary, a trust maintained for the benefit of one or more designated beneficiaries shall be treated in the same manner as a trust designated beneficiary.*

* * *

[CCH Explanation at ¶ 940 and ¶ 945. Committee Reports at ¶ 10,630 and ¶ 10,700.]

Amendments

• **2006, Pension Protection Act of 2006 (H.R. 4)**

H.R. 4, § 822(a)(1)-(2):

Amended Code Sec. 402(c)(2)(A) by striking "which is part of a plan which is a defined contribution plan and which agrees to separately account" and inserting "or to an annuity contract described in section 403(b) and such trust or contract provides for separate accounting"; and by inserting "(and earnings thereon)" after "so transferred". **Effective** for tax years beginning after 12-31-2006.

H.R. 4, § 829(a)(1):

Amended Code Sec. 402(c) by adding at the end a new paragraph (11). **Effective** for distributions after 12-31-2006.

»»→ Caution: Code Sec. 402(l), below, as added by H.R. 4, applies to distributions in tax years beginning after December 31, 2006.

(l) DISTRIBUTIONS FROM GOVERNMENTAL PLANS FOR HEALTH AND LONG-TERM CARE INSURANCE.—

(1) IN GENERAL.—In the case of an employee who is an eligible retired public safety officer who makes the election described in paragraph (6) with respect to any taxable year of such employee, gross income of such employee for such taxable year does not include any distribution from an eligible retirement plan to the extent that the aggregate amount of such distributions does not exceed the amount paid by such employee for qualified health insurance premiums of the employee, his spouse, or dependents (as defined in section 152) for such taxable year.

(2) LIMITATION.—The amount which may be excluded from gross income for the taxable year by reason of paragraph (1) shall not exceed $3,000.

(3) DISTRIBUTIONS MUST OTHERWISE BE INCLUDIBLE.—

(A) IN GENERAL.—An amount shall be treated as a distribution for purposes of paragraph (1) only to the extent that such amount would be includible in gross income without regard to paragraph (1).

(B) APPLICATION OF SECTION 72.—Notwithstanding section 72, in determining the extent to which an amount is treated as a distribution for purposes of subparagraph (A), the aggregate amounts distributed from an eligible retirement plan in a taxable year (up to the amount excluded under paragraph (1)) shall be treated as includible in gross income (without regard to subparagraph (A)) to the extent that such amount does not exceed the aggregate amount which would have been so includible if all amounts distributed from all eligible retirement plans were treated as 1 contract for purposes of determining the inclusion of such distribution under section 72. Proper adjustments shall be made in applying section 72 to other distributions in such taxable year and subsequent taxable years.

(4) DEFINITIONS.—For purposes of this subsection—

(A) ELIGIBLE RETIREMENT PLAN.—For purposes of paragraph (1), the term "eligible retirement plan" means a governmental plan (within the meaning of section 414(d)) which is described in clause (iii), (iv), (v), or (vi) of subsection (c)(8)(B).

(B) ELIGIBLE RETIRED PUBLIC SAFETY OFFICER.—The term "eligible retired public safety officer" means an individual who, by reason of disability or attainment of normal retirement age, is separated from service as a public safety officer with the employer who maintains the eligible retirement plan from which distributions subject to paragraph (1) are made.

(C) PUBLIC SAFETY OFFICER.—The term "public safety officer" shall have the same meaning given such term by section 1204(9)(A) of the Omnibus Crime Control and Safe Streets Act of 1968 (42 U.S.C. 3796b(9)(A)).

(D) QUALIFIED HEALTH INSURANCE PREMIUMS.—The term "qualified health insurance premiums" means premiums for coverage for the eligible retired public safety officer, his spouse, and dependents, by an accident or health insurance plan or qualified long-term care insurance contract (as defined in section 7702B(b)).

(5) SPECIAL RULES.—For purposes of this subsection—

(A) DIRECT PAYMENT TO INSURER REQUIRED.—Paragraph (1) shall only apply to a distribution if payment of the premiums is made directly to the provider of the accident or health insurance plan or

qualified long-term care insurance contract by deduction from a distribution from the eligible retirement plan.

(B) RELATED PLANS TREATED AS 1.—All eligible retirement plans of an employer shall be treated as a single plan.

(6) ELECTION DESCRIBED.—

(A) IN GENERAL.—For purposes of paragraph (1), an election is described in this paragraph if the election is made by an employee after separation from service with respect to amounts not distributed from an eligible retirement plan to have amounts from such plan distributed in order to pay for qualified health insurance premiums.

(B) SPECIAL RULE.—A plan shall not be treated as violating the requirements of section 401, or as engaging in a prohibited transaction for purposes of section 503(b), merely because it provides for an election with respect to amounts that are otherwise distributable under the plan or merely because of a distribution made pursuant to an election described in subparagraph (A).

(7) COORDINATION WITH MEDICAL EXPENSE DEDUCTION.—The amounts excluded from gross income under paragraph (1) shall not be taken into account under section 213.

(8) COORDINATION WITH DEDUCTION FOR HEALTH INSURANCE COSTS OF SELF-EMPLOYED INDIVIDUALS.—The amounts excluded from gross income under paragraph (1) shall not be taken into account under section 162(l).

[CCH Explanation at ¶ 825. Committee Reports at ¶ 10,790.]

Amendments

• 2006, Pension Protection Act of 2006 (H.R. 4)

H.R. 4, § 845(a):

Amended Code Sec. 402 by adding at the end a new subsection (l). **Effective** for distributions in tax years beginning after 12-31-2006.

[¶ 5040] CODE SEC. 403. TAXATION OF EMPLOYEE ANNUITIES.

(a) TAXABILITY OF BENEFICIARY UNDER A QUALIFIED ANNUITY PLAN.—

* * *

➾ *Caution: Code Sec. 403(a)(2), below, as added by H.R. 4, applies to distributions in tax years beginning after December 31, 2006.*

(2) SPECIAL RULE FOR HEALTH AND LONG-TERM CARE INSURANCE.—To the extent provided in section 402(l), paragraph (1) shall not apply to the amount distributed under the contract which is otherwise includible in gross income under this subsection.

* * *

(4) ROLLOVER AMOUNTS.—

* * *

➾ *Caution: Code Sec. 403(a)(4)(B), below, as amended by H.R. 4, applies to distributions after December 31, 2006.*

(B) CERTAIN RULES MADE APPLICABLE.—The rules of paragraphs (2) through (7) *and (11)* and (9) of section 402(c) and section 402(f) shall apply for purposes of subparagraph *(A)*.

* * *

[CCH Explanation at ¶ 825 and ¶ 945. Committee Reports at ¶ 10,700 and ¶ 10,790.]

Amendments

• 2006, Pension Protection Act of 2006 (H.R. 4)

H.R. 4, § 829(a)(2):

Amended Code Sec. 403(a)(4)(B) by inserting "and (11)" after "(7)". **Effective** for distributions after 12-31-2006.

H.R. 4, § 845(b)(1):

Amended Code Sec. 403(a) by inserting after paragraph (1) a new paragraph (2). **Effective** for distributions in tax years beginning after 12-31-2006.

(b) TAXABILITY OF BENEFICIARY UNDER ANNUITY PURCHASED BY SECTION 501(c)(3) ORGANIZATION OR PUBLIC SCHOOL.—

* * *

»»→ Caution: Code Sec. 403(b)(2), below, as added by H.R. 4, applies to distributions in tax years beginning after December 31, 2006.

(2) SPECIAL RULE FOR HEALTH AND LONG-TERM CARE INSURANCE.—To the extent provided in section 402(l), paragraph (1) shall not apply to the amount distributed under the contract which is otherwise includible in gross income under this subsection.

* * *

(7) CUSTODIAL ACCOUNTS FOR REGULATED INVESTMENT COMPANY STOCK.—

(A) AMOUNTS PAID TREATED AS CONTRIBUTIONS.—For purposes of this title, amounts paid by an employer described in paragraph (1)(A) to a custodial account which satisfies the requirements of section 401(f)(2) shall be treated as amounts contributed by him for an annuity contract for his employee if—

(i) the amounts are to be invested in regulated investment company stock to be held in that custodial account, and

(ii) under the custodial account no such amounts may be paid or made available to any distributee *(unless such amount is a distribution to which section 72(t)(2)(G) applies)* before the employee dies, attains age 59½, has a severance from employment, becomes disabled (within the meaning of section 72(m)(7)), or in the case of contributions made pursuant to a salary reduction agreement (within the meaning of section 3121(a)(5)(D)), encounters financial hardship.

* * *

(8) ROLLOVER AMOUNTS.—

* * *

»»→ Caution: Code Sec. 403(b)(8)(B), below, as amended by H.R. 4, applies to distributions after December 31, 2006.

(B) CERTAIN RULES MADE APPLICABLE.—The rules of paragraphs (2) through (7), *(9), and (11)* of section 402(c) and section 402(f) shall apply for purposes of subparagraph (A), except that section 402(f) shall be applied to the payor in lieu of the plan administrator.

* * *

(11) REQUIREMENT THAT DISTRIBUTIONS NOT BEGIN BEFORE AGE 59 ½, SEVERANCE FROM EMPLOYMENT, DEATH, OR DISABILITY.—This subsection shall not apply to any annuity contract unless under such contract distributions attributable to contributions made pursuant to a salary reduction agreement (within the meaning of section 402(g)(3)(C)) may be paid only—

(A) when the employee attains age 59½, has a severance from employment, dies, or becomes disabled (within the meaning of section 72(m)(7)),

(B) in the case of hardship*, or*

(C) for distributions to which section 72(t)(2)(G) applies.

* * *

[CCH Explanation at ¶ 825, ¶ 917 and ¶ 945. Committee Reports at ¶ 10,680, ¶ 10,700 and ¶ 10,790.]

Amendments

• 2006, Pension Protection Act of 2006 (H.R. 4)

H.R. 4, §827(b)(2):

Amended Code Sec. 403(b)(7)(A)(ii) by inserting "(unless such amount is a distribution to which section 72(t)(2)(G) applies)" after "distributee". **Effective** for distributions after 9-11-2001. For a waiver of limitations, see Act Sec. 827(c)(2), below.

H.R. 4, §827(b)(3):

Amended Code Sec. 403(b)(11) by striking "or" at the end of subparagraph (A), by striking the period at the end of subparagraph (B) and inserting ", or", and by inserting after subparagraph (B) a new subparagraph (C). **Effective** for distributions after 9-11-2001. For a waiver of limitations, see Act Sec. 827(c)(2), below.

H.R. 4, §827(c)(2), provides:

(2) WAIVER OF LIMITATIONS.—If refund or credit of any overpayment of tax resulting from the amendments made by this section is prevented at any time before the close of the 1-year period beginning on the date of the enactment of this Act by the operation of any law or rule of law (including res judicata), such refund or credit may nevertheless be made or allowed if claim therefor is filed before the close of such period.

H.R. 4, §829(a)(3):

Amended Code Sec. 403(b)(8)(B) by striking "and (9)" and inserting ", (9), and (11)". **Effective** for distributions after 12-31-2006.

H.R. 4, §845(b)(2):

Amended Code Sec. 403(b) by inserting after paragraph (1) a new paragraph (2). **Effective** for distributions in tax years beginning after 12-31-2006.

[¶5045] CODE SEC. 404. DEDUCTION FOR CONTRIBUTIONS OF AN EMPLOYER TO AN EMPLOYEES' TRUST OR ANNUITY PLAN AND COMPENSATION UNDER A DEFERRED-PAYMENT PLAN.

(a) GENERAL RULE.—If contributions are paid by an employer to or under a stock bonus, pension, profit-sharing, or annuity plan, or if compensation is paid or accrued on account of any employee under a plan deferring the receipt of such compensation, such contributions or compensation shall not be deductible under this chapter; but if they would otherwise be deductible, they shall be deductible under this section, subject, however, to the following limitations as to the amounts deductible in any year:

(1) PENSION TRUSTS.—

»»→ Caution: Code Sec. 404(a)(1)(A), below, as amended by H.R. 4, applies to years beginning after December 31, 2007.

(A) IN GENERAL.—In the taxable year when paid, if the contributions are paid into a pension trust (other than a trust to which paragraph (3) applies), and if such taxable year ends within or with a taxable year of the trust for which the trust is exempt under section 501(a), *in the case of a defined benefit plan other than a multiemployer plan, in an amount determined under subsection (o), and in the case of any other plan* in an amount determined as follows:

(i) the amount necessary to satisfy the minimum funding standard provided by section 412(a) for plan years ending within or with such taxable year (or for any prior plan year), if such amount is greater than the amount determined under clause (ii) or (iii) (whichever is applicable with respect to the plan),

(ii) the amount necessary to provide with respect to all of the employees under the trust the remaining unfunded cost of their past and current service credits distributed as a level amount, or a level percentage of compensation, over the remaining future service of each such employee, as determined under regulations prescribed by the Secretary, but if such remaining unfunded cost with respect to any 3 individuals is more than 50 percent of such remaining unfunded cost, the amount of such unfunded cost attributable to such individuals shall be distributed over a period of at least 5 taxable years,

(iii) an amount equal to the normal cost of the plan, as determined under regulations prescribed by the Secretary, plus, if past service or other supplementary pension or annuity credits are provided by the plan, an amount necessary to amortize the unfunded costs attributable to such credits in equal annual payments (until fully amortized) over 10 years, as determined under regulations prescribed by the Secretary.

In determining the amount deductible in such year under the foregoing limitations the funding method and the actuarial assumptions used shall be those used for such year under *section 431*, and the maximum amount deductible for such year shall be an amount equal to the full funding limitation for such year determined under *section 431*.

»»→ Caution: Code Sec. 404(a)(1)(B), below, as amended by H.R. 4, applies to years beginning after December 31, 2007.

(B) SPECIAL RULE IN CASE OF CERTAIN AMENDMENTS.— *In the case of a multiemployer plan* which the Secretary of Labor finds to be collectively bargained which makes an election under this subparagraph (in such manner and at such time as may be provided under regulations prescribed by the Secretary), if the full funding limitation determined under *section 431(c)(6)* for such year is zero, if as a result of any plan amendment applying to such plan year, the amount determined under *section 431(c)(6)(A)(ii)* exceeds the amount determined under *section 431(c)(6)(A)(i)*, and if the funding method and the actuarial assumptions used are those used for such year under *section 431*, the maximum amount deductible in such year under the limitations of this paragraph shall be an amount equal to the lesser of—

(i) the full funding limitation for such year determined by applying *section 431(c)(6)* but increasing the amount referred to in subparagraph (A) thereof by the decrease in the present value of all unamortized liabilities resulting from such amendment, or

(ii) the normal cost under the plan reduced by the amount necessary to amortize in equal annual installments over 10 years (until fully amortized) the decrease described in clause (i).

* * *

»»→ Caution: Code Sec. 404(a)(1)(D), below, as amended by H.R. 4, §801(d)(1), but prior to amendment by §802(a), applies to years beginning on or before December 31, 2007.

(D) SPECIAL RULE IN CASE OF CERTAIN PLANS.—

(i) IN GENERAL.—In the case of any defined benefit plan, except as provided in regulations, the maximum amount deductible under the limitations of this paragraph shall not be less than the unfunded current liability determined under *section 412(l)(8)(A), except that section 412(l)(8)(A) shall be applied for purposes of this clause by substituting "150 percent (140 percent in the case of a multiemployer plan) of current liability" for "the current liability" in clause (i).*

(ii) PLANS WITH 100 OR LESS PARTICIPANTS.—For purposes of this subparagraph, in the case of a plan which has 100 or less participants for the plan year, unfunded current liability shall not include the liability attributable to benefit increases for highly compensated employees (as defined in section 414(q)) resulting from a plan amendment which is made or becomes effective, whichever is later, within the last 2 years.

(iii) RULE FOR DETERMINING NUMBER OF PARTICIPANTS.—For purposes of determining the number of plan participants, all defined benefit plans maintained by the same employer (or any member of such employer's controlled group (within the meaning of section 412(l)(8)(C))) shall be treated as one plan, but only employees of such member or employer shall be taken into account.

(iv) SPECIAL RULE FOR TERMINATING PLANS.—In the case of a plan which, subject to section 4041 of the Employee Retirement Income Security Act of 1974, terminates during the plan year, clause (i) shall be applied by substituting for unfunded current liability the amount required to make the plan sufficient for benefit liabilities (within the meaning of section 4041(d) of such Act).

»»→ Caution: Code Sec. 404(a)(1)(D), below, as amended by H.R. 4, §802(a), applies to years beginning after December 31, 2007.

(D) AMOUNT DETERMINED ON BASIS OF UNFUNDED CURRENT LIABILITY.—In the case of a defined benefit plan which is a multiemployer plan, except as provided in regulations, the maximum amount deductible under the limitations of this paragraph shall not be less than the excess (if any) of—

(i) 140 percent of the current liability of the plan determined under section 431(c)(6)(C), over

(ii) the value of the plan's assets determined under section 431(c)(2).

* * *

(F) [*Stricken.*]

* * *

(7) LIMITATION ON DEDUCTIONS WHERE COMBINATION OF DEFINED CONTRIBUTION PLAN AND DEFINED BENEFIT PLAN.—

»»→ *Caution: Code Sec. 404(a)(7)(A), below, as amended by H.R. 4, applies to years beginning after December 31, 2007.*

(A) IN GENERAL.—If amounts are deductible under the foregoing paragraphs of this subsection (other than paragraph (5)) in connection with 1 or more defined contribution plans and 1 or more defined benefit plans or in connection with trusts or plans described in 2 or more of such paragraphs, the total amount deductible in a taxable year under such plans shall not exceed the greater of—

(i) 25 percent of the compensation otherwise paid or accrued during the taxable year to the beneficiaries under such plans, or

(ii) the amount of contributions made to or under the defined benefit plans to the extent such contributions do not exceed the amount of employer contributions necessary to satisfy the minimum funding standard provided by section 412 with respect to any such defined benefit plans for the plan year which ends with or within such taxable year (or for any prior plan year).

A defined contribution plan which is a pension plan shall not be treated as failing to provide definitely determinable benefits merely by limited employer contributions to amounts deductible under this section. For purposes of clause (ii), if paragraph (1)(D) applies to a defined benefit plan for any plan year, the amount necessary to satisfy the minimum funding standard provided by section 412 with respect to such plan for such plan year shall not be less than the unfunded current liability of such plan under section 412(l). *In the case of a defined benefit plan which is a single employer plan, the amount necessary to satisfy the minimum funding standard provided by section 412 shall not be less than the plan's funding shortfall determined under section 430.*

* * *

(C) PARAGRAPH NOT TO APPLY IN CERTAIN CASES.—

* * *

(iii) LIMITATION.—In the case of employer contributions to 1 or more defined contribution plans, this paragraph shall only apply to the extent that such contributions exceed 6 percent of the compensation otherwise paid or accrued during the taxable year to the beneficiaries under such plans. For purposes of this clause, amounts carried over from preceding taxable years under subparagraph (B) shall be treated as employer contributions to 1 or more defined contributions to the extent attributable to employer contributions to such plans in such preceding taxable years.

»»→ *Caution: Code Sec. 404(a)(7)(C)(iv), below, as added by H.R. 4, applies to years beginning after December 31, 2007.*

(iv) GUARANTEED PLANS.—In applying this paragraph, any single-employer plan covered under section 4021 of the Employee Retirement Income Security Act of 1974 shall not be taken into account.

(v) MULTIEMPLOYER PLANS.—In applying this paragraph, any multiemployer plan shall not be taken into account.

»»→ *Caution: Code Sec. 404(a)(7)(D), below, as amended by H.R. 4, applies to years beginning after December 31, 2007.*

(D) INSURANCE CONTRACT PLANS.—For purposes of this paragraph, a plan described in section 412(e)(3) shall be treated as a defined benefit plan.

* * *

[CCH Explanation at ¶ 705, ¶ 710 and ¶ 715. Committee Reports at ¶ 10,570 and ¶ 10,580,.]

Amendments

• **2006, Pension Protection Act of 2006 (H.R. 4)**

H.R. 4, § 801(a)(1):

Amended Code Sec. 404(a)(1)(A) by inserting "in the case of a defined benefit plan other than a multiemployer plan, in an amount determined under subsection (o), and in the case of any other plan" after "section 501(a),". **Effective** for years beginning after 12-31-2007.

H.R. 4, § 801(b):

Amended Code Sec. 404(a)(7)(C), as amended by this Act, by adding at the end a new clause (iv). **Effective** for years beginning after 12-31-2007.

H.R. 4, § 801(c)(1):

Amended the last sentence of Code Sec. 404(a)(1)(A) by striking "section 412" each place it appears and inserting "section 431". **Effective** for years beginning after 12-31-2007.

H.R. 4, § 801(c)(2)(A)-(E):

Amended Code Sec. 404(a)(1)(B) by striking "In the case of a plan" and inserting "In the case of a multiemployer plan", by striking "section 412(c)(7)" each place it appears and inserting "section 431(c)(6)", by striking "section 412(c)(7)(B)" and inserting "section 431(c)(6)(A)(ii)", by striking "412(c)(7)(A)" and inserting "section 431(c)(6)(A)(i)", and by striking "section 412" and inserting "section 431". **Effective** for years beginning after 12-31-2007.

H.R. 4, § 801(c)(3)(A)-(B):

Amended Code Sec. 404(a)(7), as amended by this Act, by adding at the end of subparagraph (A) a new sentence, and by striking subparagraph (D) and inserting a new subparagraph (D). **Effective** for years beginning after 12-31-2007. Prior to being stricken, Code Sec. 404(a)(7)(D) read as follows:

(D) SECTION 412(i) PLANS.—For purposes of this paragraph, any plan described in section 412(i) shall be treated as a defined benefit plan.

H.R. 4, § 801(d)(1):

Amended Code Sec. 404(a)(1)(D)(i) by striking "section 412(l)" and inserting "section 412(l)(8)(A), except that section 412(l)(8)(A) shall be applied for purposes of this clause by substituting '150 percent (140 percent in the case of a multiemployer plan) of current liability' for 'the current liability' in clause (i)". **Effective** for years beginning after 12-31-2005.

H.R. 4, § 801(d)(2):

Amended Code Sec. 404(a)(1) by striking subparagraph (F). **Effective** for years beginning after 12-31-2005. Prior to being stricken, Code Sec. 404(a)(1)(F) read as follows:

(F) ELECTION TO DISREGARD MODIFIED INTEREST RATE.—An employer may elect to disregard subsections (b)(5)(B)(ii)(II) and (l)(7)(C)(i)(IV) of section 412 solely for purposes of determining the interest rate used in calculating the maximum amount of the deduction allowable under this paragraph.

H.R. 4, § 802(a):

Amended Code Sec. 404(a)(1)(D), as amended by this Act. **Effective** for years beginning after 12-31-2007. Prior to amendment, Code Sec. 404(a)(1)(D) read as follows:

(D) SPECIAL RULE IN CASE OF CERTAIN PLANS.—

(i) IN GENERAL.—In the case of any defined benefit plan, except as provided in regulations, the maximum amount deductible under the limitations of this paragraph shall not be less than the unfunded current liability determined under section 412(l)(8)(A), except that section 412(l)(8)(A) shall be applied for purposes of this clause by substituting "150 percent (140 percent in the case of a multiemployer plan) of current liability" for "the current liability" in clause (i).

(ii) PLANS WITH 100 OR LESS PARTICIPANTS.—For purposes of this subparagraph, in the case of a plan which has 100 or less participants for the plan year, unfunded current liability shall not include the liability attributable to benefit increases for highly compensated employees (as defined in section 414(q)) resulting from a plan amendment which is made or becomes effective, whichever is later, within the last 2 years.

(iii) RULE FOR DETERMINING NUMBER OF PARTICIPANTS.—For purposes of determining the number of plan participants, all defined benefit plans maintained by the same employer (or any member of such employer's controlled group (within the meaning of section 412(l)(8)(C))) shall be treated as one plan, but only employees of such member or employer shall be taken into account.

(iv) SPECIAL RULE FOR TERMINATING PLANS.—In the case of a plan which, subject to section 4041 of the Employee Retirement Income Security Act of 1974, terminates during the plan year, clause (i) shall be applied by substituting for unfunded current liability the amount required to make the plan sufficient for benefit liabilities (within the meaning of section 4041(d) of such Act).

H.R. 4, § 803(a):

Amended Code Sec. 404(a)(7)(C) by adding after clause (ii) a new clause (iii). **Effective** for contributions for tax years beginning after 12-31-2005.

H.R. 4, § 803(b):

Amended Code Sec. 404(a)(7)(C), as amended by this Act, by adding at the end a new clause (v). **Effective** for contributions for tax years beginning after 12-31-2005.

»»→ Caution: Code Sec. 404(o), below, as added by H.R. 4, applies to years beginning after December 31, 2007.

(o) DEDUCTION LIMIT FOR SINGLE-EMPLOYER PLANS.—For purposes of subsection (a)(1)(A)—

(1) IN GENERAL.—In the case of a defined benefit plan to which subsection (a)(1)(A) applies (other than a multiemployer plan), the amount determined under this subsection for any taxable year shall be equal to the greater of—

(A) the sum of the amounts determined under paragraph (2) with respect to each plan year ending with or within the taxable year, or

(B) the sum of the minimum required contributions under section 430 for such plan years.

(2) DETERMINATION OF AMOUNT.—

(A) IN GENERAL.—The amount determined under this paragraph for any plan year shall be equal to the excess (if any) of—

(i) the sum of—

(I) the funding target for the plan year,

(II) the target normal cost for the plan year, and

(III) the cushion amount for the plan year, over

(ii) the value (determined under section 430(g)(2)) of the assets of the plan which are held by the plan as of the valuation date for the plan year.

(B) SPECIAL RULE FOR CERTAIN EMPLOYERS.—If section 430(i) does not apply to a plan for a plan year, the amount determined under subparagraph (A)(i) for the plan year shall in no event be less than the sum of—

(i) the funding target for the plan year (determined as if section 430(i) applied to the plan), plus

(ii) the target normal cost for the plan year (as so determined).

(3) CUSHION AMOUNT.—For purposes of paragraph (2)(A)(i)(III)—

(A) IN GENERAL.—The cushion amount for any plan year is the sum of—

(i) 50 percent of the funding target for the plan year, and

(ii) the amount by which the funding target for the plan year would increase if the plan were to take into account—

(I) increases in compensation which are expected to occur in succeeding plan years, or

(II) if the plan does not base benefits for service to date on compensation, increases in benefits which are expected to occur in succeeding plan years (determined on the basis of the average annual increase in benefits over the 6 immediately preceding plan years).

(B) LIMITATIONS.—

(i) IN GENERAL.—In making the computation under subparagraph (A)(ii), the plan's actuary shall assume that the limitations under subsection (l) and section 415(b) shall apply.

(ii) EXPECTED INCREASES.—In the case of a plan year during which a plan is covered under section 4021 of the Employee Retirement Income Security Act of 1974, the plan's actuary may, notwithstanding subsection (l), take into account increases in the limitations which are expected to occur in succeeding plan years.

(4) SPECIAL RULES FOR PLANS WITH 100 OR FEWER PARTICIPANTS.—

(A) IN GENERAL.—For purposes of determining the amount under paragraph (3) for any plan year, in the case of a plan which has 100 or fewer participants for the plan year, the liability of the plan attributable to benefit increases for highly compensated employees (as defined in section 414(q)) resulting from a plan amendment which is made or becomes effective, whichever is later, within the last 2 years shall not be taken into account in determining the target liability.

(B) RULE FOR DETERMINING NUMBER OF PARTICIPANTS.—For purposes of determining the number of plan participants, all defined benefit plans maintained by the same employer (or any member of such employer's controlled group (within the meaning of section 412(f)(4))) shall be treated as one plan, but only participants of such member or employer shall be taken into account.

(5) SPECIAL RULE FOR TERMINATING PLANS.—In the case of a plan which, subject to section 4041 of the Employee Retirement Income Security Act of 1974, terminates during the plan year, the amount determined under paragraph (2) shall in no event be less than the amount required to make the plan sufficient for benefit liabilities (within the meaning of section 4041(d) of such Act).

(6) ACTUARIAL ASSUMPTIONS.—Any computation under this subsection for any plan year shall use the same actuarial assumptions which are used for the plan year under section 430.

(7) DEFINITIONS.—Any term used in this subsection which is also used in section 430 shall have the same meaning given such term by section 430.

[CCH Explanation at ¶ 705. Committee Reports at ¶ 10,570.]

Amendments

• **2006, Pension Protection Act of 2006 (H.R. 4)**

H.R. 4, §801(a)(2):

Amended Code Sec. 404 by inserting at the end a new subsection (o). **Effective** for years beginning after 12-31-2007.

[¶ 5050] CODE SEC. 404A. DEDUCTION FOR CERTAIN FOREIGN DEFERRED COMPENSATION PLANS.

* * *

(g) OTHER SPECIAL RULES.—

* * *

(3) ACTUARIAL ASSUMPTIONS MUST BE REASONABLE; FULL FUNDING.—

»»→ *Caution: Code Sec. 404A(g)(3)(A), below, as amended by H.R. 4, applies to years beginning after December 31, 2007.*

(A) IN GENERAL.—Except as provided in subparagraph (B), principles similar to those set forth in *paragraphs (3) and (6) of section 431(c)* shall apply for purposes of this section.

(B) INTEREST RATE FOR RESERVE PLAN.—

(i) IN GENERAL.—In the case of a qualified reserve plan, in lieu of taking rates of interest into account under subparagraph (A), the rate of interest for the plan shall be the rate selected by the taxpayer which is within the permissible range.

(ii) RATE REMAINS IN EFFECT SO LONG AS IT FALLS WITHIN PERMISSIBLE RANGE.—Any rate selected by the taxpayer for the plan under this subparagraph shall remain in effect for such plan until the first taxable year for which such rate is no longer within the permissible range. At such time, the taxpayer shall select a new rate of interest which is within the permissible range applicable at such time.

(iii) PERMISSIBLE RANGE.—For purposes of this subparagraph, the term "permissible range" means a rate of interest which is not more than 20 percent above, and not more than 20 percent below, the average rate of interest for long-term corporate bonds in the appropriate country for the 15-year period ending on the last day before the beginning of the taxable year.

* * *

[CCH Explanation at ¶ 705. Committee Reports at ¶ 10,570.]

Amendments

• **2006, Pension Protection Act of 2006 (H.R. 4)**

H.R. 4, §801(c)(4):

Amended Code Sec. 404A(g)(3)(A) by striking "paragraphs (3) and (7) of section 412(c)" and inserting "paragraphs (3) and (6) of section 431(c)". **Effective** for years beginning after 12-31-2007.

[¶ 5055] CODE SEC. 408. INDIVIDUAL RETIREMENT ACCOUNTS.

* * *

(d) TAX TREATMENT OF DISTRIBUTIONS.—

* * *

(8) DISTRIBUTIONS FOR CHARITABLE PURPOSES.—

(A) IN GENERAL.—So much of the aggregate amount of qualified charitable distributions with respect to a taxpayer made during any taxable year which does not exceed $100,000 shall not be includible in gross income of such taxpayer for such taxable year.

(B) QUALIFIED CHARITABLE DISTRIBUTION.—For purposes of this paragraph, the term "qualified charitable distribution" means any distribution from an individual retirement plan (other than a plan described in subsection (k) or (p))—

(i) which is made directly by the trustee to an organization described in section 170(b)(1)(A) (other than any organization described in section 509(a)(3) or any fund or account described in section 4966(d)(2)), and

(ii) which is made on or after the date that the individual for whose benefit the plan is maintained has attained age 70½.

A distribution shall be treated as a qualified charitable distribution only to the extent that the distribution would be includible in gross income without regard to subparagraph (A).

(C) CONTRIBUTIONS MUST BE OTHERWISE DEDUCTIBLE.—For purposes of this paragraph, a distribution to an organization described in subparagraph (B)(i) shall be treated as a qualified charitable distribution only if a deduction for the entire distribution would be allowable under section 170 (determined without regard to subsection (b) thereof and this paragraph).

(D) APPLICATION OF SECTION 72.—Notwithstanding section 72, in determining the extent to which a distribution is a qualified charitable distribution, the entire amount of the distribution shall be treated as includible in gross income without regard to subparagraph (A) to the extent that such amount does not exceed the aggregate amount which would have been so includible if all amounts distributed from all individual retirement plans were treated as 1 contract under paragraph (2)(A) for purposes of determining the inclusion of such distribution under section 72. Proper adjustments shall be made in applying section 72 to other distributions in such taxable year and subsequent taxable years.

(E) DENIAL OF DEDUCTION.—Qualified charitable distributions which are not includible in gross income pursuant to subparagraph (A) shall not be taken into account in determining the deduction under section 170.

(F) TERMINATION.—This paragraph shall not apply to distributions made in taxable years beginning after December 31, 2007.

* * *

[CCH Explanation at ¶ 1105. Committee Reports at ¶ 10,600 and ¶ 11,110.]

Amendments

• **2006, Pension Protection Act of 2006 (H.R. 4)**

H.R. 4, §1201(a):

Amended Code Sec. 408(d) by adding at the end a new paragraph (8). **Effective** for distributions made in tax years beginning after 12-31-2005.

[¶ 5060] CODE SEC. 408A. ROTH IRAS.

* * *

(c) TREATMENT OF CONTRIBUTIONS.—

* * *

(3) LIMITS BASED ON MODIFIED ADJUSTED GROSS INCOME.—

* * *

»»→ Caution: Code Sec. 408A(c)(3)(B), below, as amended by H.R. 4, but prior to being stricken by P.L. 109-222, applies to distributions after December 31, 2007, and tax years beginning on or before December 31, 2009.

(B) ROLLOVER FROM *ELIGIBLE RETIREMENT PLAN*.—A taxpayer shall not be allowed to make a qualified rollover contribution to a Roth IRA from an *an* [sic] *eligible retirement plan (as defined by section 402(c)(8)(B))* other than a Roth IRA during any taxable year if, for the taxable year of the distribution to which such contribution relates—

(i) the taxpayer's adjusted gross income exceeds $100,000, or

(ii) the taxpayer is a married individual filing a separate return.

»»→ Caution: Code Sec. 408(c)(3)(C), below, as added by H.R. 4, applies to tax years beginning after 2006.

(C) INFLATION ADJUSTMENT.—In the case of any taxable year beginning in a calendar year after 2006, the dollar amounts in subclauses (I) and (II) of subparagraph (C)(ii) [sic] *shall each be increased by an amount equal to—*

(i) such dollar amount, multiplied by

(ii) the cost-of-living adjustment determined under section 1(f)(3) for the calendar year in which the taxable year begins, determined by substituting "calendar year 2005" for "calendar year 1992" in subparagraph (B) thereof.

Any increase determined under the preceding sentence shall be rounded to the nearest multiple of $1,000.

* * *

[CCH Explanation at ¶ 935 and ¶ 1320. Committee Reports at ¶ 10,650 and ¶ 10,740.]

Amendments

• 2006, Pension Protection Act of 2006 (H.R. 4)

H.R. 4, § 824(b)(1)(A)-(B):

Amended Code Sec. 408A(c)(3)(B), as in effect before the Tax Increase Prevention and Reconciliation Act of 2005 (P.L. 109-222), in the text by striking "individual retirement plan" and inserting "an eligible retirement plan (as defined by section 402(c)(8)(B))", and in the heading by striking "IRA" the first place it appears [sic] and inserting "ELIGIBLE RETIREMENT PLAN". **Effective** for distributions after 12-31-2007.

H.R. 4, § 833(c):

Amended Code Sec. 408A(c)(3) by adding at the end a new subparagraph (C). **Effective** for tax years beginning after 2006.

(d) DISTRIBUTION RULES.—For purposes of this title—

* * *

»»→ Caution: Code Sec. 408A(d)(3), below, as amended by H.R. 4, applies to distributions after December 31, 2007.

(3) ROLLOVERS FROM AN *ELIGIBLE RETIREMENT PLAN* OTHER THAN A ROTH IRA.—

(A) IN GENERAL.—Notwithstanding *sections 402(c), 403(b)(8), 408(d)(3), and 457(e)(16)*, in the case of any distribution to which this paragraph applies—

* * *

(B) DISTRIBUTIONS TO WHICH PARAGRAPH APPLIES.—This paragraph shall apply to a distribution from an *eligible retirement plan (as defined by section 402(c)(8)(B))* (other than a Roth IRA) maintained for the benefit of an individual which is contributed to a Roth IRA maintained for the benefit of such individual in a qualified rollover contribution.

* * *

(D) ADDITIONAL REPORTING REQUIREMENTS.—Trustees of Roth IRAs, trustees of individual retirement plans, *persons subject to section 6047(d)(1), or all of the foregoing persons*, whichever is appropriate, shall include such additional information in reports required under section 408(i) *or 6047* as the Secretary may require to ensure that amounts required to be included in gross income under subparagraph (A) are so included.

* * *

[CCH Explanation at ¶ 935. Committee Reports at ¶ 10,650.]

Amendments

• 2006, Pension Protection Act of 2006 (H.R. 4)

H.R. 4, § 824(b)(2)(A)-(E):

Amended Code Sec. 408A(d)(3) by striking "section 408(d)(3)" [and] inserting "sections 402(c), 403(b)(8), 408(d)(3), and 457(e)(16)" in subparagraph (A), by striking "individual retirement plan" and inserting "eligible retirement plan (as defined by section 402(c)(8)(B))" in subparagraph (B), by inserting "or 6047" after "408(i)" in subparagraph (D), by striking "or both" and inserting "persons subject to section 6047(d)(1), or all of the foregoing persons" in subparagraph (D), and by striking "IRA" the first place it appears in the heading and inserting "ELIGIBLE RETIREMENT PLAN". **Effective** for distributions after 12-31-2007.

»»→ Caution: Code Sec. 408A(e), below, as amended by H.R. 4, applies to distributions after December 31, 2007.

(e) QUALIFIED ROLLOVER CONTRIBUTION.—For purposes of this section, the term "qualified rollover contribution" means a rollover contribution—

(1) to a Roth IRA from another such account,

(2) from an eligible retirement plan, but only if—

(A) in the case of an individual retirement plan, such rollover contribution meets the requirements of section 408(d)(3), and

(B) in the case of any eligible retirement plan (as defined in section 402(c)(8)(B) other than clauses (i) and (ii) thereof), such rollover contribution meets the requirements of section 402(c), 403(b)(8), or 457(e)(16), as applicable.

For purposes of section 408(d)(3)(B), there shall be disregarded any qualified rollover contribution from an individual retirement plan (other than a Roth IRA) to a Roth IRA.

* * *

[CCH Explanation at ¶ 935. Committee Reports at ¶ 10,650.]

Amendments

• 2006, Pension Protection Act of 2006 (H.R. 4)

H.R. 4, § 824(a):

Amended Code Sec. 408A(e). **Effective** for distributions after 12-31-2007. Prior to amendment, Code Sec. 408A(e) read as follows:

(e) QUALIFIED ROLLOVER CONTRIBUTION.—For purposes of this section, the term "qualified rollover contribution" means a rollover contribution to a Roth IRA from another such account, or from an individual retirement plan, but only if such rollover contribution meets the requirements of section 408(d)(3). Such term includes a rollover contribution described in section 402A(c)(3)(A). For purposes of section 408(d)(3)(B), there shall be disregarded any qualified rollover contribution from an individual retirement plan (other than a Roth IRA) to a Roth IRA.

[¶ 5065] CODE SEC. 409. QUALIFICATIONS FOR TAX CREDIT EMPLOYEE STOCK OWNERSHIP PLANS.

* * *

(h) RIGHT TO DEMAND EMPLOYER SECURITIES; PUT OPTION.—

* * *

»»→ Caution: Code Sec. 409(h)(7), below, as amended by H.R. 4, applies generally to plan years beginning after December 31, 2006.

(7) EXCEPTION WHERE EMPLOYEE ELECTED DIVERSIFICATION.—Paragraph (1)(A) shall not apply with respect to the portion of the participant's account which the employee elected to have reinvested under section 401(a)(28)(B) *or subparagraph (B) or (C) of section 401(a)(35).*

* * *

[CCH Explanation at ¶ 605. Committee Reports at ¶ 10,950.]

Amendments

• 2006, Pension Protection Act of 2006 (H.R. 4)

H.R. 4, § 901(a)(2)(B):

Amended Code Sec. 409(h)(7) by inserting "or subparagraph (B) or (C) of section 401(a)(35)" before the period at the end. For the **effective** date, see Act Sec. 901(c), below.

H.R. 4, § 901(c), provides:

(c) EFFECTIVE DATES.—

(1) IN GENERAL.—Except as provided in paragraphs (2) and (3), the amendments made by this section shall apply to plan years beginning after December 31, 2006.

(2) SPECIAL RULE FOR COLLECTIVELY BARGAINED AGREEMENTS.—In the case of a plan maintained pursuant to 1 or more collective bargaining agreements between employee representatives and 1 or more employers ratified on or before the date of the enactment of this Act, paragraph (1) shall be applied to benefits pursuant to, and individuals covered by, any such agreement by substituting for "December 31, 2006" the earlier of—

(A) the later of—

(i) December 31, 2007, or

(ii) the date on which the last of such collective bargaining agreements terminates (determined without regard to any extension thereof after such date of enactment), or

(B) December 31, 2008.

(3) SPECIAL RULE FOR CERTAIN EMPLOYER SECURITIES HELD IN AN ESOP.—

(A) IN GENERAL.—In the case of employer securities to which this paragraph applies, the amendments made by this section shall apply to plan years beginning after the earlier of—

(i) December 31, 2007, or

(ii) the first date on which the fair market value of such securities exceeds the guaranteed minimum value described in subparagraph (B)(ii).

(B) APPLICABLE SECURITIES.—This paragraph shall apply to employer securities which are attributable to employer contributions other than elective deferrals, and which, on September 17, 2003—

(i) consist of preferred stock, and

(ii) are within an employee stock ownership plan (as defined in section 4975(e)(7) of the Internal Revenue Code of 1986), the terms of which provide that the value of the securities cannot be less than the guaranteed minimum value specified by the plan on such date.

(C) COORDINATION WITH TRANSITION RULE.—In applying section 401(a)(35)(H) of the Internal Revenue Code of 1986 and section 204(j)(7) of the Employee Retirement Income Security Act of 1974 (as added by this section) to employer securities to which this paragraph applies, the applicable percentage shall be determined without regard to this paragraph.

[¶ 5070] CODE SEC. 409A. INCLUSION IN GROSS INCOME OF DEFERRED COMPENSATION UNDER NONQUALIFIED DEFERRED COMPENSATION PLANS.

* * *

(b) RULES RELATING TO FUNDING.—

* * *

(3) TREATMENT OF EMPLOYER'S DEFINED BENEFIT PLAN DURING RESTRICTED PERIOD.—

(A) IN GENERAL.—If-

(i) during any restricted period with respect to a single-employer defined benefit plan, assets are set aside or reserved (directly or indirectly) in a trust (or other arrangement as determined by the Secretary) or transferred to such a trust or other arrangement for purposes of paying deferred compensation of an applicable covered employee under a nonqualified deferred compensation plan of the plan sponsor or member of a controlled group which includes the plan sponsor, or

(ii) a nonqualified deferred compensation plan of the plan sponsor or member of a controlled group which includes the plan sponsor provides that assets will become restricted to the provision of benefits under the plan in connection with such restricted period (or other similar financial measure determined by the Secretary) with respect to the defined benefit plan, or assets are so restricted,

such assets shall, for purposes of section 83, be treated as property transferred in connection with the performance of services whether or not such assets are available to satisfy claims of general creditors. Clause (i) shall not apply with respect to any assets which are so set aside before the restricted period with respect to the defined benefit plan.

(B) RESTRICTED PERIOD.—For purposes of this section, the term "restricted period" means, with respect to any plan described in subparagraph (A)—

(i) any period during which the plan is in at-risk status (as defined in section 430(i));

(ii) any period the plan sponsor is a debtor in a case under title 11, United States Code, or similar Federal or State law, and

(iii) the 12-month period beginning on the date which is 6 months before the termination date of the plan if, as of the termination date, the plan is not sufficient for benefit liabilities (within the meaning of section 4041 of the Employee Retirement Income Security Act of 1974).

(C) SPECIAL RULE FOR PAYMENT OF TAXES ON DEFERRED COMPENSATION INCLUDED IN INCOME.—If an employer provides directly or indirectly for the payment of any Federal, State, or local income taxes

with respect to any compensation required to be included in gross income by reason of this paragraph—

(i) interest shall be imposed under subsection (a)(1)(B)(i)(I) on the amount of such payment in the same manner as if such payment was part of the deferred compensation to which it relates,

(ii) such payment shall be taken into account in determining the amount of the additional tax under subsection (a)(1)(B)(i)(II) in the same manner as if such payment was part of the deferred compensation to which it relates, and

(iii) no deduction shall be allowed under this title with respect to such payment.

(D) OTHER DEFINITIONS.—For purposes of this section—

(i) APPLICABLE COVERED EMPLOYEE.—The term "applicable covered employee" means any—

(I) covered employee of a plan sponsor,

(II) covered employee of a member of a controlled group which includes the plan sponsor, and

(III) former employee who was a covered employee at the time of termination of employment with the plan sponsor or a member of a controlled group which includes the plan sponsor.

(ii) COVERED EMPLOYEE.—The term "covered employee" means an individual described in section 162(m)(3) or an individual subject to the requirements of section 16(a) of the Securities Exchange Act of 1934.

(4) INCOME INCLUSION FOR OFFSHORE TRUSTS AND EMPLOYER'S FINANCIAL HEALTH.—For each taxable year that assets treated as transferred under this subsection remain set aside in a trust or other arrangement subject to *paragraph (1), (2), or (3)*, any increase in value in, or earnings with respect to, such assets shall be treated as an additional transfer of property under this subsection (to the extent not previously included in income).

(5) INTEREST ON TAX LIABILITY PAYABLE WITH RESPECT TO TRANSFERRED PROPERTY.—

(A) IN GENERAL.—If amounts are required to be included in gross income by reason of *paragraph (1), (2), or (3)* for a taxable year, the tax imposed by this chapter for such taxable year shall be increased by the sum of—

(i) the amount of interest determined under subparagraph (B), and

(ii) an amount equal to 20 percent of the amounts required to be included in gross income.

(B) INTEREST.—For purposes of subparagraph (A), the interest determined under this subparagraph for any taxable year is the amount of interest at the underpayment rate plus 1 percentage point on the underpayments that would have occurred had the amounts so required to be included in gross income by *paragraph (1), (2), or (3)* been includible in gross income for the taxable year in which first deferred or, if later, the first taxable year in which such amounts are not subject to a substantial risk of forfeiture.

* * *

[CCH Explanation at ¶ 220. Committee Reports at ¶ 10,070.]

Amendments

• 2006, Pension Protection Act of 2006 (H.R. 4)

H.R. 4, §116(a):

Amended Code Sec. 409A(b) by redesignating paragraphs (3) and (4) as paragraphs (4) and (5), respectively, and by inserting after paragraph (2) a new paragraph (3). **Effective** for transfers or other reservation of assets after 8-17-2006.

H.R. 4, §116(b):

Amended Code Sec. 409A(b)(4)-(5), as redesignated by Act Sec. 116(a), by striking "paragraph (1) or (2)" each place it appears and inserting "paragraph (1), (2), or (3)". **Effective** for transfers or other reservation of assets after 8-17-2006.

[¶ 5075] CODE SEC. 410. MINIMUM PARTICIPATION STANDARDS

* * *

(b) MINIMUM COVERAGE REQUIREMENTS.—

* * *

(3) EXCLUSION OF CERTAIN EMPLOYEES.—For purposes of this subsection, there shall be excluded from consideration—

(A) employees who are included in a unit of employees covered by an agreement which the Secretary of Labor finds to be a collective bargaining agreement between employee representatives and one or more employers, if there is evidence that retirement benefits were the subject of good faith bargaining between such employee representatives and such employer or employers,

(B) in the case of a trust established or maintained pursuant to an agreement which the Secretary of Labor finds to be a collective bargaining agreement between air pilots represented in accordance with title II of the Railway Labor Act and one or more employers, all employees not covered by such agreement, and

(C) employees who are nonresident aliens and who receive no earned income (within the meaning of section 911(d)(2)) from the employer which constitutes income from sources within the United States (within the meaning of section 861(a)(3)).

Subparagraph (A) shall not apply with respect to coverage of employees under a plan pursuant to an agreement under such subparagraph. *For purposes of subparagraph (B), management pilots who are not represented in accordance with title II of the Railway Labor Act shall be treated as covered by a collective bargaining agreement described in such subparagraph if the management pilots manage the flight operations of air pilots who are so represented and the management pilots are, pursuant to the terms of the agreement, included in the group of employees benefitting under the trust described in such subparagraph. Subparagraph (B) shall not apply in the case of a plan which provides contributions or benefits for employees whose principal duties are not customarily performed aboard an aircraft in flight (other than management pilots described in the preceding sentence).*

* * *

[CCH Explanation at ¶ 245. Committee Reports at ¶ 10,230.]

Amendments

• 2006, Pension Protection Act of 2006 (H.R. 4)

H.R. 4, § 402(h)(1):

Amended Code Sec. 410(b)(3) by striking the last sentence and inserting two new sentences in its place. **Effective** for years beginning before, on, or after 8-17-2006. Prior to being stricken, the last sentence of Code Sec. 410(b)(3) read as follows:

Subparagraph (B) shall not apply in the case of a plan which provides contributions or benefits for employees whose principal duties are not customarily performed aboard aircraft in flight.

[¶ 5080] CODE SEC. 411. MINIMUM VESTING STANDARDS.

(a) GENERAL RULE.—A trust shall not constitute a qualified trust under section 401(a) unless the plan of which such trust is a part provides that an employee's right to his normal retirement benefit is nonforfeitable upon the attainment of normal retirement age (as defined in paragraph (8)) and in addition satisfies the requirements of paragraphs (1), (2), and (11) of this subsection and the requirements of subsection (b)(3), and also satisfies, in the case of a defined benefit plan, the requirements of subsection (b)(1) and, in the case of a defined contribution plan, the requirements of subsection (b)(2).

* * *

»»→ Caution: Code Sec. 411(a)(2), below, as amended by H.R. 4, applies generally to contributions for plan years beginning after December 31, 2006.

(2) EMPLOYER CONTRIBUTIONS.—

(A) DEFINED BENEFIT PLANS.—

(i) IN GENERAL.—In the case of a defined benefit plan, a plan satisfies the requirements of this paragraph if it satisfies the requirements of clause (ii) or (iii).

(ii) 5-YEAR VESTING.—A plan satisfies the requirements of this clause if an employee who has completed at least 5 years of service has a nonforfeitable right to 100 percent of the employee's accrued benefit derived from employer contributions.

(iii) 3 TO 7 YEAR VESTING.—A plan satisfies the requirements of this clause if an employee has a nonforfeitable right to a percentage of the employee's accrued benefit derived from employer contributions determined under the following table:

Years of service:	*The nonforfeitable percentage is:*
3	20
4	40
5	60
6	80
7 or more	100 .

(B) DEFINED CONTRIBUTION PLANS.—

(i) IN GENERAL.—In the case of a defined contribution plan, a plan satisfies the requirements of this paragraph if it satisfies the requirements of clause (ii) or (iii).

(ii) 3-YEAR VESTING.—A plan satisfies the requirements of this clause if an employee who has completed at least 3 years of service has a nonforfeitable right to 100 percent of the employee's accrued benefit derived from employer contributions.

(iii) 2 TO 6 YEAR VESTING.—A plan satisfies the requirements of this clause if an employee has a nonforfeitable right to a percentage of the employee's accrued benefit derived from employer contributions determined under the following table:

Years of service:	*The nonforfeitable percentage is:*
2	20
3	40
4	60
5	80
6 or more	100 .

(3) CERTAIN PERMITTED FORFEITURES, SUSPENSIONS, ETC.—For purposes of this subsection—

* * *

(C) EFFECT OF RETROACTIVE PLAN AMENDMENTS.—A right to an accrued benefit derived from employer contributions shall not be treated as forfeitable solely because plan amendments may be given retroactive application as provided in *section 412(c)(2).*

* * *

Caution: Code Sec. 411(a)(3)(G), below, as amended by H.R. 4, applies to plan years beginning after December 31, 2007.

(G) TREATMENT OF MATCHING CONTRIBUTIONS FORFEITED BY REASON OF EXCESS DEFERRAL OR CONTRIBUTION *OR ERRONEOUS AUTOMATIC CONTRIBUTION*.—A matching contribution (within the meaning of section 401(m)) shall not be treated as forfeitable merely because such contribution is forfeitable if the contribution to which the matching contribution relates is treated as an excess contribution under section 401(k)(8)(B), an excess deferral under section 402(g)(2)(A), *an erroneous automatic contribution under section 414(w),* or an excess aggregate contribution under section 401(m)(6)(B).

* * *

»»→ *Caution: Code Sec. 411(a)(12), below, was stricken by H.R. 4, generally applicable to contributions for plan years beginning after December 31, 2006.*

(12) FASTER VESTING FOR MATCHING CONTRIBUTIONS.—In the case of matching contributions (as defined in section 401(m)(4)(A)), paragraph (2) shall be applied—

(A) by substituting "3 years" for "5 years" in subparagraph (A), and

(B) by substituting the following table for the table contained in subparagraph (B):

Years of service:	*The nonforfeitable percentage is:*
2	20
3	40
4	60
5	80
6 or more	100.

(13) SPECIAL RULES FOR PLANS COMPUTING ACCRUED BENEFITS BY REFERENCE TO HYPOTHETICAL ACCOUNT BALANCE OR EQUIVALENT AMOUNTS.—

(A) IN GENERAL.—An applicable defined benefit plan shall not be treated as failing to meet—

(i) subject to paragraph (2) [subparagraph (B)], the requirements of subsection (a)(2), or

(ii) the requirements of subsection (c) or section 417(e) with respect to contributions other than employee contributions,

solely because the present value of the accrued benefit (or any portion thereof) of any participant is, under the terms of the plan, equal to the amount expressed as the balance in the hypothetical account described in paragraph (3) [subparagraph (C)] or as an accumulated percentage of the participant's final average compensation.

(B) 3-YEAR VESTING.—In the case of an applicable defined benefit plan, such plan shall be treated as meeting the requirements of subsection (a)(2) only if an employee who has completed at least 3 years of service has a nonforfeitable right to 100 percent of the employee's accrued benefit derived from employer contributions.

(C) APPLICABLE DEFINED BENEFIT PLAN AND RELATED RULES.—For purposes of this subsection—

(i) IN GENERAL.—The term "applicable defined benefit plan" means a defined benefit plan under which the accrued benefit (or any portion thereof) is calculated as the balance of a hypothetical account maintained for the participant or as an accumulated percentage of the participant's final average compensation.

(ii) REGULATIONS TO INCLUDE SIMILAR PLANS.—The Secretary shall issue regulations which include in the definition of an applicable defined benefit plan any defined benefit plan (or any portion of such a plan) which has an effect similar to an applicable defined benefit plan.

[CCH Explanation at ¶ 205, ¶ 720, ¶ 1005 and ¶ 1015. Committee Reports at ¶ 10,010, ¶ 10,560, ¶ 10,960 and ¶ 10,980.]

Amendments

• **2006, Pension Protection Act of 2006 (H.R. 4)**

H.R. 4, §114(b)(1):

Amended Code Sec. 411(a)(3)(C) by striking "section 412(c)(8)" and inserting "section 412(c)(2)". **Effective** 8-17-2006.

H.R. 4, §701(b)(2):

Amended Code Sec. 411(a) by adding at the end a new paragraph (13). **Effective** generally for distributions made after 8-17-2006. For special rules, see Act Sec. 701(d) and (e)(3)-(5), below.

H.R. 4, §701(d), provides:

(d) NO INFERENCE.—Nothing in the amendments made by this section shall be construed to create an inference with respect to—

(1) the treatment of applicable defined benefit plans or conversions to applicable defined benefit plans under sections 204(b)(1)(H) of the Employee Retirement Income Security Act of 1974, 4(i)(1) of the Age Discrimination in Employment Act of 1967, and 411(b)(1)(H) of the Internal Revenue Code of 1986, as in effect before such amendments, or

(2) the determination of whether an applicable defined benefit plan fails to meet the requirements of sections 203(a)(2), 204(c), or 204(g) of the Employee Retirement Income Security Act of 1974 or sections 411(a)(2), 411(c), or 417(e) of such Code, as in effect before such amendments, solely because the present value of the accrued benefit (or any portion thereof) of any participant is, under the terms of the plan, equal to the amount expressed as the balance in a hypothetical account or as an accumulated percentage of the participant's final average compensation.

For purposes of this subsection, the term "applicable defined benefit plan" has the meaning given such term by section 203(f)(3) of the Employee Retirement Income Security Act of 1974 and section 411(a)(13)(C) of such Code, as in effect after such amendments.

H.R. 4, §701(e)(3)-(5), provides:

(3) VESTING AND INTEREST CREDIT REQUIREMENTS.—In the case of a plan in existence on June 29, 2005, the requirements of clause (i) of section 411(b)(5)(B) of the Internal Revenue Code of 1986, clause (i) of section 204(b)(5)(B) of the Employee Retirement Income Security Act of 1974, and clause (i) of section 4(i)(10)(B) of the Age Discrimination in Employment Act of 1967 (as added by this Act) and the requirements of 203(f)(2) of the Employee Retirement Income Security Act of 1974 and section 411(a)(13)(B) of the Internal Revenue Code of 1986 (as so added) shall, for purposes of applying the amendments made by subsections (a) and (b), apply to years beginning after December 31, 2007, unless the plan sponsor elects the application of such requirements for any period after June 29, 2005, and before the first year beginning after December 31, 2007.

(4) SPECIAL RULE FOR COLLECTIVELY BARGAINED PLANS.—In the case of a plan maintained pursuant to 1 or more collective bargaining agreements between employee representatives and 1 or more employers ratified on or before the date of the enactment of this Act, the requirements described in paragraph (3) shall, for purposes of applying the amendments made by subsections (a) and (b), not apply to plan years beginning before—

(A) the earlier of—

(i) the date on which the last of such collective bargaining agreements terminates (determined without regard to any extension thereof on or after such date of enactment), or

(ii) January 1, 2008, or

(B) January 1, 2010.

(5) CONVERSIONS.—The requirements of clause (ii) of section 411(b)(5)(B) of the Internal Revenue Code of 1986, clause (ii) of section 204(b)(5)(B) of the Employee Retirement Income Security Act of 1974, and clause (ii) of section 4(i)(10)(B) of the Age Discrimination in Employment Act of 1967 (as added by this Act), shall apply to plan amendments adopted after, and taking effect after, June 29, 2005, except that the plan sponsor may elect to have such amendments apply to plan amendments adopted before, and taking effect after, such date.

H.R. 4, §902(d)(2)(A):

Amended Code Sec. 411(a)(3)(G) by inserting "an erroneous automatic contribution under section 414(w)," after "402(g)(2)(A),". **Effective** for plan years beginning after 12-31-2007.

H.R. 4, §902(d)(2)(B):

Amended the heading of Code Sec. 411(a)(3)(G) by inserting "OR ERRONEOUS AUTOMATIC CONTRIBUTION" before the period. **Effective** for plan years beginning after 12-31-2007.

H.R. 4, §904(a)(1):

Amended Code Sec. 411(a)(2). For the **effective** date, see Act Sec. 904(c), below. Prior to amendment, Code Sec. 411(a)(2) read as follows:

(2) EMPLOYER CONTRIBUTIONS.—Except as provided in paragraph (12), a plan satisfies the requirements of this paragraph if it satisfies the requirements of subparagraph (A) or (B).

(A) 5-YEAR VESTING.—A plan satisfies the requirements of this subparagraph if an employee who has completed at least 5 years of service has a nonforfeitable right to 100 percent of the employee's accrued benefit derived from employer contributions.

(B) 3 TO 7 YEAR VESTING.—A plan satisfies the requirements of this subparagraph if an employee has a nonforfeitable right to a percentage of the employee's accrued benefit derived from employer contributions determined under the following table:

Years of service:	*The nonforfeitable percentage is:*
3	20
4	40
5	60
6	80
7 or more	100

H.R. 4, §904(a)(2):

Amended Code Sec. 411(a) by striking paragraph (12). For the **effective** date, see Act Sec. 904(c), below. Prior to being stricken, Code Sec. 411(a)(12) read as follows:

(12) FASTER VESTING FOR MATCHING CONTRIBUTIONS.—In the case of matching contributions (as defined in section 401(m)(4)(A)), paragraph (2) shall be applied—

(A) by substituting "3 years" for "5 years" in subparagraph (A), and

(B) by substituting the following table for the table contained in subparagraph (B):

Years of service:	*The nonforfeitable percentage is:*
2	20
3	40
4	60
5	80
6 or more	100.

H.R. 4, §904(c), provides:

(c) EFFECTIVE DATES.—

(1) IN GENERAL.—Except as provided in paragraphs (2) and (4), the amendments made by this section shall apply to contributions for plan years beginning after December 31, 2006.

(2) COLLECTIVE BARGAINING AGREEMENTS.—In the case of a plan maintained pursuant to one or more collective bargaining agreements between employee representatives and one or more employers ratified before the date of the enactment of this Act, the amendments made by this section shall not apply to contributions on behalf of employees covered by any such agreement for plan years beginning before the earlier of—

(A) the later of—

(i) the date on which the last of such collective bargaining agreements terminates (determined without regard to any extension thereof on or after such date of the enactment); or

(ii) January 1, 2007; or

(B) January 1, 2009.

(3) SERVICE REQUIRED.—With respect to any plan, the amendments made by this section shall not apply to any employee before the date that such employee has 1 hour of service under such plan in any plan year to which the amendments made by this section apply.

(4) SPECIAL RULE FOR STOCK OWNERSHIP PLANS.—Notwithstanding paragraph (1) or (2), in the case of an employee stock ownership plan (as defined in section 4975(e)(7) of the Internal Revenue Code of 1986) which had outstanding on September 26, 2005, a loan incurred for the purpose of acquiring qualifying employer securities (as defined in section 4975(e)(8) of such Code), the amendments made by this section shall not apply to any plan year beginning before the earlier of—

(A) the date on which the loan is fully repaid, or

(B) the date on which the loan was, as of September 26, 2005, scheduled to be fully repaid.

(b) ACCRUED BENEFIT REQUIREMENTS.—

(1) DEFINED BENEFIT PLANS.—

* * *

(F) CERTAIN INSURED DEFINED BENEFIT PLANS.—Notwithstanding subparagraphs (A), (B), and (C), a defined benefit plan satisfies the requirements of this paragraph if such plan—

(i) is funded exclusively by the purchase of insurance contracts, and

(ii) satisfies the requirements of *subparagraphs (B) and (C) of section 412(e)(3)* (relating to certain insurance contract plans),

but only if an employee's accrued benefit as of any applicable date is not less than the cash surrender value his insurance contracts would have on such applicable date if the requirements of *subparagraphs (D), (E), and (F) of section 412(e)(3)* were satisfied.

* * *

(5) SPECIAL RULES RELATING TO AGE.—

(A) COMPARISON TO SIMILARLY SITUATED YOUNGER INDIVIDUAL.—

(i) IN GENERAL.—A plan shall not be treated as failing to meet the requirements of paragraph (1)(H)(i) if a participant's accrued benefit, as determined as of any date under the terms of the plan, would be equal to or greater than that of any similarly situated, younger individual who is or could be a participant.

(ii) SIMILARLY SITUATED.—For purposes of this subparagraph, a participant is similarly situated to any other individual if such participant is identical to such other individual in every respect (including period of service, compensation, position, date of hire, work history, and any other respect) except for age.

(iii) DISREGARD OF SUBSIDIZED EARLY RETIREMENT BENEFITS.—In determining the accrued benefit as of any date for purposes of this clause, the subsidized portion of any early retirement benefit or retirement-type subsidy shall be disregarded.

(iv) ACCRUED BENEFIT.—For purposes of this subparagraph, the accrued benefit may, under the terms of the plan, be expressed as an annuity payable at normal retirement age, the balance of a hypothetical account, or the current value of the accumulated percentage of the employee's final average compensation.

(B) APPLICABLE DEFINED BENEFIT PLANS.—

(i) INTEREST CREDITS.—

(I) IN GENERAL.—An applicable defined benefit plan shall be treated as failing to meet the requirements of paragraph (1)(H) unless the terms of the plan provide that any interest credit (or an equivalent amount) for any plan year shall be at a rate which is not greater than a market rate of return. A plan shall not be treated as failing to meet the requirements of this subclause merely because the plan provides for a reasonable minimum guaranteed rate of return or for a rate of return that is equal to the greater of a fixed or variable rate of return.

(II) PRESERVATION OF CAPITAL.—An interest credit (or an equivalent amount) of less than zero shall in no event result in the account balance or similar amount being less than the aggregate amount of contributions credited to the account.

(III) MARKET RATE OF RETURN.—The Secretary may provide by regulation for rules governing the calculation of a market rate of return for purposes of subclause (I) and for permissible methods of crediting interest to the account (including fixed or variable interest rates) resulting in effective rates of return meeting the requirements of subclause (I).

(ii) SPECIAL RULE FOR PLAN CONVERSIONS.—If, after June 29, 2005, an applicable plan amendment is adopted, the plan shall be treated as failing to meet the requirements of paragraph (1)(H) unless the requirements of clause (iii) are met with respect to each individual who was a participant in the plan immediately before the adoption of the amendment.

(iii) RATE OF BENEFIT ACCRUAL.—Subject to clause (iv), the requirements of this clause are met with respect to any participant if the accrued benefit of the participant under the terms of the plan as in effect after the amendment is not less than the sum of—

(I) the participant's accrued benefit for years of service before the effective date of the amendment, determined under the terms of the plan as in effect before the amendment, plus

(II) the participant's accrued benefit for years of service after the effective date of the amendment, determined under the terms of the plan as in effect after the amendment.

(iv) SPECIAL RULES FOR EARLY RETIREMENT SUBSIDIES.—For purposes of clause (iii)(I), the plan shall credit the accumulation account or similar amount with the amount of any early retirement benefit or retirement-type subsidy for the plan year in which the participant retires if, as of such time, the participant has met the age, years of service, and other requirements under the plan for entitlement to such benefit or subsidy.

(v) APPLICABLE PLAN AMENDMENT.—For purposes of this subparagraph—

(I) IN GENERAL.—The term "applicable plan amendment" means an amendment to a defined benefit plan which has the effect of converting the plan to an applicable defined benefit plan.

(II) SPECIAL RULE FOR COORDINATED BENEFITS.—If the benefits of 2 or more defined benefit plans established or maintained by an employer are coordinated in such a manner as to have the effect of the adoption of an amendment described in subclause (I), the sponsor of the defined benefit plan or plans providing for such coordination shall be treated as having adopted such a plan amendment as of the date such coordination begins.

(III) MULTIPLE AMENDMENTS.—The Secretary shall issue regulations to prevent the avoidance of the purposes of this subparagraph through the use of 2 or more plan amendments rather than a single amendment.

(IV) APPLICABLE DEFINED BENEFIT PLAN.—For purposes of this subparagraph, the term "applicable defined benefit plan" has the meaning given such term by section 411(a)(13).

(vi) TERMINATION REQUIREMENTS.—An applicable defined benefit plan shall not be treated as meeting the requirements of clause (i) unless the plan provides that, upon the termination of the plan—

(I) if the interest credit rate (or an equivalent amount) under the plan is a variable rate, the rate of interest used to determine accrued benefits under the plan shall be equal to the average of the rates of interest used under the plan during the 5-year period ending on the termination date, and

(II) the interest rate and mortality table used to determine the amount of any benefit under the plan payable in the form of an annuity payable at normal retirement age shall be the rate and table specified under the plan for such purpose as of the termination date, except that if such interest rate is a variable rate, the interest rate shall be determined under the rules of subclause (I).

(C) CERTAIN OFFSETS PERMITTED.—A plan shall not be treated as failing to meet the requirements of paragraph (1)(H)(i) solely because the plan provides offsets against benefits under the plan to the extent such offsets are allowable in applying the requirements of section 401(a).

(D) PERMITTED DISPARITIES IN PLAN CONTRIBUTIONS OR BENEFITS.—A plan shall not be treated as failing to meet the requirements of paragraph (1)(H) solely because the plan provides a disparity in contributions or benefits with respect to which the requirements of section 401(l) are met.

(E) INDEXING PERMITTED.—

(i) IN GENERAL.—A plan shall not be treated as failing to meet the requirements of paragraph (1)(H) solely because the plan provides for indexing of accrued benefits under the plan.

(ii) PROTECTION AGAINST LOSS.—Except in the case of any benefit provided in the form of a variable annuity, clause (i) shall not apply with respect to any indexing which results in an accrued benefit less than the accrued benefit determined without regard to such indexing.

(iii) INDEXING.—For purposes of this subparagraph, the term "indexing" means, in connection with an accrued benefit, the periodic adjustment of the accrued benefit by means of the application of a recognized investment index or methodology.

(F) EARLY RETIREMENT BENEFIT OR RETIREMENT-TYPE SUBSIDY.—For purposes of this paragraph, the terms "early retirement benefit" and "retirement-type subsidy" have the meaning given such terms in subsection (d)(6)(B)(i).

(G) BENEFIT ACCRUED TO DATE.—For purposes of this paragraph, any reference to the accrued benefit shall be a reference to such benefit accrued to date.

* * *

[CCH Explanation at ¶ 205 and ¶ 1005. Committee Reports at ¶ 10,010 and ¶ 10,560.]

Amendments

• 2006, Pension Protection Act of 2006 (H.R. 4)

H.R. 4, §114(b)(2)(A)-(B):

Amended Code Sec. 411(b)(1)(F) by striking "paragraphs (2) and (3) of section 412(i)" in clause (ii) and inserting "subparagraphs (B) and (C) of section 412(e)(3)", and by striking "paragraphs (4), (5), and (6) of section 412(i)" and inserting "subparagraphs (D), (E), and (F) of section 412(e)(3)". **Effective** 8-17-2006.

H.R. 4, §701(b)(1):

Amended Code Sec. 411(b) by adding at the end a new paragraph (5). **Effective** generally for periods beginning on or after 6-29-2005. For special rules, see Act Sec. 701(d) in the amendment notes following Code Sec. 411(a), above, and see Act Sec. 701(e)(3)-(5), below.

H.R. 4, §701(e)(3)-(5), provides:

(3) VESTING AND INTEREST CREDIT REQUIREMENTS.—In the case of a plan in existence on June 29, 2005, the requirements of clause (i) of section 411(b)(5)(B) of the Internal Revenue Code of 1986, clause (i) of section 204(b)(5)(B) of the Employee Retirement Income Security Act of 1974, and clause (i) of section 4(i)(10)(B) of the Age Discrimination in Employment Act of 1967 (as added by this Act) and the requirements of 203(f)(2) of the Employee Retirement Income Security Act of 1974 and section 411(a)(13)(B) of the Internal Revenue Code of 1986 (as so added) shall, for purposes of applying the amendments made by subsections (a) and (b), apply to years beginning after December 31, 2007, unless the plan sponsor elects the application of such requirements for any period after June 29, 2005, and before the first year beginning after December 31, 2007.

(4) SPECIAL RULE FOR COLLECTIVELY BARGAINED PLANS.—In the case of a plan maintained pursuant to 1 or more collective bargaining agreements between employee representatives and 1 or more employers ratified on or before the date of the enactment of this Act, the requirements described in paragraph (3) shall, for purposes of applying the amendments made by subsections (a) and (b), not apply to plan years beginning before—

(A) the earlier of—

(i) the date on which the last of such collective bargaining agreements terminates (determined without regard to any extension thereof on or after such date of enactment), or

(ii) January 1, 2008, or

(B) January 1, 2010.

(5) CONVERSIONS.—The requirements of clause (ii) of section 411(b)(5)(B) of the Internal Revenue Code of 1986, clause (ii) of section 204(b)(5)(B) of the Employee Retirement Income Security Act of 1974, and clause (ii) of section 4(i)(10)(B) of the Age Discrimination in Employment Act of 1967 (as added by this Act), shall apply to plan amendments adopted after, and taking effect after, June 29, 2005, except that the plan sponsor may elect to have such amendments apply to plan amendments adopted before, and taking effect after, such date.

(d) SPECIAL RULES.—

* * *

(6) ACCRUED BENEFIT NOT TO BE DECREASED BY AMENDMENT.—

(A) IN GENERAL.—A plan shall be treated as not satisfying the requirements of this section if the accrued benefit of a participant is decreased by an amendment of the plan, other than an amendment described in *section 412(e)(2)*, or section 4281 of the Employee Retirement Income Security Act of 1974.

* * *

[CCH Explanation at ¶ 205. Committee Reports at ¶ 10,010.]

Amendments

• 2006, Pension Protection Act of 2006 (H.R. 4)

H.R. 4, §114(b)(3):

Amended Code Sec. 411(d)(6)(A) by striking "section 412(c)(8)" and inserting "section 412(e)(2)". **Effective** 8-17-2006.

Caution: Code Sec. 412, below, as amended by H.R. 4, §301, but prior to the amendment of Code Sec. 412 by §111(a), applies to plan years beginning on or before December 31, 2007.

[¶ 5085] CODE SEC. 412. MINIMUM FUNDING STANDARDS.

* * *

(b) FUNDING STANDARD ACCOUNT.—

* * *

(5) INTEREST.—

* * *

(B) REQUIRED CHANGE OF INTEREST RATE.—For purposes of determining a plan's current liability and for purposes of determining a plan's required contribution under section 412(l) for any plan year—

* * *

(ii) PERMISSIBLE RANGE.—For purposes of this subparagraph—

(I) IN GENERAL.—Except as provided in subclause (II) or (III), the term "permissible range" means a rate of interest which is not more than 10 percent above, and not more than 10 percent below, the weighted average of the rates of interest on 30-year Treasury securities during the 4-year period ending on the last day before the beginning of the plan year.

(II) SPECIAL RULE FOR YEARS 2004, *2005, 2006,* AND *2007*.—In the case of plan years beginning after December 31, 2003, and before January 1, *2008*, the term "permissible range" means a rate of interest which is not above, and not more than 10 percent below, the weighted average of the rates of interest on amounts invested conservatively in long-term investment grade corporate bonds during the 4-year period ending on the last day before the beginning of the plan year. Such rates shall be determined by the Secretary on the basis of 2 or more indices that are selected periodically by the Secretary and that are in the top 3 quality levels available. The Secretary shall make the permissible range, and the indices and methodology used to determine the average rate, publicly available.

(III) SECRETARIAL AUTHORITY.—If the Secretary finds that the lowest rate of interest permissible under subclause (I) or (II) is unreasonably high, the Secretary may prescribe a lower rate of interest, except that such rate may not be less than 80 percent of the average rate determined under such subclause.

* * *

[CCH Explanation at ¶ 205. Committee Reports at ¶ 10,190.]

Amendments

• 2006, Pension Protection Act of 2006 (H.R. 4)

H.R. 4, §301(b)(1)(A)-(B):

Amended Code Sec. 412(b)(5)(B)(ii)(II) by striking "2006" and inserting "2008", and by striking "AND 2005" in the heading and inserting ", 2005, 2006, AND 2007". **Effective** 8-17-2006.

(l) ADDITIONAL FUNDING REQUIREMENTS FOR PLANS WHICH ARE NOT MULTIEMPLOYER PLANS.—

* * *

(7) CURRENT LIABILITY.—For purposes of this subsection—

* * *

(C) INTEREST RATE AND MORTALITY ASSUMPTIONS USED.—Effective for plan years beginning after December 31, 1994—

(i) INTEREST RATE.—

* * *

(IV) SPECIAL RULE FOR 2004, *2005, 2006,* AND *2007*.—For plan years beginning in 2004, *2005, 2006, or 2007*, notwithstanding subclause (I), the rate of interest used to determine current liability under this subsection shall be the rate of interest under subsection (b)(5).

* * *

[CCH Explanation at ¶ 235. Committee Reports at ¶ 10,190.]

Amendments

• **2006, Pension Protection Act of 2006 (H.R. 4)**

H.R. 4, §301(b)(2)(A)-(B):

Amended Code Sec. 412(l)(7)(C)(i)(IV) by striking "or 2005" and inserting ", 2005, 2006, or 2007", and by striking "AND 2005" in the heading and inserting ", 2005, 2006, AND 2007". **Effective** 8-17-2006.

➳ Caution: Code Sec. 412, below, as amended by H.R. 4, §111(a), applies to plan years beginning after December 31, 2007.

[¶ 5085A] *CODE SEC. 412. MINIMUM FUNDING STANDARDS.*

(a) REQUIREMENT TO MEET MINIMUM FUNDING STANDARD.—

(1) IN GENERAL.—A plan to which this section applies shall satisfy the minimum funding standard applicable to the plan for any plan year.

(2) MINIMUM FUNDING STANDARD.—For purposes of paragraph (1), a plan shall be treated as satisfying the minimum funding standard for a plan year if—

(A) in the case of a defined benefit plan which is not a multiemployer plan, the employer makes contributions to or under the plan for the plan year which, in the aggregate, are not less than the minimum required contribution determined under section 430 for the plan for the plan year,

(B) in the case of a money purchase plan which is not a multiemployer plan, the employer makes contributions to or under the plan for the plan year which are required under the terms of the plan, and

(C) in the case of a multiemployer plan, the employers make contributions to or under the plan for any plan year which, in the aggregate, are sufficient to ensure that the plan does not have an accumulated funding deficiency under section 431 as of the end of the plan year.

(b) LIABILITY FOR CONTRIBUTIONS.—

(1) IN GENERAL.—Except as provided in paragraph (2), the amount of any contribution required by this section (including any required installments under paragraphs (3) and (4) of section 430(j)) shall be paid by the employer responsible for making contributions to or under the plan.

(2) JOINT AND SEVERAL LIABILITY WHERE EMPLOYER MEMBER OF CONTROLLED GROUP.—If the employer referred to in paragraph (1) is a member of a controlled group, each member of such group shall be jointly and severally liable for payment of such contributions.

»»→ Caution: Code Sec. 412(b)(3), below, as added by H.R. 4, §212(c), applies generally with respect to plan years beginning after 2007. For sunset provision, see H.R. 4, §221(c), in the amendment notes.

(3) MULTIEMPLOYER PLANS IN CRITICAL STATUS.—Paragraph (1) shall not apply in the case of a multiemployer plan for any plan year in which the plan is in critical status pursuant to section 432. This paragraph shall only apply if the plan adopts a rehabilitation plan in accordance with section 432(e) and complies with such rehabilitation plan (and any modifications of the plan).

[CCH Explanation at ¶310. Committee Reports at ¶10,090.]

Amendments

• 2006, Pension Protection Act of 2006 (H.R. 4)

H.R. 4, §212(c):

Amended Code Sec. 412(b), as amended by this Act, by adding at the end a new paragraph (3). **Effective** generally with respect to plan years beginning after 2007. For special rules, see Act Sec. 212(e)(2)-(3), below.

H.R. 4, §212(e)(2)-(3), provides:

(2) SPECIAL RULE FOR CERTAIN NOTICES.—In any case in which a plan's actuary certifies that it is reasonably expected that a multiemployer plan will be in critical status under section 305(b)(3) of the Employee Retirement Income Security Act of 1974, as added by this section, with respect to the first plan year beginning after 2007, the notice required under subparagraph (D) of such section may be provided at any time after the date of enactment, so long as it is provided on or before the last date for providing the notice under such subparagraph.

(3) SPECIAL RULE FOR CERTAIN RESTORED BENEFITS.—In the case of a multiemployer plan—

(A) with respect to which benefits were reduced pursuant to a plan amendment adopted on or after January 1, 2002, and before June 30, 2005, and

(B) which, pursuant to the plan document, the trust agreement, or a formal written communication from the plan sponsor to participants provided before June 30, 2005, provided for the restoration of such benefits,

the amendments made by this section shall not apply to such benefit restorations to the extent that any restriction on the providing or accrual of such benefits would otherwise apply by reason of such amendments.

H.R. 4, §221(c), provides:

(c) SUNSET.—

(1) IN GENERAL.—Except as provided in this subsection, notwithstanding any other provision of this Act, the provisions of, and the amendments made by, sections 201(b), 202, and 212 shall not apply to plan years beginning after December 31, 2014.

(2) FUNDING IMPROVEMENT AND REHABILITATION PLANS.—If a plan is operating under a funding improvement or rehabilitation plan under section 305 of such Act or 432 of such Code for its last year beginning before January 1, 2015, such plan shall continue to operate under such funding improvement or rehabilitation plan during any period after December 31, 2014, such funding improvement or rehabilitation plan is in effect and all provisions of such Act or Code relating to the operation of such funding improvement or rehabilitation plan shall continue in effect during such period.

(c) VARIANCE FROM MINIMUM FUNDING STANDARDS.—

(1) WAIVER IN CASE OF BUSINESS HARDSHIP.—

(A) IN GENERAL.—If—

(i) an employer is (or in the case of a multiemployer plan, 10 percent or more of the number of employers contributing to or under the plan is) unable to satisfy the minimum funding standard for a plan year without temporary substantial business hardship (substantial business hardship in the case of a multiemployer plan), and

(ii) application of the standard would be adverse to the interests of plan participants in the aggregate,

the Secretary may, subject to subparagraph (C), waive the requirements of subsection (a) for such year with respect to all or any portion of the minimum funding standard. The Secretary shall not waive the minimum funding standard with respect to a plan for more than 3 of any 15 (5 of any 15 in the case of a multiemployer plan) consecutive plan years

(B) EFFECTS OF WAIVER.—If a waiver is granted under subparagraph (A) for any plan year—

(i) in the case of a defined benefit plan which is not a multiemployer plan, the minimum required contribution under section 430 for the plan year shall be reduced by the amount of the waived funding deficiency and such amount shall be amortized as required under section 430(e), and

(ii) in the case of a multiemployer plan, the funding standard account shall be credited under section 431(b)(3)(C) with the amount of the waived funding deficiency and such amount shall be amortized as required under section 431(b)(2)(C).

(C) WAIVER OF AMORTIZED PORTION NOT ALLOWED.—The Secretary may not waive under subparagraph (A) any portion of the minimum funding standard under subsection (a) for a plan year which is attributable to any waived funding deficiency for any preceding plan year.

(2) DETERMINATION OF BUSINESS HARDSHIP.—For purposes of this subsection, the factors taken into account in determining temporary substantial business hardship (substantial business hardship in the case of a multiemployer plan) shall include (but shall not be limited to) whether or not—

(A) the employer is operating at an economic loss,

(B) there is substantial unemployment or underemployment in the trade or business and in the industry concerned,

(C) the sales and profits of the industry concerned are depressed or declining, and

(D) it is reasonable to expect that the plan will be continued only if the waiver is granted.

(3) WAIVED FUNDING DEFICIENCY.—For purposes of this section and part III of this subchapter, the term "waived funding deficiency" means the portion of the minimum funding standard under subsection (a) (determined without regard to the waiver) for a plan year waived by the Secretary and not satisfied by employer contributions.

(4) SECURITY FOR WAIVERS FOR SINGLE-EMPLOYER PLANS, CONSULTATIONS.—

(A) SECURITY MAY BE REQUIRED.—

(i) IN GENERAL.—Except as provided in subparagraph (C), the Secretary may require an employer maintaining a defined benefit plan which is a single-employer plan (within the meaning of section 4001(a)(15) of the Employee Retirement Income Security Act of 1974) to provide security to such plan as a condition for granting or modifying a waiver under paragraph (1).

(ii) SPECIAL RULES.—Any security provided under clause (i) may be perfected and enforced only by the Pension Benefit Guaranty Corporation, or at the direction of the Corporation, by a contributing sponsor (within the meaning of section 4001(a)(13) of the Employee Retirement Income Security Act of 1974), or a member of such sponsor's controlled group (within the meaning of section 4001(a)(14) of such Act).

(B) CONSULTATION WITH THE PENSION BENEFIT GUARANTY CORPORATION.—Except as provided in subparagraph (C), the Secretary shall, before granting or modifying a waiver under this subsection with respect to a plan described in subparagraph (A)(i)—

(i) provide the Pension Benefit Guaranty Corporation with—

(I) notice of the completed application for any waiver or modification, and

(II) an opportunity to comment on such application within 30 days after receipt of such notice, and

(ii) consider—

(I) any comments of the Corporation under clause (i)(II), and

(II) any views of any employee organization (within the meaning of section 3(4) of the Employee Retirement Income Security Act of 1974) representing participants in the plan which are submitted in writing to the Secretary in connection with such application.

Information provided to the Corporation under this subparagraph shall be considered tax return information and subject to the safeguarding and reporting requirements of section 6103(p).

(C) EXCEPTION FOR CERTAIN WAIVERS.—

(i) IN GENERAL.—The preceding provisions of this paragraph shall not apply to any plan with respect to which the sum of—

(I) the aggregate unpaid minimum required contributions (within the meaning of section 4971(c)(4)) for the plan year and all preceding plan years, and

(II) the present value of all waiver amortization installments determined for the plan year and succeeding plan years under section 430(e)(2),

is less than $1,000,000.

(ii) TREATMENT OF WAIVERS FOR WHICH APPLICATIONS ARE PENDING.—*The amount described in clause (i)(I) shall include any increase in such amount which would result if all applications for waivers of the minimum funding standard under this subsection which are pending with respect to such plan were denied.*

(5) SPECIAL RULES FOR SINGLE-EMPLOYER PLANS.—

(A) APPLICATION MUST BE SUBMITTED BEFORE DATE 2½ MONTHS AFTER CLOSE OF YEAR.—*In the case of a defined benefit plan which is not a multiemployer plan, no waiver may be granted under this subsection with respect to any plan for any plan year unless an application therefor is submitted to the Secretary not later than the 15th day of the 3rd month beginning after the close of such plan year.*

(B) SPECIAL RULE IF EMPLOYER IS MEMBER OF CONTROLLED GROUP.—*In the case of a defined benefit plan which is not a multiemployer plan, if an employer is a member of a controlled group, the temporary substantial business hardship requirements of paragraph (1) shall be treated as met only if such requirements are met—*

(i) with respect to such employer, and

(ii) with respect to the controlled group of which such employer is a member (determined by treating all members of such group as a single employer).

The Secretary may provide that an analysis of a trade or business or industry of a member need not be conducted if the Secretary determines such analysis is not necessary because the taking into account of such member would not significantly affect the determination under this paragraph.

(6) ADVANCE NOTICE.—

(A) IN GENERAL.—*The Secretary shall, before granting a waiver under this subsection, require each applicant to provide evidence satisfactory to the Secretary that the applicant has provided notice of the filing of the application for such waiver to each affected party (as defined in section 4001(a)(21) of the Employee Retirement Income Security Act of 1974). Such notice shall include a description of the extent to which the plan is funded for benefits which are guaranteed under title IV of the Employee Retirement Income Security Act of 1974 and for benefit liabilities.*

(B) CONSIDERATION OF RELEVANT INFORMATION.—*The Secretary shall consider any relevant information provided by a person to whom notice was given under subparagraph (A).*

(7) RESTRICTION ON PLAN AMENDMENTS.—

(A) IN GENERAL.—*No amendment of a plan which increases the liabilities of the plan by reason of any increase in benefits, any change in the accrual of benefits, or any change in the rate at which benefits become nonforfeitable under the plan shall be adopted if a waiver under this subsection or an extension of time under section 431(d) is in effect with respect to the plan, or if a plan amendment described in subsection (d)(2) has been made at any time in the preceding 12 months (24 months in the case of a multiemployer plan). If a plan is amended in violation of the preceding sentence, any such waiver, or extension of time, shall not apply to any plan year ending on or after the date on which such amendment is adopted.*

(B) EXCEPTION.—*Subparagraph (A) shall not apply to any plan amendment which—*

(i) the Secretary determines to be reasonable and which provides for only de minimis increases in the liabilities of the plan,

(ii) only repeals an amendment described in subsection (d)(2), or

(iii) is required as a condition of qualification under part I of subchapter D, of chapter 1.

(d) MISCELLANEOUS RULES.—

(1) CHANGE IN METHOD OR YEAR.—*If the funding method, the valuation date, or a plan year for a plan is changed, the change shall take effect only if approved by the Secretary.*

(2) CERTAIN RETROACTIVE PLAN AMENDMENTS.—*For purposes of this section, any amendment applying to a plan year which—*

(A) is adopted after the close of such plan year but no later than 2½ months after the close of the plan year (or, in the case of a multiemployer plan, no later than 2 years after the close of such plan year),

(B) does not reduce the accrued benefit of any participant determined as of the beginning of the first plan year to which the amendment applies, and

(C) does not reduce the accrued benefit of any participant determined as of the time of adoption except to the extent required by the circumstances,

shall, at the election of the plan administrator, be deemed to have been made on the first day of such plan year. No amendment described in this paragraph which reduces the accrued benefits of any participant shall take effect unless the plan administrator files a notice with the Secretary notifying him of such amendment and the Secretary has approved such amendment, or within 90 days after the date on which such notice was filed, failed to disapprove such amendment. No amendment described in this subsection shall be approved by the Secretary unless the Secretary determines that such amendment is necessary because of a temporary substantial business hardship (as determined under subsection (c)(2)) or a substantial business hardship (as so determined) in the case of a multiemployer plan and that a waiver under subsection (c) (or, in the case of a multiemployer plan, any extension of the amortization period under section 431(d)) is unavailable or inadequate.

(3) CONTROLLED GROUP.—For purposes of this section, the term "controlled group" means any group treated as a single employer under subsection (b), (c), (m), or (o) of section 414.

(e) PLANS TO WHICH SECTION APPLIES.—

(1) IN GENERAL.—Except as provided in paragraphs (2) and (4), this section applies to a plan if, for any plan year beginning on or after the effective date of this section for such plan under the Employee Retirement Income Security Act of 1974—

(A) such plan included a trust which qualified (or was determined by the Secretary to have qualified) under section 401(a), or

(B) such plan satisfied (or was determined by the Secretary to have satisfied) the requirements of section 403(a).

(2) EXCEPTIONS.—This section shall not apply to—

(A) any profit-sharing or stock bonus plan,

(B) any insurance contract plan described in paragraph (3),

(C) any governmental plan (within the meaning of section 414(d)),

(D) any church plan (within the meaning of section 414(e)) with respect to which the election provided by section 410(d) has not been made,

(E) any plan which has not, at any time after September 2, 1974, provided for employer contributions, or

(F) any plan established and maintained by a society, order, or association described in section 501(c)(8) or (9), if no part of the contributions to or under such plan are made by employers of participants in such plan.

No plan described in subparagraph (C), (D), or (F) shall be treated as a qualified plan for purposes of section 401(a) unless such plan meets the requirements of section 401(a)(7) as in effect on September 1, 1974.

(3) CERTAIN INSURANCE CONTRACT PLANS.—A plan is described in this paragraph if—

(A) the plan is funded exclusively by the purchase of individual insurance contracts,

(B) such contracts provide for level annual premium payments to be paid extending not later than the retirement age for each individual participating in the plan, and commencing with the date the individual became a participant in the plan (or, in the case of an increase in benefits, commencing at the time such increase becomes effective),

(C) benefits provided by the plan are equal to the benefits provided under each contract at normal retirement age under the plan and are guaranteed by an insurance carrier (licensed under the laws of a State to do business with the plan) to the extent premiums have been paid,

(D) premiums payable for the plan year, and all prior plan years, under such contracts have been paid before lapse or there is reinstatement of the policy,

(E) no rights under such contracts have been subject to a security interest at any time during the plan year, and

(F) no policy loans are outstanding at any time during the plan year.

A plan funded exclusively by the purchase of group insurance contracts which is determined under regulations prescribed by the Secretary to have the same characteristics as contracts described in the preceding sentence shall be treated as a plan described in this paragraph.

(4) CERTAIN TERMINATED MULTIEMPLOYER PLANS.—This section applies with respect to a terminated multiemployer plan to which section 4021 of the Employee Retirement Income Security Act of 1974 applies until the last day of the plan year in which the plan terminates (within the meaning of section 4041A(a)(2) of such Act).

[CCH Explanation at ¶235. Committee Reports at ¶10,010.]

Amendments

• 2006, Pension Protection Act of 2006 (H.R. 4)

H.R. 4, §111(a):

Amended Code Sec. 412. **Effective** for plan years beginning after 12-31-2007. Prior to amendment, Code Sec. 412 read as follows:

SEC. 412. MINIMUM FUNDING STANDARDS.

(a) GENERAL RULE.—Except as provided in subsection (h), this section applies to a plan if, for any plan year beginning on or after the effective date of this section for such plan—

(1) such plan included a trust which qualified (or was determined by the Secretary to have qualified) under section 401(a), or

(2) such plan satisfied (or was determined by the Secretary to have satisfied) the requirements of section 403(a).

A plan to which this section applies shall have satisfied the minimum funding standard for such plan for a plan year if as of the end of such plan year, the plan does not have an accumulated funding deficiency. For purposes of this section and section 4971, the term "accumulated funding deficiency" means for any plan the excess of the total charges to the funding standard account for all plan years (beginning with the first plan year to which this section applies) over the total credits to such account for such years or, if less, the excess of the total charges to the alternative minimum funding standard account for such plan years over the total credits to such account for such years. In any plan year in which a multiemployer plan is in reorganization, the accumulated funding deficiency of the plan shall be determined under section 418B.

(b) FUNDING STANDARD ACCOUNT.—

(1) ACCOUNT REQUIRED.—Each plan to which this section applies shall establish and maintain a funding standard account. Such account shall be credited and charged solely as provided in this section.

(2) CHARGES TO ACCOUNT.—For a plan year, the funding standard account shall be charged with the sum of—

(A) the normal cost of the plan for the plan year,

(B) the amounts necessary to amortize in equal annual installments (until fully amortized)—

(i) in the case of a plan in existence on January 1, 1974, the unfunded past service liability under the plan on the first day of the first plan year to which this section applies, over a period of 40 plan years,

(ii) in the case of a plan which comes into existence after January 1, 1974, the unfunded past service liability under the plan on the first day of the first plan year to which this section applies, over a period of 30 plan years,

(iii) separately, with respect to each plan year, the net increase (if any) in unfunded past service liability under the plan arising from plan amendments adopted in such year, over a period of 30 plan years,

(iv) separately, with respect to each plan year, the net experience loss (if any) under the plan, over a period of 5 plan years (15 plan years in the case of a multiemployer plan), and

(v) separately, with respect to each plan year, the net loss (if any) resulting from changes in actuarial assumptions used under the plan, over a period of 10 plan years (30 plan years in the case of a multiemployer plan),

(C) the amount necessary to amortize each waived funding deficiency (within the meaning of subsection (d)(3)) for each prior plan year in equal annual installments (until fully amortized) over a period of 5 plan years (15 plan years in the case of a multiemployer plan),

(D) the amount necessary to amortize in equal annual installments (until fully amortized) over a period of 5 plan years any amount credited to the funding standard account under paragraph (3)(D), and

(E) the amount necessary to amortize in equal annual installments (until fully amortized) over a period of 20 years the contributions which would be required to be made under the plan but for the provisions of subsection (c)(7)(A)(i)(I).

For additional requirements in the case of plans other than multiemployer plans, see subsection (l).

(3) CREDITS TO ACCOUNT.—For a plan year, the funding standard account shall be credited with the sum of—

(A) the amount considered contributed by the employer to or under the plan for the plan year,

(B) the amount necessary to amortize in equal annual installments (until fully amortized)—

(i) separately, with respect to each plan year, the net decrease (if any) in unfunded past service liability under the plan arising from plan amendments adopted in such year, over a period of 30 plan years,

(ii) separately, with respect to each plan year, the net experience gain (if any) under the plan, over a period of 5 plan years (15 plan years in the case of a multiemployer plan), and

(iii) separately, with respect to each plan year, the net gain (if any) resulting from changes in actuarial assumptions used under the plan, over a period of 10 plan years (30 plan years in the case of a multiemployer plan),

(C) the amount of the waived funding deficiency (within the meaning of subsection (d)(3)) for the plan year, and

(D) in the case of a plan year for which the accumulated funding deficiency is determined under the funding standard account if such plan year follows a plan year for which such deficiency was determined under the alternative minimum funding standard, the excess (if any) of any debit balance in the funding standard account (determined without regard to this subparagraph) over any debit balance in the alternative minimum funding standard account.

(4) COMBINING AND OFFSETTING AMOUNTS TO BE AMORTIZED.—Under regulations prescribed by the Secretary, amounts required to be amortized under paragraph (2) or paragraph (3), as the case may be—

(A) may be combined into one amount under such paragraph to be amortized over a period determined on the basis of the remaining amortization period for all items entering into such combined amount, and

(B) may be offset against amounts required to be amortized under the other such paragraph, with the resulting amount to be amortized over a period determined on the basis of the remaining amortization periods for all items entering into whichever of the two amounts being offset is the greater.

(5) INTEREST.—

(A) IN GENERAL.—The funding standard account (and items therein) shall be charged or credited (as determined under regulations prescribed by the Secretary) with interest at the appropriate rate consistent with the rate or rates of interest used under the plan to determine costs.

(B) REQUIRED CHANGE OF INTEREST RATE.—For purposes of determining a plan's current liability and for purposes of determining a plan's required contribution under section 412(l) for any plan year—

(i) IN GENERAL.—If any rate of interest used under the plan to determine cost is not within the permissible range, the plan shall establish a new rate of interest within the permissible range.

(ii) PERMISSIBLE RANGE.—For purposes of this subparagraph—

(I) IN GENERAL.—Except as provided in subclause (II) or (III), the term "permissible range" means a rate of interest which is not more than 10 percent above, and not more than 10 percent below, the weighted average of the rates of interest on 30-year Treasury securities during the 4-year period ending on the last day before the beginning of the plan year.

(II) SPECIAL RULE FOR YEARS 2004, 2005, 2006, AND 2007.—In the case of plan years beginning after December 31, 2003, and before January 1, 2008, the term "permissible range" means a rate of interest which is not above, and not more than 10 percent below, the weighted average of the rates of interest on amounts invested conservatively in long-term investment grade corporate bonds during the 4-year period ending on the last day before the beginning of the plan year. Such rates shall be determined by the Secretary on the basis of 2 or more indices that are selected periodically by the Secretary and that are in the top 3 quality levels available. The Secretary shall make the permissible range, and the indices and methodology used to determine the average rate, publicly available.

(III) SECRETARIAL AUTHORITY.—If the Secretary finds that the lowest rate of interest permissible under subclause (I) or (II) is unreasonably high, the Secretary may prescribe a lower rate of interest, except that such rate may not be less than 80 percent of the average rate determined under such subclause.

(iii) ASSUMPTIONS.—Notwithstanding subsection (c)(3)(A)(i), the interest rate used under the plan shall be—

(I) determined without taking into account the experience of the plan and reasonable expectations, but

(II) consistent with the assumptions which reflect the purchase rates which would be used by insurance companies to satisfy the liabilities under the plan.

(6) CERTAIN AMORTIZATION CHARGES AND CREDITS.—In the case of a plan which, immediately before the date of the enactment of the Multiemployer Pension Plan Amendments Act of 1980, was a multiemployer plan (within the meaning of section 414(f) as in effect immediately before such date)—

(A) any amount described in paragraph (2)(B)(ii), (2)(B)(iii), or (3)(B)(i) of this subsection which arose in a plan year beginning before such date shall be amortized in equal annual installments (until fully amortized) over 40 plan years, beginning with the plan year in which the amount arose;

(B) any amount described in paragraph (2)(B)(iv) or (3)(B)(ii) of this subsection which arose in a plan year beginning before such date shall be amortized in equal annual installments (until fully amortized) over 20 plan years, beginning with the plan year in which the amount arose;

(C) any change in past service liability which arises during the period of 3 plan years beginning on or after such date, and results from a plan amendment adopted before such date, shall be amortized in equal annual installments (until fully amortized) over 40 plan years, beginning with the plan year in which the change arises; and

(D) any change in past service liability which arises during the period of 2 plan years beginning on or after such date, and results from the changing of a group of participants from one benefit level to another benefit level under a schedule of plan benefits which—

(i) was adopted before such date, and

(ii) was effective for any plan participant before the beginning of the first plan year beginning on or after such date,

shall be amortized in equal annual installments (until fully amortized) over 40 plan years, beginning with the plan year in which the change arises.

(7) SPECIAL RULES FOR MULTIEMPLOYER PLANS.—For purposes of this section—

(A) WITHDRAWAL LIABILITY.—Any amount received by a multiemployer plan in payment of all or part of an employer's withdrawal liability under part 1 of subtitle E of title IV of the Employee Retirement Income Security Act of 1974 shall be considered an amount contributed by the employer to or under the plan. The Secretary may prescribe by regulation additional charges and credits to a multiemployer plan's funding standard account to the extent necessary to prevent withdrawal liability payments from being unduly reflected as advance funding for plan liabilities.

(B) ADJUSTMENTS WHEN A MULTIEMPLOYER PLAN LEAVES REORGANIZATION.—If a multiemployer plan is not in reorganization in the plan year but was in reorganization in the immediately preceding plan year, any balance in the funding standard account at the close of such immediately preceding plan year—

(i) shall be eliminated by an offsetting credit or charge (as the case may be), but

(ii) shall be taken into account in subsequent plan years by being amortized in equal annual installments (until fully amortized) over 30 plan years.

The preceding sentence shall not apply to the extent of any accumulated funding deficiency under section 418B(a) as of the end of the last plan year that the plan was in reorganization.

(C) PLAN PAYMENTS TO SUPPLEMENTAL PROGRAM OR WITHDRAWAL LIABILITY PAYMENT FUND.—Any amount paid by a plan during a plan year to the Pension Benefit Guaranty Corporation pursuant to section 4222 of such Act or to a fund exempt under section 501(c)(22) pursuant to section 4223 of such Act shall reduce the amount of contributions considered received by the plan for the plan year.

(D) INTERIM WITHDRAWAL LIABILITY PAYMENTS.—Any amount paid by an employer pending a final determination of the employer's withdrawal liability under part 1 of subtitle E of title IV of such Act and subsequently refunded to the employer by the plan shall be charged to the funding standard account in accordance with regulations prescribed by the Secretary.

(E) For purposes of the full funding limitation under subsection (c)(7), unless otherwise provided by the plan, the accrued liability under a multiemployer plan shall not include benefits which are not nonforfeitable under the plan after the termination of the plan (taking into consideration section 411(d)(3)).

(F) ELECTION FOR DEFERRAL OF CHARGE FOR PORTION OF NET EXPERIENCE LOSS.—

(i) IN GENERAL.—With respect to the net experience loss of an eligible multiemployer plan for the first plan year beginning after December 31, 2001, the plan sponsor may elect to defer up to 80 percent of the amount otherwise required to be charged under paragraph (2)(B)(iv) for any plan year beginning after June 30, 2003, and before July 1, 2005, to any plan year selected by the plan from either of the 2 immediately succeeding plan years.

(ii) INTEREST.—For the plan year to which a charge is deferred pursuant to an election under clause (i), the funding standard account shall be charged with interest on the deferred charge for the period of deferral at the rate determined under subsection (d) for multiemployer plans.

(iii) RESTRICTIONS ON BENEFIT INCREASES.—No amendment which increases the liabilities of the plan by reason of any increase in benefits, any change in the accrual of benefits, or any change in the rate at which benefits become nonforfeitable under the plan shall be adopted during any period for which a charge is deferred pursuant to an election under clause (i), unless—

(I) the plan's enrolled actuary certifies (in such form and manner prescribed by the Secretary) that the amendment provides for an increase in annual contributions which will exceed the increase in annual charges to the funding standard account attributable to such amendment, or

(II) the amendment is required by a collective bargaining agreement which is in effect on the date of enactment of this subparagraph.

If a plan is amended during any such plan year in violation of the preceding sentence, any election under this paragraph shall not apply to any such plan year ending on or after the date on which such amendment is adopted.

(iv) ELIGIBLE MULTIEMPLOYER PLAN.—For purposes of this subparagraph, the term "eligible multiemployer plan" means a multiemployer plan—

(I) which had a net investment loss for the first plan year beginning after December 31, 2001, of at least 10 percent of the average fair market value of the plan assets during the plan year, and

(II) with respect to which the plan's enrolled actuary certifies (not taking into account the application of this subparagraph), on the basis of the acutuarial assumptions used for the last plan year ending before the date of the enactment of this subparagraph, that the plan is projected to have an accumulated funding deficiency (within the meaning of subsection (a)) for any plan year beginning after June 30, 2003, and before July 1, 2006.

For purposes of subclause (I), a plan's net investment loss shall be determined on the basis of the actual loss and not under any actuarial method used under subsection (c)(2).

(v) EXCEPTION TO TREATMENT OF ELIGIBLE MULTIEMPLOYER PLAN.—In no event shall a plan be treated as an eligible multiemployer plan under clause (iv) if—

(I) for any taxable year beginning during the 10-year period preceding the first plan year for which an election is made under clause (i), any employer required to contribute to the plan failed to timely pay any excise tax imposed under section 4971 with respect to the plan,

(II) for any plan year beginning after June 30, 1993, and before the first plan year for which an election is made under clause (i), the average contribution required to be made by all employers to the plan does not exceed 10 cents per hour or no employer is required to make contributions to the plan, or

(III) with respect to any of the plan years beginning after June 30, 1993, and before the first plan year for which an election is made under clause (i), a waiver was granted under section 412(d) or section 303 of the Employee Retirement Income Security Act of 1974 with respect to the plan or an extension of an amortization period was granted under subsection (e) or section 304 of such Act with respect to the plan.

(vi) ELECTION.—An election under this subparagraph shall be made at such time and in such manner as the Secretary may prescribe.

(c) SPECIAL RULES.—

(1) DETERMINATIONS TO BE MADE UNDER FUNDING METHOD.—For purposes of this section, normal costs, accrued liability, past service liabilities, and experience gains and losses shall be determined under the funding method used to determine costs under the plan.

(2) VALUATION OF ASSETS.—

(A) IN GENERAL.—For purposes of this section, the value of the plan's assets shall be determined on the basis of any reasonable actuarial method of valuation which takes into account fair market value and which is permitted under regulations prescribed by the Secretary.

(B) ELECTION WITH RESPECT TO BONDS.—The value of a bond or other evidence of indebtedness which is not in default as to principal or interest may, at the election of the plan administrator, be determined on an amortized basis running from initial cost at purchase to par value at maturity or earliest call date. Any election under this subparagraph shall be made at such time and in such manner as the Secretary shall by regulations provide, shall apply to all such evidences of indebtedness, and may be revoked only with the consent of the Secretary. In the case of a plan other than a multiemployer plan, this subparagraph shall not apply, but the Secretary may by regulations provide that the value of any dedicated bond portfolio of such plan shall be determined by using the interest rate under subsection (b)(5).

(3) ACTUARIAL ASSUMPTIONS MUST BE REASONABLE.—For purposes of this section, all costs, liabilities, rates of interest, and other factors under the plan shall be determined on the basis of actuarial assumptions and methods—

(A) in the case of—

(i) a plan other than a multiemployer plan, each of which is reasonable (taking into account the experience of the plan and reasonable expectations) or which, in the aggregate, result in a total contribution equivalent to that which would be determined if each such assumption and method were reasonable, or

(ii) a multiemployer plan, which, in the aggregate, are reasonable (taking into account the experiences of the plan and reasonable expectations), and

(B) which, in combination, offer the actuary's best estimate of anticipated experience under the plan.

(4) TREATMENT OF CERTAIN CHANGES AS EXPERIENCE GAIN OR LOSS.—For purposes of this section, if—

(A) a change in benefits under the Social Security Act or in other retirement benefits created under Federal or State law, or

(B) a change in the definition of the term "wages" under section 3121, or a change in the amount of such wages taken into account under regulations prescribed for purposes of section 401(a)(5),

results in an increase or decrease in accrued liability under a plan, such increase or decrease shall be treated as an experience loss or gain.

(5) CHANGE IN FUNDING METHOD OR IN PLAN YEAR REQUIRES APPROVAL.—(A) IN GENERAL.—If the funding method for a plan is changed, the new funding method shall become the funding method used to determine costs and liabilities under the plan only if the change is approved by the Secretary. If the plan year for a plan is changed, the new plan year shall become the plan year for the plan only if the change is approved by the Secretary.

(B) APPROVAL REQUIRED FOR CERTAIN CHANGES IN ASSUMPTIONS BY CERTAIN SINGLE-EMPLOYER PLANS SUBJECT TO ADDITIONAL FUNDING REQUIREMENT.—

(i) IN GENERAL.—No actuarial assumption (other than the assumptions described in subsection (l)(7)(C) used to determine the current liability for a plan to which this subparagraph applies may be changed without the approval of the Secretary.

(ii) PLANS TO WHICH SUBPARAGRAPH APPLIES.—This subparagraph shall apply to a plan only if—

(I) the plan is a defined benefit plan (other than a multiemployer plan) to which title IV of the Employee Retirement Income Security Act of 1974 applies;

(II) the aggregate unfunded vested benefits as of the close of the preceding plan year (as determined under section 4006(a)(3)(E)(iii) of the Employee Retirement Income Security Act of 1974) of such plan and all other plans maintained by the contributing sponsors (as defined in section 4001(a)(13) of such Act) and members of such sponsors' controlled groups (as defined in section 4001(a)(14) of such Act) which are covered by title IV of such Act (disregarding plans with no unfunded vested benefits) exceed $50,000,000; and

(III) the change in assumptions (determined after taking into account any changes in interest rate and mortality table) results in a decrease in the unfunded current liability of the plan for the current plan year that exceeds $50,000,000, or that exceeds $5,000,000 and that is 5 percent or more of the current liability of the plan before such change.

(6) FULL FUNDING.—If, as of the close of a plan year, a plan would (without regard to this paragraph) have an accumulated funding deficiency (determined without regard to the alternative minimum funding standard account permitted under subsection (g)) in excess of the full funding limitation—

(A) the funding standard account shall be credited with the amount of such excess, and

(B) all amounts described in paragraphs (2)(B), (C), and (D) and (3)(B) of subsection (b) which are required to be amortized shall be considered fully amortized for purposes of such paragraphs.

(7) FULL-FUNDING LIMITATION.—

(A) IN GENERAL.—For purposes of paragraph (6), the term "full-funding limitation" means the excess (if any) of—

(i) the lesser of (I) in the case of plan years beginning before January 1, 2004, the applicable percentage of current liability (including the expected increase in current liability due to benefits accruing during the plan year), or (II) the accrued liability (including normal cost) under the plan (determined under the entry age normal funding method if such accrued liability cannot be directly calculated under the funding method used for the plan), over

(ii) the lesser of—

(I) the fair market value of the plan's assets, or

(II) the value of such assets determined under paragraph (2).

(B) CURRENT LIABILITY.—For purposes of subparagraph (D) and subclause (I) of subparagraph (A)(i), the term "current liability" has the meaning given such term by subsection (l)(7) (without regard to subparagraphs (C) and (D) thereof) and using the rate of interest used under subsection (b)(5)(B).

(C) SPECIAL RULE FOR PARAGRAPH (6)(B).—For purposes of paragraph (6)(B), subparagraph (A)(i) shall be applied without regard to subclause (I) thereof.

(D) REGULATORY AUTHORITY.—The Secretary may by regulations provide—

(i) for adjustments to the percentage contained in subparagraph (A)(i) to take into account the respective ages or lengths of service of the participants, and

(ii) alternative methods based on factors other than current liability for the determination of the amount taken into account under subparagraph (A)(i).

(E) MINIMUM AMOUNT.—

(i) IN GENERAL.—In no event shall the full-funding limitation determined under subparagraph (A) be less than the excess (if any) of—

(I) 90 percent of the current liability of the plan (including the expected increase in current liability due to benefits accruing during the plan year), over

(II) the value of the plan's assets determined under paragraph (2).

(ii) CURRENT LIABILITY; ASSETS.—For purposes of clause (i)—

(I) the term "current liability" has the meaning given such term by subsection (l)(7) (without regard to subparagraph (D) thereof), and

(II) assets shall not be reduced by any credit balance in the funding standard account.

(F) APPLICABLE PERCENTAGE.—For purposes of subparagraph (A)(i)(I), the applicable percentage shall be determined in accordance with the following table:

In the case of any plan year beginning in—	*The applicable percentage is—*
2002	165
2003	170 .

(8) CERTAIN RETROACTIVE PLAN AMENDMENTS.—For purposes of this section, any amendment applying to a plan year which—

(A) is adopted after the close of such plan year but no later than 2 and one-half months after the close of the plan year (or, in the case of a multiemployer plan, no later than 2 years after the close of such plan year),

(B) does not reduce the accrued benefit of any participant determined as of the beginning of the first plan year to which the amendment applies, and

(C) does not reduce the accrued benefit of any participant determined as of the time of adoption except to the extent required by the circumstances,

shall, at the election of the plan administrator, be deemed to have been made on the first day of such plan year. No amendment described in this paragraph which reduces the accrued benefits of any participant shall take effect unless the plan administrator files a notice with the Secretary of Labor notifying him of such amendment and the Secretary of Labor has approved such amendment, or within 90 days after the date on which such notice was filed, failed to disapprove such amendment. No amendment described in this subsection shall be approved by the Secretary of Labor unless he determines that such amendment is necessary because of a substantial business hardship (as determined under subsection (d)(2)) and that a waiver under subsection (d)(1) is unavailable or inadequate.

(9) ANNUAL VALUATION.—

(A) IN GENERAL.—For purposes of this section, a determination of experience gains and losses and a valuation of the plan's liability shall be made not less frequently than once every year, except that such determination shall be made more frequently to the extent required in particular cases under regulations prescribed by the Secretary.

(B) VALUATION DATE.—

(i) CURRENT YEAR.—Except as provided in clause (ii), the valuation referred to in subparagraph (A) shall be made as of a date within the plan year to which the valuation refers or within one month prior to the beginning of such year.

(ii) USE OF PRIOR YEAR VALUATION.—The valuation referred to in subparagraph (A) may be made as of a date within the plan year prior to the year to which the valuation refers if, as of such date, the value of the assets of the plan are not less than 100 percent of the plan's current liability (as defined in paragraph (7)(B)).

(iii) ADJUSTMENTS.—Information under clause (ii) shall, in accordance with regulations, be actuarially adjusted to reflect significant differences in participants.

(iv) LIMITATION.—A change in funding method to use a prior year valuation, as provided in clause (ii), may not be made unless as of the valuation date within the prior plan year, the value of the assets of the plan are not less than 125 percent of the plan's current liability (as defined in paragraph (7)(B)).

(10) TIME WHEN CERTAIN CONTRIBUTIONS DEEMED MADE.—For purposes of this section—

(A) DEFINED BENEFIT PLANS OTHER THAN MULTIEMPLOYER PLANS.—In the case of a defined benefit plan other than a multiemployer plan, any contributions for a plan year made by an employer during the period—

(i) beginning on the day after the last day of such plan year, and

(ii) ending on the day which is 8½ months after the close of the plan year,

shall be deemed to have been made on such last day.

(B) OTHER PLANS.—In the case of a plan not described in subparagraph (A), any contributions for a plan year made by an employer after the last day of such plan year, but not later than two and one-half months after such day, shall be deemed to have been made on such last day. For purposes of this subparagraph, such two and one-half month period may be extended for not more than six months under regulations prescribed by the Secretary.

(11) LIABILITY FOR CONTRIBUTIONS.—

(A) IN GENERAL.—Except as provided in subparagraph (B), the amount of any contribution required by this section and any required installments under subsection (m) shall be paid by the employer responsible for contributing to or under the plan the amount described in subsection (b)(3)(A).

(B) JOINT AND SEVERAL LIABILITY WHERE EMPLOYER MEMBER OF CONTROLLED GROUP.—

(i) IN GENERAL.—In the case of a plan other than a multiemployer plan, if the employer referred to in subparagraph (A) is a member of a controlled group, each member of such group shall be jointly and severally liable for payment of such contribution or required installment.

(ii) CONTROLLED GROUP.—For purposes of clause (i), the term "controlled group" means any group treated as a single employer under subsection (b), (c), (m), or (o) of section 414.

(12) ANTICIPATION OF BENEFIT INCREASES EFFECTIVE IN THE FUTURE.—In determining projected benefits, the funding method of a collectively bargained plan described in section 413(a) (other than a multiemployer plan) shall anticipate benefit increases scheduled to take effect during the term of the collective bargaining agreement applicable to the plan.

(d) VARIANCE FROM MINIMUM FUNDING STANDARD.—

(1) WAIVER IN CASE OF BUSINESS HARDSHIP.—If an employer or in the case of a multiemployer plan, 10 percent or more of the number of employers contributing to or under the plan, are unable to satisfy the minimum funding standard for a plan year without temporary substantial business hardship (substantial business hardship in the case of a multiemployer plan) and if application of the standard would be adverse to the interests of plan participants in the aggregate, the Secretary may waive the requirements of subsection (a) for such year with respect to all or any portion of the minimum funding standard other than the portion thereof determined under subsection (b)(2)(C). The Secretary shall not waive the minimum funding standard with respect to a plan for more than 3 of any 15 (5 of any 15 in the case of a multiemployer plan) consecutive plan years. The interest rate used for purposes of computing the amortization charge described in subsection (b)(2)(C) for any plan year shall be—

(A) in the case of a plan other than a multiemployer plan, the greater of (i) 150 percent of the Federal mid-term rate (as in effect under section 1274 for the 1st month of such plan year), or (ii) the rate of interest used under the plan in determining costs (including adjustments under subsection (b)(5)(B)), and

(B) in the case of a multiemployer plan, the rate determined under section 6621(b).

(2) DETERMINATION OF BUSINESS HARDSHIP.—For purposes of this section, the factors taken into account in determining temporary substantial business hardship (substantial business hardship in the case of a multiemployer plan) shall include (but shall not be limited to) whether or not—

(A) the employer is operating at an economic loss,

(B) there is substantial unemployment or underemployment in the trade or business and in the industry concerned,

(C) the sales and profits of the industry concerned are depressed or declining, and

(D) it is reasonable to expect that the plan will be continued only if the waiver is granted.

(3) WAIVED FUNDING DEFICIENCY.—For purposes of this section, the term "waived funding deficiency" means the portion of the minimum funding standard (determined without regard to subsection (b)(3)(C)) for a plan year waived by the Secretary and not satisfied by employer contributions.

(4) APPLICATION MUST BE SUBMITTED BEFORE DATE 2½ MONTHS AFTER CLOSE OF YEAR.—In the case of a plan other than a multiemployer plan, no waiver may be granted under this subsection with respect to any plan for any plan year unless an application therefor is submitted to the Secretary not later than the 15th day of the 3rd month beginning after the close of such plan year.

(5) SPECIAL RULE IF EMPLOYER IS MEMBER OF CONTROLLED GROUP.—

(A) IN GENERAL.—In the case of a plan other than a multiemployer plan, if an employer is a member of a controlled group, the temporary substantial business hardship requirements of paragraph (1) shall be treated as met only if such requirements are met—

(i) with respect to such employer, and

(ii) with respect to the controlled group of which such employer is a member (determined by treating all members of such group as a single employer).

The Secretary may provide that an analysis of a trade or business or industry of a member need not be conducted if the Secretary determines such analysis is not necessary because the taking into account of such member would not significantly affect the determination under this subsection.

(B) CONTROLLED GROUP.—For purposes of subparagraph (A), the term "controlled group" means any group treated as a single employer under subsection (b), (c), (m), or (o) of section 414.

(e) EXTENSION OF AMORTIZATION PERIODS.—The period of years required to amortize any unfunded liability (described in any clause of subsection (b)(2)(B)) of any plan may be extended by the Secretary of Labor for a period of time (not in excess of 10 years) if he determines that such extension would carry out the purposes of the Employee Retirement Income Security Act of 1974 and would provide adequate protection for participants under the plan and their beneficiaries and if he determines that the failure to permit such extension would—

(1) result in—

(A) a substantial risk to the voluntary continuation of the plan, or

(B) a substantial curtailment of pension benefit levels or employee compensation, and

(2) be adverse to the interests of plan participants in the aggregate.

In the case of a plan other than a multiemployer plan, the interest rate applicable for any plan year under any arrangement entered into by the Secretary in connection with an extension granted under this subsection shall be the greater of (A) 150 percent of the Federal mid-term rate (as in effect under section 1274 for the 1st month of such plan year), or (B) the rate of interest used under the plan in determining costs. In the case of a multiemployer plan, such rate shall be the rate determined under section 6621(b).

(f) REQUIREMENTS RELATING TO WAIVERS AND EXTENSIONS.—

(1) BENEFITS MAY NOT BE INCREASED DURING WAIVER OR EXTENSION PERIOD.—No amendment of the plan which increases the liabilities of the plan by reason of any increase in benefits, any change in the accrual of benefits, or any change in the rate at which benefits become nonforfeitable under the plan shall be adopted if a waiver under subsection (d)(1) or an extension of time under subsection (e) is in effect with respect to the plan, or if a plan amendment described in subsection (c)(8) has been made at any time in the preceding 12 months (24 months for multiemployer plans). If a plan is amended in violation of the preceding sentence, any such waiver or extension of time shall not apply to any plan year ending on or after the date on which such amendment is adopted.

(2) EXCEPTION.—Paragraph (1) shall not apply to any plan amendment which—

(A) the Secretary of Labor determines to be reasonable and which provides for only de minimis increases in the liabilities of the plan,

(B) only repeals an amendment described in subsection (c)(8), or

(C) is required as a condition of qualification under this part.

(3) SECURITY FOR WAIVERS AND EXTENSIONS; CONSULTATIONS.—

(A) SECURITY MAY BE REQUIRED.—

(i) IN GENERAL.—Except as provided in subparagraph (C), the Secretary may require an employer maintaining a defined benefit plan which is a single-employer plan (within the meaning of section 4001(a)(15) of the Employee Retirement Income Security Act of 1974) to provide security to such plan as a condition for granting or modifying a waiver under subsection (d) or an extension under subsection (e).

(ii) SPECIAL RULES.—Any security provided under clause (i) may be perfected and enforced only by the Pension Benefit Guaranty Corporation, or at the direction of the Corporation, by a contributing sponsor (within the meaning of section 4001(a)(13) of such Act), or a member of such sponsor's controlled group (within the meaning of section 4001(a)(14) of such Act).

(B) CONSULTATION WITH THE PENSION BENEFIT GUARANTY CORPORATION.—Except as provided in subparagraph (C), the Secretary shall, before granting or modifying a waiver under subsection (d) or an extension under subsection (e) with respect to a plan described in subparagraph (A)(i)—

(i) provide the Pension Benefit Guaranty Corporation with—

(I) notice of the completed application for any waiver, extension, or modification, and

(II) an opportunity to comment on such application within 30 days after receipt of such notice, and

(ii) consider—

(I) any comments of the Corporation under clause (i)(II), and

(II) any views of any employee organization (within the meaning of section 3(4) of the Employee Retirement Income Security Act of 1974) representing participants in the plan which are submitted in writing to the Secretary in connection with such application.

Information provided to the corporation under this subparagraph shall be considered tax return information and subject to the safeguarding and reporting requirements of section 6103(p).

(C) EXCEPTION FOR CERTAIN WAIVERS AND EXTENSIONS.

(i) IN GENERAL.—The preceding provisions of this paragraph shall not apply to any plan with respect to which the sum of—

(I) the outstanding balance of the accumulated funding deficiencies (within the meaning of subsection (a) and section 302(a) of such Act) of the plan,

(II) the outstanding balance of the amount of waived funding deficiencies of the plan waived under subsection (d) or section 303 of such Act, and

(III) the outstanding balance of the amount of decreases in the minimum funding standard allowed under subsection (e) or section 304 of such Act,

is less than $1,000,000.

(ii) ACCUMULATED FUNDING DEFICIENCIES.—For purposes of clause (i)(I), accumulated funding deficiencies shall include any increase in such amount which would result if all applications for waivers of the minimum funding standard under subsection (d) or section 303 of such Act and for extensions of the amortization period under subsection (e) or section 304 of such Act which are pending with respect to such plan were denied.

(4) ADDITIONAL REQUIREMENTS.—

(A) ADVANCE NOTICE.—The Secretary shall, before granting a waiver under subsection (d) or an extension under subsection (e), require each applicant to provide evidence satisfactory to the Secretary that the applicant has provided notice of the filing of the application for such waiver or extension to each employee organization representing employees covered by the affected plan, and each participant, beneficiary, and alternate payee (within the meaning of section 414(p)(8)). Such notice shall include a description of the extent to which the plan is funded for benefits which are guaranteed under title IV of such Act and for benefit liabilities.

(B) CONSIDERATION OF RELEVANT INFORMATION.—The Secretary shall consider any relevant information provided by a person to whom notice was given under subparagraph (A).

(g) ALTERNATIVE MINIMUM FUNDING STANDARD.—

(1) IN GENERAL.—A plan which uses a funding method that requires contributions in all years not less than those required under the entry age normal funding method may maintain an alternative minimum funding standard account for any plan year. Such account shall be credited and charged solely as provided in this subsection.

(2) CHARGES AND CREDITS TO ACCOUNT.—For a plan year the alternative minimum funding standard account shall be—

(A) charged with the sum of—

(i) the lesser of normal cost under the funding method used under the plan or normal cost determined under the unit credit method,

(ii) the excess, if any, of the present value of accrued benefits under the plan over the fair market value of the assets, and

(iii) an amount equal to the excess (if any) of credits to the alternative minimum standard account for all prior plan years over charges to such account for all such years, and

(B) credited with the amount considered contributed by the employer to or under the plan for the plan year.

(3) SPECIAL RULES.—The alternative minimum funding standard account (and items therein) shall be charged or credited with interest in the manner provided under subsection (b)(5) with respect to the funding standard account.

(h) EXCEPTIONS.—This section shall not apply to—

(1) any profit-sharing or stock bonus plan,

(2) any insurance contract plan described in subsection (i),

(3) any governmental plan (within the meaning of section 414(d)),

(4) any church plan (within the meaning of section 414(e)) with respect to which the election provided by section 410(d) has not been made,

(5) any plan which has not, at any time after September 2, 1974, provided for employer contributions, or

(6) any plan established and maintained by a society, order, or association described in section 501(c)(8) or (9), if no part of the contributions to or under such plan are made by employers of participants in such plan.

No plan described in paragraph (3), (4), or (6) shall be treated as a qualified plan for purposes of section 401(a) unless such plan meets the requirements of section 401(a)(7) as in effect on September 1, 1974.

(i) CERTAIN INSURANCE CONTRACT PLANS.—A plan is described in this subsection if—

(1) the plan is funded exclusively by the purchase of individual insurance contracts,

(2) such contracts provide for level annual premium payments to be paid extending not later than the retirement age for each individual participating in the plan, and commencing with the date the individual became a participant in the plan (or, in the case of an increase in benefits, commencing at the time such increase becomes effective),

(3) benefits provided by the plan are equal to the benefits provided under each contract at normal retirement age under the plan and are guaranteed by an insurance carrier (licensed under the laws of a State to do business with the plan) to the extent premiums have been paid,

(4) premiums payable for the plan year, and all prior plan years, under such contracts have been paid before lapse or there is reinstatement of the policy,

(5) no rights under such contracts have been subject to a security interest at any time during the plan year, and

(6) no policy loans are outstanding at any time during the plan year.

A plan funded exclusively by the purchase of group insurance contracts which is determined under regulations prescribed by the Secretary to have the same characteristics as contracts described in the preceding sentence shall be treated as a plan described in this subsection.

(j) CERTAIN TERMINATED MULTIEMPLOYER PLANS.—This section applies with respect to a terminated multiemployer plan to which section 4021 of the Employee Retirement Income Security Act of 1974 applies, until the last day of the plan year in which the plan terminates, within the meaning of section 4041A(a)(2) of that Act.

(k) FINANCIAL ASSISTANCE.—Any amount of any financial assistance from the Pension Benefit Guaranty Corporation to any plan, and any repayment of such amount, shall be taken into account under this section in such manner as determined by the Secretary.

(l) ADDITIONAL FUNDING REQUIREMENTS FOR PLANS WHICH ARE NOT MULTIEMPLOYER PLANS.—

(1) IN GENERAL.—In the case of a defined benefit plan (other than a multiemployer plan) to which this subsection applies under paragraph (9) for any plan year, the amount charged to the funding standard account for such plan year shall be increased by the sum of—

(A) the excess (if any) of—

(i) the deficit reduction contribution determined under paragraph (2) for such plan year, over

(ii) the sum of the charges for such plan year under subsection (b)(2), reduced by the sum of the credits for such plan year under subparagraph (B) of subsection (b)(3), plus

(B) the unpredictable contingent event amount (if any) for such plan year.

Such increase shall not exceed the amount which, after taking into account charges (other than the additional charge under this subsection) and credits under subsection (b), is necessary to increase the funded current liability percentage (taking into account the expected increase in current liability due to benefits accruing during the plan year) to 100 percent.

(2) DEFICIT REDUCTION CONTRIBUTION.—For purposes of paragraph (1), the deficit reduction contribution determined under this paragraph for any plan year is the sum of—

(A) the unfunded old liability amount,

(B) the unfunded new liability amount,

(C) the expected increase in current liability due to benefits accruing during the plan year, and

(D) the aggregate of the unfunded mortality increase amounts.

(3) UNFUNDED OLD LIABILITY AMOUNT.—For purposes of this subsection—

(A) IN GENERAL.—The unfunded old liability amount with respect to any plan for any plan year is the amount necessary to amortize the unfunded old liability under the plan in equal annual installments over a period of 18 plan years (beginning with the 1st plan year beginning after December 31, 1988).

(B) UNFUNDED OLD LIABILITY.—The term "unfunded old liability" means the unfunded current liability of the plan as of the beginning of the 1st plan year beginning after December 31, 1987 (determined without regard to any plan amendment increasing liabilities adopted after October 16, 1987).

(C) SPECIAL RULES FOR BENEFIT INCREASES UNDER EXISTING COLLECTIVE BARGAINING AGREEMENTS.—

(i) IN GENERAL.—In the case of a plan maintained pursuant to 1 or more collective bargaining agreements between employee representatives and the employer ratified before October 29, 1987, the unfunded old liability amount with respect to such plan for any plan year shall be increased by the amount necessary to amortize the unfunded existing benefit increase liability in equal annual installments over a period of 18 plan years beginning with—

(I) the plan year in which the benefit increase with respect to such liability occurs, or

(II) if the taxpayer elects, the 1st plan year beginning after December 31, 1988.

(ii) Unfunded existing benefit increase liabilities.—For purposes of clause (i), the unfunded existing benefit increase liability means, with respect to any benefit increase under the agreements described in clause (i) which takes effect during or after the 1st plan year beginning after December 31, 1987, the unfunded current liability determined—

(I) by taking into account only liabilities attributable to such benefit increase, and

(II) by reducing (but not below zero) the amount determined under paragraph (8)(A)(ii) by the current liability determined without regard to such benefit increase.

(iii) EXTENSIONS, MODIFICATIONS, ETC. NOT TAKEN INTO ACCOUNT.—For purposes of this subparagraph, any extension, amendment, or other modification of an agreement after October 28, 1987, shall not be taken into account.

(D) SPECIAL RULE FOR REQUIRED CHANGES IN ACTUARIAL ASSUMPTIONS.—

(i) IN GENERAL.—The unfunded old liability amount with respect to any plan for any plan year shall be increased by the amount necessary to amortize the amount of additional unfunded old liability under the plan in equal annual installments over a period of 12 plan years (beginning with the first plan year beginning after December 31, 1994).

(ii) ADDITIONAL UNFUNDED OLD LIABILITY.—For purposes of clause (i), the term "additional unfunded old liability" means the amount (if any) by which—

(I) the current liability of the plan as of the beginning of the first plan year beginning after December 31, 1994, valued using the assumptions required by paragraph (7)(C) as in effect for plan years beginning after December 31, 1994, exceeds

(II) the current liability of the plan as of the beginning of such first plan year, valued using the same assumptions used under subclause (I) (other than the assumptions required by paragraph (7)(C)), using the prior interest rate, and using such mortality assumptions as were used to determine current liability for the first plan year beginning after December 31, 1992.

(iii) PRIOR INTEREST RATE.—For purposes of clause (ii), the term "prior interest rate" means the rate of interest that is the same percentage of the weighted average under subsection (b)(5)(B)(ii)(I) for the first plan year beginning after December 31, 1994, as the rate of interest used by the plan to determine current liability for the first plan year beginning after December 31, 1992, is of the weighted average under subsection (b)(5)(B)(ii)(I) for such first plan year beginning after December 31, 1992.

(E) OPTIONAL RULE FOR ADDITIONAL UNFUNDED OLD LIABILITY.—

(i) IN GENERAL.—If an employer makes an election under clause (ii), the additional unfunded old liability for purposes of subparagraph (D) shall be the amount (if any) by which—

(I) the unfunded current liability of the plan as of the beginning of the first plan year beginning after December 31, 1994, valued using the assumptions required by paragraph (7)(C) as in effect for plan years beginning after December 31, 1994, exceeds

(II) the unamortized portion of the unfunded old liability under the plan as of the beginning of the first plan year beginning after December 31, 1994.

(ii) ELECTION.—

(I) An employer may irrevocably elect to apply the provisions of this subparagraph as of the beginning of the first plan year beginning after December 31, 1994.

(II) If an election is made under this clause, the increase under paragraph (1) for any plan year beginning after December 31, 1994, and before January 1, 2002, to which this subsection applies (without regard to this subclause) shall not be less than the increase that would be required under paragraph (1) if the provisions of this title as in effect for the last plan year beginning before January 1, 1995, had remained in effect.

(4) UNFUNDED NEW LIABILITY AMOUNT.—For purposes of this subsection—

(A) IN GENERAL.—The unfunded new liability amount with respect to any plan for any plan year is the applicable percentage of the unfunded new liability.

(B) UNFUNDED NEW LIABILITY.—The term "unfunded new liability" means the unfunded current liability of the plan for the plan year determined without regard to—

(i) the unamortized portion of the unfunded old liability, the unamortized portion of the additional unfunded old liability, the unamortized portion of each unfunded mortality increase, and the unamortized portion of the unfunded existing benefit increase liability, and

(ii) the liability with respect to any unpredictable contingent event benefits (without regard to whether the event has occurred).

(C) APPLICABLE PERCENTAGE.—The term "applicable percentage" means, with respect to any plan year, 30 percent, reduced by the product of—

(i) .40 multiplied by

(ii) the number of percentage points (if any) by which the funded current liability percentage exceeds 60 percent.

(5) UNPREDICTABLE CONTINGENT EVENT AMOUNT.—

(A) IN GENERAL.—The unpredictable contingent event amount with respect to a plan for any plan year is an amount equal to the greatest of—

(i) the applicable percentage of the product of—

(I) 100 percent, reduced (but not below zero) by the funded current liability percentage for the plan year, multiplied by

(II) the amount of unpredictable contingent event benefits paid during the plan year, including (except as provided by the Secretary) any payment for the purchase of an annuity contract for a participant or beneficiary with respect to such benefits,

(ii) the amount which would be determined for the plan year if the unpredictable contingent event benefit liabilites were amortized in equal annual installments over 7 plan years (beginning with the plan year in which such event occurs), or

(iii) the additional amount that would be determined under paragraph (4)(A) if the unpredictable contingent event benefit liabilities were included in unfunded new liability notwithstanding paragraph (4)(B)(ii).

(B) APPLICABLE PERCENTAGE.—

In the case of plan years beginning in:	*The applicable percentage is:*
1989 and 1990	5
1991	10
1992	15
1993	20
1994	30
1995	40
1996	50
1997	60
1998	70
1999	80
2000	90
2001 and thereafter	100

(C) PARAGRAPH NOT TO APPLY TO EXISTING BENEFITS.—This paragraph shall not apply to unpredictable contingent event benefits (and liabilities attributable thereto) for which the event occurred before the first plan year beginning after December 31, 1988.

(D) SPECIAL RULE FOR FIRST YEAR OF AMORTIZATION.—Unless the employer elects otherwise, the amount determined under subparagraph (A) for the plan year in which the event occurs shall be equal to 150 percent of the amount determined under subparagraph (A)(i). The amount under subparagraph (A)(ii) for subsequent plan years in the amortization period shall be adjusted in the manner provided by the Secretary to reflect the application of this subparagraph.

(E) LIMITATION.—The present value of the amounts described in subparagraph (A) with respect to any one event shall not exceed the unpredictable contingent event benefit liabilities attributable to that event.

(6) SPECIAL RULES FOR SMALL PLANS.—

(A) PLANS WITH 100 OR FEWER PARTICIPANTS.—This subsection shall not apply to any plan for any plan year if on each day during the preceding plan year such plan had no more than 100 participants.

(B) PLANS WITH MORE THAN 100 BUT NOT MORE THAN 150 PARTICIPANTS.—In the case of a plan to which subparagraph (A) does not apply and which on each day during the preceding plan year had no more than 150 participants, the amount of the increase under paragraph (1) for such plan year shall be equal to the product of—

(i) such increase determined without regard to this subparagraph, multiplied by

(ii) 2 percent for the highest number of participants in excess of 100 on any such day.

(C) AGGREGATION OF PLANS.—For purposes of this paragraph, all defined benefit plans maintained by the same employer (or any member of such employer's controlled group) shall be treated as 1 plan, but only employees of such employer or member shall be taken into account.

(7) CURRENT LIABILITY.—For purposes of this subsection—

(A) IN GENERAL.—The term "current liability" means all liabilities to employees and their beneficiaries under the plan.

(B) TREATMENT OF UNPREDICTABLE CONTINGENT EVENT BENEFITS.—

(i) IN GENERAL.—For purposes of subparagraph (A), any unpredictable contingent event benefit shall not be taken into account until the event on which the benefit is contingent occurs.

(ii) UNPREDICTABLE CONTINGENT EVENT BENEFIT.—The term "unpredictable contingent event benefit" means any benefit contingent on an event other than—

(I) age, service, compensation, death, or disability, or

(II) an event which is reasonably and reliably predictable (as determined by the Secretary).

(C) INTEREST RATE AND MORTALITY ASSUMPTIONS USED.—Effective for plan years beginning after December 31, 1994—

(i) INTEREST RATE.—

(I) IN GENERAL.—The rate of interest used to determine current liability under this subsection shall be the rate of interest used under subsection (b)(5), except that the highest rate in the permissible range under subparagraph (B)(ii) thereof shall not exceed the specified percentage under subclause (II) of the weighted average referred to in such subparagraph.

(II) SPECIFIED PERCENTAGE.—For purposes of subclause (I), the specified percentage shall be determined as follows:

In the case of plan years beginning in calendar year:	*The specified percentage is:*
1995	109
1996	108
1997	107
1998	106
1999 and thereafter	105

(III) SPECIAL RULE FOR 2002 AND 2003.—For a plan year beginning in 2002 or 2003, notwithstanding subclause (I), in the case that the rate of interest used under subsection (b)(5) exceeds the highest rate permitted under subclause (I), the rate of interest used to determine current liability under this subsection may exceed the rate of interest otherwise permitted under subclause (I); except that such rate of interest shall not exceed 120 percent of the weighted average referred to in subsection (b)(5)(B)(ii).

(IV) SPECIAL RULE FOR 2004, 2005, 2006, AND 2007.—For plan years beginning in 2004, 2005, 2006, or 2007, notwithstanding subclause (I), the rate of interest used to determine current liability under this subsection shall be the rate of interest under subsection (b)(5).

(ii) MORTALITY TABLES.—

(I) COMMISSIONER'S STANDARD TABLE.—In the case of plan years beginning before the first plan year to which the first tables prescribed under subclause (II) apply, the mortality table used in determining current liability under this subsection shall be the table prescribed by the Secretary which is based on the prevailing commissioners' standard table (described in section 807(d)(5)(A)) used to determine reserves for group annuity contracts issued on January 1, 1993.

(II) SECRETARIAL AUTHORITY.—The Secretary may by regulation prescribe for plan years beginning after December 31, 1999, mortality tables to be used in determining current liability under this subsection. Such tables shall be based upon the actual experience of pension plans and projected trends in such experience. In prescribing such tables, the Secretary shall take into account results of available independent studies of mortality of individuals covered by pension plans.

(III) PERIODIC REVIEW.—The Secretary shall periodically (at least every 5 years) review any tables in effect under this subsection and shall, to the extent the Secretary determines necessary, by regulation update the tables to reflect the actual experience of pension plans and projected trends in such experience.

(iii) SEPARATE MORTALITY TABLES FOR THE DISABLED.—Notwithstanding clause (ii)—

(I) IN GENERAL.—In the case of plan years beginning after December 31, 1995, the Secretary shall establish mortality tables which may be used (in lieu of the tables under clause (ii)) to determine current liability under this subsection for individuals who are entitled to benefits under the plan on account of disability. The Secretary shall establish separate tables for individuals whose disabilities occur in plan years beginning before January 1, 1995, and for individuals whose disabilities occur in plan years beginning on or after such date.

(II) SPECIAL RULE FOR DISABILITIES OCCURRING AFTER 1994.—In the case of disabilities occurring in plan years beginning after December 31, 1994, the tables under subclause (I) shall apply only with respect to individuals described in such subclause who are disabled within the meaning of title II of the Social Security Act and the regulations thereunder.

(III) PLAN YEARS BEGINNING IN 1995.—In the case of any plan year beginning in 1995, a plan may use its own mortality assumptions for individuals who are entitled to benefits under the plan on account of disability.

(D) CERTAIN SERVICE DISREGARDED.—

(i) IN GENERAL.—In the case of a participant to whom this subparagraph applies, only the applicable percentage of the years of service before such individual became a participant shall be taken into account in computing the current liability of the plan.

(ii) APPLICABLE PERCENTAGE.—For purposes of this subparagraph, the applicable percentage shall be determined as follows:

If the years of participation are:	*The applicable percentage is:*
1	20
2	40
3	60
4	80
5 or more	100

(iii) PARTICIPANTS TO WHOM SUBPARAGRAPH APPLIES.—This subparagraph shall apply to any participant who, at the time of becoming a participant—

(I) has not accrued any other benefit under any defined benefit plan (whether or not terminated) maintained by the employer or a member of the same controlled group of which the employer is a member,

(II) who first becomes a participant under the plan in a plan year beginning after December 31, 1987, and

(III) has years of service greater than the minimum years of service necessary for eligibility to participate in the plan.

(iv) ELECTION.—An employer may elect not to have this subparagraph apply. Such an election, once made, may be revoked only with the consent of the Secretary.

(8) OTHER DEFINITIONS.—For purposes of this subsection—

(A) UNFUNDED CURRENT LIABILITY.—The term "unfunded current liability" means, with respect to any plan year, the excess (if any) of—

(i) the current liability under the plan, over

(ii) value of the plan's assets determined under subsection (c)(2).

(B) FUNDED CURRENT LIABILITY PERCENTAGE.—The term "funded current liability percentage" means, with respect to any plan year, the percentage which—

(i) the amount determined under subparagraph (A)(ii), is of

(ii) the current liability under the plan.

(C) CONTROLLED GROUP.—The term "controlled group" means any group treated as a single employer under subsection (b), (c), (m), and (o) of section 414.

(D) ADJUSTMENTS TO PREVENT OMISSIONS AND DUPLICATIONS.—The Secretary shall provide such adjustments in the unfunded old liability amount, the unfunded new liability amount, the unpredictable contingent event amount, the current payment amount, and any other charges or credits under this section as are necessary to avoid duplication or omission of any factors in the determination of such amounts, charges, or credits.

(E) DEDUCTION FOR CREDIT BALANCES.—For purposes of this subsection, the amount determined under subparagraph (A)(ii) shall be reduced by any credit balance in the funding standard account. The Secretary may provide for such reduction for purposes of any other provision which references this subsection.

(9) APPLICABILITY OF SUBSECTION.—

(A) IN GENERAL.—Except as provided in paragraph (6)(A), this subsection shall apply to a plan for any plan year if its funded current liability percentage for such year is less than 90 percent.

(B) EXCEPTION FOR CERTAIN PLANS AT LEAST 80 PERCENT FUNDED.—Subparagraph (A) shall not apply to a plan for a plan year if—

(i) the funded current liability percentage for the plan year is at least 80 percent, and

(ii) such percentage for each of the 2 immediately preceding plan years (or each of the 2d and 3d immediately preceding plan years) is at least 90 percent.

(C) FUNDED CURRENT LIABILITY PERCENTAGE.—For purposes of subparagraphs (A) and (B), the term "funded current liability percentage" has the meaning given such term by paragraph (8)(B), except that such percentage shall be determined for any plan year—

(i) without regard to paragraph (8)(E), and

(ii) by using the rate of interest which is the highest rate allowable for the plan year under paragraph (7)(C).

(D) TRANSITION RULES.—For purposes of this paragraph:

(i) FUNDED PERCENTAGE FOR YEARS BEFORE 1995.—The funded current liability percentage for any plan year beginning before January 1, 1995, shall be treated as not less than 90 percent only if for such plan year the plan met one of the following requirements (as in effect for such year):

(I) The full-funding limitation under subsection (c)(7) for the plan was zero.

(II) The plan had no additional funding requirement under this subsection (or would have had no such requirement if its funded current liability percentage had been determined under subparagraph (C)).

(III) The plan's additional funding requirement under this subsection did not exceed the lesser of 0.5 percent of current liability or $5,000,000.

(ii) SPECIAL RULE FOR 1995 AND 1996.—For purposes of determining whether subparagraph (B) applies to any plan year beginning in 1995 or 1996, a plan shall be treated as meeting the requirements of subparagraph (B)(ii) if the plan met the requirements of clause (i) of this subparagraph for any two of the plan years beginning in 1992, 1993, and 1994 (whether or not consecutive).

(10) UNFUNDED MORTALITY INCREASE AMOUNT.—

(A) IN GENERAL.—The unfunded mortality increase amount with respect to each unfunded mortality increase is the amount necessary to amortize such increase in equal annual installments over a period of 10 plan years (beginning with the first plan year for which a plan uses any new mortality table issued under paragraph (7)(C)(ii)(II) or (III)).

(B) UNFUNDED MORTALITY INCREASE.—For purposes of subparagraph (A), the term "unfunded mortality increase" means an amount equal to the excess of—

(i) the current liability of the plan for the first plan year for which a plan uses any new mortality table issued under paragraph (7)(C)(ii)(II) or (III), over

(ii) the current liability of the plan for such plan year which would have been determined if the mortality table in effect for the preceding plan year had been used.

(11) PHASE-IN OF INCREASES IN FUNDING REQUIRED BY RETIREMENT PROTECTION ACT OF 1994.—

(A) IN GENERAL.—For any applicable plan year, at the election of the employer, the increase under paragraph (1) shall not exceed the greater of—

(i) the increase that would be required under paragraph (1) if the provisions of this title as in effect for plan years beginning before January 1, 1995, had remained in effect, or

(ii) the amount which, after taking into account charges (other than the additional charge under this subsection) and credits under subsection (b), is necessary to increase the funded current liability percentage (taking into account the expected increase in current liability due to benefits accruing during the plan year) for the applicable plan year to a percentage equal to the sum of the initial funded current liability percentage of the plan plus the applicable number of percentage points for such applicable plan year.

(B) APPLICABLE NUMBER OF PERCENTAGE POINTS.—

(i) INITIAL FUNDED CURRENT LIABILITY PERCENTAGE OF 75 PERCENTOR LESS.—Except as provided in clause (ii), for plans with an initial funded current liability percentage of 75 percent or less, the applicable number of percentage points for the applicable plan year is:

In the case of applicable plan years beginning in:	*The applicable number of percentage points is:*
1995	3
1996	6
1997	9
1998	12
1999	15
2000	19
2001	24

(ii) OTHER CASES.—In the case of a plan to which this clause applies, the applicable number of percentage points for any such applicable plan year is the sum of—

(I) 2 percentage points;

(II) the applicable number of percentage points (if any) under this clause for the preceding applicable plan year;

(III) the product of .10 multiplied by the excess (if any) of (a) 85 percentage points over (b) the sum of the initial funded current liability percentage and the number determined under subclause (II);

(IV) for applicable plan years beginning in 2000, 1 percentage point; and

(V) for applicable plan years beginning in 2001, 2 percentage points.

(iii) PLANS TO WHICH CLAUSE (ii) APPLIES.—

(I) IN GENERAL.—Clause (ii) shall apply to a plan for an applicable plan year if the initial funded current liability percentage of such plan is more than 75 percent.

(II) PLANS INITIALLY UNDER CLAUSE (i).—In the case of a plan which (but for this subclause) has an initial funded current liability percentage of 75 percent or less, clause (ii) (and not clause (i)) shall apply to such plan with respect to applicable plan years beginning after the first applicable plan year for which the sum of the initial funded current liability percentage and the applicable number of percentage points (determined under clause (i)) exceeds 75 percent. For purposes of applying clause (ii) to such a plan, the initial funded current liability percentage of such plan shall be treated as being the sum referred to in the preceding sentence.

(C) DEFINITIONS.—For purposes of this paragraph:

(i) The term "applicable plan year" means a plan year beginning after December 31, 1994, and before January 1, 2002.

(ii) The term "initial funded current liability percentage" means the funded current liability percentage as of the first day of the first plan year beginning after December 31, 1994.

(12) ELECTION FOR CERTAIN PLANS.—

(A) IN GENERAL.—In the case of a defined benefit plan established and maintained by an applicable employer, if this subsection did not apply to the plan for the plan year beginning in 2000 (determined without regard to paragraph (6)), then, at the election of the employer, the increased amount under paragraph (1) for any applicable plan year shall be the greater of—

(i) 20 percent of the increased amount under paragraph (1) determined without regard to this paragraph, or

(ii) the increased amount which would be determined under paragraph (1) if the deficit reduction contribution under paragraph (2) for the applicable plan year were determined without regard to subparagraphs (A), (B), and (D) of paragraph (2).

(B) RESTRICTIONS ON BENEFIT INCREASES.—No amendment which increases the liabilities of the plan by reason of any increase in benefits, any change in the accrual of benefits, or any change in the rate at which benefits become nonforfeitable under the plan shall be adopted during any applicable plan year, unless—

(i) the plan's enrolled actuary certifies (in such form and manner prescribed by the Secretary) that the amendment provides for an increase in annual contributions which will exceed the increase in annual charges to the funding standard account attributable to such amendment, or

(ii) the amendment is required by a collective bargaining agreement which is in effect on the date of enactment of this subparagraph.

If a plan is amended during any applicable plan year in violation of the preceding sentence, any election under this paragraph shall not apply to any applicable plan year ending on or after the date on which such amendment is adopted.

(C) APPLICABLE EMPLOYER.—For purposes of this paragraph, the term "applicable employer" means an employer which is—

(i) a commercial passenger airline,

(ii) primarily engaged in the production or manufacture of a steel mill product or the processing of iron ore pellets, or

(iii) an organization described in section 501(c)(5) and which established the plan to which this paragraph applies on June 30, 1955.

(D) APPLICABLE PLAN YEAR.—For purposes of this paragraph—

(i) IN GENERAL.—The term "applicable plan year" means any plan year beginning after December 27, 2003, and before December 28, 2005, for which the employer elects the application of this paragraph.

(ii) LIMITATION ON NUMBER OF YEARS WHICH MAY BE ELECTED.—An election may not be made under this paragraph with respect to more than 2 plan years.

(E) ELECTION.—An election under this paragraph shall be made at such time and in such manner as the Secretary may prescribe.

(m) QUARTERLY CONTRIBUTIONS REQUIRED.—

(1) IN GENERAL.—If a defined benefit plan (other than a multiemployer plan) which has a funded current liability percentage (as defined in subsection (l)(8)) for the preceding plan year of less than 100 percent fails to pay the full amount of a required installment for any plan year, then the rate of interest charged to the funding standard account under subsection (b)(5) with respect to the amount of the underpayment for the period of the underpayment shall be equal to the greater of—

(A) 175 percent of the Federal mid-term rate (as in effect under section 1274 for the 1st month of such plan year), or

(B) the rate of interest used under the plan in determining costs (including adjustments under subsection (b)(5)(B)).

(2) AMOUNT OF UNDERPAYMENT, PERIOD OF UNDERPAYMENT.—For purposes of paragraph (1)—

(A) AMOUNT.—The amount of the underpayment shall be the excess of—

(i) the required installment, over

(ii) the amount (if any) of the installment contributed to or under the plan on or before the due date for the installment.

(B) PERIOD OF UNDERPAYMENT.—The period for which interest is charged under this subsection with regard to any portion of the underpayment shall run from the due date for the installment to the date on which such portion is contributed to or under the plan (determined without regard to subsection (c)(10)).

(C) ORDER OF CREDITING CONTRIBUTIONS.—For purposes of subparagraph (A)(ii), contributions shall be credited against unpaid required installments in the order in which such installments are required to be paid.

(3) NUMBER OF REQUIRED INSTALLMENTS; DUE DATES.—For purposes of this subsection—

(A) PAYABLE IN 4 INSTALLMENTS.—There shall be 4 required installments for each plan year.

(B) TIME FOR PAYMENT OF INSTALLMENTS.—

In the case of the following required installments:	*The due date is:*
1st	April 15
2nd	July 15
3rd	October 15
4th	January 15 of the following year

(4) AMOUNT OF REQUIRED INSTALLMENT.—For purposes of this subsection—

(A) IN GENERAL.—The amount of any required installment shall be the applicable percentage of the required annual payment.

(B) REQUIRED ANNUAL PAYMENT.—For purposes of subparagraph (A), the term "required annual payment" means the lesser of—

(i) 90 percent of the amount required to be contributed to or under the plan by the employer for the plan year under section 412 (without regard to any waiver under subsection (d) thereof), or

(ii) 100 percent of the amount so required for the preceding plan year.

Clause (ii) shall not apply if the preceding plan year was not a year of 12 months.

(C) APPLICABLE PERCENTAGE.—For purposes of subparagraph (A), the applicable percentage shall be determined in accordance with the following table:

For plan years beginning in:	*The applicable percentage is:*
1989	6.25
1990	12.5
1991	18.75
1992 and thereafter	25.

(D) SPECIAL RULES FOR UNPREDICTABLE CONTINGENT EVENT BENEFITS.—In the case of a plan to which subsection (1) applies for any calendar year and which has any unpredictable contingent event benefit liabilities—

(i) LIABILITIES NOT TAKEN INTO ACCOUNT.—Such liabilities shall not be taken into account in computing the required annual payment under subparagraph (B).

(ii) INCREASE IN INSTALLMENTS.—Each required installment shall be increased by the greatest of—

(I) the unfunded percentage of the amount of benefits described in subsection (l)(5)(A)(i) paid during the 3-month period preceding the month in which the due date for such installment occurs,

(II) 25 percent of the amount determined under subsection (1)(5)(A)(ii) for the plan year, or

(III) 25 percent of the amount determined under subsection (l)(5)(A)(iii) for the plan year.

(iii) UNFUNDED PERCENTAGE.—For purposes of clause (ii)(I), the term "unfunded percentage" means the percentage determined under subsection (1)(5)(A)(i)(I) for the plan year.

(iv) LIMITATION ON INCREASE.—In no event shall the increases under clause (ii) exceed the amount necessary to increase the funded current liability percentage (within the meaning of subsection (l)(8)(B)) for the plan year to 100 percent.

(5) LIQUIDITY REQUIREMENT.—

(A) IN GENERAL.—A plan to which this paragraph applies shall be treated as failing to pay the full amount of any required installment to the extent that the value of the liquid assets paid in such installment is less than the liquidity shortfall (whether or not such liquidity shortfall exceeds the amount of such installment required to be paid but for this paragraph).

(B) PLANS TO WHICH PARAGRAPH APPLIES.—This paragraph shall apply to a defined benefit plan (other than a multiemployer plan or a plan described in subsection (l)(6)(A)) which—

(i) is required to pay installments under this subsection for a plan year, and

(ii) has a liquidity shortall for any quarter during such plan year.

(C) PERIOD OF UNDERPAYMENT.—For purposes of paragraph (1), any portion of an installment that is treated as not paid under subparagraph (A) shall continue to be treated as unpaid until the close of the quarter in which the due date for such installment occurs.

(D) LIMITATION ON INCREASE.—If the amount of any required installment is increased by reason of subparagraph (A), in no event shall such increase exceed the amount which, when added to prior installments for the plan year, is necessary to increase the funded current liability percentage (taking into account the expected increase in current liability due to benefits accruing during the plan year) to 100 percent.

(E) DEFINITIONS.—For purposes of this paragraph:

(i) LIQUIDITY SHORTFALL.—The term "liquidity shortfall" means, with respect to any required installment, an amount equal to the excess (as of the last day of the quarter for which such installment is made) of the base amount with respect to such quarter over the value (as of such last day) of the plan's liquid assets.

(ii) BASE AMOUNT.—

(I) IN GENERAL.—The term "base amount" means, with respect to any quarter, an amount equal to 3 times the sum of the adjusted disbursements from the plan for the 12 months ending on the last day of such quarter.

(II) SPECIAL RULE.—If the amount determined under subclause (I) exceeds an amount equal to 2 times the sum of the adjusted disbursements from the plan for the 36 months ending on the last day of the quarter and an enrolled actuary certifies to the satisfaction of the Secretary that such excess is the result of nonrecurring circumstances, the base amount with respect to such quarter shall be determined without regard to amounts related to those nonrecurring circumstances.

(iii) DISBURSEMENTS FROM THE PLAN.—The term "disbursements from the plan" means all disbursements from the trust, including purchase of annuities, payments of single sums and other benefits, and administrative expenses.

(iv) ADJUSTED DISBURSEMENTS.—The term "adjusted disbursements" means disbursements from the plan reduced by the product of—

(I) the plan's funded current liability percentage (as defined in subsection (l)(8)) for the plan year, and

(II) the sum of the purchases of annuities, payments of single sums, and such other disbursements as the Secretary shall provide in regulations.

(v) LIQUID ASSETS.—The term "liquid assets" means cash, marketable securities and such other assets as specified by the Secretary in regulations.

(vi) QUARTER.—The term "quarter" means, with respect to any required installment, the 3-month period preceding the month in which the due date for such installment occurs.

(F) REGULATIONS.—The Secretary may prescribe such regulations as are necessary to carry out this paragraph.

(6) FISCAL YEARS AND SHORT YEARS.—

(A) FISCAL YEARS.—In applying this subsection to a plan year beginning on any date other than January 1, there shall be substituted for the months specified in this subsection, the months which correspond thereto.

(B) SHORT PLAN YEAR.—This subsection shall be applied to plan years of less than 12 months in accordance with regulations prescribed by the Secretary.

(7) SPECIAL RULE FOR 2002.—In any case in which the interest rate used to determine current liability is determined under subsection (l)(7)(C)(i)(III), for purposes of applying paragraphs (1) and (4)(B)(ii) for plan years beginning in 2002, the current liability for the preceding plan year shall be redetermined using 120 percent as the specified percentage determined under subsection (l)(7)(C)(i)(II).

(n) IMPOSITION OF LIEN WHERE FAILURE TO MAKE REQUIRED CONTRIBUTIONS.—

(1) IN GENERAL.—In the case of a plan to which this section applies, if—

(A) any person fails to make a required installment under subsection (m) or any other payment required under this section before the due date for such installment or other payment, and

(B) the unpaid balance of such installment or other payment (including interest), when added to the aggregate unpaid balance of all preceding such installments or other payments for which payment was not made before the due date (including interest), exceeds $1,000,000,

then there shall be a lien in favor of the plan in the amount determined under paragraph (3) upon all property and rights to property, whether real or personal, belonging to such person and any other person who is a member of the same controlled group of which such person is a member.

(2) PLANS TO WHICH SUBSECTION APPLIES.—This subsection shall apply to a defined benefit plan (other than a multiemployer plan) for any plan year for which the funded current liability percentage (within the meaning of subsection (l)(8)(B)) of such plan is less than 100 percent. This subsection shall not apply to any plan to which section 4021 of the Employee Retirement Income Security Act of 1974 does not apply (as such section is in effect on the date of the enactment of the Retirement Protection Act of 1994).

(3) AMOUNT OF LIEN.—For purposes of paragraph (1), the amount of the lien shall be equal to the aggregate unpaid balance of required installments and other payments required under this section (including interest)—

(A) for plan years beginning after 1987, and

(B) for which payment has not been made before the due date.

(4) NOTICE OF FAILURE; LIEN.—

(A) NOTICE OF FAILURE.—A person committing a failure described in paragraph (1) shall notify the Pension Benefit Guaranty Corporation of such failure within 10 days of the due date for the required installment or other payment.

(B) PERIOD OF LIEN.—The lien imposed by paragraph (1) shall arise on the due date for the required installment or other payment and shall continue until the last day of the first plan year in which the plan ceases to be described in paragraph (1)(B). Such lien shall continue to run without regard to whether such plan continues to be described in paragraph (2) during the period referred to in the preceding sentence.

(C) CERTAIN RULES TO APPLY.—Any amount with respect to which a lien is imposed under paragraph (1) shall be treated as taxes due and owing the United States and rules similar to the rules of subsections (c), (d), and (e) of section 4068 of the Employee Retirement Income Security Act of 1974 shall apply with respect to a lien imposed by subsection (a) and the amount with respect to such lien.

(5) ENFORCEMENT.—Any lien created under paragraph (1) may be perfected and enforced only by the Pension Benefit Guaranty Corporation, or at the direction of the Pension Benefit Guaranty Corporation, by the contributing sponsor (or any member of the controlled group of the contributing sponsor).

(6) DEFINITIONS.—For purposes of this subsection—

(A) DUE DATE; REQUIRED INSTALLMENT.—The terms "due date" and "required installment" have the meanings given such terms by subsection (m), except that in the case of a payment other than a required installment, the due date shall be the date such payment is required to be made under this section.

(B) CONTROLLED GROUP.—The term "controlled group" means any group treated as a single employer under subsections (b), (c), (m), and (o) of section 414.

[¶ 5090] CODE SEC. 414. DEFINITIONS AND SPECIAL RULES.

* * *

(d) GOVERNMENTAL PLAN.—For purposes of this part, the term "governmental plan" means a plan established and maintained for its employees by the Government of the United States, by the government of any State or political subdivision thereof, or by any agency or instrumentality of any of the foregoing. The term "governmental plan" also includes any plan to which the Railroad Retirement Act of 1935 or 1937 applies and which is financed by contributions required under that Act and any plan of an international organization which is exempt from taxation by reason of the International Organizations Immunities Act (59 Stat. 669). *The term "governmental plan" includes a plan which is established and maintained by an Indian tribal government (as defined in section 7701(a)(40)), a subdivision of an Indian tribal government (determined in accordance with section 7871(d)), or an agency or instrumentality of either, and all of the participants of which are employees of such entity substantially all of whose services as such an employee are in the performance of essential governmental functions but not in the performance of commercial activities (whether or not an essential government function).*

* * *

[CCH Explanation at ¶ 1065. Committee Reports at ¶ 11,000.]

Amendments

• 2006, Pension Protection Act of 2006 (H.R. 4)

H.R. 4, § 906(a)(1):

Amended Code Sec. 414(d) by adding at the end a new sentence. **Effective** for any year beginning on or after 8-17-2006.

(f) MULTIEMPLOYER PLAN.—

* * *

(6) ELECTION WITH REGARD TO MULTIEMPLOYER STATUS.—

(A) Within 1 year after the enactment of the Pension Protection Act of 2006—

(i) An election under paragraph (5) may be revoked, pursuant to procedures prescribed by the Pension Benefit Guaranty Corporation, if, for each of the 3 plan years prior to the date of the enactment of that Act, the plan would have been a multiemployer plan but for the election under paragraph (5), and

(ii) a plan that meets the criteria in subparagraph (A) and (B) of paragraph (1) of this subsection or that is described in subparagraph (E) may, pursuant to procedures prescribed by the Pension Benefit Guaranty Corporation, elect to be a multiemployer plan, if—

(I) for each of the 3 plan years immediately before the date of enactment of the Pension Protection Act of 2006, the plan has met those criteria or is so described,

(II) substantially all of the plan's employer contributions for each of those plan years were made or required to be made by organizations that were exempt from tax under section 501, and

(III) the plan was established prior to September 2, 1974.

(B) An election under this paragraph shall be effective for all purposes under this Act and under the Employee Retirement Income Security Act of 1974, starting with the first plan year ending after the date of the enactment of the Pension Protection Act of 2006.

(C) Once made, an election under this paragraph shall be irrevocable, except that a plan described in subparagraph (A)(ii) shall cease to be a multiemployer plan as of the plan year beginning immediately after the first plan year for which the majority of its employer contributions were made or required to be made by organizations that were not exempt from tax under section 501.

(D) The fact that a plan makes an election under subparagraph (A)(ii) does not imply that the plan was not a multiemployer plan prior to the date of the election or would not be a multiemployer plan without regard to the election.

(E) A plan is described in this subparagraph if it is a plan—

(i) that was established in Chicago, Illinois, on August 12, 1881; and

(ii) sponsored by an organization described in section 501(c)(5) and exempt from tax under section 501(a).

* * *

[CCH Explanation at ¶ 325. Committee Reports at ¶ 11,090.]

Amendments

• **2006, Pension Protection Act of 2006 (H.R. 4)**

H.R. 4, § 1106(b):

Amended Code Sec. 414(f) by adding at the end a new paragraph (6). **Effective** 8-17-2006.

(h) TAX TREATMENT OF CERTAIN CONTRIBUTIONS.—

* * *

(2) DESIGNATION BY UNITS OF GOVERNMENT.—For purposes of paragraph (1), in the case of any plan established by the government of any State or political subdivision thereof, or by any agency or instrumentality of any of the foregoing, *or a governmental plan described in the last sentence of section 414(d) (relating to plans of Indian tribal governments),* where the contributions of employing units are designated as employee contributions but where any employing unit picks up the contributions, the contributions so picked up shall be treated as employer contributions.

* * *

[CCH Explanation at ¶ 1065. Committee Reports at ¶ 11,000.]

Amendments

• **2006, Pension Protection Act of 2006 (H.R. 4)**

H.R. 4, § 906(b)(1)(C):

Amended Code Sec. 414(h)(2) by inserting "or a governmental plan described in the last sentence of section 414(d) (relating to plans of Indian tribal governments)," after "foregoing,". **Effective** for any year beginning on or after 8-17-2006.

(l) MERGER AND CONSOLIDATIONS OF PLANS OR TRANSFERS OF PLAN ASSETS.—

* * *

(2) ALLOCATION OF ASSETS IN PLAN SPIN-OFFS, ETC.—

(A) IN GENERAL.—In the case of a plan spin-off of a defined benefit plan, a trust which forms part of—

(i) the original plan, or

(ii) any plan spun off from such plan, shall not constitute a qualified trust under this section unless the applicable percentage of excess assets are allocated to each of such plans.

(B) APPLICABLE PERCENTAGE.—For purposes of subparagraph (A), the term "applicable percentage" means, with respect to each of the plans described in clauses (i) and (ii) of subparagraph (A), the percentage determined by dividing—

(i) the excess (if any) of—

(I) the amount determined under section 431(c)(6)(A)(i) in the case of a multiemployer plan (and the sum of the funding shortfall and target normal cost determined under section 430 in the case of any other plan), over

(II) the amount of the assets required to be allocated to the plan after the spin-off (without regard to this paragraph), by

(ii) the sum of the excess amounts determined separately under clause (i) for all such plans.

* * *

[CCH Explanation at ¶ 205 and ¶ 305. Committee Reports at ¶ 10,010.]

Amendments

• 2006, Pension Protection Act of 2006 (H.R. 4)

H.R. 4, § 114(c):

Amended Code Sec. 414(l)(2)(B)(i)(I). **Effective** 8-17-2006. Prior to amendment, Code Sec. 414(l)(2)(B)(i)(I) read as follows:

(I) the amount determined under section 412(c)(7)(A)(i) with respect to the plan, over

»»→ Caution: Code Sec. 414(w), below, as added by H.R. 4, applies to plan years beginning after December 31, 2007.

(w) SPECIAL RULES FOR CERTAIN WITHDRAWALS FROM ELIGIBLE AUTOMATIC CONTRIBUTION ARRANGEMENTS.—

(1) IN GENERAL.—If an eligible automatic contribution arrangement allows an employee to elect to make permissible withdrawals—

(A) the amount of any such withdrawal shall be includible in the gross income of the employee for the taxable year of the employee in which the distribution is made,

(B) no tax shall be imposed under section 72(t) with respect to the distribution, and

(C) the arrangement shall not be treated as violating any restriction on distributions under this title solely by reason of allowing the withdrawal.

In the case of any distribution to an employee by reason of an election under this paragraph, employer matching contributions shall be forfeited or subject to such other treatment as the Secretary may prescribe.

(2) PERMISSIBLE WITHDRAWAL.—For purposes of this subsection—

(A) IN GENERAL.—The term "permissible withdrawal" means any withdrawal from an eligible automatic contribution arrangement meeting the requirements of this paragraph which—

(i) is made pursuant to an election by an employee, and

(ii) consists of elective contributions described in paragraph (3)(B) (and earnings attributable thereto).

(B) TIME FOR MAKING ELECTION.—Subparagraph (A) shall not apply to an election by an employee unless the election is made no later than the date which is 90 days after the date of the first elective contribution with respect to the employee under the arrangement.

(C) AMOUNT OF DISTRIBUTION.—Subparagraph (A) shall not apply to any election by an employee unless the amount of any distribution by reason of the election is equal to the amount of elective contributions made with respect to the first payroll period to which the eligible automatic contribution arrangement applies to the employee and any succeeding payroll period beginning before the effective date of the election (and earnings attributable thereto).

(3) ELIGIBLE AUTOMATIC CONTRIBUTION ARRANGEMENT.—For purposes of this subsection, the term "eligible automatic contribution arrangement" means an arrangement under an applicable employer plan—

(A) under which a participant may elect to have the employer make payments as contributions under the plan on behalf of the participant, or to the participant directly in cash,

(B) under which the participant is treated as having elected to have the employer make such contributions in an amount equal to a uniform percentage of compensation provided under the plan until the participant specifically elects not to have such contributions made (or specifically elects to have such contributions made at a different percentage),

(C) under which, in the absence of an investment election by the participant, contributions described in subparagraph (B) are invested in accordance with regulations prescribed by the Secretary of Labor under section 404(c)(5) of the Employee Retirement Income Security Act of 1974, and

(D) which meets the requirements of paragraph (4).

(4) NOTICE REQUIREMENTS.—

(A) IN GENERAL.—The administrator of a plan containing an arrangement described in paragraph (3) shall, within a reasonable period before each plan year, give to each employee to whom an arrangement described in paragraph (3) applies for such plan year notice of the employee's rights and obligations under the arrangement which—

(i) is sufficiently accurate and comprehensive to apprise the employee of such rights and obligations, and

(ii) is written in a manner calculated to be understood by the average employee to whom the arrangement applies.

(B) TIME AND FORM OF NOTICE.—A notice shall not be treated as meeting the requirements of subparagraph (A) with respect to an employee unless—

(i) the notice includes an explanation of the employee's right under the arrangement to elect not to have elective contributions made on the employee's behalf (or to elect to have such contributions made at a different percentage),

(ii) the employee has a reasonable period of time after receipt of the notice described in clause (i) and before the first elective contribution is made to make such election, and

(iii) the notice explains how contributions made under the arrangement will be invested in the absence of any investment election by the employee.

(5) APPLICABLE EMPLOYER PLAN.—For purposes of this subsection, the term "applicable employer plan" means—

(A) an employees' trust described in section 401(a) which is exempt from tax under section 501(a),

(B) a plan under which amounts are contributed by an individual's employer for an annuity contract described in section 403(b), and

(C) an eligible deferred compensation plan described in section 457(b) which is maintained by an eligible employer described in section 457(e)(1)(A).

(6) SPECIAL RULE.—A withdrawal described in paragraph (1) (subject to the limitation of paragraph (2)(C)) shall not be taken into account for purposes of section 401(k)(3).

[CCH Explanation at ¶1015. Committee Reports at ¶10,960.]

Amendments

• 2006, Pension Protection Act of 2006 (H.R. 4)

H.R. 4, §902(d)(1):

Amended Code Sec. 414 by adding at the end a new subsection (w). **Effective** for plan years beginning after 12-31-2007.

»» Caution: Code Sec. 414(x), below, as added by H.R. 4, applies to plan years beginning after December 31, 2009.

(x) SPECIAL RULES FOR ELIGIBLE COMBINED DEFINED BENEFIT PLANS AND QUALIFIED CASH OR DEFERRED ARRANGEMENTS.—

(1) GENERAL RULE.—Except as provided in this subsection, the requirements of this title shall be applied to any defined benefit plan or applicable defined contribution plan which are part of an eligible combined plan in the same manner as if each such plan were not a part of the eligible combined plan.

(2) ELIGIBLE COMBINED PLAN.—For purposes of this subsection—

(A) IN GENERAL.—The term "eligible combined plan" means a plan—

(i) which is maintained by an employer which, at the time the plan is established, is a small employer,

(ii) which consists of a defined benefit plan and an applicable defined contribution plan,

(iii) the assets of which are held in a single trust forming part of the plan and are clearly identified and allocated to the defined benefit plan and the applicable defined contribution plan to the extent necessary for the separate application of this title under paragraph (1), and

(iv) with respect to which the benefit, contribution, vesting, and nondiscrimination requirements of subparagraphs (B), (C), (D), (E), and (F) are met.

For purposes of this subparagraph, the term "small employer" has the meaning given such term by section 4980D(d)(2), except that such section shall be applied by substituting "500" for "50" each place it appears.

(B) BENEFIT REQUIREMENTS.—

(i) IN GENERAL.—The benefit requirements of this subparagraph are met with respect to the defined benefit plan forming part of the eligible combined plan if the accrued benefit of each participant derived from employer contributions, when expressed as an annual retirement benefit, is not less than the applicable percentage of the participant's final average pay. For purposes of this clause, final average pay shall be determined using the period of consecutive years (not exceeding 5) during which the participant had the greatest aggregate compensation from the employer.

(ii) APPLICABLE PERCENTAGE.—For purposes of clause (i), the applicable percentage is the lesser of—

(I) 1 percent multiplied by the number of years of service with the employer, or

(II) 20 percent.

(iii) SPECIAL RULE FOR APPLICABLE DEFINED BENEFIT PLANS.—If the defined benefit plan under clause (i) is an applicable defined benefit plan as defined in section 411(a)(13)(B) which meets the interest credit requirements of section 411(b)(5)(B)(i), the plan shall be treated as meeting the requirements of clause (i) with respect to any plan year if each participant receives a pay credit for the year which is not less than the percentage of compensation determined in accordance with the following table:

If the participant's age as of the beginning of the year is—	*The percentage is—*
30 or less	2
Over 30 but less than 40	4
40 or over but less than 50	6
50 or over	8 .

(iv) YEARS OF SERVICE.—For purposes of this subparagraph, years of service shall be determined under the rules of paragraphs (4), (5), and (6) of section 411(a), except that the plan may not disregard any year of service because of a participant making, or failing to make, any elective deferral with respect to the qualified cash or deferred arrangement to which subparagraph (C) applies.

(C) CONTRIBUTION REQUIREMENTS.—

(i) IN GENERAL.—The contribution requirements of this subparagraph with respect to any applicable defined contribution plan forming part of an eligible combined plan are met if—

(I) the qualified cash or deferred arrangement included in such plan constitutes an automatic contribution arrangement, and

(II) the employer is required to make matching contributions on behalf of each employee eligible to participate in the arrangement in an amount equal to 50 percent of the elective contributions of the employee to the extent such elective contributions do not exceed 4 percent of compensation.

Rules similar to the rules of clauses (ii) and (iii) of section 401(k)(12)(B) shall apply for purposes of this clause.

(ii) NONELECTIVE CONTRIBUTIONS.—An applicable defined contribution plan shall not be treated as failing to meet the requirements of clause (i) because the employer makes nonelective

contributions under the plan but such contributions shall not be taken into account in determining whether the requirements of clause (i)(II) are met.

(D) VESTING REQUIREMENTS.—The vesting requirements of this subparagraph are met if—

(i) in the case of a defined benefit plan forming part of an eligible combined plan an employee who has completed at least 3 years of service has a nonforfeitable right to 100 percent of the employee's accrued benefit under the plan derived from employer contributions, and

(ii) in the case of an applicable defined contribution plan forming part of eligible combined plan—

(I) an employee has a nonforfeitable right to any matching contribution made under the qualified cash or deferred arrangement included in such plan by an employer with respect to any elective contribution, including matching contributions in excess of the contributions required under subparagraph (C)(i)(II), and

(II) an employee who has completed at least 3 years of service has a nonforfeitable right to 100 percent of the employee's accrued benefit derived under the arrangement from nonelective contributions of the employer.

For purposes of this subparagraph, the rules of section 411 shall apply to the extent not inconsistent with this subparagraph.

(E) UNIFORM PROVISION OF CONTRIBUTIONS AND BENEFITS.—In the case of a defined benefit plan or applicable defined contribution plan forming part of an eligible combined plan, the requirements of this subparagraph are met if all contributions and benefits under each such plan, and all rights and features under each such plan, must be provided uniformly to all participants.

(F) REQUIREMENTS MUST BE MET WITHOUT TAKING INTO ACCOUNT SOCIAL SECURITY AND SIMILAR CONTRIBUTIONS AND BENEFITS OR OTHER PLANS.—

(i) IN GENERAL.—The requirements of this subparagraph are met if the requirements of clauses (ii) and (iii) are met.

(ii) SOCIAL SECURITY AND SIMILAR CONTRIBUTIONS.—The requirements of this clause are met if—

(I) the requirements of subparagraphs (B) and (C) are met without regard to section 401(l), and

(II) the requirements of sections 401(a)(4) and 410(b) are met with respect to both the applicable defined contribution plan and defined benefit plan forming part of an eligible combined plan without regard to section 401(l).

(iii) OTHER PLANS AND ARRANGEMENTS.—The requirements of this clause are met if the applicable defined contribution plan and defined benefit plan forming part of an eligible combined plan meet the requirements of sections 401(a)(4) and 410(b) without being combined with any other plan.

(3) NONDISCRIMINATION REQUIREMENTS FOR QUALIFIED CASH OR DEFERRED ARRANGEMENT.—

(A) IN GENERAL.—A qualified cash or deferred arrangement which is included in an applicable defined contribution plan forming part of an eligible combined plan shall be treated as meeting the requirements of section 401(k)(3)(A)(ii) if the requirements of paragraph (2)(C) are met with respect to such arrangement.

(B) MATCHING CONTRIBUTIONS.—In applying section 401(m)(11) to any matching contribution with respect to a contribution to which paragraph (2)(C) applies, the contribution requirement of paragraph (2)(C) and the notice requirements of paragraph (5)(B) shall be substituted for the requirements otherwise applicable under clauses (i) and (ii) of section 401(m)(11)(A).

(4) SATISFACTION OF TOP-HEAVY RULES.—A defined benefit plan and applicable defined contribution plan forming part of an eligible combined plan for any plan year shall be treated as meeting the requirements of section 416 for the plan year.

(5) AUTOMATIC CONTRIBUTION ARRANGEMENT.—For purposes of this subsection—

(A) IN GENERAL.—A qualified cash or deferred arrangement shall be treated as an automatic contribution arrangement if the arrangement—

(i) provides that each employee eligible to participate in the arrangement is treated as having elected to have the employer make elective contributions in an amount equal to 4 percent of the employee's compensation unless the employee specifically elects not to have such contributions made or to have such contributions made at a different rate, and

(ii) meets the notice requirements under subparagraph (B).

(B) NOTICE REQUIREMENTS.—

(i) IN GENERAL.—The requirements of this subparagraph are met if the requirements of clauses (ii) and (iii) are met.

(ii) REASONABLE PERIOD TO MAKE ELECTION.—The requirements of this clause are met if each employee to whom subparagraph (A)(i) applies—

(I) receives a notice explaining the employee's right under the arrangement to elect not to have elective contributions made on the employee's behalf or to have the contributions made at a different rate, and

(II) has a reasonable period of time after receipt of such notice and before the first elective contribution is made to make such election.

(iii) ANNUAL NOTICE OF RIGHTS AND OBLIGATIONS.—The requirements of this clause are met if each employee eligible to participate in the arrangement is, within a reasonable period before any year, given notice of the employee's rights and obligations under the arrangement.

The requirements of clauses (i) and (ii) of section 401(k)(12)(D) shall be met with respect to the notices described in clauses (ii) and (iii) of this subparagraph.

(6) COORDINATION WITH OTHER REQUIREMENTS.—

(A) TREATMENT OF SEPARATE PLANS.—Section 414(k) shall not apply to an eligible combined plan.

(B) REPORTING.—An eligible combined plan shall be treated as a single plan for purposes of sections 6058 and 6059.

(7) APPLICABLE DEFINED CONTRIBUTION PLAN.—For purposes of this subsection—

(A) IN GENERAL.—The term "applicable defined contribution plan" means a defined contribution plan which includes a qualified cash or deferred arrangement.

(B) QUALIFIED CASH OR DEFERRED ARRANGEMENT.—The term "qualified cash or deferred arrangement" has the meaning given such term by section 401(k)(2).

[CCH Explanation at ¶1020. Committee Reports at ¶10,970.]

Amendments

• 2006, Pension Protection Act of 2006 (H.R. 4)

H.R. 4, §903(a):

Amended Code Sec. 414, as amended by this Act, by adding at the end a new subsection (x). **Effective** for plan years beginning after 12-31-2009.

[¶5095] CODE SEC. 415. LIMITATIONS ON BENEFITS AND CONTRIBUTION UNDER QUALIFIED PLANS.

* * *

(b) LIMITATION FOR DEFINED BENEFIT PLANS.—

* * *

(2) ANNUAL BENEFIT.—

* * *

(E) LIMITATION ON CERTAIN ASSUMPTIONS.—

(i) For purposes of adjusting any limitation under subparagraph (C) and, except as provided in clause (ii), for purposes of adjusting any benefit under subparagraph (B), the interest rate assumption shall not be less than the greater of 5 percent or the rate specified in the plan.

(ii) For purposes of adjusting any benefit under subparagraph (B) for any form of benefit subject to section 417(e)(3), the interest rate assumption shall not be less than the greatest of—

(I) 5.5 percent,

(II) the rate that provides a benefit of not more than 105 percent of the benefit that would be provided if the applicable interest rate (as defined in section 417(e)(3)) were the interest rate assumption, or

(III) the rate specified under the plan.

(iii) For purposes of adjusting any limitation under subparagraph (D), the interest rate assumption shall not be greater than the lesser of 5 percent or the rate specified in the plan.

(iv) For purposes of this subsection, no adjustments under subsection (d)(1) shall be taken into account before the year for which such adjustment first takes effect.

(v) For purposes of adjusting any benefit or limitation under subparagraph (B), (C), or (D), the mortality table used shall be the table prescribed by the Secretary. Such table shall be based on the prevailing commissioners' standard table (described in section 807(d)(5)(A)) used to determine reserves for group annuity contracts issued on the date the adjustment is being made (without regard to any other subparagraph of section 807(d)(5)).

* * *

(H) QUALIFIED PARTICIPANT DEFINED.—For purposes of subparagraph (G), the term "qualified participant" means a participant—

(i) in a defined benefit plan which is maintained by a *State, Indian tribal government (as defined in section 7701(a)(4)), or any political subdivision* thereof,

(ii) with respect to whom the period of service taken into account in determining the amount of the benefit under such defined benefit plan includes at least 15 years of service of the participant—

(I) as a full-time employee of any police department or fire department which is organized and operated by the *State, Indian tribal government (as so defined), or any political subdivision* maintaining such defined benefit plan to provide police protection, firefighting services, or emergency medical services for any area within the jurisdiction of such *State, Indian tribal government (as so defined), or any political subdivision*, or

(II) as a member of the Armed Forces of the United States.

* * *

(3) AVERAGE COMPENSATION FOR HIGH 3 YEARS.—For purposes of paragraph (1), a participant's high 3 years shall be the period of consecutive calendar years (not more than 3) during which the participant had the greatest aggregate compensation from the employer. In the case of an employee within the meaning of section 401(c)(1), the preceding sentence shall be applied by substituting for "compensation from the employer" the following: "the participant's earned income (within the meaning of section 401(c)(2) but determined without regard to any exclusion under section 911)".

* * *

(10) *SPECIAL RULE FOR STATE, INDIAN TRIBAL, AND* LOCAL GOVERNMENT PLANS.—

(A) LIMITATION TO EQUAL ACCRUED BENEFIT.—In the case of a plan maintained for its employees by any State or political subdivision thereof, or by any agency or instrumentality of the foregoing, *or a governmental plan described in the last sentence of section 414(d) (relating to plans of Indian tribal governments),* the limitation with respect to a qualified participant under this subsection shall not be less than the accrued benefit of the participant under the plan (determined without regard to any amendment of the plan made after October 14, 1987).

* * *

»»→ *Caution: Code Sec. 415(b)(11), below, as amended by H.R. 4, applies to years beginning after December 31, 2006.*

(11) SPECIAL LIMITATION RULE FOR GOVERNMENTAL AND MULTIEMPLOYER PLANS.—In the case of a governmental plan (as defined in section 414(d)) or a multiemployer plan (as defined in section 414(f)), subparagraph (B) of paragraph (1) shall not apply. *Subparagraph (B) of paragraph (1) shall not apply to a plan maintained by an organization described in section 3121(w)(3)(A) except with respect to highly compensated benefits. For purposes of this paragraph, the term "highly compensated benefits" means any benefits accrued for an employee in any year on or after the first year in which such employee is a highly compensated employee (as defined in section 414(q)) of the organization described in section 3121(w)(3)(A). For purposes of applying paragraph (1)(B) to highly compensated benefits, all benefits of the employee otherwise taken into account (without regard to this paragraph) shall be taken into account.*

* * *

[CCH Explanation at ¶735, ¶740, ¶1055 and ¶1065. Committee Reports at ¶10,210, ¶10,730, ¶10,930 and ¶11,000.]

Amendments

• 2006, Pension Protection Act of 2006 (H.R. 4)

H.R. 4, §303(a):

Amended Code Sec. 415(b)(2)(E)(ii). **Effective** for distributions made in years beginning after 12-31-2005. Prior to amendment, Code Sec. 415(b)(2)(E)(ii) read as follows:

(ii) For purposes of adjusting any benefit under subparagraph (B) for any form of benefit subject to section 417(e)(3), the applicable interest rate (as defined in section 417(e)(3)) shall be substituted for "5 percent" in clause (i), except that in the case of plan years beginning in 2004 or 2005, "5.5 percent" shall be substituted for "5 percent" in clause (i).

H.R. 4, §832(a):

Amended Code Sec. 415(b)(3) by striking "both was an active participant in the plan and" following "during which the participant". **Effective** for years beginning after 12-31-2005.

H.R. 4, §867(a):

Amended Code Sec. 415(b)(11) by adding at the end three new sentences. **Effective** for years beginning after 12-31-2006.

H.R. 4, §906(b)(1)(A)(i)-(ii):

Amended Code Sec. 415(b)(2)(H) by striking "State or political subdivision" and inserting "State, Indian tribal government (as defined in section 7701(a)(40)), or any political subdivision" in clause (i); and by striking "State or political subdivision" each place it appears and inserting "State, Indian tribal government (as so defined), or any political subdivision" in clause (ii)(I). **Effective** for any year beginning on or after 8-17-2006.

H.R. 4, §906(b)(1)(B)(i):

Amended Code Sec. 415(b)(10)(A) by inserting "or a governmental plan described in the last sentence of section 414(d) (relating to plans of Indian tribal governments)," after "foregoing,". **Effective** for any year beginning on or after 8-17-2006.

H.R. 4, §906(b)(1)(B)(ii):

Amended the heading of Code Sec. 415(b)(1)[(10)] by striking "SPECIAL RULE FOR STATE AND" and inserting "SPECIAL RULE FOR STATE, INDIAN TRIBAL, AND". **Effective** for any year beginning on or after 8-17-2006.

(n) SPECIAL RULES RELATING TO PURCHASE OF PERMISSIVE SERVICE CREDIT.—

(1) IN GENERAL.—If *a participant* makes 1 or more contributions to a defined benefit governmental plan (within the meaning of section 414(d)) to purchase permissive service credit under such plan, then the requirements of this section shall be treated as met only if—

(A) the requirements of subsection (b) are met, determined by treating the accrued benefit derived from all such contributions as an annual benefit for purposes of subsection (b), or

(B) the requirements of subsection (c) are met, determined by treating all such contributions as annual additions for purposes of subsection (c).

* * *

(3) PERMISSIVE SERVICE CREDIT.—For purposes of this subsection—

(A) IN GENERAL.—The term "permissive service credit" means service credit—

(i) recognized by the governmental plan for purposes of calculating a participant's benefit under the plan,

(ii) which such participant has not received under such governmental plan, and

(iii) which such participant may receive only by making a voluntary additional contribution, in an amount determined under such governmental plan, which does not exceed the amount necessary to fund the benefit attributable to such service credit.

Such term may include service credit for periods for which there is no performance of service, and, notwithstanding clause (ii), may include service credited in order to provide an increased benefit for service credit which a participant is receiving under the plan.

(B) LIMITATION ON NONQUALIFIED SERVICE CREDIT.—A plan shall fail to meet the requirements of this section if—

(i) more than 5 years of *nonqualified service credit* are taken into account for purposes of this subsection, or

(ii) any *nonqualified service credit* is taken into account under this subsection before the employee has at least 5 years of participation under the plan.

(C) *NONQUALIFIED SERVICE CREDIT.—For purposes of subparagraph (B), the term "nonqualified service credit" means permissive service credit other than that allowed with respect to—*

(i) service (including parental, medical, sabbatical, and similar leave) as an employee of the Government of the United States, any State or political subdivision thereof, or any agency or instrumentality of any of the foregoing (other than military service or service for credit which was obtained as a result of a repayment described in subsection (k)(3)),

(ii) service (including parental, medical, sabbatical, and similar leave) as an employee (other than as an employee described in clause (i)) of an educational organization described in section 170(b)(1)(A)(ii) which is a public, private, or sectarian school which provides *elementary or secondary education (through grade 12), or a comparable level of education, as determined under the applicable law of the jurisdiction in which the service was performed,*

(iii) service as an employee of an association of employees who are described in clause (i), or

(iv) military service (other than qualified military service under section 414(u)) recognized by such governmental plan.

In the case of service described in clause (i), (ii), or (iii), such service will be nonqualified service if recognition of such service would cause a participant to receive a retirement benefit for the same service under more than one plan.

(D) SPECIAL RULES FOR TRUSTEE-TO-TRUSTEE TRANSFERS.—In the case of a trustee-to-trustee transfer to which section 403(b)(13)(A) or 457(e)(17)(A) applies (without regard to whether the transfer is made between plans maintained by the same employer)—

(i) the limitations of subparagraph (B) shall not apply in determining whether the transfer is for the purchase of permissive service credit, and

(ii) the distribution rules applicable under this title to the defined benefit governmental plan to which any amounts are so transferred shall apply to such amounts and any benefits attributable to such amounts.

[CCH Explanation at ¶ 745. Committee Reports at ¶ 10,620.]

Amendments

• **2006, Pension Protection Act of 2006 (H.R. 4)**

H.R. 4, §821(a)(1)-(2):

Amended Code Sec. 415(n) by striking "an employee" and inserting "a participant" in paragraph (1), and by adding a new flush sentence at the end of paragraph (3)(A). **Effective** as if included in the amendments made by section 1526 of the Taxpayer Relief Act of 1997 (P.L. 105-34) [**effective** for permissive service credit contributions made in years beginning after 12-31-1997.—CCH].

H.R. 4, §821(b):

Amended Code Sec. 415(n)(3) by adding at the end a new subparagraph (D). **Effective** as if included in the amendments made by section 647 of the Economic Growth and Tax Relief Reconciliation Act of 2001 (P.L. 107-16) [**effective** for trustee-to-trustee transfers after 12-31-2001.—CCH].

H.R. 4, §821(c)(1)-(3):

Amended Code Sec. 415(n)(3) by striking "permissive service credit attributable to nonqualified service" each place it appears in subparagraph (B) and inserting "nonqualified service credit", by striking so much of subparagraph (C) as precedes clause (i) and inserting "(C) NONQUALIFIED SERVICE CREDIT.—For purposes of subparagraph (B), the term 'nonqualified service credit' means permissive service credit other than that allowed with respect to—", and by striking "elementary or secondary education (through grade 12), as determined under State law" in subparagraph (C)(ii) and inserting "elementary or secondary education (through grade 12), or a comparable level of education, as determined under the applicable law of the jurisdiction in which the service was performed". **Effective** as if included in the amendments made by section 1526 of the Taxpayer Relief Act of 1997 (P.L. 105-34) [**effective** for permissive service credit contributions made in years beginning after 12-31-1997.—CCH]. Prior to being stricken, so much of Code Sec. 415(n)(3)(C) as precedes clause (i) read as follows:

(C) NONQUALIFIED SERVICE.—For purposes of subparagraph (B), the term "nonqualified service" means service for which permissive service credit is allowed other than—

[¶ 5100] CODE SEC. 416. SPECIAL RULES FOR TOP-HEAVY PLANS.

* * *

(g) TOP-HEAVY PLAN DEFINED.—For purposes of this section—

* * *

(4) OTHER SPECIAL RULES.—For purposes of this subsection—

* * *

»»→ *Caution: Code Sec. 416(g)(4)(H), below, as amended by H.R. 4, applies to plan years beginning after December 31, 2007.*

(H) CASH OR DEFERRED ARRANGEMENTS USING ALTERNATIVE METHODS OF MEETING NONDISCRIMINATION REQUIREMENTS.—The term "top-heavy plan" shall not include a plan which consists solely of—

(i) a cash or deferred arrangement which meets the requirements of section 401(k)(12) *or 401(k)(13)*, and

(ii) matching contributions with respect to which the requirements of section 401(m)(11) *or 401(m)(12)* are met.

If, but for this subparagraph, a plan would be treated as a top-heavy plan because it is a member of an aggregation group which is a top-heavy group, contributions under the plan may be taken into account in determining whether any other plan in the group meets the requirements of subsection (c)(2).

* * *

[CCH Explanation at ¶ 1015. Committee Reports at ¶ 10,960.]

Amendments

• **2006, Pension Protection Act of 2006 (H.R. 4)**

H.R. 4, § 902(c)(1):

Amended Code Sec. 416(g)(4)(H)(i) by inserting "or 401(k)(13)" after "section 401(k)(12)". **Effective** for plan years beginning after 12-31-2007.

H.R. 4, § 902(c)(2):

Amended Code Sec. 416(g)(4)(H)(ii) by inserting "or 401(m)(12)" after "section 401(m)(11)". **Effective** for plan years beginning after 12-31-2007.

[¶ 5105] CODE SEC. 417. DEFINITIONS AND SPECIAL RULES FOR PURPOSES OF MINIMUM SURVIVOR ANNUITY REQUIREMENTS.

(a) ELECTION TO WAIVE QUALIFIED JOINT AND SURVIVOR ANNUITY OR QUALIFIED PRERETIREMENT SURVIVOR ANNUITY.—

(1) IN GENERAL.—A plan meets the requirements of section 401(a)(11) only if—

»»→ *Caution: Code Sec. 417(a)(1)(A), below, as amended by H.R. 4, applies generally to plan years beginning after December 31, 2007.*

(A) under the plan, each participant—

(i) may elect at any time during the applicable election period to waive the qualified joint and survivor annuity form of benefit or the qualified preretirement survivor annuity form of benefit (or both),

(ii) if the participant elects a waiver under clause (i), may elect the qualified optional survivor annuity at any time during the applicable election period, and

(iii) may revoke any such election at any time during the applicable election period, and

(B) the plan meets the requirements of paragraphs (2), (3), and (4) of this subsection.

* * *

(3) PLAN TO PROVIDE WRITTEN EXPLANATIONS.—

(A) EXPLANATION OF JOINT AND SURVIVOR ANNUITY.—Each plan shall provide to each participant, within a reasonable period of time before the annuity starting date (and consistent with such regulations as the Secretary may prescribe), a written explanation of—

»»→ Caution: Code Sec. 417(a)(3)(A)(i), below, as amended by H.R. 4, applies generally to plan years beginning after December 31, 2007.

(i) the terms and conditions of the qualified joint and survivor annuity *and of the qualified optional survivor annuity*,

(ii) the participant's right to make, and the effect of, an election under paragraph (1) to waive the joint and survivor annuity form of benefit,

(iii) the rights of the participant's spouse under paragraph (2), and

(iv) the right to make, and the effect of, a revocation of an election under paragraph (1).

* * *

(6) APPLICABLE ELECTION PERIOD DEFINED.—For purposes of this subsection, the term "applicable election period" means—

»»→ Caution: Code Sec. 417(a)(6)(A), below, as amended by H.R. 4, applies to years beginning after December 31, 2006.

(A) in the case of an election to waive the qualified joint and survivor annuity form of benefit, the *180-day* period ending on the annuity starting date, or

(B) in the case of an election to waive the qualified preretirement survivor annuity, the period which begins on the first day of the plan year in which the participant attains age 35 and ends on the date of the participant's death.

In the case of a participant who is separated from service, the applicable election period under subparagraph (B) with respect to benefits accrued before the date of such separation from service shall not begin later than such date.

* * *

[CCH Explanation at ¶925 and ¶1040. Committee Reports at ¶11,030 and ¶11,050.]

Amendments

• 2006, Pension Protection Act of 2006 (H.R. 4)

H.R. 4, §1004(a)(1)(A)-(C):

Amended Code Sec. 417(a)(1)(A) by striking ", and" and inserting a comma in clause (i); by redesignating clause (ii) as clause (iii); and by inserting after clause (i) a new clause (ii). **Effective** generally for plan years beginning after 12-31-2007. For a special rule, see Act Sec. 1004(c)(2), below.

H.R. 4, §1004(a)(3):

Amended Code Sec. 417(a)(3)(A)(i) by inserting "and of the qualified optional survivor annuity" after "annuity". **Effective** generally for plan years beginning after 12-31-2007. For a special rule, see Act Sec. 1004(c)(2), below.

H.R. 4, §1004(c)(2), provides:

(2) SPECIAL RULE FOR COLLECTIVELY BARGAINED PLANS.—In the case of a plan maintained pursuant to 1 or more collective bargaining agreements between employee representatives and 1 or more employers ratified on or before the date of the enactment of this Act, the amendments made by this section shall not apply to plan years beginning before the earlier of—

(A) the later of—

(i) January 1, 2008, or

(ii) the date on which the last collective bargaining agreement related to the plan terminates (determined without regard to any extension thereof after the date of enactment of this Act), or

(B) January 1, 2009.

H.R. 4, §1102(a)(1)(A):

Amended Code Sec. 417(a)(6)(A) by striking "90-day" and inserting "180-day". **Effective** for years beginning after 12-31-2006.

(e) RESTRICTIONS ON CASH-OUTS.—

* * *

»»→ Caution: Code Sec. 417(e)(3), below, as amended by H.R. 4, applies with respect to plan years beginning after December 31, 2007.

(3) DETERMINATION OF PRESENT VALUE.—

(A) IN GENERAL.—For purposes of paragraphs (1) and (2), the present value shall not be less than the present value calculated by using the applicable mortality table and the applicable interest rate.

(B) APPLICABLE MORTALITY TABLE.—For purposes of subparagraph (A), the term "applicable mortality table" means a mortality table, modified as appropriate by the Secretary, based on the mortality table specified for the plan year under subparagraph (A) of section 430(h)(3) (without regard to subparagraph (C) or (D) of such section).

(C) APPLICABLE INTEREST RATE.—For purposes of subparagraph (A), the term "applicable interest rate" means the adjusted first, second, and third segment rates applied under rules similar to the rules of section 430(h)(2)(C) for the month before the date of the distribution or such other time as the Secretary may by regulations prescribe.

(D) APPLICABLE SEGMENT RATES.—For purposes of subparagraph (C), the adjusted first, second, and third segment rates are the first, second, and third segment rates which would be determined under section 430(h)(2)(C) if—

(i) section 430(h)(2)(D) were applied by substituting the average yields for the month described in clause (ii) for the average yields for the 24-month period described in such section,

(ii) section 430(h)(2)(G)(i)(II) were applied by substituting "section 417(e)(3)(A)(ii)(II)" for "section 412(b)(5)(B)(ii)(II)", and

(iii) the applicable percentage under section 430(h)(2)(G) were determined in accordance with the following table:

In the case of plan years beginning in:	*The applicable percentage is:*
2008	*20 percent*
2009	*40 percent*
2010	*60 percent*
2011	*80 percent*

* * *

[CCH Explanation at ¶ 905. Committee Reports at ¶ 10,200.]

Amendments

• 2006, Pension Protection Act of 2006 (H.R. 4)

H.R. 4, § 302(b):

Amended Code Sec. 417(e)(3). **Effective** with respect to plan years beginning after 12-31-2007. Prior to amendment, Code Sec. 417(e)(3) read as follows:

(3) DETERMINATION OF PRESENT VALUE.—

(A) IN GENERAL.—

(i) PRESENT VALUE.—Except as provided in subparagraph (B), for purposes of paragraphs (1) and (2), the present value shall not be less than the present value calculated by using the applicable mortality table and the applicable interest rate.

(ii) DEFINITIONS.—For purposes of clause (i)—

(I) APPLICABLE MORTALITY TABLE.—The term "applicable mortality table" means the table prescribed by the Secretary. Such table shall be based on the prevailing commissioners' standard table (described in section 807(d)(5)(A)) used to determine reserves for group annuity contracts issued on the date as of which present value is being determined (without regard to any other subparagraph of section 807(d)(5)).

(II) APPLICABLE INTEREST RATE.—The term "applicable interest rate" means the annual rate of interest on 30-year Treasury securities for the month before the date of distribution or such other time as the Secretary may by regulations prescribe.

(B) EXCEPTION.—In the case of a distribution from a plan that was adopted and in effect before the date of the enactment of the Retirement Protection Act of 1994, the present value of any distribution made before the earlier of—

(i) the later of the date a plan amendment applying subparagraph (A) is adopted or made effective, or

(ii) the first day of the first plan year beginning after December 31, 1999,

shall be calculated, for purposes of paragraphs (1) and (2), using the interest rate determined under the regulations of the Pension Benefit Guaranty Corporation for determining the present value of a lump sum distribution on plan termination that were in effect on September 1, 1993, and using the provisions of the plan as in effect on the day before such date of enactment; but only if such provisions of the plan met the requirements of section 417(e)(3) as in effect on the day before such date of enactment.

»»→ Caution: Code Sec. 417(g), below, as added by H.R. 4, applies generally to plan years beginning after December 31, 2007.

(g) DEFINITION OF QUALIFIED OPTIONAL SURVIVOR ANNUITY.—

(1) IN GENERAL.—For purposes of this section, the term "qualified optional survivor annuity" means an annuity—

(A) for the life of the participant with a survivor annuity for the life of the spouse which is equal to the applicable percentage of the amount of the annuity which is payable during the joint lives of the participant and the spouse, and

(B) which is the actuarial equivalent of a single annuity for the life of the participant.

Such term also includes any annuity in a form having the effect of an annuity described in the preceding sentence.

(2) APPLICABLE PERCENTAGE.—

(A) IN GENERAL.—For purposes of paragraph (1), if the survivor annuity percentage—

(i) is less than 75 percent, the applicable percentage is 75 percent, and

(ii) is greater than or equal to 75 percent, the applicable percentage is 50 percent.

(B) SURVIVOR ANNUITY PERCENTAGE.—For purposes of subparagraph (A), the term "survivor annuity percentage" means the percentage which the survivor annuity under the plan's qualified joint and survivor annuity bears to the annuity payable during the joint lives of the participant and the spouse.

[CCH Explanation at ¶1040. Committee Reports at ¶11,030.]

Amendments

• 2006, Pension Protection Act of 2006 (H.R. 4)

H.R. 4, §1004(a)(2):

Amended Code Sec. 417 by adding at the end a new subsection (g). **Effective** generally for plan years beginning after 12-31-2007. For a special rule, see Act Sec. 1004(c)(2), below.

H.R. 4, §1004(c)(2), provides:

(2) SPECIAL RULE FOR COLLECTIVELY BARGAINED PLANS.—In the case of a plan maintained pursuant to 1 or more collective bargaining agreements between employee representatives and 1 or more employers ratified on or before the date of the enactment of this Act, the amendments made by this section shall not apply to plan years beginning before the earlier of—

(A) the later of—

(i) January 1, 2008, or

(ii) the date on which the last collective bargaining agreement related to the plan terminates (determined without regard to any extension thereof after the date of enactment of this Act), or

(B) January 1, 2009.

[¶5110] CODE SEC. 418E. INSOLVENT PLANS.

* * *

(d) PLAN SPONSOR DETERMINATION.—

»»→ Caution: Code Sec. 418E(d)(1), below, as amended by H.R. 4, applies with respect to the determinations made in plan years beginning after 2007.

(1) TRIENNIAL TEST.—As of the end of the first plan year in which a plan is in reorganization, and at least every 3 plan years thereafter (unless the plan is no longer in reorganization), the plan sponsor shall compare the value of plan assets (determined in accordance with section 418B(b)(3)(B)(ii)) for that plan year with the total amount of benefit payments made under the plan for that plan year. Unless the plan sponsor determines that the value of plan assets exceeds 3 times the total amount of benefit payments, the plan sponsor shall determine whether the plan will be insolvent in any of the next *5 plan years. If the plan sponsor makes such a determination that the plan will be insolvent in any of the next 5 plan years, the plan sponsor shall make the comparison under this paragraph at least annually until the plan sponsor makes a determination that the plan will not be insolvent in any of the next 5 plan years.*

* * *

[CCH Explanation at ¶ 315. Committee Reports at ¶ 10,100.]

Amendments

• 2006, Pension Protection Act of 2006 (H.R. 4)

H.R. 4, § 213(a)(1)-(2):

Amended Code Sec. 418E(d)(1) by striking "3 plan years" the second place it appears and inserting "5 plan years"; and by adding at the end a new sentence. **Effective** with respect to the determinations made in plan years beginning after 2007.

[¶ 5112] CODE SEC. 419A. QUALIFIED ASSET ACCOUNT; LIMITATION ON ADDITIONS TO ACCOUNT.

* * *

(c) ACCOUNT LIMIT.—For purposes of this section—

* * *

»»→ Caution: Code Sec. 419A(c)(6), below, as added by H.R. 4, applies to tax years beginning after December 31, 2006.

(6) ADDITIONAL RESERVE FOR MEDICAL BENEFITS OF BONA FIDE ASSOCIATION PLANS.—

(A) IN GENERAL.—An applicable account limit for any taxable year may include a reserve in an amount not to exceed 35 percent of the sum of—

(i) the qualified direct costs, and

(ii) the change in claims incurred but unpaid,

for such taxable year with respect to medical benefits (other than post-retirement medical benefits).

(B) APPLICABLE ACCOUNT LIMIT.—For purposes of this subsection, the term "applicable account limit" means an account limit for a qualified asset account with respect to medical benefits provided through a plan maintained by a bona fide association (as defined in section 2791(d)(3) of the Public Health Service Act (42 U.S.C. 300gg-91(d)(3)).

* * *

[CCH Explanation at ¶ 815. Committee Reports at ¶ 10,770.]

Amendments

• 2006, Pension Protection Act of 2006 (H.R. 4)

H.R. 4, § 843(a):

Amended Code Sec. 419A(c) by adding at the end a new paragraph (6). **Effective** for tax years beginning after 12-31-2006.

[¶ 5115] CODE SEC. 420. TRANSFERS OF EXCESS PENSION ASSETS TO RETIREE HEALTH ACCOUNTS.

»»→ Caution: Code Sec. 420(a), below, as amended by H.R. 4, applies to transfers made in tax years beginning after December 31, 2006.

(a) GENERAL RULE.—If there is a qualified transfer of any excess pension assets of a defined benefit plan to a health benefits account which is part of such plan—

(1) a trust which is part of such plan shall not be treated as failing to meet the requirements of subsection (a) or (h) of section 401 solely by reason of such transfer (or any other action authorized under this section),

(2) no amount shall be includible in the gross income of the employer maintaining the plan solely by reason of such transfer,

(3) such transfer shall not be treated—

(A) as an employer reversion for purposes of section 4980, or

(B) as a prohibited transaction for purposes of section 4975, and

(4) the limitations of subsection (d) shall apply to such employer.

* * *

[CCH Explanation at ¶ 810. Committee Reports at ¶ 10,760.]

Amendments

• 2006, Pension Protection Act of 2006 (H.R. 4)

H.R. 4, § 842(a)(1):

Amended Code Sec. 420(a) by striking "(other than a multiemployer plan)" following "of a defined benefit plan" in the material preceding paragraph (1). **Effective** for transfers made in tax years beginning after 12-31-2006.

(e) DEFINITION AND SPECIAL RULES.—For purposes of this section—

* * *

(2) EXCESS PENSION ASSETS.—The term "excess pension assets" means the excess (if any) of—

(A) the lesser of—

(i) the fair market value of the plan's assets (reduced by the prefunding balance and funding standard carryover balance determined under section 430(f)), or

(ii) the value of plan assets as determined under section 430(g)(3) after reduction under section 430(f), over

(B) 125 percent of the sum of the funding shortfall and the target normal cost determined under section 430 for such plan year.

* * *

(4) COORDINATION WITH SECTION 430.—In the case of a qualified transfer, any assets so transferred shall not, for purposes of this section and section 430, be treated as assets in the plan.

»»→ Caution: Code Sec. 420(e)(5), below, as added by H.R. 4, applies to transfers made in tax years beginning after December 31, 2006.

(5) APPLICATION TO MULTIEMPLOYER PLANS.—In the case of a multiemployer plan, this section shall be applied to any such plan—

(A) by treating any reference in this section to an employer as a reference to all employers maintaining the plan (or, if appropriate, the plan sponsor), and

(B) in accordance with such modifications of this section (and the provisions of this title relating to this section) as the Secretary determines appropriate to reflect the fact the plan is not maintained by a single employer.

[CCH Explanation at ¶ 205 and ¶ 810. Committee Reports at ¶ 10,010 and ¶ 10,760.]

Amendments

• 2006, Pension Protection Act of 2006 (H.R. 4)

H.R. 4, § 114(d)(1):

Amended Code Sec. 420(e)(2). **Effective** 8-17-2006. Prior to amendment, Code Sec. 420(e)(2) read as follows:

(2) EXCESS PENSION ASSETS.—The term "excess pension assets" means the excess (if any) of—

(A) the amount determined under section 412(c)(7)(A)(ii), over

(B) the greater of—

(i) the amount determined under section 412(c)(7)(A)(i), or

(ii) 125 percent of current liability (as defined in section 412(c)(7)(B)).

The determination under this paragraph shall be made as of the most recent valuation date of the plan preceding the qualified transfer.

H.R. 4, § 114(d)(2):

Amended Code Sec. 420(e)(4). **Effective** 8-17-2006. Prior to amendment, Code Sec. 420(e)(4) read as follows:

(4) COORDINATION WITH SECTION 412.—In the case of a qualified transfer to a health benefits account—

(A) any assets transferred in a plan year on or before the valuation date for such year (and any income allocable thereto) shall, for purposes of section 412, be treated as assets in the plan as of the valuation date for such year, and

(B) the plan shall be treated as having a net experience loss under section 412(b)(2)(B)(iv) in an amount equal to the amount of such transfer (reduced by any amounts transferred back to the pension plan under subsection (c)(1)(B)) and for which amortization charges begin for the first plan year after the plan year in which such transfer occurs, except that such section shall be applied to such amount by substituting "10 plan years" for "5 plan years".

H.R. 4, § 842(a)(2):

Amended Code Sec. 420(e) by adding at the end a new paragraph (5). **Effective** for transfers made in tax years beginning after 12-31-2006.

(f) QUALIFIED TRANSFERS TO COVER FUTURE RETIREE HEALTH COSTS AND COLLECTIVELY BARGAINED RETIREE HEALTH BENEFITS.—

(1) IN GENERAL.—An employer maintaining a defined benefit plan (other than a multiemployer plan) may, in lieu of a qualified transfer, elect for any taxable year to have the plan make—

(A) a qualified future transfer, or

(B) a collectively bargained transfer.

Except as provided in this subsection, a qualified future transfer and a collectively bargained transfer shall be treated for purposes of this title and the Employee Retirement Income Security Act of 1974 as if it were a qualified transfer.

(2) QUALIFIED FUTURE AND COLLECTIVELY BARGAINED TRANSFERS.—For purposes of this subsection—

(A) IN GENERAL.—The terms "qualified future transfer" and "collectively bargained transfer" mean a transfer which meets all of the requirements for a qualified transfer, except that—

(i) the determination of excess pension assets shall be made under subparagraph (B),

(ii) the limitation on the amount transferred shall be determined under subparagraph (C),

(iii) the minimum cost requirements of subsection (c)(3) shall be modified as provided under subparagraph (D), and

(iv) in the case of a collectively bargained transfer, the requirements of subparagraph (E) shall be met with respect to the transfer.

(B) EXCESS PENSION ASSETS.—

(i) IN GENERAL.—In determining excess pension assets for purposes of this subsection, subsection (e)(2) shall be applied by substituting "120 percent" for "125 percent".

(ii) REQUIREMENT TO MAINTAIN FUNDED STATUS.—If, as of any valuation date of any plan year in the transfer period, the amount determined under subsection (e)(2)(B) (after application of clause (i)) exceeds the amount determined under subsection (e)(2)(A), either—

(I) the employer maintaining the plan shall make contributions to the plan in an amount not less than the amount required to reduce such excess to zero as of such date, or

(II) there is transferred from the health benefits account to the plan an amount not less than the amount required to reduce such excess to zero as of such date.

(C) LIMITATION ON AMOUNT TRANSFERRED.-—Notwithstanding subsection (b)(3), the amount of the excess pension assets which may be transferred—

(i) in the case of a qualified future transfer shall be equal to the sum of—

(I) if the transfer period includes the taxable year of the transfer, the amount determined under subsection (b)(3) for such taxable year, plus

(II) in the case of all other taxable years in the transfer period, the sum of the qualified current retiree health liabilities which the plan reasonably estimates, in accordance with guidance issued by the Secretary, will be incurred for each of such years, and

(ii) in the case of a collectively bargained transfer, shall not exceed the amount which is reasonably estimated, in accordance with the provisions of the collective bargaining agreement and generally accepted accounting principles, to be the amount the employer maintaining the plan will pay (whether directly or through reimbursement) out of such account during the collectively bargained cost maintenance period for collectively bargained retiree health liabilities.

(D) MINIMUM COST REQUIREMENTS.—

(i) IN GENERAL.—The requirements of subsection (c)(3) shall be treated as met if—

(I) in the case of a qualified future transfer, each group health plan or arrangement under which applicable health benefits are provided provides applicable health benefits during the period beginning with the first year of the transfer period and ending with the last day of the 4th year following the transfer period such that the annual average amount of such the applicable employer cost during such period is not less than the applicable employer cost determined under subsection (c)(3)(A) with respect to the transfer, and

(II) in the case of a collectively bargained transfer, each collectively bargained group health plan under which collectively bargained health benefits are provided provides that the collectively bargained employer cost for each taxable year during the collectively bargained cost maintenance period shall not be less than the amount specified by the collective bargaining agreement.

(ii) ELECTION TO MAINTAIN BENEFITS FOR FUTURE TRANSFERS.—An employer may elect, in lieu of the requirements of clause (i)(I), to meet the requirements of subsection (c)(3) by meeting the requirements of such subsection (as in effect before the amendments made by section 535 of the Tax Relief Extension Act of 1999) for each of the years described in the period under clause (i)(I).

(iii) COLLECTIVELY BARGAINED EMPLOYER COST.—For purposes of this subparagraph, the term "collectively bargained employer cost" means the average cost per covered individual of providing collectively bargained retiree health benefits as determined in accordance with the applicable collective bargaining agreement. Such agreement may provide for an appropriate reduction in the collectively bargained employer cost to take into account any portion of the collectively bargained retiree health benefits that is provided or financed by a government program or other source.

(E) SPECIAL RULES FOR COLLECTIVELY BARGAINED TRANSFERS.—

(i) IN GENERAL.—A collectively bargained transfer shall only include a transfer which—

(I) is made in accordance with a collective bargaining agreement,

(II) before the transfer, the employer designates, in a written notice delivered to each employee organization that is a party to the collective bargaining agreement, as a collectively bargained transfer in accordance with this section, and

(III) involves a plan maintained by an employer which, in its taxable year ending in 2005, provided health benefits or coverage to retirees and their spouses and dependents under all of the benefit plans maintained by the employer, but only if the aggregate cost (including administrative expenses) of such benefits or coverage which would have been allowable as a deduction to the employer (if such benefits or coverage had been provided directly by the employer and the employer used the cash receipts and disbursements method of accounting) is at least 5 percent of the gross receipts of the employer (determined in accordance with the last sentence of subsection (c)(2)(E)(ii)(II)) for such taxable year, or a plan maintained by a successor to such employer.

(ii) USE OF ASSETS.—Any assets transferred to a health benefits account in a collectively bargained transfer (and any income allocable thereto) shall be used only to pay collectively bargained retiree health liabilities (other than liabilities of key employees not taken into account under paragraph (6)(B)(iii)) for the taxable year of the transfer or for any subsequent taxable year during the collectively bargained cost maintenance period (whether directly or through reimbursement).

(3) COORDINATION WITH OTHER TRANSFERS.—In applying subsection (b)(3) to any subsequent transfer during a taxable year in a transfer period or collectively bargained cost maintenance period, qualified current retiree health liabilities shall be reduced by any such liabilities taken into account with respect to the qualified future transfer or collectively bargained transfer to which such period relates.

(4) SPECIAL DEDUCTION RULES FOR COLLECTIVELY BARGAINED TRANSFERS.—In the case of a collectively bargained transfer—

(A) the limitation under subsection (d)(1)(C) shall not apply, and

(B) notwithstanding subsection (d)(2), an employer may contribute an amount to a health benefits account or welfare benefit fund (as defined in section 419(e)(1)) with respect to collectively bargained retiree health liabilities for which transferred assets are required to be used under subsection (c)(1)(B), and the deductibility of any such contribution shall be governed by the limits applicable to the deductibility of contributions to a welfare benefit fund under a collective bargaining agreement (as determined under section 419A(f)(5)(A)) without regard to whether such contributions are made to a health benefits account or welfare benefit fund and without regard to the provisions of section 404 or the other provisions of this section.

The Secretary shall provide rules to ensure that the application of this paragraph does not result in a deduction being allowed more than once for the same contribution or for 2 or more contributions or expenditures relating to the same collectively bargained retiree health liabilities.

(5) TRANSFER PERIOD.—For purposes of this subsection, the term "transfer period" means, with respect to any transfer, a period of consecutive taxable years (not less than 2) specified in the election under paragraph (1) which begins and ends during the 10-taxable-year period beginning with the taxable year of the transfer.

(6) TERMS RELATING TO COLLECTIVELY BARGAINED TRANSFERS.—For purposes of this subsection—

(A) COLLECTIVELY BARGAINED COST MAINTENANCE PERIOD.—The term "collectively bargained cost maintenance period" means, with respect to each covered retiree and his covered spouse and dependents, the shorter of—

(i) the remaining lifetime of such covered retiree and his covered spouse and dependents, or

(ii) the period of coverage provided by the collectively bargained health plan (determined as of the date of the collectively bargained transfer) with respect to such covered retiree and his covered spouse and dependents.

(B) COLLECTIVELY BARGAINED RETIREE HEALTH LIABILITIES.—

(i) IN GENERAL.—The term "collectively bargained retiree health liabilities" means the present value, as of the beginning of a taxable year and determined in accordance with the applicable collective bargaining agreement, of all collectively bargained health benefits (including administrative expenses) for such taxable year and all subsequent taxable years during the collectively bargained cost maintenance period.

(ii) REDUCTION FOR AMOUNTS PREVIOUSLY SET ASIDE.—The amount determined under clause (i) shall be reduced by the value (as of the close of the plan year preceding the year of the collectively bargained transfer) of the assets in all health benefits accounts or welfare benefit funds (as defined in section 419(e)(1)) set aside to pay for the collectively bargained retiree health liabilities.

(iii) KEY EMPLOYEES EXCLUDED.—If an employee is a key employee (within the meaning of section 416(I)(1)) with respect to any plan year ending in a taxable year, such employee shall not be taken into account in computing collectively bargained retiree health liabilities for such taxable year or in calculating collectively bargained employer cost under subsection (c)(3)(C).

(C) COLLECTIVELY BARGAINED HEALTH BENEFITS.—The term "collectively bargained health benefits" means health benefits or coverage which are provided to—

(i) retired employees who, immediately before the collectively bargained transfer, are entitled to receive such benefits upon retirement and who are entitled to pension benefits under the plan, and their spouses and dependents, and

(ii) if specified by the provisions of the collective bargaining agreement governing the collectively bargained transfer, active employees who, following their retirement, are entitled to receive such benefits and who are entitled to pension benefits under the plan, and their spouses and dependents.

(D) COLLECTIVELY BARGAINED HEALTH PLAN.—The term "collectively bargained health plan" means a group health plan or arrangement for retired employees and their spouses and dependents that is maintained pursuant to 1 or more collective bargaining agreements.

[CCH Explanation at ¶ 805. Committee Reports at ¶ 10,750.]

Amendments

• 2006, Pension Protection Act of 2006 (H.R. 4)

H.R. 4, §841(a):

Amended Code Sec. 420 by adding at the end a new subsection (f). **Effective** for transfers after 8-17-2006.

»»→ Caution: Code Sec. 430, below, as added by H.R. 4, applies with respect to plan years beginning after December 31, 2007.

[¶ 5120] *CODE SEC. 430. MINIMUM FUNDING STANDARDS FOR SINGLE-EMPLOYER DEFINED BENEFIT PENSION PLANS.*

(a) MINIMUM REQUIRED CONTRIBUTION.—For purposes of this section and section 412(a)(2)(A), except as provided in subsection (f), the term "minimum required contribution" means, with respect to any plan year of a defined benefit plan which is not a multiemployer plan—

(1) in any case in which the value of plan assets of the plan (as reduced under subsection (f)(4)(B)) is less than the funding target of the plan for the plan year, the sum of—

(A) the target normal cost of the plan for the plan year,

(B) the shortfall amortization charge (if any) for the plan for the plan year determined under subsection (c), and

(C) the waiver amortization charge (if any) for the plan for the plan year as determined under subsection (e);

(2) in any case in which the value of plan assets of the plan (as reduced under subsection (f)(4)(B)) equals or exceeds the funding target of the plan for the plan year, the target normal cost of the plan for the plan year reduced (but not below zero) by such excess.

(b) TARGET NORMAL COST.—For purposes of this section, except as provided in subsection (i)(2) with respect to plans in at-risk status, the term "target normal cost" means, for any plan year, the present value of all benefits which are expected to accrue or to be earned under the plan during the plan year. For purposes of this subsection, if any benefit attributable to services performed in a preceding plan year is increased by reason of any increase in compensation during the current plan year, the increase in such benefit shall be treated as having accrued during the current plan year.

(c) SHORTFALL AMORTIZATION CHARGE.—

(1) IN GENERAL.—For purposes of this section, the shortfall amortization charge for a plan for any plan year is the aggregate total (not less than zero) of the shortfall amortization installments for such plan year with respect to the shortfall amortization bases for such plan year and each of the 6 preceding plan years.

(2) SHORTFALL AMORTIZATION INSTALLMENT.—For purposes of paragraph (1)—

(A) DETERMINATION.—The shortfall amortization installments are the amounts necessary to amortize the shortfall amortization base of the plan for any plan year in level annual installments over the 7-plan-year period beginning with such plan year.

(B) SHORTFALL INSTALLMENT.—The shortfall amortization installment for any plan year in the 7-plan-year period under subparagraph (A) with respect to any shortfall amortization base is the annual installment determined under subparagraph (A) for that year for that base.

(C) SEGMENT RATES.—In determining any shortfall amortization installment under this paragraph, the plan sponsor shall use the segment rates determined under subparagraph (C) of subsection (h)(2), applied under rules similar to the rules of subparagraph (B) of subsection (h)(2).

(3) SHORTFALL AMORTIZATION BASE.—For purposes of this section, the shortfall amortization base of a plan for a plan year is—

(A) the funding shortfall of such plan for such plan year, minus

(B) the present value (determined using the segment rates determined under subparagraph (C) of subsection (h)(2), applied under rules similar to the rules of subparagraph (B) of subsection (h)(2)) of the aggregate total of the shortfall amortization installments and waiver amortization installments which have been determined for such plan year and any succeeding plan year with respect to the shortfall amortization bases and waiver amortization bases of the plan for any plan year preceding such plan year.

(4) FUNDING SHORTFALL.—For purposes of this section, the funding shortfall of a plan for any plan year is the excess (if any) of—

(A) the funding target of the plan for the plan year, over

(B) the value of plan assets of the plan (as reduced under subsection (f)(4)(B)) for the plan year which are held by the plan on the valuation date.

(5) EXEMPTION FROM NEW SHORTFALL AMORTIZATION BASE.—

(A) IN GENERAL.—In any case in which the value of plan assets of the plan (as reduced under subsection (f)(4)(A)) is equal to or greater than the funding target of the plan for the plan year, the shortfall amortization base of the plan for such plan year shall be zero.

(B) TRANSITION RULE.—

(i) IN GENERAL.—Except as provided in clauses (iii) and (iv), in the case of plan years beginning after 2007 and before 2011, only the applicable percentage of the funding target shall be taken into account under paragraph (3)(A) in determining the funding shortfall for the plan year for purposes of subparagraph (A).

(ii) APPLICABLE PERCENTAGE.—For purposes of subparagraph (A), the applicable percentage shall be determined in accordance with the following table:

In the case of a plan year beginning in calendar year:	*The applicable percentage is*
2008	*92*
2009	*94*
2010	*96*

(iii) LIMITATION.—Clause (i) shall not apply with respect to any plan year after 2008 unless the shortfall amortization base for each of the preceding years beginning after 2007 was zero (determined after application of this subparagraph).

(iv) TRANSITION RELIEF NOT AVAILABLE FOR NEW OR DEFICIT REDUCTION PLANS.—Clause (i) shall not apply to a plan—

(I) which was not in effect for a plan year beginning in 2007, or

(II) which was in effect for a plan year beginning in 2007 and which was subject to section 412(l) (as in effect for plan years beginning in 2007), determined after the application of paragraphs (6) and (9) thereof.

(6) EARLY DEEMED AMORTIZATION UPON ATTAINMENT OF FUNDING TARGET.—In any case in which the funding shortfall of a plan for a plan year is zero, for purposes of determining the shortfall amortization charge for such plan year and succeeding plan years, the shortfall amortization bases for all preceding plan years (and all shortfall amortization installments determined with respect to such bases) shall be reduced to zero.

(d) RULES RELATING TO FUNDING TARGET.—For purposes of this section—

(1) FUNDING TARGET.—Except as provided in subsection (i)(1) with respect to plans in at-risk status, the funding target of a plan for a plan year is the present value of all benefits accrued or earned under the plan as of the beginning of the plan year.

(2) FUNDING TARGET ATTAINMENT PERCENTAGE.—The "funding target attainment percentage" of a plan for a plan year is the ratio (expressed as a percentage) which—

(A) the value of plan assets for the plan year (as reduced under subsection (f)(4)(B)), bears to

(B) the funding target of the plan for the plan year (determined without regard to subsection (i)(1)).

(e) WAIVER AMORTIZATION CHARGE.—

(1) DETERMINATION OF WAIVER AMORTIZATION CHARGE.—The waiver amortization charge (if any) for a plan for any plan year is the aggregate total of the waiver amortization installments for such plan year with respect to the waiver amortization bases for each of the 5 preceding plan years.

(2) WAIVER AMORTIZATION INSTALLMENT.—For purposes of paragraph (1)—

(A) DETERMINATION.—The waiver amortization installments are the amounts necessary to amortize the waiver amortization base of the plan for any plan year in level annual installments over a period of 5 plan years beginning with the succeeding plan year.

(B) WAIVER INSTALLMENT.—The waiver amortization installment for any plan year in the 5-year period under subparagraph (A) with respect to any waiver amortization base is the annual installment determined under subparagraph (A) for that year for that base.

(3) INTEREST RATE.—In determining any waiver amortization installment under this subsection, the plan sponsor shall use the segment rates determined under subparagraph (C) of subsection (h)(2), applied under rules similar to the rules of subparagraph (B) of subsection (h)(2).

(4) WAIVER AMORTIZATION BASE.—The waiver amortization base of a plan for a plan year is the amount of the waived funding deficiency (if any) for such plan year under section 412(c).

(5) EARLY DEEMED AMORTIZATION UPON ATTAINMENT OF FUNDING TARGET.—In any case in which the funding shortfall of a plan for a plan year is zero, for purposes of determining the waiver amortization charge for such plan year and succeeding plan years, the waiver amortization bases for all preceding plan years (and all waiver amortization installments determined with respect to such bases) shall be reduced to zero.

(f) REDUCTION OF MINIMUM REQUIRED CONTRIBUTION BY PREFUNDING BALANCE AND FUNDING STANDARD CARRYOVER BALANCE.—

(1) ELECTION TO MAINTAIN BALANCES.—

(A) PREFUNDING BALANCE.—The plan sponsor of a defined benefit plan which is not a multiemployer plan may elect to maintain a prefunding balance.

(B) FUNDING STANDARD CARRYOVER BALANCE.—

(i) IN GENERAL.—In the case of a defined benefit plan (other than a multiemployer plan) described in clause (ii), the plan sponsor may elect to maintain a funding standard carryover balance, until such balance is reduced to zero.

(ii) PLANS MAINTAINING FUNDING STANDARD ACCOUNT IN 2007.—A plan is described in this clause if the plan—

(I) was in effect for a plan year beginning in 2007, and

(II) had a positive balance in the funding standard account under section 412(b) as in effect for such plan year and determined as of the end of such plan year.

(2) APPLICATION OF BALANCES.—A prefunding balance and a funding standard carryover balance maintained pursuant to this paragraph—

(A) shall be available for crediting against the minimum required contribution, pursuant to an election under paragraph (3),

(B) shall be applied as a reduction in the amount treated as the value of plan assets for purposes of this section, to the extent provided in paragraph (4), and

(C) may be reduced at any time, pursuant to an election under paragraph (5).

(3) ELECTION TO APPLY BALANCES AGAINST MINIMUM REQUIRED CONTRIBUTION.—

(A) IN GENERAL.—Except as provided in subparagraphs (B) and (C), in the case of any plan year in which the plan sponsor elects to credit against the minimum required contribution for the current plan year all or a portion of the prefunding balance or the funding standard carryover balance for the current plan year (not in excess of such minimum required contribution), the minimum required contribution for the plan year shall be reduced as of the first day of the plan year by the amount so credited by the plan sponsor as of the first day of the plan year. For purposes of the preceding sentence, the minimum required contribution shall be determined after taking into account any waiver under section 412(c).

(B) COORDINATION WITH FUNDING STANDARD CARRYOVER BALANCE.—To the extent that any plan has a funding standard carryover balance greater than zero, no amount of the prefunding balance of such plan may be credited under this paragraph in reducing the minimum required contribution.

(C) LIMITATION FOR UNDERFUNDED PLANS.—The preceding provisions of this paragraph shall not apply for any plan year if the ratio (expressed as a percentage) which—

(i) the value of plan assets for the preceding plan year (as reduced under paragraph (4)(C)), bears to

(ii) the funding target of the plan for the preceding plan year (determined without regard to subsection (i)(1)),

is less than 80 percent. In the case of plan years beginning in 2008, the ratio under this subparagraph may be determined using such methods of estimation as the Secretary may prescribe.

(4) EFFECT OF BALANCES ON AMOUNTS TREATED AS VALUE OF PLAN ASSETS.—In the case of any plan maintaining a prefunding balance or a funding standard carryover balance pursuant to this subsection, the amount treated as the value of plan assets shall be deemed to be such amount, reduced as provided in the following subparagraphs:

(A) APPLICABILITY OF SHORTFALL AMORTIZATION BASE.—For purposes of subsection (c)(5), the value of plan assets is deemed to be such amount, reduced by the amount of the prefunding balance, but only if an election under paragraph (2) applying any portion of the prefunding balance in reducing the minimum required contribution is in effect for the plan year.

(B) DETERMINATION OF EXCESS ASSETS, FUNDING SHORTFALL, AND FUNDING TARGET ATTAINMENT PERCENTAGE.—

(i) IN GENERAL.—For purposes of subsections (a), (c)(4)(B), and (d)(2)(A), the value of plan assets is deemed to be such amount, reduced by the amount of the prefunding balance and the funding standard carryover balance.

(ii) SPECIAL RULE FOR CERTAIN BINDING AGREEMENTS WITH PBGC.—For purposes of subsection (c)(4)(B), the value of plan assets shall not be deemed to be reduced for a plan year by the amount of the specified balance if, with respect to such balance, there is in effect for a plan year a binding written agreement with the Pension Benefit Guaranty Corporation which provides that such balance is not available to reduce the minimum required contribution for the plan year. For purposes of the preceding sentence, the term "specified balance" means the prefunding balance or the funding standard carryover balance, as the case may be.

(C) AVAILABILITY OF BALANCES IN PLAN YEAR FOR CREDITING AGAINST MINIMUM REQUIRED CONTRIBUTION.—For purposes of paragraph (3)(C)(i) of this subsection, the value of plan assets is deemed to be such amount, reduced by the amount of the prefunding balance.

(5) ELECTION TO REDUCE BALANCE PRIOR TO DETERMINATIONS OF VALUE OF PLAN ASSETS AND CREDITING AGAINST MINIMUM REQUIRED CONTRIBUTION.—

(A) IN GENERAL.—The plan sponsor may elect to reduce by any amount the balance of the prefunding balance and the funding standard carryover balance for any plan year (but not below zero). Such reduction shall be effective prior to any determination of the value of plan assets for such plan year under this section and application of the balance in reducing the minimum required contribution for such plan for such plan year pursuant to an election under paragraph (2).

(B) COORDINATION BETWEEN PREFUNDING BALANCE AND FUNDING STANDARD CARRYOVER BALANCE.—To the extent that any plan has a funding standard carryover balance greater than zero, no election may be made under subparagraph (A) with respect to the prefunding balance.

(6) PREFUNDING BALANCE.—

(A) IN GENERAL.—A prefunding balance maintained by a plan shall consist of a beginning balance of zero, increased and decreased to the extent provided in subparagraphs (B) and (C), and adjusted further as provided in paragraph (8).

(B) INCREASES.—

(i) IN GENERAL.—As of the first day of each plan year beginning after 2008, the prefunding balance of a plan shall be increased by the amount elected by the plan sponsor for the plan year. Such amount shall not exceed the excess (if any) of—

(I) the aggregate total of employer contributions to the plan for the preceding plan year, over—

(II) the minimum required contribution for such preceding plan year.

(ii) ADJUSTMENTS FOR INTEREST.—Any excess contributions under clause (i) shall be properly adjusted for interest accruing for the periods between the first day of the current plan year and the dates on which the excess contributions were made, determined by using the effective interest rate for the preceding plan year and by treating contributions as being first used to satisfy the minimum required contribution.

(iii) CERTAIN CONTRIBUTIONS NECESSARY TO AVOID BENEFIT LIMITATIONS DISREGARDED.—The excess described in clause (i) with respect to any preceding plan year shall be reduced (but not below zero) by the amount of contributions an employer would be required to make under paragraph (1), (2), or (4) of section 206(g) to avoid a benefit limitation which would otherwise be imposed under such paragraph for the preceding plan year. Any contribution which may be taken into account in satisfying the requirements of more than 1 of such paragraphs shall be taken into account only once for purposes of this clause.

(C) DECREASES.—The prefunding balance of a plan shall be decreased (but not below zero) by the sum of—

(i) as of the first day of each plan year after 2008, the amount of such balance credited under paragraph (2) (if any) in reducing the minimum required contribution of the plan for the preceding plan year, and

(ii) as of the time specified in paragraph (5)(A), any reduction in such balance elected under paragraph (5).

(7) FUNDING STANDARD CARRYOVER BALANCE.—

(A) IN GENERAL.—A funding standard carryover balance maintained by a plan shall consist of a beginning balance determined under subparagraph (B), decreased to the extent provided in subparagraph (C), and adjusted further as provided in paragraph (8).

(B) BEGINNING BALANCE.—The beginning balance of the funding standard carryover balance shall be the positive balance described in paragraph (1)(B)(ii)(II).

(C) DECREASES.—The funding standard carryover balance of a plan shall be decreased (but not below zero) by—

(i) as of the first day of each plan year after 2008, the amount of such balance credited under paragraph (2) (if any) in reducing the minimum required contribution of the plan for the preceding plan year, and

(ii) as of the time specified in paragraph (5)(A), any reduction in such balance elected under paragraph (5).

(8) ADJUSTMENTS FOR INVESTMENT EXPERIENCE.—In determining the prefunding balance or the funding standard carryover balance of a plan as of the first day of the plan year, the plan sponsor shall, in accordance with regulations prescribed by the Secretary of the Treasury, adjust such balance to reflect the rate of return on plan assets for the preceding plan year. Notwithstanding subsection (g)(3), such rate of return shall be determined on the basis of fair market value and shall properly take into account, in accordance with such regulations, all contributions, distributions, and other plan payments made during such period.

(9) ELECTIONS.—Elections under this subsection shall be made at such times, and in such form and manner, as shall be prescribed in regulations of the Secretary.

(g) VALUATION OF PLAN ASSETS AND LIABILITIES.—

(1) TIMING OF DETERMINATIONS.—Except as otherwise provided under this subsection, all determinations under this section for a plan year shall be made as of the valuation date of the plan for such plan year.

(2) VALUATION DATE.—For purposes of this section—

(A) IN GENERAL.—Except as provided in subparagraph (B), the valuation date of a plan for any plan year shall be the first day of the plan year.

(B) EXCEPTION FOR SMALL PLANS.—If, on each day during the preceding plan year, a plan had 100 or fewer participants, the plan may designate any day during the plan year as its valuation date for such plan year and succeeding plan years. For purposes of this subparagraph, all defined benefit plans (other than multiemployer plans) maintained by the same employer (or any member of such employer's controlled group) shall be treated as 1 plan, but only participants with respect to such employer or member shall be taken into account.

(C) APPLICATION OF CERTAIN RULES IN DETERMINATION OF PLAN SIZE.—For purposes of this paragraph—

(i) PLANS NOT IN EXISTENCE IN PRECEDING YEAR.—In the case of the first plan year of any plan, subparagraph (B) shall apply to such plan by taking into account the number of participants that the plan is reasonably expected to have on days during such first plan year.

(ii) PREDECESSORS.—Any reference in subparagraph (B) to an employer shall include a reference to any predecessor of such employer.

(3) DETERMINATION OF VALUE OF PLAN ASSETS.—For purposes of this section—

(A) IN GENERAL.—Except as provided in subparagraph (B), the value of plan assets shall be the fair market value of the assets.

(B) AVERAGING ALLOWED.—A plan may determine the value of plan assets on the basis of the averaging of fair market values, but only if such method—

(i) is permitted under regulations prescribed by the Secretary,

(ii) does not provide for averaging of such values over more than the period beginning on the last day of the 25th month preceding the month in which the valuation date occurs and ending on the valuation date (or a similar period in the case of a valuation date which is not the 1st day of a month), and

(iii) does not result in a determination of the value of plan assets which, at any time, is lower than 90 percent or greater than 110 percent of the fair market value of such assets at such time.

Any such averaging shall be adjusted for contributions and distributions (as provided by the Secretary).

(4) ACCOUNTING FOR CONTRIBUTION RECEIPTS.—For purposes of determining the value of assets under paragraph (3)—

(A) PRIOR YEAR CONTRIBUTIONS.—If—

(i) an employer makes any contribution to the plan after the valuation date for the plan year in which the contribution is made, and

(ii) the contribution is for a preceding plan year,

the contribution shall be taken into account as an asset of the plan as of the valuation date, except that in the case of any plan year beginning after 2008, only the present value (determined as of the valuation date) of such contribution may be taken into account. For purposes of the preceding sentence, present value shall be determined using the effective interest rate for the preceding plan year to which the contribution is properly allocable.

(B) SPECIAL RULE FOR CURRENT YEAR CONTRIBUTIONS MADE BEFORE VALUATION DATE.—If any contributions for any plan year are made to or under the plan during the plan year but before the valuation date for the plan year, the assets of the plan as of the valuation date shall not include—

(i) such contributions, and

(ii) interest on such contributions for the period between the date of the contributions and the valuation date, determined by using the effective interest rate for the plan year.

(h) ACTUARIAL ASSUMPTIONS AND METHODS.—

(1) IN GENERAL.—Subject to this subsection, the determination of any present value or other computation under this section shall be made on the basis of actuarial assumptions and methods—

(A) each of which is reasonable (taking into account the experience of the plan and reasonable expectations), and

(B) which, in combination, offer the actuary's best estimate of anticipated experience under the plan.

(2) INTEREST RATES.—

(A) EFFECTIVE INTEREST RATE.—For purposes of this section, the term "effective interest rate" means, with respect to any plan for any plan year, the single rate of interest which, if used to determine the present value of the plan's accrued or earned benefits referred to in subsection (d)(1), would result in an amount equal to the funding target of the plan for such plan year.

(B) INTEREST RATES FOR DETERMINING FUNDING TARGET.—For purposes of determining the funding target of a plan for any plan year, the interest rate used in determining the present value of the liabilities of the plan shall be—

(i) in the case of benefits reasonably determined to be payable during the 5-year period beginning on the first day of the plan year, the first segment rate with respect to the applicable month,

(ii) in the case of benefits reasonably determined to be payable during the 15-year period beginning at the end of the period described in clause (i), the second segment rate with respect to the applicable month, and

(iii) in the case of benefits reasonably determined to be payable after the period described in clause (ii), the third segment rate with respect to the applicable month.

(C) SEGMENT RATES.—For purposes of this paragraph—

(i) FIRST SEGMENT RATE.—The term "first segment rate" means, with respect to any month, the single rate of interest which shall be determined by the Secretary for such month on the basis of the corporate bond yield curve for such month, taking into account only that portion of such yield curve which is based on bonds maturing during the 5-year period commencing with such month.

(ii) SECOND SEGMENT RATE.—The term "second segment rate" means, with respect to any month, the single rate of interest which shall be determined by the Secretary for such month on the basis of the corporate bond yield curve for such month, taking into account only that portion of such yield curve which is based on bonds maturing during the 15-year period beginning at the end of the period described in clause (i).

(iii) THIRD SEGMENT RATE.—The term "third segment rate" means, with respect to any month, the single rate of interest which shall be determined by the Secretary for such month on the basis of the corporate bond yield curve for such month, taking into account only that portion of such yield curve which is based on bonds maturing during periods beginning after the period described in clause (ii).

(D) CORPORATE BOND YIELD CURVE.—For purposes of this paragraph—

(i) IN GENERAL.—The term "corporate bond yield curve" means, with respect to any month, a yield curve which is prescribed by the Secretary for such month and which reflects the average, for the 24-month period ending with the month preceding such month, of monthly yields on investment grade corporate bonds with varying maturities and that are in the top 3 quality levels available.

(ii) ELECTION TO USE YIELD CURVE.—*Solely for purposes of determining the minimum required contribution under this section, the plan sponsor may, in lieu of the segment rates determined under subparagraph (C), elect to use interest rates under the corporate bond yield curve. For purposes of the preceding sentence such curve shall be determined without regard to the 24-month averaging described in clause (i). Such election, once made, may be revoked only with the consent of the Secretary.*

(E) APPLICABLE MONTH.—*For purposes of this paragraph, the term "applicable month" means, with respect to any plan for any plan year, the month which includes the valuation date of such plan for such plan year or, at the election of the plan sponsor, any of the 4 months which precede such month. Any election made under this subparagraph shall apply to the plan year for which the election is made and all succeeding plan years, unless the election is revoked with the consent of the Secretary.*

(F) PUBLICATION REQUIREMENTS.—*The Secretary shall publish for each month the corporate bond yield curve (and the corporate bond yield curve reflecting the modification described in section 417(e)(3)(D)(i)) for such month and each of the rates determined under subparagraph (B) for such month. The Secretary shall also publish a description of the methodology used to determine such yield curve and such rates which is sufficiently detailed to enable plans to make reasonable projections regarding the yield curve and such rates for future months based on the plan's projection of future interest rates.*

(G) TRANSITION RULE.—

(i) IN GENERAL.—*Notwithstanding the preceding provisions of this paragraph, for plan years beginning in 2008 or 2009, the first, second, or third segment rate for a plan with respect to any month shall be equal to the sum of—*

(I) the product of such rate for such month determined without regard to this subparagraph, multiplied by the applicable percentage, and

(II) the product of the rate determined under the rules of section 412(b)(5)(B)(ii)(II) (as in effect for plan years beginning in 2007), multiplied by a percentage equal to 100 percent minus the applicable percentage.

(ii) APPLICABLE PERCENTAGE.—*For purposes of clause (i), the applicable percentage is 33⅓ percent for plan years beginning in 2008 and 66⅔ percent for plan years beginning in 2009.*

(iii) NEW PLANS INELIGIBLE.—*Clause (i) shall not apply to any plan if the first plan year of the plan begins after December 31, 2007.*

(iv) ELECTION.—*The plan sponsor may elect not to have this subparagraph apply. Such election, once made, may be revoked only with the consent of the Secretary.*

(3) MORTALITY TABLES.—

(A) IN GENERAL.—*Except as provided in subparagraph (C) or (D), the Secretary shall by regulation prescribe mortality tables to be used in determining any present value or making any computation under this section. Such tables shall be based on the actual experience of pension plans and projected trends in such experience. In prescribing such tables, the Secretary shall take into account results of available independent studies of mortality of individuals covered by pension plans.*

(B) PERIODIC REVISION.—*The Secretary shall (at least every 10 years) make revisions in any table in effect under subparagraph (A) to reflect the actual experience of pension plans and projected trends in such experience.*

(C) SUBSTITUTE MORTALITY TABLE.—

(i) IN GENERAL.—*Upon request by the plan sponsor and approval by the Secretary, a mortality table which meets the requirements of clause (iii) shall be used in determining any present value or making any computation under this section during the period of consecutive plan years (not to exceed 10) specified in the request.*

(ii) EARLY TERMINATION OF PERIOD.—*Notwithstanding clause (i), a mortality table described in clause (i) shall cease to be in effect as of the earliest of—*

(I) the date on which there is a significant change in the participants in the plan by reason of a plan spinoff or merger or otherwise, or

(II) the date on which the plan actuary determines that such table does not meet the requirements of clause (iii).

(iii) REQUIREMENTS.—A mortality table meets the requirements of this clause if—

(I) there is a sufficient number of plan participants, and the pension plans have been maintained for a sufficient period of time, to have credible information necessary for purposes of subclause (II), and

(II) such table reflects the actual experience of the pension plans maintained by the sponsor and projected trends in general mortality experience.

(iv) ALL PLANS IN CONTROLLED GROUP MUST USE SEPARATE TABLE.—Except as provided by the Secretary, a plan sponsor may not use a mortality table under this subparagraph for any plan maintained by the plan sponsor unless—

(I) a separate mortality table is established and used under this subparagraph for each other plan maintained by the plan sponsor and if the plan sponsor is a member of a controlled group, each member of the controlled group, and

(II) the requirements of clause (iii) are met separately with respect to the table so established for each such plan, determined by only taking into account the participants of such plan, the time such plan has been in existence, and the actual experience of such plan.

(v) DEADLINE FOR SUBMISSION AND DISPOSITION OF APPLICATION.—

(I) SUBMISSION.—The plan sponsor shall submit a mortality table to the Secretary for approval under this subparagraph at least 7 months before the 1st day of the period described in clause (i).

(II) DISPOSITION.—Any mortality table submitted to the Secretary for approval under this subparagraph shall be treated as in effect as of the 1st day of the period described in clause (i) unless the Secretary, during the 180-day period beginning on the date of such submission, disapproves of such table and provides the reasons that such table fails to meet the requirements of clause (iii). The 180-day period shall be extended upon mutual agreement of the Secretary and the plan sponsor.

(D) SEPARATE MORTALITY TABLES FOR THE DISABLED.—Notwithstanding subparagraph (A)—

(i) IN GENERAL.—The Secretary shall establish mortality tables which may be used (in lieu of the tables under subparagraph (A)) under this subsection for individuals who are entitled to benefits under the plan on account of disability. The Secretary shall establish separate tables for individuals whose disabilities occur in plan years beginning before January 1, 1995, and for individuals whose disabilities occur in plan years beginning on or after such date.

(ii) SPECIAL RULE FOR DISABILITIES OCCURRING AFTER 1994.—In the case of disabilities occurring in plan years beginning after December 31, 1994, the tables under clause (i) shall apply only with respect to individuals described in such subclause who are disabled within the meaning of title II of the Social Security Act and the regulations thereunder.

(iii) PERIODIC REVISION.—The Secretary shall (at least every 10 years) make revisions in any table in effect under clause (i) to reflect the actual experience of pension plans and projected trends in such experience.

(4) PROBABILITY OF BENEFIT PAYMENTS IN THE FORM OF LUMP SUMS OR OTHER OPTIONAL FORMS.—For purposes of determining any present value or making any computation under this section, there shall be taken into account—

(A) the probability that future benefit payments under the plan will be made in the form of optional forms of benefits provided under the plan (including lump sum distributions, determined on the basis of the plan's experience and other related assumptions), and

(B) any difference in the present value of such future benefit payments resulting from the use of actuarial assumptions, in determining benefit payments in any such optional form of benefits, which are different from those specified in this subsection.

(5) APPROVAL OF LARGE CHANGES IN ACTUARIAL ASSUMPTIONS.—

(A) IN GENERAL.—No actuarial assumption used to determine the funding target for a plan to which this paragraph applies may be changed without the approval of the Secretary.

(B) PLANS TO WHICH PARAGRAPH APPLIES.—This paragraph shall apply to a plan only if—

(i) the plan is a defined benefit plan (other than a multiemployer plan) to which title IV of the Employee Retirement Income Security Act of 1974 applies,

(ii) the aggregate unfunded vested benefits as of the close of the preceding plan year (as determined under section 4006(a)(3)(E)(iii) of the Employee Retirement Income Security Act of 1974) of such plan and all other plans maintained by the contributing sponsors (as defined in section 4001(a)(13) of such Act) and members of such sponsors' controlled groups (as defined in section 4001(a)(14) of such Act) which are covered by title IV (disregarding plans with no unfunded vested benefits) exceed $50,000,000, and

(iii) the change in assumptions (determined after taking into account any changes in interest rate and mortality table) results in a decrease in the funding shortfall of the plan for the current plan year that exceeds $50,000,000, or that exceeds $5,000,000 and that is 5 percent or more of the funding target of the plan before such change.

(i) SPECIAL RULES FOR AT-RISK PLANS.—

(1) FUNDING TARGET FOR PLANS IN AT-RISK STATUS.—

(A) IN GENERAL.—In the case of a plan which is in at-risk status for a plan year, the funding target of the plan for the plan year shall be equal to the sum of—

(i) the present value of all benefits accrued or earned under the plan as of the beginning of the plan year, as determined by using the additional actuarial assumptions described in subparagraph (B), and

(ii) in the case of a plan which also has been in at-risk status for at least 2 of the 4 preceding plan years, a loading factor determined under subparagraph (C).

(B) ADDITIONAL ACTUARIAL ASSUMPTIONS.—The actuarial assumptions described in this subparagraph are as follows:

(i) All employees who are not otherwise assumed to retire as of the valuation date but who will be eligible to elect benefits during the plan year and the 10 succeeding plan years shall be assumed to retire at the earliest retirement date under the plan but not before the end of the plan year for which the at-risk funding target and at-risk target normal cost are being determined.

(ii) All employees shall be assumed to elect the retirement benefit available under the plan at the assumed retirement age (determined after application of clause (i)) which would result in the highest present value of benefits.

(C) LOADING FACTOR.—The loading factor applied with respect to a plan under this paragraph for any plan year is the sum of—

(i) $700, times the number of participants in the plan, plus

(ii) 4 percent of the funding target (determined without regard to this paragraph) of the plan for the plan year.

(2) TARGET NORMAL COST OF AT-RISK PLANS.—In the case of a plan which is in at-risk status for a plan year, the target normal cost of the plan for such plan year shall be equal to the sum of—

(A) the present value of all benefits which are expected to accrue or be earned under the plan during the plan year, determined using the additional actuarial assumptions described in paragraph (1)(B), plus

(B) in the case of a plan which also has been in at-risk status for at least 2 of the 4 preceding plan years, a loading factor equal to 4 percent of the target normal cost (determined without regard to this paragraph) of the plan for the plan year.

(3) MINIMUM AMOUNT.—In no event shall—

(A) the at-risk funding target be less than the funding target, as determined without regard to this subsection, or

(B) the at-risk target normal cost be less than the target normal cost, as determined without regard to this subsection.

(4) DETERMINATION OF AT-RISK STATUS.—For purposes of this subsection—

(A) IN GENERAL.—A plan is in at-risk status for a plan year if—

(i) the funding target attainment percentage for the preceding plan year (determined under this section without regard to this subsection) is less than 80 percent, and

(ii) the funding target attainment percentage for the preceding plan year (determined under this section by using the additional actuarial assumptions described in paragraph (1)(B) in computing the funding target) is less than 70 percent.

(B) TRANSITION RULE.—In the case of plan years beginning in 2008, 2009, and 2010, subparagraph (A)(i) shall be applied by substituting the following percentages for "80 percent":

(i) 65 percent in the case of 2008.

(ii) 70 percent in the case of 2009.

(iii) 75 percent in the case of 2010.

In the case of plan years beginning in 2008, the funding target attainment percentage for the preceding plan year under subparagraph (A)(ii) may be determined using such methods of estimation as the Secretary may provide.

(C) SPECIAL RULE FOR EMPLOYEES OFFERED EARLY RETIREMENT IN 2006.—

(i) IN GENERAL.—For purposes of subparagraph (A)(ii), the additional actuarial assumptions described in paragraph (1)(B) shall not be taken into account with respect to any employee if—

(I) such employee is employed by a specified automobile manufacturer,

(II) such employee is offered a substantial amount of additional cash compensation, substantially enhanced retirement benefits under the plan, or materially reduced employment duties on the condition that by a specified date (not later than December 31, 2010) the employee retires (as defined under the terms of the plan),

(III) such offer is made during 2006 and pursuant to a bona fide retirement incentive program and requires, by the terms of the offer, that such offer can be accepted not later than a specified date (not later than December 31, 2006), and

(IV) such employee does not elect to accept such offer before the specified date on which the offer expires.

(ii) SPECIFIED AUTOMOBILE MANUFACTURER.—For purposes of clause (i), the term "specified automobile manufacturer" means—

(I) any manufacturer of automobiles, and

(II) any manufacturer of automobile parts which supplies such parts directly to a manufacturer of automobiles and which, after a transaction or series of transactions ending in 1999, ceased to be a member of a controlled group which included such manufacturer of automobiles.

(5) TRANSITION BETWEEN APPLICABLE FUNDING TARGETS AND BETWEEN APPLICABLE TARGET NORMAL COSTS.—

(A) IN GENERAL.—In any case in which a plan which is in at-risk status for a plan year has been in such status for a consecutive period of fewer than 5 plan years, the applicable amount of the funding target and of the target normal cost shall be, in lieu of the amount determined without regard to this paragraph, the sum of—

(i) the amount determined under this section without regard to this subsection, plus

(ii) the transition percentage for such plan year of the excess of the amount determined under this subsection (without regard to this paragraph) over the amount determined under this section without regard to this subsection.

(B) TRANSITION PERCENTAGE.—For purposes of subparagraph (A), the transition percentage shall be determined in accordance with the following table:

If the consecutive number of years (including the plan year) the plan is in at-risk status is—	*The transition percentage is—*
1	20
2	40
3	60
4	80 .

(C) YEARS BEFORE EFFECTIVE DATE.—For purposes of this paragraph, plan years beginning before 2008 shall not be taken into account.

(6) SMALL PLAN EXCEPTION.—If, on each day during the preceding plan year, a plan had 500 or fewer participants, the plan shall not be treated as in at-risk status for the plan year. For purposes of this paragraph, all defined benefit plans (other than multiemployer plans) maintained by the same employer (or any member of such employer's controlled group) shall be treated as 1 plan, but only participants with respect to such employer or member shall be taken into account and the rules of subsection (g)(2)(C) shall apply.

(j) PAYMENT OF MINIMUM REQUIRED CONTRIBUTIONS.—

(1) IN GENERAL.—For purposes of this section, the due date for any payment of any minimum required contribution for any plan year shall be 8½ months after the close of the plan year.

(2) INTEREST.—Any payment required under paragraph (1) for a plan year that is made on a date other than the valuation date for such plan year shall be adjusted for interest accruing for the period between the valuation date and the payment date, at the effective rate of interest for the plan for such plan year.

(3) ACCELERATED QUARTERLY CONTRIBUTION SCHEDULE FOR UNDERFUNDED PLANS.—

(A) FAILURE TO TIMELY MAKE REQUIRED INSTALLMENT.—In any case in which the plan has a funding shortfall for the preceding plan year, the employer maintaining the plan shall make the required installments under this paragraph and if the employer fails to pay the full amount of a required installment for the plan year, then the amount of interest charged under paragraph (2) on the underpayment for the period of underpayment shall be determined by using a rate of interest equal to the rate otherwise used under paragraph (2) plus 5 percentage points.

(B) AMOUNT OF UNDERPAYMENT, PERIOD OF UNDERPAYMENT.—For purposes of subparagraph (A)—

(i) AMOUNT.—The amount of the underpayment shall be the excess of—

(I) the required installment, over

(II) the amount (if any) of the installment contributed to or under the plan on or before the due date for the installment.

(ii) PERIOD OF UNDERPAYMENT.—The period for which any interest is charged under this paragraph with respect to any portion of the underpayment shall run from the due date for the installment to the date on which such portion is contributed to or under the plan.

(iii) ORDER OF CREDITING CONTRIBUTIONS.—For purposes of clause (i)(II), contributions shall be credited against unpaid required installments in the order in which such installments are required to be paid.

(C) NUMBER OF REQUIRED INSTALLMENTS; DUE DATES.—For purposes of this paragraph—

(i) PAYABLE IN 4 INSTALLMENTS.—There shall be 4 required installments for each plan year.

(ii) TIME FOR PAYMENT OF INSTALLMENTS.—*The due dates for required installments are set forth in the following table:*

In the case of the following required installment:	*The due date is:*
1st	*April 15*
2nd	*July 15*
3rd	*October 15*
4th	*January 15 of the following year.*

(D) AMOUNT OF REQUIRED INSTALLMENT.—*For purposes of this paragraph—*

(i) IN GENERAL.—*The amount of any required installment shall be 25 percent of the required annual payment.*

(ii) REQUIRED ANNUAL PAYMENT.—*For purposes of clause (i), the term "required annual payment" means the lesser of—*

(I) 90 percent of the minimum required contribution (determined without regard to this subsection) to the plan for the plan year under this section, or

(II) 100 percent of the minimum required contribution (determined without regard to this subsection or to any waiver under section 302(c)) to the plan for the preceding plan year.

Subclause (II) shall not apply if the preceding plan year referred to in such clause was not a year of 12 months.

(E) FISCAL YEARS AND SHORT YEARS.—

(i) FISCAL YEARS.—*In applying this paragraph to a plan year beginning on any date other than January 1, there shall be substituted for the months specified in this paragraph, the months which correspond thereto.*

(ii) SHORT PLAN YEAR.—*This subparagraph shall be applied to plan years of less than 12 months in accordance with regulations prescribed by the Secretary.*

(4) LIQUIDITY REQUIREMENT IN CONNECTION WITH QUARTERLY CONTRIBUTIONS.—

(A) IN GENERAL.—*A plan to which this paragraph applies shall be treated as failing to pay the full amount of any required installment under paragraph (3) to the extent that the value of the liquid assets paid in such installment is less than the liquidity shortfall (whether or not such liquidity shortfall exceeds the amount of such installment required to be paid but for this paragraph).*

(B) PLANS TO WHICH PARAGRAPH APPLIES.—*This paragraph shall apply to a plan (other than a plan described in subsection (g)(2)(B)) which—*

(i) is required to pay installments under paragraph (3) for a plan year, and

(ii) has a liquidity shortfall for any quarter during such plan year.

(C) PERIOD OF UNDERPAYMENT.—*For purposes of paragraph (3)(A), any portion of an installment that is treated as not paid under subparagraph (A) shall continue to be treated as unpaid until the close of the quarter in which the due date for such installment occurs.*

(D) LIMITATION ON INCREASE.—*If the amount of any required installment is increased by reason of subparagraph (A), in no event shall such increase exceed the amount which, when added to prior installments for the plan year, is necessary to increase the funding target attainment percentage of the plan for the plan year (taking into account the expected increase in funding target due to benefits accruing or earned during the plan year) to 100 percent.*

(E) DEFINITIONS.—*For purposes of this paragraph—*

(i) LIQUIDITY SHORTFALL.—*The term "liquidity shortfall" means, with respect to any required installment, an amount equal to the excess (as of the last day of the quarter for which such installment is made) of—*

(I) the base amount with respect to such quarter, over

(II) the value (as of such last day) of the plan's liquid assets.

(ii) BASE AMOUNT.—

(I) IN GENERAL.—The term "base amount" means, with respect to any quarter, an amount equal to 3 times the sum of the adjusted disbursements from the plan for the 12 months ending on the last day of such quarter.

(II) SPECIAL RULE.—If the amount determined under subclause (I) exceeds an amount equal to 2 times the sum of the adjusted disbursements from the plan for the 36 months ending on the last day of the quarter and an enrolled actuary certifies to the satisfaction of the Secretary that such excess is the result of nonrecurring circumstances, the base amount with respect to such quarter shall be determined without regard to amounts related to those nonrecurring circumstances.

(iii) DISBURSEMENTS FROM THE PLAN.—The term "disbursements from the plan" means all disbursements from the trust, including purchases of annuities, payments of single sums and other benefits, and administrative expenses.

(iv) ADJUSTED DISBURSEMENTS.—The term "adjusted disbursements" means disbursements from the plan reduced by the product of—

(I) the plan's funding target attainment percentage for the plan year, and

(II) the sum of the purchases of annuities, payments of single sums, and such other disbursements as the Secretary shall provide in regulations.

(v) LIQUID ASSETS.—The term "liquid assets" means cash, marketable securities, and such other assets as specified by the Secretary in regulations.

(vi) QUARTER.—The term "quarter" means, with respect to any required installment, the 3-month period preceding the month in which the due date for such installment occurs.

(F) REGULATIONS.—The Secretary may prescribe such regulations as are necessary to carry out this paragraph.

(k) IMPOSITION OF LIEN WHERE FAILURE TO MAKE REQUIRED CONTRIBUTIONS.—

(1) IN GENERAL.—In the case of a plan to which this subsection applies, if—

(A) any person fails to make a contribution payment required by section 412 and this section before the due date for such payment, and

(B) the unpaid balance of such payment (including interest), when added to the aggregate unpaid balance of all preceding such payments for which payment was not made before the due date (including interest), exceeds $1,000,000,

then there shall be a lien in favor of the plan in the amount determined under paragraph (3) upon all property and rights to property, whether real or personal, belonging to such person and any other person who is a member of the same controlled group of which such person is a member.

(2) PLANS TO WHICH SUBSECTION APPLIES.—This subsection shall apply to a defined benefit plan (other than a multiemployer plan) covered under section 4021 of the Employee Retirement Income Security Act of 1974 for any plan year for which the funding target attainment percentage (as defined in subsection (d)(2)) of such plan is less than 100 percent.

(3) AMOUNT OF LIEN.—For purposes of paragraph (1), the amount of the lien shall be equal to the aggregate unpaid balance of contribution payments required under this section and section 412 for which payment has not been made before the due date.

(4) NOTICE OF FAILURE; LIEN.—

(A) NOTICE OF FAILURE.—A person committing a failure described in paragraph (1) shall notify the Pension Benefit Guaranty Corporation of such failure within 10 days of the due date for the required contribution payment.

(B) PERIOD OF LIEN.—The lien imposed by paragraph (1) shall arise on the due date for the required contribution payment and shall continue until the last day of the first plan year in which the plan ceases to be described in paragraph (1)(B). Such lien shall continue to run without regard to whether such plan continues to be described in paragraph (2) during the period referred to in the preceding sentence.

(C) CERTAIN RULES TO APPLY.—Any amount with respect to which a lien is imposed under paragraph (1) shall be treated as taxes due and owing the United States and rules similar to the rules of subsections (c), (d), and (e) of section 4068 of the Employee Retirement Income Security Act of 1974 shall apply with respect to a lien imposed by subsection (a) and the amount with respect to such lien.

(5) ENFORCEMENT.—Any lien created under paragraph (1) may be perfected and enforced only by the Pension Benefit Guaranty Corporation, or at the direction of the Pension Benefit Guaranty Corporation, by the contributing sponsor (or any member of the controlled group of the contributing sponsor).

(6) DEFINITIONS.—For purposes of this subsection—

(A) CONTRIBUTION PAYMENT.—The term "contribution payment" means, in connection with a plan, a contribution payment required to be made to the plan, including any required installment under paragraphs (3) and (4) of subsection (j).

(B) DUE DATE; REQUIRED INSTALLMENT.—The terms "due date" and "required installment" have the meanings given such terms by subsection (j), except that in the case of a payment other than a required installment, the due date shall be the date such payment is required to be made under section 430.

(C) CONTROLLED GROUP.—The term "controlled group" means any group treated as a single employer under subsections (b), (c), (m), and (o) of section 414.

(l) QUALIFIED TRANSFERS TO HEALTH BENEFIT ACCOUNTS.—In the case of a qualified transfer (as defined in section 420), any assets so transferred shall not, for purposes of this section, be treated as assets in the plan.

[CCH Explanation at ¶210. Committee Reports at ¶10,010.]

Amendments

• 2006, Pension Protection Act of 2006 (H.R. 4)

H.R. 4, §112(a):

Amended subchapter D of chapter 1 by adding at the end a new part III (Code Sec. 430). **Effective** with respect to plan years beginning after 12-31-2007.

→ Caution: *Code Sec. 431, below, as added by H.R. 4, applies generally to plan years beginning after 2007.*

[¶5125] *CODE SEC. 431. MINIMUM FUNDING STANDARDS FOR MULTIEMPLOYER PLANS.*

(a) IN GENERAL.—For purposes of section 412, the accumulated funding deficiency of a multiemployer plan for any plan year is—

(1) except as provided in paragraph (2), the amount, determined as of the end of the plan year, equal to the excess (if any) of the total charges to the funding standard account of the plan for all plan years (beginning with the first plan year for which this part applies to the plan) over the total credits to such account for such years, and

(2) if the multiemployer plan is in reorganization for any plan year, the accumulated funding deficiency of the plan determined under section 4243 of the Employee Retirement Income Security Act of 1974.

(b) FUNDING STANDARD ACCOUNT.—

(1) ACCOUNT REQUIRED.—Each multiemployer plan to which this part applies shall establish and maintain a funding standard account. Such account shall be credited and charged solely as provided in this section.

(2) CHARGES TO ACCOUNT.—For a plan year, the funding standard account shall be charged with the sum of—

(A) the normal cost of the plan for the plan year,

(B) the amounts necessary to amortize in equal annual installments (until fully amortized)—

(i) in the case of a plan which comes into existence on or after January 1, 2008, the unfunded past service liability under the plan on the first day of the first plan year to which this section applies, over a period of 15 plan years,

(ii) separately, with respect to each plan year, the net increase (if any) in unfunded past service liability under the plan arising from plan amendments adopted in such year, over a period of 15 plan years,

(iii) separately, with respect to each plan year, the net experience loss (if any) under the plan, over a period of 15 plan years, and

(iv) separately, with respect to each plan year, the net loss (if any) resulting from changes in actuarial assumptions used under the plan, over a period of 15 plan years,

(C) the amount necessary to amortize each waived funding deficiency (within the meaning of section 412(c)(3)) for each prior plan year in equal annual installments (until fully amortized) over a period of 15 plan years,

(D) the amount necessary to amortize in equal annual installments (until fully amortized) over a period of 5 plan years any amount credited to the funding standard account under section 412(b)(3)(D) (as in effect on the day before the date of the enactment of the Pension Protection Act of 2006), and

(E) the amount necessary to amortize in equal annual installments (until fully amortized) over a period of 20 years the contributions which would be required to be made under the plan but for the provisions of section 412(c)(7)(A)(i)(I) (as in effect on the day before the date of the enactment of the Pension Protection Act of 2006).

(3) CREDITS TO ACCOUNT.—For a plan year, the funding standard account shall be credited with the sum of—

(A) the amount considered contributed by the employer to or under the plan for the plan year,

(B) the amount necessary to amortize in equal annual installments (until fully amortized)—

(i) separately, with respect to each plan year, the net decrease (if any) in unfunded past service liability under the plan arising from plan amendments adopted in such year, over a period of 15 plan years,

(ii) separately, with respect to each plan year, the net experience gain (if any) under the plan, over a period of 15 plan years, and

(iii) separately, with respect to each plan year, the net gain (if any) resulting from changes in actuarial assumptions used under the plan, over a period of 15 plan years,

(C) the amount of the waived funding deficiency (within the meaning of section 412(c)(3)) for the plan year, and

(D) in the case of a plan year for which the accumulated funding deficiency is determined under the funding standard account if such plan year follows a plan year for which such deficiency was determined under the alternative minimum funding standard under section 412(g) (as in effect on the day before the date of the enactment of the Pension Protection Act of 2006), the excess (if any) of any debit balance in the funding standard account (determined without regard to this subparagraph) over any debit balance in the alternative minimum funding standard account.

(4) SPECIAL RULE FOR AMOUNTS FIRST AMORTIZED IN PLAN YEARS BEFORE 2008.—In the case of any amount amortized under section 412(b) (as in effect on the day before the date of the enactment of the Pension Protection Act of 2006) over any period beginning with a plan year beginning before 2008 in lieu of the amortization described in paragraphs (2)(B) and (3)(B), such amount shall continue to be amortized under such section as so in effect.

(5) COMBINING AND OFFSETTING AMOUNTS TO BE AMORTIZED.—Under regulations prescribed by the Secretary, amounts required to be amortized under paragraph (2) or paragraph (3), as the case may be—

(A) may be combined into one amount under such paragraph to be amortized over a period determined on the basis of the remaining amortization period for all items entering into such combined amount, and

(B) may be offset against amounts required to be amortized under the other such paragraph, with the resulting amount to be amortized over a period determined on the basis of the remaining amortization periods for all items entering into whichever of the two amounts being offset is the greater.

(6) INTEREST.—The funding standard account (and items therein) shall be charged or credited (as determined under regulations prescribed by the Secretary of the Treasury) with interest at the appropriate rate consistent with the rate or rates of interest used under the plan to determine costs.

(7) SPECIAL RULES RELATING TO CHARGES AND CREDITS TO FUNDING STANDARD ACCOUNT.—For purposes of this part—

(A) WITHDRAWAL LIABILITY.—Any amount received by a multiemployer plan in payment of all or part of an employer's withdrawal liability under part 1 of subtitle E of title IV of the Employee Retirement Income Security Act of 1974 shall be considered an amount contributed by the employer to or under the plan. The Secretary may prescribe by regulation additional charges and credits to a multiemployer plan's funding standard account to the extent necessary to prevent withdrawal liability payments from being unduly reflected as advance funding for plan liabilities.

(B) ADJUSTMENTS WHEN A MULTIEMPLOYER PLAN LEAVES REORGANIZATION.—If a multiemployer plan is not in reorganization in the plan year but was in reorganization in the immediately preceding plan year, any balance in the funding standard account at the close of such immediately preceding plan year—

(i) shall be eliminated by an offsetting credit or charge (as the case may be), but

(ii) shall be taken into account in subsequent plan years by being amortized in equal annual installments (until fully amortized) over 30 plan years.

The preceding sentence shall not apply to the extent of any accumulated funding deficiency under section 4243(a) of such Act as of the end of the last plan year that the plan was in reorganization.

(C) PLAN PAYMENTS TO SUPPLEMENTAL PROGRAM OR WITHDRAWAL LIABILITY PAYMENT FUND.—Any amount paid by a plan during a plan year to the Pension Benefit Guaranty Corporation pursuant to section 4222 of such Act or to a fund exempt under section 501(c)(22) pursuant to section 4223 of such Act shall reduce the amount of contributions considered received by the plan for the plan year.

(D) INTERIM WITHDRAWAL LIABILITY PAYMENTS.—Any amount paid by an employer pending a final determination of the employer's withdrawal liability under part 1 of subtitle E of title IV of such Act and subsequently refunded to the employer by the plan shall be charged to the funding standard account in accordance with regulations prescribed by the Secretary.

(E) ELECTION FOR DEFERRAL OF CHARGE FOR PORTION OF NET EXPERIENCE LOSS.—If an election is in effect under section 412(b)(7)(F) (as in effect on the day before the date of the enactment of the Pension Protection Act of 2006) for any plan year, the funding standard account shall be charged in the plan year to which the portion of the net experience loss deferred by such election was deferred with the amount so deferred (and paragraph (2)(B)(iii) shall not apply to the amount so charged).

(F) FINANCIAL ASSISTANCE.—Any amount of any financial assistance from the Pension Benefit Guaranty Corporation to any plan, and any repayment of such amount, shall be taken into account under this section and section 412 in such manner as is determined by the Secretary.

(G) SHORT-TERM BENEFITS.—To the extent that any plan amendment increases the unfunded past service liability under the plan by reason of an increase in benefits which are not payable as a life annuity but are payable under the terms of the plan for a period that does not exceed 14 years from the effective date of the amendment, paragraph (2)(B)(ii) shall be applied separately with respect to such increase in unfunded past service liability by substituting the number of years of the period during which such benefits are payable for "15".

(c) Additional Rules.—

(1) Determinations to be made under funding method.—For purposes of this part, normal costs, accrued liability, past service liabilities, and experience gains and losses shall be determined under the funding method used to determine costs under the plan.

(2) Valuation of assets.—

(A) In general.—For purposes of this part, the value of the plan's assets shall be determined on the basis of any reasonable actuarial method of valuation which takes into account fair market value and which is permitted under regulations prescribed by the Secretary.

(B) Election with respect to bonds.—The value of a bond or other evidence of indebtedness which is not in default as to principal or interest may, at the election of the plan administrator, be determined on an amortized basis running from initial cost at purchase to par value at maturity or earliest call date. Any election under this subparagraph shall be made at such time and in such manner as the Secretary shall by regulations provide, shall apply to all such evidences of indebtedness, and may be revoked only with the consent of the Secretary.

(3) Actuarial assumptions must be reasonable.—For purposes of this section, all costs, liabilities, rates of interest, and other factors under the plan shall be determined on the basis of actuarial assumptions and methods—

(A) each of which is reasonable (taking into account the experience of the plan and reasonable expectations), and

(B) which, in combination, offer the actuary's best estimate of anticipated experience under the plan.

(4) Treatment of certain changes as experience gain or loss.—For purposes of this section, if—

(A) a change in benefits under the Social Security Act or in other retirement benefits created under Federal or State law, or

(B) a change in the definition of the term "wages" under section 3121, or a change in the amount of such wages taken into account under regulations prescribed for purposes of section 401(a)(5),

results in an increase or decrease in accrued liability under a plan, such increase or decrease shall be treated as an experience loss or gain.

(5) Full funding.—If, as of the close of a plan year, a plan would (without regard to this paragraph) have an accumulated funding deficiency in excess of the full funding limitation—

(A) the funding standard account shall be credited with the amount of such excess, and

(B) all amounts described in subparagraphs (B), (C), and (D) of subsection (b) (2) and subparagraph (B) of subsection (b)(3) which are required to be amortized shall be considered fully amortized for purposes of such subparagraphs.

(6) Full-funding limitation.—

(A) In general.—For purposes of paragraph (5), the term "full-funding limitation" means the excess (if any) of—

(i) the accrued liability (including normal cost) under the plan (determined under the entry age normal funding method if such accrued liability cannot be directly calculated under the funding method used for the plan), over

(ii) the lesser of—

(I) the fair market value of the plan's assets, or

(II) the value of such assets determined under paragraph (2).

(B) Minimum amount.—

(i) In general.—In no event shall the full-funding limitation determined under subparagraph (A) be less than the excess (if any) of—

(I) 90 percent of the current liability of the plan (including the expected increase in current liability due to benefits accruing during the plan year), over

(II) the value of the plan's assets determined under paragraph (2).

(ii) ASSETS.—For purposes of clause (i), assets shall not be reduced by any credit balance in the funding standard account.

(C) FULL FUNDING LIMITATION.—For purposes of this paragraph, unless otherwise provided by the plan, the accrued liability under a multiemployer plan shall not include benefits which are not nonforfeitable under the plan after the termination of the plan (taking into consideration section 411(d)(3)).

(D) CURRENT LIABILITY.—For purposes of this paragraph—

(i) IN GENERAL.—The term "current liability" means all liabilities to employees and their beneficiaries under the plan.

(ii) TREATMENT OF UNPREDICTABLE CONTINGENT EVENT BENEFITS.—For purposes of clause (i), any benefit contingent on an event other than—

(I) age, service, compensation, death, or disability, or

(II) an event which is reasonably and reliably predictable (as determined by the Secretary),

shall not be taken into account until the event on which the benefit is contingent occurs.

(iii) INTEREST RATE USED.—The rate of interest used to determine current liability under this paragraph shall be the rate of interest determined under subparagraph (E).

(iv) MORTALITY TABLES.—

(I) COMMISSIONERS' STANDARD TABLE.—In the case of plan years beginning before the first plan year to which the first tables prescribed under subclause (II) apply, the mortality table used in determining current liability under this paragraph shall be the table prescribed by the Secretary which is based on the prevailing commissioners' standard table (described in section 807(d)(5)(A)) used to determine reserves for group annuity contracts issued on January 1, 1993.

(II) SECRETARIAL AUTHORITY.—The Secretary may by regulation prescribe for plan years beginning after December 31, 1999, mortality tables to be used in determining current liability under this subsection. Such tables shall be based upon the actual experience of pension plans and projected trends in such experience. In prescribing such tables, the Secretary shall take into account results of available independent studies of mortality of individuals covered by pension plans.

(v) SEPARATE MORTALITY TABLES FOR THE DISABLED.—Notwithstanding clause (iv)—

(I) IN GENERAL.—The Secretary shall establish mortality tables which may be used (in lieu of the tables under clause (iv)) to determine current liability under this subsection for individuals who are entitled to benefits under the plan on account of disability. The Secretary shall establish separate tables for individuals whose disabilities occur in plan years beginning before January 1, 1995, and for individuals whose disabilities occur in plan years beginning on or after such date.

(II) SPECIAL RULE FOR DISABILITIES OCCURRING AFTER 1994.—In the case of disabilities occurring in plan years beginning after December 31, 1994, the tables under subclause (I) shall apply only with respect to individuals described in such subclause who are disabled within the meaning of title II of the Social Security Act and the regulations thereunder.

(vi) PERIODIC REVIEW.—The Secretary shall periodically (at least every 5 years) review any tables in effect under this subparagraph and shall, to the extent such Secretary determines necessary, by regulation update the tables to reflect the actual experience of pension plans and projected trends in such experience.

(E) Required change of interest rate.—For purposes of determining a plan's current liability for purposes of this paragraph—

(i) In general.—If any rate of interest used under the plan under subsection (b)(6) to determine cost is not within the permissible range, the plan shall establish a new rate of interest within the permissible range.

(ii) Permissible range.—For purposes of this subparagraph—

(I) In general.—Except as provided in subclause (II), the term "permissible range" means a rate of interest which is not more than 5 percent above, and not more than 10 percent below, the weighted average of the rates of interest on 30-year Treasury securities during the 4-year period ending on the last day before the beginning of the plan year.

(II) Secretarial authority.—If the Secretary finds that the lowest rate of interest permissible under subclause (I) is unreasonably high, the Secretary may prescribe a lower rate of interest, except that such rate may not be less than 80 percent of the average rate determined under such subclause.

(iii) Assumptions.—Notwithstanding paragraph (3)(A), the interest rate used under the plan shall be—

(I) determined without taking into account the experience of the plan and reasonable expectations, but

(II) consistent with the assumptions which reflect the purchase rates which would be used by insurance companies to satisfy the liabilities under the plan.

(7) Annual valuation.—

(A) In general.—For purposes of this section, a determination of experience gains and losses and a valuation of the plan's liability shall be made not less frequently than once every year, except that such determination shall be made more frequently to the extent required in particular cases under regulations prescribed by the Secretary.

(B) Valuation date.—

(i) Current year.—Except as provided in clause (ii), the valuation referred to in subparagraph (A) shall be made as of a date within the plan year to which the valuation refers or within one month prior to the beginning of such year.

(ii) Use of prior year valuation.—The valuation referred to in subparagraph (A) may be made as of a date within the plan year prior to the year to which the valuation refers if, as of such date, the value of the assets of the plan are not less than 100 percent of the plan's current liability (as defined in paragraph (6)(D) without regard to clause (iv) thereof).

(iii) Adjustments.—Information under clause (ii) shall, in accordance with regulations, be actuarially adjusted to reflect significant differences in participants.

(iv) Limitation.—A change in funding method to use a prior year valuation, as provided in clause (ii), may not be made unless as of the valuation date within the prior plan year, the value of the assets of the plan are not less than 125 percent of the plan's current liability (as defined in paragraph (6)(D) without regard to clause (iv) thereof).

(8) Time when certain contributions deemed made.—For purposes of this section, any contributions for a plan year made by an employer after the last day of such plan year, but not later than two and one-half months after such day, shall be deemed to have been made on such last day. For purposes of this subparagraph, such two and one-half month period may be extended for not more than six months under regulations prescribed by the Secretary.

(d) Extension of Amortization Periods for Multiemployer Plans.—

(1) Automatic extension upon application by certain plans.—

(A) In general.—If the plan sponsor of a multiemployer plan—

(i) submits to the Secretary an application for an extension of the period of years required to amortize any unfunded liability described in any clause of subsection (b)(2)(B) or described in subsection (b)(4), and

(ii) includes with the application a certification by the plan's actuary described in subparagraph (B),

the Secretary shall extend the amortization period for the period of time (not in excess of 5 years) specified in the application. Such extension shall be in addition to any extension under paragraph (2).

(B) CRITERIA.—A certification with respect to a multiemployer plan is described in this subparagraph if the plan's actuary certifies that, based on reasonable assumptions—

(i) absent the extension under subparagraph (A), the plan would have an accumulated funding deficiency in the current plan year or any of the 9 succeeding plan years,

(ii) the plan sponsor has adopted a plan to improve the plan's funding status,

(iii) the plan is projected to have sufficient assets to timely pay expected benefits and anticipated expenditures over the amortization period as extended, and

(iv) the notice required under paragraph (3)(A) has been provided.

(C) TERMINATION.—The preceding provisions of this paragraph shall not apply with respect to any application submitted after December 31, 2014.

(2) ALTERNATIVE EXTENSION.—

(A) IN GENERAL.—If the plan sponsor of a multiemployer plan submits to the Secretary an application for an extension of the period of years required to amortize any unfunded liability described in any clause of subsection (b)(2)(B) or described in subsection (b)(4), the Secretary may extend the amortization period for a period of time (not in excess of 10 years reduced by the number of years of any extension under paragraph (1) with respect to such unfunded liability) if the Secretary makes the determination described in subparagraph (B). Such extension shall be in addition to any extension under paragraph (1).

(B) DETERMINATION.—The Secretary may grant an extension under subparagraph (A) if the Secretary determines that—

(i) such extension would carry out the purposes of this Act and would provide adequate protection for participants under the plan and their beneficiaries, and

(ii) the failure to permit such extension would—

(I) result in a substantial risk to the voluntary continuation of the plan, or a substantial curtailment of pension benefit levels or employee compensation, and

(II) be adverse to the interests of plan participants in the aggregate.

(C) ACTION BY SECRETARY.—The Secretary shall act upon any application for an extension under this paragraph within 180 days of the submission of such application. If the Secretary rejects the application for an extension under this paragraph, the Secretary shall provide notice to the plan detailing the specific reasons for the rejection, including references to the criteria set forth above.

(3) ADVANCE NOTICE.—

(A) IN GENERAL.—The Secretary shall, before granting an extension under this subsection, require each applicant to provide evidence satisfactory to such Secretary that the applicant has provided notice of the filing of the application for such extension to each affected party (as defined in section 4001(a)(21) of the Employee Retirement Income Security Act of 1974) with respect to the affected plan. Such notice shall include a description of the extent to which the plan is funded for benefits which are guaranteed under title IV of such Act and for benefit liabilities.

(B) CONSIDERATION OF RELEVANT INFORMATION.—The Secretary shall consider any relevant information provided by a person to whom notice was given under paragraph (1).

[CCH Explanation at ¶305. Committee Reports at ¶10,080.]

Amendments

• 2006, Pension Protection Act of 2006 (H.R. 4)

H.R. 4, §211(a):

Amended subpart A of part III of subchapter D of chapter 1, as added by this Act, by inserting after Code Sec. 430 a new Code Sec. 431. **Effective** generally for plan years beginning after 2007. For a special rule, see Act Sec. 211(b)(2), below.

H.R. 4, §211(b)(2), provides:

(2) SPECIAL RULE FOR CERTAIN AMORTIZATION EXTENSIONS.—If the Secretary of the Treasury grants an extension under section 304 of the Employee Retirement Income Security Act of 1974 and section 412(e) of the Internal Revenue Code of 1986 with respect to any application filed with the Secretary of the Treasury on or before June 30, 2005, the extension (and any modification thereof) shall be applied and administered under the rules of such sections as in effect before the enactment of this Act, including the use of the rate of interest determined under section 6621(b) of such Code.

»»→ Caution: Code Sec. 432, below, as added by H.R. 4, applies generally to plan years beginning after 2007. For sunset provision, see H.R. 4, §221(c), in the amendment notes.

[¶5130] *CODE SEC. 432. ADDITIONAL FUNDING RULES FOR MULTIEMPLOYER PLANS IN ENDANGERED STATUS OR CRITICAL STATUS.*

(a) GENERAL RULE.—For purposes of this part, in the case of a multiemployer plan in effect on July 16, 2006 —

(1) if the plan is in endangered status—

(A) the plan sponsor shall adopt and implement a funding improvement plan in accordance with the requirements of subsection (c), and

(B) the requirements of subsection (d) shall apply during the funding plan adoption period and the funding improvement period, and

(2) if the plan is in critical status—

(A) the plan sponsor shall adopt and implement a rehabilitation plan in accordance with the requirements of subsection (e), and

(B) the requirements of subsection (f) shall apply during the rehabilitation plan adoption period and the rehabilitation period.

(b) DETERMINATION OF ENDANGERED AND CRITICAL STATUS.—For purposes of this section—

(1) ENDANGERED STATUS.—A multiemployer plan is in endangered status for a plan year if, as determined by the plan actuary under paragraph (3), the plan is not in critical status for the plan year and, as of the beginning of the plan year, either—

(A) the plan's funded percentage for such plan year is less than 80 percent, or

(B) the plan has an accumulated funding deficiency for such plan year, or is projected to have such an accumulated funding deficiency for any of the 6 succeeding plan years, taking into account any extension of amortization periods under section 431(d).

For purposes of this section, a plan shall be treated as in seriously endangered status for a plan year if the plan is described in both subparagraphs (A) and (B).

(2) CRITICAL STATUS.—A multiemployer plan is in critical status for a plan year if, as determined by the plan actuary under paragraph (3), the plan is described in 1 or more of the following subparagraphs as of the beginning of the plan year:

(A) A plan is described in this subparagraph if—

(i) the funded percentage of the plan is less than 65 percent, and

(ii) the sum of—

(I) the fair market value of plan assets, plus

(II) the present value of the reasonably anticipated employer contributions for the current plan year and each of the 6 succeeding plan years, assuming that the terms of all collective bargaining agreements pursuant to which the plan is maintained for the current plan year continue in effect for succeeding plan years,

is less than the present value of all nonforfeitable benefits projected to be payable under the plan during the current plan year and each of the 6 succeeding plan years (plus administrative expenses for such plan years).

(B) A plan is described in this subparagraph if—

(i) the plan has an accumulated funding deficiency for the current plan year, not taking into account any extension of amortization periods under section 431(d), or

(ii) the plan is projected to have an accumulated funding deficiency for any of the 3 succeeding plan years (4 succeeding plan years if the funded percentage of the plan is 65 percent or less), not taking into account any extension of amortization periods under section 431(d).

(C) A plan is described in this subparagraph if—

(i)(I) the plan's normal cost for the current plan year, plus interest (determined at the rate used for determining costs under the plan) for the current plan year on the amount of unfunded benefit liabilities under the plan as of the last date of the preceding plan year, exceeds

(II) the present value of the reasonably anticipated employer and employee contributions for the current plan year,

(ii) the present value, as of the beginning of the current plan year, of nonforfeitable benefits of inactive participants is greater than the present value of nonforfeitable benefits of active participants, and

(iii) the plan has an accumulated funding deficiency for the current plan year, or is projected to have such a deficiency for any of the 4 succeeding plan years, not taking into account any extension of amortization periods under section 431(d).

(D) A plan is described in this subparagraph if the sum of—

(i) the fair market value of plan assets, plus

(ii) the present value of the reasonably anticipated employer contributions for the current plan year and each of the 4 succeeding plan years, assuming that the terms of all collective bargaining agreements pursuant to which the plan is maintained for the current plan year continue in effect for succeeding plan years,

is less than the present value of all benefits projected to be payable under the plan during the current plan year and each of the 4 succeeding plan years (plus administrative expenses for such plan years).

(3) ANNUAL CERTIFICATION BY PLAN ACTUARY.—

(A) IN GENERAL.—Not later than the 90th day of each plan year of a multiemployer plan, the plan actuary shall certify to the Secretary and to the plan sponsor—

(i) whether or not the plan is in endangered status for such plan year and whether or not the plan is or will be in critical status for such plan year, and

(ii) in the case of a plan which is in a funding improvement or rehabilitation period, whether or not the plan is making the scheduled progress in meeting the requirements of its funding improvement or rehabilitation plan.

(B) ACTUARIAL PROJECTIONS OF ASSETS AND LIABILITIES.—

(i) IN GENERAL.—In making the determinations and projections under this subsection, the plan actuary shall make projections required for the current and succeeding plan years of the current value of the assets of the plan and the present value of all liabilities to participants and beneficiaries under the plan for the current plan year as of the beginning of such year. The actuary's projections shall be based on reasonable actuarial estimates, assumptions, and methods that, except as provided in clause (iii), offer the actuary's best estimate of anticipated experience under the plan. The projected present value of liabilities as of the beginning of such year shall be determined based on the most recent of either—

(I) the actuarial statement required under section 103(d) of the Employee Retirement Income Security Act of 1974 with respect to the most recently filed annual report, or

(II) the actuarial valuation for the preceding plan year.

(ii) DETERMINATIONS OF FUTURE CONTRIBUTIONS.—Any actuarial projection of plan assets shall assume—

(I) reasonably anticipated employer contributions for the current and succeeding plan years, assuming that the terms of the one or more collective bargaining agreements pursuant to which the plan is maintained for the current plan year continue in effect for succeeding plan years, or

(II) that employer contributions for the most recent plan year will continue indefinitely, but only if the plan actuary determines there have been no significant demographic changes that would make such assumption unreasonable.

(iii) PROJECTED INDUSTRY ACTIVITY.—Any projection of activity in the industry or industries covered by the plan, including future covered employment and contribution levels, shall be based on information provided by the plan sponsor, which shall act reasonably and in good faith.

(C) PENALTY FOR FAILURE TO SECURE TIMELY ACTUARIAL CERTIFICATION.—Any failure of the plan's actuary to certify the plan's status under this subsection by the date specified in subparagraph (A) shall be treated for purposes of section 502(c)(2) of the Employee Retirement Income Security Act of 1974 as a failure or refusal by the plan administrator to file the annual report required to be filed with the Secretary under section 101(b)(4) of such Act.

(D) NOTICE.—

(i) IN GENERAL.—In any case in which it is certified under subparagraph (A) that a multiemployer plan is or will be in endangered or critical status for a plan year, the plan sponsor shall, not later than 30 days after the date of the certification, provide notification of the endangered or critical status to the participants and beneficiaries, the bargaining parties, the Pension Benefit Guaranty Corporation, and the Secretary of Labor.

(ii) PLANS IN CRITICAL STATUS.—If it is certified under subparagraph (A) that a multiemployer plan is or will be in critical status, the plan sponsor shall include in the notice under clause (i) an explanation of the possibility that—

(I) adjustable benefits (as defined in subsection (e)(8)) may be reduced, and

(II) such reductions may apply to participants and beneficiaries whose benefit commencement date is on or after the date such notice is provided for the first plan year in which the plan is in critical status.

(iii) MODEL NOTICE.—The Secretary of Labor shall prescribe a model notice that a multiemployer plan may use to satisfy the requirements under clause (ii).

(c) FUNDING IMPROVEMENT PLAN MUST BE ADOPTED FOR MULTIEMPLOYER PLANS IN ENDANGERED STATUS.—

(1) IN GENERAL.—In any case in which a multiemployer plan is in endangered status for a plan year, the plan sponsor, in accordance with this subsection—

(A) shall adopt a funding improvement plan not later than 240 days following the required date for the actuarial certification of endangered status under subsection (b)(3)(A), and

(B) within 30 days after the adoption of the funding improvement plan—

(i) shall provide to the bargaining parties 1 or more schedules showing revised benefit structures, revised contribution structures, or both, which, if adopted, may reasonably be expected to enable the multiemployer plan to meet the applicable benchmarks in accordance with the funding improvement plan, including—

(I) one proposal for reductions in the amount of future benefit accruals necessary to achieve the applicable benchmarks, assuming no amendments increasing contributions under the plan (other than amendments increasing contributions necessary to achieve the applicable benchmarks after amendments have reduced future benefit accruals to the maximum extent permitted by law), and

(II) one proposal for increases in contributions under the plan necessary to achieve the applicable benchmarks, assuming no amendments reducing future benefit accruals under the plan, and

(ii) may, if the plan sponsor deems appropriate, prepare and provide the bargaining parties with additional information relating to contribution rates or benefit reductions, alternative

schedules, or other information relevant to achieving the applicable benchmarks in accordance with the funding improvement plan.

For purposes of this section, the term "applicable benchmarks" means the requirements applicable to the multiemployer plan under paragraph (3) (as modified by paragraph (5)).

(2) EXCEPTION FOR YEARS AFTER PROCESS BEGINS.—Paragraph (1) shall not apply to a plan year if such year is in a funding plan adoption period or funding improvement period by reason of the plan being in endangered status for a preceding plan year. For purposes of this section, such preceding plan year shall be the initial determination year with respect to the funding improvement plan to which it relates.

(3) FUNDING IMPROVEMENT PLAN.—For purposes of this section—

(A) IN GENERAL.—A funding improvement plan is a plan which consists of the actions, including options or a range of options to be proposed to the bargaining parties, formulated to provide, based on reasonably anticipated experience and reasonable actuarial assumptions, for the attainment by the plan during the funding improvement period of the following requirements:

(i) INCREASE IN PLAN'S FUNDING PERCENTAGE.—The plan's funded percentage as of the close of the funding improvement period equals or exceeds a percentage equal to the sum of—

(I) such percentage as of the beginning of such period, plus

(II) 33 percent of the difference between 100 percent and the percentage under subclause (I).

(ii) AVOIDANCE OF ACCUMULATED FUNDING DEFICIENCIES.—No accumulated funding deficiency for any plan year during the funding improvement period (taking into account any extension of amortization periods under section 304(d)).

(B) SERIOUSLY ENDANGERED PLANS.—In the case of a plan in seriously endangered status, except as provided in paragraph (5), subparagraph (A)(i)(II) shall be applied by substituting "20 percent" for "33 percent".

(4) FUNDING IMPROVEMENT PERIOD.—For purposes of this section—

(A) IN GENERAL.—The funding improvement period for any funding improvement plan adopted pursuant to this subsection is the 10-year period beginning on the first day of the first plan year of the multiemployer plan beginning after the earlier of—

(i) the second anniversary of the date of the adoption of the funding improvement plan, or

(ii) the expiration of the collective bargaining agreements in effect on the due date for the actuarial certification of endangered status for the initial determination year under subsection (b)(3)(A) and covering, as of such due date, at least 75 percent of the active participants in such multiemployer plan.

(B) SERIOUSLY ENDANGERED PLANS.—In the case of a plan in seriously endangered status, except as provided in paragraph (5), subparagraph (A) shall be applied by substituting "15-year period" for "10-year period".

(C) COORDINATION WITH CHANGES IN STATUS.—

(i) PLANS NO LONGER IN ENDANGERED STATUS.—If the plan's actuary certifies under subsection (b)(3)(A) for a plan year in any funding plan adoption period or funding improvement period that the plan is no longer in endangered status and is not in critical status, the funding plan adoption period or funding improvement period, whichever is applicable, shall end as of the close of the preceding plan year.

(ii) PLANS IN CRITICAL STATUS.—If the plan's actuary certifies under subsection (b)(3)(A) for a plan year in any funding plan adoption period or funding improvement period that the plan is in critical status, the funding plan adoption period or funding improvement period, whichever is applicable, shall end as of the close of the plan year preceding the first plan year in the rehabilitation period with respect to such status.

(D) PLANS IN ENDANGERED STATUS AT END OF PERIOD.—If the plan's actuary certifies under subsection (b)(3)(A) for the first plan year following the close of the period described in subparagraph

(A) that the plan is in endangered status, the provisions of this subsection and subsection (d) shall be applied as if such first plan year were an initial determination year, except that the plan may not be amended in a manner inconsistent with the funding improvement plan in effect for the preceding plan year until a new funding improvement plan is adopted.

(5) SPECIAL RULES FOR SERIOUSLY ENDANGERED PLANS MORE THAN 70 PERCENT FUNDED.—

(A) IN GENERAL.—If the funded percentage of a plan in seriously endangered status was more than 70 percent as of the beginning of the initial determination year—

(i) paragraphs (3)(B) and (4)(B) shall apply only if the plan's actuary certifies, within 30 days after the certification under subsection (b)(3)(A) for the initial determination year, that, based on the terms of the plan and the collective bargaining agreements in effect at the time of such certification, the plan is not projected to meet the requirements of paragraph (3)(A) (without regard to paragraphs (3)(B) and (4)(B)), and

(ii) if there is a certification under clause (i), the plan may, in formulating its funding improvement plan, only take into account the rules of paragraph (3)(B) and (4)(B) for plan years in the funding improvement period beginning on or before the date on which the last of the collective bargaining agreements described in paragraph (4)(A)(ii) expires.

(B) SPECIAL RULE AFTER EXPIRATION OF AGREEMENTS.—Notwithstanding subparagraph (A)(ii), if, for any plan year ending after the date described in subparagraph (A)(ii), the plan actuary certifies (at the time of the annual certification under subsection (b)(3)(A) for such plan year) that, based on the terms of the plan and collective bargaining agreements in effect at the time of that annual certification, the plan is not projected to be able to meet the requirements of paragraph (3)(A) (without regard to paragraphs (3)(B) and (4)(B)), paragraphs (3)(B) and (4)(B) shall continue to apply for such year.

(6) UPDATES TO FUNDING IMPROVEMENT PLAN AND SCHEDULES.—

(A) FUNDING IMPROVEMENT PLAN.—The plan sponsor shall annually update the funding improvement plan and shall file the update with the plan's annual report under section 104 of the Employee Retirement Income Security Act of 1974.

(B) SCHEDULES.—The plan sponsor shall annually update any schedule of contribution rates provided under this subsection to reflect the experience of the plan.

(C) DURATION OF SCHEDULE.—A schedule of contribution rates provided by the plan sponsor and relied upon by bargaining parties in negotiating a collective bargaining agreement shall remain in effect for the duration of that collective bargaining agreement.

(7) IMPOSITION OF DEFAULT SCHEDULE WHERE FAILURE TO ADOPT FUNDING IMPROVEMENT PLAN.—

(A) IN GENERAL.—If—

(i) a collective bargaining agreement providing for contributions under a multiemployer plan that was in effect at the time the plan entered endangered status expires, and

(ii) after receiving one or more schedules from the plan sponsor under paragraph (1)(B), the bargaining parties with respect to such agreement fail to agree on changes to contribution or benefit schedules necessary to meet the applicable benchmarks in accordance with the funding improvement plan,

the plan sponsor shall implement the schedule described in paragraph (1)(B)(i)(I) beginning on the date specified in subparagraph (B).

(B) DATE OF IMPLEMENTATION.—The date specified in this subparagraph is the earlier of the date—

(i) on which the Secretary certifies that the parties are at an impasse, or

(ii) which is 180 days after the date on which the collective bargaining agreement described in subparagraph (A) expires.

(8) FUNDING PLAN ADOPTION PERIOD.—For purposes of this section, the term "funding plan adoption period" means the period beginning on the date of the certification under subsection (b)(3)(A) for the initial determination year and ending on the day before the first day of the funding improvement period.

(d) RULES FOR OPERATION OF PLAN DURING ADOPTION AND IMPROVEMENT PERIODS.—

(1) SPECIAL RULES FOR PLAN ADOPTION PERIOD.—During the funding plan adoption period—

(A) the plan sponsor may not accept a collective bargaining agreement or participation agreement with respect to the multiemployer plan that provides for—

(i) a reduction in the level of contributions for any participants,

(ii) a suspension of contributions with respect to any period of service, or

(iii) any new direct or indirect exclusion of younger or newly hired employees from plan participation,

(B) no amendment of the plan which increases the liabilities of the plan by reason of any increase in benefits, any change in the accrual of benefits, or any change in the rate at which benefits become nonforfeitable under the plan may be adopted unless the amendment is required as a condition of qualification under part I of subchapter D of chapter 1 of the Internal Revenue Code of 1986 or to comply with other applicable law, and

(C) in the case of a plan in seriously endangered status, the plan sponsor shall take all reasonable actions which are consistent with the terms of the plan and applicable law and which are expected, based on reasonable assumptions, to achieve—

(i) an increase in the plan's funded percentage, and

(ii) postponement of an accumulated funding deficiency for at least 1 additional plan year.

Actions under subparagraph (C) include applications for extensions of amortization periods under section 304(d), use of the shortfall funding method in making funding standard account computations, amendments to the plan's benefit structure, reductions in future benefit accruals, and other reasonable actions consistent with the terms of the plan and applicable law.

(2) COMPLIANCE WITH FUNDING IMPROVEMENT PLAN.—

(A) IN GENERAL.—A plan may not be amended after the date of the adoption of a funding improvement plan so as to be inconsistent with the funding improvement plan.

(B) NO REDUCTION IN CONTRIBUTIONS.—A plan sponsor may not during any funding improvement period accept a collective bargaining agreement or participation agreement with respect to the multiemployer plan that provides for—

(i) a reduction in the level of contributions for any participants,

(ii) a suspension of contributions with respect to any period of service, or

(iii) "any new direct or indirect exclusion of younger or newly hired employees from plan participation.

(C) SPECIAL RULES FOR BENEFIT INCREASES.—A plan may not be amended after the date of the adoption of a funding improvement plan so as to increase benefits, including future benefit accruals, unless the plan actuary certifies that the benefit increase is consistent with the funding improvement plan and is paid for out of contributions not required by the funding improvement plan to meet the applicable benchmark in accordance with the schedule contemplated in the funding improvement plan.

(e) REHABILITATION PLAN MUST BE ADOPTED FOR MULTIEMPLOYER PLANS IN CRITICAL STATUS.—

(1) IN GENERAL.—In any case in which a multiemployer plan is in critical status for a plan year, the plan sponsor, in accordance with this subsection—

(A) shall adopt a rehabilitation plan not later than 240 days following the required date for the actuarial certification of critical status under subsection (b)(3)(A), and

(B) within 30 days after the adoption of the rehabilitation plan—

(i) shall provide to the bargaining parties 1 or more schedules showing revised benefit structures, revised contribution structures, or both, which, if adopted, may reasonably be expected to enable the multiemployer plan to emerge from critical status in accordance with the rehabilitation plan, and

(ii) may, if the plan sponsor deems appropriate, prepare and provide the bargaining parties with additional information relating to contribution rates or benefit reductions, alternative schedules, or other information relevant to emerging from critical status in accordance with the rehabilitation plan.

The schedule or schedules described in subparagraph (B)(i) shall reflect reductions in future benefit accruals and adjustable benefits, and increases in contributions, that the plan sponsor determines are reasonably necessary to emerge from critical status. One schedule shall be designated as the default schedule and such schedule shall assume that there are no increases in contributions under the plan other than the increases necessary to emerge from critical status after future benefit accruals and other benefits (other than benefits the reduction or elimination of which are not permitted under section 411(d)(6)) have been reduced to the maximum extent permitted by law.

(2) EXCEPTION FOR YEARS AFTER PROCESS BEGINS.—Paragraph (1) shall not apply to a plan year if such year is in a rehabilitation plan adoption period or rehabilitation period by reason of the plan being in critical status for a preceding plan year. For purposes of this section, such preceding plan year shall be the initial critical year with respect to the rehabilitation plan to which it relates.

(3) REHABILITATION PLAN.—For purposes of this section—

(A) IN GENERAL.—A rehabilitation plan is a plan which consists of—

(i) actions, including options or a range of options to be proposed to the bargaining parties, formulated, based on reasonably anticipated experience and reasonable actuarial assumptions, to enable the plan to cease to be in critical status by the end of the rehabilitation period and may include reductions in plan expenditures (including plan mergers and consolidations), reductions in future benefit accruals or increases in contributions, if agreed to by the bargaining parties, or any combination of such actions, or

(ii) if the plan sponsor determines that, based on reasonable actuarial assumptions and upon exhaustion of all reasonable measures, the plan can not reasonably be expected to emerge from critical status by the end of the rehabilitation period, reasonable measures to emerge from critical status at a later time or to forestall possible insolvency (within the meaning of section 4245 of the Employee Retirement Income Security Act of 1974).

A rehabilitation plan must provide annual standards for meeting the requirements of such rehabilitation plan. Such plan shall also include the schedules required to be provided under paragraph (1)(B)(i) and if clause (ii) applies, shall set forth the alternatives considered, explain why the plan is not reasonably expected to emerge from critical status by the end of the rehabilitation period, and specify when, if ever, the plan is expected to emerge from critical status in accordance with the rehabilitation plan.

(B) UPDATES TO REHABILITATION PLAN AND SCHEDULES.—

(i) REHABILITATION PLAN.—The plan sponsor shall annually update the rehabilitation plan and shall file the update with the plan's annual report under section 104 of the Employee Retirement Income Security Act of 1974.

(ii) SCHEDULES.—The plan sponsor shall annually update any schedule of contribution rates provided under this subsection to reflect the experience of the plan.

(iii) DURATION OF SCHEDULE.—A schedule of contribution rates provided by the plan sponsor and relied upon by bargaining parties in negotiating a collective bargaining agreement shall remain in effect for the duration of that collective bargaining agreement.

(C) IMPOSITION OF DEFAULT SCHEDULE WHERE FAILURE TO ADOPT REHABILITATION PLAN.—

(i) IN GENERAL.—If—

(I) a collective bargaining agreement providing for contributions under a multiemployer plan that was in effect at the time the plan entered critical status expires, and

(II) after receiving one or more schedules from the plan sponsor under paragraph (1)(B), the bargaining parties with respect to such agreement fail to adopt a contribution or benefit schedules with terms consistent with the rehabilitation plan and the schedule from the plan sponsor under paragraph (1)(B)(i),

the plan sponsor shall implement the default schedule described in the last sentence of paragraph (1) beginning on the date specified in clause (ii).

(ii) DATE OF IMPLEMENTATION.—The date specified in this clause is the earlier of the date—

(I) on which the Secretary of Labor certifies that the parties are at an impasse, or

(II) which is 180 days after the date on which the collective bargaining agreement described in clause (i) expires.

(4) REHABILITATION PERIOD.—For purposes of this section—

(A) IN GENERAL.—The rehabilitation period for a plan in critical status is the 10-year period beginning on the first day of the first plan year of the multiemployer plan following the earlier of—

(i) the second anniversary of the date of the adoption of the rehabilitation plan, or

(ii) the expiration of the collective bargaining agreements in effect on the date of the due date for the actuarial certification of critical status for the initial critical year under subsection (a)(1) and covering, as of such date at least 75 percent of the active participants in such multiemployer plan.

If a plan emerges from critical status as provided under subparagraph (B) before the end of such 10-year period, the rehabilitation period shall end with the plan year preceding the plan year for which the determination under subparagraph (B) is made.

(B) EMERGENCE.—A plan in critical status shall remain in such status until a plan year for which the plan actuary certifies, in accordance with subsection (b)(3)(A), that the plan is not projected to have an accumulated funding deficiency for the plan year or any of the 9 succeeding plan years, without regard to the use of the shortfall method and taking into account any extension of amortization periods under section 431(d).

(5) REHABILITATION PLAN ADOPTION PERIOD.—For purposes of this section, the term "rehabilitation plan adoption period" means the period beginning on the date of the certification under subsection (b)(3)(A) for the initial critical year and ending on the day before the first day of the rehabilitation period.

(6) LIMITATION ON REDUCTION IN RATES OF FUTURE ACCRUALS.—Any reduction in the rate of future accruals under the default schedule described in paragraph (1)(B)(i) shall not reduce the rate of future accruals below—

(A) a monthly benefit (payable as a single life annuity commencing at the participant's normal retirement age) equal to 1 percent of the contributions required to be made with respect to a participant, or the equivalent standard accrual rate for a participant or group of participants under the collective bargaining agreements in effect as of the first day of the initial critical year, or

(B) if lower, the accrual rate under the plan on such first day.

The equivalent standard accrual rate shall be determined by the plan sponsor based on the standard or average contribution base units which the plan sponsor determines to be representative for active participants and such other factors as the plan sponsor determines to be relevant. Nothing in this paragraph shall be construed as limiting the ability of the plan sponsor to prepare and provide the bargaining parties with alternative schedules to the default schedule that established lower or higher accrual and contribution rates than the rates otherwise described in this paragraph.

(7) AUTOMATIC EMPLOYER SURCHARGE.—

(A) IMPOSITION OF SURCHARGE.—Each employer otherwise obligated to make a contribution for the initial critical year shall be obligated to pay to the plan for such year a surcharge equal to 5 percent of the contribution otherwise required under the applicable collective bargaining agreement (or other agreement pursuant to which the employer contributes). For each succeeding plan year in which the plan is in critical status for a consecutive period of years beginning with the initial critical year, the surcharge shall be 10 percent of the contribution otherwise so required.

(B) ENFORCEMENT OF SURCHARGE.—The surcharges under subparagraph (A) shall be due and payable on the same schedule as the contributions on which the surcharges are based. Any failure to make a surcharge payment shall be treated as a delinquent contribution under section 515 of the Employee Retirement Income Security Act of 1974 and shall be enforceable as such.

(C) SURCHARGE TO TERMINATE UPON COLLECTIVE BARGAINING AGREEMENT RENEGOTIATION.—*The surcharge under this paragraph shall cease to be effective with respect to employees covered by a collective bargaining agreement (or other agreement pursuant to which the employer contributes), beginning on the effective date of a collective bargaining agreement (or other such agreement) that includes terms consistent with a schedule presented by the plan sponsor under paragraph (1)(B)(i), as modified under subparagraph (B) of paragraph (3).*

(D) SURCHARGE NOT TO APPLY UNTIL EMPLOYER RECEIVES NOTICE.—*The surcharge under this paragraph shall not apply to an employer until 30 days after the employer has been notified by the plan sponsor that the plan is in critical status and that the surcharge is in effect.*

(E) SURCHARGE NOT TO GENERATE INCREASED BENEFIT ACCRUALS.—*Notwithstanding any provision of a plan to the contrary, the amount of any surcharge under this paragraph shall not be the basis for any benefit accrual under the plan.*

(8) BENEFIT ADJUSTMENTS.—

(A) ADJUSTABLE BENEFITS.—

(i) IN GENERAL.—*Notwithstanding section 204(g), the plan sponsor shall, subject to the notice requirement under subparagraph (C), make any reductions to adjustable benefits which the plan sponsor deems appropriate, based upon the outcome of collective bargaining over the schedule or schedules provided under paragraph (1)(B)(i).*

(ii) EXCEPTION FOR RETIREES.—*Except in the case of adjustable benefits described in clause (iv)(III), the plan sponsor of a plan in critical status shall not reduce adjustable benefits of any participant or beneficiary whose benefit commencement date is before the date on which the plan provides notice to the participant or beneficiary under subsection (b)(3)(D) for the initial critical year.*

(iii) PLAN SPONSOR FLEXIBILITY.—*The plan sponsor shall include in the schedules provided to the bargaining parties an allowance for funding the benefits of participants with respect to whom contributions are not currently required to be made, and shall reduce their benefits to the extent permitted under this title and considered appropriate by the plan sponsor based on the plan's then current overall funding status.*

(iv) ADJUSTABLE BENEFIT DEFINED.—*For purposes of this paragraph, the term "adjustable benefit" means—*

(I) benefits, rights, and features under the plan, including post-retirement death benefits, 60-month guarantees, disability benefits not yet in pay status, and similar benefits,

(II) any early retirement benefit or retirement-type subsidy (within the meaning of section 411(d)(6)(B)(i)) and any benefit payment option (other than the qualified joint-and survivor annuity), and

(III) benefit increases that would not be eligible for a guarantee under section 4022A of the Employee Retirement Income Security Act of 1974 on the first day of initial critical year because the increases were adopted (or, if later, took effect) less than 60 months before such first day.

(B) NORMAL RETIREMENT BENEFITS PROTECTED.—*Except as provided in subparagraph (A)(iv)(III), nothing in this paragraph shall be construed to permit a plan to reduce the level of a participant's accrued benefit payable at normal retirement age.*

(C) NOTICE REQUIREMENTS.—

(i) IN GENERAL.—*No reduction may be made to adjustable benefits under subparagraph (A) unless notice of such reduction has been given at least 30 days before the general effective date of such reduction for all participants and beneficiaries to—*

(I) plan participants and beneficiaries,

(II) each employer who has an obligation to contribute (within the meaning of section 4212(a)) under the plan, and

(III) each employee organization which, for purposes of collective bargaining, represents plan participants employed by such an employer.

(ii) Content of notice.—The notice under clause (i) shall contain—

(I) sufficient information to enable participants and beneficiaries to understand the effect of any reduction on their benefits, including an estimate (on an annual or monthly basis) of any affected adjustable benefit that a participant or beneficiary would otherwise have been eligible for as of the general effective date described in clause (i), and

(II) information as to the rights and remedies of plan participants and beneficiaries as well as how to contact the Department of Labor for further information and assistance where appropriate.

(iii) Form and manner.—Any notice under clause (i)—

(I) shall be provided in a form and manner prescribed in regulations of the Secretary of Labor,

(II) shall be written in a manner so as to be understood by the average plan participant, and

(III) may be provided in written, electronic, or other appropriate form to the extent such form is reasonably accessible to persons to whom the notice is required to be provided.

The Secretary of Labor shall in the regulations prescribed under subclause (I) establish a model notice that a plan sponsor may use to meet the requirements of this subparagraph.

(9) Adjustments disregarded in withdrawal liability determination.—

(A) Benefit reductions.—Any benefit reductions under this subsection shall be disregarded in determining a plan's unfunded vested benefits for purposes of determining an employer's withdrawal liability under section 4201 of the Employee Retirement Income Security Act of 1974.

(B) Surcharges.—Any surcharges under paragraph (7) shall be disregarded in determining an employer's withdrawal liability under section 4211 of such Act, except for purposes of determining the unfunded vested benefits attributable to an employer under section 4211(c)(4) of such Act or a comparable method approved under section 4211(c)(5) of such Act.

(C) Simplified calculations.—The Pension Benefit Guaranty Corporation shall prescribe simplified methods for the application of this paragraph in determining withdrawal liability.

(f) Rules for Operation of Plan During Adoption and Rehabilitation Period.—

(1) Compliance with rehabilitation plan.—

(A) In general.—A plan may not be amended after the date of the adoption of a rehabilitation plan under subsection (e) so as to be inconsistent with the rehabilitation plan.

(B) Special rules for benefit increases.—A plan may not be amended after the date of the adoption of a rehabilitation plan under subsection (e) so as to increase benefits, including future benefit accruals, unless the plan actuary certifies that such increase is paid for out of additional contributions not contemplated by the rehabilitation plan, and, after taking into account the benefit increase, the multiemployer plan still is reasonably expected to emerge from critical status by the end of the rehabilitation period on the schedule contemplated in the rehabilitation plan.

(2) Restriction on lump sums and similar benefits.—

(A) In general.—Effective on the date the notice of certification of the plan's critical status for the initial critical year under subsection (b)(3)(D) is sent, and notwithstanding section 411(d)(6), the plan shall not pay—

(i) any payment, in excess of the monthly amount paid under a single life annuity (plus any social security supplements described in the last sentence of section 411(b)(1)(A)),

(ii) any payment for the purchase of an irrevocable commitment from an insurer to pay benefits, and

(iii) any other payment specified by the Secretary by regulations.

(B) EXCEPTION.—Subparagraph (A) shall not apply to a benefit which under section 411(a)(11) may be immediately distributed without the consent of the participant or to any makeup payment in the case of a retroactive annuity starting date or any similar payment of benefits owed with respect to a prior period.

(3) ADJUSTMENTS DISREGARDED IN WITHDRAWAL LIABILITY DETERMINATION.—Any benefit reductions under this subsection shall be disregarded in determining a plan's unfunded vested benefits for purposes of determining an employer's withdrawal liability under section 4201 of the Employee Retirement Income Security Act of 1974.

(4) SPECIAL RULES FOR PLAN ADOPTION PERIOD.—During the rehabilitation plan adoption period—

(A) the plan sponsor may not accept a collective bargaining agreement or participation agreement with respect to the multiemployer plan that provides for—

(i) a reduction in the level of contributions for any participants,

(ii) a suspension of contributions with respect to any period of service, or

(iii) any new direct or indirect exclusion of younger or newly hired employees from plan participation, and

(B) no amendment of the plan which increases the liabilities of the plan by reason of any increase in benefits, any change in the accrual of benefits, or any change in the rate at which benefits become nonforfeitable under the plan may be adopted unless the amendment is required as a condition of qualification under part I of subchapter D of chapter 1 or to comply with other applicable law.

(g) EXPEDITED RESOLUTION OF PLAN SPONSOR DECISIONS.—If, within 60 days of the due date for adoption of a funding improvement plan or a rehabilitation plan under subsection (e), the plan sponsor of a plan in endangered status or a plan in critical status has not agreed on a funding improvement plan or rehabilitation plan, then any member of the board or group that constitutes the plan sponsor may require that the plan sponsor enter into an expedited dispute resolution procedure for the development and adoption of a funding improvement plan or rehabilitation plan.

(h) NONBARGAINED PARTICIPATION.—

(1) BOTH BARGAINED AND NONBARGAINED EMPLOYEE-PARTICIPANTS.—In the case of an employer that contributes to a multiemployer plan with respect to both employees who are covered by one or more collective bargaining agreements and employees who are not so covered, if the plan is in endangered status or in critical status, benefits of and contributions for the nonbargained employees, including surcharges on those contributions, shall be determined as if those nonbargained employees were covered under the first to expire of the employer's collective bargaining agreements in effect when the plan entered endangered or critical status.

(2) NONBARGAINED EMPLOYEES ONLY.—In the case of an employer that contributes to a multiemployer plan only with respect to employees who are not covered by a collective bargaining agreement, this section shall be applied as if the employer were the bargaining party, and its participation agreement with the plan were a collective bargaining agreement with a term ending on the first day of the plan year beginning after the employer is provided the schedule or schedules described in subsections (c) and (e).

(i) DEFINITIONS; ACTUARIAL METHOD.—For purposes of this section—

(1) BARGAINING PARTY.—The term "bargaining party" means—

(A)(i) except as provided in clause (ii), an employer who has an obligation to contribute under the plan; or

(ii) in the case of a plan described under section 404(c), or a continuation of such a plan, the association of employers that is the employer settlor of the plan; and

(B) an employee organization which, for purposes of collective bargaining, represents plan participants employed by an employer who has an obligation to contribute under the plan.

(2) FUNDED PERCENTAGE.—The term "funded percentage" means the percentage equal to a fraction—

(A) the numerator of which is the value of the plan's assets, as determined under section 431(c)(2), and

(B) the denominator of which is the accrued liability of the plan, determined using actuarial assumptions described in section 431(c)(3).

(3) ACCUMULATED FUNDING DEFICIENCY.—The term "accumulated funding deficiency" has the meaning given such term in section 412(a).

(4) ACTIVE PARTICIPANT.—The term "active participant" means, in connection with a multiemployer plan, a participant who is in covered service under the plan.

(5) INACTIVE PARTICIPANT.—The term "inactive participant" means, in connection with a multiemployer plan, a participant, or the beneficiary or alternate payee of a participant, who—

(A) is not in covered service under the plan, and

(B) is in pay status under the plan or has a nonforfeitable right to benefits under the plan.

(6) PAY STATUS.—A person is in pay status under a multiemployer plan if—

(A) at any time during the current plan year, such person is a participant or beneficiary under the plan and is paid an early, late, normal, or disability retirement benefit under the plan (or a death benefit under the plan related to a retirement benefit), or

(B) to the extent provided in regulations of the Secretary, such person is entitled to such a benefit under the plan.

(7) OBLIGATION TO CONTRIBUTE.—The term "obligation to contribute" has the meaning given such term under section 4212(a) of the Employee Retirement Income Security Act of 1974.

(8) ACTUARIAL METHOD.—Notwithstanding any other provision of this section, the actuary's determinations with respect to a plan's normal cost, actuarial accrued liability, and improvements in a plan's funded percentage under this section shall be based upon the unit credit funding method (whether or not that method is used for the plan's actuarial valuation).

(9) PLAN SPONSOR.—In the case of a plan described under section 404(c), or a continuation of such a plan, the term "plan sponsor" means the bargaining parties described under paragraph (1).

(10) BENEFIT COMMENCEMENT DATE.—The term "benefit commencement date" means the annuity starting date (or in the case of a retroactive annuity starting date, the date on which benefit payments begin).

[CCH Explanation at ¶ 310. Committee Reports at ¶ 10,090.]

Amendments

• 2006, Pension Protection Act of 2006 (H.R. 4)

H.R. 4, § 212(a):

Amended subpart A of part III of subchapter D of chapter 1, as amended by this Act, by inserting after Code Sec. 431 a new Code Sec. 432. **Effective** generally with respect to plan years beginning after 2007. For special rules, see Act Sec. 212(e)(2) and (3), below.

H.R. 4, § 212(e)(2)-(3), provides:

(2) SPECIAL RULE FOR CERTAIN NOTICES.—In any case in which a plan's actuary certifies that it is reasonably expected that a multiemployer plan will be in critical status under section 305(b)(3) of the Employee Retirement Income Security Act of 1974, as added by this section, with respect to the first plan year beginning after 2007, the notice required under subparagraph (D) of such section may be provided at any time after the date of enactment, so long as it is provided on or before the last date for providing the notice under such subparagraph.

(3) SPECIAL RULE FOR CERTAIN RESTORED BENEFITS.—In the case of a multiemployer plan—

(A) with respect to which benefits were reduced pursuant to a plan amendment adopted on or after January 1, 2002, and before June 30, 2005, and

(B) which, pursuant to the plan document, the trust agreement, or a formal written communication from the plan sponsor to participants provided before June 30, 2005, provided for the restoration of such benefits,

the amendments made by this section shall not apply to such benefit restorations to the extent that any restriction on the providing or accrual of such benefits would otherwise apply by reason of such amendments.

H.R. 4, § 221(c), provides:

(c) SUNSET.—

(1) IN GENERAL.—Except as provided in this subsection, notwithstanding any other provision of this Act, the provisions of, and the amendments made by, sections 201(b), 202, and 212 shall not apply to plan years beginning after December 31, 2014.

(2) FUNDING IMPROVEMENT AND REHABILITATION PLANS.—If a plan is operating under a funding improvement or rehabilitation plan under section 305 of such Act or 432 of such

Code for its last year beginning before January 1, 2015, such plan shall continue to operate under such funding improvement or rehabilitation plan during any period after December 31, 2014, such funding improvement or rehabilitation plan is in effect and all provisions of such Act or Code relating to the operation of such funding improvement or rehabilitation plan shall continue in effect during such period.

»»→ Caution: Code Sec. 436, below, as added by H.R. 4, applies generally to plan years beginning after December 31, 2007.

[¶5135] *CODE SEC. 436. FUNDING-BASED LIMITS ON BENEFITS AND BENEFIT ACCRUALS UNDER SINGLE-EMPLOYER PLANS.*

(a) GENERAL RULE.—For purposes of section 401(a)(29), a defined benefit plan which is a single-employer plan shall be treated as meeting the requirements of this section if the plan meets the requirements of subsections (b), (c), (d), and (e).

(b) FUNDING-BASED LIMITATION ON SHUTDOWN BENEFITS AND OTHER UNPREDICTABLE CONTINGENT EVENT BENEFITS UNDER SINGLE-EMPLOYER PLANS.—

(1) IN GENERAL.—If a participant of a defined benefit plan which is a single-employer plan is entitled to an unpredictable contingent event benefit payable with respect to any event occurring during any plan year, the plan shall provide that such benefit may not be provided if the adjusted funding target attainment percentage for such plan year—

(A) is less than 60 percent, or

(B) would be less than 60 percent taking into account such occurrence.

(2) EXEMPTION.—Paragraph (1) shall cease to apply with respect to any plan year, effective as of the first day of the plan year, upon payment by the plan sponsor of a contribution (in addition to any minimum required contribution under section 303) equal to—

(A) in the case of paragraph (1)(A), the amount of the increase in the funding target of the plan (under section 430) for the plan year attributable to the occurrence referred to in paragraph (1), and

(B) in the case of paragraph (1)(B), the amount sufficient to result in a funding target attainment percentage of 60 percent.

(3) UNPREDICTABLE CONTINGENT EVENT.—For purposes of this subsection, the term 'unpredictable contingent event benefit' means any benefit payable solely by reason of—

(A) a plant shutdown (or similar event, as determined by the Secretary), or

(B) any event other than the attainment of any age, performance of any service, receipt or derivation of any compensation, or occurrence of death or disability.

(c) LIMITATIONS ON PLAN AMENDMENTS INCREASING LIABILITY FOR BENEFITS.—

(1) IN GENERAL.—No amendment to a defined benefit plan which is a single-employer plan which has the effect of increasing liabilities of the plan by reason of increases in benefits, establishment of new benefits, changing the rate of benefit accrual, or changing the rate at which benefits become nonforfeitable may take effect during any plan year if the adjusted funding target attainment percentage for such plan year is—

(A) less than 80 percent, or

(B) would be less than 80 percent taking into account such amendment.

(2) EXEMPTION.—Paragraph (1) shall cease to apply with respect to any plan year, effective as of the first day of the plan year (or if later, the effective date of the amendment), upon payment by the plan sponsor of a contribution (in addition to any minimum required contribution under section 430) equal to—

(A) in the case of paragraph (1)(A), the amount of the increase in the funding target of the plan (under section 430) for the plan year attributable to the amendment, and

(B) in the case of paragraph (1)(B), the amount sufficient to result in an adjusted funding target attainment percentage of 80 percent.

(3) EXCEPTION FOR CERTAIN BENEFIT INCREASES.—Paragraph (1) shall not apply to any amendment which provides for an increase in benefits under a formula which is not based on a participant's

compensation, but only if the rate of such increase is not in excess of the contemporaneous rate of increase in average wages of participants covered by the amendment.

(d) LIMITATIONS ON ACCELERATED BENEFIT DISTRIBUTIONS.—

(1) FUNDING PERCENTAGE LESS THAN 60 PERCENT.—A defined benefit plan which is a single-employer plan shall provide that, in any case in which the plan's adjusted funding target attainment percentage for a plan year is less than 60 percent, the plan may not pay any prohibited payment after the valuation date for the plan year.

(2) BANKRUPTCY.—A defined benefit plan which is a single-employer plan shall provide that, during any period in which the plan sponsor is a debtor in a case under title 11, United States Code, or similar Federal or State law, the plan may not pay any prohibited payment. The preceding sentence shall not apply on or after the date on which the enrolled actuary of the plan certifies that the adjusted funding target attainment percentage of such plan is not less than 100 percent.

(3) LIMITED PAYMENT IF PERCENTAGE AT LEAST 60 PERCENT BUT LESS THAN 80 PERCENT.—

(A) IN GENERAL.—A defined benefit plan which is a single-employer plan shall provide that, in any case in which the plan's adjusted funding target attainment percentage for a plan year is 60 percent or greater but less than 80 percent, the plan may not pay any prohibited payment after the valuation date for the plan year to the extent the amount of the payment exceeds the lesser of—

(i) 50 percent of the amount of the payment which could be made without regard to this section, or

(ii) the present value (determined under guidance prescribed by the Pension Benefit Guaranty Corporation, using the interest and mortality assumptions under section 417(e)) of the maximum guarantee with respect to the participant under section 4022 of the Employee Retirement Income Security Act of 1974.

(B) ONE-TIME APPLICATION.—

(i) IN GENERAL.—The plan shall also provide that only 1 prohibited payment meeting the requirements of subparagraph (A) may be made with respect to any participant during any period of consecutive plan years to which the limitations under either paragraph (1) or (2) or this paragraph applies.

(ii) TREATMENT OF BENEFICIARIES.—For purposes of this subparagraph, a participant and any beneficiary on his behalf (including an alternate payee, as defined in section 414(p)(8)) shall be treated as 1 participant. If the accrued benefit of a participant is allocated to such an alternate payee and 1 or more other persons, the amount under subparagraph (A) shall be allocated among such persons in the same manner as the accrued benefit is allocated unless the qualified domestic relations order (as defined in section 414(p)(1)(A)) provides otherwise.

(4) EXCEPTION.—This subsection shall not apply to any plan for any plan year if the terms of such plan (as in effect for the period beginning on September 1, 2005, and ending with such plan year) provide for no benefit accruals with respect to any participant during such period.

(5) PROHIBITED PAYMENT.—For purpose of this subsection, the term "prohibited payment" means—

(A) any payment, in excess of the monthly amount paid under a single life annuity (plus any social security supplements described in the last sentence of section 411(a)(9)), to a participant or beneficiary whose annuity starting date (as defined in section 417(f)(2)) occurs during any period a limitation under paragraph (1) or (2) is in effect,

(B) any payment for the purchase of an irrevocable commitment from an insurer to pay benefits, and

(C) any other payment specified by the Secretary by regulations.

(e) LIMITATION ON BENEFIT ACCRUALS FOR PLANS WITH SEVERE FUNDING SHORTFALLS.—

(1) IN GENERAL.—A defined benefit plan which is a single-employer plan shall provide that, in any case in which the plan's adjusted funding target attainment percentage for a plan year is less than 60 percent, benefit accruals under the plan shall cease as of the valuation date for the plan year.

(2) EXEMPTION.—*Paragraph (1) shall cease to apply with respect to any plan year, effective as of the first day of the plan year, upon payment by the plan sponsor of a contribution (in addition to any minimum required contribution under section 430) equal to the amount sufficient to result in an adjusted funding target attainment percentage of 60 percent.*

(f) RULES RELATING TO CONTRIBUTIONS REQUIRED TO AVOID BENEFIT LIMITATIONS.—

(1) SECURITY MAY BE PROVIDED.—

(A) IN GENERAL.—*For purposes of this section, the adjusted funding target attainment percentage shall be determined by treating as an asset of the plan any security provided by a plan sponsor in a form meeting the requirements of subparagraph (B).*

(B) FORM OF SECURITY.—*The security required under subparagraph (A) shall consist of—*

(i) a bond issued by a corporate surety company that is an acceptable surety for purposes of section 412 of the Employee Retirement Income Security Act of 1974,

(ii) cash, or United States obligations which mature in 3 years or less, held in escrow by a bank or similar financial institution, or

(iii) such other form of security as is satisfactory to the Secretary and the parties involved.

(C) ENFORCEMENT.—*Any security provided under subparagraph (A) may be perfected and enforced at any time after the earlier of—*

(i) the date on which the plan terminates,

(ii) if there is a failure to make a payment of the minimum required contribution for any plan year beginning after the security is provided, the due date for the payment under section 430(j), or

(iii) if the adjusted funding target attainment percentage is less than 60 percent for a consecutive period of 7 years, the valuation date for the last year in the period.

(D) RELEASE OF SECURITY.—*The security shall be released (and any amounts thereunder shall be refunded together with any interest accrued thereon) at such time as the Secretary may prescribe in regulations, including regulations for partial releases of the security by reason of increases in the funding target attainment percentage.*

(2) PREFUNDING BALANCE OR FUNDING STANDARD CARRYOVER BALANCE MAY NOT BE USED.—*No prefunding balance under section 430(f) or funding standard carryover balance may be used under subsection (b), (c), or (e) to satisfy any payment an employer may make under any such subsection to avoid or terminate the application of any limitation under such subsection.*

(3) DEEMED REDUCTION OF FUNDING BALANCES.—

(A) IN GENERAL.—*Subject to subparagraph (C), in any case in which a benefit limitation under subsection (b), (c), (d), or (e) would (but for this subparagraph and determined without regard to subsection (b)(2), (c)(2), or (e)(2)) apply to such plan for the plan year, the plan sponsor of such plan shall be treated for purposes of this title as having made an election under section 430(f) to reduce the prefunding balance or funding standard carryover balance by such amount as is necessary for such benefit limitation to not apply to the plan for such plan year.*

(B) EXCEPTION FOR INSUFFICIENT FUNDING BALANCES.—*Subparagraph (A) shall not apply with respect to a benefit limitation for any plan year if the application of subparagraph (A) would not result in the benefit limitation not applying for such plan year.*

(C) RESTRICTIONS OF CERTAIN RULES TO COLLECTIVELY BARGAINED PLANS.—*With respect to any benefit limitation under subsection (b), (c), or (e), subparagraph (A) shall only apply in the case of a plan maintained pursuant to 1 or more collective bargaining agreements between employee representatives and 1 or more employers.*

(g) NEW PLANS.—*Subsections (b), (c), and (e) shall not apply to a plan for the first 5 plan years of the plan. For purposes of this subsection, the reference in this subsection to a plan shall include a reference to any predecessor plan.*

(h) PRESUMED UNDERFUNDING FOR PURPOSES OF BENEFIT LIMITATIONS.—

(1) PRESUMPTION OF CONTINUED UNDERFUNDING.—In any case in which a benefit limitation under subsection (b), (c), (d), or (e) has been applied to a plan with respect to the plan year preceding the current plan year, the adjusted funding target attainment percentage of the plan for the current plan year shall be presumed to be equal to the adjusted funding target attainment percentage of the plan for the preceding plan year until the enrolled actuary of the plan certifies the actual adjusted funding target attainment percentage of the plan for the current plan year.

(2) PRESUMPTION OF UNDERFUNDING AFTER 10TH MONTH.—In any case in which no certification of the adjusted funding target attainment percentage for the current plan year is made with respect to the plan before the first day of the 10th month of such year, for purposes of subsections (b), (c), (d), and (e), such first day shall be deemed, for purposes of such subsection, to be the valuation date of the plan for the current plan year and the plan's adjusted funding target attainment percentage shall be conclusively presumed to be less than 60 percent as of such first day.

(3) PRESUMPTION OF UNDERFUNDING AFTER 4TH MONTH FOR NEARLY UNDERFUNDED PLANS.—In any case in which—

(A) a benefit limitation under subsection (b), (c), (d), or (e) did not apply to a plan with respect to the plan year preceding the current plan year, but the adjusted funding target attainment percentage of the plan for such preceding plan year was not more than 10 percentage points greater than the percentage which would have caused such subsection to apply to the plan with respect to such preceding plan year, and

(B) as of the first day of the 4th month of the current plan year, the enrolled actuary of the plan has not certified the actual adjusted funding target attainment percentage of the plan for the current plan year,

until the enrolled actuary so certifies, such first day shall be deemed, for purposes of such subsection, to be the valuation date of the plan for the current plan year and the adjusted funding target attainment percentage of the plan as of such first day shall, for purposes of such subsection, be presumed to be equal to 10 percentage points less than the adjusted funding target attainment percentage of the plan for such preceding plan year.

(i) TREATMENT OF PLAN AS OF CLOSE OF PROHIBITED OR CESSATION PERIOD.—For purposes of applying this title—

(1) OPERATION OF PLAN AFTER PERIOD.—Unless the plan provides otherwise, payments and accruals will resume effective as of the day following the close of the period for which any limitation of payment or accrual of benefits under subsection (d) or (e) applies.

(2) TREATMENT OF AFFECTED BENEFITS.—Nothing in this subsection shall be construed as affecting the plan's treatment of benefits which would have been paid or accrued but for this section.

(j) TERMS RELATING TO FUNDING TARGET ATTAINMENT PERCENTAGE.—For purposes of this section—

(1) IN GENERAL.—The term "funding target attainment percentage" has the same meaning given such term by section 430(d)(2).

(2) ADJUSTED FUNDING TARGET ATTAINMENT PERCENTAGE.—The term "adjusted funding target attainment percentage" means the funding target attainment percentage which is determined under paragraph (1) by increasing each of the amounts under subparagraphs (A) and (B) of section 430(d)(2) by the aggregate amount of purchases of annuities for employees other than highly compensated employees (as defined in section 414(q)) which were made by the plan during the preceding 2 plan years.

(3) APPLICATION TO PLANS WHICH ARE FULLY FUNDED WITHOUT REGARD TO REDUCTIONS FOR FUNDING BALANCES.—

(A) IN GENERAL.—In the case of a plan for any plan year, if the funding target attainment percentage is 100 percent or more (determined without regard to this paragraph and without regard to the reduction in the value of assets under section 430(f)(4)(A)), the funding target attainment percentage for purposes of paragraph (1) shall be determined without regard to such reduction.

(B) TRANSITION RULE.—Subparagraph (A) shall be applied to plan years beginning after 2007 and before 2011 by substituting for "100 percent" the applicable percentage determined in accordance with the following table:

In the case of a plan year beginning in calendar year:	*The applicable percentage is*
2008	*92*
2009	*94*
2010	*96 .*

(C) LIMITATION.—Subparagraph (B) shall not apply with respect to any plan year after 2008 unless the funding target attainment percentage (determined without regard to this paragraph) of the plan for each preceding plan year after 2007 was not less than the applicable percentage with respect to such preceding plan year determined under subparagraph (B).

(k) SPECIAL RULE FOR 2008.—For purposes of this section, in the case of plan years beginning in 2008, the funding target attainment percentage for the preceding plan year may be determined using such methods of estimation as the Secretary may provide.

[CCH Explanation at ¶ 215. Committee Reports at ¶ 10,020.]

Amendments

• 2006, Pension Protection Act of 2006 (H.R. 4)

H.R. 4, § 113(a)(1)(B):

Amended part III of subchapter D of chapter 1 by adding at the end a new subpart B (Code Sec. 436). **Effective** generally for plan years beginning after 12-31-2007. For an exception, see Act Sec. 113(b)(2), below.

H.R. 4, § 113(b)(2), provides:

(2) COLLECTIVE BARGAINING EXCEPTION.—In the case of a plan maintained pursuant to 1 or more collective bargaining agreements between employee representatives and 1 or more employers ratified before January 1, 2008, the amendments made by this section shall not apply to plan years beginning before the earlier of—

(A) the later of—

(i) the date on which the last collective bargaining agreement relating to the plan terminates (determined without regard to any extension thereof agreed to after the date of the enactment of this Act), or

(ii) the first day of the first plan year to which the amendments made by this subsection would (but for this subparagraph) apply, or

(B) January 1, 2010.

For purposes of subparagraph (A)(i), any plan amendment made pursuant to a collective bargaining agreement relating to the plan which amends the plan solely to conform to any requirement added by this section shall not be treated as a termination of such collective bargaining agreement.

[¶ 5140] CODE SEC. 457. DEFERRED COMPENSATION PLANS OF STATE AND LOCAL GOVERNMENTS AND TAX-EXEMPT ORGANIZATIONS.

(a) YEAR OF INCLUSION IN GROSS INCOME.—

* * *

Caution: Code Sec. 457(a)(3), below, as added by H.R. 4, applies to distributions in tax years beginning after December 31, 2006.

(3) SPECIAL RULE FOR HEALTH AND LONG-TERM CARE INSURANCE.—In the case of a plan of an eligible employer described in subsection (e)(1)(A), to the extent provided in section 402(l), paragraph (1) shall not apply to amounts otherwise includible in gross income under this subsection.

* * *

[CCH Explanation at ¶ 825. Committee Reports at ¶ 10,790.]

Amendments

• 2006, Pension Protection Act of 2006 (H.R. 4)

H.R. 4, § 845(b)(3):

Amended Code Sec. 457(a) by adding at the end a new paragraph (3). **Effective** for distributions in tax years beginning after 12-31-2006.

(e) OTHER DEFINITIONS AND SPECIAL RULES.—For purposes of this section—

* * *

(11) CERTAIN PLANS EXCLUDED.—

* * *

(D) CERTAIN VOLUNTARY EARLY RETIREMENT INCENTIVE PLANS.—

(i) IN GENERAL.—If an applicable voluntary early retirement incentive plan—

(I) makes payments or supplements as an early retirement benefit, a retirement-type subsidy, or a benefit described in the last sentence of section 411(a)(9), and

(II) such payments or supplements are made in coordination with a defined benefit plan which is described in section 401(a) and includes a trust exempt from tax under section 501(a) and which is maintained by an eligible employer described in paragraph (1)(A) or by an education association described in clause (ii)(II),

such applicable plan shall be treated for purposes of subparagraph (A)(i) as a bona fide severance pay plan with respect to such payments or supplements to the extent such payments or supplements could otherwise have been provided under such defined benefit plan (determined as if section 411 applied to such defined benefit plan).

(ii) APPLICABLE VOLUNTARY EARLY RETIREMENT INCENTIVE PLAN.—For purposes of this subparagraph, the term "applicable voluntary early retirement incentive plan" means a voluntary early retirement incentive plan maintained by—

(I) a local educational agency (as defined in section 9101 of the Elementary and Secondary Education Act of 1965 (20 U.S.C. 7801)), or

(II) "an education association which principally represents employees of 1 or more agencies described in subclause (I) and which is described in section 501(c)(5) or (6) and exempt from tax under section 501(a)."

* * *

(16) ROLLOVER AMOUNTS.—

* * *

→ *Caution: Code Sec. 457(e)(16)(B), below, as amended by H.R. 4, applies to distributions after December 31, 2006.*

(B) CERTAIN RULES MADE APPLICABLE.—The rules of paragraphs (2) through (7), *(9), and (11)* of section 402(c) and section 402(f) shall apply for purposes of subparagraph (A).

* * *

[CCH Explanation at ¶ 945 and ¶ 1070. Committee Reports at ¶ 10,700 and ¶ 11,070.]

Amendments

• **2006, Pension Protection Act of 2006 (H.R. 4)**

H.R. 4, § 829(a)(4):

Amended Code Sec. 457(e)(16)(B) by striking "and (9)" and inserting ", (9), and (11)". **Effective** for distributions after 12-31-2006.

H.R. 4, § 1104(a)(1):

Amended Code Sec. 457(e)(11) by adding at the end a new subparagraph (D). **Effective** generally for tax years ending after 8-17-2006. For a special rule, see Act Sec. 1104(d)(4), below.

H.R. 4, § 1104(d)(4), provides:

(4) CONSTRUCTION.—Nothing in the amendments made by this section shall alter or affect the construction of the Internal Revenue Code of 1986, the Employee Retirement Income Security Act of 1974, or the Age Discrimination in Employment Act of 1967 as applied to any plan, arrangement, or conduct to which such amendments do not apply.

(f) TAX TREATMENT OF PARTICIPANTS WHERE PLAN OR ARRANGEMENT OF EMPLOYER IS NOT ELIGIBLE.—

* * *

(2) EXCEPTIONS.—Paragraph (1) shall not apply to—

(A) a plan described in section 401(a) which includes a trust exempt from tax under section 501(a),

(B) an annuity plan or contract described in section 403,

(C) that portion of any plan which consists of a transfer of property described in section 83,

(D) that portion of any plan which consists of a trust to which section 402(b) applies,

(E) a qualified governmental excess benefit arrangement described in section 415(m) *, and*

(F) that portion of any applicable employment retention plan described in paragraph (4) with respect to any participant.

* * *

(4) EMPLOYMENT RETENTION PLANS.—For purposes of paragraph (2)(F)—

(A) IN GENERAL.—The portion of an applicable employment retention plan described in this paragraph with respect to any participant is that portion of the plan which provides benefits payable to the participant not in excess of twice the applicable dollar limit determined under subsection (e)(15).

(B) OTHER RULES.—

(i) LIMITATION.—Paragraph (2)(F) shall only apply to the portion of the plan described in subparagraph (A) for years preceding the year in which such portion is paid or otherwise made available to the participant.

(ii) TREATMENT.—A plan shall not be treated for purposes of this title as providing for the deferral of compensation for any year with respect to the portion of the plan described in subparagraph (A).

(C) APPLICABLE EMPLOYMENT RETENTION PLAN.—The term "applicable employment retention plan" means an employment retention plan maintained by—

(i) a local educational agency (as defined in section 9101 of the Elementary and Secondary Education Act of 1965 (20 U.S.C. 7801), or

(ii) an education association which principally represents employees of 1 or more agencies described in clause (i) and which is described in section 501(c) (5) or (6) and exempt from taxation under section 501(a).

(D) EMPLOYMENT RETENTION PLAN.—The term "employment retention plan" means a plan to pay, upon termination of employment, compensation to an employee of a local educational agency or education association described in subparagraph (C) for purposes of—

(i) retaining the services of the employee, or

(ii) rewarding such employee for the employee's service with 1 or more such agencies or associations.

[CCH Explanation at ¶ 1070. Committee Reports at ¶ 11,070.]

Amendments

• 2006, Pension Protection Act of 2006 (H.R. 4)

H.R. 4, § 1104(b)(1):

Amended Code Sec. 457(f)(2) by striking "and" at the end of subparagraph (D), by striking the period at the end of subparagraph (E) and inserting ", and", and by adding at the end a new subparagraph (F). **Effective** for tax years ending after 8-17-2006. For a special rule, see Act Sec. 1104(d)(4), below.

H.R. 4, § 1104(b)(2):

Amended Code Sec. 457(f) by adding at the end a new paragraph (4). **Effective** for tax years ending after 8-17-2006. For a special rule, see Act Sec. 1104(d)(4), below.

H.R. 4, § 1104(d)(4), provides:

(4) CONSTRUCTION.—Nothing in the amendments made by this section shall alter or affect the construction of the Internal Revenue Code of 1986, the Employee Retirement Income Security Act of 1974, or the Age Discrimination in Employment Act of 1967 as applied to any plan, arrangement, or conduct to which such amendments do not apply.

[¶ 5145] CODE SEC. 501. EXEMPTION FROM TAX ON CORPORATIONS, CERTAIN TRUSTS, ETC.

* * *

(c) LIST OF EXEMPT ORGANIZATIONS.—The following organizations are referred to in subsection (a):

* * *

(21)(A) A trust or trusts established in writing, created or organized in the United States, and contributed to by any person (except an insurance company) if—

(i) the purpose of such trust or trusts is exclusively—

(I) to satisfy, in whole or in part, the liability of such person for, or with respect to, claims for compensation for disability or death due to pneumoconiosis under Black Lung Acts,

(II) to pay premiums for insurance exclusively covering such liability,

(III) to pay administrative and other incidental expenses of such trust in connection with the operation of the trust and the processing of claims against such person under Black Lung Acts, and

(IV) to pay accident or health benefits for retired miners and their spouses and dependents (including administrative and other incidental expenses of such trust in connection therewith) or premiums for insurance exclusively covering such benefits; and

(ii) no part of the assets of the trust may be used for, or diverted to, any purpose other than—

(I) the purposes described in clause (i),

(II) investment (but only to the extent that the trustee determines that a portion of the assets is not currently needed for the purposes described in clause (i)) in qualified investments, or

(III) payment into the Black Lung Disability Trust Fund established under section 9501, or into the general fund of the United States Treasury (other than in satisfaction of any tax or other civil or criminal liability of the person who established or contributed to the trust).

(B) No deduction shall be allowed under this chapter for any payment described in subparagraph (A)(i)(IV) from such trust.

»»→ Caution: Code Sec. 501(c)(21)(C), below, as amended by H.R. 4, applies to tax years beginning after December 31, 2006.

(C) Payments described in subparagraph (A)(i)(IV) may be made from such trust during a taxable year only to the extent that the aggregate amount of such payments during such taxable year does not exceed the excess (if any), as of the close of the preceding taxable year, of—

(i) the fair market value of the assets of the trust, over

(ii) 110 percent of the present value of the liability described in subparagraph (A)(i)(I) of such person.

The determinations under the preceding sentence shall be made by an independent actuary using actuarial methods and assumptions (not inconsistent with the regulations prescribed under section 192(c)(1)(A)) each of which is reasonable and which are reasonable in the aggregate.

* * *

[CCH Explanation at ¶ 1220. Committee Reports at ¶ 10,880.]

Amendments

• **2006, Pension Protection Act of 2006 (H.R. 4)**

H.R. 4, § 862(a):

Amended so much of Code Sec. 501(c)(21)(C) as precedes the last sentence. **Effective** for tax years beginning after 12-31-2006. Prior to amendment, so much of Code Sec. 501(c)(21)(C) as precedes the last sentence read as follows:

(C) Payments described in subparagraph (A)(i)(IV) may be made from such trust during a taxable year only to the extent that the aggregate amount of such payments during such taxable year does not exceed the lesser of—

(i) the excess (if any) (as of the close of the preceding taxable year) of—

(I) the fair market value of the assets of the trust, over

(II) 110 percent of the present value of the liability described in subparagraph (A)(i)(I) of such person, or

(ii) the excess (if any) of—

(I) the sum of a similar excess determined as of the close of the last taxable year ending before the date of the enactment of this subparagraph plus earnings thereon as of the close of the taxable year preceding the taxable year involved, over

(II) the aggregate payments described in subparagraph (A)(i)(IV) made from the trust during all taxable years beginning after the date of the enactment of this subparagraph.

(q) SPECIAL RULES FOR CREDIT COUNSELING ORGANIZATIONS.—

(1) IN GENERAL.—An organization with respect to which the provision of credit counseling services is a substantial purpose shall not be exempt from tax under subsection (a) unless such organization is described in paragraph (3) or (4) of subsection (c) and such organization is organized and operated in accordance with the following requirements:

(A) The organization—

(i) provides credit counseling services tailored to the specific needs and circumstances of consumers,

(ii) makes no loans to debtors (other than loans with no fees or interest) and does not negotiate the making of loans on behalf of debtors,

(iii) provides services for the purpose of improving a consumer's credit record, credit history, or credit rating only to the extent that such services are incidental to providing credit counseling services, and

(iv) does not charge any separately stated fee for services for the purpose of improving any consumer's credit record, credit history, or credit rating.

(B) The organization does not refuse to provide credit counseling services to a consumer due to the inability of the consumer to pay, the ineligibility of the consumer for debt management plan enrollment, or the unwillingness of the consumer to enroll in a debt management plan.

(C) The organization establishes and implements a fee policy which—

(i) requires that any fees charged to a consumer for services are reasonable,

(ii) allows for the waiver of fees if the consumer is unable to pay, and

(iii) except to the extent allowed by State law, prohibits charging any fee based in whole or in part on a percentage of the consumer's debt, the consumer's payments to be made pursuant to a debt management plan, or the projected or actual savings to the consumer resulting from enrolling in a debt management plan.

(D) At all times the organization has a board of directors or other governing body—

(i) which is controlled by persons who represent the broad interests of the public, such as public officials acting in their capacities as such, persons having special knowledge or expertise in credit or financial education, and community leaders,

(ii) not more than 20 percent of the voting power of which is vested in persons who are employed by the organization or who will benefit financially, directly or indirectly, from the organization's activities (other than through the receipt of reasonable directors' fees or the repayment of consumer debt to creditors other than the credit counseling organization or its affiliates), and

(iii) not more than 49 percent of the voting power of which is vested in persons who are employed by the organization or who will benefit financially, directly or indirectly, from the organization's activities (other than through the receipt of reasonable directors' fees).

(E) The organization does not own more than 35 percent of—

(i) the total combined voting power of any corporation (other than a corporation which is an organization described in subsection (c)(3) and exempt from tax under subsection (a)) which is in the trade or business of lending money, repairing credit, or providing debt management plan services, payment processing, or similar services,

(ii) the profits interest of any partnership (other than a partnership which is an organization described in subsection (c)(3) and exempt from tax under subsection (a)) which is in the trade or business of lending money, repairing credit, or providing debt management plan services, payment processing, or similar services, and

(iii) the beneficial interest of any trust or estate (other than a trust which is an organization described in subsection (c)(3) and exempt from tax under subsection (a)) which is in the trade or business of lending money, repairing credit, or providing debt management plan services, payment processing, or similar services.

(F) The organization receives no amount for providing referrals to others for debt management plan services, and pays no amount to others for obtaining referrals of consumers.

(2) ADDITIONAL REQUIREMENTS FOR ORGANIZATIONS DESCRIBED IN SUBSECTION (c)(3).—

(A) IN GENERAL.—In addition to the requirements under paragraph (1), an organization with respect to which the provision of credit counseling services is a substantial purpose and which is described in paragraph (3) of subsection (c) shall not be exempt from tax under subsection (a) unless such organization is organized and operated in accordance with the following requirements:

(i) The organization does not solicit contributions from consumers during the initial counseling process or while the consumer is receiving services from the organization.

(ii) The aggregate revenues of the organization which are from payments of creditors of consumers of the organization and which are attributable to debt management plan services do not exceed the applicable percentage of the total revenues of the organization.

(B) APPLICABLE PERCENTAGE.—

(i) IN GENERAL.—For purposes of subparagraph (A)(ii), the applicable percentage is 50 percent.

(ii) TRANSITION RULE.—Notwithstanding clause (i), in the case of an organization with respect to which the provision of credit counseling services is a substantial purpose and which is described in paragraph (3) of subsection (c) and exempt from tax under subsection (a) on the date of the enactment of this subsection, the applicable percentage is—

(I) 80 percent for the first taxable year of such organization beginning after the date which is 1 year after the date of the enactment of this subsection, and

(II) 70 percent for the second such taxable year beginning after such date, and

(III) 60 percent for the third such taxable year beginning after such date.

(3) ADDITIONAL REQUIREMENT FOR ORGANIZATIONS DESCRIBED IN SUBSECTION (c)(4).—In addition to the requirements under paragraph (1), an organization with respect to which the provision of credit counseling services is a substantial purpose and which is described in paragraph (4) of subsection (c) shall not be exempt from tax under subsection (a) unless such organization notifies the Secretary, in such manner as the Secretary may by regulations prescribe, that it is applying for recognition as a credit counseling organization.

(4) CREDIT COUNSELING SERVICES; DEBT MANAGEMENT PLAN SERVICES.—For purposes of this subsection—

(A) CREDIT COUNSELING SERVICES.—The term "credit counseling services" means—

(i) the providing of educational information to the general public on budgeting, personal finance, financial literacy, saving and spending practices, and the sound use of consumer credit,

(ii) the assisting of individuals and families with financial problems by providing them with counseling, or

(iii) a combination of the activities described in clauses (i) and (ii).

(B) DEBT MANAGEMENT PLAN SERVICES.—The term "debt management plan services" means services related to the repayment, consolidation, or restructuring of a consumer's debt, and includes the negotiation with creditors of lower interest rates, the waiver or reduction of fees, and the marketing and processing of debt management plans.

[CCH Explanation at ¶ 1215. Committee Reports at ¶ 11,280.]

Amendments

• 2006, Pension Protection Act of 2006 (H.R. 4)

H.R. 4, § 1220(a):

Amended Code Sec. 501 by redesignating subsection (q) as subsection (r) and by inserting after subsection (p) a new subsection (q). **Effective** generally for tax years beginning after 8-17-2006. For a transition rule, see Act Sec. 1220(c)(2), below.

H.R. 4, § 1220(c)(2), provides:

(2) TRANSITION RULE FOR EXISTING ORGANIZATIONS.—In the case of any organization described in paragraph (3) or (4) [of] section 501(c) of the Internal Revenue Code of 1986 and with respect to which the provision of credit counseling services is a substantial purpose on the date of the enactment of this Act, the amendments made by this section shall apply to taxable years beginning after the date which is 1 year after the date of the enactment of this Act.

(r) CROSS REFERENCE.—

For nonexemption of Communist-controlled organizations, see section 11(b) of the Internal Security Act of 1950 (64 Stat. 997; 50 U. S. C. 790 (b)).

[CCH Explanation at ¶ 1215. Committee Reports at ¶ 11,280.]

Amendments

• 2006, Pension Protection Act of 2006 (H.R. 4)

H.R. 4, §1220(a):

Amended Code Sec. 501 by redesignating subsection (q) as subsection (r). **Effective** generally for tax years beginning after 8-17-2006. For a transition rule, see Act Sec. 1220(c)(2) in the amendment notes following Code Sec. 501(q).

[¶ 5150] CODE SEC. 508. SPECIAL RULES WITH RESPECT TO SECTION 501(c)(3) ORGANIZATIONS.

* * *

(f) ADDITIONAL PROVISIONS RELATING TO SPONSORING ORGANIZATIONS.—A sponsoring organization (as defined in section 4966(d)(1)) shall give notice to the Secretary (in such manner as the Secretary may provide) whether such organization maintains or intends to maintain donor advised funds (as defined in section 4966(d)(2)) and the manner in which such organization plans to operate such funds.

[CCH Explanation at ¶ 1265. Committee Reports at ¶ 11,350.]

Amendments

• 2006, Pension Protection Act of 2006 (H.R. 4)

H.R. 4, §1235(b)(1):

Amended Code Sec. 508 by adding at the end a new subsection (f). **Effective** for organizations applying for tax-exempt status after 8-17-2006.

[¶ 5155] CODE SEC. 509. PRIVATE FOUNDATION DEFINED.

(a) GENERAL RULE.—For purposes of this title, the term "private foundation" means a domestic or foreign organization described in section 501(c)(3) other than—

* * *

(3) an organization which—

(A) is organized, and at all times thereafter is operated, exclusively for the benefit of, to perform the functions of, or to carry out the purposes of one or more specified organizations described in paragraph (1) or (2),

(B) is—

(i) operated, supervised, or controlled by one or more organizations described in paragraph (1) or (2),

(ii) supervised or controlled in connection with one or more such organizations, or

(iii) operated in connection with one or more such organizations, and

(C) is not controlled directly or indirectly by one or more disqualified persons (as defined in section 4946) other than foundation managers and other than one or more organizations described in paragraph (1) or (2); and

(4) an organization which is organized and operated exclusively for testing for public safety.

For purposes of paragraph (3), an organization described in paragraph (2) shall be deemed to include an organization described in section 501(c)(4), (5), or (6) which would be described in paragraph (2) if it were an organization described in section 501(c)(3).

* * *

[CCH Explanation at ¶1225. Committee Reports at ¶11,360.]

Amendments

• 2006, Pension Protection Act of 2006 (H.R. 4)

H.R. 4, §1241(a):

Amended Code Sec. 509(a)(3)(B). **Effective** 8-17-2006. Prior to amendment, Code Sec. 509(a)(3)(B) read as follows:

(B) is operated, supervised, or controlled by or in connection with one or more organizations, described in paragraph (1) or (2), and

(e) DEFINITION OF GROSS INVESTMENT INCOME.—For purposes of subsection (d), the term "gross investment income" means the gross amount of income from interest, dividends, payments with respect to securities loans (as defined in section 512(a)(5)), rents, and royalties, but not including any such income to the extent included in computing the tax imposed by section 511. *Such term shall also include income from sources similar to those in the preceding sentence.*

[CCH Explanation at ¶1250. Committee Reports at ¶11,290.]

Amendments

• 2006, Pension Protection Act of 2006 (H.R. 4)

H.R. 4, §1221(a)(2):

Amended Code Sec. 509(e) by adding at the end a new sentence. **Effective** for tax years beginning after 8-17-2006.

(f) REQUIREMENTS FOR SUPPORTING ORGANIZATIONS.—

(1) TYPE III SUPPORTING ORGANIZATIONS.—For purposes of subsection (a)(3)(B)(iii), an organization shall not be considered to be operated in connection with any organization described in paragraph (1) or (2) of subsection (a) unless such organization meets the following requirements:

(A) RESPONSIVENESS.—For each taxable year beginning after the date of the enactment of this subsection, the organization provides to each supported organization such information as the Secretary may require to ensure that such organization is responsive to the needs or demands of the supported organization.

(B) FOREIGN SUPPORTED ORGANIZATIONS.—

(i) IN GENERAL.—The organization is not operated in connection with any supported organization that is not organized in the United States.

(ii) TRANSITION RULE FOR EXISTING ORGANIZATIONS.—If the organization is operated in connection with an organization that is not organized in the United States on the date of the enactment of this subsection, clause (i) shall not apply until the first day of the third taxable year of the organization beginning after the date of the enactment of this subsection.

(2) ORGANIZATIONS CONTROLLED BY DONORS.—

(A) IN GENERAL.—For purposes of subsection (a)(3)(B), an organization shall not be considered to be—

(i) operated, supervised, or controlled by any organization described in paragraph (1) or (2) of subsection (a), or

(ii) operated in connection with any organization described in paragraph (1) or (2) of subsection (a),

if such organization accepts any gift or contribution from any person described in subparagraph (B).

(B) PERSON DESCRIBED.—A person is described in this subparagraph if, with respect to a supported organization of an organization described in subparagraph (A), such person is—

(i) a person (other than an organization described in paragraph (1), (2), or (4) of section 509(a)) who directly or indirectly controls, either alone or together with persons described in clauses (ii) and (iii), the governing body of such supported organization,

(ii) a member of the family (determined under section 4958(f)(4)) of an individual described in clause (i), or

(iii) a 35-percent controlled entity (as defined in section 4958(f)(3) by substituting "persons described in clause (i) or (ii) of section 509(f)(2)(B)" for "persons described in subparagraph (A) or (B) of paragraph (1)" in subparagraph (A)(i) thereof).

(3) SUPPORTED ORGANIZATION.—For purposes of this subsection, the term "supported organization" means, with respect to an organization described in subsection (a)(3), an organization described in paragraph (1) or (2) of subsection (a)—

(A) for whose benefit the organization described in subsection (a)(3) is organized and operated, or

(B) with respect to which the organization performs the functions of, or carries out the purposes of.

[CCH Explanation at ¶ 1225. Committee Reports at ¶ 11,360.]

Amendments

• 2006, Pension Protection Act of 2006 (H.R. 4)

H.R. 4, § 1241(b):

Amended Code Sec. 509 by adding at the end a new subsection (f). **Effective** 8-17-2006.

[¶ 5160] CODE SEC. 512. UNRELATED BUSINESS TAXABLE INCOME.

* * *

(b) MODIFICATIONS.—The modifications referred to in subsection (a) are the following:

* * *

(13) SPECIAL RULES FOR CERTAIN AMOUNTS RECEIVED FROM CONTROLLED ENTITIES.—

* * *

(E) PARAGRAPH TO APPLY ONLY TO CERTAIN EXCESS PAYMENTS.—

(i) IN GENERAL.—Subparagraph (A) shall apply only to the portion of a qualifying specified payment received or accrued by the controlling organization that exceeds the amount which would have been paid or accrued if such payment met the requirements prescribed under section 482.

(ii) ADDITION TO TAX FOR VALUATION MISSTATEMENTS.—The tax imposed by this chapter on the controlling organization shall be increased by an amount equal to 20 percent of the larger of—

(I) such excess determined without regard to any amendment or supplement to a return of tax, or

(II) such excess determined with regard to all such amendments and supplements.

(iii) QUALIFYING SPECIFIED PAYMENT.—The term "qualifying specified payment" means a specified payment which is made pursuant to—

(I) a binding written contract in effect on the date of the enactment of this subparagraph, or

(II) a contract which is a renewal, under substantially similar terms, of a contract described in subclause (I).

(iv) TERMINATION.—This subparagraph shall not apply to payments received or accrued after December 31, 2007.

(F) RELATED PERSONS.—The Secretary shall prescribe such rules as may be necessary or appropriate to prevent avoidance of the purposes of this paragraph through the use of related persons.

* * *

[CCH Explanation at ¶1210. Committee Reports at ¶11,150.]

Amendments

• 2006, Pension Protection Act of 2006 (H.R. 4)

H.R. 4, §1205(a):

Amended Code Sec. 512(b)(13) by redesignating subparagraph (E) as subparagraph (F) and by inserting after subparagraph (D) a new subparagraph (E). **Effective** for payments received or accrued after 12-31-2005.

[¶5165] CODE SEC. 513. UNRELATED TRADE OR BUSINESS.

* * *

(j) DEBT MANAGEMENT PLAN SERVICES.—The term "unrelated trade or business" includes the provision of debt management plan services (as defined in section 501(q)(4)(B)) by any organization other than an organization which meets the requirements of section 501(q).

[CCH Explanation at ¶1215. Committee Reports at ¶11,280.]

Amendments

• 2006, Pension Protection Act of 2006 (H.R. 4)

H.R. 4, §1220(b):

Amended Code Sec. 513 by adding at the end a new subsection (j). **Effective** generally for tax years beginning after 8-17-2006. For a transition rule, see Act Sec. 1220(c)(2), below.

H.R. 4, §1220(c)(2), provides:

(2) TRANSITION RULE FOR EXISTING ORGANIZATIONS.—In the case of any organization described in paragraph (3) or (4) [of] section 501(c) of the Internal Revenue Code of 1986 and with respect to which the provision of credit counseling services is a substantial purpose on the date of the enactment of this Act, the amendments made by this section shall apply to taxable years beginning after the date which is 1 year after the date of the enactment of this Act.

[¶5170] CODE SEC. 514. UNRELATED DEBT-FINANCED INCOME.

* * *

(c) ACQUISITION INDEBTEDNESS.—

* * *

(9) REAL PROPERTY ACQUIRED BY A QUALIFIED ORGANIZATION.—

* * *

(C) QUALIFIED ORGANIZATION.—For purposes of this paragraph, the term "qualified organization" means—

(i) an organization described in section 170(b)(1)(A)(ii) and its affiliated support organizations described in section 509(a)(3);

(ii) any trust which constitutes a qualified trust under section 401;

(iii) an organization described in section 501(c)(25)*; or*

(iv) a retirement income account described in section 403(b)(9).

* * *

[CCH Explanation at ¶1050. Committee Reports at ¶10,920.]

Amendments

• 2006, Pension Protection Act of 2006 (H.R. 4)

H.R. 4, §866(a):

Amended Code Sec. 514(c)(9)(C) by striking "or" after clause (ii), by striking the period at the end of clause (iii) and inserting "; or", and by inserting after clause (iii) a new clause (iv). **Effective** for tax years beginning on or after 8-17-2006.

[¶5175] CODE SEC. 529. QUALIFIED TUITION PROGRAMS.

* * *

(f) REGULATIONS.—Notwithstanding any other provision of this section, the Secretary shall prescribe such regulations as may be necessary or appropriate to carry out the purposes of this section and to prevent abuse of such purposes, including regulations under chapters 11, 12, and 13 of this title.

[CCH Explanation at ¶1310. Committee Reports at ¶11,400.]

Amendments

• 2006, Pension Protection Act of 2006 (H.R. 4)

H.R. 4, §1304(b):

Amended Code Sec. 529 by adding at the end a new subsection (f). **Effective** 8-17-2006.

[¶5180] CODE SEC. 545. UNDISTRIBUTED PERSONAL HOLDING COMPANY INCOME.

* * *

(b) ADJUSTMENTS TO TAXABLE INCOME.—For the purposes of subsection (a), the taxable income shall be adjusted as follows:

* * *

(2) CHARITABLE CONTRIBUTIONS.—The deduction for charitable contributions provided under section 170 shall be allowed, but in computing such deduction the limitations in section 170(b)(1)(A), (B), *(D), and (E)* shall apply, and section 170(b)(2) and (d)(1) shall not apply. For purposes of this paragraph, the term "contribution base" when used in section 170(b)(1) means the taxable income computed with the adjustments (other than the 10-percent limitation) provided in section 170(b)(2) and (d)(1) and without deduction of the amount disallowed under paragraph (6) of this subsection.

* * *

[CCH Explanation at ¶1125. Committee Reports at ¶11,160.]

• 2006, Pension Protection Act of 2006 (H.R. 4)

H.R. 4, §1206(b)(2):

Amended Code Sec. 545(b)(2) by striking "and (D)" and inserting "(D), and (E)". **Effective** for contributions made in tax years beginning after 12-31-2005.

[¶5185] CODE SEC. 664. CHARITABLE REMAINDER TRUSTS.

* * *

(g) QUALIFIED GRATUITOUS TRANSFER OF QUALIFIED EMPLOYER SECURITIES.—

* * *

(3) PLAN REQUIREMENTS.—A plan contains the provisions required by this paragraph if such plan provides that—

* * *

(E) such securities are held in a suspense account under the plan to be allocated each year, up to the applicable limitation under paragraph (7) *(determined on the basis of fair market value of securities when allocated to participants)*, after first allocating all other annual additions for the limitation year, up to the limitations under sections 415(c) and (e), and

* * *

[CCH Explanation at ¶1155. Committee Reports at ¶10,940.]

Amendments

• 2006, Pension Protection Act of 2006 (H.R. 4)

H.R. 4, §868(a):

Amended Code Sec. 664(g)(3)(E) by inserting "(determined on the basis of fair market value of securities when allocated to participants)" after "paragraph (7)". **Effective** 8-17-2006.

[¶ 5190] CODE SEC. 848. CAPITALIZATION OF CERTAIN POLICY ACQUISITION EXPENSES.

* * *

(e) CLASSIFICATION OF CONTRACTS.—For purposes of this section—

* * *

»»→ *Caution: Code Sec. 848(e)(6), below, as added by H.R. 4, applies to specified policy acquisition expenses determined for tax years beginning after December 31, 2009.*

(6) TREATMENT OF CERTAIN QUALIFIED LONG-TERM CARE INSURANCE CONTRACT ARRANGEMENTS.—An annuity or life insurance contract which includes a qualified long-term care insurance contract as a part of or a rider on such annuity or life insurance contract shall be treated as a specified insurance contract not described in subparagraph (A) or (B) of subsection (c)(1).

* * *

[CCH Explanation at ¶ 820. Committee Reports at ¶ 10,780.]

Amendments

• 2006, Pension Protection Act of 2006 (H.R. 4)

H.R. 4, § 844(e):

Amended Code Sec. 848(e) by adding at the end a new paragraph (6). **Effective** for specified policy acquisition expenses determined for tax years beginning after 12-31-2009.

[¶ 5195] CODE SEC. 1035. CERTAIN EXCHANGES OF INSURANCE POLICIES.

»»→ *Caution: Code Sec. 1035(a), below, as amended by H.R. 4, applies with respect to exchanges occurring after December 31, 2009.*

(a) GENERAL RULES.—No gain or loss shall be recognized on the exchange of—

(1) a contract of life insurance for another contract of life insurance or for an endowment or annuity contract *or for a qualified long-term care insurance contract*; or

(2) a contract of endowment insurance (A) for another contract of endowment insurance which provides for regular payments beginning at a date not later than the date payments would have begun under the contract exchanged, or (B) for an annuity contract, *or (C) for a qualified long-term care insurance contract;*

(3) an annuity contract for an annuity contract *or for a qualified long-term care insurance contract; or*

(4) a qualified long-term care insurance contract for a qualified long-term care insurance contract.

[CCH Explanation at ¶ 820. Committee Reports at ¶ 10,780.]

Amendments

• 2006, Pension Protection Act of 2006 (H.R. 4)

H.R. 4, § 844(b)(3)(A)-(C):

Amended Code Sec. 1035(a) by inserting "or for a qualified long-term care insurance contract" before the semicolon at the end of paragraph (1), by inserting ", or (C) for a qualified long-term care insurance contract" before the semicolon at the end of paragraph (2), and by inserting "or for a qualified long-term care insurance contract" before the period at the end of paragraph (3). **Effective** with respect to exchanges occurring after 12-31-2009.

H.R. 4, § 844(b)(4):

Amended Code Sec. 1035(a) by striking "or" at the end the end of paragraph (2), by striking the period at the end of paragraph (3) and inserting "; or", and by inserting after paragraph (3) a new paragraph (4). **Effective** with respect to exchanges occurring after 12-31-2009.

(b) DEFINITIONS.—For the purpose of this section—

* * *

»»→ *Caution: Code Sec. 1035(b)(2)-(3), below, as amended by H.R. 4, applies with respect to exchanges occurring after December 31, 2009.*

(2) ANNUITY CONTRACT.—An annuity contract is a contract to which paragraph (1) applies but which may be payable during the life of the annuitant only in installments. *For purposes of the preceding sentence, a contract shall not fail to be treated as an annuity contract solely because a qualified long-term care insurance contract is a part of or a rider on such contract.*

(3) LIFE INSURANCE CONTRACT.—A contract of life insurance is a contract to which paragraph (1) applies but which is not ordinarily payable in full during the life of the insured. *For purposes of the preceding sentence, a contract shall not fail to be treated as a life insurance contract solely because a qualified long-term care insurance contract is a part of or a rider on such contract.*

* * *

[CCH Explanation at ¶ 820. Committee Reports at ¶ 10,780.]

Amendments

• **2006, Pension Protection Act of 2006 (H.R. 4)**

H.R. 4, § 844(b)(1):

Amended Code Sec. 1035(b)(2) by adding at the end a new sentence. **Effective** with respect to exchanges occurring after 12-31-2009.

H.R. 4, § 844(b)(2):

Amended Code Sec. 1035(b)(3) by adding at the end a new sentence. **Effective** with respect to exchanges occurring after 12-31-2009.

[¶ 5200] CODE SEC. 1367. ADJUSTMENTS TO BASIS OF STOCK OF SHAREHOLDERS, ETC.

(a) GENERAL RULE.—

* * *

(2) DECREASES IN BASIS.—The basis of each shareholder's stock in an S corporation shall be decreased for any period (but not below zero) by the sum of the following items determined with respect to the shareholder for such period:

(A) distributions by the corporation which were not includible in the income of the shareholder by reason of section 1368,

(B) the items of loss and deduction described in subparagraph (A) of section 1366(a)(1),

(C) any nonseparately computed loss determined under subparagraph (B) of section 1366(a)(1),

(D) any expense of the corporation not deductible in computing its taxable income and not properly chargeable to capital account, and

(E) the amount of the shareholder's deduction for depletion for any oil and gas property held by the S corporation to the extent such deduction does not exceed the proportionate share of the adjusted basis of such property allocated to such shareholder under section 613A(c)(11)(B).

The decrease under subparagraph (B) by reason of a charitable contribution (as defined in section 170(c)) of property shall be the amount equal to the shareholder's pro rata share of the adjusted basis of such property. The preceding sentence shall not apply to contributions made in taxable years beginning after December 31, 2007.

* * *

[CCH Explanation at ¶ 1135. Committee Reports at ¶ 11,130.]

Amendments

• **2006, Pension Protection Act of 2006 (H.R. 4)**

H.R. 4, § 1203(a):

Amended Code Sec. 1367(a)(2) by adding at the end a new flush sentence. **Effective** for contributions made in tax years beginning after 12-31-2005.

[¶ 5205] CODE SEC. 2055. TRANSFERS FOR PUBLIC, CHARITABLE, AND RELIGIOUS USES.

* * *

(e) DISALLOWANCE OF DEDUCTIONS IN CERTAIN CASES.—

»»→ *Caution: Code Sec. 2055(e)(5), below, as added by H.R. 4, applies to contributions made after the date which is 180 days after August 17, 2006.*

(5) CONTRIBUTIONS TO DONOR ADVISED FUNDS.—A deduction otherwise allowed under subsection (a) for any contribution to a donor advised fund (as defined in section 4966(d)(2)) shall only be allowed if—

(A) the sponsoring organization (as defined in section 4966(d)(1)) with respect to such donor advised fund is not—

(i) described in paragraph (3) or (4) of subsection (a), or

(ii) a type III supporting organization (as defined in section 4943(f)(5)(A)) which is not a functionally integrated type III supporting organization (as defined in section 4943(f)(5)(B)), and

(B) the taxpayer obtains a contemporaneous written acknowledgment (determined under rules similar to the rules of section 170(f)(8)(C)) from the sponsoring organization (as so defined) of such donor advised fund that such organization has exclusive legal control over the assets contributed.

* * *

[CCH Explanation at ¶1180. Committee Reports at ¶11,350.]

Amendments

• 2006, Pension Protection Act of 2006 (H.R. 4)

H.R. 4, §1234(b):

Amended Code Sec. 2055(e) by adding at the end a new paragraph (5). **Effective** for contributions made after the date which is 180 days after 8-17-2006.

(g) VALUATION OF SUBSEQUENT GIFTS.—

(1) IN GENERAL.—In the case of any additional contribution, the fair market value of such contribution shall be determined by using the lesser of—

(A) the fair market value of the property at the time of the initial fractional contribution, or

(B) the fair market value of the property at the time of the additional contribution.

(2) DEFINITIONS.—For purposes of this paragraph—

(A) ADDITIONAL CONTRIBUTION.—The term "additional contribution" means a bequest, legacy, devise, or transfer described in subsection (a) of any interest in a property with respect to which the decedent had previously made an initial fractional contribution.

(B) INITIAL FRACTIONAL CONTRIBUTION.—The term "initial fractional contribution" means, with respect to any decedent, any charitable contribution of an undivided portion of the decedent's entire interest in any tangible personal property for which a deduction was allowed under section 170.

[CCH Explanation at ¶1115. Committee Reports at ¶11,260.]

Amendments

• 2006, Pension Protection Act of 2006 (H.R. 4)

H.R. 4, §1218(b):

Amended Code Sec. 2055 by redesignating subsection (g) as subsection (h) and by inserting after subsection (f) a new subsection (g). **Effective** for contributions, bequests, and gifts made after 8-17-2006.

(h) CROSS REFERENCES.—

* * *

[CCH Explanation at ¶1115. Committee Reports at ¶11,260.]

Amendments

• 2006, Pension Protection Act of 2006 (H.R. 4)

H.R. 4, §1218(b):

Amended Code Sec. 2055 by redesignating subsection (g) as subsection (h). **Effective** for contributions, bequests, and gifts made after 8-17-2006.

[¶ 5210] CODE SEC. 2522. CHARITABLE AND SIMILAR GIFTS.

* * *

(c) DISALLOWANCE OF DEDUCTIONS IN CERTAIN CASES.—

* * *

Caution: Code Sec. 2522(c)(5), below, as added by H.R. 4, applies to contributions made after the date which is 180 days after August 17, 2006.

(5) CONTRIBUTIONS TO DONOR ADVISED FUNDS.—A deduction otherwise allowed under subsection (a) for any contribution to a donor advised fund (as defined in section 4966(d)(2)) shall only be allowed if—

(A) the sponsoring organization (as defined in section 4966(d)(1)) with respect to such donor advised fund is not—

(i) described in paragraph (3) or (4) of subsection (a), or

(ii) a type III supporting organization (as defined in section 4943(f)(5)(A)) which is not a functionally integrated type III supporting organization (as defined in section 4943(f)(5)(B)), and

(B) the taxpayer obtains a contemporaneous written acknowledgment (determined under rules similar to the rules of section 170(f)(8)(C)) from the sponsoring organization (as so defined) of such donor advised fund that such organization has exclusive legal control over the assets contributed.

* * *

[CCH Explanation at ¶ 1180. Committee Reports at ¶ 11,350.]

Amendments

• 2006, Pension Protection Act of 2006 (H.R. 4)

H.R. 4, § 1234(c):

Amended Code Sec. 2522(c) by adding at the end a new paragraph (5). **Effective** for contributions made after the date which is 180 days after 8-17-2006.

(e) SPECIAL RULES FOR FRACTIONAL GIFTS.—

(1) DENIAL OF DEDUCTION IN CERTAIN CASES.—

(A) IN GENERAL.—No deduction shall be allowed for a contribution of an undivided portion of a taxpayer's entire interest in tangible personal property unless all interest in the property is held immediately before such contribution by—

(i) the taxpayer, or

(ii) the taxpayer and the donee.

(B) EXCEPTIONS.—The Secretary may, by regulation, provide for exceptions to subparagraph (A) in cases where all persons who hold an interest in the property make proportional contributions of an undivided portion of the entire interest held by such persons.

(2) VALUATION OF SUBSEQUENT GIFTS.—In the case of any additional contribution, the fair market value of such contribution shall be determined by using the lesser of—

(A) the fair market value of the property at the time of the initial fractional contribution, or

(B) the fair market value of the property at the time of the additional contribution.

(3) RECAPTURE OF DEDUCTION IN CERTAIN CASES; ADDITION TO TAX.—

(A) IN GENERAL.—The Secretary shall provide for the recapture of an amount equal to any deduction allowed under this section (plus interest) with respect to any contribution of an undivided portion of a taxpayer's entire interest in tangible personal property—

(i) in any case in which the donor does not contribute all of the remaining interest in such property to the donee (or, if such donee is no longer in existence, to any person described in section 170(c)) before the earlier of—

(I) the date that is 10 years after the date of the initial fractional contribution, or

(II) the date of the death of the donor, and

(ii) in any case in which the donee has not, during the period beginning on the date of the initial fractional contribution and ending on the date described in clause (i)—

(I) had substantial physical possession of the property, and

(II) used the property in a use which is related to a purpose or function constituting the basis for the organizations' exemption under section 501.

(B) ADDITION TO TAX.—The tax imposed under this chapter for any taxable year for which there is a recapture under subparagraph (A) shall be increased by 10 percent of the amount so recaptured.

(4) DEFINITIONS.—For purposes of this subsection—

(A) ADDITIONAL CONTRIBUTION.—The term "additional contribution" means any gift for which a deduction is allowed under subsection (a) or (b) of any interest in a property with respect to which the donor has previously made an initial fractional contribution.

(B) INITIAL FRACTIONAL CONTRIBUTION.—The term "initial fractional contribution" means, with respect to any donor, the first gift of an undivided portion of the donor's entire interest in any tangible personal property for which a deduction is allowed under subsection (a) or (b).

[CCH Explanation at ¶ 1115. Committee Reports at ¶ 11,260.]

Amendments

• 2006, Pension Protection Act of 2006 (H.R. 4)

H.R. 4, § 1218(c):

Amended Code Sec. 2522 by redesignating subsection (e) as subsection (f) and by inserting after subsection (d) a new subsection (e). **Effective** for contributions, bequests, and gifts made after 8-17-2006.

(*f*) CROSS REFERENCES.—

* * *

[CCH Explanation at ¶ 1115. Committee Reports at ¶ 11,260.]

Amendments

• 2006, Pension Protection Act of 2006 (H.R. 4)

H.R. 4, § 1218(c):

Amended Code Sec. 2522 by redesignating subsection (e) as subsection (f). **Effective** for contributions, bequests, and gifts made after 8-17-2006.

[¶ 5215] CODE SEC. 3121. DEFINITIONS.

* * *

(b) EMPLOYMENT.—For purposes of this chapter, the term "employment" means any service, of whatever nature, performed (A) by an employee for the person employing him, irrespective of the citizenship or residence of either, (i) within the United States, or (ii) on or in connection with an American vessel or American aircraft under a contract of service which is entered into within the United States or during the performance of which and while the employee is employed on the vessel or aircraft it touches at a port in the United States, if the employee is employed on and in connection with such vessel or aircraft when outside the United States, or (B) outside the United States by a citizen of the United States [a citizen or resident of the United States (effective for remuneration paid after December 31, 1983)] as an employee for an American employer (as defined in subsection (h)), or (C) if it is service, regardless of where or by whom performed, which is designated as employment or recognized as equivalent to employment under an agreement entered into under section 233 of the Social Security Act; except that such term shall not include—

* * *

(5) service performed in the employ of the United States or any instrumentality of the United States, if such service—

* * *

(E) service performed as the Chief Justice of the United States, an Associate Justice of the Supreme Court, a judge of a United States court of appeals, a judge of a United States district court (including the district court of a territory), a judge of the United States Claims Court, a judge of the United States Court of International Trade, a judge *or special trial judge* of the United States Tax Court, a United States magistrate, or a referee in bankruptcy or United States bankruptcy judge,

* * *

[CCH Explanation at ¶ 1445. Committee Reports at ¶ 10,810.]

Amendments

• **2006, Pension Protection Act of 2006 (H.R. 4)**

H.R. 4, §854(c)(8):

Amended Code Sec. 3121(b)(5)(E) by inserting "or special trial judge" before "of the United States Tax Court". **Effective** 8-17-2006.

[¶ 5220] CODE SEC. 3304. APPROVAL OF STATE LAWS.

(a) REQUIREMENTS.—The Secretary of Labor shall approve any State law submitted to him, within 30 days of such submission, which he finds provides that—

* * *

(15) the amount of compensation payable to an individual for any week which begins after March 31, 1980, and which begins in a period with respect to which such individual is receiving a governmental or other pension, retirement or retired pay, annuity, or any other similar periodic payment which is based on the previous work of such individual shall be reduced (but not below zero) by an amount equal to the amount of such pension, retirement or retired pay, annuity, or other payment, which is reasonably attributable to such week except that—

(A) the requirements of this paragraph shall apply to any pension, retirement or retired pay, annuity, or other similar periodic payment only if—

(i) such pension, retirement or retired pay, annuity, or similar payment is under a plan maintained (or contributed to) by a base period employer or chargeable employer (as determined under applicable law), and

(ii) in the case of such a payment not made under the Social Security Act or the Railroad Retirement Act of 1974 (or the corresponding provisions of prior law), services performed for such employer by the individual after the beginning of the base period (or remuneration for such services) affect eligibility for, or increase the amount of, such pension, retirement or retired pay, annuity, or similar payment, and

(B) the State law may provide for limitations on the amount of any such a reduction to take into account contributions made by the individual for the pension, retirement or retired pay, annuity, or other similar periodic payment;

* * *

Compensation shall not be reduced under paragraph (15) for any pension, retirement or retired pay, annuity, or similar payment which is not includible in gross income of the individual for the taxable year in which paid because it was part of a rollover distribution.

* * *

[CCH Explanation at ¶ 1325. Committee Reports at ¶ 11,080.]

Amendments

• **2006, Pension Protection Act of 2006 (H.R. 4)**

H.R. 4, §1105(a):

Amended Code Sec. 3304(a) by adding at the end a new flush sentence. **Effective** for weeks beginning on or after 8-17-2006.

[¶ 5225] CODE SEC. 4041. IMPOSITION OF TAX.

* * *

→ Caution: Code Sec. 4041(g), below, as amended by H.R. 4, is effective January 1, 2007.

(g) OTHER EXEMPTIONS.—Under regulations prescribed by the Secretary, no tax shall be imposed under this section—

(1) on any liquid sold for use or used as supplies for vessels or aircraft (within the meaning of section 4221(d)(3));

(2) with respect to the sale of any liquid for the exclusive use of any State, any political subdivision of a State, or the District of Columbia, or with respect to the use by any of the foregoing of any liquid as a fuel;

(3) upon the sale of any liquid for export, or for shipment to a possession of the United States, and in due course so exported or shipped;

(4) with respect to the sale of any liquid to a nonprofit educational organization for its exclusive use, or with respect to the use by a nonprofit educational organization of any liquid as a fuel*; and*

(5) with respect to the sale of any liquid to a qualified blood collector organization (as defined in section 7701(a)(49)) for such organization's exclusive use in the collection, storage, or transportation of blood.

For purposes of paragraph (4), the term "nonprofit educational organization" means an educational organization described in section 170(b)(1)(A)(ii) which is exempt from income tax under section 501(a). The term also includes a school operated as an activity of an organization described in section 501(c)(3) which is exempt from income tax under section 501(a), if such school normally maintains a regular faculty and curriculum and normally has a regularly enrolled body of pupils or students in attendance at the place where its educational activities are regularly carried on.

* * *

[CCH Explanation at ¶ 1255. Committee Reports at ¶ 11,170.]

Amendments

• **2006, Pension Protection Act of 2006 (H.R. 4)**

H.R. 4, § 1207(a):

Amended Code Sec. 4041(g) by striking "and" at the end of paragraph (3), by striking the period in paragraph (4) and inserting "; and", and by inserting after paragraph (4) a new paragraph (5). **Effective** 1-1-2007.

[¶ 5230] CODE SEC. 4221. CERTAIN TAX-FREE SALES.

→ Caution: Code Sec. 4221(a), below, as amended by H.R. 4, is effective January 1, 2007.

(a) GENERAL RULE.—Under regulations prescribed by the Secretary, no tax shall be imposed under this chapter (other than under section 4121 or 4081) on the sale by the manufacturer (or under subchapter A or C of chapter 31 on the first retail sale) of an article—

(1) for use by the purchaser for further manufacture, or for resale by the purchaser to a second purchaser for use by such second purchaser in further manufacture,

(2) for export, or for resale by the purchaser to a second purchaser for export,

(3) for use by the purchaser as supplies for vessels or aircraft,

(4) to a State or local government for the exclusive use of a State or local government,

(5) to a nonprofit educational organization for its exclusive use, *or*

(6) to a qualified blood collector organization (as defined in section 7701(a)(49)) for such organization's exclusive use in the collection, storage, or transportation of blood,

but only if such exportation or use is to occur before any other use. *Paragraphs (4), (5), and (6)* shall not apply to the tax imposed by section 4064. In the case of taxes imposed by section 4051 or 4071, paragraphs (4) and (5) shall not apply on and after October 1, 2011. In the case of the tax imposed by section 4131, paragraphs (3), (4), and (5) shall not apply and paragraph (2) shall apply only if the use of the exported vaccine meets such requirements as the Secretary may by regulations prescribe. In the case of taxes imposed by subchapter A of chapter 31, paragraphs (1), (3), (4), and (5) shall not apply. *In the case of taxes imposed by subchapter C or D, paragraph (6) shall not apply.*

* * *

[CCH Explanation at ¶1255. Committee Reports at ¶11,170.]

Amendments

• 2006, Pension Protection Act of 2006 (H.R. 4)

H.R. 4, §1207(b)(1):

Amended Code Sec. 4221(a) by striking "or" at the end of paragraph (4), by adding "or" at the end of paragraph (5), and by inserting after paragraph (5) a new paragraph (6). **Effective** 1-1-2007.

H.R. 4, §1207(b)(2):

Amended Code Sec. 4221(a) by adding at the end a new sentence. **Effective** 1-1-2007.

H.R. 4, §1207(b)(3)(A):

Amended the second sentence of Code Sec. 4221(a) by striking "Paragraphs (4) and (5)" and inserting "Paragraphs (4), (5), and (6)". **Effective** 1-1-2007.

[¶5235] CODE SEC. 4253. EXEMPTIONS.

* * *

»»→ Caution: Code Sec. 4253(k), below, as added by H.R. 4, is effective January 1, 2007.

(k) EXEMPTION FOR QUALIFIED BLOOD COLLECTOR ORGANIZATIONS.—Under regulations provided by the Secretary, no tax shall be imposed under section 4251 on any amount paid by a qualified blood collector organization (as defined in section 7701(a)(49)) for services or facilities furnished to such organization.

[CCH Explanation at ¶1255. Committee Reports at ¶11,170.]

Amendments

• 2006, Pension Protection Act of 2006 (H.R. 4)

H.R. 4, §1207(c)(1):

Amended Code Sec. 4253 by redesignating subsection (k) as subsection (l) and inserting after subsection (j) a new subsection (k). **Effective** 1-1-2007.

»»→ Caution: Former Code Sec. 4253(k) was redesignated as Code Sec. 4253(l), below, and further amended by H.R. 4, effective January 1, 2007.

(l) FILING OF EXEMPTION CERTIFICATES.—

(1) IN GENERAL.—In order to claim an exemption under subsection (c), (h), (i), *(j), or (k)*, a person shall provide to the provider of communications services a statement (in such form and manner as the Secretary may provide) certifying that such person is entitled to such exemption.

(2) DURATION OF CERTIFICATE.—Any statement provided under paragraph (1) shall remain in effect until—

(A) the provider of communications services has actual knowledge that the information provided in such statement is false, or

(B) such provider is notified by the Secretary that the provider of the statement is no longer entitled to an exemption described in paragraph (1).

If any information provided in such statement is no longer accurate, the person providing such statement shall inform the provider of communications services within 30 days of any change of information.

[CCH Explanation at ¶1255. Committee Reports at ¶11,170.]

Amendments

• 2006, Pension Protection Act of 2006 (H.R. 4)

H.R. 4, §1207(c)(1):

Amended Code Sec. 4253 by redesignating subsection (k) as subsection (l). **Effective** 1-1-2007.

H.R. 4, §1207(c)(2):

Amended Code Sec. 4253(l), as redesignated by Act Sec. 1207(c)(1), by striking "or (j)" and inserting "(j), or (k)". **Effective** 1-1-2007.

[¶5240] CODE SEC. 4483. EXEMPTIONS.

* * *

Caution: Code Sec. 4483(h), below, as added by H.R. 4, applies to tax periods beginning on or after July 1, 2007.

(h) EXEMPTION FOR VEHICLES USED IN BLOOD COLLECTION.—

(1) IN GENERAL.—No tax shall be imposed by section 4481 on the use of any qualified blood collector vehicle by a qualified blood collector organization.

(2) QUALIFIED BLOOD COLLECTOR VEHICLE.—For purposes of this subsection, the term "qualified blood collector vehicle" means a vehicle at least 80 percent of the use of which during the prior taxable period was by a qualified blood collector organization in the collection, storage, or transportation of blood.

(3) SPECIAL RULE FOR VEHICLES FIRST PLACED IN SERVICE IN A TAXABLE PERIOD.—In the case of a vehicle first placed in service in a taxable period, a vehicle shall be treated as a qualified blood collector vehicle for such taxable period if such qualified blood collector organization certifies to the Secretary that the organization reasonably expects at least 80 percent of the use of such vehicle by the organization during such taxable period will be in the collection, storage, or transportation of blood.

(4) QUALIFIED BLOOD COLLECTOR ORGANIZATION.—The term "qualified blood collector organization" has the meaning given such term by section 7701(a)(49).

[CCH Explanation at ¶1255. Committee Reports at ¶11,170.]

Amendments

• 2006, Pension Protection Act of 2006 (H.R. 4)

H.R. 4, §1207(d):

Amended Code Sec. 4483 by redesignating subsection (h) as subsection (i) and by inserting after subsection (g) a new subsection (h). **Effective** for tax periods beginning on or after 7-1-2007.

Caution: Former Code Sec. 4483(h) was redesignated as Code Sec. 4483(i), below, by H.R. 4, applicable to tax periods beginning on or after July 1, 2007.

(i) TERMINATION OF EXEMPTIONS.—Subsections (a) and (c) shall not apply on and after October 1, 2011.

[CCH Explanation at ¶1255. Committee Reports at ¶11,170.]

Amendments

• 2006, Pension Protection Act of 2006 (H.R. 4)

H.R. 4, §1207(d):

Amended Code Sec. 4483, by redesignating subsection (h) as subsection (i). **Effective** for tax periods beginning on or after 7-1-2007.

[¶5245] CODE SEC. 4940. EXCISE TAX BASED ON INVESTMENT INCOME.

* * *

(c) NET INVESTMENT INCOME DEFINED.—

* * *

(2) GROSS INVESTMENT INCOME.—For purposes of paragraph (1), the term "gross investment income" means the gross amount of income from interest, dividends, rents, payments with respect to securities loans (as defined in section 512(a)(5)), and royalties, but not including any such income to the extent included in computing the tax imposed by section 511. *Such term shall also include income from sources similar to those in the preceding sentence.*

* * *

(4) CAPITAL GAINS AND LOSSES.—For purposes of paragraph (1) in determining capital gain net income—

(A) There shall be taken into account only gains and losses from the sale or other disposition of property *used for the production of gross investment income (as defined in paragraph (2))*, and property used for the production of income included in computing the tax imposed by section 511 (except to the extent gain or loss from the sale or other disposition of such property is taken into account for purposes of such tax).

(B) The basis for determining gain in the case of property held by the private foundation on December 31, 1969, and continuously thereafter to the date of its disposition shall be deemed to be not less than the fair market value of such property on December 31, 1969.

(C) Losses from sales or other dispositions of property shall be allowed only to the extent of gains from such sales or other dispositions, and there shall be no capital loss carryovers *or carrybacks*.

(D) Except to the extent provided by regulation, under rules similar to the rules of section 1031 (including the exception under subsection (a)(2) thereof), no gain or loss shall be taken into account with respect to any portion of property used for a period of not less than 1 year for a purpose or function constituting the basis of the private foundation's exemption if the entire property is exchanged immediately following such period solely for property of like kind which is to be used primarily for a purpose or function constituting the basis for such foundation's exemption.

* * *

[CCH Explanation at ¶1250. Committee Reports at ¶11,290.]

Amendments

• **2006, Pension Protection Act of 2006 (H.R. 4)**

H.R. 4, §1221(a)(1):

Amended Code Sec. 4940(c)(2) by adding at the end a new sentence. **Effective** for tax years beginning after 8-17-2006.

H.R. 4, §1221(b)(1)-(3):

Amended Code Sec. 4940(c)(4) by striking "used for the production of interest, dividends, rents, and royalties" and inserting "used for the production of gross investment income (as defined in paragraph (2))" in subparagraph (A), by inserting "or carrybacks" after "carryovers" in subparagraph (C), and by adding at the end a new subparagraph (D). **Effective** for tax years beginning after 8-17-2006.

[¶5250] CODE SEC. 4941. TAXES ON SELF-DEALING.

(a) INITIAL TAXES.—

(1) ON SELF-DEALER.—There is hereby imposed a tax on each act of self-dealing between a disqualified person and a private foundation. The rate of tax shall be equal to *10 percent* of the amount involved with respect to the act of self-dealing for each year (or part thereof) in the taxable period. The tax imposed by this paragraph shall be paid by any disqualified person (other than a foundation manager acting only as such) who participates in the act of self-dealing. In the case of a government official (as defined in section 4946(c)), a tax shall be imposed by this paragraph only if such disqualified person participates in the act of self-dealing knowing that it is such an act.

(2) ON FOUNDATION MANAGER.—In any case in which a tax is imposed by paragraph (1), there is hereby imposed on the participation of any foundation manager in an act of self-dealing between a disqualified person and a private foundation, knowing that it is such an act, a tax equal to *5 percent* of the amount involved with respect to the act of self-dealing for each year (or part thereof) in the taxable period, unless such participation is not willful and is due to reasonable cause. The tax imposed by this paragraph shall be paid by any foundation manager who participated in the act of self-dealing.

* * *

[CCH Explanation at ¶1245. Committee Reports at ¶11,200.]

Amendments

• **2006, Pension Protection Act of 2006 (H.R. 4)**

H.R. 4, §1212(a)(1)(A)-(B):

Amended Code Sec. 4941(a) by striking "5 percent" and inserting "10 percent" in paragraph (1), and by striking "2½ percent" and inserting "5 percent" in paragraph (2). **Effective** for tax years beginning after 8-17-2006.

(c) SPECIAL RULES.—For purposes of subsections (a) and (b)—

* * *

(2) *$20,000* LIMIT FOR MANAGEMENT.—With respect to any one act of self-dealing, the maximum amount of the tax imposed by subsection (a)(2) shall not exceed *$20,000*, and the maximum amount of the tax imposed by subsection (b)(2) shall not exceed *$20,000*.

* * *

[CCH Explanation at ¶ 1245. Committee Reports at ¶ 11,200.]

Amendments

• **2006, Pension Protection Act of 2006 (H.R. 4)**

H.R. 4, §1212(a)(2):

Amended Code Sec. 4941(c)(2) by striking "$10,000" each place it appears in the text and heading thereof and inserting "$20,000". **Effective** for tax years beginning after 8-17-2006.

[¶ 5255] CODE SEC. 4942. TAXES ON FAILURE TO DISTRIBUTE INCOME.

(a) INITIAL TAX.—There is hereby imposed on the undistributed income of a private foundation for any taxable year, which has not been distributed before the first day of the second (or any succeeding) taxable year following such taxable year (if such first day falls within the taxable period), a tax equal to *30 percent* of the amount of such income remaining undistributed at the beginning of such second (or succeeding) taxable year. The tax imposed by this subsection shall not apply to the undistributed income of a private foundation—

(1) for any taxable year for which it is an operating foundation (as defined in subsection (j)(3)), or

(2) to the extent that the foundation failed to distribute any amount solely because of an incorrect valuation of assets under subsection (e), if—

(A) the failure to value the assets properly was not willful and was due to reasonable cause,

(B) such amount is distributed as qualifying distributions (within the meaning of subsection (g)) by the foundation during the allowable distribution period (as defined in subsection (j)(2)),

(C) the foundation notifies the Secretary that such amount has been distributed (within the meaning of subparagraph (B)) to correct such failure, and

(D) such distribution is treated under subsection (h)(2) as made out of the undistributed income for the taxable year for which a tax would (except for this paragraph) have been imposed under this subsection.

* * *

[CCH Explanation at ¶ 1245. Committee Reports at ¶ 11,200.]

Amendments

• **2006, Pension Protection Act of 2006 (H.R. 4)**

H.R. 4, §1212(b):

Amended Code Sec. 4942(a) by striking "15 percent" and inserting "30 percent". **Effective** for tax years beginning after 8-17-2006.

(g) QUALIFYING DISTRIBUTIONS DEFINED.—

* * *

(4) LIMITATION ON DISTRIBUTIONS BY NONOPERATING PRIVATE FOUNDATIONS TO SUPPORTING ORGANIZATIONS.—

(A) IN GENERAL.—For purposes of this section, the term "qualifying distribution" shall not include any amount paid by a private foundation which is not an operating foundation to—

(i) any type III supporting organization (as defined in section 4943(f)(5)(A)) which is not a functionally integrated type III supporting organization (as defined in section 4943(f)(5)(B)), and

(ii) any organization which is described in subparagraph (B) or (C) if—

(I) a disqualified person of the private foundation directly or indirectly controls such organization or a supported organization (as defined in section 509(f)(3)) of such organization, or

(II) the Secretary determines by regulations that a distribution to such organization otherwise is inappropriate.

(B) TYPE I AND TYPE II SUPPORTING ORGANIZATIONS.—An organization is described in this subparagraph if the organization meets the requirements of subparagraphs (A) and (C) of section 509(a)(3) and is—

(i) operated, supervised, or controlled by one or more organizations described in paragraph (1) or (2) of section 509(a), or

(ii) supervised or controlled in connection with one or more such organizations.

(C) FUNCTIONALLY INTEGRATED TYPE III SUPPORTING ORGANIZATIONS.—An organization is described in this subparagraph if the organization is a functionally integrated type III supporting organization (as defined under section 4943(f)(5)(B)).

* * *

[CCH Explanation at ¶ 1240. Committee Reports at ¶ 11,360.]

Amendments

• **2006, Pension Protection Act of 2006 (H.R. 4)**

H.R. 4, § 1244(a):

Amended Code Sec. 4942(g)(4). **Effective** for distributions and expenditures after 8-17-2006. Prior to amendment, Code Sec. 4942(g)(4) read as follows:

(4) LIMITATION ON ADMINISTRATIVE EXPENSES ALLOCABLE TO MAKING OF CONTRIBUTIONS, GIFTS, AND GRANTS.—

(A) IN GENERAL.—The amount of the grant administrative expenses paid during any taxable year which may be taken into account as qualifying distributions shall not exceed the excess (if any) of—

(i) .65 percent of the sum of the net assets of the private foundation for such taxable year and the immediately preceding 2 taxable years, over

(ii) the aggregate amount of grant administrative expenses paid during the 2 preceding taxable years which were taken into account as qualifying distributions.

(B) GRANT ADMINISTRATIVE EXPENSES.—For purposes of this paragraph, the term "grant administrative expenses" means any administrative expenses which are allocable to the making of qualified grants.

(C) QUALIFIED GRANTS.—For purposes of this paragraph, the term "qualified grant" means any contribution, gift, or grant which is a qualifying distribution.

(D) NET ASSET.—For purposes of this paragraph, the term "net assets" means, with respect to any taxable year, the excess determined under subsection (e)(1) for such taxable year.

(E) TRANSITIONAL RULE.—In the case of any preceding taxable year which begins before January 1, 1985, the amount of the grant administrative expenses taken into account under subparagraph (A)(ii) shall not exceed .65 percent of the net assets of the private foundation for such taxable year.

(F) TERMINATION.—This paragraph shall not apply to taxable years beginning after December 31, 1990.

[¶ 5260] CODE SEC. 4943. TAXES ON EXCESS BUSINESS HOLDINGS.

(a) INITIAL TAX.—

(1) IMPOSITION.—There is hereby imposed on the excess business holdings of any private foundation in a business enterprise during any taxable year which ends during the taxable period a tax equal to *10 percent* of the value of such holdings.

* * *

[CCH Explanation at ¶ 1245. Committee Reports at ¶ 11,200.]

Amendments

• **2006, Pension Protection Act of 2006 (H.R. 4)**

H.R. 4, § 1212(c):

Amended Code Sec. 4943(a)(1) by striking "5 percent" and inserting "10 percent". **Effective** for tax years beginning after 8-17-2006.

(e) APPLICATION OF TAX TO DONOR ADVISED FUNDS.—

(1) IN GENERAL.—For purposes of this section, a donor advised fund (as defined in section 4966(d)(2)) shall be treated as a private foundation.

(2) DISQUALIFIED PERSON.—In applying this section to any donor advised fund (as so defined), the term "disqualified person" means, with respect to the donor advised fund, any person who is—

(A) described in section 4966(d)(2)(A)(iii),

(B) a member of the family of an individual described in subparagraph (A), or

(C) a 35-percent controlled entity (as defined in section 4958(f)(3) by substituting "persons described in subparagraph (A) or (B) of section 4943(e)(2)" for "persons described in subparagraph (A) or (B) of paragraph (1)" in subparagraph (A)(i) thereof).

(3) PRESENT HOLDINGS.—For purposes of this subsection, rules similar to the rules of paragraphs (4), (5), and (6) of subsection (c) shall apply to donor advised funds (as so defined), except that—

(A) "the date of the enactment of this subsection" shall be substituted for "May 26, 1969" each place it appears in paragraphs (4), (5), and (6), and

(B) "January 1, 2007" shall be substituted for "January 1, 1970" in paragraph (4)(E).

[CCH Explanation at ¶1175. Committee Reports at ¶11,350.]

Amendments

• 2006, Pension Protection Act of 2006 (H.R. 4)

H.R. 4, §1233(a):

Amended Code Sec. 4943 by adding at the end a new subsection (e). **Effective** for tax years beginning after 8-17-2006.

(f) APPLICATION OF TAX TO SUPPORTING ORGANIZATIONS.—

(1) IN GENERAL.—For purposes of this section, an organization which is described in paragraph (3) shall be treated as a private foundation.

(2) EXCEPTION.—The Secretary may exempt the excess business holdings of any organization from the application of this subsection if the Secretary determines that such holdings are consistent with the purpose or function constituting the basis for its exemption under section 501.

(3) ORGANIZATIONS DESCRIBED.—An organization is described in this paragraph if such organization is—

(A) a type III supporting organization (other than a functionally integrated type III supporting organization), or

(B) an organization which meets the requirements of subparagraphs (A) and (C) of section 509(a)(3) and which is supervised or controlled in connection with or one or more organizations described in paragraph (1) or (2) of section 509(a), but only if such organization accepts any gift or contribution from any person described in section 509(f)(2)(B).

(4) DISQUALIFIED PERSON.—

(A) IN GENERAL.—In applying this section to any organization described in paragraph (3), the term "disqualified person" means, with respect to the organization—

(i) any person who was, at any time during the 5-year period ending on the date described in subsection (a)(2)(A), in a position to exercise substantial influence over the affairs of the organization,

(ii) any member of the family (determined under section 4958(f)(4)) of an individual described in clause (i),

(iii) any 35-percent controlled entity (as defined in section 4958(f)(3) by substituting "persons described in clause (i) or (ii) of section 4943(f)(4)(A)" for "persons described in subparagraph (A) or (B) of paragraph (1)" in subparagraph (A)(i) thereof),

(iv) any person described in section 4958(c)(3)(B), and

(v) any organization—

(I) which is effectively controlled (directly or indirectly) by the same person or persons who control the organization in question, or

(II) substantially all of the contributions to which were made (directly or indirectly) by the same person or persons described in subparagraph (B) or a member of the family (within the meaning of section 4946(d)) of such a person.

(B) PERSONS DESCRIBED.—A person is described in this subparagraph if such person is—

(i) a substantial contributor to the organization (as defined in section 4958(c)(3)(C)),

(ii) an officer, director, or trustee of the organization (or an individual having powers or responsibilities similar to those of the officers, directors, or trustees of the organization), or

(iii) an owner of more than 20 percent of—

(I) the total combined voting power of a corporation,

(II) the profits interest of a partnership, or

(III) the beneficial interest of a trust or unincorporated enterprise,

which is a substantial contributor (as so defined) to the organization.

(5) TYPE III SUPPORTING ORGANIZATION; FUNCTIONALLY INTEGRATED TYPE III SUPPORTING ORGANIZATION.—For purposes of this subsection—

(A) TYPE III SUPPORTING ORGANIZATION.—The term "type III supporting organization" means an organization which meets the requirements of subparagraphs (A) and (C) of section 509(a)(3) and which is operated in connection with one or more organizations described in paragraph (1) or (2) of section 509(a).

(B) FUNCTIONALLY INTEGRATED TYPE III SUPPORTING ORGANIZATION.—The term "functionally integrated type III supporting organization" means a type III supporting organization which is not required under regulations established by the Secretary to make payments to supported organizations (as defined under section 509(f)(3)) due to the activities of the organization related to performing the functions of, or carrying out the purposes of, such supported organizations.

(6) SPECIAL RULE FOR CERTAIN HOLDINGS OF TYPE III SUPPORTING ORGANIZATIONS.—For purposes of this subsection, the term "excess business holdings" shall not include any holdings of a type III supporting organization in any business enterprise if, as of November 18, 2005, the holdings were held (and at all times thereafter, are held) for the benefit of the community pursuant to the direction of a State attorney general or a State official with jurisdiction over such organization.

(7) PRESENT HOLDINGS.—For purposes of this subsection, rules similar to the rules of paragraphs (4), (5), and (6) of subsection (c) shall apply to organizations described in section 509(a)(3), except that—

(A) "the date of the enactment of this subsection" shall be substituted for "May 26, 1969" each place it appears in paragraphs (4), (5), and (6), and

(B) "January 1, 2007" shall be substituted for "January 1, 1970" in paragraph (4)(E).

[CCH Explanation at ¶1235. Committee Reports at ¶11,360.]

Amendments

• **2006, Pension Protection Act of 2006 (H.R. 4)**

H.R. 4, §1243(a):

Amended Code Sec. 4943, as amended by this Act, by adding at the end a new subsection (f). **Effective** for tax years beginning after 8-17-2006.

[¶5265] CODE SEC. 4944. TAXES ON INVESTMENTS WHICH JEOPARDIZE CHARITABLE PURPOSE.

(a) INITIAL TAXES.—

(1) ON THE PRIVATE FOUNDATION.—If a private foundation invests any amount in such a manner as to jeopardize the carrying out of any of its exempt purposes, there is hereby imposed on the making of such investment a tax equal to *10 percent* of the amount so invested for each year (or part thereof) in the taxable period. The tax imposed by this paragraph shall be paid by the private foundation.

(2) ON THE MANAGEMENT.—In any case in which a tax is imposed by paragraph (1), there is hereby imposed on the participation of any foundation manager in the making of the investment, knowing that it is jeopardizing the carrying out of any of the foundation's exempt purposes, a tax equal to *10 percent* of the amount so invested for each year (or part thereof) in the taxable period, unless such participation is not willful and is due to reasonable cause. The tax imposed by this paragraph shall be paid by any foundation manager who participated in the making of the investment.

* * *

[CCH Explanation at ¶1245. Committee Reports at ¶11,200.]

Amendments

• **2006, Pension Protection Act of 2006 (H.R. 4)**

H.R. 4, §1212(d)(1):

Amended Code Sec. 4944(a) by striking "5 percent" both places it appears and inserting "10 percent". **Effective** for tax years beginning after 8-17-2006.

(d) SPECIAL RULES.—For purposes of subsections (a) and (b)—

* * *

(2) LIMIT FOR MANAGEMENT.—With respect to any one investment, the maximum amount of the tax imposed by subsection (a)(2) shall not exceed *$10,000*, and the maximum amount of the tax imposed by subsection (b)(2) shall not exceed *$20,000*.

[CCH Explanation at ¶1245. Committee Reports at ¶11,200.]

Amendments

• **2006, Pension Protection Act of 2006 (H.R. 4)**

H.R. 4, §1212(d)(2)(A)-(B):

Amended Code Sec. 4944(d)(2) by striking "$5,000," and inserting "$10,000,", and by striking "$10,000." and inserting "$20,000.". **Effective** for tax years beginning after 8-17-2006.

[¶5270] CODE SEC. 4945. TAXES ON TAXABLE EXPENDITURES.

(a) INITIAL TAXES.—

(1) ON THE FOUNDATION.—There is hereby imposed on each taxable expenditure (as defined in subsection (d)) a tax equal to *20 percent* of the amount thereof. The tax imposed by this paragraph shall be paid by the private foundation.

(2) ON THE MANAGEMENT.—There is hereby imposed on the agreement of any foundation manager to the making of an expenditure, knowing that it is a taxable expenditure, a tax equal to *5 percent* percent of the amount thereof, unless such agreement is not willful and is due to reasonable cause. The tax imposed by this paragraph shall be paid by any foundation manager who agreed to the making of the expenditure.

* * *

[CCH Explanation at ¶1245. Committee Reports at ¶11,200.]

Amendments

• **2006, Pension Protection Act of 2006 (H.R. 4)**

H.R. 4, §1212(e)(1)(A)-(B):

Amended Code Sec. 4945(a) by striking "10 percent" and inserting "20 percent" in paragraph (1), and by striking "2½ percent" and inserting "5 percent" in paragraph (2). **Effective** for tax years beginning after 8-17-2006.

(c) SPECIAL RULES.—For purposes of subsections (a) and (b)—

* * *

(2) LIMIT FOR MANAGEMENT.—With respect to any one taxable expenditure, the maximum amount of the tax imposed by subsection (a)(2) shall not exceed *$10,000*, and the maximum amount of the tax imposed by subsection (b)(2) shall not exceed *$20,000*.

* * *

[CCH Explanation at ¶1245. Committee Reports at ¶11,200.]

Amendments

• 2006, Pension Protection Act of 2006 (H.R. 4)

H.R. 4, §1212(e)(2)(A)-(B):

Amended Code Sec. 4945(c)(2) by striking "$5,000," and inserting "$10,000,", and by striking "$10,000." and inserting "$20,000.". **Effective** for tax years beginning after 8-17-2006.

(d) TAXABLE EXPENDITURE.—For purposes of this section, the term "taxable expenditure" means any amount paid or incurred by a private foundation—

* * *

(4) as a grant to an organization unless—

(A) such organization—

(i) is described in paragraph (1) or (2) of section 509(a),

(ii) is an organization described in section 509(a)(3) (other than an organization described in clause (i) or (ii) of section 4942(g)(4)(A)), or

(iii) is an exempt operating foundation (as defined in section 4940(d)(2)), or

(B) the private foundation exercises expenditure responsibility with respect to such grant in accordance with subsection (h), or

* * *

[CCH Explanation at ¶1240. Committee Reports at ¶11,360.]

Amendments

• 2006, Pension Protection Act of 2006 (H.R. 4)

H.R. 4, §1244(b):

Amended Code Sec. 4945(d)(4)(A). **Effective** for distributions and expenditures after 8-17-2006. Prior to amendment, Code Sec. 4945(d)(4)(A) read as follows:

(A) such organization is described in paragraph (1), (2), or (3) of section 509(a) or is an exempt operating foundation (as defined in section 4940(d)(2)), or

[¶5275] CODE SEC. 4958. TAXES ON EXCESS BENEFIT TRANSACTIONS.

* * *

(c) EXCESS BENEFIT TRANSACTION; EXCESS BENEFIT.—For purposes of this section—

* * *

(2) SPECIAL RULES FOR DONOR ADVISED FUNDS.—In the case of any donor advised fund (as defined in section 4966(d)(2))—

(A) the term "excess benefit transaction" includes any grant, loan, compensation, or other similar payment from such fund to a person described in subsection (f)(7) with respect to such fund, and

(B) the term "excess benefit" includes, with respect to any transaction described in subparagraph (A), the amount of any such grant, loan, compensation, or other similar payment.

(3) SPECIAL RULES FOR SUPPORTING ORGANIZATIONS.—

(A) IN GENERAL.—In the case of any organization described in section 509(a)(3)—

(i) the term "excess benefit transaction" includes—

(I) any grant, loan, compensation, or other similar payment provided by such organization to a person described in subparagraph (B), and

(II) any loan provided by such organization to a disqualified person (other than an organization described in paragraph (1), (2), or (4) of section 509(a)), and

(ii) the term "excess benefit" includes, with respect to any transaction described in clause (i), the amount of any such grant, loan, compensation, or other similar payment.

(B) PERSON DESCRIBED.—A person is described in this subparagraph if such person is—

(i) a substantial contributor to such organization,

(ii) a member of the family (determined under section 4958(f)(4)) of an individual described in clause (i), or

(iii) a 35-percent controlled entity (as defined in section 4958(f)(3) by substituting "persons described in clause (i) or (ii) of section 4958(c)(3)(B)" for "persons described in subparagraph (A) or (B) of paragraph (1)" in subparagraph (A)(i) thereof).

(C) SUBSTANTIAL CONTRIBUTOR.—For purposes of this paragraph—

(i) IN GENERAL.—The term "substantial contributor" means any person who contributed or bequeathed an aggregate amount of more than $5,000 to the organization, if such amount is more than 2 percent of the total contributions and bequests received by the organization before the close of the taxable year of the organization in which the contribution or bequest is received by the organization from such person. In the case of a trust, such term also means the creator of the trust. Rules similar to the rules of subparagraphs (B) and (C) of section 507(d)(2) shall apply for purposes of this subparagraph.

(ii) EXCEPTION.—Such term shall not include any organization described in paragraph (1), (2), or (4) of section 509(a).

(4) AUTHORITY TO INCLUDE CERTAIN OTHER PRIVATE INUREMENT.—To the extent provided in regulations prescribed by the Secretary, the term "excess benefit transaction" includes any transaction in which the amount of any economic benefit provided to or for the use of a disqualified person is determined in whole or in part by the revenues of 1 or more activities of the organization but only if such transaction results in inurement not permitted under paragraph (3) or (4) of section 501(c), as the case may be. In the case of any such transaction, the excess benefit shall be the amount of the inurement not so permitted.

[CCH Explanation at ¶1170 and ¶1230. Committee Reports at ¶11,350 and ¶11,360.]

Amendments

• 2006, Pension Protection Act of 2006 (H.R. 4)

H.R. 4, §1232(b)(1):

Amended Code Sec. 4958(c) by redesignating paragraph (2) as paragraph (3) and by inserting after paragraph (1) a new paragraph (2). **Effective** for transactions occurring after 8-17-2006.

H.R. 4, §1242(b):

Amended Code Sec. 4958(c), as amended by this Act, by redesignating paragraph (3) as paragraph (4) and by inserting after paragraph (2) a new paragraph (3). **Effective** for transactions occurring after 7-25-2006.

(d) SPECIAL RULES.—For purposes of this section—

* * *

(2) LIMIT FOR MANAGEMENT.—With respect to any 1 excess benefit transaction, the maximum amount of the tax imposed by subsection (a)(2) shall not exceed *$20,000*.

* * *

[CCH Explanation at ¶1245. Committee Reports at ¶11,200.]

Amendments

• 2006, Pension Protection Act of 2006 (H.R. 4)

H.R. 4, §1212(a)(3):

Amended Code Sec. 4958(d)(2) by striking "$10,000" and inserting "$20,000". **Effective** for tax years beginning after 8-17-2006.

(f) OTHER DEFINITIONS.—For purposes of this section—

(1) DISQUALIFIED PERSON.—The term "disqualified person" means, with respect to any transaction—

(A) any person who was, at any time during the 5-year period ending on the date of such transaction, in a position to exercise substantial influence over the affairs of the organization,

(B) a member of the family of an individual described in subparagraph (A),

(C) a 35-percent controlled entity,

(D) any person who is described in subparagraph (A), (B), or (C) with respect to an organization described in section 509(a)(3) and organized and operated exclusively for the benefit of, to perform the functions of, or to carry out the purposes of the applicable tax-exempt organization.

(E) which involves a donor advised fund (as defined in section 4966(d)(2)), any person who is described in paragraph (7) with respect to such donor advised fund (as so defined), and

(F) which involves a sponsoring organization (as defined in section 4966(d)(1)), any person who is described in paragraph (8) with respect to such sponsoring organization (as so defined).

* * *

(6) CORRECTION.—The terms "correction" and "correct" mean, with respect to any excess benefit transaction, undoing the excess benefit to the extent possible, and taking any additional measures necessary to place the organization in a financial position not worse than that in which it would be if the disqualified person were dealing under the highest fiduciary standards, *except that in the case of any correction of an excess benefit transaction described in subsection (c)(2), no amount repaid in a manner prescribed by the Secretary may be held in any donor advised fund.*

(7) DONORS AND DONOR ADVISORS.—For purposes of paragraph (1)(E), a person is described in this paragraph if such person—

(A) is described in section 4966(d)(2)(A)(iii),

(B) is a member of the family of an individual described in subparagraph (A), or

(C) is a 35-percent controlled entity (as defined in paragraph (3) by substituting "persons described in subparagraph (A) or (B) of paragraph (7)" for "persons described in subparagraph (A) or (B) of paragraph (1)" in subparagraph (A)(i) thereof).

(8) INVESTMENT ADVISORS.—For purposes of paragraph (1)(F)—

(A) IN GENERAL.—A person is described in this paragraph if such person—

(i) is an investment advisor,

(ii) is a member of the family of an individual described in clause (i), or

(iii) is a 35-percent controlled entity (as defined in paragraph (3) by substituting "persons described in clause (i) or (ii) of paragraph (8)(A)" for "persons described in subparagraph (A) or (B) of paragraph (1)" in subparagraph (A)(i) thereof).

(B) INVESTMENT ADVISOR DEFINED.—For purposes of subparagraph (A), the term "investment advisor" means, with respect to any sponsoring organization (as defined in section 4966(d)(1)), any person (other than an employee of such organization) compensated by such organization for managing the investment of, or providing investment advice with respect to, assets maintained in donor advised funds (as defined in section 4966(d)(2)) owned by such organization.

[CCH Explanation at ¶1170 and ¶1230. Committee Reports at ¶11,350 and ¶11,360.]

Amendments

• 2006, Pension Protection Act of 2006 (H.R. 4)

H.R. 4, §1232(a)(1):

Amended Code Sec. 4958(f)(1) by striking "and" at the end of subparagraph (B), by striking the period at the end of subparagraph (C) and inserting a comma, and by adding after subparagraph (C) new subparagraphs (D) and (E). **Effective** for transactions occurring after 8-17-2006.

H.R. 4, §1232(a)(2):

Amended Code Sec. 4958(f) by adding at the end new paragraphs (7) and (8). **Effective** for transactions occurring after 8-17-2006.

H.R. 4, §1232(b)(2):

Amended Code Sec. 4958(f)(6) by inserting ", except that in the case of any correction of an excess benefit transaction described in subsection (c)(2), no amount repaid in a manner prescribed by the Secretary may be held in any donor advised fund" after "standards". **Effective** for transactions occurring after 8-17-2006.

H.R. 4, §1242(a):

Amended Code Sec. 4958(f)(1), as amended by this Act, by redesignating subparagraphs (D) and (E) as subparagraphs (E) and (F), respectively, and by adding after subparagraph (C) a new subparagraph (D). **Effective** for transactions occurring after 8-17-2006.

[¶5280] CODE SEC. 4963. DEFINITIONS.

(a) FIRST TIER TAX.—For purposes of this subchapter, the term "first tier tax" means any tax imposed by subsection (a) of section 4941, 4942, 4943, 4944, 4945, 4951, 4952, 4955, 4958, *4966, 4967,* 4971, or 4975.

* * *

[CCH Explanation at ¶1160 and ¶1165. Committee Reports at ¶11,350.]

Amendments

- **2006, Pension Protection Act of 2006 (H.R. 4)**

H.R. 4, §1231(b)(1):

Amended Code Sec. 4963(a) by inserting "4966, 4967," after "4958,". **Effective** for tax years beginning after 8-17-2006.

(c) TAXABLE EVENT.—For purposes of this subchapter, the term "taxable event" means any act (or failure to act) giving rise to liability for tax under section 4941, 4942, 4943, 4944, 4945, 4951, 4952, 4955, 4958, *4966, 4967,* 4971, or 4975.

* * *

[CCH Explanation at ¶1160 and ¶1165. Committee Reports at ¶11,350.]

Amendments

- **2006, Pension Protection Act of 2006 (H.R. 4)**

H.R. 4, §1231(b)(1):

Amended Code Sec. 4963(c) by inserting "4966, 4967," after "4958,". **Effective** for tax years beginning after 8-17-2006.

[¶5285] *CODE SEC. 4966. TAXES ON TAXABLE DISTRIBUTIONS.*

(a) IMPOSITION OF TAXES.—

(1) ON THE SPONSORING ORGANIZATION.—There is hereby imposed on each taxable distribution a tax equal to 20 percent of the amount thereof. The tax imposed by this paragraph shall be paid by the sponsoring organization with respect to the donor advised fund.

(2) ON THE FUND MANAGEMENT.—There is hereby imposed on the agreement of any fund manager to the making of a distribution, knowing that it is a taxable distribution, a tax equal to 5 percent of the amount thereof. The tax imposed by this paragraph shall be paid by any fund manager who agreed to the making of the distribution.

(b) SPECIAL RULES.—For purposes of subsection (a)—

(1) JOINT AND SEVERAL LIABILITY.—If more than one person is liable under subsection (a)(2) with respect to the making of a taxable distribution, all such persons shall be jointly and severally liable under such paragraph with respect to such distribution.

(2) LIMIT FOR MANAGEMENT.—With respect to any one taxable distribution, the maximum amount of the tax imposed by subsection (a)(2) shall not exceed $10,000.

(c) TAXABLE DISTRIBUTION.—For purposes of this section—

(1) IN GENERAL.—The term "taxable distribution" means any distribution from a donor advised fund—

(A) to any natural person, or

(B) to any other person if—

(i) such distribution is for any purpose other than one specified in section 170(c)(2)(B), or

(ii) the sponsoring organization does not exercise expenditure responsibility with respect to such distribution in accordance with section 4945(h).

(2) EXCEPTIONS.—Such term shall not include any distribution from a donor advised fund—

(A) to any organization described in section 170(b)(1)(A) (other than a disqualified supporting organization),

(B) to the sponsoring organization of such donor advised fund, or

(C) to any other donor advised fund.

(d) DEFINITIONS.—For purposes of this subchapter—

(1) SPONSORING ORGANIZATION.—The term "sponsoring organization" means any organization which—

(A) is described in section 170(c) (other than in paragraph (1) thereof, and without regard to paragraph (2)(A) thereof),

(B) is not a private foundation (as defined in section 509(a)), and

(C) maintains 1 or more donor advised funds.

(2) DONOR ADVISED FUND.—

(A) IN GENERAL.—Except as provided in subparagraph (B) or (C), the term "donor advised fund" means a fund or account—

(i) which is separately identified by reference to contributions of a donor or donors,

(ii) which is owned and controlled by a sponsoring organization, and

(iii) with respect to which a donor (or any person appointed or designated by such donor) has, or reasonably expects to have, advisory privileges with respect to the distribution or investment of amounts held in such fund or account by reason of the donor's status as a donor.

(B) EXCEPTIONS.—The term "donor advised fund" shall not include any fund or account—

(i) which makes distributions only to a single identified organization or governmental entity, or

(ii) with respect to which a person described in subparagraph (A)(iii) advises as to which individuals receive grants for travel, study, or other similar purposes, if—

(I) such person's advisory privileges are performed exclusively by such person in the person's capacity as a member of a committee all of the members of which are appointed by the sponsoring organization,

(II) no combination of persons described in subparagraph (A)(iii) (or persons related to such persons) control, directly or indirectly, such committee, and

(III) all grants from such fund or account are awarded on an objective and nondiscriminatory basis pursuant to a procedure approved in advance by the board of directors of the sponsoring organization, and such procedure is designed to ensure that all such grants meet the requirements of paragraphs (1), (2), or (3) of section 4945(g).

(C) SECRETARIAL AUTHORITY.—The Secretary may exempt a fund or account not described in subparagraph (B) from treatment as a donor advised fund—

(i) if such fund or account is advised by a committee not directly or indirectly controlled by the donor or any person appointed or designated by the donor for the purpose of advising with respect to distributions from such fund (and any related parties), or

(ii) if such fund benefits a single identified charitable purpose.

(3) FUND MANAGER.—The term "fund manager" means, with respect to any sponsoring organization—

(A) an officer, director, or trustee of such sponsoring organization (or an individual having powers or responsibilities similar to those of officers, directors, or trustees of the sponsoring organization), and

(B) with respect to any act (or failure to act), the employees of the sponsoring organization having authority or responsibility with respect to such act (or failure to act).

(4) DISQUALIFIED SUPPORTING ORGANIZATION.—

(A) IN GENERAL.—The term "disqualified supporting organization" means, with respect to any distribution—

(i) any type III supporting organization (as defined in section 4943(f)(5)(A)) which is not a functionally integrated type III supporting organization (as defined in section 4943(f)(5)(B)), and

(ii) any organization which is described in subparagraph (B) or (C) if—

(I) the donor or any person designated by the donor for the purpose of advising with respect to distributions from a donor advised fund (and any related parties) directly or indirectly controls a supported organization (as defined in section 509(f)(3)) of such organization, or

(II) the Secretary determines by regulations that a distribution to such organization otherwise is inappropriate.

(B) TYPE I AND TYPE II SUPPORTING ORGANIZATIONS.—An organization is described in this subparagraph if the organization meets the requirements of subparagraphs (A) and (C) of section 509(a)(3) and is—

(i) operated, supervised, or controlled by one or more organizations described in paragraph (1) or (2) of section 509(a), or

(ii) supervised or controlled in connection with one or more such organizations.

(C) FUNCTIONALLY INTEGRATED TYPE III SUPPORTING ORGANIZATIONS.—An organization is described in this subparagraph if the organization is a functionally integrated type III supporting organization (as defined under section 4943(f)(5)(B)).

[CCH Explanation at ¶1160. Committee Reports at ¶11,350.]

Amendments

• 2006, Pension Protection Act of 2006 (H.R. 4)

H.R. 4, §1231(a):

Amended chapter 42, as amended by the Tax Increase Prevention and Reconciliation Act of 2005 (P.L. 109-222), by adding at the end a new subchapter G (Code Secs. 4966-4967). **Effective** for tax years beginning after 8-17-2006.

[¶5290] *CODE SEC. 4967. TAXES ON PROHIBITED BENEFITS.*

(a) IMPOSITION OF TAXES.—

(1) ON THE DONOR, DONOR ADVISOR, OR RELATED PERSON.—There is hereby imposed on the advice of any person described in subsection (d) to have a sponsoring organization make a distribution from a donor advised fund which results in such person or any other person described in subsection (d) receiving, directly or indirectly, a more than incidental benefit as a result of such distribution, a tax equal to 125 percent of such benefit. The tax imposed by this paragraph shall be paid by any person described in subsection (d) who advises as to the distribution or who receives such a benefit as a result of the distribution.

(2) ON THE FUND MANAGEMENT.—There is hereby imposed on the agreement of any fund manager to the making of a distribution, knowing that such distribution would confer a benefit described in paragraph (1), a tax equal to 10 percent of the amount of such benefit. The tax imposed by this paragraph shall be paid by any fund manager who agreed to the making of the distribution.

(b) EXCEPTION.—No tax shall be imposed under this section with respect to any distribution if a tax has been imposed with respect to such distribution under section 4958.

(c) SPECIAL RULES.—For purposes of subsection (a)—

(1) JOINT AND SEVERAL LIABILITY.—If more than one person is liable under paragraph (1) or (2) of subsection (a) with respect to a distribution described in subsection (a), all such persons shall be jointly and severally liable under such paragraph with respect to such distribution.

(2) LIMIT FOR MANAGEMENT.—With respect to any one distribution described in subsection (a), the maximum amount of the tax imposed by subsection (a)(2) shall not exceed $10,000.

(d) PERSON DESCRIBED.—A person is described in this subsection if such person is described in section 4958(f)(7) with respect to a donor advised fund.

[CCH Explanation at ¶1165. Committee Reports at ¶11,350.]

Amendments

• 2006, Pension Protection Act of 2006 (H.R. 4)

H.R. 4, §1231(a):

Amended chapter 42, as amended by the Tax Increase Prevention and Reconciliation Act of 2005 (P.L. 109-222), by adding at the end a new subchapter G (Code Secs. 4966-4967). **Effective** for tax years beginning after 8-17-2006.

[¶5295] CODE SEC. 4971. TAXES ON FAILURE TO MEET MINIMUM FUNDING STANDARDS.

(a) INITIAL TAX.—If at any time during any taxable year an employer maintains a plan to which section 412 applies, there is hereby imposed for the taxable year a tax equal to—

(1) in the case of a single-employer plan, 10 percent of the aggregate unpaid minimum required contributions for all plan years remaining unpaid as of the end of any plan year ending with or within the taxable year, and

(2) in the case of a multiemployer plan, 5 percent of the accumulated funding deficiency determined under section 431 as of the end of any plan year ending with or within the taxable year.

[CCH Explanation at ¶210 and ¶305. Committee Reports at ¶10,010.]

Amendments

• 2006, Pension Protection Act of 2006 (H.R. 4)

H.R. 4, §114(e)(1):

Amended Code Sec. 4971(a). **Effective** 8-17-2006. Prior to amendment, Code Sec. 4971(a) read as follows:

(a) INITIAL TAX.—For each taxable year of an employer who maintains a plan to which section 412 applies, there is hereby imposed a tax of 10 percent (5 percent in the case of a multiemployer plan) on the amount of the accumulated funding deficiency under the plan, determined as of the end of the plan year ending with or within such taxable year.

(b) ADDITIONAL TAX.—If—

(1) a tax is imposed under subsection (a)(1) on any unpaid required minimum contribution and such amount remains unpaid as of the close of the taxable period, or

(2) a tax is imposed under subsection (a)(2) on any accumulated funding deficiency and the accumulated funding deficiency is not corrected within the taxable period,

there is hereby imposed a tax equal to 100 percent of the unpaid minimum required contribution or accumulated funding deficiency, whichever is applicable, to the extent not so paid or corrected.

[CCH Explanation at ¶210 and ¶305. Committee Reports at ¶10,010.]

Amendments

• 2006, Pension Protection Act of 2006 (H.R. 4)

H.R. 4, §114(e)(1):

Amended Code Sec. 4971(b). **Effective** 8-17-2006. Prior to amendment, Code Sec. 4971(b) read as follows:

(b) ADDITIONAL TAX.—In any case in which an initial tax is imposed by subsection (a) on an accumulated funding deficiency and such accumulated funding deficiency is not corrected within the taxable period, there is hereby imposed a tax equal to 100 percent of such accumulated funding deficiency to the extent not corrected.

(c) DEFINITIONS.—For purposes of this section—

(1) ACCUMULATED FUNDING DEFICIENCY.—The term "accumulated funding deficiency" has the meaning given to such term by *section 431*.

* * *

(4) UNPAID MINIMUM REQUIRED CONTRIBUTION.—

(A) IN GENERAL.—The term "unpaid minimum required contribution" means, with respect to any plan year, any minimum required contribution under section 430 for the plan year which is not paid on or before the due date (as determined under section 430(j)(1)) for the plan year.

(B) ORDERING RULE.—Any payment to or under a plan for any plan year shall be allocated first to unpaid minimum required contributions for all preceding plan years on a first-in, first-out basis and then to the minimum required contribution under section 430 for the plan year.

* * *

[CCH Explanation at ¶ 210 and ¶ 305. Committee Reports at ¶ 10,010 and ¶ 10,090.]

Amendments

• 2006, Pension Protection Act of 2006 (H.R. 4)

H.R. 4, § 114(e)(2)(A)-(B):

Amended Code Sec. 4971(c) by striking "the last two sentences of section 412(a)" in paragraph (1) and inserting "section 431", and by adding at the end a new paragraph (4). **Effective** 8-17-2006.

(e) LIABILITY FOR TAX.—

(1) IN GENERAL.—Except as provided in paragraph (2), the tax imposed by subsection (a), (b), or (f) shall be paid by the employer responsible for contributing to or under the plan the amount described in *section 412(a)(1)(A).*

»»→ Caution: Code Sec. 4971(e)(2), below, as amended by H.R. 4, applies generally with respect to plan years beginning after 2007. For sunset provision, see H.R. 4, § 221(c), in the amendment notes.

(2) JOINT AND SEVERAL LIABILITY WHERE EMPLOYER MEMBER OF CONTROLLED GROUP.—

(A) IN GENERAL.—*If an* employer referred to in paragraph (1) is a member of a controlled group, each member of such group shall be jointly and severally liable for the tax imposed by subsection (a), (b), *(f), or (g).*

(B) CONTROLLED GROUP.—For purposes of subparagraph (A), the term "controlled group" means any group treated as a single employer under subsection (b), (c), (m), or (o) of section 414.

[CCH Explanation at ¶ 210 and ¶ 305. Committee Reports at ¶ 10,010.]

Amendments

• 2006, Pension Protection Act of 2006 (H.R. 4)

H.R. 4, § 114(e)(3):

Amended Code Sec. 4971(e)(1) by striking "section 412(b)(3)(A)" and inserting "section 412(a)(1)(A)". **Effective** 8-17-2006.

H.R. 4, § 212(b)(2)(A)-(B):

Amended Code Sec. 4971(c)(2) [4971(e)(2)] by striking "In the case of a plan other than a multiemployer plan, if the" and inserting "If an", and by striking "or (f)" and inserting "(f), or (g)". **Effective** generally with respect to plan years beginning after 2007. For special rules, see Act Sec. 212(e)(2)-(3) in the amendment notes following Code Sec. 4971(g), below.

H.R. 4, § 221(c), provides:

(c) SUNSET.—

(1) IN GENERAL.—Except as provided in this subsection, notwithstanding any other provision of this Act, the provisions of, and the amendments made by, sections 201(b), 202, and 212 shall not apply to plan years beginning after December 31, 2014.

(2) FUNDING IMPROVEMENT AND REHABILITATION PLANS.—If a plan is operating under a funding improvement or rehabilitation plan under section 305 of such Act or 432 of such Code for its last year beginning before January 1, 2015, such plan shall continue to operate under such funding improvement or rehabilitation plan during any period after December 31, 2014, such funding improvement or rehabilitation plan is in effect and all provisions of such Act or Code relating to the operation of such funding improvement or rehabilitation plan shall continue in effect during such period.

(f) FAILURE TO PAY LIQUIDITY SHORTFALL.—

(1) IN GENERAL.—In the case of a plan to which *section 430(j)(4)* applies, there is hereby imposed a tax of 10 percent of the excess (if any) of—

(A) the amount of the liquidity shortfall for any quarter, over

(B) the amount of such shortfall which is paid by the required installment under *section 430(j)* for such quarter (but only if such installment is paid on or before the due date for such installment).

* * *

[CCH Explanation at ¶ 210 and ¶ 305. Committee Reports at ¶ 10,010.]

Amendments

• 2006, Pension Protection Act of 2006 (H.R. 4)

H.R. 4, §114(e)(4)(A)-(B):

Amended Code Sec. 4971(f)(1) by striking "section 412(m)(5)" and inserting "section 430(j)(4)", and by striking "section 412(m)" and inserting "section 430(j)". **Effective** 8-17-2006.

»»→ Caution: Code Sec. 4971(g), below, as added by H.R. 4, applies generally with respect to plan years beginning after 2007. For sunset provision, see H.R. 4, §221(c), in the amendment notes.

(g) MULTIEMPLOYER PLANS IN ENDANGERED OR CRITICAL STATUS.—

(1) IN GENERAL.—Except as provided in this subsection—

(A) no tax shall be imposed under this section for a taxable year with respect to a multiemployer plan if, for the plan years ending with or within the taxable year, the plan is in critical status pursuant to section 432, and

(B) any tax imposed under this subsection for a taxable year with respect to a multiemployer plan if, for the plan years ending with or within the taxable year, the plan is in endangered status pursuant to section 432 shall be in addition to any other tax imposed by this section.

(2) FAILURE TO COMPLY WITH FUNDING IMPROVEMENT OR REHABILITATION PLAN.—

(A) IN GENERAL.—If any funding improvement plan or rehabilitation plan in effect under section 432 with respect to a multiemployer plan requires an employer to make a contribution to the plan, there is hereby imposed a tax on each failure of the employer to make the required contribution within the time required under such plan.

(B) AMOUNT OF TAX.—The amount of the tax imposed by subparagraph (A) shall be equal to the amount of the required contribution the employer failed to make in a timely manner.

(C) LIABILITY FOR TAX.—The tax imposed by subparagraph (A) shall be paid by the employer responsible for contributing to or under the rehabilitation plan which fails to make the contribution.

(3) FAILURE TO MEET REQUIREMENTS FOR PLANS IN ENDANGERED OR CRITICAL STATUS.—If—

(A) a plan which is in seriously endangered status fails to meet the applicable benchmarks by the end of the funding improvement period, or

(B) a plan which is in critical status either—

(i) fails to meet the requirements of section 432(e) by the end of the rehabilitation period, or

(ii) has received a certification under section 432(b)(3)(A)(ii) for 3 consecutive plan years that the plan is not making the scheduled progress in meeting its requirements under the rehabilitation plan,

the plan shall be treated as having an accumulated funding deficiency for purposes of this section for the last plan year in such funding improvement, rehabilitation, or 3-consecutive year period (and each succeeding plan year until such benchmarks or requirements are met) in an amount equal to the greater of the amount of the contributions necessary to meet such benchmarks or requirements or the amount of such accumulated funding deficiency without regard to this paragraph.

(4) FAILURE TO ADOPT REHABILITATION PLAN.—

(A) IN GENERAL.—In the case of a multiemployer plan which is in critical status, there is hereby imposed a tax on the failure of such plan to adopt a rehabilitation plan within the time prescribed under section 432.

(B) AMOUNT OF TAX.—The amount of the tax imposed under subparagraph (A) with respect to any plan sponsor for any taxable year shall be the greater of—

(i) the amount of tax imposed under subsection (a) for the taxable year (determined without regard to this subsection), or

(ii) the amount equal to $1,100 multiplied by the number of days during the taxable year which are included in the period beginning on the first day of the 240-day period described in section 432(e)(1)(A) and ending on the day on which the rehabilitation plan is adopted.

(C) LIABILITY FOR TAX.—

(i) IN GENERAL.—The tax imposed by subparagraph (A) shall be paid by each plan sponsor.

(ii) PLAN SPONSOR.—For purposes of clause (i), the term "plan sponsor" in the case of a multiemployer plan means the association, committee, joint board of trustees, or other similar group of representatives of the parties who establish or maintain the plan.

(5) WAIVER.—In the case of a failure described in paragraph (2) or (3) which is due to reasonable cause and not to willful neglect, the Secretary may waive part or all of the tax imposed by this subsection. For purposes of this paragraph, reasonable cause includes unanticipated and material market fluctuations, the loss of a significant contributing employer, or other factors to the extent that the payment of tax under this subsection with respect to the failure would be excessive or otherwise inequitable relative to the failure involved.

(6) TERMS USED IN SECTION 432.—For purposes of this subsection, any term used in this subsection which is also used in section 432 shall have the meaning given such term by section 432.

[CCH Explanation at ¶310. Committee Reports at ¶10,090.]

Amendments

• 2006, Pension Protection Act of 2006 (H.R. 4)

H.R. 4, §212(b)(1):

Amended Code Sec. 4971 by redesignating subsection (g) as subsection (h) and by inserting after subsection (f) a new subsection (g). **Effective** generally with respect to plan years beginning after 2007. For special rules, see Act Sec. 212(e)(2)-(3), below.

H.R. 4, §212(e)(2)-(3), provides:

(2) SPECIAL RULE FOR CERTAIN NOTICES.—In any case in which a plan's actuary certifies that it is reasonably expected that a multiemployer plan will be in critical status under section 305(b)(3) of the Employee Retirement Income Security Act of 1974, as added by this section, with respect to the first plan year beginning after 2007, the notice required under subparagraph (D) of such section may be provided at any time after the date of enactment, so long as it is provided on or before the last date for providing the notice under such subparagraph.

(3) SPECIAL RULE FOR CERTAIN RESTORED BENEFITS.—In the case of a multiemployer plan—

(A) with respect to which benefits were reduced pursuant to a plan amendment adopted on or after January 1, 2002, and before June 30, 2005, and

(B) which, pursuant to the plan document, the trust agreement, or a formal written communication from the plan sponsor to participants provided before June 30, 2005, provided for the restoration of such benefits,

the amendments made by this section shall not apply to such benefit restorations to the extent that any restriction on the providing or accrual of such benefits would otherwise apply by reason of such amendments.

H.R. 4, §221(c), provides:

(c) SUNSET.—

(1) IN GENERAL.—Except as provided in this subsection, notwithstanding any other provision of this Act, the provisions of, and the amendments made by, sections 201(b), 202, and 212 shall not apply to plan years beginning after December 31, 2014.

(2) FUNDING IMPROVEMENT AND REHABILITATION PLANS.—If a plan is operating under a funding improvement or rehabilitation plan under section 305 of such Act or 432 of such Code for its last year beginning before January 1, 2015, such plan shall continue to operate under such funding improvement or rehabilitation plan during any period after December 31, 2014, such funding improvement or rehabilitation plan is in effect and all provisions of such Act or Code relating to the operation of such funding improvement or rehabilitation plan shall continue in effect during such period.

»»→ Caution: Former Code Sec. 4971(g) was redesignated as Code Sec. 4971(h), below, by H.R. 4, generally applicable with respect to plan years beginning after 2007. For sunset provision, see H.R. 4, §221(c), in the amendment notes.

(h) CROSS REFERENCES.—

* * *

[CCH Explanation at ¶310. Committee Reports at ¶10,090.]

Amendments

• 2006, Pension Protection Act of 2006 (H.R. 4)

H.R. 4, §212(b)(1):

Amended Code Sec. 4971 by redesignating subsection (g) as subsection (h). **Effective** generally with respect to plan years beginning after 2007. For special rules, see Act Sec. 212(e)(2)-(3) in the amendment notes following Code Sec. 4971(g), above.

H.R. 4, §221(c), provides:

(c) SUNSET.—

(1) IN GENERAL.—Except as provided in this subsection, notwithstanding any other provision of this Act, the provisions of, and the amendments made by, sections 201(b), 202, and 212 shall not apply to plan years beginning after December 31, 2014.

(2) FUNDING IMPROVEMENT AND REHABILITATION PLANS.—If a plan is operating under a funding improvement or rehabilitation plan under section 305 of such Act or 432 of such Code for its last year beginning before January 1, 2015, such plan shall continue to operate under such funding improvement or rehabilitation plan during any period after December 31, 2014, such funding improvement or rehabilitation plan is in effect and all provisions of such Act or Code relating to the operation of such funding improvement or rehabilitation plan shall continue in effect during such period.

[¶5300] CODE SEC. 4972. TAX ON NONDEDUCTIBLE CONTRIBUTIONS TO QUALIFIED EMPLOYER PLANS.

* * *

(c) NONDEDUCTIBLE CONTRIBUTIONS.—For purposes of this section—

* * *

(6) EXCEPTIONS.—In determining the amount of nondeductible contributions for any taxable year, there shall not be taken into account—

(A) so much of the contributions to 1 or more defined contribution plans which are not deductible when contributed solely because of section 404(a)(7) as does not exceed the amount of contributions described in section 401(m)(4)(A), or

* * *

(7) DEFINED BENEFIT PLAN EXCEPTION.—In determining the amount of nondeductible contributions for any taxable year, an employer may elect for such year not to take into account any contributions to a defined benefit plan *except, in the case of a multiemployer plan, to the extent that such contributions exceed the full-funding limitation (as defined in section 431(c)(6))*. For purposes of this paragraph, the deductible limits under section 404(a)(7) shall first be applied to amounts contributed to defined contribution plans and then to amounts described in this paragraph. If an employer makes an election under this paragraph for a taxable year, paragraph (6) shall not apply to such employer for such taxable year.

* * *

[CCH Explanation at ¶210 and ¶715. Committee Reports at ¶10,010 and ¶10,580.]

Amendments

• 2006, Pension Protection Act of 2006 (H.R. 4)

H.R. 4, §114(e)(5):

Amended Code Sec. 4972(c)(7) by striking "except to the extent that such contributions exceed the full-funding limitation (as defined in section 412(c)(7), determined without regard to subparagraph (A)(i)(I) thereof)" and inserting "except, in the case of a multiemployer plan, to the extent that such contributions exceed the full-funding limitation (as defined in section 431(c)(6))". **Effective** 8-17-2006.

H.R. 4, §803(c):

Amended Code Sec. 4972(c)(6)(A). **Effective** for contributions for tax years beginning after 12-31-2005. Prior to amendment, Code Sec. 4972(c)(6)(A) read as follows:

(A) so much of the contributions to 1 or more defined contribution plans which are not deductible when contributed solely because of section 404(a)(7) as does not exceed the greater of—

(i) the amount of contributions not in excess of 6 percent of compensation (within the meaning of section 404(a) and as adjusted under section 404(a)(12)) paid or accrued (during the taxable year for which the contributions were made) to beneficiaries under the plans, or

(ii) the amount of contributions described in section 401(m)(4)(A), or

[¶5305] CODE SEC. 4975. TAX ON PROHIBITED TRANSACTIONS.

* * *

(d) EXEMPTIONS.—Except as provided in subsection (f)(6), the prohibitions provided in subsection (c) shall not apply to—

* * *

(15) a merger of multiemployer plans, or the transfer of assets or liabilities between multiemployer plans, determined by the Pension Benefit Guaranty Corporation to meet the requirements of section 4231 of such Act, but this paragraph shall not apply with respect to the application of subsection (c)(1)(E) or (F);

(16) a sale of stock held by a trust which constitutes an individual retirement account under section 408(a) to the individual for whose benefit such account is established if—

(A) such stock is in a bank (as defined in section 581) or a depository institution holding company (as defined in section 3(w)(1) of the Federal Deposit Insurance Act (12 U.S.C. 1813(w)(1)),

(B) such stock is held by such trust as of the date of the enactment of this paragraph,

(C) such sale is pursuant to an election under section 1362(a) by such bank or company,

(D) such sale is for fair market value at the time of sale (as established by an independent appraiser) and the terms of the sale are otherwise at least as favorable to such trust as the terms that would apply on a sale to an unrelated party,

(E) such trust does not pay any commissions, costs, or other expenses in connection with the sale, and

(F) the stock is sold in a single transaction for cash not later than 120 days after the S corporation election is made;

→ Caution: Code Sec. 4975(d)(17), below, as added by H.R. 4, applies with respect to advice referred to in Code Sec. 4975(c)(3)(B) provided after December 31, 2006.

(17) Any transaction in connection with the provision of investment advice described in subsection (e)(3)(B) to a participant or beneficiary in a plan and that permits such participant or beneficiary to direct the investment of plan assets in an individual account, if—

(A) the transaction is—

(i) the provision of the investment advice to the participant or beneficiary of the plan with respect to a security or other property available as an investment under the plan,

(ii) the acquisition, holding, or sale of a security or other property available as an investment under the plan pursuant to the investment advice, or

(iii) the direct or indirect receipt of fees or other compensation by the fiduciary adviser or an affiliate thereof (or any employee, agent, or registered representative of the fiduciary adviser or affiliate) in connection with the provision of the advice or in connection with an acquisition, holding, or sale of a security or other property available as an investment under the plan pursuant to the investment advice; and

(B) the requirements of subsection (f)(8) are met,

(18) any transaction involving the purchase or sale of securities, or other property (as determined by the Secretary of Labor), between a plan and a party in interest (other than a fiduciary described in subsection (e)(3)(B)) with respect to a plan if—

(A) the transaction involves a block trade,

(B) at the time of the transaction, the interest of the plan (together with the interests of any other plans maintained by the same plan sponsor), does not exceed 10 percent of the aggregate size of the block trade,

(C) the terms of the transaction, including the price, are at least as favorable to the plan as an arm's length transaction, and

(D) the compensation associated with the purchase and sale is not greater than the compensation associated with an arm's length transaction with an unrelated party,

(19) any transaction involving the purchase or sale of securities, or other property (as determined by the Secretary of Labor), between a plan and a party in interest if—

(A) the transaction is executed through an electronic communication network, alternative trading system, or similar execution system or trading venue subject to regulation and oversight by—

(i) the applicable Federal regulating entity, or

(ii) such foreign regulatory entity as the Secretary of Labor may determine by regulation,

(B) either—

(i) the transaction is effected pursuant to rules designed to match purchases and sales at the best price available through the execution system in accordance with applicable rules of the Securities and Exchange Commission or other relevant governmental authority, or

(ii) neither the execution system nor the parties to the transaction take into account the identity of the parties in the execution of trades,

(C) the price and compensation associated with the purchase and sale are not greater than the price and compensation associated with an arm's length transaction with an unrelated party,

(D) if the party in interest has an ownership interest in the system or venue described in subparagraph (A), the system or venue has been authorized by the plan sponsor or other independent fiduciary for transactions described in this paragraph, and

(E) not less than 30 days prior to the initial transaction described in this paragraph executed through any system or venue described in subparagraph (A), a plan fiduciary is provided written or electronic notice of the execution of such transaction through such system or venue,

(20) transactions described in subparagraphs (A), (B), and (D) of subsection (c)(1) between a plan and a person that is a party in interest other than a fiduciary (or an affiliate) who has or exercises any discretionary authority or control with respect to the investment of the plan assets involved in the transaction or renders investment advice (within the meaning of subsection (e)(3)(B)) with respect to those assets, solely by reason of providing services to the plan or solely by reason of a relationship to such a service provider described in subparagraph (F), (G), (H), or (I) of subsection (e)(2), or both, but only if in connection with such transaction the plan receives no less, nor pays no more, than adequate consideration,

(21) any foreign exchange transactions, between a bank or broker-dealer (or any affiliate of either) and a plan (as defined in this section) with respect to which such bank or broker-dealer (or affiliate) is a trustee, custodian, fiduciary, or other party in interest person, if—

(A) the transaction is in connection with the purchase, holding, or sale of securities or other investment assets (other than a foreign exchange transaction unrelated to any other investment in securities or other investment assets),

(B) at the time the foreign exchange transaction is entered into, the terms of the transaction are not less favorable to the plan than the terms generally available in comparable arm's length foreign exchange transactions between unrelated parties, or the terms afforded by the bank or broker-dealer (or any affiliate of either) in comparable arm's-length foreign exchange transactions involving unrelated parties,

(C) the exchange rate used by such bank or broker-dealer (or affiliate) for a particular foreign exchange transaction does not deviate by more or less than 3 percent from the interbank bid and asked rates for transactions of comparable size and maturity at the time of the transaction as displayed on an independent service that reports rates of exchange in the foreign currency market for such currency, and

(D) the bank or broker-dealer (or any affiliate of either) does not have investment discretion, or provide investment advice, with respect to the transaction,

(22) any transaction described in subsection (c)(1)(A) involving the purchase and sale of a security between a plan and any other account managed by the same investment manager, if—

(A) the transaction is a purchase or sale, for no consideration other than cash payment against prompt delivery of a security for which market quotations are readily available,

(B) the transaction is effected at the independent current market price of the security (within the meaning of section 270.17a-7(b) of title 17, Code of Federal Regulations),

(C) no brokerage commission, fee (except for customary transfer fees, the fact of which is disclosed pursuant to subparagraph (D)), or other remuneration is paid in connection with the transaction,

(D) a fiduciary (other than the investment manager engaging in the cross-trades or any affiliate) for each plan participating in the transaction authorizes in advance of any cross-trades (in a document that is separate from any other written agreement of the parties) the investment manager to engage in cross trades at the investment manager's discretion, after such fiduciary has received disclosure regarding the conditions under which cross trades may take place (but only if such

disclosure is separate from any other agreement or disclosure involving the asset management relationship), including the written policies and procedures of the investment manager described in subparagraph (H),

(E) each plan participating in the transaction has assets of at least $100,000,000, except that if the assets of a plan are invested in a master trust containing the assets of plans maintained by employers in the same controlled group (as defined in section 407(d)(7) of the Employee Retirement Income Security Act of 1974), the master trust has assets of at least $100,000,000,

(F) the investment manager provides to the plan fiduciary who authorized cross trading under subparagraph (D) a quarterly report detailing all cross trades executed by the investment manager in which the plan participated during such quarter, including the following information, as applicable: (i) the identity of each security bought or sold; (ii) the number of shares or units traded, (iii) the parties involved in the cross-trade; and (iv) trade price and the method used to establish the trade price,

(G) the investment manager does not base its fee schedule on the plan's consent to cross trading, and no other service (other than the investment opportunities and cost savings available through a cross trade) is conditioned on the plan's consent to cross trading,

(H) the investment manager has adopted, and cross-trades are effected in accordance with, written cross-trading policies and procedures that are fair and equitable to all accounts participating in the cross-trading program, and that include a description of the manager's pricing policies and procedures, and the manager's policies and procedures for allocating cross trades in an objective manner among accounts participating in the cross-trading program, and

(I) the investment manager has designated an individual responsible for periodically reviewing such purchases and sales to ensure compliance with the written policies and procedures described in subparagraph (H), and following such review, the individual shall issue an annual written report no later than 90 days following the period to which it relates signed under penalty of perjury to the plan fiduciary who authorized cross trading under subparagraph (D) describing the steps performed during the course of the review, the level of compliance, and any specific instances of non-compliance.

The written report shall also notify the plan fiduciary of the plan's right to terminate participation in the investment manager's cross-trading program at any time, or

(23) except as provided in subsection (f)(11), a transaction described in subparagraph (A), (B), (C), or (D) of subsection (c)(1) in connection with the acquisition, holding, or disposition of any security or commodity, if the transaction is corrected before the end of the correction period.

* * *

[CCH Explanation at ¶625, ¶630 and ¶635. Committee Reports at ¶10,420, ¶10,430, ¶10,450, ¶10,460, ¶10,470, ¶10,490 and ¶10,500.]

Amendments

• **2006, Pension Protection Act of 2006 (H.R. 4)**

H.R. 4, §601(b)(1)(A)-(C):

Amended Code Sec. 4975(d) by striking "or" at the end of paragraph (15); by striking the period at the end of paragraph (16) and inserting ";or" [sic]; and by adding at the end a new paragraph (17). **Effective** with respect to advice referred to in Code Sec. 4975(c)(3)(B) provided after 12-31-2006.

H.R. 4, §611(a)(2)(A):

Amended Code Sec. 4975(d), as amended by Act Sec. 601, by striking "or" at the end of paragraph (16), by striking the period at the end of paragraph (17) and inserting ", or", and by adding at the end a new paragraph (18). **Effective** for transactions occurring after 8-17-2006.

H.R. 4, §611(c)(2):

Amended Code Sec. 4975(d), as amended by Act Sec. 611(a), by striking "or" at the end of paragraph (17), by striking the period at the end of paragraph (18) and inserting ", or", and by adding at the end a new paragraph (19). **Effective** for transactions occurring after 8-17-2006.

H.R. 4, §611(d)(2)(A):

Amended Code Sec. 4975(d), as amended by Act Sec. 611(c), by striking "or" at the end of paragraph (18), by striking the period at the end of paragraph (19) and inserting ", or", and by adding at the end a new paragraph (20). **Effective** for transactions occurring after 8-17-2006.

H.R. 4, §611(e)(2):

Amended Code Sec. 4975(d), as amended by Act Sec. 611(d), by striking "or" at the end of paragraph (19), by striking the period at the end of paragraph (20) and inserting ", or", and by adding at the end a new paragraph (21). **Effective** for transactions occurring after 8-17-2006.

H.R. 4, §611(g)(2):

Amended Code Sec. 4975(d), as amended by Act Sec. 611(e), by striking "or" at the end of paragraph (20), by striking the period at the end of paragraph (21) and inserting ", or", and by adding at the end a new paragraph (22). **Effective** for transactions occurring after 8-17-2006.

H.R. 4, §612(b)(1):

Amended Code Sec. 4975(d), as amended by Act Secs. 601 and 611, by striking "or" at the end of paragraph (21), by striking the period at the end of paragraph (22) and inserting ", or", and by adding at the end a new paragraph (23). **Effective** for any transaction which the fiduciary or disqualified person discovers, or reasonably should have discovered, after 8-17-2006 constitutes a prohibited transaction.

(f) OTHER DEFINITIONS AND SPECIAL RULES.—For purposes of this section—

* * *

»»→ Caution: Code Sec. 4975(f)(8), below, as added by H.R. 4, applies with respect to advice referred to in Code Sec. 4975(c)(3)(B) provided after December 31, 2006.

(8) PROVISION OF INVESTMENT ADVICE TO PARTICIPANT AND BENEFICIARIES.—

(A) IN GENERAL.—The prohibitions provided in subsection (c) shall not apply to transactions described in subsection (b)(14) if the investment advice provided by a fiduciary adviser is provided under an eligible investment advice arrangement.

(B) ELIGIBLE INVESTMENT ADVICE ARRANGEMENT.—For purposes of this paragraph, the term "eligible investment advice arrangement" means an arrangement—

(i) which either—

(I) provides that any fees (including any commission or other compensation) received by the fiduciary adviser for investment advice or with respect to the sale, holding, or acquisition of any security or other property for purposes of investment of plan assets do not vary depending on the basis of any investment option selected, or

(II) uses a computer model under an investment advice program meeting the requirements of subparagraph (C) in connection with the provision of investment advice by a fiduciary adviser to a participant or beneficiary, and

(ii) with respect to which the requirements of subparagraphs (D), (E), (F), (G), (H), and (I) are met.

(C) INVESTMENT ADVICE PROGRAM USING COMPUTER MODEL.—

(i) IN GENERAL.—An investment advice program meets the requirements of this subparagraph if the requirements of clauses (ii), (iii), and (iv) are met.

(ii) COMPUTER MODEL.—The requirements of this clause are met if the investment advice provided under the investment advice program is provided pursuant to a computer model that—

(I) applies generally accepted investment theories that take into account the historic returns of different asset classes over defined periods of time,

(II) utilizes relevant information about the participant, which may include age, life expectancy, retirement age, risk tolerance, other assets or sources of income, and preferences as to certain types of investments,

(III) utilizes prescribed objective criteria to provide asset allocation portfolios comprised of investment options available under the plan,

(IV) operates in a manner that is not biased in favor of investments offered by the fiduciary adviser or a person with a material affiliation or contractual relationship with the fiduciary adviser, and

(V) takes into account all investment options under the plan in specifying how a participant's account balance should be invested and is not inappropriately weighted with respect to any investment option.

(iii) CERTIFICATION.—

(I) IN GENERAL.—The requirements of this clause are met with respect to any investment advice program if an eligible investment expert certifies, prior to the utilization of the computer model and in accordance with rules prescribed by the Secretary of Labor, that the computer model meets the requirements of clause (ii).

(II) RENEWAL OF CERTIFICATIONS.—If, as determined under regulations prescribed by the Secretary of Labor, there are material modifications to a computer model, the requirements of this clause are met only if a certification described in subclause (I) is obtained with respect to the computer model as so modified.

(III) Eligible investment expert.—The term "eligible investment expert" means any person which meets such requirements as the Secretary of Labor may provide and which does not bear any material affiliation or contractual relationship with any investment adviser or a related person thereof (or any employee, agent, or registered representative of the investment adviser or related person).

(iv) Exclusivity of recommendation.—The requirements of this clause are met with respect to any investment advice program if—

(I) the only investment advice provided under the program is the advice generated by the computer model described in clause (ii), and

(II) any transaction described in subsection (b)(14)(B)(ii) occurs solely at the direction of the participant or beneficiary.

Nothing in the preceding sentence shall preclude the participant or beneficiary from requesting investment advice other than that described in clause (i), but only if such request has not been solicited by any person connected with carrying out the arrangement.

(D) Express authorization by separate fiduciary.—The requirements of this subparagraph are met with respect to an arrangement if the arrangement is expressly authorized by a plan fiduciary other than the person offering the investment advice program, any person providing investment options under the plan, or any affiliate of either.

(E) Audits.—

(i) In general.—The requirements of this subparagraph are met if an independent auditor, who has appropriate technical training or experience and proficiency and so represents in writing—

(I) conducts an annual audit of the arrangement for compliance with the requirements of this paragraph, and

(II) following completion of the annual audit, issues a written report to the fiduciary who authorized use of the arrangement which presents its specific findings regarding compliance of the arrangement with the requirements of this paragraph.

(ii) Special rule for individual retirement and similar plans.—In the case of a plan described in subparagraphs (B) through (F) (and so much of subparagraph (G) as relates to such subparagraphs) of subsection (e)(1), in lieu of the requirements of clause (i), audits of the arrangement shall be conducted at such times and in such manner as the Secretary of Labor may prescribe.

(iii) Independent auditor.—For purposes of this subparagraph, an auditor is considered independent if it is not related to the person offering the arrangement to the plan and is not related to any person providing investment options under the plan.

(F) Disclosure.—The requirements of this subparagraph are met if—

(i) the fiduciary adviser provides to a participant or a beneficiary before the initial provision of the investment advice with regard to any security or other property offered as an investment option, a written notification (which may consist of notification by means of electronic communication)—

(I) of the role of any party that has a material affiliation or contractual relationship with the financial adviser in the development of the investment advice program and in the selection of investment options available under the plan,

(II) of the past performance and historical rates of return of the investment options available under the plan,

(III) of all fees or other compensation relating to the advice that the fiduciary adviser or any affiliate thereof is to receive (including compensation provided by any third party) in connection with the provision of the advice or in connection with the sale, acquisition, or holding of the security or other property,

(IV) of any material affiliation or contractual relationship of the fiduciary adviser or affiliates thereof in the security or other property,

(V) the manner, and under what circumstances, any participant or beneficiary information provided under the arrangement will be used or disclosed,

(VI) of the types of services provided by the fiduciary adviser in connection with the provision of investment advice by the fiduciary adviser,

(VII) that the adviser is acting as a fiduciary of the plan in connection with the provision of the advice, and

(VIII) that a recipient of the advice may separately arrange for the provision of advice by another adviser, that could have no material affiliation with and receive no fees or other compensation in connection with the security or other property, and

(ii) at all times during the provision of advisory services to the participant or beneficiary, the fiduciary adviser—

(I) maintains the information described in clause (i) in accurate form and in the manner described in subparagraph (H),

(II) provides, without charge, accurate information to the recipient of the advice no less frequently than annually,

(III) provides, without charge, accurate information to the recipient of the advice upon request of the recipient, and

(IV) provides, without charge, accurate information to the recipient of the advice concerning any material change to the information required to be provided to the recipient of the advice at a time reasonably contemporaneous to the change in information.

(G) OTHER CONDITIONS.—The requirements of this subparagraph are met if—

(i) the fiduciary adviser provides appropriate disclosure, in connection with the sale, acquisition, or holding of the security or other property, in accordance with all applicable securities laws,

(ii) the sale, acquisition, or holding occurs solely at the direction of the recipient of the advice,

(iii) the compensation received by the fiduciary adviser and affiliates thereof in connection with the sale, acquisition, or holding of the security or other property is reasonable, and

(iv) the terms of the sale, acquisition, or holding of the security or other property are at least as favorable to the plan as an arm's length transaction would be.

(H) STANDARDS FOR PRESENTATION OF INFORMATION.—

(i) IN GENERAL.—The requirements of this subparagraph are met if the notification required to be provided to participants and beneficiaries under subparagraph (F)(i) is written in a clear and conspicuous manner and in a manner calculated to be understood by the average plan participant and is sufficiently accurate and comprehensive to reasonably apprise such participants and beneficiaries of the information required to be provided in the notification.

(ii) MODEL FORM FOR DISCLOSURE OF FEES AND OTHER COMPENSATION.—The Secretary of Labor shall issue a model form for the disclosure of fees and other compensation required in subparagraph (F)(i)(III) which meets the requirements of clause (i).

(I) MAINTENANCE FOR 6 YEARS OF EVIDENCE OF COMPLIANCE.—The requirements of this subparagraph are met if a fiduciary adviser who has provided advice referred to in subparagraph (A) maintains, for a period of not less than 6 years after the provision of the advice, any records necessary for determining whether the requirements of the preceding provisions of this paragraph and of subsection (d)(17) have been met. A transaction prohibited under section 406 shall not be considered to have occurred solely because the records are lost or destroyed prior to the end of the 6-year period due to circumstances beyond the control of the fiduciary adviser.

(J) DEFINITIONS.—For purposes of this paragraph and subsection (d)(17)—

(i) FIDUCIARY ADVISER.—The term "fiduciary adviser" means, with respect to a plan, a person who is a fiduciary of the plan by reason of the provision of investment advice by the person to the participant or beneficiary of the plan and who is—

(I) registered as an investment adviser under the Investment Advisers Act of 1940 (15 U.S.C. 80b-1 et seq.) or under the laws of the State in which the fiduciary maintains its principal office and place of business,

(II) a bank or similar financial institution referred to in section 408(b)(4) or a savings association (as defined in section 3(b)(1) of the Federal Deposit Insurance Act (12 U.S.C. 1813(b)(1)), but only if the advice is provided through a trust department of the bank or similar financial institution or savings association which is subject to periodic examination and review by Federal or State banking authorities,

(III) an insurance company qualified to do business under the laws of a State,

(IV) a person registered as a broker or dealer under the Securities Exchange Act of 1934 (15 U.S.C. 78a et seq.),

(V) an affiliate of a person described in any of subclauses (I) through (IV), or

(VI) an employee, agent, or registered representative of a person described in subclauses (I) through (V) who satisfies the requirements of applicable insurance, banking, and securities laws relating to the provision of the advice.

For purposes of this title, a person who develops the computer model described in subparagraph (C)(ii) or markets the investment advice program or computer model shall be treated as a person who is a fiduciary of the plan by reason of the provision of investment advice referred to in subsection (e)(3)(B) to the participant or beneficiary and shall be treated as a fiduciary adviser for purposes of this paragraph and subsection (d)(17), except that the Secretary of Labor may prescribe rules under which only 1 fiduciary adviser may elect to be treated as a fiduciary with respect to the plan.

(ii) AFFILIATE.—The term "affiliate" of another entity means an affiliated person of the entity (as defined in section 2(a)(3) of the Investment Company Act of 1940 (15 U.S.C. 80a-2(a)(3))).

(iii) REGISTERED REPRESENTATIVE.—The term "registered representative" of another entity means a person described in section 3(a)(18) of the Securities Exchange Act of 1934 (15 U.S.C. 78c(a)(18)) (substituting the entity for the broker or dealer referred to in such section) or a person described in section 202(a)(17) of the Investment Advisers Act of 1940 (15 U.S.C. 80b-2(a)(17)) (substituting the entity for the investment adviser referred to in such section).

(9) BLOCK TRADE.—The term "block trade" means any trade of at least 10,000 shares or with a market value of at least $200,000 which will be allocated across two or more unrelated client accounts of a fiduciary.

(10) ADEQUATE CONSIDERATION.—The term "adequate consideration" means—

(A) in the case of a security for which there is a generally recognized market—

(i) the price of the security prevailing on a national securities exchange which is registered under section 6 of the Securities Exchange Act of 1934, taking into account factors such as the size of the transaction and marketability of the security, or

(ii) if the security is not traded on such a national securities exchange, a price not less favorable to the plan than the offering price for the security as established by the current bid and asked prices quoted by persons independent of the issuer and of the party in interest, taking into account factors such as the size of the transaction and marketability of the security, and

(B) in the case of an asset other than a security for which there is a generally recognized market, the fair market value of the asset as determined in good faith by a fiduciary or fiduciaries in accordance with regulations prescribed by the Secretary of Labor.

(11) CORRECTION PERIOD.—

(A) IN GENERAL.—For purposes of subsection (d)(23), the term "correction period" means the 14-day period beginning on the date on which the disqualified person discovers, or reasonably should have discovered, that the transaction would (without regard to this paragraph and subsection (d)(23)) constitute a prohibited transaction.

(B) EXCEPTIONS.—

(i) EMPLOYER SECURITIES.—*Subsection (d)(23) does not apply to any transaction between a plan and a plan sponsor or its affiliates that involves the acquisition or sale of an employer security (as defined in section 407(d)(1)) or the acquisition, sale, or lease of employer real property (as defined in section 407(d)(2)).*

(ii) KNOWING PROHIBITED TRANSACTION.—*In the case of any disqualified person, subsection (d)(23) does not apply to a transaction if, at the time the transaction is entered into, the disqualified person knew (or reasonably should have known) that the transaction would (without regard to this paragraph) constitute a prohibited transaction.*

(C) ABATEMENT OF TAX WHERE THERE IS A CORRECTION.—*If a transaction is not treated as a prohibited transaction by reason of subsection (d)(23), then no tax under subsection (a) and (b) shall be assessed with respect to such transaction, and if assessed the assessment shall be abated, and if collected shall be credited or refunded as an overpayment.*

(D) DEFINITIONS.—*For purposes of this paragraph and subsection (d)(23)—*

(i) SECURITY.—*The term "security" has the meaning given such term by section 475(c)(2) (without regard to subparagraph (F)(iii) and the last sentence thereof).*

(ii) COMMODITY.—*The term "commodity" has the meaning given such term by section 475(e)(2) (without regard to subparagraph (D)(iii) thereof).*

(iii) CORRECT.—*The term "correct" means, with respect to a transaction—*

(I) to undo the transaction to the extent possible and in any case to make good to the plan or affected account any losses resulting from the transaction, and

(II) to restore to the plan or affected account any profits made through the use of assets of the plan.

* * *

[CCH Explanation at ¶ 625, ¶ 630 and ¶ 635. Committee Reports at ¶ 10,420, ¶ 10,430, ¶ 10,460 and ¶ 10,500.]

Amendments

• 2006, Pension Protection Act of 2006 (H.R. 4)

H.R. 4, § 601(b)(2):

Amended Code Sec. 4975(f) by adding at the end a new paragraph (8). **Effective** with respect to advice referred to in Code Sec. 4975(c)(3)(B) provided after 12-31-2006.

H.R. 4, § 611(a)(2)(B):

Amended Code Sec. 4975(f), as amended by Act Sec. 601, by adding at the end a new paragraph (9). **Effective** for transactions occurring after 8-17-2006.

H.R. 4, § 611(d)(2)(B):

Amended Code Sec. 4975(f), as amended by Act Sec. 611(a), by adding at the end a new paragraph (10). **Effective** for transactions occurring after 8-17-2006.

H.R. 4, § 612(b)(2):

Amended Code Sec. 4975(f), as amended by Act Secs. 601 and 611, by adding at the end a new paragraph (11). **Effective** for any transaction which the fiduciary or disqualified person discovers, or reasonably should have discovered, after 8-17-2006 constitutes a prohibited transaction.

[¶ 5310] CODE SEC. 4979. TAX ON CERTAIN EXCESS CONTRIBUTIONS.

* * *

»»→ Caution: Code Sec. 4979(f), as amended by H.R. 4, applies to plan years beginning after December 31, 2007.

(f) NO TAX WHERE EXCESS DISTRIBUTED WITHIN *SPECIFIED PERIOD AFTER* CLOSE OF YEAR.—

(1) IN GENERAL.—No tax shall be imposed under this section on any excess contribution or excess aggregate contribution, as the case may be, to the extent such contribution (together with any income allocable thereto *through the end of the plan year for which the contribution was made*) is distributed (or, if forfeitable, is forfeited) before the close of the first 2½ months *(6 months in the case of an excess contribution or excess aggregate contribution to an eligible automatic contribution arrangement (as defined in section 414(w)(3)))* of the following plan year.

(2) YEAR OF INCLUSION.—*Any amount distributed as provided in paragraph (1) shall be treated as earned and received by the recipient in the recipient's taxable year in which such distributions were made.*

[CCH Explanation at ¶ 1015. Committee Reports at ¶ 10,960.]

Amendments

• 2006, Pension Protection Act of 2006 (H.R. 4)

H.R. 4, § 902(e)(1)(A)-(B):

Amended Code Sec. 4979(f) by inserting "(6 months in the case of an excess contribution or excess aggregate contribution to an eligible automatic contribution arrangement (as defined in section 414(w)(3)))" after "2½ months" in paragraph (1), and by striking "2½ MONTHS OF" in the heading and inserting "SPECIFIED PERIOD AFTER". **Effective** for plan years beginning after 12-31-2007.

H.R. 4, § 902(e)(2):

Amended Code Sec. 4979(f)(2). **Effective** for plan years beginning after 12-31-2007. Prior to amendment, Code Sec. 4979(f)(2) read as follows:

(2) YEAR OF INCLUSION.—

(A) IN GENERAL.—Except as provided in subparagraph (B), any amount distributed as provided in paragraph (1) shall be treated as received and earned by the recipient in his taxable year for which such contribution was made.

(B) DE MINIMIS DISTRIBUTIONS.—If the total excess contributions and excess aggregate contributions distributed to a recipient under a plan for any plan year are less than $100, such distributions (and any income allocable thereto) shall be treated as earned and received by the recipient in his taxable year in which such distributions were made.

H.R. 4, § 902(e)(3)(A):

Amended Code Sec. 4979(f)(1) by adding "through the end of the plan year for which the contribution was made" after "thereto". **Effective** for plan years beginning after 12-31-2007.

[¶ 5315] CODE SEC. 4980. TAX ON REVERSION OF QUALIFIED PLAN ASSETS TO EMPLOYER.

* * *

(c) DEFINITIONS AND SPECIAL RULES.—For purposes of this section—

* * *

(3) EXCEPTION FOR EMPLOYEE STOCK OWNERSHIP PLANS.—

→ *Caution: Code Sec. 4980(c)(3)(A), below, as amended by H.R. 4, applies generally to plan years beginning after December 31, 2006.*

(A) IN GENERAL.—If upon an employer reversion from a qualified plan, any applicable amount is transferred from such plan to an employee stock ownership plan described in section 4975(e)(7) or a tax credit employee stock ownership plan (as described in section 409), such amount shall not be treated as an employer reversion for purposes of this section (or includible in the gross income of the employer) *if the requirements of subparagraphs (B), (C), and (D) are met.*

* * *

[CCH Explanation at ¶ 605. Committee Reports at ¶ 10,950.]

Amendments

• 2006, Pension Protection Act of 2006 (H.R. 4)

H.R. 4, § 901(a)(2)(C):

Amended Code Sec. 4980(c)(3)(A) by striking "if—" and all that follows and inserting "if the requirements of subparagraphs (B), (C), and (D) are met.". For the **effective** date, see Act Sec. 901(c), below. Prior to being stricken, all that follows "if—" in Code Sec. 4980(c)(3)(A) read as follows:

(i) the requirements of subparagraphs (B), (C), and (D) are met, and

(ii) under the plan, employer securities to which subparagraph (B) applies must, except to the extent necessary to meet the requirements of section 401(a)(28), remain in the plan until distribution to participants in accordance with the provisions of such plan.

H.R. 4, § 901(c), provides:

(c) EFFECTIVE DATES.—

(1) IN GENERAL.—Except as provided in paragraphs (2) and (3), the amendments made by this section shall apply to plan years beginning after December 31, 2006.

(2) SPECIAL RULE FOR COLLECTIVELY BARGAINED AGREEMENTS.—In the case of a plan maintained pursuant to 1 or more collective bargaining agreements between employee representatives and 1 or more employers ratified on or before the date of the enactment of this Act, paragraph (1) shall be applied to benefits pursuant to, and individuals covered by, any such agreement by substituting for "December 31, 2006" the earlier of—

(A) the later of—

(i) December 31, 2007, or

(ii) the date on which the last of such collective bargaining agreements terminates (determined without regard to any extension thereof after such date of enactment), or

(B) December 31, 2008.

(3) SPECIAL RULE FOR CERTAIN EMPLOYER SECURITIES HELD IN AN ESOP.—

(A) IN GENERAL.—In the case of employer securities to which this paragraph applies, the amendments made by this section shall apply to plan years beginning after the earlier of—

(i) December 31, 2007, or

(ii) the first date on which the fair market value of such securities exceeds the guaranteed minimum value described in subparagraph (B)(ii).

(B) APPLICABLE SECURITIES.—This paragraph shall apply to employer securities which are attributable to employer contributions other than elective deferrals, and which, on September 17, 2003—

(i) consist of preferred stock, and

(ii) are within an employee stock ownership plan (as defined in section 4975(e)(7) of the Internal Revenue Code of 1986), the terms of which provide that the value of the securities cannot be less than the guaranteed minimum value specified by the plan on such date.

(C) COORDINATION WITH TRANSITION RULE.—In applying section 401(a)(35)(H) of the Internal Revenue Code of 1986 and section 204(j)(7) of the Employee Retirement Income Security Act of 1974 (as added by this section) to employer securities to which this paragraph applies, the applicable percentage shall be determined without regard to this paragraph.

[¶ 5320] CODE SEC. 4980F. FAILURE OF APPLICABLE PLANS REDUCING BENEFIT ACCRUALS TO SATISFY NOTICE REQUIREMENTS.

* * *

(e) NOTICE REQUIREMENTS FOR PLANS SIGNIFICANTLY REDUCING BENEFIT ACCRUALS.—

»»→ Caution: Code Sec. 4980F(e)(1), below, as amended by H.R. 4, applies to plan years beginning after December 31, 2007.

(1) IN GENERAL.—If an applicable pension plan is amended to provide for a significant reduction in the rate of future benefit accrual, the plan administrator shall provide the notice described in paragraph (2) to each applicable individual (and to each employee organization representing applicable individuals) *and to each employer who has an obligation to contribute to the plan*.

* * *

[CCH Explanation at ¶ 410. Committee Reports at ¶ 10,350.]

Amendments

• 2006, Pension Protection Act of 2006 (H.R. 4)

H.R. 4, § 502(c)(2):

Amended Code Sec. 4980F(e)(1) by adding at the end before the period the following: "and to each employer who has an obligation to contribute to the plan". **Effective** for plan years beginning after 12-31-2007.

[¶ 5325] CODE SEC. 6033. RETURNS BY EXEMPT ORGANIZATIONS.

(a) ORGANIZATIONS REQUIRED TO FILE.—

* * *

(3) EXCEPTIONS FROM FILING.—

* * *

(B) DISCRETIONARY EXCEPTIONS.—The Secretary may relieve any organization required under paragraph (1) *(other than an organization described in section 509(a)(3))* to file an information return from filing such a return where he determines that such filing is not necessary to the efficient administration of the internal revenue laws.

* * *

[CCH Explanation at ¶ 1270. Committee Reports at ¶ 11,360.]

Amendments

• 2006, Pension Protection Act of 2006 (H.R. 4)

H.R. 4, § 1245(a):

Amended Code Sec. 6033(a)(3)(B) by inserting "(other than an organization described in section 509(a)(3))" after "paragraph (1)". **Effective** for returns filed for tax years ending after 8-17-2006.

(h) CONTROLLING ORGANIZATIONS.—Each controlling organization (within the meaning of section 512(b)(13)) which is subject to the requirements of subsection (a) shall include on the return required under subsection (a)—

(1) any interest, annuities, royalties, or rents received from each controlled entity (within the meaning of section 512(b)(13)),

(2) any loans made to each such controlled entity, and

(3) any transfers of funds between such controlling organization and each such controlled entity.

[CCH Explanation at ¶1210. Committee Reports at ¶11,150.]

Amendments

• 2006, Pension Protection Act of 2006 (H.R. 4)

H.R. 4, §1205(b)(1):

Amended Code Sec. 6033 by redesignating subsection (h) as subsection (i) and by inserting after subsection (g) a new subsection (h). **Effective** for returns the due date (determined without regard to extensions) of which is after 8-17-2006.

»»→ *Caution: Code Sec. 6033(i), below, as added by H.R. 4, applies to notices and returns with respect to annual periods beginning after 2006.*

(i) ADDITIONAL NOTIFICATION REQUIREMENTS.—Any organization the gross receipts of which in any taxable year result in such organization being referred to in subsection (a)(3)(A)(ii) or (a)(3)(B)—

(1) shall furnish annually, in electronic form, and at such time and in such manner as the Secretary may by regulations prescribe, information setting forth—

(A) the legal name of the organization,

(B) any name under which such organization operates or does business,

(C) the organization's mailing address and Internet web site address (if any),

(D) the organization's taxpayer identification number,

(E) the name and address of a principal officer, and

(F) evidence of the continuing basis for the organization's exemption from the filing requirements under subsection (a)(1), and

(2) upon the termination of the existence of the organization, shall furnish notice of such termination.

[CCH Explanation at ¶1210 and ¶1260. Committee Reports at ¶11,150 and ¶11,310.]

Amendments

• 2006, Pension Protection Act of 2006 (H.R. 4)

H.R. 4, §1223(a):

Amended Code Sec. 6033, as amended by this Act, by redesignating subsection (i) as subsection (j) and by inserting after subsection (h) a new subsection (i). **Effective** for notices and returns with respect to annual periods beginning after 2006.

»»→ *Caution: Code Sec. 6033(j), below, as added by H.R. 4, applies to notices and returns with respect to annual periods beginning after 2006.*

(j) LOSS OF EXEMPT STATUS FOR FAILURE TO FILE RETURN OR NOTICE.—

(1) IN GENERAL.—If an organization described in subsection (a)(1) or (i) fails to file an annual return or notice required under either subsection for 3 consecutive years, such organization's status as an organization exempt from tax under section 501(a) shall be considered revoked on and after the date set by the Secretary for the filing of the third annual return or notice. The Secretary shall publish and maintain a list of any organization the status of which is so revoked.

(2) APPLICATION NECESSARY FOR REINSTATEMENT.—Any organization the tax-exempt status of which is revoked under paragraph (1) must apply in order to obtain reinstatement of such status regardless of whether such organization was originally required to make such an application.

(3) RETROACTIVE REINSTATEMENT IF REASONABLE CAUSE SHOWN FOR FAILURE.—If, upon application for reinstatement of status as an organization exempt from tax under section 501(a), an organization described in paragraph (1) can show to the satisfaction of the Secretary evidence of reasonable cause for the failure described in such paragraph, the organization's exempt status may, in the discretion of the Secretary, be reinstated effective from the date of the revocation under such paragraph.

[CCH Explanation at ¶ 1260. Committee Reports at ¶ 11,310.]

Amendments

• 2006, Pension Protection Act of 2006 (H.R. 4)

H.R. 4, §1223(b):

Amended Code Sec. 6033, as amended by Act Sec. 1223(a), by redesignating subsection (j) as subsection (k) and by inserting after subsection (i) a new subsection (j). **Effective** for notices and returns with respect to annual periods beginning after 2006.

(k) Additional Provisions Relating to Sponsoring Organizations.—Every organization described in section 4966(d)(1) shall, on the return required under subsection (a) for the taxable year—

(1) list the total number of donor advised funds (as defined in section 4966(d)(2)) it owns at the end of such taxable year,

(2) indicate the aggregate value of assets held in such funds at the end of such taxable year, and

(3) indicate the aggregate contributions to and grants made from such funds during such taxable year.

[CCH Explanation at ¶ 1260 and ¶ 1265. Committee Reports at ¶ 11,310 and ¶ 11,350.]

Amendments

• 2006, Pension Protection Act of 2006 (H.R. 4)

H.R. 4, §1235(a)(1):

Amended Code Sec. 6033, as amended by this Act, by redesignating subsection (k) as subsection (l) and by inserting after subsection (j) a new subsection (k). **Effective** for returns filed for tax years ending after 8-17-2006.

(l) Additional Provisions Relating to Supporting Organizations.—Every organization described in section 509(a)(3) shall, on the return required under subsection (a)—

(1) list the supported organizations (as defined in section 509(f)(3)) with respect to which such organization provides support,

(2) indicate whether the organization meets the requirements of clause (i), (ii), or (iii) of section 509(a)(3)(B), and

(3) certify that the organization meets the requirements of section 509(a)(3)(C).

[CCH Explanation at ¶ 1265 and ¶ 1270. Committee Reports at ¶ 11,350 and ¶ 11,360.]

Amendments

• 2006, Pension Protection Act of 2006 (H.R. 4)

H.R. 4, §1245(b):

Amended Code Sec. 6033, as amended by this Act, by redesignating subsection (l) as subsection (m) and by inserting after subsection (k) a new subsection (l). **Effective** for returns filed for tax years ending after 8-17-2006.

(m) Cross Reference.—

* * *

Amendments

• 2006, Pension Protection Act of 2006 (H.R. 4)

H.R. 4, §1205(b)(1):

Amended Code Sec. 6033, by redesignating subsection (h) as subsection (i). **Effective** for returns the due date (determined without regard to extensions) of which is after 8-17-2006.

H.R. 4, §1223(a):

Amended Code Sec. 6033, as amended by this Act, by redesignating subsection (i) as subsection (j). **Effective** for notices and returns with respect to annual periods beginning after 2006.

H.R. 4, §1223(b):

Amended Code Sec. 6033, as amended by Act Sec. 1223(a), by redesignating subsection (j) as subsection (k). **Effective** for notices and returns with respect to annual periods beginning after 2006.

H.R. 4, §1235(a)(1):

Amended Code Sec. 6033, as amended by this Act, by redesignating subsection (k) as subsection (l). **Effective** for returns filed for tax years ending after 8-17-2006.

H.R. 4, §1245(b):

Amended Code Sec. 6033, as amended by this Act, by redesignating subsection (l) as subsection (m). **Effective** for returns filed for tax years ending after 8-17-2006.

»»→ *Caution: Code Sec. 6034, below, as amended by H.R. 4, applies to returns for tax years beginning after December 31, 2006.*

[¶ 5330] *CODE SEC. 6034. RETURNS BY CERTAIN TRUSTS.*

(a) SPLIT-INTEREST TRUSTS.—*Every trust described in section 4947(a)(2) shall furnish such information with respect to the taxable year as the Secretary may by forms or regulations require.*

(b) TRUSTS CLAIMING CERTAIN CHARITABLE DEDUCTIONS.—

(1) IN GENERAL.—*Every trust not required to file a return under subsection (a) but claiming a deduction under section 642(c) for the taxable year shall furnish such information with respect to such taxable year as the Secretary may by forms or regulations prescribe, including—*

(A) *the amount of the deduction taken under section 642(c) within such year,*

(B) *the amount paid out within such year which represents amounts for which deductions under section 642(c) have been taken in prior years,*

(C) *the amount for which such deductions have been taken in prior years but which has not been paid out at the beginning of such year,*

(D) *the amount paid out of principal in the current and prior years for the purposes described in section 642(c),*

(E) *the total income of the trust within such year and the expenses attributable thereto, and*

(F) *a balance sheet showing the assets, liabilities, and net worth of the trust as of the beginning of such year.*

(2) EXCEPTIONS.—*Paragraph (1) shall not apply to a trust for any taxable year if—*

(A) *all the net income for such year, determined under the applicable principles of the law of trusts, is required to be distributed currently to the beneficiaries, or*

(B) *the trust is described in section 4947(a)(1).*

[CCH Explanation at ¶ 1190. Committee Reports at ¶ 11,110.]

Amendments

• **2006, Pension Protection Act of 2006 (H.R. 4)**

H.R. 4, § 1201(b)(1):

Amended Code Sec. 6034. **Effective** for returns for tax years beginning after 12-31-2006. Prior to amendment, Code Sec. 6034 read as follows:

SEC. 6034. RETURNS BY TRUSTS DESCRIBED IN SECTION 4947(a)(2) OR CLAIMING CHARITABLE DEDUCTIONS UNDER SECTION 642(c) .

(a) GENERAL RULE.—Every trust described in section 4947(a)(2) or claiming a charitable, etc., deduction under section 642(c) for the taxable year shall furnish such information with respect to such taxable year as the Secretary may by forms or regulations prescribe, including—

(1) the amount of the charitable, etc., deduction taken under section 642(c) within such year,

(2) the amount paid out within such year which represents amounts for which charitable, etc., deductions under section 642(c) have been taken in prior years,

(3) the amount for which charitable, etc., deductions have been taken in prior years but which has not been paid out at the beginning of such year,

(4) the amount paid out of principal in the current and prior years for charitable, etc., purposes,

(5) the total income of the trust within such year and the expenses attributable thereto, and

(6) a balance sheet showing the assets, liabilities, and net worth of the trust as of the beginning of such year.

(b) EXCEPTIONS.—This section shall not apply in the case of a taxable year if all the net income for such year, determined under the applicable principles of the law of trusts, is required to be distributed currently to the beneficiaries. This section shall not apply in the case of a trust described in section 4947(a)(1).

(c) CROSS REFERENCE.—

For provisions relating to penalties for failure to file a return required by this section, see section 6652(c).

[¶ 5335] *CODE SEC. 6039I. RETURNS AND RECORDS WITH RESPECT TO EMPLOYER-OWNED LIFE INSURANCE CONTRACTS.*

(a) IN GENERAL.—Every applicable policyholder owning 1 or more employer-owned life insurance contracts issued after the date of the enactment of this section shall file a return (at such time and in such manner as the Secretary shall by regulations prescribe) showing for each year such contracts are owned—

(1) the number of employees of the applicable policyholder at the end of the year,

(2) the number of such employees insured under such contracts at the end of the year,

(3) the total amount of insurance in force at the end of the year under such contracts,

(4) the name, address, and taxpayer identification number of the applicable policyholder and the type of business in which the policyholder is engaged, and

(5) that the applicable policyholder has a valid consent for each insured employee (or, if all such consents are not obtained, the number of insured employees for whom such consent was not obtained).

(b) RECORDKEEPING REQUIREMENT.—Each applicable policyholder owning 1 or more employer-owned life insurance contracts during any year shall keep such records as may be necessary for purposes of determining whether the requirements of this section and section 101(j) are met.

(c) DEFINITIONS.—Any term used in this section which is used in section 101(j) shall have the same meaning given such term by section 101(j).

[CCH Explanation at ¶1330. Committee Reports at ¶10,890.]

Amendments

• 2006, Pension Protection Act of 2006 (H.R. 4)

H.R. 4, §863(b):

Amended subpart A of part III of subchapter A of chapter 61 by inserting after Code Sec. 6039H a new Code Sec. 6039I. **Effective** for life insurance contracts issued after 8-17-2006, except for a contract issued after such date pursuant to an exchange described in Code Sec. 1035 for a contract issued on or prior to that date. For purposes of the preceding sentence, any material increase in the death benefit or other material change shall cause the contract to be treated as a new contract except that, in the case of a master contract (within the meaning of Code Sec. 264(f)(4)(E)), the addition of covered lives shall be treated as a new contract only with respect to such additional covered lives.

[¶5340] CODE SEC. 6050L. RETURNS RELATING TO CERTAIN DONATED PROPERTY.

(a) DISPOSITIONS OF DONATED PROPERTY.—

(1) IN GENERAL.—If the donee of any charitable deduction property sells, exchanges, or otherwise disposes of such property within *3 years* after its receipt, the donee shall make a return (in accordance with forms and regulations prescribed by the Secretary) showing—

(A) the name, address, and TIN of the donor,

(B) a description of the property,

(C) the date of the contribution,

(D) the amount received on the disposition,

(E) the date of such disposition,

(F) a description of the donee's use of the property, and

(G) a statement indicating whether the use of the property was related to the purpose or function constituting the basis for the donee's exemption under section 501.

In any case in which the donee indicates that the use of applicable property (as defined in section 170(e)(7)(C)) was related to the purpose or function constituting the basis for the exemption of the donee under section 501 under subparagraph (G), the donee shall include with the return the certification described in section 170(e)(7)(D) if such certification is made under section 170(e)(7).

* * *

[CCH Explanation at ¶1150. Committee Reports at ¶11,230.]

Amendments

• 2006, Pension Protection Act of 2006 (H.R. 4)

H.R. 4, §1215(b)(1)-(2):

Amended Code Sec. 6050L(a)(1) by striking "2 years" and inserting "3 years", and by striking "and" at the end of subparagraph (D), by striking the period at the end of subparagraph (E) and inserting a comma, and by inserting at the end new subparagraphs (F) and (G) and a new flush sentence. **Effective** for returns filed after 9-1-2006.

→ Caution: Code Sec. 6050U, below, as added by H.R. 4, applies to charges made after December 31, 2009.

[¶5345] *CODE SEC. 6050U. CHARGES OR PAYMENTS FOR QUALIFIED LONG-TERM CARE INSURANCE CONTRACTS UNDER COMBINED ARRANGEMENTS.*

(a) REQUIREMENT OF REPORTING.—Any person who makes a charge against the cash value of an annuity contract, or the cash surrender value of a life insurance contract, which is excludible from gross income under section 72(e)(11) shall make a return, according to the forms or regulations prescribed by the Secretary, setting forth—

(1) the amount of the aggregate of such charges against each such contract for the calendar year,

(2) the amount of the reduction in the investment in each such contract by reason of such charges, and

(3) the name, address, and TIN of the individual who is the holder of each such contract.

(b) STATEMENTS TO BE FURNISHED TO PERSONS WITH RESPECT TO WHOM INFORMATION IS REQUIRED.—Every person required to make a return under subsection (a) shall furnish to each individual whose name is required to be set forth in such return a written statement showing—

(1) the name, address, and phone number of the information contact of the person making the payments, and

(2) the information required to be shown on the return with respect to such individual.

The written statement required under the preceding sentence shall be furnished to the individual on or before January 31 of the year following the calendar year for which the return under subsection (a) was required to be made.

[CCH Explanation at ¶820. Committee Reports at ¶10,780.]

Amendments

• 2006, Pension Protection Act of 2006 (H.R. 4)

H.R. 4, §844(d)(1):

Amended subpart B of part III of subchapter A of chapter 61 by adding at the end a new Code Sec. 6050U. **Effective** for charges made after 12-31-2009.

[¶5350] *CODE SEC. 6050V. RETURNS RELATING TO APPLICABLE INSURANCE CONTRACTS IN WHICH CERTAIN EXEMPT ORGANIZATIONS HOLD INTERESTS.*

(a) IN GENERAL.—Each applicable exempt organization which makes a reportable acquisition shall make the return described in subsection (c).

(b) TIME FOR MAKING RETURN.—Any applicable exempt organization required to make a return under subsection (a) shall file such return at such time as may be established by the Secretary.

(c) FORM AND MANNER OF RETURNS.—A return is described in this subsection if such return—

(1) is in such form as the Secretary prescribes,

(2) contains the name, address, and taxpayer identification number of the applicable exempt organization and the issuer of the applicable insurance contract, and

(3) contains such other information as the Secretary may prescribe.

(d) DEFINITIONS.—For purposes of this section—

(1) REPORTABLE ACQUISITION.—The term "reportable acquisition" means the acquisition by an applicable exempt organization of a direct or indirect interest in any applicable insurance contract in any case in which such acquisition is a part of a structured transaction involving a pool of such contracts.

(2) APPLICABLE INSURANCE CONTRACT.—

(A) IN GENERAL.—The term "applicable insurance contract" means any life insurance, annuity, or endowment contract with respect to which both an applicable exempt organization and a person other than an applicable exempt organization have directly or indirectly held an interest in the contract (whether or not at the same time).

(B) EXCEPTIONS.—Such term shall not include a life insurance, annuity, or endowment contract if—

(i) all persons directly or indirectly holding any interest in the contract (other than applicable exempt organizations) have an insurable interest in the insured under the contract independent of any interest of an applicable exempt organization in the contract,

(ii) the sole interest in the contract of an applicable exempt organization or each person other than an applicable exempt organization is as a named beneficiary, or

(iii) the sole interest in the contract of each person other than an applicable exempt organization is—

(I) as a beneficiary of a trust holding an interest in the contract, but only if the person's designation as such beneficiary was made without consideration and solely on a purely gratuitous basis, or

(II) as a trustee who holds an interest in the contract in a fiduciary capacity solely for the benefit of applicable exempt organizations or persons otherwise described in subclause (I) or clause (i) or (ii).

(3) APPLICABLE EXEMPT ORGANIZATION.—The term "applicable exempt organization" means—

(A) an organization described in section 170(c),

(B) an organization described in section 168(h)(2)(A)(iv), or

(C) an organization not described in paragraph (1) or (2) which is described in section 2055(a) or section 2522(a).

(e) TERMINATION.—This section shall not apply to reportable acquisitions occurring after the date which is 2 years after the date of the enactment of this section.

[CCH Explanation at ¶ 1285. Committee Reports at ¶ 11,190.]

Amendments

• 2006, Pension Protection Act of 2006 (H.R. 4)

H.R. 4, § 1211(a)(1):

Amended subpart B of part III of subchapter A of chapter 61, as amended by this Act, by adding at the end a new Code Sec. 6050V. **Effective** for acquisitions of contracts after 8-17-2006.

[¶ 5355] CODE SEC. 6059. PERIODIC REPORT OF ACTUARY.

* * *

(b) ACTUARIAL REPORT.—The actuarial report of a plan required by subsection (a) shall be prepared and signed by an enrolled actuary (within the meaning of section 7701(a)(35)) and shall contain—

(1) a description of the funding method and actuarial assumptions used to determine costs under the plan,

(2) a certification of the contribution necessary to reduce *the minimum required contribution determined under section 430, or the accumulated funding deficiency determined under section 431,* to zero,

(3) a statement—

(A) that to the best of his knowledge the report is complete and accurate, and

(B) the requirements for reasonable actuarial assumptions under section 430(h)(1) or 431(c)(3), whichever are applicable, have been complied with. [sic]

(4) such other information as may be necessary to fully and fairly disclose the actuarial position of the plan, and

(5) such other information regarding the plan as the Secretary may by regulations require.

* * *

[CCH Explanation at ¶210 and ¶305. Committee Reports at ¶10,010.]

Amendments

• 2006, Pension Protection Act of 2006 (H.R. 4)

H.R. 4, §114(f)(1)-(2):

Amended Code Sec. 6059(b) by striking "the accumulated funding deficiency (as defined in section 412(a))" in paragraph (2) and inserting "the minimum required contribution determined under section 430, or the accumulated funding deficiency determined under section 431,", and by striking paragraph (3)(B) and inserting a new paragraph (3)(B). **Effective** 8-17-2006. Prior to being stricken, Code Sec. 6059(b)(3)(B) read as follows:

(B) the requirements of section 412(c) (relating to reasonable actuarial assumptions) have been complied with,

[¶5360] CODE SEC. 6103. CONFIDENTIALITY AND DISCLOSURE OF RETURNS AND RETURN INFORMATION.

(a) GENERAL RULE.—Returns and return information shall be confidential, and except as authorized by this title—

(1) no officer or employee of the United States,

(2) no officer or employee of any State, any local law enforcement agency receiving information under subsection (i)(7)(A), any local child support enforcement agency, or any local agency administering a program listed in subsection (l)(7)(D) who has or had access to returns or return information under this section *or section 6104(c)*, and

(3) no other person (or officer or employee thereof) who has or had access to returns or return information under subsection (e)(1)(D)(iii), paragraph (6), (12), (16), (19), or (20) of subsection (l), paragraph (2) or (4)(B) of subsection (m), or subsection (n),

shall disclose any return or return information obtained by him in any manner in connection with his service as such an officer or an employee or otherwise or under the provisions of this section. For purposes of this subsection, the term "officer or employee" includes a former officer or employee.

* * *

[CCH Explanation at ¶1280. Committee Reports at ¶11,320.]

Amendments

• 2006, Pension Protection Act of 2006 (H.R. 4)

H.R. 4, §1224(b)(1):

Amended Code Sec. 6103(a)(2) by inserting "or section 6104(c)" after "this section". **Effective** 8-17-2006 but shall not apply to requests made before such date.

(p) PROCEDURE AND RECORDKEEPING.—

* * *

(3) RECORDS OF INSPECTION AND DISCLOSURE.—

(A) SYSTEM OF RECORDKEEPING.—Except as otherwise provided by this paragraph, the Secretary shall maintain a permanent system of standardized records or accountings of all requests for inspection or disclosure of returns and return information (including the reasons for and dates of such requests) and of returns and return information inspected or disclosed under this section *and section 6104(c)*. Notwithstanding the provisions of section 552a(c) of title 5, United States Code, the Secretary shall not be required to maintain a record or accounting of requests for inspection or disclosure of returns and return information, or of returns and return information inspected or disclosed, under the authority of subsections (c), (e), (f)(5), (h)(1), (3)(A), or (4), (i)(4), or (8)(A)(ii), (k)(1), (2), (6), (8), or (9), (l)(1), (4)(B), (5), (7), (8), (9), (10), (11), (12), (13)[,] (14), (15), (16), (17), or (18), (m), or (n). The records or accountings required to be maintained under this paragraph shall be available for examination by the Joint Committee on Taxation or the Chief of Staff of such joint committee. Such record or accounting shall also be available for examination by such person or persons as may be, but only to the extent, authorized to make such examination under section 552a(c)(3) of title 5, United States Code.

* * *

(4) SAFEGUARDS.—Any Federal agency described in subsection (h)(2), (h)(5), (i)(1), (2), (3), (5), or (7), (j)(1), (2), or (5), (k)(8), (l)(1), (2), (3), (5), (10), (11), (13), (14), or (17) or (o)(1), the Government Accountability Office, the Congressional Budget Office, or any agency, body, or commission described in subsection (d), (i)(3)(B)(i) or 7(A)(ii), or (l)(6), (7), (8), (9), (12), (15), or (16), *any appropriate State officer (as defined in section 6104(c)),* or any other person described in subsection (l)(16), (18), (19), or (20) shall, as a condition for receiving returns or return information—

(A) establish and maintain, to the satisfaction of the Secretary, a permanent system of standardized records with respect to any request, the reason for such request, and the date of such request made by or of it and any disclosure of return or return information made by or to it;

(B) establish and maintain, to the satisfaction of the Secretary, a secure area or place in which such returns or return information shall be stored;

(C) restrict, to the satisfaction of the Secretary, access to the returns or return information only to persons whose duties or responsibilities require access and to whom disclosure may be made under the provisions of this title;

(D) provide such other safeguards which the Secretary determines (and which he prescribes in regulations) to be necessary or appropriate to protect the confidentiality of the returns or return information;

(E) furnish a report to the Secretary, at such time and containing such information as the Secretary may prescribe, which describes the procedures established and utilized by such agency, body, or commission, the Government Accountability Office, or the Congressional Budget Office for ensuring the confidentiality of returns and return information required by this paragraph; and

(F) upon completion of use of such returns or return information—

(i) in the case of an agency, body, or commission described in subsection (d), (i)(3)(B)(i), or (l)(6), (7), (8), (9), or (16), *any appropriate State officer (as defined in section 6104(c)),* or any other person described in subsection (l)(16), (18), (19), or (20) return to the Secretary such returns or return information (along with any copies made therefrom) or make such returns or return information undisclosable in any manner and furnish a written report to the Secretary describing such manner,

(ii) in the case of an agency described in subsections (h)(2), (h)(5), (i)(1), (2), (3), (5) or (7), (j)(1), (2), or (5), (k)(8), (l)(1), (2), (3), (5), (10), (11), (12), (13), (14), (15), or (17) or (o)(1), the Government Accountability Office, or the Congressional Budget Office, either—

(I) return to the Secretary such returns or return information (along with any copies made therefrom),

(II) otherwise make such returns or return information undisclosable, or

(III) to the extent not so returned or made undisclosable, ensure that the conditions of subparagraphs (A), (B), (C), (D), and (E) of this paragraph continue to be met with respect to such returns or return information, and

(iii) in the case of the Department of Health and Human Services for purposes of subsection (m)(6), destroy all such return information upon completion of its use in providing the notification for which the information was obtained, so as to make such information undisclosable;

except that the conditions of subparagraphs (A), (B), (C), (D), and (E) shall cease to apply with respect to any return or return information if, and to the extent that, such return or return information is disclosed in the course of any judicial or administrative proceeding and made a part of the public record thereof. If the Secretary determines that any such agency, body, or commission, including an agency, *an appropriate State officer (as defined in section 6104(c)),* or any other person described in subsection (l)(16), (18), (19), or (20), or the Government Accountability Office or the Congressional Budget Office, has failed to, or does not, meet the requirements of this paragraph, he may, after any proceedings for review established under paragraph (7), take such actions as are necessary to ensure such requirements are met, including refusing to disclose returns or return information to such agency, body, or commission, including an agency, *an appropriate State officer (as defined in section 6104(c)),* or any other person described in subsection (l)(16), (18), (19), or (20), or the Government Accountability Office or the Congressional Budget Office, until he determines that such requirements have been or will be met. In the case of any agency which receives any mailing address under paragraph (2), (4), (6), or (7) of subsection (m) and which discloses any such mailing address to any agent or which receives any information under paragraph (6)(A), (12)(B), or (16) of subsection (l) and which discloses any such information to any agent, or any person including an agent described in subsection (l)(16), this paragraph shall apply to such agency and each such agent or other person (except that, in the case of an agent, or any person including an agent described in subsection (l)(16), any report to the Secretary or other action with respect to the Secretary shall be made or taken through such agency). For purposes of applying this paragraph in any case to which subsection (m)(6) applies, the term "return information" includes related blood donor records (as defined in section 1141(h)(2) of the Social Security Act).

* * *

[CCH Explanation at ¶1280. Committee Reports at ¶11,320.]

Amendments

- **2006, Pension Protection Act of 2006 (H.R. 4)**

H.R. 4, §1224(b)(2):

Amended Code Sec. 6103(p)(3)(A) by inserting "and section 6104(c)" after "section" in the first sentence. **Effective** 8-17-2006 but shall not apply to requests made before such date.

H.R. 4, §1224(b)(3)(A)-(C):

Amended Code Sec. 6103(p)(4) by inserting ", any appropriate State officer (as defined in section 6104(c))," before "or any other person" in the matter preceding subparagraph (A), by inserting "any appropriate State officer (as defined in section 6104(c))," before "or any other person" in subparagraph (F)(i), and by inserting ", an appropriate State officer (as defined in section 6104(c))," after "including an agency" each place it appears in the matter following subparagraph (F). **Effective** 8-17-2006 but shall not apply to requests made before such date.

[¶5365] CODE SEC. 6104. PUBLICITY OF INFORMATION REQUIRED FROM CERTAIN EXEMPT ORGANIZATIONS AND CERTAIN TRUSTS.

* * *

»»→ Caution: Code Sec. 6104(b), below, as amended by H.R. 4, applies to returns for tax years beginning after December 31, 2006.

(b) INSPECTION OF ANNUAL INFORMATION RETURNS.—The information required to be furnished by sections 6033, 6034, and 6058, together with the names and addresses of such organizations and trusts, shall be made available to the public at such times and in such places as the Secretary may prescribe. Nothing in this subsection shall authorize the Secretary to disclose the name or address of any contributor to any organization or trust (other than a private foundation, as defined in section 509(a) or a political organization exempt from taxation under section 527) which is required to furnish such information. In the case of an organization described in section 501(d), this subsection shall not apply to copies referred to in section 6031(b) with respect to such organization. *In the case of a trust which is required to file a return under section 6034(a), this subsection shall not apply to information regarding beneficiaries which are not organizations described in section 170(c).*

[CCH Explanation at ¶1190. Committee Reports at ¶11,110.]

Amendments

- **2006, Pension Protection Act of 2006 (H.R. 4)**

H.R. 4, §1201(b)(3):

Amended Code Sec. 6104(b) by adding at the end a new sentence. **Effective** for returns for tax years beginning after 12-31-2006.

(c) PUBLICATION TO STATE OFFICIALS.—

(1) GENERAL RULE *FOR CHARITABLE ORGANIZATIONS*.—In the case of any organization which is described in section 501(c)(3) and exempt from taxation under section 501(a), or has applied

under section 508(a) for recognition as an organization described in section 501(c)(3), the Secretary at such times and in such manner as he may by regulations prescribe shall—

(A) notify the appropriate State officer of a refusal to recognize such organization as an organization described in section 501(c)(3), or of the operation of such organization in a manner which does not meet, or no longer meets, the requirements of its exemption,

(B) notify the appropriate State officer of the mailing of a notice of deficiency of tax imposed under section 507 or chapter 41 or 42, and

(C) at the request of such appropriate State officer, make available for inspection and copying such returns, filed statements, records, reports, and other information, relating to a determination under subparagraph (A) or (B) as are relevant to any determination under State law.

(2) DISCLOSURE OF PROPOSED ACTIONS RELATED TO CHARITABLE ORGANIZATIONS.—

(A) SPECIFIC NOTIFICATIONS.—In the case of an organization to which paragraph (1) applies, the Secretary may disclose to the appropriate State officer—

(i) a notice of proposed refusal to recognize such organization as an organization described in section 501(c)(3) or a notice of proposed revocation of such organization's recognition as an organization exempt from taxation,

(ii) the issuance of a letter of proposed deficiency of tax imposed under section 507 or chapter 41 or 42, and

(iii) the names, addresses, and taxpayer identification numbers of organizations which have applied for recognition as organizations described in section 501(c)(3).

(B) ADDITIONAL DISCLOSURES.—Returns and return information of organizations with respect to which information is disclosed under subparagraph (A) may be made available for inspection by or disclosed to an appropriate State officer.

(C) PROCEDURES FOR DISCLOSURE.—Information may be inspected or disclosed under subparagraph (A) or (B) only—

(i) upon written request by an appropriate State officer, and

(ii) for the purpose of, and only to the extent necessary in, the administration of State laws regulating such organizations.

Such information may only be inspected by or disclosed to a person other than the appropriate State officer if such person is an officer or employee of the State and is designated by the appropriate State officer to receive the returns or return information under this paragraph on behalf of the appropriate State officer.

(D) DISCLOSURES OTHER THAN BY REQUEST.—The Secretary may make available for inspection or disclose returns and return information of an organization to which paragraph (1) applies to an appropriate State officer of any State if the Secretary determines that such returns or return information may constitute evidence of noncompliance under the laws within the jurisdiction of the appropriate State officer.

(3) DISCLOSURE WITH RESPECT TO CERTAIN OTHER EXEMPT ORGANIZATIONS.—Upon written request by an appropriate State officer, the Secretary may make available for inspection or disclosure returns and return information of any organization described in section 501(c) (other than organizations described in paragraph (1) or (3) thereof) for the purpose of, and only to the extent necessary in, the administration of State laws regulating the solicitation or administration of the charitable funds or charitable assets of such organizations. Such information may only be inspected by or disclosed to a person other than the appropriate State officer if such person is an officer or employee of the State and is designated by the appropriate State officer to receive the returns or return information under this paragraph on behalf of the appropriate State officer.

(4) USE IN CIVIL JUDICIAL AND ADMINISTRATIVE PROCEEDINGS.—Returns and return information disclosed pursuant to this subsection may be disclosed in civil administrative and civil judicial proceedings pertaining to the enforcement of State laws regulating such organizations in a manner prescribed by the Secretary similar to that for tax administration proceedings under section 6103(h)(4).

(5) NO DISCLOSURE IF IMPAIRMENT.—Returns and return information shall not be disclosed under this subsection, or in any proceeding described in paragraph (4), to the extent that the Secretary determines that such disclosure would seriously impair Federal tax administration.

(6) DEFINITIONS.—For purposes of this subsection—

(A) RETURN AND RETURN INFORMATION.—The terms "return" and "return information" have the respective meanings given to such terms by section 6103(b).

(B) APPROPRIATE STATE OFFICER.—The term "appropriate State officer" means—

(i) the State attorney general,

(ii) the State tax officer,

(iii) in the case of an organization to which paragraph (1) applies, any other State official charged with overseeing organizations of the type described in section 501(c)(3), and

(iv) in the case of an organization to which paragraph (3) applies, the head of an agency designated by the State attorney general as having primary responsibility for overseeing the solicitation of funds for charitable purposes.

[CCH Explanation at ¶1280. Committee Reports at ¶11,320.]

Amendments

• 2006, Pension Protection Act of 2006 (H.R. 4)

H.R. 4, §1224(a):

Amended Code Sec. 6104(c) by striking paragraph (2) and inserting new paragraphs (2)-(6). **Effective** 8-17-2006 but shall not apply to requests made before such date. Prior to being stricken, Code Sec. 6104(c)(2) read as follows:

(2) APPROPRIATE STATE OFFICER.—For purposes of this subsection, the term "appropriate State officer" means the State attorney general, State tax officer, or any State official charged with overseeing organizations of the type described in section 501(c)(3).

H.R. 4, §1224(b)(4):

Amended the heading for Code Sec. 6104(c)(1) by inserting "FOR CHARITABLE ORGANIZATIONS" after "RULE". **Effective** 8-17-2006 but shall not apply to requests made before such date.

(d) PUBLIC INSPECTION OF CERTAIN ANNUAL RETURNS, REPORTS, APPLICATIONS FOR EXEMPTION, AND NOTICES OF STATUS.—

(1) IN GENERAL.—In the case of an organization described in subsection (c) or (d) of section 501 and exempt from taxation under section 501(a) or an organization exempt from taxation under section 527(a)—

(A) a copy of—

(i) the annual return filed under section 6033 (relating to returns by exempt organizations) by such organization,

(ii) any annual return filed under section 6011 which relates to any tax imposed by section 511 (relating to imposition of tax on unrelated business income of charitable, etc., organizations) by such organization, but only if such organization is described in section 501(c)(3),

(iii) if the organization filed an application for recognition of exemption under section 501 or notice of status under section 527(i), the exempt status application materials or any notice materials of such organization, and

(iv) the reports filed under section 527(j) (relating to required disclosure of expenditures and contributions) by such organization,

shall be made available by such organization for inspection during regular business hours by any individual at the principal office of such organization and, if such organization regularly maintains 1 or more regional or district offices having 3 or more employees, at each such regional or district office, and

(B) upon request of an individual made at such principal office or such a regional or district office, a copy of such annual return, reports, and exempt status application materials or such notice materials shall be provided to such individual without charge other than a reasonable fee for any reproduction and mailing costs.

The request described in subparagraph (B) must be made in person or in writing. If such request is made in person, such copy shall be provided immediately and, if made in writing, shall be provided within 30 days.

* * *

[CCH Explanation at ¶ 1275. Committee Reports at ¶ 11,330.]

Amendments

• 2006, Pension Protection Act of 2006 (H.R. 4)

H.R. 4, §1225(a):

Amended Code Sec. 6104(d)(1)(A) by redesignating clauses (ii) and (iii) as clauses (iii) and (iv), respectively, and by inserting after clause (i) a new clause (ii). **Effective** for returns filed after 8-17-2006.

[¶ 5370] CODE SEC. 6214. DETERMINATIONS BY TAX COURT.

* * *

(b) JURISDICTION OVER OTHER YEARS AND QUARTERS.—The Tax Court in redetermining a deficiency of income tax for any taxable year or of gift tax for any calendar year or calendar quarter shall consider such facts with relation to the taxes for other years or calendar quarters as may be necessary correctly to redetermine the amount of such deficiency, but in so doing shall have no jurisdiction to determine whether or not the tax for any other year or calendar quarter has been overpaid or underpaid. *Notwithstanding the preceding sentence, the Tax Court may apply the doctrine of equitable recoupment to the same extent that it is available in civil tax cases before the district courts of the United States and the United States Court of Federal Claims.*

* * *

[CCH Explanation at ¶ 1415. Committee Reports at ¶ 10,840.]

Amendments

• 2006, Pension Protection Act of 2006 (H.R. 4)

H.R. 4, §858(a):

Amended Code Sec. 6214(b) by adding at the end a new sentence. **Effective** for any action or proceeding in the United States Tax Court with respect to which a decision has not become final (as determined under Code Sec. 7481) as of 8-17-2006.

[¶ 5375] CODE SEC. 6330. NOTICE AND OPPORTUNITY FOR HEARING BEFORE LEVY.

* * *

(d) PROCEEDING AFTER HEARING.—

(1) JUDICIAL REVIEW OF DETERMINATION.—The person may, within 30 days of a determination under this section, appeal such determination to the Tax Court (and the Tax Court shall have jurisdiction with respect to such matter).

* * *

[CCH Explanation at ¶ 1405. Committee Reports at ¶ 10,820.]

Amendments

• 2006, Pension Protection Act of 2006 (H.R. 4)

H.R. 4, §855(a):

Amended Code Sec. 6330(d)(1). **Effective** for determinations made after the date which is 60 days after 8-17-2006. Prior to amendment, Code Sec. 6330(d)(1) read as follows:

(1) JUDICIAL REVIEW OF DETERMINATION.—The person may, within 30 days of a determination under this section, appeal such determination—

(A) to the Tax Court (and the Tax Court shall have jurisdiction with respect to such matter); or

(B) if the Tax Court does not have jurisdiction of the underlying tax liability, to a district court of the United States.

If a court determines that the appeal was to an incorrect court, a person shall have 30 days after the court determination to file such appeal with the correct court.

[¶ 5380] CODE SEC. 6416. CERTAIN TAXES ON SALES AND SERVICES.

* * *

(b) SPECIAL CASES IN WHICH TAX PAYMENTS CONSIDERED OVERPAYMENTS.—Under regulations prescribed by the Secretary, credit or refund (without interest) shall be allowed or made in respect of the overpayments determined under the following paragraphs:

* * *

»»→ *Caution: Code Sec. 6416(b)(2), below, as amended by H.R. 4, is effective January 1, 2007.*

(2) SPECIFIED USES AND RESALES.—The tax paid under chapter 32 (or under subsection (a) or (d) of section 4041 in respect of sales or under section 4051) in respect of any article shall be deemed to be an overpayment if such article was, by any person—

(A) exported;

(B) used or sold for use as supplies for vessels or aircraft;

(C) sold to a State or local government for the exclusive use of a State or local government;

(D) sold to a nonprofit educational organization for its exclusive use;

(E) sold to a qualified blood collector organization (as defined in section 7701(a)(49)) for such organization's exclusive use in the collection, storage, or transportation of blood;

(F) in the case of any tire taxable under section 4071(a), sold to any person for use as described in section 4221(e)(3); or

(G) in the case of gasoline, used or sold for use in the production of special fuels referred to in section 4041.

Subparagraphs (C), (D), and (E) shall not apply in the case of any tax paid under section 4064. This paragraph shall not apply in the case of any tax imposed under section 4041(a)(1) or 4081 on diesel fuel or kerosene and any tax paid under section 4121. In the case of the tax imposed by section 4131, subparagraphs *(B), (C), (D), and (E)* shall not apply and subparagraph (A) shall apply only if the use of the exported vaccine meets such requirements as the Secretary may by regulations prescribe. Subparagraphs (C) and (D) shall not apply in the case of any tax imposed on gasoline under section 4081 if the requirements of subsection (a)(4) are not met. *In the case of taxes imposed by subchapter C or D of chapter 32, subparagraph (E) shall not apply.*

* * *

(4) TIRES.—If—

(A) the tax imposed by section 4071 has been paid with respect to the sale of any tire by the manufacturer, producer, or importer thereof, and

»»→ *Caution: Code Sec. 6416(b)(4)(B), below, as amended by H.R. 4, is effective January 1, 2007.*

(B) such tire is sold by any person on or in connection with, or with the sale of, any other article, such tax shall be deemed to be an overpayment by such person if such other article is—

(i) an automobile bus chassis or an automobile bus body,

(ii) by such person exported, sold to a State or local government for the exclusive use of a State or local government, sold to a nonprofit educational organization for its exclusive use, or used or sold for use as supplies for vessels or aircraft*, or*

(iii) sold to a qualified blood collector organization for its exclusive use in connection with a vehicle the organization certifies will be primarily used in the collection, storage, or transportation of blood.

* * *

[CCH Explanation at ¶1255. Committee Reports at ¶11,170.]

Amendments

• **2006, Pension Protection Act of 2006 (H.R. 4)**

H.R. 4, §1207(e)(1)(A):

Amended Code Sec. 6416(b)(2) by redesignating subparagraphs (E) and (F) as subparagraphs (F) and (G), respectively, and by inserting after subparagraph (D) a new subparagraph (E). **Effective** 1-1-2007.

H.R. 4, §1207(e)(1)(B):

Amended Code Sec. 6416(b)(2) by adding at the end a new sentence. **Effective** 1-1-2007.

H.R. 4, §1207(e)(1)(C)(i)-(ii):

Amended Code Sec. 6416(b)(2) by striking "Subparagraphs (C) and (D)" in the second sentence and inserting "Subparagraphs (C), (D), and (E)", and by striking "(B), (C), and (D)" and inserting "(B), (C), (D), and (E)". **Effective** 1-1-2007.

H.R. 4, §1207(e)(2):

Amended Code Sec. 6416(b)(4)(B) by striking "or" at the end of clause (i), by striking the period at the end of clause (ii) and inserting ", or", and by adding after clause (ii) a new clause (iii). **Effective** 1-1-2007.

[¶5385] CODE SEC. 6421. GASOLINE USED FOR CERTAIN NONHIGHWAY PURPOSES, USED BY LOCAL TRANSIT SYSTEMS, OR SOLD FOR CERTAIN EXEMPT PURPOSES.

* * *

»»→ Caution: Code Sec. 6421(c), below, as amended by H.R. 4, is effective January 1, 2007.

(c) EXEMPT PURPOSES.—If gasoline is sold to any person for any purpose described in paragraph (2), (3), (4), *(5), or (6)* of section 4221(a), the Secretary shall pay (without interest) to such person an amount equal to the product of the number of gallons of gasoline so sold multiplied by the rate at which tax was imposed on such gasoline by section 4081. The preceding sentence shall apply notwithstanding paragraphs (2) and (3) of subsection (f). Subsection (a) shall not apply to gasoline to which this subsection applies.

* * *

[CCH Explanation at ¶1255. Committee Reports at ¶11,170.]

Amendments

• 2006, Pension Protection Act of 2006 (H.R. 4)

H.R. 4, §1207(b)(3)(B):

Amended Code Sec. 6421(c) by striking "or (5)" and inserting "(5), or (6)". **Effective** 1-1-2007.

[¶5390] CODE SEC. 6652. FAILURE TO FILE CERTAIN INFORMATION RETURNS, REGISTRATION STATEMENTS, ETC.

* * *

(c) RETURNS BY EXEMPT ORGANIZATIONS AND BY CERTAIN TRUSTS.—

(1) ANNUAL RETURNS UNDER SECTION 6033(a)(1) OR 6012(a)(6).—

* * *

»»→ Caution: Code Sec. 6652(c)(1)(E), below, as added by H.R. 4, applies to notices and returns with respect to annual periods beginning after 2006.

(E) NO PENALTY FOR CERTAIN ANNUAL NOTICES.—This paragraph shall not apply with respect to any notice required under section 6033(i).

(2) RETURNS UNDER SECTION 6034 OR 6043.—

* * *

»»→ Caution: Code Sec. 6652(c)(2)(C), below, as added by H.R. 4, applies to returns for tax years beginning after December 31, 2006.

(C) SPLIT-INTEREST TRUSTS.—In the case of a trust which is required to file a return under section 6034(a), subparagraphs (A) and (B) of this paragraph shall not apply and paragraph (1) shall apply in the same manner as if such return were required under section 6033, except that—

(i) the 5 percent limitation in the second sentence of paragraph (1)(A) shall not apply,

(ii) in the case of any trust with gross income in excess of $250,000, the first sentence of paragraph (1)(A) shall be applied by substituting "$100" for "$20", and the second sentence thereof shall be applied by substituting "$50,000" for "$10,000", and

(iii) the third sentence of paragraph (1)(A) shall be disregarded.

In addition to any penalty imposed on the trust pursuant to this subparagraph, if the person required to file such return knowingly fails to file the return, such penalty shall also be imposed on such person who shall be personally liable for such penalty.

* * *

[CCH Explanation at ¶ 1190 and ¶ 1260. Committee Reports at ¶ 11,110 and ¶ 11,310.]

Amendments

• 2006, Pension Protection Act of 2006 (H.R. 4)

H.R. 4, § 1201(b)(2):

Amended Code Sec. 6652(c)(2) by adding at the end a new subparagraph (C). **Effective** for returns for tax years beginning after 12-31-2006.

H.R. 4, § 1223(d):

Amended Code Sec. 6652(c)(1) by adding at the end a new subparagraph (E). **Effective** for notices and returns with respect to annual periods beginning after 2006.

[¶ 5395] CODE SEC. 6662. IMPOSITION OF ACCURACY-RELATED PENALTY ON UNDERPAYMENTS.

* * *

(e) SUBSTANTIAL VALUATION MISSTATEMENT UNDER CHAPTER 1.—

(1) IN GENERAL.—For purposes of this section, there is a substantial valuation misstatement under chapter 1 if—

(A) the value of any property (or the adjusted basis of any property) claimed on any return of tax imposed by chapter 1 is *150 percent* or more of the amount determined to be the correct amount of such valuation or adjusted basis (as the case may be), or

(B)(i) the price for any property or services (or for the use of property) claimed on any such return in connection with any transaction between persons described in section 482 is 200 percent or more (or 50 percent or less) of the amount determined under section 482 to be the correct amount of such price, or

(ii) the net section 482 transfer price adjustment for the taxable year exceeds the lesser of $5,000,000 or 10 percent of the taxpayer's gross receipts.

* * *

[CCH Explanation at ¶ 1345. Committee Reports at ¶ 11,270.]

Amendments

• 2006, Pension Protection Act of 2006 (H.R. 4)

H.R. 4, § 1219(a)(1)(A):

Amended Code Sec. 6662(e)(1)(A) by striking "200 percent" and inserting "150 percent". **Effective** generally for returns filed after 8-17-2006. For a special rule, see Act Sec. 1219(e)(3), below.

H.R. 4, § 1219(e)(3), provides:

(3) SPECIAL RULE FOR CERTAIN EASEMENTS.—In the case of a contribution of a qualified real property interest which is a restriction with respect to the exterior of a building described in section 170(h)(4)(C)(ii) of the Internal Revenue Code of 1986, and an appraisal with respect to the contribution, the amendments made by subsections (a) and (b) shall apply to returns filed after July 25, 2006.

(g) SUBSTANTIAL ESTATE OR GIFT TAX VALUATION UNDERSTATEMENT.—

(1) IN GENERAL.—For purposes of this section, there is a substantial estate or gift tax valuation understatement if the value of any property claimed on any return of tax imposed by subtitle B is *65 percent* or less of the amount determined to be the correct amount of such valuation.

* * *

[CCH Explanation at ¶ 1345. Committee Reports at ¶ 11,270.]

Amendments

• 2006, Pension Protection Act of 2006 (H.R. 4)

H.R. 4, § 1219(a)(1)(B):

Amended Code Sec. 6662(g)(1) by striking "50 percent" and inserting "65 percent". **Effective** generally for returns filed after 8-17-2006. For a special rule, see Act Sec. 1219(e)(3), below.

H.R. 4, § 1219(e)(3), provides:

(3) SPECIAL RULE FOR CERTAIN EASEMENTS.—In the case of a contribution of a qualified real property interest which is a restriction with respect to the exterior of a building described in section 170(h)(4)(C)(ii) of the Internal Revenue Code of 1986, and an appraisal with respect to the contribution, the amendments made by subsections (a) and (b) shall apply to returns filed after July 25, 2006.

(h) INCREASE IN PENALTY IN CASE OF GROSS VALUATION MISSTATEMENTS.—

* * *

(2) GROSS VALUATION MISSTATEMENTS.—The term "gross valuation misstatements" means—

(A) any substantial valuation misstatement under chapter 1 as determined under subsection (e) by substituting—

(i) in paragraph (1)(A), "200 percent" for "150 percent",

(ii) in paragraph (1)(B)(i)—

(I) "400 percent" for "200 percent", and

(II) "25 percent" for "50 percent", and

(iii) in paragraph (1)(B)(ii)—

(I) "$20,000,000" for "$5,000,000", and

(II) "20 percent" for "10 percent".

(B) any substantial overstatement of pension liabilities as determined under subsection (f) by substituting "400 percent" for "200 percent", and

(C) any substantial estate or gift tax valuation understatement as determined under subsection (g) by substituting *"40 percent" for "65 percent"*.

[CCH Explanation at ¶ 1345. Committee Reports at ¶ 11,270.]

Amendments

• 2006, Pension Protection Act of 2006 (H.R. 4)

H.R. 4, § 1219(a)(2)(A):

Amended Code Sec. 6662(h)(2)(A)(i)-(ii). **Effective** generally for returns filed after 8-17-2006. For a special rule, see Act Sec. 1219(e)(3), below. Prior to amendment, Code Sec. 6662(h)(2)(A)(i)-(ii) read as follows:

(i) "400 percent" for "200 percent" each place it appears,

(ii) "25 percent" for "50 percent", and

H.R. 4, § 1219(a)(2)(B):

Amended Code Sec. 6662(h)(2)(C) by striking "'25 percent' for '50 percent'" and inserting "'40 percent' for '65 percent'". **Effective** generally for returns filed after 8-17-2006. For a special rule, see Act Sec. 1219(e)(3), below.

H.R. 4, § 1219(e)(3), provides:

(3) SPECIAL RULE FOR CERTAIN EASEMENTS.—In the case of a contribution of a qualified real property interest which is a restriction with respect to the exterior of a building described in section 170(h)(4)(C)(ii) of the Internal Revenue Code of 1986, and an appraisal with respect to the contribution, the amendments made by subsections (a) and (b) shall apply to returns filed after July 25, 2006.

[¶ 5400] CODE SEC 6664. DEFINITIONS AND SPECIAL RULES.

* * *

(c) REASONABLE CAUSE EXCEPTION FOR UNDERPAYMENTS.—

(1) IN GENERAL.—No penalty shall be imposed under section 6662 or 6663 with respect to any portion of an underpayment if it is shown that there was a reasonable cause for such portion and that the taxpayer acted in good faith with respect to such portion.

(2) SPECIAL RULE FOR CERTAIN VALUATION OVERSTATEMENTS.—In the case of any underpayment attributable to a substantial or gross valuation over statement under chapter 1 with respect to charitable deduction property, *paragraph (1) shall not apply. The preceding sentence shall not apply to a substantial valuation overstatement under chapter 1 if*—

(A) the claimed value of the property was based on a qualified appraisal made by a qualified appraiser, and

(B) in addition to obtaining such appraisal, the taxpayer made a good faith investigation of the value of the contributed property.

(3) DEFINITIONS.—For purposes of this subsection—

* * *

(B) QUALIFIED APPRAISAL.—The term "qualified appraisal" has the meaning given such term by section 170(f)(11)(E)(i).

(C) QUALIFIED APPRAISER.—The term "qualified appraiser" has the meaning given such term by section 170(f)(11)(E)(ii).

* * *

[CCH Explanation at ¶1345 and ¶1355. Committee Reports at ¶11,270.]

Amendments

• **2006, Pension Protection Act of 2006 (H.R. 4)**

H.R. 4, §1219(a)(3):

Amended Code Sec. 6664(c)(2) by striking "paragraph (1) shall not apply unless" and inserting "paragraph (1) shall not apply. The preceding sentence shall not apply to a substantial valuation overstatement under chapter 1 if". **Effective** generally for returns filed after 8-17-2006. For a special rule, see Act Sec. 1219(e)(3), below.

H.R. 4, §1219(c)(2):

Amended Code Sec. 6664(c)(3)(B)-(C). **Effective** generally for appraisals prepared with respect to returns or submissions filed after 8-17-2006. Prior to amendment, Code Sec. 6664(c)(3)(B)-(C) read as follows:

(B) QUALIFIED APPRAISER.—The term "qualified appraiser" means any appraiser meeting the requirements of the regulations prescribed under section 170(a)(1).

(C) QUALIFIED APPRAISAL.—The term "qualified appraisal" means any appraisal meeting the requirements of the regulations prescribed under section 170(a)(1).

H.R. 4, §1219(e)(3), provides:

(3) SPECIAL RULE FOR CERTAIN EASEMENTS.—In the case of a contribution of a qualified real property interest which is a restriction with respect to the exterior of a building described in section 170(h)(4)(C)(ii) of the Internal Revenue Code of 1986, and an appraisal with respect to the contribution, the amendments made by subsections (a) and (b) shall apply to returns filed after July 25, 2006.

[¶5405] *CODE SEC. 6695A. SUBSTANTIAL AND GROSS VALUATION MISSTATEMENTS ATTRIBUTABLE TO INCORRECT APPRAISALS.*

(a) IMPOSITION OF PENALTY.—If—

(1) a person prepares an appraisal of the value of property and such person knows, or reasonably should have known, that the appraisal would be used in connection with a return or a claim for refund, and

(2) the claimed value of the property on a return or claim for refund which is based on such appraisal results in a substantial valuation misstatement under chapter 1 (within the meaning of section 6662(e)), or a gross valuation misstatement (within the meaning of section 6662(h)), with respect to such property, then such person shall pay a penalty in the amount determined under subsection (b).

(b) AMOUNT OF PENALTY.—The amount of the penalty imposed under subsection (a) on any person with respect to an appraisal shall be equal to the lesser of—

(1) the greater of—

(A) 10 percent of the amount of the underpayment (as defined in section 6664(a)) attributable to the misstatement described in subsection (a)(2), or

(B) $1,000, or

(2) 125 percent of the gross income received by the person described in subsection (a)(1) from the preparation of the appraisal.

(c) EXCEPTION.—No penalty shall be imposed under subsection (a) if the person establishes to the satisfaction of the Secretary that the value established in the appraisal was more likely than not the proper value.

[CCH Explanation at ¶1350. Committee Reports at ¶11,270.]

Amendments

• **2006, Pension Protection Act of 2006 (H.R. 4)**

H.R. 4, §1219(b)(1):

Amended part I of subchapter B of chapter 68 by inserting after Code Sec. 6695 a new Code Sec. 6695A. **Effective** generally for appraisals prepared with respect to returns or submissions filed after 8-17-2006. For a special rule, see Act Sec. 1219(e)(3), below.

H.R. 4, §1219(e)(3), provides:

(3) SPECIAL RULE FOR CERTAIN EASEMENTS.—In the case of a contribution of a qualified real property interest which is a restriction with respect to the exterior of a building described in section 170(h)(4)(C)(ii) of the Internal Revenue Code of 1986, and an appraisal with respect to the contribution, the amendments made by subsections (a) and (b) shall apply to returns filed after July 25, 2006.

[¶5410] CODE SEC. 6696. RULES APPLICABLE WITH RESPECT TO SECTIONS *6694, 6695, and 6695A.*

(a) PENALTIES TO BE ADDITIONAL TO ANY OTHER PENALTIES.—The penalties provided by section[s] *6694, 6695, and 6695A* shall be in addition to any other penalties provided by law.

[CCH Explanation at ¶ 1350. Committee Reports at ¶ 11,270.]

Amendments

• 2006, Pension Protection Act of 2006 (H.R. 4)

H.R. 4, § 1219(b)(2)(A):

Amended Code Sec. 6696 by striking "6694 and 6695" each place it appears in the text and heading thereof and inserting "6694, 6695, and 6695A". **Effective** generally for appraisals prepared with respect to returns or submissions filed after 8-17-2006. For a special rule, see Act Sec. 1219(e)(3), below.

H.R. 4, § 1219(e)(3), provides:

(3) SPECIAL RULE FOR CERTAIN EASEMENTS.—In the case of a contribution of a qualified real property interest which is a restriction with respect to the exterior of a building described in section 170(h)(4)(C)(ii) of the Internal Revenue Code of 1986, and an appraisal with respect to the contribution, the amendments made by subsections (a) and (b) shall apply to returns filed after July 25, 2006.

(b) DEFICIENCY PROCEDURES NOT TO APPLY.—Subchapter B of chapter 63 (relating to deficiency procedures for income, estate, gift, and certain excise taxes) shall not apply with respect to the assessment or collection of the penalties provided by sections *6694, 6695, and 6695A*.

[CCH Explanation at ¶ 1350. Committee Reports at ¶ 11,270.]

Amendments

• 2006, Pension Protection Act of 2006 (H.R. 4)

H.R. 4, § 1219(b)(2)(A):

Amended Code Sec. 6696 by striking "6694 and 6695" each place it appears in the text and inserting "6694, 6695, and 6695A". **Effective** generally for appraisals prepared with respect to returns or submissions filed after 8-17-2006. For a special rule, see Act Sec. 1219(e)(3) in the amendment notes following Code Sec. 6696(a), above.

(c) PROCEDURE FOR CLAIMING REFUND.—Any claim for credit or refund of any penalty paid under section *6694, 6695, or 6695A* shall be filed in accordance with regulations prescribed by the Secretary.

[CCH Explanation at ¶ 1350. Committee Reports at ¶ 11,270.]

Amendments

• 2006, Pension Protection Act of 2006 (H.R. 4)

H.R. 4, § 1219(b)(2)(B):

Amended Code Sec. 6696 by striking "6694 or 6695" each place it appears in the text and inserting "6694, 6695, or 6695A". **Effective** generally for appraisals prepared with respect to returns or submissions filed after 8-17-2006. For a special rule, see Act Sec. 1219(e)(3) in the amendment notes following Code Sec. 6696(a), above.

(d) PERIODS OF LIMITATION.—

(1) ASSESSMENT.—The amount of any penalty under section 6694(a) or under section 6695 shall be assessed within 3 years after the return or claim for refund with respect to which the penalty is assessed was filed, and no proceeding in court without assessment for the collection of such tax shall be begun after the expiration of such period. In the case of any penalty under section 6694(b), the penalty may be assessed, or a proceeding in court for the collection of the penalty may be begun without assessment, at any time.

(2) CLAIM FOR REFUND.—Except as provided in section 6694(d), any claim for refund of an overpayment of any penalty assessed under section *6694, 6695, or 6695A* shall be filed within 3 years from the time the penalty was paid.

[CCH Explanation at ¶ 1350. Committee Reports at ¶ 11,270.]

Amendments

• 2006, Pension Protection Act of 2006 (H.R. 4)

H.R. 4, § 1219(b)(2)(B):

Amended Code Sec. 6696 by striking "6694 or 6695" each place it appears in the text and inserting "6694, 6695, or 6695A". **Effective** generally for appraisals prepared with respect to returns or submissions filed after 8-17-2006. For a special rule, see Act Sec. 1219(e)(3) in the amendment notes following Code Sec. 6696(a), above.

(e) DEFINITIONS.—For purposes of sections *6694, 6695, and 6695A*—

(1) RETURN.—The term "return" means any return of any tax imposed by subtitle A.

(2) CLAIM FOR REFUND.—The term "claim for refund" means a claim for refund of, or credit against, any tax imposed by subtitle A.

[CCH Explanation at ¶ 1350. Committee Reports at ¶ 11,270.]

Amendments

• 2006, Pension Protection Act of 2006 (H.R. 4)

H.R. 4, § 1219(b)(2)(A):

Amended Code Sec. 6696 by striking "6694 and 6695" each place it appears in the text and heading thereof and inserting "6694, 6695, and 6695A". **Effective** generally for appraisals prepared with respect to returns or submissions filed after 8-17-2006. For a special rule, see Act Sec. 1219(e)(3) in the amendment notes following Code Sec. 6696(a), above.

[¶ 5415] *CODE SEC. 6720B. FRAUDULENT IDENTIFICATION OF EXEMPT USE PROPERTY.*

In addition to any criminal penalty provided by law, any person who identifies applicable property (as defined in section 170(e)(7)(C)) as having a use which is related to a purpose or function constituting the basis for the donee's exemption under section 501 and who knows that such property is not intended for such a use shall pay a penalty of $10,000.

[CCH Explanation at ¶ 1150. Committee Reports at ¶ 11,230.]

Amendments

• 2006, Pension Protection Act of 2006 (H.R. 4)

H.R. 4, § 1215(c)(1):

Amended part I of subchapter B of chapter 68 by inserting after Code Sec. 6720A a new Code Sec. 6720B. **Effective** for identifications made after 8-17-2006.

[¶ 5420] CODE SEC. 6721. FAILURE TO FILE CORRECT INFORMATION RETURNS.

* * *

(e) PENALTY IN CASE OF INTENTIONAL DISREGARD.—If 1 or more failures described in subsection (a)(2) are due to intentional disregard of the filing requirement (or the correct information reporting requirement), then, with respect to each such failure—

(1) subsections (b), (c), and (d) shall not apply,

(2) the penalty imposed under subsection (a) shall be $100, or, if greater—

(A) in the case of a return other than a return required under section 6045(a), 6041A(b), 6050H, 6050I, 6050J, 6050K, or 6050L, 10 percent of the aggregate amount of the items required to be reported correctly,

(B) in the case of a return required to be filed by section 6045(a), 6050K, or 6050L, 5 percent of the aggregate amount of the items required to be reported correctly,

(C) in the case of a return required to be filed under section 6050I(a) with respect to any transaction (or related transactions), the greater of—

(i) $25,000, or

(ii) the amount of cash (within the meaning of section 6050I(d)) received in such transaction (or related transactions) to the extent the amount of such cash does not exceed $100,000, *or*

(D) in the case of a return required to be filed under section 6050V, 10 percent of the value of the benefit of any contract with respect to which information is required to be included on the return, and

(3) in the case of any penalty determined under paragraph (2)—

(A) the $250,000 limitation under subsection (a) shall not apply, and

(B) such penalty shall not be taken into account in applying such limitation (or any similar limitation under subsection (b)) to penalties not determined under paragraph (2).

[CCH Explanation at ¶ 1285. Committee Reports at ¶ 11,190.]

Amendments

• 2006, Pension Protection Act of 2006 (H.R. 4)

H.R. 4, § 1211(b)(2):

Amended Code Sec. 6721(e)(2) by striking "or" at the end of subparagraph (B), by striking "and" at the end of subparagraph (C) and inserting "or", and by adding at the end a new subparagraph (D). **Effective** for acquisitions of contracts after 8-17-2006.

[¶ 5425] CODE SEC. 6724. WAIVER; DEFINITIONS AND SPECIAL RULES.

* * *

(d) DEFINITIONS.—For purposes of this part—

(1) INFORMATION RETURN.—The term "information return" means—

* * *

(B) any return required by—

* * *

(xiii) section 6052(a) (relating to reporting payment of wages in the form of group-life insurance),

(xiv) section 6050V (relating to returns relating to applicable insurance contracts in which certain exempt organizations hold interests),

(xv) section 6053(c)(1) (relating to reporting with respect to certain tips),

(xvi) subsection (b) or (e) of section 1060 (relating to reporting requirements of transferors and transferees in certain asset acquisitions),

(xvii) section 4101(d) (relating to information reporting with respect to fuels taxes),

(xviii) subparagraph (C) of section 338(h)(10) (relating to information required to be furnished to the Secretary in case of elective recognition of gain or loss),

(xix) section 264(f)(5)(A)(iv) (relating to reporting with respect to certain life insurance and annuity contracts), *or*

»»→ Caution: Former Code Sec. 6724(d)(1)(B)(xix), below, as added by H.R. 4, §844(d)(2)(A), and redesignated as Code Sec. 6724(d)(1)(B)(xx) by §1211(b)(1), applies to charges made after December 31, 2009.

(xx) section 6050U (relating to charges or payments for qualified long-term care insurance contracts under combined arrangements), and

* * *

Such term also includes any form, statement, or schedule required to be filed with the Secretary with respect to any amount from which tax was required to be deducted and withheld under chapter 3 (or from which tax would be required to be so deducted and withheld but for an exemption under this title or any treaty obligation of the United States).

(2) PAYEE STATEMENT.—The term "payee statement" means any statement required to be furnished under—

* * *

(AA) section 264(f)(5)(A)(iv) (relating to reporting with respect to certain life insurance and annuity contracts),

(BB) section 6050T (relating to returns relating to credit for health insurance costs of eligible individuals) [, or]

»»→ Caution: Code Sec. 6724(d)(2)(CC), below, as added by H.R. 4, applies to charges made after December 31, 2009.

(CC) section 6050U (relating to charges or payments for qualified long-term care insurance contracts under combined arrangements).

Such term also includes any form, statement, or schedule required to be furnished to the recipient of any amount from which tax was required to be deducted and withheld under chapter 3 (or from which tax would be required to be so deducted and withheld but for an exemption under this title or any treaty obligation of the United States).

* * *

[CCH Explanation at ¶820 and ¶1285. Committee Reports at ¶10,780 and ¶11,190.]

Amendments

• **2006, Pension Protection Act of 2006 (H.R. 4)**

H.R. 4, §844(d)(2)(A):

Amended Code Sec. 6724(d)(1)(B) by striking "or" at the end of clause (xvii), by striking "and" at the end of clause (xviii) and inserting "or", and by adding at the end a new clause (xix). **Effective** for charges made after 12-31-2009.

H.R. 4, §844(d)(2)(B):

Amended Code Sec. 6724(d)(2) by striking "or" at the end of subparagraph (AA), by striking the period at the end of subparagraph (BB), and by inserting after subparagraph (BB) a new subparagraph (CC). **Effective** for charges made after 12-31-2009.

H.R. 4, §1211(b)(1):

Amended Code Sec. 6724(d)(1)(B), as amended by this Act, by redesignating clauses (xiv) through (xix) as clauses (xv) through (xx) and by inserting after clause (xiii) a new clause (xiv). **Effective** for acquisitions of contracts after 8-17-2006.

[¶5430] CODE SEC. 7213. UNAUTHORIZED DISCLOSURE OF INFORMATION.

(a) RETURNS AND RETURN INFORMATION.—

* * *

(2) STATE AND OTHER EMPLOYEES.—It shall be unlawful for any person (not described in paragraph (1)) willfully to disclose to any person, except as authorized in this title, any return or return information (as defined in section 6103(b)) acquired by him or another person under subsection (d), (i)(3)(B)(i) or (7)(A)(ii), (l)(6), (7), (8), (9), (10), (12), (15), (16), (19), or (20) or (m)(2), (4), (5), (6), or (7) of section 6103 *or under section 6104(c)*. Any violation of this paragraph shall be a felony punishable by a fine in any amount not exceeding $5,000, or imprisonment of not more than 5 years, or both, together with the costs of prosecution.

* * *

[CCH Explanation at ¶1280. Committee Reports at ¶11,320.]

Amendments

• **2006, Pension Protection Act of 2006 (H.R. 4)**

H.R. 4, §1224(b)(5):

Amended Code Sec. 7213(a)(2) by inserting "or under section 6104(c)" after "6103". **Effective** 8-17-2006 but shall not apply to requests made before such date.

[¶5435] CODE SEC. 7213A. UNAUTHORIZED INSPECTION OF RETURNS OR RETURN INFORMATION.

(a) PROHIBITIONS.—

* * *

(2) STATE AND OTHER EMPLOYEES.—It shall be unlawful for any person (not described in paragraph (1)) willfully to inspect, except as authorized in this title, any return or return information acquired by such person or another person under a provision of section 6103 referred to in section 7213(a)(2) *or under section 6104(c)*.

* * *

[CCH Explanation at ¶1280. Committee Reports at ¶11,320.]

Amendments

• **2006, Pension Protection Act of 2006 (H.R. 4)**

H.R. 4, §1224(b)(6):

Amended Code Sec. 7213A(a)(2) by inserting "or under section 6104(c)" after "7213(a)(2)". **Effective** 8-17-2006 but shall not apply to requests made before such date.

[¶ 5440] CODE SEC. 7428. DECLARATORY JUDGMENTS RELATING TO STATUS AND CLASSIFICATION OF ORGANIZATIONS UNDER SECTION 501(c)(3), ETC.

* * *

(b) LIMITATIONS.—

* * *

➾ *Caution: Code Sec. 7428(b)(4), below, as added by H.R. 4, applies to notices and returns with respect to annual periods beginning after 2006.*

(4) NONAPPLICATION FOR CERTAIN REVOCATIONS.—No action may be brought under this section with respect to any revocation of status described in section 6033(j)(1).

* * *

[CCH Explanation at ¶ 1260. Committee Reports at ¶ 11,310.]

Amendments

• 2006, Pension Protection Act of 2006 (H.R. 4)

H.R. 4, § 1223(c):

Amended Code Sec. 7428(b) by adding at the end a new paragraph (4). **Effective** for notices and returns with respect to annual periods beginning after 2006.

[¶ 5445] CODE SEC. 7431. CIVIL DAMAGES FOR UNAUTHORIZED INSPECTION OR DISCLOSURE OF RETURNS AND RETURN INFORMATION.

(a) IN GENERAL.—

* * *

(2) INSPECTION OR DISCLOSURE BY A PERSON WHO IS NOT AN EMPLOYEE OF UNITED STATES.—If any person who is not an officer or employee of the United States knowingly, or by reason of negligence, inspects or discloses any return or return information with respect to a taxpayer in violation of any provision of section 6103 *or in violation of section 6104(c)*, such taxpayer may bring a civil action for damages against such person in a district court of the United States.

* * *

[CCH Explanation at ¶ 1280. Committee Reports at ¶ 11,320.]

Amendments

• 2006, Pension Protection Act of 2006 (H.R. 4)

H.R. 4, § 1224(b)(7):

Amended Code Sec. 7431(a)(2) by inserting "or in violation of section 6104(c)" after "6103". **Effective** 8-17-2006 but shall not apply to requests made before such date.

[¶ 5450] CODE SEC. 7443A. SPECIAL TRIAL JUDGES.

* * *

(b) PROCEEDINGS WHICH MAY BE ASSIGNED TO SPECIAL TRIAL JUDGES.—The chief judge may assign—

(1) any declaratory judgment proceeding,

(2) any proceeding under section 7463,

(3) any proceeding where neither the amount of the deficiency placed in dispute (within the meaning of section 7463) nor the amount of any claimed overpayment exceeds $50,000,

(4) any proceeding under section 6320 or 6330,

(5) any proceeding under section 7436(c), and

(6) any other proceeding which the chief judge may designate,

to be heard by the special trial judges of the court.

[CCH Explanation at ¶1410. Committee Reports at ¶10,830.]

Amendments

• **2006, Pension Protection Act of 2006 (H.R. 4)**

H.R. 4, §857(a):

Amended Code Sec. 7443A(b) by striking "and" at the end of paragraph (4), by redesignating paragraph (5) as paragraph (6), and by inserting after paragraph (4) a new paragraph (5). **Effective** for any proceeding under Code Sec. 7436(c) with respect to which a decision has not become final (as determined under Code Sec. 7481) before 8-17-2006.

(c) AUTHORITY TO MAKE COURT DECISIONS.—The court may authorize a special trial judge to make the decision of the court with respect to any proceeding described in paragaph (1), (2), (3), *(4), or (5)* of subsection (b), subject to such conditions and review as the court may provide.

* * *

[CCH Explanation at ¶1410. Committee Reports at ¶10,830.]

Amendments

• **2006, Pension Protection Act of 2006 (H.R. 4)**

H.R. 4, §857(b):

Amended Code Sec. 7443A(c) by striking "or 4" and inserting "(4), or (5)". **Effective** for any proceeding under Code Sec. 7436(c) with respect to which a decision has not become final (as determined under Code Sec. 7481) before 8-17-2006.

[¶5455] *CODE SEC. 7443B. RECALL OF SPECIAL TRIAL JUDGES OF THE TAX COURT.*

(a) RECALLING OF RETIRED SPECIAL TRIAL JUDGES.—Any individual who has retired pursuant to the applicable provisions of title 5, United States Code, upon reaching the age and service requirements established therein, may at or after retirement be called upon by the chief judge of the Tax Court to perform such judicial duties with the Tax Court as may be requested of such individual for any period or periods specified by the chief judge; except that in the case of any such individual—

(1) the aggregate of such periods in any 1 calendar year shall not (without such individual's consent) exceed 90 calendar days, and

(2) such individual shall be relieved of performing such duties during any period in which illness or disability precludes the performance of such duties.

Any act, or failure to act, by an individual performing judicial duties pursuant to this subsection shall have the same force and effect as if it were the act (or failure to act) of a special trial judge of the Tax Court.

(b) COMPENSATION.—For the year in which a period of recall occurs, the special trial judge shall receive, in addition to the annuity provided under the applicable provisions of title 5, United States Code, an amount equal to the difference between that annuity and the current salary of the office to which the special trial judge is recalled.

(c) RULEMAKING AUTHORITY.—The provisions of this section may be implemented under such rules as may be promulgated by the Tax Court.

[CCH Explanation at ¶1450. Committee Reports at ¶10,810.]

Amendments

• **2006, Pension Protection Act of 2006 (H.R. 4)**

H.R. 4, §856(a):

Amended part I of subchapter C of chapter 76 by inserting after Code Sec. 7443A a new Code Sec. 7443B. **Effective** 8-17-2006.

[¶5460] CODE SEC. 7447. RETIREMENT.

* * *

(j) THRIFT SAVINGS PLAN.—

(1) ELECTION TO CONTRIBUTE.—

(A) IN GENERAL.—A judge of the Tax Court may elect to contribute to the Thrift Savings Fund established by section 8437 of title 5, United States Code.

(B) Period of election.—An election may be made under this paragraph only during a period provided under section 8432(b) of title 5, United States Code, for individuals subject to chapter 84 of such title.

(2) Applicability of title 5 provisions.—Except as otherwise provided in this subsection, the provisions of subchapters III and VII of chapter 84 of title 5, United States Code, shall apply with respect to a judge who makes an election under paragraph (1).

(3) Special rules.—

(A) Amount contributed.—The amount contributed by a judge to the Thrift Savings Fund in any pay period shall not exceed the maximum percentage of such judge's basic pay for such period as allowable under section 8440f of title 5, United States Code. Basic pay does not include any retired pay paid pursuant to this section.

(B) Contributions for benefit of judge.—No contributions may be made for the benefit of a judge under section 8432(c) of title 5, United States Code.

(C) Applicability of section 8433(b) of title 5 whether or not judge retires.—Section 8433(b) of title 5, United States Code, applies with respect to a judge who makes an election under paragraph (1) and who either—

(i) retires under subsection (b), or

(ii) ceases to serve as a judge of the Tax Court but does not retire under subsection (b).

Retirement under subsection (b) is a separation from service for purposes of subchapters III and VII of chapter 84 of that title.

(D) Applicability of section 8351(b)(5) of title 5.—The provisions of section 8351(b)(5) of title 5, United States Code, shall apply with respect to a judge who makes an election under paragraph (1).

(E) Exception.—Notwithstanding subparagraph (C), if any judge retires under this section, or resigns without having met the age and service requirements set forth under subsection (b)(2), and such judge's nonforfeitable account balance is less than an amount that the Executive Director of the Federal Retirement Thrift Investment Board prescribes by regulation, the Executive Director shall pay the nonforfeitable account balance to the participant in a single payment.

[CCH Explanation at ¶ 1440. Committee Reports at ¶ 10,800.]

Amendments

• 2006, Pension Protection Act of 2006 (H.R. 4)

H.R. 4, § 853(a):

Amended Code Sec. 7447 by adding at the end a new subsection (j). **Effective** 8-17-2006, except that United States Tax Court judges may only begin to participate in the Thrift Savings Plan at the next open season beginning after such date.

[¶ 5465] CODE SEC. 7448. ANNUITIES TO SURVIVING SPOUSES AND DEPENDENT CHILDREN OF JUDGES *AND SPECIAL TRIAL JUDGES*.

(a) Definitions.—For purposes of this section—

* * *

(5) The term "special trial judge" means a judicial officer appointed pursuant to section 7443A, including any individual receiving an annuity under chapter 83 or 84 of title 5, United States Code, whether or not performing judicial duties under section 7443B.

(6) The term "special trial judge's salary" means the salary of a special trial judge received under section 7443A(d), any amount received as an annuity under chapter 83 or 84 of title 5, United States Code, and compensation received under section 7443B.

(7) The term "survivors annuity fund" means the Tax Court judges survivors annuity fund established by this section.

(8) The term "surviving spouse" means a surviving spouse of an individual, who either (A) shall have been married to such individual for at least 2 years immediately preceding his death or (B) is a parent of issue by such marriage, and who has not remarried.

(9) The term "dependent child" means an unmarried child, including a dependent stepchild or an adopted child, who is under the age of 18 years or who because of physical or mental disability is incapable of self-support.

[CCH Explanation at ¶ 1445. Committee Reports at ¶ 10,810.]

Amendments

• 2006, Pension Protection Act of 2006 (H.R. 4)

H.R. 4, § 854(a):

Amended Code Sec. 7448(a), as amended by this Act, by redesignating paragraphs (5), (6), (7), and (8) [sic] as paragraphs (7), (8), (9), and (10) [sic], respectively, and by inserting after paragraph (4) new paragraphs (5) and (6). **Effective** 8-17-2006.

H.R. 4, § 854(c)(1):

Amended the heading of Code Sec. 7448 by inserting "AND SPECIAL TRIAL JUDGES" after "JUDGES". **Effective** 8-17-2006.

(b) *ELECTION.—*

(1) *JUDGES.*—Any judge may by written election filed while he is a judge (except that in the case of an individual who is not reappointed following expiration of his term of office, it may be made at any time before the day after the day on which his successor takes office) bring himself within the purview of this section. In the case of any judge other than the chief judge the election shall be filed with the chief judge; in the case of the chief judge the election shall be filed as prescribed by the Tax Court.

(2) SPECIAL TRIAL JUDGES.—Any special trial judge may by written election filed with the chief judge bring himself or herself within the purview of this section. Such election shall be filed not later than the later of 6 months after—

(A) 6 months after the date of the enactment of this paragraph,

(B) the date the judge takes office, or

(C) the date the judge marries.

[CCH Explanation at ¶ 1445. Committee Reports at ¶ 10,810.]

Amendments

• 2006, Pension Protection Act of 2006 (H.R. 4)

H.R. 4, § 854(b)(1)-(3):

Amended Code Sec. 7448(b) by striking the subsection heading and inserting "(b) ELECTION.—(1) JUDGES.—", by moving the text 2 ems to the right, and by adding at the end a new paragraph (2). **Effective** 8-17-2006. Prior to being stricken, the subsection heading for Code Sec. 7448(b) read as follows:

(b) ELECTION.—

(c) SURVIVORS ANNUITY FUND.—

(1) SALARY DEDUCTIONS.—There shall be deducted and withheld from the salary of each judge *or special trial judge* electing under subsection (b) a sum equal to 3.5 percent of such judge's *or special trial judge's* salary. The amounts so deducted and withheld from such judge's *or special trial judge's* salary, in accordance with such procedure as may be prescribed by the Comptroller General of the United States, be deposited in the Treasury of the United States to the credit of a fund to be known as the "*Tax Court judicial officers* survivors annuity fund" and said fund is appropriated for the payment of annuities, refunds, and allowances as provided by this section. Each judge *or special trial judge* electing under subsection (b) shall be deemed thereby to consent and agree to the deductions from his salary as provided in this subsection, and payment less such deductions shall be a full and complete discharge and acquittance of all claims and demands whatsoever for all judicial services rendered by such judge *or special trial judge* during the period covered by such payment, except the right to the benefits to which he or his survivors shall be entitled under the provisions of this section.

(2) APPROPRIATIONS WHERE UNFUNDED LIABILITY.—

(A) IN GENERAL.—Not later than the close of each fiscal year, there shall be deposited in the Treasury of the United States to the credit of the survivors annuity fund, in accordance with such procedures as may be prescribed by the Comptroller General of [the] United States, amounts required to reduce to zero the unfunded liability (if any) of such fund. Subject to appropriation Acts, such deposits shall be taken from sums available for such fiscal year for the payment of amounts described in subsection (a)(4) *and section 7443A(d)*, and shall immediately become an integrated part of such fund.

(B) EXCEPTION.—The amount required by subparagraph (A) to be deposited in any fiscal year shall not exceed an amount equal to 11 percent of the aggregate amounts described in *subsections (a)(4) and (a)(6)* paid during such fiscal year.

* * *

[CCH Explanation at ¶ 1445. Committee Reports at ¶ 10,810.]

Amendments

• 2006, Pension Protection Act of 2006 (H.R. 4)

H.R. 4, §854(c)(3)(A)-(B):

Amended Code Sec. 7448(c)(1) by inserting "or special trial judge" after "judge" each place it appears other than in the phrase "chief judge", and by inserting "or special trial judge's" after "judge's" each place it appears. **Effective** 8-17-2006.

H.R. 4, §854(c)(4)(A)-(B):

Amended Code Sec. 7448(c) by striking "Tax Court judges" and inserting "Tax Court judicial officers" in paragraph (1), by inserting "and section 7443A(d)" after "(a)(4)" in paragraph (2)(A), and by striking "subsection (a)(4)" and inserting "subsections (a)(4) and (a)(6)" in paragraph (2)(B). **Effective** 8-17-2006.

(d) DEPOSITS IN SURVIVORS ANNUITY FUND.—Each judge *or special trial judge* electing under subsection (b) shall deposit, with interest at 4 percent per annum to December 31, 1947, and 3 percent per annum thereafter, compounded on December 31 of each year, to the credit of the survivors annuity fund, a sum equal to 3.5 percent of his judge's *or special trial judge's* salary and of his basic salary, pay, or compensation for service as a Senator, Representative, Delegate, or Resident Commissioner in Congress, and for any other civilian service within the purview of section 8332 of title 5 of the United States Code. Each such judge *or special trial judge* may elect to make such deposits in installments during the continuance of his service as a judge *or special trial judge* in such amount and under such conditions as may be determined in each instance by the chief judge. Notwithstanding the failure of a judge *or special trial judge* to make such deposit, credit shall be allowed for the service rendered, but the annuity of the surviving spouse of such judge *or special trial judge* shall be reduced by an amount equal to 10 percent of the amount of such deposit, computed as of the date of the death of such judge *or special trial judge*, unless such surviving spouse shall elect to eliminate such service entirely from credit under subsection (n), except that no deposit shall be required from a judge *or special trial judge* for any year with respect to which deductions from his salary were actually made under the civil service retirement laws and no deposit shall be required for any honorable service in the Army, Navy, Air Force, Marine Corps, or Coast Guard of the United States.

* * *

[CCH Explanation at ¶ 1445. Committee Reports at ¶ 10,810.]

Amendments

• 2006, Pension Protection Act of 2006 (H.R. 4)

H.R. 4, §854(c)(3)(A)-(B):

Amended Code Sec. 7448(d) by inserting "or special trial judge" after "judge" each place it appears other than in the phrase "chief judge", and by inserting "or special trial judge's" after "judge's" each place it appears. **Effective** 8-17-2006.

(f) CREDITING OF DEPOSITS.—The amount deposited by or deducted and withheld from the salary of each judge *or special trial judge* electing to bring himself within the purview of this section for credit to the survivors annuity fund shall be credited to an individual account of such judge *or special trial judge*.

[CCH Explanation at ¶ 1445. Committee Reports at ¶ 10,810.]

Amendments

• 2006, Pension Protection Act of 2006 (H.R. 4)

H.R. 4, §854(c)(3)(A)-(B):

Amended Code Sec. 7448(f) by inserting "or special trial judge" after "judge" each place it appears other than in the phrase "chief judge", and by inserting "or special trial judge's" after "judge's" each place it appears. **Effective** 8-17-2006.

(g) TERMINATION.—If the service of any judge *or special trial judge* electing under subsection (b) terminates other than pursuant to the provisions of section 7447 or other than pursuant to section 1106 of the Internal Revenue Code of 1939 or if any judge *or special trial judge* ceases to be married after making the election under subsection (b) and revokes (in a writing filed as provided in subsection (b)) such election, the amount credited to his individual account, together with interest at 4 percent per annum to December 31, 1947, and 3 percent per annum thereafter, compounded on

December 31 of each year, to the date of his relinquishment of office, shall be returned to him. For the purpose of this section, the service of any judge *or special trial judge* electing under subsection (b) who is not reappointed following expiration of his term but who, at the time of such expiration, is eligible for and elects to receive retired pay under section 7447 shall be deemed to have terminated pursuant to said section.

[CCH Explanation at ¶1445. Committee Reports at ¶10,810.]

Amendments

• 2006, Pension Protection Act of 2006 (H.R. 4)

H.R. 4, §854(c)(3)(A)-(B):

Amended Code Sec. 7448(g) by inserting "or special trial judge" after "judge" each place it appears other than in the phrase "chief judge", and by inserting "or special trial judge's" after "judge's" each place it appears. **Effective** 8-17-2006.

(h) ENTITLEMENT TO ANNUITY.—In case any judge *or special trial judge* electing under subsection (b) shall die while a judge *or special trial judge* after having rendered at least 5 years of civilian service computed as prescribed in subsection (n), for the last 5 years of which the salary deductions provided for by subsection (c)(1) or the deposits required by subsection (d) have actually been made or the salary deductions required by the civil service retirement laws have actually been made—

(1) if such judge *or special trial judge* is survived by a surviving spouse but not by a dependent child, there shall be paid to such surviving spouse an annuity beginning with the day of the death of the judge *or special trial judge* or following the surviving spouse's attainment of the age of 50 years, whichever is the later, in an amount computed as provided in subsection (m); or

(2) if such judge *or special trial judge* is survived by a surviving spouse and a dependent child or children, there shall be paid to such surviving spouse an immediate annuity in an amount computed as provided in subsection (m), and there shall also be paid to or on behalf of each such child an immediate annuity equal to the lesser of—

(A) 10 percent of the average annual salary of such judge *or special trial judge* (determined in accordance with subsection (m)), or

(B) 20 percent of such average annual salary, divided by the number of such children; or

(3) if such judge *or special trial judge* leaves no surviving spouse but leaves a surviving dependent child or children, there shall be paid to or on behalf of each such child an immediate annuity equal to the lesser of—

(A) 20 percent of the average annual salary of such judge *or special trial judge* (determined in accordance with subsection (m)), or

(B) 40 percent of such average annual salary, divided by the number of such children.

The annuity payable to a surviving spouse under this subsection shall be terminable upon such surviving spouse's death or such surviving spouse's remarriage before attaining age 55. The annuity payable to a child under this subsection shall be terminable upon (A) his attaining the age of 18 years, (B) his marriage, or (C) his death, whichever first occurs, except that if such child is incapable of self-support by reason of mental or physical disability his annuity shall be terminable only upon death, marriage or recovery from such disability. In case of the death of a surviving spouse of a judge *or special trial judge* leaving a dependent child or children of the judge *or special trial judge* surviving such spouse, the annuity of such child or children shall be recomputed and paid as provided in paragraph (3) of this subsection. In any case in which the annuity of a dependent child is terminated under this subsection, the annuities of any remaining dependent child or children, based upon the service of the same judge *or special trial judge*, shall be recomputed and paid as though the child whose annuity was so terminated had not survived such judge *or special trial judge*.

* * *

[CCH Explanation at ¶1445. Committee Reports at ¶10,810.]

Amendments

• 2006, Pension Protection Act of 2006 (H.R. 4)

H.R. 4, §854(c)(3)(A)-(B):

Amended Code Sec. 7448(h) by inserting "or special trial judge" after "judge" each place it appears other than in the phrase "chief judge", and by inserting "or special trial judge's" after "judge's" each place it appears. **Effective** 8-17-2006.

(j) PAYMENTS IN CERTAIN CASES.—

(1) In any case in which—

(A) a judge *or special trial judge* electing under subsection (b) shall die while in office (whether in regular active *service, retired* from such service under section 7447 *, or receiving any annuity under chapter 83 or 84 of title 5, United States Code,* [sic]), before having rendered 5 years of civilian service computed as prescribed in subsection (n), or after having rendered 5 years of such civilian service but without a survivor or survivors entitled to annuity benefits provided by subsection (h), or

(B) the right of all persons entitled to annuity under subsection (h) based on the service of such judge *or special trial judge* shall terminate before a valid claim therefor shall have been established,

the total amount credited to the individual account of such judge *or special trial judge*, with interest at 4 percent per annum to December 31, 1947, and 3 percent per annum thereafter, compounded on December 31 of each year, to the date of the death of such judge *or special trial judge*, shall be paid, upon the establishment of a valid claim therefor, to the person or persons surviving at the date title to the payment arises, in the following order of precedence, and such payment shall be a bar to recovery by any other person:

(i) to the beneficiary or beneficiaries whom the judge *or special trial judge* may have designated by a writing filed prior to his death with the chief judge, except that in the case of the chief judge such designation shall be by a writing filed by him, prior to his death, as prescribed by the Tax Court;

(ii) if there be no such beneficiary, to the surviving spouse of such judge *or special trial judge* ;

(iii) if none of the above, to the child or children of such judge *or special trial judge* and the descendants of any deceased children by representation;

(iv) if none of the above, to the parents of such judge *or special trial judge* or the survivor of them;

(v) if none of the above, to the duly appointed executor or administrator of the estate of such judge *or special trial judge* ; and

(vi) if none of the above, to such other next of kin of such judge *or special trial judge* as may be determined by the chief judge to be entitled under the laws of the domicile of such judge *or special trial judge* at the time of his death.

Determination as to the surviving spouse, child, or parent of a judge *or special trial judge* for the purposes of this paragraph shall be made by the chief judge without regard to the definitions in *paragraphs (8) and (9) of subsection (a).*

(2) In any case in which the annuities of all persons entitled to annuity based upon the service of a judge *or special trial judge* shall terminate before the aggregate amount of annuity paid equals the total amount credited to the individual account of such judge *or special trial judge*, with interest at 4 percent per annum to December 31, 1947, and 3 percent per annum thereafter, compounded on December 31 of each year, to the date of the death of such judge *or special trial judge*, the difference shall be paid, upon establishment of a valid claim therefor, in the order of precedence prescribed in paragraph (1).

(3) Any accrued annuity remaining unpaid upon the termination (other than by death) of the annuity of any person based upon the service of a judge *or special trial judge* shall be paid to such person. Any accrued annuity remaining unpaid upon the death of any person receiving annuity based upon the service of a judge *or special trial judge* shall be paid, upon the establishment of a valid claim therefor, in the following order of precedence:

* * *

[CCH Explanation at ¶ 1445. Committee Reports at ¶ 10,810.]

Amendments

• **2006, Pension Protection Act of 2006 (H.R. 4)**

H.R. 4, § 854(c)(3)(A)-(B):

Amended Code Sec. 7448(j) by inserting "or special trial judge" after "judge" each place it appears other than in the phrase "chief judge", and by inserting "or special trial judge's" after "judge's" each place it appears. **Effective** 8-17-2006.

H.R. 4, §854(c)(5)(A)-(B):

Amended Code Sec. 7448(j)(1) by striking "service or retired" and inserting "service, retired", and by inserting ", or receiving any annuity under chapter 83 or 84 of title 5, United States Code, [sic]" after "section 7447" in subparagraph (A), and by striking "subsections (a) (6) [sic] and (7)" and inserting "paragraphs (8) and (9) of subsection (a)" in the last sentence. **Effective** 8-17-2006.

(m) COMPUTATION OF ANNUITIES.—The annuity of the surviving spouse of a judge *or special trial judge* electing under subsection (b) shall be an amount equal to the sum of (1) 1.5 percent of the average annual salary (whether judge's *or special trial judge's* salary or compensation for other allowable service) received by such judge *or special trial judge* for judicial service (including periods in which he received retired pay under section 7447(d) *or any annuity under chapter 83 or 84 of title 5, United States Code*) or for any other prior allowable service during the period of 3 consecutive years in which he received the largest such average annual salary, multiplied by the sum of his years of such judicial service, his years of prior allowable service as a Senator, Representative, Delegate, or Resident Commissioner in Congress, his years of prior allowable service performed as a member of the Armed Forces of the United States, and his years, not exceeding 15, of prior allowable service performed as a congressional employee (as defined in section 2107 of title 5 of the United States Code), and (2) three-fourths of 1 percent of such average annual salary multiplied by his years of any other prior allowable service, except that such annuity shall not exceed an amount equal to 50 percent of such average annual salary, nor be less than an amount equal to 25 percent of such average annual salary, and shall be further reduced in accordance with subsection (d) (if applicable). In determining the period of 3 consecutive years referred to in the preceding sentence, there may not be taken into account any period for which an election under section 7447(f)(4) is in effect.

[CCH Explanation at ¶1445. Committee Reports at ¶10,810.]

Amendments

• 2006, Pension Protection Act of 2006 (H.R. 4)

H.R. 4, §854(c)(3)(A)-(B):

Amended Code Sec. 7448(m) by inserting "or special trial judge" after "judge" each place it appears other than in the phrase "chief judge", and by inserting "or special trial judge's" after "judge's" each place it appears. **Effective** 8-17-2006.

H.R. 4, §854(c)(6):

Amended Code Sec. 7448(m)(1), as amended by this Act, by inserting "or any annuity under chapter 83 or 84 of title 5, United States Code," after "7447(d)". **Effective** 8-17-2006.

(n) INCLUDIBLE SERVICE.—Subject to the provisions of subsection (d), the years of service of a judge *or special trial judge* which are allowable as the basis for calculating the amount of the annuity of his surviving spouse shall include his years of service as a member of the United States Board of Tax Appeals, as a judge *or special trial judge* of the Tax Court of the United States, and as a judge *or special trial judge* of the Tax Court, *his years of service pursuant to any appointment under section 7443A,* his years of service as a Senator, Representative, Delegate, or Resident Commissioner in Congress, his years of active service as a member of the Armed Forces of the United States not exceeding 5 years in the aggregate and not including any such service for which credit is allowed for the purposes of retirement or retired pay under any other provision of law, and his years of any other civilian service within the purview of section 8332 of title 5 of the United States Code.

* * *

[CCH Explanation at ¶1445. Committee Reports at ¶10,810.]

Amendments

• 2006, Pension Protection Act of 2006 (H.R. 4)

H.R. 4, §854(c)(3)(A)-(B):

Amended Code Sec. 7448(n) by inserting "or special trial judge" after "judge" each place it appears other than in the phrase "chief judge", and by inserting "or special trial judge's" after "judge's" each place it appears. **Effective** 8-17-2006.

H.R. 4, §854(c)(7):

Amended Code Sec. 7448(n) by inserting "his years of service pursuant to any appointment under section 7443A," after "of the Tax Court,". **Effective** 8-17-2006.

(s) INCREASES IN SURVIVOR ANNUITIES.—Each time that an increase is made under section 8340(b) of title 5, United States Code, in annuities payable under subchapter III of chapter 83 of that title, each annuity payable from the survivors annuity fund under this section shall be increased at the same time by the same percentage by which annuities are increased under such section 8340(b).

* * *

[CCH Explanation at ¶ 1430. Committee Reports at ¶ 10,800.]

Amendments

• 2006, Pension Protection Act of 2006 (H.R. 4)

H.R. 4, §851(a):

Amended Code Sec. 7448(s). **Effective** with respect to increases made under section 8340(b) of title 5, United States Code, in annuities payable under subchapter III of chapter 83 of that title, taking effect after 8-17-2006. Prior to amendment, Code Sec. 7448(s) read as follows:

(s) INCREASES ATTRIBUTABLE TO INCREASED PAY.—Whenever the salary of a judge under section 7443(c) is increased, each annuity payable from the survivors annuity fund which is based, in whole or in part, upon a deceased judge having rendered some portion of his or her final 18 months of service as a judge of the Tax Court, shall also be increased. The amount of the increase in such an annuity shall be determined by multiplying the amount of the annuity, on the date on which the increase in salary becomes effective, by 3 percent for each full 5 percent by which such salary has been increased.

H.R. 4, §854(c)(3)(A)-(B):

Amended Code Sec. 7448(u) by inserting "or special trial judge" after "judge" each place it appears other than in the phrase "chief judge", and by inserting "or special trial judge's" after "judge's" each place it appears [This amendment cannot be made, as Code Sec. 7448(u) does not exist.—CCH]. **Effective** 8-17-2006.

[¶ 5470] CODE SEC. 7451. FEE FOR FILING PETITION.

The Tax Court is authorized to impose a fee in an amount not in excess of $60 to be fixed by the Tax Court for the filing of any petition.

[CCH Explanation at ¶ 1420. Committee Reports at ¶ 10,850.]

Amendments

• 2006, Pension Protection Act of 2006 (H.R. 4)

H.R. 4, §859(a):

Amended Code Sec. 7451 by striking all that follows "petition" and inserting a period. **Effective** 8-17-2006. Prior to being amended, the text of Code Sec. 7451 read as follows:

The Tax Court is authorized to impose a fee in an amount not in excess of $60 to be fixed by the Tax Court for the filing of any petition for the redetermination of a deficiency or for a declaratory judgment under part IV of this subchapter or under section 7428 or for judicial review under section 6226 or section 6228(a).

[¶ 5475] CODE SEC. 7472. EXPENDITURES.

The Tax Court is authorized to make such expenditures (including expenditures for personal services and rent at the seat of Government and elsewhere, and for law books, books of reference, and periodicals), as may be necessary efficiently to execute the functions vested in the Tax Court. *Notwithstanding any other provision of law, the Tax Court is authorized to pay on behalf of its judges, age 65 or over, any increase in the cost of Federal Employees' Group Life Insurance imposed after the date of the enactment of the Pension Protection Act of 2006, including any expenses generated by such payments, as authorized by the chief judge in a manner consistent with such payments authorized by the Judicial Conference of the United States pursuant to section 604(a)(5) of title 28, United States Code.* Except as provided in section 7475, all expenditures of the Tax Court shall be allowed and paid, out of any moneys appropriated for purposes of the Tax Court, upon presentation of itemized vouchers therefor signed by the certifying officer designated by the chief judge.

[CCH Explanation at ¶ 1435. Committee Reports at ¶ 10,800.]

Amendments

• 2006, Pension Protection Act of 2006 (H.R. 4)

H.R. 4, §852:

Amended Code Sec. 7472 by inserting after the first sentence a new sentence. **Effective** 8-17-2006.

[¶ 5480] CODE SEC. 7475. PRACTICE FEE.

* * *

(b) USE OF FEES.—The fees described in subsection (a) shall be available to the Tax Court to employ independent counsel to pursue disciplinary matters *and to provide services to pro se taxpayers*.

[CCH Explanation at ¶ 1425. Committee Reports at ¶ 10,860.]

Amendments

• 2006, Pension Protection Act of 2006 (H.R. 4)

H.R. 4, §860(a):

Amended Code Sec. 7475(b) by inserting before the period at the end "and to provide services to pro se taxpayers". **Effective** 8-17-2006.

[¶ 5485] CODE SEC. 7701. DEFINITIONS.

(a) When used in this title, where not otherwise distinctly expressed or manifestly incompatible with the intent thereof—

* * *

»»→ Caution: Code Sec. 7701(a)(49), below, as added by H.R. 4, is effective January 1, 2007.

(49) QUALIFIED BLOOD COLLECTOR ORGANIZATION.—The term "qualified blood collector organization" means an organization which is—

(A) described in section 501(c)(3) and exempt from tax under section 501(a),

(B) primarily engaged in the activity of the collection of human blood,

(C) registered with the Secretary for purposes of excise tax exemptions, and

(D) registered by the Food and Drug Administration to collect blood.

* * *

[CCH Explanation at ¶ 1255. Committee Reports at ¶ 11,170.]

Amendments

• 2006, Pension Protection Act of 2006 (H.R. 4)

H.R. 4, §1207(f):

Amended Code Sec. 7701(a) by inserting at the end a new paragraph (49). **Effective** 1-1-2007.

(o) CONVENTION OR ASSOCIATION OF CHURCHES.—For purposes of this title, any organization which is otherwise a convention or association of churches shall not fail to so qualify merely because the membership of such organization includes individuals as well as churches or because individuals have voting rights in such organization.

[CCH Explanation at ¶ 1205. Committee Reports at ¶ 11,300.]

Amendments

• 2006, Pension Protection Act of 2006 (H.R. 4)

H.R. 4, §1222:

Amended Code Sec. 7701 by redesignating subsection (o) as subsection (p) and by inserting after subsection (n) a new subsection (o). **Effective** 8-17-2006.

(p) CROSS REFERENCES.—

* * *

[CCH Explanation at ¶ 1205. Committee Reports at ¶ 11,300.]

Amendments

• 2006, Pension Protection Act of 2006 (H.R. 4)

H.R. 4, §1222:

Amended Code Sec. 7701 by redesignating subsection (o) as subsection (p). **Effective** 8-17-2006.

[¶5490] CODE SEC. 7702B. TREATMENT OF QUALIFIED LONG-TERM CARE INSURANCE.

* * *

»»→ Caution: Code Sec. 7702B(e), below, as amended by H.R. 4, §844(f), but prior to amendment by §844(c), applies to contracts issued after December 31, 1996, but only with respect to tax years beginning on or before December 31, 2009.

(e) TREATMENT OF COVERAGE PROVIDED AS PART OF A LIFE INSURANCE CONTRACT.—Except as otherwise provided in regulations prescribed by the Secretary, in the case of any long-term care insurance coverage (whether or not qualified) provided by a rider on or as part of a life insurance contract—

(1) IN GENERAL.—This *title* shall apply as if the portion of the contract providing such coverage is a separate contract.

(2) APPLICATION OF SECTION 7702.—Section 7702(c)(2) (relating to the guideline premium limitation) shall be applied by increasing the guideline premium limitation with respect to a life insurance contract, as of any date—

(A) by the sum of any charges (but not premium payments) against the life insurance contract's cash surrender value (within the meaning of section 7702(f)(2)(A)) for such coverage made to that date under the contract, less

(B) any such charges the imposition of which reduces the premiums paid for the contract (within the meaning of section 7702(f)(1)).

(3) APPLICATION OF SECTION 213.—No deduction shall be allowed under section 213(a) for charges against the life insurance contract's cash surrender value described in paragraph (2), unless such charges are includible in income as a result of the application of section 72(e)(10) and the rider is a qualified long-term care insurance contract under subsection (b).

(4) PORTION DEFINED.—For purposes of this subsection, the term "portion" means only the terms and benefits under a life insurance contract that are in addition to the terms and benefits under the contract without regard to long-term care insurance coverage.

»»→ Caution: Code Sec. 7702B(e), below, as amended by H.R. 4, §844(c) and (f), applies to contracts issued after December 31, 1996, but only with respect to tax years beginning after December 31, 2009.

(e) TREATMENT OF COVERAGE PROVIDED AS PART OF A LIFE INSURANCE OR ANNUITY CONTRACT.—Except as otherwise provided in regulations prescribed by the Secretary, in the case of any long-term care insurance coverage (whether or not qualified) provided by a rider on or as part of a life insurance contract or an annuity contract—

(1) IN GENERAL.—This title shall apply as if the portion of the contract providing such coverage is a separate contract.

(2) DENIAL OF DEDUCTION UNDER SECTION 213.—No deduction shall be allowed under section 213(a) for any payment made for coverage under a qualified long-term care insurance contract if such payment is made as a charge against the cash surrender value of a life insurance contract or the cash value of an annuity contract.

(3) PORTION DEFINED.—For purposes of this subsection, the term "portion" means only the terms and benefits under a life insurance contract or annuity contract that are in addition to the terms and benefits under the contract without regard to long-term care insurance coverage.

(4) ANNUITY CONTRACTS TO WHICH PARAGRAPH (1) DOES NOT APPLY.—For purposes of this subsection, none of the following shall be treated as an annuity contract:

(A) A trust described in section 401(a) which is exempt from tax under section 501(a).

(B) A contract—

(i) purchased by a trust described in subparagraph (A),

(ii) purchased as part of a plan described in section 403(a),

(iii) described in section 403(b),

(iv) provided for employees of a life insurance company under a plan described in section 818(a)(3), or

(v) from an individual retirement account or an individual retirement annuity.

(C) A contract purchased by an employer for the benefit of the employee (or the employee's spouse).

Any dividend described in section 404(k) which is received by a participant or beneficiary shall, for purposes of this paragraph, be treated as paid under a separate contract to which subparagraph (B)(i) applies.

* * *

[CCH Explanation at ¶ 820. Committee Reports at ¶ 10,780.]

Amendments

• 2006, Pension Protection Act of 2006 (H.R. 4)

H.R. 4, § 844(c):

Amended Code Sec. 7702B(e). **Effective** for contracts issued after 12-31-1996, but only with respect to tax years beginning after 12-31-2009. Prior to amendment, Code Sec. 7702B(e) read as follows:

(e) TREATMENT OF COVERAGE PROVIDED AS PART OF A LIFE INSURANCE CONTRACT.—Except as otherwise provided in regulations prescribed by the Secretary, in the case of any long-term care insurance coverage (whether or not qualified) provided by a rider on or as part of a life insurance contract—

(1) IN GENERAL.—This title shall apply as if the portion of the contract providing such coverage is a separate contract.

(2) APPLICATION OF SECTION 7702.—Section 7702(c)(2) (relating to the guideline premium limitation) shall be applied by increasing the guideline premium limitation with respect to a life insurance contract, as of any date—

(A) by the sum of any charges (but not premium payments) against the life insurance contract's cash surrender value (within the meaning of section 7702(f)(2)(A)) for such coverage made to that date under the contract, less

(B) any such charges the imposition of which reduces the premiums paid for the contract (within the meaning of section 7702(f)(1)).

(3) APPLICATION OF SECTION 213.—No deduction shall be allowed under section 213(a) for charges against the life insurance contract's cash surrender value described in paragraph (2), unless such charges are includible in income as a result of the application of section 72(e)(10) and the rider is a qualified long-term care insurance contract under subsection (b).

(4) PORTION DEFINED.—For purposes of this subsection, the term "portion" means only the terms and benefits under a life insurance contract that are in addition to the terms and benefits under the contract without regard to long-term care insurance coverage.

H.R. 4, § 844(f):

Amended Code Sec. 7702B(e)(1), as in effect before amendment by Act Sec. 844(c), by striking "section" and inserting "title". **Effective** as if included in section 321(a) of the Health Insurance Portability and Accountability Act of 1996 [**effective** for contracts issued after 12-31-96.—CCH].

Act Sections Not Amending Code Sections

PENSION PROTECTION ACT OF 2006

[¶7003] ACT SEC. 1. SHORT TITLE AND TABLE OF CONTENTS.

(a) SHORT TITLE.—This Act may be cited as the "Pension Protection Act of 2006".

* * *

TITLE I—REFORM OF FUNDING RULES FOR SINGLE-EMPLOYER DEFINED BENEFIT PENSION PLANS

Subtitle A—Amendments to Employee Retirement Income Security Act of 1974

[¶7006] ACT SEC. 101. MINIMUM FUNDING STANDARDS.

(a) REPEAL OF EXISTING FUNDING RULES.—Sections 302 through 308 of the Employee Retirement Income Security Act of 1974 (29 U.S.C. 1082 through 1086) are repealed.

(b) NEW MINIMUM FUNDING STANDARDS.—Part 3 of subtitle B of title I of such Act (as amended by subsection (a)) is amended by inserting after section 301 the following new section:

"SEC. 302. MINIMUM FUNDING STANDARDS.

"(a) REQUIREMENT TO MEET MINIMUM FUNDING STANDARD.—

"(1) IN GENERAL.—A plan to which this part applies shall satisfy the minimum funding standard applicable to the plan for any plan year.

"(2) MINIMUM FUNDING STANDARD.—For purposes of paragraph (1), a plan shall be treated as satisfying the minimum funding standard for a plan year if—

"(A) in the case of a defined benefit plan which is a single-employer plan, the employer makes contributions to or under the plan for the plan year which, in the aggregate, are not less than the minimum required contribution determined under section 303 for the plan for the plan year,

"(B) in the case of a money purchase plan which is a single-employer plan, the employer makes contributions to or under the plan for the plan year which are required under the terms of the plan, and

"(C) in the case of a multiemployer plan, the employers make contributions to or under the plan for any plan year which, in the aggregate, are sufficient to ensure that the plan does not have an accumulated funding deficiency under section 304 as of the end of the plan year.

"(b) LIABILITY FOR CONTRIBUTIONS.—

"(1) IN GENERAL.—Except as provided in paragraph (2), the amount of any contribution required by this section (including any required installments under paragraphs (3) and (4) of section 303(j)) shall be paid by the employer responsible for making contributions to or under the plan.

"(2) JOINT AND SEVERAL LIABILITY WHERE EMPLOYER MEMBER OF CONTROLLED GROUP.—If the employer referred to in paragraph (1) is a member of a controlled group, each member of such group shall be jointly and severally liable for payment of such contributions.

"(c) VARIANCE FROM MINIMUM FUNDING STANDARDS.—

"(1) WAIVER IN CASE OF BUSINESS HARDSHIP.—

"(A) IN GENERAL.—If—

"(i) an employer is (or in the case of a multiemployer plan, 10 percent or more of the number of employers contributing to or under the plan is) unable to satisfy the minimum funding standard for a plan year without temporary substantial business hardship (substantial business hardship in the case of a multiemployer plan), and

"(ii) application of the standard would be adverse to the interests of plan participants in the aggregate,

the Secretary of the Treasury may, subject to subparagraph (C), waive the requirements of subsection (a) for such year with respect to all or any portion of the minimum funding standard. The Secretary of the Treasury shall not waive the minimum funding standard with respect to a plan for more than 3 of any 15 (5 of any 15 in the case of a multiemployer plan) consecutive plan years.

"(B) EFFECTS OF WAIVER.—If a waiver is granted under subparagraph (A) for any plan year—

"(i) in the case of a single-employer plan, the minimum required contribution under section 303 for the plan year shall be reduced by the amount of the waived funding deficiency and such amount shall be amortized as required under section 303(e), and

"(ii) in the case of a multiemployer plan, the funding standard account shall be credited under section 304(b)(3)(C) with the amount of the waived funding deficiency and such amount shall be amortized as required under section 304(b)(2)(C).

"(C) WAIVER OF AMORTIZED PORTION NOT ALLOWED.—The Secretary of the Treasury may not waive under subparagraph (A) any portion of the minimum funding standard under subsection (a) for a plan year which is attributable to any waived funding deficiency for any preceding plan year.

"(2) DETERMINATION OF BUSINESS HARDSHIP.—For purposes of this subsection, the factors taken into account in determining temporary substantial business hardship (substantial business hardship in the case of a multiemployer plan) shall include (but shall not be limited to) whether or not—

"(A) the employer is operating at an economic loss,

"(B) there is substantial unemployment or underemployment in the trade or business and in the industry concerned,

"(C) the sales and profits of the industry concerned are depressed or declining, and

"(D) it is reasonable to expect that the plan will be continued only if the waiver is granted.

"(3) WAIVED FUNDING DEFICIENCY.—For purposes of this part, the term 'waived funding deficiency' means the portion of the minimum funding standard under subsection (a) (determined without regard to the waiver) for a plan year waived by the Secretary of the Treasury and not satisfied by employer contributions.

"(4) SECURITY FOR WAIVERS FOR SINGLE-EMPLOYER PLANS, CONSULTATIONS.—

"(A) SECURITY MAY BE REQUIRED.—

"(i) IN GENERAL.—Except as provided in subparagraph (C), the Secretary of the Treasury may require an employer maintaining a defined benefit plan which is a single-employer plan (within the meaning of section 4001(a)(15)) to provide security to such plan as a condition for granting or modifying a waiver under paragraph (1).

"(ii) SPECIAL RULES.—Any security provided under clause (i) may be perfected and enforced only by the Pension Benefit Guaranty Corporation, or at the direction of the Corporation, by a contributing sponsor (within the meaning of section 4001(a)(13)), or a member of such sponsor's controlled group (within the meaning of section 4001(a)(14)).

"(B) CONSULTATION WITH THE PENSION BENEFIT GUARANTY CORPORATION.—Except as provided in subparagraph (C), the Secretary of the Treasury shall, before granting or modifying a waiver under this subsection with respect to a plan described in subparagraph (A)(i)—

"(i) provide the Pension Benefit Guaranty Corporation with—

"(I) notice of the completed application for any waiver or modification, and

"(II) an opportunity to comment on such application within 30 days after receipt of such notice, and

"(ii) consider—

"(I) any comments of the Corporation under clause (i)(II), and

"(II) any views of any employee organization (within the meaning of section 3(4)) representing participants in the plan which are submitted in writing to the Secretary of the Treasury in connection with such application.

Information provided to the Corporation under this subparagraph shall be considered tax return information and subject to the safeguarding and reporting requirements of section 6103(p) of the Internal Revenue Code of 1986.

"(C) EXCEPTION FOR CERTAIN WAIVERS.—

"(i) IN GENERAL.—The preceding provisions of this paragraph shall not apply to any plan with respect to which the sum of—

"(I) the aggregate unpaid minimum required contributions for the plan year and all preceding plan years, and

"(II) the present value of all waiver amortization installments determined for the plan year and succeeding plan years under section 303(e)(2),

is less than $1,000,000.

"(ii) TREATMENT OF WAIVERS FOR WHICH APPLICATIONS ARE PENDING.—The amount described in clause (i)(I) shall include any increase in such amount which would result if all applications for waivers of the minimum funding standard under this subsection which are pending with respect to such plan were denied.

"(iii) UNPAID MINIMUM REQUIRED CONTRIBUTION.—For purposes of this subparagraph—

"(I) IN GENERAL.—The term 'unpaid minimum required contribution' means, with respect to any plan year, any minimum required contribution under section 303 for the plan year which is not paid on or before the due date (as determined under section 303(j)(1)) for the plan year.

"(II) ORDERING RULE.—For purposes of subclause (I), any payment to or under a plan for any plan year shall be allocated first to unpaid minimum required contributions for all preceding plan years on a first-in, first-out basis and then to the minimum required contribution under section 303 for the plan year.

"(5) SPECIAL RULES FOR SINGLE-EMPLOYER PLANS.—

"(A) APPLICATION MUST BE SUBMITTED BEFORE DATE 2½ MONTHS AFTER CLOSE OF YEAR.—In the case of a single-employer plan, no waiver may be granted under this subsection with respect to any plan for any plan year unless an application therefor is submitted to the Secretary of the Treasury not later than the 15th day of the 3rd month beginning after the close of such plan year.

"(B) SPECIAL RULE IF EMPLOYER IS MEMBER OF CONTROLLED GROUP.—In the case of a single-employer plan, if an employer is a member of a controlled group, the temporary substantial business hardship requirements of paragraph (1) shall be treated as met only if such requirements are met—

"(i) with respect to such employer, and

"(ii) with respect to the controlled group of which such employer is a member (determined by treating all members of such group as a single employer).

The Secretary of the Treasury may provide that an analysis of a trade or business or industry of a member need not be conducted if such Secretary determines such analysis is not necessary because the taking into account of such member would not significantly affect the determination under this paragraph.

"(6) ADVANCE NOTICE.—

"(A) IN GENERAL.—The Secretary of the Treasury shall, before granting a waiver under this subsection, require each applicant to provide evidence satisfactory to such Secretary that the applicant has provided notice of the filing of the application for such waiver to each affected party (as defined in section 4001(a)(21)). Such notice shall include a description of the extent to which the plan is funded for benefits which are guaranteed under title IV and for benefit liabilities.

"(B) CONSIDERATION OF RELEVANT INFORMATION.—The Secretary of the Treasury shall consider any relevant information provided by a person to whom notice was given under subparagraph (A).

"(7) RESTRICTION ON PLAN AMENDMENTS.—

"(A) IN GENERAL.—No amendment of a plan which increases the liabilities of the plan by reason of any increase in benefits, any change in the accrual of benefits, or any change in the rate at which benefits become nonforfeitable under the plan shall be adopted if a waiver under this subsection or an extension of time under section 304(d) is in effect with respect to the plan, or if a plan amendment described in subsection (d)(2) has been made at any time in the preceding 12 months (24 months in the case of a multiemployer plan). If a plan is amended in violation of the preceding sentence, any such waiver, or extension of time, shall not apply to any plan year ending on or after the date on which such amendment is adopted.

"(B) EXCEPTION.—Subparagraph (A) shall not apply to any plan amendment which—

"(i) the Secretary of the Treasury determines to be reasonable and which provides for only de minimis increases in the liabilities of the plan,

"(ii) only repeals an amendment described in subsection (d)(2), or

"(iii) is required as a condition of qualification under part I of subchapter D of chapter 1 of the Internal Revenue Code of 1986.

"(8) CROSS REFERENCE.—For corresponding duties of the Secretary of the Treasury with regard to implementation of the Internal Revenue Code of 1986, see section 412(c) of such Code.

"(d) MISCELLANEOUS RULES.—

"(1) CHANGE IN METHOD OR YEAR.—If the funding method, the valuation date, or a plan year for a plan is changed, the change shall take effect only if approved by the Secretary of the Treasury.

"(2) CERTAIN RETROACTIVE PLAN AMENDMENTS.—For purposes of this section, any amendment applying to a plan year which—

"(A) is adopted after the close of such plan year but no later than 2½ months after the close of the plan year (or, in the case of a multiemployer plan, no later than 2 years after the close of such plan year),

"(B) does not reduce the accrued benefit of any participant determined as of the beginning of the first plan year to which the amendment applies, and

"(C) does not reduce the accrued benefit of any participant determined as of the time of adoption except to the extent required by the circumstances,

shall, at the election of the plan administrator, be deemed to have been made on the first day of such plan year. No amendment described in this paragraph which reduces the accrued benefits of any participant shall take effect unless the plan administrator files a notice with the Secretary of the Treasury notifying him of such amendment and such Secretary has approved such amendment, or within 90 days after the date on which such notice was filed, failed to disapprove such amendment. No amendment described in this subsection shall be approved by the Secretary of the Treasury unless such Secretary determines that such amendment is necessary because of a temporary substantial business hardship (as determined under subsection (c)(2)) or a substantial business hardship (as so determined) in the case of a multiemployer plan and that a waiver under subsection (c) (or, in the case of a multiemployer plan, any extension of the amortization period under section 304(d)) is unavailable or inadequate.

"(3) CONTROLLED GROUP.—For purposes of this section, the term 'controlled group' means any group treated as a single employer under subsection (b), (c), (m), or (o) of section 414 of the Internal Revenue Code of 1986.".

(c) CLERICAL AMENDMENT.—The table of contents in section 1 of such Act is amended by striking the items relating to sections 302 through 308 and inserting the following new item:

"Sec. 302. Minimum funding standards.".

(d) EFFECTIVE DATE.—The amendments made by this section shall apply to plan years beginning after 2007.

[CCH Explanation at ¶ 205. Committee Reports at ¶ 10,010.]

[¶ 7009] ACT SEC. 102. FUNDING RULES FOR SINGLE-EMPLOYER DEFINED BENEFIT PENSION PLANS.

(a) IN GENERAL.—Part 3 of subtitle B of title I of the Employee Retirement Income Security Act of 1974 (as amended by section 101 of this Act) is amended by inserting after section 302 the following new section:

"SEC. 303. MINIMUM FUNDING STANDARDS FOR SINGLE-EMPLOYER DEFINED BENEFIT PENSION PLANS.

"(a) MINIMUM REQUIRED CONTRIBUTION.—For purposes of this section and section 302(a)(2)(A), except as provided in subsection (f), the term 'minimum required contribution' means, with respect to any plan year of a single-employer plan—

"(1) in any case in which the value of plan assets of the plan (as reduced under subsection (f)(4)(B)) is less than the funding target of the plan for the plan year, the sum of—

"(A) the target normal cost of the plan for the plan year,

"(B) the shortfall amortization charge (if any) for the plan for the plan year determined under subsection (c), and

"(C) the waiver amortization charge (if any) for the plan for the plan year as determined under subsection (e); or

"(2) in any case in which the value of plan assets of the plan (as reduced under subsection (f)(4)(B)) equals or exceeds the funding target of the plan for the plan year, the target normal cost of the plan for the plan year reduced (but not below zero) by such excess.

"(b) TARGET NORMAL COST.—For purposes of this section, except as provided in subsection (i)(2) with respect to plans in at-risk status, the term 'target normal cost' means, for any plan year, the present value of all benefits which are expected to accrue or to be earned under the plan during the plan year. For purposes of this subsection, if any benefit attributable to services performed in a preceding plan year is increased by reason of any increase in compensation during the current plan year, the increase in such benefit shall be treated as having accrued during the current plan year.

"(c) SHORTFALL AMORTIZATION CHARGE.—

"(1) IN GENERAL.—For purposes of this section, the shortfall amortization charge for a plan for any plan year is the aggregate total (not less than zero) of the shortfall amortization installments for such plan year with respect to the shortfall amortization bases for such plan year and each of the preceding plan years.

"(2) SHORTFALL AMORTIZATION INSTALLMENT.—For purposes of paragraph (1)—

"(A) DETERMINATION.—The shortfall amortization installments are the amounts necessary to amortize the shortfall amortization base of the plan for any plan year in level annual installments over the 7-plan-year period beginning with such plan year.

"(B) SHORTFALL INSTALLMENT.—The shortfall amortization installment for any plan year in the 7-plan-year period under subparagraph (A) with respect to any shortfall amortization base is the annual installment determined under subparagraph (A) for that year for that base.

"(C) SEGMENT RATES.—In determining any shortfall amortization installment under this paragraph, the plan sponsor shall use the segment rates determined under subparagraph (C) of subsection (h)(2), applied under rules similar to the rules of subparagraph (B) of subsection (h)(2).

"(3) SHORTFALL AMORTIZATION BASE.—For purposes of this section, the shortfall amortization base of a plan for a plan year is—

"(A) the funding shortfall of such plan for such plan year, minus

"(B) the present value (determined using the segment rates determined under subparagraph (C) of subsection (h)(2), applied under rules similar to the rules of subparagraph (B) of subsection (h)(2)) of the aggregate total of the shortfall amortization installments and waiver amortization installments which have been determined for such plan year and any succeeding plan year with respect to the shortfall amortization bases and waiver amortization bases of the plan for any plan year preceding such plan year.

"(4) FUNDING SHORTFALL.—For purposes of this section, the funding shortfall of a plan for any plan year is the excess (if any) of—

"(A) the funding target of the plan for the plan year, over

"(B) the value of plan assets of the plan (as reduced under subsection (f)(4)(B)) for the plan year which are held by the plan on the valuation date.

"(5) EXEMPTION FROM NEW SHORTFALL AMORTIZATION BASE.—

"(A) IN GENERAL.—In any case in which the value of plan assets of the plan (as reduced under subsection (f)(4)(A)) is equal to or greater than the funding target of the plan for the plan year, the shortfall amortization base of the plan for such plan year shall be zero.

"(B) TRANSITION RULE.—

"(i) IN GENERAL.—Except as provided in clauses (iii) and (iv), in the case of plan years beginning after 2007 and before 2011, only the applicable percentage of the funding target shall be taken into account under paragraph (3)(A) in determining the funding shortfall for the plan year for purposes of subparagraph (A).

"(ii) APPLICABLE PERCENTAGE.—For purposes of subparagraph (A), the applicable percentage shall be determined in accordance with the following table:

"In the case of a plan year beginning in calendar year:	The applicable percentage is
2008	92
2009	94
2010	96 .

"(iii) LIMITATION.—Clause (i) shall not apply with respect to any plan year after 2008 unless the shortfall amortization base for each of the preceding years beginning after 2007 was zero (determined after application of this subparagraph).

"(iv) TRANSITION RELIEF NOT AVAILABLE FOR NEW OR DEFICIT REDUCTION PLANS.—Clause (i) shall not apply to a plan—

"(I) which was not in effect for a plan year beginning in 2007, or

"(II) which was in effect for a plan year beginning in 2007 and which was subject to section 302(d) (as in effect for plan years beginning in 2007), determined after the application of paragraphs (6) and (9) thereof.

"(6) EARLY DEEMED AMORTIZATION UPON ATTAINMENT OF FUNDING TARGET.—In any case in which the funding shortfall of a plan for a plan year is zero, for purposes of determining the shortfall amortization charge for such plan year and succeeding plan years, the shortfall amortization bases for all preceding plan years (and all shortfall amortization installments determined with respect to such bases) shall be reduced to zero.

"(d) RULES RELATING TO FUNDING TARGET.—For purposes of this section—

"(1) FUNDING TARGET.—Except as provided in subsection (i)(1) with respect to plans in at-risk status, the funding target of a plan for a plan year is the present value of all benefits accrued or earned under the plan as of the beginning of the plan year.

"(2) FUNDING TARGET ATTAINMENT PERCENTAGE.—The 'funding target attainment percentage' of a plan for a plan year is the ratio (expressed as a percentage) which—

"(A) the value of plan assets for the plan year (as reduced under subsection (f)(4)(B)), bears to

"(B) the funding target of the plan for the plan year (determined without regard to subsection (i)(1)).

"(e) WAIVER AMORTIZATION CHARGE.—

"(1) DETERMINATION OF WAIVER AMORTIZATION CHARGE.—The waiver amortization charge (if any) for a plan for any plan year is the aggregate total of the waiver amortization installments for such plan year with respect to the waiver amortization bases for each of the 5 preceding plan years.

"(2) WAIVER AMORTIZATION INSTALLMENT.—For purposes of paragraph (1)—

"(A) DETERMINATION.—The waiver amortization installments are the amounts necessary to amortize the waiver amortization base of the plan for any plan year in level annual installments over a period of 5 plan years beginning with the succeeding plan year.

"(B) WAIVER INSTALLMENT.—The waiver amortization installment for any plan year in the 5-year period under subparagraph (A) with respect to any waiver amortization base is the annual installment determined under subparagraph (A) for that year for that base.

"(3) INTEREST RATE.—In determining any waiver amortization installment under this subsection, the plan sponsor shall use the segment rates determined under subparagraph (C) of subsection (h)(2), applied under rules similar to the rules of subparagraph (B) of subsection (h)(2).

"(4) WAIVER AMORTIZATION BASE.—The waiver amortization base of a plan for a plan year is the amount of the waived funding deficiency (if any) for such plan year under section 302(c).

"(5) EARLY DEEMED AMORTIZATION UPON ATTAINMENT OF FUNDING TARGET.—In any case in which the funding shortfall of a plan for a plan year is zero, for purposes of determining the waiver amortization charge for such plan year and succeeding plan years, the waiver amortization bases for all preceding plan years (and all waiver amortization installments determined with respect to such bases) shall be reduced to zero.

"(f) REDUCTION OF MINIMUM REQUIRED CONTRIBUTION BY PREFUNDING BALANCE AND FUNDING STANDARD CARRYOVER BALANCE.—

"(1) ELECTION TO MAINTAIN BALANCES.—

"(A) PREFUNDING BALANCE.—The plan sponsor of a single-employer plan may elect to maintain a prefunding balance.

"(B) FUNDING STANDARD CARRYOVER BALANCE.—

"(i) IN GENERAL.—In the case of a single-employer plan described in clause (ii), the plan sponsor may elect to maintain a funding standard carryover balance, until such balance is reduced to zero.

"(ii) PLANS MAINTAINING FUNDING STANDARD ACCOUNT IN 2007.—A plan is described in this clause if the plan—

"(I) was in effect for a plan year beginning in 2007, and

"(II) had a positive balance in the funding standard account under section 302(b) as in effect for such plan year and determined as of the end of such plan year.

"(2) APPLICATION OF BALANCES.—A prefunding balance and a funding standard carryover balance maintained pursuant to this paragraph—

"(A) shall be available for crediting against the minimum required contribution, pursuant to an election under paragraph (3),

"(B) shall be applied as a reduction in the amount treated as the value of plan assets for purposes of this section, to the extent provided in paragraph (4), and

"(C) may be reduced at any time, pursuant to an election under paragraph (5).

"(3) ELECTION TO APPLY BALANCES AGAINST MINIMUM REQUIRED CONTRIBUTION.—

"(A) IN GENERAL.—Except as provided in subparagraphs (B) and (C), in the case of any plan year in which the plan sponsor elects to credit against the minimum required contribution for the current plan year all or a portion of the prefunding balance or the funding standard carryover balance for the current plan year (not in excess of such minimum required contribution), the minimum required contribution for the plan year shall be reduced as of the first day of the plan year by the amount so credited by the plan sponsor. For purposes of the preceding sentence, the minimum required contribution shall be determined after taking into account any waiver under section 302(c).

"(B) COORDINATION WITH FUNDING STANDARD CARRYOVER BALANCE.—To the extent that any plan has a funding standard carryover balance greater than zero, no amount of the prefunding balance of such plan may be credited under this paragraph in reducing the minimum required contribution.

"(C) LIMITATION FOR UNDERFUNDED PLANS.—The preceding provisions of this paragraph shall not apply for any plan year if the ratio (expressed as a percentage) which—

"(i) the value of plan assets for the preceding plan year (as reduced under paragraph (4)(C)), bears to

"(ii) the funding target of the plan for the preceding plan year (determined without regard to subsection (i)(1)),

is less than 80 percent. In the case of plan years beginning in 2008, the ratio under this subparagraph may be determined using such methods of estimation as the Secretary of the Treasury may prescribe.

"(4) EFFECT OF BALANCES ON AMOUNTS TREATED AS VALUE OF PLAN ASSETS.—In the case of any plan maintaining a prefunding balance or a funding standard carryover balance pursuant to this subsection, the amount treated as the value of plan assets shall be deemed to be such amount, reduced as provided in the following subparagraphs:

"(A) APPLICABILITY OF SHORTFALL AMORTIZATION BASE.—For purposes of subsection (c)(5), the value of plan assets is deemed to be such amount, reduced by the amount of the prefunding balance, but only if an election under paragraph (2) applying any portion of the prefunding balance in reducing the minimum required contribution is in effect for the plan year.

"(B) DETERMINATION OF EXCESS ASSETS, FUNDING SHORTFALL, AND FUNDING TARGET ATTAINMENT PERCENTAGE.—

"(i) IN GENERAL.—For purposes of subsections (a), (c)(4)(B), and (d)(2)(A), the value of plan assets is deemed to be such amount, reduced by the amount of the prefunding balance and the funding standard carryover balance.

"(ii) SPECIAL RULE FOR CERTAIN BINDING AGREEMENTS WITH PBGC.—For purposes of subsection (c)(4)(B), the value of plan assets shall not be deemed to be reduced for a plan year by the amount of the specified balance if, with respect to such balance, there is in effect for a plan year a binding written agreement with the Pension Benefit Guaranty Corporation which provides that such balance is not available to reduce the minimum required contribution for the plan year. For purposes of the preceding sentence, the term 'specified balance' means the prefunding balance or the funding standard carryover balance, as the case may be.

"(C) AVAILABILITY OF BALANCES IN PLAN YEAR FOR CREDITING AGAINST MINIMUM REQUIRED CONTRIBUTION.—For purposes of paragraph (3)(C)(i) of this subsection, the value of plan assets is deemed to be such amount, reduced by the amount of the prefunding balance.

"(5) ELECTION TO REDUCE BALANCE PRIOR TO DETERMINATIONS OF VALUE OF PLAN ASSETS AND CREDITING AGAINST MINIMUM REQUIRED CONTRIBUTION.—

"(A) IN GENERAL.—The plan sponsor may elect to reduce by any amount the balance of the prefunding balance and the funding standard carryover balance for any plan year (but not below zero). Such reduction shall be effective prior to any determination of the value of plan assets for such plan year under this section and application of the balance in reducing the minimum required contribution for such plan for such plan year pursuant to an election under paragraph (2).

"(B) COORDINATION BETWEEN PREFUNDING BALANCE AND FUNDING STANDARD CARRYOVER BALANCE.—To the extent that any plan has a funding standard carryover balance greater than zero, no election may be made under subparagraph (A) with respect to the prefunding balance.

"(6) PREFUNDING BALANCE.—

"(A) IN GENERAL.—A prefunding balance maintained by a plan shall consist of a beginning balance of zero, increased and decreased to the extent provided in subparagraphs (B) and (C), and adjusted further as provided in paragraph (8).

"(B) INCREASES.—

"(i) IN GENERAL.—As of the first day of each plan year beginning after 2008, the prefunding balance of a plan shall be increased by the amount elected by the plan sponsor for the plan year. Such amount shall not exceed the excess (if any) of—

"(I) the aggregate total of employer contributions to the plan for the preceding plan year, over—

"(II) the minimum required contribution for such preceding plan year.

"(ii) ADJUSTMENTS FOR INTEREST.—Any excess contributions under clause (i) shall be properly adjusted for interest accruing for the periods between the first day of the current plan year and the dates on which the excess contributions were made, determined by using the effective interest rate for the preceding plan year and by treating contributions as being first used to satisfy the minimum required contribution.

"(iii) CERTAIN CONTRIBUTIONS NECESSARY TO AVOID BENEFIT LIMITATIONS DISREGARDED.—The excess described in clause (i) with respect to any preceding plan year shall be reduced (but not below zero) by the amount of contributions an employer would be required to make under paragraph (1), (2), or (4) of section 206(g) to avoid a benefit limitation which would otherwise be imposed under such paragraph for the preceding plan year. Any contribution which may be taken into account in satisfying the requirements of more than 1 of such paragraphs shall be taken into account only once for purposes of this clause.

"(C) DECREASE.—The prefunding balance of a plan shall be decreased (but not below zero) by—

"(i) as of the first day of each plan year after 2008, the amount of such balance credited under paragraph (2) (if any) in reducing the minimum required contribution of the plan for the preceding plan year, and

"(ii) as of the time specified in paragraph (5))(A), any reduction in such balance elected under paragraph (5).

"(7) FUNDING STANDARD CARRYOVER BALANCE.—

"(A) IN GENERAL.—A funding standard carryover balance maintained by a plan shall consist of a beginning balance determined under subparagraph (B), decreased to the extent provided in subparagraph (C), and adjusted further as provided in paragraph (8).

"(B) BEGINNING BALANCE.—The beginning balance of the funding standard carryover balance shall be the positive balance described in paragraph (1)(B)(ii)(II).

"(C) DECREASES.—The funding standard carryover balance of a plan shall be decreased (but not below zero) by—

"(i) as of the first day of each plan year after 2008, the amount of such balance credited under paragraph (2) (if any) in reducing the minimum required contribution of the plan for the preceding plan year, and

"(ii) as of the time specified in paragraph (5))(A), any reduction in such balance elected under paragraph (5).

"(8) ADJUSTMENTS FOR INVESTMENT EXPERIENCE.—In determining the prefunding balance or the funding standard carryover balance of a plan as of the first day of the plan year, the plan sponsor shall, in accordance with regulations prescribed by the Secretary of the Treasury, adjust such balance to reflect the rate of return on plan assets for the preceding plan year. Notwithstanding subsection (g)(3), such rate of return shall be determined on the basis of fair market value and shall properly take into account, in accordance with such regulations, all contributions, distributions, and other plan payments made during such period.

"(9) ELECTIONS.—Elections under this subsection shall be made at such times, and in such form and manner, as shall be prescribed in regulations of the Secretary of the Treasury.

"(g) VALUATION OF PLAN ASSETS AND LIABILITIES.—

"(1) TIMING OF DETERMINATIONS.—Except as otherwise provided under this subsection, all determinations under this section for a plan year shall be made as of the valuation date of the plan for such plan year.

"(2) VALUATION DATE.—For purposes of this section—

"(A) IN GENERAL.—Except as provided in subparagraph (B), the valuation date of a plan for any plan year shall be the first day of the plan year.

"(B) EXCEPTION FOR SMALL PLANS.—If, on each day during the preceding plan year, a plan had 100 or fewer participants, the plan may designate any day during the plan year as its valuation date for such plan year and succeeding plan years. For purposes of this subparagraph, all defined benefit plans which are single-employer plans and are maintained by the same employer (or any member of such employer's controlled group) shall be treated as 1 plan, but only participants with respect to such employer or member shall be taken into account.

"(C) APPLICATION OF CERTAIN RULES IN DETERMINATION OF PLAN SIZE.—For purposes of this paragraph—

"(i) PLANS NOT IN EXISTENCE IN PRECEDING YEAR.—In the case of the first plan year of any plan, subparagraph (B) shall apply to such plan by taking into account the number of participants that the plan is reasonably expected to have on days during such first plan year.

"(ii) PREDECESSORS.—Any reference in subparagraph (B) to an employer shall include a reference to any predecessor of such employer.

"(3) DETERMINATION OF VALUE OF PLAN ASSETS.—For purposes of this section—

"(A) IN GENERAL.—Except as provided in subparagraph (B), the value of plan assets shall be the fair market value of the assets.

"(B) AVERAGING ALLOWED.—A plan may determine the value of plan assets on the basis of the averaging of fair market values, but only if such method—

"(i) is permitted under regulations prescribed by the Secretary of the Treasury,

"(ii) does not provide for averaging of such values over more than the period beginning on the last day of the 25th month preceding the month in which the valuation date occurs and ending on the valuation date (or a similar period in the case of a valuation date which is not the 1st day of a month), and

"(iii) does not result in a determination of the value of plan assets which, at any time, is lower than 90 percent or greater than 110 percent of the fair market value of such assets at such time.

Any such averaging shall be adjusted for contributions and distributions (as provided by the Secretary of the Treasury).

"(4) ACCOUNTING FOR CONTRIBUTION RECEIPTS.—For purposes of determining the value of assets under paragraph (3)—

"(A) PRIOR YEAR CONTRIBUTIONS.—If—

"(i) an employer makes any contribution to the plan after the valuation date for the plan year in which the contribution is made, and

"(ii) the contribution is for a preceding plan year,

the contribution shall be taken into account as an asset of the plan as of the valuation date, except that in the case of any plan year beginning after 2008, only the present value (determined as of the valuation date) of such contribution may be taken into account. For purposes of the preceding sentence, present value shall be determined using the effective interest rate for the preceding plan year to which the contribution is properly allocable.

"(B) SPECIAL RULE FOR CURRENT YEAR CONTRIBUTIONS MADE BEFORE VALUATION DATE.—If any contributions for any plan year are made to or under the plan during the plan year but before the valuation date for the plan year, the assets of the plan as of the valuation date shall not include—

"(i) such contributions, and

"(ii) interest on such contributions for the period between the date of the contributions and the valuation date, determined by using the effective interest rate for the plan year.

"(h) ACTUARIAL ASSUMPTIONS AND METHODS.—

"(1) IN GENERAL.—Subject to this subsection, the determination of any present value or other computation under this section shall be made on the basis of actuarial assumptions and methods—

"(A) each of which is reasonable (taking into account the experience of the plan and reasonable expectations), and

"(B) which, in combination, offer the actuary's best estimate of anticipated experience under the plan.

"(2) INTEREST RATES.—

"(A) EFFECTIVE INTEREST RATE.—For purposes of this section, the term 'effective interest rate' means, with respect to any plan for any plan year, the single rate of interest which, if used to determine the present value of the plan's accrued or earned benefits referred to in subsection (d)(1), would result in an amount equal to the funding target of the plan for such plan year.

"(B) INTEREST RATES FOR DETERMINING FUNDING TARGET.—For purposes of determining the funding target and normal cost of a plan for any plan year, the interest rate used in determining the present value of the benefits of the plan shall be—

"(i) in the case of benefits reasonably determined to be payable during the 5-year period beginning on the first day of the plan year, the first segment rate with respect to the applicable month,

"(ii) in the case of benefits reasonably determined to be payable during the 15-year period beginning at the end of the period described in clause (i), the second segment rate with respect to the applicable month, and

"(iii) in the case of benefits reasonably determined to be payable after the period described in clause (ii), the third segment rate with respect to the applicable month.

"(C) SEGMENT RATES.—For purposes of this paragraph—

"(i) FIRST SEGMENT RATE.—The term 'first segment rate' means, with respect to any month, the single rate of interest which shall be determined by the Secretary of the Treasury for such month on the basis of the corporate bond yield curve for such month, taking into account only that portion of such yield curve which is based on bonds maturing during the 5-year period commencing with such month.

"(ii) SECOND SEGMENT RATE.—The term 'second segment rate' means, with respect to any month, the single rate of interest which shall be determined by the Secretary of the Treasury for such month on the basis of the corporate bond yield curve for such month, taking into account only that portion of such yield curve which is based on bonds maturing during the 15-year period beginning at the end of the period described in clause (i).

"(iii) THIRD SEGMENT RATE.—The term 'third segment rate' means, with respect to any month, the single rate of interest which shall be determined by the Secretary of the Treasury for such month on the basis of the corporate bond yield curve for such month, taking into account only that portion of such yield curve which is based on bonds maturing during periods beginning after the period described in clause (ii).

"(D) CORPORATE BOND YIELD CURVE.—For purposes of this paragraph—

"(i) IN GENERAL.—The term 'corporate bond yield curve' means, with respect to any month, a yield curve which is prescribed by the Secretary of the Treasury for such month and which reflects the average, for the 24-month period ending with the month preceding such month, of monthly yields on investment grade corporate bonds with varying maturities and that are in the top 3 quality levels available.

"(ii) ELECTION TO USE YIELD CURVE.—Solely for purposes of determining the minimum required contribution under this section, the plan sponsor may, in lieu of the segment rates determined under subparagraph (C), elect to use interest rates under the corporate bond yield curve. For purposes of the preceding sentence such curve shall be determined without regard to the 24-month averaging described in clause (i). Such election, once made, may be revoked only with the consent of the Secretary of the Treasury.

"(E) APPLICABLE MONTH.—For purposes of this paragraph, the term 'applicable month' means, with respect to any plan for any plan year, the month which includes the valuation date of such plan for such plan year or, at the election of the plan sponsor, any of the 4 months which precede such month. Any election made under this subparagraph shall apply to the plan year for which the election is made and all succeeding plan years, unless the election is revoked with the consent of the Secretary of the Treasury.

"(F) PUBLICATION REQUIREMENTS.—The Secretary of the Treasury shall publish for each month the corporate bond yield curve (and the corporate bond yield curve reflecting the modification described in section 205(g)(3)(B)(iii)(I)) for such month and each of the rates determined under subparagraph (B) for such month. The Secretary of the Treasury shall also publish a description of the methodology used to determine such yield curve and such rates which is sufficiently detailed to enable plans to make reasonable projections regarding the yield curve and such rates for future months based on the plan's projection of future interest rates.

"(G) TRANSITION RULE.—

"(i) IN GENERAL.—Notwithstanding the preceding provisions of this paragraph, for plan years beginning in 2008 or 2009, the first, second, or third segment rate for a plan with respect to any month shall be equal to the sum of—

"(I) the product of such rate for such month determined without regard to this subparagraph, multiplied by the applicable percentage, and

"(II) the product of the rate determined under the rules of section 302(b)(5)(B)(ii)(II) (as in effect for plan years beginning in 2007), multiplied by a percentage equal to 100 percent minus the applicable percentage.

"(ii) APPLICABLE PERCENTAGE.—For purposes of clause (i), the applicable percentage is 33⅓ percent for plan years beginning in 2008 and 66⅔ percent for plan years beginning in 2009.

"(iii) NEW PLANS INELIGIBLE.—Clause (i) shall not apply to any plan if the first plan year of the plan begins after December 31, 2007.

"(iv) ELECTION.—The plan sponsor may elect not to have this subparagraph apply. Such election, once made, may be revoked only with the consent of the Secretary of the Treasury.

"(3) MORTALITY TABLES.—

"(A) IN GENERAL.—Except as provided in subparagraph (C) or (D), the Secretary of the Treasury shall by regulation prescribe mortality tables to be used in determining any present value or making any computation under this section. Such tables shall be based on the actual experience of pension plans and projected trends in such experience. In prescribing such tables, the Secretary of the Treasury shall take into account results of available independent studies of mortality of individuals covered by pension plans.

"(B) PERIODIC REVISION.—The Secretary of the Treasury shall (at least every 10 years) make revisions in any table in effect under subparagraph (A) to reflect the actual experience of pension plans and projected trends in such experience.

"(C) SUBSTITUTE MORTALITY TABLE.—

"(i) IN GENERAL.—Upon request by the plan sponsor and approval by the Secretary of the Treasury, a mortality table which meets the requirements of clause (iii) shall be used in determining any present value or making any computation under this section during the period of consecutive plan years (not to exceed 10) specified in the request.

"(ii) EARLY TERMINATION OF PERIOD.—Notwithstanding clause (i), a mortality table described in clause (i) shall cease to be in effect as of the earliest of—

"(I) the date on which there is a significant change in the participants in the plan by reason of a plan spinoff or merger or otherwise, or

"(II) the date on which the plan actuary determines that such table does not meet the requirements of clause (iii).

"(iii) REQUIREMENTS.—A mortality table meets the requirements of this clause if—

"(I) there is a sufficient number of plan participants, and the pension plans have been maintained for a sufficient period of time, to have credible information necessary for purposes of subclause (II), and

"(II) such table reflects the actual experience of the pension plans maintained by the sponsor and projected trends in general mortality experience.

"(iv) ALL PLANS IN CONTROLLED GROUP MUST USE SEPARATE TABLE.—Except as provided by the Secretary of the Treasury, a plan sponsor may not use a mortality table under this subparagraph for any plan maintained by the plan sponsor unless—

"(I) a separate mortality table is established and used under this subparagraph for each other plan maintained by the plan sponsor and if the plan sponsor is a member of a controlled group, each member of the controlled group, and

"(II) the requirements of clause (iii) are met separately with respect to the table so established for each such plan, determined by only taking into account the participants of such plan, the time such plan has been in existence, and the actual experience of such plan.

"(v) DEADLINE FOR SUBMISSION AND DISPOSITION OF APPLICATION.—

"(I) SUBMISSION.—The plan sponsor shall submit a mortality table to the Secretary of the Treasury for approval under this subparagraph at least 7 months before the 1st day of the period described in clause (i).

"(II) DISPOSITION.—Any mortality table submitted to the Secretary of the Treasury for approval under this subparagraph shall be treated as in effect as of the 1st day of the period described in clause (i) unless the Secretary of the Treasury, during the 180-day period beginning on the date of such submission, disapproves of such table and provides the reasons that such table fails to meet the requirements of clause (iii). The 180-day period shall be extended upon mutual agreement of the Secretary of the Treasury and the plan sponsor.

"(D) SEPARATE MORTALITY TABLES FOR THE DISABLED.—Notwithstanding subparagraph (A)—

"(i) IN GENERAL.—The Secretary of the Treasury shall establish mortality tables which may be used (in lieu of the tables under subparagraph (A)) under this subsection for individuals who are entitled to benefits under the plan on account of disability. The Secretary of the Treasury shall establish separate tables for individuals whose disabilities occur in plan years beginning before January 1, 1995, and for individuals whose disabilities occur in plan years beginning on or after such date.

"(ii) SPECIAL RULE FOR DISABILITIES OCCURRING AFTER 1994.—In the case of disabilities occurring in plan years beginning after December 31, 1994, the tables under clause (i) shall apply only with respect to individuals described in such subclause who are disabled within the meaning of title II of the Social Security Act and the regulations thereunder.

"(iii) PERIODIC REVISION.—The Secretary of the Treasury shall (at least every 10 years) make revisions in any table in effect under clause (i) to reflect the actual experience of pension plans and projected trends in such experience.

"(4) PROBABILITY OF BENEFIT PAYMENTS IN THE FORM OF LUMP SUMS OR OTHER OPTIONAL FORMS.—For purposes of determining any present value or making any computation under this section, there shall be taken into account—

"(A) the probability that future benefit payments under the plan will be made in the form of optional forms of benefits provided under the plan (including lump sum distributions, determined on the basis of the plan's experience and other related assumptions), and

"(B) any difference in the present value of such future benefit payments resulting from the use of actuarial assumptions, in determining benefit payments in any such optional form of benefits, which are different from those specified in this subsection.

"(5) APPROVAL OF LARGE CHANGES IN ACTUARIAL ASSUMPTIONS.—

"(A) IN GENERAL.—No actuarial assumption used to determine the funding target for a plan to which this paragraph applies may be changed without the approval of the Secretary of the Treasury.

"(B) PLANS TO WHICH PARAGRAPH APPLIES.—This paragraph shall apply to a plan only if—

"(i) the plan is a single-employer plan to which title IV applies,

"(ii) the aggregate unfunded vested benefits as of the close of the preceding plan year (as determined under section 4006(a)(3)(E)(iii)) of such plan and all other plans maintained by the contributing sponsors (as defined in section 4001(a)(13)) and members of such sponsors' controlled groups (as defined in section 4001(a)(14)) which are covered by title IV (disregarding plans with no unfunded vested benefits) exceed $50,000,000, and

"(iii) the change in assumptions (determined after taking into account any changes in interest rate and mortality table) results in a decrease in the funding shortfall of the plan for the current plan year that exceeds $50,000,000, or that exceeds $5,000,000 and that is 5 percent or more of the funding target of the plan before such change.

"(i) SPECIAL RULES FOR AT-RISK PLANS.—

"(1) FUNDING TARGET FOR PLANS IN AT-RISK STATUS.—

"(A) IN GENERAL.—In the case of a plan which is in at-risk status for a plan year, the funding target of the plan for the plan year shall be equal to the sum of—

"(i) the present value of all benefits accrued or earned under the plan as of the beginning of the plan year, as determined by using the additional actuarial assumptions described in subparagraph (B), and

"(ii) in the case of a plan which also has been in at-risk status for at least 2 of the 4 preceding plan years, a loading factor determined under subparagraph (C).

"(B) ADDITIONAL ACTUARIAL ASSUMPTIONS.—The actuarial assumptions described in this subparagraph are as follows:

"(i) All employees who are not otherwise assumed to retire as of the valuation date but who will be eligible to elect benefits during the plan year and the 10 succeeding plan years shall be assumed to retire at the earliest retirement date under the plan but not before the end of the plan year for which the at-risk funding target and at-risk target normal cost are being determined.

"(ii) All employees shall be assumed to elect the retirement benefit available under the plan at the assumed retirement age (determined after application of clause (i)) which would result in the highest present value of benefits.

"(C) LOADING FACTOR.—The loading factor applied with respect to a plan under this paragraph for any plan year is the sum of—

"(i) $700, times the number of participants in the plan, plus

"(ii) 4 percent of the funding target (determined without regard to this paragraph) of the plan for the plan year.

"(2) TARGET NORMAL COST OF AT-RISK PLANS.—In the case of a plan which is in at-risk status for a plan year, the target normal cost of the plan for such plan year shall be equal to the sum of—

"(A) the present value of all benefits which are expected to accrue or be earned under the plan during the plan year, determined using the additional actuarial assumptions described in paragraph (1)(B), plus

"(B) in the case of a plan which also has been in at-risk status for at least 2 of the 4 preceding plan years, a loading factor equal to 4 percent of the target normal cost (determined without regard to this paragraph) of the plan for the plan year.

"(3) MINIMUM AMOUNT.—In no event shall—

"(A) the at-risk funding target be less than the funding target, as determined without regard to this subsection, or

"(B) the at-risk target normal cost be less than the target normal cost, as determined without regard to this subsection.

"(4) DETERMINATION OF AT-RISK STATUS.—For purposes of this subsection—

"(A) IN GENERAL.—A plan is in at-risk status for a plan year if—

"(i) the funding target attainment percentage for the preceding plan year (determined under this section without regard to this subsection) is less than 80 percent, and

"(ii) the funding target attainment percentage for the preceding plan year (determined under this section by using the additional actuarial assumptions described in paragraph (1)(B) in computing the funding target) is less than 70 percent.

"(B) TRANSITION RULE.—In the case of plan years beginning in 2008, 2009, and 2010, subparagraph (A)(i) shall be applied by substituting the following percentages for '80 percent':

"(i) 65 percent in the case of 2008.

"(ii) 70 percent in the case of 2009.

"(iii) 75 percent in the case of 2010.

In the case of plan years beginning in 2008, the funding target attainment percentage for the preceding plan year under subparagraph (A)(ii) may be determined using such methods of estimation as the Secretary of the Treasury may provide.

"(C) SPECIAL RULE FOR EMPLOYEES OFFERED EARLY RETIREMENT IN 2006.—

"(i) IN GENERAL.—For purposes of subparagraph (A)(ii), the additional actuarial assumptions described in paragraph (1)(B) shall not be taken into account with respect to any employee if—

"(I) such employee is employed by a specified automobile manufacturer,

"(II) such employee is offered a substantial amount of additional cash compensation, substantially enhanced retirement benefits under the plan, or materially reduced employment duties on the condition that by a specified date (not later than December 31, 2010) the employee retires (as defined under the terms of the plan),

"(III) such offer is made during 2006 and pursuant to a bona fide retirement incentive program and requires, by the terms of the offer, that such offer can be accepted not later than a specified date (not later than December 31, 2006), and

"(IV) such employee does not elect to accept such offer before the specified date on which the offer expires.

"(ii) SPECIFIED AUTOMOBILE MANUFACTURER.—For purposes of clause (i), the term 'specified automobile manufacturer' means—

"(I) any manufacturer of automobiles, and

"(II) any manufacturer of automobile parts which supplies such parts directly to a manufacturer of automobiles and which, after a transaction or series of transactions ending in 1999, ceased to be a member of a controlled group which included such manufacturer of automobiles.

"(5) TRANSITION BETWEEN APPLICABLE FUNDING TARGETS AND BETWEEN APPLICABLE TARGET NORMAL COSTS.—

"(A) IN GENERAL.—In any case in which a plan which is in at-risk status for a plan year has been in such status for a consecutive period of fewer than 5 plan years, the applicable amount of the funding target and of the target normal cost shall be, in lieu of the amount determined without regard to this paragraph, the sum of—

"(i) the amount determined under this section without regard to this subsection, plus

"(ii) the transition percentage for such plan year of the excess of the amount determined under this subsection (without regard to this paragraph) over the amount determined under this section without regard to this subsection.

"(B) TRANSITION PERCENTAGE.—For purposes of subparagraph (A), the transition percentage shall be determined in accordance with the following table:

"If the consecutive number of years (including the plan year) the plan is in at-risk status is—	The transition percentage is—
1	20
2	40
3	60
4	80 .

"(C) YEARS BEFORE EFFECTIVE DATE.—For purposes of this paragraph, plan years beginning before 2008 shall not be taken into account.

"(6) SMALL PLAN EXCEPTION.—If, on each day during the preceding plan year, a plan had 500 or fewer participants, the plan shall not be treated as in at-risk status for the plan year. For purposes of this paragraph, all defined benefit plans (other than multiemployer plans) maintained by the same employer (or any member of such employer's controlled group) shall be treated as 1 plan, but only participants with respect to such employer or member shall be taken into account and the rules of subsection (g)(2)(C) shall apply.

"(j) PAYMENT OF MINIMUM REQUIRED CONTRIBUTIONS.—

"(1) IN GENERAL.—For purposes of this section, the due date for any payment of any minimum required contribution for any plan year shall be 8½ months after the close of the plan year.

"(2) INTEREST.—Any payment required under paragraph (1) for a plan year that is made on a date other than the valuation date for such plan year shall be adjusted for interest accruing for the period between the valuation date and the payment date, at the effective rate of interest for the plan for such plan year.

"(3) ACCELERATED QUARTERLY CONTRIBUTION SCHEDULE FOR UNDERFUNDED PLANS.—

"(A) FAILURE TO TIMELY MAKE REQUIRED INSTALLMENT.—In any case in which the plan has a funding shortfall for the preceding plan year, the employer maintaining the plan shall make the required installments under this paragraph and if the employer fails to pay the full amount of a required installment for the plan year, then the amount of interest charged under paragraph (2) on the underpayment for the period of underpayment shall be determined by using a rate of interest equal to the rate otherwise used under paragraph (2) plus 5 percentage points.

"(B) AMOUNT OF UNDERPAYMENT, PERIOD OF UNDERPAYMENT.—For purposes of subparagraph (A)—

"(i) AMOUNT.—The amount of the underpayment shall be the excess of—

"(I) the required installment, over

"(II) the amount (if any) of the installment contributed to or under the plan on or before the due date for the installment.

"(ii) PERIOD OF UNDERPAYMENT.—The period for which any interest is charged under this paragraph with respect to any portion of the underpayment shall run from the due date for the installment to the date on which such portion is contributed to or under the plan.

"(iii) ORDER OF CREDITING CONTRIBUTIONS.—For purposes of clause (i)(II), contributions shall be credited against unpaid required installments in the order in which such installments are required to be paid.

"(C) NUMBER OF REQUIRED INSTALLMENTS; DUE DATES.—For purposes of this paragraph—

"(i) PAYABLE IN 4 INSTALLMENTS.—There shall be 4 required installments for each plan year.

"(ii) TIME FOR PAYMENT OF INSTALLMENTS.—The due dates for required installments are set forth in the following table:

In the case of the following required installment:	The due date is:
1st	April 15
2nd	July 15
3rd	October 15
4th	January 15 of the following year.

"(D) AMOUNT OF REQUIRED INSTALLMENT.—For purposes of this paragraph—

"(i) IN GENERAL.—The amount of any required installment shall be 25 percent of the required annual payment.

"(ii) REQUIRED ANNUAL PAYMENT.—For purposes of clause (i), the term 'required annual payment' means the lesser of—

"(I) 90 percent of the minimum required contribution (determined without regard to this subsection) to the plan for the plan year under this section, or

"(II) 100 percent of the minimum required contribution (determined without regard to this subsection or to any waiver under section 302(c)) to the plan for the preceding plan year.

Subclause (II) shall not apply if the preceding plan year referred to in such clause was not a year of 12 months.

"(E) FISCAL YEARS AND SHORT YEARS.—

"(i) FISCAL YEARS.—In applying this paragraph to a plan year beginning on any date other than January 1, there shall be substituted for the months specified in this paragraph, the months which correspond thereto.

"(ii) SHORT PLAN YEAR.—This subparagraph shall be applied to plan years of less than 12 months in accordance with regulations prescribed by the Secretary of the Treasury.

"(4) LIQUIDITY REQUIREMENT IN CONNECTION WITH QUARTERLY CONTRIBUTIONS.—

"(A) IN GENERAL.—A plan to which this paragraph applies shall be treated as failing to pay the full amount of any required installment under paragraph (3) to the extent that the value of the liquid assets paid in such installment is less than the liquidity shortfall (whether or not such liquidity shortfall exceeds the amount of such installment required to be paid but for this paragraph).

"(B) PLANS TO WHICH PARAGRAPH APPLIES.—This paragraph shall apply to a plan (other than a plan described in subsection (g)(2)(B)) which—

"(i) is required to pay installments under paragraph (3) for a plan year, and

"(ii) has a liquidity shortfall for any quarter during such plan year.

"(C) PERIOD OF UNDERPAYMENT.—For purposes of paragraph (3)(A), any portion of an installment that is treated as not paid under subparagraph (A) shall continue to be treated as unpaid until the close of the quarter in which the due date for such installment occurs.

"(D) LIMITATION ON INCREASE.—If the amount of any required installment is increased by reason of subparagraph (A), in no event shall such increase exceed the amount which, when added to prior installments for the plan year, is necessary to increase the funding target attainment percentage of the plan for the plan year (taking into account the expected increase in funding target due to benefits accruing or earned during the plan year) to 100 percent.

"(E) DEFINITIONS.—For purposes of this paragraph—

"(i) LIQUIDITY SHORTFALL.—The term 'liquidity shortfall' means, with respect to any required installment, an amount equal to the excess (as of the last day of the quarter for which such installment is made) of—

"(I) the base amount with respect to such quarter, over

"(II) the value (as of such last day) of the plan's liquid assets.

"(ii) BASE AMOUNT.—

"(I) IN GENERAL.—The term 'base amount' means, with respect to any quarter, an amount equal to 3 times the sum of the adjusted disbursements from the plan for the 12 months ending on the last day of such quarter.

"(II) SPECIAL RULE.—If the amount determined under subclause (I) exceeds an amount equal to 2 times the sum of the adjusted disbursements from the plan for the 36 months ending on the last day of the quarter and an enrolled actuary certifies to the satisfaction of the Secretary of the Treasury that such excess is the result of nonrecurring circumstances, the base amount with respect to such quarter shall be determined without regard to amounts related to those nonrecurring circumstances.

"(iii) DISBURSEMENTS FROM THE PLAN.—The term 'disbursements from the plan' means all disbursements from the trust, including purchases of annuities, payments of single sums and other benefits, and administrative expenses.

"(iv) ADJUSTED DISBURSEMENTS.—The term 'adjusted disbursements' means disbursements from the plan reduced by the product of—

"(I) the plan's funding target attainment percentage for the plan year, and

"(II) the sum of the purchases of annuities, payments of single sums, and such other disbursements as the Secretary of the Treasury shall provide in regulations.

"(v) LIQUID ASSETS.—The term 'liquid assets' means cash, marketable securities, and such other assets as specified by the Secretary of the Treasury in regulations.

"(vi) QUARTER.—The term 'quarter' means, with respect to any required installment, the 3-month period preceding the month in which the due date for such installment occurs.

"(F) REGULATIONS.—The Secretary of the Treasury may prescribe such regulations as are necessary to carry out this paragraph.

"(k) IMPOSITION OF LIEN WHERE FAILURE TO MAKE REQUIRED CONTRIBUTIONS.—

"(1) IN GENERAL.—In the case of a plan to which this subsection applies (as provided under paragraph (2)), if—

"(A) any person fails to make a contribution payment required by section 302 and this section before the due date for such payment, and

"(B) the unpaid balance of such payment (including interest), when added to the aggregate unpaid balance of all preceding such payments for which payment was not made before the due date (including interest), exceeds $1,000,000,

then there shall be a lien in favor of the plan in the amount determined under paragraph (3) upon all property and rights to property, whether real or personal, belonging to such person and any other person who is a member of the same controlled group of which such person is a member.

"(2) PLANS TO WHICH SUBSECTION APPLIES.—This subsection shall apply to a single-employer plan covered under section 4021 for any plan year for which the funding target attainment percentage (as defined in subsection (d)(2)) of such plan is less than 100 percent.

"(3) AMOUNT OF LIEN.—For purposes of paragraph (1), the amount of the lien shall be equal to the aggregate unpaid balance of contribution payments required under this section and section 302 for which payment has not been made before the due date.

"(4) NOTICE OF FAILURE; LIEN.—

"(A) NOTICE OF FAILURE.—A person committing a failure described in paragraph (1) shall notify the Pension Benefit Guaranty Corporation of such failure within 10 days of the due date for the required contribution payment.

"(B) PERIOD OF LIEN.—The lien imposed by paragraph (1) shall arise on the due date for the required contribution payment and shall continue until the last day of the first plan year in which the plan ceases to be described in paragraph (1)(B). Such lien shall continue to run without regard to whether such plan continues to be described in paragraph (2) during the period referred to in the preceding sentence.

"(C) CERTAIN RULES TO APPLY.—Any amount with respect to which a lien is imposed under paragraph (1) shall be treated as taxes due and owing the United States and rules similar to the rules of subsections (c), (d), and (e) of section 4068 shall apply with respect to a lien imposed by subsection (a) and the amount with respect to such lien.

"(5) ENFORCEMENT.—Any lien created under paragraph (1) may be perfected and enforced only by the Pension Benefit Guaranty Corporation, or at the direction of the Pension Benefit Guaranty Corporation, by the contributing sponsor (or any member of the controlled group of the contributing sponsor).

"(6) DEFINITIONS.—For purposes of this subsection—

"(A) CONTRIBUTION PAYMENT.—The term 'contribution payment' means, in connection with a plan, a contribution payment required to be made to the plan, including any required installment under paragraphs (3) and (4) of subsection (j).

"(B) DUE DATE; REQUIRED INSTALLMENT.—The terms 'due date' and 'required installment' have the meanings given such terms by subsection (j), except that in the case of a payment other than a required installment, the due date shall be the date such payment is required to be made under section 303.

"(C) CONTROLLED GROUP.—The term 'controlled group' means any group treated as a single employer under subsections (b), (c), (m), and (o) of section 414 of the Internal Revenue Code of 1986.

"(l) QUALIFIED TRANSFERS TO HEALTH BENEFIT ACCOUNTS.—In the case of a qualified transfer (as defined in section 420 of the Internal Revenue Code of 1986), any assets so transferred shall not, for purposes of this section, be treated as assets in the plan.".

(b) CLERICAL AMENDMENT.—The table of sections in section 1 of such Act (as amended by section 101) is amended by inserting after the item relating to section 302 the following new item:

"Sec. 303. Minimum funding standards for single-employer defined benefit pension plans.".

(c) EFFECTIVE DATE.—The amendments made by this section shall apply with respect to plan years beginning after 2007.

[CCH Explanation at ¶210. Committee Reports at ¶10,010.]

[¶7012] ACT SEC. 103. BENEFIT LIMITATIONS UNDER SINGLE-EMPLOYER PLANS.

(a) FUNDING-BASED LIMITS ON BENEFITS AND BENEFIT ACCRUALS UNDER SINGLE-EMPLOYER PLANS.—Section 206 of the Employee Retirement Income Security Act of 1974 (29 U.S.C. 1056) is amended by adding at the end the following new subsection:

"(g) FUNDING-BASED LIMITS ON BENEFITS AND BENEFIT ACCRUALS UNDER SINGLE-EMPLOYER PLANS.—

"(1) FUNDING-BASED LIMITATION ON SHUTDOWN BENEFITS AND OTHER UNPREDICTABLE CONTINGENT EVENT BENEFITS UNDER SINGLE-EMPLOYER PLANS.—

"(A) IN GENERAL.—If a participant of a defined benefit plan which is a single-employer plan is entitled to an unpredictable contingent event benefit payable with respect to any event occurring during any plan year, the plan shall provide that such benefit may not be provided if the adjusted funding target attainment percentage for such plan year—

"(i) is less than 60 percent, or

"(ii) would be less than 60 percent taking into account such occurrence.

"(B) EXEMPTION.—Subparagraph (A) shall cease to apply with respect to any plan year, effective as of the first day of the plan year, upon payment by the plan sponsor of a contribution (in addition to any minimum required contribution under section 303) equal to—

"(i) in the case of subparagraph (A)(i), the amount of the increase in the funding target of the plan (under section 303) for the plan year attributable to the occurrence referred to in subparagraph (A), and "(ii) in the case of subparagraph (A)(ii), the amount sufficient to result in a funding target attainment percentage of 60 percent.

"(C) UNPREDICTABLE CONTINGENT EVENT.—For purposes of this paragraph, the term 'unpredictable contingent event benefit' means any benefit payable solely by reason of—

"(i) a plant shutdown (or similar event, as determined by the Secretary of the Treasury), or

"(ii) an event other than the attainment of any age, performance of any service, receipt or derivation of any compensation, or occurrence of death or disability.

"(2) LIMITATIONS ON PLAN AMENDMENTS INCREASING LIABILITY FOR BENEFITS.—

"(A) IN GENERAL.—No amendment to a defined benefit plan which is a single-employer plan which has the effect of increasing liabilities of the plan by reason of increases in benefits, establishment of new benefits, changing the rate of benefit accrual, or changing the rate at which benefits become nonforfeitable may take effect during any plan year if the adjusted funding target attainment percentage for such plan year is—

"(i) less than 80 percent, or

"(ii) would be less than 80 percent taking into account such amendment.

"(B) EXEMPTION.—Subparagraph (A) shall cease to apply with respect to any plan year, effective as of the first day of the plan year (or if later, the effective date of the amendment), upon payment by the plan sponsor of a contribution (in addition to any minimum required contribution under section 303) equal to—

"(i) in the case of subparagraph (A)(i), the amount of the increase in the funding target of the plan (under section 303) for the plan year attributable to the amendment, and

"(ii) in the case of subparagraph (A)(ii), the amount sufficient to result in an adjusted funding target attainment percentage of 80 percent.

"(C) EXCEPTION FOR CERTAIN BENEFIT INCREASES.—Subparagraph (A) shall not apply to any amendment which provides for an increase in benefits under a formula which is not based on a participant's compensation, but only if the rate of such increase is not in excess of the contemporaneous rate of increase in average wages of participants covered by the amendment.

"(3) LIMITATIONS ON ACCELERATED BENEFIT DISTRIBUTIONS.—

"(A) FUNDING PERCENTAGE LESS THAN 60 PERCENT.—A defined benefit plan which is a single-employer plan shall provide that, in any case in which the plan's adjusted funding target attainment percentage for a plan year is less than 60 percent, the plan may not pay any prohibited payment after the valuation date for the plan year.

"(B) BANKRUPTCY.—A defined benefit plan which is a single-employer plan shall provide that, during any period in which the plan sponsor is a debtor in a case under title 11, United States Code, or similar Federal or State law, the plan may not pay any prohibited payment. The preceding sentence shall not apply on or after the date on which the enrolled actuary of the plan certifies that the adjusted funding target attainment percentage of such plan is not less than 100 percent.

"(C) LIMITED PAYMENT IF PERCENTAGE AT LEAST 60 PERCENT BUT LESS THAN 80 PERCENT.—

"(i) IN GENERAL.—A defined benefit plan which is a single-employer plan shall provide that, in any case in which the plan's adjusted funding target attainment percentage for a plan year is 60 percent or greater but less than 80 percent, the plan may not pay any prohibited payment after the valuation date for the plan year to the extent the amount of the payment exceeds the lesser of—

"(I) 50 percent of the amount of the payment which could be made without regard to this subsection, or

"(II) the present value (determined under guidance prescribed by the Pension Benefit Guaranty Corporation, using the interest and mortality assumptions under section 205(g)) of the maximum guarantee with respect to the participant under section 4022.

"(ii) ONE-TIME APPLICATION.—

"(I) IN GENERAL.—The plan shall also provide that only 1 prohibited payment meeting the requirements of clause (i) may be made with respect to any participant during any period of consecutive plan years to which the limitations under either subparagraph (A) or (B) or this subparagraph applies.

"(II) TREATMENT OF BENEFICIARIES.—For purposes of this clause, a participant and any beneficiary on his behalf (including an alternate payee, as defined in section 206(d)(3)(K)) shall be treated as 1 participant. If the accrued benefit of a participant is allocated to such an alternate payee and 1 or more other persons, the amount under clause (i) shall be allocated among such persons in the same manner as the accrued benefit is allocated unless the qualified domestic relations order (as defined in section 206(d)(3)(B)(i)) provides otherwise.

"(D) EXCEPTION.—This paragraph shall not apply to any plan for any plan year if the terms of such plan (as in effect for the period beginning on September 1, 2005, and ending with such plan year) provide for no benefit accruals with respect to any participant during such period.

"(E) PROHIBITED PAYMENT.—For purpose of this paragraph, the term 'prohibited payment' means—

"(i) any payment, in excess of the monthly amount paid under a single life annuity (plus any social security supplements described in the last sentence of section 204(b)(1)(G)), to a participant or beneficiary whose annuity starting date (as defined in section 205(h)(2)) occurs during any period a limitation under subparagraph (A) or (B) is in effect,

"(ii) any payment for the purchase of an irrevocable commitment from an insurer to pay benefits, and

"(iii) any other payment specified by the Secretary of the Treasury by regulations.

"(4) LIMITATION ON BENEFIT ACCRUALS FOR PLANS WITH SEVERE FUNDING SHORTFALLS.—

"(A) IN GENERAL.—A defined benefit plan which is a single-employer plan shall provide that, in any case in which the plan's adjusted funding target attainment percentage for a plan year is less than 60 percent, benefit accruals under the plan shall cease as of the valuation date for the plan year.

"(B) EXEMPTION.—Subparagraph (A) shall cease to apply with respect to any plan year, effective as of the first day of the plan year, upon payment by the plan sponsor of a contribution (in addition to any minimum required contribution under section 303) equal to the amount sufficient to result in an adjusted funding target attainment percentage of 60 percent.

"(5) RULES RELATING TO CONTRIBUTIONS REQUIRED TO AVOID BENEFIT LIMITATIONS.—

"(A) SECURITY MAY BE PROVIDED.—

"(i) IN GENERAL.—For purposes of this subsection, the adjusted funding target attainment percentage shall be determined by treating as an asset of the plan any security provided by a plan sponsor in a form meeting the requirements of clause (ii).

"(ii) FORM OF SECURITY.—The security required under clause (i) shall consist of—

"(I) a bond issued by a corporate surety company that is an acceptable surety for purposes of section 412 of this Act,

"(II) cash, or United States obligations which mature in 3 years or less, held in escrow by a bank or similar financial institution, or

"(III) such other form of security as is satisfactory to the Secretary of the Treasury and the parties involved.

"(iii) ENFORCEMENT.—Any security provided under clause (i) may be perfected and enforced at any time after the earlier of—

"(I) the date on which the plan terminates,

"(II) if there is a failure to make a payment of the minimum required contribution for any plan year beginning after the security is provided, the due date for the payment under section 303(j), or

"(III) if the adjusted funding target attainment percentage is less than 60 percent for a consecutive period of 7 years, the valuation date for the last year in the period.

"(iv) RELEASE OF SECURITY.—The security shall be released (and any amounts thereunder shall be refunded together with any interest accrued thereon) at such time as the Secretary of the Treasury may prescribe in regulations, including regulations for partial releases of the security by reason of increases in the funding target attainment percentage.

"(B) PREFUNDING BALANCE OR FUNDING STANDARD CARRYOVER BALANCE MAY NOT BE USED.—No prefunding balance or funding standard carryover balance under section 303(f) may be used under paragraph (1), (2), or (4) to satisfy any payment an employer may make under any such paragraph to avoid or terminate the application of any limitation under such paragraph.

"(C) DEEMED REDUCTION OF FUNDING BALANCES.—

"(i) IN GENERAL.—Subject to clause (iii), in any case in which a benefit limitation under paragraph (1), (2), (3), or (4) would (but for this subparagraph and determined without regard to paragraph (1)(B), (2)(B), or (4)(B)) apply to such plan for the plan year, the plan sponsor of such plan shall be treated for purposes of this Act as having made an election under section 303(f) to reduce the prefunding balance or funding standard carryover balance by such amount as is necessary for such benefit limitation to not apply to the plan for such plan year.

"(ii) EXCEPTION FOR INSUFFICIENT FUNDING BALANCES.—Clause (i) shall not apply with respect to a benefit limitation for any plan year if the application of clause (i) would not result in the benefit limitation not applying for such plan year.

"(iii) RESTRICTIONS OF CERTAIN RULES TO COLLECTIVELY BARGAINED PLANS.—With respect to any benefit limitation under paragraph (1), (2), or (4), clause (i) shall only apply in the case of a plan maintained pursuant to 1 or more collective bargaining agreements between employee representatives and 1 or more employers.

"(6) NEW PLANS.—Paragraphs (1), (2) and (4) shall not apply to a plan for the first 5 plan years of the plan. For purposes of this paragraph, the reference in this paragraph to a plan shall include a reference to any predecessor plan.

"(7) PRESUMED UNDERFUNDING FOR PURPOSES OF BENEFIT LIMITATIONS.—

"(A) PRESUMPTION OF CONTINUED UNDERFUNDING.—In any case in which a benefit limitation under paragraph (1), (2), (3), or (4) has been applied to a plan with respect to the plan year preceding the current plan year, the adjusted funding target attainment percentage of the plan for the current plan year shall be presumed to be equal to the adjusted funding target attainment percentage of the plan for the preceding plan year until the enrolled actuary of the plan certifies the actual adjusted funding target attainment percentage of the plan for the current plan year.

"(B) PRESUMPTION OF UNDERFUNDING AFTER 10TH MONTH.—In any case in which no certification of the adjusted funding target attainment percentage for the current plan year is made with respect to the plan before the first day of the 10th month of such year, for purposes of paragraphs (1), (2), (3), and (4), such first day shall be deemed, for purposes of such paragraph, to be the valuation date of the plan for the current plan year and the plan's adjusted funding target attainment percentage shall be conclusively presumed to be less than 60 percent as of such first day.

"(C) PRESUMPTION OF UNDERFUNDING AFTER 4TH MONTH FOR NEARLY UNDERFUNDED PLANS.—In any case in which—

"(i) a benefit limitation under paragraph (1), (2), (3), or (4) did not apply to a plan with respect to the plan year preceding the current plan year, but the adjusted funding target attainment percentage of the plan for such preceding plan year was not more than 10 percentage points greater than the percentage which would have caused such paragraph to apply to the plan with respect to such preceding plan year, and

"(ii) as of the first day of the 4th month of the current plan year, the enrolled actuary of the plan has not certified the actual adjusted funding target attainment percentage of the plan for the current plan year,

until the enrolled actuary so certifies, such first day shall be deemed, for purposes of such paragraph, to be the valuation date of the plan for the current plan year and the adjusted funding target attainment percentage of the plan as of such first day shall, for purposes of such paragraph, be presumed to be equal to 10 percentage points less than the adjusted funding target attainment percentage of the plan for such preceding plan year.

"(8) TREATMENT OF PLAN AS OF CLOSE OF PROHIBITED OR CESSATION PERIOD.—For purposes of applying this part—

"(A) OPERATION OF PLAN AFTER PERIOD.—Unless the plan provides otherwise, payments and accruals will resume effective as of the day following the close of the period for which any limitation of payment or accrual of benefits under paragraph (3) or (4) applies.

"(B) TREATMENT OF AFFECTED BENEFITS.—Nothing in this paragraph shall be construed as affecting the plan's treatment of benefits which would have been paid or accrued but for this subsection.

"(9) TERMS RELATING TO FUNDING TARGET ATTAINMENT PERCENTAGE.—For purposes of this subsection—

"(A) IN GENERAL.—The term 'funding target attainment percentage' has the same meaning given such term by section 303(d)(2).

"(B) ADJUSTED FUNDING TARGET ATTAINMENT PERCENTAGE.—The term 'adjusted funding target attainment percentage' means the funding target attainment percentage which is determined under subparagraph (A) by increasing each of the amounts under subparagraphs (A) and (B) of section 303(d)(2) by the aggregate amount of purchases of annuities for employees other than highly compensated employees (as defined in section 414(q) of the Internal Revenue Code of 1986) which were made by the plan during the preceding 2 plan years.

"(C) APPLICATION TO PLANS WHICH ARE FULLY FUNDED WITHOUT REGARD TO REDUCTIONS FOR FUNDING BALANCES.—

"(i) IN GENERAL.—In the case of a plan for any plan year, if the funding target attainment percentage is 100 percent or more (determined without regard to this subparagraph and without regard to the reduction in the value of assets under section 303(f)(4)), the funding target attainment percentage for purposes of subparagraphs (A) and (B) shall be determined without regard to such reduction.

"(ii) TRANSITION RULE.—Clause (i) shall be applied to plan years beginning after 2007 and before 2011 by substituting for '100 percent' the applicable percentage determined in accordance with the following table:

"In the case of a plan year beginning in calendar year:	The applicable percentage is
2008	92
2009	94
2010	96 .

"(iii) LIMITATION.—Clause (ii) shall not apply with respect to any plan year after 2008 unless the funding target attainment percentage (determined without regard to this subparagraph) of the plan for each preceding plan year after 2007 was not less than the applicable percentage with respect to such preceding plan year determined under clause (ii).

"(10) SPECIAL RULE FOR 2008.—For purposes of this subsection, in the case of plan years beginning in 2008, the funding target attainment percentage for the preceding plan year may be determined using such methods of estimation as the Secretary of the Treasury may provide.".

(b) NOTICE REQUIREMENT.—

(1) IN GENERAL.—Section 101 of such Act (29 U.S.C. 1021) is amended—

(A) by redesignating subsection (j) as subsection (k); and

(B) by inserting after subsection (i) the following new subsection:

"(j) NOTICE OF FUNDING-BASED LIMITATION ON CERTAIN FORMS OF DISTRIBUTION.—The plan administrator of a single-employer plan shall provide a written notice to plan participants and beneficiaries within 30 days—

"(1) after the plan has become subject to a restriction described in paragraph (1) or (3) of section 206(g)),

"(2) in the case of a plan to which section 206(g)(4) applies, after the valuation date for the plan year described in section 206(g)(4)(B) for which the plan's adjusted funding target attainment percentage for the plan year is less than 60 percent (or, if earlier, the date such percentage is deemed to be less than 60 percent under section 206(g)(7)), and

"(3) at such other time as may be determined by the Secretary of the Treasury.

The notice required to be provided under this subsection shall be in writing, except that such notice may be in electronic or other form to the extent that such form is reasonably accessible to the recipient.".

(2) ENFORCEMENT.—Section 502(c)(4) of such Act (29 U.S.C. 1132(c)(4)) is amended by striking "section 302(b)(7)(F)(iv)" and inserting "section 101(j) or 302(b)(7)(F)(iv)".

(c) EFFECTIVE DATES.—

(1) IN GENERAL.—The amendments made by this section shall apply to plan years beginning after December 31, 2007.

(2) COLLECTIVE BARGAINING EXCEPTION.—In the case of a plan maintained pursuant to 1 or more collective bargaining agreements between employee representatives and 1 or more employers ratified before January 1, 2008, the amendments made by this section shall not apply to plan years beginning before the earlier of—

(A) the later of—

(i) the date on which the last collective bargaining agreement relating to the plan terminates (determined without regard to any extension thereof agreed to after the date of the enactment of this Act), or

(ii) the first day of the first plan year to which the amendments made by this subsection would (but for this subparagraph) apply, or

(B) January 1, 2010.

For purposes of subparagraph (A)(i), any plan amendment made pursuant to a collective bargaining agreement relating to the plan which amends the plan solely to conform to any requirement added by this section shall not be treated as a termination of such collective bargaining agreement.

[CCH Explanation at ¶ 215. Committee Reports at ¶ 10,020.]

[¶ 7015] ACT SEC. 104. SPECIAL RULES FOR MULTIPLE EMPLOYER PLANS OF CERTAIN COOPERATIVES.

(a) GENERAL RULE.—Except as provided in this section, if a plan in existence on July 26, 2005, was an eligible cooperative plan for its plan year which includes such date, the amendments made by this subtitle and subtitle B shall not apply to plan years beginning before the earlier of—

(1) the first plan year for which the plan ceases to be an eligible cooperative plan, or

(2) January 1, 2017.

(b) INTEREST RATE.—In applying section 302(b)(5)(B) of the Employee Retirement Income Security Act of 1974 and section 412(b)(5)(B) of the Internal Revenue Code of 1986 (as in effect before the amendments made by this subtitle and subtitle B) to an eligible cooperative plan for plan years beginning after December 31, 2007, and before the first plan year to which such amendments apply, the third segment rate determined under section 303(h)(2)(C)(iii) of such Act and section 430(h)(2)(C)(iii) of such Code (as added by such amendments) shall be used in lieu of the interest rate otherwise used.

(c) ELIGIBLE COOPERATIVE PLAN DEFINED.—For purposes of this section, a plan shall be treated as an eligible cooperative plan for a plan year if the plan is maintained by more than 1 employer and at least 85 percent of the employers are—

(1) rural cooperatives (as defined in section 401(k)(7)(B) of such Code without regard to clause (iv) thereof), or

(2) organizations which are—

(A) cooperative organizations described in section 1381(a) of such Code which are more than 50-percent owned by agricultural producers or by cooperatives owned by agricultural producers, or

(B) more than 50-percent owned, or controlled by, one or more cooperative organizations described in subparagraph (A).

A plan shall also be treated as an eligible cooperative plan for any plan year for which it is described in section 210(a) of the Employee Retirement Income Security Act of 1974 and is maintained by a rural telephone cooperative association described in section 3(40)(B)(v) of such Act.

[CCH Explanation at ¶ 240. Committee Reports at ¶ 10,030.]

[¶ 7018] ACT SEC. 105. TEMPORARY RELIEF FOR CERTAIN PBGC SETTLEMENT PLANS.

(a) GENERAL RULE.—Except as provided in this section, if a plan in existence on July 26, 2005, was a PBGC settlement plan as of such date, the amendments made by this subtitle and subtitle B shall not apply to plan years beginning before January 1, 2014.

(b) INTEREST RATE.—In applying section 302(b)(5)(B) of the Employee Retirement Income Security Act of 1974 and section 412(b)(5)(B) of the Internal Revenue Code of 1986 (as in effect before the amendments made by this subtitle and subtitle B), to a PBGC settlement plan for plan years beginning after December 31, 2007, and before January 1, 2014, the third segment rate determined under section 303(h)(2)(C)(iii) of such Act and section 430(h)(2)(C)(iii) of such Code (as added by such amendments) shall be used in lieu of the interest rate otherwise used.

(c) PBGC SETTLEMENT PLAN.—For purposes of this section, the term "PBGC settlement plan" means a defined benefit plan (other than a multiemployer plan) to which section 302 of such Act and section 412 of such Code apply and—

(1) which was sponsored by an employer which was in bankruptcy, giving rise to a claim by the Pension Benefit Guaranty Corporation of not greater than $150,000,000, and the sponsorship of which was assumed by another employer that was not a member of the same controlled group as the bankrupt sponsor and the claim of the Pension Benefit Guaranty Corporation was settled or withdrawn in connection with the assumption of the sponsorship, or

(2) which, by agreement with the Pension Benefit Guaranty Corporation, was spun off from a plan subsequently terminated by such Corporation under section 4042 of the Employee Retirement Income Security Act of 1974.

[CCH Explanation at ¶ 240. Committee Reports at ¶ 10,040.]

[¶ 7021] ACT SEC. 106. SPECIAL RULES FOR PLANS OF CERTAIN GOVERNMENT CONTRACTORS.

(a) GENERAL RULE.—Except as provided in this section, if a plan is an eligible government contractor plan, this subtitle and subtitle B shall not apply to plan years beginning before the earliest of—

(1) the first plan year for which the plan ceases to be an eligible government contractor plan,

(2) the effective date of the Cost Accounting Standards Pension Harmonization Rule, or

(3) January 1, 2011.

(b) INTEREST RATE.—In applying section 302(b)(5)(B) of the Employee Retirement Income Security Act of 1974 and section 412(b)(5)(B) of the Internal Revenue Code of 1986 (as in effect before the amendments made by this subtitle and subtitle B) to an eligible government contractor plan for plan years beginning after December 31, 2007, and before the first plan year to which such amendments apply, the third segment rate determined under section 303(h)(2)(C)(iii) of such Act and section 430(h)(2)(C)(iii) of such Code (as added by such amendments) shall be used in lieu of the interest rate otherwise used.

(c) ELIGIBLE GOVERNMENT CONTRACTOR PLAN DEFINED.—For purposes of this section, a plan shall be treated as an eligible government contractor plan if it is maintained by a corporation or a member of the same affiliated group (as defined by section 1504(a) of the Internal Revenue Code of 1986), whose primary source of revenue is derived from business performed under contracts with the United States that are subject to the Federal Acquisition Regulations (Chapter 1 of Title 48, C.F.R.) and that are also subject to the Defense Federal Acquisition Regulation Supplement (Chapter 2 of Title 48, C.F.R.), and whose revenue derived from such business in the previous fiscal year exceeded $5,000,000,000, and whose pension plan costs that are assignable under those contracts are subject to sections 412 and 413 of the Cost Accounting Standards (48 C.F.R. 9904.412 and 9904.413).

(d) COST ACCOUNTING STANDARDS PENSION HARMONIZATION RULE.—The Cost Accounting Standards Board shall review and revise sections 412 and 413 of the Cost Accounting Standards (48 C.F.R. 9904.412 and 9904.413) to harmonize the minimum required contribution under the Employee Retirement Income Security Act of 1974 of eligible government contractor plans and government reimbursable pension plan costs not later than January 1, 2010. Any final rule adopted by the Cost Accounting Standards Board shall be deemed the Cost Accounting Standards Pension Harmonization Rule.

[CCH Explanation at ¶ 240. Committee Reports at ¶ 10,050.]

[¶ 7024] ACT SEC. 107. TECHNICAL AND CONFORMING AMENDMENTS.

(a) MISCELLANEOUS AMENDMENTS TO TITLE I.—Subtitle B of title I of such Act (29 U.S.C. 1021 et seq.) is amended—

(1) in section 101(d)(3), by striking "section 302(e)" and inserting "section 303(j)";

(2) in section 103(d)(8)(B), by striking "the requirements of section 302(c)(3)" and inserting "the applicable requirements of sections 303(h) and 304(c)(3)";

(3) in section 103(d), by striking paragraph (11) and inserting the following:

"(11) If the current value of the assets of the plan is less than 70 percent of—

"(A) in the case of a single-employer plan, the funding target (as defined in section 303(d)(1)) of the plan, or

"(B) in the case of a multiemployer plan, the current liability (as defined in section 304(c)(6)(D)) under the plan,

the percentage which such value is of the amount described in subparagraph (A) or (B).";

(4) in section 203(a)(3)(C), by striking "section 302(c)(8)" and inserting "section 302(d)(2)";

(5) in section 204(g)(1), by striking "section 302(c)(8)" and inserting "section 302(d)(2)";

(6) in section 204(i)(2)(B), by striking "section 302(c)(8)" and inserting "section 302(d)(2)";

(7) in section 204(i)(3), by striking "funded current liability percentage (within the meaning of section 302(d)(8) of this Act)" and inserting "funding target attainment percentage (as defined in section 303(d)(2))";

(8) in section 204(i)(4), by striking "section 302(c)(11)(A), without regard to section 302(c)(11)(B)" and inserting "section 302(b)(1), without regard to section 302(b)(2)";

(9) in section 206(e)(1), by striking "section 302(d)" and inserting "section 303(j)(4)", and by striking "section 302(e)(5)" and inserting "section 303(j)(4)(E)(i)";

(10) in section 206(e)(3), by striking "section 302(e) by reason of paragraph (5)(A) thereof" and inserting "section 303(j)(3) by reason of section 303(j)(4)(A)"; and

(11) in sections 101(e)(3), 403(c)(1), and 408(b)(13), by striking "American Jobs Creation Act of 2004" and inserting "Pension Protection Act of 2006".

(b) MISCELLANEOUS AMENDMENTS TO TITLE IV.—Title IV of such Act is amended—

(1) in section 4001(a)(13) (29 U.S.C. 1301(a)(13)), by striking "302(c)(11)(A)" and inserting "302(b)(1)", by striking "412(c)(11)(A)" and inserting "412(b)(1)", by striking "302(c)(11)(B)" and inserting "302(b)(2)", and by striking "412(c)(11)(B)" and inserting "412(b)(2)";

(2) in section 4003(e)(1) (29 U.S.C. 1303(e)(1)), by striking "302(f)(1)(A) and (B)" and inserting "303(k)(1)(A) and (B)", and by striking "412(n)(1)(A) and (B)" and inserting "430(k)(1)(A) and (B)";

(3) in section 4010(b)(2) (29 U.S.C. 1310(b)(2)), by striking "302(f)(1)(A) and (B)" and inserting "303(k)(1)(A) and (B)", and by striking "412(n)(1)(A) and (B)" and inserting "430(k)(1)(A) and (B)";

(4) in section 4062(c) (29 U.S.C. 1362(c)), by striking paragraphs (1), (2), and (3) and inserting the following:

"(1) the sum of the shortfall amortization charge (within the meaning of section 303(c)(1) of this Act and 430(d)(1) of the Internal Revenue Code of 1986) with respect to the plan (if any) for the plan year in which the termination date occurs, plus the aggregate total of shortfall amortization installments (if any) determined for succeeding plan years under section 303(c)(2) of this Act and section 430(d)(2) of such Code (which, for purposes of this subparagraph, shall include any increase in such sum which would result if all applications for waivers of the minimum funding standard under section 302(c) of this Act and section 412(c) of such Code which are pending with respect to such plan were denied and if no additional contributions (other than those already made by the termination date) were made for the plan year in which the termination date occurs or for any previous plan year), and

"(2) the sum of the waiver amortization charge (within the meaning of section 303(e)(1) of this Act and 430(e)(1) of the Internal Revenue Code of 1986) with respect to the plan (if any) for the plan year in which the termination date occurs, plus the aggregate total of waiver amortization installments (if any) determined for succeeding plan years under section 303(e)(2) of this Act and section 430(e)(2) of such Code,";

(5) in section 4071 (29 U.S.C. 1371), by striking "302(f)(4)" and inserting "303(k)(4)";

(6) in section 4243(a)(1)(B) (29 U.S.C. 1423(a)(1)(B)), by striking "302(a)" and inserting "304(a)", and, in clause (i), by striking "302(a)" and inserting "304(a)";

(7) in section 4243(f)(1) (29 U.S.C. 1423(f)(1)), by striking "303(a)" and inserting "302(c)";

(8) in section 4243(f)(2) (29 U.S.C. 1423(f)(2)), by striking "303(c)" and inserting "302(c)(3)"; and

(9) in section 4243(g) (29 U.S.C. 1423(g)), by striking "302(c)(3)" and inserting "304(c)(3)".

(c) AMENDMENTS TO REORGANIZATION PLAN NO. 4 OF 1978.—Section 106(b)(ii) of Reorganization Plan No. 4 of 1978 (ratified and affirmed as law by Public Law 98-532 (98 Stat. 2705)) is amended by striking "302(c)(8)" and inserting "302(d)(2)", by striking "304(a) and (b)(2)(A)" and inserting "304(d)(1), (d)(2), and (e)(2)(A)", and by striking "412(c)(8), (e), and (f)(2)(A)" and inserting "412(c)(2) and 431(d)(1), (d)(2), and (e)(2)(A)".

(d) REPEAL OF EXPIRED AUTHORITY FOR TEMPORARY VARIANCES.—Section 207 of such Act (29 U.S.C. 1057) is repealed.

(e) EFFECTIVE DATE.—The amendments made by this section shall apply to plan years beginning after 2007.

[CCH Explanation at ¶ 205. Committee Reports at ¶ 10,010.]

Subtitle B—Amendments to Internal Revenue Code of 1986

* * *

[¶7027] ACT SEC. 115. MODIFICATION OF TRANSITION RULE TO PENSION FUNDING REQUIREMENTS.

(a) IN GENERAL.—In the case of a plan that—

(1) was not required to pay a variable rate premium for the plan year beginning in 1996,

(2) has not, in any plan year beginning after 1995, merged with another plan (other than a plan sponsored by an employer that was in 1996 within the controlled group of the plan sponsor); and

(3) is sponsored by a company that is engaged primarily in the interurban or interstate passenger bus service,

the rules described in subsection (b) shall apply for any plan year beginning after December 31, 2007.

(b) MODIFIED RULES.—The rules described in this subsection are as follows:

(1) For purposes of section 430(j)(3) of the Internal Revenue Code of 1986 and section 303(j)(3) of the Employee Retirement Income Security Act of 1974, the plan shall be treated as not having a funding shortfall for any plan year.

(2) For purposes of—

(A) determining unfunded vested benefits under section 4006(a)(3)(E)(iii) of such Act, and

(B) determining any present value or making any computation under section 412 of such Code or section 302 of such Act,

the mortality table shall be the mortality table used by the plan.

(3) Section 430(c)(5)(B) of such Code and section 303(c)(5)(B) of such Act (relating to phase-in of funding target for exemption from new shortfall amortization base) shall each be applied by substituting "2012" for "2011" therein and by substituting for the table therein the following:

In the case of a plan year beginning in calendar year:	The applicable percentage is:
2008	90 percent
2009	92 percent
2010	94 percent
2011	96 percent.

(c) DEFINITIONS.—Any term used in this section which is also used in section 430 of such Code or section 303 of such Act shall have the meaning provided such term in such section. If the same term has a different meaning in such Code and such Act, such term shall, for purposes of this section, have the meaning provided by such Code when applied with respect to such Code and the meaning provided by such Act when applied with respect to such Act.

(d) SPECIAL RULE FOR 2006 AND 2007.—

(1) IN GENERAL.—Section 769(c)(3) of the Retirement Protection Act of 1994, as added by section 201 of the Pension Funding Equity Act of 2004, is amended by striking "and 2005" and inserting ", 2005, 2006, and 2007".

(2) EFFECTIVE DATE.—The amendment made by paragraph (1) shall apply to plan years beginning after December 31, 2005.

(e) CONFORMING AMENDMENT.—

(1) Section 769 of the Retirement Protection Act of 1994 is amended by striking subsection (c).

(2) The amendment made by paragraph (1) shall take effect on December 31, 2007, and shall apply to plan years beginning after such date.

* * *

[CCH Explanation at ¶ 230. Committee Reports at ¶ 10,060.]

TITLE II—FUNDING RULES FOR MULTIEMPLOYER DEFINED BENEFIT PLANS AND RELATED PROVISIONS

Subtitle A—Amendments to Employee Retirement Income Security Act of 1974

[¶ 7030] ACT SEC. 201. FUNDING RULES FOR MULTIEMPLOYER DEFINED BENEFIT PLANS.

(a) IN GENERAL.—Part 3 of subtitle B of title I of the Employee Retirement Income Security Act of 1974 (as amended by this Act) is amended by inserting after section 303 the following new section:

"Minimum Funding Standards for Multiemployer Plans

"SEC. 304. (a) IN GENERAL.—For purposes of section 302, the accumulated funding deficiency of a multiemployer plan for any plan year is—

"(1) except as provided in paragraph (2), the amount, determined as of the end of the plan year, equal to the excess (if any) of the total charges to the funding standard account of the plan for all plan years (beginning with the first plan year for which this part applies to the plan) over the total credits to such account for such years, and

"(2) if the multiemployer plan is in reorganization for any plan year, the accumulated funding deficiency of the plan determined under section 4243.

"(b) FUNDING STANDARD ACCOUNT.—

"(1) ACCOUNT REQUIRED.—Each multiemployer plan to which this part applies shall establish and maintain a funding standard account. Such account shall be credited and charged solely as provided in this section.

"(2) CHARGES TO ACCOUNT.—For a plan year, the funding standard account shall be charged with the sum of—

"(A) the normal cost of the plan for the plan year,

"(B) the amounts necessary to amortize in equal annual installments (until fully amortized)—

"(i) in the case of a plan which comes into existence on or after January 1, 2008, the unfunded past service liability under the plan on the first day of the first plan year to which this section applies, over a period of 15 plan years,

"(ii) separately, with respect to each plan year, the net increase (if any) in unfunded past service liability under the plan arising from plan amendments adopted in such year, over a period of 15 plan years,

"(iii) separately, with respect to each plan year, the net experience loss (if any) under the plan, over a period of 15 plan years, and

"(iv) separately, with respect to each plan year, the net loss (if any) resulting from changes in actuarial assumptions used under the plan, over a period of 15 plan years,

"(C) the amount necessary to amortize each waived funding deficiency (within the meaning of section 302(c)(3)) for each prior plan year in equal annual installments (until fully amortized) over a period of 15 plan years,

"(D) the amount necessary to amortize in equal annual installments (until fully amortized) over a period of 5 plan years any amount credited to the funding standard account under section 302(b)(3)(D) (as in effect on the day before the date of the enactment of the Pension Protection Act of 2006), and

"(E) the amount necessary to amortize in equal annual installments (until fully amortized) over a period of 20 years the contributions which would be required to be made under the plan but for the provisions of section 302(c)(7)(A)(i)(I) (as in effect on the day before the date of the enactment of the Pension Protection Act of 2006).

"(3) CREDITS TO ACCOUNT.—For a plan year, the funding standard account shall be credited with the sum of—

"(A) the amount considered contributed by the employer to or under the plan for the plan year,

"(B) the amount necessary to amortize in equal annual installments (until fully amortized)—

"(i) separately, with respect to each plan year, the net decrease (if any) in unfunded past service liability under the plan arising from plan amendments adopted in such year, over a period of 15 plan years,

"(ii) separately, with respect to each plan year, the net experience gain (if any) under the plan, over a period of 15 plan years, and

"(iii) separately, with respect to each plan year, the net gain (if any) resulting from changes in actuarial assumptions used under the plan, over a period of 15 plan years,

"(C) the amount of the waived funding deficiency (within the meaning of section 302(c)(3)) for the plan year, and

"(D) in the case of a plan year for which the accumulated funding deficiency is determined under the funding standard account if such plan year follows a plan year for which such deficiency was determined under the alternative minimum funding standard under section 305 (as in effect on the day before the date of the enactment of the Pension Protection Act of 2006), the excess (if any) of any debit balance in the funding standard account (determined without regard to this subparagraph) over any debit balance in the alternative minimum funding standard account.

"(4) SPECIAL RULE FOR AMOUNTS FIRST AMORTIZED IN PLAN YEARS BEFORE 2008.—In the case of any amount amortized under section 302(b) (as in effect on the day before the date of the enactment of the Pension Protection Act of 2006) over any period beginning with a plan year beginning before 2008, in lieu of the amortization described in paragraphs (2)(B) and (3)(B), such amount shall continue to be amortized under such section as so in effect.

"(5) COMBINING AND OFFSETTING AMOUNTS TO BE AMORTIZED.—Under regulations prescribed by the Secretary of the Treasury, amounts required to be amortized under paragraph (2) or paragraph (3), as the case may be—

"(A) may be combined into one amount under such paragraph to be amortized over a period determined on the basis of the remaining amortization period for all items entering into such combined amount, and

"(B) may be offset against amounts required to be amortized under the other such paragraph, with the resulting amount to be amortized over a period determined on the basis of the remaining amortization periods for all items entering into whichever of the two amounts being offset is the greater.

"(6) INTEREST.—The funding standard account (and items therein) shall be charged or credited (as determined under regulations prescribed by the Secretary of the Treasury) with interest at the appropriate rate consistent with the rate or rates of interest used under the plan to determine costs.

"(7) SPECIAL RULES RELATING TO CHARGES AND CREDITS TO FUNDING STANDARD ACCOUNT.—For purposes of this part—

"(A) WITHDRAWAL LIABILITY.—Any amount received by a multiemployer plan in payment of all or part of an employer's withdrawal liability under part 1 of subtitle E of title IV shall be considered an amount contributed by the employer to or under the plan. The Secretary of the Treasury may prescribe by regulation additional charges and credits to a multiemployer plan's funding standard account to the extent necessary to prevent withdrawal liability payments from being unduly reflected as advance funding for plan liabilities.

"(B) ADJUSTMENTS WHEN A MULTIEMPLOYER PLAN LEAVES REORGANIZATION.—If a multiemployer plan is not in reorganization in the plan year but was in reorganization in the immediately preceding plan year, any balance in the funding standard account at the close of such immediately preceding plan year—

"(i) shall be eliminated by an offsetting credit or charge (as the case may be), but

"(ii) shall be taken into account in subsequent plan years by being amortized in equal annual installments (until fully amortized) over 30 plan years.

The preceding sentence shall not apply to the extent of any accumulated funding deficiency under section 4243(a) as of the end of the last plan year that the plan was in reorganization.

"(C) PLAN PAYMENTS TO SUPPLEMENTAL PROGRAM OR WITHDRAWAL LIABILITY PAYMENT FUND.—Any amount paid by a plan during a plan year to the Pension Benefit Guaranty Corporation pursuant to section 4222 of this Act or to a fund exempt under section 501(c)(22) of the Internal Revenue Code of 1986 pursuant to section 4223 of this Act shall reduce the amount of contributions considered received by the plan for the plan year.

"(D) INTERIM WITHDRAWAL LIABILITY PAYMENTS.—Any amount paid by an employer pending a final determination of the employer's withdrawal liability under part 1 of subtitle E of title IV and subsequently refunded to the employer by the plan shall be charged to the funding standard account in accordance with regulations prescribed by the Secretary of the Treasury.

"(E) ELECTION FOR DEFERRAL OF CHARGE FOR PORTION OF NET EXPERIENCE.—If an election is in effect under section 302(b)(7)(F) (as in effect on the day before the date of the enactment of the Pension Protection Act of 2006) for any plan year, the funding standard account shall be charged in the plan year to which the portion of the net experience loss deferred by such election was deferred with the amount so deferred (and paragraph (2)(B)(iii) shall not apply to the amount so charged).

"(F) FINANCIAL ASSISTANCE.—Any amount of any financial assistance from the Pension Benefit Guaranty Corporation to any plan, and any repayment of such amount, shall be taken into account under this section and section 302 in such manner as is determined by the Secretary of the Treasury.

"(G) SHORT-TERM BENEFITS.—To the extent that any plan amendment increases the unfunded past service liability under the plan by reason of an increase in benefits which are not payable as a life annuity but are payable under the terms of the plan for a period that does not exceed 14 years from the effective date of the amendment, paragraph (2)(B)(ii) shall be applied separately with respect to such increase in unfunded past service liability by substituting the number of years of the period during which such benefits are payable for '15'.

"(c) ADDITIONAL RULES.—

"(1) DETERMINATIONS TO BE MADE UNDER FUNDING METHOD.—For purposes of this part, normal costs, accrued liability, past service liabilities, and experience gains and losses shall be determined under the funding method used to determine costs under the plan.

"(2) VALUATION OF ASSETS.—

"(A) IN GENERAL.—For purposes of this part, the value of the plan's assets shall be determined on the basis of any reasonable actuarial method of valuation which takes into account fair market value and which is permitted under regulations prescribed by the Secretary of the Treasury.

"(B) ELECTION WITH RESPECT TO BONDS.—The value of a bond or other evidence of indebtedness which is not in default as to principal or interest may, at the election of the plan administrator, be determined on an amortized basis running from initial cost at purchase to par value at maturity or earliest call date. Any election under this subparagraph shall be made at such time and in such manner as the Secretary of the Treasury shall by regulations provide, shall apply to all such evidences of indebtedness, and may be revoked only with the consent of such Secretary.

"(3) ACTUARIAL ASSUMPTIONS MUST BE REASONABLE.—For purposes of this section, all costs, liabilities, rates of interest, and other factors under the plan shall be determined on the basis of actuarial assumptions and methods—

"(A) each of which is reasonable (taking into account the experience of the plan and reasonable expectations), and

"(B) which, in combination, offer the actuary's best estimate of anticipated experience under the plan.

"(4) TREATMENT OF CERTAIN CHANGES AS EXPERIENCE GAIN OR LOSS.—For purposes of this section, if—

"(A) a change in benefits under the Social Security Act or in other retirement benefits created under Federal or State law, or

"(B) a change in the definition of the term 'wages' under section 3121 of the Internal Revenue Code of 1986, or a change in the amount of such wages taken into account under regulations prescribed for purposes of section 401(a)(5) of such Code,

results in an increase or decrease in accrued liability under a plan, such increase or decrease shall be treated as an experience loss or gain.

"(5) FULL FUNDING.—If, as of the close of a plan year, a plan would (without regard to this paragraph) have an accumulated funding deficiency in excess of the full funding limitation—

"(A) the funding standard account shall be credited with the amount of such excess, and

"(B) all amounts described in subparagraphs (B), (C), and (D) of subsection (b) (2) and subparagraph (B) of subsection (b)(3) which are required to be amortized shall be considered fully amortized for purposes of such subparagraphs.

"(6) FULL-FUNDING LIMITATION.—

"(A) IN GENERAL.—For purposes of paragraph (5), the term 'full-funding limitation' means the excess (if any) of—

"(i) the accrued liability (including normal cost) under the plan (determined under the entry age normal funding method if such accrued liability cannot be directly calculated under the funding method used for the plan), over

"(ii) the lesser of—

"(I) the fair market value of the plan's assets, or

"(II) the value of such assets determined under paragraph (2).

"(B) MINIMUM AMOUNT.—

"(i) IN GENERAL.—In no event shall the full-funding limitation determined under subparagraph (A) be less than the excess (if any) of—

"(I) 90 percent of the current liability of the plan (including the expected increase in current liability due to benefits accruing during the plan year), over

"(II) the value of the plan's assets determined under paragraph (2).

"(ii) ASSETS.—For purposes of clause (i), assets shall not be reduced by any credit balance in the funding standard account.

"(C) FULL FUNDING LIMITATION.—For purposes of this paragraph, unless otherwise provided by the plan, the accrued liability under a multiemployer plan shall not include benefits which are not nonforfeitable under the plan after the termination of the plan (taking into consideration section 411(d)(3) of the Internal Revenue Code of 1986).

"(D) CURRENT LIABILITY.—For purposes of this paragraph—

"(i) IN GENERAL.—The term 'current liability' means all liabilities to employees and their beneficiaries under the plan.

"(ii) TREATMENT OF UNPREDICTABLE CONTINGENT EVENT BENEFITS.—For purposes of clause (i), any benefit contingent on an event other than—

"(I) age, service, compensation, death, or disability, or

"(II) an event which is reasonably and reliably predictable (as determined by the Secretary of the Treasury), shall not be taken into account until the event on which the benefit is contingent occurs.

"(iii) INTEREST RATE USED.—The rate of interest used to determine current liability under this paragraph shall be the rate of interest determined under subparagraph (E).

"(iv) MORTALITY TABLES.—

"(I) COMMISSIONERS' STANDARD TABLE.—In the case of plan years beginning before the first plan year to which the first tables prescribed under subclause (II) apply, the mortality table used in determining current liability under this paragraph shall be the table prescribed by the Secretary of the Treasury which is based on the prevailing commissioners' standard table (described in section 807(d)(5)(A) of the Internal Revenue Code of 1986) used to determine reserves for group annuity contracts issued on January 1, 1993.

"(II) SECRETARIAL AUTHORITY.—The Secretary of the Treasury may by regulation prescribe for plan years beginning after December 31, 1999, mortality tables to be used in determining current liability under this subsection. Such tables shall be based upon the actual experience of pension plans and projected trends in such experience. In prescribing such tables, such Secretary shall take into account results of available independent studies of mortality of individuals covered by pension plans.

"(v) SEPARATE MORTALITY TABLES FOR THE DISABLED.—Notwithstanding clause (iv)—

"(I) IN GENERAL.—The Secretary of the Treasury shall establish mortality tables which may be used (in lieu of the tables under clause (iv)) to determine current liability under this subsection for individuals who are entitled to benefits under the plan on account of disability. Such Secretary shall establish separate tables for individuals whose disabilities occur in plan years beginning before January 1, 1995, and for individuals whose disabilities occur in plan years beginning on or after such date.

"(II) SPECIAL RULE FOR DISABILITIES OCCURRING AFTER 1994.—In the case of disabilities occurring in plan years beginning after December 31, 1994, the tables under subclause (I) shall apply only with respect to individuals described in such subclause who are disabled within the meaning of title II of the Social Security Act and the regulations thereunder.

"(vi) PERIODIC REVIEW.—The Secretary of the Treasury shall periodically (at least every 5 years) review any tables in effect under this subparagraph and shall, to the extent such Secretary determines necessary, by regulation update the tables to reflect the actual experience of pension plans and projected trends in such experience.

"(E) REQUIRED CHANGE OF INTEREST RATE.—For purposes of determining a plan's current liability for purposes of this paragraph—

"(i) IN GENERAL.—If any rate of interest used under the plan under subsection (b)(6) to determine cost is not within the permissible range, the plan shall establish a new rate of interest within the permissible range.

"(ii) PERMISSIBLE RANGE.—For purposes of this subparagraph—

"(I) IN GENERAL.—Except as provided in subclause (II), the term 'permissible range' means a rate of interest which is not more than 5 percent above, and not more than 10 percent below, the weighted average of the rates of interest on 30-year Treasury securities during the 4-year period ending on the last day before the beginning of the plan year.

"(II) SECRETARIAL AUTHORITY.—If the Secretary of the Treasury finds that the lowest rate of interest permissible under subclause (I) is unreasonably high, such Secretary may prescribe a lower rate of interest, except that such rate may not be less than 80 percent of the average rate determined under such subclause.

"(iii) ASSUMPTIONS.—Notwithstanding paragraph (3)(A), the interest rate used under the plan shall be—

"(I) determined without taking into account the experience of the plan and reasonable expectations, but

"(II) consistent with the assumptions which reflect the purchase rates which would be used by insurance companies to satisfy the liabilities under the plan.

"(7) ANNUAL VALUATION.—

"(A) IN GENERAL.—For purposes of this section, a determination of experience gains and losses and a valuation of the plan's liability shall be made not less frequently than once every year, except that such determination shall be made more frequently to the extent required in particular cases under regulations prescribed by the Secretary of the Treasury.

"(B) VALUATION DATE.—

"(i) CURRENT YEAR.—Except as provided in clause (ii), the valuation referred to in subparagraph (A) shall be made as of a date within the plan year to which the valuation refers or within one month prior to the beginning of such year.

"(ii) USE OF PRIOR YEAR VALUATION.—The valuation referred to in subparagraph (A) may be made as of a date within the plan year prior to the year to which the valuation refers if, as of such date, the value of the assets of the plan are not less than 100 percent of the plan's current liability (as defined in paragraph (6)(D) without regard to clause (iv) thereof).

"(iii) ADJUSTMENTS.—Information under clause (ii) shall, in accordance with regulations, be actuarially adjusted to reflect significant differences in participants.

"(iv) LIMITATION.—A change in funding method to use a prior year valuation, as provided in clause (ii), may not be made unless as of the valuation date within the prior plan year, the value of the assets of the plan are not less than 125 percent of the plan's current liability (as defined in paragraph (6)(D) without regard to clause (iv) thereof).

"(8) TIME WHEN CERTAIN CONTRIBUTIONS DEEMED MADE.—For purposes of this section, any contributions for a plan year made by an employer after the last day of such plan year, but not later than two and one-half months after such day, shall be deemed to have been made on such last day. For purposes of this subparagraph, such two and one-half month period may be extended for not more than six months under regulations prescribed by the Secretary of the Treasury.

"(d) EXTENSION OF AMORTIZATION PERIODS FOR MULTIEMPLOYER PLANS.—

"(1) AUTOMATIC EXTENSION UPON APPLICATION BY CERTAIN PLANS.—

"(A) IN GENERAL.—If the plan sponsor of a multiemployer plan—

"(i) submits to the Secretary of the Treasury an application for an extension of the period of years required to amortize any unfunded liability described in any clause of subsection (b)(2)(B) or described in subsection (b)(4), and

"(ii) includes with the application a certification by the plan's actuary described in subparagraph (B),

the Secretary of the Treasury shall extend the amortization period for the period of time (not in excess of 5 years) specified in the application. Such extension shall be in addition to any extension under paragraph (2).

"(B) CRITERIA.—A certification with respect to a multiemployer plan is described in this subparagraph if the plan's actuary certifies that, based on reasonable assumptions—

"(i) absent the extension under subparagraph (A), the plan would have an accumulated funding deficiency in the current plan year or any of the 9 succeeding plan years,

"(ii) the plan sponsor has adopted a plan to improve the plan's funding status,

"(iii) the plan is projected to have sufficient assets to timely pay expected benefits and anticipated expenditures over the amortization period as extended, and

"(iv) the notice required under paragraph (3)(A) has been provided.

"(C) TERMINATION.—The preceding provisions of this paragraph shall not apply with respect to any application submitted after December 31, 2014.

"(2) ALTERNATIVE EXTENSION.—

"(A) IN GENERAL.—If the plan sponsor of a multiemployer plan submits to the Secretary of the Treasury an application for an extension of the period of years required to amortize any unfunded liability described in any clause of subsection (b)(2)(B) or described in subsection (b)(4), the Secretary of the Treasury may extend the amortization period for a period of time (not in excess of 10 years reduced by the number of years of any extension under paragraph (1) with respect to such unfunded liability) if the Secretary of the Treasury makes the determination described in subparagraph (B). Such extension shall be in addition to any extension under paragraph (1).

"(B) DETERMINATION.—The Secretary of the Treasury may grant an extension under subparagraph (A) if such Secretary determines that—

"(i) such extension would carry out the purposes of this Act and would provide adequate protection for participants under the plan and their beneficiaries, and

"(ii) the failure to permit such extension would—

"(I) result in a substantial risk to the voluntary continuation of the plan, or a substantial curtailment of pension benefit levels or employee compensation, and

"(II) be adverse to the interests of plan participants in the aggregate.

"(C) ACTION BY SECRETARY OF THE TREASURY.—The Secretary of the Treasury shall act upon any application for an extension under this paragraph within 180 days of the submission of such application. If such Secretary rejects the application for an extension under this paragraph, such Secretary shall provide notice to the plan detailing the specific reasons for the rejection, including references to the criteria set forth above.

"(3) ADVANCE NOTICE.—

"(A) IN GENERAL.—The Secretary of the Treasury shall, before granting an extension under this subsection, require each applicant to provide evidence satisfactory to such Secretary that the applicant has provided notice of the filing of the application for such extension to each affected party (as defined in section 4001(a)(21)) with respect to the affected plan. Such notice shall include a description of the extent to which the plan is funded for benefits which are guaranteed under title IV and for benefit liabilities.

"(B) CONSIDERATION OF RELEVANT INFORMATION.—The Secretary of the Treasury shall consider any relevant information provided by a person to whom notice was given under paragraph (1).".

(b) SHORTFALL FUNDING METHOD.—

(1) IN GENERAL.—A multiemployer plan meeting the criteria of paragraph (2) may adopt, use, or cease using, the shortfall funding method and such adoption, use, or cessation of use of such method, shall be deemed approved by the Secretary of the Treasury under section 302(d)(1) of the Employee Retirement Income Security Act of 1974 and section 412(d)(1) of the Internal Revenue Code of 1986.

(2) CRITERIA.—A multiemployer pension plan meets the criteria of this clause if—

(A) the plan has not used the shortfall funding method during the 5-year period ending on the day before the date the plan is to use the method under paragraph (1); and

(B) the plan is not operating under an amortization period extension under section 304(d) of such Act and did not operate under such an extension during such 5-year period.

(3) SHORTFALL FUNDING METHOD DEFINED.—For purposes of this subsection, the term "shortfall funding method" means the shortfall funding method described in Treasury Regulations section 1.412(c)(1)-2 (26 CFR 1.412(c)(1)-2).

(4) BENEFIT RESTRICTIONS TO APPLY.—The benefit restrictions under section 302(c)(7) of such Act and section 412(c)(7) of such Code shall apply during any period a multiemployer plan is on the shortfall funding method pursuant to this subsection.

(5) USE OF SHORTFALL METHOD NOT TO PRECLUDE OTHER OPTIONS.—Nothing in this subsection shall be construed to affect a multiemployer plan's ability to adopt the shortfall funding method with the Secretary's permission under otherwise applicable regulations or to affect a multiemployer plan's right to change funding methods, with or without the Secretary's consent, as provided in applicable rules and regulations.

(c) CONFORMING AMENDMENTS.—

(1) Section 301 of the Employee Retirement Income Security Act of 1974 (29 U.S.C. 1081) is amended by striking subsection (d).

(2) The table of contents in section 1 of such Act (as amended by this Act) is amended by inserting after the item relating to section 303 the following new item:

"Sec. 304. Minimum funding standards for multiemployer plans.".

(d) EFFECTIVE DATE.—

(1) IN GENERAL.—The amendments made by this section shall apply to plan years beginning after 2007.

(2) SPECIAL RULE FOR CERTAIN AMORTIZATION EXTENSIONS.—If the Secretary of the Treasury grants an extension under section 304 of the Employee Retirement Income Security Act of 1974 and section 412(e) of the Internal Revenue Code of 1986 with respect to any application filed with the Secretary of the Treasury on or before June 30, 2005, the extension (and any modification thereof) shall be applied and administered under the rules of such sections as in effect before the enactment of this Act, including the use of the rate of interest determined under section 6621(b) of such Code.

[CCH Explanation at ¶ 305. Committee Reports at ¶ 10,080.]

[¶ 7033] ACT SEC. 202. ADDITIONAL FUNDING RULES FOR MULTIEMPLOYER PLANS IN ENDANGERED OR CRITICAL STATUS.

(a) IN GENERAL.—Part 3 of subtitle B of title I of the Employee Retirement Income Security Act of 1974 (as amended by the preceding provisions of this Act) is amended by inserting after section 304 the following new section:

"ADDITIONAL FUNDING RULES FOR MULTIEMPLOYER PLANS IN ENDANGERED STATUS OR CRITICAL STATUS

"SEC. 305. (a) GENERAL RULE.—For purposes of this part, in the case of a multiemployer plan in effect on July 16, 2006—

"(1) if the plan is in endangered status—

"(A) the plan sponsor shall adopt and implement a funding improvement plan in accordance with the requirements of subsection (c), and

"(B) the requirements of subsection (d) shall apply during the funding plan adoption period and the funding improvement period, and

"(2) if the plan is in critical status—

"(A) the plan sponsor shall adopt and implement a rehabilitation plan in accordance with the requirements of subsection (e), and

"(B) the requirements of subsection (f) shall apply during the rehabilitation plan adoption period and the rehabilitation period.

"(b) DETERMINATION OF ENDANGERED AND CRITICAL STATUS.—For purposes of this section—

"(1) ENDANGERED STATUS.—A multiemployer plan is in endangered status for a plan year if, as determined by the plan actuary under paragraph (3), the plan is not in critical status for the plan year and, as of the beginning of the plan year, either—

"(A) the plan's funded percentage for such plan year is less than 80 percent, or

"(B) the plan has an accumulated funding deficiency for such plan year, or is projected to have such an accumulated funding deficiency for any of the 6 succeeding plan years, taking into account any extension of amortization periods under section 304(d).

For purposes of this section, a plan shall be treated as in seriously endangered status for a plan year if the plan is described in both subparagraphs (A) and (B).

"(2) CRITICAL STATUS.—A multiemployer plan is in critical status for a plan year if, as determined by the plan actuary under paragraph (3), the plan is described in 1 or more of the following subparagraphs as of the beginning of the plan year:

"(A) A plan is described in this subparagraph if—

"(i) the funded percentage of the plan is less than 65 percent, and

"(ii) the sum of—

"(I) the fair market value of plan assets, plus

"(II) the present value of the reasonably anticipated employer contributions for the current plan year and each of the 6 succeeding plan years, assuming that the terms of all collective bargaining agreements pursuant to which the plan is maintained for the current plan year continue in effect for succeeding plan years,

is less than the present value of all nonforfeitable benefits projected to be payable under the plan during the current plan year and each of the 6 succeeding plan years (plus administrative expenses for such plan years).

"(B) A plan is described in this subparagraph if—

"(i) the plan has an accumulated funding deficiency for the current plan year, not taking into account any extension of amortization periods under section 304(d), or

"(ii) the plan is projected to have an accumulated funding deficiency for any of the 3 succeeding plan years (4 succeeding plan years if the funded percentage of the plan is 65 percent or less), not taking into account any extension of amortization periods under section 304(d).

"(C) A plan is described in this subparagraph if—

"(i)(I) the plan's normal cost for the current plan year, plus interest (determined at the rate used for determining costs under the plan) for the current plan year on the amount of unfunded benefit liabilities under the plan as of the last date of the preceding plan year, exceeds

"(II) the present value of the reasonably anticipated employer and employee contributions for the current plan year,

"(ii) the present value, as of the beginning of the current plan year, of nonforfeitable benefits of inactive participants is greater than the present value of nonforfeitable benefits of active participants, and

"(iii) the plan has an accumulated funding deficiency for the current plan year, or is projected to have such a deficiency for any of the 4 succeeding plan years, not taking into account any extension of amortization periods under section 304(d).

"(D) A plan is described in this subparagraph if the sum of—

"(i) the fair market value of plan assets, plus

"(ii) the present value of the reasonably anticipated employer contributions for the current plan year and each of the 4 succeeding plan years, assuming that the terms of all collective bargaining agreements pursuant to which the plan is maintained for the current plan year continue in effect for succeeding plan years,

is less than the present value of all benefits projected to be payable under the plan during the current plan year and each of the 4 succeeding plan years (plus administrative expenses for such plan years).

"(3) ANNUAL CERTIFICATION BY PLAN ACTUARY.—

"(A) IN GENERAL.—Not later than the 90th day of each plan year of a multiemployer plan, the plan actuary shall certify to the Secretary of the Treasury and to the plan sponsor—

"(i) whether or not the plan is in endangered status for such plan year and whether or not the plan is or will be in critical status for such plan year, and

"(ii) in the case of a plan which is in a funding improvement or rehabilitation period, whether or not the plan is making the scheduled progress in meeting the requirements of its funding improvement or rehabilitation plan.

"(B) ACTUARIAL PROJECTIONS OF ASSETS AND LIABILITIES.—

"(i) IN GENERAL.—In making the determinations and projections under this subsection, the plan actuary shall make projections required for the current and succeeding plan years of the current value of the assets of the plan and the present value of all liabilities to participants and beneficiaries under the plan for the current plan year as of the beginning of such year. The actuary's projections shall be based on reasonable actuarial estimates, assumptions, and methods that, except as provided in clause (iii), offer the actuary's best estimate of anticipated experience under the plan. The projected present value of liabilities as of the beginning of such year shall be determined based on the most recent of either—

"(I) the actuarial statement required under section 103(d) with respect to the most recently filed annual report, or

"(II) the actuarial valuation for the preceding plan year.

"(ii) DETERMINATIONS OF FUTURE CONTRIBUTIONS.—Any actuarial projection of plan assets shall assume—

"(I) reasonably anticipated employer contributions for the current and succeeding plan years, assuming that the terms of the one or more collective bargaining agreements pursuant to which the plan is maintained for the current plan year continue in effect for succeeding plan years, or

"(II) that employer contributions for the most recent plan year will continue indefinitely, but only if the plan actuary determines there have been no significant demographic changes that would make such assumption unreasonable.

"(iii) PROJECTED INDUSTRY ACTIVITY.—Any projection of activity in the industry or industries covered by the plan, including future covered employment and contribution levels, shall be based on information provided by the plan sponsor, which shall act reasonably and in good faith.

"(C) PENALTY FOR FAILURE TO SECURE TIMELY ACTUARIAL CERTIFICATION.—Any failure of the plan's actuary to certify the plan's status under this subsection by the date specified in subparagraph (A) shall be treated for purposes of section 502(c)(2) as a failure or refusal by the plan administrator to file the annual report required to be filed with the Secretary under section 101(b)(4).

"(D) NOTICE.—

"(i) IN GENERAL.—In any case in which it is certified under subparagraph (A) that a multiemployer plan is or will be in endangered or critical status for a plan year, the plan sponsor shall, not later than 30 days after the date of the certification, provide notification of the endangered or critical status to the participants and beneficiaries, the bargaining parties, the Pension Benefit Guaranty Corporation, and the Secretary.

"(ii) PLANS IN CRITICAL STATUS.—If it is certified under subparagraph (A) that a multiemployer plan is or will be in critical status, the plan sponsor shall include in the notice under clause (i) an explanation of the possibility that—

"(I) adjustable benefits (as defined in subsection (e)(8)) may be reduced, and

"(II) such reductions may apply to participants and beneficiaries whose benefit commencement date is on or after the date such notice is provided for the first plan year in which the plan is in critical status.

"(iii) MODEL NOTICE.—The Secretary shall prescribe a model notice that a multiemployer plan may use to satisfy the requirements under clause (ii).

"(c) FUNDING IMPROVEMENT PLAN MUST BE ADOPTED FOR MULTIEMPLOYER PLANS IN ENDANGERED STATUS.—

"(1) IN GENERAL.—In any case in which a multiemployer plan is in endangered status for a plan year, the plan sponsor, in accordance with this subsection—

"(A) shall adopt a funding improvement plan not later than 240 days following the required date for the actuarial certification of endangered status under subsection (b)(3)(A), and

"(B) within 30 days after the adoption of the funding improvement plan—

"(i) shall provide to the bargaining parties 1 or more schedules showing revised benefit structures, revised contribution structures, or both, which, if adopted, may reasonably be expected to enable the multiemployer plan to meet the applicable benchmarks in accordance with the funding improvement plan, including—

"(I) one proposal for reductions in the amount of future benefit accruals necessary to achieve the applicable benchmarks, assuming no amendments increasing contributions under the plan (other than amendments increasing contributions necessary to achieve the applicable benchmarks after amendments have reduced future benefit accruals to the maximum extent permitted by law), and

"(II) one proposal for increases in contributions under the plan necessary to achieve the applicable benchmarks, assuming no amendments reducing future benefit accruals under the plan, and

"(ii) may, if the plan sponsor deems appropriate, prepare and provide the bargaining parties with additional information relating to contribution rates or benefit reductions, alternative schedules, or other information relevant to achieving the applicable benchmarks in accordance with the funding improvement plan.

For purposes of this section, the term 'applicable benchmarks' means the requirements applicable to the multiemployer plan under paragraph (3) (as modified by paragraph (5)).

"(2) EXCEPTION FOR YEARS AFTER PROCESS BEGINS.—Paragraph (1) shall not apply to a plan year if such year is in a funding plan adoption period or funding improvement period by reason of the plan being in endangered status for a preceding plan year. For purposes of this section, such preceding plan year shall be the initial determination year with respect to the funding improvement plan to which it relates.

"(3) FUNDING IMPROVEMENT PLAN.—For purposes of this section—

"(A) IN GENERAL.—A funding improvement plan is a plan which consists of the actions, including options or a range of options to be proposed to the bargaining parties, formulated to provide, based on reasonably anticipated experience and reasonable actuarial assumptions, for the attainment by the plan during the funding improvement period of the following requirements:

"(i) INCREASE IN PLAN'S FUNDING PERCENTAGE.—The plan's funded percentage as of the close of the funding improvement period equals or exceeds a percentage equal to the sum of—

"(I) such percentage as of the beginning of such period, plus

"(II) 33 percent of the difference between 100 percent and the percentage under subclause (I).

"(ii) AVOIDANCE OF ACCUMULATED FUNDING DEFICIENCIES.—No accumulated funding deficiency for any plan year during the funding improvement period (taking into account any extension of amortization periods under section 304(d)).

"(B) SERIOUSLY ENDANGERED PLANS.—In the case of a plan in seriously endangered status, except as provided in paragraph (5), subparagraph (A)(i)(II) shall be applied by substituting '20 percent' for '33 percent'.

"(4) FUNDING IMPROVEMENT PERIOD.—For purposes of this section—

"(A) IN GENERAL.—The funding improvement period for any funding improvement plan adopted pursuant to this subsection is the 10-year period beginning on the first day of the first plan year of the multiemployer plan beginning after the earlier of—

"(i) the second anniversary of the date of the adoption of the funding improvement plan, or

"(ii) the expiration of the collective bargaining agreements in effect on the due date for the actuarial certification of endangered status for the initial determination year under subsection (b)(3)(A) and covering, as of such due date, at least 75 percent of the active participants in such multiemployer plan.

"(B) SERIOUSLY ENDANGERED PLANS.—In the case of a plan in seriously endangered status, except as provided in paragraph (5), subparagraph (A) shall be applied by substituting '15-year period' for '10-year period'.

"(C) COORDINATION WITH CHANGES IN STATUS.—

"(i) PLANS NO LONGER IN ENDANGERED STATUS.—If the plan's actuary certifies under subsection (b)(3)(A) for a plan year in any funding plan adoption period or funding improvement period that the plan is no longer in endangered status and is not in critical status, the funding plan adoption period or funding improvement period, whichever is applicable, shall end as of the close of the preceding plan year.

"(ii) PLANS IN CRITICAL STATUS.—If the plan's actuary certifies under subsection (b)(3)(A) for a plan year in any funding plan adoption period or funding improvement period that the plan is in critical status, the funding plan adoption period or funding improvement period, whichever is applicable, shall end as of the close of the plan year preceding the first plan year in the rehabilitation period with respect to such status.

"(D) PLANS IN ENDANGERED STATUS AT END OF PERIOD.—If the plan's actuary certifies under subsection (b)(3)(A) for the first plan year following the close of the period described in subparagraph (A) that the plan is in endangered status, the provisions of this subsection and subsection (d) shall be applied as if such first plan year were an initial determination year, except that the plan may not be amended in a manner inconsistent with the funding improvement plan in effect for the preceding plan year until a new funding improvement plan is adopted.

"(5) SPECIAL RULES FOR SERIOUSLY ENDANGERED PLANS MORE THAN 70 PERCENT FUNDED.—

"(A) IN GENERAL.—If the funded percentage of a plan in seriously endangered status was more than 70 percent as of the beginning of the initial determination year—

"(i) paragraphs (3)(B) and (4)(B) shall apply only if the plan's actuary certifies, within 30 days after the certification under subsection (b)(3)(A) for the initial determination year, that, based on the terms of the plan and the collective bargaining agreements in effect at the time of such certification, the plan is not projected to meet the requirements of paragraph (3)(A) (without regard to paragraphs (3)(B) and (4)(B)), and

"(ii) if there is a certification under clause (i), the plan may, in formulating its funding improvement plan, only take into account the rules of paragraph (3)(B) and (4)(B) for plan years in the funding improvement period beginning on or before the date on which the last of the collective bargaining agreements described in paragraph (4)(A)(ii) expires.

"(B) SPECIAL RULE AFTER EXPIRATION OF AGREEMENTS.—Notwithstanding subparagraph (A)(ii), if, for any plan year ending after the date described in subparagraph (A)(ii), the plan actuary certifies (at the time of the annual certification under subsection (b)(3)(A) for such plan year) that, based on the terms of the plan and collective bargaining agreements in effect at the time of that annual certification, the plan is not projected to be able to meet the requirements of paragraph (3)(A) (without regard to paragraphs (3)(B) and (4)(B)), paragraphs (3)(B) and (4)(B) shall continue to apply for such year.

"(6) UPDATES TO FUNDING IMPROVEMENT PLAN AND SCHEDULES.—

"(A) FUNDING IMPROVEMENT PLAN.—The plan sponsor shall annually update the funding improvement plan and shall file the update with the plan's annual report under section 104.

"(B) SCHEDULES.—The plan sponsor shall annually update any schedule of contribution rates provided under this subsection to reflect the experience of the plan.

"(C) DURATION OF SCHEDULE.—A schedule of contribution rates provided by the plan sponsor and relied upon by bargaining parties in negotiating a collective bargaining agreement shall remain in effect for the duration of that collective bargaining agreement.

"(7) IMPOSITION OF DEFAULT SCHEDULE WHERE FAILURE TO ADOPT FUNDING IMPROVEMENT PLAN.—

"(A) IN GENERAL.—If—

"(i) a collective bargaining agreement providing for contributions under a multiemployer plan that was in effect at the time the plan entered endangered status expires, and

"(ii) after receiving one or more schedules from the plan sponsor under paragraph (1)(B), the bargaining parties with respect to such agreement fail to agree on changes to contribution or benefit schedules necessary to meet the applicable benchmarks in accordance with the funding improvement plan, the plan sponsor shall implement the schedule described in paragraph (1)(B)(i)(I) beginning on the date specified in subparagraph (B).

"(B) DATE OF IMPLEMENTATION.—The date specified in this subparagraph is the earlier of the date—

"(i) on which the Secretary certifies that the parties are at an impasse, or

"(ii) which is 180 days after the date on which the collective bargaining agreement described in subparagraph (A) expires.

"(8) FUNDING PLAN ADOPTION PERIOD.—For purposes of this section, the term 'funding plan adoption period' means the period beginning on the date of the certification under subsection (b)(3)(A) for the initial determination year and ending on the day before the first day of the funding improvement period.

"(d) RULES FOR OPERATION OF PLAN DURING ADOPTION AND IMPROVEMENT PERIODS.—

"(1) SPECIAL RULES FOR PLAN ADOPTION PERIOD.—During the funding plan adoption period—

"(A) the plan sponsor may not accept a collective bargaining agreement or participation agreement with respect to the multiemployer plan that provides for—

"(i) a reduction in the level of contributions for any participants,

"(ii) a suspension of contributions with respect to any period of service, or

"(iii) any new direct or indirect exclusion of younger or newly hired employees from plan participation,

"(B) no amendment of the plan which increases the liabilities of the plan by reason of any increase in benefits, any change in the accrual of benefits, or any change in the rate at which benefits become nonforfeitable under the plan may be adopted unless the amendment is required as a condition of qualification under part I of subchapter D of chapter 1 of the Internal Revenue Code of 1986 or to comply with other applicable law, and

"(C) in the case of a plan in seriously endangered status, the plan sponsor shall take all reasonable actions which are consistent with the terms of the plan and applicable law and which are expected, based on reasonable assumptions, to achieve—

"(i) an increase in the plan's funded percentage, and

"(ii) postponement of an accumulated funding deficiency for at least 1 additional plan year.

Actions under subparagraph (C) include applications for extensions of amortization periods under section 304(d), use of the shortfall funding method in making funding standard account computations, amendments to the plan's benefit structure, reductions in future benefit accruals, and other reasonable actions consistent with the terms of the plan and applicable law.

"(2) COMPLIANCE WITH FUNDING IMPROVEMENT PLAN.—

"(A) IN GENERAL.—A plan may not be amended after the date of the adoption of a funding improvement plan so as to be inconsistent with the funding improvement plan.

"(B) NO REDUCTION IN CONTRIBUTIONS.—A plan sponsor may not during any funding improvement period accept a collective bargaining agreement or participation agreement with respect to the multiemployer plan that provides for—

"(i) a reduction in the level of contributions for any participants,

"(ii) a suspension of contributions with respect to any period of service, or

"(iii) any new direct or indirect exclusion of younger or newly hired employees from plan participation.

"(C) SPECIAL RULES FOR BENEFIT INCREASES.—A plan may not be amended after the date of the adoption of a funding improvement plan so as to increase benefits, including future benefit accruals, unless the plan actuary certifies that the benefit increase is consistent with the funding improvement plan and is paid for out of contributions not required by the funding improvement plan to meet the applicable benchmark in accordance with the schedule contemplated in the funding improvement plan.

"(e) REHABILITATION PLAN MUST BE ADOPTED FOR MULTIEMPLOYER PLANS IN CRITICAL STATUS.—

"(1) IN GENERAL.—In any case in which a multiemployer plan is in critical status for a plan year, the plan sponsor, in accordance with this subsection—

"(A) shall adopt a rehabilitation plan not later than 240 days following the required date for the actuarial certification of critical status under subsection (b)(3)(A), and

"(B) within 30 days after the adoption of the rehabilitation plan—

"(i) shall provide to the bargaining parties 1 or more schedules showing revised benefit structures, revised contribution structures, or both, which, if adopted, may reasonably be expected to enable the multiemployer plan to emerge from critical status in accordance with the rehabilitation plan, and

"(ii) may, if the plan sponsor deems appropriate, prepare and provide the bargaining parties with additional information relating to contribution rates or benefit reductions, alternative schedules, or other information relevant to emerging from critical status in accordance with the rehabilitation plan.

The schedule or schedules described in subparagraph (B)(i) shall reflect reductions in future benefit accruals and adjustable benefits, and increases in contributions, that the plan sponsor determines are reasonably necessary to emerge from critical status. One schedule shall be designated as the default schedule and such schedule shall assume that there are no increases in contributions under the plan other than the increases necessary to emerge from critical status after future benefit accruals and other benefits (other than benefits the reduction or elimination of which are not permitted under section 204(g)) have been reduced to the maximum extent permitted by law.

"(2) EXCEPTION FOR YEARS AFTER PROCESS BEGINS.—Paragraph (1) shall not apply to a plan year if such year is in a rehabilitation plan adoption period or rehabilitation period by reason of the plan being in critical status for a preceding plan year. For purposes of this section, such preceding plan year shall be the initial critical year with respect to the rehabilitation plan to which it relates.

"(3) REHABILITATION PLAN.—For purposes of this section—

"(A) IN GENERAL.—A rehabilitation plan is a plan which consists of—

"(i) actions, including options or a range of options to be proposed to the bargaining parties, formulated, based on reasonably anticipated experience and reasonable actuarial assumptions, to enable the plan to cease to be in critical status by the end of the rehabilitation period and may include reductions in plan expenditures (including plan mergers and consolidations), reductions in future benefit accruals or increases in contributions, if agreed to by the bargaining parties, or any combination of such actions, or

"(ii) if the plan sponsor determines that, based on reasonable actuarial assumptions and upon exhaustion of all reasonable measures, the plan can not reasonably be expected to emerge from critical status by the end of the rehabilitation period, reasonable measures to emerge from critical status at a later time or to forestall possible insolvency (within the meaning of section 4245).

A rehabilitation plan must provide annual standards for meeting the requirements of such rehabilitation plan. Such plan shall also include the schedules required to be provided under paragraph (1)(B)(i) and if clause (ii) applies, shall set forth the alternatives considered, explain why the plan is not reasonably expected to emerge from critical status by the end of the rehabilitation period, and specify when, if ever, the plan is expected to emerge from critical status in accordance with the rehabilitation plan.

"(B) UPDATES TO REHABILITATION PLAN AND SCHEDULES.—

"(i) REHABILITATION PLAN.—The plan sponsor shall annually update the rehabilitation plan and shall file the update with the plan's annual report under section 104.

"(ii) SCHEDULES.—The plan sponsor shall annually update any schedule of contribution rates provided under this subsection to reflect the experience of the plan.

"(iii) DURATION OF SCHEDULE.—A schedule of contribution rates provided by the plan sponsor and relied upon by bargaining parties in negotiating a collective bargaining agreement shall remain in effect for the duration of that collective bargaining agreement.

"(C) IMPOSITION OF DEFAULT SCHEDULE WHERE FAILURE TO ADOPT REHABILITATION PLAN.—

"(i) IN GENERAL.—If—

"(I) a collective bargaining agreement providing for contributions under a multiemployer plan that was in effect at the time the plan entered critical status expires, and

"(II) after receiving one or more schedules from the plan sponsor under paragraph (1)(B), the bargaining parties with respect to such agreement fail to adopt a contribution or benefit schedules with terms consistent with the rehabilitation plan and the schedule from the plan sponsor under paragraph (1)(B)(i),

the plan sponsor shall implement the default schedule described in the last sentence of paragraph (1) beginning on the date specified in clause (ii).

"(ii) DATE OF IMPLEMENTATION.—The date specified in this clause is the earlier of the date—

"(I) on which the Secretary certifies that the parties are at an impasse, or

"(II) which is 180 days after the date on which the collective bargaining agreement described in clause (i) expires.

"(4) REHABILITATION PERIOD.—For purposes of this section—

"(A) IN GENERAL.—The rehabilitation period for a plan in critical status is the 10-year period beginning on the first day of the first plan year of the multiemployer plan following the earlier of—

"(i) the second anniversary of the date of the adoption of the rehabilitation plan, or

"(ii) the expiration of the collective bargaining agreements in effect on the date of the due date for the actuarial certification of critical status for the initial critical year under subsection (a)(1) and covering, as of such date at least 75 percent of the active participants in such multiemployer plan.

If a plan emerges from critical status as provided under subparagraph (B) before the end of such 10-year period, the rehabilitation period shall end with the plan year preceding the plan year for which the determination under subparagraph (B) is made.

"(B) EMERGENCE.—A plan in critical status shall remain in such status until a plan year for which the plan actuary certifies, in accordance with subsection (b)(3)(A), that the plan is not projected to have an accumulated funding deficiency for the plan year or any of the 9 succeeding plan years, without regard to the use of the shortfall method and taking into account any extension of amortization periods under section 304(d).

"(5) REHABILITATION PLAN ADOPTION PERIOD.—For purposes of this section, the term 'rehabilitation plan adoption period' means the period beginning on the date of the certification under subsection (b)(3)(A) for the initial critical year and ending on the day before the first day of the rehabilitation period.

"(6) LIMITATION ON REDUCTION IN RATES OF FUTURE ACCRUALS.—Any reduction in the rate of future accruals under the default schedule described in paragraph (1)(B)(i) shall not reduce the rate of future accruals below—

"(A) a monthly benefit (payable as a single life annuity commencing at the participant's normal retirement age) equal to 1 percent of the contributions required to be made with respect to a participant, or the equivalent standard accrual rate for a participant or group of participants under the collective bargaining agreements in effect as of the first day of the initial critical year, or

"(B) if lower, the accrual rate under the plan on such first day.

The equivalent standard accrual rate shall be determined by the plan sponsor based on the standard or average contribution base units which the plan sponsor determines to be representative for active participants and such other factors as the plan sponsor determines to be relevant. Nothing in this paragraph shall be construed as limiting the ability of the plan sponsor to prepare and provide the bargaining parties with alternative schedules to the default schedule that established lower or higher accrual and contribution rates than the rates otherwise described in this paragraph.

"(7) AUTOMATIC EMPLOYER SURCHARGE.—

"(A) IMPOSITION OF SURCHARGE.—Each employer otherwise obligated to make contributions for the initial critical year shall be obligated to pay to the plan for such year a surcharge equal to 5 percent of the contributions otherwise required under the applicable collective bargaining agreement (or other agreement pursuant to which the employer contributes). For each succeeding plan year in which the plan is in critical status for a consecutive period of years beginning with the initial critical year, the surcharge shall be 10 percent of the contributions otherwise so required.

"(B) ENFORCEMENT OF SURCHARGE.—The surcharges under subparagraph (A) shall be due and payable on the same schedule as the contributions on which the surcharges are based. Any failure to make a surcharge payment shall be treated as a delinquent contribution under section 515 and shall be enforceable as such.

"(C) SURCHARGE TO TERMINATE UPON COLLECTIVE BARGAINING AGREEMENT RENEGOTIATION.—The surcharge under this paragraph shall cease to be effective with respect to employees covered by a collective bargaining agreement (or other agreement pursuant to which the employer contributes), beginning on the effective date of a collective bargaining agreement (or other such agreement) that includes terms consistent with a schedule presented by the plan sponsor under paragraph (1)(B)(i), as modified under subparagraph (B) of paragraph (3).

"(D) SURCHARGE NOT TO APPLY UNTIL EMPLOYER RECEIVES NOTICE.—The surcharge under this paragraph shall not apply to an employer until 30 days after the employer has been notified by the plan sponsor that the plan is in critical status and that the surcharge is in effect.

"(E) SURCHARGE NOT TO GENERATE INCREASED BENEFIT ACCRUALS.—Notwithstanding any provision of a plan to the contrary, the amount of any surcharge under this paragraph shall not be the basis for any benefit accrual under the plan.

"(8) BENEFIT ADJUSTMENTS.—

"(A) ADJUSTABLE BENEFITS.—

"(i) IN GENERAL.—Notwithstanding section 204(g), the plan sponsor shall, subject to the notice requirements in subparagraph (C), make any reductions to adjustable benefits which the plan sponsor deems appropriate, based upon the outcome of collective bargaining over the schedule or schedules provided under paragraph (1)(B)(i).

"(ii) EXCEPTION FOR RETIREES.—Except in the case of adjustable benefits described in clause (iv)(III), the plan sponsor of a plan in critical status shall not reduce adjustable benefits of any participant or beneficiary whose benefit commencement date is before the date on which the plan provides notice to the participant or beneficiary under subsection (b)(3)(D) for the initial critical year.

"(iii) PLAN SPONSOR FLEXIBILITY.—The plan sponsor shall include in the schedules provided to the bargaining parties an allowance for funding the benefits of participants with respect to whom contributions are not currently required to be made, and shall reduce their benefits to the extent permitted under this title and considered appropriate by the plan sponsor based on the plan's then current overall funding status.

"(iv) ADJUSTABLE BENEFIT DEFINED.—For purposes of this paragraph, the term 'adjustable benefit' means—

"(I) benefits, rights, and features under the plan, including post-retirement death benefits, 60-month guarantees, disability benefits not yet in pay status, and similar benefits,

"(II) any early retirement benefit or retirement-type subsidy (within the meaning of section 204(g)(2)(A)) and any benefit payment option (other than the qualified joint-and survivor annuity), and

"(III) benefit increases that would not be eligible for a guarantee under section 4022A on the first day of initial critical year because the increases were adopted (or, if later, took effect) less than 60 months before such first day.

"(B) NORMAL RETIREMENT BENEFITS PROTECTED.—Except as provided in subparagraph (A)(iv)(III), nothing in this paragraph shall be construed to permit a plan to reduce the level of a participant's accrued benefit payable at normal retirement age.

"(C) NOTICE REQUIREMENTS.—

"(i) IN GENERAL.—No reduction may be made to adjustable benefits under subparagraph (A) unless notice of such reduction has been given at least 30 days before the general effective date of such reduction for all participants and beneficiaries to—

"(I) plan participants and beneficiaries,

"(II) each employer who has an obligation to contribute (within the meaning of section 4212(a)) under the plan, and

"(III) each employee organization which, for purposes of collective bargaining, represents plan participants employed by such an employer.

"(ii) CONTENT OF NOTICE.—The notice under clause (i) shall contain—

"(I) sufficient information to enable participants and beneficiaries to understand the effect of any reduction on their benefits, including an estimate (on an annual or monthly basis) of any affected adjustable benefit that a participant or beneficiary would otherwise have been eligible for as of the general effective date described in clause (i), and

"(II) information as to the rights and remedies of plan participants and beneficiaries as well as how to contact the Department of Labor for further information and assistance where appropriate.

"(iii) FORM AND MANNER.—Any notice under clause (i)—

"(I) shall be provided in a form and manner prescribed in regulations of the Secretary,

"(II) shall be written in a manner so as to be understood by the average plan participant, and

"(III) may be provided in written, electronic, or other appropriate form to the extent such form is reasonably accessible to persons to whom the notice is required to be provided.

The Secretary shall in the regulations prescribed under subclause (I) establish a model notice that a plan sponsor may use to meet the requirements of this subparagraph.

"(9) ADJUSTMENTS DISREGARDED IN WITHDRAWAL LIABILITY DETERMINATION.—

"(A) BENEFIT REDUCTIONS.—Any benefit reductions under this subsection shall be disregarded in determining a plan's unfunded vested benefits for purposes of determining an employer's withdrawal liability under section 4201.

"(B) SURCHARGES.—Any surcharges under paragraph (7) shall be disregarded in determining an employer's withdrawal liability under section 4211, except for purposes of determining the unfunded vested benefits attributable to an employer under section 4211(c)(4) or a comparable method approved under section 4211(c)(5).

"(C) SIMPLIFIED CALCULATIONS.—The Pension Benefit Guaranty Corporation shall prescribe simplified methods for the application of this paragraph in determining withdrawal liability.

"(f) RULES FOR OPERATION OF PLAN DURING ADOPTION AND REHABILITATION PERIOD.—

"(1) COMPLIANCE WITH REHABILITATION PLAN.—

"(A) IN GENERAL.—A plan may not be amended after the date of the adoption of a rehabilitation plan under subsection (e) so as to be inconsistent with the rehabilitation plan.

"(B) SPECIAL RULES FOR BENEFIT INCREASES.—A plan may not be amended after the date of the adoption of a rehabilitation plan under subsection (e) so as to increase benefits, including future benefit accruals, unless the plan actuary certifies that such increase is paid for out of additional contributions not contemplated by the rehabilitation plan, and, after taking into account the benefit increase, the multiemployer plan still is reasonably expected to emerge from critical status by the end of the rehabilitation period on the schedule contemplated in the rehabilitation plan.

"(2) RESTRICTION ON LUMP SUMS AND SIMILAR BENEFITS.—

"(A) IN GENERAL.—Effective on the date the notice of certification of the plan's critical status for the initial critical year under subsection (b)(3)(D) is sent, and notwithstanding section 204(g), the plan shall not pay—

"(i) any payment, in excess of the monthly amount paid under a single life annuity (plus any social security supplements described in the last sentence of section 204(b)(1)(G)),

"(ii) any payment for the purchase of an irrevocable commitment from an insurer to pay benefits, and

"(iii) any other payment specified by the Secretary of the Treasury by regulations.

"(B) EXCEPTION.—Subparagraph (A) shall not apply to a benefit which under section 203(e) may be immediately distributed without the consent of the participant or to any makeup payment in the case of a retroactive annuity starting date or any similar payment of benefits owed with respect to a prior period.

"(3) ADJUSTMENTS DISREGARDED IN WITHDRAWAL LIABILITY DETERMINATION.—Any benefit reductions under this subsection shall be disregarded in determining a plan's unfunded vested benefits for purposes of determining an employer's withdrawal liability under section 4201.

"(4) SPECIAL RULES FOR PLAN ADOPTION PERIOD.—During the rehabilitation plan adoption period—

"(A) the plan sponsor may not accept a collective bargaining agreement or participation agreement with respect to the multiemployer plan that provides for—

"(i) a reduction in the level of contributions for any participants,

"(ii) a suspension of contributions with respect to any period of service, or

"(iii) any new direct or indirect exclusion of younger or newly hired employees from plan participation, and

"(B) no amendment of the plan which increases the liabilities of the plan by reason of any increase in benefits, any change in the accrual of benefits, or any change in the rate at which benefits become nonforfeitable under the plan may be adopted unless the amendment is required as a condition of qualification under part I of subchapter D of chapter 1 of the Internal Revenue Code of 1986 or to comply with other applicable law.

"(g) EXPEDITED RESOLUTION OF PLAN SPONSOR DECISIONS.—If, within 60 days of the due date for adoption of a funding improvement plan or a rehabilitation plan under subsection (e), the plan sponsor of a plan in endangered status or a plan in critical status has not agreed on a funding improvement plan or rehabilitation plan, then any member of the board or group that constitutes the plan sponsor may require that the plan sponsor enter into an expedited dispute resolution procedure for the development and adoption of a funding improvement plan or rehabilitation plan.

"(h) NONBARGAINED PARTICIPATION.—

"(1) BOTH BARGAINED AND NONBARGAINED EMPLOYEE-PARTICIPANTS.—In the case of an employer that contributes to a multiemployer plan with respect to both employees who are covered by one or more collective bargaining agreements and employees who are not so covered, if the plan is in endangered status or in critical status, benefits of and contributions for the nonbargained employees, including surcharges on those contributions, shall be determined as if those nonbargained employees were covered under the first to expire of the employer's collective bargaining agreements in effect when the plan entered endangered or critical status.

"(2) NONBARGAINED EMPLOYEES ONLY.—In the case of an employer that contributes to a multiemployer plan only with respect to employees who are not covered by a collective bargaining agreement, this section shall be applied as if the employer were the bargaining party, and its participation agreement with the plan were a collective bargaining agreement with a term ending on the first day of the plan year beginning after the employer is provided the schedule or schedules described in subsections (c) and (e).

"(i) DEFINITIONS; ACTUARIAL METHOD.—For purposes of this section—

"(1) BARGAINING PARTY.—The term 'bargaining party' means—

"(A)(i) except as provided in clause (ii), an employer who has an obligation to contribute under the plan; or

"(ii) in the case of a plan described under section 404(c) of the Internal Revenue Code of 1986, or a continuation of such a plan, the association of employers that is the employer settlor of the plan; and

"(B) an employee organization which, for purposes of collective bargaining, represents plan participants employed by an employer who has an obligation to contribute under the plan.

"(2) FUNDED PERCENTAGE.—The term 'funded percentage' means the percentage equal to a fraction—

"(A) the numerator of which is the value of the plan's assets, as determined under section 304(c)(2), and

"(B) the denominator of which is the accrued liability of the plan, determined using actuarial assumptions described in section 304(c)(3).

"(3) ACCUMULATED FUNDING DEFICIENCY.—The term 'accumulated funding deficiency' has the meaning given such term in section 304(a).

"(4) ACTIVE PARTICIPANT.—The term 'active participant' means, in connection with a multiemployer plan, a participant who is in covered service under the plan.

"(5) INACTIVE PARTICIPANT.—The term 'inactive participant' means, in connection with a multiemployer plan, a participant, or the beneficiary or alternate payee of a participant, who—

"(A) is not in covered service under the plan, and

"(B) is in pay status under the plan or has a nonforfeitable right to benefits under the plan.

"(6) PAY STATUS.—A person is in pay status under a multiemployer plan if—

"(A) at any time during the current plan year, such person is a participant or beneficiary under the plan and is paid an early, late, normal, or disability retirement benefit under the plan (or a death benefit under the plan related to a retirement benefit), or

"(B) to the extent provided in regulations of the Secretary of the Treasury, such person is entitled to such a benefit under the plan.

"(7) OBLIGATION TO CONTRIBUTE.—The term 'obligation to contribute' has the meaning given such term under section 4212(a).

"(8) ACTUARIAL METHOD.—Notwithstanding any other provision of this section, the actuary's determinations with respect to a plan's normal cost, actuarial accrued liability, and improvements in a plan's funded percentage under this section shall be based upon the unit credit funding method (whether or not that method is used for the plan's actuarial valuation).

"(9) PLAN SPONSOR.—In the case of a plan described under section 404(c) of the Internal Revenue Code of 1986, or a continuation of such a plan, the term 'plan sponsor' means the bargaining parties described under paragraph (1).

"(10) BENEFIT COMMENCEMENT DATE.—The term 'benefit commencement date' means the annuity starting date (or in the case of a retroactive annuity starting date, the date on which benefit payments begin).".

(b) ENFORCEMENT.—Section 502 of the Employee Retirement Income Security Act of 1974 (29 U.S.C. 1132) is amended—

(1) in subsection (a)(6) by striking "(6), or (7)" and inserting "(6), (7), or (8)";

(2) by redesignating subsection (c)(8) as subsection (c)(9); and

(3) by inserting after subsection (c)(7) the following new paragraph:

"(8) The Secretary may assess against any plan sponsor of a multiemployer plan a civil penalty of not more than $1,100 per day—

"(A) for each violation by such sponsor of the requirement under section 305 to adopt by the deadline established in that section a funding improvement plan or rehabilitation plan with respect to a multiemployer which is in endangered or critical status, or

"(B) in the case of a plan in endangered status which is not in seriously endangered status, for failure by the plan to meet the applicable benchmarks under section 305 by the end of the funding improvement period with respect to the plan.".

(c) CAUSE OF ACTION TO COMPEL ADOPTION OR IMPLEMENTATION OF FUNDING IMPROVEMENT OR REHABILITATION PLAN.—Section 502(a) of the Employee Retirement Income Security Act of 1974 is amended by striking "or" at the end of paragraph (8), by striking the period at the end of paragraph (9) and inserting "; or" and by adding at the end the following:

"(10) in the case of a multiemployer plan that has been certified by the actuary to be in endangered or critical status under section 305, if the plan sponsor—

"(A) has not adopted a funding improvement or rehabilitation plan under that section by the deadline established in such section, or

"(B) fails to update or comply with the terms of the funding improvement or rehabilitation plan in accordance with the requirements of such section,

by an employer that has an obligation to contribute with respect to the multiemployer plan or an employee organization that represents active participants in the multiemployer plan, for an order compelling the plan sponsor to adopt a funding improvement or rehabilitation plan or to update or comply with the terms of the funding improvement or rehabilitation plan in accordance with the requirements of such section and the funding improvement or rehabilitation plan.".

(d) NO ADDITIONAL CONTRIBUTIONS REQUIRED.—Section 302(b) of the Employee Retirement Income Security Act of 1974, as amended by this Act, is amended by adding at the end the following new paragraph:

"(3) MULTIEMPLOYER PLANS IN CRITICAL STATUS.—Paragraph (1) shall not apply in the case of a multiemployer plan for any plan year in which the plan is in critical status pursuant to section 305. This paragraph shall only apply if the plan adopts a rehabilitation plan in accordance with section 305(e) and complies with the terms of such rehabilitation plan (and any updates or modifications of the plan).".

(e) CONFORMING AMENDMENT.—The table of contents in section 1 of such Act (as amended by the preceding provisions of this Act) is amended by inserting after the item relating to section 304 the following new item:

"Sec. 305. Additional funding rules for multiemployer plans in endangered status or critical status.".

(f) EFFECTIVE DATES.—

(1) IN GENERAL.—The amendments made by this section shall apply with respect to plan years beginning after 2007.

(2) SPECIAL RULE FOR CERTAIN NOTICES.—In any case in which a plan's actuary certifies that it is reasonably expected that a multiemployer plan will be in critical status under section 305(b)(3) of the Employee Retirement Income Security Act of 1974, as added by this section, with respect to the first plan year beginning after 2007, the notice required under subparagraph (D) of such section may be provided at any time after the date of enactment, so long as it is provided on or before the last date for providing the notice under such subparagraph.

(3) SPECIAL RULE FOR CERTAIN RESTORED BENEFITS.—In the case of a multiemployer plan—

(A) with respect to which benefits were reduced pursuant to a plan amendment adopted on or after January 1, 2002, and before June 30, 2005, and

(B) which, pursuant to the plan document, the trust agreement, or a formal written communication from the plan sponsor to participants provided before June 30, 2005, provided for the restoration of such benefits, the amendments made by this section shall not apply to such benefit restorations to the extent that any restriction on the providing or accrual of such benefits would otherwise apply by reason of such amendments.

[CCH Explanation at ¶310. Committee Reports at ¶10,090.]

[¶7036] ACT SEC. 203. MEASURES TO FORESTALL INSOLVENCY OF MULTIEMPLOYER PLANS.

(a) ADVANCE DETERMINATION OF IMPENDING INSOLVENCY OVER 5 YEARS.—Section 4245(d)(1) of the Employee Retirement Income Security Act of 1974 (29 U.S.C. 1426(d)(1)) is amended—

(1) by striking "3 plan years" the second place it appears and inserting "5 plan years"; and

(2) by adding at the end the following new sentence: "If the plan sponsor makes such a determination that the plan will be insolvent in any of the next 5 plan years, the plan sponsor shall make the comparison under this paragraph at least annually until the plan sponsor makes a determination that the plan will not be insolvent in any of the next 5 plan years.".

(b) EFFECTIVE DATE.—The amendments made by this section shall apply with respect to determinations made in plan years beginning after 2007.

[CCH Explanation at ¶315. Committee Reports at ¶10,100.]

[¶7039] ACT SEC. 204. WITHDRAWAL LIABILITY REFORMS.

(a) UPDATE OF RULES RELATING TO LIMITATIONS ON WITHDRAWAL LIABILITY.—

(1) INCREASE IN LIMITS.—Section 4225(a)(2) of such Act (29 U.S.C. 1405(a)(2)) is amended by striking the table contained therein and inserting the following new table:

"If the liquidation or distribution value of the employer after the sale or exchange is—	The portion is—
Not more than $5,000,000	30 percent of the amount.
More than $5,000,000, but not more than $10,000,000.	$1,500,000, plus 35 percent of the amount in excess of $5,000,000.
More than $10,000,000, but not more than $15,000,000.	$3,250,000, plus 40 percent of the amount in excess of $10,000,000.
More than $15,000,000, but not more than $17,500,000.	$5,250,000, plus 45 percent of the amount in excess of $15,000,000.
More than $17,500,000, but not more than $20,000,000.	$6,375,000, plus 50 percent of the amount in excess of $17,500,000.
More than $20,000,000, but not more than $22,500,000.	$7,625,000, plus 60 percent of the amount in excess of $20,000,000.
More than $22,500,000, but not more than $25,000,000.	$9,125,000, plus 70 percent of the amount in excess of $22,500,000.
More than $25,000,000	$10,875,000, plus 80 percent of the amount in excess of $25,000,000.".

(2) PLANS USING ATTRIBUTABLE METHOD.—Section 4225(a)(1)(B) of such Act (29 U.S.C. 1405(a)(1)(B)) is amended to read as follows:

"(B) in the case of a plan using the attributable method of allocating withdrawal liability, the unfunded vested benefits attributable to employees of the employer.".

(3) EFFECTIVE DATE.—The amendments made by this subsection shall apply to sales occurring on or after January 1, 2007.

(b) WITHDRAWAL LIABILITY CONTINUES IF WORK CONTRACTED OUT.—

(1) IN GENERAL.—Clause (i) of section 4205(b)(2)(A) of such Act (29 U.S.C. 1385(b)(2)(A)) is amended by inserting "or to an entity or entities owned or controlled by the employer" after "to another location".

(2) EFFECTIVE DATE.—The amendment made by this subsection shall apply with respect to work transferred on or after the date of the enactment of this Act.

(c) APPLICATION OF RULES TO PLANS PRIMARILY COVERING EMPLOYEES IN THE BUILDING AND CONSTRUCTION INDUSTRY.—

(1) IN GENERAL.—Section 4210(b) of such Act (29 U.S.C. 1390(b)) is amended—

(A) by striking paragraph (1); and

(B) by redesignating paragraphs (2) through (4) as paragraphs (1) through (3), respectively.

(2) FRESH START OPTION.—Section 4211(c)(5) of such Act (29 U.S.C. 1391(c)(5)) is amended by adding at the end the following new subparagraph:

"(E) FRESH START OPTION.—Notwithstanding paragraph (1), a plan may be amended to provide that the withdrawal liability method described in subsection (b) shall be applied by substituting the plan year which is specified in the amendment and for which the plan has no unfunded vested benefits for the plan year ending before September 26, 1980.".

(3) EFFECTIVE DATE.—The amendments made by this subsection shall apply with respect to plan withdrawals occurring on or after January 1, 2007.

(d) PROCEDURES APPLICABLE TO DISPUTES INVOLVING PENSION PLAN WITHDRAWAL LIABILITY.—

(1) IN GENERAL.—Section 4221 of Employee Retirement Income Security Act of 1974 (29 U.S.C. 1401) is amended by adding at the end the following:

"(g) PROCEDURES APPLICABLE TO CERTAIN DISPUTES.—

"(1) IN GENERAL.—If—

"(A) a plan sponsor of a plan determines that—

"(i) a complete or partial withdrawal of an employer has occurred, or

"(ii) an employer is liable for withdrawal liability payments with respect to such complete or partial withdrawal, and

"(B) such determination is based in whole or in part on a finding by the plan sponsor under section 4212(c) that a principal purpose of any transaction which occurred after December 31, 1998, and at least 5 years (2 years in the case of a small employer) before the date of the complete or partial withdrawal was to evade or avoid withdrawal liability under this subtitle,

then the person against which the withdrawal liability is assessed based solely on the application of section 4212(c) may elect to use the special rule under paragraph (2) in applying subsection (d) of this section and section 4219(c) to such person.

"(2) SPECIAL RULE.—Notwithstanding subsection (d) and section 4219(c), if an electing person contests the plan sponsor's determination with respect to withdrawal liability payments under paragraph (1) through an arbitration proceeding pursuant to subsection (a), through an action brought in a court of competent jurisdiction for review of such an arbitration decision, or as otherwise permitted by law, the electing person shall not be obligated to make the withdrawal liability payments until a final decision in the arbitration proceeding, or in court, upholds the plan sponsor's determination, but only if the electing person—

"(A) provides notice to the plan sponsor of its election to apply the special rule in this paragraph within 90 days after the plan sponsor notifies the electing person of its liability by reason of the application of section 4212(c); and

"(B) if a final decision in the arbitration proceeding, or in court, of the withdrawal liability dispute has not been rendered within 12 months from the date of such notice, the electing person provides to the plan, effective as of the first day following the 12-month period, a bond issued by a corporate surety company that is an acceptable surety for purposes of section 412 of this Act, or an amount held in escrow by a bank or similar financial institution satisfactory to the plan, in an amount equal to the sum of the withdrawal liability payments that would otherwise be due under subsection (d) and section 4219(c) for the 12-month period beginning with the first anniversary of such notice. Such bond or escrow shall remain in effect until there is a final decision in the arbitration proceeding, or in court, of the withdrawal liability dispute, at which time such bond or escrow shall be paid to the plan if such final decision upholds the plan sponsor's determination.

"(3) DEFINITION OF SMALL EMPLOYER.—For purposes of this subsection—

"(A) IN GENERAL.—The term 'small employer' means any employer which, for the calendar year in which the transaction referred to in paragraph (1)(B) occurred and for each of the 3 preceding years, on average—

"(i) employs not more than 500 employees, and

"(ii) is required to make contributions to the plan for not more than 250 employees.

"(B) CONTROLLED GROUP.—Any group treated as a single employer under subsection (b)(1) of section 4001, without regard to any transaction that was a basis for the plan's finding under section 4212, shall be treated as a single employer for purposes of this subparagraph.

"(4) ADDITIONAL SECURITY PENDING RESOLUTION OF DISPUTE.—If a withdrawal liability dispute to which this subsection applies is not concluded by 12 months after the electing person posts the bond or escrow described in paragraph (2), the electing person shall, at the start of each succeeding 12month period, provide an additional bond or amount held in escrow equal to the sum of the withdrawal liability payments that would otherwise be payable to the plan during that period.

"(5) The liability of the party furnishing a bond or escrow under this subsection shall be reduced, upon the payment of the bond or escrow to the plan, by the amount thereof."

(2) EFFECTIVE DATE.—The amendments made by this subsection shall apply to any person that receives a notification under section 4219(b)(1) of the Employee Retirement Income Security Act of 1974 on or after the date of enactment of this Act with respect to a transaction that occurred after December 31, 1998.

[CCH Explanation at ¶ 320. Committee Reports at ¶ 10,110, ¶ 10,120, ¶ 10,130 and ¶ 10,140.]

[¶ 7042] ACT SEC. 205. PROHIBITION ON RETALIATION AGAINST EMPLOYERS EXERCISING THEIR RIGHTS TO PETITION THE FEDERAL GOVERNMENT.

Section 510 of the Employee Retirement Income Security Act of 1974 (29 U.S.C. 1140) is amended by inserting before the last sentence thereof the following new sentence: "In the case of a multiemployer plan, it shall be unlawful for the plan sponsor or any other person to discriminate against any contributing employer for exercising rights under this Act or for giving information or testifying in any inquiry or proceeding relating to this Act before Congress."

[CCH Explanation at ¶ 330. Committee Reports at ¶ 10,150.]

[¶ 7045] ACT SEC. 206. SPECIAL RULE FOR CERTAIN BENEFITS FUNDED UNDER AN AGREEMENT APPROVED BY THE PENSION BENEFIT GUARANTY CORPORATION.

In the case of a multiemployer plan that is a party to an agreement that was approved by the Pension Benefit Guaranty Corporation prior to June 30, 2005, and that—

(1) increases benefits, and

(2) provides for special withdrawal liability rules under section 4203(f) of the Employee Retirement Income Security Act of 1974 (29 U.S.C. 1383),

the amendments made by sections 201, 202, 211, and 212 of this Act shall not apply to the benefit increases under any plan amendment adopted prior to June 30, 2005, that are funded pursuant to such agreement if the plan is funded in compliance with such agreement (and any amendments thereto).

[CCH Explanation at ¶ 305 and ¶ 310. Committee Reports at ¶ 10,160.]

Subtitle B—Amendments to Internal Revenue Code of 1986

* * *

[¶7048] ACT SEC. 214. EXEMPTION FROM EXCISE TAXES FOR CERTAIN MULTIEMPLOYER PENSION PLANS.

(a) IN GENERAL.—Notwithstanding any other provision of law, no tax shall be imposed under subsection (a) or (b) of section 4971 of the Internal Revenue Code of 1986 with respect to any accumulated funding deficiency of a plan described in subsection (b) of this section for any taxable year beginning before the earlier of—

(1) the taxable year in which the plan sponsor adopts a rehabilitation plan under section 305(e) of the Employee Retirement Income Security Act of 1974 and section 432(e) of such Code (as added by this Act); or

(2) the taxable year that contains January 1, 2009.

(b) PLAN DESCRIBED.—A plan described under this subsection is a multiemployer pension plan—

(1) with less than 100 participants;

(2) with respect to which the contributing employers participated in a Federal fishery capacity reduction program;

(3) with respect to which employers under the plan participated in the Northeast Fisheries Assistance Program; and

(4) with respect to which the annual normal cost is less than $100,000 and the plan is experiencing a funding deficiency on the date of enactment of this Act.

[CCH Explanation at ¶310. Committee Reports at ¶10,170.]

Subtitle C—Sunset of Additional Funding Rules

[¶7051] ACT SEC. 221. SUNSET OF ADDITIONAL FUNDING RULES.

(a) REPORT.—Not later than December 31, 2011, the Secretary of Labor, the Secretary of the Treasury, and the Executive Director of the Pension Benefit Guaranty Corporation shall conduct a study of the effect of the amendments made by this subtitle on the operation and funding status of multiemployer plans and shall report the results of such study, including any recommendations for legislation, to the Congress.

(b) MATTERS INCLUDED IN STUDY.—The study required under subsection (a) shall include—

(1) the effect of funding difficulties, funding rules in effect before the date of the enactment of this Act, and the amendments made by this subtitle on small businesses participating in multiemployer plans,

(2) the effect on the financial status of small employers of—

(A) funding targets set in funding improvement and rehabilitation plans and associated contribution increases,

(B) funding deficiencies,

(C) excise taxes,

(D) withdrawal liability,

(E) the possibility of alternatives schedules and procedures for financially-troubled employers, and

(F) other aspects of the multiemployer system, and

(3) the role of the multiemployer pension plan system in helping small employers to offer pension benefits.

(c) SUNSET.—

(1) IN GENERAL.—Except as provided in this subsection, notwithstanding any other provision of this Act, the provisions of, and the amendments made by, sections 201(b), 202, and 212 shall not apply to plan years beginning after December 31, 2014.

(2) FUNDING IMPROVEMENT AND REHABILITATION PLANS.—If a plan is operating under a funding improvement or rehabilitation plan under section 305 of such Act or 432 of such Code for its last year beginning before January 1, 2015, such plan shall continue to operate under such funding improvement or rehabilitation plan during any period after December 31, 2014, such funding improvement or rehabilitation plan is in effect and all provisions of such Act or Code relating to the operation of such funding improvement or rehabilitation plan shall continue in effect during such period.

[CCH Explanation at ¶335. Committee Reports at ¶10,180.]

TITLE III—INTEREST RATE ASSUMPTIONS

[¶7054] ACT SEC. 301. EXTENSION OF REPLACEMENT OF 30-YEAR TREASURY RATES.

(a) AMENDMENTS OF ERISA.—

(1) DETERMINATION OF RANGE.—Subclause (II) of section 302(b)(5)(B)(ii) of the Employee Retirement Income Security Act of 1974 is amended—

(A) by striking "2006" and inserting "2008", and

(B) by striking "**AND 2005**" in the heading and inserting "**, 2005, 2006, AND 2007**".

(2) DETERMINATION OF CURRENT LIABILITY.—Subclause (IV) of section 302(d)(7)(C)(i) of such Act is amended—

(A) by striking "or 2005" and inserting ", 2005, 2006, or 2007", and

(B) by striking "**AND 2005**" in the heading and inserting "**, 2005, 2006, AND 2007**".

(3) PBGC PREMIUM RATE.—Subclause (V) of section 4006(a)(3)(E)(iii) of such Act is amended by striking "2006" and inserting "2008".

* * *

(c) PLAN AMENDMENTS.—Clause (ii) of section 101(c)(2)(A) of the Pension Funding Equity Act of 2004 is amended by striking "2006" and inserting "2008".

• • PENSION FUNDING EQUITY ACT OF 2004 ACT SEC. 101(c)(2)(A)(ii) AS AMENDED

ACT SEC. 101. TEMPORARY REPLACEMENT OF 30-YEAR TREASURY RATE.

* * *

(c) PROVISIONS RELATING TO PLAN AMENDMENTS.—

* * *

(2) AMENDMENTS TO WHICH SECTION APPLIES.—

(A) IN GENERAL.—This subsection shall apply to any amendment to any plan or annuity contract which is made—

* * *

(ii) on or before the last day of the first plan year beginning on or after January 1, *2008*.

[CCH Explanation at ¶235. Committee Reports at ¶10,190.]

[¶7057] ACT SEC. 302. INTEREST RATE ASSUMPTION FOR DETERMINATION OF LUMP SUM DISTRIBUTIONS.

(a) AMENDMENT TO EMPLOYEE RETIREMENT INCOME SECURITY ACT OF 1974.—Paragraph (3) of section 205(g) of the Employee Retirement Income Security Act of 1974 (29 U.S.C. 1055(g)(3)) is amended to read as follows:

"(3)(A) For purposes of paragraphs (1) and (2), the present value shall not be less than the present value calculated by using the applicable mortality table and the applicable interest rate.

"(B) For purposes of subparagraph (A)—

"(i) The term 'applicable mortality table' means a mortality table, modified as appropriate by the Secretary of the Treasury, based on the mortality table specified for the plan year under subparagraph (A) of section 303(h)(3) (without regard to subparagraph (C) or (D) of such section).

"(ii) The term 'applicable interest rate' means the adjusted first, second, and third segment rates applied under rules similar to the rules of section 303(h)(2)(C) for the month before the date of the distribution or such other time as the Secretary of the Treasury may by regulations prescribe.

"(iii) For purposes of clause (ii), the adjusted first, second, and third segment rates are the first, second, and third segment rates which would be determined under section 303(h)(2)(C) if—

"(I) section 303(h)(2)(D) were applied by substituting the average yields for the month described in clause (ii) for the average yields for the 24-month period described in such section,

"(II) section 303(h)(2)(G)(i)(II) were applied by substituting 'section 205(g)(3)(B)(iii)(II)' for 'section 302(b)(5)(B)(ii)(II)', and

"(III) the applicable percentage under section 303(h)(2)(G) were determined in accordance with the following table:

In the case of plan years beginning in:	The applicable percentage is:
2008	20 percent
2009	40 percent
2010	60 percent
2011	80 percent.".

* * *

(c) EFFECTIVE DATE.—The amendments made by this section shall apply with respect to plan years beginning after December 31, 2007.

* * *

[CCH Explanation at ¶905. Committee Reports at ¶10,200.]

TITLE IV—PBGC GUARANTEE AND RELATED PROVISIONS

[¶7060] ACT SEC. 401. PBGC PREMIUMS.

(a) VARIABLE-RATE PREMIUMS.—

(1) CONFORMING AMENDMENTS RELATED TO FUNDING RULES FOR SINGLE-EMPLOYER PLANS.—Section 4006(a)(3)(E) of the Employee Retirement Income and Security Act of 1974 (29 U.S.C. 1306(a)(3)(E)) is amended by striking clauses (iii) and (iv) and inserting the following:

"(iii) For purposes of clause (ii), the term 'unfunded vested benefits' means, for a plan year, the excess (if any) of—

"(I) the funding target of the plan as determined under section 303(d) for the plan year by only taking into account vested benefits and by using the interest rate described in clause (iv), over

"(II) the fair market value of plan assets for the plan year which are held by the plan on the valuation date.

"(iv) The interest rate used in valuing benefits for purposes of subclause (I) of clause (iii) shall be equal to the first, second, or third segment rate for the month preceding the month in which the plan year begins, which would be determined under section 303(h)(2)(C) if section 303(h)(2)(D) were applied by using the monthly yields for the month preceding the month in which the plan year begins on investment grade corporate bonds with varying maturities and in the top 3 quality levels rather than the average of such yields for a 24-month period.".

(2) EFFECTIVE DATE.—The amendments made by paragraph (1) shall apply with respect to plan years beginning after 2007.

(b) TERMINATION PREMIUMS.—

(1) REPEAL OF SUNSET PROVISION.—Subparagraph (E) of section 4006(a)(7) of such Act is repealed.

(2) TECHNICAL CORRECTION.—

(A) IN GENERAL.—Section 4006(a)(7)(C)(ii) of such Act is amended by striking "subparagraph (B)(i)(I)" and inserting "subparagraph (B)".

(B) EFFECTIVE DATE.—The amendment made by this paragraph shall take effect as if included in the provision of the Deficit Reduction Act of 2005 to which it relates.

[CCH Explanation at ¶ 505. Committee Reports at ¶ 10,220.]

[¶ 7063] ACT SEC. 402. SPECIAL FUNDING RULES FOR CERTAIN PLANS MAINTAINED BY COMMERCIAL AIRLINES.

(a) IN GENERAL.—The plan sponsor of an eligible plan may elect to either—

(1) have the rules of subsection (b) apply, or

(2) have section 303 of the Employee Retirement Income Security Act of 1974 and section 430 of the Internal Revenue Code of 1986 applied to its first taxable year beginning in 2008 by amortizing the shortfall amortization base for such taxable year over a period of 10 plan years (rather than 7 plan years) beginning with such plan year.

(b) ALTERNATIVE FUNDING SCHEDULE.—

(1) IN GENERAL.—If an election is made under subsection (a)(1) to have this subsection apply to an eligible plan and the requirements of paragraphs (2) and (3) are met with respect to the plan—

(A) in the case of any applicable plan year beginning before January 1, 2008, the plan shall not have an accumulated funding deficiency for purposes of section 302 of the Employee Retirement Income Security Act of 1974 and sections 412 and 4971 of the Internal Revenue Code of 1986 if contributions to the plan for the plan year are not less than the minimum required contribution determined under subsection (e) for the plan for the plan year, and

(B) in the case of any applicable plan year beginning on or after January 1, 2008, the minimum required contribution determined under sections 303 of such Act and 430 of such Code shall, for purposes of sections 302 and 303 of such Act and sections 412, 430, and 4971 of such Code, be equal to the minimum required contribution determined under subsection (e) for the plan for the plan year.

(2) ACCRUAL RESTRICTIONS.—

(A) IN GENERAL.—The requirements of this paragraph are met if, effective as of the first day of the first applicable plan year and at all times thereafter while an election under this section is in effect, the plan provides that—

(i) the accrued benefit, any death or disability benefit, and any social security supplement described in the last sentence of section 411(a)(9) of such Code and section 204(b)(1)(G) of such Act, of each participant are frozen at the amount of such benefit or supplement immediately before such first day, and

(ii) all other benefits under the plan are eliminated,

but only to the extent the freezing or elimination of such benefits would have been permitted under section 411(d)(6) of such Code and section 204(g) of such Act if they had been implemented by a plan amendment adopted immediately before such first day.

(B) INCREASES IN SECTION 415 LIMITS.—If a plan provides that an accrued benefit of a participant which has been subject to any limitation under section 415 of such Code will be increased if such limitation is increased, the plan shall not be treated as meeting the requirements of this section unless, effective as of the first day of the first applicable plan year (or, if later, the date of the enactment of this Act) and at all times thereafter while an election under this section is in effect, the plan provides that any such increase shall not take effect. A plan shall not fail to meet the requirements of section 411(d)(6) of such Code and section 204(g) of such Act solely because the plan is amended to meet the requirements of this subparagraph.

(3) RESTRICTION ON APPLICABLE BENEFIT INCREASES.—

(A) IN GENERAL.—The requirements of this paragraph are met if no applicable benefit increase takes effect at any time during the period beginning on July 26, 2005, and ending on the day before the first day of the first applicable plan year.

(B) APPLICABLE BENEFIT INCREASE.—For purposes of this paragraph, the term "applicable benefit increase" means, with respect to any plan year, any increase in liabilities of the plan by plan amendment (or otherwise provided in regulations provided by the Secretary) which, but for this paragraph, would occur during the plan year by reason of—

(i) any increase in benefits,

(ii) any change in the accrual of benefits, or

(iii) any change in the rate at which benefits become nonforfeitable under the plan.

(4) EXCEPTION FOR IMPUTED DISABILITY SERVICE.—Paragraphs (2) and (3) shall not apply to any accrual or increase with respect to imputed service provided to a participant during any period of the participant's disability occurring on or after the effective date of the plan amendment providing the restrictions under paragraph (2) (or on or after July 26, 2005, in the case of the restrictions under paragraph (3)) if the participant—

(A) was receiving disability benefits as of such date, or

(B) was receiving sick pay and subsequently determined to be eligible for disability benefits as of such date.

(c) DEFINITIONS.—For purposes of this section—

(1) ELIGIBLE PLAN.—The term "eligible plan" means a defined benefit plan (other than a multiemployer plan) to which sections 302 of such Act and 412 of such Code applies which is sponsored by an employer—

(A) which is a commercial airline passenger airline, or

(B) the principal business of which is providing catering services to a commercial passenger airline.

(2) APPLICABLE PLAN YEAR.—The term "applicable plan year" means each plan year to which the election under subsection (a)(1) applies under subsection (d)(1)(A).

(d) ELECTIONS AND RELATED TERMS.—

(1) YEARS FOR WHICH ELECTION MADE.—

(A) ALTERNATIVE FUNDING SCHEDULE.—If an election under subsection (a)(1) was made with respect to an eligible plan, the plan sponsor may select either a plan year beginning in 2006 or a plan year beginning in 2007 as the first plan year to which such election applies. The election shall apply to such plan year and all subsequent years. The election shall be made—

(i) not later than December 31, 2006, in the case of an election for a plan year beginning in 2006, or

(ii) not later than December 31, 2007, in the case of an election for a plan year beginning in 2007.

(B) 10 YEAR AMORTIZATION.—An election under subsection (a)(2) shall be made not later than December 31, 2007.

(C) ELECTION OF NEW PLAN YEAR FOR ALTERNATIVE FUNDING SCHEDULE.—In the case of an election under subsection (a)(1), the plan sponsor may specify a new plan year in such election and the plan year of the plan may be changed to such new plan year without the approval of the Secretary of the Treasury.

(2) MANNER OF ELECTION.—A plan sponsor shall make any election under subsection (a) in such manner as the Secretary of the Treasury may prescribe. Such election, once made, may be revoked only with the consent of such Secretary.

(e) MINIMUM REQUIRED CONTRIBUTION.—In the case of an eligible plan with respect to which an election is made under subsection (a)(1)—

(1) IN GENERAL.—In the case of any applicable plan year during the amortization period, the minimum required contribution shall be the amount necessary to amortize the unfunded liability of the plan, determined as of the first day of the plan year, in equal annual installments (until fully amortized) over the remainder of the amortization period. Such amount shall be separately determined for each applicable plan year.

(2) YEARS AFTER AMORTIZATION PERIOD.—In the case of any plan year beginning after the end of the amortization period, section 302(a)(2)(A) of such Act and section 412(a)(2)(A) of such Code shall apply to such plan, but the prefunding balance and funding standard carryover balance as of the first day of the first of such years under section 303(f) of such Act and section 430(f) of such Code shall be zero.

(3) DEFINITIONS.—For purposes of this section—

(A) UNFUNDED LIABILITY.—The term "unfunded liability" means the unfunded accrued liability under the plan, determined under the unit credit funding method.

(B) AMORTIZATION PERIOD.—The term "amortization period" means the 17-plan year period beginning with the first applicable plan year.

(4) OTHER RULES.—In determining the minimum required contribution and amortization amount under this subsection—

(A) the provisions of section 302(c)(3) of such Act and section 412(c)(3) of such Code, as in effect before the date of enactment of this section, shall apply,

(B) a rate of interest of 8.85 percent shall be used for all calculations requiring an interest rate, and

(C) the value of plan assets shall be equal to their fair market value.

(5) SPECIAL RULE FOR CERTAIN PLAN SPINOFFS.—For purposes of subsection (b), if, with respect to any eligible plan to which this subsection applies—

(A) any applicable plan year includes the date of the enactment of this Act,

(B) a plan was spun off from the eligible plan during the plan year but before such date of enactment,

the minimum required contribution under paragraph (1) for the eligible plan for such applicable plan year shall be an aggregate amount determined as if the plans were a single plan for that plan year (based on the full 12-month plan year in effect prior to the spin-off). The employer shall designate the allocation of such aggregate amount between such plans for the applicable plan year.

(f) SPECIAL RULES FOR CERTAIN BALANCES AND WAIVERS.—In the case of an eligible plan with respect to which an election is made under subsection (a)(1)—

(1) FUNDING STANDARD ACCOUNT AND CREDIT BALANCES.—Any charge or credit in the funding standard account under section 302 of such Act or section 412 of such Code, and any prefunding balance or funding standard carryover balance under section 303 of such Act or section 430 of such Code, as of the day before the first day of the first applicable plan year, shall be reduced to zero.

(2) WAIVED FUNDING DEFICIENCIES.—Any waived funding deficiency under sections 302 and 303 of such Act or section 412 of such Code, as in effect before the date of enactment of this section, shall be deemed satisfied as of the first day of the first applicable plan year and the amount of such waived funding deficiency shall be taken into account in determining the plan's unfunded liability under subsection (e)(3)(A). In the case of a plan amendment adopted to satisfy the requirements of subsection (b)(2), the plan shall not be deemed to violate section 304(b) of such Act or section 412(f) of such Code, as so in effect, by reason of such amendment or any increase in benefits provided to such plan's participants under a separate plan that is a defined contribution plan or a multiemployer plan.

(g) OTHER RULES FOR PLANS MAKING ELECTION UNDER THIS SECTION.—

(1) SUCCESSOR PLANS TO CERTAIN PLANS.—If—

(A) an election under paragraph (1) or (2) of subsection (a) is in effect with respect to any eligible plan, and

(B) the eligible plan is maintained by an employer that establishes or maintains 1 or more other defined benefit plans (other than any multiemployer plan), and such other plans in combination provide benefit accruals to any substantial number of successor employees,

the Secretary of the Treasury may, in the Secretary's discretion, determine that any trust of which any other such plan is a part does not constitute a qualified trust under section 401(a) of the Internal Revenue Code of 1986 unless all benefit obligations of the eligible plan have been satisfied. For purposes of this paragraph, the term "successor employee" means any employee who is or was covered by the eligible plan and any employees who perform substantially the same type of work with respect to the same business operations as an employee covered by such eligible plan.

(2) SPECIAL RULES FOR TERMINATIONS.—

(A) PBGC LIABILITY LIMITED.—Section 4022 of the Employee Retirement Income Security Act of 1974, as amended by this Act, is amended by adding at the end the following new subsection:

"(h) SPECIAL RULE FOR PLANS ELECTING CERTAIN FUNDING REQUIREMENTS.—If any plan makes an election under section 402(a)(1) of the Pension Protection Act of 2006 and is terminated effective before the end of the 10-year period beginning on the first day of the first applicable plan year—

"(1) this section shall be applied—

"(A) by treating the first day of the first applicable plan year as the termination date of the plan, and

"(B) by determining the amount of guaranteed benefits on the basis of plan assets and liabilities as of such assumed termination date, and

"(2) notwithstanding section 4044(a), plan assets shall first be allocated to pay the amount, if any, by which—

"(A) the amount of guaranteed benefits under this section (determined without regard to paragraph (1) and on the basis of plan assets and liabilities as of the actual date of plan termination), exceeds

"(B) the amount determined under paragraph (1).".

(B) TERMINATION PREMIUM.—In applying section 4006(a)(7)(A) of the Employee Retirement Income Security Act of 1974 to an eligible plan during any period in which an election under subsection (a)(1) is in effect—

(i) "$2,500" shall be substituted for"$1,250" in such section if such plan terminates during the 5-year period beginning on the first day of the first applicable plan year with respect to such plan, and

(ii) such section shall be applied without regard to subparagraph (B) of section 8101(d)(2) of the Deficit Reduction Act of 2005 (relating to special rule for plans terminated in bankruptcy).

The substitution described in clause (i) shall not apply with respect to any plan if the Secretary of Labor determines that such plan terminated as a result of extraordinary circumstances such as a terrorist attack or other similar event.

(3) LIMITATION ON DEDUCTIONS UNDER CERTAIN PLANS.—Section 404(a)(7)(C)(iv) of the Internal Revenue Code of 1986, as added by this Act, shall not apply with respect to any taxable year of a plan sponsor of an eligible plan if any applicable plan year with respect to such plan ends with or within such taxable year.

(4) NOTICE.—In the case of a plan amendment adopted in order to comply with this section, any notice required under section 204(h) of such Act or section 4980F(e) of such Code shall be provided within 15 days of the effective date of such plan amendment. This subsection shall not apply to any plan unless such plan is maintained pursuant to one or more collective bargaining agreements between employee representatives and 1 or more employers.

* * *

(i) EXTENSION OF SPECIAL RULE FOR ADDITIONAL FUNDING REQUIREMENTS.—In the case of an employer which is a commercial passenger airline, section 302(d)(12) of the Employee Retirement Income Security Act of 1974 and section 412(l)(12) of the Internal Revenue Code of 1986, as in effect before the date of the enactment of this Act, shall each be applied—

(1) by substituting "December 28, 2007" for "December 28, 2005" in subparagraph (D)(i) thereof, and

(2) without regard to subparagraph (D)(ii).

(j) EFFECTIVE DATE.—Except as otherwise provided in this section, the provisions of and amendments made by this section shall apply to plan years ending after the date of the enactment of this Act.

[CCH Explanation at ¶ 245. Committee Reports at ¶ 10,230.]

[¶ 7066] ACT SEC. 403. LIMITATION ON PBGC GUARANTEE OF SHUTDOWN AND OTHER BENEFITS.

(a) IN GENERAL.—Section 4022(b) of the Employee Retirement Income Security Act of 1974 (29 U.S.C. 1322(b)) is amended by adding at the end the following:

"(8) If an unpredictable contingent event benefit (as defined in section 206(g)(1)) is payable by reason of the occurrence of any event, this section shall be applied as if a plan amendment had been adopted on the date such event occurred.".

(b) EFFECTIVE DATE.—The amendment made by this section shall apply to benefits that become payable as a result of an event which occurs after July 26, 2005.

[CCH Explanation at ¶ 520. Committee Reports at ¶ 10,240.]

[¶ 7069] ACT SEC. 404. RULES RELATING TO BANKRUPTCY OF EMPLOYER.

(a) GUARANTEE.—Section 4022 of the Employee Retirement Income Security Act of 1974 (29 U.S.C. 1322) is amended by adding at the end the following:

"(g) BANKRUPTCY FILING SUBSTITUTED FOR TERMINATION DATE.—If a contributing sponsor of a plan has filed or has had filed against such person a petition seeking liquidation or reorganization in a case under title 11, United States Code, or under any similar Federal law or law of a State or political subdivision, and the case has not been dismissed as of the termination date of the plan, then this section shall be applied by treating the date such petition was filed as the termination date of the plan.".

(b) ALLOCATION OF ASSETS AMONG PRIORITY GROUPS IN BANKRUPTCY PROCEEDINGS.—Section 4044 of the Employee Retirement Income Security Act of 1974 (29 U.S.C. 1344) is amended by adding at the end the following:

"(e) BANKRUPTCY FILING SUBSTITUTED FOR TERMINATION DATE.—If a contributing sponsor of a plan has filed or has had filed against such person a petition seeking liquidation or reorganization in a case under title 11, United States Code, or under any similar Federal law or law of a State or political subdivision, and the case has not been dismissed as of the termination date of the plan, then subsection (a)(3) shall be applied by treating the date such petition was filed as the termination date of the plan.".

(c) EFFECTIVE DATE.—The amendments made this section shall apply with respect to proceedings initiated under title 11, United States Code, or under any similar Federal law or law of a State or political subdivision, on or after the date that is 30 days after the date of enactment of this Act.

[CCH Explanation at ¶ 525. Committee Reports at ¶ 10,250.]

[¶ 7072] ACT SEC. 405. PBGC PREMIUMS FOR SMALL PLANS.

(a) SMALL PLANS.—Paragraph (3) of section 4006(a) of the Employee Retirement Income Security Act of 1974 (29 U.S.C. 1306(a)) is amended—

(1) by striking "The additional" in subparagraph (E)(i) and inserting "Except as provided in subparagraph (H), the additional", and

(2) by inserting after subparagraph (G) the following new subparagraph:

"(H)(i) In the case of an employer who has 25 or fewer employees on the first day of the plan year, the additional premium determined under subparagraph (E) for each participant shall not exceed $5 multiplied by the number of participants in the plan as of the close of the preceding plan year."

"(ii) For purposes of clause (i), whether an employer has 25 or fewer employees on the first day of the plan year is determined by taking into consideration all of the employees of all members of the contributing sponsor's controlled group. In the case of a plan maintained by two or more contributing sponsors, the employees of all contributing sponsors and their controlled groups shall be aggregated for purposes of determining whether the 25-or-fewer-employees limitation has been satisfied."

(b) EFFECTIVE DATES.—The amendment made by this section shall apply to plan years beginning after December 31, 2006.

[CCH Explanation at ¶ 510. Committee Reports at ¶ 10,260.]

[¶ 7075] ACT SEC. 406. AUTHORIZATION FOR PBGC TO PAY INTEREST ON PREMIUM OVERPAYMENT REFUNDS.

(a) IN GENERAL.—Section 4007(b) of the Employment Retirement Income Security Act of 1974 (29 U.S.C. 1307(b)) is amended—

(1) by striking "(b)" and inserting "(b)(1)", and

(2) by inserting at the end the following new paragraph:

"(2) The corporation is authorized to pay, subject to regulations prescribed by the corporation, interest on the amount of any overpayment of premium refunded to a designated payor. Interest under this paragraph shall be calculated at the same rate and in the same manner as interest is calculated for underpayments under paragraph (1)."

(b) EFFECTIVE DATE.—The amendments made by subsection (a) shall apply to interest accruing for periods beginning not earlier than the date of the enactment of this Act.

[CCH Explanation at ¶ 515. Committee Reports at ¶ 10,270.]

[¶ 7078] ACT SEC. 407. RULES FOR SUBSTANTIAL OWNER BENEFITS IN TERMINATED PLANS.

(a) MODIFICATION OF PHASE-IN OF GUARANTEE.—Section 4022(b)(5) of the Employee Retirement Income Security Act of 1974 (29 U.S.C. 1322(b)(5)) is amended to read as follows:

"(5)(A) For purposes of this paragraph, the term 'majority owner' means an individual who, at any time during the 60-month period ending on the date the determination is being made—

"(i) owns the entire interest in an unincorporated trade or business,

"(ii) in the case of a partnership, is a partner who owns, directly or indirectly, 50 percent or more of either the capital interest or the profits interest in such partnership, or

"(iii) in the case of a corporation, owns, directly or indirectly, 50 percent or more in value of either the voting stock of that corporation or all the stock of that corporation.

For purposes of clause (iii), the constructive ownership rules of section 1563(e) of the Internal Revenue Code of 1986 (other than paragraph (3)(C) thereof) shall apply, including the application of such rules under section 414(c) of such Code.

"(B) In the case of a participant who is a majority owner, the amount of benefits guaranteed under this section shall equal the product of—

"(i) a fraction (not to exceed 1) the numerator of which is the number of years from the later of the effective date or the adoption date of the plan to the termination date, and the denominator of which is 10, and

"(ii) the amount of benefits that would be guaranteed under this section if the participant were not a majority owner."

(b) MODIFICATION OF ALLOCATION OF ASSETS.—

(1) Section 4044(a)(4)(B) of the Employee Retirement Income Security Act of 1974 (29 U.S.C. 1344(a)(4)(B)) is amended by striking "section 4022(b)(5)" and inserting "section 4022(b)(5)(B)".

(2) Section 4044(b) of such Act (29 U.S.C. 1344(b)) is amended—

(A) by striking "(5)" in paragraph (2) and inserting "(4), (5),", and

(B) by redesignating paragraphs (3) through (6) as paragraphs (4) through (7), respectively, and by inserting after paragraph (2) the following new paragraph:

"(3) If assets available for allocation under paragraph (4) of subsection (a) are insufficient to satisfy in full the benefits of all individuals who are described in that paragraph, the assets shall be allocated first to benefits described in subparagraph (A) of that paragraph. Any remaining assets shall then be allocated to benefits described in subparagraph (B) of that paragraph. If assets allocated to such subparagraph (B) are insufficient to satisfy in full the benefits described in that subparagraph, the assets shall be allocated pro rata among individuals on the basis of the present value (as of the termination date) of their respective benefits described in that subparagraph."

(c) CONFORMING AMENDMENTS.—

(1) Section 4021 of the Employee Retirement Income Security Act of 1974 (29 U.S.C. 1321) is amended—

(A) in subsection (b)(9), by striking "as defined in section 4022(b)(6)", and

(B) by adding at the end the following new subsection:

"(d) For purposes of subsection (b)(9), the term 'substantial owner' means an individual who, at any time during the 60-month period ending on the date the determination is being made—

"(1) owns the entire interest in an unincorporated trade or business,

"(2) in the case of a partnership, is a partner who owns, directly or indirectly, more than 10 percent of either the capital interest or the profits interest in such partnership, or

"(3) in the case of a corporation, owns, directly or indirectly, more than 10 percent in value of either the voting stock of that corporation or all the stock of that corporation.

For purposes of paragraph (3), the constructive ownership rules of section 1563(e) of the Internal Revenue Code of 1986 (other than paragraph (3)(C) thereof) shall apply, including the application of such rules under section 414(c) of such Code."

(2) Section 4043(c)(7) of such Act (29 U.S.C. 1343(c)(7)) is amended by striking "section 4022(b)(6)" and inserting "section 4021(d)".

(d) EFFECTIVE DATES.—

(1) IN GENERAL.—Except as provided in paragraph (2), the amendments made by this section shall apply to plan terminations—

(A) under section 4041(c) of the Employee Retirement Income Security Act of 1974 (29 U.S.C. 1341(c)) with respect to which notices of intent to terminate are provided under section 4041(a)(2) of such Act (29 U.S.C. 1341(a)(2)) after December 31, 2005, and

(B) under section 4042 of such Act (29 U.S.C. 1342) with respect to which notices of determination are provided under such section after such date.

(2) CONFORMING AMENDMENTS.—The amendments made by subsection (c) shall take effect on January 1, 2006.

[CCH Explanation at ¶530. Committee Reports at ¶10,280.]

[¶7081] ACT SEC. 408. ACCELERATION OF PBGC COMPUTATION OF BENEFITS ATTRIBUTABLE TO RECOVERIES FROM EMPLOYERS.

(a) MODIFICATION OF AVERAGE RECOVERY PERCENTAGE OF OUTSTANDING AMOUNT OF BENEFIT LIABILITIES PAYABLE BY CORPORATION TO PARTICIPANTS AND BENEFICIARIES.—Section 4022(c)(3)(B)(ii) of the Employee Retirement Income Security Act of 1974 (29 U.S.C. 1322(c)(3)(B)(ii)) is amended to read as follows:

"(ii) notices of intent to terminate were provided (or in the case of a termination by the corporation, a notice of determination under section 4042 was issued) during the 5-Federal fiscal year period ending with the third fiscal year preceding the fiscal year in which occurs the date of the notice of intent to terminate (or the notice of determination under section 4042) with respect to the plan termination for which the recovery ratio is being determined."

(b) VALUATION OF SECTION 4062(C) LIABILITY FOR DETERMINING AMOUNTS PAYABLE BY CORPORATION TO PARTICIPANTS AND BENEFICIARIES.—

(1) SINGLE-EMPLOYER PLAN BENEFITS GUARANTEED.—Section 4022(c)(3)(A) of the Employee Retirement Income Security Act of 1974 (29 U.S.C. 13) is amended to read as follows:

"(A) IN GENERAL.—Except as provided in subparagraph (C), the term 'recovery ratio' means the ratio which—

"(i) the sum of the values of all recoveries under section 4062, 4063, or 4064, determined by the corporation in connection with plan terminations described under subparagraph (B), bears to

"(ii) the sum of all unfunded benefit liabilities under such plans as of the termination date in connection with any such prior termination.".

(2) ALLOCATION OF ASSETS.—Section 4044 of the Employee Retirement Income Security Act of 1974 (29 U.S.C. 1362) is amended by adding at the end the following new subsection:

"(e) VALUATION OF SECTION 4062(C) LIABILITY FOR DETERMINING AMOUNTS PAYABLE BY CORPORATION TO PARTICIPANTS AND BENEFICIARIES.—

"(1) IN GENERAL.—In the case of a terminated plan, the value of the recovery of liability under section 4062(c) allocable as a plan asset under this section for purposes of determining the amount of benefits payable by the corporation shall be determined by multiplying—

"(A) the amount of liability under section 4062(c) as of the termination date of the plan, by

"(B) the applicable section 4062(c) recovery ratio.

"(2) SECTION 4062(C) RECOVERY RATIO.—For purposes of this subsection—

"(A) IN GENERAL.—Except as provided in subparagraph (C), the term 'section 4062(c) recovery ratio' means the ratio which—

"(i) the sum of the values of all recoveries under section 4062(c) determined by the corporation in connection with plan terminations described under subparagraph (B), bears to

"(ii) the sum of all the amounts of liability under section 4062(c) with respect to such plans as of the termination date in connection with any such prior termination.

"(B) PRIOR TERMINATIONS.—A plan termination described in this subparagraph is a termination with respect to which—

"(i) the value of recoveries under section 4062(c) have been determined by the corporation, and

"(ii) notices of intent to terminate were provided (or in the case of a termination by the corporation, a notice of determination under section 4042 was issued) during the 5-Federal fiscal year period ending with the third fiscal year preceding the fiscal year in which occurs the date of the notice of intent to terminate (or the notice of determination under section 4042) with respect to the plan termination for which the recovery ratio is being determined.

"(C) EXCEPTION.—In the case of a terminated plan with respect to which the outstanding amount of benefit liabilities exceeds $20,000,000, the term 'section 4062(c) recovery ratio' means, with respect to the termination of such plan, the ratio of—

"(i) the value of the recoveries on behalf of the plan under section 4062(c), to

"(ii) the amount of the liability owed under section 4062(c) as of the date of plan termination to the trustee appointed under section 4042 (b) or (c).

"(3) SUBSECTION NOT TO APPLY.—This subsection shall not apply with respect to the determination of—

"(A) whether the amount of outstanding benefit liabilities exceeds $20,000,000, or

"(B) the amount of any liability under section 4062 to the corporation or the trustee appointed under section 4042 (b) or (c).

"(4) DETERMINATIONS.—Determinations under this subsection shall be made by the corporation. Such determinations shall be binding unless shown by clear and convincing evidence to be unreasonable.".

(c) EFFECTIVE DATE.—The amendments made by this section shall apply for any termination for which notices of intent to terminate are provided (or in the case of a termination by the corporation, a notice of determination under section 4042 under the Employee Retirement Income Security Act of 1974 is issued) on or after the date which is 30 days after the date of enactment of this section.

[CCH Explanation at ¶ 535. Committee Reports at ¶ 10,290.]

[¶ 7084] ACT SEC. 409. TREATMENT OF CERTAIN PLANS WHERE CESSATION OR CHANGE IN MEMBERSHIP OF A CONTROLLED GROUP.

(a) IN GENERAL.—Section 4041(b) of the Employee Retirement Income Security Act of 1974 (29 U.S.C. 1341(b)) is amended by adding at the end the following new paragraph:

"(5) SPECIAL RULE FOR CERTAIN PLANS WHERE CESSATION OR CHANGE IN MEMBERSHIP OF A CONTROLLED GROUP.—

"(A) IN GENERAL.—Except as provided in subparagraph (B), if—

"(i) there is transaction or series of transactions which result in a person ceasing to be a member of a controlled group, and

"(ii) such person immediately before the transaction or series of transactions maintained a single-employer plan which is a defined benefit plan which is fully funded,

then the interest rate used in determining whether the plan is sufficient for benefit liabilities or to otherwise assess plan liabilities for purposes of this subsection or section 4042(a)(4) shall be not less than the interest rate used in determining whether the plan is fully funded.

"(B) LIMITATIONS.—Subparagraph (A) shall not apply to any transaction or series of transactions unless—

"(i) any employer maintaining the plan immediately before or after such transaction or series of transactions—

"(I) has an outstanding senior unsecured debt instrument which is rated investment grade by each of the nationally recognized statistical rating organizations for corporate bonds that has issued a credit rating for such instrument, or

"(II) if no such debt instrument of such employer has been rated by such an organization but 1 or more of such organizations has made an issuer credit rating for such employer, all such organizations which have so rated the employer have rated such employer investment grade, and

"(ii) the employer maintaining the plan after the transaction or series of transactions employs at least 20 percent of the employees located in the United States who were employed by such employer immediately before the transaction or series of transactions.

"(C) FULLY FUNDED.—For purposes of subparagraph (A), a plan shall be treated as fully funded with respect to any transaction or series of transactions if—

"(i) in the case of a transaction or series of transactions which occur in a plan year beginning before January 1, 2008, the funded current liability percentage determined under section 302(d) for the plan year is at least 100 percent, and

"(ii) in the case of a transaction or series of transactions which occur in a plan year beginning on or after such date, the funding target attainment percentage determined under section 303 is, as of the valuation date for such plan year, at least 100 percent.

"(D) 2 YEAR LIMITATION.—Subparagraph (A) shall not apply to any transaction or series of transaction if the plan referred to in subparagraph (A)(ii) is terminated under section 4041(c) or 4042 after the close of the 2-year period beginning on the date on which the first such transaction occurs.".

(b) EFFECTIVE DATE.—The amendments made by this section shall apply to any transaction or series of transactions occurring on and after the date of the enactment of this Act.

[CCH Explanation at ¶ 225. Committee Reports at ¶ 10,300.]

[¶ 7087] ACT SEC. 410. MISSING PARTICIPANTS.

(a) IN GENERAL.—Section 4050 of the Employee Retirement Income Security Act of 1974 (29 U.S.C. 1350) is amended by redesignating subsection (c) as subsection (e) and by inserting after subsection (b) the following new subsections:

"(c) MULTIEMPLOYER PLANS.—The corporation shall prescribe rules similar to the rules in subsection (a) for multiemployer plans covered by this title that terminate under section 4041A.

"(d) PLANS NOT OTHERWISE SUBJECT TO TITLE.—

"(1) TRANSFER TO CORPORATION.—The plan administrator of a plan described in paragraph (4) may elect to transfer a missing participant's benefits to the corporation upon termination of the plan.

"(2) INFORMATION TO THE CORPORATION.—To the extent provided in regulations, the plan administrator of a plan described in paragraph (4) shall, upon termination of the plan, provide the corporation information with respect to benefits of a missing participant if the plan transfers such benefits—

"(A) to the corporation, or

"(B) to an entity other than the corporation or a plan described in paragraph (4)(B)(ii).

"(3) PAYMENT BY THE CORPORATION.—If benefits of a missing participant were transferred to the corporation under paragraph (1), the corporation shall, upon location of the participant or beneficiary, pay to the participant or beneficiary the amount transferred (or the appropriate survivor benefit) either—

"(A) in a single sum (plus interest), or

"(B) in such other form as is specified in regulations of the corporation.

"(4) PLANS DESCRIBED.—A plan is described in this paragraph if—

"(A) the plan is a pension plan (within the meaning of section 3(2))—

"(i) to which the provisions of this section do not apply (without regard to this subsection), and

"(ii) which is not a plan described in paragraphs (2) through (11) of section 4021(b), and

"(B) at the time the assets are to be distributed upon termination, the plan—

"(i) has missing participants, and

"(ii) has not provided for the transfer of assets to pay the benefits of all missing participants to another pension plan (within the meaning of section 3(2)).

"(5) CERTAIN PROVISIONS NOT TO APPLY.—Subsections (a)(1) and (a)(3) shall not apply to a plan described in paragraph (4).".

(b) CONFORMING AMENDMENTS.—Section 206(f) of such Act (29 U.S.C. 1056(f)) is amended—

(1) by striking "title IV" and inserting "section 4050"; and

(2) by striking "the plan shall provide that,".

(c) EFFECTIVE DATE.—The amendments made by this section shall apply to distributions made after final regulations implementing subsections (c) and (d) of section 4050 of the Employee Retirement Income Security Act of 1974 (as added by subsection (a)), respectively, are prescribed.

[CCH Explanation at ¶ 540. Committee Reports at ¶ 10,310.]

[¶ 7090] ACT SEC. 411. DIRECTOR OF THE PENSION BENEFIT GUARANTY CORPORATION.

(a) IN GENERAL.—Title IV of the Employee Retirement Income Security Act of 1974 (29 U.S.C. 1301 et seq.) is amended—

(1) by striking the second sentence of section 4002(a) and inserting the following: "In carrying out its functions under this title, the corporation shall be administered by a Director, who shall be appointed by the President, by and with the advice and consent of the Senate, and who shall act in accordance with the policies established by the board."; and

(2) in section 4003(b), by—

(A) striking "under this title, any member" and inserting "under this title, the Director, any member"; and

(B) striking "designated by the chairman" and inserting "designated by the Director or chairman".

(b) COMPENSATION OF DIRECTOR.—Section 5314 of title 5, United States Code, is amended by adding at the end the following new item:

"Director, Pension Benefit Guaranty Corporation.".

(c) JURISDICTION OF NOMINATION.—

(1) IN GENERAL.—The Committee on Finance of the Senate and the Committee on Health, Education, Labor, and Pensions of the Senate shall have joint jurisdiction over the nomination of a person nominated by the President to fill the position of Director of the Pension Benefit Guaranty Corporation under section 4002 of the Employee Retirement Income Security Act of 1974 (29 U.S.C. 1302) (as amended by this Act), and if one committee votes to order reported such a nomination, the other shall report within 30 calendar days, or be automatically discharged.

(2) RULEMAKING OF THE SENATE.—This subsection is enacted by Congress—

(A) as an exercise of rulemaking power of the Senate, and as such it is deemed a part of the rules of the Senate, but applicable only with respect to the procedure to be followed in the Senate in the case of a nomination described in such sentence, and it supersedes other rules only to the extent that it is inconsistent with such rules; and

(B) with full recognition of the constitutional right of the Senate to change the rules (so far as relating to the procedure of the Senate) at any time, in the same manner and to the same extent as in the case of any other rule of the Senate.

(d) TRANSITION.—The term of the individual serving as Executive Director of the Pension Benefit Guaranty Corporation on the date of enactment of this Act shall expire on such date of enactment. Such individual, or any other individual, may serve as interim Director of such Corporation until an individual is appointed as Director of such Corporation under section 4002 of the Employee Retirement Income Security Act of 1974 (29 U.S.C. 1302) (as amended by this Act).

[CCH Explanation at ¶ 545. Committee Reports at ¶ 10,320.]

[¶ 7093] ACT SEC. 412. INCLUSION OF INFORMATION IN THE PBGC ANNUAL REPORT.

Section 4008 of the Employee Retirement Income Security Act of 1974 (29 U.S.C. 1308) is amended by—

(1) striking "As soon as practicable" and inserting "(a) As soon as practicable"; and

(2) adding at the end the following:

"(b) The report under subsection (a) shall include—

"(1) a summary of the Pension Insurance Modeling System microsimulation model, including the specific simulation parameters, specific initial values, temporal parameters, and policy parameters used to calculate the financial statements for the corporation;

"(2) a comparison of—

"(A) the average return on investments earned with respect to assets invested by the corporation for the year to which the report relates; and

"(B) an amount equal to 60 percent of the average return on investment for such year in the Standard & Poor's 500 Index, plus 40 percent of the average return on investment for such year in the Lehman Aggregate Bond Index (or in a similar fixed income index); and

"(3) a statement regarding the deficit or surplus for such year that the corporation would have had if the corporation had earned the return described in paragraph (2)(B) with respect to assets invested by the corporation.".

[CCH Explanation at ¶ 550. Committee Reports at ¶ 10,330.]

TITLE V—DISCLOSURE

[¶ 7096] ACT SEC. 501. DEFINED BENEFIT PLAN FUNDING NOTICE.

(a) IN GENERAL.—Section 101(f) of the Employee Retirement Income Security Act of 1974 (29 U.S.C. 1021(f)) is amended to read as follows:

"(f) DEFINED BENEFIT PLAN FUNDING NOTICES.—

"(1) IN GENERAL.—The administrator of a defined benefit plan to which title IV applies shall for each plan year provide a plan funding notice to the Pension Benefit Guaranty Corporation, to each plan participant and beneficiary, to each labor organization representing such participants or beneficiaries, and, in the case of a multiemployer plan, to each employer that has an obligation to contribute to the plan.

"(2) INFORMATION CONTAINED IN NOTICES.—

"(A) IDENTIFYING INFORMATION.—Each notice required under paragraph (1) shall contain identifying information, including the name of the plan, the address and phone number of the plan administrator and the plan's principal administrative officer, each plan sponsor's employer identification number, and the plan number of the plan.

"(B) SPECIFIC INFORMATION.—A plan funding notice under paragraph (1) shall include—

"(i)(I) in the case of a single-employer plan, a statement as to whether the plan's funding target attainment percentage (as defined in section 303(d)(2)) for the plan year to which the notice relates, and for the 2 preceding plan years, is at least 100 percent (and, if not, the actual percentages), or

"(II) in the case of a multiemployer plan, a statement as to whether the plan's funded percentage (as defined in section 305(i)) for the plan year to which the notice relates, and for the 2 preceding plan years, is at least 100 percent (and, if not, the actual percentages),

"(ii)(I) in the case of a single-employer plan, a statement of—

"(aa) the total assets (separately stating the prefunding balance and the funding standard carryover balance) and liabilities of the plan, determined in the same manner as under section 303, for the plan year for which the latest annual report filed under section 104(a) was filed and for the 2 preceding plan years, as reported in the annual report for each such plan year, and

"(bb) the value of the plan's assets and liabilities for the plan year to which the notice relates as of the last day of the plan year to which the notice relates determined using the asset valuation under subclause (II) of section 4006(a)(3)(E)(iii) and the interest rate under section 4006(a)(3)(E)(iv), and

"(II) in the case of a multiemployer plan, a statement of the value of the plan's assets and liabilities for the plan year to which the notice relates as the last day of such plan year and the preceding 2 plan years,

"(iii) a statement of the number of participants who are—

"(I) retired or separated from service and are receiving benefits,

"(II) retired or separated participants entitled to future benefits, and

"(III) active participants under the plan,

"(iv) a statement setting forth the funding policy of the plan and the asset allocation of investments under the plan (expressed as percentages of total assets) as of the end of the plan year to which the notice relates,

"(v) in the case of a multiemployer plan, whether the plan was in critical or endangered status under section 305 for such plan year and, if so—

"(I) a statement describing how a person may obtain a copy of the plan's funding improvement or rehabilitation plan, as appropriate, adopted under section 305 and the actuarial and financial data that demonstrate any action taken by the plan toward fiscal improvement, and

"(II) a summary of any funding improvement plan, rehabilitation plan, or modification thereof adopted under section 305 during the plan year to which the notice relates,

"(vi) in the case of any plan amendment, scheduled benefit increase or reduction, or other known event taking effect in the current plan year and having a material effect on plan liabilities or assets for the year (as defined in regulations by the Secretary), an explanation of the amendment, schedule increase or reduction, or event, and a projection to the end of such plan year of the effect of the amendment, scheduled increase or reduction, or event on plan liabilities,

"(vii)(I) in the case of a single-employer plan, a summary of the rules governing termination of single-employer plans under subtitle C of title IV, or

"(II) in the case of a multiemployer plan, a summary of the rules governing reorganization or insolvency, including the limitations on benefit payments,

"(viii) a general description of the benefits under the plan which are eligible to be guaranteed by the Pension Benefit Guaranty Corporation, along with an explanation of the limitations on the guarantee and the circumstances under which such limitations apply,

"(ix) a statement that a person may obtain a copy of the annual report of the plan filed under section 104(a) upon request, through the Internet website of the Department of Labor, or through an Intranet website maintained by the applicable plan sponsor (or plan administrator on behalf of the plan sponsor), and

"(x) if applicable, a statement that each contributing sponsor, and each member of the contributing sponsor's controlled group, of the single-employer plan was required to provide the information under section 4010 for the plan year to which the notice relates.

"(C) OTHER INFORMATION.—Each notice under paragraph (1) shall include—

"(i) in the case of a multiemployer plan, a statement that the plan administrator shall provide, upon written request, to any labor organization representing plan participants and beneficiaries and any employer that has an obligation to contribute to the plan, a copy of the annual report filed with the Secretary under section 104(a), and

"(ii) any additional information which the plan administrator elects to include to the extent not inconsistent with regulations prescribed by the Secretary.

"(3) TIME FOR PROVIDING NOTICE.—

"(A) IN GENERAL.—Any notice under paragraph (1) shall be provided not later than 120 days after the end of the plan year to which the notice relates.

"(B) EXCEPTION FOR SMALL PLANS.—In the case of a small plan (as such term is used under section 303(g)(2)(B)) any notice under paragraph (1) shall be provided upon filing of the annual report under section 104(a).

"(4) FORM AND MANNER.—Any notice under paragraph (1)—

"(A) shall be provided in a form and manner prescribed in regulations of the Secretary,

"(B) shall be written in a manner so as to be understood by the average plan participant, and

"(C) may be provided in written, electronic, or other appropriate form to the extent such form is reasonably accessible to persons to whom the notice is required to be provided.".

(b) REPEAL OF NOTICE TO PARTICIPANTS OF FUNDING STATUS.—

(1) IN GENERAL.—Title IV of such Act (29 U.S.C. 1301 et seq.) is amended by striking section 4011.

(2) CLERICAL AMENDMENT.—Section 1 of such Act is amended in the table of contents by striking the item relating to section 4011.

(c) MODEL NOTICE.—Not later than 1 year after the date of the enactment of this Act, the Secretary of Labor shall publish a model version of the notice required by section 101(f) of the Employee Retirement Income Security Act of 1974. The Secretary of Labor may promulgate any interim final rules as the Secretary determines appropriate to carry out the provisions of this subsection.

(d) EFFECTIVE DATE.—

(1) IN GENERAL.—The amendments made by this section shall apply to plan years beginning after December 31, 2007, except that the amendment made by subsection (b) shall apply to plan years beginning after December 31, 2006.

(2) TRANSITION RULE.—Any requirement under section 101(f) of the Employee Retirement Income Security Act of 1974 (as amended by this section) to report the funding target attainment percentage or funded percentage of a plan with respect to any plan year beginning before January 1, 2008, shall be treated as met if the plan reports—

(A) in the case of a plan year beginning in 2006, the funded current liability percentage (as defined in section 302(d)(8) of such Act) of the plan for such plan year, and

(B) in the case of a plan year beginning in 2007, the funding target attainment percentage or funded percentage as determined using such methods of estimation as the Secretary of the Treasury may provide.

[CCH Explanation at ¶405. Committee Reports at ¶10,340.]

[¶7099] ACT SEC. 502. ACCESS TO MULTIEMPLOYER PENSION PLAN INFORMATION.

(a) FINANCIAL INFORMATION WITH RESPECT TO MULTIEMPLOYER PLANS.—

(1) IN GENERAL.—Section 101 of the Employee Retirement Income Security Act of 1974 (29 U.S.C. 1021), as amended by section 103, is amended—

(A) by redesignating subsection (k) as subsection (l); and

(B) by inserting after subsection (j) the following new subsection:

"(k) MULTIEMPLOYER PLAN INFORMATION MADE AVAILABLE ON REQUEST.—

"(1) IN GENERAL.—Each administrator of a multiemployer plan shall, upon written request, furnish to any plan participant or beneficiary, employee representative, or any employer that has an obligation to contribute to the plan—

"(A) a copy of any periodic actuarial report (including any sensitivity testing) received by the plan for any plan year which has been in the plan's possession for at least 30 days,

"(B) a copy of any quarterly, semi-annual, or annual financial report prepared for the plan by any plan investment manager or advisor or other fiduciary which has been in the plan's possession for at least 30 days, and

"(C) a copy of any application filed with the Secretary of the Treasury requesting an extension under section 304 of this Act or section 431(d) of the Internal Revenue Code of 1986 and the determination of such Secretary pursuant to such application.

"(2) COMPLIANCE.—Information required to be provided under paragraph (1) —

"(A) shall be provided to the requesting participant, beneficiary, or employer within 30 days after the request in a form and manner prescribed in regulations of the Secretary,

"(B) may be provided in written, electronic, or other appropriate form to the extent such form is reasonably accessible to persons to whom the information is required to be provided, and

"(C) shall not—

"(i) include any individually identifiable information regarding any plan participant, beneficiary, employee, fiduciary, or contributing employer, or

"(ii) reveal any proprietary information regarding the plan, any contributing employer, or entity providing services to the plan.

"(3) LIMITATIONS.—In no case shall a participant, beneficiary, or employer be entitled under this subsection to receive more than one copy of any report or application described in paragraph (1) during any one 12-month period. The administrator may make a reasonable charge to cover copying, mailing, and other costs of furnishing copies of information pursuant to paragraph (1). The Secretary may by regulations prescribe the maximum amount which will constitute a reasonable charge under the preceding sentence.".

(2) ENFORCEMENT.—Section 502(c)(4) of such Act (29 U.S.C. 1132(c)(4)) is amended by striking "section 101(j)" and inserting "subsection (j) or (k) of section 101".

(3) REGULATIONS.—The Secretary shall prescribe regulations under section 101(k)(2) of the Employee Retirement Income Security Act of 1974 (as added by paragraph (1)) not later than 1 year after the date of the enactment of this Act.

(b) NOTICE OF POTENTIAL WITHDRAWAL LIABILITY TO MULTIEMPLOYER PLANS.—

(1) IN GENERAL.—Section 101 of such Act (as amended by subsection (a)) is amended—

(A) by redesignating subsection (l) as subsection (m); and

(B) by inserting after subsection (k) the following new subsection:

"(l) NOTICE OF POTENTIAL WITHDRAWAL LIABILITY.—

"(1) IN GENERAL.—The plan sponsor or administrator of a multiemployer plan shall, upon written request, furnish to any employer who has an obligation to contribute to the plan a notice of—

"(A) the estimated amount which would be the amount of such employer's withdrawal liability under part 1 of subtitle E of title IV if such employer withdrew on the last day of the plan year preceding the date of the request, and

"(B) an explanation of how such estimated liability amount was determined, including the actuarial assumptions and methods used to determine the value of the plan liabilities and assets, the data regarding employer contributions, unfunded vested benefits, annual changes in the plan's unfunded vested benefits, and the application of any relevant limitations on the estimated withdrawal liability.

For purposes of subparagraph (B), the term 'employer contribution' means, in connection with a participant, a contribution made by an employer as an employer of such participant.

"(2) COMPLIANCE.—Any notice required to be provided under paragraph (1)—

"(A) shall be provided in a form and manner prescribed in regulations of the Secretary to the requesting employer within—

"(i) 180 days after the request, or

"(ii) subject to regulations of the Secretary, such longer time as may be necessary in the case of a plan that determines withdrawal liability based on any method described under paragraph (4) or (5) of section 4211(c); and

"(B) may be provided in written, electronic, or other appropriate form to the extent such form is reasonably accessible to employers to whom the information is required to be provided.

"(3) LIMITATIONS.—In no case shall an employer be entitled under this subsection to receive more than one notice described in paragraph (1) during any one 12-month period. The person required to provide such notice may make a reasonable charge to cover copying, mailing, and other costs of furnishing such notice pursuant to paragraph (1). The Secretary may by regulations prescribe the maximum amount which will constitute a reasonable charge under the preceding sentence.".

(2) ENFORCEMENT.—Section 502(c)(4) of such Act (29 U.S.C. 1132(c)(4)) is amended by striking "section 101(j) or (k)" and inserting "subsection (j), (k), or (l) of section 101".

(c) NOTICE OF AMENDMENT REDUCING FUTURE ACCRUALS.—

(1) AMENDMENT OF ERISA.—Section 204(h)(1) of such Act (29 U.S.C. 1054(h)(1)) is amended by inserting at the end before the period the following: "and to each employer who has an obligation to contribute to the plan.".

* * *

(d) EFFECTIVE DATE.—The amendments made by this section shall apply to plan years beginning after December 31, 2007.

[CCH Explanation at ¶ 410. Committee Reports at ¶ 10,350.]

[¶ 7102] ACT SEC. 503. ADDITIONAL ANNUAL REPORTING REQUIREMENTS.

(a) ADDITIONAL ANNUAL REPORTING REQUIREMENTS WITH RESPECT TO DEFINED BENEFIT PLANS.—

(1) IN GENERAL.—Section 103 of the Employee Retirement Income Security Act of 1974 (29 U.S.C. 1023) is amended—

(A) in subsection (a)(1)(B), by striking "subsections (d) and (e)" and inserting "subsections (d), (e), and (f)"; and

(B) by adding at the end the following new subsection:

"(f) ADDITIONAL INFORMATION WITH RESPECT TO DEFINED BENEFIT PLANS.—

"(1) LIABILITIES UNDER 2 OR MORE PLANS.—

"(A) IN GENERAL.—In any case in which any liabilities to participants or their beneficiaries under a defined benefit plan as of the end of a plan year consist (in whole or in part) of liabilities to such participants and beneficiaries under 2 or more pension plans as of immediately before such plan year, an annual report under this section for such plan year shall include the funded percentage of each of such 2 or more pension plans as of the last day of such plan year and the funded percentage of the plan with respect to which the annual report is filed as of the last day of such plan year.

"(B) FUNDED PERCENTAGE.—For purposes of this paragraph, the term 'funded percentage'—

"(i) in the case of a single-employer plan, means the funding target attainment percentage, as defined in section 303(d)(2), and

"(ii) in the case of a multiemployer plan, has the meaning given such term in section 305(i)(2).

"(2) ADDITIONAL INFORMATION FOR MULTIEMPLOYER PLANS.—With respect to any defined benefit plan which is a multiemployer plan, an annual report under this section for a plan year shall include, in addition to the information required under paragraph (1), the following, as of the end of the plan year to which the report relates:

"(A) The number of employers obligated to contribute to the plan.

"(B) A list of the employers that contributed more than 5 percent of the total contributions to the plan during such plan year.

"(C) The number of participants under the plan on whose behalf no contributions were made by an employer as an employer of the participant for such plan year and for each of the 2 preceding plan years.

"(D) The ratios of—

"(i) the number of participants under the plan on whose behalf no employer had an obligation to make an employer contribution during the plan year, to

"(ii) the number of participants under the plan on whose behalf no employer had an obligation to make an employer contribution during each of the 2 preceding plan years.

"(E) Whether the plan received an amortization extension under section 304(d) of this Act or section 431(d) of the Internal Revenue Code of 1986 for such plan year and, if so, the amount of the difference between the minimum required contribution for the year and the minimum required contribution which would have been required without regard to the extension, and the period of such extension.

"(F) Whether the plan used the shortfall funding method (as such term is used in section 305) for such plan year and, if so, the amount of the difference between the minimum required contribution for the year and the minimum required contribution which would have been required without regard to the use of such method, and the period of use of such method.

"(G) Whether the plan was in critical or endangered status under section 305 for such plan year, and if so, a summary of any funding improvement or rehabilitation plan (or modification thereto) adopted during the plan year, and the funded percentage of the plan.

"(H) The number of employers that withdrew from the plan during the preceding plan year and the aggregate amount of withdrawal liability assessed, or estimated to be assessed, against such withdrawn employers.

"(I) In the case of a multiemployer plan that has merged with another plan or to which assets and liabilities have been transferred, the actuarial valuation of the assets and liabilities of each affected plan during the year preceding the effective date of the merger or transfer, based upon the most recent data available as of the day before the first day of the plan year, or other valuation method performed under standards and procedures as the Secretary may prescribe by regulation.".

(2) GUIDANCE BY SECRETARY OF LABOR.—Not later than 1 year after the date of enactment of this Act, the Secretary of Labor shall publish guidance to assist multiemployer defined benefit plans to—

(A) identify and enumerate plan participants for whom there is no employer with an obligation to make an employer contribution under the plan; and

(B) report such information under section 103(f)(2)(D) of the Employee Retirement Income Security Act of 1974 (as added by this section).

(b) ADDITIONAL INFORMATION IN ANNUAL ACTUARIAL STATEMENT REGARDING PLAN RETIREMENT PROJECTIONS.—Section 103(d) of such Act (29 U.S.C. 1023(d)) is amended—

(1) by redesignating paragraphs (12) and (13) as paragraphs (13) and (14), respectively; and

(2) by inserting after paragraph (11) the following new paragraph:

"(12) A statement explaining the actuarial assumptions and methods used in projecting future retirements and forms of benefit distributions under the plan.".

(c) REPEAL OF SUMMARY ANNUAL REPORT REQUIREMENT FOR DEFINED BENEFIT PLANS.—

(1) IN GENERAL.—Section 104(b)(3) of such Act (29 U.S.C. 1024(b)(3)) is amended by inserting "(other than an administrator of a defined benefit plan to which the requirements of section 103(f) applies)" after "the administrators".

(2) CONFORMING AMENDMENT.—Section 101(a)(2) of such Act (29 U.S.C. 1021(a)(2)) is amended by inserting "subsection (f) and" before "sections 104(b)(3) and 105(a) and (c)".

(d) FURNISHING SUMMARY PLAN INFORMATION TO EMPLOYERS AND EMPLOYEE REPRESENTATIVES OF MULTIEMPLOYER PLANS.—Section 104 of such Act (29 U.S.C. 1024) is amended—

(1) in the header, by striking "**participants**" and inserting "**participants and certain employers**";

(2) redesignating subsection (d) as subsection (e); and

(3) inserting after subsection (c) the following:

"(d) FURNISHING SUMMARY PLAN INFORMATION TO EMPLOYERS AND EMPLOYEE REPRESENTATIVES OF MULTIEMPLOYER PLANS.—

"(1) IN GENERAL.—With respect to a multiemployer plan subject to this section, within 30 days after the due date under subsection (a)(1) for the filing of the annual report for the fiscal year of the plan, the administrators shall furnish to each employee organization and to each employer with an obligation to contribute to the plan a report that contains—

"(A) a description of the contribution schedules and benefit formulas under the plan, and any modification to such schedules and formulas, during such plan year;

"(B) the number of employers obligated to contribute to the plan;

"(C) a list of the employers that contributed more than 5 percent of the total contributions to the plan during such plan year;

"(D) the number of participants under the plan on whose behalf no contributions were made by an employer as an employer of the participant for such plan year and for each of the 2 preceding plan years;

"(E) whether the plan was in critical or endangered status under section 305 for such plan year and, if so, include—

"(i) a list of the actions taken by the plan to improve its funding status; and

"(ii) a statement describing how a person may obtain a copy of the plan's improvement or rehabilitation plan, as applicable, adopted under section 305 and the actuarial and financial data that demonstrate any action taken by the plan toward fiscal improvement;

"(F) the number of employers that withdrew from the plan during the preceding plan year and the aggregate amount of withdrawal liability assessed, or estimated to be assessed, against such withdrawn employers, as reported on the annual report for the plan year to which the report under this subsection relates;

"(G) in the case of a multiemployer plan that has merged with another plan or to which assets and liabilities have been transferred, the actuarial valuation of the assets and liabilities of each affected plan during the year preceding the effective date of the merger or transfer, based upon the most recent data available as of the day before the first day of the plan year, or other valuation method performed under standards and procedures as the Secretary may prescribe by regulation;

"(H) a description as to whether the plan—

"(i) sought or received an amortization extension under section 304(d) of this Act or section 431(d) of the Internal Revenue Code of 1986 for such plan year; or

"(ii) used the shortfall funding method (as such term is used in section 305) for such plan year; and

"(I) notification of the right under this section of the recipient to a copy of the annual report filed with the Secretary under subsection (a), summary plan description, summary of any material modification of the plan, upon written request, but that—

"(i) in no case shall a recipient be entitled to receive more than one copy of any such document described during any one 12-month period; and

"(ii) the administrator may make a reasonable charge to cover copying, mailing, and other costs of furnishing copies of information pursuant to this subparagraph.

"(2) EFFECT OF SUBSECTION.—Nothing in this subsection waives any other provision under this title requiring plan administrators to provide, upon request, information to employers that have an obligation to contribute under the plan.".

(e) MODEL FORM.—Not later than 1 year after the date of the enactment of this Act, the Secretary of Labor shall publish a model form for providing the statements, schedules, and other material required to be provided under section 101(f) of the Employee Retirement Income Security Act of 1974, as amended by this section. The Secretary of Labor may promulgate any interim final rules as the Secretary determines appropriate to carry out the provisions of this subsection.

(f) EFFECTIVE DATE.—The amendments made by this section shall apply to plan years beginning after December 31, 2007.

[CCH Explanation at ¶415. Committee Reports at ¶10,360.]

[¶7105] ACT SEC. 504. ELECTRONIC DISPLAY OF ANNUAL REPORT INFORMATION.

(a) ELECTRONIC DISPLAY OF INFORMATION.—Section 104(b) of such Act (29 U.S.C. 1024(b)) is amended by adding at the end the following:

"(5) Identification and basic plan information and actuarial information included in the annual report for any plan year shall be filed with the Secretary in an electronic format which accommodates display on the Internet, in accordance with regulations which shall be prescribed by the Secretary. The Secretary shall provide for display of such information included in the annual report, within 90 days after the date of the filing of the annual report, on an Internet website maintained by the Secretary and other appropriate media. Such information shall also be displayed on any Intranet website maintained by the plan sponsor (or by the plan administrator on behalf of the plan sponsor) for the purpose of communicating with employees and not the public, in accordance with regulations which shall be prescribed by the Secretary.".

(b) EFFECTIVE DATE.—The amendments made by this section shall apply to plan years beginning after December 31, 2007.

[CCH Explanation at ¶ 420. Committee Reports at ¶ 10,360.]

[¶ 7108] ACT SEC. 505. SECTION 4010 FILINGS WITH THE PBGC.

(a) CHANGE IN CRITERIA FOR PERSONS REQUIRED TO PROVIDE INFORMATION TO PBGC.—Section 4010(b) of the Employee Retirement Income Security Act of 1974 (29 U.S.C. 1310(b)) is amended by striking paragraph (1) and inserting the following:

"(1) the funding target attainment percentage (as defined in subsection (d)) at the end of the preceding plan year of a plan maintained by the contributing sponsor or any member of its controlled group is less than 80 percent;".

(b) ADDITIONAL INFORMATION REQUIRED.—Section 4010 of the Employee Retirement Income Security Act of 1974 (29 U.S.C. 1310) is amended by adding at the end the following new subsection:

"(d) ADDITIONAL INFORMATION REQUIRED.—

"(1) IN GENERAL.—The information submitted to the corporation under subsection (a) shall include—

"(A) the amount of benefit liabilities under the plan determined using the assumptions used by the corporation in determining liabilities;

"(B) the funding target of the plan determined as if the plan has been in at-risk status for at least 5 plan years; and

"(C) the funding target attainment percentage of the plan.

"(2) DEFINITIONS.—For purposes of this subsection:

"(A) FUNDING TARGET.—The term 'funding target' has the meaning provided under section 303(d)(1).

"(B) FUNDING TARGET ATTAINMENT PERCENTAGE.—The term 'funding target attainment percentage' has the meaning provided under section 302(d)(2).

"(C) AT-RISK STATUS.—The term 'at-risk status' has the meaning provided in section 303(i)(4).

"(e) NOTICE TO CONGRESS.—The corporation shall, on an annual basis, submit to the Committee on Health, Education, Labor, and Pensions and the Committee on Finance of the Senate and the Committee on Education and the Workforce and the Committee on Ways and Means of the House of Representatives, a summary report in the aggregate of the information submitted to the corporation under this section.".

(c) EFFECTIVE DATE.—The amendments made by this section shall apply with respect to years beginning after 2007.

[CCH Explanation at ¶ 425. Committee Reports at ¶ 10,370.]

[¶ 7111] ACT SEC. 506. DISCLOSURE OF TERMINATION INFORMATION TO PLAN PARTICIPANTS.

(a) DISTRESS TERMINATIONS.—

(1) IN GENERAL.—Section 4041(c)(2) of the Employee Retirement Income Security Act of 1974 (29 U.S.C. 1341(c)(2)) is amended by adding at the end the following:

"(D) DISCLOSURE OF TERMINATION INFORMATION.—

"(i) IN GENERAL.—A plan administrator that has filed a notice of intent to terminate under subsection (a)(2) shall provide to an affected party any information provided to the corporation under subsection (a)(2) not later than 15 days after—

"(I) receipt of a request from the affected party for the information; or

"(II) the provision of new information to the corporation relating to a previous request.

"(ii) CONFIDENTIALITY.—

"(I) IN GENERAL.—The plan administrator shall not provide information under clause (i) in a form that includes any information that may directly or indirectly be associated with, or otherwise identify, an individual participant or beneficiary.

"(II) LIMITATION.—A court may limit disclosure under this subparagraph of confidential information described in section 552(b) of title 5, United States Code, to any authorized representative of the participants or beneficiaries that agrees to ensure the confidentiality of such information.

"(iii) FORM AND MANNER OF INFORMATION; CHARGES.—

"(I) FORM AND MANNER.—The corporation may prescribe the form and manner of the provision of information under this subparagraph, which shall include delivery in written, electronic, or other appropriate form to the extent that such form is reasonably accessible to individuals to whom the information is required to be provided.

"(II) REASONABLE CHARGES.—A plan administrator may charge a reasonable fee for any information provided under this subparagraph in other than electronic form.

"(iv) AUTHORIZED REPRESENTATIVE.—For purposes of this subparagraph, the term 'authorized representative' means any employee organization representing participants in the pension plan.".

(2) CONFORMING AMENDMENT.—Section 4041(c)(1) of the Employee Retirement Income Security Act of 1974 (29 U.S.C. 1341(c)(1)) is amended in subparagraph (C) by striking "subparagraph (B)" and inserting "subparagraphs (B) and (D)".

(b) INVOLUNTARY TERMINATIONS.—

(1) IN GENERAL.—Section 4042(c) of the Employee Retirement Income Security Act of 1974 (29 U.S.C. 1342(c)) is amended by—

(A) striking "(c) If the" and inserting "(c)(1) If the";

(B) redesignating paragraph (3) as paragraph (2); and

(C) adding at the end the following:

"(3) DISCLOSURE OF TERMINATION INFORMATION.—

"(A) IN GENERAL.—

"(i) INFORMATION FROM PLAN SPONSOR OR ADMINISTRATOR.—A plan sponsor or plan administrator of a single-employer plan that has received a notice from the corporation of a determination that the plan should be terminated under this section shall provide to an affected party any information provided to the corporation in connection with the plan termination.

"(ii) INFORMATION FROM CORPORATION.—The corporation shall provide a copy of the administrative record, including the trusteeship decision record of a termination of a plan described under clause (i).

"(B) TIMING OF DISCLOSURE.—The plan sponsor, plan administrator, or the corporation, as applicable, shall provide the information described in subparagraph (A) not later than 15 days after—

"(i) receipt of a request from an affected party for such information; or "(ii) in the case of information described under subparagraph (A)(i), the provision of any new information to the corporation relating to a previous request by an affected party.

"(C) CONFIDENTIALITY.—

"(i) IN GENERAL.—The plan administrator and plan sponsor shall not provide information under subparagraph (A)(i) in a form which includes any information that may directly or indirectly be associated with, or otherwise identify, an individual participant or beneficiary.

"(ii) LIMITATION.—A court may limit disclosure under this paragraph of confidential information described in section 552(b) of title 5, United States Code, to authorized representatives (within the meaning of section 4041(c)(2)(D)(iv)) of the participants or beneficiaries that agree to ensure the confidentiality of such information.

"(D) FORM AND MANNER OF INFORMATION; CHARGES.—

"(i) FORM AND MANNER.—The corporation may prescribe the form and manner of the provision of information under this paragraph, which shall include delivery in written, electronic, or other appropriate form to the extent that such form is reasonably accessible to individuals to whom the information is required to be provided.

"(ii) REASONABLE CHARGES.—A plan sponsor may charge a reasonable fee for any information provided under this paragraph in other than electronic form.".

(c) EFFECTIVE DATE.—

(1) IN GENERAL.—The amendments made by this section shall apply to any plan termination under title IV of the Employee Retirement Income Security Act of 1974 (29 U.S.C. 1301 et seq.) with respect to which the notice of intent to terminate (or in the case of a termination by the Pension Benefit Guaranty Corporation, a notice of determination under section 4042 of such Act (29 U.S.C. 1342)) occurs after the date of enactment of this Act.

(2) TRANSITION RULE.—If notice under section 4041(c)(2)(D) or 4042(c)(3) of the Employee Retirement Income Security Act of 1974 (as added by this section) would otherwise be required to be provided before the 90th day after the date of the enactment of this Act, such notice shall not be required to be provided until such 90th day.

[CCH Explanation at ¶430. Committee Reports at ¶10,380.]

[¶7114] ACT SEC. 507. NOTICE OF FREEDOM TO DIVEST EMPLOYER SECURITIES.

(a) IN GENERAL.—Section 101 of the Employee Retirement Income Security Act of 1974 (29 U.S.C. 1021), as amended by this Act, is amended by redesignating subsection (m) as subsection (n) and by inserting after subsection (l) the following:

"(m) NOTICE OF RIGHT TO DIVEST.—Not later than 30 days before the first date on which an applicable individual of an applicable individual account plan is eligible to exercise the right under section 204(j) to direct the proceeds from the divestment of employer securities with respect to any type of contribution, the administrator shall provide to such individual a notice—

"(1) setting forth such right under such section, and

"(2) describing the importance of diversifying the investment of retirement account assets.

The notice required by this subsection shall be written in a manner calculated to be understood by the average plan participant and may be delivered in written, electronic, or other appropriate form to the extent that such form is reasonably accessible to the recipient."

(b) PENALTIES.—Section 502(c)(7) of the Employee Retirement Income Security Act of 1974 (29 U.S.C. 1132(c)(7)) is amended by striking "section 101(i)" and inserting "subsection (i) or (m) of section 101".

(c) MODEL NOTICE.—The Secretary of the Treasury shall, within 180 days after the date of the enactment of this subsection, prescribe a model notice for purposes of satisfying the requirements of the amendments made by this section.

(d) EFFECTIVE DATES.—

(1) IN GENERAL.—The amendments made by this section shall apply to plan years beginning after December 31, 2006.

(2) TRANSITION RULE.—If notice under section 101(m) of the Employee Retirement Income Security Act of 1974 (as added by this section) would otherwise be required to be provided before the 90th day after the date of the enactment of this Act, such notice shall not be required to be provided until such 90th day.

[CCH Explanation at ¶ 610. Committee Reports at ¶ 10,390.]

[¶ 7117] ACT SEC. 508. PERIODIC PENSION BENEFIT STATEMENTS.

(a) AMENDMENTS OF ERISA.—

(1) IN GENERAL.—Section 105(a) of the Employee Retirement Income Security Act of 1974 (29 U.S.C. 1025(a)) is amended to read as follows:

"(a) REQUIREMENTS TO PROVIDE PENSION BENEFIT STATEMENTS.—

"(1) REQUIREMENTS.—

"(A) INDIVIDUAL ACCOUNT PLAN.—The administrator of an individual account plan (other than a one-participant retirement plan described in section 101(i)(8)(B)) shall furnish a pension benefit statement—

"(i) at least once each calendar quarter to a participant or beneficiary who has the right to direct the investment of assets in his or her account under the plan,

"(ii) at least once each calendar year to a participant or beneficiary who has his or her own account under the plan but does not have the right to direct the investment of assets in that account, and

"(iii) upon written request to a plan beneficiary not described in clause (i) or (ii).

"(B) DEFINED BENEFIT PLAN.—The administrator of a defined benefit plan (other than a one-participant retirement plan described in section 101(i)(8)(B)) shall furnish a pension benefit statement—

"(i) at least once every 3 years to each participant with a nonforfeitable accrued benefit and who is employed by the employer maintaining the plan at the time the statement is to be furnished, and

"(ii) to a participant or beneficiary of the plan upon written request.

Information furnished under clause (i) to a participant may be based on reasonable estimates determined under regulations prescribed by the Secretary, in consultation with the Pension Benefit Guaranty Corporation.

"(2) STATEMENTS.—

"(A) IN GENERAL.—A pension benefit statement under paragraph (1)—

"(i) shall indicate, on the basis of the latest available information—

"(I) the total benefits accrued, and

"(II) the nonforfeitable pension benefits, if any, which have accrued, or the earliest date on which benefits will become nonforfeitable,

"(ii) shall include an explanation of any permitted disparity under section 401(l) of the Internal Revenue Code of 1986 or any floor-offset arrangement that may be applied in determining any accrued benefits described in clause (i),

"(iii) shall be written in a manner calculated to be understood by the average plan participant, and

"(iv) may be delivered in written, electronic, or other appropriate form to the extent such form is reasonably accessible to the participant or beneficiary.

"(B) ADDITIONAL INFORMATION.—In the case of an individual account plan, any pension benefit statement under clause (i) or (ii) of paragraph (1)(A) shall include—

"(i) the value of each investment to which assets in the individual account have been allocated, determined as of the most recent valuation date under the plan, including the value of any assets held in the form of employer securities, without regard to whether such securities were contributed by the plan sponsor or acquired at the direction of the plan or of the participant or beneficiary, and

"(ii) in the case of a pension benefit statement under paragraph (1)(A)(i)—

"(I) an explanation of any limitations or restrictions on any right of the participant or beneficiary under the plan to direct an investment,

"(II) an explanation, written in a manner calculated to be understood by the average plan participant, of the importance, for the long-term retirement security of participants and beneficiaries, of a well-balanced and diversified investment portfolio, including a statement of the risk that holding more than 20 percent of a portfolio in the security of one entity (such as employer securities) may not be adequately diversified, and

"(III) a notice directing the participant or beneficiary to the Internet website of the Department of Labor for sources of information on individual investing and diversification.

"(C) ALTERNATIVE NOTICE.—The requirements of subparagraph (A)(i)(II) are met if, at least annually and in accordance with requirements of the Secretary, the plan—

"(i) updates the information described in such paragraph which is provided in the pension benefit statement, or

"(ii) provides in a separate statement such information as is necessary to enable a participant or beneficiary to determine their nonforfeitable vested benefits.

"(3) DEFINED BENEFIT PLANS.—

"(A) ALTERNATIVE NOTICE.—In the case of a defined benefit plan, the requirements of paragraph (1)(B)(i) shall be treated as met with respect to a participant if at least once each year the administrator provides to the participant notice of the availability of the pension benefit statement and the ways in which the participant may obtain such statement. Such notice may be delivered in written, electronic, or other appropriate form to the extent such form is reasonably accessible to the participant.

"(B) YEARS IN WHICH NO BENEFITS ACCRUE.—The Secretary may provide that years in which no employee or former employee benefits (within the meaning of section 410(b) of the Internal Revenue Code of 1986) under the plan need not be taken into account in determining the 3-year period under paragraph (1)(B)(i)."

(2) CONFORMING AMENDMENTS.—

(A) Section 105 of the Employee Retirement Income Security Act of 1974 (29 U.S.C. 1025) is amended by striking subsection (d).

(B) Section 105(b) of such Act (29 U.S.C. 1025(b)) is amended to read as follows:

"(b) LIMITATION ON NUMBER OF STATEMENTS.—In no case shall a participant or beneficiary of a plan be entitled to more than 1 statement described in subparagraph (A)(iii) or (B)(ii) of subsection (a)(1), whichever is applicable, in any 12-month period."

(C) Section 502(c)(1) of such Act (29 U.S.C. 1132(c)(1)) is amended by striking "or section 101(f)" and inserting "section 101(f), or section 105(a)".

(b) MODEL STATEMENTS.—

(1) IN GENERAL.—The Secretary of Labor shall, within 1 year after the date of the enactment of this section, develop 1 or more model benefit statements that are written in a manner calculated to be understood by the average plan participant and that may be used by plan administrators in complying with the requirements of section 105 of the Employee Retirement Income Security Act of 1974.

(2) INTERIM FINAL RULES.—The Secretary of Labor may promulgate any interim final rules as the Secretary determines appropriate to carry out the provisions of this subsection.

(c) EFFECTIVE DATE.—

(1) IN GENERAL.—The amendments made by this section shall apply to plan years beginning after December 31, 2006.

(2) SPECIAL RULE FOR COLLECTIVELY BARGAINED AGREEMENTS.—In the case of a plan maintained pursuant to 1 or more collective bargaining agreements between employee representatives and 1 or more employers ratified on or before the date of the enactment of this Act, paragraph (1) shall be applied to benefits pursuant to, and individuals covered by, any such agreement by substituting for "December 31, 2006" the earlier of—

(A) the later of—

(i) December 31, 2007, or

(ii) the date on which the last of such collective bargaining agreements terminates (determined without regard to any extension thereof after such date of enactment), or

(B) December 31, 2008.

[CCH Explanation at ¶615. Committee Reports at ¶10,400.]

[¶7120] ACT SEC. 509. NOTICE TO PARTICIPANTS OR BENEFICIARIES OF BLACKOUT PERIODS.

(a) IN GENERAL.—Section 101(i)(8)(B) of the Employee Retirement Income Security Act of 1974 (29 U.S.C. 1021(i)(8)(B)) is amended by striking clauses (i) through (iv), by redesignating clause (v) as clause (ii), and by inserting before clause (ii), as so redesignated, the following new clause:

"(i) on the first day of the plan year—

"(I) covered only one individual (or the individual and the individual's spouse) and the individual (or the individual and the individual's spouse) owned 100 percent of the plan sponsor (whether or not incorporated), or

"(II) covered only one or more partners (or partners and their spouses) in the plan sponsor, and".

(b) EFFECTIVE DATE.—The amendments made by this subsection shall take effect as if included in the provisions of section 306 of Public Law 107-204 (116 Stat. 745 et seq.).

[CCH Explanation at ¶620. Committee Reports at ¶10,410.]

TITLE VI—INVESTMENT ADVICE, PROHIBITED TRANSACTIONS, AND FIDUCIARY RULES

Subtitle A—Investment Advice

[¶7123] ACT SEC. 601. PROHIBITED TRANSACTION EXEMPTION FOR PROVISION OF INVESTMENT ADVICE.

(a) AMENDMENTS TO THE EMPLOYEE RETIREMENT INCOME SECURITY ACT OF 1974.—

(1) EXEMPTION FROM PROHIBITED TRANSACTIONS.—Section 408(b) of the Employee Retirement Income Security Act of 1974 (29 U.S.C. 1108(b)) is amended by adding at the end the following new paragraph:

"(14) Any transaction in connection with the provision of investment advice described in section 3(21)(A)(ii) to a participant or beneficiary of an individual account plan that permits such participant or beneficiary to direct the investment of assets in their individual account, if—

"(A) the transaction is—

"(i) the provision of the investment advice to the participant or beneficiary of the plan with respect to a security or other property available as an investment under the plan, "(ii) the acquisition, holding, or sale of a security or other property available as an investment under the plan pursuant to the investment advice, or

"(iii) the direct or indirect receipt of fees or other compensation by the fiduciary adviser or an affiliate thereof (or any employee, agent, or registered representative of the fiduciary adviser or affiliate) in connection with the provision of the advice or in connection with an acquisition, holding, or sale of a security or other property available as an investment under the plan pursuant to the investment advice; and

"(B) the requirements of subsection (g) are met.".

(2) REQUIREMENTS.—Section 408 of such Act is amended further by adding at the end the following new subsection:

"(g) PROVISION OF INVESTMENT ADVICE TO PARTICIPANT AND BENEFICIARIES.—

"(1) IN GENERAL.—The prohibitions provided in section 406 shall not apply to transactions described in subsection (b)(14) if the investment advice provided by a fiduciary adviser is provided under an eligible investment advice arrangement.

"(2) ELIGIBLE INVESTMENT ADVICE ARRANGEMENT.—For purposes of this subsection, the term 'eligible investment advice arrangement' means an arrangement—

"(A) which either—

"(i) provides that any fees (including any commission or other compensation) received by the fiduciary adviser for investment advice or with respect to the sale, holding, or acquisition of any security or other property for purposes of investment of plan assets do not vary depending on the basis of any investment option selected, or

"(ii) uses a computer model under an investment advice program meeting the requirements of paragraph (3) in connection with the provision of investment advice by a fiduciary adviser to a participant or beneficiary, and

"(B) with respect to which the requirements of paragraph (4), (5), (6), (7), (8), and (9) are met.

"(3) INVESTMENT ADVICE PROGRAM USING COMPUTER MODEL.—

"(A) IN GENERAL.—An investment advice program meets the requirements of this paragraph if the requirements of subparagraphs (B), (C), and (D) are met.

"(B) COMPUTER MODEL.—The requirements of this subparagraph are met if the investment advice provided under the investment advice program is provided pursuant to a computer model that—

"(i) applies generally accepted investment theories that take into account the historic returns of different asset classes over defined periods of time,

"(ii) utilizes relevant information about the participant, which may include age, life expectancy, retirement age, risk tolerance, other assets or sources of income, and preferences as to certain types of investments,

"(iii) utilizes prescribed objective criteria to provide asset allocation portfolios comprised of investment options available under the plan,

"(iv) operates in a manner that is not biased in favor of investments offered by the fiduciary adviser or a person with a material affiliation or contractual relationship with the fiduciary adviser, and

"(v) takes into account all investment options under the plan in specifying how a participant's account balance should be invested and is not inappropriately weighted with respect to any investment option.

"(C) CERTIFICATION.—

"(i) IN GENERAL.—The requirements of this subparagraph are met with respect to any investment advice program if an eligible investment expert certifies, prior to the utilization of the computer model and in accordance with rules prescribed by the Secretary, that the computer model meets the requirements of subparagraph (B).

"(ii) RENEWAL OF CERTIFICATIONS.—If, as determined under regulations prescribed by the Secretary, there are material modifications to a computer model, the requirements of this subparagraph are met only if a certification described in clause (i) is obtained with respect to the computer model as so modified.

"(iii) ELIGIBLE INVESTMENT EXPERT.—The term 'eligible investment expert' means any person—

"(I) which meets such requirements as the Secretary may provide, and

"(II) does not bear any material affiliation or contractual relationship with any investment adviser or a related person thereof (or any employee, agent, or registered representative of the investment adviser or related person).

"(D) EXCLUSIVITY OF RECOMMENDATION.—The requirements of this subparagraph are met with respect to any investment advice program if—

"(i) the only investment advice provided under the program is the advice generated by the computer model described in subparagraph (B), and

"(ii) any transaction described in subsection (b)(14)(B)(ii) occurs solely at the direction of the participant or beneficiary.

Nothing in the preceding sentence shall preclude the participant or beneficiary from requesting investment advice other than that described in subparagraph (A), but only if such request has not been solicited by any person connected with carrying out the arrangement.

"(4) EXPRESS AUTHORIZATION BY SEPARATE FIDUCIARY.—The requirements of this paragraph are met with respect to an arrangement if the arrangement is expressly authorized by a plan fiduciary other than the person offering the investment advice program, any person providing investment options under the plan, or any affiliate of either.

"(5) ANNUAL AUDIT.—The requirements of this paragraph are met if an independent auditor, who has appropriate technical training or experience and proficiency and so represents in writing—

"(A) conducts an annual audit of the arrangement for compliance with the requirements of this subsection, and

"(B) following completion of the annual audit, issues a written report to the fiduciary who authorized use of the arrangement which presents its specific findings regarding compliance of the arrangement with the requirements of this subsection.

For purposes of this paragraph, an auditor is considered independent if it is not related to the person offering the arrangement to the plan and is not related to any person providing investment options under the plan.

"(6) DISCLOSURE.—The requirements of this paragraph are met if—

"(A) the fiduciary adviser provides to a participant or a beneficiary before the initial provision of the investment advice with regard to any security or other property offered as an investment option, a written notification (which may consist of notification by means of electronic communication)—

"(i) of the role of any party that has a material affiliation or contractual relationship with the financial adviser in the development of the investment advice program and in the selection of investment options available under the plan,

"(ii) of the past performance and historical rates of return of the investment options available under the plan,

"(iii) of all fees or other compensation relating to the advice that the fiduciary adviser or any affiliate thereof is to receive (including compensation provided by any third party) in connection with the provision of the advice or in connection with the sale, acquisition, or holding of the security or other property,

"(iv) of any material affiliation or contractual relationship of the fiduciary adviser or affiliates thereof in the security or other property,

"(v) the manner, and under what circumstances, any participant or beneficiary information provided under the arrangement will be used or disclosed,

"(vi) of the types of services provided by the fiduciary adviser in connection with the provision of investment advice by the fiduciary adviser, "(vii) that the adviser is acting as a fiduciary of the plan in connection with the provision of the advice, and

"(viii) that a recipient of the advice may separately arrange for the provision of advice by another adviser, that could have no material affiliation with and receive no fees or other compensation in connection with the security or other property, and

"(B) at all times during the provision of advisory services to the participant or beneficiary, the fiduciary adviser—

"(i) maintains the information described in subparagraph (A) in accurate form and in the manner described in paragraph (8),

"(ii) provides, without charge, accurate information to the recipient of the advice no less frequently than annually,

"(iii) provides, without charge, accurate information to the recipient of the advice upon request of the recipient, and

"(iv) provides, without charge, accurate information to the recipient of the advice concerning any material change to the information required to be provided to the recipient of the advice at a time reasonably contemporaneous to the change in information.

"(7) OTHER CONDITIONS.—The requirements of this paragraph are met if—

"(A) the fiduciary adviser provides appropriate disclosure, in connection with the sale, acquisition, or holding of the security or other property, in accordance with all applicable securities laws,

"(B) the sale, acquisition, or holding occurs solely at the direction of the recipient of the advice,

"(C) the compensation received by the fiduciary adviser and affiliates thereof in connection with the sale, acquisition, or holding of the security or other property is reasonable, and

"(D) the terms of the sale, acquisition, or holding of the security or other property are at least as favorable to the plan as an arm's length transaction would be.

"(8) STANDARDS FOR PRESENTATION OF INFORMATION.—

"(A) IN GENERAL.—The requirements of this paragraph are met if the notification required to be provided to participants and beneficiaries under paragraph (6)(A) is written in a clear and conspicuous manner and in a manner calculated to be understood by the average plan participant and is sufficiently accurate and comprehensive to reasonably apprise such participants and beneficiaries of the information required to be provided in the notification.

"(B) MODEL FORM FOR DISCLOSURE OF FEES AND OTHER COMPENSATION.—The Secretary shall issue a model form for the disclosure of fees and other compensation required in paragraph (6)(A)(iii) which meets the requirements of subparagraph (A).

"(9) MAINTENANCE FOR 6 YEARS OF EVIDENCE OF COMPLIANCE.—The requirements of this paragraph are met if a fiduciary adviser who has provided advice referred to in paragraph (1) maintains, for a period of not less than 6 years after the provision of the advice, any records necessary for determining whether the requirements of the preceding provisions of this subsection and of subsection (b)(14) have been met. A transaction prohibited under section 406 shall not be considered to have occurred solely because the records are lost or destroyed prior to the end of the 6-year period due to circumstances beyond the control of the fiduciary adviser.

"(10) EXEMPTION FOR PLAN SPONSOR AND CERTAIN OTHER FIDUCIARIES.—

"(A) IN GENERAL.—Subject to subparagraph (B), a plan sponsor or other person who is a fiduciary (other than a fiduciary adviser) shall not be treated as failing to meet the requirements of this part solely by reason of the provision of investment advice referred to in section 3(21)(A)(ii) (or solely by reason of contracting for or otherwise arranging for the provision of the advice), if—

"(i) the advice is provided by a fiduciary adviser pursuant to an eligible investment advice arrangement between the plan sponsor or other fiduciary and the fiduciary adviser for the provision by the fiduciary adviser of investment advice referred to in such section,

"(ii) the terms of the eligible investment advice arrangement require compliance by the fiduciary adviser with the requirements of this subsection, and

"(iii) the terms of the eligible investment advice arrangement include a written acknowledgment by the fiduciary adviser that the fiduciary adviser is a fiduciary of the plan with respect to the provision of the advice.

"(B) CONTINUED DUTY OF PRUDENT SELECTION OF ADVISER AND PERIODIC REVIEW.—Nothing in subparagraph (A) shall be construed to exempt a plan sponsor or other person who is a fiduciary from any requirement of this part for the prudent selection and periodic review of a fiduciary adviser with whom the plan sponsor or other person enters into an eligible investment advice arrangement for the provision of investment advice referred to in section 3(21)(A)(ii). The plan sponsor or other person who is a fiduciary has no duty under this part to monitor the specific investment advice given by the fiduciary adviser to any particular recipient of the advice.

"(C) AVAILABILITY OF PLAN ASSETS FOR PAYMENT FOR ADVICE.—Nothing in this part shall be construed to preclude the use of plan assets to pay for reasonable expenses in providing investment advice referred to in section 3(21)(A)(ii).

"(11) DEFINITIONS.—For purposes of this subsection and subsection (b)(14)—

"(A) FIDUCIARY ADVISER.—The term 'fiduciary adviser' means, with respect to a plan, a person who is a fiduciary of the plan by reason of the provision of investment advice referred to in section 3(21)(A)(ii) by the person to the participant or beneficiary of the plan and who is—

"(i) registered as an investment adviser under the Investment Advisers Act of 1940 (15 U.S.C. 80b-1 et seq.) or under the laws of the State in which the fiduciary maintains its principal office and place of business,

"(ii) a bank or similar financial institution referred to in section 408(b)(4) or a savings association (as defined in section 3(b)(1) of the Federal Deposit Insurance Act (12 U.S.C. 1813(b)(1)), but only if the advice is provided through a trust department of the bank or similar financial institution or savings association which is subject to periodic examination and review by Federal or State banking authorities,

"(iii) an insurance company qualified to do business under the laws of a State,

"(iv) a person registered as a broker or dealer under the Securities Exchange Act of 1934 (15 U.S.C. 78a et seq.),

"(v) an affiliate of a person described in any of clauses (i) through (iv), or

"(vi) an employee, agent, or registered representative of a person described in clauses (i) through (v) who satisfies the requirements of applicable insurance, banking, and securities laws relating to the provision of the advice.

For purposes of this part, a person who develops the computer model described in paragraph (3)(B) or markets the investment advice program or computer model shall be treated as a person who is a fiduciary of the plan by reason of the provision of investment advice referred to in section 3(21)(A)(ii) to the participant or beneficiary and shall be treated as a fiduciary adviser for purposes of this subsection and subsection (b)(14), except that the Secretary may prescribe rules under which only 1 fiduciary adviser may elect to be treated as a fiduciary with respect to the plan.

"(B) AFFILIATE.—The term 'affiliate' of another entity means an affiliated person of the entity (as defined in section 2(a)(3) of the Investment Company Act of 1940 (15 U.S.C. 80a-2(a)(3))).

"(C) REGISTERED REPRESENTATIVE.—The term 'registered representative' of another entity means a person described in section 3(a)(18) of the Securities Exchange Act of 1934 (15 U.S.C. 78c(a)(18)) (substituting the entity for the broker or dealer referred to in such section) or a person described in section 202(a)(17) of the Investment Advisers Act of 1940 (15 U.S.C. 80b-2(a)(17)) (substituting the entity for the investment adviser referred to in such section).".

(3) EFFECTIVE DATE.—The amendments made by this subsection shall apply with respect to advice referred to in section 3(21)(A)(ii) of the Employee Retirement Income Security Act of 1974 provided after December 31, 2006.

(b) AMENDMENTS TO INTERNAL REVENUE CODE OF 1986.—

* * *

(3) DETERMINATION OF FEASIBILITY OF APPLICATION OF COMPUTER MODEL INVESTMENT ADVICE PROGRAMS FOR INDIVIDUAL RETIREMENT AND SIMILAR PLANS.—

(A) SOLICITATION OF INFORMATION.—As soon as practicable after the date of the enactment of this Act, the Secretary of Labor, in consultation with the Secretary of the Treasury, shall—

(i) solicit information as to the feasibility of the application of computer model investment advice programs for plans described in subparagraphs (B) through (F) (and so much of subparagraph (G) as relates to such subparagraphs) of section 4975(e)(1) of the Internal Revenue Code of 1986, including soliciting information from—

(I) at least the top 50 trustees of such plans, determined on the basis of assets held by such trustees, and

(II) other persons offering computer model investment advice programs based on nonproprietary products, and

(ii) shall on the basis of such information make the determination under subparagraph (B).

The information solicited by the Secretary of Labor under clause (i) from persons described in subclauses (I) and (II) of clause (i) shall include information on computer modeling capabilities of such persons with respect to the current year and preceding year, including such capabilities for investment accounts maintained by such persons.

(B) DETERMINATION OF FEASIBILITY.—The Secretary of Labor, in consultation with the Secretary of the Treasury, shall, on the basis of information received under subparagraph (A), determine whether there is any computer model investment advice program which may be utilized by a plan described in subparagraph (A)(i) to provide investment advice to the account beneficiary of the plan which—

(i) utilizes relevant information about the account beneficiary, which may include age, life expectancy, retirement age, risk tolerance, other assets or sources of income, and preferences as to certain types of investments,

(ii) takes into account the full range of investments, including equities and bonds, in determining the options for the investment portfolio of the account beneficiary, and

(iii) allows the account beneficiary, in directing the investment of assets, sufficient flexibility in obtaining advice to evaluate and select investment options.

The Secretary of Labor shall report the results of such determination to the committees of Congress referred to in subparagraph (D)(ii) not later than December 31, 2007.

(C) APPLICATION OF COMPUTER MODEL INVESTMENT ADVICE PROGRAM.—

(i) CERTIFICATION REQUIRED FOR USE OF COMPUTER MODEL.—

(I) RESTRICTION ON USE.—Subclause (II) of section 4975(f)(8)(B)(i) of the Internal Revenue Code of 1986 shall not apply to a plan described in subparagraph (A)(i).

(II) RESTRICTION LIFTED IF MODEL CERTIFIED.—If the Secretary of Labor determines under subparagraph (B) or (D) that there is a computer model investment advice program described in subparagraph (B), subclause (I) shall cease to apply as of the date of such determination.

(ii) CLASS EXEMPTION IF NO INITIAL CERTIFICATION BY SECRETARY.—If the Secretary of Labor determines under subparagraph (B) that there is no computer model investment advice program described in subparagraph (B), the Secretary of Labor shall grant a class exemption from treatment as a prohibited transaction under section 4975(c) of the Internal Revenue Code of 1986 to any transaction described in section 4975(d)(17)(A) of such Code with respect to plans described in subparagraph (A)(i), subject to such conditions as set forth in such exemption as are in the interests of the plan and its account beneficiary and protective of the rights of the account beneficiary and as are necessary to—

(I) ensure the requirements of sections 4975(d)(17) and 4975(f)(8) (other than subparagraph (C) thereof) of the Internal Revenue Code of 1986 are met, and

(II) ensure the investment advice provided under the investment advice program utilizes prescribed objective criteria to provide asset allocation portfolios comprised of securities or other property available as investments under the plan.

If the Secretary of Labor solicits any information under subparagraph (A) from a person and such person does not provide such information within 60 days after the solicitation, then, unless such failure was due to reasonable cause and not wilful neglect, such person shall not be entitled to utilize the class exemption under this clause.

(D) SUBSEQUENT DETERMINATION.—

(i) IN GENERAL.—If the Secretary of Labor initially makes a determination described in subparagraph (C)(ii), the Secretary may subsequently determine that there is a computer model investment advice program described in subparagraph (B). If the Secretary makes such subsequent determination, then the class exemption described in subparagraph (C)(ii) shall cease to apply after the later of—

(I) the date which is 2 years after such subsequent determination, or

(II) the date which is 3 years after the first date on which such exemption took effect.

(ii) REQUESTS FOR DETERMINATION.—Any person may request the Secretary of Labor to make a determination under this subparagraph with respect to any computer model investment advice program, and the Secretary of Labor shall make a determination with respect to such request within 90 days. If the Secretary of Labor makes a determination that such program is not described in subparagraph (B), the Secretary shall, within 10 days of such determination, notify the Committee on Ways and Means and the Committee on Education and the Workforce of the House of Representatives and the Committee on Finance and the Committee on Health, Education, Labor, and Pensions of the Senate of such determination and the reasons for such determination.

(E) EFFECTIVE DATE.—The provisions of this paragraph shall take effect on the date of the enactment of this Act.

* * *

(c) COORDINATION WITH EXISTING EXEMPTIONS.—Any exemption under section 408(b) of the Employee Retirement Income Security Act of 1974 and section 4975(d) of the Internal Revenue Code of 1986 provided by the amendments made by this section shall not in any manner alter existing individual or class exemptions, provided by statute or administrative action.

[CCH Explanation at ¶625. Committee Reports at ¶10,420.]

Subtitle B—Prohibited Transactions

[¶7126] ACT SEC. 611. PROHIBITED TRANSACTION RULES RELATING TO FINANCIAL INVESTMENTS.

(a) EXEMPTION FOR BLOCK TRADING.—

(1) AMENDMENTS TO EMPLOYEE RETIREMENT INCOME SECURITY ACT OF 1974.—Section 408(b) of such Act (29 U.S.C. 1108(b)), as amended by section 601, is amended by adding at the end the following new paragraph:

"(15)(A) Any transaction involving the purchase or sale of securities, or other property (as determined by the Secretary), between a plan and a party in interest (other than a fiduciary described in section 3(21)(A)) with respect to a plan if—

"(i) the transaction involves a block trade,

"(ii) at the time of the transaction, the interest of the plan (together with the interests of any other plans maintained by the same plan sponsor), does not exceed 10 percent of the aggregate size of the block trade,

"(iii) the terms of the transaction, including the price, are at least as favorable to the plan as an arm's length transaction, and

"(iv) the compensation associated with the purchase and sale is not greater than the compensation associated with an arm's length transaction with an unrelated party.

"(B) For purposes of this paragraph, the term 'block trade' means any trade of at least 10,000 shares or with a market value of at least $200,000 which will be allocated across two or more unrelated client accounts of a fiduciary.".

* * *

(b) BONDING RELIEF.—Section 412(a) of such Act (29 U.S.C. 1112(a)) is amended—

(1) by redesignating paragraph (2) as paragraph (3),

(2) by striking "and" at the end of paragraph (1), and

(3) by inserting after paragraph (1) the following new paragraph:

"(2) no bond shall be required of any entity which is registered as a broker or a dealer under section 15(b) of the Securities Exchange Act of 1934 (15 U.S.C. 78o(b)) if the broker or dealer is subject to the fidelity bond requirements of a self-regulatory organization (within the meaning of section 3(a)(26) of such Act (15 U.S.C. 78c(a)(26)).".

(c) EXEMPTION FOR ELECTRONIC COMMUNICATION NETWORK.—

(1) AMENDMENTS TO EMPLOYEE RETIREMENT INCOME SECURITY ACT OF 1974.—Section 408(b) of such Act, as amended by subsection (a), is amended by adding at the end the following:

"(16) Any transaction involving the purchase or sale of securities, or other property (as determined by the Secretary), between a plan and a party in interest if—

"(A) the transaction is executed through an electronic communication network, alternative trading system, or similar execution system or trading venue subject to regulation and oversight by—

"(i) the applicable Federal regulating entity, or

"(ii) such foreign regulatory entity as the Secretary may determine by regulation,

"(B) either—

"(i) the transaction is effected pursuant to rules designed to match purchases and sales at the best price available through the execution system in accordance with applicable rules of the Securities and Exchange Commission or other relevant governmental authority, or

"(ii) neither the execution system nor the parties to the transaction take into account the identity of the parties in the execution of trades,

"(C) the price and compensation associated with the purchase and sale are not greater than the price and compensation associated with an arm's length transaction with an unrelated party,

"(D) if the party in interest has an ownership interest in the system or venue described in subparagraph (A), the system or venue has been authorized by the plan sponsor or other independent fiduciary for transactions described in this paragraph, and

"(E) not less than 30 days prior to the initial transaction described in this paragraph executed through any system or venue described in subparagraph (A), a plan fiduciary is provided written or electronic notice of the execution of such transaction through such system or venue.".

* * *

(d) EXEMPTION FOR SERVICE PROVIDERS.—

(1) AMENDMENTS TO EMPLOYEE RETIREMENT INCOME SECURITY ACT OF 1974.—Section 408(b) of such Act (29 U.S.C. 1106), as amended by subsection (c), is amended by adding at the end the following new paragraph:

"(17)(A) Transactions described in subparagraphs (A), (B), and (D) of section 406(a)(1) between a plan and a person that is a party in interest other than a fiduciary (or an affiliate) who has or exercises any discretionary authority or control with respect to the investment of the plan assets involved in the transaction or renders investment advice (within the meaning of section 3(21)(A)(ii)) with respect to those assets, solely by reason of providing services to the plan or solely by reason of a relationship to such a service provider described in subparagraph (F), (G), (H), or (I) of section 3(14), or both, but only if in connection with such transaction the plan receives no less, nor pays no more, than adequate consideration.

"(B) For purposes of this paragraph, the term 'adequate consideration' means—

"(i) in the case of a security for which there is a generally recognized market—

"(I) the price of the security prevailing on a national securities exchange which is registered under section 6 of the Securities Exchange Act of 1934, taking into account factors such as the size of the transaction and marketability of the security, or

"(II) if the security is not traded on such a national securities exchange, a price not less favorable to the plan than the offering price for the security as established by the current bid and asked prices quoted by persons independent of the issuer and of the party in interest, taking into account factors such as the size of the transaction and marketability of the security, and

"(ii) in the case of an asset other than a security for which there is a generally recognized market, the fair market value of the asset as determined in good faith by a fiduciary or fiduciaries in accordance with regulations prescribed by the Secretary.".

* * *

(e) RELIEF FOR FOREIGN EXCHANGE TRANSACTIONS.—

(1) AMENDMENTS TO EMPLOYEE RETIREMENT INCOME SECURITY ACT OF 1974.—Section 408(b) of such Act (29 U.S.C. 1108(b)), as amended by subsection (d), is amended by adding at the end the following new paragraph:

"(18) FOREIGN EXCHANGE TRANSACTIONS.—Any foreign exchange transactions, between a bank or broker-dealer (or any affiliate of either), and a plan (as defined in section 3(3)) with respect to which such bank or broker-dealer (or affiliate) is a trustee, custodian, fiduciary, or other party in interest, if—

"(A) the transaction is in connection with the purchase, holding, or sale of securities or other investment assets (other than a foreign exchange transaction unrelated to any other investment in securities or other investment assets),

"(B) at the time the foreign exchange transaction is entered into, the terms of the transaction are not less favorable to the plan than the terms generally available in comparable arm's length foreign exchange transactions between unrelated parties, or the terms afforded by the bank or broker-dealer (or any affiliate of either) in comparable arm's-length foreign exchange transactions involving unrelated parties,

"(C) the exchange rate used by such bank or broker-dealer (or affiliate) for a particular foreign exchange transaction does not deviate by more or less than 3 percent from the interbank bid and asked rates for transactions of comparable size and maturity at the time of the transaction as displayed on an independent service that reports rates of exchange in the foreign currency market for such currency, and

"(D) the bank or broker-dealer (or any affiliate of either) does not have investment discretion, or provide investment advice, with respect to the transaction.".

* * *

(f) DEFINITION OF PLAN ASSET VEHICLE.—Section 3 of such Act (29 U.S.C. 1002) is amended by adding at the end the following new paragraph:

"(42) the term 'plan assets' means plan assets as defined by such regulations as the Secretary may prescribe, except that under such regulations the assets of any entity shall not be treated as plan assets if, immediately after the most recent acquisition of any equity interest in the entity, less than 25 percent of the total value of each class of equity interest in the entity is held by benefit plan investors. For purposes of determinations pursuant to this paragraph, the value of any equity interest held by a person (other than such a benefit plan investor) who has discretionary authority or control with respect to the assets of the entity or any person who provides investment advice for a fee (direct or indirect) with respect to such assets, or any affiliate of such a person, shall be disregarded for purposes of calculating the 25 percent threshold. An entity shall be considered to hold plan assets only to the extent of the percentage of the equity interest held by benefit plan investors. For purposes of this paragraph, the term 'benefit plan investor' means an employee benefit plan subject to part 4, any plan to which section 4975 of the Internal Revenue Code of 1986 applies, and any entity whose underlying assets include plan assets by reason of a plan's investment in such entity.".

(g) EXEMPTION FOR CROSS TRADING.—

(1) AMENDMENTS TO EMPLOYEE RETIREMENT INCOME SECURITY ACT OF 1974.—Section 408(b) of such Act (29 U.S.C. 1108(b)), as amended by subsection (e), is amended by adding at the end the following new paragraph:

"(19) CROSS TRADING.—Any transaction described in sections 406(a)(1)(A) and 406(b)(2) involving the purchase and sale of a security between a plan and any other account managed by the same investment manager, if—

"(A) the transaction is a purchase or sale, for no consideration other than cash payment against prompt delivery of a security for which market quotations are readily available,

"(B) the transaction is effected at the independent current market price of the security (within the meaning of section 270.17a-7(b) of title 17, Code of Federal Regulations),

"(C) no brokerage commission, fee (except for customary transfer fees, the fact of which is disclosed pursuant to subparagraph (D)), or other remuneration is paid in connection with the transaction,

"(D) a fiduciary (other than the investment manager engaging in the cross-trades or any affiliate) for each plan participating in the transaction authorizes in advance of any crosstrades (in a document that is separate from any other written agreement of the parties) the investment manager to engage in cross trades at the investment manager's discretion, after such fiduciary has received disclosure regarding the conditions under which cross trades may take place (but only if such disclosure is separate from any other agreement or disclosure involving the asset management relationship), including the written policies and procedures of the investment manager described in subparagraph (H),

"(E) each plan participating in the transaction has assets of at least $100,000,000, except that if the assets of a plan are invested in a master trust containing the assets of plans maintained by employers in the same controlled group (as defined in section 407(d)(7)), the master trust has assets of at least $100,000,000,

"(F) the investment manager provides to the plan fiduciary who authorized cross trading under subparagraph (D) a quarterly report detailing all cross trades executed by the investment manager in which the plan participated during such quarter, including the following information, as applicable: (i) the identity of each security bought or sold; (ii) the number of shares or units traded, (iii) the parties involved in the cross-trade; and (iv) trade price and the method used to establish the trade price,

"(G) the investment manager does not base its fee schedule on the plan's consent to cross trading, and no other service (other than the investment opportunities and cost savings available through a cross trade) is conditioned on the plan's consent to cross trading,

"(H) the investment manager has adopted, and cross-trades are effected in accordance with, written cross-trading policies and procedures that are fair and equitable to all accounts participating in the cross-trading program, and that include a description of the manager's pricing policies and procedures, and the manager's policies and procedures for allocating cross trades in an objective manner among accounts participating in the cross-trading program, and

"(I) the investment manager has designated an individual responsible for periodically reviewing such purchases and sales to ensure compliance with the written policies and procedures described in subparagraph (H), and following such review, the individual shall issue an annual written report no later than 90 days following the period to which it relates signed under penalty of perjury to the plan fiduciary who authorized cross trading under subparagraph (D) describing the steps performed during the course of the review, the level of compliance, and any specific instances of non-compliance.

The written report under subparagraph (I) shall also notify the plan fiduciary of the plan's right to terminate participation in the investment manager's cross-trading program at any time.".

* * *

(3) REGULATIONS.—No later than 180 days after the date of the enactment of this Act, the Secretary of Labor, after consultation with the Securities and Exchange Commission, shall issue regulations regarding the content of policies and procedures required to be adopted by an investment manager under section 408(b)(19) of the Employee Retirement Income Security Act of 1974.

(h) EFFECTIVE DATES.—

(1) IN GENERAL.—Except as provided in paragraph (2), the amendments made by this section shall apply to transactions occurring after the date of the enactment of this Act.

(2) BONDING RULE.—The amendments made by subsection (b) shall apply to plan years beginning after such date.

[CCH Explanation at ¶630. Committee Reports at ¶10,430, ¶10,440, ¶10,450, ¶10,460, ¶10,470, ¶10,480 and ¶10,490.]

[¶7129] ACT SEC. 612. CORRECTION PERIOD FOR CERTAIN TRANSACTIONS INVOLVING SECURITIES AND COMMODITIES.

(a) AMENDMENT OF EMPLOYEE RETIREMENT INCOME SECURITY ACT OF 1974.—Section 408(b) of the Employee Retirement Income Security Act of 1974 (29 U.S.C. 1108(b)), as amended by sections 601 and 611, is further amended by adding at the end the following new paragraph:

"(20)(A) Except as provided in subparagraphs (B) and (C), a transaction described in section 406(a) in connection with the acquisition, holding, or disposition of any security or commodity, if the transaction is corrected before the end of the correction period.

"(B) Subparagraph (A) does not apply to any transaction between a plan and a plan sponsor or its affiliates that involves the acquisition or sale of an employer security (as defined in section 407(d)(1)) or the acquisition, sale, or lease of employer real property (as defined in section 407(d)(2)).

"(C) In the case of any fiduciary or other party in interest (or any other person knowingly participating in such transaction), subparagraph (A) does not apply to any transaction if, at the time the transaction occurs, such fiduciary or party in interest (or other person) knew (or reasonably should have known) that the transaction would (without regard to this paragraph) constitute a violation of section 406(a).

"(D) For purposes of this paragraph, the term 'correction period' means, in connection with a fiduciary or party in interest (or other person knowingly participating in the transaction), the 14-day period beginning on the date on which such fiduciary or party in interest (or other person) discovers, or reasonably should have discovered, that the transaction would (without regard to this paragraph) constitute a violation of section 406(a).

"(E) For purposes of this paragraph—

"(i) The term 'security' has the meaning given such term by section 475(c)(2) of the Internal Revenue Code of 1986 (without regard to subparagraph (F)(iii) and the last sentence thereof).

"(ii) The term 'commodity' has the meaning given such term by section 475(e)(2) of such Code (without regard to subparagraph (D)(iii) thereof).

"(iii) The term 'correct' means, with respect to a transaction—

"(I) to undo the transaction to the extent possible and in any case to make good to the plan or affected account any losses resulting from the transaction, and

"(II) to restore to the plan or affected account any profits made through the use of assets of the plan.".

* * *

(c) EFFECTIVE DATE.—The amendments made by this section shall apply to any transaction which the fiduciary or disqualified person discovers, or reasonably should have discovered, after the date of the enactment of this Act constitutes a prohibited transaction.

[CCH Explanation at ¶ 635. Committee Reports at ¶ 10,500.]

Subtitle C—Fiduciary and Other Rules

[¶ 7132] ACT SEC. 621. INAPPLICABILITY OF RELIEF FROM FIDUCIARY LIABILITY DURING SUSPENSION OF ABILITY OF PARTICIPANT OR BENEFICIARY TO DIRECT INVESTMENTS.

(a) IN GENERAL.—Section 404(c) of the Employee Retirement Income Security Act of 1974 (29 U.S.C. 1104(c)) is amended—

(1) in paragraph (1)—

(A) by redesignating subparagraphs (A) and (B) as clauses (i) and (ii), respectively, and by inserting "(A)" after "(c)(1)",

(B) in subparagraph (A)(ii) (as redesignated by paragraph (1)), by inserting before the period the following: ", except that this clause shall not apply in connection with such participant or beneficiary for any blackout period during which the ability of such participant or beneficiary to direct the investment of the assets in his or her account is suspended by a plan sponsor or fiduciary", and

(C) by adding at the end the following new subparagraphs:

"(B) If a person referred to in subparagraph (A)(ii) meets the requirements of this title in connection with authorizing and implementing the blackout period, any person who is otherwise a fiduciary shall not be liable under this title for any loss occurring during such period.

"(C) For purposes of this paragraph, the term 'blackout period' has the meaning given such term by section 101(i)(7)."; and

(2) by adding at the end the following:

"(4)(A) In any case in which a qualified change in investment options occurs in connection with an individual account plan, a participant or beneficiary shall not be treated for purposes of paragraph (1) as not exercising control over the assets in his account in connection with such change if the requirements of subparagraph (C) are met in connection with such change.

"(B) For purposes of subparagraph (A), the term 'qualified change in investment options' means, in connection with an individual account plan, a change in the investment options offered to the participant or beneficiary under the terms of the plan, under which—

"(i) the account of the participant or beneficiary is reallocated among one or more remaining or new investment options which are offered in lieu of one or more investment options offered immediately prior to the effective date of the change, and

"(ii) the stated characteristics of the remaining or new investment options provided under clause (i), including characteristics relating to risk and rate of return, are, as of immediately after the change, reasonably similar to those of the existing investment options as of immediately before the change.

"(C) The requirements of this subparagraph are met in connection with a qualified change in investment options if—

"(i) at least 30 days and no more than 60 days prior to the effective date of the change, the plan administrator furnishes written notice of the change to the participants and beneficiaries, including information comparing the existing and new investment options and an explanation that, in the absence of affirmative investment instructions from the participant or beneficiary to the contrary, the account of the participant or beneficiary will be invested in the manner described in subparagraph (B),

"(ii) the participant or beneficiary has not provided to the plan administrator, in advance of the effective date of the change, affirmative investment instructions contrary to the change, and

"(iii) the investments under the plan of the participant or beneficiary as in effect immediately prior to the effective date of the change were the product of the exercise by such participant or beneficiary of control over the assets of the account within the meaning of paragraph (1).".

(b) EFFECTIVE DATE.—

(1) IN GENERAL.—The amendments made by this section shall apply to plan years beginning after December 31, 2007.

(2) SPECIAL RULE FOR COLLECTIVELY BARGAINED AGREEMENTS.—In the case of a plan maintained pursuant to 1 or more collective bargaining agreements between employee representatives and 1 or more employers ratified on or before the date of the enactment of this Act, paragraph (1) shall be applied to benefits pursuant to, and individuals covered by, any such agreement by substituting for "December 31, 2007" the earlier of—

(A) the later of—

(i) December 31, 2008, or

(ii) the date on which the last of such collective bargaining agreements terminates (determined without regard to any extension thereof after such date of enactment), or

(B) December 31, 2009.

[CCH Explanation at ¶640. Committee Reports at ¶10,510.]

[¶7135] ACT SEC. 622. INCREASE IN MAXIMUM BOND AMOUNT.

(a) IN GENERAL.—Section 412(a) of the Employee Retirement Income Security Act of 1974 (29 U.S.C. 1112), as amended by section 611(b), is amended by adding at the end the following: "In the case of a plan that holds employer securities (within the meaning of section 407(d)(1)), this subsection shall be applied by substituting '$1,000,000' for '$500,000' each place it appears."

(b) EFFECTIVE DATE.—The amendment made by this section shall apply to plan years beginning after December 31, 2007.

[CCH Explanation at ¶645. Committee Reports at ¶10,520.]

[¶7138] ACT SEC. 623. INCREASE IN PENALTIES FOR COERCIVE INTERFERENCE WITH EXERCISE OF ERISA RIGHTS.

(a) IN GENERAL.—Section 511 of the Employment Retirement Income Security Act of 1974 (29 U.S.C. 1141) is amended—

(1) by striking "$10,000" and inserting"$100,000", and

(2) by striking "one year" and inserting "10 years".

(b) EFFECTIVE DATE.—The amendments made by this section shall apply to violations occurring on and after the date of the enactment of this Act.

[CCH Explanation at ¶650. Committee Reports at ¶10,530.]

[¶7141] ACT SEC. 624. TREATMENT OF INVESTMENT OF ASSETS BY PLAN WHERE PARTICIPANT FAILS TO EXERCISE INVESTMENT ELECTION.

(a) IN GENERAL.—Section 404(c) of the Employee Retirement Income Security Act of 1974 (29 U.S.C. 1104(c)), as amended by section 622, is amended by adding at the end the following new paragraph:

"(5) DEFAULT INVESTMENT ARRANGEMENTS.—

"(A) IN GENERAL.—For purposes of paragraph (1), a participant in an individual account plan meeting the notice requirements of subparagraph (B) shall be treated as exercising control over the assets in the account with respect to the amount of contributions and earnings which, in the absence of an investment election by the participant, are invested by the plan in accordance with regulations prescribed by the Secretary. The regulations under this subparagraph shall provide guidance on the appropriateness of designating default investments that include a mix of asset classes consistent with capital preservation or long-term capital appreciation, or a blend of both.

"(B) NOTICE REQUIREMENTS.—

"(i) IN GENERAL.—The requirements of this subparagraph are met if each participant—

"(I) receives, within a reasonable period of time before each plan year, a notice explaining the employee's right under the plan to designate how contributions and earnings will be invested and explaining how, in the absence of any investment election by the participant, such contributions and earnings will be invested, and

"(II) has a reasonable period of time after receipt of such notice and before the beginning of the plan year to make such designation.

"(ii) FORM OF NOTICE.—The requirements of clauses (i) and (ii) of section 401(k)(12)(D) of the Internal Revenue Code of 1986 shall apply with respect to the notices described in this subparagraph.".

(b) EFFECTIVE DATE.—

(1) IN GENERAL.—The amendments made by this section shall apply to plan years beginning after December 31, 2006.

(2) REGULATIONS.—Final regulations under section 404(c)(5)(A) of the Employee Retirement Income Security Act of 1974 (as added by this section) shall be issued no later than 6 months after the date of the enactment of this Act.

[CCH Explanation at ¶655. Committee Reports at ¶10,540.]

[¶7144] ACT SEC. 625. CLARIFICATION OF FIDUCIARY RULES.

(a) IN GENERAL.—Not later than 1 year after the date of the enactment of this Act, the Secretary of Labor shall issue final regulations clarifying that the selection of an annuity contract as an optional form of distribution from an individual account plan to a participant or beneficiary—

(1) is not subject to the safest available annuity standard under Interpretive Bulletin 95-1 (29 C.F.R. 2509.95-1), and

(2) is subject to all otherwise applicable fiduciary standards.

(b) EFFECTIVE DATE.—This section shall take effect on the date of enactment of this Act.

[CCH Explanation at ¶660. Committee Reports at ¶10,550.]

TITLE VII—BENEFIT ACCRUAL STANDARDS

[¶7147] ACT SEC. 701. BENEFIT ACCRUAL STANDARDS.

(a) AMENDMENTS TO THE EMPLOYEE RETIREMENT INCOME SECURITY ACT OF 1974.—

(1) RULES RELATING TO REDUCTION IN RATE OF BENEFIT ACCRUAL.—Section 204(b) of the Employee Retirement Income Security Act of 1974 (29 U.S.C. 1054(b)) is amended by adding at the end the following new paragraph:

"(5) SPECIAL RULES RELATING TO AGE.—

"(A) COMPARISON TO SIMILARLY SITUATED YOUNGER INDIVIDUAL.—

"(i) IN GENERAL.—A plan shall not be treated as failing to meet the requirements of paragraph (1)(H)(i) if a participant's accrued benefit, as determined as of any date under the terms of the plan, would be equal to or greater than that of any similarly situated, younger individual who is or could be a participant.

"(ii) SIMILARLY SITUATED.—For purposes of this subparagraph, a participant is similarly situated to any other individual if such participant is identical to such other individual in every respect (including period of service, compensation, position, date of hire, work history, and any other respect) except for age.

"(iii) DISREGARD OF SUBSIDIZED EARLY RETIREMENT BENEFITS.—In determining the accrued benefit as of any date for purposes of this clause, the subsidized portion of any early retirement benefit or retirement-type subsidy shall be disregarded.

"(iv) ACCRUED BENEFIT.—For purposes of this subparagraph, the accrued benefit may, under the terms of the plan, be expressed as an annuity payable at normal retirement age, the balance of a hypothetical account, or the current value of the accumulated percentage of the employee's final average compensation.

"(B) APPLICABLE DEFINED BENEFIT PLANS.—

"(i) INTEREST CREDITS.—

"(I) IN GENERAL.—An applicable defined benefit plan shall be treated as failing to meet the requirements of paragraph (1)(H) unless the terms of the plan provide that any interest credit (or an equivalent amount) for any plan year shall be at a rate which is not greater than a market rate of return. A plan shall not be treated as failing to meet the requirements of this subclause merely because the plan provides for a reasonable minimum guaranteed rate of return or for a rate of return that is equal to the greater of a fixed or variable rate of return.

"(II) PRESERVATION OF CAPITAL.—An interest credit (or an equivalent amount) of less than zero shall in no event result in the account balance or similar amount being less than the aggregate amount of contributions credited to the account.

"(III) MARKET RATE OF RETURN.—The Secretary of the Treasury may provide by regulation for rules governing the calculation of a market rate of return for purposes of subclause (I) and for permissible methods of crediting interest to the account (including fixed or variable interest rates) resulting in effective rates of return meeting the requirements of subclause (I).

"(ii) SPECIAL RULE FOR PLAN CONVERSIONS.—If, after June 29, 2005, an applicable plan amendment is adopted, the plan shall be treated as failing to meet the requirements of paragraph (1)(H) unless the requirements of clause (iii) are met with respect to each individual who was a participant in the plan immediately before the adoption of the amendment.

"(iii) RATE OF BENEFIT ACCRUAL.—Subject to clause (iv), the requirements of this clause are met with respect to any participant if the accrued benefit of the participant under the terms of the plan as in effect after the amendment is not less than the sum of—

"(I) the participant's accrued benefit for years of service before the effective date of the amendment, determined under the terms of the plan as in effect before the amendment, plus

"(II) the participant's accrued benefit for years of service after the effective date of the amendment, determined under the terms of the plan as in effect after the amendment.

"(iv) SPECIAL RULES FOR EARLY RETIREMENT SUBSIDIES.—For purposes of clause (iii)(I), the plan shall credit the accumulation account or similar amount with the amount of any early retirement benefit or retirement-type subsidy for the plan year in which the participant retires if, as of such time, the participant has met the age, years of service, and other requirements under the plan for entitlement to such benefit or subsidy.

"(v) APPLICABLE PLAN AMENDMENT.—For purposes of this subparagraph—

"(I) IN GENERAL.—The term 'applicable plan amendment' means an amendment to a defined benefit plan which has the effect of converting the plan to an applicable defined benefit plan.

"(II) SPECIAL RULE FOR COORDINATED BENEFITS.—If the benefits of 2 or more defined benefit plans established or maintained by an employer are coordinated in such a manner as to have the effect of the adoption of an amendment described in subclause (I), the sponsor of the defined benefit plan or plans providing for such coordination shall be treated as having adopted such a plan amendment as of the date such coordination begins.

"(III) MULTIPLE AMENDMENTS.—The Secretary of the Treasury shall issue regulations to prevent the avoidance of the purposes of this subparagraph through the use of 2 or more plan amendments rather than a single amendment.

"(IV) APPLICABLE DEFINED BENEFIT PLAN.—For purposes of this subparagraph, the term 'applicable defined benefit plan' has the meaning given such term by section 203(f)(3).

"(vi) TERMINATION REQUIREMENTS.—An applicable defined benefit plan shall not be treated as meeting the requirements of clause (i) unless the plan provides that, upon the termination of the plan—

"(I) if the interest credit rate (or an equivalent amount) under the plan is a variable rate, the rate of interest used to determine accrued benefits under the plan shall be equal to the average of the rates of interest used under the plan during the 5-year period ending on the termination date, and

"(II) the interest rate and mortality table used to determine the amount of any benefit under the plan payable in the form of an annuity payable at normal retirement age shall be the rate and table specified under the plan for such purpose as of the termination date, except that if such interest rate is a variable rate, the interest rate shall be determined under the rules of subclause (I).

"(C) CERTAIN OFFSETS PERMITTED.—A plan shall not be treated as failing to meet the requirements of paragraph (1)(H)(i) solely because the plan provides offsets against benefits under the plan to the extent such offsets are allowable in applying the requirements of section 401(a) of the Internal Revenue Code of 1986.

"(D) PERMITTED DISPARITIES IN PLAN CONTRIBUTIONS OR BENEFITS.—A plan shall not be treated as failing to meet the requirements of paragraph (1)(H) solely because the plan provides a disparity in contributions or benefits with respect to which the requirements of section 401(l) of the Internal Revenue Code of 1986 are met.

"(E) INDEXING PERMITTED.—

"(i) IN GENERAL.—A plan shall not be treated as failing to meet the requirements of paragraph (1)(H) solely because the plan provides for indexing of accrued benefits under the plan.

"(ii) PROTECTION AGAINST LOSS.—Except in the case of any benefit provided in the form of a variable annuity, clause (i) shall not apply with respect to any indexing which results in an accrued benefit less than the accrued benefit determined without regard to such indexing.

"(iii) INDEXING.—For purposes of this subparagraph, the term 'indexing' means, in connection with an accrued benefit, the periodic adjustment of the accrued benefit by means of the application of a recognized investment index or methodology.

"(F) EARLY RETIREMENT BENEFIT OR RETIREMENT-TYPE SUBSIDY.—For purposes of this paragraph, the terms 'early retirement benefit' and 'retirement-type subsidy' have the meaning given such terms in subsection (g)(2)(A).

"(G) BENEFIT ACCRUED TO DATE.—For purposes of this paragraph, any reference to the accrued benefit shall be a reference to such benefit accrued to date.".

(2) DETERMINATIONS OF ACCRUED BENEFIT AS BALANCE OF BENEFIT ACCOUNT OR EQUIVALENT AMOUNTS.—Section 203 of such Act (29 U.S.C. 1053) is amended by adding at the end the following new subsection:

"(f) SPECIAL RULES FOR PLANS COMPUTING ACCRUED BENEFITS BY REFERENCE TO HYPOTHETICAL ACCOUNT BALANCE OR EQUIVALENT AMOUNTS.—

"(1) IN GENERAL.—An applicable defined benefit plan shall not be treated as failing to meet—

"(A) subject to paragraph (2), the requirements of subsection (a)(2), or

"(B) the requirements of section 204(c) or section 205(g) with respect to contributions other than employee contributions,

solely because the present value of the accrued benefit (or any portion thereof) of any participant is, under the terms of the plan, equal to the amount expressed as the balance in the hypothetical account described in paragraph (3) or as an accumulated percentage of the participant's final average compensation.

"(2) 3-YEAR VESTING.—In the case of an applicable defined benefit plan, such plan shall be treated as meeting the requirements of subsection (a)(2) only if an employee who has completed at least 3 years of service has a nonforfeitable right to 100 percent of the employee's accrued benefit derived from employer contributions.

"(3) APPLICABLE DEFINED BENEFIT PLAN AND RELATED RULES.—For purposes of this subsection—

"(A) IN GENERAL.—The term 'applicable defined benefit plan' means a defined benefit plan under which the accrued benefit (or any portion thereof) is calculated as the balance of a hypothetical account maintained for the participant or as an accumulated percentage of the participant's final average compensation.

"(B) REGULATIONS TO INCLUDE SIMILAR PLANS.—The Secretary of the Treasury shall issue regulations which include in the definition of an applicable defined benefit plan any defined benefit plan (or any portion of such a plan) which has an effect similar to an applicable defined benefit plan.".

* * *

(c) AMENDMENTS TO AGE DISCRIMINATION IN EMPLOYMENT ACT.—Section 4(i) of the Age Discrimination in Employment Act of 1967 (29 U.S.C. 623(i)) is amended by adding at the end the following new paragraph:

"(10) SPECIAL RULES RELATING TO AGE.—

"(A) COMPARISON TO SIMILARLY SITUATED YOUNGER INDIVIDUAL.—

"(i) IN GENERAL.—A plan shall not be treated as failing to meet the requirements of paragraph (1) if a participant's accrued benefit, as determined as of any date under the terms of the plan, would be equal to or greater than that of any similarly situated, younger individual who is or could be a participant.

"(ii) SIMILARLY SITUATED.—For purposes of this subparagraph, a participant is similarly situated to any other individual if such participant is identical to such other individual in every respect (including period of service, compensation, position, date of hire, work history, and any other respect) except for age.

"(iii) DISREGARD OF SUBSIDIZED EARLY RETIREMENT BENEFITS.—In determining the accrued benefit as of any date for purposes of this clause, the subsidized portion of any early retirement benefit or retirement-type subsidy shall be disregarded.

"(iv) ACCRUED BENEFIT.—For purposes of this subparagraph, the accrued benefit may, under the terms of the plan, be expressed as an annuity payable at normal retirement age, the balance of a hypothetical account, or the current value of the accumulated percentage of the employee's final average compensation.

"(B) APPLICABLE DEFINED BENEFIT PLANS.—

"(i) INTEREST CREDITS.—

"(I) IN GENERAL.—An applicable defined benefit plan shall be treated as failing to meet the requirements of paragraph (1) unless the terms of the plan provide that any interest credit (or an equivalent amount) for any plan year shall be at a rate which is not greater than a market rate of return. A plan shall not be treated as failing to meet the requirements of this subclause merely because the plan provides for a reasonable minimum guaranteed rate of return or for a rate of return that is equal to the greater of a fixed or variable rate of return.

"(II) PRESERVATION OF CAPITAL.—An interest credit (or an equivalent amount) of less than zero shall in no event result in the account balance or similar amount being less than the aggregate amount of contributions credited to the account.

"(III) MARKET RATE OF RETURN.—The Secretary of the Treasury may provide by regulation for rules governing the calculation of a market rate of return for purposes of subclause (I) and for permissible methods of crediting interest to the account (including fixed or variable interest rates) resulting in effective rates of return meeting the requirements of subclause (I).

"(ii) SPECIAL RULE FOR PLAN CONVERSIONS.—If, after June 29, 2005, an applicable plan amendment is adopted, the plan shall be treated as failing to meet the requirements of paragraph (1)(H) unless the requirements of clause (iii) are met with respect to each individual who was a participant in the plan immediately before the adoption of the amendment.

"(iii) RATE OF BENEFIT ACCRUAL.—Subject to clause (iv), the requirements of this clause are met with respect to any participant if the accrued benefit of the participant under the terms of the plan as in effect after the amendment is not less than the sum of—

"(I) the participant's accrued benefit for years of service before the effective date of the amendment, determined under the terms of the plan as in effect before the amendment, plus

"(II) the participant's accrued benefit for years of service after the effective date of the amendment, determined under the terms of the plan as in effect after the amendment.

"(iv) SPECIAL RULES FOR EARLY RETIREMENT SUBSIDIES.—For purposes of clause (iii)(I), the plan shall credit the accumulation account or similar amount with the amount of any early retirement benefit or retirement-type subsidy for the plan year in which the participant retires if, as of such time, the participant has met the age, years of service, and other requirements under the plan for entitlement to such benefit or subsidy.

"(v) APPLICABLE PLAN AMENDMENT.—For purposes of this subparagraph—

"(I) IN GENERAL.—The term 'applicable plan amendment' means an amendment to a defined benefit plan which has the effect of converting the plan to an applicable defined benefit plan.

"(II) SPECIAL RULE FOR COORDINATED BENEFITS.—If the benefits of 2 or more defined benefit plans established or maintained by an employer are coordinated in such a manner as to have the effect of the adoption of an amendment described in subclause (I), the sponsor of the defined benefit plan or plans providing for such coordination shall be treated as having adopted such a plan amendment as of the date such coordination begins.

"(III) MULTIPLE AMENDMENTS.—The Secretary of the Treasury shall issue regulations to prevent the avoidance of the purposes of this subparagraph through the use of 2 or more plan amendments rather than a single amendment.

"(IV) APPLICABLE DEFINED BENEFIT PLAN.—For purposes of this subparagraph, the term 'applicable defined benefit plan' has the meaning given such term by section 203(f)(3) of the Employee Retirement Income Security Act of 1974.

"(vi) TERMINATION REQUIREMENTS.—An applicable defined benefit plan shall not be treated as meeting the requirements of clause (i) unless the plan provides that, upon the termination of the plan—

"(I) if the interest credit rate (or an equivalent amount) under the plan is a variable rate, the rate of interest used to determine accrued benefits under the plan shall be equal to the average of the rates of interest used under the plan during the 5-year period ending on the termination date, and

"(II) the interest rate and mortality table used to determine the amount of any benefit under the plan payable in the form of an annuity payable at normal retirement age shall be the rate and table specified under the plan for such purpose as of the termination date, except that if such interest rate is a variable rate, the interest rate shall be determined under the rules of subclause (I).

"(C) CERTAIN OFFSETS PERMITTED.—A plan shall not be treated as failing to meet the requirements of paragraph (1) solely because the plan provides offsets against benefits under the plan to the extent such offsets are allowable in applying the requirements of section 401(a) of the Internal Revenue Code of 1986.

"(D) PERMITTED DISPARITIES IN PLAN CONTRIBUTIONS OR BENEFITS.—A plan shall not be treated as failing to meet the requirements of paragraph (1) solely because the plan provides a disparity in contributions or benefits with respect to which the requirements of section 401(l) of the Internal Revenue Code of 1986 are met.

"(E) INDEXING PERMITTED.—

"(i) IN GENERAL.—A plan shall not be treated as failing to meet the requirements of paragraph (1) solely because the plan provides for indexing of accrued benefits under the plan.

"(ii) PROTECTION AGAINST LOSS.—Except in the case of any benefit provided in the form of a variable annuity, clause (i) shall not apply with respect to any indexing which results in an accrued benefit less than the accrued benefit determined without regard to such indexing.

"(iii) INDEXING.—For purposes of this subparagraph, the term 'indexing' means, in connection with an accrued benefit, the periodic adjustment of the accrued benefit by means of the application of a recognized investment index or methodology.

"(F) EARLY RETIREMENT BENEFIT OR RETIREMENT-TYPE SUBSIDY.—For purposes of this paragraph, the terms 'early retirement benefit' and 'retirement-type subsidy' have the meaning given such terms in section 203(g)(2)(A) of the Employee Retirement Income Security Act of 1974.

"(G) BENEFIT ACCRUED TO DATE.—For purposes of this paragraph, any reference to the accrued benefit shall be a reference to such benefit accrued to date.".

(d) NO INFERENCE.—Nothing in the amendments made by this section shall be construed to create an inference with respect to—

(1) the treatment of applicable defined benefit plans or conversions to applicable defined benefit plans under sections 204(b)(1)(H) of the Employee Retirement Income Security Act of 1974, 4(i)(1) of the Age Discrimination in Employment Act of 1967, and 411(b)(1)(H) of the Internal Revenue Code of 1986, as in effect before such amendments, or

(2) the determination of whether an applicable defined benefit plan fails to meet the requirements of sections 203(a)(2), 204(c), or 204(g) of the Employee Retirement Income Security Act of 1974 or sections 411(a)(2), 411(c), or 417(e) of such Code, as in effect before such amendments, solely because the present value of the accrued benefit (or any portion thereof) of any participant is, under the terms of the plan, equal to the amount expressed as the balance in a

hypothetical account or as an accumulated percentage of the participant's final average compensation.

For purposes of this subsection, the term "applicable defined benefit plan" has the meaning given such term by section 203(f)(3) of the Employee Retirement Income Security Act of 1974 and section 411(a)(13)(C) of such Code, as in effect after such amendments.

(e) EFFECTIVE DATE.—

(1) IN GENERAL.—The amendments made by this section shall apply to periods beginning on or after June 29, 2005.

(2) PRESENT VALUE OF ACCRUED BENEFIT.—The amendments made by subsections (a)(2) and (b)(2) shall apply to distributions made after the date of the enactment of this Act.

(3) VESTING AND INTEREST CREDIT REQUIREMENTS.—In the case of a plan in existence on June 29, 2005, the requirements of clause (i) of section 411(b)(5)(B) of the Internal Revenue Code of 1986, clause (i) of section 204(b)(5)(B) of the Employee Retirement Income Security Act of 1974, and clause (i) of section 4(i)(10)(B) of the Age Discrimination in Employment Act of 1967 (as added by this Act) and the requirements of 203(f)(2) of the Employee Retirement Income Security Act of 1974 and section 411(a)(13)(B) of the Internal Revenue Code of 1986 (as so added) shall, for purposes of applying the amendments made by subsections (a) and (b), apply to years beginning after December 31, 2007, unless the plan sponsor elects the application of such requirements for any period after June 29, 2005, and before the first year beginning after December 31, 2007.

(4) SPECIAL RULE FOR COLLECTIVELY BARGAINED PLANS.—In the case of a plan maintained pursuant to 1 or more collective bargaining agreements between employee representatives and 1 or more employers ratified on or before the date of the enactment of this Act, the requirements described in paragraph (3) shall, for purposes of applying the amendments made by subsections (a) and (b), not apply to plan years beginning before—

(A) the earlier of—

(i) the date on which the last of such collective bargaining agreements terminates (determined without regard to any extension thereof on or after such date of enactment), or

(ii) January 1, 2008, or

(B) January 1, 2010.

(5) CONVERSIONS.—The requirements of clause (ii) of section 411(b)(5)(B) of the Internal Revenue Code of 1986, clause (ii) of section 204(b)(5)(B) of the Employee Retirement Income Security Act of 1974, and clause (ii) of section 4(i)(10)(B) of the Age Discrimination in Employment Act of 1967 (as added by this Act), shall apply to plan amendments adopted after, and taking effect after, June 29, 2005, except that the plan sponsor may elect to have such amendments apply to plan amendments adopted before, and taking effect after, such date.

[CCH Explanation at ¶ 1005. Committee Reports at ¶ 10,560.]

[¶ 7150] ACT SEC. 702. REGULATIONS RELATING TO MERGERS AND ACQUISITIONS.

The Secretary of the Treasury or his delegate shall, not later than 12 months after the date of the enactment of this Act, prescribe regulations for the application of the amendments made by, and the provisions of, this title in cases where the conversion of a plan to an applicable defined benefit plan is made with respect to a group of employees who become employees by reason of a merger, acquisition, or similar transaction.

[CCH Explanation at ¶ 1010. Committee Reports at ¶ 10,560.]

TITLE VIII—PENSION RELATED REVENUE PROVISIONS

* * *

Subtitle B—Certain Pension Provisions Made Permanent

[¶7153] ACT SEC. 811. PENSIONS AND INDIVIDUAL RETIREMENT ARRANGEMENT PROVISIONS OF ECONOMIC GROWTH AND TAX RELIEF RECONCILIATION ACT OF 2001 MADE PERMANENT.

Title IX of the Economic Growth and Tax Relief Reconciliation Act of 2001 shall not apply to the provisions of, and amendments made by, subtitles A through F of title VI of such Act (relating to pension and individual retirement arrangement provisions).

* * *

[CCH Explanation at ¶1305. Committee Reports at ¶10,600.]

Subtitle C—Improvements in Portability, Distribution, and Contribution Rules

* * *

[¶7156] ACT SEC. 823. CLARIFICATION OF MINIMUM DISTRIBUTION RULES FOR GOVERNMENTAL PLANS.

The Secretary of the Treasury shall issue regulations under which a governmental plan (as defined in section 414(d) of the Internal Revenue Code of 1986) shall, for all years to which section 401(a)(9) of such Code applies to such plan, be treated as having complied with such section 401(a)(9) if such plan complies with a reasonable good faith interpretation of such section 401(a)(9).

* * *

[CCH Explanation at ¶930. Committee Reports at ¶10,640.]

[¶7159] ACT SEC. 825. ELIGIBILITY FOR PARTICIPATION IN RETIREMENT PLANS.

An individual shall not be precluded from participating in an eligible deferred compensation plan by reason of having received a distribution under section 457(e)(9) of the Internal Revenue Code of 1986, as in effect prior to the enactment of the Small Business Job Protection Act of 1996.

[CCH Explanation at ¶1075. Committee Reports at ¶10,660.]

[¶7162] ACT SEC. 826. MODIFICATIONS OF RULES GOVERNING HARDSHIPS AND UNFORSEEN FINANCIAL EMERGENCIES.

Within 180 days after the date of the enactment of this Act, the Secretary of the Treasury shall modify the rules for determining whether a participant has had a hardship for purposes of section 401(k)(2)(B)(i)(IV) of the Internal Revenue Code of 1986 to provide that if an event (including the occurrence of a medical expense) would constitute a hardship under the plan if it occurred with respect to the participant's spouse or dependent (as defined in section 152 of such Code), such event shall, to the extent permitted under a plan, constitute a hardship if it occurs with respect to a person who is a beneficiary under the plan with respect to the participant. The Secretary of the Treasury shall issue similar rules for purposes of determining whether a participant has had—

(1) a hardship for purposes of section 403(b)(11)(B) of such Code; or

(2) an unforeseen financial emergency for purposes of sections 409A(a)(2)(A)(vi), 409A(a)(2)(B)(ii), and 457(d)(1)(A)(iii) of such Code.

* * *

[CCH Explanation at ¶910. Committee Reports at ¶10,670.]

[¶7165] ACT SEC. 830. DIRECT PAYMENT OF TAX REFUNDS TO INDIVIDUAL RETIREMENT PLANS.

(a) IN GENERAL.—The Secretary of the Treasury (or the Secretary's delegate) shall make available a form (or modify existing forms) for use by individuals to direct that a portion of any refund of overpayment of tax imposed by chapter 1 of the Internal Revenue Code of 1986 be paid directly to an individual retirement plan (as defined in section 7701(a)(37) of such Code) of such individual.

(b) EFFECTIVE DATE.—The form required by subsection (a) shall be made available for taxable years beginning after December 31, 2006.

* * *

[CCH Explanation at ¶725. Committee Reports at ¶10,710.]

Subtitle E—United States Tax Court Modernization

* * *

[¶7168] ACT SEC. 854. ANNUITIES TO SURVIVING SPOUSES AND DEPENDENT CHILDREN OF SPECIAL TRAIL JUDGES OF THE TAX COURT.

* * *

(c) CONFORMING AMENDMENTS.—

* * *

(9) Section 210(a)(5)(E) of the Social Security Act is amended by inserting "or special trial judge" before "of the United States Tax Court".

* * *

[CCH Explanation at ¶1445. Committee Reports at ¶10,810.]

Subtitle F—Other Provisions

[¶7171] ACT SEC. 861. EXTENSION TO ALL GOVERNMENTAL PLANS OF CURRENT MORATORIUM ON APPLICATION OF CERTAIN NONDISCRIMINATION RULES APPLICABLE TO STATE AND LOCAL PLANS.

(a) IN GENERAL.—

* * *

(2) Subparagraph (G) of section 401(k)(3) of such Code and paragraph (2) of section 1505(d) of the Taxpayer Relief Act of 1997 (Public Law 105-34; 111 Stat. 1063) are each amended by striking "maintained by a State or local government or political subdivision thereof (or agency or instrumentality thereof)".

• • *TAXPAYER RELIEF ACT OF 1997 ACT SEC. 1505(d)(2) BEFORE AMENDMENT*—

ACT SEC. 1505. EXTENSION OF MORATORIUM ON APPLICATION OF CERTAIN NONDISCRIMINATION RULES TO STATE AND LOCAL GOVERNMENTS.

* * *

(d) EFFECTIVE DATES.—

* * *

(2) TREATMENT FOR YEARS BEGINNING BEFORE DATE OF ENACTMENT.—A governmental plan (within the meaning of section 414(d) of the Internal Revenue Code of 1986) maintained by a State or local government or political subdivision thereof (or agency or instrumentality thereof) shall be treated as satisfying the requirements of sections 401(a)(3), 401(a)(4),

• • *TAXPAYER RELIEF ACT OF 1997 ACT SEC. 1505(d)(2) BEFORE AMENDMENT*—

401(a)(26), 401(k), 401(m), 403(b)(1)(D) and (b)(12), and 410 of such Code for all taxable years beginning before the date of enactment of this Act.

---

* * *

(c) EFFECTIVE DATE.—The amendments made by this section shall apply to any year beginning after the date of the enactment of this Act.

* * *

[CCH Explanation at ¶ 1060. Committee Reports at ¶ 10,870.]

[¶ 7174] ACT SEC. 864. TREATMENT OF TEST ROOM SUPERVISORS AND PROCTORS WHO ASSIST IN THE ADMINISTRATION OF COLLEGE ENTRANCE AND PLACEMENT EXAMS.

(a) IN GENERAL.—Section 530 of the Revenue Reconciliation Act of 1978 is amended by adding at the end the following new subsection:

"(f) TREATMENT OF TEST ROOM SUPERVISORS AND PROCTORS WHO ASSIST IN THE ADMINISTRATION OF COLLEGE ENTRANCE AND PLACEMENT EXAMS.—

"(1) IN GENERAL.—In the case of an individual described in paragraph (2) who is providing services as a test proctor or room supervisor by assisting in the administration of college entrance or placement examinations, this section shall be applied to such services performed after December 31, 2006 (and remuneration paid for such services) without regard to subsection (a)(3) thereof.

"(2) APPLICABILITY.—An individual is described in this paragraph if the individual—

"(A) is providing the services described in subsection (a) to an organization described in section 501(c), and exempt from tax under section 501(a), of the Internal Revenue Code of 1986, and

"(B) is not otherwise treated as an employee of such organization for purposes of subtitle C of such Code (relating to employment taxes).".

(b) EFFECTIVE DATE.—The amendment made by this section shall apply to remuneration for services performed after December 31, 2006.

[CCH Explanation at ¶ 1335. Committee Reports at ¶ 10,900.]

[¶ 7177] ACT SEC. 865. GRANDFATHER RULE FOR CHURCH PLANS WHICH SELF-ANNUITIZE.

(a) IN GENERAL.—In the case of any plan year ending after the date of the enactment of this Act, annuity payments provided with respect to any account maintained for a participant or beneficiary under a qualified church plan shall not fail to satisfy the requirements of section 401(a)(9) of the Internal Revenue Code of 1986 merely because the payments are not made under an annuity contract purchased from an insurance company if such payments would not fail such requirements if provided with respect to a retirement income account described in section 403(b)(9) of such Code.

(b) QUALIFIED CHURCH PLAN.—For purposes of this section, the term "qualified church plan" means any money purchase pension plan described in section 401(a) of such Code which—

(1) is a church plan (as defined in section 414(e) of such Code) with respect to which the election provided by section 410(d) of such Code has not been made, and

(2) was in existence on April 17, 2002.

* * *

[CCH Explanation at ¶ 1045. Committee Reports at ¶ 10,910.]

TITLE IX—INCREASE IN PENSION PLAN DIVERSIFICATION AND PARTICIPATION AND OTHER PENSION PROVISIONS

[¶7180] ACT SEC. 901. DEFINED CONTRIBUTION PLANS REQUIRED TO PROVIDE EMPLOYEES WITH FREEDOM TO INVEST THEIR PLAN ASETS.

* * *

(b) AMENDMENTS OF ERISA.—

(1) IN GENERAL.—Section 204 of the Employee Retirement Income Security Act of 1974 (29 U.S.C. 1054) is amended by redesignating subsection (j) as subsection (k) and by inserting after subsection (i) the following new subsection:

"(j) DIVERSIFICATION REQUIREMENTS FOR CERTAIN INDIVIDUAL ACCOUNT PLANS.—

"(1) IN GENERAL.—An applicable individual account plan shall meet the diversification requirements of paragraphs (2), (3), and (4).

"(2) EMPLOYEE CONTRIBUTIONS AND ELECTIVE DEFERRALS INVESTED IN EMPLOYER SECURITIES.—In the case of the portion of an applicable individual's account attributable to employee contributions and elective deferrals which is invested in employer securities, a plan meets the requirements of this paragraph if the applicable individual may elect to direct the plan to divest any such securities and to reinvest an equivalent amount in other investment options meeting the requirements of paragraph (4).

"(3) EMPLOYER CONTRIBUTIONS INVESTED IN EMPLOYER SECURITIES.—In the case of the portion of the account attributable to employer contributions other than elective deferrals which is invested in employer securities, a plan meets the requirements of this paragraph if each applicable individual who—

"(A) is a participant who has completed at least 3 years of service, or

"(B) is a beneficiary of a participant described in subparagraph (A) or of a deceased participant,

may elect to direct the plan to divest any such securities and to reinvest an equivalent amount in other investment options meeting the requirements of paragraph (4).

"(4) INVESTMENT OPTIONS.—

"(A) IN GENERAL.—The requirements of this paragraph are met if the plan offers not less than 3 investment options, other than employer securities, to which an applicable individual may direct the proceeds from the divestment of employer securities pursuant to this subsection, each of which is diversified and has materially different risk and return characteristics.

"(B) TREATMENT OF CERTAIN RESTRICTIONS AND CONDITIONS.—

"(i) TIME FOR MAKING INVESTMENT CHOICES.—A plan shall not be treated as failing to meet the requirements of this paragraph merely because the plan limits the time for divestment and reinvestment to periodic, reasonable opportunities occurring no less frequently than quarterly.

"(ii) CERTAIN RESTRICTIONS AND CONDITIONS NOT ALLOWED.—Except as provided in regulations, a plan shall not meet the requirements of this paragraph if the plan imposes restrictions or conditions with respect to the investment of employer securities which are not imposed on the investment of other assets of the plan. This subparagraph shall not apply to any restrictions or conditions imposed by reason of the application of securities laws.

"(5) APPLICABLE INDIVIDUAL ACCOUNT PLAN.—For purposes of this subsection—

"(A) IN GENERAL.—The term 'applicable individual account plan' means any individual account plan (as defined in section 3(34)) which holds any publicly traded employer securities.

"(B) EXCEPTION FOR CERTAIN ESOPS.—Such term does not include an employee stock ownership plan if—

"(i) there are no contributions to such plan (or earnings thereunder) which are held within such plan and are subject to subsection (k) or (m) of section 401 of the Internal Revenue Code of 1986, and

"(ii) such plan is a separate plan (for purposes of section 414(l) of such Code) with respect to any other defined benefit plan or individual account plan maintained by the same employer or employers.

"(C) EXCEPTION FOR ONE PARTICIPANT PLANS.—Such term shall not include a one-participant retirement plan (as defined in section 101(i)(8)(B)).

"(D) CERTAIN PLANS TREATED AS HOLDING PUBLICLY TRADED EMPLOYER SECURITIES.—

"(i) IN GENERAL.—Except as provided in regulations or in clause (ii), a plan holding employer securities which are not publicly traded employer securities shall be treated as holding publicly traded employer securities if any employer corporation, or any member of a controlled group of corporations which includes such employer corporation, has issued a class of stock which is a publicly traded employer security.

"(ii) EXCEPTION FOR CERTAIN CONTROLLED GROUPS WITH PUBLICLY TRADED SECURITIES.—Clause (i) shall not apply to a plan if—

"(I) no employer corporation, or parent corporation of an employer corporation, has issued any publicly traded employer security, and

"(II) no employer corporation, or parent corporation of an employer corporation, has issued any special class of stock which grants particular rights to, or bears particular risks for, the holder or issuer with respect to any corporation described in clause (i) which has issued any publicly traded employer security.

"(iii) DEFINITIONS.—For purposes of this subparagraph, the term—

"(I) 'controlled group of corporations' has the meaning given such term by section 1563(a) of the Internal Revenue Code of 1986, except that '50 percent' shall be substituted for '80 percent' each place it appears,

"(II) 'employer corporation' means a corporation which is an employer maintaining the plan, and

"(III) 'parent corporation' has the meaning given such term by section 424(e) of such Code.

"(6) OTHER DEFINITIONS.—For purposes of this paragraph—

"(A) APPLICABLE INDIVIDUAL.—The term 'applicable individual' means—

"(i) any participant in the plan, and

"(ii) any beneficiary who has an account under the plan with respect to which the beneficiary is entitled to exercise the rights of a participant.

"(B) ELECTIVE DEFERRAL.—The term 'elective deferral' means an employer contribution described in section 402(g)(3)(A) of the Internal Revenue Code of 1986.

"(C) EMPLOYER SECURITY.—The term 'employer security' has the meaning given such term by section 407(d)(1).

"(D) EMPLOYEE STOCK OWNERSHIP PLAN.—The term 'employee stock ownership plan' has the meaning given such term by section 4975(e)(7) of such Code.

"(E) PUBLICLY TRADED EMPLOYER SECURITIES.—The term 'publicly traded employer securities' means employer securities which are readily tradable on an established securities market.

"(F) YEAR OF SERVICE.—The term 'year of service' has the meaning given such term by section 203(b)(2).

"(7) TRANSITION RULE FOR SECURITIES ATTRIBUTABLE TO EMPLOYER CONTRIBUTIONS.—

"(A) RULES PHASED IN OVER 3 YEARS.—

"(i) IN GENERAL.—In the case of the portion of an account to which paragraph (3) applies and which consists of employer securities acquired in a plan year beginning before January 1, 2007, paragraph (3) shall only apply to the applicable percentage of such securities. This subparagraph shall be applied separately with respect to each class of securities.

"(ii) EXCEPTION FOR CERTAIN PARTICIPANTS AGED 55 OR OVER.—Clause (i) shall not apply to an applicable individual who is a participant who has attained age 55 and completed at least 3 years of service before the first plan year beginning after December 31, 2005.

"(B) APPLICABLE PERCENTAGE.—For purposes of subparagraph (A), the applicable percentage shall be determined as follows:

"Plan year to which paragraph (3) applies:	The applicable percentage is:
1st	33
2d	66
3d	100 .".

(2) CONFORMING AMENDMENT.—Section 407(b)(3) of such Act (29 U.S.C. 1107(b)(3)) is amended by adding at the end the following:

"(D) For diversification requirements for qualifying employer securities held in certain individual account plans, see section 204(j).".

(c) EFFECTIVE DATES.—

(1) IN GENERAL.—Except as provided in paragraphs (2) and (3), the amendments made by this section shall apply to plan years beginning after December 31, 2006.

(2) SPECIAL RULE FOR COLLECTIVELY BARGAINED AGREEMENTS.—In the case of a plan maintained pursuant to 1 or more collective bargaining agreements between employee representatives and 1 or more employers ratified on or before the date of the enactment of this Act, paragraph (1) shall be applied to benefits pursuant to, and individuals covered by, any such agreement by substituting for "December 31, 2006" the earlier of—

(A) the later of—

(i) December 31, 2007, or

(ii) the date on which the last of such collective bargaining agreements terminates (determined without regard to any extension thereof after such date of enactment), or

(B) December 31, 2008.

(3) SPECIAL RULE FOR CERTAIN EMPLOYER SECURITIES HELD IN AN ESOP.—

(A) IN GENERAL.—In the case of employer securities to which this paragraph applies, the amendments made by this section shall apply to plan years beginning after the earlier of—

(i) December 31, 2007, or

(ii) the first date on which the fair market value of such securities exceeds the guaranteed minimum value described in subparagraph (B)(ii).

(B) APPLICABLE SECURITIES.—This paragraph shall apply to employer securities which are attributable to employer contributions other than elective deferrals, and which, on September 17, 2003—

(i) consist of preferred stock, and

(ii) are within an employee stock ownership plan (as defined in section 4975(e)(7) of the Internal Revenue Code of 1986), the terms of which provide that the value of the securities cannot be less than the guaranteed minimum value specified by the plan on such date.

(C) COORDINATION WITH TRANSITION RULE.—In applying section 401(a)(35)(H) of the Internal Revenue Code of 1986 and section 204(j)(7) of the Employee Retirement Income Security

Act of 1974 (as added by this section) to employer securities to which this paragraph applies, the applicable percentage shall be determined without regard to this paragraph.

[CCH Explanation at ¶ 605. Committee Reports at ¶ 10,950.]

[¶ 7183] ACT SEC. 902. INCREASING PARTICIPATION THROUGH AUTOMATIC CONTRIBUTION ARRANGEMENTS.

* * *

(d) TREATMENT OF WITHDRAWALS OF CONTRIBUTIONS DURING FIRST 90 DAYS.—

* * *

(2) VESTING CONFORMING AMENDMENTS.—

* * *

(E) Section 203(a)(3)(F) of the Employee Retirement Income Security Act of 1974 (29 U.S.C. 1053(a)(3)(F)) is amended by inserting "an erroneous automatic contribution under section 414(w) of such Code," after "402(g)(2)(A) of such Code,".

* * *

(f) PREEMPTION OF CONFLICTING STATE REGULATION.—

(1) IN GENERAL.—Section 514 of the Employee Retirement Income Security Act of 1974 (29 U.S.C. 1144) is amended by adding at the end the following new subsection:

"(e)(1) Notwithstanding any other provision of this section, this title shall supersede any law of a State which would directly or indirectly prohibit or restrict the inclusion in any plan of an automatic contribution arrangement. The Secretary may prescribe regulations which would establish minimum standards that such an arrangement would be required to satisfy in order for this subsection to apply in the case of such arrangement.

"(2) For purposes of this subsection, the term 'automatic contribution arrangement' means an arrangement——

"(A) under which a participant may elect to have the plan sponsor make payments as contributions under the plan on behalf of the participant, or to the participant directly in cash,

"(B) under which a participant is treated as having elected to have the plan sponsor make such contributions in an amount equal to a uniform percentage of compensation provided under the plan until the participant specifically elects not to have such contributions made (or specifically elects to have such contributions made at a different percentage), and

"(C) under which such contributions are invested in accordance with regulations prescribed by the Secretary under section 404(c)(5).

"(3)(A) The plan administrator of an automatic contribution arrangement shall, within a reasonable period before such plan year, provide to each participant to whom the arrangement applies for such plan year notice of the participant's rights and obligations under the arrangement which—

"(i) is sufficiently accurate and comprehensive to apprise the participant of such rights and obligations, and

"(ii) is written in a manner calculated to be understood by the average participant to whom the arrangement applies.

"(B) A notice shall not be treated as meeting the requirements of subparagraph (A) with respect to a participant unless—

"(i) the notice includes an explanation of the participant's right under the arrangement not to have elective contributions made on the participant's behalf (or to elect to have such contributions made at a different percentage), "(ii) the participant has a reasonable period of time, after receipt of the notice described in clause (i) and before the first elective contribution is made, to make such election, and

"(iii) the notice explains how contributions made under the arrangement will be invested in the absence of any investment election by the participant.".

(2) ENFORCEMENT.—Section 502(c)(4) of such Act (29 U.S.C. 1132(c)(4)) is amended by striking "or section 302(b)(7)(F)(vi)" inserting ", section 302(b)(7)(F)(vi), or section 514(e)(3)".

(g) EFFECTIVE DATE.—The amendments made by this section shall apply to plan years beginning after December 31, 2007, except that the amendments made by subsection (f) shall take effect on the date of the enactment of this Act.

[CCH Explanation at ¶1015. Committee Reports at ¶10,960.]

[¶7186] ACT SEC. 903. TREATMENT OF ELIGIBLE COMBINED DEFINED BENEFIT PLANS AND QUALIFIED CASH OR DEFERRED ARRANGEMENTS.

* * *

(b) AMENDMENTS TO THE EMPLOYEE RETIREMENT INCOME SECURITY ACT OF 1974.—

(1) IN GENERAL.—Section 210 of the Employee Retirement Income Security Act of 1974 is amended by adding at the end the following new subsection:

"(e) SPECIAL RULES FOR ELIGIBLE COMBINED DEFINED BENEFIT PLANS AND QUALIFIED CASH OR DEFERRED ARRANGEMENTS.—

"(1) GENERAL RULE.—Except as provided in this subsection, this Act shall be applied to any defined benefit plan or applicable individual account plan which are part of an eligible combined plan in the same manner as if each such plan were not a part of the eligible combined plan.

"(2) ELIGIBLE COMBINED PLAN.—For purposes of this subsection—

"(A) IN GENERAL.—The term 'eligible combined plan' means a plan—

"(i) which is maintained by an employer which, at the time the plan is established, is a small employer,

"(ii) which consists of a defined benefit plan and an applicable individual account plan each of which qualifies under section 401(a) of the Internal Revenue Code of 1986,

"(iii) the assets of which are held in a single trust forming part of the plan and are clearly identified and allocated to the defined benefit plan and the applicable individual account plan to the extent necessary for the separate application of this Act under paragraph (1), and

"(iv) with respect to which the benefit, contribution, vesting, and nondiscrimination requirements of subparagraphs (B), (C), (D), (E), and (F) are met.

For purposes of this subparagraph, the term 'small employer' has the meaning given such term by section 4980D(d)(2) of the Internal Revenue Code of 1986, except that such section shall be applied by substituting '500' for '50' each place it appears.

"(B) BENEFIT REQUIREMENTS.—

"(i) IN GENERAL.—The benefit requirements of this subparagraph are met with respect to the defined benefit plan forming part of the eligible combined plan if the accrued benefit of each participant derived from employer contributions, when expressed as an annual retirement benefit, is not less than the applicable percentage of the participant's final average pay. For purposes of this clause, final average pay shall be determined using the period of consecutive years (not exceeding 5) during which the participant had the greatest aggregate compensation from the employer.

"(ii) APPLICABLE PERCENTAGE.—For purposes of clause (i), the applicable percentage is the lesser of—

"(I) 1 percent multiplied by the number of years of service with the employer, or

"(II) 20 percent.

"(iii) SPECIAL RULE FOR APPLICABLE DEFINED BENEFIT PLANS.—If the defined benefit plan under clause (i) is an applicable defined benefit plan as defined in section 203(f)(3)(B) which meets the interest credit requirements of section 204(b)(5)(B)(i), the plan shall be treated as meeting the requirements of clause (i) with respect to any plan year if each participant receives pay credit for the year which is not less than the percentage of compensation determined in accordance with the following table:

"If the participant's age as of the beginning of the year is—	The percentage is—
30 or less	2
Over 30 but less than 40	4
40 or over but less than 50	6
50 or over	8 .

"(iv) YEARS OF SERVICE.—For purposes of this subparagraph, years of service shall be determined under the rules of paragraphs (1), (2), and (3) of section 203(b), except that the plan may not disregard any year of service because of a participant making, or failing to make, any elective deferral with respect to the qualified cash or deferred arrangement to which subparagraph (C) applies.

"(C) CONTRIBUTION REQUIREMENTS.—

"(i) IN GENERAL.—The contribution requirements of this subparagraph with respect to any applicable individual account plan forming part of an eligible combined plan are met if—

"(I) the qualified cash or deferred arrangement included in such plan constitutes an automatic contribution arrangement, and

"(II) the employer is required to make matching contributions on behalf of each employee eligible to participate in the arrangement in an amount equal to 50 percent of the elective contributions of the employee to the extent such elective contributions do not exceed 4 percent of compensation.

Rules similar to the rules of clauses (ii) and (iii) of section 401(k)(12)(B) of the Internal Revenue Code of 1986 shall apply for purposes of this clause.

"(ii) NONELECTIVE CONTRIBUTIONS.—An applicable individual account plan shall not be treated as failing to meet the requirements of clause (i) because the employer makes nonelective contributions under the plan but such contributions shall not be taken into account in determining whether the requirements of clause (i)(II) are met.

"(D) VESTING REQUIREMENTS.—The vesting requirements of this subparagraph are met if—

"(i) in the case of a defined benefit plan forming part of an eligible combined plan an employee who has completed at least 3 years of service has a nonforfeitable right to 100 percent of the employee's accrued benefit under the plan derived from employer contributions, and

"(ii) in the case of an applicable individual account plan forming part of eligible combined plan—

"(I) an employee has a nonforfeitable right to any matching contribution made under the qualified cash or deferred arrangement included in such plan by an employer with respect to any elective contribution, including matching contributions in excess of the contributions required under subparagraph (C)(i)(II), and

"(II) an employee who has completed at least 3 years of service has a nonforfeitable right to 100 percent of the employee's accrued benefit derived under the arrangement from nonelective contributions of the employer.

For purposes of this subparagraph, the rules of section 203 shall apply to the extent not inconsistent with this subparagraph.

"(E) UNIFORM PROVISION OF CONTRIBUTIONS AND BENEFITS.—In the case of a defined benefit plan or applicable individual account plan forming part of an eligible combined plan, the requirements of this subparagraph are met if all contributions and benefits under each such plan, and all rights and features under each such plan, must be provided uniformly to all participants.

"(F) REQUIREMENTS MUST BE MET WITHOUT TAKING INTO ACCOUNT SOCIAL SECURITY AND SIMILAR CONTRIBUTIONS AND BENEFITS OR OTHER PLANS.—

"(i) IN GENERAL.—The requirements of this subparagraph are met if the requirements of clauses (ii) and (iii) are met.

"(ii) SOCIAL SECURITY AND SIMILAR CONTRIBUTIONS.—The requirements of this clause are met if—

"(I) the requirements of subparagraphs (B) and (C) are met without regard to section 401(l) of the Internal Revenue Code of 1986, and

"(II) the requirements of sections 401(a)(4) and 410(b) of the Internal Revenue Code of 1986 are met with respect to both the applicable defined contribution plan and defined benefit plan forming part of an eligible combined plan without regard to section 401(l) of the Internal Revenue Code of 1986.

"(iii) OTHER PLANS AND ARRANGEMENTS.—The requirements of this clause are met if the applicable defined contribution plan and defined benefit plan forming part of an eligible combined plan meet the requirements of sections 401(a)(4) and 410(b) of the Internal Revenue Code of 1986 without being combined with any other plan.

"(3) NONDISCRIMINATION REQUIREMENTS FOR QUALIFIED CASH OR DEFERRED ARRANGEMENT.—

"(A) IN GENERAL.—A qualified cash or deferred arrangement which is included in an applicable individual account plan forming part of an eligible combined plan shall be treated as meeting the requirements of section 401(k)(3)(A)(ii) of the Internal Revenue Code of 1986 if the requirements of paragraph (2) are met with respect to such arrangement.

"(B) MATCHING CONTRIBUTIONS.—In applying section 401(m)(11) of such Code to any matching contribution with respect to a contribution to which paragraph (2)(C) applies, the contribution requirement of paragraph (2)(C) and the notice requirements of paragraph (5)(B) shall be substituted for the requirements otherwise applicable under clauses (i) and (ii) of section 401(m)(11)(A) of such Code.

"(4) AUTOMATIC CONTRIBUTION ARRANGEMENT.—For purposes of this subsection—

"(A) IN GENERAL.—A qualified cash or deferred arrangement shall be treated as an automatic contribution arrangement if the arrangement—

"(i) provides that each employee eligible to participate in the arrangement is treated as having elected to have the employer make elective contributions in an amount equal to 4 percent of the employee's compensation unless the employee specifically elects not to have such contributions made or to have such contributions made at a different rate, and

"(ii) meets the notice requirements under subparagraph (B).

"(B) NOTICE REQUIREMENTS.—

"(i) IN GENERAL.—The requirements of this subparagraph are met if the requirements of clauses (ii) and (iii) are met.

"(ii) REASONABLE PERIOD TO MAKE ELECTION.—The requirements of this clause are met if each employee to whom subparagraph (A)(i) applies—

"(I) receives a notice explaining the employee's right under the arrangement to elect not to have elective contributions made on the employee's behalf or to have the contributions made at a different rate, and

"(II) has a reasonable period of time after receipt of such notice and before the first elective contribution is made to make such election.

"(iii) ANNUAL NOTICE OF RIGHTS AND OBLIGATIONS.—The requirements of this clause are met if each employee eligible to participate in the arrangement is, within a reasonable period before any year, given notice of the employee's rights and obligations under the arrangement.

The requirements of this subparagraph shall not be treated as met unless the requirements of clauses (i) and (ii) of section 401(k)(12)(D) of the Internal Revenue Code of 1986 are met with respect to the notices described in clauses (ii) and (iii) of this subparagraph.

"(5) COORDINATION WITH OTHER REQUIREMENTS.—

"(A) TREATMENT OF SEPARATE PLANS.—The except clause in section 3(35) shall not apply to an eligible combined plan.

"(B) REPORTING.—An eligible combined plan shall be treated as a single plan for purposes of section 103.

"(6) APPLICABLE INDIVIDUAL ACCOUNT PLAN.—For purposes of this subsection—

"(A) IN GENERAL.—The term 'applicable individual account plan' means an individual account plan which includes a qualified cash or deferred arrangement.

"(B) QUALIFIED CASH OR DEFERRED ARRANGEMENT.—The term 'qualified cash or deferred arrangement' has the meaning given such term by section 401(k)(2) of the Internal Revenue Code of 1986.".

(2) CONFORMING CHANGES.—

(A) The heading for section 210 of such Act is amended to read as follows:

"SEC. 210. MULTIPLE EMPLOYER PLANS AND OTHER SPECIAL RULES.".

(B) The table of contents in section 1 of such Act is amended by striking the item relating to section 210 and inserting the following new item:

"Sec. 210. Multiple employer plans and other special rules.".

(c) EFFECTIVE DATE.—The amendments made by this section shall apply to plan years beginning after December 31, 2009.

[CCH Explanation at ¶ 1020. Committee Reports at ¶ 10,970.]

[¶ 7189] ACT SEC. 904. FASTER VESTING OF EMPLOYER NONELECTIVE CONTRIBUTIONS.

* * *

(b) AMENDMENTS TO THE EMPLOYEE RETIREMENT INCOME SECURITY ACT OF 1974

(1) IN GENERAL.—Paragraph (2) of section 203(a) of the Employee Retirement Income Security Act of 1974 (29 U.S.C. 1053(a)(2)) is amended to read as follows:

"(2)(A)(i) In the case of a defined benefit plan, a plan satisfies the requirements of this paragraph if it satisfies the requirements of clause (ii) or (iii).

"(ii) A plan satisfies the requirements of this clause if an employee who has completed at least 5 years of service has a nonforfeitable right to 100 percent of the employee's accrued benefit derived from employer contributions.

"(iii) A plan satisfies the requirements of this clause if an employee has a nonforfeitable right to a percentage of the employee's accrued benefit derived from employer contributions determined under the following table:

" Years of service:	The nonforfeitable percentage is:
3	20
4	40
5	60
6	80
7 or more	100 .

"(B)(i) In the case of an individual account plan, a plan satisfies the requirements of this paragraph if it satisfies the requirements of clause (ii) or (iii).

"(ii) A plan satisfies the requirements of this clause if an employee who has completed at least 3 years of service has a nonforfeitable right to 100 percent of the employee's accrued benefit derived from employer contributions.

"(iii) A plan satisfies the requirements of this clause if an employee has a nonforfeitable right to a percentage of the employee's accrued benefit derived from employer contributions determined under the following table:

" Years of service:	The nonforfeitable percentage is:
2	20
3	40
4	60
5	80
6 or more	100 .".

(2) CONFORMING AMENDMENT.—Section 203(a) of such Act is amended by striking paragraph (4).

(c) EFFECTIVE DATES

(1) IN GENERAL.—Except as provided in paragraphs (2) and (4), the amendments made by this section shall apply to contributions for plan years beginning after December 31, 2006.

(2) COLLECTIVE BARGAINING AGREEMENTS.—In the case of a plan maintained pursuant to one or more collective bargaining agreements between employee representatives and one or more employers ratified before the date of the enactment of this Act, the amendments made by this section shall not apply to contributions on behalf of employees covered by any such agreement for plan years beginning before the earlier of—

(A) the later of—

(i) the date on which the last of such collective bargaining agreements terminates (determined without regard to any extension thereof on or after such date of the enactment); or

(ii) January 1, 2007; or

(B) January 1, 2009.

(3) SERVICE REQUIRED.—With respect to any plan, the amendments made by this section shall not apply to any employee before the date that such employee has 1 hour of service under such plan in any plan year to which the amendments made by this section apply.

(4) SPECIAL RULE FOR STOCK OWNERSHIP PLANS.—Notwithstanding paragraph (1) or (2), in the case of an employee stock ownership plan (as defined in section 4975(e)(7) of the Internal Revenue Code of 1986) which had outstanding on September 26, 2005, a loan incurred for the purpose of acquiring qualifying employer securities (as defined in section 4975(e)(8) of such Code), the amendments made by this section shall not apply to any plan year beginning before the earlier of—

(A) the date on which the loan is fully repaid, or

(B) the date on which the loan was, as of September 26, 2005, scheduled to be fully repaid.

[CCH Explanation at ¶720. Committee Reports at ¶10,980.]

[¶7192] ACT SEC. 905. DISTRIBUTIONS DURING WORKING RETIREMENT.

(a) AMENDMENT TO THE EMPLOYEE RETIREMENT INCOME SECURITY ACT OF 1974.—Subparagraph (A) of section 3(2) of the Employee Retirement Income Security Act of 1974 (29 U.S.C. 1002(2)) is amended by adding at the end the following new sentence: "A distribution from a plan, fund, or program shall not be treated as made in a form other than retirement income or as a distribution prior to termination of covered employment solely because such distribution is made to an employee who has attained age 62 and who is not separated from employment at the time of such distribution.".

* * *

(c) EFFECTIVE DATE.—The amendments made by this section shall apply to distributions in plan years beginning after December 31, 2006.

[CCH Explanation at ¶ 920. Committee Reports at ¶ 10,990.]

[¶ 7195] ACT SEC. 906. TREATMENT OF CERTAIN PENSION PLANS OF INDIAN TRIBAL GOVERNMENTS.

(a) DEFINITION OF GOVERNMENT PLAN TO INCLUDE CERTAIN PENSION PLANS OF INDIAN TRIBAL GOVERNMENTS.

* * *

(2) AMENDMENT TO EMPLOYEE RETIREMENT INCOME SECURITY ACT OF 1974.

(A) Section 3(32) of the Employee Retirement Income Security Act of 1974 (29 U.S.C. 1002(32)) is amended by adding at the end the following: "The term 'governmental plan' includes a plan which is established and maintained by an Indian tribal government (as defined in section 7701(a)(40) of the Internal Revenue Code of 1986), a subdivision of an Indian tribal government (determined in accordance with section 7871(d) of such Code), or an agency or instrumentality of either, and all of the participants of which are employees of such entity substantially all of whose services as such an employee are in the performance of essential governmental functions but not in the performance of commercial activities (whether or not an essential government function)".

(B) Section 4021(b)(2) of such Act is amended by adding at the end the following: "or which is described in the last sentence of section 3(32)".

(b) CLARIFICATION THAT TRIBAL GOVERNMENTS ARE SUBJECT TO THE SAME PENSION PLAN RULES AND REGULATIONS APPLIED TO STATE AND OTHER LOCAL GOVERNMENTS AND THEIR POLICE AND FIREFIGHTERS.

* * *

(2) AMENDMENTS TO EMPLOYEE RETIREMENT INCOME SECURITY ACT OF 1974.—Section 4021(b) of the Employee Retirement Income Security Act of 1974 (29 U.S.C. 1321(b)) is amended—

(A) in paragraph (12), by striking "or" at the end;

(B) in paragraph (13), by striking "plan." and inserting "plan; or"; and

(C) by adding at the end the following:

"(14) established and maintained by an Indian tribal government (as defined in section 7701(a)(40) of the Internal Revenue Code of 1986), a subdivision of an Indian tribal government (determined in accordance with section 7871(d) of such Code), or an agency or instrumentality of either, and all of the participants of which are employees of such entity substantially all of whose services as such an employee are in the performance of essential governmental functions but not in the performance of commercial activities (whether or not an essential government function).".

(c) EFFECTIVE DATE.—The amendments made by this section shall apply to any year beginning on or after the date of the enactment of this Act.

[CCH Explanation at ¶ 1065. Committee Reports at ¶ 11,000.]

TITLE X—PROVISIONS RELATING TO SPOUSAL PENSION PROTECTION

[¶7198] ACT SEC. 1001. REGULATIONS ON TIME AND ORDER OF ISSUANCE OF DOMESTIC RELATIONS ORDERS.

Not later than 1 year after the date of the enactment of this Act, the Secretary of Labor shall issue regulations under section 206(d)(3) of the Employee Retirement Security Act of 1974 and section 414(p) of the Internal Revenue Code of 1986 which clarify that—

(1) a domestic relations order otherwise meeting the requirements to be a qualified domestic relations order, including the requirements of section 206(d)(3)(D) of such Act and section 414(p)(3) of such Code, shall not fail to be treated as a qualified domestic relations order solely because—

(A) the order is issued after, or revises, another domestic relations order or qualified domestic relations order; or

(B) of the time at which it is issued; and

(2) any order described in paragraph (1) shall be subject to the same requirements and protections which apply to qualified domestic relations orders, including the provisions of section 206(d)(3)(H) of such Act and section 414(p)(7) of such Code.

[CCH Explanation at ¶1025. Committee Reports at ¶11,010.]

[¶7201] ACT SEC. 1002. ENTITLEMENT OF DIVORCED SPOUSES TO RAILROAD RETIREMENT ANNUITIES INDEPENDENT OF ACTUAL ENTITLEMENT OF EMPLOYEE.

(a) IN GENERAL.—Section 2 of the Railroad Retirement Act of 1974 (45 U.S.C. 231a) is amended—

(1) in subsection (c)(4)(i), by striking "(A) is entitled to an annuity under subsection (a)(1) and (B)"; and

(2) in subsection (e)(5), by striking "or divorced wife" the second place it appears.

(b) EFFECTIVE DATE.—The amendments made by this section shall take effect 1 year after the date of the enactment of this Act.

[CCH Explanation at ¶1030. Committee Reports at ¶11,020.]

[¶7204] ACT SEC. 1003. EXTENSION OF TIER II RAILROAD RETIREMENT BENEFITS TO SURVIVING FORMER SPOUSES PURSUANT TO DIVORCE AGREEMENTS.

(a) IN GENERAL.—Section 5 of the Railroad Retirement Act of 1974 (45 U.S.C. 231d) is amended by adding at the end the following:

"(d) Notwithstanding any other provision of law, the payment of any portion of an annuity computed under section 3(b) to a surviving former spouse in accordance with a court decree of divorce, annulment, or legal separation or the terms of any court-approved property settlement incident to any such court decree shall not be terminated upon the death of the individual who performed the service with respect to which such annuity is so computed unless such termination is otherwise required by the terms of such court decree."

(b) EFFECTIVE DATE.—The amendment made by this section shall take effect 1 year after the date of the enactment of this Act.

[CCH Explanation at ¶1035. Committee Reports at ¶11,020.]

[¶7207] ACT SEC. 1004. REQUIREMENT FOR ADDITIONAL SURVIVOR ANNUITY OPTION.

* * *

(b) AMENDMENTS TO ERISA.—

(1) ELECTION OF SURVIVOR ANNUITY.—Section 205(c)(1)(A) of the Employee Retirement Income Security Act of 1974 (29 U.S.C. 1055(c)(1)(A)) is amended—

(A) in clause (i), by striking ", and" and inserting a comma;

(B) by redesignating clause (ii) as clause (iii); and

(C) by inserting after clause (i) the following:

"(ii) if the participant elects a waiver under clause (i), may elect the qualified optional survivor annuity at any time during the applicable election period, and".

(2) DEFINITION.—Section 205(d) of such Act (29 U.S.C. 1055(d)) is amended—

(A) by inserting "(1)" after "(d)";

(B) by redesignating paragraphs (1) and (2) as subparagraphs (A) and (B), respectively; and

(C) by adding at the end the following:

"(2)(A) For purposes of this section, the term 'qualified optional survivor annuity' means an annuity—

"(i) for the life of the participant with a survivor annuity for the life of the spouse which is equal to the applicable percentage of the amount of the annuity which is payable during the joint lives of the participant and the spouse, and

"(ii) which is the actuarial equivalent of a single annuity for the life of the participant.

Such term also includes any annuity in a form having the effect of an annuity described in the preceding sentence.

"(B)(i) For purposes of subparagraph (A), if the survivor annuity percentage—

"(I) is less than 75 percent, the applicable percentage is 75 percent, and

"(II) is greater than or equal to 75 percent, the applicable percentage is 50 percent.

"(ii) For purposes of clause (i), the term 'survivor annuity percentage' means the percentage which the survivor annuity under the plan's qualified joint and survivor annuity bears to the annuity payable during the joint lives of the participant and the spouse.".

(3) NOTICE.—Section 205(c)(3)(A)(i) of such Act (29 U.S.C. 1055(c)(3)(A)(i)) is amended by inserting "and of the qualified optional survivor annuity" after "annuity".

(c) EFFECTIVE DATES.—

(1) IN GENERAL.—The amendments made by this section shall apply to plan years beginning after December 31, 2007.

(2) SPECIAL RULE FOR COLLECTIVELY BARGAINED PLANS.—In the case of a plan maintained pursuant to 1 or more collective bargaining agreements between employee representatives and 1 or more employers ratified on or before the date of the enactment of this Act, the amendments made by this section shall not apply to plan years beginning before the earlier of—

(A) the later of—

(i) January 1, 2008, or

(ii) the date on which the last collective bargaining agreement related to the plan terminates (determined without regard to any extension thereof after the date of enactment of this Act), or

(B) January 1, 2009.

[CCH Explanation at ¶1040. Committee Reports at ¶11,030.]

TITLE XI—ADMINISTRATIVE PROVISIONS

[¶7210] ACT SEC. 1101. EMPLOYEE PLANS COMPLIANCE RESOLUTION SYSTEM.

(a) IN GENERAL.—The Secretary of the Treasury shall have full authority to establish and implement the Employee Plans Compliance Resolution System (or any successor program) and any other employee plans correction policies, including the authority to waive income, excise, or other taxes to ensure that any tax, penalty, or sanction is not excessive and bears a reasonable relationship to the nature, extent, and severity of the failure.

(b) IMPROVEMENTS.—The Secretary of the Treasury shall continue to update and improve the Employee Plans Compliance Resolution System (or any successor program), giving special attention to—

(1) increasing the awareness and knowledge of small employers concerning the availability and use of the program;

(2) taking into account special concerns and circumstances that small employers face with respect to compliance and correction of compliance failures;

(3) extending the duration of the self-correction period under the Self-Correction Program for significant compliance failures;

(4) expanding the availability to correct insignificant compliance failures under the Self-Correction Program during audit; and

(5) assuring that any tax, penalty, or sanction that is imposed by reason of a compliance failure is not excessive and bears a reasonable relationship to the nature, extent, and severity of the failure.

[CCH Explanation at ¶1085. Committee Reports at ¶11,040.]

[¶7213] ACT SEC. 1102. NOTICE AND CONSENT PERIOD REGARDING DISTRIBUTIONS.

(a) EXPANSION OF PERIOD.—

* * *

(2) AMENDMENT OF ERISA.—

(A) IN GENERAL.—Section 205(c)(7)(A) of the Employee Retirement Income Security Act of 1974 (29 U.S.C. 1055(c)(7)(A)) is amended by striking "90-day" and inserting "180-day".

(B) MODIFICATION OF REGULATIONS.—The Secretary of the Treasury shall modify the regulations under part 2 of subtitle B of title I of the Employee Retirement Income Security Act of 1974 relating to sections 203(e) and 205 of such Act by substituting "180 days" for "90 days" each place it appears.

(3) EFFECTIVE DATE.—The amendments and modifications made or required by this subsection shall apply to years beginning after December 31, 2006.

(b) NOTIFICATION OF RIGHT TO DEFER.—

(1) IN GENERAL.—The Secretary of the Treasury shall modify the regulations under section 411(a)(11) of the Internal Revenue Code of 1986 and under section 205 of the Employee Retirement Income Security Act of 1974 to provide that the description of a participant's right, if

any, to defer receipt of a distribution shall also describe the consequences of failing to defer such receipt.

(2) EFFECTIVE DATE.—

(A) IN GENERAL.—The modifications required by paragraph (1) shall apply to years beginning after December 31, 2006.

(B) REASONABLE NOTICE.—A plan shall not be treated as failing to meet the requirements of section 411(a)(11) of such Code or section 205 of such Act with respect to any description of consequences described in paragraph (1) made within 90 days after the Secretary of the Treasury issues the modifications required by paragraph (1) if the plan administrator makes a reasonable attempt to comply with such requirements.

[CCH Explanation at ¶ 925. Committee Reports at ¶ 11,050.]

[¶ 7216] ACT SEC. 1103. REPORTING SIMPLIFICATION.

(a) SIMPLIFIED ANNUAL FILING REQUIREMENT FOR OWNERS AND THEIR SPOUSES.—

(1) IN GENERAL.—The Secretary of the Treasury shall modify the requirements for filing annual returns with respect to one-participant retirement plans to ensure that such plans with assets of $250,000 or less as of the close of the plan year need not file a return for that year.

(2) ONE-PARTICIPANT RETIREMENT PLAN DEFINED.—For purposes of this subsection, the term "one-participant retirement plan" means a retirement plan with respect to which the following requirements are met:

(A) on the first day of the plan year—

(i) the plan covered only one individual (or the individual and the individual's spouse) and the individual owned 100 percent of the plan sponsor (whether or not incorporated), or

(ii) the plan covered only one or more partners (or partners and their spouses) in the plan sponsor;

(B) the plan meets the minimum coverage requirements of section 410(b) of the Internal Revenue Code of 1986 without being combined with any other plan of the business that covers the employees of the business;

(C) the plan does not provide benefits to anyone except the individual (and the individual's spouse) or the partners (and their spouses);

(D) the plan does not cover a business that is a member of an affiliated service group, a controlled group of corporations, or a group of businesses under common control; and

(E) the plan does not cover a business that uses the services of leased employees (within the meaning of section 414(n) of such Code).

For purposes of this paragraph, the term "partner" includes a 2-percent shareholder (as defined in section 1372(b) of such Code) of an S corporation.

(3) OTHER DEFINITIONS.—Terms used in paragraph (2) which are also used in section 414 of the Internal Revenue Code of 1986 shall have the respective meanings given such terms by such section.

(4) EFFECTIVE DATE.—The provisions of this subsection shall apply to plan years beginning on or after January 1, 2007.

(b) SIMPLIFIED ANNUAL FILING REQUIREMENT FOR PLANS WITH FEWER THAN 25 PARTICIPANTS.—In the case of plan years beginning after December 31, 2006, the Secretary of the Treasury and the Secretary of Labor shall provide for the filing of a simplified annual return for any retirement plan which covers less than 25 participants on the first day of a plan year and which meets the requirements described in subparagraphs (B), (D), and (E) of subsection (a)(2).

[CCH Explanation at ¶ 1080. Committee Reports at ¶ 11,060.]

[¶ 7219] ACT SEC. 1104. VOLUNTARY EARLY RETIREMENT INCENTIVE AND EMPLOYMENT RETENTION PLANS MAINTAINED BY LOCAL EDUCATIONAL AGENCIES AND OTHER ENTITIES.

(a) VOLUNTARY EARLY RETIREMENT INCENTIVE PLANS.—

* * *

(2) AGE DISCRIMINATION IN EMPLOYMENT ACT.—Section 4(l)(1) of the Age Discrimination in Employment Act of 1967 (29 U.S.C. 623(l)(1)) is amended—

(A) by inserting "(A)" after "(1)",

(B) by redesignating subparagraphs (A) and (B) as clauses (i) and (ii), respectively,

(C) by redesignating clauses (i) and (ii) of subparagraph (B) (as in effect before the amendments made by subparagraph (B)) as subclauses (I) and (II), respectively, and

(D) by adding at the end the following:

"(B) A voluntary early retirement incentive plan that—

"(i) is maintained by—

"(I) a local educational agency (as defined in section 9101 of the Elementary and Secondary Education Act of 1965 (20 U.S.C. 7801), or

"(II) an education association which principally represents employees of 1 or more agencies described in subclause (I) and which is described in section 501(c) (5) or (6) of the Internal Revenue Code of 1986 and exempt from taxation under section 501(a) of such Code, and

"(ii) makes payments or supplements described in subclauses (I) and (II) of subparagraph (A)(ii) in coordination with a defined benefit plan (as so defined) maintained by an eligible employer described in section 457(e)(1)(A) of such Code or by an education association described in clause (i)(II),

shall be treated solely for purposes of subparagraph (A)(ii) as if it were a part of the defined benefit plan with respect to such payments or supplements. Payments or supplements under such a voluntary early retirement incentive plan shall not constitute severance pay for purposes of paragraph (2).".

* * *

(c) COORDINATION WITH ERISA.—Section 3(2)(B) of the Employee Retirement Income Security Act of 1974 (29 U.S.C. 1002(2)(B)) is amended by adding at the end the following: "An applicable voluntary early retirement incentive plan (as defined in section 457(e)(11)(D)(ii) of the Internal Revenue Code of 1986) making payments or supplements described in section 457(e)(11)(D)(i) of such Code, and an applicable employment retention plan (as defined in section 457(f)(4)(C) of such Code) making payments of benefits described in section 457(f)(4)(A) of such Code, shall, for purposes of this title, be treated as a welfare plan (and not a pension plan) with respect to such payments and supplements."

(d) EFFECTIVE DATES.—

(1) IN GENERAL.—The amendments made by this Act shall take effect on the date of the enactment of this Act.

* * *

(3) ERISA AMENDMENTS.—The amendment made by subsection (c) shall apply to plan years ending after the date of the enactment of this Act.

(4) CONSTRUCTION.—Nothing in the amendments made by this section shall alter or affect the construction of the Internal Revenue Code of 1986, the Employee Retirement Income Security Act of 1974, or the Age Discrimination in Employment Act of 1967 as applied to any plan, arrangement, or conduct to which such amendments do not apply.

* * *

[CCH Explanation at ¶ 1070. Committee Reports at ¶ 11,070.]

[¶7222] ACT SEC. 1106. REVOCATION OF ELECTION RELATING TO TREATMENT AS MULTIEMPLOYER PLAN.

(a) AMENDMENT TO ERISA.—Section 3(37) of the Employee Retirement Income Security Act of 1974 is amended by adding at the end the following new subparagraph (G):

"(G)(i) Within 1 year after the enactment of the Pension Protection Act of 2006—

"(I) an election under subparagraph (E) may be revoked, pursuant to procedures prescribed by the Pension Benefit Guaranty Corporation, if, for each of the 3 plan years prior to the date of the enactment of that Act, the plan would have been a multiemployer plan but for the election under subparagraph (E), and

"(II) a plan that meets the criteria in clauses (i) and (ii) of subparagraph (A) of this paragraph or that is described in clause (vi) may, pursuant to procedures prescribed by the Pension Benefit Guaranty Corporation, elect to be a multiemployer plan, if—

"(aa) for each of the 3 plan years immediately before the date of the enactment of the Pension Protection Act of 2006, the plan has met those criteria or is so described,

"(bb) substantially all of the plan's employer contributions for each of those plan years were made or required to be made by organizations that were exempt from tax under section 501 of the Internal Revenue Code of 1986, and

"(cc) the plan was established prior to September 2, 1974.

"(ii) An election under this paragraph shall be effective for all purposes under this Act and under the Internal Revenue Code of 1986, starting with the first plan year ending after the date of the enactment of the Pension Protection Act of 2006.

"(iii) Once made, an election under this paragraph shall be irrevocable, except that a plan described in subclause (i)(II) shall cease to be a multiemployer plan as of the plan year beginning immediately after the first plan year for which the majority of its employer contributions were made or required to be made by organizations that were not exempt from tax under section 501 of the Internal Revenue Code of 1986.

"(iv) The fact that a plan makes an election under clause (i)(II) does not imply that the plan was not a multiemployer plan prior to the date of the election or would not be a multiemployer plan without regard to the election.

"(v)(I) No later than 30 days before an election is made under this paragraph, the plan administrator shall provide notice of the pending election to each plan participant and beneficiary, each labor organization representing such participants or beneficiaries, and each employer that has an obligation to contribute to the plan, describing the principal differences between the guarantee programs under title IV and the benefit restrictions under this title for single employer and multiemployer plans, along with such other information as the plan administrator chooses to include.

"(II) Within 180 days after the date of enactment of the Pension Protection Act of 2006, the Secretary shall prescribe a model notice under this subparagraph.

"(III) A plan administrator's failure to provide the notice required under this subparagraph shall be treated for purposes of section 502(c)(2) as a failure or refusal by the plan administrator to file the annual report required to be filed with the Secretary under section 101(b)(4).

"(vi) A plan is described in this clause if it is a plan—

"(I) that was established in Chicago, Illinois, on August 12, 1881; and

"(II) sponsored by an organization described in section 501(c)(5) of the Internal Revenue Code of 1986 and exempt from tax under section 501(a) of such Code.".

* * *

[CCH Explanation at ¶325. Committee Reports at ¶11,090.]

[¶ 7225] ACT SEC. 1107. PROVISIONS RELATING TO PLAN AMENDMENTS.

(a) IN GENERAL.—If this section applies to any pension plan or contract amendment—

(1) such pension plan or contract shall be treated as being operated in accordance with the terms of the plan during the period described in subsection (b)(2)(A), and

(2) except as provided by the Secretary of the Treasury, such pension plan shall not fail to meet the requirements of section 411(d)(6) of the Internal Revenue Code of 1986 and section 204(g) of the Employee Retirement Income Security Act of 1974 by reason of such amendment.

(b) AMENDMENTS TO WHICH SECTION APPLIES.—

(1) IN GENERAL.—This section shall apply to any amendment to any pension plan or annuity contract which is made—

(A) pursuant to any amendment made by this Act or pursuant to any regulation issued by the Secretary of the Treasury or the Secretary of Labor under this Act, and

(B) on or before the last day of the first plan year beginning on or after January 1, 2009.

In the case of a governmental plan (as defined in section 414(d) of the Internal Revenue Code of 1986), this paragraph shall be applied by substituting "2011" for "2009".

(2) CONDITIONS.—This section shall not apply to any amendment unless—

(A) during the period—

(i) beginning on the date the legislative or regulatory amendment described in paragraph (1)(A) takes effect (or in the case of a plan or contract amendment not required by such legislative or regulatory amendment, the effective date specified by the plan), and

(ii) ending on the date described in paragraph (1)(B) (or, if earlier, the date the plan or contract amendment is adopted), the plan or contract is operated as if such plan or contract amendment were in effect; and

(B) such plan or contract amendment applies retroactively for such period.

[CCH Explanation at ¶ 1090. Committee Reports at ¶ 11,100.]

TITLE XII—PROVISIONS RELATING TO EXEMPT ORGANIZATIONS

Subtitle A—Charitable Giving Incentives

* * *

[¶ 7228] ACT SEC. 1205. MODIFICATION OF TAX TREATMENT OF CERTAIN PAYMENTS TO CONTROLLING EXEMPT ORGANIZATIONS.

* * *

(b) REPORTING.—

* * *

(2) REPORT TO CONGRESS.—Not later than January 1, 2009, the Secretary of the Treasury shall submit to the Committee on Finance of the Senate and the Committee on Ways and Means of the House of Representatives a report on the effectiveness of the Internal Revenue Service in administering the amendments made by subsection (a) and on the extent to which payments by controlled entities (within the meaning of section 512(b)(13) of the Internal Revenue Code of 1986) to controlling organizations (within the meaning of section 512(b)(13) of such Code) meet the requirements under section 482 of such Code. Such report shall include the results of any audit of any controlling organization or controlled entity and recommendations relating to the tax treatment of payments from controlled entities to controlling organizations.

* * *

[CCH Explanation at ¶ 1210. Committee Reports at ¶ 11,150.]

Subtitle B—Reforming Exempt Organizations

PART 1—GENERAL REFORMS

[¶7231] ACT SEC. 1211. REPORTING ON CERTAIN ACQUISITIONS OF INTERESTS IN INSURANCE CONTRACTS IN WHICH CERTAIN EXEMPT ORGANIZATIONS HOLD AN INTEREST.

* * *

(c) STUDY.—

(1) IN GENERAL.—The Secretary of the Treasury shall undertake a study on—

(A) the use by tax exempt organizations of applicable insurance contracts (as defined under section 6050V(d)(2) of the Internal Revenue Code of 1986, as added by subsection (a)) for the purpose of sharing the benefits of the organization's insurable interest in individuals insured under such contracts with investors, and

(B) whether such activities are consistent with the tax exempt status of such organizations.

(2) REPORT.—Not later than 30 months after the date of the enactment of this Act, the Secretary of the Treasury shall report on the study conducted under paragraph (1) to the Committee on Finance of the Senate and the Committee on Ways and Means of the House of Representatives.

* * *

[CCH Explanation at ¶1285. Committee Reports at ¶11,190.]

[¶7234] ACT SEC. 1219. PROVISIONS RELATING TO SUBSTANTIAL AND GROSS OVERSTATEMENTS OF VALUATIONS.

* * *

(d) DISCIPLINARY ACTIONS AGAINST APPRAISERS.—Section 330(c) of title 31, United States Code, is amended by striking "with respect to whom a penalty has been assessed under section 6701(a) of the Internal Revenue Code of 1986".

(e) EFFECTIVE DATES.—

* * *

(2) APPRAISER PROVISIONS.—Except as provided in paragraph (3), the amendments made by subsections (b), (c), and (d) shall apply to appraisals prepared with respect to returns or submissions filed after the date of the enactment of this Act.

* * *

[CCH Explanation at ¶1350. Committee Reports at ¶11,270.]

[¶7237] ACT SEC. 1223. NOTIFICATION REQUIREMENT FOR ENTITIES NOT CURRENTLY REQUIRED TO FILE.

* * *

(e) SECRETARIAL OUTREACH REQUIREMENTS.

(1) NOTICE REQUIREMENT.—The Secretary of the Treasury shall notify in a timely manner every organization described in section 6033(i) of the Internal Revenue Code of 1986 (as added by this section) of the requirement under such section 6033(i) and of the penalty established under section 6033(j) of such Code—

(A) by mail, in the case of any organization the identity and address of which is included in the list of exempt organizations maintained by the Secretary, and

(B) by Internet or other means of outreach, in the case of any other organization.

(2) LOSS OF STATUS PENALTY FOR FAILURE TO FILE RETURN.—The Secretary of the Treasury shall publicize, in a timely manner in appropriate forms and instructions and through other appropriate means, the penalty established under section 6033(j) of such Code for the failure to file a return under subsection (a)(1) or (i) of section 6033 of such Code.

* * *

[CCH Explanation at ¶1260. Committee Reports at ¶11,310.]

[¶7240] ACT SEC. 1226. STUDY ON DONOR ADVISED FUNDS AND SUPPORTING ORGANIZATIONS.

(a) STUDY.—The Secretary of the Treasury shall undertake a study on the organization and operation of donor advised funds (as defined in section 4966(d)(2) of the Internal Revenue Code of 1986, as added by this Act) and of organizations described in section 509(a)(3) of such Code. The study shall specifically consider—

(1) whether the deductions allowed for the income, gift, or estate taxes for charitable contributions to sponsoring organizations (as defined in section 4966(d)(1) of such Code, as added by this Act) of donor advised funds or to organizations described in section 509(a)(3) of such Code are appropriate in consideration of—

(A) the use of contributed assets (including the type, extent, and timing of such use), or

(B) the use of the assets of such organizations for the benefit of the person making the charitable contribution (or a person related to such person),

(2) whether donor advised funds should be required to distribute for charitable purposes a specified amount (whether based on the income or assets of the fund) in order to ensure that the sponsoring organization with respect to such donor advised fund is operating consistent with the purposes or functions constituting the basis for its exemption under section 501, or its status as an organization described in section 509(a), of such Code,

(3) whether the retention by donors to organizations described in paragraph (1) of rights or privileges with respect to amounts transferred to such organizations (including advisory rights or privileges with respect to the making of grants or the investment of assets) is consistent with the treatment of such transfers as completed gifts that qualify for a deduction for income, gift, or estate taxes, and

(4) whether the issues raised by paragraphs (1), (2), and (3) are also issues with respect to other forms of charities or charitable donations.

(b) REPORT.—Not later than 1 year after the date of the enactment of this Act, the Secretary of the Treasury shall submit to the Committee on Finance of the Senate and the Committee on Ways and Means of the House of Representatives a report on the study conducted under subsection (a) and make such recommendations as the Secretary of the Treasury considers appropriate.

* * *

[CCH Explanation at ¶1290. Committee Reports at ¶11,340.]

PART 3—IMPROVED ACCOUNTABILITY OF SUPPORTING ORGANIZATIONS

[¶7243] ACT SEC. 1241. REQUIREMENTS FOR SUPPORTING ORGANIZATIONS.

* * *

(c) CHARITABLE TRUSTS WHICH ARE TYPE III SUPPORTING ORGANIZATIONS.—For purposes of section 509(a)(3)(B)(iii) of the Internal Revenue Code of 1986, an organization which is a trust shall not be considered to be operated in connection with any organization described in paragraph (1) or (2) of section 509(a) of such Code solely because—

(1) it is a charitable trust under State law,

(2) the supported organization (as defined in section 509(f)(3) of such Code) is a beneficiary of such trust, and

(3) the supported organization (as so defined) has the power to enforce the trust and compel an accounting.

(d) PAYOUT REQUIREMENTS FOR TYPE III SUPPORTING ORGANIZATIONS.—

(1) IN GENERAL.—The Secretary of the Treasury shall promulgate new regulations under section 509 of the Internal Revenue Code of 1986 on payments required by type III supporting organizations which are not functionally integrated type III supporting organizations. Such regulations shall require such organizations to make distributions of a percentage of either income or assets to supported organizations (as defined in section 509(f)(3) of such Code) in order to ensure that a significant amount is paid to such organizations.

(2) TYPE III SUPPORTING ORGANIZATION; FUNCTIONALLY INTEGRATED TYPE III SUPPORTING ORGANIZATION.—For purposes of paragraph (1), the terms "type III supporting organization" and "functionally integrated type III supporting organization" have the meanings given such terms under subparagraphs (A) and (B) section 4943(f)(5) of the Internal Revenue Code of 1986 (as added by this Act), respectively.

(e) EFFECTIVE DATES.—

* * *

(2) CHARITABLE TRUSTS WHICH ARE TYPE III SUPPORTING ORGANIZATIONS.—Subsection (c) shall take effect—

(A) in the case of trusts operated in connection with an organization described in paragraph (1) or (2) of section 509(a) of the Internal Revenue Code of 1986 on the date of the enactment of this Act, on the date that is one year after the date of the enactment of this Act, and

(B) in the case of any other trust, on the date of the enactment of this Act.

* * *

[CCH Explanation at ¶ 1225. Committee Reports at ¶ 11,360.]

TITLE XIII—OTHER PROVISIONS

* * *

[¶ 7252] ACT SEC. 1303. EXCEPTION TO THE LOCAL FURNISHING REQUIREMENT OF THE TAX-EXEMPT BOND RULES.

(a) SNETTISHAM HYDROELECTRIC FACILITY.—For purposes of determining whether any private activity bond issued before May 31, 2006, and used to finance the acquisition of the Snettisham hydroelectric facility is a qualified bond for purposes of section 142(a)(8) of the Internal Revenue Code of 1986, the electricity furnished by such facility to the City of Hoonah, Alaska, shall not be taken into account for purposes of section 142(f)(1) of such Code.

(b) LAKE DOROTHY HYDROELECTRIC FACILITY.—For purposes of determining whether any private activity bond issued before May 31, 2006, and used to finance the Lake Dorothy hydroelectric facility is a qualified bond for purposes of section 142(a)(8) of the Internal Revenue Code of 1986, the electricity furnished by such facility to the City of Hoonah, Alaska, shall not be taken into account for purposes of paragraphs (1) and (3) of section 142(f) of such Code.

(c) DEFINITIONS.—For purposes of this section—

(1) LAKE DOROTHY HYDROELECTRIC FACILITY.—The term "Lake Dorothy hydroelectric facility" means the hydroelectric facility located approximately 10 miles south of Juneau, Alaska, and commonly referred to as the "Lake Dorothy project".

(2) SNETTISHAM HYDROELECTRIC FACILITY.—The term "Snettisham hydroelectric facility" means the hydroelectric project described in section 1804 of the Small Business Job Protection Act of 1996.

[CCH Explanation at ¶ 1340. Committee Reports at ¶ 11,390.]

[¶ 7255] ACT SEC. 1304. QUALIFIED TUITION PROGRAMS.

(a) PERMANENT EXTENSION OF MODIFICATIONS.—Section 901 of the Economic Growth and Tax Relief Reconciliation Act of 2001 (relating to sunset provisions) shall not apply to section 402 of such Act (relating to modifications to qualified tuition programs).

* * *

[CCH Explanation at ¶ 1310. Committee Reports at ¶ 11,400.]

Committee Reports

Pension Protection Act of 2006

¶10,001 Introduction

The description and technical explanation of the Pension Protection Act of 2006, prepared by the Staff of the Joint Committee on Taxation, explains the intent of Congress regarding the provisions in the Act. Reports of the Joint Committee on Taxation are included in this section to aid in the reader's understanding of the relevant provisions, but may not be cited as the official Conference Committee Report accompanying the Pension Protection Act. At the end of the Joint Committee Report text, references are provided to corresponding explanations and Code provisions. Subscribers to the electronic version can link from these references to the corresponding material. *The pertinent sections of the Technical Explanation appear in Act Section order beginning at ¶10,010.*

¶10,005 Background

The Pension Protection Act of 2006 (H.R. 4) was introduced in the House on July 28, 2006, after House leaders dismissed conferees on a pension reform bill (H.R. 2830) earlier that morning. H.R. 4 went to the House floor without committee hearings or markups by the House leadership. On the same day, the House passed H.R. 4 by a vote of 279 to 131.

On August 3, 2006, the Senate passed H.R. 6 by a vote of 93 to 5. In floor debate, Sen. William Frist (R-Tenn.) asked for and received unanimous consent that the Senate not consider any conference report on H.R. 2830, effectively blocking that bill from any future consideration. President Bush signed the bill into law on August 17, 2006.

Without a conference report or controlling committee reports, the staff of the Joint Committee on Taxation released its Technical Explanation of H.R. 4 on August 3, 2006.

The following material includes the pertinent texts of the committee reports and the description and technical explanation of the conference agreement prepared by the Staff of the Joint Committee on Taxation for the Pension Protection Act of 2006 that explains the intent of Congress regarding the revenue-related provisions of the Act. References are to the following report:

- The Joint Committee on Taxation, Technical Explanation of H.R. 4, the "Pension Protection Act of 2006," as passed by the House on July 28, 2006, and as considered by the Senate on August 3, 2006 (JCX-38-06) (H.R. 4, August 3, 2006) is referred to as Joint Committee on Taxation (J.C.T. REP. NO. JCX-38-06).

[¶10,010] Act Secs. 101, 102, 107, 111, 112 and 114. Minimum funding standards for single-employer defined benefit pension plans

Joint Committee Taxation (J.C.T. REP. NO. JCX-38-06)

[Code Sec. 412 and New Code Sec. 430]

Present Law

In general

Single-employer defined benefit pension plans are subject to minimum funding requirements under the Employee Retirement Income Security Act of 1974 ("ERISA") and the Internal Revenue Code (the "Code").[3] The amount of contributions required for a plan year under the minimum funding rules is generally the amount needed to fund benefits earned during that year plus that year's portion of other liabilities that are amortized over a period of years, such as benefits resulting from a grant of past service credit. The amount of required annual contributions is determined under one of a number of acceptable actuarial cost methods. Additional contributions are required under the deficit reduction contribution rules in the case of certain underfunded plans. No contribution is required under the minimum funding rules in excess of the full funding limit (described below).

General minimum funding rules

Funding standard account

As an administrative aid in the application of the funding requirements, a defined benefit pension plan is required to maintain a special account called a "funding standard account" to which specified charges and credits are made for each plan year, including a charge for normal cost and credits for contributions to the plan. Other charges or credits may apply as a result of decreases or increases in past service liability as a result of plan amendments, experience gains or losses, gains or losses resulting from a change in actuarial assumptions, or a waiver of minimum required contributions.

In determining plan funding under an actuarial cost method, a plan's actuary generally makes certain assumptions regarding the future experience of a plan. These assumptions typically involve rates of interest, mortality, disability, salary increases, and other factors affecting the value of assets and liabilities. If the plan's actual unfunded liabilities are less than those anticipated by the actuary on the basis of these assumptions, then the excess is an experience gain. If the actual unfunded liabilities are greater than those anticipated, then the difference is an experience loss. Experience gains and losses for a year are generally amortized as credits or charges to the funding standard account over five years.

If the actuarial assumptions used for funding a plan are revised and, under the new assumptions, the accrued liability of a plan is less than the accrued liability computed under the previous assumptions, the decrease is a gain from changes in actuarial assumptions. If the new assumptions result in an increase in the plan's accrued liability, the plan has a loss from changes in actuarial assumptions. The accrued liability of a plan is the actuarial present value of projected pension benefits under the plan that will not be funded by future contributions to meet normal cost or future employee contributions. The gain or loss for a year from changes in actuarial assumptions is amortized as credits or charges to the funding standard account over ten years.

If minimum required contributions are waived (as discussed below), the waived amount (referred to as a "waived funding deficiency") is credited to the funding standard account. The waived funding deficiency is then amortized over a period of five years, beginning with the year following the year in which the waiver is granted. Each year, the funding standard account is charged with the amortization amount for that year unless the plan becomes fully funded.

If, as of the close of a plan year, the funding standard account reflects credits at least equal to charges, the plan is generally treated as meeting the minimum funding standard for the year. If, as of the close of the plan year, charges to the funding standard account exceed credits to the account, then the excess is referred to as an "ac-

[3] Multiemployer defined benefit pension plans are also subject to the minimum funding requirements, but the rules for multiemployer plans differ in various respects from the rules applicable to single-employer plans. Governmental plans and church plans are generally exempt from the minimum funding requirements.

cumulated funding deficiency." Thus, as a general rule, the minimum contribution for a plan year is determined as the amount by which the charges to the funding standard account would exceed credits to the account if no contribution were made to the plan. For example, if the balance of charges to the funding standard account of a plan for a year would be $200,000 without any contributions, then a minimum contribution equal to that amount would be required to meet the minimum funding standard for the year to prevent an accumulated funding deficiency.

Credit balances

If credits to the funding standard account exceed charges, a "credit balance" results. A credit balance results, for example, if contributions in excess of minimum required contributions are made. Similarly, a credit balance may result from large net experience gains. The amount of the credit balance, increased with interest at the rate used under the plan to determine costs, is applied against charges to the funding standard account, thus reducing required contributions.

Funding methods and general concepts

A defined benefit pension plan is required to use an acceptable actuarial cost method to determine the elements included in its funding standard account for a year. Generally, an actuarial cost method breaks up the cost of benefits under the plan into annual charges consisting of two elements for each plan year. These elements are referred to as: (1) normal cost; and (2) supplemental cost.

The plan's normal cost for a plan year generally represents the cost of future benefits allocated to the year by the funding method used by the plan for current employees and, under some funding methods, for separated employees. Specifically, it is the amount actuarially determined that would be required as a contribution by the employer for the plan year in order to maintain the plan if the plan had been in effect from the beginning of service of the included employees and if the costs for prior years had been paid, and all assumptions as to interest, mortality, time of payment, etc., had been fulfilled. The normal cost will be funded by future contributions to the plan: (1) in level dollar amounts; (2) as a uniform percentage of payroll; (3) as a uniform amount per unit of service (e.g., $1 per hour); or (4) on the basis of the actuarial present values of benefits considered accruing in particular plan years.

The supplemental cost for a plan year is the cost of future benefits that would not be met by future normal costs, future employee contributions, or plan assets. The most common supplemental cost is that attributable to past service liability, which represents the cost of future benefits under the plan: (1) on the date the plan is first effective; or (2) on the date a plan amendment increasing plan benefits is first effective. Other supplemental costs may be attributable to net experience losses, changes in actuarial assumptions, and amounts necessary to make up funding deficiencies for which a waiver was obtained. Supplemental costs must be amortized (i.e., recognized for funding purposes) over a specified number of years, depending on the source. For example, the cost attributable to a past service liability is generally amortized over 30 years.

Normal costs and supplemental costs under a plan are computed on the basis of an actuarial valuation of the assets and liabilities of a plan. An actuarial valuation is generally required annually and is made as of a date within the plan year or within one month before the beginning of the plan year. However, a valuation date within the preceding plan year may be used if, as of that date, the value of the plan's assets is at least 100 percent of the plan's current liability (i.e., the present value of benefits under the plan, as described below).

For funding purposes, the actuarial value of plan assets may be used, rather than fair market value. The actuarial value of plan assets is the value determined on the basis of a reasonable actuarial valuation method that takes into account fair market value and is permitted under Treasury regulations. Any actuarial valuation method used must result in a value of plan assets that is not less than 80 percent of the fair market value of the assets and not more than 120 percent of the fair market value. In addition, if the valuation method uses average value of the plan assets, values may be used for a stated period not to exceed the five most recent plan years, including the current year.

In applying the funding rules, all costs, liabilities, interest rates, and other factors are required to be determined on the basis of actuarial assumptions and methods, each of which is reasonable (taking into account the experience of the plan and reasonable expectations), or which, in the aggregate, result in a total plan contribution equivalent to a contribution that would be determined if each assumption and method were reasonable. In addition, the assumptions are required to offer the actuary's best estimate of anticipated experience under the plan.[4]

Additional contributions for underfunded plans

In general

Under special funding rules (referred to as the "deficit reduction contribution" rules),[5] an additional charge to a plan's funding standard account is generally required for a plan year if the plan's funded current liability percentage for the plan year is less than 90 percent.[6] A plan's "funded current liability percentage" is generally the actuarial value of plan assets as a percentage of the plan's current liability.[7] In general, a plan's current liability means all liabilities to employees and their beneficiaries under the plan, determined on a present-value basis.

The amount of the additional charge required under the deficit reduction contribution rules is the sum of two amounts: (1) the excess, if any, of (a) the deficit reduction contribution (as described below), over (b) the contribution required under the normal funding rules; and (2) the amount (if any) required with respect to unpredictable contingent event benefits. The amount of the additional charge cannot exceed the amount needed to increase the plan's funded current liability percentage to 100 percent (taking into account the expected increase in current liability due to benefits accruing during the plan year).

The deficit reduction contribution is generally the sum of (1) the "unfunded old liability amount," (2) the "unfunded new liability amount," and (3) the expected increase in current liability due to benefits accruing during the plan year.[8] The "unfunded old liability amount" is the amount needed to amortize certain unfunded liabilities under 1987 and 1994 transition rules. The "unfunded new liability amount" is the applicable percentage of the plan's unfunded new liability. Unfunded new liability generally means the unfunded current liability of the plan (i.e., the amount by which the plan's current liability exceeds the actuarial value of plan assets), but determined without regard to certain liabilities (such as the plan's unfunded old liability and unpredictable contingent event benefits). The applicable percentage is generally 30 percent, but decreases by .40 of one percentage point for each percentage point by which the plan's funded current liability percentage exceeds 60 percent. For example, if a plan's funded current liability percentage is 85 percent (i.e., it exceeds 60 percent by 25 percentage points), the applicable percentage is 20 percent (30 percent minus 10 percentage points (25 multiplied by .4)).[9]

A plan may provide for unpredictable contingent event benefits, which are benefits that depend on contingencies that are not reliably and reasonably predictable, such as facility shutdowns or reductions in workforce. The value of any unpredictable contingent event benefit is not considered in determining additional contributions until the event has occurred. The event on which an unpredictable contingent event benefit is contingent is generally not considered to have occurred until all events on which the benefit is contingent have occurred.

Required interest rate and mortality table

Specific interest rate and mortality assumptions must be used in determining a plan's current liability for purposes of the special funding rule. For plans years beginning before January 1, 2004, and after December 31, 2005, the interest rate used to determine a plan's current liability must be within a permissible range of the weighted average of the interest rates on 30-year Treasury securities for the four-year period end-

---

[4] Under present law, certain changes in actuarial assumptions that decrease the liabilities of an underfunded single-employer plan must be approved by the Secretary of the Treasury.

[5] The deficit reduction contribution rules apply to single-employer plans, other than single-employer plans with no more than 100 participants on any day in the preceding plan year. Single-employer plans with more than 100 but not more than 150 participants are generally subject to lower contribution requirements under these rules.

[6] Under an alternative test, a plan is not subject to the deficit reduction contribution rules for a plan year if (1) the plan's funded current liability percentage for the plan year is at least 80 percent, and (2) the plan's funded current liability percentage was at least 90 percent for each of the two immediately preceding plan years or each of the second and third immediately preceding plan years.

[7] In determining a plan's funded current liability percentage for a plan year, the value of the plan's assets is generally reduced by the amount of any credit balance under the plan's funding standard account. However, this reduction does not apply in determining the plan's funded current liability percentage for purposes of whether an additional charge is required under the deficit reduction contribution rules.

[8] The deficit reduction contribution may also include an additional amount as a result of the use of a new mortality table prescribed by the Secretary of the Treasury in determining current liability for plan years beginning after 2006, as described below.

[9] In making these computations, the value of the plan's assets is reduced by the amount of any credit balance under the plan's funding standard account.

ing on the last day before the plan year begins.[10] The permissible range is generally from 90 percent to 105 percent (120 percent for plan years beginning in 2002 or 2003).[11] The interest rate used under the plan generally must be consistent with the assumptions which reflect the purchase rates that would be used by insurance companies to satisfy the liabilities under the plan.[12]

Under the Pension Funding Equity Act of 2004 ("PFEA 2004"),[13] a special interest rate applies in determining current liability for plan years beginning in 2004 or 2005.[14] For these years, the interest rate used must be within a permissible range of the weighted average of the rates of interest on amounts invested conservatively in long-term investment-grade corporate bonds during the four-year period ending on the last day before the plan year begins. The permissible range for these years is from 90 percent to 100 percent. The interest rate is to be determined by the Secretary of the Treasury on the basis of two or more indices that are selected periodically by the Secretary and are in the top three quality levels available.

In determining current liability, the 1983 Group Annuity Mortality Table has been used since 1995.[15] Under present law, the Secretary of the Treasury may prescribe other tables to be used based on the actual experience of pension plans and projected trends in such experience. In addition, the Secretary of the Treasury is required to periodically review (at least every five years) any tables in effect and, to the extent the Secretary determines necessary, update such tables to reflect the actuarial experience of pension plans and projected trends in such experience.[16]

Under Prop. Treas. Reg. 1.412(l)(7)-1, beginning in 2007, RP-2000 Mortality Tables are used with improvements in mortality (including future improvements) projected to the current year and with separate tables for annuitants and nonannuitants.[17]

Other rules

Full funding limitation

No contributions are required under the minimum funding rules in excess of the full funding limitation. The full funding limitation is the excess, if any, of (1) the accrued liability under the plan (including normal cost), over (2) the lesser of (a) the market value of plan assets or (b) the actuarial value of plan assets.[18] However, the full funding limitation may not be less than the excess, if any, of 90 percent of the plan's current liability (including the expected increase in current liability due to benefits accruing during the plan year) over the actuarial value of plan assets. In general, current liability is all liabilities to plan participants and beneficiaries accrued to date, whereas the accrued liability under the full funding limitation may be based on projected future benefits, including future salary increases.

Timing of plan contributions

In general, plan contributions required to satisfy the funding rules must be made within 8½ months after the end of the plan year. If the contribution is made by such due date, the contribution is treated as if it were made on the last day of the plan year.

---

[10] The weighting used for this purpose is 40 percent, 30 percent, 20 percent and 10 percent, starting with the most recent year in the four-year period. Notice 88-73, 1988-2 C.B. 383.

[11] If the Secretary of the Treasury determines that the lowest permissible interest rate in this range is unreasonably high, the Secretary may prescribe a lower rate, but not less than 80 percent of the weighted average of the 30-year Treasury rate.

[12] Code sec. 412(b)(5)(B)(iii)(II); ERISA sec. 302(b)(5)(B)(iii)(II). Under Notice 90-11, 1990-1 C.B. 319, the interest rates in the permissible range are deemed to be consistent with the assumptions reflecting the purchase rates that would be used by insurance companies to satisfy the liabilities under the plan.

[13] Pub. L. No. 108-218 (2004).

[14] In addition, under PFEA 2004, if certain requirements are met, reduced contributions under the deficit reduction contribution rules apply for plan years beginning after December 27, 2003, and before December 28, 2005, in the case of plans maintained by commercial passenger airlines, employers primarily engaged in the production or manufacture of a steel mill product or in the processing of iron ore pellets, or a certain labor organization.

[15] Rev. Rul. 95-28, 1995-1 C.B. 74. Separate mortality tables are required to be used with respect to disabled participants.

[16] Code sec. 412(l)(7)(C)(ii)(III); ERISA sec. 302(d)(7)(C)(ii)(III).

[17] Separate tables continue to apply with respect to disabled participants.

[18] For plan years beginning before 2004, the full funding limitation was generally defined as the excess, if any, of (1) the lesser of (a) the accrued liability under the plan (including normal cost) or (b) a percentage (170 percent for 2003) of the plan's current liability (including the current liability normal cost), over (2) the lesser of (a) the market value of plan assets or (b) the actuarial value of plan assets, but in no case less than the excess, if any, of 90 percent of the plan's current liability over the actuarial value of plan assets. Under the Economic Growth and Tax Relief Reconciliation Act of 2001 ("EGTRRA"), the full funding limitation based on 170 percent of current liability is repealed for plan years beginning in 2004 and thereafter. The provisions of EGTRRA generally do not apply for years beginning after December 31, 2010.

In the case of a plan with a funded current liability percentage of less than 100 percent for the preceding plan year, estimated contributions for the current plan year must be made in quarterly installments during the current plan year.[19] The amount of each required installment is generally 25 percent of the lesser of (1) 90 percent of the amount required to be contributed for the current plan year or (2) 100 percent of the amount required to be contributed for the preceding plan year.[20] If a required installment is not made, interest applies for the period of underpayment at a rate of the greater of (1) 175 percent of the Federal mid-term rate, or (2) the plan rate.

Funding waivers

Within limits, the Secretary of the Treasury is permitted to waive all or a portion of the contributions required under the minimum funding standard for a plan year (a "waived funding deficiency").[21] A waiver may be granted if the employer (or employers) responsible for the contribution could not make the required contribution without temporary substantial business hardship and if requiring the contribution would be adverse to the interests of plan participants in the aggregate. Generally, no more than three waivers may be granted within any period of 15 consecutive plan years.

The IRS is authorized to require security to be provided as a condition of granting a waiver of the minimum funding standard if the sum of the plan's accumulated funding deficiency and the balance of any outstanding waived funding deficiencies exceeds $1 million.

Failure to make required contributions

An employer is generally subject to an excise tax if it fails to make minimum required contributions and fails to obtain a waiver from the IRS.[22] The excise tax is 10 percent of the amount of the accumulated funding deficiency. In addition, a tax of 100 percent may be imposed if the accumulated funding deficiency is not corrected within a certain period.

If the total of the contributions the employer fails to make (plus interest) exceeds $1 million and the plan's funded current liability percentage is less than 100 percent, a lien arises in favor of the plan with respect to all property of the employer and the members of the employer's controlled group. The amount of the lien is the total amount of the missed contributions (plus interest).

Explanation of Provision

Interest rate required for plan years beginning in 2006 and 2007

For plan years beginning after December 31, 2005, and before January 1, 2008, the provision applies the present-law funding rules, with an extension of the interest rate applicable in determining current liability for plan years beginning in 2004 and 2005. Thus, in determining current liability for funding purposes for plan years beginning in 2006 and 2007, the interest rate used must be within the permissible range (90 to 100 percent) of the weighted average of the rates of interest on amounts invested conservatively in long-term investment-grade corporate bonds during the four-year period ending on the last day before the plan year begins.

Funding rules for plan years beginning after 2007 - in general

For plan years beginning after December 31, 2007, in the case of single-employer defined benefit plans, the provision repeals the present-law funding rules (including the requirement that a funding standard account be maintained) and provides a new set of rules for determining minimum required contributions.[23] Under the provision, the minimum required contribution to a single-employer defined benefit pension plan for a plan year generally depends on a comparison of the value of the plan's assets with the plan's funding target and target normal cost. As described in more detail below, under the provision, credit balances generated under present law are carried over (into a "funding standard

---

[19] Code sec. 412(m); ERISA sec. 302(e).

[20] If quarterly contributions are required with respect to a plan, the amount of a quarterly installment must also be sufficient to cover any shortfall in the plan's liquid assets (a "liquidity shortfall").

[21] Code sec. 412(d); ERISA sec. 303. Under similar rules, the amortization period applicable to an unfunded past service liability or loss may also be extended.

[22] Code sec. 4971. An excise tax applies also if a quarterly installment is less than the amount required to cover the plan's liquidity shortfall.

[23] A delayed effective date applies to certain plans as discussed in Items C, D and E below. Changes to the funding rules for multiemployer plans are discussed in Title II below. Governmental plans and church plans continue to be exempt from the funding rules to the extent provided under present law.

carryover balance") and generally may be used in certain circumstances to reduce otherwise required minimum contributions. In addition, as described more fully below, contributions in excess of the minimum contributions required under the provision for plan years beginning after 2007 generally are credited to a prefunding balance that may be used in certain circumstances to reduce otherwise required minimum contributions. To facilitate the use of such balances to reduce minimum required contributions, while avoiding use of such balances for more than one purpose, in some circumstances the value of plan assets is reduced by the prefunding balance and/or the funding standard carryover balance.

The minimum required contribution for a plan year, based on the value of plan assets (reduced by any prefunding balance and funding standard carryover balance) compared to the funding target, is shown in the following table:

If:	*The minimum required contribution is:*
the value of plan assets (reduced by any prefunding balance and funding standard carryover balance) is less than the funding target,	the sum of: (1) target normal cost; (2) any shortfall amortization charge; and (3) any waiver amortization charge.
the value of plan assets (reduced by any prefunding balance and funding standard carryover balance) equals or exceeds the funding target,	the target normal cost, reduced (but not below zero) by the excess of (1) the value of plan assets (reduced by any prefunding balance and funding standard carryover balance), over (2) the funding target.

Under the provision, a plan's funding target is the present value of all benefits accrued or earned as of the beginning of the plan year. A plan's target normal cost for a plan year is the present value of benefits expected to accrue or be earned during the plan year. A shortfall amortization charge is generally the sum of the amounts required to amortize any shortfall amortization bases for the plan year and the six preceding plan years. A shortfall amortization base is generally required to be established for a plan year if the plan has a funding shortfall for a plan year.[24] A shortfall amortization base may be positive or negative, i.e., an offsetting amortization base is established for gains. In general, a plan has a funding shortfall if the plan's funding target for the year exceeds the value of the plan's assets (reduced by any prefunding balance and funding standard carryover balance). A waiver amortization charge is the amount required to amortize a waived funding deficiency.

The provision specifies the interest rates and mortality table that must be used in determining a plan's target normal cost and funding target, as well as certain other actuarial assumptions, including special assumptions ("at-risk" assumptions) for a plan in at-risk status. A plan is in at-risk status for a year if the value of the plan's assets (reduced by any prefunding and funding standard carryover balances) for the preceding year was less than (1) 80 percent of the plan's funding target determined without regard to the at-risk assumptions, and (2) 70 percent of the plan's funding target determined using the at-risk assumptions. Under a transition rule, instead of 80 percent, the following percentages apply: 65 percent for 2008, 70 percent for 2009, and 75 percent for 2010.

Target normal cost

Under the provision, the minimum required contribution for a plan year generally includes the plan's target normal cost for the plan year. A plan's target normal cost is the present value of all benefits expected to accrue or be earned under the plan during the plan year (the "current" year). For this purpose, an increase in any benefit attributable to services performed in a preceding year by reason of a compensation increase during the current year is treated as having accrued during the current year.

If the value of a plan's assets (reduced by any funding standard carryover balance and prefunding balance) exceeds the plan's funding target for a plan year, the minimum required contribution for the plan year is target normal cost reduced by such excess (but not below zero).

Funding target and shortfall amortization charges

In general

If the value of a plan's assets (reduced by any funding standard carryover balance and prefunding balance) is less than the plan's funding target for a plan year, so that the plan has a

[24] Under a special rule, discussed below, a shortfall amortization base does not have to be established if the value of a plan's assets (reduced by any prefunding balance, but only if the employer elects to use any portion of the prefunding balance to reduce required contributions for the year) is at least equal to the plan's funding target for the plan year.

funding shortfall,[25] the minimum required contribution is generally increased by a shortfall amortization charge. As discussed more fully below, the shortfall amortization charge is the aggregate total (not less than zero) of the shortfall amortization installments for the plan year with respect to any shortfall amortization bases for the plan year and the six preceding plan years.

Funding target

A plan's funding target for a plan year is the present value of all benefits accrued or earned under the plan as of the beginning of the plan year. For this purpose, all benefits (including early retirement or similar benefits) are taken into account. Benefits accruing in the plan year are not taken into account in determining the plan's funding target, regardless of whether the valuation date for the plan year is later than the first day of the plan year.[26]

Shortfall amortization charge

The shortfall amortization charge for a plan year is the aggregate total (not less than zero) of the shortfall amortization installments for the plan year with respect to any shortfall amortization bases for that plan year and the six preceding plan years. The shortfall amortization installments with respect to a shortfall amortization base for a plan year are the amounts necessary to amortize the shortfall amortization base in level annual installments over the seven-plan-year period beginning with the plan year. The shortfall amortization installment with respect to a shortfall amortization base for any plan year in the seven-year period is the annual installment determined for that year for that shortfall amortization base. Shortfall amortization installments are determined using the appropriate segment interest rates (discussed below).

Shortfall amortization base and phase-in of funding target

A shortfall amortization base is determined for a plan year based on the plan's funding shortfall for the plan year. The funding shortfall is the amount (if any) by which the plan's funding target for the year exceeds the value of the plan's assets (reduced by any funding standard carryover balance and prefunding balance).

The shortfall amortization base for a plan year is (1) the plan's funding shortfall, minus (2) the present value, determined using the segment interest rates (discussed below), of the aggregate total of the shortfall amortization installments and waiver amortization installments that have been determined for the plan year and any succeeding plan year with respect to any shortfall amortization bases and waiver amortization bases for preceding plan years.

A shortfall amortization base may be positive or negative, depending on whether the present value of remaining installments with respect to prior year amortization bases is more or less than the plan's funding shortfall. In either case, the shortfall amortization base is amortized over seven years. Shortfall amortization installments for a particular plan year with respect to positive and negative shortfall amortization bases are netted in determining the shortfall amortization charge for the plan year, but the resulting shortfall amortization charge cannot be less than zero. Thus, negative amortization installments may not offset waiver amortization installments or normal cost.

Under a special rule, a shortfall amortization base does not have to be established for a plan year if the value of a plan's assets (reduced by any prefunding balance, but only if the employer elects to use any portion of the prefunding balance to reduce required contributions for the year) is at least equal to the plan's funding target for the plan year. For purposes of the special rule, a transition rule applies for plan years beginning after 2007 and before 2011. The transition rule does not apply to a plan that (1) is not in effect for 2007, or (2) is subject to the present-law deficit reduction contribution rules for 2007 (i.e., a plan covering more than 100 participants and with a funded current liability below the applicable threshold).

Under the transition rule, a shortfall amortization base does not have to be established for a plan year during the transition period if the value of plan assets (reduced by any prefunding balance, but only if the employer elects to use the prefunding balance to reduce required contributions for the year) for the plan year is at least equal to the applicable percentage of the plan's funding target for the year. The applicable percentage is 92 percent for 2008, 94 percent for 2009, and 96 percent for 2010. However, the transition rule does not apply to a plan for any plan

[25] Under a special rule, in determining a plan's funding shortfall, the value of plan assets is not reduced by any funding standard carryover balance or prefunding balance if, with respect to the funding standard carryover balance or prefunding balance, there is in effect for the year a binding written with the Pension Benefit Guaranty Corporation which provides that such balance is not available to reduce the minimum required contribution for the plan year.

[26] Benefits accruing during the plan year are taken into account in determining normal cost for the plan year.

year after 2008 unless, for each preceding plan year after 2007, the plan's shortfall amortization base was zero (i.e., the plan was eligible for the special rule each preceding year).

Early deemed amortization of funding shortfalls for preceding years

If a plan's funding shortfall for a plan year is zero (i.e., the value of the plan's assets, reduced by any funding standard carryover balance and prefunding balance, is at least equal to the plan's funding target for the year), any shortfall amortization bases for preceding plan years are eliminated. That is, for purposes of determining any shortfall amortization charges for that year and succeeding years, the shortfall amortization bases for all preceding years (and all shortfall amortization installments determined with respect to such bases) are reduced to zero.

Waiver amortization charges

The provision retains the present-law rules under which the Secretary of the Treasury may waive all or a portion of the contributions required under the minimum funding standard for a plan year (referred to as a "waived funding deficiency").[27] If a plan has a waived funding deficiency for any of the five preceding plan years, the minimum required contribution for the plan year is increased by the waiver amortization charge for the plan year.

The waiver amortization charge for a plan year is the aggregate total of the waiver amortization installments for the plan year with respect to any waiver amortization bases for the five preceding plan years. The waiver amortization installments with respect to a waiver amortization base for a plan year are the amounts necessary to amortize the waiver amortization base in level annual installments over the five-year plan period beginning with the succeeding plan year. The waiver amortization installment with respect to that waiver amortization base for any plan year in the five-year period is the annual installment determined for the shortfall amortization base. Waiver amortization installments are determined using the appropriate segment interest rates (discussed below). The waiver amortization base for a plan year is the amount of the waived funding deficiency (if any) for the plan year.

If a plan's funding shortfall for a plan year is zero (i.e., the value of the plan's assets, reduced by any funding standard carryover balance and prefunding balance, is at least equal to the plan's funding target for the year), any waiver amortization bases for preceding plan years are eliminated. That is, for purposes of determining any waiver amortization charges for that year and succeeding years, the waiver amortization bases for all preceding years (and all waiver amortization installments determined with respect to such bases) are reduced to zero.

Actuarial assumptions used in determining a plan's target normal cost and funding target

Interest rates

The provision specifies the interest rates that must be used in determining a plan's target normal cost and funding target. Under the provision, present value is determined using three interest rates ("segment" rates), each of which applies to benefit payments expected to be made from the plan during a certain period. The first segment rate applies to benefits reasonably determined to be payable during the five-year period beginning on the first day of the plan year; the second segment rate applies to benefits reasonably determined to be payable during the 15-year period following the initial five-year period; and the third segment rate applies to benefits reasonably determined to be payable the end of the 15-year period. Each segment rate is a single interest rate determined monthly by the Secretary of the Treasury on the basis of a corporate bond yield curve, taking into account only the portion of the yield curve based on corporate bonds maturing during the particular segment rate period.

The corporate bond yield curve used for this purpose is to be prescribed on a monthly basis by the Secretary of the Treasury and reflect the average, for the 24-month period ending with the preceding month, of yields on investment grade corporate bonds with varying maturities and that are in the top three quality levels available. The yield curve should reflect the average of the rates on all bonds in the top three quality levels on which the yield curve is based.

The Secretary of the Treasury is directed to publish each month the corporate bond yield curve and each of the segment rates for the month. In addition, such Secretary is directed to publish a description of the methodology used to determine the yield curve and segment rates, which is sufficiently detailed to enable plans to make reasonable projections regarding the yield curve and segment rates for future months,

[27] In the case of single-employer plans, the provision repeals the present-law rules under which the amortization period applicable to an unfunded past service liability or loss may be extended.

based on a plan's projection of future interest rates.

Under the provision, the present value of liabilities under a plan is determined using the segment rates for the "applicable month" for the plan year. The applicable month is the month that includes the plan's valuation date for the plan year, or, at the election of the plan sponsor, any of the four months preceding the month that includes the valuation date. An election of a preceding month applies to the plan year for which it is made and all succeeding plan years unless revoked with the consent of the Secretary of the Treasury.

Solely for purposes of determining minimum required contributions, in lieu of the segment rates described above, an employer may elect to use interest rates on a yield curve based on the yields on investment grade corporate bonds for the month preceding the month in which the plan year begins (i.e., without regard to the 24-month averaging described above). Such an election may be revoked only with consent of the Secretary of the Treasury.

The provision provides a transition rule for plan years beginning in 2008 and 2009 (other than for plans first effective after December 31, 2007). Under this rule, for plan years beginning in 2008, the first, second, or third segment rate with respect to any month is the sum of: (1) the product of the segment rate otherwise determined for the month, multiplied by 33-⅓ percent; and (2) the product of the applicable long-term corporate bond rate,[28] multiplied by 66-⅔ percent. For plan years beginning in 2009, the first, second, or third segment rate with respect to any month is the sum of: (1) the product of the segment rate otherwise determined for the month, multiplied by 66⅔ percent; and (2) the product of applicable long-term corporate bond rate multiplied by 33⅓ percent. An employer may elect not to have the transition rule apply with respect to a plan. Such an election may be revoked only with consent of the Secretary of the Treasury.

Under the provision, certain amounts are determined using the plan's "effective interest rate" for a plan year. The effective interest rate with respect to a plan for a plan year is the single rate of interest which, if used to determine the present value of the benefits taken into account in determining the plan's funding target for the year, would result in an amount equal to the plan's funding target (as determined using the first, second, and third segment rates).

Mortality table

Under the provision, the Secretary of the Treasury is directed to prescribe by regulation the mortality tables to be used in determining present value or making any computation under the funding rules.[29] Such tables are to be based on the actual experience of pension plans and projected trends in such experience. In prescribing tables, the Secretary is to take into account results of available independent studies of mortality of individuals covered by pension plans. In addition, the Secretary is required (at least every 10 years) to revise any table in effect to reflect the actual experience of pension plans and projected trends in such experience.

The provision also provides for the use of a separate mortality table upon request of the plan sponsor and approval by the Secretary of the Treasury in accordance with procedures described below. In order for the table to be used: (1) the table must reflect the actual experience of the pension plans maintained by the plan sponsor and projected trends in general mortality experience, and (2) there must be a sufficient number of plan participants, and the pension plans must have been maintained for a sufficient period of time, to have credible information necessary for that purpose. A separate mortality table can be a mortality table constructed by the plan's enrolled actuary from the plan's own experience or a table that is an adjustment to the table prescribed by the Secretary which sufficiently reflects the plan's experience. Except as provided by the Secretary, a separate table may not be used for any plan unless (1) a separate table is established and used for each other plan maintained by the plan sponsor and, if the plan sponsor is a member of a controlled group, each member of the controlled group,[30] and (2) the requirements for using a separate table are met with respect to the table established for each plan, taking into account only the participants of that plan, the time that plan has been in existence, and the actual experience of that plan. In general, a separate plan may be used during the

[28] The applicable long-term corporate bond rate is a rate that is from 90 to 100 percent of the weighted average of the rates of interest on amounts invested conservatively in long-term investment-grade corporate bonds during the four-year period ending on the last day before the plan year begins as determined by the Secretary under the method in effect for 2007.

[29] As under present law, separate mortality tables are required to be used with respect to disabled participants.

[30] For example, the Secretary may deem it appropriate to provide an exception in the case of a small plan.

period of consecutive year plan years (not to exceed 10) specified in the request. However, a separate mortality table ceases to be in effect as of the earlier of (1) the date on which there is a significant change in the participants in the plan by reason of a plan spinoff or merger or otherwise, or (2) the date on which the plan actuary determines that the table does not meet the requirements for being used.

A plan sponsor must submit a separate mortality table to the Secretary for approval at least seven months before the first day of the period for which the table is to be used. A mortality table submitted to the Secretary for approval is treated as in effect as of the first day of the period unless the Secretary, during the 180-day period beginning on the date of the submission, disapproves of the table and provides the reasons that the table fails to meet the applicable criteria. The 180-day period is to be extended upon mutual agreement of the Secretary and the plan sponsor.

Other assumptions

Under the provision, in determining any present value or making any computation, the probability that future benefits will be paid in optional forms of benefit provided under the plan must be taken into account (including the probability of lump-sum distributions determined on the basis of the plan's experience and other related assumptions). The assumptions used to determine optional forms of benefit under a plan may differ from the assumptions used to determine present value for purposes of the funding rules under the provision. Differences in the present value of future benefit payments that result from the different assumptions used to determine optional forms of benefit under a plan must be taken into account in determining any present value or making any computation for purposes of the funding rules.

The provision generally does not require other specified assumptions to be used in determining the plan's target normal cost and funding target except in the case of at-risk plans (discussed below). However, similar to present law, the determination of present value or other computation must be made on the basis of actuarial assumptions and methods, each of which is reasonable (taking into account the experience of the plan and reasonable expectations), and which, in combination, offer the actuary's best estimate of anticipated experience under the plan.[31]

Special assumptions for at-risk plans

The provision applies special assumptions ("at-risk" assumptions) in determining the funding target and normal cost of a plan in at-risk status. Whether a plan is in at-risk status for a plan year depends on its funding target attainment percentage for the preceding year. A plan's funding target attainment percentage for a plan year is the ratio, expressed as a percentage, that the value of the plan's assets (reduced by any funding standard carryover balance and prefunding balance) bears to the plan's funding target for the year. For this purpose, the plan's funding target is determined using the actuarial assumptions for plans that are not at-risk.

Under the provision, a plan is in at-risk status for a year if, for the preceding year: (1) the plan's funding target attainment percentage, determined without regard to the at-risk assumptions, was less than 80 percent (with a transition rule discussed below), and (2) the plan's funding target attainment percentage, determined using the at-risk assumptions (without regard to whether the plan was in at-risk status for the preceding year), was less than 70 percent. Under a transition rule applicable for plan years beginning in 2008, 2009, and 2010, instead of 80 percent, the following percentages apply: 65 percent for 2008, 70 percent for 2009, and 75 percent for 2010. In the case of plan years beginning in 2008, the plan's funding target attainment percentage for the preceding plan year may be determined using such methods of estimation as the Secretary of Treasury may provide.

Under the provision, the at-risk rules do not apply if a plan had 500 or fewer participants on each day during the preceding plan year. For this purpose, all defined benefit pension plans (other than multiemployer plans) maintained by the same employer (or a predecessor employer), or by any member of such employer's controlled group, are treated as a single plan, but only participants with respect to such employer or controlled group member are taken into account.

If a plan is in at-risk status, the plan's funding target and normal cost are determined using the assumptions that: (1) all employees who are not otherwise assumed to retire as of the valuation date, but who will be eligible to elect benefits in the current and 10 succeeding years, are assumed to retire at the earliest retirement date under plan, but not before the end of the plan year; and (2) all employees are assumed to elect the retirement benefit available under the plan at

[31] The provision retains the present-law rule under which certain changes in actuarial assumptions that decrease the liabilities of an underfunded single-employer plan must be approved by the Secretary of the Treasury.

the assumed retirement age that results in the highest present value. In some cases, a loading factor also applies.

The at-risk assumptions are not applied to certain employees of specified automobile manufacturers for purposes of determining whether a plan is in at-risk status, i.e., whether the plan's funding target attainment percentage, determined using the at-risk assumptions, was less than 70 percent for the preceding plan year. An employee is disregarded for this purpose if: (1) the employee is employed by a specified automobile manufacturer; (2) the employee is offered, pursuant to a bona fide retirement incentive program, a substantial amount of additional cash compensation, substantially enhanced retirement benefits under the plan, or materially reduced employment duties, on the condition that by a specified date no later than December 31, 2010, the employee retires (as defined under the terms of the plan; (3) the offer is made during 2006 pursuant to a bona fide retirement incentive program and requires that the offer can be accepted no later than a specified date (not later than December 31, 2006); and (4) the employee does not accept the offer before the specified date on which the offer expires. For this purpose, a specified automobile manufacturer is (1) any automobile manufacturer and (2) any manufacturer of automobile parts that supplies parts directly to an automobile manufacturer and which, after a transaction or series of transactions ending in 1999, ceased to be a member of the automobile manufacturer's controlled group.

The funding target of a plan in at-risk status for a plan year is generally the sum of: (1) the present value of all benefits accrued or earned as of the beginning of the plan year, determined using the at-risk assumptions described above, and (2) in the case of a plan that has also been in at-risk status for at least two of the four preceding plans years, a loading factor. The loading factor is the sum of (1) $700 times the number of participants in the plan, plus (2) four percent of the funding target determined without regard to the loading factor.[32] The at-risk funding target is in no event less than the funding target determined without regard to the at-risk rules.

The target normal cost of a plan in at-risk status for a plan year is generally the sum of: (1) the present value of benefits expected to accrue or be earned under the plan during the plan year, determined using the special assumptions described above, and (2) in the case of a plan that has also been in at-risk status for at least two of the four preceding plans years, a loading factor of four percent of the target normal cost determined without regard to the loading factor.[33] The at-risk target normal is in no event less than at-risk normal cost determined without regard to the at-risk rules.

If a plan has been in at-risk status for fewer than five consecutive plan years, the amount of a plan's funding target for a plan year is the sum of: (1) the amount of the funding target determined without regard to the at-risk rules, plus (2) the transition percentage for the plan year of the excess of the amount of the funding target determined under the at-risk rules over the amount determined without regard to the at-risk rules. Similarly, if a plan has been in at-risk status for fewer than five consecutive plan years, the amount of a plan's target normal cost for a plan year is the sum of: (1) the amount of the target normal cost determined without regard to the at-risk rules, plus (2) the transition percentage for the plan year of the excess of the amount of the target normal cost determined under the at-risk rules over the amount determined without regard to the at-risk rules. The transition percentage is the product of 20 percent times the number of consecutive plan years for which the plan has been in at-risk status. In applying this rule, plan years beginning before 2008 are not taken into account.

Funding standard carryover balance or prefunding balance

In general

The provision preserves credit balances that have accumulated under present law (referred to as "funding standard carryover balances"). In addition, for plan years beginning after 2007, new credit balances (referred to as "prefunding balances") result if an employer makes contributions greater than those required under the new funding rules. In general, under the bill, employers may choose whether to count funding standard carryover balances and prefunding balances in determining the value of plan assets or to use the balances to reduce required contributions, but not both. In this regard, the provision provides more favorable rules with respect to the use of funding standard carryover balances.

Under the provision, if the value of a plan's assets (reduced by any prefunding balance) is at

32 This loading factor is intended to reflect the cost of purchasing group annuity contracts in the case of termination of the plan.

33 Target normal cost for a plan in at-risk status does not include a loading factor of $700 per plan participant.

least 80 percent of the plan's funding target (determined without regard to the at-risk rules) for the preceding plan year,[34] the plan sponsor may elect to credit all or a portion of the funding standard carryover balance or prefunding balance against the minimum required contribution for the current plan year (determined after any funding waiver), thus reducing the amount that must be contributed for the current plan year.

The value of plan assets is generally reduced by any funding standard carryover balance or prefunding balance for purposes of determining minimum required contributions, including a plan's funding shortfall, and a plan's funding target attainment percentage (discussed above). However, the plan sponsor may elect to permanently reduce a funding standard carryover balance or prefunding balance, so that the value of plan assets is not required to be reduced by that amount in determining the minimum required contribution for the plan year. Any reduction of a funding standard carryover balance or prefunding balance applies before determining the balance that is available for crediting against minimum required contributions for the plan year.

Funding standard carryover balance

In the case of a single-employer plan that is in effect for a plan year beginning in 2007 and, as of the end of the 2007 plan year, has a positive balance in the funding standard account maintained under the funding rules as in effect for 2007, the plan sponsor may elect to maintain a funding standard carryover balance. The funding standard carryover balance consists of a beginning balance in the amount of the positive balance in the funding standard account as of the end of the 2007 plan year, decreased (as described below) and adjusted to reflect the rate of net gain or loss on plan assets.

For subsequent years (i.e., as of the first day of each plan year beginning after 2008), the funding standard carryover balance of a plan is decreased (but not below zero) by the sum of: (1) any amount credited to reduce the minimum required contribution for the preceding plan year, plus (2) any amount elected by the plan sponsor as a reduction in the funding standard carryover balance (thus reducing the amount by which the value of plan assets must be reduced in determining minimum required contributions).

Prefunding balance

The plan sponsor may elect to maintain a prefunding balance, which consists of a beginning balance of zero for the 2008 plan year, increased and decreased (as described below) and adjusted to reflect the rate of net gain or loss on plan assets.

For subsequent years, i.e., as of the first day of plan year beginning after 2008 (the "current" plan year), the plan sponsor may increase the prefunding balance by an amount, not to exceed (1) the excess (if any) of the aggregate total employer contributions for the preceding plan year, over (2) the minimum required contribution for the preceding plan year. For this purpose, any excess contribution for the preceding plan year is adjusted for interest accruing for the periods between the first day of the current plan year and the dates on which the excess contributions were made, determined using the effective interest rate of the plan for the preceding plan year and treating contributions as being first used to satisfy the minimum required contribution.

The amount by which the aggregate total employer contributions for the preceding plan year exceeds the minimum required contribution for the preceding plan year is reduced (but not below zero) by the amount of contributions an employer would need to make to avoid a benefit limitation that would otherwise be imposed for the preceding plan year under the provisions of the provision relating to benefit limitations for single-employer plans.[35] Thus, contributions needed to avoid a benefit limitation do not result in an increase in the plan's prefunding balance.[36]

As of the first day of each plan year beginning after 2008, the prefunding balance of a plan is decreased (but not below zero) by the sum of: (1) any amount credited to reduce the minimum required contribution for the preceding plan year, plus (2) any amount elected by the plan sponsor as a reduction in the prefunding balance (thus reducing the amount by which the value of plan assets must be reduced in determining minimum required contributions). As discussed above, if any portion of the prefunding balance is used to reduce a minimum required contribu-

[34] In the case of plan years beginning in 2008, the percentage for the preceding plan year may be determined using such methods of estimation as the Secretary of Treasury may provide.

[35] Any contribution that may be taken into account in satisfying the requirement to make additional contributions with respect to more than one type of benefit limitation is taken into account only once for purposes of this reduction.

[36] The benefit limitations are discussed in Part B below.

tion, the value of plan assets must be reduced by the prefunding balance in determining whether a shortfall amortization base must be established for the plan year (i.e., whether the value of plan assets for a plan year is less than the plan's funding target for the plan year). Thus, the prefunding balance may not be included in the value of plan assets in order to avoid a shortfall amortization base for a plan year and also used to reduce the minimum required contribution for the same year.

Other rules

In determining the prefunding balance or funding standard carryover balance as of the first day of a plan year, the plan sponsor must adjust the balance in accordance with regulations prescribed by the Secretary of the Treasury to reflect the rate of return on plan assets for the preceding year. The rate of return is determined on the basis of the fair market value of the plan assets and must properly take into account, in accordance with regulations, all contributions, distributions, and other plan payments made during the period.

To the extent that a plan has a funding standard carryover balance of more than zero for a plan year, none of the plan's prefunding balance may be credited to reduce a minimum required contribution, nor may an election be made to reduce the prefunding balance for purposes of determining the value of plan assets. Thus, the funding standard carryover balance must be used for these purposes before the prefunding balance may be used.

Any election relating to the prefunding balance and funding standard carryover balance is to be made in such form and manner as the Secretary of the Treasury prescribes.

Other rules and definitions

Valuation date

Under the provision, all determinations made with respect to minimum required contributions for a plan year (such as the value of plan assets and liabilities) must be made as of the plan's valuation date for the plan year. In general, the valuation date for a plan year must be the first day of the plan year. However, any day in the plan year may be designated as the plan's valuation date if, on each day during the preceding plan year, the plan had 100 or fewer participants.[37] For this purpose, all defined benefit pension plans (other than multiemployer plans) maintained by the same employer (or a predecessor employer), or by any member of such employer's controlled group, are treated as a single plan, but only participants with respect to such employer or controlled group member are taken into account.

Value of plan assets

Under the provision, the value of plan assets is generally fair market value. However, the value of plan assets may be determined on the basis of the averaging of fair market values, but only if such method: (1) is permitted under regulations; (2) does not provide for averaging of fair market values over more than the period beginning on the last day of the 25th month preceding the month in which the plan's valuation date occurs and ending on the valuation date (or similar period in the case of a valuation date that's not the first day of a month); and (3) does not result in a determination of the value of plan assets that at any time is less than 90 percent or more than 110 percent of the fair market value of the assets at that time. Any averaging must be adjusted for contributions and distributions as provided by the Secretary of the Treasury.

If a required contribution for a preceding plan year is made after the valuation date for the current year, the contribution is taken into account in determining the value of plan assets for the current plan year. For plan years beginning after 2008, only the present value of the contribution is taken into account, determined as of the valuation date for the current plan year, using the plan's effective interest rate for the preceding plan year. In addition, any required contribution for the current plan year is not taken into account in determining the value of plan assets. If any contributions for the current plan year are made before the valuation date, plan assets as of the valuation date does not include (1) the contributions, and (2) interest on the contributions for the period between the date of the contributions and the valuation date, determined using the plan's effective interest rate for the current plan year.

Timing rules for contributions

As under present law, the due date for the payment of a minimum required contribution for a plan year is generally 8½ months after the end of the plan year. Any payment made on a date other than the valuation date for the plan

[37] In the case of a plan's first plan year, the ability to use a valuation date other than the first day of the plan year is determined by taking into account the number of participants the plan is reasonably expected to have on each day during that first plan year.

year must be adjusted for interest accruing at the plan's effective interest rate for the plan year for the period between the valuation date and the payment date. Quarterly contributions must be made during a plan year if the plan had a funding shortfall for the preceding plan year (that is, if the value of the plan's assets, reduced by the funding standard carryover balance and prefunding balance, was less than the plan's funding target for the preceding plan year).[38] If a quarterly installment is not made, interest applies for the period of underpayment at the rate of interest otherwise applicable (i.e., the plan's effective interest rate) plus 5 percentage points.

Excise tax on failure to make minimum required contributions

The provision retains the present-law rules under which an employer is generally subject to an excise tax if it fails to make minimum required contributions and fails to obtain a waiver from the IRS.[39] The excise tax is 10 percent of the aggregate unpaid minimum required contributions for all plan years remaining unpaid as of the end of any plan year. In addition, a tax of 100 percent may be imposed if any unpaid minimum required contributions remain unpaid after a certain period.

Conforming changes

The provision makes various technical and conforming changes to reflect the new funding requirements.

Effective Date

The extension of the interest rate applicable in determining current liability for plan years beginning in 2004 and 2005 is effective for plan years beginning after December 31, 2005, and before January 1, 2008. The modifications to the single-employer plan funding rules are effective for plan years beginning after December 31, 2007.

[Law at ¶ 5030, ¶ 5080, ¶ 5085, ¶ 5090, ¶ 5115, ¶ 5120, ¶ 5295, ¶ 5300, ¶ 5355, ¶ 7006, ¶ 7009 and ¶ 7024. CCH Explanation at ¶ 205, ¶ 210, ¶ 305 and ¶ 805.]

[¶ 10,020] Act Secs. 103 and 113. Benefit limitations under single-employer defined benefit pension plans

Joint Committee Taxation (J.C.T. Rep. No. JCX-38-06)

[New Code Secs. 436 and 437]

Present Law

Plant shutdown and other unpredictable contingent event benefits

A plan may provide for unpredictable contingent event benefits, which are benefits that depend on contingencies other than age, service, compensation, death or disability or that are not reliably and reasonably predictable as determined by the Secretary. Some of these benefits are commonly referred to as "plant shutdown" benefits. Under present law, unpredictable contingent event benefits generally are not taken into account for funding purposes until the event has occurred.

Defined benefit pension plans are not permitted to provide "layoff" benefits (i.e., severance benefits).[40] However, defined benefit pension plans may provide subsidized early retirement benefits, including early retirement window benefits.[41]

Limitation on certain benefit increases while funding waivers in effect

Within limits, the IRS is permitted to waive all or a portion of the contributions required under the minimum funding standard for a plan year.[42] In the case of a single-employer plan, a waiver may be granted if the employer responsible for the contribution could not make the required contribution without temporary substantial business hardship for the employer (and members of the employer's controlled group) and if requiring the contribution would be adverse to the interests of plan participants in the aggregate.

---

[38] The provision retains the present-law rules under which the amount of any quarterly installment must be sufficient to cover any liquidity shortfall.

[39] The provision retains the present-law rules under which a lien in favor of the plan with respect to property of the employer (and members of the employer's controlled group) arises in certain circumstances in which the employer fails to make required contributions.

[40] Treas. Reg. sec. 1.401-1(b)(1)(i).

[41] See, e.g., Treas. Reg. secs. 1.401(a)(4)-3(f)(4) and 1.411(a)-7(c).

[42] Code sec. 412(d); ERISA sec. 303.

If a funding waiver is in effect for a plan, subject to certain exceptions, no plan amendment may be adopted that increases the liabilities of the plan by reason of any increase in benefits, any change in the accrual of benefits, or any change in the rate at which benefits vest under the plan.[43]

Security for certain plan amendments

In the case of a single-employer defined benefit pension plan, if a plan amendment increasing current liability is adopted and the plan's funded current liability percentage is less than 60 percent (taking into account the effect of the amendment, but disregarding any unamortized unfunded old liability), the employer and members of the employer's controlled group must provide security in favor of the plan.[44] The amount of security required is the excess of: (1) the lesser of (a) the amount by which the plan's assets are less than 60 percent of current liability, taking into account the benefit increase, or (b) the amount of the benefit increase and prior benefit increases after December 22, 1987, over (2) $10 million. The amendment is not effective until the security is provided.

The security must be in the form of a surety bond, cash, certain U.S. government obligations, or such other form as is satisfactory to the Secretary of the Treasury and the parties involved. The security is released after the funded liability of the plan reaches 60 percent.

Prohibition on benefit increases during bankruptcy

Subject to certain exceptions, if an employer maintaining a single-employer defined benefit pension plan is involved in bankruptcy proceedings, no plan amendment may be adopted that increases the liabilities of the plan by reason of any increase in benefits, any change in the accrual of benefits, or any change in the rate at which benefits vest under the plan.[45] This limitation does not apply if the plan's funded current liability percentage is at least 100 percent, taking into account the amendment.

Restrictions on benefit payments due to liquidity shortfalls

In the case of a single-employer plan with a funded current liability percentage of less than 100 percent for the preceding plan year, estimated contributions for the current plan year must be made in quarterly installments during the current plan year. If quarterly contributions are required with respect to a plan, the amount of a quarterly installment must also be sufficient to cover any shortfall in the plan's liquid assets (a "liquidity shortfall"). In general, a plan has a liquidity shortfall for a quarter if the plan's liquid assets (such as cash and marketable securities) are less than a certain amount (generally determined by reference to disbursements from the plan in the preceding 12 months).

If a quarterly installment is less than the amount required to cover the plan's liquidity shortfall, limits apply to the benefits that can be paid from a plan during the period of underpayment. During that period, the plan may not make any prohibited payment, defined as: (1) any payment in excess of the monthly amount paid under a single life annuity (plus any social security supplement provided under the plan) to a participant or beneficiary whose annuity starting date occurs during the period; (2) any payment for the purchase of an irrevocable commitment from an insurer to pay benefits (e.g., an annuity contract); or (3) any other payment specified by the Secretary of the Treasury by regulations.[46]

Explanation of Provision

Plant shutdown and other unpredictable contingent event benefits

Under the provision, if a participant is entitled to an unpredictable contingent event benefit payable with respect to any event occurring during any plan year, the plan must provide that such benefits may not be provided if the plan's adjusted funding target attainment percentage for that plan year: (1) is less than 60 percent; or (2) would be less than 60 percent taking into account the occurrence of the event. For this purpose, the term unpredictable contingent event benefit means any benefit payable solely by reason of: (1) a plant shutdown (or similar event, as determined by the Secretary of the Treasury); or (2) any event other than attainment of any age, performance of any service, receipt or derivation of any compensation, or the occurrence of death or disability.

The determination of whether the limitation applies is made in the year the unpredictable contingent event occurs. For example, suppose a plan provides for benefits upon the occurrence of a plant shutdown, and a plant shut down occurs in 2010. Taking into account the plan shutdown, the plan's adjusted funding target attainment percentage is less than 60 percent. Thus, the limi-

43 Code sec. 412(f); ERISA sec. 304(b)(1).

44 Code sec. 401(a)(29); ERISA sec. 307.

45 Code sec. 401(a)(33); ERISA sec. 204(i).

46 Code sec. 401(a)(32); ERISA sec. 206(e).

tation applies, and benefits payable solely by reason of the plant shutdown may not be paid (unless the employer makes contributions to the plan as described below), regardless of whether the benefits will be paid in the 2010 plan year or a later plan year.[47]

The limitation ceases to apply with respect to any plan year, effective as of the first day of the plan year, if the plan sponsor makes a contribution (in addition to any minimum required contribution for the plan year) equal to: (1) if the plan's adjusted funding target attainment percentage is less than 60 percent, the amount of the increase in the plan's funding target for the plan year attributable to the occurrence of the event; or (2) if the plan's adjusted funding target attainment percentage would be less than 60 percent taking into account the occurrence of the event, the amount sufficient to result in a adjusted funding target attainment percentage of 60 percent.

The limitation does not apply for the first five years a plan (or a predecessor plan) is in effect.

Plan amendments increasing benefit liabilities

Certain plan amendments may not take effect during a plan year if the plan's adjusted funding target attainment percentage for the plan year: (1) is less than 80 percent; or (2) would be less than 80 percent taking into account the amendment.[48] In such a case, no amendment may take effect if it has the effect of increasing the liabilities of the plan by reason of any increase in benefits, the establishment of new benefits, any change in the rate of benefit accrual, or any change in the rate at which benefits vest under the plan. The limitation does not apply to an amendment that provides for an increase in benefits under a formula which is not based on compensation, but only if the rate of increase does not exceed the contemporaneous rate of increase in average wages of the participants covered by the amendment.

The limitation ceases to apply with respect to any plan year, effective as of the first day of the plan year (or, if later, the effective date of the amendment), if the plan sponsor makes a contribution (in addition to any minimum required contribution for the plan year) equal to: (1) if the plan's adjusted funding target attainment percentage is less than 80 percent, the amount of the increase in the plan's funding target for the plan year attributable to the amendment; or (2) if the plan's adjusted funding target attainment percentage would be less than 80 percent taking into account the amendment, the amount sufficient to result in a adjusted funding target attainment percentage of 80 percent.

The limitation does not apply for the first five years a plan (or a predecessor plan) is in effect.

Prohibited payments

A plan must provide that, if the plan's adjusted funding target attainment percentage for a plan year is less than 60 percent, the plan will not make any prohibited payments after the valuation date for the plan year.

A plan must also provide that, if the plan's adjusted funding target attainment percentage for a plan year is 60 percent or greater, but less than 80 percent, the plan may not pay any prohibited payments exceeding the lesser of: (1) 50 percent of the amount otherwise payable under the plan, and (2) the present value of the maximum PBGC guarantee with respect to the participant (determined under guidance prescribed by the PBGC, using the interest rates and mortality table applicable in determining minimum lump-sum benefits). The plan must provide that only one payment under this exception may be made with respect to any participant during any period of consecutive plan years to which the limitation applies. For this purpose, a participant and any beneficiary of the participant (including an alternate payee) is treated as one participant. If the participant's accrued benefit is allocated to an alternate payee and one or more other persons, the amount that may be distributed is allocated in the same manner unless the applicable qualified domestic relations order provides otherwise.

In addition, a plan must provide that, during any period in which the plan sponsor is in bankruptcy proceedings, the plan may not pay any prohibited payment. However, this limitation does not apply on or after the date the plan's enrolled actuary certifies that the adjusted funding target attainment percentage of the plan is not less than 100 percent.

For purposes of these limitations, "prohibited payment" is defined as under the present-law rule restricting distributions during a period

[47] Benefits already being paid as a result of a plant shutdown or other event that occurred in a preceding year are not affected by the limitation.

[48] Under the provision, the present-law rules limiting benefit increases while an employer is in bankruptcy continue to apply.

of a liquidity shortfall and means (1) any payment in excess of the monthly amount paid under a single life annuity (plus any social security supplement provided under the plan) to a participant or beneficiary whose annuity starting date occurs during the period, (2) any payment for the purchase of an irrevocable commitment from an insurer to pay benefits (e.g., an annuity contract), or (3) any other payment specified by the Secretary of the Treasury by regulations.

The prohibited payment limitation does not apply to a plan for any plan year if the terms of the plan (as in effect for the period beginning on September 1, 2005, and ending with the plan year) provide for no benefit accruals with respect to any participant during the period.

Cessation of benefit accruals

A plan must provide that, if the plan's adjusted funding target attainment percentage is less than 60 percent for a plan year, all future benefit accruals under the plan must cease as of the valuation date for the plan year. The limitation applies only for purposes of the accrual of benefits; service during the freeze period is counted for other purposes. For example, if accruals are frozen under the provision, service earned during the freeze period still counts for vesting purposes. Or, as another example, suppose a plan provides that payment of benefits begins when a participant terminates employment after age 55 and with 25 years of service. Under this example, if a participant who is age 55 and has 23 years of service when the freeze on accruals becomes applicable terminates employment two years later, the participant has 25 years of service for this purpose and thus can begin receiving benefits. However (assuming the freeze on accruals is still in effect), the amount of the benefit is based on the benefit accrued before the freeze (i.e., counting only 23 years of service).

The limitation ceases to apply with respect to any plan year, effective as of the first day of the plan year, if the plan sponsor makes a contribution (in addition to any minimum required contribution for the plan year) equal to the amount sufficient to result in an adjusted funding target attainment percentage of 60 percent.

The limitation does not apply for the first five years a plan (or a predecessor plan) is in effect.

Adjusted funding target attainment percentage

In general

The term "funding target attainment percentage" is defined as under the minimum funding rules, i.e., the ratio, expressed as a percentage, that the value of the plan's assets (reduced by any funding standard carryover balance and prefunding balance) bears to the plan's funding target for the year (determined without regard to at-risk status). A plan's adjusted funding target attainment percentage is determined in the same way, except that the value of the plan's assets and the plan's funding target are both increased by the aggregate amount of purchases of annuities for employees other than highly compensated employees made by the plan during the two preceding plan years.

Special rule for fully funded plans

Under a special rule, if a plan's funding target attainment percentage is at least 100 percent, determined by not reducing the value of the plan's assets by any funding standard carryover balance or prefunding balance, the value of the plan's assets is not so reduced in determining the plan's funding target attainment percentage for purposes of whether the benefit limitations apply. Under a transition rule for a plan year beginning after 2007 and before 2011, the "applicable percentage" for the plan year is substituted for 100 percent in applying the special rule. For this purpose, the applicable percentage is 92 percent for 2007, 94 percent for 2008, 96 percent for 2009, and 98 percent for 2010. However, for any plan year beginning after 2008, the transition rule does not apply unless the plan's funding target attainment percentage (determined by not reducing the value of the plan's assets by any funding standard carryover balance or prefunding balance) for each preceding plan year in the transition period is at least equal to the applicable percentage for the preceding year.

Presumptions as to funded status

Under the provision, certain presumptions apply in determining whether limitations apply with respect to a plan, subject to certification of the plan's adjusted funding target attainment percentage by the plan's enrolled actuary.

If a plan was subject to a limitation for the preceding year, the plan's adjusted funding target attainment percentage for the current year is presumed to be the same as for the preceding year until the plan actuary certifies the plan's actual adjusted funding target attainment percentage for the current year.

If (1) a plan was not subject to a limitation for the preceding year, but its adjusted funding target attainment percentage for the preceding year was not more than 10 percentage points greater than the threshold for a limitation, and (2) as of the first day of the fourth month of the current plan year, the plan actuary has not certified the plan's actual adjusted funding target attainment percentage for the current year, the plan's funding target attainment percentage is presumed to be reduced by 10 percentage points as of that day and that day is deemed to be the plan's valuation date for purposes of applying the benefit limitation. As a result, the limitation applies as of that date until the actuary certifies the plan's actual adjusted funding target attainment percentage.

In any other case, if the plan actuary has not certified the plan's actual adjusted funding target attainment percentage by the first day of the tenth month of the current plan year, for purposes of the limitations, the plan's adjusted funding target attainment percentage is conclusively presumed to be less than 60 percent as of that day and that day is deemed to be the valuation date for purposes of applying the benefit limitations.[49]

Reduction of funding standard carryover and prefunding balances

Election to reduce balances

As discussed above, the value of plan assets is generally reduced by any funding standard carryover or prefunding in determining a plan's funding target attainment percentage. As provided for under the funding rules applicable to single-employer plans, a plan sponsor may elect to reduce a funding standard carryover balance or prefunding balance, so that the value of plan assets is not required to be reduced by that amount in determining the plan's funding target attainment percentage.

Deemed reduction of balances in the case of collectively bargained plans

If a benefit limitation would otherwise apply to a plan maintained pursuant to one or more collective bargaining agreements between employee representatives and one or more employers, the plan sponsor is treated as having made an election to reduce any prefunding balance or funding standard carryover balance by the amount necessary to prevent the benefit limitation from applying. However, the employer is not treated as having made such an election if the election would not prevent the benefit limitation from applying to the plan.

Deemed reduction of balances in the case of other plans

If the prohibited payment limitation would otherwise apply to a plan that is not maintained pursuant to a collective bargaining agreement, the plan sponsor is treated as having made an election to reduce any prefunding balance or funding standard carryover balance by the amount necessary to prevent the benefit limitation from applying. However, the employer is not treated as having made such an election if the election would not prevent the benefit limitation from applying to the plan.

Contributions made to avoid a benefit limitation

Under the provision, an employer may make contributions (in addition to any minimum required contribution) in an amount sufficient to increase the plan's adjusted funding target attainment percentage to a level to avoid a limitation on unpredictable contingent event benefits, a plan amendment increasing benefits, or additional accruals. An employer may not use a prefunding balance or funding standard carryover balance in lieu of such a contribution, and such a contribution does not result in an increase in any prefunding balance.

Instead of making additional contributions to avoid a benefit limitation, an employer may provide security in the form of a surety bond, cash, certain U.S. government obligations, or such other form as is satisfactory to the Secretary of the Treasury and the parties involved. In such a case, the plan's adjusted funding target attainment percentage is determined by treating the security as a plan asset. Any such security may be perfected and enforced at any time after the earlier of: (1) the date on which the plan terminates; (2) if the plan sponsor fails to make a required contribution for any subsequent plan year, the due date for the contribution; or (3) if the plan's adjusted funding target attainment percentage is less than 60 percent for a consecutive period of seven years, the valuation date for the last year in the period. The security will be released (and any related amounts will be refunded with any accrued interest) at such time as the Secretary of the Treasury may prescribe in regulations (including partial releases by reason

---

[49] For purposes of applying the presumptions to plan years beginning in 2008, the funding target attainment percentage for the preceding year may be determined using such methods of estimation as the Secretary of Treasury may provide.

of increases in the plan's funding target attainment percentage).

Treatment of plan as of close of prohibited or cessation period

Under the provision, if a limitation on prohibited payments or future benefit accruals ceases to apply to a plan, all such payments and benefit accruals resume, effective as of the day following the close of the period for which the limitation applies.[50] Nothing in this rule is to be construed as affecting a plan's treatment of benefits which would have been paid or accrued but for the limitation.

Notice to participants

The plan administrator must provide written notice to participants and beneficiaries within 30 days: (1) after the plan has become subject to the limitation on unpredictable uncontingent event benefits or prohibited payments; (2) in the case of a plan to which the limitation on benefit accruals applies, after the valuation date for the plan year in which the plan's adjusted target attainment percentage is less than 60 percent (or, if earlier, the date the adjusted target attainment percentage is deemed to be less than 60 percent). Notice must also be provided at such other times as may be determined by the Secretary of the Treasury. The notice may be in electronic or other form to the extent such form is reasonably accessible to the recipient.

If the plan administrator fails to provide the required notice, the Secretary of Labor may impose a civil penalty of up to $1,000 a day from the time of the failure.

Effective Date

The provision generally applies with respect to plan years beginning after December 31, 2007.

In the case of a plan maintained pursuant to one or more collective bargaining agreements between employee representatives and one or more employers ratified before January 1, 2008, the provision does not apply to plan years beginning before the earlier of: (1) the later of (a) the date on which the last collective bargaining agreement relating to the plan terminates (determined without regard to any extension thereof agreed to after the date of enactment), or (b) the first day of the first plan year to which the provision would otherwise apply; or (2) January 1, 2010. For this purpose, any plan amendment made pursuant to a collective bargaining agreement relating to the plan that amends the plan solely to conform to any requirement under the provision is not to be treated as a termination of the collective bargaining agreement.

[Law at ¶ 5135 and ¶ 7012. CCH Explanation at ¶ 215.]

[¶ 10,030] Act Sec. 104. Special rules for multiple-employer plans of certain cooperatives

Joint Committee Taxation (J.C.T. Rep. No. JCX-38-06)

[Act Sec. 104]

Present Law

Defined benefit pension plans are required to meet certain minimum funding rules. In some cases, additional contributions are required under the deficit reduction contribution rules if a single-employer defined benefit pension plan is underfunded. Additional contributions generally are not required in the case of a plan with a funded current liability percentage of at least 90 percent. A plan's funded current liability percentage is the value of plan assets as a percentage of current liability. In general, a plan's current liability means all liabilities to employees and their beneficiaries under the plan, determined using specified interest and mortality assumptions. In the case of a plan with a funded current liability percentage of less than 100 percent for the preceding plan year, estimated contributions for the current plan year must be made in quarterly installments during the current plan year.

The PBGC insures benefits under most single-employer defined benefit pension plans in the event the plan is terminated with insufficient assets to pay for plan benefits. The PBGC is funded in part by a flat-rate premium per plan participant, and variable-rate premiums based

[50] This rule does not apply to limitations on unpredictable contingent event benefits and plan amendments increasing liabilities.

on the amount of unfunded vested benefits under the plan. A specified interest rate and a specified mortality table apply in determining unfunded vested benefits for this purpose.

A multiple-employer plan is a plan that is maintained by more than one employer and is not maintained pursuant to a collective bargaining agreement.[51] A multiple-employer plan is subject to the minimum funding rules for single-employer plans and to PBGC variable-rate premiums.

Explanation of Provision

The provision provides a delayed effective date for the new single-employer plan funding rules in the case of a plan that was in existence on July 26, 2005, and was an eligible cooperative plan for the plan year including that date. The new funding rules do not apply with respect to such a plan for plan years beginning before the earlier of: (1) the first plan year for which the plan ceases to be an eligible cooperative plan, or (2) January 1, 2017. In addition, in applying the present-law funding rules to an eligible cooperative plan to such a plan for plan years beginning after December 31, 2007, and before the first plan year for which the new funding rules apply, the interest rate used is the interest rate applicable under the new funding rules with respect to payments expected to be made from the plan after the 20-year period beginning on the first day of the plan year (i.e., the third segment rate under the new funding rules).

A plan is treated as an eligible cooperative plan for a plan year if it is maintained by more than one employer and at least 85 percent of the employers are: (1) certain rural cooperatives;[52] or (2) certain cooperative organizations that are more than 50-percent owned by agricultural producers or by cooperatives owned by agricultural producers, or organizations that are more than 50-percent owned, or controlled by, one or more such cooperative organizations. A plan is also treated as an eligible cooperative plan for any plan year for which it is maintained by more than one employer and is maintained by a rural telephone cooperative association.

Effective Date

The provision is effective on the date of enactment.

[Law at ¶ 7015. CCH Explanation at ¶ 240.]

[¶10,040] Act Sec. 105. Temporary relief for certain PBGC settlement plans

Joint Committee Taxation (J.C.T. Rep. No. JCX-38-06)

[Act Sec. 105]

Present Law

Defined benefit pension plans are required to meet certain minimum funding rules. In some cases, additional contributions are required under the deficit reduction contribution rules if a single-employer defined benefit pension plan is underfunded. Additional contributions generally are not required in the case of a plan with a funded current liability percentage of at least 90 percent. A plan's funded current liability percentage is the value of plan assets as a percentage of current liability. In general, a plan's current liability means all liabilities to employees and their beneficiaries under the plan, determined using specified interest and mortality assumptions. In the case of a plan with a funded current liability percentage of less than 100 percent for the preceding plan year, estimated contributions for the current plan year must be made in quarterly installments during the current plan year.

The PBGC insures benefits under most single-employer defined benefit pension plans in the event the plan is terminated with insufficient assets to pay for plan benefits. The PBGC is funded in part by a flat-rate premium per plan participant, and variable-rate premiums based on the amount of unfunded vested benefits under the plan. A specified interest rate and a specified mortality table apply in determining unfunded vested benefits for this purpose.

---

[51] A plan maintained by more than one employer pursuant to a collective bargaining agreement is referred to as a multiemployer plan.

[52] This is as defined in Code section 401(k)(7)(B) without regard to (iv) thereof and includes (1) organizations engaged primarily in providing electric service on a mutual or cooperative basis, or engaged primarily in providing electric service to the public in its service area and which is exempt from tax or which is a State or local government, other than a municipality; (2) certain civic leagues and business leagues exempt from tax 80 percent of the members of which are described in (1); (3) certain cooperative telephone companies; and (4) any organization that is a national association of organizations described above.

Explanation of Provision

The provision agreement provides a delayed effective date for the new single-employer plan funding rules in the case of a plan that was in existence on July 26, 2005, and was a "PBGC settlement plan" as of that date. The new funding rules do not apply with respect to such a plan for plan years beginning before January 1, 2014. In addition, in applying the present-law funding rules to a such a plan for plan years beginning after December 31, 2007, and before January 1, 2014, the interest rate used is the interest rate applicable under the new funding rules with respect to payments expected to be made from the plan after the 20-year period beginning on the first day of the plan year (i.e., the third segment rate under the new funding rules).

Under the provision, the term "PBGC settlement plan" means a single-employer defined benefit plan: (1) that was sponsored by an employer in bankruptcy proceedings giving rise to a claim by the PBGC of not greater than $150 million, and the sponsorship of which was assumed by another employer (not a member of the same controlled group as the bankrupt sponsor) and the PBGC's claim was settled or withdrawn in connection with the assumption of the sponsorship; or (2) that, by agreement with the PBGC, was spun off from a plan subsequently terminated by the PBGC in an involuntary termination.

Effective Date

The provision is effective on the date of enactment.

[Law at ¶ 7018. CCH Explanation at ¶ 240.]

[¶ 10,050] Act Sec. 106. Special rules for plans of certain government contractors

Joint Committee Taxation (J.C.T. Rep. No. JCX-38-06)

[Act Sec. 106]

Present Law

Defined benefit pension plans are required to meet certain minimum funding rules. In some cases, additional contributions are required under the deficit reduction contribution rules if a single-employer defined benefit pension plan is underfunded. Additional contributions generally are not required in the case of a plan with a funded current liability percentage of at least 90 percent. A plan's funded current liability percentage is the value of plan assets as a percentage of current liability. In general, a plan's current liability means all liabilities to employees and their beneficiaries under the plan, determined using specified interest and mortality assumptions. In the case of a plan with a funded current liability percentage of less than 100 percent for the preceding plan year, estimated contributions for the current plan year must be made in quarterly installments during the current plan year.

The PBGC insures benefits under most single-employer defined benefit pension plans in the event the plan is terminated with insufficient assets to pay for plan benefits. The PBGC is funded in part by a flat-rate premium per plan participant, and variable-rate premiums based on the amount of unfunded vested benefits under the plan. A specified interest rate and a specified mortality table apply in determining unfunded vested benefits for this purpose.

Explanation of Provision

The provision provides a delayed effective date for the new single-employer plan funding rules in the case of an eligible government contractor plan. The new funding rules do not apply with respect to such a plan for plan years beginning before the earliest of: (1) the first plan year for which the plan ceases to be an eligible government contractor plan, (2) the effective date of the Cost Accounting Standards Pension Harmonization Rule, and (3) the first plan year beginning after December 31, 2010. In addition, in applying the present-law funding rules to a such a plan for plan years beginning after December 31, 2007, and before the first plan year for which the new funding rules apply, the interest rate used is the interest rate applicable under the new funding rules with respect to payments expected to be made from the plan after the 20-year period beginning on the first day of the plan year (i.e., the third segment rate under the new funding rules).

Under the provision, a plan is treated as an eligible government contractor plan if it is maintained by a corporation (or member of the same affiliated group): (1) whose primary source of revenue is derived from business performed under contracts with the United States that are subject to the Federal Acquisition Regulations and also to the Defense Federal Acquisition Regulation Supplement; (2) whose revenue derived from such business in the previous fiscal year exceeded $5 billion; and (3) whose pension plan costs that are assignable under those contracts are subject to certain provisions of the Cost Accounting Standards.

The provision also requires the Cost Accounting Standards Board, not later than January 1, 2010, to review and revise the relevant provisions of the Cost Accounting Standards to harmonize minimum contributions required under ERISA of eligible government contractor plans and government reimbursable pension plan costs. Any final rule adopted by the Cost Accounting Standards Board shall be deemed the Cost Accounting Standards Pension Harmonization Rule.

Effective Date

The provision is effective on the date of enactment.

[Law at ¶ 7021. CCH Explanation at ¶ 240.]

[¶ 10,060] Act Sec. 115. Modification of transition rule to pension funding requirements for interstate bus company

Joint Committee Taxation (J.C.T. Rep. No. JCX-38-06)

[Act Sec. 115]

Present Law

Defined benefit pension plans are required to meet certain minimum funding rules. In some cases, additional contributions are required under the deficit reduction contribution rules if a single-employer defined benefit pension plan is underfunded. Additional contributions generally are not required in the case of a plan with a funded current liability percentage of at least 90 percent. A plan's funded current liability percentage is the value of plan assets as a percentage of current liability. In general, a plan's current liability means all liabilities to employees and their beneficiaries under the plan, determined using specified interest and mortality assumptions. In the case of a plan with a funded current liability percentage of less than 100 percent for the preceding plan year, estimated contributions for the current plan year must be made in quarterly installments during the current plan year.

The PBGC insures benefits under most single-employer defined benefit pension plans in the event the plan is terminated with insufficient assets to pay for plan benefits. The PBGC is funded in part by a flat-rate premium per plan participant, and variable rate premiums based on the amount of unfunded vested benefits under the plan. A specified interest rate and a specified mortality table apply in determining unfunded vested benefits for this purpose.

A special rule modifies the minimum funding requirements in the case of certain plans. The special rule applies in the case of plans that: (1) were not required to pay a variable rate PBGC premium for the plan year beginning in 1996; (2) do not, in plan years beginning after 1995 and before 2009, merge with another plan (other than a plan sponsored by an employer that was a member of the controlled group of the employer in 1996); and (3) are sponsored by a company that is engaged primarily in interurban or interstate passenger bus service.

The special rule generally treats a plan to which it applies as having a funded current liability percentage of at least 90 percent for plan years beginning after 1996 and before 2004 if for such plan year the funded current liability percentage is at least 85 percent. If the funded current liability of the plan is less than 85 percent for any plan year beginning after 1996 and before 2004, the relief from the minimum funding requirements generally applies only if certain specified contributions are made.

For plan years beginning in 2004 and 2005, the funded current liability percentage of the plan is treated as at least 90 percent for purposes of determining the amount of required contributions (100 percent for purposes of determining whether quarterly contributions are required). As a result, for these years, additional contributions under the deficit reduction contribution rules and quarterly contributions are not required with respect to the plan. In addition, for these years, the mortality table used under the plan is used in calculating PBGC variable rate premiums.

For plan years beginning after 2005 and before 2010, the funded current liability percentage generally will be deemed to be at least 90 percent if the actual funded current liability percentage is at least at certain specified levels. The relief from the minimum funding requirements generally applies for a plan year beginning in 2006, 2007, or 2008 only if contributions to the plan for the plan year equal at least the expected increase in current liability due to benefits accruing during the plan year.

Explanation of Provision

The provision revises the special rule for a plan that is sponsored by a company engaged primarily in interurban or interstate passenger bus service and that meets the other requirements for the special rule under present law. The provision extends the application of the special rule under present law for plan years beginning in 2004 and 2005 to plan years beginning in 2006 and 2007. The provision also provides several special rules relating to determining minimum required contributions and variable rate premiums for plan years beginning after 2007 when the new funding rules for single-employer plans apply.

Under the provision, for the plan year beginning in 2006 or 2007, a plan's funded current liability percentage of a plan is treated as at least 90 percent for purposes of determining the amount of required contributions (100 percent for purposes of determining whether quarterly contributions are required). As a result, for the 2006 and 2007 plan years, additional contributions under the deficit reduction contribution rules and quarterly contributions are not required with respect to the plan. In addition, the mortality table used under the plan is used in calculating PBGC variable rate premiums.

Under the provision, for plan years beginning after 2007, the mortality table used under the plan is used in: (1) determining any present value or making any computation under the minimum funding rules applicable to the plan; and (2) calculating PBGC variable rate premiums. Under a special phase-in (in lieu of the phase-in otherwise applicable under the provision relating to funding rules for single-employer plans), for purposes of determining whether a shortfall amortization base is required for plan years beginning after 2007 and before 2012, the applicable percentage of the plan's funding shortfall is the following: 90 percent for 2008, 92 percent for 2009, 94 percent for 2010, and 96 percent for 2011. In addition, for purposes of the quarterly contributions requirement, the plan is treated as not having a funding shortfall for any plan year. As a result, quarterly contributions are not required with respect to the plan.

Effective Date

The provision is effective for plan years beginning after December 31, 2005.

[Law at ¶ 7027. CCH Explanation at ¶ 230.]

[¶10,070] Act Sec. 116. Restrictions on funding of nonqualified deferred compensation plans by employers maintaining underfunded or terminated single-employer plans

Joint Committee Taxation (J.C.T. REP. NO. JCX-38-06)

[Code Sec. 409A]

Present Law

Amounts deferred under a nonqualified deferred compensation plan for all taxable years are currently includible in gross income to the extent not subject to a substantial risk of forfeiture and not previously included in gross income, unless certain requirements are satisfied.[53] For example, distributions from a nonqualified deferred compensation plan may be allowed only upon certain times and events. Rules also apply for the timing of elections. If the requirements are not satisfied, in addition to current income inclusion, interest at the underpayment rate plus one percentage point is imposed on the underpayments that would have occurred had the compensation been includible in income when first deferred, or if later, when not subject to a substantial risk of forfeiture. The amount required to be included in income is also subject to a 20-percent additional tax.

In the case of assets set aside in a trust (or other arrangement) for purposes of paying nonqualified deferred compensation, such assets are treated as property transferred in connection with the performance of services under Code section 83 at the time set aside if such assets (or trust or other arrangement) are located outside

[53] Code sec. 409A.

of the United States or at the time transferred if such assets (or trust or other arrangement) are subsequently transferred outside of the United States. A transfer of property in connection with the performance of services under Code section 83 also occurs with respect to compensation deferred under a nonqualified deferred compensation plan if the plan provides that upon a change in the employer's financial health, assets will be restricted to the payment of nonqualified deferred compensation.

Explanation of Provision

Under the provision, if during any restricted period in which a defined benefit pension plan of an employer is in at-risk status,[54] assets are set aside (directly or indirectly) in a trust (or other arrangement as determined by the Secretary of the Treasury), or transferred to such a trust or other arrangement, for purposes of paying deferred compensation of an applicable covered employee, such transferred assets are treated as property transferred in connection with the performance of services (whether or not such assets are available to satisfy the claims of general creditors) under Code section 83. The rule does not apply in the case of assets that are set aside before the defined benefit pension plan is in at-risk status.

If a nonqualified deferred compensation plan of an employer provides that assets will be restricted to the provision of benefits under the plan in connection with a restricted period (or other similar financial measure determined by the Secretary of Treasury) of any defined benefit pension plan of the employer, or assets are so restricted, such assets are treated as property transferred in connection with the performance of services (whether or not such assets are available to satisfy the claims of general creditors) under Code section 83.

A restricted period is (1) any period in which a single-employer defined benefit pension plan of an employer is in at risk-status, (2) any period in which the employer is in bankruptcy, and (3) the period that begins six months before and ends six months after the date any defined benefit pension plan of the employer is terminated in an involuntary or distress termination. The provision does not apply with respect to assets set aside before a restricted period.

In general, applicable covered employees include the chief executive officer (or individual acting in such capacity), the four highest compensated officers for the taxable year (other than the chief executive officer), and individuals subject to section 16(a) of the Securities Exchange Act of 1934. An applicable covered employee includes any (1) covered employee of a plan sponsor; (2) covered employee of a member of a controlled group which includes the plan sponsor; and (3) former employee who was a covered employee at the time of termination of employment with the plan sponsor or a member of a controlled group which includes the plan sponsor.

A nonqualified deferred compensation plan is any plan that provides for the deferral of compensation other than a qualified employer plan or any bona fide vacation leave, sick leave, compensatory time, disability pay, or death benefit plan. A qualified employer plan means a qualified retirement plan, tax-deferred annuity, simplified employee pension, and SIMPLE.[55] A qualified governmental excess benefit arrangement (sec. 415(m)) is a qualified employer plan. An eligible deferred compensation plan (sec. 457(b)) is also a qualified employer plan under the provision. The term plan includes any agreement or arrangement, including an agreement or arrangement that includes one person.

Any subsequent increases in the value of, or any earnings with respect to, transferred or restricted assets are treated as additional transfers of property. Interest at the underpayment rate plus one percentage point is imposed on the underpayments that would have occurred had the amounts been includible in income for the taxable year in which first deferred or, if later, the first taxable year not subject to a substantial risk of forfeiture. The amount required to be included in income is also subject to an additional 20-percent tax.

Under the provision, if an employer provides directly or indirectly for the payment of any Federal, State or local income taxes with respect to any compensation required to be included in income under the provision, interest is imposed on the amount of such payment in the same manner as if the payment were part of the deferred compensation to which it related. As under present law, such payment is included in income; in addition, under the provision, such payment is subject to a 20 percent additional tax. The payment is also nondeductible by the employer.

---

[54] At-risk status is defined as under the provision relating to funding rules for single-employer defined benefit pension plans and applies if a plan's funding target attainment percentage for the preceding year was less than 60 percent.

[55] A qualified employer plan also includes a section 501(c)(18) trust.

Effective Date

The provision is effective for transfers or other reservations of assets after date of enactment.

[Law at ¶ 5070. CCH Explanation at ¶ 220.]

[¶ 10,080] Act Secs. 201 and 211. Funding rules for multiemployer defined benefit plans

Joint Committee Taxation (J.C.T. Rep. No. JCX-38-06)

[New Code Sec. 431]

Present Law

Multiemployer plans

A multiemployer plan is a plan to which more than one unrelated employer contributes, which is established pursuant to one or more collective bargaining agreements, and which meets such other requirements as specified by the Secretary of Labor. Multiemployer plans are governed by a board of trustees consisting of an equal number of employer and employee representatives. In general, the level of contributions to a multiemployer plan is specified in the applicable collective bargaining agreements, and the level of plan benefits is established by the plan trustees.

Defined benefit multiemployer plans are subject to the same general minimum funding rules as single-employer plans, except that different rules apply in some cases. For example, different amortization periods apply for some costs in the case of multiemployer plans. In addition, the deficit reduction contribution rules do not apply to multiemployer plans.

Funding standard account

As an administrative aid in the application of the funding requirements, a defined benefit pension plan is required to maintain a special account called a "funding standard account" to which specified charges and credits are made for each plan year, including a charge for normal cost and credits for contributions to the plan. Other credits or charges or credits may apply as a result of decreases or increases in past service liability as a result of plan amendments or experience gains or losses, gains or losses resulting from a change in actuarial assumptions, or a waiver of minimum required contributions.

If, as of the close of the plan year, charges to the funding standard account exceed credits to the account, then the excess is referred to as an "accumulated funding deficiency." For example, if the balance of charges to the funding standard account of a plan for a year would be $200,000 without any contributions, then a minimum contribution equal to that amount would be required to meet the minimum funding standard for the year to prevent an accumulated funding deficiency. If credits to the funding standard account exceed charges, a "credit balance" results. The amount of the credit balance, increased with interest, can be used to reduce future required contributions.

Funding methods and general concepts

In general

A defined benefit pension plan is required to use an acceptable actuarial cost method to determine the elements included in its funding standard account for a year. Generally, an actuarial cost method breaks up the cost of benefits under the plan into annual charges consisting of two elements for each plan year. These elements are referred to as: (1) normal cost; and (2) supplemental cost.

Normal cost

The plan's normal cost for a plan year generally represents the cost of future benefits allocated to the year by the funding method used by the plan for current employees and, under some funding methods, for separated employees. Specifically, it is the amount actuarially determined that would be required as a contribution by the employer for the plan year in order to maintain the plan if the plan had been in effect from the beginning of service of the included employees and if the costs for prior years had been paid, and all assumptions as to interest, mortality, time of payment, etc., had been fulfilled.

Supplemental cost

The supplemental cost for a plan year is the cost of future benefits that would not be met by future normal costs, future employee contributions, or plan assets. The most common supplemental cost is that attributable to past service liability, which represents the cost of future benefits under the plan: (1) on the date the plan is first effective; or (2) on the date a plan amendment increasing plan benefits is first effective. Other supplemental costs may be attributable to net experience losses, changes in actuarial assumptions, and amounts necessary to make up funding deficiencies for which a waiver was obtained. Supplemental costs must be amortized (i.e., recognized for funding purposes) over a specified number of years, depending on the source.

Valuation of assets

For funding purposes, the actuarial value of plan assets may be used, rather than fair market value. The actuarial value of plan assets is the value determined under a reasonable actuarial valuation method that takes into account fair market value and is permitted under Treasury regulations. Any actuarial valuation method used must result in a value of plan assets that is not less than 80 percent of the fair market value of the assets and not more than 120 percent of the fair market value. In addition, if the valuation method uses average value of the plan assets, values may be used for a stated period not to exceed the five most recent plan years, including the current year.

Reasonableness of assumptions

In applying the funding rules, all costs, liabilities, interest rates, and other factors are required to be determined on the basis of actuarial assumptions and methods, each of which is reasonable (taking into account the experience of the plan and reasonable expectations), or which, in the aggregate, result in a total plan contribution equivalent to a contribution that would be obtained if each assumption and method were reasonable. In addition, the assumptions are required to offer the actuary's best estimate of anticipated experience under the plan.

Charges and credits to the funding standard account

In general

Under the minimum funding standard, the portion of the cost of a plan that is required to be paid for a particular year depends upon the nature of the cost. For example, the normal cost for a year is generally required to be funded currently. Other costs are spread (or amortized) over a period of years. In the case of a multiemployer plan, past service liability is amortized over 40 or 30 years depending on how the liability arose, experience gains and losses are amortized over 15 years, gains and losses from changes in actuarial assumptions are amortized over 30 years, and waived funding deficiencies are amortized over 15 years.

Normal cost

Each plan year, a plan's funding standard account is charged with the normal cost assigned to that year under the particular acceptable actuarial cost method adopted by the plan. The charge for normal cost will require an offsetting credit in the funding standard account. Usually, an employer contribution is required to create the credit. For example, if the normal cost for a plan year is $150,000, the funding standard account would be charged with that amount for the year. Assuming that there are no other credits in the account to offset the charge for normal cost, an employer contribution of $150,000 will be required for the year to avoid an accumulated funding deficiency.

Past service liability

There are three separate charges to the funding standard account one or more of which may apply to a multiemployer plan as the result of past service liabilities. In the case of a plan in existence on January 1, 1974, past service liability under the plan on the first day on which the plan was first subject to ERISA is amortized over 40 years. In the case of a plan which was not in existence on January 1, 1974, past service liability under the plan on the first day on which the plan was first subject to ERISA is amortized over 30 years. Past service liability due to plan amendments is amortized over 30 years.

Experience gains and losses

In determining plan funding under an actuarial cost method, a plan's actuary generally makes certain assumptions regarding the future experience of a plan. These assumptions typically involve rates of interest, mortality, disability, salary increases, and other factors affecting the value of assets and liabilities. The actuarial assumptions are required to be reasonable, as discussed above. If the plan's actual unfunded liabilities are less than those anticipated by the actuary on the basis of these assumptions, then the excess is an experience gain. If the actual unfunded liabilities are greater than those anticipated, then the difference is an experience loss. In the case of a multiemployer plan, experience gains and losses for a year are generally amortized over a 15-year period, resulting in credits or charges to the funding standard account.

Gains and losses from changes in assumptions

If the actuarial assumptions used for funding a plan are revised and, under the new assumptions, the accrued liability of a plan is less than the accrued liability computed under the previous assumptions, the decrease is a gain from changes in actuarial assumptions. If the new assumptions result in an increase in the accrued liability, the plan has a loss from changes in actuarial assumptions. The accrued liability of a plan is the actuarial present value of projected pension benefits under the plan that will not be funded by future contributions to meet normal cost or future employee contributions. In the case of a multiemployer plan, the gain or loss for a year from changes in actuarial assumptions is amortized over a period of 30 years, resulting in credits or charges to the funding standard account.

Shortfall funding method

Certain plans may elect to determine the required charges to the funding standard account under the shortfall method. Under such method, the charges are computed on the basis of an estimated number of units of service or production for which a certain amount per unit is to be charged. The difference between the net amount charged under this method and the net amount that otherwise would have been charged for the same period is a shortfall loss or gain that is amortized over subsequent plan years. The use of the shortfall method and changes to use of the shortfall method are generally subject to IRS approval.

Funding waivers and amortization of waived funding deficiencies

Within limits, the Secretary of the Treasury is permitted to waive all or a portion of the contributions required under the minimum funding standard for the year (a "waived funding deficiency"). In the case of a multiemployer plan, a waiver may be granted if 10 percent or more of the number of employers contributing to the plan could not make the required contribution without temporary substantial business hardship and if requiring the contribution would be adverse to the interests of plan participants in the aggregate. The minimum funding requirements may not be waived with respect to a multiemployer plan for more five out of any 15 consecutive years.

If a funding deficiency is waived, the waived amount is credited to the funding standard account. In the case of a multiemployer plan, the waived amount is then amortized over a period of 15 years, beginning with the year following the year in which the waiver is granted. Each year, the funding standard account is charged with the amortization amount for that year unless the plan becomes fully funded. In the case of a multiemployer plan, the interest rate used for purposes of determining the amortization on the waived amount is the rate determined under section 6621(b) of the Internal Revenue Code (relating to the Federal short-term rate).

Extension of amortization periods

Amortization periods may be extended for up to 10 years by the Secretary of the Treasury if the Secretary finds that the extension would carry out the purposes of ERISA and would provide adequate protection for participants under the plan and if such Secretary determines that the failure to permit such an extension would (1) result in a substantial risk to the voluntary continuation of the plan or a substantial curtailment of pension benefit levels or employee compensation, and (2) be adverse to the interests of plan participants in the aggregate. The interest rate with respect to extensions of amortization periods is the same as that used with respect to waived funding deficiencies.

Alternative funding standard account

As an alternative to applying the rules described above, a plan which uses the entry age normal cost method may satisfy an alternative minimum funding standard. Under the alternative, the minimum required contribution for the year is generally based on the amount necessary to bring the plan's assets up to the present value of accrued benefits, determine using the actuarial assumptions that apply when a plan terminates. The alternative standard has been rarely used.

Controlled group liability for required contributions

Unlike the rule for single-employer plans which imposes liability for minimum required contributions to all members of the employer's controlled group, controlled-group liability does not apply to contributions an employer is required to make to a multiemployer plan.

Explanation of Provision

Amortization periods

The provision modifies the amortization periods applicable to multiemployer plans so that the amortization period for most charges is 15 years. Under the provision, past service liability under the plan is amortized over 15 years (rather than 30); past service liability due to plan amendments is amortized over 15 years (rather than 30); and experience gains and losses resulting from a change in actuarial assumptions are amortized over 15 years (rather than 30). As under present law, experience gains and losses and waived funding deficiencies are amortized over 15 years. The new amortization periods do not apply to amounts being amortized under present-law amortization periods, that is, no recalculation of amortization schedules already in effect is required under the provision. The provision eliminates the alternative funding standard account.

Actuarial assumptions

The provision provides that in applying the funding rules, all costs, liabilities, interest rates, and other factors are required to be determined on the basis of actuarial assumptions and methods, each of which is reasonable (taking into account the experience of the plan and reasonable expectations). In addition, as under present law, the assumptions are required to offer the actuary's best estimate of anticipated experience under the plan.

Extension of amortization periods

The provision provides that, upon application to the Secretary of the Treasury, the Secretary is required to grant an extension of the amortization period for up to five years with respect to any unfunded past service liability, investment loss, or experience loss. Included with the application must be a certification by the plan's actuary that (1) absent the extension, the plan would have an accumulated funding deficiency in the current plan year and any of the nine succeeding plan years, (2) the plan sponsor has adopted a plan to improve the plan's funding status, (3) taking into account the extension, the plan is projected to have sufficient assets to timely pay its expected benefit liabilities and other anticipated expenditures, and (4) that required notice is provided. The automatic extension provision does not apply with respect to any application submitted after December 31, 2014.

The Secretary of the Treasury may also grant an additional extension of such amortization periods for an additional five years. The standards for determining whether such an extension may be granted are the same as under present law. In addition, the provision requires the Secretary of the Treasury to act upon an application for an additional extension within 180 days after submission. If the Secretary rejects the application, the Secretary must provide notice to the plan detailing the specific reasons for the rejection.

As under present law, these extensions do not apply unless the applicant demonstrates to the satisfaction of the Treasury Secretary that notice of the application has been provided to each affected party (as defined in ERISA section 4001(a)(21)).

Interest rate applicable to funding waivers and extension of amortization periods

The provision eliminates the special interest rate rule for funding waivers and extensions of amortization periods so that the plan rate applies.

Additional provisions

Controlled group liability for required contributions

The provision imposes joint and several liability to all members of the employer's controlled group for minimum required contributions to single-employer or multiemployer plans.

Shortfall funding method

The provision provides that, for plan years beginning before January 1, 2015, certain multiemployer plans may adopt, use or cease using the shortfall funding method and such adoption, use, or cessation of use is deemed approved by the Secretary of the Treasury. Plans are eligible if (1) the plan has not used the shortfall funding method during the five-year period ending on the day before the date the plan is to use the shortfall funding method; and (2) the plan is not operating under an amortization period extension and did not operate under such an extension during such five-year period. Benefit restrictions apply during a period that a multiemployer plan is using the shortfall funding method. In general, plan amendments increasing benefits cannot be adopted while the shortfall funding method is in use. The provision is not intended to affect a plan's ability to adopt the shortfall funding method with IRS approval or to affect a plan's right to change funding methods as otherwise permitted.

Effective Date

The provision is effective for plan years beginning after 2007.

[Law at ¶5125 and ¶7030. CCH Explanation at ¶205 and ¶305.]

[¶10,090] Act Secs. 202 and 212. Additional funding rules for multiemployer plans in endangered or critical status

Joint Committee Taxation (J.C.T. Rep. No. JCX-38-06)

[New Code Sec. 432]

Present Law

In general

Multiemployer defined benefit plans are subject to minimum funding rules similar to those applicable to single-employer plans.[56] If a multiemployer plan has an accumulated funding deficiency for a year, an excise tax of five percent generally applies, increasing to 100 percent if contributions sufficient to eliminate the funding deficiency are not made within a certain period.

Additional required contributions and benefit reductions may apply if a multiemployer plan is in reorganization status or is insolvent.

Reorganization status

Certain modifications to the single-employer plan funding rules apply to multiemployer plans that experience financial difficulties, referred to as "reorganization status." A plan is in reorganization status for a year if the contribution needed to balance the charges and credits to its funding standard account exceeds its "vested benefits charge."[57] The plan's vested benefits charge is generally the amount needed to amortize, in equal annual installments, unfunded vested benefits under the plan over: (1) 10 years in the case of obligations attributable to participants in pay status; and (2) 25 years in the case of obligations attributable to other participants. A plan in reorganization status is eligible for a special funding credit. In addition, a cap on year-to-year contribution increases and other relief is available to employers that continue to contribute to the plan.

Subject to certain requirements, a multiemployer plan in reorganization status may also be amended to reduce or eliminate accrued benefits in excess of the amount of benefits guaranteed by the PBGC.[58] In order for accrued benefits to be reduced, at least six months before the beginning of the plan year in which the amendment is adopted, notice must be given that the plan is in reorganization status and that, if contributions to the plan are not increased, accrued benefits will be reduced or an excise tax will be imposed on employers obligated to contribute to the plan. The notice must be provided to plan participants and beneficiaries, any employer who has an obligation to contribute to the plan, and any employee organization representing employees in the plan.

Insolvency

In the case of multiemployer plans, the PBGC insures plan insolvency, rather than plan termination. A plan is insolvent when its available resources are not sufficient to pay the plan benefits for the plan year in question, or when the sponsor of a plan in reorganization reasonably determines, taking into account the plan's recent and anticipated financial experience, that the plan's available resources will not be sufficient to pay benefits that come due in the next plan year.[59] An insolvent plan is required to reduce benefits to the level that can be covered by the plan's assets. However, benefits cannot be reduced below the level guaranteed by the PBGC.[60] If a multiemployer plan is insolvent, the PBGC guarantee is provided in the form of loans to the plan trustees. If the plan recovers from insolvency status, loans from the PBGC can be repaid. Plans in reorganization status are required to compare assets and liabilities to determine if the plan will become insolvent in the future.

Explanation of Provision

In general

The provision provides additional funding rules for multiemployer defined benefit plans in effect on July 16, 2006, that are in endangered or critical status. The provision requires the adoption of and compliance with (1) a funding im-

[56] See the explanation of the preceding provision for a discussion of the minimum funding rules for multiemployer defined benefit plans. Under Treasury regulations, certain noncollectively bargained employees covered by a multiemployer plan may be treated as collectively bargained employees for purposes of applying the minimum coverage rules of the Code. Treas. Reg. sec. 1.410(b)-6(d)(2)(ii)(D).

[57] ERISA sec. 4241.

[58] ERISA sec. 4244A.

[59] ERISA sec. 4245.

[60] The limit of benefits that the PBGC guarantees under a multiemployer plan is the sum of 100 percent of the first $11 of monthly benefits and 75 percent of the next $33 of monthly benefits for each year of service. ERISA sec. 4022A(c).

provement plan in the case of a multiemployer plan in endangered status, and (2) a rehabilitation plan in the case of a multiemployer plan in critical status.

Under the provision, in the case of a plan in critical status, additional required contributions and benefit reductions apply and employers are relieved of liability for minimum required contributions under the otherwise applicable funding rules, provided that a rehabilitation plan is adopted and followed.

Annual certification of status; notice; annual reports

Not later than the 90th day of each plan year, the plan actuary must certify to the Secretary of the Treasury and to the plan sponsor whether or not the plan is in endangered or critical status for the plan year. In the case of a plan that is in a funding improvement or rehabilitation period, the actuary must certify whether or not the plan is making scheduled progress in meeting the requirements of its funding improvement or rehabilitation plan.

In making the determinations and projections applicable under the endangered and critical status rules, the plan actuary must make projections for the current and succeeding plan years of the current value of the assets of the plan and the present value of all liabilities to participants and beneficiaries under the plan for the current plan year as of the beginning of such year. The actuary's projections must be based on reasonable actuarial estimates, assumptions, and methods that offer the actuary's best estimate of anticipated experience under the plan. An exception to this rule applies in the case of projected industry activity. Any projection of activity in the industry or industries covered by the plan, including future covered employment and contribution levels, must be based on information provided by the plan sponsor, which shall act reasonably and in good faith. The projected present value of liabilities as of the beginning of the year must be based on the most recent actuarial statement required with respect to the most recently filed annual report or the actuarial valuation for the preceding plan year.

Any actuarial projection of plan assets must assume (1) reasonably anticipated employer contributions for the current and succeeding plan years, assuming that the terms of one or more collective bargaining agreements pursuant to which the plan is maintained for the current plan year continue in effect for the succeeding plan years, or (2) that employer contributions for the most recent plan year will continue indefinitely, but only if the plan actuary determines that there have been no significant demographic changes that would make continued application of such terms unreasonable.

Failure of the plan's actuary to certify the status of the plan is treated as a failure to file the annual report (thus, an ERISA penalty of up to $1,100 per day applies).

If a plan is certified to be in endangered or critical status, notification of the endangered or critical status must be provided within 30 days after the date of certification to the participants and beneficiaries, the bargaining parties, the PBGC and the Secretary of Labor.[61] If it is certified that a plan is or will be in critical status, the plan sponsor must included in the notice an explanation of the possibility that (1) adjustable benefits may be reduced and (2) such reductions may apply to participants and beneficiaries whose benefit commencement date is on or after the date such notice is provided for the first plan year in which the plan is in critical status. The Secretary of Labor is required to prescribe a model notice to satisfy these requirements.

The plan sponsor must annually update the funding improvement or rehabilitation plan. Updates are required to be filed with the plan's annual report.

Endangered status

Definition of endangered status

A multiemployer plan is in endangered status if the plan is not in critical status and, as of the beginning of the plan year, (1) the plan's funded percentage for the plan year is less than 80 percent, or (2) the plan has an accumulated funding deficiency for the plan year or is projected to have an accumulated funding deficiency in any of the six succeeding plan years (taking into account amortization extensions). A plan's funded percentage is the percentage of plan assets over accrued liability of the plan. A plan that meets the requirements of both (1) and (2) is treated as in seriously endangered status.

Information to be provided to bargaining parties

Within 30 days of the adoption of a funding improvement plan, the plan sponsor must pro-

[61] If a plan actuary certifies that it is reasonably expected that a plan will be in critical status with respect to the first plan year after 2007, notice may be provided at any time after date of enactment, as long as it is provided on or before the date otherwise required.

vide to the bargaining parties schedules showing revised benefit structures, revised contribution structures, or both, which, if adopted, may reasonably be expected to enable the multiemployer plan to meet the applicable benchmarks in accordance with the funding improvement plan, including (1) one proposal for reductions in the amount of future benefit accruals necessary to achieve the applicable benchmarks, assuming no amendments increasing contributions under the plan (other than amendments increasing contributions necessary to achieve the applicable benchmarks after amendments have reduced future benefit accruals to the maximum extent permitted by law) (the "default schedule"), and (2) one proposal for increases in contributions under the plan necessary to achieve the applicable benchmarks, assuming no amendments reducing future benefit accruals under the plan. The applicable benchmarks are the requirements of the funding improvement plan (discussed below). The plan sponsor may provide the bargaining parties with additional information if deemed appropriate.

The plan sponsor must annually update any schedule of contribution rates to reflect the experience of the plan.

Funding improvement plan and funding improvement period

In the case of a multiemployer plan in endangered status, a funding improvement plan must be adopted within 240 days following the deadline for certifying a plan's status.[62] A funding improvement plan is a plan which consists of the actions, including options or a range of options, to be proposed to the bargaining parties, formulated to provide, based on reasonably anticipated experience and reasonable actuarial assumptions, for the attainment by the plan of certain requirements.

The funding improvement plan must provide that during the funding improvement period, the plan will have a certain required increase in the funded percentage and no accumulated funding deficiency for any plan year during the funding improvement period, taking into account amortization extensions (the "applicable benchmarks"). In the case of a plan that is not in seriously endangered status, under the applicable benchmarks, the plan's funded percentage must increase such that the funded percentage as of the close of the funding improvement period equals or exceeds a percentage equal to the sum of (1) the funded percentage at the beginning of the period, plus (2) 33 percent of the difference between 100 percent and the percentage in (1). Thus, the difference between 100 percent and the plan's funded percentage at the beginning of the period must be reduced by at least one-third during the funding improvement period.

The funding improvement period is the 10-year period beginning on the first day of the first plan year beginning after the earlier of (1) the second anniversary of the date of adoption of the funding improvement plan, or (2) the expiration of collective bargaining agreements that were in effect on the due date for the actuarial certification of endangered status for the initial determination year and covering, as of such date, at least 75 percent of the plan's active participants. The period ends if the plan is no longer in endangered status or if the plan enters critical status.

In the case of a plan in seriously endangered status that is funded 70 percent or less, under the applicable benchmarks, the difference between 100 percent and the plan's funded percentage at the beginning of the period must be reduced by at least one-fifth during the funding improvement period. In the case of such plans, a 15-year funding improvement period is used.

In the case of a seriously endangered plan that is more than 70 percent funded as of the beginning of the initial determination year, the same benchmarks apply for plan years beginning on or before the date on which the last collective bargaining agreements in effect on the date for actuarial certification for the initial determination year and covering at least 75 percent of active employees in the multiemployer plan have expired if the plan actuary certifies within 30 days after certification of endangered status that the plan is not projected to attain the funding percentage increase otherwise required by the provision. Thus, for such plans, the difference between 100 percent and the plan's funded percentage at the beginning of the period must be reduced by at least one-fifth during the 15-year funding improvement period. For subsequent years for such plans, if the plan actuary certifies that the plan is not able to attain the increase generally required under the provision, the same benchmarks continue to apply.

As previously discussed, the plan sponsor must annually update the funding improvement

[62] This requirement applies for the initial determination year (i.e., the first plan year that the plan is in endangered status).

plan and must file the update with the plan's annual report.

If, for the first plan year following the close of the funding improvement period, the plan's actuary certifies that the plan is in endangered status, such year is treated as an initial determination year. Thus, a new funding improvement plan must be adopted within 240 days of the required certification date. In such case, the plan may not be amended in a manner inconsistent with the funding improvement plan in effect for the preceding plan year until a new funding improvement plan is adopted.

Requirements pending approval of plan and during funding improvement period

Certain restrictions apply during the period beginning on the date of certification for the initial determination year and ending on the day before the first day of the funding improvement period (the "funding plan adoption period").

During the funding plan adoption period, the plan sponsor may not accept a collective bargaining agreement or participation agreement that provides for (1) a reduction in the level of contributions for any participants; (2) a suspension of contributions with respect to any period of service; or (3) any new or indirect exclusion of younger or newly hired employees from plan participation.

In addition, during the funding plan adoption period, except in the case of amendments required as a condition of qualification under the Internal Revenue Code or to apply with other applicable law, no amendment may be adopted which increases liabilities of the plan by reason of any increase in benefits, any change in accrual of benefits, or any change in the rate at which benefits become nonforfeitable under the plan.

In the case of a plan in seriously endangered status, during the funding plan adoption period, the plan sponsor must take all reasonable actions (consistent with the terms of the plan and present law) which are expected, based on reasonable assumptions, to achieve an increase in the plan's funded percentage and a postponement of an accumulated funding deficiency for at least one additional plan year. These actions include applications for extensions of amortization periods, use of the shortfall funding method in making funding standard account computations, amendments to the plan's benefit structure, reductions in future benefit accruals, and other reasonable actions.

Upon adoption of a funding improvement plan, the plan may not be amended to be inconsistent with the funding improvement plan. During the funding improvement period, a plan sponsor may not accept a collective bargaining agreement or participation agreement with respect to the multiemployer plan that provides for (1) a reduction in the level of contributions for any participants; (2) a suspension of contributions with respect to any period of service, or (3) any new direct or indirect exclusion of younger or newly hired employees from plan participation.

After the adoption of a funding improvement plan, a plan may not be amended to increase benefits, including future benefit accruals, unless the plan actuary certifies that the benefit increase is consistent with the funding improvement plan and is paid for out of contributions not required by the funding improvement plan to meet the applicable benchmark in accordance with the schedule contemplated in the funding improvement plan.

Effect of and penalty for failure to adopt a funding improvement plan

If a collective bargaining agreement providing for contributions under a multiemployer plan that was in effect at the time the plan entered endangered status expires, and after receiving one or more schedules from the plan sponsor, the bargaining parties fail to agree on changes to contribution or benefit schedules necessary to meet the applicable benchmarks, the plan sponsor must implement the default schedule. The schedule must be implemented on the earlier of the date (1) on which the Secretary of Labor certifies that the parties are at an impasse, or (2) which is 180 days after the date on which the collective bargaining agreement expires.

In the case of the failure of a plan sponsor to adopt a funding improvement plan by the end of the 240-day period after the required certification date, an ERISA penalty of up to $1,100 a day applies.

Excise tax on employers failing to meet required contributions

If the funding improvement plan requires an employer to make contributions to the plan, an excise tax applies upon the failure of the employer to make such required contributions within the time required under the plan. The amount of tax is equal to the amount of the required contribution the employer failed to make in a timely manner.

Application of excise tax to plans in endangered status/penalty for failure to achieve benchmarks

In the case of a plan in endangered status, which is not in seriously endangered status, a civil penalty of $1,100 a day applies for the failure of the plan to meet the applicable benchmarks by the end of the funding improvement period.

In the case of a plan in seriously endangered status, an excise tax applies for the failure to meet the benchmarks by the end of the funding improvement period. In such case, an excise tax applies based on the greater of (1) the amount of the contributions necessary to meet such benchmarks or (2) the plan's accumulated funding deficiency. The excise tax applies for each succeeding plan year until the benchmarks are met.

Waiver of excise tax

In the case of a failure which is due to reasonable cause and not to willful neglect, the Secretary of the Treasury may waive all or part of the excise tax on employers failing to make required contributions and the excise tax for failure to achieve the applicable benchmarks. The party against whom the tax is imposed has the burden of establishing that the failure was due to reasonable cause and not willful neglect. Reasonable cause includes unanticipated and material market fluctuations, the loss of a significant contributing employer, or other factors to the extent that the payment of tax would be excessive or otherwise inequitable relative to the failure involved. The determination of reasonable cause is based on the facts and circumstances of each case and requires the parties to act with ordinary business care and prudence. The standard requires the funding improvement plan to be based on reasonably foreseeable events. It is expected that reasonable cause would include instances in which the plan experiences a net equity loss of at least ten percent during the funding improvement period, a change in plan demographics such as the bankruptcy of a significant contributing employer, a legal change (including the outcome of litigation) that unexpectedly increases the plan's benefit obligations, or a strike or lockout for a significant period.

Critical status

Definition of critical status

A multiemployer plan is in critical status for a plan year if as of the beginning of the plan year:

1. The funded percentage of the plan is less than 65 percent and the sum of (A) the market value of plan assets, plus (B) the present value of reasonably anticipated employer and employee contributions for the current plan year and each of the six succeeding plan years (assuming that the terms of the collective bargaining agreements continue in effect) is less than the present value of all benefits projected to be payable under the plan during the current plan year and each of the six succeeding plan years (plus administrative expenses),

2. (A) The plan has an accumulated funding deficiency for the current plan year, not taking into account any amortization extension, or (B) the plan is projected to have an accumulated funding deficiency for any of the three succeeding plan years (four succeeding plan years if the funded percentage of the plan is 65 percent or less), not taking into account any amortization extension,

3. (A) The plan's normal cost for the current plan year, plus interest for the current plan year on the amount of unfunded benefit liabilities under the plan as of the last day of the preceding year, exceeds the present value of the reasonably anticipated employer contributions for the current plan year, (B) the present value of nonforfeitable benefits of inactive participants is greater than the present value of nonforfeitable benefits of active participants, and (C) the plan has an accumulated funding deficiency for the current plan year, or is projected to have an accumulated funding deficiency for any of the four succeeding plan years (not taking into account amortization period extensions), or

4. The sum of (A) the market value of plan assets, plus (B) the present value of the reasonably anticipated employer contributions for the current plan year and each of the four succeeding plan years (assuming that the terms of the collective bargaining agreements continue in effect) is less than the present value of all benefits projected to be payable under the plan during the current plan year and each of the four succeeding plan years (plus administrative expenses).

Additional contributions during critical status

In the case of a plan in critical status, the provision imposes an additional required contribution ("surcharge") on employers otherwise obligated to make a contribution in the initial critical year, i.e., the first plan year for which the plan is in critical status. The amount of the surcharge is five percent of the contribution otherwise required to be made under the applicable collective bargaining agreement. The surcharge is 10 percent of contributions otherwise required in the case of succeeding plan years in which the plan is in critical status. The surcharge applies 30 days after the employer is notified by the plan sponsor that the plan is in critical status and the surcharge is in effect. The surcharges are due and payable on the same schedule as the contributions on which the surcharges are based. Failure to make the surcharge payment is treated as a delinquent contribution. The surcharge is not required with respect to employees covered by a collective bargaining agreement (or other agreement pursuant to which the employer contributes), beginning on the effective date of a collective bargaining agreement (or other agreement) that includes terms consistent with a schedule presented by the plan sponsor. The amount of the surcharge may not be the basis for any benefit accrual under the plan.

Surcharges are disregarded in determining an employer's withdrawal liability except for purposes of determining the unfunded vested benefits attributable to an employer under ERISA section 4211(c)(4) or a comparable method approved under ERISA section 4211(c)(5).[63]

Reductions to previously earned benefits

Notwithstanding the anti-cutback rules, the plan sponsor may make any reductions to adjustable benefits which the plan sponsor deems appropriate, based upon the outcome of collective bargaining over the schedules required to be provided by the plan sponsor as discussed below. Adjustable benefits means (1) benefits, rights, and features under the plan, including post-retirement death benefits, 60-month guarantees, disability benefits not yet in pay status, and similar benefits; (2) any early retirement benefit or retirement-type subsidy and any benefit payment option (other than the qualified joint-and-survivor annuity); and (3) benefit increase that would not be eligible for PBGC guarantee on the first day of the initial critical year because the increases were adopted (or, if later, took effect) less than 60 months before such first day. Except as provided in (3), nothing should be construed to permit a plan to reduce the level of a participant's accrued benefit payable at normal retirement age.

The plan sponsor may not reduce adjustable benefits of any participant or beneficiary whose benefit commencement date is before the date on which the plan provides notice to the participant or beneficiary that the plan is in critical status and that benefits may be reduced. An exception applies in the case of benefit increases that would not be eligible for PBGC guarantee because the increases were adopted less than 60 months before the first day of the initial critical year.

The plan sponsor must include in the schedules provided to the bargaining parties an allowance for funding the benefits of participants with respect to whom contributions are not currently required to be made, and shall reduce their benefits to the extent permitted under the Code and ERISA and considered appropriate by the plan sponsor based on the plan's then current overall funding status.

Notice of any reduction of adjustable benefits must be provided at least 30 days before the general effective date of the reduction for all participants and beneficiaries. Benefits may not be reduced until the notice requirement is satisfied. Notice must be provided to (1) plan participants and beneficiaries; (2) each employer who has an obligation to contribute under the plans; and (3) each employee organization which, for purposes of collective bargaining, represents plan participants employed by such employer. The notice must contain (1) sufficient information to enable participants and beneficiaries to understand the effect of any reduction of their benefits, including an estimate (on an annual or monthly basis) of any affected adjustable benefit that a participant or beneficiary would otherwise have been eligible for as of the general effective date for benefit reductions; and (2) information as to the rights and remedies of plan participants and beneficiaries as well as how to contact the Department of Labor for further information and assistance where appropriate. The notice must be provided in a form and manner prescribed in regulations of the Secretary of Labor. In such regulations, the Secretary of Labor must establish a model notice.

Benefit reduction are disregarded in determining a plan's unfunded vested benefits for purposes of determining an employer's withdrawal liability.[64]

Information to be provided to bargaining parties

Within 30 days after adoption of the rehabilitation plan, the plan sponsor must provide to the bargaining parties schedules showing re-

[63] The PBGC is directed to prescribe simplified methods for determining withdrawal liability in this case.

[64] The PBGC is directed to prescribe simplified methods for determining withdrawal liability in this case.

vised benefit structures, revised contribution structures, or both which, if adopted, may reasonably be expected to enable the multiemployer plan to emerge from critical status in accordance with the rehabilitation plan.[65] The schedules must reflect reductions in future benefit accruals and adjustable benefits and increases in contributions that the plan sponsor determined are reasonably necessary to emerge from critical status. One schedule must be designated as the default schedule and must assume no increases in contributions other than increases necessary to emerge from critical status after future benefit accruals and other benefits (other than benefits the reduction or elimination of which are not permitted under the anti-cutback rules) have been reduced. The plan sponsor may also provide additional information as appropriate.

The plan sponsor must periodically update any schedule of contributions rates to reflect the experience of the plan.

Rehabilitation plan

If a plan is in critical status for a plan year, the plan sponsor must adopt a rehabilitation plan within 240 days following the required date for the actuarial certification of critical status.[66]

A rehabilitation plan is a plan which consists of actions, including options or a range of options to be proposed to the bargaining parties, formulated, based on reasonable anticipated experience and reasonable actuarial assumptions, to enable the plan to cease to be in critical status by the end of the rehabilitation period and may include reductions in plan expenditures (including plan mergers and consolidations), reductions in future benefits accruals or increases in contributions, if agreed to by the bargaining parties, or any combination of such actions.

A rehabilitation plan must provide annual standards for meeting the requirements of the rehabilitation. The plan must also include the schedules required to be provided to the bargaining parties.

If the plan sponsor determines that, based on reasonable actuarial assumptions and upon exhaustion of all reasonable measures, the plan cannot reasonably be expected to emerge from critical status by the end of the rehabilitation period, the plan must include reasonable measures to emerge from critical status at a later time or to forestall possible insolvency. In such case, the plan must set forth alternatives considered, explain why the plan is not reasonable expected to emerge from critical status by the end of the rehabilitation period, and specify when, if ever, the plan is expected to emerge from critical status in accordance with the rehabilitation plan.

As previously discussed, the plan sponsor must annually update the rehabilitation plan and must file the update with the plan's annual report.

Rehabilitation period

The rehabilitation period is the 10-year period beginning on the first day of the first plan year following the earlier of (1) the second anniversary of the date of adoption of the rehabilitation plan or (2) the expiration of collective bargaining agreements that were in effect on the due date for the actuarial certification of critical status for the initial critical year and covering at least 75 percent of the active participants in the plan.

The rehabilitation period ends if the plan emerges from critical status. A plan in critical status remains in critical status until a plan year for which the plan actuary certifies that the plan is not projected to have an accumulated funding deficiency for the plan year or any of the nine succeeding plan years, without regard to the use of the shortfall method and taking into account amortization period extensions.

Rules for reductions in future benefit accrual rates

Any schedule including reductions in future benefit accruals forming part of a rehabilitation plan must not reduce the rate of benefit accruals below (1) a monthly benefit (payable as a single life annuity commencing at the participant's normal retirement age) equal to one percent of the contributions required to be made with respect to a participant or the equivalent standard accrual rate for a participant or group of participants under the collective bargaining agreements in effect as of the first day of the initial critical year, or (2) if lower, the accrual rate under the plan on such first day.

The equivalent standard accrual rate is determined by the plan sponsor based on the standard or average contribution base units which the plan sponsor determines to be representative

---

[65] A schedule of contribution rates provided by the plan sponsor and relied upon by bargaining parties in negotiating a collective bargaining agreement must remain in effect for the duration of the collective bargaining agreement.

[66] The requirement applies with respect to the initial critical year.

for active participants and such other factors that the plan sponsor determines to be relevant.

Benefit reductions are disregarded in determining an employer's withdrawal liability.

Requirements pending approval and during rehabilitation period

Rehabilitation plan adoption period.—Certain restrictions apply during the period beginning on the date of certification and ending on the day before the first day of the rehabilitation period (defined as the "rehabilitation plan adoption period").

During the rehabilitation plan adoption period, the plan sponsor may not accept a collective bargaining agreement or participation agreement that provides for (1) a reduction in the level of contributions for any participants; (2) a suspension of contributions with respect to any period of service; or (3) any new direct or indirect exclusion of younger or newly hired employees from plan participation. Except in the case of amendments required as a condition of qualification under the Internal Revenue Code or to comply with other applicable law, during the rehabilitation plan adoption period, no amendments that increase the liabilities of the plan by reason of any increase in benefits, any change in the accrual of benefits, or any change in the rate at which benefits become nonforfeitable may be adopted.

During rehabilitation period.—A plan may not be amended after the date of adoption of a rehabilitation plan to be inconsistent with the rehabilitation plan.

A plan may not be amended after the date of adoption of a rehabilitation plan to increase benefits (including future benefit accruals) unless the plan actuary certifies that such increase is paid for out of additional contributions not contemplated by the rehabilitation plan and, after taking into account the benefit increases, the plan is still reasonably expected to emerge from critical status by the end of the rehabilitation period on the schedule contemplated by the rehabilitation plan.

Beginning on the date that notice of certification of the plan's critical status is sent, lump sum and other similar benefits may not be paid. The restriction does not apply if the present value of the participant's accrued benefit does not exceed $5,000. The restriction also does not apply to any makeup payment in the case of a retroactive annuity starting date or any similar payment of benefits owed with respect to a prior period.

The plan sponsor must annually update the plan and must file updates with the plan's annual report. Schedules must be annually updated to reflect experience of the plan.

Effect and penalty for failure to adopt a rehabilitation plan

If a collective bargaining agreement providing for contributions under a multiemployer plan that was in effect at the time the plan entered endangered status expires, and after receiving one of more schedules from the plan sponsor, the bargaining parties fail to adopt a contribution or benefit schedule with terms consistent with the rehabilitation plan and the scheduled from the plan sponsor, the plan sponsor must implement the default schedule. The schedule must be implemented on the earlier of the date (1) on which the Secretary of Labor certifies that the parties are at an impasse, or (2) which is 180 days after the date on which the collective bargaining agreement expires.

Upon the failure of a plan sponsor to adopt a rehabilitation plan within 240 days after the date required for certification, an ERISA penalty of $1,100 a day applies. In addition, upon the failure to timely adopt a rehabilitation plan, an excise tax is imposed on the plan sponsor equal to the greater of (1) the present law excise tax or (2) $1,100 per day. The tax must be paid by the plan sponsor.

Excise tax on employers failing to meet required contributions

If the rehabilitation plan requires an employer to make contributions to the plan, an excise tax applies upon the failure of the employer to make such required contributions within the time required under the plan. The amount of tax is equal to the amount of the required contribution the employer failed to make in a timely manner.

Application of excise tax to plans in critical status/penalty for failure to meet benchmarks or make scheduled progress

In the case of a plan in critical status, if a rehabilitation plan is adopted and complied with, employers are not liable for contributions otherwise required under the general funding rules. In addition, the present-law excise tax does not apply.

If a plan fails to leave critical status at the end of the rehabilitation period or fails to make scheduled progress in meeting its requirements under the rehabilitation plan for three consecutive years, the present law excise tax applies based on the greater of (1) the amount of the contributions necessary to leave critical status or make scheduled progress or (2) the plan's accumulated funding deficiency. The excise tax applies for each succeeding plan year until the requirements are met.

Waiver of excise tax

In the case of a failure which is due to reasonable cause and not to willful neglect, the Secretary of the Treasury may waive all or part of the excise tax on employers failing to make required contributions and the excise tax for failure to meet the rehabilitation plan requirements or make scheduled progress. The standards applicable to waivers of the excise tax for plans in endangered status apply to waivers of plans in critical status.

Additional rules

In general

The actuary's determination with respect to a plan's normal cost, actuarial accrued liability, and improvements in a plan's funded percentage must be based on the unit credit funding method (whether or not that method is used for the plan's actuarial valuation).

In the case of a plan sponsor described under section 404(c) of the Code, the term "plan sponsor" means the bargaining parties.

Expedited resolution of plan sponsor decisions

If, within 60 days of the due date for the adoption of a funding improvement plan or a rehabilitation plan, the plan sponsor has not agreed on a funding improvement plan or a rehabilitation plan, any member of the board or group that constitutes the plan sponsor may require that the plan sponsor enter into an expedited dispute resolution procedure for the development and adoption of a funding improvement plan or rehabilitation plan.

Nonbargained participation

In the case of an employer who contributes to a multiemployer plan with respect to both employees who are covered by one or more collective bargaining agreements and to employees who are not so covered, if the plan is in endangered or critical status, benefits of and contributions for the nonbargained employees, including surcharges on those contributions, must be determined as if the nonbargained employees were covered under the first to expire of the employer's collective bargaining agreements in effect when the plan entered endangered or critical status.[67] In the case of an employer who contributes to a multiemployer plan only with respect to employees who are not covered by a collective bargaining agreement, the additional funding rules apply as if the employer were the bargaining party, and its participation agreement with the plan was a collective bargaining agreement with a term ending on the first day of the plan year beginning after the employer is provided the schedule requires to be provided by the plan sponsor.

Special rule for certain restored benefits

In the case of benefits which were reduced pursuant to a plan amendment adopted on or after January 1, 2002, and before June 30, 2005, if, pursuant to the plan document, the trust agreement, or a formal written communication from the plan sponsor to participants provided before June 30, 2005, such benefits were restored, the rules under the provision do not apply to such benefit restorations to the extent that any restriction on the providing or accrual of such benefits would otherwise apply by reason of the provision.

Cause of action to compel adoption of funding improvement or rehabilitation plan

The provision creates a cause of action under ERISA in the case that the plan sponsor of a plan certified to be endangered or critical (1) has not adopted a funding improvement or rehabilitation plan within 240 days of certification of endangered or critical or (2) fails to update or comply with the terms of the funding improvement or rehabilitation plan. In such case, a civil action may be brought by an employer that has an obligation to contribute with respect to the plan, or an employee organization that represents active participants, for an order compelling the plan sponsor to adopt a funding improvement or rehabilitation plan or to update or comply with the terms of the funding improvement or rehabilitation plan.

Effective Date

The provision is effective for plan years beginning after 2007. The additional funding rules for plans in endangered or critical status do not

[67] Treasury regulations allowing certain noncollectively bargained employees covered by a multiemployer plan to be treated as collectively bargained employees for purposes of the minimum coverage rules of the Code do not apply in making determinations under the provision.

apply to plan years beginning after December 31, 2014.

If a plan is operating under a funding improvement or rehabilitation plan for its last year beginning before January 1, 2015, the plan shall continue to operate under such funding improvement or rehabilitation plan during any period after December 31, 2014, that such funding improvement or rehabilitation plan is in effect.

[Law at ¶5085A, ¶5130, ¶5295 and ¶7033. CCH Explanation at ¶310.]

[¶10,100] Act Secs. 203 and 213. Measures to forestall insolvency of multiemployer plans

Joint Committee Taxation (J.C.T. Rep. No. JCX-38-06)

[Code Sec. 418E]

Present Law

In the case of multiemployer plans, the PBGC insures plan insolvency, rather than plan termination. A plan is insolvent when its available resources are not sufficient to pay the plan benefits for the plan year in question, or when the sponsor of a plan in reorganization reasonably determines, taking into account the plan's recent and anticipated financial experience, that the plan's available resources will not be sufficient to pay benefits that come due in the next plan year.

In order to anticipate future insolvencies, at the end of the first plan year in which a plan is in reorganization and at least every three plans year thereafter, the plan sponsor must compare the value of plan assets for the plan year with the total amount of benefit payments made under the plan for the plan year.[68] Unless the plan sponsor determines that the value of plan assets exceeds three times the total amount of benefit payments, the plan sponsor must determine whether the plan will be insolvent for any of the next three plan years.

Explanation of Provision

The provision modifies the requirements for anticipating future insolvencies of plans in reorganization status. Under the provision, unless the plan sponsor determines that the value of plan assets exceeds three times the total amount of benefit payments, the plan sponsor must determine whether the plan will be insolvent for any of the next five plan years, rather than three plan years as under present law. If the plan sponsor makes a determination that the plan will be insolvent for any of the next five plan years, the plan sponsor must make the comparison of plan assets and benefit payments under the plan at least annually until the plan sponsor makes a determination that the plan will not be insolvent in any of the next five plan years.

Effective Date

The provision is effective with respect to determinations made in plan years beginning after 2007.

[Law at ¶5110 and ¶7036. CCH Explanation at ¶315.]

[¶10,110] Act Sec. 204(a). Repeal of limitation on withdrawal liability in certain cases

Joint Committee Taxation (J.C.T. Rep. No. JCX-38-06)

[Act Sec. 204(a)]

Present Law

Under ERISA, an employer which withdraws from a multiemployer plan in a complete or partial withdrawal is liable to the plan in the amount determined to be the employer's withdrawal liability.[69] In general, a "complete withdrawal" means the employer has permanently ceased operations under the plan or has permanently ceased to have an obligation to contribute.[70] A "partial withdrawal" generally occurs if, on the last day of a plan year, there is a 70-percent contribution decline for such plan year or there is a partial cessation of the employer's contribution obligation.[71]

---

[68] Code sec. 418E(d)(1); ERISA sec. 4245(d)(1).

[69] ERISA sec. 4201.

[70] ERISA sec. 4203.

[71] ERISA sec. 4205.

When an employer withdraws from a multiemployer plan, the plan sponsor is required to determine the amount of the employer's withdrawal liability, notify the employer of the amount of the withdrawal liability, and collect the amount of the withdrawal liability from the employer.[72] The employer's withdrawal liability generally is based on the extent of the plan's unfunded vested benefits for the plan years preceding the withdrawal.[73]

ERISA section 4225 provides rules limiting or subordinating withdrawal liability in certain cases. The amount of unfunded vested benefits allocable to an employer is limited in the case of certain sales of all or substantially all of the employer's assets and in the case of an insolvent employer undergoing liquidation or dissolution.

In the case of a bona fide sale of all or substantially all of the employer's assets in an arm's length transaction to an unrelated party, the unfunded vested benefits allocable to an employer is limited to the greater of (1) a portion of the liquidation or dissolution value of the employer (determined after the sale or exchange of such assets), or (2) the unfunded vested benefits attributable to the employees of the employer. The portion to be used in (1) is determined in accordance with a table described in ERISA section 4225(a)(2). Other limitations on withdrawal liability also apply.

Explanation of Provision

The provision prescribes a new table under ERISA section 4225(a)(2) to be used in determining the portion of the liquidation or dissolution value of the employer for the calculation of the limitation of unfunded vested benefits allocable to an employer in the case of a bona fide sale of all or substantially all of the employer's assets in an arm's length transaction to an unrelated party. The provision also modifies the calculation of the limit so that the unfunded vested benefits allocable to an employer do not exceed the greater of (1) a portion of the liquidation or dissolution value of the employer (determined after the sale or exchange of such assets), or (2) in the case of a plan using the attributable method of allocating withdrawal liability, the unfunded vested benefits attributable to the employees of the employer. Present law ERISA section 4225(b) is not amended by the provision.

Effective Date

The provisions are effective for sales occurring on or after January 1, 2007.

[Law at ¶ 7039. CCH Explanation at ¶ 320.]

[¶ 10,120] Act Sec. 204(b). Withdrawal liability continues if work contracted out

Joint Committee Taxation (J.C.T. Rep. No. JCX-38-06)

[Act Sec. 204(b)]

Present Law

Under ERISA, an employer which withdraws from a multiemployer plan in a complete or partial withdrawal is liable to the plan in the amount determined to be the employer's withdrawal liability.[74] In general, a "complete withdrawal" means the employer has permanently ceased operations under the plan or has permanently ceased to have an obligation to contribute.[75]

A "partial withdrawal" generally occurs if, on the last day of a plan year, there is a 70-percent contribution decline for such plan year or there is a partial cessation of the employer's contribution obligation.[76] A partial cessation of the employer's obligation occurs if (1) the employer permanently ceases to have an obligation to contribute under one or more, but fewer than all collective bargaining agreements under which obligated to contribute, but the employer continues to perform work in the jurisdiction of the collective bargaining agreement or transfers such work to another location or (2) an employer permanently ceases to have an obligation to contribute under the plan with respect to work performed at one or more, but fewer than all of its facilities, but continues to perform work at the facility of the type for which the obligation to contribute ceased.[77]

Explanation of Provision

Under the provision, a partial withdrawal also occurs if the employer permanently ceases to have an obligation to contribute under one or

---

[72] ERISA sec. 4202.

[73] ERISA secs. 4209 and 4211.

[74] ERISA sec. 4201.

[75] ERISA sec. 4203.

[76] ERISA sec. 4205.

[77] ERISA sec. 4205(b)(2).

more, but fewer than all collective bargaining agreements under which obligated to contribute, but the employer transfers such work to an entity or entities owned or controlled by the employer.

Effective Date

The provision is effective with respect to work transferred on or after the date of enactment.

[Law at ¶ 7039. CCH Explanation at ¶ 320.]

[¶ 10,130] Act Sec. 204(c). Application of forgiveness rule to plans primarily covering employees in building and construction

Joint Committee Taxation (J.C.T. REP. No. JCX-38-06)

[Act Sec. 204(c)]

Present Law

Under ERISA, an employer which withdraws from a multiemployer plan in a complete or partial withdrawal is liable to the plan in the amount determined to be the employer's withdrawal liability.[78] A multiemployer plan, other than a plan which primarily covers employees in the building and construction industry, may adopt a rule that an employer who withdraws from the plan is not subject to withdrawal liability if certain requirements are satisfied.[79] In general, the employer is not liable if the employer (1) first had an obligation to contribute to the plan after the date of enactment of the Multiemployer Pension Plan Amendments Act of 1980; (2) contributed to the plan for no more than the lesser of six plan years or the number of years required for vesting under the plan; (3) was required to make contributions to the plan for each year in an amount equal to less than two percent of all employer contributions for the year; and (4) never avoided withdrawal liability because of the special rule.

A multiemployer plan, other than a plan that primarily covers employees in the building and construction industry, may be amended to provide that the amount of unfunded benefits allocable to an employer that withdraws from the plan is determined under an alternative method.[80]

Explanation of Provision

The provision extends the rule allowing plans to exempt certain employers from withdrawal liability to plans primarily covering employees in the building and construction industries. In addition, the provision also provides that a plan (including a plan which primarily covers employees in the building and construction industry) may be amended to provide that the withdrawal liability method otherwise applicable shall be applied by substituting the plan year which is specified in the amendment and for which the plan has no unfunded vested benefits for the plan year ending before September 26, 1980.

Effective Date

The provision is effective with respect to plan withdrawals occurring on or after January 1, 2007.

[Law at ¶ 7039. CCH Explanation at ¶ 320.]

[¶ 10,140] Act Sec. 204(d). Procedures applicable to disputes involving withdrawal liability

Joint Committee Taxation (J.C.T. REP. No. JCX-38-06)

[Act Sec. 204(d)]

Present Law

Under ERISA, when an employer withdraws from a multiemployer plan, the employer is generally liable for its share of unfunded vested benefits, determined as of the date of withdrawal (generally referred to as the "withdrawal liability"). Whether and when a withdrawal has occurred and the amount of the withdrawal liability is determined by the plan sponsor. The plan sponsor's assessment of with-

[78] ERISA sec. 4201.

[79] ERISA sec. 4210.

[80] ERISA sec. 4211(c)(1).

drawal liability is presumed correct unless the employer shows by a preponderance of the evidence that the plan sponsor's determination of withdrawal liability was unreasonable or clearly erroneous. A similar standard applies in the event the amount of the plan's unfunded vested benefits is challenged.

The first payment of withdrawal liability determined by the plan sponsor is generally due no later than 60 days after demand, even if the employer contests the determination of liability. Disputes between an employer and plan sponsor concerning withdrawal liability are resolved through arbitration, which can be initiated by either party. Even if the employer contests the determination, payments of withdrawal liability must be made by the employer until the arbitrator issues a final decision with respect to the determination submitted for arbitration.

For purposes of withdrawal liability, all trades or businesses under common control are treated as a single employer. In addition, the plan sponsor may disregard a transaction in order to assess withdrawal liability if the sponsor determines that the principal purpose of the transaction was to avoid or evade withdrawal liability. For example, if a subsidiary of a parent company is sold and the subsidiary then withdraws from a multiemployer plan, the plan sponsor may assess withdrawal liability as if the subsidiary were still part of the parent company's controlled group if the sponsor determines that a principal purpose of the sale of the subsidiary was to evade or avoid withdrawal liability.

In the case of an employer that receives a notification of withdrawal liability and demand for payment after October 31, 2003, a special rule may apply if a transaction is disregarded by a plan sponsor in determining that a withdrawal has occurred or that an employer is liable for withdrawal liability. If the transaction that is disregarded by the plan sponsor occurred before January 1, 1999, and at least five years before the date of the withdrawal, then (1) the determination by the plan sponsor that a principal purpose of the transaction was to evade or avoid withdrawal liability is not be presumed to be correct, (2) the plan sponsor, rather than the employer, has the burden to establish, by a preponderance of the evidence, the elements of the claim that a principal purpose of the transaction was to evade or avoid withdrawal liability, and (3) if an employer contests the plan sponsor's determination through an arbitration proceeding, or through a claim brought in a court of competent jurisdiction, the employer is not obligated to make any withdrawal liability payments until a final decision in the arbitration proceeding, or in court, upholds the plan sponsor's determination.

Explanation of Provision

Under the provision, if (1) a plan sponsor determines that a complete or partial withdrawal of an employer has occurred or an employer is liable for withdrawal liability payments with respect to the complete or partial withdrawal from the plan and (2) such determination is based in whole or in part on a finding by the plan sponsor that a principal purpose of any transaction that occurred after December 31, 1998, and at least five years (two years in the case of a small employer) before the date of complete or partial withdrawal was to evade or avoid withdrawal liability, the person against which the withdrawal liability is assessed may elect to use a special rule relating to required payments. Under the special rule, if the electing person contests the plan sponsor's determination with respect to withdrawal liability payments through an arbitration proceeding, through a claim brought in a court of competent jurisdiction, or as otherwise permitted by law, the electing person is not obligated to make the withdrawal liability payments until a final decision in the arbitration proceeding, or in court, upholds the plan sponsor's determination. The special rule applies only if the electing person (1) provides notice to the plan sponsor of its election to apply the special rule within 90 days after the plan sponsor notifies the electing person of its liability, and (2) if a final decision on the arbitration proceeding, or in court, of the withdrawal liability dispute has not been rendered within 12 months from the date of such notice, the electing person provides to the plan, effective as of the first day following the 12-month period, a bond issued by a corporate surety, or an amount held on escrow by a bank or similar financial institution satisfactory to the plan, in an amount equal to the sum of the withdrawal liability payments that would otherwise be due for the 12-month period beginning with the first anniversary of such notice. The bond or escrow must remain in effect until there is a final decision in the arbitration proceeding, or on court, of the withdrawal liability dispute. At such time, the bond or escrow must be paid to the plan if the final decision upholds the plan sponsor's determination. If the withdrawal liability dispute is not concluded by 12 months after the electing person posts the bond or escrow, the electing person must, at the start of each succeeding 12-month period, provide an additional bond or amount held in escrow equal to the sum of the withdrawal liability payments that would otherwise be payable to the plan during that period.

A small employer is an employer which, for the calendar year in which the transaction occurred, and for each of the three preceding years, on average (1) employs no more than 500 employees, and (2) is required to make contributions to the plan on behalf of not more than 250 employees.

Effective Date

The provision is effective for any person that receives a notification of withdrawal liability and demand for payment on or after the date of enactment with respect to a transaction that occurred after December 31, 1998.

[Law at ¶ 7039. CCH Explanation at ¶ 320.]

[¶ 10,150] Act Sec. 205. Prohibition on retaliation against employers exercising their rights to petition the federal government

Joint Committee Taxation (J.C.T. Rep. No. JCX-38-06)

[Act Sec. 205]

Present Law

Under ERISA section 510, it is unlawful for any person to discharge, fine, suspend, expel, discipline, or discriminate against a participant or beneficiary for exercising any right to which he is entitled under the provisions of an employee benefit plan, Title I or section 3001 of ERISA, or the Welfare and Pension Plans Disclosure Act, or for the purpose of interfering with the attainment of any right to which a participant may become entitled. It is also unlawful for any person to discharge, fine, suspend, expel or discriminate against any person because he has given information or has testified or is about to testify in any inquiry or proceeding relating to ERISA or the Welfare and Pension Plans Disclosure Act. The civil enforcement provisions under ERISA section 503 are applicable in the enforcement of such provisions.

Explanation of Provision

The provision provides that in the case of a multiemployer plan, it is unlawful for the plan sponsor or any other person to discriminate against any contributing employer for exercising rights under ERISA or for giving information or testifying in an inquiry or proceedings relating to ERISA before Congress. The provision amends the anti-retaliation section of ERISA to provide protection for employers who contribute to multiemployer plans and others. The provision is intended to close a loophole in the existing whistleblower protections. In June 2005, a witness who appeared on behalf of several other companies testified before the Retirement Security & Aging Subcommittee of the Senate Health, Education, Labor & Pensions Committee. Subsequent to that testimony there was an allegation that some of these companies may have been targeted for possible audits.

It is intended that retaliation against any employer who has an obligation to contribute to a plan due to testifying before Congress or exercising his or her rights to petition for redress of grievances would amount to unlawful retaliation under ERISA as amended by the provision. Exercising rights under ERISA, testifying before Congress, and giving information in any inquiry or proceeding relating to this Act are intended to be protected under the provision.

Effective Date

The provision is effective on the date of enactment.

[Law at ¶ 7042. CCH Explanation at ¶ 330.]

[¶10,160] Act Sec. 206. Special rule for certain benefits funded under an agreement approved by the PBGC

Joint Committee Taxation (J.C.T. Rep. No. JCX-38-06)

[Act Sec. 206]

Present Law

No provision.

Explanation of Provision

The provision provides that in the case of a multiemployer plan that is a party to an agreement that was approved by the PBGC before June 30, 2005, that increases benefits and provides for special withdrawal liability rules, certain benefit increases funded pursuant to the agreement are not subject to the multiemployer plan funding rules under the provision (including the additional funding rules for plans in endangered or critical status) if the multiemployer plan is funded in compliance with the agreement (or any amendment thereto).

Effective Date

The provision is effective on the date of enactment.

[Law at ¶7045. CCH Explanation at ¶310.]

[¶10,170] Act Sec. 214. Exception from excise tax for certain multiemployer pension plans

Joint Committee Taxation (J.C.T. Rep. No. JCX-38-06)

[Code Sec. 4971]

Present Law

If a multiemployer plan has an accumulated funding deficiency for a year, an excise tax of five percent generally applies, increasing to 100 percent if contributions sufficient to eliminate the funding deficiency are not made within a certain period.[81]

Explanation of Provision

Under the provision, the present-law excise tax does not apply with respect to any accumulated funding deficiency of a multiemployer plan (1) with less than 100 participants; (2) with respect to which the contributing employers participated in a Federal fishery capacity reduction program; (3) with respect to which employers under the plan participated in the Northeast Fisheries Assistance Program; and (4) with respect to which the annual normal cost is less than $100,000 and the plan is experiencing a funding deficiency on the date of enactment. The tax does not apply to any taxable year beginning before the earlier of (1) the taxable year in which the plan sponsor adopts a rehabilitation plan, or (2) the taxable year that contains January 1, 2009.

Effective Date

The provision is effective for any taxable year beginning before the earlier of (1) the taxable year in which the plan sponsor adopts a rehabilitation plan, or (2) the taxable year that contains January 1, 2009.

[Law at ¶7048. CCH Explanation at ¶310.]

[¶10,180] Act Sec. 221. Sunset of multiemployer plan funding provisions

Joint Committee Taxation (J.C.T. Rep. No. JCX-38-06)

[Act Sec. 221]

Present Law

No provision.

Explanation of Provision

The provision directs the Secretary of Labor, the Secretary of Treasury, and the Executive Di-

[81] Code sec. 4971.

rector of the PBGC, not later than December 31, 2011, to conduct a study of the effect of the changes made by the provision on the operation and funding status of multiemployer plans and report the results of the study, including recommendations for legislation, to Congress. The study must include (1) the effect of funding difficulties, funding rules in effect before the date of enactment, and the changes made by the provision on small businesses participating in multiemployer plans; (2) the effect on the financial status of small employers of funding targets set in funding improvement and rehabilitation plans and associated contribution increases, funding deficiencies, excise taxes, withdrawal liability, the possibility of alternative schedules and procedures for financially-troubled employers, and other aspects of the multiemployer system; and (3) the role of the multiemployer pension plan system in helping small employers to offer pension benefits.

The provision provides that the rules applicable to plans in endangered and critical status and the rules relating to the automatic amortization extension and shortfall funding method under the general funding rules for multiemployer plans do not apply to plan years beginning after December 31, 2014. The present-law rules are reinstated for such years except that funding improvement and rehabilitation plans and amortization schedules in effect at the time of the sunset continue.

Effective Date

The provision is effective on the date of enactment.

[Law at ¶ 7051. CCH Explanation at ¶ 335.]

[¶ 10,190] Act Sec. 301. Extension of replacement of 30-year treasury rates

Joint Committee Taxation (J.C.T. Rep. No. JCX-38-06)

[Code Sec. 412]

The provisions relating to extension of the replacement of the 30-year Treasury rate for purposes of single-employer funding rules are described above, under Title I. The provision relating to extension of the replacement of the 30-year Treasury rate for PBGC premium purposes is described below, under Title IV.

[Law at ¶ 5083, ¶ 5085A and ¶ 7054. CCH Explanation at ¶ 235.]

[¶ 10,200] Act Sec. 302. Interest rate assumption for determination of lump-sum distributions

Joint Committee Taxation (J.C.T. Rep. No. JCX-38-06)

[Code Sec. 417(e)]

Present law

Accrued benefits under a defined benefit pension plan generally must be paid in the form of an annuity for the life of the participant unless the participant consents to a distribution in another form. Defined benefit pension plans generally provide that a participant may choose among other forms of benefit offered under the plan, such as a lump-sum distribution. These optional forms of benefit generally must be actuarially equivalent to the life annuity benefit payable to the participant.

A defined benefit pension plan must specify the actuarial assumptions that will be used in determining optional forms of benefit under the plan in a manner that precludes employer discretion in the assumptions to be used. For example, a plan may specify that a variable interest rate will be used in determining actuarial equivalent forms of benefit, but may not give the employer discretion to choose the interest rate.

Statutory interest and mortality assumptions must be used in determining the minimum value of certain optional forms of benefit, such as a lump sum. That is, the lump sum payable under the plan may not be less than the amount of the lump sum that is actuarially equivalent to the life annuity payable to the participant, determined using the statutory assumptions. The statutory assumptions consist of an applicable interest rate and an applicable mortality table (as published by the IRS).

The applicable interest rate is the annual interest rate on 30-year Treasury securities for the month before the date of distribution or such other time as prescribed by Treasury regulations. The regulations provide various options for determining the interest rate to be used under the plan, such as the period for which the interest rate will remain constant ("stability period") and the use of averaging.

The applicable mortality table is a mortality table based on the 1994 Group Annuity Reserving Table ("94 GAR"), projected through 2002.

An amendment of a qualified retirement plan may not decrease the accrued benefit of a plan participant.[82] This restriction is sometimes referred to as the "anticutback" rule and applies to benefits that have already accrued. For purposes of the anticutback rule, an amendment is also treated as reducing an accrued benefit if, with respect to benefits accrued before the amendment is adopted, the amendment has the effect of either (1) eliminating or reducing an early retirement benefit or a retirement-type subsidy, or (2) except as provided by Treasury regulations, eliminating an optional form of benefit.

Explanation of Provision

The provision changes the interest rate and mortality table used in calculating the minimum value of certain optional forms of benefit, such as lump sums.[83]

Minimum value is calculated using the first, second, and third segment rates as applied under the funding rules, with certain adjustments, for the month before the date of distribution or such other time as prescribed by Treasury regulations. The adjusted first, second, and third segment rates are derived from a corporate bond yield curve prescribed by the Secretary of the Treasury for such month which reflects the yields on investment grade corporate bonds with varying maturities (rather than a 24-month average, as under the minimum funding rules). Thus, the interest rate that applies depends upon how many years in the future a participant's annuity payment will be made. Typically, a higher interest applies for payments made further out in the future.

A transition rule applies for distributions in 2008 through 2011. For distributions in 2008 through 2011, minimum lump-sum values are determined as the weighted average of two values: (1) the value of the lump sum determined under the methodology under present law (the "old" methodology); and (2) the value of the lump sum determined using the methodology applicable for 2008 and thereafter (the "new" methodology). For distributions in 2008, the weighting factor is 80 percent for the lump-sum value determined under the old methodology and 20 percent for the lump-sum determined under the new methodology. For distributions in 2009, the weighting factor is 60 percent for the lump-sum value determined under the old methodology and 40 percent for the lump-sum determined under the new methodology. For distributions in 2010, the weighting factor is 40 percent for the lump-sum value determined under the old methodology and 60 percent for the lump-sum determined under the new methodology. For distributions in 2011, the weighting factor is 20 percent for the lump-sum value determined under the old methodology and 80 percent for the lump-sum determined under the new methodology.

The mortality table that must be used for calculating lump sums under the bill is based on the mortality table required for minimum funding purposes under the bill, modified as appropriate by the Secretary of the Treasury. The Secretary is to prescribe gender-neutral tables for use in determining minimum lump sums.

Effective Date

The provision is effective for plan years beginning after December 31, 2007.

[Law at ¶ 5105 and ¶ 7057. CCH Explanation at ¶ 905.]

[82] Code sec. 411(d)(6); ERISA sec. 204(g).

[83] Under the provision of the bill relating to plan amendments, if certain requirements are met, a plan amendment to implement the changes made to the minimum value requirements may be made retroactively and without violating the anticutback rule.

[¶10,210] Act Sec. 303. Interest rate assumption for applying benefit limitations to lump-sum distributions

Joint Committee Taxation (J.C.T. Rep. No. JCX-38-06)

[Code Sec. 415(b)]

Present Law

Annual benefits payable under a defined benefit pension plan generally may not exceed the lesser of (1) 100 percent of average compensation, or (2) $175,000 (for 2006). The dollar limit generally applies to a benefit payable in the form of a straight life annuity. If the benefit is not in the form of a straight life annuity (e.g., a lump sum), the benefit generally is adjusted to an equivalent straight life annuity. For purposes of adjusting a benefit in a form that is subject to the minimum value rules, such as a lump-sum benefit, the interest rate used generally must be not less than the greater of: (1) the rate applicable in determining minimum lump sums, i.e., the interest rate on 30-year Treasury securities; or (2) the interest rate specified in the plan. In the case of plan years beginning in 2004 or 2005, the interest rate used generally must be not less than the greater of: (1) 5.5 percent; or (2) the interest rate specified in the plan.[84]

An amendment of a qualified retirement plan may not decrease the accrued benefit of a plan participant.[85] This restriction is sometimes referred to as the "anticutback" rule and applies to benefits that have already accrued. For purposes of the anticutback rule, an amendment is also treated as reducing an accrued benefit if, with respect to benefits accrued before the amendment is adopted, the amendment has the effect of either (1) eliminating or reducing an early retirement benefit or a retirement-type subsidy, or (2) except as provided by Treasury regulations, eliminating an optional form of benefit.

Explanation of Provision

Under the bill, for purposes of adjusting a benefit in a form that is subject to the minimum value rules, such as a lump-sum benefit, the interest rate used generally must be not less than the greater of: (1) 5.5 percent; (2) the rate that provides a benefit of not more than 105 percent of the benefit that would be provided if the rate (or rates) applicable in determining minimum lump sums were used; or (3) the interest rate specified in the plan.[86]

Effective Date

The provision is effective for years beginning after December 31, 2005.

[Law at ¶5095. CCH Explanation at ¶740.]

[¶10,220] Act Sec. 401. PBGC premiums

Joint Committee Taxation (J.C.T. Rep. No. JCX-38-06)

[Act Sec. 401]

Present Law

The PBGC

The minimum funding requirements permit an employer to fund defined benefit plan benefits over a period of time. Thus, it is possible that a plan may be terminated at a time when plan assets are not sufficient to provide all benefits accrued by employees under the plan. In order to protect plan participants from losing retirement benefits in such circumstances, the Pension Benefit Guaranty Corporation ("PBGC"), a corporation within the Department of Labor, was created in 1974 under ERISA to provide an insurance program for benefits under most defined benefit plans maintained by private employers.

---

[84] In the case of a plan under which lump-sum benefits are determined solely as required under the minimum value rules (rather than using an interest rate that results in larger lump-sum benefits), the interest rate specified in the plan is the interest rate applicable under the minimum value rules. Thus, for purposes of applying the benefit limits to lump-sum benefits under the plan, the interest rate used must be not less than the greater of: (1) 5.5 percent; or (2) the interest rate applicable under the minimum value rules.

[85] Code sec. 411(d)(6); ERISA sec. 204(g).

[86] Under the provision of the bill relating to plan amendments, if certain requirements are met, a plan amendment to implement the change made to the interest rate used in adjusting a benefit in a form that is subject to the minimum value rules may be made retroactively and without violating the anticutback rule.

Termination of single-employer defined benefit plans

An employer may voluntarily terminate a single-employer plan only in a standard termination or a distress termination. The PBGC may also involuntarily terminate a plan (that is, the termination is not voluntary on the part of the employer).

A standard termination is permitted only if plan assets are sufficient to cover benefit liabilities. If assets in a defined benefit plan are not sufficient to cover benefit liabilities, the employer may not terminate the plan unless the employer (and members of the employer's controlled group) meets one of four criteria of financial distress.[87]

The PBGC may institute proceedings to terminate a plan if it determines that the plan in question has not met the minimum funding standards, will be unable to pay benefits when due, has a substantial owner who has received a distribution greater than $10,000 (other than by reason of death) while the plan has unfunded nonforfeitable benefits, or may reasonably be expected to increase PBGC's long-run loss unreasonably. The PBGC must institute proceedings to terminate a plan if the plan is unable to pay benefits that are currently due.

Guaranteed benefits

When an underfunded plan terminates, the amount of benefits that the PBGC will pay depends on legal limits, asset allocation, and recovery on the PBGC's employer liability claim. The PBGC guarantee applies to "basic benefits." Basic benefits generally are benefits accrued before a plan terminates, including (1) benefits at normal retirement age; (2) most early retirement benefits; (3) disability benefits for disabilities that occurred before the plan was terminated; and (4) certain benefits for survivors of plan participants. Generally only that part of the retirement benefit that is payable in monthly installments (rather than, for example, lump-sum benefits payable to encourage early retirement) is guaranteed.[88]

Retirement benefits that begin before normal retirement age are guaranteed, provided they meet the other conditions of guarantee (such as that before the date the plan terminates, the participant had satisfied the conditions of the plan necessary to establish the right to receive the benefit other than application for the benefit). Contingent benefits (for example, subsidized early retirement benefits) are guaranteed only if the triggering event occurs before plan termination.

For plans terminating in 2006, the maximum guaranteed benefit for an individual retiring at age 65 and receiving a single life annuity is $3,971.59 per month or $47,659.08 per year.[89] The dollar limit is indexed annually for inflation. The guaranteed amount is reduced for benefits starting before age 65.

The dollar limit is indexed annually for wage inflation. The guaranteed amount is reduced for benefits starting before age 65.

In the case of a plan or a plan amendment that has been in effect for less than five years before a plan termination, the amount guaranteed is phased in by 20 percent a year.[90]

PBGC premiums

In general

The PBGC is funded by assets in terminated plans, amounts recovered from employers who terminate underfunded plans, premiums paid with respect to covered plans, and investment earnings. All covered single-employer plans are

---

[87] The four criteria for a distress termination are: (1) the contributing sponsor, and every member of the controlled group of which the sponsor is a member, is being liquidated in bankruptcy or any similar Federal law or other similar State insolvency proceedings; (2) the contributing sponsor and every member of the sponsor's controlled group is being reorganized in bankruptcy or similar State proceeding; (3) the PBGC determines that termination is necessary to allow the employer to pay its debts when due; or (4) the PBGC determines that termination is necessary to avoid unreasonably burdensome pension costs caused solely by a decline in the employer's work force.

[88] ERISA sec. 4022(b) and (c).

[89] The PBGC generally pays the greater of the guaranteed benefit amount and the amount that was covered by plan assets when it terminated. Thus, depending on the amount of assets in the terminating plan, participants may receive more than the amount guaranteed by PBGC.

Special rules limit the guaranteed benefits of individuals who are substantial owners covered by a plans whose benefits have not been increased by reason of any plan amendment. A substantial owner generally is an individual who: (1) owns the entire interest in an unincorporated trade or business; (2) in the case of a partnership, is a partner who owns, directly or indirectly, more than 10 percent of either the capital interest or the profits interest in the partnership; (3) in the case of a corporation, owns, directly or indirectly, more than 10 percent in value of either the voting stock of the corporation or all the stock of the corporation; or (4) at any time within the preceding 60 months was a substantial owner under the plan. ERISA sec. 4022(b)(5).

[90] The phase in does not apply if the benefit is less than $20 per month.

required to pay a flat per-participant premium and underfunded plans are subject to an additional variable rate premium based on the level of underfunding. The amount of both the flat rate premium and the variable rate premium are set by statute; the premiums are not indexed for inflation.

Flat rate premium

Under the Deficit Reduction Act of 2005,[91] the flat-rate premium is $30 for plan years beginning after December, 31, 2005, with indexing after 2006 based on increases in average wages.

Variable rate premium

The variable rate premium is equal to $9 per $1,000 of unfunded vested benefits. "Unfunded vested benefits" is the amount which would be the unfunded current liability (as defined under the minimum funding rules) if only vested benefits were taken into account and if benefits were valued at the variable premium interest rate. No variable rate premium is imposed for a year if contributions to the plan for the prior year were at least equal to the full funding limit for that year.

In determining the amount of unfunded vested benefits, the interest rate used is generally 85 percent of the interest rate on 30 year Treasury securities for the month preceding the month in which the plan year begins (100 percent of the interest rate on 30 year Treasury securities for plan years beginning in 2002 and 2003). Under the Pension Funding Equity Act of 2004, in determining the amount of unfunded vested benefits for plan years beginning after December 31, 2003, and before January 1, 2006, the interest rate used is 85 percent of the annual rate of interest determined by the Secretary of the Treasury on amounts invested conservatively in long term investment-grade corporate bonds for the month preceding the month in which the plan year begins.

Termination premium

Under the Deficit Reduction Act of 2005, a new premium generally applies in the case of certain plan terminations occurring after 2005 and before 2011. A premium of $1,250 per participant is imposed generally for the year of the termination and each of the following two years. The premium applies in the case of a plan termination by the PBGC or a distress termination due to reorganization in bankruptcy, the inability of the employer to pay its debts when due, or a determination that a termination is necessary to avoid unreasonably burdensome pension costs caused solely by a decline in the workforce. In the case of a termination due to reorganization, the liability for the premium does not arise until the employer is discharged from the reorganization proceeding. The premium does not apply with respect to a plan terminated during bankruptcy reorganization proceedings pursuant to a bankruptcy filing before October 18, 2005.

Explanation of Provision

Variable rate premium

For 2006 and 2007, the bill extends the present-law rule under which, in determining the amount of unfunded vested benefits for variable rate premium purposes, the interest rate used is 85 percent of the annual rate of interest determined by the Secretary of the Treasury on amounts invested conservatively in long term investment-grade corporate bonds for the month preceding the month in which the plan year begins.

Beginning in 2008, the determination of unfunded vested benefits for purposes of the variable rate premium is modified to reflect the changes to the funding rules of the provision. Thus, under the provision, unfunded vested benefits are equal to the excess (if any) of (1) the plan's funding target[92] for the year determined as under the minimum funding rules, but taking into account only vested benefits over (2) the fair market value of plan assets. In valuing unfunded vested benefits the interest rate is the first, second, and third segment rates which would be determined under the funding rules of the provision, if the segment rates were based on the yields of corporate bond rates, rather than a 24-month average of such rates. Under the bill, deductible contributions are no longer limited by the full funding limit; thus, the rule providing that no variable rate premium is required if contributions for the prior plan year were at least equal to the full funding limit no longer applies under the provision.

Termination premium

The bill makes permanent the termination premium enacted in the Deficit Reduction Act of 2005.

---

[91] Pub. L. No. 109-171, enacted February 8, 2006.

[92] The assumptions used in determining funded target are the same as under the minimum funding rules. Thus, for a plan in at-risk status, the at-risk assumptions are used.

Effective Date

The extension of the present-law interest rate for purposes of calculating the variable rate premium is effective for plan years beginning in 2006 and 2007. The modifications to the variable rate premium are effective for plan years beginning after December 31, 2007. The provision extending the termination premium is effective on the date of enactment.

[Law at ¶7060. CCH Explanation at ¶505.]

[¶10,230] Act Sec. 402. Special funding rules for plans maintained by commercial airlines

Joint Committee Taxation (J.C.T. REP. NO. JCX-38-06)

[Code Sec. 410(b)(3)]

Present Law

Minimum funding rules in general

Single-employer defined benefit pension plans are subject to minimum funding requirements under the Employee Retirement Income Security Act of 1974 ("ERISA") and the Internal Revenue Code (the "Code").[93] The amount of contributions required for a plan year under the minimum funding rules is generally the amount needed to fund benefits earned during that year plus that year's portion of other liabilities that are amortized over a period of years, such as benefits resulting from a grant of past service credit. The amount of required annual contributions is determined under one of a number of acceptable actuarial cost methods. Additional contributions are required under the deficit reduction contribution rules in the case of certain underfunded plans. No contribution is required under the minimum funding rules in excess of the full funding limit. A detailed description of the present-law funding rules is provided in Title I, above.

Notice of certain plan amendments

A notice requirement must be met if an amendment to a defined benefit pension plan provides for a significant reduction in the rate of future benefit accrual. In that case, the plan administrator must furnish a written notice concerning the amendment. Notice may also be required if a plan amendment eliminates or reduces an early retirement benefit or retirement-type subsidy. The plan administrator is required to provide the notice to any participant or alternate payee whose rate of future benefit accrual may reasonably be expected to be significantly reduced by the plan amendment (and to any employee organization representing affected participants). The notice must be written in a manner calculated to be understood by the average plan participant and must provide sufficient information to allow recipients to understand the effect of the amendment. In the case of a single-employer plan, the plan administrator is generally required to provide the notice at least 45 days before the effective date of the plan amendment. In the case of a multiemployer plan, the notice is generally required to be provided 15 days before the effective date of the plan amendment.

PBGC termination insurance program

The minimum funding requirements permit an employer to fund defined benefit plan benefits over a period of time. Thus, it is possible that a plan may be terminated at a time when plan assets are not sufficient to provide all benefits accrued by employees under the plan. In order to protect plan participants from losing retirement benefits in such circumstances, the PBGC guarantees basic benefits under most defined benefit plans. When an underfunded plan terminates, the amount of benefits that the PBGC will pay depends on legal limits, asset allocation, and recovery on the PBGC's employer liability claim. There is a dollar limit on the amount of otherwise guaranteed benefits based on the year in which the plan terminates. For plans terminating in 2006, the maximum guaranteed benefit for an individual retiring at age 65 and receiving a single life annuity is $3,971.59 per month or $47,659.08 per year.[94] The dollar limit is indexed annually for inflation. The guaranteed amount is

---

[93] Code sec. 412. The minimum funding rules also apply to multiemployer plans, but the rules for multiemployer plans differ in various respects from the rules applicable to single-employer plans.

[94] The PBGC generally pays the greater of the guaranteed benefit amount and the amount that was covered by plan assets when it terminated. Thus, depending on the amount of assets in the terminating plan, participants may receive more than the amount guaranteed by PBGC.

Special rules limit the guaranteed benefits of individuals who are substantial owners covered by a plans whose benefits have not been increased by reason of any plan amendment. A substantial owner generally is an individual who: (1) owns the entire interest in an unincorporated trade

reduced for benefits starting before age 65. In the case of a plan or a plan amendment that has been in effect for less than five years before a plan termination, the amount guaranteed is phased in by 20 percent a year.[95]

Termination premiums

Under the Deficit Reduction Act of 2005, a new premium generally applies in the case of certain plan terminations occurring after 2005 and before 2011. A premium of $1,250 per participant is imposed generally for the year of the termination and each of the following two years. The premium applies in the case of a plan termination by the PBGC or a distress termination due to reorganization in bankruptcy, the inability of the employer to pay its debts when due, or a determination that a termination is necessary to avoid unreasonably burdensome pension costs caused solely by a decline in the workforce. In the case of a termination due to reorganization, the liability for the premium does not arise until the employer is discharged from the reorganization proceeding. The premium does not apply with respect to a plan terminated during bankruptcy reorganization proceedings pursuant to a bankruptcy filing before October 18, 2005.

Minimum coverage requirements

The Code imposes minimum coverage requirements on qualified retirement plans in order to ensure that plans cover a broad cross section of employees.[96] In general, the minimum coverage requirements are satisfied if one of the following criteria are met: (1) the plan benefits at least 70 percent of employees who are not highly compensated employees; (2) the plan benefits a percentage of employees who are not highly compensated employees which is at least 70 percent of the percentage of highly compensated employees participating under the plan; or (3) the plan meets the average benefits test.

Certain employees may be disregarded in applying the minimum coverage requirements. Under one exclusion, in the case of a plan established or maintained pursuant to an agreement which the Secretary of Labor finds to be a collective bargaining agreement between air pilots represented in accordance with title II of the Railway Labor Act and one or more employers, all employees not covered by such agreement may be disregarded. This exclusion does not apply in the case of a plan which provides contributions or benefits for employees whose principal duties are not customarily performed aboard aircraft in flight.

Alternative deficit reduction contribution for certain plans

Under present law, certain employers ("applicable employers") may elect a reduced amount of additional required contribution under the deficit reduction contribution rules (an "alternative deficit reduction contribution") with respect to certain plans for applicable plan years. An applicable plan year is a plan year beginning after December 27, 2003, and before December 28, 2005, for which the employer elects a reduced contribution. If an employer so elects, the amount of the additional deficit reduction contribution for an applicable plan year is the greater of: (1) 20 percent of the amount of the additional contribution that would otherwise be required; or (2) the additional contribution that would be required if the deficit reduction contribution for the plan year were determined as the expected increase in current liability due to benefits accruing during the plan year.

An applicable employer is an employer that is: (1) a commercial passenger airline; (2) primarily engaged in the production or manufacture of a steel mill product, or the processing of iron ore pellets; or (3) an organization described in section 501(c)(5) that established the plan for which an alternative deficit reduction contribution is elected on June 30, 1955.

Explanation of Provision

In general

The provision provides special funding rules for certain eligible plans. For purposes of the provision, an eligible plan is a single-employer defined benefit pension plan sponsored by an employer that is a commercial passenger airline or the principal business of which is providing catering services to a commercial passenger airline.

The plan sponsor of an eligible plan may make one of two alternative elections. In the case of a plan that meets certain benefit accrual and

(Footnote Continued)

or business; (2) in the case of a partnership, is a partner who owns, directly or indirectly, more than 10 percent of either the capital interest or the profits interest in the partnership; (3) in the case of a corporation, owns, directly or indirectly, more than 10 percent in value of either the voting stock of the corporation or all the stock of the corporation; or (4) at any time within the preceding 60 months was a substantial owner under the plan. ERISA sec. 4022(b)(5).

[95] The phase in does not apply if the benefit is less than $20 per month.

[96] Code sec. 410(b).

benefit increase restrictions, an election allowing a 17-year amortization of the plan's unfunded liability is available. A plan that does not meet such requirements may elect to use a 10-year amortization period in amortizing the plan's shortfall amortization base for the first taxable year beginning in 2008.

Election for plans that meet benefit accrual and benefit increase restriction requirements

In general

Under the provision, if an election of a 17-year amortization period is made with respect to an eligible plan for a plan year (an "applicable" plan year), the minimum required contribution is determined under a special method.[97] If minimum required contributions as determined under the provision are made: (1) for an applicable plan year beginning before January 1, 2008 (for which the present-law funding rules apply), the plan does not have an accumulated funding deficiency; and (2) for an applicable plan year beginning on or after January 1, 2008 (for which the funding rules under the provision apply), the minimum required contribution is the contribution determined under the provision.

The employer may select either a plan year beginning in 2006 or 2007 as the first plan year to which the election applies. The election applies to such plan year and all subsequent plan years, unless the election is revoked with the approval of the Secretary of the Treasury. The election must be made (1) no later than December 31, 2006, in the case of an election for a plan year beginning in 2006, or (2) not later than December 31, 2007, in the case of a plan year beginning in 2007. An election under the provision must be made in such manner as prescribed by the Secretary of the Treasury. The employer may change the plan year with respect to the plan by specifying a new plan year in the election. Such a change in plan year does not require approval of the Secretary of the Treasury.

Determination of required contribution

Under the provision, the minimum required contribution for any applicable plan year during the amortization period is the amount required to amortize the plan's unfunded liability, determined as of the first day of the plan year, in equal annual installments over the remaining amortization period. For this purpose, the amortization period is the 17-plan-year period beginning with the first applicable plan year. Thus, the annual amortization amount is redetermined each year, based on the plan's unfunded liability at that time and the remainder of the amortization period. For any plan years beginning after the end of the amortization period, the plan is subject to the generally applicable minimum funding rules (as provided under the bill, including the benefit limitations applicable to underfunded plans). The plan's prefunding balance and funding standard carryover balance as of the first day of the first year beginning after the end of the amortization period is zero.[98]

Any waived funding deficiency as of the day before the first day of the first applicable plan year is deemed satisfied and the amount of such waived funding deficiency must be taken into account in determining the plan's unfunded liability under the provision. Any plan amendment adopted to satisfy the benefit accrual restrictions of the provision (discussed below) or any increase in benefits provided to such plan's participants under a defined contribution or multiemployer plan will not be deemed to violate the prohibition against benefit increases during a waiver period.[99]

For purposes of the provision, a plan's unfunded liability is the unfunded accrued liability under the plan, determined under the unit credit funding method. As under present law, minimum required contributions (including the annual amortization amount) under the provision must be determined using actuarial assumptions and methods, each of which is reasonable (taking into account the experience of the plan and reasonable expectations), or which, in the aggregate, result in a total plan contribution equivalent to a contribution that would be obtained if each assumption and method were reasonable. The assumptions are required also to offer the actuary's best estimate of anticipated experience under the plan. Under the election, a rate of interest of 8.85 percent is used in determining the plan's accrued

[97] Any charge or credit in the funding standard account determined under the present-law rules or any prefunding balance or funding standard carryover balance (determined under the funding provisions of the bill) as of the end of the last year preceding the first applicable year is reduced to zero.

[98] If an election to use the special method is revoked before the end of the amortization period, the plan is subject to the generally applicable minimum funding rules beginning with the first plan year for which the election is revoked, and the plan's prefunding balance as of the beginning of that year is zero.

[99] ERISA sec. 304(b); Code sec. 412(f).

liability. The value of plan assets used must be the fair market value.

If any applicable plan year with respect to an eligible plan using the special method includes the date of enactment of the provision and a plan was spun off from such eligible plan during the plan year, but before the date of enactment, the minimum required contribution under the special method for the applicable plan year is an aggregate amount determined as if the plans were a single plan for that plan year (based on the full 12-month plan year in effect prior to the spin off). The employer is to designate the allocation of the aggregate amount between the plans for the applicable plan year.

Benefit accrual and benefit increase restrictions

Benefit accrual restrictions. —Under the provision, effective as of the first day of the first applicable plan year and at all times thereafter while an election under the provision is in effect, an eligible plan must include two accrual restrictions. First, the plan must provide that, with respect to each participant: (1) the accrued benefit, any death or disability benefit, and any social security supplement are frozen at the amount of the benefit or supplement immediately before such first day; and (2) all other benefits under the plan are eliminated. However, such freezing or elimination of benefits or supplements is required only to the extent that it would be permitted under the anticutback rule if implemented by a plan amendment adopted immediately before such first day.

Second, if an accrued benefit of a participant has been subject to the limitations on benefits under section 415 of the Code and would otherwise be increased if such limitation is increased, the plan must provide that, effective as of the first day of the first applicable plan year (or, if later, the date of enactment) any such increase will not take effect. The plan does not fail to meet the anticutback rule solely because the plan is amended to meet this requirement.

Benefit increase restriction. — No applicable benefit increase under an eligible plan may take effect at any time during the period beginning on July 26, 2005, and ending on the day before the first day of the first applicable plan year. For this purpose, an applicable benefit increase is any increase in liabilities of the plan by plan amendment (or otherwise as specified by the Secretary) which would occur by reason of: (1) any increase in benefits; (2) any change in the accrual of benefits; or (3) any change in the rate at which benefits become nonforfeitable under the plan.

Exception for imputed disability service.—The benefit accrual and benefit increase restrictions do not apply to any accrual or increase with respect to imputed serviced provided to a participant during any period of the participant's disability occurring on or after the effective date of the plan amendment providing for the benefit accrual restrictions (on or after July 26, 2005, in the case of benefit increase restrictions) if the participant was: (1) was receiving disability benefits as of such date or (2) was receiving sick pay and subsequently determined to be eligible for disability benefits as of such date.

Rules relating to PBGC guarantee and plan terminations

Under the provision, if a plan to which an election applies is terminated before the end of the 10-year period beginning on the first day of the first applicable plan year, certain aspects of the PBGC guarantee provisions are applied as if the plan terminated on the first day of the first applicable plan year. Specifically, the amount of guaranteed benefits payable by the PBGC is determined based on plan assets and liabilities as of the assumed termination date. The difference between the amount of guaranteed benefits determined as of the assumed termination date and the amount of guaranteed benefits determined as of the actual termination date is to be paid from plan assets before other benefits.

The provision of the bill under which defined benefit plans that are covered by the PBGC insurance program are not taken into account in applying the overall limit on deductions for contributions to combinations of defined benefit and defined contribution plans, does not apply to an eligible plan to which the special method applies. Thus, the overall deduction limit applies.

In the case of notice required with respect to an amendment that is made to an eligible plan maintained pursuant to one or more collective bargaining agreements in order to comply with the benefit accrual and benefit increase restrictions under the provision, the provision allows the notice to be provided 15 days before the effective date of the plan amendment.

Termination premiums

If a plan terminates during the five-year period beginning on the first day of the first applicable plan year, termination premiums are imposed at a rate of $2,500 per participant (in lieu of the present-law $1,250 amount). The increased termination premium applies notwithstanding that a plan was terminated during bankruptcy reorganization proceedings pursuant to a bankruptcy filing before October 18, 2005 (i.e., the present-law grandfather rule does not apply).

The Secretary of Labor may waive the additional termination premium if the Secretary determines that the termination occurred as the result of extraordinary circumstances such as a terrorist attack or other similar event. It is intended that extraordinary circumstances means a substantial, system-wide adverse effect on the airline industry such as the terrorist attack which occurred on September 11, 2001. It is intended that the waiver of the additional premiums occur only in rare and unpredictable events. Extraordinary circumstances would not include a mere economic event such as the high price of oil or fuel, or a downturn in the market.

Alternative election in the case of plans not meeting benefit accrual and benefit increase restrictions

In lieu of the election above, a plan sponsor may elect, for the first taxable year beginning in 2008, to amortize the shortfall amortization base for such taxable year over a period of 10 plan years (rather than seven plan years) beginning with such plan year. Under such election, the benefit accrual, benefit increase and other restrictions discussed above do not apply. This 10-year amortization election must be made by December 31, 2007.

Authority of Treasury to disqualify successor plans

If either election is made under the provision and the eligible plan is maintained by an employer that establishes or maintains one or more other single-employer defined benefit plans, and such other plans in combination provide benefit accruals to any substantial number of successor employees, the Secretary of Treasury may disqualify such successor plans unless all benefit obligations of the eligible plan have been satisfied. Successor employees include any employee who is or was covered by the eligible plan and any employee who performs substantially the same type of work with respect to the same business operations as an employee covered by the eligible plan.

Alternative deficit reduction contribution for certain plans

In the case of an employer which is a commercial passenger airline, the provision extends the alternative deficit reduction contributions rules to plan years beginning before December 28, 2007.

Application of minimum coverage rules

In applying the minimum coverage rules to a plan, management pilots who are not represented in accordance with title II of the Railway Labor Act are treated as covered by a collective bargaining agreement if the management pilots manage the flight operations of air pilots who are so represented and the management pilots are, pursuant to the terms of the agreement, included in the group of employees benefiting under the plan.

The exclusion under the minimum coverage rules for air pilots represented in accordance with title II of the Railway Labor Act does not apply in the case of a plan which provides contributions or benefits for employees whose principal duties are not customarily performed aboard an aircraft in flight (other than management pilots described above).

Effective Date

The provision is effective for plan years ending after the date of enactment except that the modifications to the minimum coverage rules apply to years beginning before, on, or after the date of enactment.

[Law at ¶ 5075 and ¶ 7063. CCH Explanation at ¶ 245.]

[¶ 10,240] Act Sec. 403. Limitations on PBGC guarantee of shutdown and other benefits

Joint Committee Taxation (J.C.T. Rep. No. JCX-38-06)

[Act Sec. 403]

Present Law

A plan may provide for unpredictable contingent event benefits, which are benefits that depend on contingencies that are not reliably and reasonably predictable, such as facility shutdowns or reductions in workforce. Under present law, unpredictable contingent event benefits generally are not taken into account for funding purposes until the event has occurred.

Under present law, defined benefit pension plans are not permitted to provide "layoff" benefits (i.e., severance benefits).[100] However, defined benefit pension plans may provide subsidized early retirement benefits, including early retirement window benefits.[101]

Within certain limits, the PBGC guarantees any retirement benefit that was vested on the date of plan termination (other than benefits that vest solely on account of the termination), and any survivor or disability benefit that was owed or was in payment status at the date of plan termination.[102] Generally only that part of the retirement benefit that is payable in monthly installments is guaranteed.[103]

Retirement benefits that begin before normal retirement age are guaranteed, provided they meet the other conditions of guarantee (such as that, before the date the plan terminates, the participant had satisfied the conditions of the plan necessary to establish the right to receive the benefit other than application for the benefit). Contingent benefits (for example, early retirement benefits provided only if a plant shuts down) are guaranteed only if the triggering event occurs before plan termination.

In the case of a plan or a plan amendment that has been in effect for less than five years before a plan termination, the amount guaranteed is phased in by 20 percent a year.

Explanation of Provision

Under the bill, the PBGC guarantee applies to unpredictable contingent event benefits as if a plan amendment had been adopted on the date the event giving rise to the benefits occurred. An unpredictable contingent event benefit is defined as under the benefit limitations applicable to single-employer plans (described above) and means a benefit payable solely by reason of (1) a plant shutdown (or similar event as determined by the Secretary of the Treasury), or (2) an event other than the attainment of any age, performance of any service, receipt or derivation of any compensation, or occurrence of death or disability.

Effective Date

The provision applies to benefits that become payable as a result of an event which occurs after July 26, 2005.

[Law at ¶ 7066. CCH Explanation at ¶ 520.]

[¶ 10,250] Act Sec. 404. Rules relating to bankruptcy of the employer

Joint Committee Taxation (J.C.T. REP. NO. JCX-38-06)

[Act Sec. 404]

Present Law

Guaranteed benefits

When an underfunded plan terminates, the amount of benefits that the PBGC will pay depends on legal limits, asset allocation, and recovery on the PBGC's employer liability claim. The PBGC guarantee applies to "basic benefits." Basic benefits generally are benefits accrued before a plan terminates, including (1) benefits at normal retirement age; (2) most early retirement benefits; (3) disability benefits for disabilities that occurred before the plan was terminated; and (4) certain benefits for survivors of plan participants. Generally only that part of the retirement benefit that is payable in monthly installments is guaranteed.[104]

Retirement benefits that begin before normal retirement age are guaranteed, provided they meet the other conditions of guarantee (such as that before the date the plan terminates, the participant had satisfied the conditions of the plan necessary to establish the right to receive the benefit other than application for the benefit). Contingent benefits (for example, subsidized early retirement benefits) are guaranteed only if the triggering event occurs before plan termination.

For plans terminating in 2006, the maximum guaranteed benefit for an individual retiring at age 65 and receiving a single life annuity is $3,971.59 per month or $47,659.08 per year.[105] The dollar limit is indexed annually for inflation. The guaranteed amount is reduced for benefits starting before age 65.

---

[100] Treas. Reg. sec. 1.401-1(b)(1)(i).

[101] Treas. Reg. secs. 1.401(a)(4)-3(f)(4) and 1.411(a)-7(c).

[102] ERISA sec. 4022(a).

[103] ERISA sec. 4022(b) and (c).

[104] ERISA sec. 4022(b) and (c).

[105] The PBGC generally pays the greater of the guaranteed benefit amount and the amount that was covered by plan assets when it terminated. Thus, depending on the

In the case of a plan or a plan amendment that has been in effect for less than five years before a plan termination, the amount guaranteed is phased in by 20 percent a year.[106]

Asset allocation

ERISA contains rules for allocating the assets of a single-employer plan when the plan terminates. Plan assets available to pay for benefits under a terminating plan include all plan assets remaining after subtracting all liabilities (other than liabilities for future benefit payments), paid or payable from plan assets under the provisions of the plan. On termination, the plan administrator must allocate plan assets available to pay for benefits under the plan in the manner prescribed by ERISA. In general, plan assets available to pay for benefits under the plan are allocated to six priority categories. If the plan has sufficient assets to pay for all benefits in a particular priority category, the remaining assets are allocated to the next lower priority category. This process is repeated until all benefits in the priority categories are provided or until all available plan assets have been allocated.

Explanation of Provision

Under the bill, the amount of guaranteed benefits payable by the PBGC is frozen when a contributing sponsor enters bankruptcy or a similar proceeding.[107] If the plan terminates during the contributing sponsor's bankruptcy, the amount of guaranteed benefits payable by the PBGC is determined based on plan provisions, salary, service, and the guarantee in effect on the date the employer entered bankruptcy. The priority among participants for purposes of allocating plan assets and employer recoveries to non-guaranteed benefits in the event of plan termination is determined as of the date the sponsor enters bankruptcy or a similar proceeding.

A contributing sponsor of a single-employer plan is required to notify the plan administrator when the sponsor enters bankruptcy or a similar proceeding. Within a reasonable time after a plan administrator knows or has reason to know that a contributing sponsor has entered bankruptcy (or similar proceeding), the administrator is required to notify plan participants and beneficiaries of the bankruptcy and the limitations on benefit guarantees if the plan is terminated while underfunded, taking into account the bankruptcy.

The Secretary of Labor is to prescribe the form and manner of notices required under this provision. The notice is to be written in a manner calculated to be understood by the average plan participant and may be delivered in written, electronic, or other appropriate form to the extent that such form is reasonably accessible to the applicable individual.

The Secretary of Labor may assess a civil penalty of up to $100 a day for each failure to provide the notice required by the provision. Each violation with respect to any single participant or beneficiary is treated as a separate violation.

Effective Date

The provision is effective with respect to Federal bankruptcy or similar proceedings or arrangements for the benefit of creditors which are initiated on or after the date that is 30 days after enactment.

[Law at ¶ 7069. CCH Explanation at ¶ 525.]

(Footnote Continued)

amount of assets in the terminating plan, participants may receive more than the amount guaranteed by PBGC.

Special rules limit the guaranteed benefits of individuals who are substantial owners covered by a plans whose benefits have not been increased by reason of any plan amendment. A substantial owner generally is an individual who: (1) owns the entire interest in an unincorporated trade or business; (2) in the case of a partnership, is a partner who owns, directly or indirectly, more than 10 percent of either the capital interest or the profits interest in the partnership; (3) in the case of a corporation, owns, directly or indirectly, more than 10 percent in value of either the voting stock of the corporation or all the stock of the corporation; or (4) at any time within the preceding 60 months was a substantial owner under the plan. ERISA sec. 4022(b)(5).

[106] The phase in does not apply if the benefit is less than $20 per month.

[107] For purposes of the provision, a contributing sponsor is considered to have entered bankruptcy if the sponsor files or has had filed against it a petition seeking liquidation or reorganization in a case under title 11 of the United States Code or under any similar Federal law or law of a State or political subdivision.

[¶10,260] Act Sec. 405. PBGC premiums for small plans

Joint Committee Taxation (J.C.T. REP. NO. JCX-38-06)

[Act Sec. 405]

Present Law

Under present law, the Pension Benefit Guaranty Corporation ("PBGC") provides insurance protection for participants and beneficiaries under certain defined benefit pension plans by guaranteeing certain basic benefits under the plan in the event the plan is terminated with insufficient assets to pay benefits promised under the plan. The guaranteed benefits are funded in part by premium payments from employers who sponsor defined benefit pension plans. The amount of the required annual PBGC premium for a single-employer plan is generally a flat rate premium of $19 per participant and an additional variable-rate premium based on a charge of $9 per $1,000 of unfunded vested benefits. Unfunded vested benefits under a plan generally means (1) the unfunded current liability for vested benefits under the plan, over (2) the value of the plan's assets, reduced by any credit balance in the funding standard account. No variable-rate premium is imposed for a year if contributions to the plan were at least equal to the full funding limit.

The PBGC guarantee is phased in ratably in the case of plans that have been in effect for less than five years, and with respect to benefit increases from a plan amendment that was in effect for less than five years before termination of the plan.

Explanation of Provision

In the case of a plan of a small employer, the per participant variable-rate premium is no more than $5 multiplied by the number of plan participants in the plan at the end of the preceding plan year. For purposes of the provision, a small employer is a contributing sponsor that, on the first day of the plan year, has 25 or fewer employees. For this purpose, all employees of the members of the controlled group of the contributing sponsor are to be taken into account. In the case of a plan to which more than one unrelated contributing sponsor contributed, employees of all contributing sponsors (and their controlled group members) are to be taken into account in determining whether the plan was a plan of a small employer. For example, under the provision, in the case of a plan with 20 participants, the total variable rate premium is not more than $2,000, that is, (20 × $5) × 20.

Effective Date

The provision applies to plan years beginning after December 31, 2006.

[Law at ¶7072. CCH Explanation at ¶510.]

[¶10,270] Act Sec. 406. Authorization for PBGC to pay interest on premium overpayment refunds

Joint Committee Taxation (J.C.T. REP. NO. JCX-38-06)

[Act Sec. 406]

Present Law

The PBGC charges interest on underpayments of premiums, but is not authorized to pay interest on overpayments.

Explanation of Provision

The provision allows the PBGC to pay interest on overpayments made by premium payors. Interest paid on overpayments is to be calculated at the same rate and in the same manner as interest charged on premium underpayments.

Effective Date

The provision is effective with respect to interest accruing for periods beginning not earlier than the date of enactment.

[Law at ¶7075. CCH Explanation at ¶515.]

[¶10,280] Act Sec. 407. Rules for substantial owner benefits in terminated plans

Joint Committee Taxation (J.C.T. Rep. No. JCX-38-06)

[Act Sec. 407]

Present Law

Under present law, the Pension Benefit Guaranty Corporation ("PBGC") provides participants and beneficiaries in a defined benefit pension plan with certain minimal guarantees as to the receipt of benefits under the plan in case of plan termination. The employer sponsoring the defined benefit pension plan is required to pay premiums to the PBGC to provide insurance for the guaranteed benefits. In general, the PBGC will guarantee all basic benefits which are payable in periodic installments for the life (or lives) of the participant and his or her beneficiaries and are non-forfeitable at the time of plan termination. The amount of the guaranteed benefit is subject to certain limitations. One limitation is that the plan (or an amendment to the plan which increases benefits) must be in effect for 60 months before termination for the PBGC to guarantee the full amount of basic benefits for a plan participant, other than a substantial owner. In the case of a substantial owner, the guaranteed basic benefit is phased in over 30 years beginning with participation in the plan. A substantial owner is one who owns, directly or indirectly, more than 10 percent of the voting stock of a corporation or all the stock of a corporation. Special rules restricting the amount of benefit guaranteed and the allocation of assets also apply to substantial owners.

Explanation of Provision

The provision provides that the 60-month phase-in of guaranteed benefits applies to a substantial owner with less than 50 percent ownership interest. For a substantial owner with a 50 percent or more ownership interest ("majority owner"), the phase-in occurs over a 10-year period and depends on the number of years the plan has been in effect. The majority owner's guaranteed benefit is limited so that it cannot be more than the amount phased in over 60 months for other participants. The rules regarding allocation of assets apply to substantial owners, other than majority owners, in the same manner as other participants.

Effective Date

The provision is effective for plan terminations with respect to which notices of intent to terminate are provided, or for which proceedings for termination are instituted by the PBGC, after December 31, 2005.

[Law at ¶7078. CCH Explanation at ¶530.]

[¶10,290] Act Sec. 408. Acceleration of PBGC computation of benefits attributable to recoveries from employers

Joint Committee Taxation (J.C.T. Rep. No. JCX-38-06)

[Act Sec. 408]

Present Law

In general

The Pension Benefit Guaranty Corporation ("PBGC") provides insurance protection for participants and beneficiaries under certain defined benefit pension plans by guaranteeing certain basic benefits under the plan in the event the plan is terminated with insufficient assets to pay promised benefits.[108] The guaranteed benefits are funded in part by premium payments from employers who sponsor defined benefit plans. In general, the PBGC guarantees all basic benefits which are payable in periodic installments for the life (or lives) of the participant and his or her beneficiaries and are non-forfeitable at the time of plan termination. For plans terminating in 2006, the maximum guaranteed benefit for an individual retiring at age 65 and receiving a straight life annuity is $3971.59 per month, or $47,659.08 per year.

---

[108] The PBGC termination insurance program does not cover plans of professional service employers that have fewer than 25 participants.

The PBGC pays plan benefits, subject to the guarantee limits, when it becomes trustee of a terminated plan. The PBGC also pays amounts in addition to the guarantee limits ("additional benefits") if there are sufficient plan assets, including amounts recovered from the employer for unfunded benefit liabilities and contributions owed to the plan. The employer (including members of its controlled group) is statutorily liable for these amounts.

Plan underfunding recoveries

The PBGC's recoveries on its claims for unfunded benefit liabilities are shared between the PBGC and plan participants. The amounts recovered are allocated partly to the PBGC to help cover its losses for paying unfunded guaranteed benefits and partly to participants to help cover the loss of benefits that are above the PBGC's guarantees and are not funded. In determining the portion of the recovered amounts that will be allocated to participants, present law specifies the use of a recovery ratio based on plan terminations during a specified period, rather than the actual amount recovered for each specific plan. The recovery ratio that applies to a plan includes the PBGC's actual recovery experience for plan terminations in the five-Federal fiscal year period immediately preceding the Federal fiscal year in which falls the notice of intent to terminate for the particular plan.

The recovery ratio is used for all but very large plans taken over by the PBGC. For a very large plan (i.e., a plan for which participants' benefit losses exceed $20 million) actual recovery amounts with respect to the specific plan are used to determine the portion of the amounts recovered that will be allocated to participants.

Recoveries for due and unpaid employer contributions

Amounts recovered from an employer for contributions owed to the plan are treated as plan assets and are allocated to plan benefits in the same manner as other assets in the plan's trust on the plan termination date. The amounts recovered are determined on a plan-specific basis rather than based on an historical average recovery ratio.

Explanation of Provision

The bill changes the five-year period used to determine the recovery ratio for unfunded benefit liabilities so that the period begins two years earlier. Thus, under the bill, the recovery ratio that applies to a plan includes the PBGC's actual recovery experience for plan terminations in the five-Federal fiscal year period ending with the third fiscal year preceding the fiscal year in which falls the notice of intent to terminate for the particular plan.

In addition, the provision creates a recovery ratio for determining amounts recovered for contributions owed to the plan, based on the PBGC's recovery experience over the same five-year period.

The provision does not apply to very large plans (i.e., plans for which participants' benefit losses exceed $20 million). As under present law, in the case of a very large plan, actual amounts recovered for unfunded benefit liabilities and for contributions owed to the plan are used to determine the amount available to provide additional benefits to participants.

Effective Date

The provision is effective for any plan termination for which notices of intent to terminate are provided (or, in the case of a termination by the PBGC, a notice of determination that the plan must be terminated is issued) on or after the date that is 30 days after the date of enactment.

[Law at ¶ 7081. CCH Explanation at ¶ 535.]

[¶ 10,300] Act Sec. 409. Treatment of certain plans where there is a cessation or change in membership of a controlled group

Joint Committee Taxation (J.C.T. Rep. No. JCX-38-06)

[Act Sec. 409]

Present Law

An employer may voluntarily terminate a single-employer plan only in a standard termination or a distress termination. A standard termination is permitted only if plan assets are sufficient to cover benefit liabilities. Benefit liabilities are defined generally as the present value of all benefits due under the plan (this amount is referred to as "termination liability"). This present value is determined using interest and mortality assumptions prescribed by the PBGC.

Explanation of Provision

Under the bill, if: (1) there is a transaction or series of transactions which result in a person ceasing to be a member of a controlled group; (2) such person, immediately before the transaction or series of transactions maintained a single-employer defined benefit plan which is fully funded then the interest rate used in determining whether the plan is sufficient for benefit liabilities or to otherwise assess plan liabilities for purposes of section 4041(b) or section 4042(a)(4) shall not be less than the interest rate used in determining whether the plan is fully funded.

The provision does not apply to any transaction or series of transactions unless (1) any employer maintaining the plan immediately before or after such transactions or series of transactions (a) has a outstanding senior unsecured debt instrument which is rated investment grade by each of the nationally recognized statistical rating organizations for corporate bonds that has issued a credit rating for such instrument, or (b) if no such debt instrument of such employer has been rated by such an organization but one or more of such organizations has made an issuer credit rating for such employer, all such organizations which have so rated the employer have rated such employer investment grade and (2) the employer maintaining the plan after the transaction or series of transaction employs at least 20 percent of the employees located within United States who were employed by such employer immediately before the transaction or series of transactions.

The provision does not apply in the case of determinations of liabilities by the PBGC or a court if the plan is terminated within two years of the transaction (or first transaction in a series of transactions).

For purposes of the provision, a plan is considered fully funded with respect to a transaction or series of transactions if (1) in the case of a transaction or series of transactions which occur in a plan year beginning before January 1, 2008, the funded current liability percentage for the plan year (determined under the minimum funding rules) is at least 100 percent, or (2) in the case of a transaction or series of transactions which occur on or after January 1, 2008, the funding target attainment percentage (as determined under the minimum funding rules) as of the valuation date for the plan year is at least 100 percent.

Effective Date

The provision applies to transactions or series of transactions occurring on or after the date of enactment.

[Law at ¶ 7084. CCH Explanation at ¶ 225.]

[¶ 10,310] Act Sec. 410. Missing participants

Joint Committee Taxation (J.C.T. Rep. No. JCX-38-06)

[Act Sec. 410]

Present Law

In the case of a defined benefit pension plan that is subject to the plan termination insurance program under Title IV of the Employee Retirement Income Security Act of 1974 ("ERISA"), is maintained by a single employer, and terminates under a standard termination, the plan administrator generally must purchase annuity contracts from a private insurer to provide the benefits to which participants are entitled and distribute the annuity contracts to the participants.

If the plan administrator of a terminating single employer plan cannot locate a participant after a diligent search (a "missing participant"), the plan administrator may satisfy the distribution requirement only by purchasing an annuity from an insurer or transferring the participant's designated benefit to the Pension Benefit Guaranty Corporation ("PBGC"), which holds the benefit of the missing participant as trustee until the PBGC locates the missing participant and distributes the benefit.[109]

The PBGC missing participant program is not available to multiemployer plans or defined contribution plans and other plans not covered by Title IV of ERISA.

Explanation of Provision

Under the bill, the PBGC is directed to prescribe rules for terminating multiemployer plans similar to the present-law missing participant rules applicable to terminating single-employer plans that are subject to Title IV of ERISA.

---

[109] Secs. 4041(b)(3)(A) and 4050 of ERISA.

In addition, under the bill, plan administrators of certain types of plans not subject to the PBGC termination insurance program under present law are permitted, but not required, to elect to transfer missing participants' benefits to the PBGC upon plan termination. Specifically, the provision extends the missing participants program (in accordance with regulations) to defined contribution plans, defined benefit pension plans that have no more than 25 active participants and are maintained by professional service employers, and the portion of defined benefit pension plans that provide benefits based upon the separate accounts of participants and therefore are treated as defined contribution plans under ERISA.

Effective Date

The provision is effective for distributions made after final regulations implementing the provision are prescribed.

[Law at ¶ 7087. CCH Explanation at ¶ 540.]

[¶ 10,320] Act Sec. 411. Director of the PBGC

Joint Committee Taxation (J.C.T. Rep. No. JCX-38-06)

[Act Sec. 411]

Present Law

The PBGC is a corporation within the Department of Labor. In carrying out its functions, the PBGC is administered by the chairman of the board of directors in accordance with the policies established by the board. The board of directors consists of the Secretaries of Labor, Treasury and Commerce.[110] The Secretary of Labor is the chairman of the board. The executive director of the PBGC is selected by the chairman of the board.

The PBGC is authorized to make such investigations as it deems necessary to enforce any provisions of title IV of ERISA or any rule or regulation thereunder. For the purpose of any such investigation (or any other proceeding under title IV or ERISA), any member of the board of directors or any officer designated by the chairman of the board may administer oaths, subpoena witnesses and take other actions as provided by ERISA as the corporation deems relevant or material to the inquiry.[111]

Explanation of Provision

The bill provides that, in carrying out its functions, the PBGC will be administered by a Director, who is appointed by the President by and with the advice and consent of the Senate. The Director is to act in accordance with the policies established by the PBGC board. The Senate Committees on Finance and on Health, Education, Labor, and Pensions are given joint jurisdiction over the nomination of a person nominated by the President to be Director of the PBGC. If one of such Committees votes to order reported such a nomination, the other such Committee is to report on the nomination within 30 calendar days, or it is automatically discharged.[112]

The Director, and any officer designated by the chairman, is given the authority with respect to investigations that is provided under present law to members of the PBGC board and officers designated by the chairman of the board.

The Director is to be compensated at the rate of compensation provided under Level III of the Executive Schedule.[113] Effective January 1, 2006, such annual rate of pay is $152,000.

Effective Date

The provision is effective on the date of enactment. The term of the individual serving as Executive Director of the PBGC on the date of enactment expires on the date of enactment. Such individual, or any other individual, may serve as interim Director of the PBGC until an individual is appointed as Director in accordance with the provision.

[Law at ¶ 7090. CCH Explanation at ¶ 545.]

---

[110] ERISA sec. 4002.

[111] ERISA sec. 4003.

[112] The provision relating to the Senate committees is treated as an exercise of rulemaking power of the Senate and is deemed a part of the rules of the Senate. It is applicable only with respect to the procedure to be followed in the case of a nomination of the Director of the PBGC and it supersedes other Senate rules only to the extent that it is inconsistent with such rules. The provision does not change the constitutional right of the Senate to change its rules (so far as relating to the procedure of the Senate) at any time, in the same manner and to the same extent as in the case of any other rule of the Senate.

[113] 5 U.S.C. sec. 5314.

[¶10,330] Act Sec. 412. Inclusion of information in the PBGC annual report

Joint Committee Taxation (J.C.T. REP. NO. JCX-38-06)

[Act Sec. 412]

Present Law

As soon as practicable after the close of each fiscal year, the PBGC is required to transmit to the President and Congress a report relative to the conduct of its business for the year. The report must include (1) financial statements setting forth its finances and the result of its operations and (2) an actuarial evaluation of the expected operations and status of the four revolving funds used by the PBGC in carrying out its operations.

Explanation of Provision

Under the bill, additional information is required to be provided in the PBGC's annual report. The report must include (1) a summary of the Pension Insurance Modeling System microsimulation model, including the specific simulation parameters, specific initial values, temporal parameters, and policy parameters used to calculate the PBGC's financial statements; (2) a comparison of (a) the average return on investments earned with respect to assets invested by the PBGC for the year to which the report relates and (b) an amount equal to 60 percent of the average return on investment for the year in the Standard & Poor's 500 Index, plus 40 percent of the average return on investment for such year in the Lehman Aggregate Bond Index (or in a similar fixed income index), and (3) a statement regarding the deficit or surplus for the year that the PBGC would have had if it had earned the return described in (2) with respect to its invested assets.

Effective Date

The provision is effective on the date of enactment.

[Law at ¶7093. CCH Explanation at ¶550.]

[¶10,340] Act Sec. 501. Defined benefit plan funding notice

Joint Committee Taxation (J.C.T. REP. NO. JCX-38-06)

[Act Sec. 501]

Present Law

Defined benefit pension plans are generally required to meet certain minimum funding requirements. These requirements are designed to help ensure that such plans are adequately funded. In addition, the Pension Benefit Guaranty Corporation ("PBGC") guarantees benefits under defined benefit pension plans, subject to limits.

Certain notices must be provided to participants in a single-employer defined benefit pension plan relating to the funding status of the plan. For example, ERISA requires an employer of a single-employer defined benefit plan to notify plan participants if the employer fails to make required contributions (unless a request for a funding waiver is pending).[114] In addition, in the case of an underfunded single-employer plan for which PBGC variable rate premiums are required, the plan administrator generally must notify plan participants of the plan's funding status and the limits on the PBGC benefit guarantee if the plan terminates while underfunded.[115]

Effective for plan years beginning after December 31, 2004, the plan administrator of a multiemployer defined benefit pension plan must provide an annual funding notice to: (1) each participant and beneficiary; (2) each labor organization representing such participants or beneficiaries; (3) each employer that has an obligation to contribute under the plan; and (4) the PBGC.

Such a notice must include: (1) identifying information, including the name of the plan, the address and phone number of the plan administrator and the plan's principal administrative officer, each plan sponsor's employer identification number, and the plan identification number; (2) a statement as to whether the plan's funded current liability percentage for the plan year to which the notice relates is at least 100 percent (and if not, a statement of the percentage); (3) a statement of the value of the

[114] ERISA sec. 101(d).

[115] ERISA sec. 4011.

plan's assets, the amount of benefit payments, and the ratio of the assets to the payments for the plan year to which the notice relates; (4) a summary of the rules governing insolvent multiemployer plans, including the limitations on benefit payments and any potential benefit reductions and suspensions (and the potential effects of such limitations, reductions, and suspensions on the plan); (5) a general description of the benefits under the plan that are eligible to be guaranteed by the PBGC and the limitations of the guarantee and circumstances in which such limitations apply; and (6) any additional information the plan administrator elects to include to the extent it is not inconsistent with regulations prescribed by the Secretary of Labor.

The annual funding notice must be provided no later than two months after the deadline (including extensions) for filing the plan's annual report for the plan year to which the notice relates (i.e., nine months after the end of the plan year unless the due date for the annual report is extended). The funding notice must be provided in a form and manner prescribed in regulations by the Secretary of Labor. Additionally, it must be written so as to be understood by the average plan participant and may be provided in written, electronic, or some other appropriate form to the extent that it is reasonably accessible to persons to whom the notice is required to be provided.

A plan administrator that fails to provide the required notice to a participant or beneficiary may be liable to the participant or beneficiary in the amount of up to $100 a day from the time of the failure and for such other relief as a court may deem proper.

Explanation of Provision

The provision expands the annual funding notice requirement that applies under present law to multiemployer plans, so that it applies also to single-employer plans and, in the case of a single-employer plan, includes a summary of the PBGC rules governing plan termination. The provision also changes the information that must be provided in the notice and accelerates the time when the notice must be provided.

In addition to the information required under present law, an annual funding notice with respect to either a single-employer or multiemployer plan must include the following additional information, as of the end of the plan year to which the notice relates: (1) a statement of the number of participants who are retired or separated from service and receiving benefits, retired or separated participants who are entitled to future benefits, and active participants); (2) a statement setting forth the funding policy of the plan and the asset allocation of investments under the plan (expressed as percentages of total assets); (3) an explanation containing specific information of any plan amendment, scheduled benefit increase or reduction, or other known event taking effect in the current plan year and having a material effect on plan liabilities or assets for the year (as defined in regulations by the Secretary); and (4) a statement that a person may obtain a copy of the plan's annual report upon request, through the Department of Labor Internet website, or through an Intranet website maintained by the applicable plan sponsor.

In the case of a single-employer plan, the notice must provide: (1) a statement as to whether the plan's funding target attainment percentage (as defined under the minimum funding rules for single-employer plans) for the plan year to which the notice relates and the two preceding plan years, is at least 100 percent (and, if not, the actual percentages); (2) a statement of (a) the total assets (separately stating any funding standard carryover or prefunding balance) and the plan's liabilities for the plan year and the two preceding years, determined in the same manner as under the funding rules, and (b) the value of the plan's assets and liabilities as of the last day of the plan year to which the notice relates, determined using fair market value and the interest rate used in determining variable rate premiums; and (3) if applicable, a statement that each contributing sponsor, and each member of the sponsor's controlled group, was required to provide the information under section 4010 for the plan year to which the notice relates.

In the case of a multiemployer plan, the notice must provide: (1) a statement as to whether the plan's funded percentage (as defined under the minimum funding rules for multiemployer plans) for the plan year to which the notice relates and the two preceding plan years, is at least 100 percent (and, if not, the actual percentages); (2) a statement of the value of the plan's assets and liabilities for the plan year to which the notice relates and the two preceding plan years; (3) whether the plan was in endangered or critical status and, if so, a summary of the plan's funding improvement or rehabilitation plan and a statement describing how a person can obtain a copy of the plan's funding improvement or rehabilitation plan and the actuarial or financial data that demonstrate any action taken by the plan toward fiscal improvement; and (4) a statement that the plan administrator will provide, on written request, a copy of the plan's annual report to any labor organization representing participants and beneficiaries and any employer that has an obligation to contribute to the plan.

The annual funding notice must be provided within 120 days after the end of the plan year to which it relates. In the case of a plan covering not more than 100 employees for the preceding year, the annual funding notice must be provided upon filing of the annual report with respect to the plan (i.e., within seven months after the end of the plan year unless the due date for the annual report is extended).

The Secretary of Labor is required to publish a model notice not later than one year after the date of enactment. In addition, the Secretary of Labor is given the authority to promulgate any interim final rules as appropriate to carry out the requirement that a model notice be published.

Under the provision, the annual funding notice includes the information provided in the notice required under present law in the case of a single-employer plan that is subject to PBGC variable rate premiums. Accordingly, that present-law notice requirement is repealed under the provision.

Effective Date

The provision is effective for plan years beginning after December 31, 2007, except that the repeal of the notice required under present law in the case of a single-employer plan that is subject to PBGC variable rate premiums is effective for plan years beginning after December 31, 2006. Under a transition rule, any requirement to report a plan's funding target attainment percentage or funded percentage for a plan year beginning before January 1, 2008, is met if (1) in the case of a plan year beginning in 2006, the plan's funded current liability percentage is reported, and (2) in the case of a plan year beginning in 2007, the funding target attainment percentage or funded percentage as determined using such methods of estimation as the Secretary of the Treasury may provide is reported.

[Law at ¶ 7096. CCH Explanation at ¶ 405.]

[¶ 10,350] Act Sec. 502. Access to multiemployer pension plan information

Joint Committee Taxation (J.C.T. Rep. No. JCX-38-06)

[Code Sec. 4980F]

Present Law

Annual report

The plan administrator of a pension plan generally must file an annual return with the Secretary of the Treasury, an annual report with the Secretary of Labor, and certain information with the Pension Benefit Guaranty Corporation ("PBGC"). Form 5500, which consists of a primary form and various schedules, includes the information required to be filed with all three agencies. The plan administrator satisfies the reporting requirement with respect to each agency by filing the Form 5500 with the Department of Labor.

In the case of a defined benefit pension plan, the annual report must include an actuarial statement. The actuarial statement must include, for example, information as to the value of plan assets, the plan's accrued and current liabilities, the plan's actuarial cost method and actuarial assumptions, and plan contributions. The report must be signed by an actuary enrolled to practice before the IRS, Department of Labor and the PBGC.

The Form 5500 is due by the last day of the seventh month following the close of the plan year. The due date generally may be extended up to two and one-half months. Copies of filed Form 5500s are available for public examination at the U.S. Department of Labor.

Notice of significant reduction in benefit accruals

If an amendment to a defined benefit pension plan provides for a significant reduction in the rate of future benefit accrual, the plan administrator must furnish a written notice concerning the amendment. Notice may also be required if a plan amendment eliminates or reduces an early retirement benefit or retirement-type subsidy. The plan administrator is required to provide the notice to any participant or alternate payee whose rate of future benefit accrual may reasonably be expected to be significantly reduced by the plan amendment (and to any employee organization representing affected participants). The notice must be written in a manner calculated to be understood by the average plan participant and must provide sufficient information to allow recipients to understand the effect of the amendment. The plan administrator is generally required to provide the notice at least 45 days before the effective date of the plan amendment.

Explanation of Provision

Under the provision, a plan administrator of a multiemployer plan must, within 30 days of a written request, provide a plan participant or beneficiary, employee organization or employer that has an obligation to contribute to the plan with a copy of: (1) any periodic actuarial report (including any sensitivity testing) for any plan year that has been in the plan's possession for at least 30 days; (2) a copy of any quarterly, semi-annual, or annual financial report prepared for the plan by any plan investment manager or advisor or other person who is a plan fiduciary that has been in the plan's possession for at least 30 days; and (3) a copy of any application for an amortization extension filed with the Secretary of the Treasury. Any actuarial report or financial report provided to a participant, beneficiary, or employer must not include any individually identifiable information regarding any participant, beneficiary, employee, fiduciary, or contributing employer, or reveal any proprietary information regarding the plan, any contributing employer, or any entity providing services to the plan. Regulations relating to the requirement to provide actuarial or financial reports on request must be issued within one year after the date of enactment.

In addition, the plan sponsor or administrator of a multiemployer plan must provide to any employer having an obligation to contribute to the plan, within 180 days of a written request, notice of: (1) the estimated amount that would be the employer's withdrawal liability with respect to the plan if the employer withdrew from the plan on the last day of the year preceding the date of the request; and (2) an explanation of how the estimated liability amount was determined, including the actuarial assumptions and methods used to determine the value of plan liabilities and assets, the data regarding employer contributions, unfunded vested benefits, annual changes in the plan's unfunded vested benefits, and the application of any relevant limitations on the estimated withdrawal liability. Regulations may permit a longer time than 180 days as may be necessary in the case of a plan that determines withdrawal liability using certain methods.

A person is not entitled to receive more than one copy of any actuary or financial report or more than one notice of withdrawal liability during any 12-month period. The plan administrator may make a reasonable charge to cover copying, mailing, and other costs of furnishing copies or notices, subject to a maximum amount that may be prescribed by regulations. Any information required to be provided under the provision may be provided in written, electronic, or other appropriate form to the extent such form is reasonably available to the persons to whom the information is required to be provided.

In the case of a failure to comply with these requirements, the Secretary of Labor may assess a civil penalty of up to $1,000 per day for each failure to provide a notice.

Under the provision, notice of an amendment that provides for a significant reduction in the rate of future benefit accrual must be provided also to each employer that has an obligation to contribute to the plan.

Effective Date

The provision is effective for plan years beginning after December 31, 2007.

[Law at ¶ 5320 and ¶ 7099. CCH Explanation at ¶ 410.]

[¶ 10,360] Act Secs. 503 and 504. Additional annual reporting requirements and electronic display of annual report information

Joint Committee Taxation (J.C.T. Rep. No. JCX-38-06)

[Act Secs. 503 and 504]

Present Law

Annual report

The plan administrator of a pension plan generally must file an annual return with the Secretary of the Treasury, an annual report with the Secretary of Labor, and certain information with the Pension Benefit Guaranty Corporation ("PBGC"). Form 5500, which consists of a primary form and various schedules, includes the information required to be filed with all three agencies. The plan administrator satisfies the reporting requirement with respect to each agency by filing the Form 5500 with the Department of Labor.

In the case of a defined benefit pension plan, the annual report must include an actuarial statement. The actuarial statement must include, for example, information as to the value of plan assets, the plan's accrued and current liabilities, the plan's actuarial cost method and actuarial assumptions, and plan contributions. The report must be signed by an actuary enrolled to practice before the IRS, Department of Labor and the PBGC.

The Form 5500 is due by the last day of the seventh month following the close of the plan year. The due date generally may be extended up to two and one-half months. Copies of filed Form 5500s are available for public examination at the U.S. Department of Labor.

Summary annual report

A participant must be provided with a copy of the full annual report on written request. In addition, the plan administrator must automatically provide participants with a summary of the annual report within two months after the due date of the annual report (i.e., by the end of the ninth month after the end of the plan year unless an extension applies). The summary annual report must include a statement whether contributions were made to keep the plan funded in accordance with minimum funding requirements, or whether contributions were not made and the amount of the deficit. The current value of plan assets is also required to be disclosed. If an extension applies for the Form 5500, the summary annual report must be provided within two months after the extended due date. A plan administrator who fails to provide a summary annual report to a participant within 30 days of the participant making a request for the report may be liable to the participant for a civil penalty of up to $100 a day from the date of the failure.

Explanation of Provision

Annual report

The provision requires additional information to be provided in the annual report filed with respect to a defined benefit pension plan. In a case in which the liabilities under the plan as of the end of a plan year consist (in whole or in part) of liabilities under two or more other pension plans as of immediately before the plan year, the annual report must include the plan's funded percentage as of the last day of the plan year and the funded percentage of each of such other plans. Funded percentage is defined as: (1) in the case of a single-employer plan, the plan's funded target attainment percentage (as defined under the minimum funding rules for single-employer plans); and (2) in the case of a multiemployer plan, the plan's funded percentage (as defined under the minimum funding rules for multiemployer plans).

An annual report filed with respect to a multiemployer plan must include, as of the end of the plan year, the following additional information: (1) the number of employers obligated to contribute to the plan; (2) a list of the employers that contributed more than five percent of the total contributions to the plan during the plan year; (3) the number of participants on whose behalf no contributions were made by an employer as an employer of the participant for the plan year and two preceding years; (4) the ratio of the number of participants under the plan on whose behalf no employer had an obligation to make an employer contribution during the plan year, to the number of participants under the plan on whose behalf no employer had an obligation to make an employer contribution during each of the two preceding plan years; (5) whether the plan received an amortization extension for the plan year and, if so, the amount by which it changed the minimum required contribution for the year, what minimum contribution would have been required without the extension, and the period of the extension; (6) whether the plan used the shortfall funding method and, if so, the amount by which it changed the minimum required contribution for the year, what minimum contribution would have been required without the use of this method, and the period for which the method is used; (7) whether the plan was in critical or endangered status for the plan year, and if so, a summary of any funding improvement or rehabilitation plan (or modification thereto) adopted during the plan year, and the funding percentage of the plan; (8) the number of employers that withdrew from the plan during the preceding plan year and the aggregate amount of withdrawal liability assessed, or estimated to be assessed, against the withdrawn employers; (9) if the plan that has merged with another plan or if assets and liabilities have been transferred to the plan, the actuarial valuation of the assets and liabilities of each affected plan during the year preceding the effective date of the merger or transfer, based upon the most recent data available as of the day before the first day of the plan year, or other valuation method performed under standards and procedures as prescribed by regulation.

The Secretary of Labor is required, not later than one year after the date of enactment, to publish guidance to assist multiemployer plans to identify and enumerate plan participants for whom there is no employer with an obligation to make an employer contribution under the plan and report such information in the annual report. The Secretary may provide rules as needed to apply this requirement with respect to contributions made on a basis other than hours worked, such as on the basis of units of production.

The actuarial statement filed with the annual return must include a statement explaining the actuarial assumptions and methods used in projecting future retirements and asset distributions under the plan.

Electronic display of annual report

Identification and basic plan information and actuarial information included in the annual report must be filed with the Secretary of Labor in an electronic format that accommodates display on the Internet (in accordance with regulations). The Secretary of Labor is to provide for the display of such information, within 90 days after the filing of the annual report, on a website maintained by the Secretary of Labor on the Internet and other appropriate media. Such information is also required to be displayed on any Intranet website maintained by the plan sponsor (or by the plan administrator on behalf of the plan sponsor) in accordance with regulations.

Summary annual report

Under the provision, the requirement to provide a summary annual report to participants applies does not apply to defined benefit pension plans.[116]

Multiemployer plan summary report

The provision requires the plan administrator of a multiemployer plan to provide a report containing certain summary plan information to each employee organization and each employer with an obligation to contribute to the plan within 30 days after the due date of the plan's annual report. The report must contain: (1) a description of the contribution schedules and benefit formulas under the plan, and any modification to such schedules and formulas, during such plan year; (2) the number of employers obligated to contribute to the plan; (3) a list of the employers that contributed more than 5 percent of the total contributions to the plan during such plan year; (4) the number of participants under the plan on whose behalf no employer contributions have been made to the plan for such plan year and for each of the two preceding plan years; (5) whether the plan was in critical or endangered status for the plan year and, if so, a list of the actions taken by the plan to improve its funding status and a statement describing how to obtain a copy of the plan's improvement or rehabilitation plan, as appropriate, and the actuarial and financial data that demonstrate any action taken by the plan toward fiscal improvement; (6) the number of employers that withdrew from the plan during the preceding plan year and the aggregate amount of withdrawal liability assessed, or estimated to be assessed, against such withdrawn employers, as reported on the annual report for the plan year; (7) if the plan that has merged with another plan or if assets and liabilities have been transferred to the plan, the actuarial valuation of the assets and liabilities of each affected plan during the year preceding the effective date of the merger or transfer, based upon the most recent data available as of the day before the first day of the plan year, or other valuation method performed under standards and procedures as prescribed by regulation; (8) a description as to whether the plan sought or received an amortization extension or used the shortfall funding method for the plan year; and (9) notification of the right to obtain upon written request a copy of the annual report filed with respect to the plan, the summary annual report, the summary plan description, and the summary of any material modification of the plan, subject to a limitation of one copy of any such document in any 12-month period and any reasonable charge to cover copying, mailing, and other costs of furnishing the document. Nothing in this report requirement waives any other ERISA provision requiring plan administrators to provide, upon request, information to employers that have an obligation to contribute under the plan.

Effective Date

The provisions are effective for plan years beginning after December 31, 2007.

[Law at ¶7102 and ¶7105. CCH Explanation at ¶415 and ¶420.]

[116] As discussed in Part A above, detailed information about a defined benefit pension plan must be provided to participants in an annual funding notice.

[¶10,370] Act Sec. 505. Section 4010 filings with the PBGC

Joint Committee Taxation (J.C.T. Rep. No. JCX-38-06)

[Act Sec. 505]

Present Law

Present law provides that, in certain circumstances, the contributing sponsor of a single-employer plan defined benefit pension plan covered by the PBGC (and members of the contributing sponsor's controlled group) must provide certain information to the PBGC (referred to as "section 4010 reporting"). This information includes financial information with respect to the contributing sponsor (and controlled group members) and actuarial information with respect to single-employer plans maintained by the sponsor (and controlled group members).[117] Section 4010 reporting is required if: (1) the aggregate unfunded vested benefits (determined using the interest rate used in determining variable-rate premiums) as of the end of the preceding plan year under all plans maintained by members of the controlled group exceed $50 million (disregarding plans with no unfunded vested benefits); (2) the conditions for imposition of a lien (i.e., required contributions totaling more than $1 million have not been made) have occurred with respect to an underfunded plan maintained by a member of the controlled group; or (3) minimum funding waivers in excess of $1 million have been granted with respect to a plan maintained by any member of the controlled group and any portion of the waived amount is still outstanding. Information provided to the PBGC in accordance with these requirements is not available to the public.

The PBGC may assess a penalty for a failure to provide the required information in the amount of up to $1,000 a day for each day the failure continues.[118]

Explanation of Provision

Under the provision, the requirement of section 4010 reporting applicable under present law if aggregate unfunded vested benefits exceed $50 million is replaced with a requirement of section 4010 reporting if: (1) the funding target attainment percentage at the end of the preceding plan year of a plan maintained by a contributing sponsor or any member of its controlled group is less than 80 percent. It is intended that the PBGC may waive the requirement in appropriate circumstances, such as in the case of small plans.

The provision also requires the information provided to the PBGC to include the following: (1) the amount of benefit liabilities under the plan determined using the assumptions used by the PBGC in determining liabilities; (2) the funding target of the plan determined as if the plan has been in at-risk status for at least 5 plan years; and (3) the funding target attainment percentage of the plan.

The value of plan assets, a plan's funding target, a plan's funding target attainment percentage, and at-risk status are determined under the provision relating to funding rules applicable to single-employer plans under the provision. Thus, a plan's funding target for a plan year is the present value of the benefits earned or accrued under the plan as of the beginning of the plan year. A plan's "funding target attainment percentage" means the ratio, expressed as a percentage, that the value of the plan's assets (reduced by any funding standard carryover balance and prefunding balance) bears to the plan's funding target for the year (determined without regard to the special assumptions that apply to at-risk plans). A plan is in at-risk status for a plan year if the plan's funding target attainment percentage for the preceding year was less than (1) 80 percent, determined without regard to the special at-risk assumptions, and (2) 70 percent, determined using the special at-risk assumptions.

The provision requires the PBGC to provide the Senate Committees on Health, Education, Labor, and Pensions and Finance and the House Committees on Education and the Workforce and Ways and Means with a summary report in the aggregate of the information submitted to the PBGC under section 4010.

Effective Date

The provision is effective for filings for years beginning after December 31, 2007.

[Law at ¶7108. CCH Explanation at ¶425.]

---

[117] ERISA sec. 4010.

[118] ERISA sec. 4071.

[¶10,380] Act Sec. 506. Disclosure of plan termination information to plan participants

Joint Committee Taxation (J.C.T. Rep. No. JCX-38-06)

[Act Sec. 506]

Present Law

In the case of a single-employer defined benefit pension plan covered under the PBGC insurance program, the plan sponsor may voluntarily terminate the plan in a standard termination or a distress termination.[119] A standard termination is permitted only if plan assets are sufficient to cover benefit liabilities.

If assets in a defined benefit plan are not sufficient to cover benefit liabilities, the plan sponsor may not terminate the plan unless the plan sponsor (and members of the plan sponsor's controlled group) meets one of four criteria of financial distress. The four criteria for a distress termination are: (1) the plan sponsor, and every member of the controlled group of which the sponsor is a member, is being liquidated in bankruptcy or any similar Federal law or other similar State insolvency proceedings; (2) the plan sponsor and every member of the sponsor's controlled group is being reorganized in bankruptcy or similar State proceeding; (3) the PBGC determines that termination is necessary to allow the plan sponsor to pay its debts when due; or (4) the PBGC determines that termination is necessary to avoid unreasonably burdensome pension costs caused solely by a decline in the plan sponsor's work force.

In order for a plan sponsor to terminate a plan, the plan administrator must provide each affected party with advance written notice of the intent to terminate at least 60 days before the proposed termination date. Additional information must be included as required by the PBGC. For this purpose, an affected party is: (1) a plan participant; (2) a beneficiary of a deceased participant or an alternate payee under a qualified domestic relations order; (3) any employee organization representing plan participants; and (4) the PBGC (except in the case of a standard termination). In the case of a proposed distress termination, as soon as practicable after providing notice, the plan administrator must provide the PBGC with certain information, including information necessary for the PBGC to determine whether any of the criteria for a distress termination is met.

The PBGC may institute proceedings to terminate a single-employer plan if it determines that the plan in question: (1) has not met the minimum funding standards; (2) will be unable to pay benefits when due; (3) has a substantial owner who has received a distribution greater than $10,000 (other than by reason of death) while the plan has unfunded vested benefits; or (4) may reasonably be expected to increase the PBGC's long-run loss with respect to the plan unreasonably if the plan is not terminated. The PBGC must institute proceedings to terminate a plan if the plan is unable to pay benefits that are currently due.

If the PBGC determines that the requirements for an involuntary plan termination are met, it must provide notice to the plan.

Explanation of Provision

The provision revises the rules applicable in the case of a distress termination to require a plan administrator to provide an affected party with any information provided to the PBGC in connection with the proposed plan termination. The plan administrator must provide the information not later than 15 days after: (1) the receipt of a request for the information from the affected party; or (2) the provision of new information to the PBGC relating to a previous request.

The provision also requires the plan sponsor or plan administrator of a plan that has received notice from the PBGC of a determination that the plan should be involuntarily terminated to provide an affected party with any information provided to the PBGC in connection with the plan termination. In addition, the PBGC is required to provide a copy of the administrative record, including the trusteeship decision record in connection with a plan termination. The plan sponsor, plan administrator, or PBGC must provide the required information not later than 15 days after: (1) the receipt of a request for the information from the affected party; or (2) in the case of information provided to the PBGC, the

---

[119] The PBGC may not proceed with a voluntary termination if the termination would violate an existing collective bargaining agreement.

provision of new information to the PBGC relating to a previous request.

The PBGC may prescribe the form and manner in which information is to be provided, which is to include delivery in written, electronic, or other appropriate form to the extent such form is reasonably accessible to individuals to whom the information is required to be provided. A plan administrator or plan sponsor may charge a reasonable fee for any information provided under this subparagraph in other than electronic form.

A plan administrator or plan sponsor may not provide the relevant information in a form that includes any information that may directly or indirectly be associated with, or otherwise identify, an individual participant or beneficiary. In addition, a court may limit disclosure of confidential information (as described under the Freedom of Information Act) to any authorized representative of the participants or beneficiaries that agrees to ensure the confidentiality of such information. For this purposes, an authorized representative means any employee organization representing participants in the pension plan.

Effective Date

The provision generally applies with respect to any plan termination, with respect to which the notice of intent to terminate, or notice that the PBGC has determined that the requirements for an involuntary plan termination are met, occurs after the date of enactment. Under a transition rule, if notice under the provision would otherwise be required before the 90th day after the date of enactment, such notice is not required to be provided until the 90th day.

[Law at ¶7111. CCH Explanation at ¶430.]

[¶10,390] Act Sec. 507. Notice of freedom to divest employer securities

Joint Committee Taxation (J.C.T. Rep. No. JCX-38-06)

[Act Sec. 507]

Present Law

Under ERISA, a plan administrator is required to furnish participants with certain notices and information about the plan. This information includes, for example, a summary plan description that includes certain information, including administrative information about the plan, the plan's requirements as to eligibility for participation and benefits, the plan's vesting provisions, and the procedures for claiming benefits under the plan. Under ERISA, if a plan administrator fails or refuses to furnish to a participant information required to be provided to the participant within 30 days of the participant's written request, the participant generally may bring a civil action to recover from the plan administrator $100 a day, within the court's discretion, or other relief that the court deems proper.

Explanation of Provision

The provision requires a new notice in connection with the right of an applicable individual to divest his or her account under an applicable defined contribution plan of employer securities, as required under the provision of the provision relating to diversification rights with respect to amounts invested in employer securities. Not later than 30 days before the first date on which an applicable individual is eligible to exercise such right with respect to any type of contribution, the administrator of the plan must provide the individual with a notice setting forth such right and describing the importance of diversifying the investment of retirement account assets. Under the diversification provision, an applicable individual's right to divest his or her account of employer securities attributable to elective deferrals and employee after-tax contributions and the right to divest his or her account of employer securities attributable to other contributions (i.e., nonelective employer contributions and employer matching contributions) may become exercisable at different times. Thus, to the extent the applicable individual is first eligible to exercise such rights at different times, separate notices are required.

The notice must be written in a manner calculated to be understood by the average plan participant and may be delivered in written, electronic, or other appropriate form to the extent such form is reasonably accessible to the applicable individual. The Secretary of Treasury has regulatory authority over the required notice and is directed to prescribe a model notice to be used for this purpose within 180 days of the date of enactment of the provision. It is expected that the Secretary of Treasury will consult with the Secretary of Labor on the description of the importance of diversifying the investment of retirement account assets. In addition, it is intended that the Secretary of Treasury will prescribe rules to enable the notice to be provided at reduced administrative expense, such as allowing the notice to be provided with the summary plan description, with a reminder of these rights within a reasonable period before they become exercisable.

In the case of a failure to provide a required notice of diversification rights, the Secretary of Labor may assess a civil penalty against the plan administrator of up to $100 a day from the date of the failure. For this purpose, each violation with respect to any single applicable individual is treated as a separate violation.

Effective Date

The provision generally applies to plan years beginning after December 31, 2006. Under a transition rule, if notice would otherwise be required to be provided before 90 days after the date of enactment, notice is not required until 90 days after the date of enactment.

[Law at ¶ 7114. CCH Explanation at ¶ 610.]

[¶ 10,400] Act Sec. 508. Periodic pension benefit statements

Joint Committee Taxation (J.C.T. Rep. No. JCX-38-06)

[Act Sec. 508]

Present Law

ERISA provides that the administrator of a defined contribution or defined benefit pension plan must furnish a benefit statement to any participant or beneficiary who makes a written request for such a statement. The benefit statement must indicate, on the basis of the latest available information: (1) the participant's or beneficiary's total accrued benefit; and (2) the participant's or beneficiary's vested accrued benefit or the earliest date on which the accrued benefit will become vested. A participant or beneficiary is not entitled to receive more than one benefit statement during any 12-month period. If a plan administrator fails or refuses to furnish a benefit statement to a participant or beneficiary within 30 days of a written request, the participant or beneficiary may bring a civil action to recover from the plan administrator $100 a day, within the court's discretion, or other relief that the court deems proper.

A benefit statement is required to indicate, on the basis of the latest available information: (1) the total benefits accrued; (2) the vested accrued benefit or the earliest date on which the accrued benefit will become vested; and (3) an explanation of any permitted disparity or floor-offset arrangement that may be applied in determining accrued benefits under the plan.[121] With respect to information on vested benefits, the Secretary of Labor is required to provide that the requirements are met if, at least annually, the plan: (1) updates the information on vested benefits that is provided in the benefit statement; or (2) provides in a separate statement information as is necessary to enable participants and beneficiaries to determine their vested benefits.

If a plan administrator fails to provide a required benefit statement to a participant or beneficiary, the participant or beneficiary may bring a civil action to recover from the plan administrator $100 a day, within the court's discretion, or other relief that the court deems proper.

Explanation of Provision

In general

The provision revises the benefit statement requirements under ERISA. The new requirements depend in part on the type of plan and the individual to whom the statement is provided. The benefit statement requirements do not apply to a one-participant retirement plan.[120]

Requirements for defined contribution plans

The administrator of a defined contribution plan is required to provide a benefit statement (1) to a participant or beneficiary who has the right to direct the investment of the assets in his or her account, at least quarterly, (2) to any other participant or other beneficiary who has his or

[120] A one-participant retirement plan is defined as under the provision of ERISA that requires advance notice of a blackout period to be provided to participants and beneficiaries affected by the blackout period, as discussed in Part H below.

[121] Under the permitted disparity rules, contributions or benefits may be provided at a higher rate with respect to compensation above a specified level and at a lower rate with respect to compensation up to the specified level. In addition, benefits under a defined benefit plan may be offset by a portion of a participant's expected social security benefits. Under a floor-offset arrangement, benefits under a defined benefit pension plan are reduced by benefits under a defined contribution plan.

her own account under the plan, at least annually, and (3) to other beneficiaries, upon written request, but limited to one request during any 12-month period.

A benefit statement provided with respect to a defined contribution plan must include the value of each investment to which assets in the individual's account are allocated (determined as of the plan's most recent valuation date), including the value of any assets held in the form of employer securities (without regard to whether the securities were contributed by the employer or acquired at the direction of the individual). A quarterly benefit statement provided to a participant or beneficiary who has the right to direct investments must also provide: (1) an explanation of any limitations or restrictions on any right of the individual to direct an investment; (2) an explanation, written in a manner calculated to be understood by the average plan participant, of the importance, for the long-term retirement security of participants and beneficiaries, of a well-balanced and diversified investment portfolio, including a statement of the risk that holding more than 20 percent of a portfolio in the security of one entity (such as employer securities) may not be adequately diversified; and (3) a notice directing the participant or beneficiary to the Internet website of the Department of Labor for sources of information on individual investing and diversification.

Requirements for defined benefit plans

The administrator of a defined benefit plan is required either: (1) to furnish a benefit statement at least once every three years to each participant who has a vested accrued benefit under the plan and who is employed by the employer at the time the benefit statements are furnished to participants; or (2) to furnish at least annually to each such participant notice of the availability of a benefit statement and the manner in which the participant can obtain it. The Secretary of Labor is authorized to provide that years in which no employee or former employee benefits under the plan need not be taken into account in determining the three-year period. It is intended that the annual notice of the availability of a benefit statement may be included with other communications to the participant if done in a manner reasonably designed to attract the attention of the participant.

The administrator of a defined benefit pension plan is also required to furnish a benefit statement to a participant or beneficiary upon written request, limited to one request during any 12-month period.

In the case of a statement provided to a participant with respect to a defined benefit plan (other than at the participant's request), information may be based on reasonable estimates determined under regulations prescribed by the Secretary of Labor in consultation with the Pension Benefit Guaranty Corporation.

Form of benefit statement

A benefit statement must be written in a manner calculated to be understood by the average plan participant. It may be delivered in written, electronic, or other appropriate form to the extent such form is reasonably accessible to the recipient. For example, regulations could permit current benefit statements to be provided on a continuous basis through a secure plan website for a participant or beneficiary who has access to the website.

The Secretary of Labor is directed, within one year after the date of enactment, to develop one or more model benefit statements that may be used by plan administrators in complying with the benefit statement requirements. The use of the model statement is optional. It is intended that the model statement include items such as the amount of vested accrued benefits as of the statement date that are payable at normal retirement age under the plan, the amount of accrued benefits that are forfeitable but that may become vested under the terms of the plan, information on how to contact the Social Security Administration to obtain a participant's personal earnings and benefit estimate statement, and other information that may be important to understanding benefits earned under the plan. The Secretary of Labor is also given the authority to promulgate any interim final rules as determined appropriate to carry out the benefit statement requirements.

Effective Date

The provision is generally effective for plan years beginning after December 31, 2006. In the case of a plan maintained pursuant to one or more collective bargaining agreements, the provision is effective for plan years beginning after the earlier of (1) the later of December 31, 2007, or the date on which the last of such collective bargaining agreements terminates (determined without regard to any extension thereof after the date of enactment), or (2) December 31, 2008.

[Law at ¶ 7117. CCH Explanation at ¶ 615.]

[¶10,410] Act Sec. 509. Notice to participants or beneficiaries of blackout periods

Joint Committee Taxation (J.C.T. Rep. No. JCX-38-06)

[Act Sec. 509]

Present Law

In general

The Sarbanes-Oxley Act of 2002[122] amended ERISA to require that the plan administrator of an individual account plan[123] provide advance notice of a blackout period (a "blackout notice") to plan participants and beneficiaries to whom the blackout period applies.[124] Generally, notice must be provided at least 30 days before the beginning of the blackout period. In the case of a blackout period that applies with respect to employer securities, the plan administrator must also provide timely notice of the blackout period to the employer (or the affiliate of the employer that issued the securities, if applicable).

The blackout notice requirement does not apply to a one-participant retirement plan, which is defined as a plan that (1) on the first day of the plan year, covered only the employer (and the employer's spouse) and the employer owns the entire business (whether or not incorporated) or covers only one or more partners (and their spouses) in a business partnership (including partners in an S or C corporation as defined in section 1361(a) of the Code), (2) meets the minimum coverage requirements without being combined with any other plan that covers employees of the business, (3) does not provide benefits to anyone except the employer (and the employer's spouse) or the partners (and their spouses), (4) does not cover a business that is a member of an affiliated service group, a controlled group of corporations, or a group of corporations under common control, and (5) does not cover a business that leases employees.[125]

Definition of blackout period

A blackout period is any period during which any ability of participants or beneficiaries under the plan, which is otherwise available under the terms of the plan, to direct or diversify assets credited to their accounts, or to obtain loans or distributions from the plan, is temporarily suspended, limited, or restricted if the suspension, limitation, or restriction is for any period of more than three consecutive business days. However, a blackout period does not include a suspension, limitation, or restriction that (1) occurs by reason of the application of securities laws, (2) is a change to the plan providing for a regularly scheduled suspension, limitation, or restriction that is disclosed through a summary of material modifications to the plan or materials describing specific investment options under the plan, or changes thereto, or (3) applies only to one or more individuals, each of whom is a participant, alternate payee, or other beneficiary under a qualified domestic relations order.

Timing of notice

Notice of a blackout period is generally required at least 30 days before the beginning of the period. The 30-day notice requirement does not apply if (1) deferral of the blackout period would violate the fiduciary duty requirements of ERISA and a plan fiduciary so determines in writing, or (2) the inability to provide the 30-day advance notice is due to events that were unforeseeable or circumstances beyond the reasonable control of the plan administrator and a plan fiduciary so determines in writing. In those cases, notice must be provided as soon as reasonably practicable under the circumstances unless notice in advance of the termination of the blackout period is impracticable.

Another exception to the 30-day period applies in the case of a blackout period that applies only to one or more participants or beneficiaries in connection with a merger, acquisition, divestiture, or similar transaction involving the plan or the employer and that occurs solely in connection with becoming or ceasing to be a participant or beneficiary under the plan by reason of the merger, acquisition, divestiture, or similar transaction. Under the exception, the blackout notice requirement is treated as met if notice is pro-

[122] Pub. L. No. 107-204 (2002).

[123] An "individual account plan" is the term generally used under ERISA for a defined contribution plan.

[124] ERISA sec. 101(i), as enacted by section 306(b) of the Sarbanes-Oxley Act of 2002. Under section 306(a), a director or executive officer of a publicly-traded corporation is prohibited from trading in employer stock during blackout periods in certain circumstances. Section 306 is effective 180 days after enactment.

[125] Governmental plans and church plans are exempt from ERISA. Accordingly, the blackout notice requirement does not apply to these plans.

vided to the participants or beneficiaries to whom the blackout period applies as soon as reasonably practicable.

The Secretary of Labor may provide additional exceptions to the notice requirement that the Secretary determines are in the interests of participants and beneficiaries.

Form and content of notice

A blackout notice must be written in a manner calculated to be understood by the average plan participant and must include (1) the reasons for the blackout period, (2) an identification of the investments and other rights affected, (3) the expected beginning date and length of the blackout period, and (4) in the case of a blackout period affecting investments, a statement that the participant or beneficiary should evaluate the appropriateness of current investment decisions in light of the inability to direct or diversify assets during the blackout period, and (5) other matters as required by regulations. If the expected beginning date or length of the blackout period changes after notice has been provided, the plan administrator must provide notice of the change (and specify any material change in other matters related to the blackout) to affected participants and beneficiaries as soon as reasonably practicable.

Notices provided in connection with a blackout period (or changes thereto) must be provided in writing and may be delivered in electronic or other form to the extent that the form is reasonably accessible to the recipient. The Secretary of Labor is required to issue guidance regarding the notice requirement and a model blackout notice.

Penalty for failure to provide notice

In the case of a failure to provide notice of a blackout period, the Secretary of Labor may assess a civil penalty against a plan administrator of up to $100 per day for each failure to provide a blackout notice. For this purpose, each violation with respect to a single participant or beneficiary is treated as a separate violation.

Explanation of Provision

The provision modifies the definition of a one-participant retirement plan to be consistent with Department of Labor regulations under which certain business owners and their spouses are not treated as employees.[126] As modified, a one-participant retirement plan is a plan that: (1) on the first day of the plan year, either covered only one individual (or the individual and his or her spouse) and the individual owned 100 percent of the plan sponsor, whether or not incorporated, or covered only one or more partners (or partners and their spouses) in the plan sponsor; and (2) does not cover a business that leases employees.

Effective Date

The provision is effective as if included in section 306 of the Sarbanes-Oxley Act of 2002.

[Law at ¶ 7120. CCH Explanation at ¶ 620.]

[¶ 10,420] Act Sec. 601. Investment advice

Joint Committee Taxation (J.C.T. REP. NO. JCX-38-06)

[Code Sec. 4975]

Present Law

ERISA and the Code prohibit certain transactions between an employer-sponsored retirement plan and a disqualified person (referred to as a "party in interest" under ERISA).[127] Under ERISA, the prohibited transaction rules apply to employer-sponsored retirement plans and welfare benefit plans. Under the Code, the prohibited transaction rules apply to qualified retirement plans and qualified retirement annuities, as well as individual retirement accounts and annuities ("IRAs"), health savings accounts ("HSAs"), Archer MSAs, and Coverdell education savings accounts.[128]

Disqualified persons include a fiduciary of the plan, a person providing services to the plan, and an employer with employees covered by the plan. For this purpose, a fiduciary includes any person who (1) exercises any authority or control respecting management or disposition of the plan's assets, (2) renders investment advice for a

[126] 29 C.F.R. sec. 2510.3-3(c) (2006).

[127] ERISA sec. 406; Code sec. 4975.

[128] The prohibited transaction rules under ERISA and the Code generally do not apply to governmental plans or church plans.

fee or other compensation with respect to any plan moneys or property, or has the authority or responsibility to do so, or (3) has any discretionary authority or responsibility in the administration of the plan.

Prohibited transactions include (1) the sale, exchange or leasing of property, (2) the lending of money or other extension of credit, (3) the furnishing of goods, services or facilities, (4) the transfer to, or use by or for the benefit of, the income or assets of the plan, (5) in the case of a fiduciary, any act that deals with the plan's income or assets for the fiduciary's own interest or account, and (6) the receipt by a fiduciary of any consideration for the fiduciary's own personal account from any party dealing with the plan in connection with a transaction involving the income or assets of the plan. However, certain transactions are exempt from prohibited transaction treatment, for example, certain loans to plan participants.

Under ERISA, the Secretary of Labor may assess a civil penalty against a person who engages in a prohibited transaction, other than a transaction with a plan covered by the prohibited transaction rules of the Code. The penalty may not exceed five percent of the amount involved in the transaction for each year or part of a year that the prohibited transaction continues. If the prohibited transaction is not corrected within 90 days after notice from the Secretary of Labor, the penalty may be up to 100 percent of the amount involved in the transaction. Under the Code, if a prohibited transaction occurs, the disqualified person who participates in the transaction is subject to a two-tier excise tax. The first level tax is 15 percent of the amount involved in the transaction. The second level tax is imposed if the prohibited transaction is not corrected within a certain period and is 100 percent of the amount involved.

Explanation of Provision

In general

The provision adds a new category of prohibited transaction exemption under ERISA and the Code in connection with the provision of investment advice through an "eligible investment advice arrangement" to participants and beneficiaries of a defined contribution plan who direct the investment of their accounts under the plan and to beneficiaries of IRAs.[129] If the requirements under the provision are met, the following are exempt from prohibited transaction treatment: (1) the provision of investment advice; (2) an investment transaction (i.e., a sale, acquisition, or holding of a security or other property) pursuant to the advice; and (3) the direct or indirect receipt of fees or other compensation in connection with the provision of the advice or an investment transaction pursuant to the advice. The prohibited transaction exemptions provided under the provision do not in any manner alter existing individual or class exemptions provided by statute or administrative action.

The provision also directs the Secretary of Labor, in consultation with the Secretary of the Treasury, to determine, based on certain information to be solicited by the Secretary of Labor, whether there is any computer model investment advice program that meets the requirements of the provision and may be used by IRAs. The determination is to be made by December 31, 2007. If the Secretary of Labor determines there is such a program, the exemptions described above apply in connection with the use of the program with respect to IRA beneficiaries. If the Secretary of Labor determines that there is not such a program, such Secretary is directed to grant a class exemption from prohibited transaction treatment (as discussed below) for the provision of investment advice, investment transactions pursuant to such advice, and related fees to beneficiaries of such arrangements.

Eligible investment advice arrangements

In general

The exemptions provided under the provision apply in connection with the provision of investment advice by a fiduciary adviser under an eligible investment advice arrangement. An eligible investment advice arrangement is an arrangement (1) meeting certain requirements (discussed below) and (2) which either (a) provides that any fees (including any commission or compensation) received by the fiduciary adviser for investment advice or with respect to an investment transaction with respect to plan assets do not vary depending on the basis of any investment option selected, or (b) uses a computer model under an investment advice program as described below in connection with the provision of investment advice to a participant or beneficiary. In the case of an eligible investment advice arrangement with respect to a defined contribution plan, the arrangement must be ex-

[129] The portions of the provision relating to IRAs apply to HSAs, Archer MSAs, and Coverdell education savings accounts. References here to IRAs include such other arrangements as well.

pressly authorized by a plan fiduciary other than (1) the person offering the investment advice program, (2) any person providing investment options under the plan, or (3) any affiliate of (1) or (2).

Investment advice program using computer model

If an eligible investment advice arrangement provides investment advice pursuant to a computer model, the model must (1) apply generally accepted investment theories that take into account the historic returns of different asset classes over defined periods of time, (2) use relevant information about the participant or beneficiary, (3) use prescribed objective criteria to provide asset allocation portfolios comprised of investment options under the plan, (4) operate in a manner that is not biased in favor of any investment options offered by the fiduciary adviser or related person, and (5) take into account all the investment options under the plan in specifying how a participant's or beneficiary's account should be invested without inappropriate weighting of any investment option. An eligible investment expert must certify, before the model is used and in accordance with rules prescribed by the Secretary, that the model meets these requirements. The certification must be renewed if there are material changes to the model as determined under regulations. For this purpose, an eligible investment expert is a person who meets requirements prescribed by the Secretary and who does not bear any material affiliation or contractual relationship with any investment adviser or related person.

In addition, if a computer model is used, the only investment advice that may be provided under the arrangement is the advice generated by the computer model, and any investment transaction pursuant the advice must occur solely at the direction of the participant or beneficiary. This requirement does not preclude the participant or beneficiary from requesting other investment advice, but only if the request has not been solicited by any person connected with carrying out the investment advice arrangement.

Audit requirements

In the case of an eligible investment advice arrangement with respect to a defined contribution plan, an annual audit of the arrangement for compliance with applicable requirements must be conducted by an independent auditor (i.e., unrelated to the person offering the investment advice arrangement or any person providing investment options under the plan) who has appropriate technical training or experience and proficiency and who so represents in writing. The auditor must issue a report of the audit results to the fiduciary that authorized use of the arrangement. In the case of an eligible investment advice arrangement with respect to IRAs, an audit is required at such times and in such manner as prescribed by the Secretary of Labor.

Notice requirements

Before the initial provision of investment advice, the fiduciary adviser must provide written notice (which may be in electronic form) containing various information to the recipient of the advice, including information relating to: (1) the role of any related party in the development of the investment advice program or the selection of investment options under the plan; (2) past performance and rates of return for each investment option offered under the plan; (3) any fees or other compensation to be received by the fiduciary adviser or affiliate; (4) any material affiliation or contractual relationship of the fiduciary adviser or affiliates in the security or other property involved in the investment transaction; (5) the manner and under what circumstances any participant or beneficiary information will be used or disclosed; (6) the types of services provided by the fiduciary adviser in connection with the provision of investment advice; (7) the adviser's status as a fiduciary of the plan in connection with the provision of the advice; and (8) the ability of the recipient of the advice separately to arrange for the provision of advice by another adviser that could have no material affiliation with and receive no fees or other compensation in connection with the security or other property. This information must be maintained in accurate form and must be provided to the recipient of the investment advice, without charge, on an annual basis, on request, or in the case of any material change.

Any notification must be written in a clear and conspicuous manner, calculated to be understood by the average plan participant, and sufficiently accurate and comprehensive so as to reasonably apprise participants and beneficiaries of the required information. The Secretary is directed to issue a model form for the disclosure of fees and other compensation as required by the provision. The fiduciary adviser must maintain for at least six years any records necessary for determining whether the requirements for the prohibited transaction exemption were met. A prohibited transaction will not be considered to have occurred solely because records were lost or destroyed before the end of six years due to circumstances beyond the adviser's control.

Other requirements

In order for the exemption to apply, the following additional requirements must be satisfied: (1) the fiduciary adviser must provide disclosures applicable under securities laws; (2) an investment transaction must occur solely at the direction of the recipient of the advice; (3) compensation received by the fiduciary adviser or affiliates in connection with an investment transaction must be reasonable; and (4) the terms of the investment transaction must be at least as favorable to the plan as an arm's length transaction would be.

Fiduciary adviser

For purposes of the provision, "fiduciary adviser" is defined as a person who is a fiduciary of the plan by reason of the provision of investment advice to a participant or beneficiary and who is also: (1) registered as an investment adviser under the Investment Advisers Act of 1940 or under State laws; (2) a bank, a similar financial institution supervised by the United States or a State, or a savings association (as defined under the Federal Deposit Insurance Act), but only if the advice is provided through a trust department that is subject to periodic examination and review by Federal or State banking authorities; (3) an insurance company qualified to do business under State law; (4) registered as a broker or dealer under the Securities Exchange Act of 1934; (5) an affiliate of any of the preceding; or (6) an employee, agent or registered representative of any of the preceding who satisfies the requirements of applicable insurance, banking and securities laws relating to the provision of advice. A person who develops the computer model or markets the investment advice program or computer model is treated as a person who is a plan fiduciary by reason of the provision of investment advice and is treated as a fiduciary adviser, except that the Secretary may prescribe rules under which only one fiduciary adviser may elect treatment as a plan fiduciary. "Affiliate" means an affiliated person as defined under section 2(a)(3) of the Investment Company Act of 1940. "Registered representative" means a person described in section 3(a)(18) of the Securities Exchange Act of 1934 or a person described in section 202(a)(17) of the Investment Advisers Act of 1940.

Fiduciary rules

Subject to certain requirements, an employer or other person who is a plan fiduciary, other than a fiduciary adviser, is not treated as failing to meet the fiduciary requirements of ERISA, solely by reason of the provision of investment advice as permitted under the provision or of contracting for or otherwise arranging for the provision of the advice. This rule applies if: (1) the advice is provided under an arrangement between the employer or plan fiduciary and the fiduciary adviser for the provision of investment advice by the fiduciary adviser as permitted under the provision; (2) the terms of the arrangement require compliance by the fiduciary adviser with the requirements of the provision; and (3) the terms of the arrangement include a written acknowledgement by the fiduciary adviser that the fiduciary adviser is a plan fiduciary with respect to the provision of the advice.

The provision does not exempt the employer or a plan fiduciary from fiduciary responsibility under ERISA for the prudent selection and periodic review of a fiduciary adviser with whom the employer or plan fiduciary has arranged for the provision of investment advice. The employer or plan fiduciary does not have the duty to monitor the specific investment advice given by a fiduciary adviser. The provision also provides that nothing in the fiduciary responsibility provisions of ERISA is to be construed to preclude the use of plan assets to pay for reasonable expenses in providing investment advice.

Study and determination by the Secretary of Labor; class exemption

Under the provision, the Secretary of Labor must determine, in consultation with the Secretary of the Treasury, whether there is any computer model investment advice program that can be used by IRAs and that meets the requirements of the provision. The determination is to be made on the basis of information to be solicited by the Secretary of Labor as described below. Under the provision, a computer model investment advice program must (1) use relevant information about the beneficiary, (2) take into account the full range of investments, including equities and bonds, in determining the options for the investment portfolio of the beneficiary, and (3) allow the account beneficiary, in directing the investment of assets, sufficient flexibility in obtaining advice to evaluate and select options. The Secretary of Labor must report the results of this determination to the House Committees on Ways and Means and Education and the Workforce and the Senate Committees on Finance and Health, Education, Labor, and Pensions no later than December 31, 2007.

As soon as practicable after the date of enactment, the Secretary of Labor, in consultation with the Secretary of the Treasury, must solicit information as to the feasibility of the application of computer model investment advice programs for IRAs, including from (1) at least the top 50 trustees of IRAs, determined on the basis of assets held by such trustees, and (2) other persons offering such programs based on nonproprietary products. The information solicited by the Secretary of Labor from such trustees and other persons is to include information on their computer modeling capabilities with respect to the current year and the preceding year, including their capabilities for investment accounts they maintain. If a person from whom the Secretary of Labor solicits information does not provide such information within 60 days after the solicitation, the person is not entitled to use any class exemption granted by the Secretary of Labor as required under the provision (as discussed below) unless such failure is due to reasonable cause and not willful neglect.

The exemptions provided under the provision with respect to an eligible investment advice arrangement involving a computer model do not apply to IRAs. If the Secretary of Labor determines that there is a computer model investment advice program that can be used by IRAs, the exemptions provided under the provision with respect to an eligible investment advice arrangement involving a computer model can apply to IRAs.

If, as a result of the study of this issue as directed by the provision, the Secretary of Labor determines that there is not such a program, the Secretary of Labor must grant a class exemption from prohibited transaction treatment for (1) the provision of investment advice by a fiduciary adviser to beneficiaries of IRAs; (2) investment transactions pursuant to the advice; and (3) the direct or indirect receipt of fees or other compensation in connection with the provision of the advice or an investment transaction pursuant to the advice. Application of the exemptions are to be subject to conditions as are set forth in the class exemption and as are (1) in the interests of the IRA and its beneficiary and protective of the rights of the beneficiary, and (2) necessary to ensure the requirements of the applicable exemptions and the investment advice provided utilizes prescribed objective criteria to provide asset allocation portfolios comprised of securities or other property available as investments under the IRA. Such conditions could require that the fiduciary adviser providing the advice (1) adopt written policies and procedures that ensure the advice provided is not biased in favor of investments offered by the fiduciary adviser or a related person, and (2) appoint an individual responsible for annually reviewing the advice provided to determine that the advice is provided in accordance with the policies and procedures in (1).

If the Secretary of Labor later determines that there is any computer model investment advice program that can be used by IRAs, the class exemption ceases to apply after the later of (1) the date two years after the Secretary's later determination, or (2) the date three years after the date the exemption first took effect.

Any person may request the Secretary of Labor to make a determination with respect to any computer model investment advice program as to whether it can be used by IRAs, and the Secretary must make such determination within 90 days of the request. If the Secretary determines that the program cannot be so used, within 10 days of the determination, the Secretary must notify the House Committees on Ways and Means and Education and the Workforce and the Senate Committees on Finance and Health, Education, Labor, and Pensions thereof and the reasons for the determination.

Effective Date

The provisions are effective with respect to investment advice provided after December 31, 2006. The provision relating to the study by the Secretary of Labor is effective on the date of enactment.

[Law at ¶5305 and ¶7123. CCH Explanation at ¶625.]

[¶10,430] Act Sec. 611(a). Exemption for block trading

Joint Committee Taxation (J.C.T. REP. NO. JCX-38-06)

[Code Sec. 4975]

Present Law

Present law provides statutory exemptions from the prohibited transaction rules for certain transactions.[130] Present law does not provide a statutory prohibited transaction exemption for block trades. For purposes of the prohibited transaction rules, a fiduciary means any person who (1) exercises any authority or control respecting management or disposition of the plan's assets, (2) renders investment advice for a fee or other compensation with respect to any plan moneys or property, or has the authority or responsibility to do so, or (3) has any discretionary authority or responsibility in the administration of the plan.

Explanation of Provision

The provision provides prohibited transaction exemptions under ERISA and the Code for a purchase or sale of securities or other property (as determined by the Secretary of Labor) between a plan and a disqualified person (other than a fiduciary) involving a block trade if: (1) the transaction involves a block trade; (2) at the time of the transaction, the interest of the plan (together with the interests of any other plans maintained by the same plan sponsor) does not exceed 10 percent of the aggregate size of the block trade; (3) the terms of the transaction, including the price, are at least as favorable to the plan as an arm's length transaction with an unrelated party; and (4) the compensation associated with the transaction must be no greater than the compensation associated with an arm's length transaction with an unrelated party. For purposes of the provision, block trade is defined as any trade of at least 10,000 shares or with a market value of at least $200,000 that will be allocated across two or more unrelated client accounts of a fiduciary. Examples of property other than securities that the Secretary of labor may apply the exemption to include (but are not limited to) future contracts and currency.

Effective Date

The provision is effective with respect to transactions occurring after the date of enactment.

[Law at ¶ 5305 and ¶ 7126. CCH Explanation at ¶ 630.]

[¶ 10,440] Act Sec. 611(b). Bonding relief

Joint Committee Taxation (J.C.T. Rep. No. JCX-38-06)

[Act Sec. 611(b)]

Present Law

Subject to certain exceptions, ERISA requires a plan fiduciary and any person handling plan assets to be bonded, generally in an amount between $1,000 and $500,000. An exception to the bonding requirement generally applies for a fiduciary (or a director, officer, or employee of the fiduciary) that is a corporation authorized to exercise trust powers or conduct an insurance business if the corporation is subject to supervision or examination by Federal or State regulators and meets certain financial requirements.

Explanation of Provision

The provision provides an exception to the ERISA bonding requirement for an entity registered as a broker or a dealer under the Securities Exchange Act of 1934 if the broker or dealer is subject to the fidelity bond requirements of a self-regulatory organization (within the meaning of the Securities Exchange Act of 1934).

Effective Date

The provision is effective for plan years beginning after the date of enactment.

[Law at ¶ 7126. CCH Explanation at ¶ 630.]

---

[130] In addition, under ERISA section 408(a), the Secretary of Labor may grant exemptions with respect to particular transactions or classes of transactions after consultation and coordination with the Secretary of Treasury. An exemption may not be granted unless the Secretary of Labor finds that the exemption is administratively feasible, in the interests of the plan and its participants and beneficiaries, and protective of the rights of plan participants and beneficiaries.

[¶10,450] Act Sec. 611(c). Exemption for electronic communication network

Joint Committee Taxation (J.C.T. REP. NO. JCX-38-06)

[Code Sec. 4975]

Present Law

Present law provides statutory exemptions from the prohibited transaction rules for certain transactions.[131] Present law does not provide a statutory prohibited transaction exemption for transactions made through an electronic communication network, but such transactions may be permitted if the parties are not known to each other (a "blind" transaction).

Explanation of Provision

The provision provides a prohibited transaction exemption under ERISA and the Code for a transaction involving the purchase or sale of securities (or other property as determined under regulations) between a plan and a party in interest if: (1) the transaction is executed through an electronic communication network, alternative trading system, or similar execution system or trading venue that is subject to regulation and oversight by (a) the applicable Federal regulating entity or (b) a foreign regulatory entity as the Secretary may determine under regulations; (2) either (a) neither the execution system nor the parties to the transaction take into account the identity of the parties in the execution of trades, or (b) the transaction is effected under rules designed to match purchases and sales at the best price available through the execution system in accordance with applicable rules of the SEC or other relevant governmental authority; (3) the price and compensation associated with the purchase and sale are not greater than an arm's length transaction with an unrelated party; (4) if the disqualified person has an ownership interest in the system or venue, the system or venue has been authorized by the plan sponsor or other independent fiduciary for this type of transaction; and (5) not less than 30 days before the first transaction of this type executed through any such system or venue, a plan fiduciary is provided written notice of the execution of the transaction through the system or venue.

Examples of other property for purposes of the exemption include (but are not limited to) futures contracts and currency.

Effective Date

The provision is effective with respect to transactions occurring after the date of enactment.

[Law at ¶5305 and ¶7126. CCH Explanation at ¶630.]

[¶10,460] Act Sec. 611(d). Exemption for service providers

Joint Committee Taxation (J.C.T. REP. NO. JCX-38-06)

[Code Sec. 4975]

Present Law

Certain transactions are exempt from prohibited transaction treatment if made for adequate consideration. For this purpose, adequate consideration means: (1) in the case of a security for which there is a generally recognized market, either the price of the security prevailing on a national securities exchange registered under the Securities Exchange Act of 1934, or, if the security is not traded on such a national securities exchange, a price not less favorable to the plan than the offering price for the security as established by the current bid and asked prices quoted by persons independent of the issuer and of any disqualified person; and (2) in the case of an asset other than a security for which there is a generally recognized market, the fair market value of the asset as determined in good faith by a trustee or named fiduciary pursuant to the terms of the plan and in accordance with regulations.[132]

[131] In addition, under ERISA section 408(a), the Secretary of Labor may grant exemptions with respect to particular transactions or classes of transactions after consultation and coordination with the Secretary of Treasury. An exemption may not be granted unless the Secretary of Labor finds that the exemption is administratively feasible, in the interests of the plan and its participants and beneficiaries, and protective of the rights of plan participants and beneficiaries.

[132] ERISA sec. 3(18).

Explanation of Provision

The provision provides a prohibited transaction exemption under ERISA for certain transactions (such as sales of property, loans, and transfers or use of plan assets) between a plan and a person that is a party in interest solely by reason of providing services (or solely by reason of having certain relationships with a service provider), but only if, in connection with the transaction, the plan receives no less, nor pays no more, than adequate consideration. For this purpose, adequate consideration means: (1) in the case of a security for which there is a generally recognized market, the price of the security prevailing on a national securities exchange registered under the Securities Exchange Act of 1934, taking into account factors such as the size of the transaction and marketability of the security, or, if the security is not traded on such a national securities exchange, a price not less favorable to the plan than the offering price for the security as established by the current bid and asked prices quoted by persons independent of the issuer and of any disqualified person, taking into account factors such as the size of the transaction and marketability of the security; and (2) in the case of an asset other than a security for which there is a generally recognized market, the fair market value of the asset as determined in good faith by a fiduciary or named fiduciaries in accordance with regulations. The exemption does not apply to a fiduciary (or an affiliate) who has or exercises any discretionary authority or control with respect to the investment of the assets involved in the transaction or provides investment advice with respect to the assets.

Effective Date

The provision is effective with respect to transactions occurring after the date of enactment.

[Law at ¶ 5305 and ¶ 7126. CCH Explanation at ¶ 630.]

[¶ 10,470] Act Sec. 611(e). Relief for foreign exchange transactions

Joint Committee Taxation (J.C.T. Rep. No. JCX-38-06)

[Code Sec. 4975]

Present Law

Present law provides statutory exemptions from the prohibited transaction rules for certain transactions.[133] Present law does not provide a statutory prohibited transaction exemption for foreign exchange transactions.

Explanation of Provision

The provision provides a prohibited transaction exemption under ERISA and the Code for foreign exchange transactions between a bank or broker-dealer (or an affiliate of either) and a plan in connection with the sale, purchase, or holding of securities or other investment assets (other than a foreign exchange transaction unrelated to any other investment in securities or other investment assets) if: (1) at the time the foreign exchange transaction is entered into, the terms of the transaction are not less favorable to the plan than the terms generally available in comparable arm's length foreign exchange transactions between unrelated parties or the terms afforded by the bank or the broker-dealer (or any affiliate thereof) in comparable arm's-length foreign exchange transactions involving unrelated parties; (2) the exchange rate used for a particular foreign exchange transaction may not deviate by more than three percent from the interbank bid and asked rates at the time of the transaction for transactions of comparable size and maturity as displayed on an independent service that reports rates of exchange in the foreign currency market for such currency; and (3) the bank, broker-dealer (and any affiliate of either) does not have investment discretion or provide investment advice with respect to the transaction.

Effective Date

The provision is effective with respect to transactions occurring after the date of enactment.

[Law at ¶ 5305 and ¶ 7126. CCH Explanation at ¶ 630.]

---

[133] In addition, under ERISA section 408(a), the Secretary of Labor may grant exemptions with respect to particular transactions or classes of transactions after consultation and coordination with the Secretary of Treasury. An exemption may not be granted unless the Secretary of Labor finds that the exemption is administratively feasible, in the interests of the plan and its participants and beneficiaries, and protective of the rights of plan participants and beneficiaries.

[¶10,480] Act Sec. 611(f). Definition of plan asset vehicle

Joint Committee Taxation (J.C.T. Rep. No. JCX-38-06)

[Act Sec. 611(f)]

Present Law

Under ERISA regulations, applicable also for purposes of the prohibited transaction rules of the Code, when a plan holds a non-publicly-traded equity interest in an entity, the assets of the entity may be considered plan assets in certain circumstances unless equity participation in the entity by benefit plan inventors is not significant.[134] In general, such equity participation is significant if, immediately after the most recent acquisition of any equity interest in the entity, 25 percent or more of the value of any class of equity interest in the entity (disregarding certain interests) is held by benefit plan investors, defined as (1) employer-sponsored plans (including those exempt from ERISA, such as governmental plans), (2) other arrangements, such as IRAs, that are subject only to the prohibited transaction rules of the Code, and (3) any entity whose assets are plan assets by reason of a plan's investment in the entity.[135] In that case, unless an exception applies, plan assets include the plan's equity interest in the entity and an undivided interest in each of the underlying assets of the entity.

Explanation of Provision

Under the provision, the term "plan assets" means plan assets as defined under regulations prescribed by the Secretary of Labor. Under the regulations, the assets of any entity are not to be treated as plan assets if, immediately after the most recent acquisition of any equity interest in the entity, less than 25 percent of the total value of each class of equity interest in the entity (disregarding certain interests) is held by benefit plan investors. For this purpose, an entity is considered to hold plan assets only to the extent of the percentage of the equity interest held by benefit plan investors, which means an employee benefit plan subject to the fiduciary rules of ERISA, any plan to which the prohibited transaction rules of the Code applies, and any entity whose underlying assets include plan assets by reason of a plan's investment in such entity.

Effective Date

The provision is effective with respect to transactions occurring after the date of enactment.

[Law at ¶7126. CCH Explanation at ¶630.]

[¶10,490] Act Sec. 611(g). Exemption for cross trading

Joint Committee Taxation (J.C.T. Rep. No. JCX-38-06)

[Code Sec. 4975]

Present Law

Present law provides statutory exemptions from the prohibited transaction rules for certain transactions.[136] Present law does not provide a statutory prohibited transaction exemption for cross trades.

Explanation of Provision

The provision provides prohibited transaction exemptions under ERISA and the Code for a transaction involving the purchase and sale of a security between a plan and any other account managed by the same investment manager if certain requirements are met. These requirements are—

- the transaction is a purchase or sale, for no consideration other than cash payment against prompt delivery of a security for which market quotations are readily available;
- the transaction is effected at the independent current market price of the security;
- no brokerage commission fee (except for customary transfer fees, the fact of which is

---

[134] 29 C.F.R. sec. 2510.3-101(a) (2005). As a result, a person who exercises authority or control respecting management or disposition of the assets of the entity or renders investment advice with respect to the assets for a fee (direct or indirect) is a plan fiduciary.

[135] 29 C.F.R. sec. 2510.3-101(f) (2005).

[136] In addition, under ERISA section 408(a), the Secretary of Labor may grant exemptions with respect to particular transactions or classes of transactions after consultation and coordination with the Secretary of Treasury. An exemption may not be granted unless the Secretary of Labor finds that the exemption is administratively feasible, in the interests of the plan and its participants and beneficiaries, and protective of the rights of plan participants and beneficiaries.

disclosed) or other remuneration is paid in connection with the transaction;

• a fiduciary (other than the investment manager engaging in the cross trades or any affiliate) for each plan participating in the transaction authorizes in advance of any cross-trades (in a document that is separate from any other written agreement of the parties) the investment manager to engage in cross trades at the investment manager's discretion, after the fiduciary has received disclosure regarding the conditions under which cross trades may take place (but only if the disclosure is separate from any other agreement or disclosure involving the asset management relationship), including the written policies and procedures of the investment manager;

• each plan participating in the transaction has assets of at least $100,000,000, except that, if the assets of a plan are invested in a master trust containing the assets of plans maintained by employers in the same controlled group, the master trust has assets of at least $100,000,000;

• the investment manager provides to the plan fiduciary who has authorized cross trading a quarterly report detailing all cross trades executed by the investment manager in which the plan participated during such quarter, including the following information as applicable: the identity of each security bought or sold, the number of shares or units traded, the parties involved in the cross trade, and the trade price and the method used to establish the trade price;

• the investment manager does not base its fee schedule on the plan's consent to cross trading and no other service (other than the investment opportunities and cost savings available through a cross trade) is conditioned on the plan's consent to cross trading;

• the investment manager has adopted, and cross trades are effected in accordance with, written cross-trading policies and procedures that are fair and equitable to all accounts participating in the cross-trading program and that include a description of the manager's pricing policies and procedures, and the manager's policies and procedures for allocating cross trades in an objective manner among accounts participating in the cross-trading program; and

• the investment manager has designated an individual responsible for periodically reviewing purchases and sales to ensure compliance with the written policies and procedures and, following such review, the individual must issue an annual written report no later than 90 days following the period to which it relates, signed under penalty of perjury, to the plan fiduciary who authorized the cross trading, describing the steps performed during the course of the review, the level of compliance, and any specific instances of noncompliance.

The written report must also notify the plan fiduciary of the plan's right to terminate participation in the investment manager's cross-trading program at any time.

No later than 180 days after the date of enactment, the Secretary of Labor, after consultation with the Securities and Exchange Commission, is directed to issue regulations regarding the content of policies and procedures required to be adopted by an investment manager under the requirements for the exemption.

Effective Date

The provision is effective with respect to transactions occurring after the date of enactment.

[Law at ¶ 5305 and ¶ 7126. CCH Explanation at ¶ 630.]

[¶ 10,500] Act Sec. 612. Correction period for certain transactions involving securities and commodities

Joint Committee Taxation (J.C.T. Rep. No. JCX-38-06)

[Code Sec. 4975]

Present Law

ERISA and the Code prohibit certain transactions between an employer-sponsored retirement plan and a disqualified person (referred to as a "party in interest" under ERISA).[137] Disqualified persons include a fiduciary of the plan, a person providing services to the plan, and an employer with employees covered by the plan.

---

[137] Under ERISA, the prohibited transaction rules apply to employer-sponsored retirement plans and welfare benefit plans. Under the Code, the prohibited transaction rules apply to qualified retirement plans and qualified retirement annuities, as well as individual retirement accounts and annuities, Archer MSAs, health savings accounts, and Cov-

For this purpose, a fiduciary includes any person who (1) exercises any authority or control respecting management or disposition of the plan's assets, (2) renders investment advice for a fee or other compensation with respect to any plan moneys or property, or has the authority or responsibility to do so, or (3) has any discretionary authority or responsibility in the administration of the plan.

Prohibited transactions include (1) the sale, exchange or leasing of property, (2) the lending of money or other extension of credit, (3) the furnishing of goods, services or facilities, (4) the transfer to, or use by or for the benefit of, the income or assets of the plan, (5) in the case of a fiduciary, any act that deals with the plan's income or assets for the fiduciary's own interest or account, and (6) the receipt by a fiduciary of any consideration for the fiduciary's own personal account from any party dealing with the plan in connection with a transaction involving the income or assets of the plan. However, certain transactions are exempt from prohibited transaction treatment, for example, certain loans to plan participants.

Under the Code, if a prohibited transaction occurs, the disqualified person who participates in the transaction is subject to a two-tier excise tax. The first level tax is 15 percent of the amount involved in the transaction. The second level tax is imposed if the prohibited transaction is not corrected within a certain period and is 100 percent of the amount involved. Under ERISA, the Secretary of Labor may assess a civil penalty against a person who engages in a prohibited transaction, other than a transaction with a plan covered by the prohibited transaction rules of the Code (i.e., involving a qualified retirement plan or annuity). The penalty may not exceed five percent of the amount involved in the transaction. If the prohibited transaction is not corrected within 90 days after notice from the Secretary of Labor, the penalty may be up to 100 percent of the amount involved in the transaction.[138] For purposes of these rules, the "amount involved" generally means the greater of (1) the amount of money and the fair market value of the other property given, or (2) the amount of money and the fair market value of other property received by the plan. The terms "correction" and "correct" mean, with respect to a prohibited transaction, undoing the transaction to the extent possible, but in any case placing the plan in a financial position not worse than the position in which it would be if the disqualified person were acting under the highest fiduciary standards.

For purposes of the prohibited transaction rules of the Code and ERISA, a transaction involving the sale of securities is considered to occur when the transaction is settled (that is, an actual change in ownership of the securities). Under current practice, securities transactions are commonly settled 3 days after the agreement to sell is made. Present law does not provide a statutory prohibited transaction exemption that is based solely on correction of the transaction.

Explanation of Provision

The bill provides a prohibited transaction exemption under ERISA and the Code for a transaction in connection with the acquisition, holding, or disposition of any security or commodity if the transaction is corrected within a certain period, generally within 14 days of the date the disqualified person (or other person knowingly participating in the transaction) discovers, or reasonably should have discovered, the transaction was a prohibited transaction. For this purpose, the term "correct" means, with respect to a transaction: (1) to undo the transaction to the extent possible and in any case to make good to the plan or affected account any losses resulting from the transaction; and (2) to restore to the plan or affected account any profits made through the use of assets of the plan. If the exemption applies, no excise tax is to be assessed with the transaction, any tax assessed is to be abated, and any tax collected is to be credited or refunded as a tax overpayment.

The exemption does not apply to any transaction between a plan and a plan sponsor or its affiliates that involves the acquisition or sale of an employer security or the acquisition, sale, or lease of employer real property. In addition, in the case of a disqualified person (or other person knowingly participating in the transaction), the exemption does not apply if, at the time of the transaction, the person knew (or reasonably should have known) that the transaction would constitute a prohibited transaction.

(Footnote Continued)

erdell education savings accounts. The prohibited transaction rules under ERISA and the Code generally do not apply to governmental plans or church plans.

[138] A prohibited transaction violates the fiduciary responsibility provisions of ERISA. Under section 502(l) of ERISA, in the case of a violation of fiduciary responsibility, a civil penalty is generally imposed of 20 percent of the amount recovered from a person with respect to the violation in a settlement agreement with the Department of Labor or a judicial proceeding, but the penalty is reduced by the amount of any excise tax or other civil penalty with respect to a prohibited transaction.

Effective Date

The provision is effective with respect to any transaction that a fiduciary or other person discovers, or reasonably should have discovered, after the date of enactment constitutes a prohibited transaction.

[Law at ¶ 5305 and ¶ 7129. CCH Explanation at ¶ 635.]

[¶ 10,510] Act Sec. 621. Inapplicability of relief from fiduciary liability during suspension of ability of participant or beneficiary to direct investments

Joint Committee Taxation (J.C.T. REP. NO. JCX-38-06)

[Act Sec. 621]

Present Law

Fiduciary rules under ERISA

ERISA contains general fiduciary duty standards that apply to all fiduciary actions, including investment decisions. ERISA requires that a plan fiduciary generally must discharge its duties solely in the interests of participants and beneficiaries and with the care, skill, prudence, and diligence under the circumstances then prevailing that a prudent man acting in a like capacity and familiar with such matters would use in the conduct of an enterprise of a like character and with like aims. With respect to plan assets, ERISA requires a fiduciary to diversify the investments of the plan so as to minimize the risk of large losses, unless under the circumstances it is clearly prudent not to do so.

A plan fiduciary that breaches any of the fiduciary responsibilities, obligations, or duties imposed by ERISA is personally liable to make good to the plan any losses to the plan resulting from such breach and to restore to the plan any profits the fiduciary has made through the use of plan assets. A plan fiduciary may be liable also for a breach of responsibility by another fiduciary (a "co-fiduciary") in certain circumstances.

Special rule for participant control of assets

ERISA provides a special rule in the case of a defined contribution plan that permits participants to exercise control over the assets in their individual accounts. Under the special rule, if a participant exercises control over the assets in his or her account (as determined under regulations), the participant is not deemed to be a fiduciary by reason of such exercise and no person who is otherwise a fiduciary is liable for any loss, or by reason of any breach, that results from the participant's exercise of control.

Regulations issued by the Department of Labor describe the requirements that must be met in order for a participant to be treated as exercising control over the assets in his or her account. With respect to investment options, the regulations provide in part:

- the plan must provide at least three different investment options, each of which is diversified and has materially different risk and return characteristics;

- the plan must allow participants to give investment instructions with respect to each investment option under the plan with a frequency that is appropriate in light of the reasonably expected market volatility of the investment option (the general volatility rule);

- at a minimum, participants must be allowed to give investment instructions at least every three months with respect to least three of the investment options, and those investment options must constitute a broad range of options (the three-month minimum rule);

- participants must be provided with detailed information about the investment options, information regarding fees, investment instructions and limitations, and copies of financial data and prospectuses; and

- specific requirements must be satisfied with respect to investments in employer stock to ensure that employees' buying, selling, and voting decisions are confidential and free from employer influence.

If these and the other requirements under the regulations are met, a plan fiduciary may be liable for the investment options made available under the plan, but not for the specific investment decisions made by participants.

Blackout notice

Under ERISA, the plan administrator of a defined contribution plan generally must provide at least 30 days advance notice of a blackout period (a "blackout notice") to plan participants and beneficiaries to whom the blackout period applies.[139] Failure to provide a blackout notice may result in a civil penalty up to $100 per day for each failure with respect to a single participant or beneficiary.

A blackout period is any period during which any ability of participants or beneficiaries under the plan, which is otherwise available under the terms of the plan, to direct or diversify assets credited to their accounts, or to obtain loans or distributions from the plan, is temporarily suspended, limited, or restricted if the suspension, limitation, or restriction is for any period of more than three consecutive business days. However, a blackout period does not include a suspension, limitation, or restriction that (1) occurs by reason of the application of securities laws, (2) is a change to the plan providing for a regularly scheduled suspension, limitation, or restriction that is disclosed through a summary of material modifications to the plan or materials describing specific investment options under the plan, or changes thereto, or (3) applies only to one or more individuals, each of whom is a participant, alternate payee, or other beneficiary under a qualified domestic relations order.

A blackout notice must be written in a manner calculated to be understood by the average plan participant and must include (1) the reasons for the blackout period, (2) an identification of the investments and other rights affected, (3) the expected beginning date and length of the blackout period, and (4) in the case of a blackout period affecting investments, a statement that the participant or beneficiary should evaluate the appropriateness of current investment decisions in light of the inability to direct or diversify assets during the blackout period, and (5) other matters as required by regulations. If the expected beginning date or length of the blackout period changes after notice has been provided, the plan administrator must provide notice of the change (and specify any material change in other matters related to the blackout) to affected participants and beneficiaries as soon as reasonably practicable.

Explanation of Provision

The bill amends the special rule applicable if a participant exercises control over the assets in his or her account with respect to a case in which a qualified change in investment options offered under the defined contribution plan occurs. In such a case, for purposes of the special rule, a participant or beneficiary who has exercised control over the assets in his or her account before a change in investment options is not treated as not exercising control over such assets in connection with the change if certain requirements are met.

For this purpose, a qualified change in investment options means a change in the investment options offered to a participant or beneficiary under the terms of the plan, under which: (1) the participant's account is reallocated among one or more new investment options offered instead of one or more investment options that were offered immediately before the effective date of the change; and (2) the characteristics of the new investment options, including characteristics relating to risk and rate of return, are, immediately after the change, reasonably similar to the characteristics of the investment options offered immediately before the change.

The following requirements must be met in order for the rule to apply: (1) at least 30 but not more than 60 days before the effective date of the change in investment options, the plan administrator furnishes written notice of the change to participants and beneficiaries, including information comparing the existing and new investment options and an explanation that, in the absence of affirmative investment instructions from the participant or beneficiary to the contrary, the account of the participant or beneficiary will be invested in new options with characteristics reasonably similar to the characteristics of the existing investment options; (2) the participant or beneficiary has not provided to the plan administrator, in advance of the effective date of the change, affirmative investment instructions contrary to the proposed reinvestment of the participant's or beneficiary's account; and (3) the investment of the participant's or beneficiary's account as in effect immediately before the effective date of the change was the product of the exercise by such participant or beneficiary of control over the assets of the account.

In addition, the provision amends the special rule applicable if a participant or beneficiary exercises control over the assets in his or her account so that the provision under which no person who is otherwise a fiduciary is liable for any loss, or by reason of any breach, that results from the participant's or beneficiary's exercise of control does not apply in connection with a

[139] ERISA sec. 101(i).

blackout period[140] in which the participant's or beneficiary's ability to direct the assets in his or her account is suspended by a plan sponsor or fiduciary. However, if a plan sponsor or fiduciary meets the requirements of ERISA in connection with authorizing and implementing a blackout period, any person who is otherwise a fiduciary is not liable under ERISA for any loss occurring during the blackout period.

Not later than one year after the date of enactment, the Secretary of Labor is to issue interim final regulations providing guidance, including safe harbors, on how plan sponsors or other affected fiduciaries can satisfy their fiduciary responsibilities during any blackout period.

Effective Date

The provision generally applies to plan years beginning after December 31, 2007. In the case of a plan maintained pursuant to one or more collective bargaining agreements, the provision is effective for plan years beginning after the earlier of (1) the later of December 31, 2008 or the date on which the last of such collective bargaining agreements terminates (determined without regard to any extension thereof after the date of enactment), or (2) December 31, 2009.

[Law at ¶ 7132. CCH Explanation at ¶ 640.]

[¶ 10,520] Act Sec. 622. Increase in maximum bond amount

Joint Committee Taxation (J.C.T. Rep. No. JCX-38-06)

[Act Sec. 622]

Present Law

ERISA generally requires every plan fiduciary and every person who handles funds or other property of a plan (a "plan official") to be bonded. The amount of the bond is fixed annually at no less than ten percent of the funds handled, but must be at least $1,000 and not more than $500,000 (unless the Secretary of Labor prescribes a larger amount after notice and an opportunity to be heard). The bond is intended to protect plans against loss from acts of fraud or dishonesty by plan officials. Qualifying bonds must have as surety a corporate surety company that is an acceptable surety on Federal bonds.

Explanation of Provision

The provision raises the maximum bond amount to $1 million in the case of a plan that holds employer securities. The provision raises the maximum bond amount to $1 million in the case of a plan that holds employer securities. A plan would not be considered to hold employer securities within the meaning of this section where the only securities held by the plan are part of a broadly diversified fund of assets, such as mutual or index funds.

Effective Date

The provision is effective for plan years beginning after December 31, 2007.

[Law at ¶ 7135. CCH Explanation at ¶ 645.]

[¶ 10,530] Act Sec. 623. Increase in penalties for coercive interference with exercise of ERISA rights

Joint Committee Taxation (J.C.T. Rep. No. JCX-38-06)

[Act Sec. 623]

Present Law

ERISA prohibits any person from using fraud, force or violence (or threatening force or violence) to restrain, coerce, or intimidate (or attempt to) any plan participant or beneficiary in order to interfere with or prevent the exercise of their rights under the plan, ERISA, or the Welfare and Pension Plans Disclosure Act ("WPPDA"). Willful violation of this prohibition is a criminal offense subject to a $10,000 fine or imprisonment of up to one year, or both.

Explanation of Provision

The provision increases the penalties for willful acts of coercive interference with participants' rights under a plan, ERISA, or the

[140] For this purpose, blackout period is defined as under the present-law provision requiring advance notice of a blackout period.

WPPDA. The amount of the fine is increased to $100,000, and the maximum term of imprisonment is increased to 10 years.

Effective Date

The provision is effective for violations occurring on and after the date of enactment.

[Law at ¶ 7138. CCH Explanation at ¶ 650.]

[¶ 10,540] Act Sec. 624. Treatment of investment of assets by plan where participant fails to exercise investment election

Joint Committee Taxation (J.C.T. REP. NO. JCX-38-06)

[Act Sec. 624]

Present Law

ERISA imposes standards on the conduct of plan fiduciaries, including persons who make investment decisions with respect to plan assets. Fiduciaries are personally liable for any losses to the plan due to a violation of fiduciary standards.

An individual account plan may permit participants to make investment decisions with respect to their accounts. ERISA fiduciary liability does not apply to investment decisions made by plan participants if participants exercise control over the investment of their individual accounts, as determined under ERISA regulations. In that case, a plan fiduciary may be responsible for the investment alternatives made available, but not for the specific investment decisions made by participants.

Explanation of Provision

Under the bill, a participant is treated as exercising control with respect to assets in an individual account plan if such amounts are invested in a default arrangement in accordance with Department of Labor regulations until the participant makes an affirmative election regarding investments. Such regulations must provide guidance on the appropriateness of certain investments for designation as default investments under the arrangement, including guidance regarding appropriate mixes of default investments and asset classes which the Secretary considers consistent with long-term capital appreciation or long-term capital preservation (or both), and the designation of other default investments. The Secretary of Labor is directed to issue regulations under the provision within six months of the date of enactment.

In order for this treatment to apply, notice of the participant's rights and obligations under the arrangement must be provided. Under the notice requirement, within a reasonable period before the plan year, the plan administrator must give each participant notice of the rights and obligations under the arrangement which is sufficiently accurate and comprehensive to apprise the participant of such rights and obligations and is written in a manner to be understood by the average participant. The notice must include an explanation of the participant's rights under the arrangement to specifically elect to exercise control over the assets in the participant's account. In addition, the participant must have a reasonable period of time after receipt of the notice and before the assets are first invested to make such an election. The notice must also explain how contributions made under the arrangement will be invested in the absence of any investment election by the employee.

Effective Date

The provision is effective for plan years beginning after December 31, 2006.

[Law at ¶ 7141. CCH Explanation at ¶ 655.]

[¶10,550] Act Sec. 625. Clarification of fiduciary rules

Joint Committee Taxation (J.C.T. REP. NO. JCX-38-06)

[Act Sec. 625]

Present Law

ERISA imposes standards on the conduct of plan fiduciaries. Fiduciaries are personally liable for any losses to the plan due to a violation of fiduciary standards.

An ERISA interpretive bulletin requires a fiduciary choosing an annuity provider for purposes of distributions from a plan (whether on separation or retirement of a participant or on termination of the plan) to take steps calculated to obtain the safest available annuity, based on the annuity provider's claims paying ability and creditworthiness, unless under the circumstances it would be in the interest of participants to do otherwise.[141]

Explanation of Provision

The bill directs the Secretary of Labor to issue final regulations within one year of the date of enactment, clarifying that the selection of an annuity contract as an optional form of distribution from a defined contribution plan is not subject to the safest available annuity requirement under the ERISA interpretive bulletin and is subject to all otherwise applicable fiduciary standards.

The regulations to be issued by the Secretary of Labor are intended to clarify that the plan sponsor or other applicable plan fiduciary is required to act in accordance with the prudence standards of ERISA section 404(a). It is not intended that there be a single safest available annuity contract since the plan fiduciary must select the most prudent option specific to its plan and its participants and beneficiaries. Furthermore, it is not intended that the regulations restate all of the factors contained in the interpretive bulletin.

Effective Date

The provision is effective on the date of enactment.

[Law at ¶7144. CCH Explanation at ¶660.]

[¶10,560] Act Sec. 701 and 702. Benefit accrual standards

Joint Committee Taxation (J.C.T. REP. NO. JCX-38-06)

[Code Secs. 411 and 417]

Present Law

Prohibition on age discrimination

In general

A prohibition on age discrimination applies to benefit accruals under a defined benefit pension plan.[142] Specifically, an employee's benefit accrual may not cease, and the rate of an employee's benefit accrual may not be reduced, because of the attainment of any age. However, this prohibition is not violated solely because the plan imposes (without regard to age) a limit on the amount of benefits that the plan provides or a limit on the number of years of service or years of participation that are taken into account for purposes of determining benefit accrual under the plan. Moreover, for purposes of this requirement, the subsidized portion of any early retirement benefit may be disregarded in determining benefit accruals.

In December 2002, the IRS issued proposed regulations that dealt with the application of the age discrimination rules.[143] The proposed regulations included rules for applying the age discrimination rules with respect to accrued benefits, optional forms of benefit, ancillary benefits, and other rights and features provided under a plan. Under the proposed regulations, for purposes of applying the prohibition on age discrimination to defined benefit pension plans, an employee's rate of benefit accrual for a year is generally the increase in the employee's accrued normal retirement benefit (i.e., the benefit payable at normal retirement age) for the plan year. In the preamble to the proposed regulations, the IRS requested comments on other approaches to determining the rate of benefit accrual, such as allowing accrual rates to be averaged over multi-

---

[141] 29 C.F.R. sec. 2509.95-1 (2005).

[142] Code sec. 411(b)(1)(H); ERISA sec. 204(b)(1)(H).

[143] 67 Fed. Reg. 76123.

ple years (for example, to accommodate plans that provide a higher rate of accrual in earlier years) or, in the case of a plan that applies an offset, determining accrual rates before application of the offset. As discussed below, in June 2004, the IRS announced the withdrawal of the proposed regulations.

Cash balance and other hybrid plans

Certain types of defined benefit pension plans, such as cash balance plans and pension equity plans, are referred to as "hybrid" plans because they combine features of a defined benefit pension plan and a defined contribution plan.

Under a cash balance plan, benefits are determined by reference to a hypothetical account balance. An employee's hypothetical account balance is determined by reference to hypothetical annual allocations to the account ("pay credits") (e.g., a certain percentage of the employee's compensation for the year) and hypothetical earnings on the account ("interest credits"). Cash balance plans are generally designed so that, when a participant receives a pay credit for a year of service, the participant also receives the right to future interest on the pay credit, regardless of whether the participant continues employment (referred to as "front-loaded" interest credits). That is, the participant's hypothetical account continues to be credited with interest after the participant stops working for the employer. As a result, if an employee terminates employment and defers distribution to a later date, interest credits will continue to be credited to that employee's hypothetical account.

Another type of hybrid plan is a pension equity plan (sometimes referred to as a "PEP"). Under a pension equity plan, benefits are generally described as a percentage of final average pay, with the percentage determined on the basis of points received for each year of service, which are often weighted for older or longer service employees. Pension equity plans commonly provide interest credits for the period between a participant's termination of employment and commencement of benefits.

Because of the front-loaded nature of accruals under cash balance plans, there is a longer time for interest credits to accrue on a pay credit to the account of a younger employee. Thus, a pay credit received at a younger age may provide a larger annuity benefit at normal retirement age than the same pay credit received at an older age. A similar effect may occur with respect to other types of hybrid plan designs, including pension equity plans.

IRS consideration of cash balance plans began in the early 1990s.[144] At that time, the focus was on the question of whether such plans satisfied the nondiscrimination requirements under section 401(a)(4), which requires that benefits or contributions not discriminate in favor of highly compensated employees. Treasury regulations issued in 1991 under section 401(a)(4) provided a safe harbor for cash balance plans that provide frontloaded interest credits and meet certain other requirements. In connection with the issuance of these regulations, Treasury spoke to the cash balance age discrimination issue. The preamble to the final regulations stated "[t]he fact that interest adjustments through normal retirement age are accrued in the year of the related hypothetical allocation will not cause a cash balance plan to fail to satisfy the requirements of section 411(b)(1)(H), relating to age-based reductions in the rate at which benefits accrue under a plan."[145] Many interpreted this language as Treasury's position that cash balance plan designs do not violate the prohibitions on age discrimination. The IRS has not to date asserted that hybrid plan formulas result in per se violations of age discrimination requirements. In 1999, Treasury and the IRS issued an announcement and a Federal Register notice stating that the question of whether cash balance conversions were age discriminatory or otherwise inconsistent with plan qualification rules was under active consideration, that further IRS determination letters on conversions to cash balance plans would therefore be suspected be referral to the IRS National Office until the IRS and Treasury had resolved the issues, and inviting public comment on the issues. Hundreds of comments were submitted. The December 2002 proposed regulations, noted above, provided that an employee's rate of benefit accrual for a year is generally the increase in the employee's accrued normal retirement benefit (i.e., the benefit payable at normal retirement age) for the plan year. However, the proposed regulations provided a special rule under which an employee's rate of benefit accrual under a cash balance plan meeting certain requirements (an "eligible" cash balance plan) was based on the rate of pay credit provided under the plan. Thus, under the proposed regulations, an eligible cash balance plan would not violate the prohibition on age discrimination solely because pay credits for younger employees earn interest credits for a longer period.

---

[144] Statement of Stuart L. Brown, Chief Counsel Internal Revenue Service, before the Senate Committee on Health, Education, Labor, and Pensions (Sept. 21, 1999).

[145] 56 Fed. Reg. 47528 (Sept. 19, 1991).

Section 205 of the Consolidated Appropriations Act, 2004 (the "2004 Appropriations Act"), enacted January 24, 2004, provides that none of the funds made available in the 2004 Appropriations Act may be used by the Secretary of the Treasury, or his designee, to issue any rule or regulation implementing the 2002 proposed Treasury age discrimination regulations or any regulation reaching similar results.[146] The 2004 Appropriations Act also required the Secretary of the Treasury within 180 days of enactment to present to Congress a legislative proposal for providing transition relief for older and longer-service participants affected by conversions of their employers' traditional pension plans to cash balance plans. The Treasury Department complied with this requirement by including in the President's budget for fiscal year 2005 a proposal relating to cash balance and other hybrid plans that specifically addresses conversions to such plans, the application of the age discrimination rules to such plans, and the determination of minimum lump sums under such plans.[147] In June 2004, the IRS announced the withdrawal of the proposed age discrimination regulations, including the special rules for eligible cash balance plans.[148] According to the Announcement, "[t]his will provide Congress an opportunity to . . . address cash balance and other hybrid plan issues through legislation."

The application of the age discrimination rules to hybrid plans has been the subject of litigation. The decisions are divided on how ERISA requires courts to calculate the rate of benefit accrual.[149]

Calculating minimum lump-sum distributions under hybrid plans

Defined benefit pension plans, including cash balance plans and other hybrid plans, are required to provide benefits in the form of a life annuity commencing at a participant's normal retirement age. If the plan permits benefits to be paid in certain other forms, such as a lump sum, minimum present value rules apply, under which the alternative form of benefit cannot be less than the present value of the life annuity payable at normal retirement age, determined using certain statutorily prescribed interest and mortality assumptions.[150]

Most cash balance plans are designed to permit a lump-sum distribution of a participant's hypothetical account balance upon termination of employment. This raises an issue as to the whether a distribution of a participant's hypothetical account balance satisfies the minimum present value rules. In 1996, the IRS issued proposed guidance (Notice 96-8) on the application of the minimum present value rules to lump-sum distributions under cash balance plans and requested public comments in anticipation of proposed regulations incorporating the proposed guidance.[151]

Under the proposed guidance, a lump-sum distribution from a cash balance plan cannot be less than the present value of the benefit payable at normal retirement age, determined using the statutory interest and mortality assumptions. For this purpose, a participant's normal retirement benefit under a cash balance plan is generally determined by projecting the participant's hypothetical account balance to normal retirement age by crediting to the account future interest credits at the plan rate, the right to which has already accrued, and converting the projected account balance to an actuarially equivalent life annuity payable at normal retirement age, using the interest and mortality assumptions specified in the plan. The proposed guidance also included rules under which cash balance plans can provide lump-sum distributions in the amount of participants' hypothetical account balances if the rate at which interest credits are provided under the plan is not greater (or is assumed not to be greater) than the statutory interest rate.

---

[146] Pub. L. No. 108-199 (2004).

[147] A similar proposal was also contained in the President's budget proposal for fiscal year 2006.

[148] IRS Announcement 2004-57, 2004-27 I.R.B. 15.

[149] Compare *Register v. PNC Financial Services Group, Inc.* No. 04-CV-6097, 2005 WL 3120268 (E.D. Pa. Nov. 21, 2005), *Tootle v. ARINC, Inc.*, 222 F.R.D. 88 (D. Md. 2004); *Eaton v. Oanan Corp.*, 117 F. Supp. 2d 812 (S.D. Ind. 2000); with *Cooper v. IBM Personal Pension Plan*, 274 F. Supp.2d 1010 (S.D. Ill. 2003), *Richards v. Fleetboston Financial Corp.*, 427 F.Supp.2d 150 (D. Conn. 2006), *Donaldson v. Pharmacia Pension Plan*, 2006 WL 1669789, 38 E.B.C. 1006 (S.D. Ill. June 14, 2006). See also *Campbell v. BankBoston*, 327 F.3d 1 (1st Cir. 2003) and *Hirt v. Equitable Retirement Plan for Employees, Managers and Agents* No. 01 Civ. 7920 (AKH), 2006 WL 2023545 (S.D.N.Y. July 20, 2006).

[150] Code sec. 417(e); ERISA sec. 205(g)(3). For years before 1995, these provisions required the use of an interest rate based on interest rates determined by the PBGC. For years after 1994, these provisions require the use of an interest rate based on interest rates on 30-year Treasury securities and a mortality table specified by the IRS.

[151] Notice 96-8, 1996-1996-1 C.B. 359. The Notice provides that regulations will be effective prospectively and, for plan years before regulations are effective, allows lump-sum distributions from cash balance plans that provide front-loaded interest credits to be based on a reasonable, good-faith interpretation of the minimum present value rules, taking into account preexisting guidance. The Notice further provides that plans that comply with the guidance in the Notice are deemed to be applying a reasonable, good-faith interpretation.

Under the approach in the proposed guidance, a difference in the rate of interest credits provided under the plan, which is used to project the account balance forward to normal retirement age, and the statutory rate used to determine the lump-sum value (i.e., present value) of the accrued benefit can cause a discrepancy between the value of the minimum lump-sum and the employee's hypothetical account balance. This effect is sometimes referred to as "whipsaw." In particular, if the plan's interest crediting rate is higher than the statutory interest rate, then the resulting lump-sum amount will generally be greater than the hypothetical account balance.

Several courts, but not all, have applied an approach similar to the approach in the proposed guidance in cases involving the determination of lump sums under cash balance plans.[152] Regulations addressing the application of the minimum present value rules to cash balance plans have not been issued.[153]

Explanation of Provision

Age discrimination rules in general

Under the provision, a plan is not treated as violating the prohibition on age discrimination under ERISA, the Code, and ADEA if a participant's accrued benefit,[154] as determined as of any date under the terms of the plan would be equal to or greater than that of any similarly situated, younger individual who is or could be a participant. For this purpose, an individual is similarly situated to a participant if the individual and the participant are (and always have been) identical in every respect (including period of service, compensation, position, date of hire, work history, and any other respect) except for age. Under the provision, the comparison of benefits for older and younger participants applies to all possible participants under all possible dates under the plan, in the same manner as the present-law application of the backloading and accrual rules.

In addition, in determining a participant's accrued benefit for this purpose, the subsidized portion of any early retirement benefit or any retirement type subsidy is disregarded. In some cases the value of an early retirement subsidy may be difficult to determine; it is therefore intended that a reasonable approximation of such value may be used for this purpose. In calculating the accrued benefit, the benefit may, under the terms of the plan, be calculated as an annuity payable at normal retirement age, the balance of a hypothetical account, or the current value of the accumulated percentage of the employee's final average compensation. That is, the age discrimination rules may be applied on the basis of the balance of the a hypothetical account or the current value of the accumulated percentage of the employee's final average compensation, but only if the plan terms provide the accrued benefit in such form. The provision is intended to apply to hybrid plans, including pension equity plans.

The provision makes it clear that a plan is not treated as age discriminatory solely because the plan provides offsets of benefits under the plan to the extent such offsets are allowable in applying the requirements under section 401(a) of the Code. It is intended that such offsets also comply with ERISA and the ADEA.

A plan is not treated as failing to meet the age discrimination requirements solely because the plan provides a disparity in contributions and benefits with respect to which the requirements of section 401(l) of the Code are met.

A plan is not treated as failing to meet the age discrimination requirements solely because the plan provides for indexing of accrued benefits under the plan. Except in the case of any benefit provided in the form of a variable annuity, this rule does not apply with respect to any indexing which results in an accrued benefit less than the accrued benefit determined without regard to such indexing. Indexing for this purpose

[152] *Berger v. Xerox Corp. Retirement Income Guarantee Plan*, 338 F.3d 755 (7th Cir. 2003); *Esden v. Bank of Boston*, 229 F.3d 154 (2d Cir. 2000), cert. dismissed, 531 U.S. 1061 (2001); *Lyons v. Georgia Pacific Salaried Employees Retirement Plan*, 221 F.3d 1235 (11th Cir. 2000) ("*Lyons II*"), cert. denied, 532 U.S. 967 (2001); and *West v. AK Steel Corp. Retirement Accumulation Plan*, 318 F. Supp.2d 579 (S.D. Ohio 2004). In *Lyons II*, the court reversed a lower court holding in *Lyons v. Georgia Pacific Salaried Employees Retirement Plan*, 66 F. Supp.2d 1328 (N.D. Ga. 1999) ("*Lyons I*"), relating to the application of the minimum present value rules in effect before 1995. The *Lyons II* court limited its analysis to the minimum present value rules in effect as of 1993 when Mr. Lyons received his lump-sum distribution; however, the court indicated that a different result could apply under the law in effect after 1994. On remand, in *Lyons v. Georgia Pacific Salaried Employees Retirement Plan*, 196 F. Supp.2d 1260 (N.D. Ga. 2002) ("*Lyons III*"), the lower court determined that payment of the hypothetical account balance did not violate the minimum present value rules in effect for years after 1994.

[153] As mentioned above, the President's budgets for fiscal years 2005 and 2006 include a proposal relating to cash balance plans that specifically addresses the determination of minimum lump sums under such plans. The President's proposal would eliminate the whipsaw effect and allow the plan to pay the hypothetical account balance, if certain requirements are satisfied.

[154] For purposes of this rule, the accrued benefit means such benefit accrued to date.

means, with respect to an accrued benefit, the periodic adjustment of the accrued benefit by means of the application of a recognized investment index or methodology. Under the provision, in no event may indexing be reduced or cease because of age.

Rules for applicable defined benefit plans

In general

Under the provision, an applicable defined benefit plan fails to satisfy the age discrimination rules unless the plan meets certain requirements with respect to interest credits and, in the case of a conversion, certain additional requirements. Applicable defined benefit plans must also satisfy certain vesting requirements.

Interest requirement

A plan satisfies the interest requirement if the terms of the plan provide that any interest credit (or equivalent amount) for any plan year is at a rate that is not less than zero and is not greater than a market rate of return. A plan does not fail to meet the interest requirement merely because the plan provides for a reasonable minimum guaranteed rate of return or for a rate or return that is equal to the greater of a fixed or variable rate of return. An interest credit (or an equivalent amount) of less than zero cannot result in the account balance or similar amount being less than the aggregate amount of contributions credited to the account. The Secretary of the Treasury may provide rules governing the calculation of a market rate of return and for permissible methods of crediting interest to the account (including fixed or variable interest rates) resulting in effective rates of return that meet the requirements of the provision.

If the interest credit rate (or equivalent amount) is a variable rate, the plan must provide that, upon termination of the plan, the rate of interest used to determine accrued benefits under the plan is equal to the average of the rates of interest used under the plan during the five-year period ending on the termination date.

Conversion rules

Under the provision, special rules apply if an amendment to a defined benefit plan is adopted which would have the effect of converting the plan into an applicable defined benefit plan (an "applicable plan amendment").[155] If an applicable plan amendment is adopted after June 29, 2005, the plan fails to satisfy the age discrimination rules unless the plan provides that the accrued benefit of any individual who was a participant immediately before the adoption of the amendment is not less than the sum of (1) the participant's accrued benefit for years of service before the effective date of the amendment, determined under the terms of the plan as in effect before the amendment; plus (2) the participant's accrued benefit for years of service after the effective date of the amendment, determined under the terms of the plan as in effect after the terms of the amendment.

For purposes of determining the amount in (1) above, the plan must credit the accumulation account or similar amount with the amount of any early retirement benefit or retirement-type subsidy for the plan year in which the participant retires if, as of such time, the participant has met the age, years of service, and other requirements under the plan for entitlement to such benefit or subsidy.

Vesting rules

The provision amends the ERISA and Code rules relating to vesting to provide that an applicable defined benefit plan must provide that each employee who has completed at least three years of serves has a nonforfeitable right to 100 percent of the employee's accrued benefit derived from employer contributions.

Minimum present value rules

The provision provides that an applicable defined benefit plan is not treated as failing to meet the minimum present value rules[156] solely because of the present value of the accrued benefit (or any portion thereof) of any participant is,

[155] If the benefits under two or more defined benefit plans established by an employer are coordinated in such a manner as to have the effect of the adoption of an applicable plan amendment, the sponsor of the defined benefit plan or plans providing for the coordination is treated as having adopted an applicable plan amendment as of the date the coordination begins. In addition, the Secretary of Treasury is directed to issue regulations to prevent the avoidance of the requirements with respect to an applicable plan amendment through the use of two or more plan amendments rather than a single amendment.

[156] ERISA sec. 205(g), Code sec. 417(e). A plan complying with the provision also does not violate certain rules relating to vesting (ERISA sec. 203(a)(2) and Code sec. 411(a)(2)) and the determination of the accrued benefit (in the case of a plan which does not provide for employee contributions) (ERISA sec. 204(c) and Code sec. 411(c)).

under the terms of the plan, equal to the amount expressed as the balance in the hypothetical account or as an accumulated percentage of the participant's final average compensation.

Rules on plan termination

The provision provides rules for making determinations of benefits upon termination of an applicable defined benefit plan. Such a plan must provide that, upon plan termination, (1) if the interest credit rate (or equivalent amount) under the plan is a variable rate, the rate of interest used to determine accrued benefits under the plan shall be equal to the average of the rates of interest used under the plan during the five-year period ending on the termination date and (2) the interest rate and mortality table used to determine the amount of any benefit under the plan payable in the form of an annuity payable at normal retirement age is the rate and table specified under the plan for such purposes as of the termination date. For purposes of (2), if the rate of interest is a variable rate, then the rate is the average of such rates during the five-year period ending on the termination date.

Definition of applicable defined benefit plan

An applicable defined benefit plan is a defined benefit plan under which the accrued benefit (or any portion thereof) is calculated as the balance of a hypothetical account maintained for the participant or as an accumulated percentage of the participant's final average compensation. The Secretary of the Treasury is to provide rules which include in the definition of an applicable defined benefit plan any defined benefit plan (or portion of such a plan) which has an effect similar to an applicable defined benefit plan.

No inference

Nothing in the provision is to be construed to infer the treatment of applicable defined benefit plans or conversions to such plans under the rules in ERISA, ADEA and the Code prohibiting age discrimination[157] as in effect before the provision is effective. In addition, no inference is to be drawn with respect to the application of the minimum benefit rules to applicable defined benefit plans before the provision is effective.

Regulations relating to mergers and acquisitions

The Secretary of the Treasury is directed to prescribe regulations for the application of the provisions relating to applicable defined benefit plans in cases where the conversion of a plan to a cash balance or similar plan is made with respect to a group of employees who become employees by reason of a merger, acquisition, or similar treatment. The regulations are to be issued not later than 12 months after the date of enactment.

Effective Date

In general, the provision is effective for periods beginning on or after June 29, 2005.

The provision relating to the minimum value rules is effective for distributions after the date of enactment.

In the case of a plan in existence on June 29, 2005, the interest credit and vesting requirements for an applicable defined benefit plan generally apply to years beginning after December 31, 2007, except that the plan sponsor may elect to have such requirements apply for any period after June 29, 2005, and before the first plan year beginning after December 31, 2007. In the case of a plan maintained pursuant to one or more collective bargaining agreements, a delayed effective date applies with respect to the interest credit and vesting requirements for an applicable defined benefit plan.

The provision relating to conversions of plans applies to plan amendments adopted after and taking effect after June 29, 2005, except that a plan sponsor may elect to have such amendments apply to plan amendments adopted before and taking affect after such date.

The direction to the Secretary of the Treasury to issue regulations relating to mergers and acquisitions is effective on the date of enactment.

[Law at ¶ 5080 ,¶ 7147 and ¶ 7150. CCH Explanation at ¶ 1005 and ¶ 1010.]

[157] ERISA sec. 204(b)(1)(H), ADEA sec. 4(i)(1), and Code sec. 411(b)(1)(H).

[¶10,570] Act Secs. 801 and 802. Increase in deduction limits applicable to single-employer and multiemployer defined benefit pension plans

Joint Committee Taxation (J.C.T. REP. NO. JCX-38-06)

[Code Sec. 404]

Present Law

In general

Employer contributions to qualified retirement plans are deductible subject to certain limits.

In the case of contributions to a defined benefit pension plan (including both single-employer and multiemployer plans), the employer generally may deduct the greater of: (1) the amount necessary to satisfy the minimum funding requirement of the plan for the year; or (2) the amount of the plan's normal cost for the year plus the amount necessary to amortize certain unfunded liabilities over 10 years, but limited to the full funding limitation for the year.[158] The maximum amount otherwise deductible generally is not less than the plan's unfunded current liability.[159] In the case of a single-employer plan covered by the PBGC insurance program that terminates during the year, the maximum deductible amount is generally not less than the amount needed to make the plan assets sufficient to fund benefit liabilities as defined for purposes of plan termination under the PBGC insurance program ("unfunded termination liability"). In applying these limits, future increases in the limits on compensation taken into account under a qualified retirement plan and on benefits payable under a defined benefit pension plan may not be taken into account.

In the case of a defined contribution plan, the employer generally may deduct contributions in an amount up to 25 percent of compensation paid or accrued during the employer's taxable year.

Overall deduction limit

If an employer sponsors one or more defined benefit pension plans and one or more defined contribution plans that cover at least one of the same employees, an overall deduction limit applies to the total contributions to all plans for a plan year. The overall deduction limit is the greater of (1) 25 percent of compensation, or (2) the amount necessary to meet the minimum funding requirement with respect to the defined benefit plan for the year. For this purpose, the amount necessary to meet the minimum funding requirement with respect to the defined benefit plan is treated as not less than the amount of the plan's unfunded current liability.

Subject to certain exceptions, an employer that makes nondeductible contributions to a plan is subject to an excise tax equal to 10 percent of the amount of the nondeductible contributions for the year.

Explanation of Provision

Single-employer defined benefit pension plans

General deduction limit

Under the bill, for taxable years beginning in 2006 and 2007, in the case of contributions to a single-employer defined benefit plan, the maximum deductible amount is not less than the excess (if any) of (1) 150 percent of the plan's current liability, over (2) the value of plan assets.

For taxable years beginning after 2007, in the case of contributions to a single-employer defined benefit pension plan, the maximum de-

158 The full funding limitation is the excess, if any, of (1) the accrued liability of the plan (including normal cost), over (2) the lesser of (a) the market value of plan assets or (b) the actuarial value of plan assets. However, the full funding limit is not less than the excess, if any, of 90 percent of the plan's current liability (including the current liability normal cost) over the actuarial value of plan assets.

159 In the case of a plan with 100 or fewer participants, unfunded current liability for this purpose does not include the liability attributable to benefit increases for highly compensated employees resulting from a plan amendment that is made or becomes effective, whichever is later, within the last two years.

ductible amount is equal to the greater of: (1) the excess (if any) of the sum of the plan's funding target, the plan's target normal cost, and a cushion amount for a plan year, over the value of plan assets (as determined under the minimum funding rules[160]); and (2) the minimum required contribution for the plan year.[161]

However, in the case of a plan that is not in at-risk status, the first amount above is not less than the excess (if any) of the sum of the plan's funding target and target normal cost, determined as if the plan was in at-risk status, over the value of plan assets.

The cushion amount for a plan year is the sum of (1) 50 percent of the plan's funding target for the plan year; and (2) the amount by which the plan's funding target would increase if determined by taking into account increases in participants' compensation for future years or, if the plan does not base benefits attributable to past service on compensation, increases in benefits that are expected to occur in succeeding plans year, determined on the basis of average annual benefit increases over the previous six years.[162] For this purpose, the dollar limits on benefits and on compensation apply, but, in the case of a plan that is covered by the PBGC insurance program, increases in the compensation limit (under sec. 401(a)(17)) that are expected to occur in succeeding plan years may be taken into account.[163] The rules relating to projecting compensation for future years are intended solely to enable employers to reduce volatility in pension contributions; the rules are not intended to create any inference that employees have any protected interest with respect to such projected increases.

Overall deduction limit

Under the bill, in applying the overall deduction limit to contributions to one or more defined benefit pension plans and one or more defined contribution plans for years beginning after December 31, 2007, single-employer defined benefit pension plans that are covered by the PBGC insurance program are not taken into account. Thus, the deduction for contributions to a defined benefit pension plan or a defined contribution plan is not affected by the overall deduction limit merely because employees are covered by both plans if the defined benefit plan is covered by the PBGC insurance program (i.e., the separate deduction limits for contributions to defined contribution plans and defined benefit pension plans apply). In addition, in applying the overall deduction limit, the amount necessary to meet the minimum funding requirement with respect to a single-employer defined benefit pension plan that is not covered by the PBGC insurance program is treated as not less than the plan's funding shortfall (as determined under the minimum funding rules).

Multiemployer defined benefit pension plans

General deduction limit

Under the bill, for taxable years beginning after 2005, in the case of contributions to a multiemployer defined benefit pension plan, the maximum deductible amount is not less than the excess (if any) of (1) 140 percent of the plan's current liability, over (2) the value of plan assets.

Overall deduction limit

Under the bill, for taxable years beginning after December 31, 2005, in applying the overall deduction limit to contributions to one or more defined benefit pension plans and one or more defined contribution plans, multiemployer plans are not taken into account. Thus, the deduction for contributions to a defined benefit pension plan or a defined contribution plan is not affected by the overall deduction limit merely because employees are covered by both plans if either plan is a multiemployer plan (i.e., the separate deduction limits for contributions to defined contribution plans and defined benefit pension plans apply).

Effective Date

The effective dates of the provisions regarding deductions are described above under each provision.

[Law at ¶ 5045 and ¶ 5050. CCH Explanation at ¶ 705 and ¶ 710.]

[160] In determining the maximum deductible amount, the value of plan assets is not reduced by any pre-funding balance or funding standard account carryover balance.

[161] The bill retains the present-law rule, under which, in the case of a single-employer plan covered by the PBGC that terminates during the year, the maximum deductible amount is generally not less than the amount needed to make the plan assets sufficient to fund benefit liabilities as defined for purposes of the PBGC termination insurance program.

[162] In determining the cushion amount for a plan with 100 or fewer participants, a plan's funding target does not include the liability attributable to benefit increases for highly compensated employees resulting from a plan amendment that is made or becomes effective, whichever is later, within the last two years.

[163] Expected increases in the limitations on benefits under section 415, however, may not be taken into account.

[¶10,580] Act Sec. 803. Updating deduction rules for combination of plans

Joint Committee Taxation (J.C.T. REP. NO. JCX-38-06)

[Code Secs. 404(a)(7) and 4972]

Present Law

Employer contributions to qualified retirement plans are deductible subject to certain limits.[164] In general, the deduction limit depends on the kind of plan.[165]

If an employer sponsors one or more defined benefit pension plans and one or more defined contribution plans that cover at least one of the same employees, an overall deduction limit applies to the total contributions to all plans for a plan year. The overall deduction limit is the greater of (1) 25 percent of compensation, or (2) the amount necessary to meet the minimum funding requirements of the defined benefit plan for the year, but not less than the amount of the plan's unfunded current liability.

Under EGTRRA, elective deferrals are not subject to the limits on deductions and are not taken into account in applying the limits to other employer contributions. The combined deduction limit of 25 percent of compensation for defined benefit and defined contribution plans does not apply if the only amounts contributed to the defined contribution plan are elective deferrals.[166]

Subject to certain exceptions, an employer that makes nondeductible contributions to a plan is subject to an excise tax equal to 10 percent of the amount of the nondeductible contributions for the year. Certain contributions to a defined contribution plan that are nondeductible solely because of the overall deduction limit are disregarded in determining the amount of nondeductible contributions for purposes of the excise tax. Contributions that are disregarded are the greater of (1) the amount of contributions not in excess of six percent of the compensation of the employees covered by the defined contribution plan, or (2) the amount of matching contributions.

Explanation of Provision

Under the bill, the overall limit on employer deductions for contributions to combinations of defined benefit and defined contribution plans applies to contributions to one or more defined contribution plans only to the extent that such contributions exceed six percent of compensation otherwise paid or accrued during the taxable year to the beneficiaries under the plans. As under present law, for purposes of determining the excise tax on nondeductible contributions, matching contributions to a defined contribution plan that are nondeductible solely because of the overall deduction limit are disregarded.

Effective Date

The provision is effective for contributions for taxable years beginning after December 31, 2005.

[Law at ¶ 5045 and ¶ 5300. CCH Explanation at ¶ 715.]

[¶10,600] Act Sec. 811. Permanency of EGTRRA pension and IRA provisions

Joint Committee Taxation (J.C.T. REP. NO. JCX-38-06)

[Act Sec. 811]

Present Law

In general

The Economic Growth and Tax Relief Reconciliation Act of 2001 ("EGTRRA") made a number of changes to the Federal tax laws, including a variety of provisions relating to pensions and individual retirement arrangements ("IRAs"). However, in order to comply with reconciliation procedures under the Congressional Budget Act of 1974 (e.g., section 313 of the

[164] Code sec. 404.

[165] See the discussion under A., above, for a description of the deduction rules for defined benefit and defined contribution plans.

[166] Under the general EGTRRA sunset, this rule expires for plan years beginning after 2010.

Budget Act, under which a point of order may be lodged in the Senate), EGTRRA included a "sunset" provision, pursuant to which the provisions of EGTRRA expire at the end of 2010. Specifically, EGTRRA's provisions do not apply for taxable, plan, or limitation years beginning after December 31, 2010, or to estates of decedents dying after, or gifts or generation-skipping transfers made after, December 31, 2010. EGTRRA provides that, as of the effective date of the sunset, both the Internal Revenue Code and the Employee Retirement Income Security Act of 1974 ("ERISA") will be applied as though EGTRRA had never been enacted.

Certain provisions contained in EGTRRA expire before the general sunset date of 2010.[167]

List of affected provisions

Following is a list of the provisions affected by the general EGTRRA sunset.

Individual retirement arrangements ("IRAs")

- Increases in the IRA contribution limits, including the ability to make catch-up contributions (secs. 219, 408, and 408A of the Code and sec. 601 of EGTRRA); and
- Rules relating to deemed IRAs under employer plans (sec. 408(q) of the Code and sec. 602 of EGTRRA).

Expanding coverage

- Increases in the limits on contributions, benefits, and compensation under qualified retirement plans, tax-sheltered annuities, and eligible deferred compensation plans (secs. 401(a)(17), 402(g), 408(p), 414(v), 415, and 457 of the Code and sec. 611 of EGTRRA);
- Application of prohibited transaction rules to plan loans of S corporation owners, partners, and sole proprietors (sec. 4975 of the Code and sec. 612 of EGTRRA);
- Modification of the top-heavy rules (sec. 416 of the Code and sec. 613 of EGTRRA);
- Elective deferrals not taken into account for purposes of deduction limits (sec. 404 of the Code and sec. 614 of EGTRRA);
- Repeal of coordination requirements for deferred compensation plans of state and local governments and tax-exempt organizations (sec. 457 of the Code and sec. 615 of EGTRRA);
- Modifications to deduction limits (sec. 404 of the Code and sec. 616 of EGTRRA);
- Option to treat elective deferrals as after-tax Roth contributions (sec. 402A of the Code and sec. 617 of EGTRRA);
- Credit for pension plan start-up costs (sec. 45E of the Code and sec. 619 of EGTRRA); and
- Certain nonresident aliens excluded in applying minimum coverage requirements (secs. 410(b)(3) and 861(a)(3) of the Code).

Enhancing fairness

- Catch-up contributions for individuals age 50 and older (sec. 414 of the Code and sec. 631 of EGTRRA);
- Equitable treatment for contributions of employees to defined contribution plans (secs. 403(b), 415, and 457 of the Code and sec. 632 of EGTRRA);
- Faster vesting of employer matching contributions (sec. 411 of the Code and sec. 633 of EGTRRA);
- Modifications to minimum distribution rules (sec. 401(a)(9) of the Code and sec. 634 of EGTRRA);
- Clarification of tax treatment of division of section 457 plan benefits upon divorce (secs. 414(p) and 457 of the Code and sec. 635 of EGTRRA);
- Provisions relating to hardship withdrawals (secs. 401(k) and 402 of the Code and sec. 636 of EGTRRA); and
- Waiver of tax on nondeductible contributions for domestic and similar workers (sec. 4972(c)(6) of the Code and sec. 637 of EGTRRA).

Increasing portability

- Rollovers of retirement plan and IRA distributions (secs. 401, 402, 403(b), 408, 457, and 3405 of the Code and secs. 641-644 of EGTRRA);
- Treatment of forms of distribution (sec. 411(d)(6) of the Code and sec. 645 of EGTRRA);
- Rationalization of restrictions on distributions (secs. 401(k), 403(b), and 457 of the Code and sec. 646 of EGTRRA):
- Purchase of service credit under governmental pension plans (secs. 403(b) and 457 of the Code and sec. 647 of EGTRRA):

---

[167] The saver's credit (sec. 25B) expires at the end of 2006. Another provision of the bill makes the saver's credit permanent.

• Employers may disregard rollovers for purposes of cash-out rules (sec. 411(a)(11) of the Code and sec. 648 of EGTRRA); and

• Minimum distribution and inclusion requirements for section 457 plans (sec. 457 of the Code and sec. 649 of EGTRRA).

Strengthening pension security and enforcement

• Phase in repeal of 160 percent of current liability funding limit; maximum deduction rules (secs. 404(a)(1), 412(c)(7), and 4972(c) of the Code and secs. 651-652 of EGTRRA);

• Excise tax relief for sound pension funding (sec. 4972 of the Code and sec. 653 of EGTRRA);

• Modifications to section 415 limits for multiemployer plans (sec. 415 of the Code and sec. 654 of EGTRRA);

• Investment of employee contributions in 401(k) plans (sec. 655 of EGTRRA);

• Prohibited allocations of stock in an S corporation ESOP (secs. 409 and 4979A of the Code and sec. 656 of EGTRRA);

• Automatic rollovers of certain mandatory distributions (secs. 401(a)(31) and 402(f)(1) of the Code and sec. 657 of EGTRRA);

• Clarification of treatment of contributions to a multiemployer plan (sec. 446 of the Code and sec. 658 of EGTRRA); and

• Treatment of plan amendments reducing future benefit accruals (sec. 4980F of the Code and sec. 659 of EGTRRA).

Reducing regulatory burdens

• Modification of timing of plan valuations (sec. 412 of the Code and sec. 661 of EGTRRA);

• ESOP dividends may be reinvested without loss of dividend deduction (sec. 404 of the Code and sec. 662 of EGTRRA);

• Repeal transition rule relating to certain highly compensated employees (sec. 663 of EGTRRA);

• Treatment of employees of tax-exempt entities for purposes of nondiscrimination rules (secs. 410, 401(k), and 401(m) of the Code and sec. 664 of EGTRRA);

• Treatment of employer-provided retirement advice (sec. 132 of the Code and sec. 665 of EGTRRA); and

• Repeal of the multiple use test (sec. 401(m) of the Code and sec. 666 of EGTRRA).

Explanation of Provision

The provision repeals the sunset provision of EGTRRA as applied to the provisions relating to pensions and IRAs.

Effective Date

The provision is effective on the date of enactment.

[Law at ¶ 5055, ¶ 5255 and ¶ 7153. CCH Explanation at ¶ 1305.]

[¶ 10,610] Act Sec. 812. Saver's credit made permanent

Joint Committee Taxation (J.C.T. Rep. No. JCX-38-06)

[Code Sec. 25B]

Present Law

Present law provides a temporary nonrefundable tax credit for eligible taxpayers for qualified retirement savings contributions. The maximum annual contribution eligible for the credit is $2,000. The credit rate depends on the adjusted gross income ("AGI") of the taxpayer. Joint returns with AGI of $50,000 or less, head of household returns of $37,500 or less, and single returns of $25,000 or less are eligible for the credit. The AGI limits applicable to single taxpayers apply to married taxpayers filing separate returns. The credit is in addition to any deduction or exclusion that would otherwise apply with respect to the contribution. The credit offsets minimum tax liability as well as regular tax liability. The credit is available to individuals who are 18 or older, other than individuals who are full-time students or claimed as a dependent on another taxpayer's return.

The credit is available with respect to: (1) elective deferrals to a qualified cash or deferred arrangement (a "section 401(k) plan"), a tax-sheltered annuity (a "section 403(b)" annuity), an eligible deferred compensation arrangement of a State or local government (a "section 457 plan"), a SIMPLE, or a simplified employee pension ("SEP"); (2) contributions to a traditional or Roth IRA; and (3) voluntary after-tax employee contributions to a tax-sheltered annuity or qualified retirement plan.

The amount of any contribution eligible for the credit is reduced by distributions received by the taxpayer (or by the taxpayer's spouse if the taxpayer filed a joint return with the spouse) from any plan or IRA to which eligible contributions can be made during the taxable year for which the credit is claimed, the two taxable years prior to the year the credit is claimed, and during the period after the end of the taxable year for which the credit is claimed and prior to the due date for filing the taxpayer's return for the year. Distributions that are rolled over to another retirement plan do not affect the credit.

The credit rates based on AGI are provided in Table 1, below.

Table 1.—Credit Rates for Saver's Credit

Joint Filers	Heads of Households	All Other Filers	Credit Rate
$0 — $30,000	$0 — $22,500	$0 — $15,000	50 percent
$30,001 — $32,500	$22,501 — $24,375	$15,001 — $16,250	20 percent
$32,501 — $50,000	$24,376 — $37,500	$16,251 — $25,000	10 percent
Over $50,000	Over $37,500	Over $25,000	0 percent

The credit does not apply to taxable years beginning after December 31, 2006.

Explanation of Provision

The provision makes the saver's credit permanent.

The provision also provides that an individual may direct that the amount of any refund attributable to the saver's credit be directly deposited by the Federal government into an applicable retirement plan, meaning an IRA, qualified retirement plan, section 403(b) annuity, or governmental section 457 plan designated by the individual (if the plan or other arrangement agrees to accept such direct deposits). In the case of a joint return, each spouse is entitled to designate an applicable retirement plan with respect to payments attributable to such spouse. The provision does not change the rules relating to the tax treatment of contributions to such plans or other arrangements.

Effective Date

The extension of the saver's credit is effective on enactment. The provision relating to direct deposit of refunds relating to the saver's credit is effective for taxable years beginning after December 31, 2006. (In addition, another provision of bill, described below, provides for indexing of the income limits on the saver's credit.)

[Law at ¶ 5005. CCH Explanation at ¶ 1315.]

[¶10,620] Act Sec. 821. Purchase of permissive service credit

Joint Committee Taxation (J.C.T. Rep. No. JCX-38-06)

[Code Secs. 403(b)(13), 415(n)(3) and 457(e)(17)]

Present Law

In general

Present law imposes limits on contributions and benefits under qualified plans.[168] The limits on contributions and benefits under qualified plans are based on the type of plan. Under a defined benefit plan, the maximum annual benefit payable at retirement is generally the lesser of (1) a certain dollar amount ($175,000 for 2006) or (2) 100 percent of the participant's average compensation for his or her high three years.

A qualified retirement plan maintained by a State or local government employer may provide that a participant may make after-tax employee contributions in order to purchase permissive service credit, subject to certain limits.[169]

In the case of any repayment of contributions and earnings to a governmental plan with respect to an amount previously refunded upon a forfeiture of service credit under the plan (or another plan maintained by a State or local government employer within the same State), any such repayment is not taken into account for purposes of the section 415 limits on contributions and benefits. Also, service credit obtained as a result of such a repayment is not considered permissive service credit for purposes of the section 415 limits.

168 Sec. 415.

169 Sec. 415(n)(3).

Permissive service credit

Definition of permissive service credit

Permissive service credit means credit for a period of service recognized by the governmental plan which the participant has not received under the plan and which the employee receives only if the employee voluntarily contributes to the plan an amount (as determined by the plan) that does not exceed the amount necessary to fund the benefit attributable to the period of service and that is in addition to the regular employee contributions, if any, under the plan.

The IRS has ruled that credit is not permissive service credit where it is purchased to provide enhanced retirement benefits for a period of service already credited under the plan, as the enhanced benefit is treated as credit for service already received.[170]

Nonqualified service

Service credit is not permissive service credit if more than five years of permissive service credit is purchased for nonqualified service or if nonqualified service is taken into account for an employee who has less than five years of participation under the plan. Nonqualified service is service other than service (1) as a Federal, State or local government employee, (2) as an employee of an association representing Federal, State or local government employees, (3) as an employee of an educational institution which provides elementary or secondary education, as determined under State law, or (4) for military service. Service under (1), (2) and (3) is nonqualified service if it enables a participant to receive a retirement benefit for the same service under more than one plan.

Trustee-to-trustee transfers to purchase permissive service credit

Under EGTRRA, a participant is not required to include in gross income a direct trustee-to-trustee transfer to a governmental defined benefit plan from a section 403(b) annuity or a section 457 plan if the transferred amount is used (1) to purchase permissive service credit under the plan, or (2) to repay contributions and earnings with respect to an amount previously refunded under a forfeiture of service credit under the plan (or another plan maintained by a State or local government employer within the same State).[171]

Explanation of Provision

Permissive service credit

The provision modifies the definition of permissive service credit by providing that permissive service credit means service credit which relates to benefits to which the participant is not otherwise entitled under such governmental plan, rather than service credit which such participant has not received under the plan. Credit qualifies as permissive service credit if it is purchased to provide an increased benefit for a period of service already credited under the plan (e.g., if a lower level of benefit is converted to a higher benefit level otherwise offered under the same plan) as long as it relates to benefits to which the participant is not otherwise entitled.

The provision allows participants to purchase credit for periods regardless of whether service is performed, subject to the limits on nonqualified service.

Under the provision, service as an employee of an educational organization providing elementary or secondary education can be determined under the law of the jurisdiction in which the service was performed. Thus, for example, permissive service credit can be granted for time spent teaching outside of the United States without being considered nonqualified service credit.

Trustee-to-trustee transfers to purchase permissive service credit

The provision provides that the limits regarding nonqualified service are not applicable in determining whether a trustee-to-trustee transfer from a section 403(b) annuity or a section 457 plan to a governmental defined benefit plan is for the purchase of permissive service credit. Thus, failure of the transferee plan to satisfy the limits does not cause the transferred amounts to be included in the participant's income. As under present law, the transferee plan must satisfy the limits in providing permissive service credit as a result of the transfer.

The provision provides that trustee-to-trustee transfers under sections 457(e)(17) and 403(b)(13) may be made regardless of whether the transfer is made between plans maintained by the same employer. The provision also provides that amounts transferred from a section 403(b) annuity or a section 457 plan to a governmental defined benefit plan to purchase permis-

---

[170] Priv. Ltr. Rul. 200229051 (April 26, 2002).

[171] Secs. 403(b)(13) and 457(e)(17).

sive service credit are subject to the distribution rules applicable under the Internal Revenue Code to the defined benefit plan.

Effective Date

The provision is generally effective as if included in the amendments made by section 1526 of the Taxpayer Relief Act of 1997, except that the provision regarding trustee-to-trustee transfers is effective as if included in the amendments made by section 647 of the Economic Growth and Tax Relief Reconciliation Act of 2001.

[Law at ¶ 5095. CCH Explanation at ¶ 745.]

[¶ 10,630] Act Sec. 822. Rollover of after-tax amounts in annuity contracts

Joint Committee Taxation (J.C.T. Rep. No. JCX-38-06)

[Code Sec. 402(c)(2)]

Present Law

Employee after-tax contributions may be rolled over from a tax-qualified retirement plan into another tax-qualified retirement plan, if the plan to which the rollover is made is a defined contribution plan, the rollover is accomplished through a direct rollover, and the plan to which the rollover is made provides for separate accounting for such contributions (and earnings thereon). After-tax contributions can also be rolled over from a tax-sheltered annuity (a "section 403(b) annuity") to another tax-sheltered annuity if the rollover is a direct rollover, and the annuity to which the rollover is made provides for separate accounting for such contributions (and earnings thereon). After-tax contributions may also be rolled over to an IRA. If the rollover is to an IRA, the rollover need not be a direct rollover and the IRA owner has the responsibility to keep track of the amount of after-tax contributions.[172]

Explanation of Provision

The provision allows after-tax contributions to be rolled over from a qualified retirement plan to another qualified retirement plan (either a defined contribution or a defined benefit plan) or to a tax-sheltered annuity. As under present law, the rollover must be a direct rollover, and the plan to which the rollover is made must separately account for after-tax contributions (and earnings thereon).

Effective Date

The provision is effective for taxable years beginning after December 31, 2006.

[Law at ¶ 5035. CCH Explanation at ¶ 940.]

[¶ 10,640] Act Sec. 823. Application of minimum distribution rules to governmental plans

Joint Committee Taxation (J.C.T. Rep. No. JCX-38-06)

[Act Sec. 823]

Present Law

Minimum distribution rules apply to tax-favored retirement arrangements, including governmental plans. In general, under these rules, distribution of minimum benefits must begin no later than the required beginning date. Minimum distribution rules also apply to benefits payable with respect to a plan participant who has died. Failure to comply with the minimum distribution rules results in an excise tax imposed on the plan participant equal to 50 percent of the required minimum distribution not distributed for the year. The excise tax may be waived in certain cases.

In the case of distributions prior to the death of the plan participant, the minimum distribution rules are satisfied if either (1) the participant's entire interest in the plan is distributed by the required beginning date, or (2) the participant's interest in the plan is to be distributed (in accordance with regulations) beginning not later than the required beginning date, over a permissible period. The permissible periods are (1) the life of the participant, (2) the lives of the participant and a designated beneficiary, (3) the life

[172] Sec. 402(c)(2); IRS Notice 2002-3, 2002-2 I.R.B. 289.

expectancy of the participant, or (4) the joint life and last survivor expectancy of the participant and a designated beneficiary. In calculating minimum required distributions from account-type arrangements (e.g., a defined contribution plan or an individual retirement arrangement), life expectancies of the participant and the participant's spouse generally may be recomputed annually.

The required beginning date generally is April 1 of the calendar year following the later of (1) the calendar year in which the participant attains age 70½ or (2) the calendar year in which the participant retires.

The minimum distribution rules also apply to distributions to beneficiaries of deceased participants. In general, if the participant dies after minimum distributions have begun, the remaining interest must be distributed at least as rapidly as under the minimum distribution method being used as of the date of death. If the participant dies before minimum distributions have begun, then the entire remaining interest must generally be distributed within five years of the participant's death. The five-year rule does not apply if distributions begin within one year of the participant's death and are payable over the life of a designated beneficiary or over the life expectancy of a designated beneficiary. A surviving spouse beneficiary is not required to begin distributions until the date the deceased participant would have attained age 70½. In addition, if the surviving spouse makes a rollover from the plan into a plan or IRA of his or her own, the minimum distribution rules apply separately to the surviving spouse.

Explanation of Provision

The provision directs the Secretary of the Treasury to issue regulations under which a governmental plan is treated as complying with the minimum distribution requirements, for all years to which such requirements apply, if the plan complies with a reasonable, good faith interpretation of the statutory requirements. It is intended that the regulations apply for periods before the date of enactment.

Effective Date

The provision is effective on the date of enactment.

[Law at ¶ 7156. CCH Explanation at ¶ 930.]

[¶ 10,650] Act Sec. 824. Allow direct rollovers from retirement plans to Roth IRAs

Joint Committee Taxation (J.C.T. REP. NO. JCX-38-06)

[Code Sec. 408A(e)]

Present Law

IRAs in general

There are two general types of individual retirement arrangements ("IRAs"): traditional IRAs, to which both deductible and nondeductible contributions may be made, and Roth IRAs.

Traditional IRAs

An individual may make deductible contributions to an IRA up to the lesser of a dollar limit (generally $4,000 for 2006)[173] or the individual's compensation if neither the individual nor the individual's spouse is an active participant in an employer-sponsored retirement plan.[174] If the individual (or the individual's spouse) is an active participant in an employer-sponsored retirement plan, the deduction limit is phased out for taxpayers with adjusted gross income ("AGI") over certain levels for the taxable year. A different, higher, income phaseout applies in the case of an individual who is not an active participant in an employer sponsored plan but whose spouse is.

To the extent an individual cannot or does not make deductible contributions to an IRA or contributions to a Roth IRA, the individual may make nondeductible contributions to a traditional IRA.

Amounts held in a traditional IRA are includible in income when withdrawn (except to the extent the withdrawal is a return of nondeductible contributions). Includible amounts withdrawn prior to attainment of age 59½ are subject to an additional 10-percent early with-

---

[173] The dollar limit is scheduled to increase until it is $5,000 in 2008-2010. Individuals age 50 and older may make additional, catch-up contributions.

[174] In the case of a married couple, deductible IRA contributions of up to the dollar limit can be made for each spouse (including, for example, a homemaker who does not work outside the home), if the combined compensation of both spouses is at least equal to the contributed amount.

drawal tax, unless the withdrawal is due to death or disability, is made in the form of certain periodic payments, or is used for certain specified purposes.

Roth IRAs

Individuals with AGI below certain levels may make nondeductible contributions to a Roth IRA. The maximum annual contributions that can be made to all of an individuals IRAs (both traditional and Roth) cannot exceed the maximum deductible IRA contribution limit. The maximum annual contribution that can be made to a Roth IRA is phased out for taxpayers with income above certain levels.

Amounts held in a Roth IRA that are withdrawn as a qualified distribution are not includible in income, or subject to the additional 10-percent tax on early withdrawals. A qualified distribution is a distribution that (1) is made after the five-taxable year period beginning with the first taxable year for which the individual made a contribution to a Roth IRA, and (2) which is made after attainment of age 59½, on account of death or disability, or is made for first-time homebuyer expenses of up to $10,000.

Distributions from a Roth IRA that are not qualified distributions are includible in income to the extent attributable to earnings, and subject to the 10-percent early withdrawal tax (unless an exception applies). The same exceptions to the early withdrawal tax that apply to IRAs apply to Roth IRAs.

Rollover contributions

If certain requirements are satisfied, a participant in a tax-qualified retirement plan, a tax-sheltered annuity (sec. 403(b)), or a governmental section 457 plan may roll over distributions from the plan or annuity into a traditional IRA. Distributions from such plans may not be rolled over into a Roth IRA.

Taxpayers with modified AGI of $100,000 or less generally may roll over amounts in a traditional IRA into a Roth IRA. The amount rolled over is includible in income as if a withdrawal had been made, except that the 10-percent early withdrawal tax does not apply. Married taxpayers who file separate returns cannot roll over amounts in a traditional IRA into a Roth IRA. Amounts that have been distributed from a tax-qualified retirement plan, a tax-sheltered annuity, or a governmental section 457 plan may be rolled over into a traditional IRA, and then rolled over from the traditional IRA into a Roth IRA.

Explanation of Provision

The provision allows distributions from tax-qualified retirement plans, tax-sheltered annuities, and governmental 457 plans to be rolled over directly from such plan into a Roth IRA, subject to the present law rules that apply to rollovers from a traditional IRA into a Roth IRA. For example, a rollover from a tax-qualified retirement plan into a Roth IRA is includible in gross income (except to the extent it represents a return of after-tax contributions), and the 10-percent early distribution tax does not apply. Similarly, an individual with AGI of $100,000 or more could not roll over amounts from a tax-qualified retirement plan directly into a Roth IRA.

Effective Date

The provision is effective for distributions made after December 31, 2007.

[Law at ¶ 5060. CCH Explanation at ¶ 935.]

[¶ 10,660] Act Sec. 825. Eligibility for participation in eligible deferred compensation plans

Joint Committee Taxation (J.C.T. REP. NO. JCX-38-06)

[Code Sec. 457]

Present Law

A section 457 plan is an eligible deferred compensation plan of a State or local government or tax-exempt employer that meets certain requirements. In some cases, different rules apply under section 457 to governmental plans and plans of tax-exempt employers.

Amounts deferred under an eligible deferred compensation plan of a non-governmental tax-exempt organization are includible in gross income for the year in which amounts are paid or made available. Under present law, if the amount payable to a participant does not exceed $5,000, a plan may allow a distribution up to $5,000 without such amount being treated as made available if the distribution can be made only if no amount has been deferred under the plan by the participant during the two-year period ending on the date of the distribution and there has been no prior distribution under the plan. Prior to the Small Business Job Protection Act of 1996, under former section 457(e)(9), benefits were not treated as made available because a participant could elect to receive a lump sum payable after separation from service and within 60 days of the election if (1) the total amount payable under the plan did not exceed $3,500 and (2) no additional amounts could be deferred under the plan.

Explanation of Provision

Under the provision, an individual is not precluded from participating in an eligible deferred compensation plan by reason of having received a distribution under section 457(e)(9) as in effect before the Small Business Job Protection Act of 1996.

Effective Date

The provision is effective on the date of enactment.

[Law at ¶7159. CCH Explanation at ¶1075.]

[¶10,670] Act Sec. 826. Modifications of rules governing hardships and unforeseen financial emergencies

Joint Committee Taxation (J.C.T. Rep. No. JCX-38-06)

[Act Sec. 826]

Present Law

Distributions from a qualified cash or deferred arrangement (a "section 401(k) plan"), a tax-shelter annuity, section 457 plan, or nonqualified deferred compensation plan subject to section 409A may not be made prior to the occurrence of one or more specified events. In the case of a section 401(k) plan or tax-sheltered annuity, one event upon which distribution is permitted is the case of a hardship. Similarly, distributions from section 457 plans and nonqualified deferred compensation plans subject to section 409A may be made in the case of an unforeseeable emergency. Under regulations, a hardship or unforeseeable emergency includes a hardship or unforeseeable emergency of a participant's spouse or dependent.

Explanation of Provision

The provision directs the Secretary of the Treasury to revise the rules for determining whether a participant has had a hardship or unforeseeable emergency to provide that if an event would constitute a hardship or unforeseeable emergency under the plan if it occurred with respect to the participant's spouse or dependent, such event shall, to the extent permitted under the plan, constitute a hardship or unforeseeable emergency if it occurs with respect to a beneficiary under the plan. The provision requires that the revised rules be issued within 180 days after the date of enactment.

Effective Date

The provision is effective on the date of enactment.

[Law at ¶7162. CCH Explanation at ¶910.]

[¶10,680] Act Sec. 827. Treatment of distributions to individuals called to active duty for at least 179 days

Joint Committee Taxation (J.C.T. Rep. No. JCX-38-06)

[Code Sec. 72(t)]

Present Law

Under present law, a taxpayer who receives a distribution from a qualified retirement plan prior to age 59½, death, or disability generally is subject to a 10-percent early withdrawal tax on the amount includible in income, unless an exception to the tax applies. Among other exceptions, the early distribution tax does not apply to distributions made to an employee who separates from service after age 55, or to distributions that are part of a series of substantially equal periodic payments made for the life (or life expectancy) of the employee or the joint lives (or life expectancies) of the employee and his or her beneficiary.

Certain amounts held in a qualified cash or deferred arrangement (a "401(k) plan") or in a tax-sheltered annuity (a "403(b) annuity") may not be distributed before severance from employment, age 59½, death, disability, or financial hardship of the employee.

Explanation of Provision

Under the provision, the 10-percent early withdrawal tax does not apply to a qualified reservist distribution. A qualified reservist distribution is a distribution (1) from an IRA or attributable to elective deferrals under a 401(k) plan, 403(b) annuity, or certain similar arrangements, (2) made to an individual who (by reason of being a member of a reserve component as defined in section 101 of title 37 of the U.S. Code) was ordered or called to active duty for a period in excess of 179 days or for an indefinite period, and (3) that is made during the period beginning on the date of such order or call to duty and ending at the close of the active duty period. A 401(k) plan or 403(b) annuity does not violate the distribution restrictions applicable to such plans by reason of making a qualified reservist distribution.

An individual who receives a qualified reservist distribution may, at any time during the two-year period beginning on the day after the end of the active duty period, make one or more contributions to an IRA of such individual in an aggregate amount not to exceed the amount of such distribution. The dollar limitations otherwise applicable to contributions to IRAs do not apply to any contribution made pursuant to the provision. No deduction is allowed for any contribution made under the provision.

This provision applies to individuals ordered or called to active duty after September 11, 2001, and before December 31, 2007. The two-year period for making recontributions of qualified reservist distributions does not end before the date that is two years after the date of enactment.

Effective Date

The provision applies to distributions after September 11, 2001. If refund or credit of any overpayment of tax resulting from the provision would be prevented at any time before the close of the one-year period beginning on the date of the enactment by the operation of any law or rule of law (including res judicata), such refund or credit may nevertheless be made or allowed if claim therefor is filed before the close of such period.

[Law at ¶ 5010, ¶ 5030 and ¶ 5040. CCH Explanation at ¶ 917.]

[¶ 10,690] Act Sec. 828. Inapplicability of 10-percent additional tax on early distributions of pension plans of public safety employees

Joint Committee Taxation (J.C.T. REP. NO. JCX-38-06)

[Code Sec. 72(t)]

Present Law

Under present law, a taxpayer who receives a distribution from a qualified retirement plan prior to age 59½, death, or disability generally is subject to a 10-percent early withdrawal tax on the amount includible in income, unless an exception to the tax applies. Among other exceptions, the early distribution tax does not apply to distributions made to an employee who separates from service after age 55, or to distributions that are part of a series of substantially equal periodic payments made for the life (or life expectancy) of the employee or the joint lives (or life expectancies) of the employee and his or her beneficiary.

Explanation of Provision

Under the provision, the 10-percent early withdrawal tax does not apply to distributions from a governmental defined benefit pension plan to a qualified public safety employee who separates from service after age 50. A qualified public safety employee is an employee of a State or political subdivision of a State if the employee provides police protection, firefighting services, or emergency medical services for any area within the jurisdiction of such State or political subdivision.

Effective Date

The provision is effective for distributions made after the date of enactment.

[Law at ¶ 5010. CCH Explanation at ¶ 915.]

[¶10,700] Act Sec. 829. Rollovers by nonspouse beneficiaries

Joint Committee Taxation (J.C.T. REP. NO. JCX-38-06)

[Code Sec. 402]

Present Law

Tax-free rollovers

Under present law, a distribution from a qualified retirement plan, a tax-sheltered annuity ("section 403(b) annuity"), an eligible deferred compensation plan of a State or local government employer (a "governmental section 457 plan"), or an individual retirement arrangement (an "IRA") generally is included in income for the year distributed. However, eligible rollover distributions may be rolled over tax free within 60 days to another plan, annuity, or IRA.[175]

In general, an eligible rollover distribution includes any distribution to the plan participant or IRA owner other than certain periodic distributions, minimum required distributions, and distributions made on account of hardship.[176] Distributions to a participant from a qualified retirement plan, a tax-sheltered annuity, or a governmental section 457 plan generally can be rolled over to any of such plans or an IRA.[177] Similarly, distributions from an IRA to the IRA owner generally are permitted to be rolled over into a qualified retirement plan, a tax-sheltered annuity, a governmental section 457 plan, or another IRA.

Similar rollovers are permitted in the case of a distribution to the surviving spouse of the plan participant or IRA owner, but not to other persons.

If an individual inherits an IRA from the individual's deceased spouse, the IRA may be treated as the IRA of the surviving spouse. This treatment does not apply to IRAs inherited from someone other than the deceased spouse. In such cases, the IRA is not treated as the IRA of the beneficiary. Thus, for example, the beneficiary may not make contributions to the IRA and cannot roll over any amounts out of the inherited IRA. Like the original IRA owner, no amount is generally included in income until distributions are made from the IRA. Distributions from the inherited IRA must be made under the rules that apply to distributions to beneficiaries, as described below.

Minimum distribution rules

Minimum distribution rules apply to tax-favored retirement arrangements. In the case of distributions prior to the death of the participant, distributions generally must begin by the April 1 of the calendar year following the later of the calendar year in which the participant (1) attains age 70½ or (2) retires.[178] The minimum distribution rules also apply to distributions following the death of the participant. If minimum distributions have begun prior to the participant's death, the remaining interest generally must be distributed at least as rapidly as under the minimum distribution method being used prior to the date of death. If the participant dies before minimum distributions have begun, then either (1) the entire remaining interest must be distributed within five years of the death, or (2) distributions must begin within one year of the death over the life (or life expectancy) of the designated beneficiary. A beneficiary who is the surviving spouse of the participant is not required to begin distributions until the date the deceased participant would have attained age 70½. Alternatively, if the surviving spouse makes a rollover from the plan into a plan or IRA of his or her own, minimum distributions generally would not need to begin until the surviving spouse attains age 70½.

Explanation of Provision

The provision provides that benefits of a beneficiary other than a surviving spouse may be transferred directly to an IRA. The IRA is treated as an inherited IRA of the nonspouse beneficiary. Thus, for example, distributions from the inherited IRA are subject to the distribution rules applicable to beneficiaries. The provision applies to amounts payable to a beneficiary under a qualified retirement plan,

175 The IRS has the authority to waive the 60-day requirement if failure to waive the requirement would be against equity or good conscience, including cases of casualty, disaster, or other events beyond the reasonable control of the individual. Sec. 402(c)(3)(B).

176 Sec. 402(c)(4). Certain other distributions also are not eligible rollover distributions, e.g., corrective distributions of elective deferrals in excess of the elective deferral limits and loans that are treated as deemed distributions.

177 Some restrictions or special rules may apply to certain distributions. For example, after-tax amounts distributed from a plan can be rolled over only to a plan of the same type or to an IRA.

178 In the case of five-percent owners and distributions from an IRA, distributions must begin by the April 1 of the calendar year following the year in which the individual attains age 70½.

governmental section 457 plan, or a tax-sheltered annuity. To the extent provided by the Secretary, the provision applies to benefits payable to a trust maintained for a designated beneficiary to the same extent it applies to the beneficiary.

Effective Date

The provision is effective for distributions after December 31, 2006.

[Law at ¶ 5035, ¶ 5040 and ¶ 5140. CCH Explanation at ¶ 945.]

[¶ 10,710] Act Sec. 830. Direct deposit of tax refunds in an IRA

Joint Committee Taxation (J.C.T. Rep. No. JCX-38-06)

[Act Sec. 830]

Present Law

Under current IRS procedures, a taxpayer may direct that his or her tax refund be deposited into a checking or savings account with a bank or other financial institution (such as a mutual fund, brokerage firm, or credit union) rather than having the refund sent to the taxpayer in the form of a check.

Explanation of Provision

The Secretary is directed to develop forms under which all or a portion of a taxpayer's refund may be deposited in an IRA of the taxpayer (or the spouse of the taxpayer in the case of a joint return). The provision does not modify the rules relating to IRAs, including the rules relating to timing and deductibility of contributions.

Effective Date

The form required by the provision is to be available for taxable years beginning after December 31, 2006.

[Law at ¶ 7165. CCH Explanation at ¶ 725.]

[¶ 10,720] Act Sec. 831. Additional IRA contributions for certain employees

Joint Committee Taxation (J.C.T. Rep. No. JCX-38-06)

[Code Secs. 25B and 219]

Present Law

Under present law, favored tax treatment applies to qualified retirement plans maintained by employers and to individual retirement arrangements ("IRAs").

Qualified defined contribution plans may permit both employees and employers to make contributions to the plan. Under a qualified cash or deferred arrangement (commonly referred to as a "section 401(k) plan"), employees may elect to make pretax contributions to a plan, referred to as elective deferrals. Employees may also be permitted to make after-tax contributions to a plan. In addition, a plan may provide for employer nonelective contributions or matching contributions. Nonelective contributions are employer contributions that are made without regard to whether the employee makes elective deferrals or after-tax contributions. Matching contributions are employer contributions that are made only if the employee makes elective deferrals or after-tax contributions. Matching contributions are sometimes made in the form of employer stock.

Under present law, an individual may generally make contributions to an IRA for a taxable year up to the lesser of a certain dollar amount or the individual's compensation. The maximum annual dollar limit on IRA contributions to IRAs is $4,000 for 2005-2007 and $5,000 for 2008, with indexing thereafter. Individuals who have attained age 50 may make additional "catch-up" contributions to an IRA for a taxable year of up to $500 for 2005 and $1,000 for 2006 and thereafter.[179]

[179] These IRA limits were enacted as part of the Economic Growth and Tax Relief Reconciliation Act of 2001 ("EGTRRA"), Pub. L. No. 107-16. The provisions of EGTRRA

Present law provides a temporary nonrefundable tax credit for eligible taxpayers for qualified retirement savings contributions ("saver's" credit). The maximum annual contribution eligible for the credit is $2,000. The credit rate depends on the adjusted gross income ("AGI") of the taxpayer. Taxpayers filing joint returns with AGI of $50,000 or less, head of household returns of $37,500 or less, and single returns of $25,000 or less are eligible for the credit. The AGI limits applicable to single taxpayers apply to married taxpayers filing separate returns. The credit is in addition to any deduction or exclusion that would otherwise apply with respect to the contribution. The credit offsets minimum tax liability as well as regular tax liability. The credit is available to individuals who are 18 or over, other than individuals who are full-time students or claimed as a dependent on another taxpayer's return. The credit is available with respect to contributions to various types of retirement savings arrangements, including contributions to a traditional or Roth IRA. The saver's credit does not apply to taxable years beginning after December 31, 2006.

Explanation of Provision

Under the provision, an applicable individual may elect to make additional IRA contributions of up to $3,000 per year for 2006-2009. An applicable individual must have been a participant in a section 401(k) plan under which the employer matched at least 50 percent of the employee's contributions to the plan with stock of the employer. In addition, in a taxable year preceding the taxable year of an additional contribution: (1) the employer (or any controlling corporation of the employer) must have been a debtor in a bankruptcy case, and (2) the employer or any other person must have been subject to an indictment or conviction resulting from business transactions related to the bankruptcy. The individual must also have been a participant in the section 401(k) plan on the date six months before the bankruptcy case was filed. An applicable individual who elects to make these additional IRA contributions is not permitted to make IRA catch-up contributions that apply to individuals age 50 and older.

Effective Date

The provision is effective for taxable years beginning after December 31, 2006, and before January 1, 2010.

[Law at ¶ 5025. CCH Explanation at ¶ 730.]

[¶ 10,730] Act Sec. 832. Special rule for computing high-three average compensation for benefit limitation purposes

Joint Committee Taxation (J.C.T. Rep. No. JCX-38-06)

[Code Sec. 415(b)(3)]

Present Law

Annual benefits payable to a participant under a defined benefit pension plan generally may not exceed the lesser of (1) 100 percent of average compensation for the participant's high three years, or (2) $175,000 (for 2006). The dollar limit is reduced proportionately for individuals with less than 10 years of participation in the plan. The compensation limit is reduced proportionately for individuals with less than 10 years of service.

For purposes of determining average compensation for a participant's high three years, the high three years are the period of consecutive calendar years (not more than three) during which the participant was both an active participant in the plan and had the greatest aggregate compensation from the employer.

Explanation of Provision

Under the bill, for purposes of determining average compensation for a participant's high three years, the high three years are the period of consecutive calendar years (not more than three) during which the participant had the greatest aggregate compensation from the employer.

Effective Date

The provision is effective for years beginning after December 31, 2005.

[Law at ¶ 5095. CCH Explanation at ¶ 735.]

(Footnote Continued)

generally do not apply for years beginning after December 31, 2010.

[¶10,740] Act Sec. 833. Inflation indexing of gross income limitations on certain retirement savings incentives

Joint Committee Taxation (J.C.T. Rep. No. JCX-38-06)

[Code Secs. 25A and 219]

Present Law

Saver's credit

Present law provides a temporary nonrefundable tax credit for eligible taxpayers for qualified retirement savings contributions. The maximum annual contribution eligible for the credit is $2,000. The credit rate depends on the adjusted gross income ("AGI") of the taxpayer. Joint returns with AGI of $50,000 or less, head of household returns of $37,500 or less, and single returns of $25,000 or less are eligible for the credit. The AGI limits applicable to single taxpayers apply to married taxpayers filing separate returns. The credit is in addition to any deduction or exclusion that would otherwise apply with respect to the contribution. The credit offsets minimum tax liability as well as regular tax liability. The credit is available to individuals who are 18 or older, other than individuals who are full-time students or claimed as a dependent on another taxpayer's return.

Under present law, the saver's credit expires after 2006.

Individual retirement arrangements

In general

There are two general types of individual retirement arrangements ("IRAs") under present law: traditional IRAs,[180] to which both deductible and nondeductible contributions may be made,[181] and Roth IRAs.[182]

The maximum annual deductible and nondeductible contributions that can be made to a traditional IRA and the maximum contribution that can be made to a Roth IRA by or on behalf of an individual varies depending on the particular circumstances, including the individual's income. However, the contribution limits for IRAs are coordinated so that the maximum annual contribution that can be made to all of an individual's IRAs is the lesser of a certain dollar amount ($4,000 for 2006) or the individual's compensation. In the case of a married couple, contributions can be made up to the dollar limit for each spouse if the combined compensation of the spouses is at least equal to the contributed amount. An individual who has attained age 50 before the end of the taxable year may also make catch-up contributions to an IRA. For this purpose, the dollar limit is increased by a certain dollar amount ($1,000 for 2006).[183]

Traditional IRAs

An individual may make deductible contributions to a traditional IRA up to the IRA contribution limit if neither the individual nor the individual's spouse is an active participant in an employer-sponsored retirement plan. If an individual (or the individual's spouse) is an active participant in an employer-sponsored retirement plan, the deduction is phased out for taxpayers with adjusted gross income over certain levels for the taxable year. The adjusted gross income phase-out ranges are: (1) for single taxpayers, $50,000 to $60,000; (2) for married taxpayers filing joint returns, $75,000 to $85,000 for 2006 and $80,000 to $100,000 for years after 2006; and (3) for married taxpayers filing separate returns, $0 to $10,000. If an individual is not an active participant in an employer-sponsored retirement plan, but the individual's spouse is, the deduction is phased out for taxpayers with adjusted gross income between $150,000 and $160,000.

To the extent an individual cannot or does not make deductible contributions to an IRA or contributions to a Roth IRA, the individual may make nondeductible contributions to a traditional IRA, subject to the same limits as deductible contributions. An individual who has attained age 50 before the end of the taxable year may also make nondeductible catch-up contributions to an IRA.

Amounts held in a traditional IRA are includible in income when withdrawn, except to the extent the withdrawal is a return of nonde-

[180] Sec. 408.

[181] Sec. 219.

[182] Sec. 408A.

[183] Under the Economic Growth and Tax Relief Reconciliation Act of 2001 ("EGTRRA"), the dollar limit on IRA contributions increases to $5,000 in 2008, with indexing for inflation thereafter. The provisions of EGTRRA generally do not apply for years beginning after December 31, 2010. As a result, the dollar limit on annual IRA contributions is $2,000 for years after 2010, and catch-ups contributions are not permitted.

ductible contributions. Withdrawals from an IRA before age 70½, death, or disability are subject to an additional 10-percent tax unless an exception applies.[184]

Roth IRAs

Individuals with adjusted gross income below certain levels may make nondeductible contributions to a Roth IRA, subject to the overall limit on IRA contributions described above. The maximum annual contribution that can be made to a Roth IRA is phased out for taxpayers with adjusted gross income over certain levels for the taxable year. The adjusted gross income phase-out ranges are: (1) for single taxpayers, $95,000 to $110,000; (2) for married taxpayers filing joint returns, $150,000 to $160,000; and (3) for married taxpayers filing separate returns, $0 to $10,000.

Taxpayers generally may convert a traditional IRA into a Roth IRA, except for married taxpayers filing separate returns. The amount converted is includible in income as if a withdrawal had been made, except that the 10-percent early withdrawal tax does not apply.

Amounts held in a Roth IRA that are withdrawn as a qualified distribution are not includible in income, or subject to the additional 10-percent tax on early withdrawals. A qualified distribution is a distribution that (1) is made after the five-taxable year period beginning with the first taxable year for which the individual made a contribution to a Roth IRA, and (2) is made after attainment of age 59½, on account of death or disability, or is made for first-time homebuyer expenses of up to $10,000.

Distributions from a Roth IRA that are not qualified distributions are includible in income to the extent attributable to earnings. The amount includible in income is also subject to the 10-percent early withdrawal tax described above.

Explanation of Provision

The bill indexes the income limits applicable to the saver's credit beginning in 2007. (Another provision of the bill, described above, permanently extends the saver's credit.) Indexed amounts are rounded to the nearest multiple of $500. Under the indexed income limits, as under present law, the income limits for single taxpayers is one-half that for married taxpayers filing a joint return and the limits for heads of household are three-fourths that for married taxpayers filing a joint return.

The bill also indexes the income limits for IRA contributions beginning in 2007. The indexing applies to the income limits for deductible contributions for active participants in an employer-sponsored plan,[185] the income limits for deductible contributions if the individual is not an active participant but the individual's spouse is, and the income limits for Roth IRA contributions. Indexed amounts are rounded to the nearest multiple of $1,000. The provision does not affect the phase-out ranges under present law. Thus, for example, in the case of an active participant in an employer-sponsored plan, the phase-out range is $20,000 in the case of a married taxpayer filing a joint return and $10,000 in the case of an individual taxpayer.

Effective Date

The provision is effective for taxable years beginning after December 31, 2006.

[Law at ¶ 5005, ¶ 5025 and ¶ 5060. CCH Explanation at ¶ 1320.]

---

[184] Sec. 72(t).

[185] Under the bill, for 2007, the lower end of the income phase out for active participants filing a joint return is $80,000 as adjusted to reflect inflation.

[¶10,750] Act Sec. 841. Ability to use excess pension assets for future retiree health benefits and collectively bargained retiree health benefits

Joint Committee Taxation (J.C.T. REP. NO. JCX-38-06)

[Code Sec. 420]

Present Law

Transfer of pension assets

Defined benefit plan assets generally may not revert to an employer prior to termination of the plan and satisfaction of all plan liabilities. In addition, a reversion may occur only if the plan so provides. A reversion prior to plan termination may constitute a prohibited transaction and may result in plan disqualification. Any assets that revert to the employer upon plan termination are includible in the gross income of the employer and subject to an excise tax. The excise tax rate is 20 percent if the employer maintains a replacement plan or makes certain benefit increases in connection with the termination; if not, the excise tax rate is 50 percent. Upon plan termination, the accrued benefits of all plan participants are required to be 100-percent vested.

A pension plan may provide medical benefits to retired employees through a separate account that is part of such plan ("retiree medical accounts"). A qualified transfer of excess assets of a defined benefit plan to such a separate account within the plan may be made in order to fund retiree health benefits.[186] A qualified transfer does not result in plan disqualification, is not a prohibited transaction, and is not treated as a reversion. Thus, transferred assets are not includible in the gross income of the employer and are not subject to the excise tax on reversions. No more than one qualified transfer may be made in any taxable year. A qualified transfer may not be made from a multiemployer plan. No qualified transfer may be made after December 31, 2013.

Excess assets generally means the excess, if any, of the value of the plan's assets[187] over the greater of (1) the accrued liability under the plan (including normal cost) or (2) 125 percent of the plan's current liability.[188] In addition, excess assets transferred in a qualified transfer may not exceed the amount reasonably estimated to be the amount that the employer will pay out of such account during the taxable year of the transfer for qualified current retiree health liabilities. No deduction is allowed to the employer for (1) a qualified transfer or (2) the payment of qualified current retiree health liabilities out of transferred funds (and any income thereon). In addition, no deduction is allowed for amounts paid other than from transferred funds for qualified current retiree health liabilities to the extent such amounts are not greater than the excess of (1) the amount transferred (and any income thereon), over (2) qualified current retiree health liabilities paid out of transferred assets (and any income thereon). An employer may not contribute any amount to a health benefits account or welfare benefit fund with respect to qualified current retiree health liabilities for which transferred assets are required to be used.

Transferred assets (and any income thereon) must be used to pay qualified current retiree health liabilities for the taxable year of the transfer. Transferred amounts generally must benefit pension plan participants, other than key employees, who are entitled upon retirement to receive retiree medical benefits through the separate account. Retiree health benefits of key employees may not be paid out of transferred assets.

Amounts not used to pay qualified current retiree health liabilities for the taxable year of the transfer are to be returned to the general assets of the plan. These amounts are not includible in the gross income of the employer, but are treated as an employer reversion and are subject to a 20-percent excise tax.

In order for the transfer to be qualified, accrued retirement benefits under the pension plan generally must be 100-percent vested as if the plan terminated immediately before the transfer (or in the case of a participant who separated in

---

[186] Sec. 420.

[187] The value of plan assets for this purpose is the lesser of fair market value or actuarial value.

[188] In the case of plan years beginning before January 1, 2004, excess assets generally means the excess, if any, of the value of the plan's assets over the greater of (1) the lesser of (a) the accrued liability under the plan (including normal cost) or (b) 170 percent of the plan's current liability (for 2003), or (2) 125 percent of the plan's current liability. The current liability full funding limit was repealed for years beginning after 2003. Under the general sunset provision of EGTRRA, the limit is reinstated for years after 2010.

the one-year period ending on the date of the transfer, immediately before the separation).

In order to a transfer to be qualified, the employer generally must maintain retiree health benefits at the same level for the taxable year of the transfer and the following four years.

In addition, ERISA provides that, at least 60 days before the date of a qualified transfer, the employer must notify the Secretary of Labor, the Secretary of the Treasury, employee representatives, and the plan administrator of the transfer, and the plan administrator must notify each plan participant and beneficiary of the transfer.[189]

Deductions for contributions

Deductions for contributions to qualified retirement plans are subject to certain limits. Deductions for contributions to funded welfare benefit plans are generally also subject to limits, including limits on the amount that may be contributed to an account to fund the expected cost of retiree medical benefits for future years. The limit on the amount that may be contributed to an account to fund the expected cost of retiree medical benefits for future years does not apply to a separate fund established under a collective bargaining agreement.

Explanation of Provision

In general

If certain requirements are satisfied, the bill permits transfers of excess pension assets under a single-employer plan to retiree medical accounts to fund the expected cost of retiree medical benefits for the current and future years (a "qualified future transfer") and also allows such transfers in the case of benefits provided under a collective bargaining agreement (a "collectively bargained transfer"). Transfers must be made for at least a two-year period. An employer can elect to make a qualified future transfer or a collectively bargained transfer rather than a qualified transfer. A qualified future transfer or collectively bargained transfer must meet the requirements applicable to qualified transfers, except that the provision modifies the rules relating to (1) the determination of excess pension assets; (2) the limitation on the amount transferred; and (3) the minimum cost requirement. Additional requirements apply in the case of collectively bargained transfer.

The general sunset applicable to qualified transfer applies (i.e., transfers can be made only before January 1, 2014).

Rule applicable to qualified future transfers and collectively bargained transfers

Qualified future transfers and collectively bargained transfers can be made to the extent that plan assets exceed the greater of (1) accrued liability, or (2) 120 percent of current liability.[190] The provision requires that, during the transfer period, the plan's funded status must be maintained at the minimum level required to make transfers. If the minimum level is not maintained, the employer must make contributions to the plan to meet the minimum level or an amount required to meet the minimum level must be transferred from the health benefits account. The transfer period is the period not to exceed a total of ten consecutive taxable years beginning with the taxable year of the transfer. As previously discussed, the period must be not less than two consecutive years.

A limit applies on the amount that can be transferred. In the case of a qualified future transfer, the amount of excess pension assets that may be transferred is limited to the sum of (1) the amount that is reasonably estimated to be the amount the employer will pay out of the account during the taxable year of the transfer for current retiree health liabilities, and (2) the sum of the qualified current retiree health liabilities which the plan reasonably estimates, in accordance with guidance issued by the Secretary, will be incurred for each additional year in the transfer period. The amount that can be transferred under a collectively bargained transfer cannot exceed the amount which is reasonably estimated, in accordance with the provisions of the collective bargaining agreement and generally accepted accounting principles, to be the amount the employer maintaining the plan will pay out of such account during the collectively bargained cost maintenance period for collectively bargained retiree health liabilities.

The provision also modifies the minimum cost requirement which requires retiree medical benefits to be maintained at a certain level. In the case of a qualified future transfer, the minimum cost requirement will be satisfied if, during the

---

[189] ERISA sec. 101(e). ERISA also provides that a qualified transfer is not a prohibited transaction under ERISA or a prohibited reversion.

[190] The single-employer plan funding concepts are updated after 2007 to reflect the changes to the single-employer plan funding rules under the bill.

transfer period and the four subsequent years, the annual average amount of employer costs is not less than applicable employer cost determined with respect to the transfer. An employer may elect to meet this minimum cost requirement by meeting the requirements as in effect before the amendments made by section 535 of the Tax Relief Extension Act of 1999 for each year during the transfer period and the four subsequent years. In the case of a collectively bargained transfer, the minimum cost requirements is satisfied if each collectively bargained group health plan under which collectively bargained health benefits are provided provides that the collectively bargained employer cost for each table year during the collectively bargained cost maintenance period is not less than the amount specified by the collective bargaining agreement. The collectively bargained employer cost is the average cost per covered individual of providing collectively bargained retiree health benefits as determined in accordance with the applicable collective bargaining agreement. Thus, retiree medical benefits must be provided at the level determined under the collective bargaining agreement for the shorter of (1) the remaining lifetime of each covered retiree (and any covered spouse and dependent), or (2) the period of coverage provided under the collectively bargained health plan for such covered retiree (and any covered spouse and dependent).

Additional requirements for collectively bargained transfers

As previously discussed, the bill imposes certain additional requirements in the case of a collectively bargained transfer. Collectively bargained transfers can be made only if (1) for the employer's taxable year ending in 2005, medical benefits are provided to retirees (and spouses and dependents) under all the employer's benefit plans, and (2) the aggregate cost of benefits for such year is at least five percent of the employer's gross receipts. The provision also applies to successors of such employers. Before a collectively bargained transfer, the employer must designate in writing to each employee organization that is a party to the collective bargaining agreement that the transfer is a collectively bargained transfer.

Collectively bargained retiree health liabilities means the present value, as of the beginning of a taxable year and determined in accordance with the applicable collective bargaining agreement, of all collectively bargained health benefits (including administrative expenses) for such taxable year and all subsequent taxable years during the collectively bargained cost maintenance period (with the exclusion of certain key employees) reduced by the value of assets in all health benefits accounts or welfare benefit funds set aside to pay for the collectively bargained retiree health liabilities. Collectively bargained health benefits are health benefits or coverage provided to retired employees who, immediately before the collectively bargained transfer, are entitled to receive such benefits upon retirement and who are entitled to pension benefits under the plan (and their spouses and dependents). If specified by the provisions of the collective bargaining agreement, collectively bargained health benefits also include active employees who, following their retirement, are entitled to receive such benefits and who are entitled to pension benefits under the plan (and their spouse and dependents).

Assets transferred in a collectively bargained transfer can be used to pay collectively bargained retiree health liabilities (other than liabilities of certain key employees not taken into account) for the taxable year of the transfer and for any subsequent taxable year during the collectively bargained cost maintenance period. The collectively bargained cost maintenance period (with respect to a retiree) is the shorter of (1) the remaining lifetime of the covered retiree (and any covered spouse and dependents) or (2) the period of coverage provided by the collectively bargained health plan with respect to such covered retiree (and any covered spouse and dependents).

The limit on deductions in the case of certain amounts paid for qualified current retiree health liabilities other than from the health benefits account does not apply in the case of a collectively bargained transfer.

An employer may contribute additional amounts to a health benefits account or welfare benefit fund with respect to collectively bargained health liabilities for which transferred assets are required to be used. The deductibility of such contributions are subject to the limits that otherwise apply to a welfare benefit fund under a collective bargaining agreements without regard to whether such contributions are made to a health benefits account or a welfare benefit fund and without regard to the limits on deductions for contributions to qualified retirement plans (under Code section 404). The Secretary of the Treasury is directed to provide rules to prevent duplicate deductions for the same contributions or for duplicate contributions to fund the same benefits.

Effective Date

The provision is effective for transfers after the date of enactment.

[Law at ¶ 5115. CCH Explanation at ¶ 805.]

[¶10,760] Act Sec. 842. Transfer of excess pension assets to multiemployer health plans

Joint Committee Taxation (J.C.T. Rep. No. JCX-38-06)

[Code Sec. 420]

Present Law

Defined benefit plan assets generally may not revert to an employer prior to termination of the plan and satisfaction of all plan liabilities. In addition, a reversion may occur only if the plan so provides. A reversion prior to plan termination may constitute a prohibited transaction and may result in plan disqualification. Any assets that revert to the employer upon plan termination are includible in the gross income of the employer and subject to an excise tax. The excise tax rate is 20 percent if the employer maintains a replacement plan or makes certain benefit increases in connection with the termination; if not, the excise tax rate is 50 percent. Upon plan termination, the accrued benefits of all plan participants are required to be 100-percent vested.

A pension plan may provide medical benefits to retired employees through a separate account that is part of such plan. A qualified transfer of excess assets of a defined benefit plan to such a separate account within the plan may be made in order to fund retiree health benefits.[191] A qualified transfer does not result in plan disqualification, is not a prohibited transaction, and is not treated as a reversion. Thus, transferred assets are not includible in the gross income of the employer and are not subject to the excise tax on reversions. No more than one qualified transfer may be made in any taxable year. A qualified transfer may not be made from a multiemployer plan. No qualified transfer may be made after December 31, 2013.

Excess assets generally means the excess, if any, of the value of the plan's assets[192] over the greater of (1) the accrued liability under the plan (including normal cost) or (2) 125 percent of the plan's current liability.[193] In addition, excess assets transferred in a qualified transfer may not exceed the amount reasonably estimated to be the amount that the employer will pay out of such account during the taxable year of the transfer for qualified current retiree health liabilities. No deduction is allowed to the employer for (1) a qualified transfer or (2) the payment of qualified current retiree health liabilities out of transferred funds (and any income thereon).

Transferred assets (and any income thereon) must be used to pay qualified current retiree health liabilities for the taxable year of the transfer. Transferred amounts generally must benefit pension plan participants, other than key employees, who are entitled upon retirement to receive retiree medical benefits through the separate account. Retiree health benefits of key employees may not be paid out of transferred assets.

Amounts not used to pay qualified current retiree health liabilities for the taxable year of the transfer are to be returned to the general assets of the plan. These amounts are not includible in the gross income of the employer, but are treated as an employer reversion and are subject to a 20-percent excise tax.

In order for the transfer to be qualified, accrued retirement benefits under the pension plan generally must be 100-percent vested as if the plan terminated immediately before the transfer (or in the case of a participant who separated in the one-year period ending on the date of the transfer, immediately before the separation).

In order to a transfer to be qualified, the employer generally must maintain retiree health benefits at the same level for the taxable year of the transfer and the following four years.

In addition, ERISA provides that, at least 60 days before the date of a qualified transfer, the employer must notify the Secretary of Labor, the Secretary of the Treasury, employee representatives, and the plan administrator of the transfer,

---

[191] Sec. 420.

[192] The value of plan assets for this purpose is the lesser of fair market value or actuarial value.

[193] In the case of plan years beginning before January 1, 2004, excess assets generally means the excess, if any, of the value of the plan's assets over the greater of (1) the lesser of (a) the accrued liability under the plan (including normal cost) or (b) 170 percent of the plan's current liability (for 2003), or (2) 125 percent of the plan's current liability. The current liability full funding limit was repealed for years beginning after 2003. Under the general sunset provision of EGTRRA, the limit is reinstated for years after 2010.

and the plan administrator must notify each plan participant and beneficiary of the transfer.[194]

Under present law, special deduction rules apply to a multiemployer defined benefit plan established before January 1, 1954, under an agreement between the Federal government and employee representatives in a certain industry.[195]

Explanation of Provision

The bill allows qualified transfers of excess defined benefit plan assets to be made by multiemployer defined benefit plans.

Effective Date

The provision is effective for transfer made in taxable years beginning after December 31, 2006.

[Law at ¶ 5115. CCH Explanation at ¶ 810.]

[¶ 10,770] Act Sec. 843. Allowance of reserve for medical benefits of plans sponsored by bona fide associations

Joint Committee Taxation (J.C.T. Rep. No. JCX-38-06)

[Code Sec. 419A]

Present Law

Under present law, deductions for contributions to funded welfare benefit plans are generally subject to limits, including limits on the amount that may be contributed to an account to fund medical benefits (other than retiree medical benefits) for future years. Deductions for contributions to a welfare benefit fund are limited to the fund's qualified cost for the taxable year. The qualified cost is the sum of (1) the qualified direct cost for the taxable year, and (2) permissible additions to a qualified asset account.

The qualified direct costs are the amount which would have been allowable as a deduction to the employer with respect to the benefits provided during the taxable year if the benefits were provided directly by the employer and the employer used the cash receipts and disbursements method of accounting. Additions to the qualified asset account are limited to the account limit. The account limit is the amount reasonably and actuarially necessary to fund claims uncured but unpaid (as of the close of the taxable year) and administrative costs with respect to such claims.

These limits do not apply to a welfare benefit fund that is part of a plan (referred to a "10-or-more employer" plan), to which (1) more than one employer contributes, and (2) no employer normally contributes more than 10 percent of the total contributions, provided that the plan may not maintain experience rating arrangements with respect to individual employers.

Explanation of Provision

The bill allows deductions for contributions to fund a reserve for medical benefits (other than retiree medical benefits) for future years provided through a bona fide association as defined in section 2791(d)(3) of the Public Health Service Act. In such case, the account limit may include a reserve not to exceed 35 percent of the sum of (1) qualified direct costs, and (2) the change in claims incurred, but unpaid for such taxable year with respect to medical benefits (other than post-retirement medical benefits).

Effective Date

The provision is effective for taxable years ending after December 31, 2006.

[Law at ¶ 5112. CCH Explanation at ¶ 815.]

---

[194] ERISA sec. 101(e). ERISA also provides that a qualified transfer is not a prohibited transaction under ERISA or a prohibited reversion.

[195] Code sec. 404(c).

[¶10,780] Act Sec. 844. Tax treatment of combined annuity or life insurance contracts with a long-term care insurance feature

Joint Committee Taxation (J.C.T. Rep. No. JCX-38-06)

[Code Secs. 72, 1035 and 7702B and New Code Sec. 6050U]

Present Law

Annuity contracts

In general, earnings and gains on amounts invested in a deferred annuity contract held by an individual are not subject to tax during the deferral period in the hands of the holder of the contract. When payout commences under a deferred annuity contract, the tax treatment of amounts distributed depends on whether the amount is received "as an annuity" (generally, as periodic payments under contract terms) or not.

For amounts received as an annuity by an individual, an "exclusion ratio" is provided for determining the taxable portion of each payment (sec. 72(b)). The portion of each payment that is attributable to recovery of the taxpayer's investment in the contract is not taxed. The taxable portion of each payment is ordinary income. The exclusion ratio is the ratio of the taxpayer's investment in the contract to the expected return under the contract, that is, the total of the payments expected to be received under the contract. The ratio is determined as of the taxpayer's annuity starting date. Once the taxpayer has recovered his or her investment in the contract, all further payments are included in income. If the taxpayer dies before the full investment in the contract is recovered, a deduction is allowed on the final return for the remaining investment in the contract (sec. 72(b)(3)).

Amounts not received as an annuity generally are included as ordinary income if received on or after the annuity starting date. Amounts not received as an annuity are included in income to the extent allocable to income on the contract if received before the annuity starting date, i.e., as income first (sec. 72(e)(2)). In general, loans under the annuity contract, partial withdrawals and partial surrenders are treated as amounts not received as an annuity and are subject to tax as income first (sec. 72(e)(4)). Exceptions are provided in some circumstances, such as for certain grandfathered contracts, certain life insurance and endowment contracts (other than modified endowment contracts), and contracts under qualified plans (sec. 72(e)(5)). Under these exceptions, the amount received is included in income, but only to the extent it exceeds the investment in the contract, i.e., as basis recovery first.

Long-term care insurance contracts

Tax treatment

Present law provides favorable tax treatment for qualified long-term care insurance contracts meeting the requirements of section 7702B.

A qualified long-term care insurance contract is treated as an accident and health insurance contract (sec. 7702B(a)(1)). Amounts received under the contract generally are excludable from income as amounts received for personal injuries or sickness (sec. 104(a)(3)). The excludable amount is subject to a dollar cap of $250 per day or $91,250 annually (for 2006), as indexed, on per diem contracts only (sec. 7702B(d)). If payments under such contracts exceed the dollar cap, then the excess is excludable only to the extent of costs in excess of the dollar cap that are incurred for long-term care services. Amounts in excess of the dollar cap, with respect to which no actual costs were incurred for long-term care services, are fully includable in income without regard to the rules relating to return of basis under section 72.

A plan of an employer providing coverage under a long-term care insurance contract generally is treated as an accident and health plan (benefits under which generally are excludable from the recipient's income under section 105).

Premiums paid for a qualified long-term care insurance contract are deductible as medical expenses, subject to a dollar cap on the deductible amount of the premium per year based on the insured person's age at the end of the taxable year (sec. 213(d)(10)). Medical expenses generally are allowed as a deduction only to the extent they exceed 7.5 percent of adjusted gross income (sec. 213(a)).

Unreimbursed expenses for qualified long-term care services provided to the taxpayer or the taxpayer's spouse or dependent are treated as medical expenses for purposes of the itemized deduction for medical expenses (subject to the floor of 7.5 percent of adjusted gross income). Amounts received under a qualified long-term care insurance contract (regardless of whether the contract reimburses expenses or pays benefits on a per diem or other periodic basis) are treated as reimbursement for expense actually incurred for medical care (sec. 7702B(a)(2)).

Definitions

A qualified long-term care insurance contract is defined as any insurance contract that provides only coverage of qualified long-term care services, and that meets additional requirements (sec. 7702B(b)). The contract is not permitted to provide for a cash surrender value or other money that can paid, assigned or pledged as collateral for a loan, or borrowed (and premium refunds are to be applied as a reduction in future premiums or to increase future benefits). Per diem-type and reimbursement-type contracts are permitted.

Qualified long-term care services are necessary diagnostic, preventive, therapeutic, curing treating, mitigating, and rehabilitative services, and maintenance or personal care services that are required by a chronically ill individual and that are provided pursuant to a plan of care prescribed by a licensed health care practitioner (sec. 7702B(c)(1)).

A chronically ill individual is generally one who has been certified within the previous 12 months by a licensed health care practitioner as being unable to perform (without substantial assistance) at least 2 activities of daily (ADLs) for at least 90 days due to a loss of functional capacity (or meeting other definitional requirements) (sec. 7702B(c)(2)).

Long-term care riders on life insurance contracts

In the case of long-term care insurance coverage provided by a rider on or as part of a life insurance contract, the requirements applicable to long-term care insurance contracts apply as if the portion of the contract providing such coverage were a separate contract (sec. 7702B(e)). The term "portion" means only the terms and benefits that are in addition to the terms and benefits under the life insurance contract without regard to long-term care coverage. As a result, if the applicable requirements are met by the long-term care portion of the contract, amounts received under the contract as provided by the rider are treated in the same manner as long-term care insurance benefits, whether or not the payment of such amounts causes a reduction in the contract's death benefit or cash surrender value.

The guideline premium limitation applicable under section 7702(c)(2) is increased by the sum of charges (but not premium payments) against the life insurance contract's cash surrender value, the imposition of which reduces premiums paid for the contract (within the meaning of sec. 7702(f)(1)). Thus, a policyholder can prefund to a greater degree a life insurance policy with a long-term care rider without causing the policy to lose its tax-favored treatment as life insurance.

No medical expense deduction generally is allowed under section 213 for charges against the life insurance contract's cash surrender value, unless such charges are includible in income because the life insurance contract is treated as a "modified endowment contract" under section 72(e)(10) and 7702A (sec. 7702B(e)((3)).

Tax-free exchanges of insurance contracts

Present law provides for the exchange of certain insurance contracts without recognition of gain or loss (sec. 1035). No gain or loss is recognized on the exchange of: (1) a life insurance contract for another life insurance contract or for an endowment or annuity contract; or (2) an endowment contract for another endowment contract (that provides for regular payments beginning no later than under the exchanged contract) or for an annuity contract; or (3) an annuity contract for an annuity contract. The basis of the contract received in the exchange generally is the same as the basis of the contract exchanged (sec. 1031(d)). Tax-free exchanges of long-term care insurance contracts are not permitted.

Capitalization of certain policy acquisition expenses of insurance companies

In the case of an insurance company, specified policy acquisition expenses for any taxable year are required to be capitalized, and are amortized generally over the 120-month period beginning with the first month in the second half of the taxable year (sec. 848). Specified policy acquisition expenses are determined as that portion of the insurance company's general deductions for the taxable year that does not exceed a specific percentage of the net premiums for the taxable year on each of three categories of insurance contracts. For annuity contracts, the percentage is 1.75; for group life insurance contracts, the percentage is 2.05; and for all other specified insurance contracts, the percentage is 7.7. With certain exceptions, a specified insurance contract is any life insurance, annuity, or noncancellable accident and health insurance contract or combination thereof.

Explanation of Provision

The provision provides tax rules for long-term care insurance that is provided by a rider on or as part of an annuity contract, and modifies the tax rules for long-term care insurance coverage provided by a rider on or as part of a life insurance contract.

Under the provision, any charge against the cash value of an annuity contract or the cash surrender value of a life insurance contract made as payment for coverage under a qualified long-term care insurance contract that is part of or a rider on the annuity or life insurance contract is not includable in income. The investment in the contract is reduced (but not below zero) by the charge.

The provision expands the rules for tax-free exchanges of certain insurance contracts. The provision provides that no gain or loss is recognized on the exchange of a life insurance contract, an endowment contract, an annuity contract, or a qualified long-term care insurance contract for a qualified long-term care insurance contract. The provision provides that a contract does not fail to be treated as an annuity contract, or as a life insurance contract, solely because a qualified long-term care insurance contract is a part of or a rider on such contract, for purposes of the rules for tax-free exchanges of certain insurance contracts.

The provision provides that, except as otherwise provided in regulations, for Federal tax purposes, in the case of a long-term care insurance contract (whether or not qualified) provided by a rider on or as part of a life insurance contract or an annuity contract, the portion of the contract providing long-term care insurance coverage is treated as a separate contract. The term "portion" means only the terms and benefits under a life insurance contract or annuity contract that are in addition to the terms and benefits under the contract without regard to long-term care coverage. As a result, if the applicable requirements are met by the long-term care portion of the contract, amounts received under the contract as provided by the rider are treated in the same manner as long-term care insurance benefits, whether or not the payment of such amounts causes a reduction in the life insurance contract's death benefit or cash surrender value or in the annuity contract's cash value.

No deduction as a medical expense is allowed for any payment made for coverage under a qualified long-term care insurance contract if the payment is made as a charge against the cash value of an annuity contract or the cash surrender value of a life insurance contract.

The provision provides that, for taxable years beginning after December 31, 2009, the guideline premium limitation is not directly increased by charges against a life insurance contract's cash surrender value for coverage under the qualified long-term care insurance portion of the contract. Rather, because such charges are not included in the holder's income by reason of new section 72(e)(11),[196] the charges reduce premiums paid under section 7702(f)(1), for purposes of the guideline premium limitation of section 7702. The amount by which premiums paid (under 7702(f)(1)) are reduced under this rule is intended to be the sum of any charges (but not premium payments) against the life insurance contract's cash surrender value (within the meaning of section 7702(f)(2)(a)) for long-term care coverage made to that date under the contract. For taxable years beginning before January 1, 2010, the present-law rule of section 7702B(e)(2) before amendment by the bill (the so-called "pay-as-you-go" rule) increases the guideline premium limitation by this same amount, reduced by charges the imposition of which reduces the premiums paid under the contract. Thus, the provision of the bill recreates the result of the "pay-as-you-go" rule (which is repealed by the provision) as a reduction in premiums paid rather than as an increase in the guideline premium limitation.

The provision provides that certain retirement-related arrangements are not treated as annuity contracts, for purposes of the provision.

The provision requires information reporting by any person who makes a charge against the cash value of an annuity contract, or the cash surrender value of a life insurance contract, that is excludible from gross income under the provision. The information required to be reported includes the amount of the aggregate of such charges against each such contract for the calendar year, the amount of the reduction in the investment in the contract by reason of the charges, and the name, address, and taxpayer identification number of the holder of the con-

---

[196] Because such charges are not included in the holder's income under new section 72(e)(11), the effect would be to increase the guideline premium limitation under present-law section 7702B(e)(2)(A) by the amount of the charges and simultaneously to reduce it by the same charges under section 7702B(e)(2)(B). Such charges that are not included in income serve to reduce premiums paid under section 7702(f)(1), and therefore would cancel each other out under 7702B(e)(2)(A) and (B).

tract. A statement is required to be furnished to each individual identified in the information report. Penalties apply for failure to file the information report or furnish the statement required under the provision.

The provision modifies the application of the rules relating to capitalization of policy acquisition expenses of insurance companies. In the case of an annuity or life insurance contract that includes a qualified long-term care insurance contract as a part of or rider on the annuity or life insurance contract, the specified policy acquisition expenses that must be capitalized is determined using 7.7 percent of the net premiums for the taxable year on such contracts.

The provision clarifies that, effective as if included in the Health Insurance Portability and Accountability Act of 1996 (when section 7702B was enacted), except as otherwise provided in regulations, for Federal tax purposes (not just for purposes of section 7702B), in the case of a long-term care insurance contract (whether or not qualified) provided by a rider on or as part of a life insurance contract, the portion of the contract providing long-term care insurance coverage is treated as a separate contract.

Effective Date

The provisions are effective generally for contracts issued after December 31, 1996, but only with respect to taxable years beginning after December 31, 2009. The provisions relating to tax-free exchanges apply with respect to exchanges occurring after December 31, 2009. The provision relating to information reporting applies to charges made after December 31, 2009. The provision relating to policy acquisition expenses applies to specified policy acquisition expenses determined for taxable years beginning after December 31, 2009. The technical amendment relating to long-term care insurance coverage under section 7702B(e) is effective as if included with the underlying provisions of the Health Insurance Portability and Accountability Act of 1996.

[Law at ¶ 5010, ¶ 5190, ¶ 5195, ¶ 5345, ¶ 5425 and ¶ 5490. CCH Explanation at ¶ 820.]

[¶ 10,790] Act Sec. 845. Permit tax-free distributions from governmental retirement plans for premiums for health and long-term care insurance for public safety officers

Joint Committee Taxation (J.C.T. Rep. No. JCX-38-06)

[Code Sec. 402]

Present Law

Under present law, a distribution from a qualified retirement plan under section 401(a), a qualified annuity plan under section 403(a), a tax-sheltered annuity under section 403(b) (a "403(b) annuity"), an eligible deferred compensation plan maintained by a State or local government under section 457 (a "governmental 457 plan"), or an individual retirement arrangement under section 408 (an "IRA") generally is included in income for the year distributed (except to the extent the amount received constitutes a return of after-tax contributions or a qualified distribution from a Roth IRA).[197] In addition, a distribution from a qualified retirement or annuity plan, a 403(b) annuity, or an IRA received before age 591/2, death, or disability generally is subject to a 10-percent early withdrawal tax on the amount includible in income, unless an exception applies.[198]

Explanation of Provision

The bill provides that certain pension distributions from an eligible retirement plan used to pay for qualified health insurance premiums are excludible from income, up to a maximum exclusion of $3,000 annually. An eligible retirement plan includes a governmental qualified retirement or annuity plan, 403(b) annuity, or 457 plan. The exclusion applies with respect to eligible retired public safety officers who make an election to have qualified health insurance premiums deducted from amounts distributed from an eligible retirement plan and paid directly to the insurer. An eligible retired public safety officer is an individual who, by reason of disability or attainment of normal retirement age, is sepa-

[197] Secs. 402(a), 403(a), 403(b), 408(d), and 457(a).

[198] Sec. 72(t).

rated from service as a public safety officer[199] with the employer who maintains the eligible retirement plan from which pension distributions are made.

Qualified health insurance premiums include premiums for accident or health insurance or qualified long-term care insurance contracts covering the taxpayer, the taxpayer's spouse, and the taxpayer's dependents. The qualified health insurance premiums do not have to be for a plan sponsored by the employer; however, the exclusion does not apply to premiums paid by the employee and reimbursed with pension distributions. Amounts excluded from income under the provision are not taken into account in determining the itemized deduction for medical expenses under section 213 or the deduction for health insurance of self-employed individuals under section 162.

Effective Date

The provision is effective for distributions in taxable years beginning after December 31, 2006.

[Law at ¶ 5035, ¶ 5040 and ¶ 5140. CCH Explanation at ¶ 825.]

[¶ 10,800] Act Secs. 851, 852 and 853. Judges of the Tax Court

Joint Committee Taxation (J.C.T. Rep. No. JCX-38-06)

[Code Secs. 7447, 7448 and 7472]

Present Law

The Tax Court is established by the Congress pursuant to Article I of the U.S. Constitution.[200] The salary of a Tax Court judge is the same salary as received by a U.S. District Court judge.[201] Present law also provides Tax Court judges with some benefits that correspond to benefits provided to U.S. District Court judges, including specific retirement and survivor benefit programs for Tax Court judges.[202]

Under the retirement program, a Tax Court judge may elect to receive retirement pay from the Tax Court in lieu of benefits under another Federal retirement program. A Tax Court judge may also elect to participate in a plan providing annuity benefits for the judge's surviving spouse and dependent children (the "survivors' annuity plan"). Generally, benefits under the survivors' annuity plan are payable only if the judge has performed at least five years of service. Cost-of-living increases in benefits under the survivors' annuity plan are generally based on increases in pay for active judges.

Tax Court judges participate in the Federal Employees Group Life Insurance program (the "FEGLI" program). Retired Tax Court judges are eligible to participate in the FEGLI program as the result of an administrative determination of their eligibility, rather than a specific statutory provision.

Tax Court judges are not covered by the leave system for Federal Executive Branch employees. As a result, an individual who works in the Federal Executive Branch before being appointed to the Tax Court does not continue to accrue annual leave under the same leave program and may not use leave accrued prior to his or her appointment to the Tax Court.

Tax Court judges are not eligible to participate in the Thrift Savings Plan.

Under the retirement program for Tax Court judges, retired judges generally receive retired pay equal to the rate of salary of an active judge and must be available for recall to perform judicial duties as needed by the court for up to 90 days a year (unless the judge consents to more). However, retired judges may elect to freeze the amount of their retired pay, and those who do so are not available for recall.

Retired Tax Court judges on recall are subject to the limitations on outside earned income that apply to active Federal employees under the Ethics in Government Act of 1978. However, retired District Court judges on recall may receive compensation for teaching without regard to the limitations on outside earned income. Retired Tax Court judges who elect to freeze the amount of their retired pay (thus making themselves unavailable for recall) are not subject to the limitations on outside earned income.

---

199 The term "public safety officer" has the same meaning as under section 1204(8)(A) of the Omnibus Crime Control and Safe Streets Act of 1986.

200 Sec. 7441.

201 Sec. 7443(c).

202 Secs. 7447 and 7448.

Explanation of Provision

Cost-of-living adjustments for survivor annuities

The bill provides that cost-of-living increases in benefits under the survivors' annuity plan are generally based on cost-of-living increases in benefits paid under the Civil Service Retirement System.

Life insurance coverage

In the case of a Tax Court judge age 65 or over, the Tax Court is authorized to pay on behalf of the judge any increase in employee premiums under the FEGLI program that occur after the date of enactment, including expenses generated by such payment, as authorized by the chief judge of the Tax Court in a manner consistent with payments authorized by the Judicial Conference of the United States (i.e., the body with policy-making authority over the administration of the courts of the Federal judicial branch).

Thrift Savings Plan participation

Under the provision, Tax Court judges are permitted to participate in the Thrift Savings Plan. A Tax Court judge is not eligible for agency contributions to the Thrift Savings Plan.

Effective Date

The provisions are effective on the date of enactment, except that the provision relating to cost-of-living increases in benefits under the survivors' annuity plan applies with respect to increases in Civil Service Retirement benefits taking effect after the date of enactment.

[Law at ¶ 5460, ¶ 5465 and ¶ 5475. CCH Explanation at ¶ 1430, ¶ 1435 and ¶ 1440.]

[¶ 10,810] Act Secs. 854 and 856. Special trial judges of the Tax Court

Joint Committee Taxation (J.C.T. Rep. No. JCX-38-06)

[Code Sec. 7448 and New Code Sec. 7443C]

Present Law

The Tax Court is established by the Congress pursuant to Article I of the U.S. Constitution.[203] The chief judge of the Tax Court may appoint special trial judges to handle certain cases.[204] Special trial judges serve for an indefinite term. Special trial judges receive a salary of 90 percent of the salary of a Tax Court judge and are generally covered by the benefit programs that apply to Federal executive branch employees, including the Civil Service Retirement System or the Federal Employees' Retirement System.

Explanation of Provision

Survivors' annuity plan

Under the provision, magistrate judges of the Tax Court may elect to participate in the survivors' annuity plan for Tax Court judges. An election to participate in the survivors' annuity plan must be filed not later than the latest of: (1) twelve months after the date of enactment of the provision; (2) six months after the date the judge takes office; or (3) six months after the date the judge marries.

Recall of retired special trial judges

The provision provides rules under which a retired special trial judge may be recalled to perform services for up to 90 days a year.

Effective Date

The provisions are effective on the date of enactment.

[Law at ¶ 5215, ¶ 5455, ¶ 5465 and ¶ 7168. CCH Explanation at ¶ 1445 and ¶ 1450.]

---

[203] Sec. 7441.

[204] Sec. 7443A.

[¶10,820] Act Sec. 855. Consolidate review of collection due process cases in the Tax Court

Joint Committee Taxation (J.C.T. Rep. No. JCX-38-06)

[Code Sec. 6330(d)]

Present Law

In general, the IRS is required to notify taxpayers that they have a right to a fair and impartial hearing before levy may be made on any property or right to property.[205] Similar rules apply with respect to liens.[206] The hearing is held by an impartial officer from the IRS Office of Appeals, who is required to issue a determination with respect to the issues raised by the taxpayer at the hearing. The taxpayer is entitled to appeal that determination to a court. The appeal must be brought to the Tax Court, unless the Tax Court does not have jurisdiction over the underlying tax liability. If that is the case, then the appeal must be brought in the district court of the United States.[207] If a court determines that an appeal was not made to the correct court, the taxpayer has 30 days after such determination to file with the correct court.

The Tax Court is established under Article I of the United States Constitution[208] and is a court of limited jurisdiction.[209] The Tax Court only has the jurisdiction that is expressly conferred on it by statute.[210] For example, the jurisdiction of the Tax Court includes the authority to hear disputes concerning notices of income tax deficiency, certain types of declaratory judgment, and worker classification status, among others, but does not include jurisdiction over most excise taxes imposed by the Internal Revenue Code. Thus, the Tax Court may not have jurisdiction over the underlying tax liability with respect to an appeal of a due process hearing relating to a collections matter. As a practical matter, many cases involving appeals of a due process hearing (whether within the jurisdiction of the Tax Court or a district court) do not involve the underlying tax liability.

Explanation of Provision

The provision modifies the jurisdiction of the Tax Court by providing that all appeals of collection due process determinations are to be made to the United States Tax Court.

Effective Date

The provision applies to determinations made after the date which is 60 days after the date of enactment.

[Law at ¶5375. CCH Explanation at ¶1405.]

[¶10,830] Act Sec. 857. Extend authority for special trial judges to hear and decide certain employment status cases

Joint Committee Taxation (J.C.T. Rep. No. JCX-38-06)

[Code Sec. 7443A]

Present Law

In connection with the audit of any person, if there is an actual controversy involving a determination by the IRS as part of an examination that (1) one or more individuals performing services for that person are employees of that person or (2) that person is not entitled to relief under section 530 of the Revenue Act of 1978, the Tax Court has jurisdiction to determine whether the IRS is correct and the proper amount of employment tax under such determination.[211] Any redetermination by the Tax Court has the force and effect of a decision of the Tax Court and is reviewable.

An election may be made by the taxpayer for small case procedures if the amount of the employment taxes in dispute is $50,000 or less for each calendar quarter involved.[212] The decision entered under the small case procedure is not reviewable in any other court and should not be cited as authority.

The chief judge of the Tax Court may assign proceedings to special trial judges. The Code

[205] Sec. 6330(a).

[206] Sec. 6320.

[207] Sec. 6330(d).

[208] Sec. 7441.

[209] Sec. 7442.

[210] Sec. 7442.

[211] Sec. 7436.

[212] Sec. 7436(c).

enumerates certain types of proceedings that may be so assigned and may be decided by a special trial judge. In addition, the chief judge may designate any other proceeding to be heard by a special trial judge.[213]

Explanation of Provision

The provision clarifies that the chief judge of the Tax Court may assign to special trial judges any employment tax cases that are subject to the small case procedure and may authorize special trial judges to decide such small tax cases.

Effective Date

The provision is effective for any action or proceeding in the Tax Court with respect to which a decision has not become final as of the date of enactment.

[Law at ¶ 5450. CCH Explanation at ¶ 1410.]

[¶ 10,840] Act Sec. 858. Confirmation of Tax Court authority to apply equitable recoupment

Joint Committee Taxation (J.C.T. REP. NO. JCX-38-06)

[Code Sec. 6214(b)]

Present Law

Equitable recoupment is a common-law equitable principle that permits the defensive use of an otherwise time-barred claim to reduce or defeat an opponent's claim if both claims arise from the same transaction. U.S. District Courts and the U.S. Court of Federal Claims, the two Federal tax refund forums, may apply equitable recoupment in deciding tax refund cases.[214] In Estate of Mueller v. Commissioner,[215] the Court of Appeals for the Sixth Circuit held that the United States Tax Court (the "Tax Court") may not apply the doctrine of equitable recoupment. More recently, the Court of Appeals for the Ninth Circuit, in Branson v. Commissioner,[216] held that the Tax Court may apply the doctrine of equitable recoupment.

Explanation of Provision

The provision confirms that the Tax Court may apply the principle of equitable recoupment to the same extent that it may be applied in Federal civil tax cases by the U.S. District Courts or the U.S. Court of Claims. No implication is intended as to whether the Tax Court has the authority to continue to apply other equitable principles in deciding matters over which it has jurisdiction.

Effective Date

The provision is effective for any action or proceeding in the Tax Court with respect to which a decision has not become final as of the date of enactment.

[Law at ¶ 5370. CCH Explanation at ¶ 1415.]

[¶ 10,850] Act Sec. 859. Tax Court filing fee

Joint Committee Taxation (J.C.T. REP. NO. JCX-38-06)

[Code Sec. 7451]

Present Law

The Tax Court is authorized to impose a fee of up to $60 for the filing of any petition for the redetermination of a deficiency or for declaratory judgments relating to the status and classification of 501(c)(3) organizations, the judicial review of final partnership administrative adjustments, and the judicial review of partnership items if an administrative adjustment request is not allowed in full.[217] The statute does not specifically authorize the Tax Court to impose a filing fee for the filing of a petition for review of the IRS's failure to abate interest or for failure to award administrative costs and other areas of jurisdiction for which a petition may be filed. The practice of the Tax Court is to impose a $60 filing fee in all cases commenced by petition.[218]

---

[213] Sec. 7443A.

[214] *See Stone v. White*, 301 U.S. 532 (1937); *Bull v. United States*, 295 U.S. 247 (1935).

[215] 153 F.3d 302 (6th Cir.), *cert. den.*, 525 U.S. 1140 (1999).

[216] 264 F.3d 904 (9th Cir.), *cert. den.*, 2002 U.S. LEXIS 1545 (U.S. Mar. 18, 2002).

[217] Sec. 7451.

[218] *See* Rule 20(b) of the Tax Court Rules of Practice and Procedure.

Explanation of Provision

The provision provides that the Tax Court is authorized to charge a filing fee of up to $60 in all cases commenced by the filing of a petition. No negative inference is to be drawn as to whether the Tax Court has the authority under present law to impose a filing fee for any case commenced by the filing of a petition.

Effective Date

The provision is effective on the date of enactment.

[Law at ¶ 5470. CCH Explanation at ¶ 1420.]

[¶ 10,860] Act Sec. 860. Use of practitioner fee

Joint Committee Taxation (J.C.T. Rep. No. JCX-38-06)

[Code Sec. 7475(b)]

Present Law

The Tax Court is authorized to impose a fee of up to $30 per year on practitioners admitted to practice before the Tax Court.[219] These fees are to be used to employ independent counsel to pursue disciplinary matters.

Explanation of Provision

The provision provides that Tax Court fees imposed on practitioners also are available to provide services to pro se taxpayers (i.e., a taxpayer representing himself) that will assist such taxpayers in controversies before the Court. For example, fees could be used for programs to educate pro se taxpayers on the procedural requirements for contesting a tax deficiency before the Tax Court.

Effective Date

The provision is effective on the date of enactment.

[Law at ¶ 5480. CCH Explanation at ¶ 1425.]

[¶ 10,870] Act Sec. 861. Extension to all governmental plans of moratorium on application of certain nondiscrimination rules

Joint Committee Taxation (J.C.T. Rep. No. JCX-38-06)

[Code Secs. 401(a) and 401(k)]

Present Law

A qualified retirement plan maintained by a State or local government is exempt from the nondiscrimination and minimum participation requirements. A cash or deferred arrangement maintained by a State or local government is also treated as meeting the participation and nondiscrimination requirements applicable to such a qualified cash or deferred arrangement. Other governmental plans are subject to these requirements.[220]

Explanation of Provision

The provision exempts all governmental plans from the nondiscrimination and minimum participation rules. The provision also treats all governmental cash or deferred arrangements as meeting the participation and nondiscrimination requirements applicable to a qualified cash or deferred arrangement.

Effective Date

The provision is effective for any year beginning after the date of enactment.

[Law at ¶ 5030 and ¶ 7171. CCH Explanation at ¶ 1060.]

---

[219] Sec. 7475.

[220] The IRS has announced that governmental plans that are subject to the nondiscrimination requirements are deemed to satisfy such requirements pending the issuance of final regulations addressing this issue. Notice 2003-6, 2003-3 I.R.B. 298; Notice 2001-46, 2001-2 C.B. 122.

[¶10,880] Act Sec. 862. Eliminate aggregate limit for usage of excess funds from black lung disability trusts to pay for retiree health

Joint Committee Taxation (J.C.T. Rep. No. JCX-38-06)

[Code Secs. 501(c)(21) and 9705]

Present Law

Qualified black lung benefit trusts

A qualified black lung benefit trust is exempt from Federal income taxation. Contributions to a qualified black lung benefit trust generally are deductible to the extent such contributions are necessary to fund the trust.

Under present law, no assets of a qualified black lung benefit trust may be used for, or diverted to, any purpose other than (1) to satisfy liabilities, or pay insurance premiums to cover liabilities, arising under the Black Lung Acts, (2) to pay administrative costs of operating the trust, (3) to pay accident and health benefits or premiums for insurance exclusively covering such benefits (including administrative and other incidental expenses relating to such benefits) for retired coal miners and their spouses and dependents (within certain limits) or (4) investment in Federal, State, or local securities and obligations, or in time demand deposits in a bank or insured credit union. Additionally, trust assets may be paid into the national Black Lung Disability Trust Fund, or into the general fund of the U.S. Treasury.

The amount of assets in qualified black lung benefit trusts available to pay accident and health benefits or premiums for insurance exclusively covering such benefits (including administrative and other incidental expenses relating to such benefits) for retired coal miners and their spouses and dependents may not exceed a yearly limit or an aggregate limit, whichever is less. The yearly limit is the amount of trust assets in excess of 110 percent of the present value of the liability for black lung benefits determined as of the close of the preceding taxable year of the trust. The aggregate limit is the excess of the sum of the yearly limit as of the close of the last taxable year ending before October 24, 1992, plus earnings thereon as of the close of the taxable year preceding the taxable year involved over the aggregate payments for accident of health benefits for retired coal miners and their spouses and dependents made from the trust since October 24, 1992. Each of these determinations is required to be made by an independent actuary.

In general, amounts used to pay retiree accident or health benefits are not includible in the income of the company, nor is a deduction allowed for such amounts.

United Mine Workers of America Combined Benefit Fund

The United Mine Workers of America ("UMWA") Combined Benefit Fund was established by the Coal Industry Retiree Health Benefit Act of 1992 to assume responsibility of payments for medical care expenses of retired miners and their dependents who were eligible for heath care from the private 1950 and 1974 UMWA Benefit Plans. The UMWA Combined Benefit Fund is financed by assessments on current and former signatories to labor agreements with the UMWA, past transfers from an overfunded United Mine Workers pension fund, and transfers from the Abandoned Mine Reclamation Fund.

Explanation of Provision

The provision eliminates the aggregate limit on the amount of excess black lung benefit trust assets that may be used to pay accident and health benefits or premiums for insurance exclusively covering such benefits (including administrative and other incidental expenses relating to such benefits) for retired coal miners and their spouses and dependents.

Effective Date

The provision is effective for taxable years beginning after December 31, 2006.

[Law at ¶ 5145. CCH Explanation at ¶ 1220.]

[¶10,890] Act Sec. 863. Tax treatment of company-owned life insurance ("COLI")

Joint Committee Taxation (J.C.T. Rep. No. JCX-38-06)

[New Code Secs. 101(j) and 6039I]

Present Law

Amounts received under a life insurance contract

Amounts received under a life insurance contract paid by reason of the death of the insured are not includible in gross income for Federal tax purposes.[221] No Federal income tax generally is imposed on a policyholder with respect to the earnings under a life insurance contract (inside buildup).[222]

Distributions from a life insurance contract (other than a modified endowment contract) that are made prior to the death of the insured generally are includible in income to the extent that the amounts distributed exceed the taxpayer's investment in the contract (i.e., basis). Such distributions generally are treated first as a tax-free recovery of basis, and then as income.[223]

Premium and interest deduction limitations[224]

Premiums

Under present law, no deduction is permitted for premiums paid on any life insurance, annuity or endowment contract, if the taxpayer is directly or indirectly a beneficiary under the contract.[225]

Interest paid or accrued with respect to the contract

No deduction generally is allowed for interest paid or accrued on any debt with respect to a life insurance, annuity or endowment contract covering the life of any individual.[226] An exception is provided under this provision for insurance of key persons.

Interest that is otherwise deductible (e.g., is not disallowed under other applicable rules or general principles of tax law) may be deductible under the key person exception, to the extent that the aggregate amount of the debt does not exceed $50,000 per insured individual. The deductible interest may not exceed the amount determined by applying a rate based on a Moody's Corporate Bond Yield Average-Monthly Average Corporates. A key person is an individual who is either an officer or a 20-percent owner of the taxpayer. The number of individuals that can be treated as key persons may not exceed the greater of (1) five individuals, or (2) the lesser of five percent of the total number of officers and employees of the taxpayer, or 20 individuals.[227]

Pro rata interest limitation

A pro rata interest deduction disallowance rule also applies. Under this rule, in the case of a taxpayer other than a natural person, no deduction is allowed for the portion of the taxpayer's interest expense that is allocable to unborrowed policy cash surrender values.[228] Interest expense is allocable to unborrowed policy cash values based on the ratio of (1) the taxpayer's average unborrowed policy cash values of life insurance, annuity and endowment contracts, to (2) the sum of the average unborrowed cash values (or average adjusted bases, for other assets) of all the taxpayer's assets.

---

[221] Sec. 101(a).

[222] This favorable tax treatment is available only if a life insurance contract meets certain requirements designed to limit the investment character of the contract (sec. 7702).

[223] Sec. 72(e). In the case of a modified endowment contract, however, in general, distributions are treated as income first, loans are treated as distributions (i.e., income rather than basis recovery first), and an additional 10-percent tax is imposed on the income portion of distributions made before age 59½ and in certain other circumstances (secs. 72(e) and (v)). A modified endowment contract is a life insurance contract that does not meet a statutory "7-pay" test, i.e., generally is funded more rapidly than seven annual level premiums (sec. 7702A).

[224] In addition to the statutory limitations described below, interest deductions under company-owned life insurance arrangements have also been limited by recent cases applying general principles of tax law. See *Winn-Dixie Stores, Inc. v. Commissioner*, 113 T.C. 254 (1999), aff'd 254 F.3d 1313 (11th Cir. 2001), cert. denied, April 15, 2002; *Internal Revenue Service v. CM Holdings, Inc.*, 254 B.R. 578 (D. Del. 2000), aff'd, 301 F.3d 96 (3d Cir. 2002); *American Electric Power, Inc. v. U.S.*, 136 F. Supp. 2d 762 (S. D. Ohio 2001), aff'd, 326 F.3d 737 (6th Cir. 2003), reh. denied, 338 F.3d 534 (6th Cir. 2003), cert. denied, U.S. No. 03-529 (Jan. 12, 2004); *Dow Chemical Company v. U.S.*, 435 F.3d 594 (6th Cir. 2006), rev'g 250 F. Supp. 2d 748 (E.D. Mich. 2003) as modified, 278 F. Supp. 2d 844 (E.D. Mich. 2003).

[225] Sec. 264(a)(1).

[226] Sec. 264(a)(4).

[227] Sec. 264(e)(3).

[228] Sec. 264(f). This applies to any life insurance, annuity or endowment contract issued after June 8, 1997.

Under the pro rata interest disallowance rule, an exception is provided for any contract owned by an entity engaged in a trade or business, if the contract covers an individual who is a 20-percent owner of the entity, or an officer, director, or employee of the trade or business. The exception also applies to a joint-life contract covering a 20-percent owner and his or her spouse.

"Single premium" and "4-out-of-7" limitations

Other interest deduction limitation rules also apply with respect to life insurance, annuity and endowment contracts. Present law provides that no deduction is allowed for any amount paid or accrued on debt incurred or continued to purchase or carry a single premium life insurance, annuity or endowment contract.[229] In addition, present law provides that no deduction is allowed for any amount paid or accrued on debt incurred or continued to purchase or carry a life insurance, annuity or endowment contract pursuant to a plan of purchase that contemplates the systematic direct or indirect borrowing of part or all of the increases in the cash value of the contract (either from the insurer or otherwise).[230] Under this rule, several exceptions are provided, including an exception if no part of four of the annual premiums due during the initial seven-year period is paid by means of such debt (known as the "4-out-of-7 rule").

Definitions of highly compensated employee

Present law defines highly compensated employees and individuals for various purposes. For purposes of nondiscrimination rules relating to qualified retirement plans, an employee, including a self-employed individual, is treated as highly compensated with respect to a year if the employee (1) was a five-percent owner of the employer at any time during the year or the preceding year or (2) either (a) had compensation for the preceding year in excess of $95,000 (for 2005) or (b) at the election of the employer had compensation in excess of $95,000 (for 2005) and was in the highest paid 20 percent of employees for such year.[231] The $95,000 dollar amount is indexed for inflation.

For purposes of nondiscrimination rules relating to self-insured medical reimbursement plans, a highly compensated individual is an employee who is one of the five highest paid officers of the employer, a shareholder who owns more than 10 percent of the value of the stock of the employer, or is among the highest paid 25 percent of all employees.[232]

Explanation of Provision

The provision provides generally that, in the case of an employer-owned life insurance contract, the amount excluded from the applicable policyholder's income as a death benefit cannot exceed the premiums and other amounts paid by such applicable policyholder for the contract. The excess death benefit is included in income.

Exceptions to this income inclusion rule are provided. In the case of an employer-owned life insurance contract with respect to which the notice and consent requirements of the provision are met, the income inclusion rule does not apply to an amount received by reason of the death of an insured individual who, with respect to the applicable policyholder, was an employee at any time during the 12-month period before the insured's death, or who, at the time the contract was issued, was a director or highly compensated employee or highly compensated individual. For this purpose, such a person is one who is either: (1) a highly compensated employee as defined under the rules relating to qualified retirement plans, determined without regard to the election regarding the top-paid 20 percent of employees; or (2) a highly compensated individual as defined under the rules relating to self-insured medical reimbursement plans, determined by substituting the highest-paid 35 percent of employees for the highest-paid 25 percent of employees.[233]

In the case of an employer-owned life insurance contract with respect to which the notice and consent requirements of the provision are met, the income inclusion rule does not apply to an amount received by reason of the death of an insured, to the extent the amount is (1) paid to a member of the family[234] of the insured, to an individual who is the designated beneficiary of

---

[229] Sec. 264(a)(2).

[230] Sec. 264(a)(3).

[231] Sec. 414(q). For purposes of determining the top-paid 20 percent of employees, certain employees, such as employees subject to a collective bargaining agreement, are disregarded.

[232] Sec. 105(h)(5). For purposes of determining the top-paid 25 percent of employees, certain employees, such as employees subject to a collective bargaining agreement, are disregarded.

[233] As under present law, certain employees are disregarded in making the determinations regarding the top-paid groups.

[234] For this purpose, a member of the family is defined in section 267(c)(4) to include only the individual's brothers

the insured under the contract (other than an applicable policyholder), to a trust established for the benefit of any such member of the family or designated beneficiary, or to the estate of the insured; or (2) used to purchase an equity (or partnership capital or profits) interest in the applicable policyholder from such a family member, beneficiary, trust or estate. It is intended that such amounts be so paid or used by the due date of the tax return for the taxable year of the applicable policyholder in which they are received as a death benefit under the insurance contract, so that the payment of the amount to such a person or persons, or the use of the amount to make such a purchase, is known in the taxable year for which the exception from the income inclusion rule is claimed.

An employer-owned life insurance contract is defined for purposes of the provision as a life insurance contract which (1) is owned by a person engaged in a trade or business and under which such person (or a related person) is directly or indirectly a beneficiary, and (2) covers the life of an individual who is an employee with respect to the trade or business of the applicable policyholder on the date the contract is issued.

An applicable policyholder means, with respect to an employer-owned life insurance contract, the person (including related persons) that owns the contract, if the person is engaged in a trade or business, and if the person (or a related person) is directly or indirectly a beneficiary under the contract.

For purposes of the provision, a related person includes any person that bears a relationship specified in section 267(b) or 707(b)(1)[235] or is engaged in trades or businesses that are under common control (within the meaning of section 52(a) or (b)).

The notice and consent requirements of the provision are met if, before the issuance of the contract, (1) the employee is notified in writing that the applicable policyholder intends to insure the employee's life, and is notified of the maximum face amount at issue of the life insurance contract that the employer might take out on the life of the employee, (2) the employee provides written consent to being insured under the contract and that such coverage may continue after the insured terminates employment, and (3) the employee is informed in writing that an applicable policyholder will be a beneficiary of any proceeds payable on the death of the employee.

For purposes of the provision, an employee includes an officer, a director, and a highly compensated employee; an insured means, with respect to an employer-owned life insurance contract, an individual covered by the contract who is a U.S. citizen or resident. In the case of a contract covering the joint lives of two individuals, references to an insured include both of the individuals.

The provision requires annual reporting and recordkeeping by applicable policyholders that own one or more employer-owned life insurance contracts. The information to be reported is (1) the number of employees of the applicable policyholder at the end of the year, (2) the number of employees insured under employer-owned life insurance contracts at the end of the year, (3) the total amount of insurance in force at the end of the year under such contracts, (4) the name, address, and taxpayer identification number of the applicable policyholder and the type of business in which it is engaged, and (5) a statement that the applicable policyholder has a valid consent (in accordance with the consent requirements under the provision) for each insured employee and, if all such consents were not obtained, the total number of insured employees for whom such consent was not obtained. The applicable policyholder is required to keep records necessary to determine whether the requirements of the reporting rule and the income inclusion rule of new section 101(j) are met.

Effective Date

The provision generally appleis to contracts issued after the date of enactment, except for contracts issued after such date pursuant to an exchange described in section 1035 of the Code. In addition, certain material increases in the death benefit or other material changes will generally cause a contract to be treated as a new contract, with an exception for existing lives under a master contract. Increases in the death benefit that occur as a result of the operation of section 7702 of the Code or the terms of the existing contract, provided that the insurer's consent to the increase is not required, will not cause

(Footnote Continued)

and sisters (whether by the whole or half blood), spouse, ancestors, and lineal descendants.

[235] The relationships include specified relationships among family members, shareholders and corporations, corporations that are members of a controlled group, trust grantors and fiduciaries, tax-exempt organizations and persons that control such organizations, commonly controlled S corporations, partnerships and C corporations, estates and beneficiaries, commonly controlled partnerships, and partners and partnerships. Detailed rules apply to determine the specific relationships.

a contract to be treated as a new contract. In addition, certain changes to a contract will not be considered material changes so as to cause a contract to be treated as a new contract. These changes include administrative changes, changes from general to separate account, or changes as a result of the exercise of an option or right granted under the contract as originally issued.

Examples of situations in which death benefit increases would not cause a contract to be treated as a new contract include the following:

1. Section 7702 provides that life insurance contracts need to either meet the cash value accumulation test of section 7702(b) or the guideline premium requirements of section 7702(c) and the cash value corridor of section 7702(d). Under the corridor test, the amount of the death benefit may not be less than the applicable percentage of the cash surrender value. Contracts may be written to comply with the corridor requirement by providing for automatic increases in the death benefit based on the cash surrender value. Death benefit increases required by the corridor test or the cash value accumulation test do not require the insurer's consent at the time of increase and occur in order to keep the contact in compliance with section 7702.

2. Death benefits may also increase due to normal operation of the contract. For example, for some contracts, policyholder dividends paid under the contract may be applied to purchase paid-up additions, which increase the death benefits. The insurer's consent is not required for these death benefit increases.

3. For variable contacts and universal life contracts, the death benefit may increase as a result of market performance or the contract design. For example, some contracts provide that the death benefit will equal the cash value plus a specified amount at risk. With these contracts, the amount of the death benefit at any time will vary depending on changes in the cash value of the contract. The insurance company's consent is not required for these death benefit increases.

[Law at ¶5015 and ¶5335. CCH Explanation at ¶1330.]

[¶10,900] Act Sec. 864. Treatment of test room supervisors and proctors who assist in the administration of college entrance and placement exams

Joint Committee Taxation (J.C.T. REP. NO. JCX-38-06)

[Act Sec. 864]

Present Law

Section 530 of the Revenue Act of 1978 prohibits the Internal Revenue Service from challenging a taxpayer's treatment of an individual as an independent contractor for employment tax purposes if the taxpayer (1) has a reasonable basis for such treatment and (2) consistently treats the individual, and any other individual holding a substantially similar position, as an independent contractor.

Explanation of Provision

Under the bill, section 530 of the Revenue Act of 1978 is amended to provide that in the case of an individual providing services as a test proctor or room supervisor by assisting in the administration of college entrance or placements examinations, the consistency requirement does not apply with respect to services performed after December 31, 2006 (and remuneration paid with respect to such services). The provision applies if the individual (1) is performing the services for a tax-exempt organization, and (2) is not otherwise treated as an employee of such organization for purposes of employment taxes. Thus, under the bill, if the requirements are satisfied, the IRS is prohibited from challenging the treatment of such individuals as independent contractors for employment tax purposes, even if the organization previously treated such individuals as employees.

Effective Date

The provision is effective for remuneration paid for services performed after December 31, 2006.

[Law at ¶7174. CCH Explanation at ¶1335.]

[¶10,910] Act Sec. 865. Rule for church plans which self-annuitize

Joint Committee Taxation (J.C.T. Rep. No. JCX-38-06)

[Code Sec. 401(a)(9)]

Present Law

Minimum distribution rules apply to qualified retirement plans (sec. 401(a)(9)). Special rules apply in the case of payments under an annuity contract purchased with the employee's benefit by the plan from an insurance company.[236] If certain requirements are satisfied, these special rules apply to annuity payments from a retirement income account maintained by a church (or certain other organizations as described in sec. 403(b)(9)) even though the payments are not made under an annuity purchased from an insurance company.[237]

Explanation of Provision

The bill provides that annuity payments provided with respect to any account maintained for a participant or beneficiary under a qualified church plan does not fail to meet the minimum distribution rules merely because the payments are not made under an annuity contract purchased from an insurance company if such payments would not fail such requirements if provided with respect to a retirement income account described in section 403(b)(9).

For purposes of the provision, a qualified church plan means any money purchase plan described in section 401(a) which (1) is a church plan (as defined in section 414(e)) with respect to which the election provided by section 410(d) has not been made, and (2) was in existence on April 17, 2002.

Effective Date

The provision is effective for years beginning after the date of enactment. No inference is intended from the provision with respect to the proper application of the minimum distribution rules to church plans before the effective date.

[Law at ¶7177. CCH Explanation at ¶1045.]

[¶10,920] Act Sec. 866. Exemption for income from leveraged real estate held by church plans

Joint Committee Taxation (J.C.T. Rep. No. JCX-38-06)

[Code Sec. 514(c)(9)]

Present Law

Debt-financed income of a tax-exempt entity is subject to unrelated business income tax ("UBIT") under section 514 of the Code. Debt-financed property generally is property that is held to produce income and with respect to which there is acquisition indebtedness.

There is an exception to the UBIT rules for debt-financed property held by qualifying organizations (sec. 514(c)(9)). Qualified organizations include retirement plans qualified under section 401(a).

Explanation of Provision

The bill provides that a retirement income account of a church (or certain other organizations) as defined in section 403(b)(9) is a qualified organization for purposes of the exemption from the UBIT debt-financed property rules.

Effective Date

The provision is effective for taxable years beginning on or after the date of enactment.

[Law at ¶5170. CCH Explanation at ¶1050.]

[¶10,930] Act Sec. 867. Church plan rule for benefit limitations

Joint Committee Taxation (J.C.T. Rep. No. JCX-38-06)

[Code Sec. 415]

Present Law

Section 415 limits the amount of benefits and contributions that may be provided under a tax-qualified plan. In the case of a defined benefit plan, the limit on annual benefits payable under the plan is the lesser of: (1) a dollar amount which is adjusted for inflation ($175,000 for 2006); and (2) 100 percent of the participant's

---

[236] Treas. Reg. sec. 1.401(a)(9)-6, A-4.

[237] Treas. Reg. sec. 1.403(b)-3, A-1(c)(3).

compensation for the highest three years. Special rules apply in some cases.

Explanation of Provision

The provision provides that the 100 percent of compensation limit does not apply to a plan maintained by a church or qualified church controlled organization defined in section 3121(w)(3)(A) except with respect to "highly compensated benefits". The term "highly compensated benefits" means any benefits accrued for an employee in any year on or after the first year in which such employee is a highly compensated employee (as defined in sec. 414(q)) of the organization. For purposes of applying the 100 percent of compensation limit to highly compensated benefits, all the benefits of the employee which would otherwise be taken into account in applying the limit shall be taken into account, i.e., the limit does not apply only to those benefits accrued on or after the first year in which the employee is a highly compensated employee.

Effective Date

The provision is effective for years beginning after December 31, 2006.

[Law at ¶ 5095. CCH Explanation at ¶ 1055.]

[¶ 10,940] Act Sec. 868. Gratuitous transfers for the benefit of employees

Joint Committee Taxation (J.C.T. Rep. No. JCX-38-06)

[Code Sec. 664]

Present Law

Present law permits certain limited transfers of qualified employer securities by charitable remainder trusts to an employee stock ownership plan ("ESOP") without adversely affecting the status of the charitable remainder trusts under section 664. In addition, the ESOP does not fail to be a qualified plan because it complies with the requirements with respect to a qualified gratuitous transfer.

A number of requirements must be satisfied for a transfer of securities to be a qualified gratuitous transfer, including the following: (1) the securities transferred to the ESOP must previously have passed from the decedent to a charitable remainder trust; (2) at the time of the transfer to the ESOP, family members own no more than a certain percentage of the outstanding stock of the company; (3) immediately after the transfer the ESOP owns at least 60 percent of the value of the outstanding stock of company; and (4) the ESOP meets certain requirements.

Among other requirements applicable to the ESOP, securities transferred to the ESOP are required to be allocated each year up to the applicable limit (after first allocating all other annual additions for the limitation year). The applicable limit is the lesser of (1) $30,000 (as indexed) or (2) 25 percent of the participant's compensation.

Explanation of Provision

The provision clarifies that, under section 664, the amount of transferred securities required to be allocated each year is determined on the basis of fair market value of the securities when allocated to participants.

Effective Date

The provision is effective on the date of enactment.

[Law at ¶ 5185. CCH Explanation at ¶ 1155.]

[¶ 10,950] Act Sec. 901. Defined contribution plans required to provide employees with freedom to invest their plan assets

Joint Committee Taxation (J.C.T. Rep. No. JCX-38-06)

[Code Sec. 401(a)(35)]

Present Law

In general

Defined contribution plans may permit both employees and employers to make contributions to the plan. Under a qualified cash or deferred arrangement (commonly referred to as a "section 401(k) plan"), employees may elect to make pretax contributions to a plan, referred to as elective deferrals. Employees may also be permitted to make after-tax contributions to a plan.

In addition, a plan may provide for employer nonelective contributions or matching contributions. Nonelective contributions are employer contributions that are made without regard to whether the employee makes elective deferrals or after-tax contributions. Matching contributions are employer contributions that are made only if the employee makes elective deferrals or after-tax contributions.

Under the Code, elective deferrals, after-tax employee contributions, and employer matching contributions are subject to special nondiscrimination tests. Certain employer nonelective contributions may be used to satisfy these special nondiscrimination tests. In addition, plans may satisfy the special nondiscrimination tests by meeting certain safe harbor contribution requirements.

The Code requires employee stock ownership plans ("ESOPs") to offer certain plan participants the right to diversify investments in employer securities. The Employee Retirement Income Security Act of 1974 ("ERISA") limits the amount of employer securities and employer real property that can be acquired or held by certain employer-sponsored retirement plans. The extent to which the ERISA limits apply depends on the type of plan and the type of contribution involved.

Diversification requirements applicable to ESOPs under the Code

An ESOP is a defined contribution plan that is designated as an ESOP and is designed to invest primarily in qualifying employer securities and that meets certain other requirements under the Code. For purposes of ESOP investments, a "qualifying employer security" is defined as: (1) publicly traded common stock of the employer or a member of the same controlled group; (2) if there is no such publicly traded common stock, common stock of the employer (or member of the same controlled group) that has both voting power and dividend rights at least as great as any other class of common stock; or (3) noncallable preferred stock that is convertible into common stock described in (1) or (2) and that meets certain requirements. In some cases, an employer may design a class of preferred stock that meets these requirements and that is held only by the ESOP.

An ESOP can be an entire plan or it can be a component of a larger defined contribution plan. An ESOP may provide for different types of contributions. For example, an ESOP may include a qualified cash or deferred arrangement that permits employees to make elective deferrals.[238]

Under the Code, ESOPs are subject to a requirement that a participant who has attained age 55 and who has at least 10 years of participation in the plan must be permitted to diversify the investment of the participant's account in assets other than employer securities.[239] The diversification requirement applies to a participant for six years, starting with the year in which the individual first meets the eligibility requirements (i.e., age 55 and 10 years of participation). The participant must be allowed to elect to diversify up to 25 percent of the participant's account (50 percent in the sixth year), reduced by the portion of the account diversified in prior years.

The participant must be given 90 days after the end of each plan year in the election period to make the election to diversify. In the case of participants who elect to diversify, the plan satisfies the diversification requirement if: (1) the plan distributes the applicable amount to the participant within 90 days after the election period; (2) the plan offers at least three investment options (not inconsistent with Treasury regulations) and, within 90 days of the election period, invests the applicable amount in accordance with the participant's election; or (3) the applicable amount is transferred within 90 days of the election period to another qualified defined contribution plan of the employer providing investment options in accordance with (2).[240]

ERISA limits on investments in employer securities and real property

ERISA imposes restrictions on the investment of retirement plan assets in employer securities or employer real property.[241] A retirement plan may hold only a "qualifying" employer security and only "qualifying" employer real property.

Under ERISA, any stock issued by the employer or an affiliate of the employer is a qualifying employer security.[242] Qualifying employer securities also include certain publicly traded

---

[238] Such an ESOP design is sometimes referred to as a "KSOP."

[239] Sec. 401(a)(28). The present-law diversification requirements do not apply to employer securities held by an ESOP that were acquired before January 1, 1987.

[240] IRS Notice 88-56, 1988-1 C.B. 540, Q&A-16.

[241] ERISA sec. 407.

[242] Certain additional requirements apply to employer stock held by a defined benefit pension plan or a money purchase pension plan (other than certain plans in existence before the enactment of ERISA).

partnership interests and certain marketable obligations (i.e., a bond, debenture, note, certificate or other evidence of indebtedness). Qualifying employer real property means parcels of employer real property: (1) if a substantial number of the parcels are dispersed geographically; (2) if each parcel of real property and the improvements thereon are suitable (or adaptable without excessive cost) for more than one use; (3) even if all of the real property is leased to one lessee (which may be an employer, or an affiliate of an employer); and (4) if the acquisition and retention of such property generally comply with the fiduciary rules of ERISA (with certain specified exceptions).

ERISA also prohibits defined benefit pension plans and money purchase pension plans (other than certain plans in existence before the enactment of ERISA) from acquiring employer securities or employer real property if, after the acquisition, more than 10 percent of the assets of the plan would be invested in employer securities and real property. Except as discussed below with respect to elective deferrals, this 10-percent limitation generally does not apply to defined contribution plans other than money purchase pension plans.[243] In addition, a fiduciary generally is deemed not to violate the requirement that plan assets be diversified with respect to the acquisition or holding of employer securities or employer real property in a defined contribution plan.[244]

The 10-percent limitation on the acquisition of employer securities and real property applies separately to the portion of a plan consisting of elective deferrals (and earnings thereon) if any portion of an individual's elective deferrals (or earnings thereon) are required to be invested in employer securities or real property pursuant to plan terms or the direction of a person other than the participant. This restriction does not apply if: (1) the amount of elective deferrals required to be invested in employer securities and real property does not exceed more than one percent of any employee's compensation; (2) the fair market value of all defined contribution plans maintained by the employer is no more than 10 percent of the fair market value of all retirement plans of the employer; or (3) the plan is an ESOP.

Explanation of Provision

In general

Under the provision, in order to satisfy the plan qualification requirements of the Code and the vesting requirements of ERISA, certain defined contribution plans are required to provide diversification rights with respect to amounts invested in employer securities. Such a plan is required to permit applicable individuals to direct that the portion of the individual's account held in employer securities be invested in alternative investments. An applicable individual includes: (1) any plan participant; and (2) any beneficiary who has an account under the plan with respect to which the beneficiary is entitled to exercise the rights of a participant. The time when the diversification requirements apply depends on the type of contributions invested in employer securities.

Plans subject to requirements

The diversification requirements generally apply to an "applicable defined contribution plan,"[245] which means a defined contribution plan holding publicly-traded employer securities (i.e., securities issued by the employer or a member of the employer's controlled group of corporations[246] that are readily tradable on an established securities market).

For this purpose, a plan holding employer securities that are not publicly traded is generally treated as holding publicly-traded employer securities if the employer (or any member of the employer's controlled group of corporations) has issued a class of stock that is a publicly-traded employer security. This treatment does not apply if neither the employer nor any parent corporation[247] of the employer has issued any publicly-traded security or any special class of stock that

---

[243] The 10-percent limitation also applies to a defined contribution plan that is part of an arrangement under which benefits payable to a participant under a defined benefit pension plan are reduced by benefits under the defined contribution plan (i.e., a "floor-offset" arrangement).

[244] Under ERISA, a defined contribution plan is generally referred to as an individual account plan. Plans that are not subject to the 10-percent limitation on the acquisition of employer securities and employer real property are referred to as "eligible individual account plans."

[245] Under ERISA, the diversification requirements apply to an "applicable individual account plan."

[246] For this purpose, "controlled group of corporations" has the same meaning as under section 1563(a), except that, in applying that section, 50 percent is substituted for 80 percent.

[247] For this purpose, "parent corporation" has the same meaning as under section 424(e), i.e., any corporation (other than the employer) in an unbroken chain of corporations ending with the employer if each corporation other than the employer owns stock possessing at least 50 percent of the total combined voting power of all classes of stock with voting rights or at least 50 percent of the total value of shares of all classes of stock in one of the other corporations in the chain.

grants particular rights to, or bears particular risks for, the holder or the issuer with respect to any member of the employer's controlled group that has issued any publicly-traded employer security. For example, a controlled group that generally consists of corporations that have not issued publicly-traded securities may include a member that has issued publicly-traded stock (the "publicly-traded member"). In the case of a plan maintained by an employer that is another member of the controlled group, the diversification requirements do not apply to the plan, provided that neither the employer nor a parent corporation of the employer has issued any publicly-traded security or any special class of stock that grants particular rights to, or bears particular risks for, the holder or issuer with respect to the member that has issued publicly-traded stock. The Secretary of the Treasury has the authority to provide other exceptions in regulations. For example, an exception may be appropriate if no stock of the employer maintaining the plan (including stock held in the plan) is publicly traded, but a member of the employer's controlled group has issued a small amount of publicly-traded stock.

The diversification requirements do not apply to an ESOP that: (1) does not hold contributions (or earnings thereon) that are subject to the special nondiscrimination tests that apply to elective deferrals, employee after-tax contributions, and matching contributions; and (2) is a separate plan from any other qualified retirement plan of the employer. Accordingly, an ESOP that holds elective deferrals, employee contributions, employer matching contributions, or nonelective employer contributions used to satisfy the special nondiscrimination tests (including the safe harbor methods of satisfying the tests) is subject to the diversification requirements under the Provision. The diversification rights applicable under the provision are broader than those applicable under the Code's present-law ESOP diversification rules. Thus, an ESOP that is subject to the new requirements is excepted from the present-law rules.[248]

The new diversification requirements also do not apply to a one-participant retirement plan. For purposes of the Code, a one-participant retirement plan is a plan that: (1) on the first day of the plan year, either covered only one individual (or the individual and his or her spouse) and the individual owned 100 percent of the plan sponsor (i.e., the employer maintaining the plan), whether or not incorporated, or covered only one or more partners (or partners and their spouses) in the plan sponsor; (2) meets the minimum coverage requirements without being combined with any other plan of the business that covers employees of the business; (3) does not provide benefits to anyone except the individuals and partners (and spouses) described in (1); (4) does not cover a business that is a member of an affiliated service group, a controlled group of corporations, or a group of corporations under common control; and (5) does not cover a business that uses the services of leased employees.[249] It is intended that, for this purpose, a "partner" includes an owner of a business that is treated as a partnership for tax purposes. In addition, it includes a two-percent shareholder of an S corporation.[250]

Elective deferrals and after-tax employee contributions

In the case of amounts attributable to elective deferrals under a qualified cash or deferred arrangement and employee after-tax contributions that are invested in employer securities, any applicable individual must be permitted to direct that such amounts be invested in alternative investments.

Other contributions

In the case of amounts attributable to contributions other than elective deferrals and after-tax employees contributions (i.e., nonelective employer contributions and employer matching contributions) that are invested in employer securities, an applicable individual who is a participant with three years of service,[251] a beneficiary of such a participant, or a beneficiary of a deceased participant must be permitted to direct that such amounts be invested in alternative investments.

A transition rule applies to amounts attributable to these other contributions that are invested in employer securities acquired before the first plan year for which the new diversification requirements apply. Under the transition rule,

[248] An ESOP will not be treated as failing to be designed to invest primarily in qualifying employer securities merely because the plan provides diversification rights as required under the provision or greater diversification rights than required under the provision.

[249] For purposes of ERISA, a one-participant retirement plan is defined as under the provision of ERISA that requires advance notice of a blackout period to be provided to participants and beneficiaries affected by the blackout period, as discussed below.

[250] Under section 1372, a two-percent shareholder of an S corporation is treated as a partner for fringe benefit purposes.

[251] Years of service is defined as under the rules relating to vesting (sec. 411(a)).

for the first three years for which the new diversification requirements apply to the plan, the applicable percentage of such amounts is subject to diversification as shown in Table 1, below. The applicable percentage applies separately to each class of employer security in an applicable individual's account. The transition rule does not apply to plan participants who have three years of service and who have attained age 55 by the beginning of the first plan year beginning after December 31, 2005.

Table 1.—Applicable Percentage for Employer Securities Held on Effective Date

Plan year for which diversification applies:	Applicable percentage:
First year	33 percent
Second year	66 percent
Third year	100 percent

The application of the transition rule is illustrated by the following example. Suppose that the account of a participant with at least three years of service held 120 shares of employer common stock contributed as matching contributions before the diversification requirements became effective. In the first year for which diversification applies, 33 percent (i.e., 40 shares) of that stock is subject to the diversification requirements. In the second year for which diversification applies, a total of 66 percent of 120 shares of stock (i.e., 79 shares, or an additional 39 shares) is subject to the diversification requirements. In the third year for which diversification applies, 100 percent of the stock, or all 120 shares, is subject to the diversification requirements. In addition, in each year, employer stock in the account attributable to elective deferrals and employee after-tax contributions is fully subject to the diversification requirements, as is any new stock contributed to the account.

Rules relating to the election of investment alternatives

A plan subject to the diversification requirements is required to give applicable individuals a choice of at least three investment options, other than employer securities, each of which is diversified and has materially different risk and return characteristics. It is intended that other investment options generally offered by the plan also must be available to applicable individuals.

A plan does not fail to meet the diversification requirements merely because the plan limits the times when divestment and reinvestment can be made to periodic, reasonable opportunities that occur at least quarterly. It is intended that applicable individuals generally be given the opportunity to make investment changes with respect to employer securities on the same basis as the opportunity to make other investment changes, except in unusual circumstances. Thus, in general, applicable individuals must be given the opportunity to request changes with respect to investments in employer securities with the same frequency as the opportunity to make other investment changes and that such changes are implemented in the same timeframe as other investment changes, unless circumstances require different treatment.

Except as provided in regulations, a plan may not impose restrictions or conditions with respect to the investment of employer securities that are not imposed on the investment of other plan assets (other than restrictions or conditions imposed by reason of the application of securities laws). For example, such a restriction or condition includes a provision under which a participant who divests his or her account of employer securities receives less favorable treatment (such as a lower rate of employer contributions) than a participant whose account remains invested in employer securities. On the other hand, such a restriction does not include the imposition of fees with respect to other investment options under the plan, merely because fees are not imposed with respect to investments in employer securities.

Effective Date

The provision is effective for plan years beginning after December 31, 2006.

In the case of a plan maintained pursuant to one or more collective bargaining agreements, the provision is effective for plan years beginning after the earlier of (1) the later of December 31, 2007, or the date on which the last of such collective bargaining agreements terminates (determined without regard to any extension thereof after the date of enactment), or (2) December 31, 2008.

A special effective date applies with respect to employer matching and nonelective contributions (and earnings thereon) that are invested in employer securities that, as of September 17, 2003: (1) consist of preferred stock; and (2) are held within an ESOP, under the terms of which the value of the preferred stock is subject to a guaranteed minimum. Under the special rule, the diversification requirements apply to such preferred stock for plan years beginning after the earlier of (1) December 31, 2007; or (2) the first date as of which the actual value of the preferred stock equals or exceeds the guaranteed minimum. When the new diversification requirements become effective for the plan under the special rule, the applicable percentage of employer securities held on the effective date that is subject to diversification is determined without regard to the special rule.

[Law at ¶ 5030, ¶ 5065, ¶ 5315 and ¶ 7180. CCH Explanation at ¶ 605.]

[¶ 10,960] Act Sec. 902. Increasing participation through automatic enrollment arrangements

Joint Committee Taxation (J.C.T. REP. NO. JCX-38-06)

[Code Secs. 401(k), 401(m), 414and 4979]

Present Law

Qualified cash or deferred arrangements-in general

Under present law, most defined contribution plans may include a qualified cash or deferred arrangement (commonly referred to as a "section 401(k)" or "401(k)" plan),[252] under which employees may elect to receive cash or to have contributions made to the plan by the employer on behalf of the employee in lieu of receiving cash. Contributions made to the plan at the election of the employee are referred to as "elective deferrals" or "elective contributions".[253] A 401(k) plan may be designed so that the employee will receive cash unless an affirmative election to make contributions is made. Alternatively, a plan may provide that elective contributions are made at a specified rate unless the employee elects otherwise (i.e., elects not to make contributions or to make contributions at a different rate). Arrangements that operate in this manner are sometimes referred to as "automatic enrollment" or "negative election" plans. In either case, the employee must have an effective opportunity to elect to receive cash in lieu of contributions.[254]

Nondiscrimination rules

A special nondiscrimination test applies to elective deferrals under a section 401(k) plan, called the actual deferral percentage test or the "ADP" test. The ADP test compares the actual deferral percentages ("ADPs") of the highly compensated employee group and the nonhighly compensated employee group. The ADP for each group generally is the average of the deferral percentages separately calculated for the employees in the group who are eligible to make elective deferrals for all or a portion of the relevant plan year. Each eligible employee's deferral percentage generally is the employee's elective deferrals for the year divided by the employee's compensation for the year.

The plan generally satisfies the ADP test if the ADP of the highly compensated employee group for the current plan year is either (1) not more than 125 percent of the ADP of the nonhighly compensated employee group for the prior plan year, or (2) not more than 200 percent of the ADP of the nonhighly compensated employee group for the prior plan year and not more than two percentage points greater than the ADP of the nonhighly compensated employee group for the prior plan year.

Under a safe harbor, a section 401(k) plan is deemed to satisfy the special nondiscrimination test if the plan satisfies one of two contribution requirements and satisfies a notice requirement (a "safe harbor section 401(k) plan"). A plan satisfies the contribution requirement under the safe harbor rule if the employer either (1) satisfies a matching contribution requirement or (2) makes a nonelective contribution to a defined contribution plan of at least three percent of an employee's compensation on behalf of each nonhighly compensated employee who is eligible to participate in the arrangement. A plan generally satisfies the matching contribution requirement if, under the arrangement: (1) the employer makes a matching contribution on behalf of each nonhighly compensated employee that is equal to (a) 100 percent of the employee's elec-

[252] Legally, a section 401(k) plan is not a separate type of plan, but is a profit-sharing, stock bonus, or pre-ERISA money purchase plan that contains a qualified cash or deferred arrangement. The terms "section 401(k) plan" and "401(k) plan" are used here for convenience.

[253] The maximum annual amount of elective deferrals that can be made by an individual is subject to a limit ($15,000 for 2006). An individual who has attained age 50 before the end of the taxable year may also make catch-up contributions to a section 401(k) plan, subject to a limit ($5,000 for 2006).

[254] Treasury regulations provide that whether an employee has an effective opportunity to receive cash is based on all the relevant facts and circumstances, including the adequacy of notice of the availability of the election, the period of time during which an election may be made, and any other conditions on elections. Treas. Reg. sec. 1.401(k)-1(e)(2).

tive deferrals up to three percent of compensation and (b) 50 percent of the employee's elective deferrals from three to five percent of compensation;[255] and (2) the rate of match with respect to any elective deferrals for highly compensated employees is not greater than the rate of match for nonhighly compensated employees.

Employer matching contributions are also subject to a special nondiscrimination test, the "ACP test," which compares the average actual contribution percentages ("ACPs") of matching contributions for the highly compensated employee group and the nonhighly compensated employee group. The plan generally satisfies the ACP test if the ACP of the highly compensated employee group for the current plan year is either (1) not more than 125 percent of the ACP of the nonhighly compensated employee group for the prior plan year, or (2) not more than 200 percent of the ACP of the nonhighly compensated employee group for the prior plan year and not more than two percentage points greater than the ACP of the nonhighly compensated employee group for the prior plan year.

A safe harbor section 401(k) plan that provides for matching contributions is deemed to satisfy the ACP test if, in addition to meeting the safe harbor contribution and notice requirements under section 401(k), (1) matching contributions are not provided with respect to elective deferrals in excess of six percent of compensation, (2) the rate of matching contribution does not increase as the rate of an employee's elective deferrals increases, and (3) the rate of matching contribution with respect to any rate of elective deferral of a highly compensated employee is no greater than the rate of matching contribution with respect to the same rate of deferral of a nonhighly compensated employee.

Top-heavy rules

Special rules apply in the case of a top-heavy plan. In general, a defined contribution plan is a top-heavy plan if the accounts of key employees account for more than 60 percent of the aggregate value of accounts under the plan. If a plan is a top-heavy plan, then certain minimum vesting standards and minimum contribution requirements apply.

A plan that consists solely of contributions that satisfy the safe harbor plan rules for elective and matching contributions is not considered a top-heavy plan.

Tax-sheltered annuities

Tax-sheltered annuities ("section 403(b) annuities") may provide for contributions on a salary reduction basis, similar to section 401(k) plans. Matching contributions under a section 403(b) annuity are subject to the same nondiscrimination rules under section 401(m) as matching contributions under a section 401(k) plan (sec. 403(b)(12)). Thus, for example, the safe harbor method of satisfying the section 401(m) rules for matching contributions under a 401(k) plan applies to section 403(b) annuities.

Erroneous automatic elective contributions

Present law provides special rules for distributions of elective contributions that exceed the amount permitted under the nondiscrimination rules or the dollar limit on such contributions.

Fiduciary rules applicable to default investments of individual account plans

ERISA imposes standards on the conduct of plan fiduciaries, including persons who make investment decisions with respect to plan assets. Fiduciaries are personally liable for any losses to the plan due to a violation of fiduciary standards.

An individual account plan may permit participants to make investment decisions with respect to their accounts. ERISA fiduciary liability does not apply to investment decisions made by plan participants if participants exercise control over the investment of their individual accounts, as determined under ERISA regulations. In that case, a plan fiduciary may be responsible for the investment alternatives made available, but not for the specific investment decisions made by participants.

Preemption of State law

ERISA generally preempts all State laws relating to employee benefit plans, other than generally applicable criminal laws and laws relating to insurance, banking, or securities.

Excess contributions

An excise tax is imposed on an employer making excess contributions or excess aggregate contributions to a qualified retirement plan. Excess contributions are elective contributions, including qualified nonelective contributions and

[255] In lieu of matching contributions at rates equal to the safe harbor rates, a plan may provide for an alternative match if (1) the rate of the matching contributions does not increase as an employee's rate of elective deferrals increases and (2) the amount of matching contributions at such rate of elective deferrals is at lest equal to the aggregate amount of contributions which would be made if rate of the matching contributions equaled the safe harbor rates.

qualified matching contributions that are treated as elective contributions, made to a plan on behalf of highly compensated employees to the extent that the contributions fail to satisfy the applicable nondiscrimination tests for such plan for the year. Excess aggregate contributions are the aggregate amount of employer matching contributions and employee after-tax contributions to a plan for highly compensated employees to the extent that the contributions fail to satisfy the applicable nondiscrimination tests for such plan for the year.

The excise tax is equal to 10 percent of the excess contributions or excess aggregate contributions under a plan for the plan year ending in the taxable year. The tax does not apply to any excess contributions or excess aggregate contributions that, together with income allocable to the contributions, are distributed or forfeited (if forfeitable) within 2½ months after the close of the plan year. Any excess contributions or excess aggregate contributions that are distributed within 2½ months after the close of the plan year are treated as received and earned by the recipient in the taxable year for which such contributions are made. If the total of such distributions to a recipient under a plan for any plan year is less than $100, such distributions (and any income allocable thereto) are treated as earned and received by the recipient in the taxable year in which the distributions are made.

Additionally, if certain requirements are met, excess contributions may be recharacterized as after-tax employee contributions, no later than 2½ months after the close of the plan year to which the excess contributions relate.[256]

Explanation of Provision

In general

Under the provision, a 401(k) plan that contains an automatic enrollment feature that satisfies certain requirements (a "qualified automatic enrollment feature") is treated as meeting the ADP test with respect to elective deferrals and the ACP test with respect to matching contributions. In addition, a plan consisting solely of contributions made pursuant to a qualified automatic enrollment feature is not subject to the top-heavy rules.

A qualified automatic enrollment feature must meet certain requirements with respect to: (1) automatic deferral; (2) matching or nonelective contributions; and (3) notice to employees.

Automatic deferral/amount of elective contributions

A qualified automatic enrollment feature must provide that, unless an employee elects otherwise, the employee is treated as making an election to make elective deferrals equal to a stated percentage of compensation not in excess of 10 percent and at least equal to: three percent of compensation for the first year the deemed election applies to the participant; four percent during the second year; five percent during the third year; and six percent during the fourth year and thereafter. The stated percentage must be applied uniformly to all eligible employees.

Eligible employees mean all employees eligible to participate in the arrangement, other than employees eligible to participate in the arrangement immediately before the date on which the arrangement became a qualified automatic contribution arrangement with an election in effect (either to participate at a certain percentage or not to participate).

Matching or nonelective contribution requirement

Contributions

An automatic enrollment feature satisfies the contribution requirement if the employer either (1) satisfies a matching contribution requirement or (2) makes a nonelective contribution to a defined contribution plan of at least three percent of an employee's compensation on behalf of each nonhighly compensated employee who is eligible to participate in the automatic enrollment feature. A plan generally satisfies the matching contribution requirement if, under the arrangement: (1) the employer makes a matching contribution on behalf of each nonhighly compensated employee that is equal to 100 percent of the employee's elective deferrals as do not exceed one percent of compensation and 50 percent of the employee's elective deferrals as exceeds one percent but does not exceed six percent of compensation and (2) the rate of match with respect to any elective deferrals for highly compensated employees is not greater than the rate of match for nonhighly compensated employees. It is intended that the provision apply to section 403(b) annuities.

A plan including an automatic enrollment feature that provides for matching contributions is deemed to satisfy the ACP test if, in addition

---

[256] Treas. Reg. sec. 1.401(k)-2(b)(3).

to meeting the safe harbor contribution requirements applicable to the qualified automatic enrollment feature: (1) matching contributions are not provided with respect to elective deferrals in excess of six percent of compensation, (2) the rate of matching contribution does not increase as the rate of an employee's elective deferrals increases, and (3) the rate of matching contribution with respect to any rate of elective deferral of a highly compensated employee is no greater than the rate of matching contribution with respect to the same rate of deferral of a nonhighly compensated employee.

Vesting

Any matching or other employer contributions taken into account in determining whether the requirements for a qualified automatic enrollment feature are satisfied must vest at least as rapidly as under two-year cliff vesting. That is, employees with at least two years of service must be 100 percent vested with respect to such contributions.

Withdrawal restrictions

Under the provision, any matching or other employer contributions taken into account in determining whether the requirements for a qualified automatic enrollment feature are satisfied are subject to the withdrawal rules applicable to elective contributions.

Notice requirement

Under a notice requirement, each employee eligible to participate in the arrangement must receive notice of the arrangement which is sufficiently accurate and comprehensive to apprise the employee of such rights and obligations and is written in a manner calculated to be understood by the average employee to whom the arrangement applies. The notice must explain: (1) the employee's right under the arrangement to elect not to have elective contributions made on the employee's behalf or to elect to have contributions made in a different amount; and (2) how contributions made under the automatic enrollment arrangement will be invested in the absence of any investment election by the employee. The employee must be given a reasonable period of time after receipt of the notice and before the first election contribution is to be made to make an election with respect to contributions and investments.

Application to tax-sheltered annuities

The new safe harbor rules for automatic contribution plans apply with respect to matching contributions under a section 403(b) annuity through the operation of section 403(b)(12).

Corrective distributions

The provision includes rules under which erroneous automatic contributions may be distributed from the plan no later than 90 days after the date of the first elective contribution with respect to the employee under the arrangement. The amount that is treated as an erroneous contribution is limited to the amount of automatic contributions made during the 90-day period that the employee elects to treat as an erroneous contribution. It is intended that distributions of such amounts are generally treated as a payment of compensation, rather than as a contribution to and then a distribution from the plan. The 10-percent early withdrawal tax does not apply to distributions of erroneous automatic contributions. In addition, it is intended that such contributions are not taken into account for purposes of applying the nondiscrimination rules, or the limit on elective deferrals. Similarly, it is intended that distributions of such contributions are not subject to the otherwise applicable withdrawal restrictions. The rules for corrective distributions apply to distributions from (1) qualified pension plans under Code section 401(a), (2) plans under which amounts are contributed by an individual's employer for Code section 403(b) annuity contract and (3) governmental eligible deferred compensation plans under Code section 457(b).

The corrective distribution rules are not limited to arrangements meeting the requirements of a qualified enrollment feature.

Excess contributions

In the case of an eligible automatic contribution arrangement, the excise tax on excess contributions does not apply to any excess contributions or excess aggregate contributions which, together with income allocable to the contributions, are distributed or forfeited (if forfeitable) within six months after the close of the plan year. Additionally, any excess contributions or excess aggregate contributions (and any income allocable thereto) that are distributed within the period required to avoid application of the excise tax are treated as earned and received by the recipient in the taxable year in which the distribution is made (regardless of the amount distributed), and the income allocable to excess contributions or excess aggregate contributions that must be distributed is determined through the end of the year for which the contributions were made.

Preemption of State law

The provision preempts any State law that would directly or indirectly prohibit or restrict the inclusion in a plan of an automatic contribution arrangement. The Labor Secretary may establish minimum standards for such arrangements in order for preemption to apply. An automatic contribution arrangement is an arrangement: (1) under which a participant may elect to have the plan sponsor make payments as contributions under the plan on behalf of the participant, or to the participant directly in cash, (2) under which a participant is treated as having elected to have the plan sponsor make such contributions in an amount equal to a uniform percentage of compensation provided under the plan until the participant specifically elects not to have such contributions made (or elects to have contributions made at a different percentage), and (3) under which contributions are invested in accordance with regulations issued by the Secretary of Labor relating to default investments as provided under the bill. The State preemption rules under the bill are not limited to arrangements that meet the requirements of a qualified enrollment feature.

A plan administrator must provide notice to each participant to whom the automatic contribution arrangement applies. If the notice requirement is not satisfied, an ERISA penalty of $1,100 per day applies.

Effective Date

The provision is effective for years beginning after December 31, 2007. The preemption of conflicting State regulations is effective on the date of enactment. No inference is intended as to the effect of conflicting State regulations prior to date of enactment.

[Law at ¶ 5030, ¶ 5080, ¶ 5090, ¶ 5100, ¶ 5310 and ¶ 7183. CCH Explanation at ¶ 1015.]

[¶ 10,970] Act Sec. 903. Treatment of eligible combined defined benefit plans and qualified cash or deferred arrangements

Joint Committee Taxation (J.C.T. Rep. No. JCX-38-06)

[Code Sec. 414(x)]

Present Law

In general

Under present law, most defined contribution plans may include a qualified cash or deferred arrangement (commonly referred to as a "section 401(k)" or "401(k)" plan),[257] under which employees may elect to receive cash or to have contributions made to the plan by the employer on behalf of the employee in lieu of receiving cash (referred to as "elective deferrals" or "elective contributions").[258] A section 401(k) plan may provide that elective deferrals are made for an employee at a specified rate unless the employee elects otherwise (i.e., elects not to make contributions or to make contributions at a different rate), provided that the employee has an effective opportunity to elect to receive cash in lieu of the default contributions. Such a design is sometimes referred to as "automatic enrollment."

Besides elective deferrals, a section 401(k) plan may provide for: (1) matching contributions, which are employer contributions that are made only if an employee makes elective deferrals; and (2) nonelective contributions, which are employer contributions that are made without regard to whether an employee makes elective deferrals. Under a section 401(k) plan, no benefit other than matching contributions can be contingent on whether an employee makes elective deferrals. Thus, for example, an employee's eligibility for benefits under a defined benefit pension plan cannot be contingent on whether the employee makes elective deferrals.

A cash balance plan is a defined benefit pension plan with benefits resembling the benefits associated with defined contribution plans. Cash balance plans are sometimes referred to as "hybrid" plans because they combine features of a defined benefit pension plan and a defined contribution plan. Under a cash balance plan, benefits are determined by reference to a hypo-

---

[257] Legally, a section 401(k) plan is not a separate type of plan, but is a profit-sharing, stock bonus, or pre-ERISA money purchase plan that contains a qualified cash or deferred arrangement. The terms "section 401(k) plan" and "401(k) plan" are used here for convenience.

[258] The maximum annual amount of elective deferrals that can be made by an individual is subject to a dollar limit ($15,000 for 2006). An individual who has attained age 50 before the end of the taxable year may also make catch-up contributions to a section 401(k) plan, subject to a limit ($5,000 for 2006).

thetical account balance. An employee's hypothetical account balance is determined by reference to hypothetical annual allocations to the account ("pay credits") (e.g., a certain percentage of the employee's compensation for the year) and hypothetical earnings on the account ("interest credits"). Other types of hybrid plans exist as well, such as so-called "pension equity" plans.

The assets of a qualified retirement plan (either a defined contribution plan or a defined benefit pension plan) must be held in trust for the exclusive benefit of participants and beneficiaries. Defined benefit pension plans are subject to funding rules, which require employers to make contributions at specified minimum levels.[259] In addition, limits apply on the extent to which defined benefit pension plan assets may be invested in employer securities or real property. The minimum funding rules and limits on investments in employer securities or real property generally do not apply to defined contribution plans.

Nondiscrimination requirements

Under a general nondiscrimination requirement, the contributions or benefits provided under a qualified retirement plan must not discriminate in favor of highly compensated employees.[260] Treasury regulations provide detailed and exclusive rules for determining whether a plan satisfies the general nondiscrimination rules. Under the regulations, the amount of contributions or benefits provided under the plan and the benefits, rights and features offered under the plan must be tested.

A special nondiscrimination test applies to elective deferrals under a section 401(k) plan, called the actual deferral percentage test or the "ADP" test. The ADP test compares the actual deferral percentages ("ADPs") of the highly compensated employee group and the nonhighly compensated employee group. The ADP for each group generally is the average of the deferral percentages separately calculated for the employees in the group who are eligible to make elective deferrals for all or a portion of the relevant plan year. Each eligible employee's deferral percentage generally is the employee's elective deferrals for the year divided by the employee's compensation for the year.

The plan generally satisfies the ADP test if the ADP of the highly compensated employee group for the current plan year is either (1) not more than 125 percent of the ADP of the nonhighly compensated employee group for the prior plan year, or (2) not more than 200 percent of the ADP of the nonhighly compensated employee group for the prior plan year and not more than two percentage points greater than the ADP of the nonhighly compensated employee group for the prior plan year.

Under a safe harbor, a section 401(k) plan is deemed to satisfy the special nondiscrimination test if the plan satisfies one of two contribution requirements and satisfies a notice requirement (a "safe harbor section 401(k) plan"). A plan satisfies the contribution requirement under the safe harbor rule if the employer either (1) satisfies a matching contribution requirement or (2) makes a nonelective contribution to a defined contribution plan of at least three percent of an employee's compensation on behalf of each nonhighly compensated employee who is eligible to participate in the arrangement. A plan generally satisfies the matching contribution requirement if, under the arrangement: (1) the employer makes a matching contribution on behalf of each nonhighly compensated employee that is equal to (a) 100 percent of the employee's elective deferrals up to three percent of compensation and (b) 50 percent of the employee's elective deferrals from three to five percent of compensation; and (2) the rate of matching contribution with respect to any rate of elective deferrals of a highly compensated employee is not greater than the rate of matching contribution with respect to the same rate of elective deferral of a nonhighly compensated employee.[261]

Employer matching contributions are also subject to a special nondiscrimination test, the "ACP test," which compares the average actual contribution percentages ("ACPs") of matching contributions for the highly compensated employee group and the nonhighly compensated employee group. The plan generally satisfies the ACP test if the ACP of the highly compensated

[259] The Pension Benefit Guaranty Corporation generally guarantees a minimum level of benefits under a defined benefit plan.

[260] Under special rules, referred to as the permitted disparity rules, higher contributions or benefits can be provided to higher-paid employees in certain circumstances without violating the general nondiscrimination rules.

[261] Alternatively, matching contributions may be provided at a different rate, provided that: (1) the rate of matching contribution doesn't increase as the rate of elective deferral increases; and (2) the aggregate amount of matching contributions with respect to each rate of elective deferral is not less than the amount that would be provided under the general rule.

employee group for the current plan year is either (1) not more than 125 percent of the ACP of the nonhighly compensated employee group for the prior plan year, or (2) not more than 200 percent of the ACP of the nonhighly compensated employee group for the prior plan year and not more than two percentage points greater than the ACP of the nonhighly compensated employee group for the prior plan year.

A safe harbor section 401(k) plan that provides for matching contributions must satisfy the ACP test. Alternatively, it is deemed to satisfy the ACP test if it satisfies a matching contribution safe harbor, under which (1) matching contributions are not provided with respect to elective deferrals in excess of six percent of compensation, (2) the rate of matching contribution does not increase as the rate of an employee's elective deferrals increases, and (3) the rate of matching contribution with respect to any rate of elective deferral of a highly compensated employee is no greater than the rate of matching contribution with respect to the same rate of deferral of a nonhighly compensated employee.

Vesting rules

A qualified retirement plan generally must satisfy one of two alternative minimum vesting schedules. A plan satisfies the first schedule if a participant acquires a nonforfeitable right to 100 percent of the participant's accrued benefit derived from employer contributions upon the completion of five years of service. A plan satisfies the second schedule if a participant has a nonforfeitable right to at least 20 percent of the participant's accrued benefit derived from employer contributions after three years of service, 40 percent after four years of service, 60 percent after five years of service, 80 percent after six years of service, and 100 percent after seven years of service.

Special vesting rules apply to elective deferrals and matching contributions. Elective deferrals must be immediately vested. Matching contributions generally must vest at least as rapidly as under one of two alternative minimum vesting schedules. A plan satisfies the first schedule if a participant acquires a nonforfeitable right to 100 percent of matching contributions upon the completion of three years of service. A plan satisfies the second schedule if a participant has a nonforfeitable right to 20 percent of matching contributions for each year of service beginning with the participant's second year of service and ending with 100 percent after six years of service. However, matching contributions under a safe harbor section 401(k) plan must be immediately vested.

Top-heavy rules

Under present law, a top-heavy plan is a qualified retirement plan under which cumulative benefits are provided primarily to key employees. An employee is considered a key employee if, during the prior year, the employee was (1) an officer with compensation in excess of a certain amount ($140,000 for 2006), (2) a five-percent owner, or (3) a one-percent owner with compensation in excess of $150,000. A plan that is top-heavy must provide (1) minimum employer contributions or benefits to participants who are not key employees and (2) more rapid vesting for participants who are not key employees (as discussed below).

In the case of a defined contribution plan, the minimum contribution is the lesser of (1) three percent of compensation, or (2) the highest percentage of compensation at which contributions were made for any key employee. In the case of a defined benefit pension, the minimum benefit is the lesser of (1) two percent of average compensation multiplied by the participant's years of service, or (2) 20 percent of average compensation. For this purpose, a participant's average compensation is generally average compensation for the consecutive-year period (not exceeding five years) during which the participant's aggregate compensation is the greatest.

Top-heavy plans must satisfy one of two alternative minimum vesting schedules. A plan satisfies the first schedule if a participant acquires a nonforfeitable right to 100 percent of contributions or benefits upon the completion of three years of service. A plan satisfies the second schedule if a participant has a nonforfeitable right to 20 percent of contributions or benefits for each year of service beginning with the participant's second year of service and ending with 100 percent after six years of service.[262]

A safe harbor section 401(k) plan is not subject to the top-heavy rules, provided that, if the plan provides for matching contributions, it must also satisfy the matching contribution safe harbor.

Other qualified retirement plan requirements

Qualified retirement plans are subject to various other requirements, some of which depend

[262] The top-heavy vesting schedules are the same as the vesting schedules that apply to matching contributions.

on whether the plan is a defined contribution plan or a defined benefit pension. Such requirements include limits on contributions and benefits and spousal protections.

In the case of a defined contribution plan, annual additions with respect to each plan participant cannot exceed the lesser of: (1) 100 percent of the participant's compensation; or (2) a dollar amount, indexed for inflation ($44,000 for 2006). Annual additions are the sum of employer contributions, employee contributions, and forfeitures with respect to an individual under all defined contribution plans of the same employer. In the case of a defined benefit pension, annual benefits payable under the plan generally may not exceed the lesser of: (1) 100 percent of average compensation; or (2) a dollar amount, indexed for inflation ($175,000 for 2006).

Defined benefit pension plans are required to provide benefits in the form of annuity unless the participant (and his or her spouse, in the case of a married participant) consents to another form of benefit. In addition, in the case of a married participant, benefits generally must be paid in the form of a qualified joint and survivor annuity ("QJSA") unless the participant and his or her spouse consent to a distribution in another form. A QJSA is an annuity for the life of the participant, with a survivor annuity for the life of the spouse which is not less than 50 percent (and not more than 100 percent) of the amount of the annuity payable during the joint lives of the participant and his or her spouse. These spousal protection requirements generally do not apply to a defined contribution plan that does not offer annuity distributions.

Annual reporting by qualified retirement plans

The plan administrator of a qualified retirement plan generally must file an annual return with the Secretary of the Treasury and an annual report with the Secretary of Labor. In addition, in the case of a defined benefit pension, certain information is generally required to be filed with the Pension Benefit Guaranty Corporation ("PBGC"). Form 5500, which consists of a primary form and various schedules, includes the information required to be filed with all three agencies. The plan administrator satisfies the reporting requirement with respect to each agency by filing the Form 5500 with the Department of Labor.

The Form 5500 is due by the last day of the seventh month following the close of the plan year. The due date may be extended up to two and one-half months. Copies of filed Form 5500s are available for public examination at the U.S. Department of Labor.

A plan administrator must automatically provide participants with a summary of the annual report within two months after the due date of the annual report (i.e., by the end of the ninth month after the end of the plan year unless an extension applies). In addition, a copy of the full annual report must be provided to participants on written request.

Explanation of Provision

In general

The provision provides rules for an "eligible combined plan." An eligible combined plan is a plan: (1) that is maintained by an employer that is a small employer at the time the plan is established; (2) that consists of a defined benefit plan and an "applicable" defined contribution plan; (3) the assets of which are held in a single trust forming part of the plan and are clearly identified and allocated to the defined benefit plan and the applicable defined contribution plan to the extent necessary for the separate application of the Code and ERISA; and (4) that meets certain benefit, contribution, vesting and nondiscrimination requirements as discussed below. For this purpose, an applicable defined contribution plan is a defined contribution plan that includes a qualified cash or deferred arrangement (i.e., a section 401(k) plan). A small employer is an employer that employed an average of at least two, but not more than 500, employees on business days during the preceding calendar year and at least two employees on the first day of the plan year.

Except as specified in the provision, the provisions of the Code and ERISA are applied to any defined benefit plan and any applicable defined contribution plan that are part of an eligible combined plan in the same manner as if each were not part of the eligible combined plan. Thus, for example, the present-law limits on contributions and benefits apply separately to contributions under an applicable defined contribution plan that is part of an eligible combined plan and to benefits under the defined benefit plan that is part of the eligible combined plan. In addition, the spousal protection rules apply to the defined benefit plan, but not to the applicable defined contribution plan except to the extent provided under present law. Moreover, although the assets of an eligible combined plan are held in a single trust, the funding rules apply to a defined benefit plan that is part of an eligible combined plan on the basis of the assets identified and allocated to the defined benefit, and the limits on investing defined benefit plan assets in employer securities or real property apply to such assets. Similarly, separate participant accounts are required to be maintained under the applicable defined contribution plan that is part of the eligible combined plan, and earnings (or losses) on participants' account are based on the earnings (or losses) with respect to the assets of the applicable defined contribution plan.

Requirements with respect to defined benefit plan

A defined benefit plan that is part of an eligible combined plan is required to provide each participant with a benefit of not less than the applicable percentage of the participant's final average pay. The applicable percentage is the lesser of: (1) one percent multiplied by the participant's years of service; or (2) 20 percent. For this purpose, final average pay is determined using the consecutive-year period (not exceeding five years) during which the participant has the greatest aggregate compensation.

If the defined benefit plan is an applicable defined benefit plan,[263] the plan is treated as meeting this benefit requirement if each participant receives a pay credit for each plan year of not less than the percentage of compensation determined in accordance with the following table:

Table 2.—Percentage of Compensation

Participant's age as of the beginning of the plan year:	Percentage:
30 or less	2 percent
Over 30 but less than 40	4 percent
Over 40 but less than 50	6 percent
50 or over	8 percent

A defined benefit that is part of an eligible combined plan must provide the required benefit to each participant, regardless of whether the participant makes elective deferrals to the applicable defined contribution plan that is part of the eligible combined plan.

Any benefits provided under the defined benefit plan (including any benefits provided in addition to required benefits) must be fully vested after three years of service.

Requirements with respect to applicable defined contribution plan

Certain automatic enrollment and matching contribution requirements must be met with respect to an applicable defined contribution plan that is part of an eligible combined plan. First, the qualified cash or deferred arrangement under the plan must constitute an automatic contribution arrangement, under which each employee eligible to participate is treated as having elected to make deferrals of four percent of compensation unless the employee elects otherwise (i.e., elects not to make deferrals or to make deferrals at a different rate). Participants must be given notice of their right to elect otherwise and must be given a reasonable period of time after receiving notice in which to make an election. In addition, participants must be given notice of their rights and obligations within a reasonable period before each year.

Under the applicable defined contribution plan, the employer must be required to make matching contributions on behalf of each employee eligible to participate in the arrangement in an amount equal to 50 percent of the employee's elective deferrals up to four percent of compensation, and the rate of matching contribution with respect to any elective deferrals for highly compensated employees must not be not greater than the rate of match for nonhighly compensated employees.[264] Matching contributions in addition to the required matching contributions may also be made. The employer may also make nonelective contributions under the applicable defined contribution plan, but any nonelective contributions are not taken into account in determining whether the matching contribution requirement is met.

Any matching contributions under the applicable defined contribution plan (including any in excess of required matching contributions) must be fully vested when made. Any nonelective contributions made under the applicable defined contribution plan must be fully vested after three years of service.

[263] Applicable defined benefit plan is defined as under the TITLE VII of the bill.

[264] As under present law, matching contributions may be provided at a different rate, provided that: (1) the rate of matching contribution doesn't increase as the rate of elective deferral increases; and (2) the aggregate amount of matching contributions with respect to each rate of elective deferral is not less than the amount that would be provided under the general rule.

Nondiscrimination and other rules

An applicable defined contribution plan satisfies the ADP test on a safe-harbor basis. Matching contributions under an applicable defined contribution plan must satisfy the ACP test or may satisfy the matching contribution safe harbor under present law, as modified to reflect the matching contribution requirements applicable under the provision.

Nonelective contributions under an applicable defined contribution plan and benefits under a defined benefit plan that are part of an eligible combined plan are generally subject to the nondiscrimination rules as under present law. However, neither a defined benefit plan nor an applicable defined contribution plan that is part of an eligible combined plan may be combined with another plan in determining whether the nondiscrimination requirements are met.[265]

An applicable defined contribution plan and a defined benefit plan that are part of an eligible combined plan are treated as meeting the top-heavy requirements.

All contributions, benefits, and other rights and features that are provided under a defined benefit plan or an applicable defined contribution plan that is part of an eligible combined plan must be provided uniformly to all participants. This requirement applies regardless of whether nonuniform contributions, benefits, or other rights or features could be provided without violating the nondiscrimination rules. However, it is intended that a plan will not violate the uniformity requirement merely because benefits accrued for periods before a defined benefit or defined contribution plan became part of an eligible combined plan are protected (as required under the anticutback rules).

Annual reporting

An eligible combined plan is treated as a single plan for purposes of annual reporting. Thus, only a single Form 5500 is required. All of the information required under present law with respect to a defined benefit plan or a defined contribution plan must be provided in the Form 5500 for the eligible combined plan. In addition, only a single summary annual report must be provided to participants.

Other rules

The provision of the bill relating to default investment options and the preemption of State laws with respect to automatic enrollment arrangements are applicable to eligible combined plans. It is intended that in the case that an eligible combined plan terminates, the PBGC guarantee applies only to benefits under the defined benefit portion of the plan.

Effective Date

The provision is effective for plan years beginning after December 31, 2009.

[Law at ¶ 5090 and ¶ 7186. CCH Explanation at ¶ 1020.]

[¶ 10,980] Act Sec. 904. Faster vesting of employer nonelective contributions

Joint Committee Taxation (J.C.T. Rep. No. JCX-38-06)

[Code Sec. 411]

Present Law

Under present law, in general, a plan is not a qualified plan unless a participant's employer-provided benefit vests at least as rapidly as under one of two alternative minimum vesting schedules. A plan satisfies the first schedule if a participant acquires a nonforfeitable right to 100 percent of the participant's accrued benefit derived from employer contributions upon the completion of five years of service. A plan satisfies the second schedule if a participant has a nonforfeitable right to at least 20 percent of the participant's accrued benefit derived from employer contributions after three years of service, 40 percent after four years of service, 60 percent after five years of service, 80 percent after six years of service, and 100 percent after seven years of service.[266]

---

[265] The permitted disparity rules do not apply in determining whether an applicable defined contribution plan or a defined benefit plan that is part of an eligible combined plan satisfies (1) the contribution or benefit requirements under the provision or (2) the nondiscrimination requirements.

[266] The minimum vesting requirements are also contained in Title I of the Employee Retirement Income Security Act of 1974 ("ERISA").

Faster vesting schedules apply to employer matching contributions. Employer matching contributions are required to vest at least as rapidly as under one of the following two alternative minimum vesting schedules. A plan satisfies the first schedule if a participant acquires a nonforfeitable right to 100 percent of employer matching contributions upon the completion of three years of service. A plan satisfies the second schedule if a participant has a nonforfeitable right to 20 percent of employer matching contributions for each year of service beginning with the participant's second year of service and ending with 100 percent after six years of service.

Explanation of Provision

The provision applies the present-law vesting schedule for matching contributions to all employer contributions to defined contribution plans.

The provision does not apply to any employee until the employee has an hour of service after the effective date. In applying the new vesting schedule, service before the effective date is taken into account.

Effective Date

The provision is generally effective for contributions for plan years beginning after December 31, 2006.

In the case of a plan maintained pursuant to one or more collective bargaining agreements, the provision is not effective for contributions (including allocations of forfeitures) for plan years beginning before the earlier of (1) the later of the date on which the last of such collective bargaining agreements terminates (determined without regard to any extension thereof on or after the date of enactment) or January 1, 2007, or (2) January 1, 2009.

In the case of an employee stock ownership plan ("ESOP") which on September 26, 2005, had outstanding a loan incurred for the purpose of acquiring qualifying employer securities, the provision does not apply to any plan year beginning before the earlier of (1) the date on which the loan is fully repaid, or (2) the date on which the loan was, as of September 26, 2005, scheduled to be fully repaid.

[Law at ¶ 5080 and ¶ 7189. CCH Explanation at ¶ 720.]

[¶ 10,990] Act Sec. 905. Distributions during working retirement

Joint Committee Taxation (J.C.T. Rep. No. JCX-38-06)

[Code Sec. 401(a)(36)]

Present Law

Under ERISA, a pension plan is a plan, fund, or program established or maintained by an employer or an employee organization, or by both, to the extent that, by its express terms or surrounding circumstances, the plan, fund, or program: (1) provides retirement income to employees, or (2) results in a deferral of income by employees for periods extending to the termination of covered employment or beyond, regardless of the method of calculating contributions made to or benefits under the plan or the method of distributing benefits from the plan.

For purposes of the qualification requirements applicable to pension plans, stock bonus plans, and profit-sharing plans under the Code, a pension plan is a plan established and maintained primarily to provide systematically for the payment of definitely determinable benefits to employees over a period of years, usually life, after retirement.[267] A pension plan (i.e., a defined benefit plan or money purchase pension plan) may not provide for distributions before the attainment of normal retirement age (commonly age 65) to participants who have not separated from employment.[268]

Under proposed regulations, in the case of a phased retirement program, a pension plan is permitted to pay a portion of a participant's benefits before attainment of normal retirement age.[269] A phased retirement program is a program under which employees who are at least

[267] Treas. Reg. sec. 1.401-1(b)(1)(i).

[268] See, e.g., Rev. Rul. 74-254.

[269] Prop. Treas. Reg. secs. 1.401(a)-1(b)(1)(iv) and 1.401(a)-3.

age 59½ and are eligible for retirement may reduce (by at least 20 percent) the number of hours they customarily work and receive a pro rata portion of their retirement benefits, based on the reduction in their work schedule.

Explanation of Provision

Under the provision, for purposes of the definition of pension plan under ERISA, a distribution from a plan, fund, or program is not treated as made in a form other than retirement income or as a distribution prior to termination of covered employment solely because the distribution is made to an employee who has attained age 62 and who is not separated from employment at the time of such distribution.

In addition, under the Code, a pension plan does not fail to be a qualified retirement plan solely because the plan provides that a distribution may be made to an employee who has attained age 62 and who is not separated from employment at the time of the distribution.

Effective Date

The provision is effective for distributions in plan years beginning after December 31, 2006.

[Law at ¶ 5030 and ¶ 7192. CCH Explanation at ¶ 920.]

[¶ 11,000] Act Sec. 906. Treatment of plans maintained by Indian tribes

Joint Committee Taxation (J.C.T. Rep. No. JCX-38-06)

[Code Sec. 414(d)]

Present Law

Governmental plans are exempt from ERISA and from Code requirements that correspond to ERISA requirements, such as the vesting rules and the funding rules. A governmental plan is generally a plan established and maintained for its employees by (1) the Federal government, (2) the government of a State or political subdivision of a State, or (3) any agency or instrumentality of any of the foregoing.

Benefits under a defined benefit pension plan generally cannot exceed the lesser of (1) 100 percent of average compensation, or (2) a dollar amount ($175,000 for 2006), subject to certain special rules for defined benefit plans maintained by State and local government employers and other special rules for employees of a police or fire department. Employee contributions to a defined benefit pension plan are generally subject to tax; however, employee contributions may be made to a State or local government defined benefit pension plan on a pretax basis (referred to as "pickup" contributions).

Governmental defined benefit pension plans are not covered by the PBGC insurance program.

Explanation of Provision

Under the provision, the term "governmental plan" for purposes of section 414 of the Code, section 3(32) of ERISA, and the PBGC termination insurance program includes a plan: (1) which is established and maintained by an Indian tribal government (as defined in Code sec. 7701(a)(40)), a subdivision of an Indian tribal government (determined in accordance with Code sec. 7871(d)), or an agency or instrumentality of either; and (2) all of the participants of which are qualified employees of such entity. A qualified employee is an employee of an entity described in (1) all of whose services for such entity are in the performance of essential governmental services and not in the performance of commercial activities (whether or not such activities are an essential governmental function). Thus, for example, a governmental plan would include a plan of a tribal government all of the participants of which are teachers in tribal schools. On the other hand, a governmental plan would not include a plan covering tribal employees who are employed by a hotel, casino, service station, convenience store, or marina operated by a tribal government.

Under the provision, the special benefit limitations applicable to employees of police and fire departments of a State or political subdivision (Code sec. 415(b)(2)(H)) apply to such employees of an Indian tribe or any political subdivision thereof. In addition, the rules relating to pick up contribution under governmental plans (Code sec. 414(h)) and special benefit limitations for governmental plans (sec. 415(b)(10)) apply to tribal plans treated as governmental plans under the provision.

Effective Date

The provision is effective for plan years beginning on or after the date of enactment.

[Law at ¶ 5090, ¶ 5095 and ¶ 7195. CCH Explanation at ¶ 1065.]

[¶11,010] Act Sec. 1001. Regulations on time and order of issuance of domestic relations orders

Joint Committee Taxation (J.C.T. REP. NO. JCX-38-06)

[Act Sec. 1001]

Present Law

Benefits provided under a qualified retirement plan for a participant may not be assigned or alienated to creditors of the participant, except in very limited circumstances.[270] One exception to the prohibition on assignment or alienation is a qualified domestic relations order ("QDRO").[271] A QDRO is a domestic relations order that creates or recognizes a right of an alternate payee, including a former spouse, to any plan benefit payable with respect to a participant and that meets certain procedural requirements. In addition, a QDRO generally may not require the plan to provide any type or form of benefit, or any option, not otherwise provided under the plan, or to provide increased benefits.

Present law also provides that a QDRO may not require the payment of benefits to an alternate payee that are required to be paid to another alternate payee under a domestic relations order previously determined to be a QDRO. This rule implicitly recognizes that a domestic relations order issued after a QDRO may also qualify as a QDRO. However, present law does not otherwise provide specific rules for the treatment of a domestic relations order as a QDRO if the order is issued after another domestic relations order or a QDRO (including an order issued after a divorce decree) or revises another domestic relations order or a QDRO.

Present law provides specific rules that apply during any period in which the status of a domestic relations order as a QDRO is being determined (by the plan administrator, by a court, or otherwise). During such a period, the plan administrator is required to account separately for the amounts that would have been payable to the alternate payee during the period if the order had been determined to be a QDRO (referred to as "segregated amounts"). If, within the 18-month period beginning with the date on which the first payment would be required to be made under the order, the order (or modification thereof) is determined to be a QDRO, the plan administrator is required to pay the segregated amounts (including any interest thereon) to the person or persons entitled thereto. If, within the 18-month period, the order is determined not to be a QDRO, or its status as a QDRO is not resolved, the plan administrator is required to pay the segregated amounts (including any interest) to the person or persons who would be entitled to such amounts if there were no order. In such a case, any subsequent determination that the order is a QDRO is applied prospectively only.

Explanation of Provision

The Secretary of Labor is directed to issue, not later than one year after the date of enactment of the provision, regulations to clarify the status of certain domestic relations orders. In particular, the regulations are to clarify that a domestic relations order otherwise meeting the QDRO requirements will not fail to be treated as a QDRO solely because of the time it is issued or because it is issued after or revises another domestic relations order or QDRO. The regulations are also to clarify that such a domestic relations order is in all respects subject to the same requirements and protections that apply to QDROs. For example, as under present law, such a domestic relations order may not require the payment of benefits to an alternate payee that are required to be paid to another alternate payee under an earlier QDRO. In addition, the present-law rules regarding segregated amounts that apply while the status of a domestic relations order as a QDRO is being determined continue to apply.

Effective Date

The provision is effective on the date of enactment.

[Law at ¶ 7198. CCH Explanation at ¶ 1025.]

[270] Code sec. 401(a)(13); ERISA sec. 206(d).

[271] Code secs. 401(a)(13)(B) and 414(p); ERISA sec. 206(d)(3).

[¶11,020] Act Secs. 1002 and 1003. Benefits under the Railroad Retirement System for former spouses

Joint Committee Taxation (J.C.T. REP. NO. JCX-38-06)

[Act Secs. 1002 and 1003]

Present Law

In general

The Railroad Retirement System has two main components. Tier I of the system is financed by taxes on employers and employees equal to the Social Security payroll tax and provides qualified railroad retirees (and their qualified spouses, dependents, widows, or widowers) with benefits that are roughly equal to Social Security. Covered railroad workers and their employers pay the Tier I tax instead of the Social Security payroll tax, and most railroad retirees collect Tier I benefits instead of Social Security. Tier II of the system replicates a private pension plan, with employers and employees contributing a certain percentage of pay toward the system to finance defined benefits to eligible railroad retirees (and qualified spouses, dependents, widows, or widowers) upon retirement; however, the Federal Government collects the Tier II payroll contribution and pays out the benefits.

Former spouses of living railroad employees

Generally, a former spouse of a railroad employee who is otherwise eligible for any Tier I or Tier II benefit cannot receive either benefit until the railroad employee actually retires and begins receiving his or her retirement benefits. This is the case regardless of whether a State divorce court has awarded such railroad retirement benefits to the former spouse.

Former spouses of deceased railroad employees

The former spouse of a railroad employee may be eligible for survivors' benefits under Tier I of the Railroad Retirement System. However, a former spouse loses eligibility for any otherwise allowable Tier II benefits upon the death of the railroad employee.

Explanation of Provision

Former spouses of living railroad employees

The provision eliminates the requirement that a railroad employee actually receive railroad retirement benefits for the former spouse to be entitled to any Tier I benefit or Tier II benefit awarded under a State divorce court decision.

Former spouses of deceased railroad employees

The provision provides that a former spouse of a railroad employee does not lose eligibility for otherwise allowable Tier II benefits upon the death of the railroad employee.

Effective Date

The provision is effective one year after the date of enactment.

[Law at ¶7201 and ¶7204. CCH Explanation at ¶1030 and ¶1035.]

[¶11,030] Act Sec. 1004. Requirement for additional survivor annuity option

Joint Committee Taxation (J.C.T. REP. NO. JCX-38-06)

[Code Sec. 417]

Present Law

Defined benefit pension plans and money purchase pension plans are required to provide benefits in the form of a qualified joint and survivor annuity ("QJSA") unless the participant and his or her spouse consent to another form of benefit. A QJSA is an annuity for the life of the participant, with a survivor annuity for the life of the spouse which is not less than 50 percent (and not more than 100 percent) of the amount of the annuity payable during the joint lives of the participant and his or her spouse.[272] In the case

[272] Thus, for example, a QJSA could consist of an annuity for the life of the participant, with a survivor annuity for the life of the spouse equal to 75 percent of the amount of the annuity payable during the joint lives of the participant and his or her spouse.

of a married participant who dies before the commencement of retirement benefits, the surviving spouse must be provided with a qualified preretirement survivor annuity ("QPSA"), which must provide the surviving spouse with a benefit that is not less than the benefit that would have been provided under the survivor portion of a QJSA.

The participant and his or her spouse may waive the right to a QJSA and QPSA provided certain requirements are satisfied. In general, these conditions include providing the participant with a written explanation of the terms and conditions of the survivor annuity, the right to make, and the effect of, a waiver of the annuity, the rights of the spouse to waive the survivor annuity, and the right of the participant to revoke the waiver. In addition, the spouse must provide a written consent to the waiver, witnessed by a plan representative or a notary public, which acknowledges the effect of the waiver.

Defined contribution plans other than money purchase pension plans are not required to provide a QJSA or QPSA if the participant does not elect an annuity as the form of payment, the surviving spouse is the beneficiary of the participant's entire vested account balance under the plan (unless the spouse consents to designation of another beneficiary),[273] and, with respect to the participant, the plan has not received a transfer from a plan to which the QJSA and QPSA requirements applied (or separately accounts for the transferred assets). In the case of a defined contribution plan subject to the QJSA and QPSA requirements, a QPSA means an annuity for the life of the surviving spouse that has an actuarial value of at least 50 percent of the participant's vested account balance as of the date of death.

Explanation of Provision

The provision revises the minimum survivor annuity requirements to require that, at the election of the participant, benefits will be paid in the form of a "qualified optional survivor annuity." A qualified optional survivor annuity means an annuity for the life of the participant with a survivor annuity for the life of the spouse which is equal to the applicable percentage of the amount of the annuity that is: (1) payable during the joint lives of the participant and the spouse; and (2) the actuarial equivalent of a single annuity for the life of the participant.

If the survivor annuity provided by the QJSA under the plan is less than 75 percent of the annuity payable during the joint lives of the participant and spouse, the applicable percentage is 75 percent. If the survivor annuity provided by the QJSA under the plan is greater than or equal to 75 percent of the annuity payable during the joint lives of the participant and spouse, the applicable percentage is 50 percent. Thus, for example, if the survivor annuity provided by the QJSA under the plan is 50 percent, the survivor annuity provided under the qualified optional survivor annuity must be 75 percent.

The written explanation required to be provided to participants explaining the terms and conditions of the qualified joint and survivor annuity must also include the terms and conditions of the qualified optional survivor annuity.

Under the provision of the bill relating to plan amendments, a plan amendment made pursuant to a provision of the bill generally will not violate the anticutback rule if certain requirements are met. Thus, a plan is not treated as having decreased the accrued benefit of a participant solely by reason of the adoption of a plan amendment pursuant to the provision requiring that the plan offer a qualified optional survivor annuity. The elimination of a subsidized QJSA is not protected by the anticutback provision in the bill unless an equivalent or greater subsidy is retained in one of the forms offered under the plan as amended. For example, if a plan that offers a subsidized 50 percent QJSA is amended to provide an unsubsidized 50 percent QJSA and an unsubsidized 75 percent joint and survivor annuity as its qualified optional survivor annuity, the replacement of the subsidized 50 percent QJSA with the unsubsidized 50 percent QJSA is not protected by the anticutback protection.

Effective Date

The provision applies generally to plan years beginning after December 31, 2007. In the case of a plan maintained pursuant to one or more collective bargaining agreements, the provision applies to plan years beginning on or after the earlier of (1) the later of January 1, 2008, and the last date on which an applicable collective bargaining agreement terminates (without regard to extensions), and (2) January 1, 2009.

[Law at ¶5105 and ¶7207. CCH Explanation at ¶1040.]

---

[273] Waiver and election rules apply to the waiver of the right of the spouse to be the beneficiary under a defined contribution plan that is not required to provide a QJSA.

[¶11,040] Act Sec. 1101. Updating of employee plans compliance resolution system

Joint Committee Taxation (J.C.T. REP. NO. JCX-38-06)

[Act Sec. 1101]

Present Law

Tax-favored treatment is provided to various retirement savings arrangements that meet certain requirements under the Code, including qualified retirement plans and annuities (secs. 401(a) and 403(a)), tax-sheltered annuities (sec. 403(b)), simplified employee pensions ("SEPs") (sec. 408(k)), and SIMPLE IRAs (sec. 408(p)). The Internal Revenue Service ("IRS") has established the Employee Plans Compliance Resolution System ("EPCRS"), which is a comprehensive system of correction programs for sponsors of retirement plans and annuities that are intended to satisfy the requirements of section 401(a), section 403(a), section 403(b), section 408(k), or section 408(p), as applicable. The IRS has updated and expanded EPCRS several times.[274]

EPCRS permits employers to correct compliance failures and continue to provide their employees with retirement benefits on a tax-favored basis. EPCRS is based on the following general principles:

- Plans sponsors and administrators should be encouraged to establish administrative practices and procedures that ensure that plans are operated properly in accordance with applicable Code requirements;
- Plans sponsors and administrators should satisfy applicable plan document requirements;
- Plans sponsors and administrators should make voluntary and timely correction of any plan failures, whether involving discrimination in favor of highly compensated employees, plan operations, the terms of the plan document, or adoption of a plan by an ineligible employer; timely and efficient correction protects participating employees by providing them with their expected retirement benefits, including favorable tax treatment;
- Voluntary compliance is promoted by providing for limited fees for voluntary corrections approved by the Service, thereby reducing employers' uncertainty regarding their potential tax liability and participants' potential tax liability;
- Fees and sanctions should be graduated in a series of steps so that there is always an incentive to correct promptly;
- Sanctions for plan failures identified on audit should be reasonable in light of the nature, extent, and severity of the violation;
- Administration of EPCRS should be consistent and uniform; and
- Sponsors should be able to rely on the availability of EPCRS in taking corrective actions to maintain the tax-favored status of their plans.

The components of EPCRS provide for self-correction, voluntary correction with IRS approval, and correction on audit. The Self-Correction Program ("SCP") generally permits a plan sponsor that has established compliance practices and procedures to correct certain insignificant failures at any time (including during an audit), and certain significant failures generally within a 2-year period, without payment of any fee or sanction. The Voluntary Correction Program ("VCP") permits an employer, at any time before an audit, to pay a limited fee and receive IRS approval of a correction. For a failure that is discovered on audit and corrected, the Audit Closing Agreement Program ("Audit CAP") provides for a sanction that bears a reasonable relationship to the nature, extent, and severity of the failure and that takes into account the extent to which correction occurred before audit.

Explanation of Provision

The provision clarifies that the Secretary has the full authority to establish and implement EPCRS (or any successor program) and any other employee plans correction policies, including the authority to waive income, excise or other taxes to ensure that any tax, penalty or sanction is not excessive and bears a reasonable relationship to the nature, extent and severity of the failure.

Under the provision, the Secretary of the Treasury is directed to continue to update and improve EPCRS (or any successor program), giving special attention to (1) increasing the awareness and knowledge of small employers concerning the availability and use of EPCRS, (2)

[274] See Rev. Proc. 2006-27, 2006-22 IRB 945.

taking into account special concerns and circumstances that small employers face with respect to compliance and correction of compliance failures, (3) extending the duration of the self-correction period under SCP for significant compliance failures, (4) expanding the availability to correct insignificant compliance failures under SCP during audit, and (5) assuring that any tax, penalty, or sanction that is imposed by reason of a compliance failure is not excessive and bears a reasonable relationship to the nature, extent, and severity of the failure.

Effective Date

The provision is effective on the date of enactment.

[Law at ¶7210. CCH Explanation at ¶1085.]

[¶11,050] Act Sec. 1102. Notice and consent period regarding distributions

Joint Committee Taxation (J.C.T. Rep. No. JCX-38-06)

[Code Sec. 417(a)]

Present Law

Notice and consent requirements apply to certain distributions from qualified retirement plans. These requirements relate to the content and timing of information that a plan must provide to a participant prior to a distribution, and to whether the plan must obtain the participant's consent to the distribution. The nature and extent of the notice and consent requirements applicable to a distribution depend upon the value of the participant's vested accrued benefit and whether the joint and survivor annuity requirements apply to the participant.

If the present value of the participant's vested accrued benefit exceeds $5,000,[275] the plan may not distribute the participant's benefit without the written consent of the participant. The participant's consent to a distribution is not valid unless the participant has received from the plan a notice that contains a written explanation of (1) the material features and the relative values of the optional forms of benefit available under the plan, (2) the participant's right to defer the receipt of a distribution, or, as applicable, to have the distribution directly transferred to another retirement plan or individual retirement arrangement ("IRA"), and (3) the rules concerning taxation of a distribution. If the joint and survivor annuity requirements are applicable, this notice also must contain a written explanation of (1) the terms and conditions of the qualified joint and survivor annuity ("QJSA"), (2) the participant's right to make, and the effect of, an election to waive the QJSA, (3) the rights of the participant's spouse with respect to a participant's waiver of the QJSA, and (4) the right to make, and the effect of, a revocation of a waiver of the QJSA. The plan generally must provide this notice to the participant no less than 30 and no more than 90 days before the date distribution commences.[276]

Explanation of Provision

Under the provision, a qualified retirement plan is required to provide the applicable distribution notice no less than 30 days and no more than 180 days before the date distribution commences. The Secretary of the Treasury is directed to modify the applicable regulations to reflect the extension of the notice period to 180 days and to provide that the description of a participant's right, if any, to defer receipt of a distribution shall also describe the consequences of failing to defer such receipt.

Effective Date

The provision and the modifications required to be made under the provision apply to years beginning after December 31, 2006. In the case of a description of the consequences of a participant's failure to defer receipt of a distribution that is made before the date 90 days after the date on which the Secretary of the Treasury makes modifications to the applicable regulations, the plan administrator is required to make a reasonable attempt to comply with the requirements of the provision.

[Law at ¶5105 and ¶7213. CCH Explanation at ¶925.]

---

[275] The portion of a participant's benefit that is attributable to amounts rolled over from another plan may be disregarded in determining the present value of the participant's vested accrued benefit.

[276] Code sec. 417(a)(6)(A); ERISA sec. 205(c)(7)(A); Treas. Reg. secs. 1.402(f)-1, 1.411(a)-11(c), and 1.417(e)-1(b).

[¶11,060] Act Sec. 1103. Pension plan reporting simplification

Joint Committee Taxation (J.C.T. REP. NO. JCX-38-06)

[Act Sec. 1103]

Present Law

The plan administrator of a pension plan generally must file an annual return with the Secretary of the Treasury, an annual report with the Secretary of Labor, and certain information with the Pension Benefit Guaranty Corporation ("PBGC"). Form 5500, which consists of a primary form and various schedules, includes the information required to be filed with all three agencies. The plan administrator satisfies the reporting requirement with respect to each agency by filing the Form 5500 with the Department of Labor.

The Form 5500 series consists of 2 different forms: Form 5500 and Form 5500-EZ. Form 5500 is the more comprehensive of the forms and requires the most detailed financial information. The plan administrator of a "one-participant plan" generally may file Form 5500-EZ. For this purpose, a plan is a one-participant plan if: (1) the only participants in the plan are the sole owner of a business that maintains the plan (and such owner's spouse), or partners in a partnership that maintains the plan (and such partners' spouses);[277] (2) the plan is not aggregated with another plan in order to satisfy the minimum coverage requirements of section 410(b); (3) the plan does not provide benefits to anyone other than the sole owner of the business (or the sole owner and spouse) or the partners in the business (or the partners and spouses); (4) the employer is not a member of a related group of employers; and (5) the employer does not use the services of leased employees. In addition, the plan administrator of a one-participant plan is not required to file a return if the plan does not have an accumulated funding deficiency and the total value of the plan assets as of the end of the plan year and all prior plan years beginning on or after January 1, 1994, does not exceed $100,000.

With respect to a plan that does not satisfy the eligibility requirements for Form 5500-EZ, the characteristics and the size of the plan determine the amount of detailed financial information that the plan administrator must provide on Form 5500. If the plan has more than 100 participants at the beginning of the plan year, the plan administrator generally must provide more information.

Explanation of Provision

The Secretary of the Treasury is directed to modify the annual return filing requirements with respect to a one-participant plan to provide that if the total value of the plan assets of such a plan as of the end of the plan year does not exceed $250,000, the plan administrator is not required to file a return. In addition, the Secretary of the Treasury and the Secretary of Labor are directed to provide simplified reporting requirements for plan years beginning after December 31, 2006, for certain plans with fewer than 25 participants.

Effective Date

The provision relating to one-participant retirement plans is effective for plan years beginning on or after January 1, 2007. The provision relating to simplified reporting for plans with fewer than 25 participants is effective on the date of enactment.

[Law at ¶7216. CCH Explanation at ¶1080.]

---

[277] Under Department of Labor regulations, certain business owners and their spouses are not treated as employees. 29 C.F.R. sec. 2510.3-3(c) (2006). Thus, plans covering only such individuals are not subject to ERISA.

[¶11,070] Act Sec. 1104. Voluntary early retirement incentive and employment retention plans maintained by local educational agencies and other entities

Joint Committee Taxation (J.C.T. REP. NO. JCX-38-06)

[Code Secs. 457(e)(11) and 457(f)]

Present Law

Eligible deferred compensation plans of State and local governments and tax-exempt employers

A "section 457 plan" is an eligible deferred compensation plan of a State or local government or tax-exempt employer that meets certain requirements. For example, the amount that can be deferred annually under section 457 cannot exceed a certain dollar limit ($14,000 for 2005). Amounts deferred under a section 457 plan are generally includible in gross income when paid or made available (or, in the case of governmental section 457 plans, when paid). Subject to certain exceptions, amounts deferred under a plan that does not comply with section 457 (an "ineligible plan") are includible in income when the amounts are not subject to a substantial risk of forfeiture. Section 457 does not apply to any bona fide vacation leave, sick leave, compensatory time, severance pay, disability pay, or death benefit plan. Additionally, section 457 does not apply to qualified retirement plans or qualified governmental excess benefit plans that provide benefits in excess of those that are provided under a qualified retirement plan maintained by the governmental employer.

ERISA

ERISA provides rules governing the operation of most employee benefit plans. The rules to which a plan is subject depend on whether the plan is an employee welfare benefit plan or an employee pension benefit plan. For example, employee pension benefit plans are subject to reporting and disclosure requirements, participation and vesting requirements, funding requirements, and fiduciary provisions. Employee welfare benefit plans are not subject to all of these requirements. Governmental plans are exempt from ERISA.

Age Discrimination in Employment Act

The Age Discrimination in Employment Act ("ADEA") generally prohibits discrimination in employment because of age. However, certain defined benefit pension plans may lawfully provide payments that constitute the subsidized portion of an early retirement benefit or social security supplements pursuant to ADEA[278], and employers may lawfully provide a voluntary early retirement incentive plan that is consistent with the purposes of ADEA.[279]

Explanation of Provision

Early retirement incentive plans of local educational agencies and education associations

In general

The provision addresses the treatment of certain voluntary early retirement incentive plans under section 457, ERISA, and ADEA.

Code section 457

Under the provision, special rules apply under section 457 to a voluntary early retirement incentive plan that is maintained by a local educational agency or a tax-exempt education association which principally represents employees of one or more such agencies and that makes payments or supplements as an early retirement benefit, a retirement-type subsidy, or a social security supplement in coordination with a defined benefit pension plan maintained by a State or local government or by such an association. Such a voluntary early retirement incentive plan is treated as a bona fide severance plan for purposes of section 457, and therefore is not subject to the limits under section 457, to the extent the payments or supplements could otherwise be provided under the defined benefit pension plan. For purposes of the provision, the payments or supplements that could otherwise be provided under the defined benefit pension plan are to be determined by applying the accrual and

[278] See ADEA sec. 4(l)(1).

[279] See ADEA sec. 4(f)(2).

vesting rules for defined benefit pension plans.[280]

ERISA

Under the provision, voluntary early retirement incentive plans (as described above) are treated as welfare benefit plans for purposes of ERISA (other than governmental plans that are exempt from ERISA).

ADEA

The provision also addresses the treatment under ADEA of voluntary early retirement incentive plans that are maintained by local educational agencies and tax-exempt education associations which principally represent employees of one or more such agencies, and that make payments or supplements that constitute the subsidized portion of an early retirement benefit or a social security supplement and that are made in coordination with a defined benefit pension plan maintained by a State or local government or by such an association. For purposes of ADEA, such a plan is treated as part of the defined benefit pension plan and the payments or supplements under the plan are not severance pay that may be subject to certain deductions under ADEA.

Employment retention plans of local educational agencies and education associations

The provision addresses the treatment of certain employment retention plans under section 457 and ERISA. The provision applies to employment retention plans that are maintained by local educational agencies or tax-exempt education associations which principally represent employees of one or more such agencies and that provide compensation to an employee (payable on termination of employment) for purposes of retaining the services of the employee or rewarding the employee for service with educational agencies or associations.

Under the provision, special tax treatment applies to the portion of an employment retention plan that provides benefits that do not exceed twice the applicable annual dollar limit on deferrals under section 457 ($14,000 for 2005). The provision provides an exception from the rules under section 457 for ineligible plans with respect to such portion of an employment retention plan. This exception applies for years preceding the year in which benefits under the employment retention plan are paid or otherwise made available to the employee. In addition, such portion of an employment retention plan is not treated as providing for the deferral of compensation for tax purposes.

Under the provision, an employment retention plan is also treated as a welfare benefit plan for purposes of ERISA (other than a governmental plan that is exempt from ERISA).

Effective Date

The provision is generally effective on the date of enactment. The amendments to section 457 apply to taxable years ending after the date of enactment. The amendments to ERISA apply to plan years ending after the date of enactment. Nothing in the provision alters or affects the construction of the Code, ERISA, or ADEA as applied to any plan, arrangement, or conduct to which the provision does not apply.

[Law at ¶ 5140 and ¶ 7219. CCH Explanation at ¶ 1070.]

[¶ 11,080] Act Sec. 1105. No reduction in unemployment compensation as a result of pension rollovers

Joint Committee Taxation (J.C.T. Rep. No. JCX-38-06)

[Code Sec. 3304(a)]

Present Law

Under present law, unemployment compensation payable by a State to an individual generally is reduced by the amount of retirement benefits received by the individual. Distributions from certain employer-sponsored retirement plans or IRAs that are transferred to a similar retirement plan or IRA ("rollover distributions") generally are not includible in income. Some States currently reduce the amount of an individual's unemployment compensation by the amount of a rollover distribution.

[280] The accrual and vesting rules have the effect of limiting the social security supplements and early retirement benefits that may be provided under a defined benefit pension plan; however, government plans are exempt from these rules.

Explanation of Provision

The provision amends the Code so that the reduction of unemployment compensation payable to an individual by reason of the receipt of retirement benefits does not apply in the case of a rollover distribution.

Effective Date

The provision is effective for weeks beginning on or after the date of enactment.

[Law at ¶ 5220. CCH Explanation at ¶ 1325.]

[¶ 11,090] Act Sec. 1106. Revocation of election relating to treatment as multiemployer plan

Joint Committee Taxation (J.C.T. Rep. No. JCX-38-06)

[Code Sec. 414(f)]

Present Law

A multiemployer plan mean a plan (1) to which more than one employer is required to contribute; (2) which is maintained pursuant to one or more collective bargaining agreements between one or more employee organizations and more than one employer; and (3) which satisfies such other requirements as the Secretary of Labor may prescribe.[281] Present law provides that within one year after the date of enactment of the Multiemployer Pension Plan Amendments Act of 1980, a multiemployer plan could irrevocably elect for the plan not to be treated as a multiemployer plan if certain requirements were satisfied.

Explanation of Provision

The provision allows multiemployer plans to revoke an existing election not to treat the plan as a multiemployer plan if, for each of the three plan years prior to the date of enactment, the plan would have been a multiemployer plan, but for the extension in place. The revocation must be pursuant to procedures prescribed by the PBGC.

The provision also provides that a plan to which more than one employer is required to contribute which is maintained pursuant to one or more collective bargaining agreements between one or more employee organizations and more than one employer (collectively the "criteria") may, pursuant to procedures prescribed by the PBGC, elect to be a multiemployer plan if (1) for each of the three plan years prior to the date of enactment, the plan has met the criteria; (2) substantially all of the plan's employer contributions for each of those plan years were made or required to be made by organizations that were tax-exempt; and (3) the plan was established prior to September 2, 1974. Such election is also available in the case of a plan sponsored by an organization that was established in Chicago, Illinois, on August 12, 1881, and is described in Code section 501(c)(5). There is no inference that a plan that makes an election to be a multiemployer plan was not a multiemployer plan prior to the date of enactment or would not be a multiemployer plan without regard to the election.

An election made under the provision is effective beginning with the first plan year ending after date of enactment and is irrevocable. A plan that elects to be a multiemployer plan under the provision will cease to be a multiemployer plan as of the plan year beginning immediately after the first plan year for which the majority of its employer contributions were made or required to be made by organizations that were not tax-exempt. Elections and revocations under the provision must be made within one year after the date of enactment.

Not later than 30 days before an election is made, the plan administrator must provide notice of the pending election to each plan participant and beneficiary, each labor organization representing such participants or beneficiaries, and to each employer that has an obligation to contribute to the plan. Such notice must include the principal differences between the guarantee programs and benefit restrictions for single employer and multiemployer plans. The Secretary of Labor must prescribe a model notice within 180 days after date of enactment. The plan administrator's failure to provide the notice is treated as a failure to file an annual report. Thus, an ERISA penalty of $1,100 per day applies.

Effective Date

The provision is effective on the date of enactment.

[Law at ¶ 5090 and ¶ 7222. CCH Explanation at ¶ 325.]

---

[281] ERISA sec. 3(36); Code sec. 414(f).

[¶11,100] Act Sec. 1107. Provisions relating to plan amendments

Joint Committee Taxation (J.C.T. Rep. No. JCX-38-06)

[Act Sec. 1107]

Present Law

Present law provides a remedial amendment period during which, under certain circumstances, a plan may be amended retroactively in order to comply with the qualification requirements.[282] In general, plan amendments to reflect changes in the law generally must be made by the time prescribed by law for filing the income tax return of the employer for the employer's taxable year in which the change in law occurs. The Secretary of the Treasury may extend the time by which plan amendments need to be made.

The Code and ERISA provide that, in general, accrued benefits cannot be reduced by a plan amendment.[283] This prohibition on the reduction of accrued benefits is commonly referred to as the "anticutback rule."

Explanation of Provision.

A plan amendment made pursuant to the changes made by the bill or regulations issued thereunder, may be retroactively effective and will not violate the anticutback rule, if, in addition to meeting the other applicable requirements, the amendment is made on or before the last day of the first plan year beginning on or after January 1, 2009 (2011 in the case of a governmental plan).

A plan amendment will not be considered to be pursuant to the bill (or applicable regulations) if it has an effective date before the effective date of the provision under the bill (or regulations) to which it relates. Similarly, the provision does not provide relief from the anticutback rule for periods prior to the effective date of the relevant provision (or regulations) or the plan amendment. The Secretary of the Treasury is authorized to provide exceptions to the relief from the prohibition on reductions in accrued benefits. It is intended that the Secretary will not permit inappropriate reductions in contributions or benefits that are not directly related to the provisions under the bill.

Effective Date

The provision is effective on the date of enactment.

[Law at ¶ 7225. CCH Explanation at ¶ 1090.]

[¶11,110] Act Sec. 1201. Tax-free distributions from individual retirement plans for charitable purposes

Joint Committee Taxation (J.C.T. Rep. No. JCX-38-06)

[Code Secs. 408, 6034, 6104 and 6652]

Present Law

In general

If an amount withdrawn from a traditional individual retirement arrangement ("IRA") or a Roth IRA is donated to a charitable organization, the rules relating to the tax treatment of withdrawals from IRAs apply to the amount withdrawn and the charitable contribution is subject to the normally applicable limitations on deductibility of such contributions.

Charitable contributions

In computing taxable income, an individual taxpayer who itemizes deductions generally is allowed to deduct the amount of cash and up to the fair market value of property contributed to a charity described in section 501(c)(3), to certain veterans' organizations, fraternal societies, and cemetery companies,[284] or to a Federal, State, or local governmental entity for exclusively public purposes.[285] The deduction also is allowed for purposes of calculating alternative minimum taxable income.

---

282 Sec. 401(b).

283 Code sec. 411(d)(6); ERISA sec. 204(g).

284 Secs. 170(c)(3)-(5).

285 Sec. 170(c)(1).

The amount of the deduction allowable for a taxable year with respect to a charitable contribution of property may be reduced depending on the type of property contributed, the type of charitable organization to which the property is contributed, and the income of the taxpayer.[286]

A taxpayer who takes the standard deduction (i.e., who does not itemize deductions) may not take a separate deduction for charitable contributions.[287]

A payment to a charity (regardless of whether it is termed a "contribution") in exchange for which the donor receives an economic benefit is not deductible, except to the extent that the donor can demonstrate, among other things, that the payment exceeds the fair market value of the benefit received from the charity. To facilitate distinguishing charitable contributions from purchases of goods or services from charities, present law provides that no charitable contribution deduction is allowed for a separate contribution of $250 or more unless the donor obtains a contemporaneous written acknowledgement of the contribution from the charity indicating whether the charity provided any good or service (and an estimate of the value of any such good or service) to the taxpayer in consideration for the contribution.[288] In addition, present law requires that any charity that receives a contribution exceeding $75 made partly as a gift and partly as consideration for goods or services furnished by the charity (a "quid pro quo" contribution) is required to inform the contributor in writing of an estimate of the value of the goods or services furnished by the charity and that only the portion exceeding the value of the goods or services may be deductible as a charitable contribution.[289]

Under present law, total deductible contributions of an individual taxpayer to public charities, private operating foundations, and certain types of private nonoperating foundations may not exceed 50 percent of the taxpayer's contribution base, which is the taxpayer's adjusted gross income for a taxable year (disregarding any net operating loss carryback). To the extent a taxpayer has not exceeded the 50-percent limitation, (1) contributions of capital gain property to public charities generally may be deducted up to 30 percent of the taxpayer's contribution base, (2) contributions of cash to private foundations and certain other charitable organizations generally may be deducted up to 30 percent of the taxpayer's contribution base, and (3) contributions of capital gain property to private foundations and certain other charitable organizations generally may be deducted up to 20 percent of the taxpayer's contribution base.

Contributions by individuals in excess of the 50-percent, 30-percent, and 20-percent limits may be carried over and deducted over the next five taxable years, subject to the relevant percentage limitations on the deduction in each of those years.

In addition to the percentage limitations imposed specifically on charitable contributions, present law imposes a reduction on most itemized deductions, including charitable contribution deductions, for taxpayers with adjusted gross income in excess of a threshold amount, which is indexed annually for inflation. The threshold amount for 2006 is $150,500 ($75,250 for married individuals filing separate returns). For those deductions that are subject to the limit, the total amount of itemized deductions is reduced by three percent of adjusted gross income over the threshold amount, but not by more than 80 percent of itemized deductions subject to the limit. Beginning in 2006, the overall limitation on itemized deductions phases-out for all taxpayers. The overall limitation on itemized deductions is reduced by one-third in taxable years beginning in 2006 and 2007, and by two-thirds in taxable years beginning in 2008 and 2009. The overall limitation on itemized deductions is eliminated for taxable years beginning after December 31, 2009; however, this elimination of the limitation sunsets on December 31, 2010.

In general, a charitable deduction is not allowed for income, estate, or gift tax purposes if the donor transfers an interest in property to a charity (e.g., a remainder) while also either retaining an interest in that property (e.g., an income interest) or transferring an interest in that property to a noncharity for less than full and adequate consideration.[290] Exceptions to this general rule are provided for, among other interests, remainder interests in charitable remainder annuity trusts, charitable remainder unitrusts, and pooled income funds, and present interests in the form of a guaranteed annuity or a fixed percentage of the annual value of the property.[291] For such interests, a charitable deduction is allowed to the extent of the present value of the interest designated for a charitable organization.

---

[286] Secs. 170(b) and (e).

[287] Sec. 170(a).

[288] Sec. 170(f)(8).

[289] Sec. 6115.

[290] Secs. 170(f), 2055(e)(2), and 2522(c)(2).

[291] Sec. 170(f)(2).

IRA rules

Within limits, individuals may make deductible and nondeductible contributions to a traditional IRA. Amounts in a traditional IRA are includible in income when withdrawn (except to the extent the withdrawal represents a return of nondeductible contributions). Individuals also may make nondeductible contributions to a Roth IRA. Qualified withdrawals from a Roth IRA are excludable from gross income. Withdrawals from a Roth IRA that are not qualified withdrawals are includible in gross income to the extent attributable to earnings. Includible amounts withdrawn from a traditional IRA or a Roth IRA before attainment of age 59-½ are subject to an additional 10-percent early withdrawal tax, unless an exception applies. Under present law, minimum distributions are required to be made from tax-favored retirement arrangements, including IRAs. Minimum required distributions from a traditional IRA must generally begin by the April 1 of the calendar year following the year in which the IRA owner attains age 70-½.[292]

If an individual has made nondeductible contributions to a traditional IRA, a portion of each distribution from an IRA is nontaxable until the total amount of nondeductible contributions has been received. In general, the amount of a distribution that is nontaxable is determined by multiplying the amount of the distribution by the ratio of the remaining nondeductible contributions to the account balance. In making the calculation, all traditional IRAs of an individual are treated as a single IRA, all distributions during any taxable year are treated as a single distribution, and the value of the contract, income on the contract, and investment in the contract are computed as of the close of the calendar year.

In the case of a distribution from a Roth IRA that is not a qualified distribution, in determining the portion of the distribution attributable to earnings, contributions and distributions are deemed to be distributed in the following order: (1) regular Roth IRA contributions; (2) taxable conversion contributions;[293] (3) nontaxable conversion contributions; and (4) earnings. In determining the amount of taxable distributions from a Roth IRA, all Roth IRA distributions in the same taxable year are treated as a single distribution, all regular Roth IRA contributions for a year are treated as a single contribution, and all conversion contributions during the year are treated as a single contribution.

Distributions from an IRA (other than a Roth IRA) are generally subject to withholding unless the individual elects not to have withholding apply.[294] Elections not to have withholding apply are to be made in the time and manner prescribed by the Secretary.

Split-interest trust filing requirements

Split-interest trusts, including charitable remainder annuity trusts, charitable remainder unitrusts, and pooled income funds, are required to file an annual information return (Form 1041A).[295] Trusts that are not split-interest trusts but that claim a charitable deduction for amounts permanently set aside for a charitable purpose[296] also are required to file Form 1041A. The returns are required to be made publicly available.[297] A trust that is required to distribute all trust net income currently to trust beneficiaries in a taxable year is exempt from this return requirement for such taxable year. A failure to file the required return may result in a penalty on the trust of $10 a day for as long as the failure continues, up to a maximum of $5,000 per return.

In addition, split-interest trusts are required to file annually Form 5227.[298] Form 5227 requires disclosure of information regarding a trust's noncharitable beneficiaries. The penalty for failure to file this return is calculated based on the amount of tax owed. A split-interest trust generally is not subject to tax and therefore, in general, a penalty may not be imposed for the failure to file Form 5227. Form 5227 is not required to be made publicly available.

Explanation of Provision

Qualified charitable distributions from IRAs

The provision provides an exclusion from gross income for otherwise taxable IRA distributions from a traditional or a Roth IRA in the case of qualified charitable distributions.[299] The ex-

292 Minimum distribution rules also apply in the case of distributions after the death of a traditional or Roth IRA owner.

293 Conversion contributions refer to conversions of amounts in a traditional IRA to a Roth IRA.

294 Sec. 3405.

295 Sec. 6034. This requirement applies to all split-interest trusts described in section 4947(a)(2).

296 Sec. 642(c).

297 Sec. 6104(b).

298 Sec. 6011; Treas. Reg. sec. 53.6011-1(d).

299 The provision does not apply to distributions from employer-sponsored retirements plans, including SIMPLE IRAs and simplified employee pensions ("SEPs").

clusion may not exceed $100,000 per taxpayer per taxable year. Special rules apply in determining the amount of an IRA distribution that is otherwise taxable. The present-law rules regarding taxation of IRA distributions and the deduction of charitable contributions continue to apply to distributions from an IRA that are not qualified charitable distributions. Qualified charitable distributions are taken into account for purposes of the minimum distribution rules applicable to traditional IRAs to the same extent the distribution would have been taken into account under such rules had the distribution not been directly distributed under the provision. An IRA does not fail to qualify as an IRA merely because qualified charitable distributions have been made from the IRA. It is intended that the Secretary will prescribe rules under which IRA owners are deemed to elect out of withholding if they designate that a distribution is intended to be a qualified charitable distribution.

A qualified charitable distribution is any distribution from an IRA directly by the IRA trustee to an organization described in section 170(b)(1)(A) (other than an organization described in section 509(a)(3) or a donor advised fund (as defined in section 4966(d)(2)). Distributions are eligible for the exclusion only if made on or after the date the IRA owner attains age 70-1/2.

The exclusion applies only if a charitable contribution deduction for the entire distribution otherwise would be allowable (under present law), determined without regard to the generally applicable percentage limitations. Thus, for example, if the deductible amount is reduced because of a benefit received in exchange, or if a deduction is not allowable because the donor did not obtain sufficient substantiation, the exclusion is not available with respect to any part of the IRA distribution.

If the IRA owner has any IRA that includes nondeductible contributions, a special rule applies in determining the portion of a distribution that is includible in gross income (but for the provision) and thus is eligible for qualified charitable distribution treatment. Under the special rule, the distribution is treated as consisting of income first, up to the aggregate amount that would be includible in gross income (but for the provision) if the aggregate balance of all IRAs having the same owner were distributed during the same year. In determining the amount of subsequent IRA distributions includible in income, proper adjustments are to be made to reflect the amount treated as a qualified charitable distribution under the special rule.

Distributions that are excluded from gross income by reason of the provision are not taken into account in determining the deduction for charitable contributions under section 170.

Qualified charitable distribution examples

The following examples illustrate the determination of the portion of an IRA distribution that is a qualified charitable distribution. In each example, it is assumed that the requirements for qualified charitable distribution treatment are otherwise met (e.g., the applicable age requirement and the requirement that contributions are otherwise deductible) and that no other IRA distributions occur during the year.

Example 1.—Individual A has a traditional IRA with a balance of $100,000, consisting solely of deductible contributions and earnings. Individual A has no other IRA. The entire IRA balance is distributed in a distribution to an organization described in section 170(b)(1)(A) (other than an organization described in section 509(a)(3) or a donor advised fund). Under present law, the entire distribution of $100,000 would be includible in Individual A's income. Accordingly, under the provision, the entire distribution of $100,000 is a qualified charitable distribution. As a result, no amount is included in Individual A's income as a result of the distribution and the distribution is not taken into account in determining the amount of Individual A's charitable deduction for the year.

Example 2.—Individual B has a traditional IRA with a balance of $100,000, consisting of $20,000 of nondeductible contributions and $80,000 of deductible contributions and earnings. Individual B has no other IRA. In a distribution to an organization described in section 170(b)(1)(A) (other than an organization described in section 509(a)(3) or a donor advised fund), $80,000 is distributed from the IRA. Under present law, a portion of the distribution from the IRA would be treated as a nontaxable return of nondeductible contributions. The nontaxable portion of the distribution would be $16,000, determined by multiplying the amount of the distribution ($80,000) by the ratio of the nondeductible contributions to the account balance ($20,000/$100,000). Accordingly, under present law, $64,000 of the distribution ($80,000 minus $16,000) would be includible in Individual B's income.

Under the provision, notwithstanding the present-law tax treatment of IRA distributions, the distribution is treated as consisting of income first, up to the total amount that would be includible in gross income (but for the provision) if all amounts were distributed from all IRAs otherwise taken into account in determining the amount of IRA distributions. The total amount that would be includible in income if all amounts were distributed from the IRA is $80,000. Accordingly, under the provision, the entire $80,000 distributed to the charitable organization is treated as includible in income (before application of the provision) and is a qualified charitable distribution. As a result, no amount is included in Individual B's income as a result of the distribution and the distribution is not taken into account in determining the amount of Individual B's charitable deduction for the year. In addition, for purposes of determining the tax treatment of other distributions from the IRA, $20,000 of the amount remaining in the IRA is treated as Individual B's nondeductible contributions (i.e., not subject to tax upon distribution).

Split-interest trust filing requirements

The provision increases the penalty on split-interest trusts for failure to file a return and for failure to include any of the information required to be shown on such return and to show the correct information. The penalty is $20 for each day the failure continues up to $10,000 for any one return. In the case of a split-interest trust with gross income in excess of $250,000, the penalty is $100 for each day the failure continues up to a maximum of $50,000. In addition, if a person (meaning any officer, director, trustee, employee, or other individual who is under a duty to file the return or include required information)[300] knowingly failed to file the return or include required information, then that person is personally liable for such a penalty, which would be imposed in addition to the penalty that is paid by the organization. Information regarding beneficiaries that are not charitable organizations as described in section 170(c) is exempt from the requirement to make information publicly available. In addition, the provision repeals the present-law exception to the filing requirement for split-interest trusts that are required in a taxable year to distribute all net income currently to beneficiaries. Such exception remains available to trusts other than split-interest trusts that are otherwise subject to the filing requirement.

Effective Date

The provision relating to qualified charitable distributions is effective for distributions made in taxable years beginning after December 31, 2005, and taxable years beginning before January 1, 2008. The provision relating to information returns of split-interest trusts is effective for returns for taxable years beginning after December 31, 2006.

[Law at ¶5055, ¶5330, ¶5365 and ¶5390. CCH Explanation at ¶1105 and ¶1190.]

[¶11,120] Act Sec. 1202. Charitable deduction for contributions of food inventory

Joint Committee Taxation (J.C.T. Rep. No. JCX-38-06)

[Code Sec. 170]

Present Law

Under present law, a taxpayer's deduction for charitable contributions of inventory generally is limited to the taxpayer's basis (typically, cost) in the inventory, or if less the fair market value of the inventory.

For certain contributions of inventory, C corporations may claim an enhanced deduction equal to the lesser of (1) basis plus one-half of the item's appreciation (i.e., basis plus one half of fair market value in excess of basis) or (2) two times basis (sec. 170(e)(3)). In general, a C corporation's charitable contribution deductions for a year may not exceed 10 percent of the corporation's taxable income (sec. 170(b)(2)). To be eligible for the enhanced deduction, the contributed property generally must be inventory of the taxpayer, contributed to a charitable organization described in section 501(c)(3) (except for private nonoperating foundations), and the donee must (1) use the property consistent with the donee's exempt purpose solely for the care of the ill, the needy, or infants, (2) not transfer the property in exchange for money, other property, or services, and (3) provide the taxpayer a written statement that the donee's use of the property will be consistent with such requirements. In the case of contributed property subject to the Federal Food,

[300] Sec. 6652(c)(4)(C).

Drug, and Cosmetic Act, the property must satisfy the applicable requirements of such Act on the date of transfer and for 180 days prior to the transfer.

A donor making a charitable contribution of inventory must make a corresponding adjustment to the cost of goods sold by decreasing the cost of goods sold by the lesser of the fair market value of the property or the donor's basis with respect to the inventory (Treas. Reg. sec. 1.170A-4A(c)(3)). Accordingly, if the allowable charitable deduction for inventory is the fair market value of the inventory, the donor reduces its cost of goods sold by such value, with the result that the difference between the fair market value and the donor's basis may still be recovered by the donor other than as a charitable contribution.

To use the enhanced deduction, the taxpayer must establish that the fair market value of the donated item exceeds basis. The valuation of food inventory has been the subject of disputes between taxpayers and the IRS.[301]

Under the Katrina Emergency Tax Relief Act of 2005, any taxpayer, whether or not a C corporation, engaged in a trade or business is eligible to claim the enhanced deduction for certain donations made after August 28, 2005, and before January 1, 2006, of food inventory. For taxpayers other than C corporations, the total deduction for donations of food inventory in a taxable year generally may not exceed 10 percent of the taxpayer's net income for such taxable year from all sole proprietorships, S corporations, or partnerships (or other entity that is not a C corporation) from which contributions of "apparently wholesome food" are made. "Apparently wholesome food" is defined as food intended for human consumption that meets all quality and labeling standards imposed by Federal, State, and local laws and regulations even though the food may not be readily marketable due to appearance, age, freshness, grade, size, surplus, or other conditions.

Explanation of Provision

The provision extends the provision enacted as part of the Katrina Emergency Tax Relief Act of 2005. As under such Act, under the provision, any taxpayer, whether or not a C corporation, engaged in a trade or business is eligible to claim the enhanced deduction for donations of food inventory. For taxpayers other than C corporations, the total deduction for donations of food inventory in a taxable year generally may not exceed 10 percent of the taxpayer's net income for such taxable year from all sole proprietorships, S corporations, or partnerships (or other non C corporation) from which contributions of apparently wholesome food are made. For example, as under the Katrina Emergency Tax Relief Act of 2005, if a taxpayer is a sole proprietor, a shareholder in an S corporation, and a partner in a partnership, and each business makes charitable contributions of food inventory, the taxpayer's deduction for donations of food inventory is limited to 10 percent of the taxpayer's net income from the sole proprietorship and the taxpayer's interests in the S corporation and partnership. However, if only the sole proprietorship and the S corporation made charitable contributions of food inventory, the taxpayer's deduction would be limited to 10 percent of the net income from the trade or business of the sole proprietorship and the taxpayer's interest in the S corporation, but not the taxpayer's interest in the partnership.[302]

Under the provision, the enhanced deduction for food is available only for food that qualifies as "apparently wholesome food." "Apparently wholesome food" is defined as it is defined under the Katrina Emergency Tax Relief Act of 2005.

Effective Date

The provision is effective for contributions made after December 31, 2005, and before January 1, 2008.

[Law at ¶ 5020. CCH Explanation at ¶ 1140.]

---

[301] *Lucky Stores Inc. v. Commissioner,* 105 T.C. 420 (1995) (holding that the value of surplus bread inventory donated to charity was the full retail price of the bread rather than half the retail price, as the IRS asserted).

[302] The 10 percent limitation does not affect the application of the generally applicable percentage limitations. For example, if 10 percent of a sole proprietor's net income from the proprietor's trade or business was greater than 50 percent of the proprietor's contribution base, the available deduction for the taxable year (with respect to contributions to public charities) would be 50 percent of the proprietor's contribution base. Consistent with present law, such contributions may be carried forward because they exceed the 50 percent limitation. Contributions of food inventory by a taxpayer that is not a C corporation that exceed the 10 percent limitation but not the 50 percent limitation could not be carried forward.

[¶11,130] Act Sec. 1203. Basis adjustment to stock of S corporation contributing property

Joint Committee Taxation (J.C.T. REP. NO. JCX-38-06)

[Code Sec. 1367]

Present Law

Under present law, if an S corporation contributes money or other property to a charity, each shareholder takes into account the shareholder's pro rata share of the contribution in determining its own income tax liability.[303] A shareholder of an S corporation reduces the basis in the stock of the S corporation by the amount of the charitable contribution that flows through to the shareholder.[304]

Explanation of Provision

The provision provides that the amount of a shareholder's basis reduction in the stock of an S corporation by reason of a charitable contribution made by the corporation will be equal to the shareholder's pro rata share of the adjusted basis of the contributed property.[305]

Thus, for example, assume an S corporation with one individual shareholder makes a charitable contribution of stock with a basis of $200 and a fair market value of $500. The shareholder will be treated as having made a $500 charitable contribution (or a lesser amount if the special rules of section 170(e) apply), and will reduce the basis of the S corporation stock by $200.[306]

Effective Date

The provision applies to contributions made in taxable years beginning after December 31, 2005, and taxable years beginning before January 1, 2008.

[Law at ¶5200. CCH Explanation at ¶1135.]

[¶11,140] Act Sec. 1204. Charitable deduction for contributions of book inventory

Joint Committee Taxation (J.C.T. REP. NO. JCX-38-06)

[Code Sec. 170]

Present Law

Under present law, a taxpayer's deduction for charitable contributions of inventory generally is limited to the taxpayer's basis (typically, cost) in the inventory, or if less the fair market value of the inventory.

For certain contributions of inventory, C corporations may claim an enhanced deduction equal to the lesser of (1) basis plus one-half of the item's appreciation (i.e., basis plus one half of fair market value in excess of basis) or (2) two times basis (sec. 170(e)(3)). In general, a C corporation's charitable contribution deductions for a year may not exceed 10 percent of the corporation's taxable income (sec. 170(b)(2)). To be eligible for the enhanced deduction, the contributed property generally must be inventory of the taxpayer, contributed to a charitable organization described in section 501(c)(3) (except for private nonoperating foundations), and the donee must (1) use the property consistent with the donee's exempt purpose solely for the care of the ill, the needy, or infants, (2) not transfer the property in exchange for money, other property, or services, and (3) provide the taxpayer a written statement that the donee's use of the property will be consistent with such requirements. In the case of contributed property subject to the Federal Food, Drug, and Cosmetic Act, the property must satisfy the applicable requirements of such Act on the date of transfer and for 180 days prior to the transfer.

A donor making a charitable contribution of inventory must make a corresponding adjustment to the cost of goods sold by decreasing the cost of goods sold by the lesser of the fair market value of the property or the donor's basis with respect to the inventory (Treas. Reg. sec. 1.170A-4A(c)(3)). Accordingly, if the allowable charitable deduction for inventory is the fair market value of the inventory, the donor reduces its cost of goods sold by such value, with the result that the difference between the fair market value and the donor's basis may still be recovered by the donor other than as a charitable contribution.

---

[303] Sec. 1366(a)(1)(A).

[304] Sec. 1367(a)(2)(B).

[305] *See* Rev. Rul. 96-11 (1996-1 C.B. 140) for a rule reaching a similar result in the case of charitable contributions made by a partnership.

[306] This example assumes that basis of the S corporation stock (before reduction) is at least $200.

To use the enhanced deduction, the taxpayer must establish that the fair market value of the donated item exceeds basis.

The Katrina Emergency Tax Relief Act of 2005 extended the present-law enhanced deduction for C corporations to certain qualified book contributions made after August 28, 2005, and before January 1, 2006. For such purposes, a qualified book contribution means a charitable contribution of books to a public school that provides elementary education or secondary education (kindergarten through grade 12) and that is an educational organization that normally maintains a regular faculty and curriculum and normally has a regularly enrolled body of pupils or students in attendance at the place where its educational activities are regularly carried on. The enhanced deduction under the Katrina Emergency Tax Relief Act of 2005 is not allowed unless the donee organization certifies in writing that the contributed books are suitable, in terms of currency, content, and quantity, for use in the donee's educational programs and that the donee will use the books in such educational programs.

Explanation of Provision

The provision extends the provision enacted as part of the Katrina Emergency Tax Relief Act of 2005. As under such Act, an enhanced deduction for C corporations for qualified book contributions is allowed.

Effective Date

The provision is effective for contributions made after December 31, 2005, and before January 1, 2008.

[Law at ¶ 5020. CCH Explanation at ¶ 1145.]

[¶11,150] Act Sec. 1205. Modify tax treatment of certain payments to controlling exempt organizations

Joint Committee Taxation (J.C.T. Rep. No. JCX-38-06)

[Code Secs. 512 and 6033]

Present Law

In general, interest, rents, royalties, and annuities are excluded from the unrelated business income of tax-exempt organizations. However, section 512(b)(13) generally treats otherwise excluded rent, royalty, annuity, and interest income as unrelated business income if such income is received from a taxable or tax-exempt subsidiary that is 50 percent controlled by the parent tax-exempt organization. In the case of a stock subsidiary, "control" means ownership by vote or value of more than 50 percent of the stock. In the case of a partnership or other entity, control means ownership of more than 50 percent of the profits, capital or beneficial interests. In addition, present law applies the constructive ownership rules of section 318 for purposes of section 512(b)(13). Thus, a parent exempt organization is deemed to control any subsidiary in which it holds more than 50 percent of the voting power or value, directly (as in the case of a first-tier subsidiary) or indirectly (as in the case of a second-tier subsidiary).

Under present law, interest, rent, annuity, or royalty payments made by a controlled entity to a tax-exempt organization are includable in the latter organization's unrelated business income and are subject to the unrelated business income tax to the extent the payment reduces the net unrelated income (or increases any net unrelated loss) of the controlled entity (determined as if the entity were tax exempt).

Explanation of Provision

The provision provides that the general rule of section 512(b)(13), which includes interest, rent, annuity, or royalty payments made by a controlled entity to the controlling tax-exempt organization in the latter organization's unrelated business income to the extent the payment reduces the net unrelated income (or increases any net unrelated loss) of the controlled entity, applies only to the portion of payments received or accrued in a taxable year that exceeds the amount of the specified payment that would have been paid or accrued if such payment had been determined under the principles of section 482. Thus, if a payment of rent by a controlled subsidiary to its tax-exempt parent organization exceeds fair market value, the excess amount of such payment over fair market value (as determined in accordance with section 482) is included in the parent organization's unrelated business income, to the extent that such excess reduced the net unrelated income (or increased any net unrelated loss) of the controlled entity (determined as if the entity were tax exempt). In addition, the provision imposes a 20-percent penalty on the larger of such excess determined without regard to any amendment or supplement to a return of tax, or such excess determined with regard to all such amendments and supplements. The provision applies only to payments made pursuant to a binding written contract in effect on the date of enactment (or renewal of such a contract on substantially similar terms). It is intended that there should be further study of such arrangements in light of the provision before any determination about whether to extend or expand the provision is made.

The provision requires that a tax-exempt organization that receives interest, rent, annuity, or royalty payments from a controlled entity report such payments on its annual information return as well as any loans made to any controlled entity and any transfers between such organization and a controlled entity.

The provision provides that, not later than January 1, 2009, the Secretary shall submit a report to the Committee on Finance of the Senate and the Committee on Ways and Means of the House of Representatives a report on the effectiveness of the Internal Revenue Service in administering the provision and on the extent to which payments by controlled entities to the controlling exempt organization meet the requirements of section 482 of the Code. Such report shall include the results of any audit of any controlling organization or controlled entity and recommendations relating to the tax treatment of payments from controlled entities to controlling organizations.

Effective Date

The provision related to payments to controlling organizations applies to payments received or accrued after December 31, 2005 and before January 1, 2008. The provision relating to reporting is effective for returns the due date (determined without regard to extensions) of which is after the date of enactment. The provision relating to a report is effective on the date of enactment.

[Law at ¶ 5160, ¶ 5325 and ¶ 7228. CCH Explanation at ¶ 1210.]

[¶ 11,160] Act Sec. 1206. Encourage contributions of real property made for conservation purposes

Joint Committee Taxation (J.C.T. REP. NO. JCX-38-06)

[Code Sec. 170]

Present Law

Charitable contributions generally

In general, a deduction is permitted for charitable contributions, subject to certain limitations that depend on the type of taxpayer, the property contributed, and the donee organization. The amount of deduction generally equals the fair market value of the contributed property on the date of the contribution. Charitable deductions are provided for income, estate, and gift tax purposes.[307]

In general, in any taxable year, charitable contributions by a corporation are not deductible to the extent the aggregate contributions exceed 10 percent of the corporation's taxable income computed without regard to net operating or capital loss carrybacks. For individuals, the amount deductible is a percentage of the taxpayer's contribution base, which is the taxpayer's adjusted gross income computed without regard to any net operating loss carryback. The applicable percentage of the contribution base varies depending on the type of donee organization and property contributed. Cash contributions of an individual taxpayer to public charities, private operating foundations, and certain types of private nonoperating foundations may not exceed 50 percent of the taxpayer's contribution base. Cash contributions to private foundations and certain other organizations generally may be deducted up to 30 percent of the taxpayer's contribution base.

In general, a charitable deduction is not allowed for income, estate, or gift tax purposes if the donor transfers an interest in property to a charity while also either retaining an interest in that property or transferring an interest in that property to a noncharity for less than full and adequate consideration. Exceptions to this general rule are provided for, among other interests, remainder interests in charitable remainder annuity trusts, charitable remainder unitrusts, and pooled income funds, present interests in the form of a guaranteed annuity or a fixed percentage of the annual value of the property, and qualified conservation contributions.

---

[307] Secs. 170, 2055, and 2522, respectively.

Capital gain property

Capital gain property means any capital asset or property used in the taxpayer's trade or business the sale of which at its fair market value, at the time of contribution, would have resulted in gain that would have been long-term capital gain. Contributions of capital gain property to a qualified charity are deductible at fair market value within certain limitations. Contributions of capital gain property to charitable organizations described in section 170(b)(1)(A) (e.g., public charities, private foundations other than private non-operating foundations, and certain governmental units) generally are deductible up to 30 percent of the taxpayer's contribution base. An individual may elect, however, to bring all these contributions of capital gain property for a taxable year within the 50-percent limitation category by reducing the amount of the contribution deduction by the amount of the appreciation in the capital gain property. Contributions of capital gain property to charitable organizations described in section 170(b)(1)(B) (e.g., private non-operating foundations) are deductible up to 20 percent of the taxpayer's contribution base.

For purposes of determining whether a taxpayer's aggregate charitable contributions in a taxable year exceed the applicable percentage limitation, contributions of capital gain property are taken into account after other charitable contributions. Contributions of capital gain property that exceed the percentage limitation may be carried forward for five years.

Qualified conservation contributions

Qualified conservation contributions are not subject to the "partial interest" rule, which generally bars deductions for charitable contributions of partial interests in property. A qualified conservation contribution is a contribution of a qualified real property interest to a qualified organization exclusively for conservation purposes. A qualified real property interest is defined as: (1) the entire interest of the donor other than a qualified mineral interest; (2) a remainder interest; or (3) a restriction (granted in perpetuity) on the use that may be made of the real property. Qualified organizations include certain governmental units, public charities that meet certain public support tests, and certain supporting organizations. Conservation purposes include: (1) the preservation of land areas for outdoor recreation by, or for the education of, the general public; (2) the protection of a relatively natural habitat of fish, wildlife, or plants, or similar ecosystem; (3) the preservation of open space (including farmland and forest land) where such preservation will yield a significant public benefit and is either for the scenic enjoyment of the general public or pursuant to a clearly delineated Federal, State, or local governmental conservation policy; and (4) the preservation of an historically important land area or a certified historic structure.

Qualified conservation contributions of capital gain property are subject to the same limitations and carryover rules of other charitable contributions of capital gain property.

Explanation of Provision

In general

Under the provision, the 30-percent contribution base limitation on contributions of capital gain property by individuals does not apply to qualified conservation contributions (as defined under present law). Instead, individuals may deduct the fair market value of any qualified conservation contribution to an organization described in section 170(b)(1)(A) to the extent of the excess of 50 percent of the contribution base over the amount of all other allowable charitable contributions. These contributions are not taken into account in determining the amount of other allowable charitable contributions.

Individuals are allowed to carryover any qualified conservation contributions that exceed the 50-percent limitation for up to 15 years.

For example, assume an individual with a contribution base of $100 makes a qualified conservation contribution of property with a fair market value of $80 and makes other charitable contributions subject to the 50-percent limitation of $60. The individual is allowed a deduction of $50 in the current taxable year for the non-conservation contributions (50 percent of the $100 contribution base) and is allowed to carryover the excess $10 for up to 5 years. No current deduction is allowed for the qualified conservation contribution, but the entire $80 qualified conservation contribution may be carried forward for up to 15 years.

Farmers and ranchers

Individuals

In the case of an individual who is a qualified farmer or rancher for the taxable year in which the contribution is made, a qualified conservation contribution is allowable up to 100 percent of the excess of the taxpayer's contribution base over the amount of all other allowable charitable contributions.

In the above example, if the individual is a qualified farmer or rancher, in addition to the $50 deduction for non-conservation contributions, an additional $50 for the qualified conservation contribution is allowed and $30 may be carried forward for up to 15 years as a contribution subject to the 100-percent limitation.

Corporations

In the case of a corporation (other than a publicly traded corporation) that is a qualified farmer or rancher for the taxable year in which the contribution is made, any qualified conservation contribution is allowable up to 100 percent of the excess of the corporation's taxable income (as computed under section 170(b)(2)) over the amount of all other allowable charitable contributions. Any excess may be carried forward for up to 15 years as a contribution subject to the 100-percent limitation.

Requirement that land be available for agriculture or livestock production

As an additional condition of eligibility for the 100 percent limitation, with respect to any contribution of property in agriculture or livestock production, or that is available for such production, by a qualified farmer or rancher, the qualified real property interest must include a restriction that the property remain generally available for such production. (There is no requirement as to any specific use in agriculture or farming, or necessarily that the property be used for such purposes, merely that the property remain available for such purposes.) Such additional condition does not apply to contributions made after December 31, 2005, and on or before the date of enactment.

Definition

A qualified farmer or rancher means a taxpayer whose gross income from the trade of business of farming (within the meaning of section 2032A(e)(5)) is greater than 50 percent of the taxpayer's gross income for the taxable year.

Effective Date

The provision applies to contributions made in taxable years beginning after December 31, 2005, and before January 1, 2008.

[Law at ¶ 5020 and ¶ 5180. CCH Explanation at ¶ 1125.]

[¶ 11,170] Act Sec. 1207. Excise tax exemptions for blood collector organizations

Joint Committee Taxation (J.C.T. REP. NO. JCX-38-06)

[Code Secs. 4041, 4221, 4253, 4483, 6416 and 7701]

Present Law

American National Red Cross

The American National Red Cross ("Red Cross") is a Congressionally chartered corporation. It is responsible for giving aid to members of the U.S. Armed Forces, to disaster victims in the United States and abroad to help people prevent, prepare for, and respond to emergencies.[308] The Red Cross is responsible for over half of the nation's blood supply and blood products.

Exemption from certain retail and manufacturers excise taxes

The Code permits the Secretary to exempt from excise tax certain articles and services to be purchased for the exclusive use of the United States (sec. 4293). This authority is conditioned upon the Secretary determining (1) that the imposition of such taxes will cause substantial burden or expense which can be avoided by granting tax exemption and (2) that full benefit of such exemption, if granted, will accrue to the United States.

On April 18, 1979, the Secretary exercised this authority to exempt, with limited exceptions, the Red Cross from the taxes imposed by chapters 31 and 32 of the Code with respect to articles sold to the Red Cross for its exclusive use.[309] An exemption is also authorized from the taxes imposed with respect to tires and inner tubes if such tire or inner tube is sold by any person on or in connection with the sale of any article to the American National Red Cross, for

---

[308] *See* 36 U.S.C. sec. 300102.

[309] Department of the Treasury, *Notice-Manufacturers and Retailers Excise Taxes -Exemption from Tax of Sales of Certain Articles to the American Red Cross*, 44 F.R. 23407, 1979-1 C.B. 478 (1979). At the time the notice was issued the following taxes were covered in Chapters 31 and 32: special fuels, automotive and related items (motor vehicles, tires and

its exclusive use.[310] No exemption is provided from the gas guzzler tax (sec. 4064), and the taxes imposed on aviation fuel, on fuel used on inland waterways (sec. 4042), and on coal (sec. 4121).[311] The exemption is subject to registration requirements for tax-free sales contained in Treasury regulations. Credit and refund of tax is subject to the requirements set forth in section 6416 relating to the exemption for taxable articles sold for the exclusive use of State and local governments.

Exemption from heavy highway motor vehicle use tax

An annual use tax is imposed on highway motor vehicles, at the rates below (sec. 4481).

Under 55,000 pounds	No tax
55,000-75,000 pounds	$100 plus $22 per 1,000 pounds over 55,000
Over 75,000 pounds	$550

The Code provides that the Secretary may authorize exemption from the heavy highway vehicle use tax as to the use by the United States of any particular highway motor vehicle or class of highway motor vehicles if the Secretary determines that the imposition of such tax with respect to such use will cause substantial burden or expense which can be avoided by granting tax exemption and that the full benefit of such exemption, if granted will accrue to the United States (sec. 4483(b)). The IRS has ruled that the Red Cross comes within the term "United States" for purposes of the exemption from the heavy highway motor vehicle use tax (Rev. Rul. 76-510).

Exemption from communications excise tax

The Code imposes a three-percent tax on amounts paid for local telephone service; toll telephone service and teletypewriter exchange service (sec. 4251). These taxes do not apply to amounts paid for services furnished to the Red Cross (sec. 4253(c)).

Certain other tax-free sales

Exemption from certain manufacturer and retail sale excise taxes

The following sales generally are exempt from certain manufacturer and retail sale excise taxes: (1) for use by the purchaser for further manufacture, or for resale to a second purchaser in further manufacture; (2) for export or for resale to a second purchaser for export; (3) for use by the purchaser as supplies for vessels or aircraft; (4) to a State or local government for the exclusive use of a State or local government; and (5) to a nonprofit educational organization for its exclusive use (sec. 4221). The exemption generally applies to manufacturers taxes imposed by chapter 32 of the Code (the gas guzzlers tax, and the taxes imposed on tires, certain vaccines, and recreational equipment) and the tax on retail sales of heavy trucks and trailers.[312]

The manufacturers excise taxes on coal (sec. 4121), on gasoline, diesel fuel, and kerosene (sec. 4081) are not covered by the exemption. The exemption for a sale to a State or local government for their exclusive use and the exemption for sales to a nonprofit educational organization does not apply to the gas guzzlers tax, and the tax on vaccines. In addition, the exemption of sales for use as supplies for vessels and aircraft does not apply to the vaccine tax.

Exempt sales of special fuels

A retail excise tax is imposed on special motor fuels, including propane, compressed natural gas, and certain alcohol mixtures (sec. 4041). Section 4041 also serves as a back-up tax for diesel fuel or kerosene that was not subject to the manufacturers taxes under section 4081 (other than the Leaking Underground Storage Tank Trust Fund tax) if such fuel is delivered into the fuel supply tank of a diesel-powered highway vehicle or train.[313] No tax is imposed on these fuels for nontaxable uses, including fuel: (1) sold for use or used as supplies for vessels or aircraft, (2) sold for the exclusive use of any State, any

(Footnote Continued)

tubes, petroleum products, coal, and recreational equipment (sporting goods and firearms).

[310] Under present law, there is no longer a tax on inner tubes.

[311] Department of the Treasury, *Notice-Manufacturers and Retailers Excise Taxes -Exemption from Tax of Sales of Certain Articles to the American Red Cross*, 44 F.R. 23407, 1979-1 C.B. 478, at 479 (1979). The Treasury notice also exempts the Red Cross from tax on aircraft tires and tubes, however, present law currently limits the tax to highway vehicle tires (sec. 4071(a)).

[312] The tax imposed by subchapter A of chapter 31 (relating to luxury passenger vehicles) are also exempt pursuant to this provision, however, this tax expired on December 31, 2002. (sec. 4001(g).)

[313] For example, tax is imposed on the delivery of any of the following into the fuel supply tank of a diesel powered highway vehicle or train of any dyed diesel or dyed kerosene for other than a nontaxable use; any undyed diesel fuel or undyed kerosene on which a credit or refund.

political subdivision of a State, or the District of Columbia or used by such entity as fuel, (3) sold for export, or for shipment to a possession of the United States and is actually exported or shipped, (4) sold to a nonprofit educational organization for its exclusive use, or used by such entity as fuel (sec. 4041(g)).

Credits and refunds

In general

A credit or refund is allowed for overpayment of manufacturers or retail excise taxes (sec. 6416). Overpayments include (1) certain uses and resales, (2) price adjustments, and (3) further manufacture.

Specified uses and rates

The special fuel taxes, the retail tax on heavy trucks and trailers, and any of the manufacturers excise taxes paid on any article will be a deemed overpayment subject to credit or refund if sold for certain specified uses (sec. 6416(b)(2)). These uses are (1) export, (2) used or sold for use as supplies for vessels or aircraft, (3) sold to a State or local government for the exclusive use of a State or local government, (4) sold to a nonprofit educational organization for its exclusive use; (5) taxable tires sold to any person for use in connection with a qualified bus, or (6) the case of gasoline used or sold for use in the production of a special fuel. Certain exceptions apply in that this deemed overpayment rule does not apply to the taxes imposed by sections 4041 and 4081 on diesel fuel and kerosene, and the coal taxes (sec. 4121). Additionally, the deemed overpayment rule does not apply to the gas guzzler tax in the case of an article sold to a state or local government for its exclusive use or sold to an educational organization for its exclusive use.

Special rule for tires sold in connection with other articles

If the tax imposed on tires (sec. 4071) has been paid with respect to the sale of any tire by the manufacturer, producer, or importer, and such tire is sold by any person in connection with the sale of any other article, such tax will be deemed an overpayment by person if such other article (1) is an automobile bus chassis or an automobile bus body, or (2) is by any person exported, sold to a State or local government for exclusive use of a State or local government, sold to a nonprofit educational organization for its exclusive use, or used or sold for use as supplies for vessels or aircraft (sec. 6416(b)(4)).

Gasoline used for exempt purposes

If gasoline is sold to any person for certain specified purposes, the Secretary is required to pay (without interest) to such person an amount equal to the product of the number of gallons of gasoline so sold multiplied by the rate at which tax was imposed on such gasoline under section 4081 (sec. 6421(c)). Under this provision, the specified purposes are (1) for export or for resale to a second purchaser for export; (2) for use by the purchaser as supplies for vessels or aircraft; (3) to a State or local government for exclusive use of a State or local government; and (4) to a nonprofit educational organization for its exclusive use (sec. 4221(a), 6421(c)).

Diesel fuel or kerosene used in a nontaxable use

If diesel fuel or kerosene, upon which tax has been imposed is used by any person in a nontaxable use, the Code authorizes the Secretary to pay (without interest) an amount equal to the aggregate amount of tax imposed on such fuel (sec. 6427(l)). Nontaxable uses include any exemption from the tax imposed by section 4041(a) (except prior taxation).

Explanation of Provision

The provision exempts qualified blood collector organizations from certain retail and manufacturers excise taxes to the extent such items are for the exclusive use of such an organization for the distribution or collection of blood. A qualified blood collector organization means an organization that is (1) described in section 501(c)(3) and exempt from tax under section 501(a), (2) primarily engaged in the activity of the collection of blood, (3) registered with the Secretary for purposes of excise tax exemptions, and (4) registered by the Food and Drug Administration to collect blood.

Under the provision, qualified blood collector organizations are exempt from the communications excise tax as provided by Treasury regulations. The provision also provides an exemption from the special fuels tax, and certain taxes imposed by chapter 32 and subchapter A and C of chapter 31 of the Code (i.e., the retail excise tax on heavy trucks and trailers, and the manufacturers excise taxes on tires).[314] The provision also makes conforming amendments to

[314] Such organizations are also exempt from the expired retail excise tax on luxury passenger vehicles. No exemption is provided from the gas guzzler tax (sec. 4064), the taxes imposed on fuel used on inland waterways (sec. 4042), on coal (sec. 4121), and on recreational equipment (sport fishing equipment, bows, arrow components, and firearms).

allow for the credit or refund of these taxes and any tax paid on gasoline for the exclusive use of the blood collector organization. The provision also permits a refund of tax for diesel fuel or kerosene used by a qualified blood collector organization. Finally, the provision provides an exemption from the heavy vehicle use tax of a "qualified blood collector vehicle" by a qualified blood collector organization. A "qualified blood collector vehicle" means a vehicle at least 80 percent of the use of which during the prior taxable period was by a qualified blood collector organization in the collection, storage, or transportation of blood. A special rule is provided for the first taxable period a vehicle is placed in service by the qualified blood collector organization. For the first taxable period a vehicle is placed in service by the organization, the vehicle will be treated as a "qualified blood collector vehicle" for that period if the organization certifies that it reasonably expects that at least 80 percent of the use of the vehicle during such taxable period will be by the organization in the collection, storage, or transportation of blood. Such certification is to be provided to the Secretary on such forms and in such manner as the Secretary may require.

It is expected that the excise tax exemptions of the Red Cross will be reexamined in conjunction with a review of its charter.

Effective Date

Generally, the provision is effective on January 1, 2007. The exemption from the heavy vehicle use tax is effective for taxable periods beginning July 1, 2007.

[Law at ¶5225, ¶5230, ¶5235, ¶5240, ¶5380, ¶5385 and ¶5485. CCH Explanation at ¶1255.]

[¶11,190] Act Sec. 1211. Reporting on certain acquisitions of interests in insurance contracts in which certain exempt organizations hold interests

Joint Committee Taxation (J.C.T. Rep. No. JCX-38-06)

[New Code Sec. 6050V]

Present Law

Amounts received under a life insurance contract

Amounts received under a life insurance contract paid by reason of the death of the insured are not includible in gross income for Federal tax purposes.[315] No Federal income tax generally is imposed on a policyholder with respect to the earnings under a life insurance contract (inside buildup).[316]

Distributions from a life insurance contract (other than a modified endowment contract) that are made prior to the death of the insured generally are includible in income to the extent that the amounts distributed exceed the taxpayer's investment in the contract (i.e., basis). Such distributions generally are treated first as a tax-free recovery of basis, and then as income.[317]

Transfers for value

A limitation on the exclusion for amounts received under a life insurance contract is provided in the case of transfers for value. If a life insurance contract (or an interest in the contract) is transferred for valuable consideration, the amount excluded from income by reason of the death of the insured is limited to the actual value of the consideration plus the premiums and other amounts subsequently paid by the acquiror of the contract.[318]

---

[315] Sec. 101(a).

[316] This favorable tax treatment is available only if a life insurance contract meets certain requirements designed to limit the investment character of the contract. Sec. 7702.

[317] Sec. 72(e). In the case of a modified endowment contract, however, in general, distributions are treated as income first, loans are treated as distributions (i.e., income rather than basis recovery first), and an additional 10-percent tax is imposed on the income portion of distributions made before age 59-½ and in certain other circumstances. Secs. 72(e) and (v). A modified endowment contract is a life insurance contract that does not meet a statutory "7-pay" test, i.e., generally is funded more rapidly than seven annual level premiums. Sec. 7702A.

[318] Section 101(a)(2). The transfer-for-value rule does not apply, however, in the case of a transfer in which the life insurance contract (or interest in the contract) transferred has a basis in the hands of the transferee that is determined by reference to the transferor's basis. Similarly, the transfer-for-value rule generally does not apply if the transfer is between certain parties (specifically, if the transfer is to the insured, a partner of the insured, a partnership in which the insured is a partner, or a corporation in which the insured is a shareholder or officer).

Tax treatment of charitable organizations and donors

Present law generally provides tax-exempt status for charitable, educational and certain other organizations, no part of the net earnings of which inures to the benefit of any private shareholder or individual, and which meet certain other requirements.[319] Governmental entities, including some educational organizations, are exempt from tax on income under other tax rules providing that gross income does not include income derived from the exercise of any essential governmental function and accruing to a State or any political subdivision thereof.[320]

In computing taxable income, a taxpayer who itemizes deductions generally is allowed to deduct the amount of cash and the fair market value of property contributed to an organization described in section 501(c)(3) or to a Federal, State, or local governmental entity for exclusively public purposes.[321]

State-law insurable interest rules

State laws generally provide that the owner of a life insurance contract must have an insurable interest in the insured person when the life insurance contract is issued. State laws vary as to the insurable interest of a charitable organization in the life of any individual. Some State laws provide that a charitable organization meeting the requirements of section 501(c)(3) of the Code is treated as having an insurable interest in the life of any donor,[322] or, in other States, in the life of any individual who consents (whether or not the individual is a donor).[323] Other States' insurable interest rules permit the purchase of a life insurance contract even though the person paying the consideration has no insurable interest in the life of the person insured if a charitable, benevolent, educational or religious institution is designated irrevocably as the beneficiary.[324]

Transactions involving charities and noncharities acquiring life insurance

Recently, there has been an increase in transactions involving the acquisition of life insurance contracts using arrangements in which both exempt organizations, primarily charities, and private investors have an interest in the contract.[325] The exempt organization has an insurable interest in the insured individuals, either because they are donors, because they consent, or otherwise under applicable State insurable interest rules. Private investors provide capital used to fund the purchase of the life insurance contracts, sometimes together with annuity contracts. Both the private investors and the charity have an interest in the contracts, directly or indirectly, through the use of trusts, partnerships, or other arrangements for sharing the rights to the contracts. Both the charity and the private investors receive cash amounts in connection with the investment in the contracts while the life insurance is in force or as the insured individuals die.

Explanation of Provision

The provision includes a temporary reporting requirement with respect to the acquisition of interests in certain life insurance contracts by certain exempt organizations, together with a Treasury study.

The provision provides that, for reportable acquisitions occurring after the date of enactment and on or before the date two years from the date of enactment, an applicable exempt organization that makes a reportable acquisition is required to file an information return. The information return is to contain the name, address, and taxpayer identification number of the organization and of the issuer of the applicable insurance contract, and such other information as the Secretary of the Treasury prescribes. It is intended that the Treasury Department may require the reporting of other information relevant to the study required under the provision. The report is to be in the form prescribed by the Treasury Secretary and is required to be filed at the time established by the Treasury Secretary. It is intended that the Treasury Department may require the report to be filed within a certain period after the reportable acquisition takes place in order to gather information in a timely

[319] Section 501(c)(3).

[320] Section 115.

[321] Section 170.

[322] See, e.g., Mass. Gen. Laws Ann. ch. 175, sec. 123A(2) (West 2005); Iowa Code Ann. sec. 511.39 (West 2004) ("a person who, when purchasing a life insurance policy, makes a donation to the charitable organization or makes the charitable organization the beneficiary of all or a part of the proceeds of the policy . . .).

[323] See, e.g., Cal. Ins. Code sec. 10110.1(f) (West 2005); 40 Pa. Cons. Stat. Ann. sec. 40-512 (2004); Fla. Stat. Ann. sec. 27.404 (2) (2004); Mich. Comp. Laws Ann. sec. 500.2212 (West 2004).

[324] Or. Rev. Stat. sec. 743.030 (2003); Del. Code Ann. Tit. 18, sec. 2705(a) (2004).

[325] Davis, Wendy, "Death-Pool Donations," Trusts and Estates, May 2004, 55; Francis, Theo, "Tax May Thwart Investment Plans Enlisting Charities," Wall St. J., Feb. 8, 2005, A-10.

manner that is relevant to the study required under the provision.

For this purpose, a reportable acquisition means the acquisition by an applicable exempt organization of a direct or indirect interest in a contract that the applicable exempt organization knows or has reason to know is an applicable insurance contract, if such acquisition is a part of a structured transaction involving a pool of such contracts.

An applicable insurance contract means any life insurance, annuity, or endowment contract with respect to which both an applicable exempt organization and a person other than an applicable exempt organization have directly or indirectly held an interest in the contract (whether or not at the same time). Exceptions apply under this definition. First, the term does not apply if each person (other than an applicable exempt organization) with a direct or indirect interest in the contract has an insurable interest in the insured independent of any interest of the exempt organization in the contract. Second, the term does not apply if the sole interest in the contract of the applicable exempt organization or each person other than the applicable exempt organization is as a named beneficiary. Third, the term does not apply if the sole interest in the contract of each person other than the applicable exempt organization is either (1) as a beneficiary of a trust holding an interest in the contract, but only if the person's designation as such a beneficiary was made without consideration and solely on a purely gratuitous basis, or (2) as a trustee who holds an interest in the contract in a fiduciary capacity solely for the benefit of applicable exempt organizations or of persons otherwise meeting one of the first two exceptions.

An applicable exempt organization is any organization described in section 170(c), 168(h)(2)(A)(iv), 2055(a), or 2522(a). Thus, for example, an applicable exempt organization generally includes an organization that is exempt from Federal income tax by reason of being described in section 501(c)(3) (including one organized outside the United States), a government or political subdivision of a government, and an Indian tribal government.

Under the provision, penalties apply for failure to file the return.

The reporting requirement terminates with respect to reportable acquisitions occurring after the date that is 2 years after the date of enactment.

The provision requires the Treasury Secretary to undertake a study on the use by tax-exempt organizations of applicable insurance contracts for the purpose of sharing the benefits of the organization's insurable interest in insured individuals under such contracts with investors, and whether such activities are consistent with the tax-exempt status of the organizations. The study may, for example, address whether certain such arrangements are or may be used to improperly shelter income from tax, and whether they should be listed transactions within the meaning of Treasury Regulation section 1.6011-4(b)(2). No later than 30 months after the date of enactment, the Treasury Secretary is required to report on the study to the Committee on Finance of the Senate and the Committee on Ways and Means of the House of Representatives.

Effective Date

The reporting provision is effective for acquisitions of contracts after the date of enactment. The study provision is effective on the date of enactment.

[Law at ¶5350, ¶5420, ¶5425 and ¶7231. CCH Explanation at ¶1285.]

[¶11,200] Act Sec. 1212. Increase the amounts of excise taxes imposed relating to public charities, social welfare organizations, and private foundations

Joint Committee Taxation (J.C.T. REP. NO. JCX-38-06)

[Code Secs. 4941, 4942, 4943, 4944, 4945 and 4958]

Present Law

Public charities and social welfare organizations

The Code imposes excise taxes on excess benefit transactions between disqualified persons (as defined in section 4958(f)) and charitable organizations (other than private foundations) or social welfare organizations (as described in section 501(c)(4)).[326] An excess benefit transaction generally is a transaction in which an economic benefit is provided by a charitable or social welfare organization directly or indirectly to or for the use of a disqualified person, if the value of the economic benefit provided exceeds the value of the consideration (including the performance of services) received for providing such benefit.

The excess benefit tax is imposed on the disqualified person and, in certain cases, on the organization manager, but is not imposed on the exempt organization. An initial tax of 25 percent of the excess benefit amount is imposed on the disqualified person that receives the excess benefit. An additional tax on the disqualified person of 200 percent of the excess benefit applies if the violation is not corrected. A tax of 10 percent of the excess benefit (not to exceed $10,000 with respect to any excess benefit transaction) is imposed on an organization manager that knowingly participated in the excess benefit transaction, if the manager's participation was willful and not due to reasonable cause, and if the initial tax was imposed on the disqualified person.[327] If more than one person is liable for the tax on disqualified persons or on management, all such persons are jointly and severally liable for the tax.[328]

Private foundations

Self-dealing by private foundations

Excise taxes are imposed on acts of self-dealing between a disqualified person (as defined in section 4946) and a private foundation.[329] In general, self-dealing transactions are any direct or indirect: (1) sale or exchange, or leasing, of property between a private foundation and a disqualified person; (2) lending of money or other extension of credit between a private foundation and a disqualified person; (3) the furnishing of goods, services, or facilities between a private foundation and a disqualified person; (4) the payment of compensation (or payment or reimbursement of expenses) by a private foundation to a disqualified person; (5) the transfer to, or use by or for the benefit of, a disqualified person of the income or assets of the private foundation; and (6) certain payments of money or property to a government official.[330] Certain exceptions apply.[331]

An initial tax of five percent of the amount involved with respect to an act of self-dealing is imposed on any disqualified person (other than a foundation manager acting only as such) who participates in the act of self-dealing. If such a tax is imposed, a 2.5-percent tax of the amount involved is imposed on a foundation manager who participated in the act of self-dealing knowing it was such an act (and such participation was not willful and was due to reasonable cause) up to $10,000 per act. Such initial taxes may not be abated.[332] Such initial taxes are imposed for each year in the taxable period, which begins on the date the act of self-dealing occurs and ends on the earliest of the date of mailing of a notice of deficiency for the tax, the date on which the tax is assessed, or the date on which correction of

---

[326] Sec. 4958. The excess benefit transaction tax commonly is referred to as "intermediate sanctions," because it imposes penalties generally considered to be less punitive than revocation of the organization's exempt status.

[327] Sec. 4958(d)(2). Taxes imposed may be abated if certain conditions are met. Secs. 4961 and 4962.

[328] Sec. 4958(d)(1).

[329] Sec. 4941.

[330] Sec. 4941(d)(1).

[331] See sec. 4941(d)(2).

[332] Sec. 4962(b).

the act of self-dealing is completed. A government official (as defined in section 4946(c)) is subject to such initial tax only if the official participates in the act of self-dealing knowing it is such an act. If the act of self-dealing is not corrected, a tax of 200 percent of the amount involved is imposed on the disqualified person and a tax of 50 percent of the amount involved (up to $10,000 per act) is imposed on a foundation manager who refused to agree to correcting the act of self-dealing. Such additional taxes are subject to abatement.[333]

Tax on failure to distribute income

Private nonoperating foundations are required to pay out a minimum amount each year as qualifying distributions. In general, a qualifying distribution is an amount paid to accomplish one or more of the organization's exempt purposes, including reasonable and necessary administrative expenses.[334] Failure to pay out the minimum results in an initial excise tax on the foundation of 15 percent of the undistributed amount. An additional tax of 100 percent of the undistributed amount applies if an initial tax is imposed and the required distributions have not been made by the end of the applicable taxable period.[335] A foundation may include as a qualifying distribution the salaries, occupancy expenses, travel costs, and other reasonable and necessary administrative expenses that the foundation incurs in operating a grant program. A qualifying distribution also includes any amount paid to acquire an asset used (or held for use) directly in carrying out one or more of the organization's exempt purposes and certain amounts set-aside for exempt purposes.[336] Private operating foundations are not subject to the payout requirements.

Tax on excess business holdings

Private foundations are subject to tax on excess business holdings.[337] In general, a private foundation is permitted to hold 20 percent of the voting stock in a corporation, reduced by the amount of voting stock held by all disqualified persons (as defined in section 4946). If it is established that no disqualified person has effective control of the corporation, a private foundation and disqualified persons together may own up to 35 percent of the voting stock of a corporation. A private foundation shall not be treated as having excess business holdings in any corporation if it owns (together with certain other related private foundations) not more than two percent of the voting stock and not more than two percent in value of all outstanding shares of all classes of stock in that corporation. Similar rules apply with respect to holdings in a partnership ("profits interest" is substituted for "voting stock" and "capital interest" for "nonvoting stock") and to other unincorporated enterprises (by substituting "beneficial interest" for "voting stock"). Private foundations are not permitted to have holdings in a proprietorship. Foundations generally have a five-year period to dispose of excess business holdings (acquired other than by purchase) without being subject to tax.[338] This five-year period may be extended an additional five years in limited circumstances.[339] The excess business holdings rules do not apply to holdings in a functionally related business or to holdings in a trade or business at least 95 percent of the gross income of which is derived from passive sources.[340]

The initial tax is equal to five percent of the value of the excess business holdings held during the foundation's applicable taxable year. An additional tax is imposed if an initial tax is imposed and at the close of the applicable taxable period, the foundation continues to hold excess business holdings. The amount of the additional tax is equal to 200 percent of such holdings.

Tax on jeopardizing investments

Private foundations and foundation managers are subject to tax on investments that jeopardize the foundation's charitable purpose.[341] In general, an initial tax of five percent of the amount of the investment applies to the foundation and to foundation managers who participated in the making of the investment knowing that it jeopardized the carrying out of the foundation's exempt purposes. The initial tax on foundation managers may not exceed $5,000 per investment. If the investment is not removed from jeopardy (e.g., sold or otherwise disposed of), an additional tax of 25 percent of the amount of the investment is imposed on the foundation

---

[333] Sec. 4961.

[334] Sec. 4942(g)(1)(A).

[335] Sec. 4942(a) and (b). Taxes imposed may be abated if certain conditions are met. Secs. 4961 and 4962.

[336] Sec. 4942(g)(1)(B) and 4942(g)(2). In general, an organization is permitted to adjust the distributable amount in those cases where distributions during the five preceding years have exceeded the payout requirements. Sec. 4942(i).

[337] Sec. 4943. Taxes imposed may be abated if certain conditions are met. Secs. 4961 and 4962.

[338] Sec. 4943(c)(6).

[339] Sec. 4943(c)(7).

[340] Sec. 4943(d)(3).

[341] Sec. 4944. Taxes imposed may be abated if certain conditions are met. Secs. 4961 and 4962.

and five percent of the amount of the investment on a foundation manager who refused to agree to removing the investment from jeopardy. The additional tax on foundation managers may not exceed $10,000 per investment. An investment, the primary purpose of which is to accomplish a charitable purpose and no significant purpose of which is the production of income or the appreciation of property, is not considered a jeopardizing investment.[342]

Tax on taxable expenditures

Certain expenditures of private foundations are subject to tax.[343] In general, taxable expenditures are expenses: (1) for lobbying; (2) to influence the outcome of a public election or carry on a voter registration drive (unless certain requirements are met); (3) as a grant to an individual for travel, study, or similar purposes unless made pursuant to procedures approved by the Secretary; (4) as a grant to an organization that is not a public charity or exempt operating foundation unless the foundation exercises expenditure responsibility[344] with respect to the grant; or (5) for any non-charitable purpose. For each taxable expenditure, a tax is imposed on the foundation of 10 percent of the amount of the expenditure, and an additional tax of 100 percent is imposed on the foundation if the expenditure is not corrected. A tax of 2.5 percent of the expenditure (up to $5,000) also is imposed on a foundation manager who agrees to making a taxable expenditure knowing that it is a taxable expenditure. An additional tax of 50 percent of the amount of the expenditure (up to $10,000) is imposed on a foundation manager who refuses to agree to correction of such expenditure.

Explanation of Provision

Self-dealing and excess benefit transaction initial taxes and dollar limitations

For acts of self-dealing by a private foundation to a disqualified person, the provision increases the initial tax on the self-dealer from five percent of the amount involved to 10 percent of the amount involved. The provision increases the initial tax on foundation managers from 2.5 percent of the amount involved to five percent of the amount involved and increases the dollar limitation on the amount of the initial and additional taxes on foundation managers per act of self-dealing from $10,000 per act to $20,000 per act. Similarly, the provision doubles the dollar limitation on organization managers of public charities and social welfare organizations for participation in excess benefit transactions from $10,000 per transaction to $20,000 per transaction.

Failure to distribute income, excess business holdings, jeopardizing investments, and taxable expenditures

The provision doubles the amounts of the initial taxes and the dollar limitations on foundation managers with respect to the private foundation excise taxes on the failure to distribute income, excess business holdings, jeopardizing investments, and taxable expenditures.

Specifically, for the failure to distribute income, the initial tax on the foundation is increased from 15 percent of the undistributed amount to 30 percent of the undistributed amount.

For excess business holdings, the initial tax on excess business holdings is increased from five percent of the value of such holdings to 10 percent of such value.

For jeopardizing investments, the initial tax of five percent of the amount of the investment that is imposed on the foundation and on foundation managers is increased to 10 percent of the amount of the investment. The dollar limitation on the initial tax on foundation managers of $5,000 per investment is increased to $10,000 and the dollar limitation on the additional tax on foundation managers of $10,000 per investment is increased to $20,000.

For taxable expenditures, the initial tax on the foundation is increased from 10 percent of the amount of the expenditure to 20 percent, the initial tax on the foundation manager is increased from 2.5 percent of the amount of the expenditure to five percent, the dollar limitation on the initial tax on foundation managers is increased from $5,000 to $10,000, and the dollar limitation on the additional tax on foundation managers is increased from $10,000 to $20,000.

Effective Date

The provision is effective for taxable years beginning after the date of enactment.

[Law at ¶ 5250, ¶ 5255, ¶ 5260, ¶ 5265, ¶ 5270 and ¶ 5275. CCH Explanation at ¶ 1245.]

---

[342] Sec. 4944(c).

[343] Sec. 4945. Taxes imposed may be abated if certain conditions are met. Secs. 4961 and 4962.

[344] In general, expenditure responsibility requires that a foundation make all reasonable efforts and establish reasonable procedures to ensure that the grant is spent solely for the purpose for which it was made, to obtain reports from the grantee on the expenditure of the grant, and to make reports to the Secretary regarding such expenditures. Sec. 4945(h).

[¶11,210] Act Sec. 1213. Reform rules for charitable contributions of easements in registered historic districts and take account of rehabilitation credit in easement donations

Joint Committee Taxation (J.C.T. REP. NO. JCX-38-06)

[Code Sec. 170]

Present Law

In general

Present law provides special rules that apply to charitable deductions of qualified conservation contributions, which include conservation easements and facade easements.[345] Qualified conservation contributions are not subject to the "partial interest" rule, which generally bars deductions for charitable contributions of partial interests in property.[346] Accordingly, qualified conservation contributions are contributions of partial interests that are eligible for a fair market value charitable deduction.

A qualified conservation contribution is a contribution of a qualified real property interest to a qualified organization exclusively for conservation purposes. A qualified real property interest is defined as: (1) the entire interest of the donor other than a qualified mineral interest; (2) a remainder interest; or (3) a restriction (granted in perpetuity) on the use that may be made of the real property.[347] Qualified organizations include certain governmental units, public charities that meet certain public support tests, and certain supporting organizations.

Conservation purposes include: (1) the preservation of land areas for outdoor recreation by, or for the education of, the general public; (2) the protection of a relatively natural habitat of fish, wildlife, or plants, or similar ecosystem; (3) the preservation of open space (including farmland and forest land) where such preservation will yield a significant public benefit and is either for the scenic enjoyment of the general public or pursuant to a clearly delineated Federal, State, or local governmental conservation policy; and (4) the preservation of an historically important land area or a certified historic structure.[348]

In general, no deduction is available if the property may be put to a use that is inconsistent with the conservation purpose of the gift.[349] A contribution is not deductible if it accomplishes a permitted conservation purpose while also destroying other significant conservation interests.[350]

Taxpayers are required to obtain a qualified appraisal for donated property with a value of $5,000 or more, and to attach an appraisal summary to the tax return.[351] Under Treasury regulations, a qualified appraisal means an appraisal document that, among other things: (1) relates to an appraisal that is made not earlier than 60 days prior to the date of contribution of the appraised property and not later than the due date (including extensions) of the return on which a deduction is first claimed under section 170;[352] (2) is prepared, signed, and dated by a qualified appraiser; (3) includes (a) a description of the property appraised; (b) the fair market value of such property on the date of contribution and the specific basis for the valuation; (c) a statement that such appraisal was prepared for income tax purposes; (d) the qualifications of the qualified appraiser; and (e) the signature and taxpayer identification number of such appraiser; and (4) does not involve an appraisal fee that violates certain prescribed rules.[353]

Valuation

The value of a conservation restriction granted in perpetuity generally is determined under the "before and after approach." Such ap-

[345] Sec. 170(h).

[346] Sec. 170(f)(3).

[347] Charitable contributions of interests that constitute the taxpayer's entire interest in the property are not regarded as qualified real property interests within the meaning of section 170(h), but instead are subject to the general rules applicable to charitable contributions of entire interests of the taxpayer (i.e., generally are deductible at fair market value, without regard to satisfaction of the requirements of section 170(h)).

[348] Sec. 170(h)(4)(A).

[349] Treas. Reg. sec. 1.170A-14(e)(2).

[350] Treas. Reg. sec. 1.170A-14(e)(2).

[351] Sec. 170(f)(11)(C).

[352] In the case of a deduction first claimed or reported on an amended return, the deadline is the date on which the amended return is filed.

[353] Treas. Reg. sec. 1.170A-13(c)(3).

proach provides that the fair market value of the restriction is equal to the difference (if any) between the fair market value of the property the restriction encumbers before the restriction is granted and the fair market value of the encumbered property after the restriction is granted.[354]

If the granting of a perpetual restriction has the effect of increasing the value of any other property owned by the donor or a related person, the amount of the charitable deduction for the conservation contribution is to be reduced by the amount of the increase in the value of the other property.[355] In addition, the donor is to reduce the amount of the charitable deduction by the amount of financial or economic benefits that the donor or a related person receives or can reasonably be expected to receive as a result of the contribution.[356] If such benefits are greater than those that will inure to the general public from the transfer, no deduction is allowed.[357] In those instances where the grant of a conservation restriction has no material effect on the value of the property, or serves to enhance, rather than reduce, the value of the property, no deduction is allowed.[358]

Preservation of a certified historic structure

A certified historic structure means any building, structure, or land which is (i) listed in the National Register, or (ii) located in a registered historic district (as defined in section 47(c)(3)(B)) and is certified by the Secretary of the Interior to the Secretary of the Treasury as being of historic significance to the district.[359] For this purpose, a structure means any structure, whether or not it is depreciable, and, accordingly, easements on private residences may qualify.[360] If restrictions to preserve a building or land area within a registered historic district permit future development on the site, a deduction will be allowed only if the terms of the restrictions require that such development conform with appropriate local, State, or Federal standards for construction or rehabilitation within the district.[361]

The IRS and the courts have held that a facade easement may constitute a qualifying conservation contribution.[362] In general, a facade easement is a restriction the purpose of which is to preserve certain architectural, historic, and cultural features of the facade, or front, of a building. The terms of a facade easement might permit the property owner to make alterations to the facade of the structure if the owner obtains consent from the qualified organization that holds the easement.

Rehabilitation credit

In general, present law allows as part of the general business credit an investment tax credit.[363] The amount of the investment tax credit includes the amount of a rehabilitation credit.[364] The rehabilitation credit for any taxable year is the sum of ten percent of the qualified rehabilitation expenditures with respect to any qualified rehabilitated building other than a certified historic structure and 20 percent of the qualified rehabilitation expenditures with respect to any certified historic structure.[365] In general, a qualified rehabilitated building is a depreciable building (and its structural components) if the building has been substantially rehabilitated, was placed in service before the beginning of the rehabilitation, and (except for a certified historic structure) in the rehabilitation process a certain percentage of the existing internal and external walls and internal structural framework are retained in place as internal and external walls and internal structural framework. A qualified rehabilitation expenditure is, in general, an amount properly chargeable to a capital account (i) for depreciable property that is nonresidential real property, residential rental property, real property that has a class life of more than 12.5 years, or an addition or improve-

---

354 Treas. Reg. sec. 1.170A-14(h)(3).

355 Treas. Reg. sec. 1.170A-14(h)(3)(i).

356 *Id.*

357 *Id.*

358 Treas. Reg. sec. 1.170A-14(h)(3)(ii).

359 Sec. 170(h)(4)(B).

360 Treas. Reg. sec. 1.170A-14(d)(5)(iii).

361 Treas. Reg. sec. 1.170A-14(d)(5)(i).

362 *Hillborn v. Commissioner*, 85 T.C. 677 (1985) (holding the fair market value of a facade donation generally is determined by applying the "before and after" valuation approach); *Richmond v. U.S.*, 699 F. Supp. 578 (E.D. La. 1988); Priv. Ltr. Rul. 199933029 (May 24, 1999) (ruling that a preservation and conservation easement relating to the facade and certain interior portions of a fraternity house was a qualified conservation contribution).

363 Sec. 38(b)(1).

364 Sec. 46.

365 Sec. 47(a).

ment to any such property and (ii) in connection with the rehabilitation of a qualified rehabilitation building.

Explanation of Provision

Easements in registered historic districts

The provision revises the rules for qualified conservation contributions with respect to property for which a charitable deduction is allowable under section 170(h)(4)(B)(ii) by reason of a property's location in a registered historic district. Under the provision, a charitable deduction is not allowable with respect to a structure or land area located in such a district (by reason of the structure or land area's location in such a district). A charitable deduction is allowable with respect to buildings (as is the case under present law) but the qualified real property interest that relates to the exterior of the building must preserve the entire exterior of the building, including the space above the building, the sides, the rear, and the front of the building. In addition, such qualified real property interest must provide that no portion of the exterior of the building may be changed in a manner inconsistent with the historical character of such exterior.

For any contribution relating to a registered historic district made after the date of enactment of the provision, taxpayers must include with the return for the taxable year of the contribution a qualified appraisal of the qualified real property interest (irrespective of the claimed value of such interest) and attach the appraisal with the taxpayer's return, photographs of the entire exterior of the building,[366] and descriptions of all current restrictions on development of the building, including, for example, zoning laws, ordinances, neighborhood association rules, restrictive covenants, and other similar restrictions. Failure to obtain and attach an appraisal or to include the required information results in disallowance of the deduction. In addition, the donor and the donee must enter into a written agreement certifying, under penalty of perjury, that the donee is a qualified organization, with a purpose of environmental protection, land conservation, open space preservation, or historic preservation, and that the donee has the resources to manage and enforce the restriction and a commitment to do so.

Taxpayers claiming a deduction for a qualified conservation contribution with respect to the exterior of a building located in a registered historic district in excess of $10,000 must pay a $500 fee to the Internal Revenue Service or the deduction is not allowed. Amounts paid are required to be dedicated to Internal Revenue Service enforcement of qualified conservation contributions.

Reduction of deduction to take account of rehabilitation credit

The provision provides that in the case of any qualified conservation contribution, the amount of the deduction is reduced by an amount that bears the same ratio to the fair market value of the contribution as the sum of the rehabilitation credits under section 47 for the preceding five taxable years with respect to a building that is part of the contribution bears to the fair market value of the building on the date of the contribution. For example, if a taxpayer makes a qualified conservation contribution with respect to a building, and such taxpayer has claimed a rehabilitation credit with respect to such building in any of the five taxable years preceding the year in which the contribution is claimed, the taxpayer must reduce the amount of the contribution. If the aggregate amount of credits claimed by the taxpayer within such five year period is $100,000, and the fair market value of the building with respect to which the contribution is made is $1,000,000, the taxpayer must reduce the amount of the deduction by 10 percent (or 100,000 over 1,000,000).

Effective Date

The provisions relating to deductions for contributions relating to structures and land areas and to the rehabilitation credit are effective for contributions made after the date of enactment. The provision relating to a filing fee is effective for contributions made 180 days after the date of enactment. The rest of the provision is effective for contributions made after July 25, 2006.

[Law at ¶ 5020. CCH Explanation at ¶ 1130.]

---

[366] Photographs of the entire exterior of the building are required to the extent practicable. For example, if the building is a skyscraper, aerial photographs of the roof would not be required, but photographs sufficient to establish the existing exterior still must be submitted.

[¶11,220] Act Sec. 1214. Reform rules relating to charitable contributions of taxidermy

Joint Committee Taxation (J.C.T. REP. NO. JCX-38-06)

[Code Sec. 170]

Present Law

In computing taxable income, a taxpayer who itemizes deductions generally is allowed to deduct the amount of cash and the fair market value of property contributed to an organization described in section 501(c)(3) or to a Federal, State, or local governmental entity.[367] The amount of the deduction allowable for a taxable year with respect to a charitable contribution of property may be reduced or limited depending on the type of property contributed, the type of charitable organization to which the property is contributed, and the income of the taxpayer.[368] In general, more generous charitable contribution deduction rules apply to gifts made to public charities than to gifts made to private foundations. Within certain limitations, donors also are entitled to deduct their contributions to section 501(c)(3) organizations for Federal estate and gift tax purposes. By contrast, contributions to nongovernmental, non-charitable tax-exempt organizations generally are not deductible by the donor,[369] though such organizations are eligible for the exemption from Federal income tax with respect to such donations.

The amount of the deduction for charitable contributions of capital gain property generally equals the fair market value of the contributed property on the date of the contribution. Capital gain property means any capital asset, or property used in the taxpayer's trade or business, the sale of which at its fair market value, at the time of contribution, would have resulted in gain that would have been long-term capital gain. Contributions of capital gain property are subject to different percentage limitations (i.e., limitations based on the donor's income) than other contributions of property.

For certain contributions of property, the deductible amount is reduced from the fair market value of the contributed property by the amount of any gain, generally resulting in a deduction equal to the taxpayer's basis. This rule applies to contributions of: (1) ordinary income property, e.g., property that, at the time of contribution, would not have resulted in long-term capital gain if the property was sold by the taxpayer on the contribution date;[370] (2) tangible personal property that is used by the donee in a manner unrelated to the donee's exempt (or governmental) purpose; and (3) property to or for the use of a private foundation (other than a foundation defined in section 170(b)(1)(E)).

Charitable contributions of taxidermy are subject to the tangible personal property rule (number (2) above). For example, for appreciated taxidermy, if the property is used to further the donee's exempt purpose, the deduction is fair market value. But if the property is not used to further the donee's exempt purpose, the deduction is the donor's basis. If the taxidermy is depreciated, i.e., the value is less than the taxpayer's basis in such property, taxpayers generally deduct the fair market value of such contributions, regardless of whether the property is used for exempt or unrelated purposes by the donee.

Explanation of Provision

In general, the provision provides that the amount allowed as a deduction for charitable contributions of taxidermy property that is contributed by the person who prepared, stuffed, or mounted the property (or by any person who paid or incurred the cost of such preparation, stuffing, or mounting) is the lesser of the taxpayer's basis in the property or the fair market value of the property. Specifically, a taxpayer that makes such a charitable contribution of taxidermy property for a use related to the donee's exempt purpose or function must, in determining the amount of the deduction, reduce the fair market value of the property by the amount of gain that would have been long-term capital gain if the property contributed had been sold by the taxpayer at its fair market value (determined at the time of the contribution). Taxidermy property is defined as any work of art that is the reproduction or preservation of an animal in whole or in part, is prepared, stuffed or mounted for purposes of recreating one or more character-

---

[367] The deduction also is allowed for purposes of calculating alternative minimum taxable income.

[368] Secs. 170(b) and (e).

[369] Exceptions to the general rule of non-deductibility include certain gifts made to a veterans' organization or to a domestic fraternal society. In addition, contributions to certain nonprofit cemetery companies are deductible for Federal income tax purposes, but generally are not deductible for Federal estate and gift tax purposes. Secs. 170(c)(3), 170(c)(4), 170(c)(5), 2055(a)(3), 2055(a)(4), 2106(a)(2)(A)(iii), 2522(a)(3), and 2522(a)(4).

[370] For certain contributions of inventory, C corporations may claim an enhanced deduction equal to the lesser of (1) basis plus one-half of the item's appreciation (i.e., basis plus one half of fair market value in excess of basis) or (2) two times basis. Sec. 170(e)(3), 170(e)(4), 170(e)(6).

istics of such animal, and contains a part of the body of the dead animal.

For purposes of determining a taxpayer's basis in taxidermy property that is contributed by the person who prepared, stuffed, or mounted the property (or by any person who paid or incurred the cost of such preparation, stuffing, or mounting), the provision provides a special rule that the basis of such property may include only the cost of the preparing, stuffing, or mounting. For purposes of the special rule, it is intended that only the direct costs of the preparing, stuffing, or mounting may be included in basis. Indirect costs, not included in the basis, include the costs of transportation relating to any aspect of the taxidermy or the hunting of the animal, and the direct or indirect costs relating to the hunting or killing of an animal (including the cost of equipment and the costs of preparing an animal carcass for taxidermy).

Effective Date

The provision is effective for contributions made after July 25, 2006.

[Law at ¶ 5020. CCH Explanation at ¶ 1120.]

[¶11,230] Act Sec. 1215. Recapture of tax benefit on property not used for an exempt use

Joint Committee Taxation (J.C.T. REP. NO. JCX-38-06)

[New Code Sec. 6720B

Present Law

Deductibility of charitable contributions

In general

In computing taxable income, a taxpayer who itemizes deductions generally is allowed to deduct the amount of cash and the fair market value of property contributed to an organization described in section 501(c)(3) or to a Federal, State, or local governmental entity.[371] The amount of the deduction allowable for a taxable year with respect to a charitable contribution of property may be reduced or limited depending on the type of property contributed, the type of charitable organization to which the property is contributed, and the income of the taxpayer.[372] In general, more generous charitable contribution deduction rules apply to gifts made to public charities than to gifts made to private foundations. Within certain limitations, donors also are entitled to deduct their contributions to section 501(c)(3) organizations for Federal estate and gift tax purposes. By contrast, contributions to nongovernmental, non-charitable tax-exempt organizations generally are not deductible by the donor,[373] though such organizations are eligible for the exemption from Federal income tax with respect to such donations.

Contribution of property

The amount of the deduction for charitable contributions of capital gain property generally equals the fair market value of the contributed property on the date of the contribution. Capital gain property means any capital asset, or property used in the taxpayer's trade or business, the sale of which at its fair market value, at the time of contribution, would have resulted in gain that would have been long-term capital gain. Contributions of capital gain property are subject to different percentage limitations (i.e., limitations based on the donor's income) than other contributions of property.

For certain contributions of property, the deductible amount is reduced from the fair market value of the contributed property by the amount of any gain, generally resulting in a deduction equal to the taxpayer's basis. This rule applies to contributions of: (1) ordinary income property, e.g., property that, at the time of contribution, would not have resulted in long-term capital gain if the property was sold by the taxpayer on the contribution date;[374] (2) tangible personal property that is used by the donee in a

---

[371] The deduction also is allowed for purposes of calculating alternative minimum taxable income.

[372] Secs. 170(b) and (e).

[373] Exceptions to the general rule of non-deductibility include certain gifts made to a veterans' organization or to a domestic fraternal society. In addition, contributions to certain nonprofit cemetery companies are deductible for Federal income tax purposes, but generally are not deductible for Federal estate and gift tax purposes. Secs. 170(c)(3), 170(c)(4), 170(c)(5), 2055(a)(3), 2055(a)(4), 2106(a)(2)(A)(iii), 2522(a)(3), and 2522(a)(4).

[374] For certain contributions of inventory, C corporations may claim an enhanced deduction equal to the lesser of (1) basis plus one-half of the item's appreciation (i.e., basis plus one half of fair market value in excess of basis) or (2) two times basis. Sec. 170(e)(3), 170(e)(4), 170(e)(6).

manner unrelated to the donee's exempt (or governmental) purpose; and (3) property to or for the use of a private foundation (other than a foundation defined in section 170(b)(1)(E)).

Substantiation

No charitable deduction is allowed for any contribution of $250 or more unless the taxpayer substantiates the contribution by a contemporaneous written acknowledgement of the contribution by the donee organization.[375] Such acknowledgement must include the amount of cash and a description (but not value) of any property other than cash contributed, whether the donee provided any goods or services in consideration for the contribution (and a good faith estimate of the value of any such goods or services).

In general, if the total charitable deduction claimed for non-cash property is more than $500, the taxpayer must attach a completed Form 8283 (Noncash Charitable Contributions) to the taxpayer's return or the deduction is not allowed.[376] C corporations (other than personal service corporations and closely-held corporations) are required to file Form 8283 only if the deduction claimed is more than $5,000. Information required on the Form 8283 includes, among other things, a description of the property, the appraised fair market value (if an appraisal is required), the donor's basis in the property, how the donor acquired the property, a declaration by the appraiser regarding the appraiser's general qualifications, an acknowledgement by the donee that it is eligible to receive deductible contributions, and an indication by the donee whether the property is intended for an unrelated use.

Taxpayers are required to obtain a qualified appraisal for donated property with a value of more than $5,000, and to attach an appraisal summary to the tax return.[377] Under Treasury regulations, a qualified appraisal means an appraisal document that, among other things: (1) relates to an appraisal that is made not earlier than 60 days prior to the date of contribution of the appraised property and not later than the due date (including extensions) of the return on which a deduction is first claimed under section 170;[378] (2) is prepared, signed, and dated by a qualified appraiser; (3) includes (a) a description of the property appraised; (b) the fair market value of such property on the date of contribution and the specific basis for the valuation; (c) a statement that such appraisal was prepared for income tax purposes; (d) the qualifications of the qualified appraiser; and (e) the signature and taxpayer identification number of such appraiser; and (4) does not involve an appraisal fee that violates certain prescribed rules.[379] In the case of contributions of art valued at more than $20,000 and other contributions of more than $500,000, taxpayers are required to attach the appraisal to the tax return. Taxpayers may request a Statement of Value from the Internal Revenue Service in order to substantiate the value of art with an appraised value of $50,000 or more for income, estate, or gift tax purposes.[380] The fee for such a Statement is $2,500 for one, two, or three items or art plus $250 for each additional item.

If a donee organization sells, exchanges, or otherwise disposes of contributed property with a claimed value of more than $5,000 (other than publicly traded securities) within two years of the property's receipt, the donee is required to file a return (Form 8282) with the Secretary, and to furnish a copy of the return to the donor, showing the name, address, and taxpayer identification number of the donor, a description of the property, the date of the contribution, the amount received on the disposition, and the date of the disposition.[381]

Explanation of Provision

In general, the provision recovers the tax benefit for charitable contributions of tangible personal property with respect to which a fair market value deduction is claimed and which is not used for exempt purposes. The provision applies to appreciated tangible personal property that is identified by the donee organization, for example on the Form 8283, as for a use related to the purpose or function constituting the donee's basis for tax exemption, and for which a deduction of more than $5,000 is claimed ("applicable property").[382]

Under the provision, if a donee organization disposes of applicable property within three years of the contribution of the property, the donor is subject to an adjustment of the tax benefit. If the disposition occurs in the tax year

---

375 Sec. 170(f)(8).

376 Sec. 170(f)(11).

377 *Id.*

378 In the case of a deduction first claimed or reported on an amended return, the deadline is the date on which the amended return is filed.

379 Treas. Reg. sec. 1.170A-13(c)(3). Sec. 170(f)(11)(E).

380 Rev. Proc. 96-15, 1996-1 C.B. 627.

381 Sec. 6050L(a)(1).

382 Present law rules continue to apply to any contribution of exempt use property for which a deduction of $5,000 or less is claimed.

of the donor in which the contribution is made, the donor's deduction generally is basis and not fair market value.[383] If the disposition occurs in a subsequent year, the donor must include as ordinary income for its taxable year in which the disposition occurs an amount equal to the excess (if any) of (i) the amount of the deduction previously claimed by the donor as a charitable contribution with respect to such property, over (ii) the donor's basis in such property at the time of the contribution.

There is no adjustment of the tax benefit if the donee organization makes a certification to the Secretary, by written statement signed under penalties of perjury by an officer of the organization. The statement must either (1) certify that the use of the property by the donee was related to the purpose or function constituting the basis for the donee's exemption, and describe how the property was used and how such use furthered such purpose or function; or (2) state the intended use of the property by the donee at the time of the contribution and certify that such use became impossible or infeasible to implement. The organization must furnish a copy of the certification to the donor (for example, as part of the Form 8282, a copy of which is supplied to the donor).

A penalty of $10,000 applies to a person that identifies applicable property as having a use that is related to a purpose or function constituting the basis for the donee's exemption knowing that it is not intended for such a use.[384]

Reporting of exempt use property contributions

The provision modifies the present-law information return requirements that apply upon the disposition of contributed property by a charitable organization (Form 8282, sec. 6050L). The return requirement is extended to dispositions made within three years after receipt (from two years). The donee organization also must provide, in addition to the information already required to be provided on the return, a description of the donee's use of the property, a statement of whether use of the property was related to the purpose or function constituting the basis for the donee's exemption, and, if applicable, a certification of any such use (described above).

Effective Date

The provision is effective for contributions made and returns filed after September 1, 2006, and with respect to the penalty, for identifications made after the date of enactment.

[Law at ¶ 5020, ¶ 5340 and ¶ 5415. CCH Explanation at ¶ 1150.]

[¶ 11,240] Act Sec. 1216. Limit charitable deduction for contributions of clothing and household items

Joint Committee Taxation (J.C.T. REP. NO. JCX-38-06)

[Code Sec. 170]

Present Law

In general

In computing taxable income, a taxpayer who itemizes deductions generally is allowed to deduct the amount of cash and the fair market value of property contributed to an organization described in section 501(c)(3) or to a Federal, State, or local governmental entity.[385] The amount of the deduction allowable for a taxable year with respect to a charitable contribution of property may be reduced or limited depending on the type of property contributed, the type of charitable organization to which the property is contributed, and the income of the taxpayer.[386] In general, more generous charitable contribution deduction rules apply to gifts made to public charities than to gifts made to private foundations. Within certain limitations, donors also are entitled to deduct their contributions to section 501(c)(3) organizations for Federal estate and gift tax purposes. By contrast, contributions to nongovernmental, non-charitable tax-exempt organizations generally are not deductible by the

---

[383] The disposition proceeds are regarded as relevant to a determination of fair market value.

[384] Other present-law penalties also may apply, such as the penalty for aiding and abetting the understatement of tax liability under section 6701.

[385] The deduction also is allowed for purposes of calculating alternative minimum taxable income.

[386] Secs. 170(b) and (e).

donor,[387] though such organizations are eligible for the exemption from Federal income tax with respect to such donations.

Contributions of property

The amount of the deduction for charitable contributions of capital gain property generally equals the fair market value of the contributed property on the date of the contribution. Capital gain property means any capital asset or property used in the taxpayer's trade or business the sale of which at its fair market value, at the time of contribution, would have resulted in gain that would have been long-term capital gain. Contributions of capital gain property are subject to different percentage limitations than other contributions of property.

For certain contributions of property, the deductible amount is reduced from the fair market value of the contributed property by the amount of any gain, generally resulting in a deduction equal to the taxpayer's basis. This rule applies to contributions of: (1) ordinary income property, e.g., property that, at the time of contribution, would not have resulted in long-term capital gain if the property was sold by the taxpayer on the contribution date;[388] (2) tangible personal property that is used by the donee in a manner unrelated to the donee's exempt (or governmental) purpose; and (3) property to or for the use of a private foundation (other than a foundation defined in section 170(b)(1)(E)).

Charitable contributions of clothing and household items are subject to the tangible personal property rule (number (2) above). If such contributed property is appreciated property in the hands of the taxpayer, and is not used to further the donee's exempt purpose, the deduction is basis. In general, however, the value of clothing and household items is less than the taxpayer's basis in such property, with the result that taxpayers generally deduct the fair market value of such contributions, regardless of whether the property is used for exempt or unrelated purposes by the donee.

Substantiation

A donor who claims a deduction for a charitable contribution must maintain reliable written records regarding the contribution, regardless of the value or amount of such contribution. For a contribution of money, the donor generally must maintain one of the following: (1) a cancelled check; (2) a receipt (or a letter or other written communication) from the donee showing the name of the donee organization, the date of the contribution, and the amount of the contribution; or (3) in the absence of a cancelled check or a receipt, other reliable written records showing the name of the donee, the date of the contribution, and the amount of the contribution. For a contribution of property other than money, the donor generally must maintain a receipt from the donee organization showing the name of the donee, the date and location of the contribution, and a detailed description (but not the value) of the property.[389] A donor of property other than money need not obtain a receipt, however, if circumstances make obtaining a receipt impracticable. Under such circumstances, the donor must maintain reliable written records regarding the contribution. The required content of such a record varies depending upon factors such as the type and value of property contributed.[390]

In addition to the foregoing recordkeeping requirements, substantiation requirements apply in the case of charitable contributions with a value of $250 or more. No charitable deduction is allowed for any contribution of $250 or more unless the taxpayer substantiates the contribution by a contemporaneous written acknowledgement of the contribution by the donee organization. Such acknowledgement must include the amount of cash and a description (but not value) of any property other than cash contributed, whether the donee provided any goods or services in consideration for the contribution, and a good faith estimate of the value of any such goods or services.[391] In general, if the total charitable deduction claimed for non-cash property is more than $500, the taxpayer must attach

---

[387] Exceptions to the general rule of non-deductibility include certain gifts made to a veterans' organization or to a domestic fraternal society. In addition, contributions to certain nonprofit cemetery companies are deductible for Federal income tax purposes, but generally are not deductible for Federal estate and gift tax purposes. Secs. 170(c)(3), 170(c)(4), 170(c)(5), 2055(a)(3), 2055(a)(4), 2106(a)(2)(A)(iii), 2522(a)(3), and 2522(a)(4).

[388] For certain contributions of inventory and other property, C corporations may claim an enhanced deduction equal to the lesser of (1) basis plus one-half of the item's appreciation (i.e., basis plus one half of fair market value in excess of basis) or (2) two times basis. Sec. 170(e)(3), 170(e)(4), 170(e)(6).

[389] Treas. Reg. sec. 1.170A-13(a).

[390] Treas. Reg. sec. 1.170A-13(b).

[391] Sec. 170(f)(8).

a completed Form 8283 (Noncash Charitable Contributions) to the taxpayer's return or the deduction is not allowed.[392] In general, taxpayers are required to obtain a qualified appraisal for donated property with a value of more than $5,000, and to attach an appraisal summary to the tax return.

Explanation of Provision

The provision provides that no deduction is allowed for a charitable contribution of clothing or household items unless the clothing or household item is in good used condition or better. The Secretary is authorized to deny by regulation a deduction for any contribution of clothing or a household item that has minimal monetary value, such as used socks and used undergarments. It is noted that the President's Advisory Panel on Federal Tax Reform and the staff of the Joint Committee on Taxation both have concluded that the fair market value-based deduction for contributions of clothing and household items present difficult tax administration issues, as determining the correct value of an item is a fact intensive, and thus also a resource intensive matter.[393] As recently reported by the IRS, the amount claimed as deductions in tax year 2003 for clothing and household items was more than $9 billion.[394] It is expected that the Secretary, in consultation with affected charities, will exercise assiduously the authority to disallow a deduction for some items of low value, consistent with the goals of improving tax administration and ensure that donated clothing and households items are of meaningful use to charitable organizations.

Under the provision, a deduction may be allowed for a charitable contribution of an item of clothing or a household item not in good used condition or better if the amount claimed for the item is more than $500 and the taxpayer includes with the taxpayer's return a qualified appraisal with respect to the property. Household items include furniture, furnishings, electronics, appliances, linens, and other similar items. Food, paintings, antiques, and other objects of art, jewelry and gems, and collections are excluded from the provision.

Effective Date

The provision is effective for contributions made after the date of enactment.

[Law at ¶ 5020. CCH Explanation at ¶ 1110.]

[¶ 11,250] Act Sec. 1217. Modify recordkeeping and substantiation requirements for certain charitable contributions

Joint Committee Taxation (J.C.T. REP. NO. JCX-38-06)

[Code Sec. 170]

Present Law

A donor who claims a deduction for a charitable contribution must maintain reliable written records regarding the contribution, regardless of the value or amount of such contribution. For a contribution of money, the donor generally must maintain one of the following: (1) a cancelled check; (2) a receipt (or a letter or other written communication) from the donee showing the name of the donee organization, the date of the contribution, and the amount of the contribution; or (3) in the absence of a cancelled check or a receipt, other reliable written records showing the name of the donee, the date of the contribution, and the amount of the contribution. For a contribution of property other than money, the donor generally must maintain a receipt from the donee organization showing the name of the donee, the date and location of the contribution, and a detailed description (but not the value) of the property.[395] A donor of property other than money need not obtain a receipt, however, if circumstances make obtaining a receipt impracticable. Under such circumstances, the donor must maintain reliable written records regarding the contribution. The required content of such a re-

---

[392] Sec. 170(f)(11).

[393] See *The President's Advisory Panel on Federal Tax Reform*, 78 (2005); Joint Committee on Taxation, *Options to Improve Tax Compliance and Reform Tax Expenditures* 288 (JCS-02-05), January 27, 2005.

[394] Internal Revenue Service, Statistics of Income Division, *Individual Noncash Charitable Contributions, 2003*, Figure A (Spring 2006).

[395] Treas. Reg. sec. 1.170A-13(a).

cord varies depending upon factors such as the type and value of property contributed.[396]

In addition to the foregoing recordkeeping requirements, substantiation requirements apply in the case of charitable contributions with a value of $250 or more. No charitable deduction is allowed for any contribution of $250 or more unless the taxpayer substantiates the contribution by a contemporaneous written acknowledgement of the contribution by the donee organization. Such acknowledgement must include the amount of cash and a description (but not value) of any property other than cash contributed, whether the donee provided any goods or services in consideration for the contribution, and a good faith estimate of the value of any such goods or services.[397] In general, if the total charitable deduction claimed for non-cash property is more than $500, the taxpayer must attach a completed Form 8283 (Noncash Charitable Contributions) to the taxpayer's return or the deduction is not allowed.[398] In general, taxpayers are required to obtain a qualified appraisal for donated property with a value of more than $5,000, and to attach an appraisal summary to the tax return.

Explanation of Provision

The provision more closely aligns the substantiation rules for money to the substantiation rules for property by providing that in the case of a charitable contribution of money, regardless of the amount, applicable recordkeeping requirements are satisfied only if the donor maintains as a record of the contribution a bank record or a written communication from the donee showing the name of the donee organization, the date of the contribution, and the amount of the contribution. The recordkeeping requirements may not be satisfied by maintaining other written records. It is noted that currently, taxpayers are required to have a contemporaneous record of contributions of money, but that many taxpayers may not be aware of the requirement and do not keep a log of such contributions. The provision is intended to provide greater certainty, both to taxpayers and to the Secretary, in determining what may be deducted as a charitable contribution.

Effective Date

The provision is effective for contributions made in taxable years beginning after the date of enactment.

[Law at ¶ 5020. CCH Explanation at ¶ 1185.]

[¶11,260] Act Sec. 1218. Contributions of fractional interests in tangible personal property

Joint Committee Taxation (J.C.T. Rep. No. JCX-38-06)

[Code Secs. 170, 2055 and 2522]

Present Law

In general, a charitable deduction is not allowable for a contribution of a partial interest in property, such as an income interest, a remainder interest, or a right to use property.[399] A gift of an undivided portion of a donor's entire interest in property generally is not treated as a nondeductible gift of a partial interest in property.[400] For this purpose, an undivided portion of a donor's entire interest in property must consist of a fraction or percentage of each and every substantial interest or right owned by the donor in such property and must extend over the entire term of the donor's interest in such property.[401] A gift generally is treated as a gift of an undivided portion of a donor's entire interest in property if the donee is given the right, as a tenant in common with the donor, to possession, dominion, and control of the property for a portion of each year appropriate to its interest in such property.[402]

A charitable contribution deduction generally is not allowable for a contribution of a future interest in tangible personal property.[403] For this purpose, a future interest is one "in which a donor purports to give tangible personal property to a charitable organization, but has an un-

---

396 Treas. Reg. sec. 1.170A-13(b).

397 Sec. 170(f)(8).

398 Sec. 170(f)(11).

399 Secs. 170(f)(3)(A) (income tax), 2055(e)(2) (estate tax), and 2522(c)(2) (gift tax).

400 Sec. 170(f)(3)(B)(ii).

401 Treas. Reg. sec. 1.170A-7(b)(1).

402 Treas. Reg. sec. 1.170A-7(b)(1).

403 Sec. 170(a)(3).

derstanding, arrangement, agreement, etc., whether written or oral, with the charitable organization which has the effect of reserving to, or retaining in, such donor a right to the use, possession, or enjoyment of the property."[404] Treasury regulations provide that section 170(a)(3), which generally denies a deduction for a contribution of a future interest in tangible personal property, "[has] no application in respect of a transfer of an undivided present interest in property. For example, a contribution of an undivided one-quarter interest in a painting with respect to which the donee is entitled to possession during three months of each year shall be treated as made upon the receipt by the donee of a formally executed and acknowledged deed of gift. However, the period of initial possession by the donee may not be deferred in time for more than one year."[405]

Explanation of Provision

In general, under present law and the provision a donor may take a deduction for a charitable contribution of a fractional interest in tangible personal property (such as an artwork), provided the donor satisfies the requirements for deductibility (including the requirements concerning contributions of partial interests and future interests in property), and in subsequent years make additional charitable contributions of interests in the same property.[406] Under the provision, the value of a donor's charitable deduction for the initial contribution of a fractional interest in an item of tangible personal property (or collection of such items) shall be determined as under current law (e.g., based upon the fair market value of the artwork at the time of the contribution of the fractional interest and considering whether the use of the artwork will be related to the donee's exempt purposes). For purposes of determining the deductible amount of each additional contribution of an interest (whether or not a fractional interest) in the same item of property, the fair market value of the item is the lesser of: (1) the value used for purposes of determining the charitable deduction for the initial fractional contribution; or (2) the fair market value of the item at the time of the subsequent contribution. This portion of the provision applies for income, gift, and estate tax purposes.

The provision provides for recapture of the income tax charitable deduction and gift tax charitable deduction under certain circumstances. First, if a donor makes an initial fractional contribution, then fails to contribute all of the donor's remaining interest in such property to the same donee before the earlier of 10 years from the initial fractional contribution or the donor's death, then the donee's charitable income and gift tax deductions for all previous contributions of interests in the item shall be recaptured (plus interest). If the donee of the initial contribution is no longer in existence as of such time, the donor's remaining interest may be contributed to another organization described in section 170(c) (which describes organizations to which contributions that are deductible for income tax purposes may be made). Second, if the donee of a fractional interest in an item of tangible personal property fails to take substantial physical possession of the item during the period described above (the possession requirement) or fails to use the property for an exempt use during the period described above (the related-use requirement), then the donee's charitable income and gift tax deductions for all previous contributions of interests in the item shall be recaptured (plus interest). If, for example, an art museum described in section 501(c)(3) that is the donee of a fractional interest in a painting includes the painting in an art exhibit sponsored by the museum, such use generally will be treated as satisfying the related-use requirement of the provision.

In any case in which there is a recapture of a deduction as described in the preceding paragraph, the provision also imposes an additional tax in an amount equal to 10 percent of the amount recaptured.

Under the provision, no income or gift tax charitable deduction is allowed for a contribution of a fractional interest in an item of tangible personal property unless immediately before such contribution all interests in the item are owned (1) by the donor or (2) by the donor and the donee organization. The Secretary is authorized to make exceptions to this rule in cases where all persons who hold an interest in the item make proportional contributions of undivided interests in their respective shares of such item to the donee organization. For example, if A owns an undivided 40 percent interest in a painting and B owns an undivided 60 percent interest in the same painting, the Secretary may provide that A may take a deduction for a charitable contribution of less than the entire interest held by A, provided that both A and B make proportional contributions of undivided fractional in-

[404] Treas. Reg. sec. 1.170A-5(a)(4).

[405] Treas. Reg. sec. 1.170A-5(a)(2).

[406] See, e.g., *Winokur v. Commissioner*, 90 T.C. 733 (1988).

terests in their respective shares of the painting to the same donee organization (e.g., if A contributes 50 percent of A's interest and B contributes 50 percent of B's interest).

It is intended that a contribution occurring before the date of enactment not be treated as an initial fractional contribution for purposes of the provision. Instead, the first fractional contribution by a taxpayer after the date of enactment would be considered the initial fractional contribution under the provision, regardless of whether the taxpayer had made a contribution of a fractional interest in the same item of tangible personal property prior to the date of enactment.

Effective Date

The provision is applicable for contributions, bequests, and gifts made after the date of enactment.

[Law at ¶ 5020, ¶ 5205 and ¶ 5210. CCH Explanation at ¶ 1115.]

[¶ 11,270] Act Sec. 1219. Proposals relating to appraisers and substantial and gross overstatement of valuations of property

Joint Committee Taxation (J.C.T. REP. NO. JCX-38-06)

[Code Secs. 170, 6662, 6664, 6696 and New Code Sec. 6695A]

Present Law

Taxpayer penalties

Present law imposes accuracy-related penalties on a taxpayer in cases involving a substantial valuation misstatement or gross valuation misstatement relating to an underpayment of income tax.[407] For this purpose, a substantial valuation misstatement generally means a value claimed that is at least twice (200 percent or more) the amount determined to be the correct value, and a gross valuation misstatement generally means a value claimed that is at least four times (400 percent or more) the amount determined to be the correct value.

The penalty is 20 percent of the underpayment of tax resulting from a substantial valuation misstatement and rises to 40 percent for a gross valuation misstatement. No penalty is imposed unless the portion of the underpayment attributable to the valuation misstatement exceeds $5,000 ($10,000 in the case of a corporation other than an S corporation or a personal holding company). Under present law, no penalty is imposed with respect to any portion of the understatement attributable to any item if (1) the treatment of the item on the return is or was supported by substantial authority, or (2) facts relevant to the tax treatment of the item were adequately disclosed on the return or on a statement attached to the return and there is a reasonable basis for the tax treatment. Special rules apply to tax shelters.

Present law also imposes an accuracy-related penalty on substantial or gross estate or gift tax valuation understatements.[408] In general, there is a substantial estate or gift tax understatement if the value of any property claimed on any return is 50 percent or less of the amount determined to be the correct amount, and a gross estate or gift tax understatement if such value is 25 percent or less of the amount determined to be the correct amount.

In addition, the accuracy-related penalties do not apply if a taxpayer shows there was reasonable cause for an underpayment and the taxpayer acted in good faith.[409]

Penalty for aiding and abetting understatement of tax

A penalty is imposed on a person who: (1) aids or assists in or advises with respect to a tax return or other document; (2) knows (or has reason to believe) that such document will be used in connection with a material tax matter; and (3) knows that this would result in an understatement of tax of another person. In general, the amount of the penalty is $1,000. If the document relates to the tax return of a corporation, the amount of the penalty is $10,000.

Qualified appraisals

Present law requires a taxpayer to obtain a qualified appraisal for donated property with a value of more than $5,000, and to attach an appraisal summary to the tax return.[410] Treasury Regulations state that a qualified appraisal means an appraisal document that, among other

[407] Sec. 6662(b)(3) and (h).

[408] Sec. 6662(g) and (h).

[409] Sec. 6664(c).

[410] Sec. 170(f)(11).

things: (1) relates to an appraisal that is made not earlier than 60 days prior to the date of contribution of the appraised property and not later than the due date (including extensions) of the return on which a deduction is first claimed under section 170; (2) is prepared, signed, and dated by a qualified appraiser; (3) includes (a) a description of the property appraised; (b) the fair market value of such property on the date of contribution and the specific basis for the valuation; (c) a statement that such appraisal was prepared for income tax purposes; (d) the qualifications of the qualified appraiser; and (e) the signature and taxpayer identification number of such appraiser; and (4) does not involve an appraisal fee that violates certain prescribed rules.[411]

Qualified appraisers

Treasury Regulations define a qualified appraiser as a person who holds himself or herself out to the public as an appraiser or performs appraisals on a regular basis, is qualified to make appraisals of the type of property being valued (as determined by the appraiser's background, experience, education and membership, if any, in professional appraisal associations), is independent, and understands that an intentionally false or fraudulent overstatement of the value of the appraised property may subject the appraiser to civil penalties.[412]

Appraiser oversight

The Secretary is authorized to regulate the practice of representatives of persons before the Department of the Treasury ("Department").[413] After notice and hearing, the Secretary is authorized to suspend or disbar from practice before the Department or the Internal Revenue Service ("IRS") a representative who is incompetent, who is disreputable, who violates the rules regulating practice before the Department or the IRS, or who (with intent to defraud) willfully and knowingly misleads or threatens the person being represented (or a person who may be represented).

The Secretary also is authorized to bar from appearing before the Department or the IRS, for the purpose of offering opinion evidence on the value of property or other assets, any individual against whom a civil penalty for aiding and abetting the understatement of tax has been assessed. Thus, an appraiser who aids or assists in the preparation or presentation of an appraisal will be subject to disciplinary action if the appraiser knows that the appraisal will be used in connection with the tax laws and will result in an understatement of the tax liability of another person. The Secretary has authority to provide that the appraisals of an appraiser who has been disciplined have no probative effect in any administrative proceeding before the Department or the IRS.

Explanation of Provision

Taxpayer penalties

The provision lowers the thresholds for imposing accuracy-related penalties on a taxpayer. Under the provision, a substantial valuation misstatement exists when the claimed value of any property is 150 percent or more of the amount determined to be the correct value. A gross valuation misstatement occurs when the claimed value of any property is 200 percent or more of the amount determined to be the correct value.

The provision tightens the thresholds for imposing accuracy-related penalties with respect to the estate or gift tax. Under the provision, a substantial estate or gift tax valuation misstatement exists when the claimed value of any property is 65 percent or less of the amount determined to be the correct value. A gross estate or gift tax valuation misstatement exists when the claimed value of any property is 40 percent or less of the amount determined to be the correct value.

Under the provision, the reasonable cause exception to the accuracy-related penalty does not apply in the case of gross valuation misstatements.

Appraiser oversight

Appraiser penalties

The provision establishes a civil penalty on any person who prepares an appraisal that is to be used to support a tax position if such appraisal results in a substantial or gross valuation misstatement. The penalty is equal to the greater of $1,000 or 10 percent of the understatement of tax resulting from a substantial or gross valuation misstatement, up to a maximum of 125 percent of the gross income derived from the appraisal. Under the provision, the penalty does not apply if the appraiser establishes that it was "more likely than not" that the appraisal was correct.

---

411 Treas. Reg. sec. 1.170A-13(c)(3).

412 Treas. Reg. sec. 1.170A-13(c)(5)(i).

413 31 U.S.C. sec. 330.

Disciplinary proceeding

The provision eliminates the requirement that the Secretary assess against an appraiser the civil penalty for aiding and abetting the understatement of tax before such appraiser may be subject to disciplinary action. Thus, the Secretary is authorized to discipline appraisers after notice and hearing. Disciplinary action may include, but is not limited to, suspending or barring an appraiser from: preparing or presenting appraisals on the value of property or other assets to the Department or the IRS; appearing before the Department or the IRS for the purpose of offering opinion evidence on the value of property or other assets; and providing that the appraisals of an appraiser who has been disciplined have no probative effect in any administrative proceeding before the Department or the IRS.

Qualified appraisers

The provision defines a qualified appraiser as an individual who (1) has earned an appraisal designation from a recognized professional appraiser organization or has otherwise met minimum education and experience requirements to be determined by the IRS in regulations; (2) regularly performs appraisals for which he or she receives compensation; (3) can demonstrate verifiable education and experience in valuing the type of property for which the appraisal is being performed; (4) has not been prohibited from practicing before the IRS by the Secretary at any time during the three years preceding the conduct of the appraisal; and (5) is not excluded from being a qualified appraiser under applicable Treasury regulations.

Qualified appraisals

The provision defines a qualified appraisal as an appraisal of property prepared by a qualified appraiser (as defined by the provision) in accordance with generally accepted appraisal standards and any regulations or other guidance prescribed by the Secretary.

Effective Date

The provision amending the accuracy-related penalty applies to returns filed after the date of enactment. The provision establishing a civil penalty that may be imposed on any person who prepares an appraisal that is to be used to support a tax position if such appraisal results in a substantial or gross valuation misstatement applies to appraisals prepared with respect to returns or submissions filed after the date of enactment. The provisions relating to appraiser oversight apply to appraisals prepared with respect to returns or submissions filed after the date of enactment. With respect to any contribution of a qualified real property interest which is a restriction with respect to the exterior of a building described in section 170(h)(4)(C)(ii) (currently designated section 170(h)(4)(B)(ii), relating to certain property located in a registered historic district and certified as being of historic significance to the district), and any appraisal with respect to such contribution, the provision generally applies to returns filed after July 25, 2006.

[Law at ¶ 5020, ¶ 5395, ¶ 5400, ¶ 5405, ¶ 5410 and ¶ 7234. CCH Explanation at ¶ 1345, ¶ 1350 and ¶ 1355.]

[¶ 11,280] Act Sec. 1220. Establish additional exemption standards for credit counseling organizations

Joint Committee Taxation (J.C.T. REP. NO. JCX-38-06)

[Code Secs. 501 and 513]

Present Law

Under present law, a credit counseling organization may be exempt as a charitable or educational organization described in section 501(c)(3), or as a social welfare organization described in section 501(c)(4). The IRS has issued two revenue rulings holding that certain credit counseling organizations are exempt as charitable or educational organizations or as social welfare organizations.

In Revenue Ruling 65-299,[414] an organization whose purpose was to assist families and individuals with financial problems, and help reduce the incidence of personal bankruptcy, was determined to be a social welfare organization described in section 501(c)(4). The organization counseled people in financial difficulties, advised applicants on payment of debts, and negotiated with creditors and set up debt repayment plans. The organization did not restrict its services to the poor, made no charge for counseling services, and made a nominal charge for

[414] Rev. Rul. 65-299, 1965-2 C.B. 165.

certain services to cover postage and supplies. For financial support, the organization relied on voluntary contributions from local businesses, lending agencies, and labor unions.

In Revenue Ruling 69-441,[415] the IRS ruled an organization was a charitable or educational organization exempt under section 501(c)(3) by virtue of aiding low-income people who had financial problems and providing education to the public. The organization in that ruling had two functions: (1) educating the public on personal money management, such as budgeting, buying practices, and the sound use of consumer credit through the use of films, speakers, and publications; and (2) providing individual counseling to low-income individuals and families without charge. As part of its counseling activities, the organization established debt management plans for clients who required such services, at no charge to the clients.[416] The organization was supported by contributions primarily from creditors, and its board of directors was comprised of representatives from religious organizations, civic groups, labor unions, business groups, and educational institutions.

In 1976, the IRS denied exempt status to an organization, Consumer Credit Counseling Service of Alabama, whose activities were distinguishable from those in Revenue Ruling 69-441 in that (1) it did not restrict its services to the poor, and (2) it charged a nominal fee for its debt management plans.[417] The organization provided free information to the general public through the use of speakers, films, and publications on the subjects of budgeting, buying practices, and the use of consumer credit. It also provided counseling to debt-distressed individuals, not necessarily poor or low-income, and provided debt management plans at the cost of $10 per month, which was waived in cases of financial hardship. Its debt management activities were a relatively small part of its overall activities. The district court determined the organization qualified as charitable and educational within section 501(c)(3), finding the debt management plans to be an integral part of the agency's counseling function, and that its debt management activities were incidental to its principal functions, as only approximately 12 percent of the counselors' time was applied to such programs and the charge for the service was nominal. The court also considered the facts that the agency was publicly supported, and that it had a board dominated by members of the general public, as factors indicating a charitable operation.[418]

A recent estimate shows the number of credit counseling organizations increased from approximately 200 in 1990 to over 1,000 in 2002.[419] During the period from 1994 to late 2003, 1,215 credit counseling organizations applied to the IRS for tax exempt status under section 501(c)(3), including 810 during 2000 to 2003.[420] The IRS has recognized more than 850 credit counseling organizations as tax exempt under section 501c)((3).[421] Few credit counseling organizations have sought section 501(c)(4) status, and the IRS reports it has not seen any significant increase in the number or activity of such organizations operating as social welfare organizations.[422] As of late 2003, there were 872 active tax-exempt credit counseling agencies operating in the United States.[423]

---

[415] Rev. Rul. 69-441, 1969-2 C.B. 115.

[416] Debt management plans are debt payment arrangements, including debt consolidation arrangements, entered into by a debtor and one or more of the debtor's creditors, generally structured to reduce the amount of a debtor's regular ongoing payment by modifying the interest rate, minimum payment, maturity or other terms of the debt. Such plans frequently are promoted as a means for a debtor to restructure debt without filing for bankruptcy.

[417] *Consumer Credit Counseling Service of Alabama, Inc. v. U.S.*, 44 A.F.T.R. 2d (RIA) 5122 (D.D.C. 1978). The case involved 24 agencies throughout the United States.

[418] *See also, Credit Counseling Centers of Oklahoma, Inc., v. U.S.*, 45 A.F.T.R. 2d (RIA) 1401 (D.D.C. 1979) (holding the same on virtually identical facts).

[419] Opening Statement of The Honorable Max Sandlin, Hearing on Non-Profit Credit Counseling Organizations, House Ways and Means Committee, Subcommittee on Oversight (November 20, 2003).

[420] United States Senate Permanent Subcommittee on Investigations, Committee on Governmental Affairs, *Profiteering in a Non-Profit Industry: Abusive Practices in Credit Counseling*, Report Prepared by the Majority & Minority Staffs of the Permanent Subcommittee on Investigations and Released in Conjunction with the Permanent Subcommittee Investigations' Hearing on March 24, 2004, p. 3 (citing letter dated December 18, 2003, to the Subcommittee from IRS Commissioner Everson).

[421] Testimony of Commissioner Mark Everson before the House Ways and Means Committee, Subcommittee on Oversight (November 20, 2003).

[422] Testimony of Commissioner Mark Everson before the House Ways and Means Committee, Subcommittee on Oversight (November 20, 2003).

[423] United States Senate Permanent Subcommittee on Investigations, Committee on Governmental Affairs, *Profiteering in a Non-Profit Industry: Abusive Practices in Credit Counseling*, Report Prepared by the Majority & Minority Staffs of the Permanent Subcommittee on Investigations and Released in Conjunction with the Permanent Subcommittee Investigations' Hearing on March 24, 2004, p. 3 (citing letter dated December 18, 2003 to the Subcommittee from IRS Commissioner Everson).

A credit counseling organization described in section 501(c)(3) is exempt from certain Federal and State consumer protection laws that provide exemptions for organizations described therein.[424] Some believe that these exclusions from Federal and State regulation may be a primary motivation for the recent increase in the number of organizations seeking and obtaining exempt status under section 501(c)(3).[425] Such regulatory exemptions generally are not available for social welfare organizations described in section 501(c)(4).

Congress recently conducted hearings investigating the activities of credit counseling organizations under various consumer protection laws,[426] such as the Federal Trade Commission Act.[427] In addition, the IRS commenced a broad examination and compliance program with respect to the credit counseling industry. On May 15, 2006, the IRS announced that over the past two years, it had been auditing 63 credit counseling agencies, representing more than 40 percent of the revenue in the industry. Audits of 41 organizations, representing more than 40 percent of the revenue in the industry have been completed as of that date. All of such completed audits resulted in revocation, proposed revocation, or other termination of tax-exempt status.[428] In addition, the IRS released two legal documents that provide a legal framework for determining the exempt status and related issues with respect to credit counseling organizations.[429] In CCA 200620001, the IRS found that "[t]he critical inquiry is whether a credit counseling organization conducts its counseling program to improve an individual debtor's understanding of his financial problems and improve his ability to address those problems." The CCA concluded that whether a credit counseling organization primarily furthers educational purposes

> can be determined by assessing the methodology by which the organization conducts its counseling activities. The process an organization uses to interview clients and develop recommendations, train its counselors and market its services can distinguish between an organization whose object is to improve a person's knowledge and skills to manage his personal debt, and an organization that is offering counseling primarily as a mechanism to enroll individuals in a specific option (e.g., debt management plans) without considering the individual's best interest.

Under the Bankruptcy Abuse Prevention and Consumer Protection Act of 2005, Public Law 109-8, an individual generally may not be a debtor in bankruptcy unless such individual has, within 180 days of filing a petition for bankruptcy, received from an approved nonprofit budget and credit counseling agency an individual or group briefing that outlines the opportunities for available credit counseling and assists the individual in performing a related budget analysis.[430] The clerk of the court must maintain a

---

[424] *E.g.*, The Credit Repair Organizations Act, 15 U.S.C. section 1679 *et seq.*, effective April 1, 1997 (imposing restrictions on credit repair organizations that are enforced by the Federal Trade Commission, including forbidding the making of untrue or misleading statements and forbidding advance payments; section 501(c)(3) organizations are explicitly exempt from such regulation). Testimony of Commissioner Mark Everson before the House Ways and Means Committee, Subcommittee on Oversight (November 20, 2003) (California's consumer protections laws that impose strict standards on credit service organizations and the credit repair industry do not apply to nonprofit organizations that have received a final determination from the IRS that they are exempt from tax under section 501(c)(3) and are not private foundations).

[425] Testimony of Commissioner Mark Everson before the House Ways and Means Committee, Subcommittee on Oversight (November 20, 2003).

[426] United States Senate Permanent Subcommittee on Investigations, Committee on Governmental Affairs, *Profiteering in a Non-Profit Industry: Abusive Practices in Credit Counseling*, Report Prepared by the Majority & Minority Staffs of the Permanent Subcommittee on Investigations and Released in Conjunction with the Permanent Subcommittee Investigations' Hearing on March 24, 2004.

[427] 15 U.S.C. sec. 45(a) (prohibiting unfair and deceptive acts or practices in or affecting commerce; although the Federal Trade Commission generally lacks jurisdiction to enforce consumer protection laws against bona fide nonprofit organizations, it may assert jurisdiction over a nonprofit, including a credit counseling organization, if it demonstrates the organization is organized to carry on business for profit, is a mere instrumentality of a for-profit entity, or operates through a common enterprise with one or more for-profit entities).

[428] IRS News Release, IR-2006-80, May 15, 2006.

[429] Chief Counsel Advice 200431023 (July 13, 2004); Chief Counsel Advice 200620001 (May 9, 2006).

[430] This requirement does not apply in certain circumstances, such as: (1) in general, where a debtor resides in a district for which the U.S. Trustee has determined that the approved counseling agencies for such district are not reasonably able to provide adequate services to additional individuals; (2) where exigent circumstances merit a waiver, the individual seeking bankruptcy protection files an appropriate certification with the court, and the certification is acceptable to the court; and (3) in general, where a court determines, after notice and hearing, that the individual is unable to complete the requirement because of incapacity, disability, or active military duty in a military combat zone.

publicly available list of nonprofit budget and credit counseling agencies approved by the U.S. Trustee (or bankruptcy administrator). In general, the U.S. Trustee (or bankruptcy administrator) shall only approve an agency that demonstrates that it will provide qualified counselors, maintain adequate provision for safekeeping and payment of client funds, provide adequate counseling with respect to client credit problems, and deal responsibly and effectively with other matters relating to the quality, effectiveness, and financial security of the services it provides. The minimum qualifications for approval of such an agency include: (1) in general, having an independent board of directors; (2) charging no more than a reasonable fee, and providing services without regard to ability to pay; (3) adequate provision for safekeeping and payment of client funds; (4) provision of full disclosures to clients; (5) provision of adequate counseling with respect to a client's credit problems; (6) trained counselors who receive no commissions or bonuses based on the outcome of the counseling services; (7) experience and background in providing credit counseling; and (8) adequate financial resources to provide continuing support services for budgeting plans over the life of any repayment plan. An individual debtor must file with the court a certificate from the approved nonprofit budget and credit counseling agency that provided the required services describing the services provided, and a copy of the debt management plan, if any, developed through the agency.[431]

Explanation of Provision

Requirements for exempt status of credit counseling organizations

The provision establishes standards that a credit counseling organization must satisfy, in addition to present law requirements, in order to be organized and operated either as an organization described in section 501(c)(3) or in section 501(c)(4). The provision does not diminish the requirements set forth recently by the IRS in Chief Counsel Advice 200431023 or Chief Counsel Advice 200620001 but builds on and is consistent with such requirements, and the analysis therein. The provision is not intended to raise any question about IRS actions taken, and the IRS is expected to continue its vigorous examination of the credit counseling industry, applying the additional standards provided by the provision. The provision does not and is not intended to affect the approval process for credit counseling agencies under Public Law 109-8. Public Law 109-8 requires that an approved credit counseling agency be a nonprofit, and does not require that an approved agency be a section 501(c)(3) organization. It is expected that the Department of Justice shall continue to approve agencies for purposes of providing pre-bankruptcy counseling based on criteria that are consistent with such Public Law.

Under the provision, an organization that provides credit counseling services as a substantial purpose of the organization ("credit counseling organization") is eligible for exemption from Federal income tax only as a charitable or educational organization under section 501(c)(3) or as a social welfare organization under section 501(c)(4), and only if (in addition to present-law requirements) the credit counseling organization is organized and operated in accordance with the following:

1. The organization provides credit counseling services tailored to the specific needs and circumstances of the consumer;

2. The organization makes no loans to debtors (other than loans with no fees or interest) and does not negotiate the making of loans on behalf of debtors;[432]

3. The organization provides services for the purpose of improving a consumer's credit record, credit history, or credit rating only to the extent that such services are incidental to providing credit counseling services and does not charge any separately stated fee for any such services;[433]

4. The organization does not refuse to provide credit counseling services to a consumer due to inability of the consumer to pay, the ineligibility of the consumer for debt management plan enrollment, or the unwillingness of a consumer to enroll in a debt management plan;

5. The organization establishes and implements a fee policy to require that any fees

---

[431] The Act also requires that, prior to discharge of indebtedness under chapter 7 or chapter 13, a debtor complete an approved instructional course concerning personal financial management, which course need not be conducted by a nonprofit agency.

[432] In general, negotiation of a loan involves negotiation of the terms of a loan, rather than the processing of a loan. Organizations that provide assistance to consumers to obtain a loan from the Department of Housing and Urban Development, for example, are not necessarily negotiating a loan for a consumer.

[433] Accordingly, a credit counseling organization may provide credit repair type services, but only to the extent that the provision of such services is a direct outgrowth of the provision of credit counseling services.

charged to a consumer for its services are reasonable,[434] allows for the waiver of fees if the consumer is unable to pay, and except to the extent allowed by State law prohibits charging any fee based in whole or in part on a percentage of the consumer's debt, the consumer's payments to be made pursuant to a debt management plan, or on the projected or actual savings to the consumer resulting from enrolling in a debt management plan;

6. The organization at all times has a board of directors or other governing body (a) that is controlled by persons who represent the broad interests of the public, such as public officials acting in their capacities as such, persons having special knowledge or expertise in credit or financial education, and community leaders; (b) not more than 20 percent of the voting power of which is vested in persons who are employed by the organization or who will benefit financially, directly or indirectly, from the organization's activities (other than through the receipt of reasonable directors' fees or the repayment of consumer debt to creditors other than the credit counseling organization or its affiliates) and (c) not more than 49 percent of the voting power of which is vested in persons who are employed by the organization or who will benefit financially, directly or indirectly, from the organization's activities (other than through the receipt of reasonable directors' fees);[435]

7. The organization does not own (except with respect to a section 501(c)(3) organization) more than 35 percent of the total combined voting power of a corporation (or profits or beneficial interest in the case of a partnership or trust or estate) that is in the trade or business of lending money, repairing credit, or providing debt management plan services, payment processing, and similar services; and

8. The organization receives no amount for providing referrals to others for debt management plan services, and pays no amount to others for obtaining referrals of consumers.[436]

Additional requirements for charitable and educational organizations

Under the provision, a credit counseling organization is described in section 501(c)(3) only if, in addition to satisfying the above requirements and the requirements of section 501(c)(3), the organization is organized and operated such that the organization (1) does not solicit contributions from consumers during the initial counseling process or while the consumer is receiving services from the organization and (2) the aggregate revenues of the organization that are from payments of creditors of consumers of the organization and that are attributable to debt management plan services do not exceed the applicable percentage of the total revenues of the organization. For credit counseling organizations in existence on the date of enactment, the applicable percentage is 80 percent for the first taxable year of the organization beginning after the date which is one year after the date of enactment, 70 percent for the second such taxable year beginning after such date, 60 percent for the third such taxable year beginning after such date, and 50 percent thereafter. For new credit counseling organizations, the applicable percentage is 50 percent for taxable years beginning after the date of enactment. Satisfaction of the aggregate revenues requirement is not a safe harbor; all other requirements of the provision (and of section 501(c)(3)) pertaining to section 501(c)(3) organizations also must be satisfied. Satisfaction of the aggregate revenues requirement means only that an organization has not automatically failed to be organized or operated consistent with exempt purposes. Compliance with the revenues test does not mean that the organization's debt management plan services activity is at a level that organizationally or operationally is consistent with exempt status. In other words, satisfaction of the aggregate revenues requirement (as a preliminary matter in an exemption application, or on an ongoing operational basis) provides no affirmative evidence that an organization's primary purpose is an exempt purpose, or that the

[434] Whether a credit counseling organization's fees are consistent with specific State law requirements is evidence of the reasonableness of fees but is not determinative.

[435] The requirements described in paragraphs 4, 5, and 6 above address core issues that are related to tax-exempt status and that have proved to be problematic in the credit counseling industry—the provision of services and waiver of fees without regard to ability to pay, the establishment of a reasonable fee policy, and the presence of independent board members. No inference is intended through the provision of these specific requirements on credit counseling organizations that similar or more stringent requirements should not be adhered to by other exempt organizations providing fees for services. Rather, the provision affirms the importance of these core issues to the matter of tax exemption, both to credit counseling organizations and to other types of exempt organizations.

[436] If a credit counseling organization pays or receives a fee, for example, for using or maintaining a locator service for consumers to find a credit counseling organization, such a fee is not considered a referral.

revenues that are subject to the limitation (or debt management plan services revenues more generally) are related to exempt purposes. As described below, whether revenues from such activity are substantially related to exempt purposes depends on the facts and circumstances, that is, satisfaction of the aggregate revenues requirement generally is not relevant for purposes of whether any of an organization's revenues are revenues from an unrelated trade or business. Failure to satisfy the aggregate revenues requirement does not disqualify the organization from recognition of exemption under section 501(c)(4).

Additional requirement for social welfare organizations

Under the provision, a credit counseling organization is described in section 501(c)(4) only if, in addition to satisfying the above requirements applicable to such organizations, the organization notifies the Secretary, in such manner as the Secretary may by regulations prescribe, that it is applying for recognition as a credit counseling organization.

Debt management plan services treated as an unrelated trade or business

Under the provision, debt management plan services are treated as an unrelated trade or business for purposes of the tax on income from an unrelated trade or business to the extent such services are provided by an organization that is not a credit counseling organization. With respect to the provision of debt management plan services by a credit counseling organization, in order for the income from such services not to be unrelated business income, it is intended that, consistent with current law, the debt management plan service with respect to such income (1) must contribute importantly to the accomplishment of credit counseling services, and (2) must not be conducted on a larger scale than reasonably is necessary for the accomplishment of such services. For example, the provision of debt management plan services would not be substantially related to accomplishing exempt purposes if the organization recommended and enrolled an individual in a debt management plan only after determining whether the individual satisfied the financial criteria established by the creditors for such plan, without (1) considering whether it was an appropriate action in light of the individual's particular needs and objectives, (2) discussing the disadvantages of a debt management plan with the consumer, and (3) presenting other possible options to such consumer.

Definitions

Credit counseling services

Credit counseling services are (a) the provision of educational information to the general public on budgeting, personal finance, financial literacy, saving and spending practices, and the sound use of consumer credit; (b) the assisting of individuals and families with financial problems by providing them with counseling; or (c) any combination of such activities.

Debt management plan services

Debt management plan services are services related to the repayment, consolidation, or restructuring of a consumer's debt, and includes the negotiation with creditors of lower interest rates, the waiver or reduction of fees, and the marketing and processing of debt management plans.

Effective Date

In general, the provision applies to taxable years beginning after the date of enactment. For a credit counseling organization that is described in section 501(c)(3) or 501(c)(4) on the date of enactment, the provision is effective for taxable years beginning after the date that is one year after the date of enactment.

[Law at ¶5145 and ¶5165. CCH Explanation at ¶1215.]

[¶11,290] Act Sec. 1221. Expand the base of the tax on private foundation net investment income

Joint Committee Taxation (J.C.T. REP. NO. JCX-38-06)

[Code Sec. 4940]

Present Law

In general

Under section 4940(a) of the Code, private foundations that are recognized as exempt from Federal income tax under section 501(a) of the Code are subject to a two-percent excise tax on their net investment income. Private foundations that are not exempt from tax, such as certain charitable trusts,[437] also are subject to an excise tax under section 4940(b) based on net investment income and unrelated business income. The two-percent rate of tax is reduced to one-percent if certain requirements are met in a taxable year.[438] Unlike certain other excise taxes imposed on private foundations, the tax based on investment income does not result from a violation of substantive law by the private foundation; it is solely an excise tax.

The tax on taxable private foundations under section 4940(b) is equal to the excess of the sum of the excise tax that would have been imposed under section 4940(a) if the foundation were tax exempt and the amount of the unrelated business income tax that would have been imposed if the foundation were tax exempt, over the income tax imposed on the foundation under subtitle A of the Code.

Net investment income

Internal Revenue Code

In general, net investment income is defined as the amount by which the sum of gross investment income and capital gain net income exceeds the deductions relating to the production of gross investment income.[439]

Gross investment income is the gross amount of income from interest, dividends, rents, payments with respect to securities loans, and royalties. Gross investment income does not include any income that is included in computing a foundation's unrelated business taxable income.[440]

Capital gain net income takes into account only gains and losses from the sale or other disposition of property used for the production of interest, dividends, rents, and royalties, and property used for the production of income included in computing the unrelated business income tax (except to the extent the gain or loss is taken into account for purposes of such tax). Losses from sales or other dispositions of property are allowed only to the extent of gains from such sales or other dispositions, and no capital loss carryovers are allowed.[441]

Treasury Regulations and case law

The Treasury regulations elaborate on the Code definition of net investment income. The regulations cite items of investment income listed in the Code, and in addition clarify that net investment income includes interest, dividends, rents, and royalties derived from all sources, including from assets devoted to charitable activities. For example, interest received on a student loan is includible in the gross investment income of a foundation making the loan.[442]

The regulations further provide that gross investment income includes certain items of investment income that are described in the unrelated business income tax regulations.[443] Such additional items include payments with respect to securities loans (an item added to the Code in 1978), annuities, income from notional principal contracts, and other substantially similar income from ordinary and routine investments to the extent determined by the Commissioner.[444] These latter three categories of income are not enumerated as net investment income in the Code.

The Treasury regulations also elaborate on the Code definition of capital gain net income. The regulations provide that the only capital gains and losses that are taken into account are (1) gains and losses from the sale or other disposition of property held by a private foundation for investment purposes (other than program related investments), and (2) property used for the production of income included in computing the unrelated business income tax (except to the extent the gain or loss is taken into account for purposes of such tax).

This definition of capital gain net income builds on the definition provided in the Code by providing an exception for gain and loss from program related investments and by stating, in addition, that "gains and losses from the sale or other disposition of property used for the exempt purposes of the private foundation are excluded."[445] As an example, the regulations provide that gain or loss on the sale of buildings used for the foundation's exempt activities are not taken into account for purposes of the section 4940 tax. If a foundation uses exempt income for exempt purposes and (other than incidentally) for investment purposes, then the portion of the gain or loss received upon sale or other disposition that is allocable to the invest-

---

437 *See* sec. 4947(a)(1).

438 Sec. 4940(e).

439 Sec. 4940(c)(1). Net investment income also is determined by applying section 103 (generally providing an exclusion for interest on certain State and local bonds) and section 265 (generally disallowing the deduction for interest and certain other expenses with respect to tax-exempt income). Sec. 4940(c)(5).

440 Sec. 4940(c)(2).

441 Sec. 4940(c)(4).

442 Treas. Reg. sec. 53.4940-1(d)(1).

443 *Id.*

444 Treas. Reg. sec. 1.512(b)-1(a)(1).

445 Treas. Reg. sec. 53.4940-1(f)(1).

ment use is taken into account for purposes of the tax.

The regulations further provide that "property shall be treated as held for investment purposes even though such property is disposed of by the foundation immediately upon its receipt, if it is property of a type which generally produces interest, dividends, rents, royalties, or capital gains through appreciation (for example, rental real estate, stock, bonds, mineral interest, mortgages, and securities)."[446]

This regulation has been challenged in the courts. The regulation says that property is treated as held for investment purposes if it is of a type that "generally produces" certain types of income. By contrast, the Code provides that the property be "used" to produce such income. In Zemurray Foundation v. United States, 687 F.2d 97 (5th Cir. 1982), the taxpayer foundation challenged the Treasury's attempt to tax under section 4940 capital gain on the sale of timber property. The taxpayer asserted that the property was not actually used to produce investment income, and that the Treasury Regulation was invalid because the regulation would subject to tax property that is of a type that could generally be used to produce investment income. On this issue, the court upheld the Treasury regulation, reasoning that the regulation's use of the phrase "generally used," though permitting taxation "so long as the property sold is usable to produce the applicable types of income, regardless of whether the property is actually used to produce income or not" was not unreasonable or plainly inconsistent with the statute.[447] However, on remand to the district court, the district court concluded that the timber property at issue, though a type of property generally used to produce investment income, was not susceptible for such use.[448] Thus, the district court concluded that the Treasury could not tax the gain under this portion of the regulation.

The question then turned to the taxpayer's second challenge to the regulation. At issue was the meaning of the regulatory phrase "capital gains through appreciation." The regulation provides that if property is of a type that generally produces capital gains through appreciation, then the gain is subject to tax. The Treasury argued that the timber property at issue, although held by the court not to be property (in this case) susceptible for use to produce interest, dividends, rents, or royalties, still was held by the taxpayer to produce capital gain through appreciation and therefore the gain should be subject to tax under the regulation.

On this issue, the court held for the taxpayer, reasoning that the language of the Code clearly is limited to certain gains and losses, e.g., the court cited the Code language providing that "there shall be taken into account only gains and losses from the sale or other disposition of property used for the production of interest, dividends, rents, and royalties . . . ."[449] The court noted that "capital gains through appreciation" is not enumerated in the statute. The court used as an example a jade figurine held by a foundation. Jade figurines do not generally produce interest, dividends, rents, or royalties, but gain on the sale of such a figurine would be taxable under the "capital gains through appreciation" standard, yet such standard does not appear in the statute. After Zemurray, the Treasury generally conceded this issue.[450]

With respect to capital losses, the Code provides that carryovers are not permitted, whereas the regulations state that neither carryovers nor carrybacks are permitted.[451]

Application of Zemurray to the Code and the regulations

Applying the Zemurray case to the Code and regulations results in a general principle for purposes of present law: private foundations are subject to tax under section 4940 only on the items of income and only on gains and losses specifically enumerated therein. Under this principle, private foundations generally are not subject to the section 4940 tax on other substantially similar types of income from ordinary and routine investments, notwithstanding Treasury regulations to the contrary. In addition, the regulations provide that gain or loss from the sale or other disposition of assets used for exempt purposes, with specific reference to program-related investments, is excluded. The Code provides for no such blanket exclusion; thus, under the language of the Code and the reasoning of Zemurray, if a foundation provided office space at below market rent to a charitable organization for use in the organization's exempt purposes, gain on the sale of the building by the

---

[446] *Id.*

[447] *Zemurray Foundation v. United States*, 687 F.2d 97, 100 (5th Cir. 1982).

[448] *Zemurray Foundation v. United States*, 53 A.F.T.R. 2d (RIA) 842 (E. D. La. 1983).

[449] *Zemurray Foundation v. United States*, 755 F.2d 404 (5th Cir. 1985), 413 (citing Code sec. 4940(c)(4)(A).

[450] G.C.M. 39538 (July 23, 1986).

[451] Treas. Reg. sec. 53.4940-1(f)(3).

foundation should be subject to the section 4940 tax despite the Treasury regulations.[452]

In addition, under the logic of Zemurray, capital loss carrybacks arguably are permitted, notwithstanding Treasury regulations to the contrary, because the Code mentions only a bar on use of carryovers and says nothing about carrybacks.

Explanation of Provision

The provision amends the definition of gross investment income (including for purposes of capital gain net income) to include items of income that are similar to the items presently enumerated in the Code. Such similar items include income from notional principal contracts, annuities, and other substantially similar income from ordinary and routine investments, and, with respect to capital gain net income, capital gains from appreciation, including capital gains and losses from the sale or other disposition of assets used to further an exempt purpose.

Certain gains and losses are not taken into account in determining capital gain net income. Specifically, under the provision, no gain or loss shall be taken into account with respect to any portion of property used for a period of not less than one year for a purpose or function constituting the basis of the private foundation's exemption, if the entire property is exchanged immediately following such period solely for property of like kind which is to be used primarily for a purpose or function constituting the basis for such foundation's exemption. Rules similar to the rules of section 1031 (relating to exchange of property held for productive use or investment) apply, including, but not limited to, the exceptions of section 1031(a)(2) and the rule of section 1031(a)(3) regarding completion of the exchange within 180 days.

The provision provides that there are no carrybacks of losses from sales or other dispositions of property.

Effective Date

The provision is effective for taxable years beginning after the date of enactment.

[Law at ¶ 5155 and ¶ 5245. CCH Explanation at ¶ 1250.]

[¶ 11,300] Act Sec. 1222. Definition of convention or association of churches

Joint Committee Taxation (J.C.T. Rep. No. JCX-38-06)

[Code Sec. 7701]

Present Law

Under present law, an organization that qualifies as a "convention or association of churches" (within the meaning of sec. 170(b)(1)(A)(i)) is not required to file an annual return,[453] is subject to the church tax inquiry and church tax examination provisions applicable to organizations claiming to be a church,[454] and is subject to certain other provisions generally applicable to churches.[455] The Internal Revenue Code does not define the term "convention or association of churches."

Explanation of Provision

The provision provides that an organization that otherwise is a convention or association of churches does not fail to so qualify merely because the membership of the organization includes individuals as well as churches, or because individuals have voting rights in the organization.

Effective Date

The provision is effective on the date of enactment.

[Law at ¶ 5485. CCH Explanation at ¶ 1205.]

---

[452] *See also* the example in Treas. Reg. sec. 53.4940-1(f)(1).

[453] Sec. 6033(a)(2)(A)(i).

[454] Sec. 7611(h)(1)(B).

[455] *See, e.g.*, Sec. 402(g)(8)(B) (limitation on elective deferrals); sec. 403(b)(9)(B) (definition of retirement income account); sec. 410(d) (election to have participation, vesting, funding, and certain other provisions apply to church plans); sec. 414(e) (definition of church plan); sec. 415(c)(7) (certain contributions by church plans); sec. 501(h)(5) (disqualification of certain organizations from making the sec. 501(h) election regarding lobbying expenditure limits); sec. 501(m)(3) (definition of commercial-type insurance); sec. 508(c)(1)(A) (exception from requirement to file application seeking recognition of exempt status); sec. 512(b)(12) (allowance of up to $1,000 deduction for purposes of determining unrelated business taxable income); sec. 514(b)(3)(E) (definition of debt-financed property); sec. 3121(w)(3)(A) (election regarding exemption from social security taxes); sec. 3309(b)(1) (application of federal unemployment tax provisions to services performed in the employ of certain organizations); sec. 6043(b)(1) (requirement to file a return upon liquidation or dissolution of the organization); and sec. 7702(j)(3)(A) (treatment of certain death benefit plans as life insurance).

[¶11,310] Act Sec. 1223. Notification requirement for exempt entities not currently required to file an annual information return

Joint Committee Taxation (J.C.T. REP. NO. JCX-38-06)

[Code Secs. 6033, 6652 and 7428]

Present Law

Under present law, the requirement that an exempt organization file an annual information return does not apply to several categories of exempt organizations. Organizations excepted from the filing requirement include organizations (other than private foundations), the gross receipts of which in each taxable year normally are not more than $25,000.[456] Also exempt from the requirement are churches, their integrated auxiliaries, and conventions or associations of churches; the exclusively religious activities of any religious order; section 501(c)(1) instrumentalities of the United States; section 501(c)(21) trusts; an interchurch organization of local units of a church; certain mission societies; certain church-affiliated elementary and high schools; certain State institutions whose income is excluded from gross income under section 115; certain governmental units and affiliates of governmental units; and other organizations that the IRS has relieved from the filing requirement pursuant to its statutory discretionary authority.

Explanation of Provision

The provision requires organizations that are excused from filing an information return by reason of normally having gross receipts below a certain specified amount (generally, under $25,000) to furnish to the Secretary annually, in electronic form, the legal name of the organization, any name under which the organization operates or does business, the organization's mailing address and Internet web site address (if any), the organization's taxpayer identification number, the name and address of a principal officer, and evidence of the organization's continuing basis for its exemption from the generally applicable information return filing requirements. Upon such organization's termination of existence, the organization is required to furnish notice of such termination.

The provision provides that if an organization fails to provide the required notice for three consecutive years, the organization's tax-exempt status is revoked. In addition, if an organization that is required to file an annual information return under section 6033(a) (Form 990) fails to file such an information return for three consecutive years, the organization's tax-exempt status is revoked. If an organization fails to meet its filing obligation to the IRS for three consecutive years in cases where the organization is subject to the information return filing requirement in one or more years during a three-year period and also is subject to the notice requirement for one or more years during the same three-year period, the organization's tax-exempt status is revoked.

A revocation under the provision is effective from the date that the Secretary determines was the last day the organization could have timely filed the third required information return or notice. To again be recognized as tax-exempt, the organization must apply to the Secretary for recognition of tax-exemption, irrespective of whether the organization was required to make an application for recognition of tax-exemption in order to gain tax-exemption originally.

If, upon application for tax-exempt status after a revocation under the provision, the organization shows to the satisfaction of the Secretary reasonable cause for failing to file the required annual notices or returns, the organization's tax-exempt status may, in the discretion of the Secretary, be reinstated retroactive to the date of revocation. An organization may not challenge under the Code's declaratory judgment procedures (section 7428) a revocation of tax-exemption made pursuant to the provision.

There is no monetary penalty for failure to file the notice under the provision. Like other information returns, the notices are subject to the public disclosure and inspection rules generally applicable to exempt organizations. The provision does not affect an organization's obligation

[456] Sec. 6033(a)(2); Treas. Reg. sec. 1.6033-2(a)(2)(i); Treas. Reg. sec. 1.6033-2(g)(1). Sec. 6033(a)(2)(A)(ii) provides a $5,000 annual gross receipts exception from the annual reporting requirements for certain exempt organizations. In Announcement 82-88, 1982-25 I.R.B. 23, the IRS exercised its discretionary authority under section 6033 to increase the gross receipts exception to $25,000, and enlarge the category of exempt organizations that are not required to file Form 990.

under present law to file required information returns or existing penalties for failure to file such returns.

The Secretary is required to notify every organization that is subject to the notice filing requirement of the new filing obligation in a timely manner. Notification by the Secretary shall be by mail, in the case of any organization the identity and address of which is included in the list of exempt organizations maintained by the Secretary, and by Internet or other means of outreach, in the case of any other organization. In addition, the Secretary is required to publicize in a timely manner in appropriate forms and instructions and other means of outreach the new penalty imposed for consecutive failures to file the information return.

The Secretary is authorized to publish a list of organizations whose exempt status is revoked under the provision.

Effective Date

The provision is effective for notices and returns with respect to annual periods beginning after 2006.

[Law at ¶ 5325, ¶ 5390, ¶ 5440 and ¶ 7237. CCH Explanation at ¶ 1260.]

[¶ 11,320] Act Sec. 1224 Disclosure to state officials relating to section 501(c) organizations

Joint Committee Taxation (J.C.T. REP. NO. JCX-38-06)

[Code Secs. 6103, 6104, 7213, 7213A and 7431]

Present Law

In the case of organizations that are described in section 501(c)(3) and exempt from tax under section 501(a) or that have applied for exemption as an organization so described, present law (sec. 6104(c)) requires the Secretary to notify the appropriate State officer of (1) a refusal to recognize such organization as an organization described in section 501(c)(3), (2) a revocation of a section 501(c)(3) organization's tax-exempt status, and (3) the mailing of a notice of deficiency for any tax imposed under section 507, chapter 41, or chapter 42.[457] In addition, at the request of such appropriate State officer, the Secretary is required to make available for inspection and copying, such returns, filed statements, records, reports, and other information relating to the above-described disclosures, as are relevant to any State law determination. An appropriate State officer is the State attorney general, State tax officer, or any State official charged with overseeing organizations of the type described in section 501(c)(3).

In general, returns and return information (as such terms are defined in section 6103(b)) are confidential and may not be disclosed or inspected unless expressly provided by law.[458] Present law requires the Secretary to keep records of disclosures and requests for inspection[459] and requires that persons authorized to receive returns and return information maintain various safeguards to protect such information against unauthorized disclosure.[460] Willful unauthorized disclosure or inspection of returns or return information is subject to a fine and/or imprisonment.[461] The knowing or negligent unauthorized inspection or disclosure of returns or return information gives the taxpayer a right to bring a civil suit.[462] Such present-law protections against unauthorized disclosure or inspection of returns and return information do not apply to the disclosures or inspections, described above, that are authorized by section 6104(c).

Explanation of Provision

The provision provides that upon written request by an appropriate State officer, the Secretary may disclose: (1) a notice of proposed refusal to recognize an organization as a section

---

457 The applicable taxes include the termination tax on private foundations; taxes on public charities for certain excess lobbying expenses; taxes on a private foundation's net investment income, self-dealing activities, undistributed income, excess business holdings, investments that jeopardize charitable purposes, and taxable expenditures (some of these taxes also apply to certain non-exempt trusts); taxes on the political expenditures and excess benefit transactions of section 501(c)(3) organizations; and certain taxes on black lung benefit trusts and foreign organizations.

458 Sec. 6103(a).

459 Sec. 6103(p)(3).

460 Sec. 6103(p)(4).

461 Secs. 7213 and 7213A.

462 Sec. 7431.

501(c)(3) organization; (2) a notice of proposed revocation of tax-exemption of a section 501(c)(3) organization; (3) the issuance of a proposed deficiency of tax imposed under section 507, chapter 41, or chapter 42; (4) the names, addresses, and taxpayer identification numbers of organizations that have applied for recognition as section 501(c)(3) organizations; and (5) returns and return information of organizations with respect to which information has been disclosed under (1) through (4) above.[463] Disclosure or inspection is permitted for the purpose of, and only to the extent necessary in, the administration of State laws regulating section 501(c)(3) organizations, such as laws regulating tax-exempt status, charitable trusts, charitable solicitation, and fraud. Such disclosure or inspection may be made only to or by an appropriate State officer or to an officer or employee of the State who is designated by the appropriate State officer, and may not be made by or to a contractor or agent. The Secretary also is permitted to disclose or open to inspection the returns and return information of an organization that is recognized as tax-exempt under section 501(c)(3), or that has applied for such recognition, to an appropriate State officer if the Secretary determines that disclosure or inspection may constitute evidence of noncompliance under the laws within the jurisdiction of the appropriate State officer. For this purpose, appropriate State officer means the State attorney general, the State tax officer, or any other State official charged with overseeing organizations of the type described in section 501(c)(3).

In addition, the provision provides that upon the written request by an appropriate State officer, the Secretary may make available for inspection or disclosure returns and return information of an organization described in section 501(c) (other than section 501(c)(1) or section 501(c)(3)). Such returns and return information are available for inspection or disclosure only for the purpose of, and to the extent necessary in, the administration of State laws regulating the solicitation or administration of the charitable funds or charitable assets of such organizations. Such disclosure or inspection may be made only to or by an appropriate State officer or to an officer or employee of the State who is designated by the appropriate State officer, and may not be made by or to a contractor or agent. For this purpose, appropriate State officer means the State attorney general, the State tax officer, and the head of an agency designated by the State attorney general as having primary responsibility for overseeing the solicitation of funds for charitable purposes of such organizations.

In addition, the provision provides that any returns and return information disclosed under section 6104(c) may be disclosed in civil administrative and civil judicial proceedings pertaining to the enforcement of State laws regulating the applicable tax-exempt organization in a manner prescribed by the Secretary. Returns and return information are not to be disclosed under section 6104(c), or in such an administrative or judicial proceeding, to the extent that the Secretary determines that such disclosure would seriously impair Federal tax administration. The provision makes disclosures of returns and return information under section 6104(c) subject to the disclosure, recordkeeping, and safeguard provisions of section 6103, including through requirements that the Secretary maintain a permanent system of records of requests for disclosure (sec. 6103(p)(3)) and that the appropriate State officer maintain various safeguards that protect against unauthorized disclosure (sec. 6103(p)(4)). The provision provides that the willful unauthorized disclosure of returns or return information described in section 6104(c) is a felony subject to a fine of up to $5,000 and/or imprisonment of up to five years (sec. 7213(a)(2)), the willful unauthorized inspection of returns or return information described in section 6104(c) is subject to a fine of up to $1,000 and/or imprisonment of up to one year (sec. 7213A), and provides the taxpayer the right to bring a civil action for damages in the case of knowing or negligent unauthorized disclosure or inspection of such information (sec. 7431(a)(2)).

Effective Date

The provision is effective on the date of enactment but does not apply to requests made before such date.

[Law at ¶ 5360, ¶ 5365, ¶ 5430, ¶ 5435 and ¶ 5445. CCH Explanation at ¶ 1280.]

[463] Such returns and return information also may be open to inspection by an appropriate State officer.

[¶11,330] Act Sec. 1225. Require that unrelated business income tax returns of section 501(c)(3) organizations be made publicly available

Joint Committee Taxation (J.C.T. REP. NO. JCX-38-06)

[Code Sec. 6104]

Present Law

In general, an organization described in section 501(c) or (d) is required to make available for public inspection a copy of its annual information return (Form 990) and exemption application materials.[464] A penalty may be imposed on any person who does not make an organization's annual returns or exemption application materials available for public inspection. The penalty amount is $20 for each day during which a failure occurs. If more than one person fails to comply, each person is jointly and severally liable for the full amount of the penalty. The maximum penalty that may be imposed on all persons for any one annual return is $10,000. There is no maximum penalty amount for failing to make exemption application materials available for public inspection. Any person who willfully fails to comply with the public inspection requirements is subject to an additional penalty of $5,000.[465]

These requirements do not apply to an organization's annual return for unrelated business income tax (generally Form 990-T).[466]

Explanation of Provision

The provision extends the present-law public inspection and disclosure requirements and penalties applicable to the Form 990 to the unrelated business income tax return (Form 990-T) of organizations described in section 501(c)(3). The provision provides that certain information may be withheld by the organization from public disclosure and inspection if public availability would adversely affect the organization, similar to the information that may be withheld under present law with respect to applications for tax exemption and the Form 990 (e.g., information relating to a trade secret, patent, process, style of work, or apparatus of the organization, if the Secretary determines that public disclosure of such information would adversely affect the organization).

Effective Date

The provision is effective for returns filed after the date of enactment.

[Law at ¶5365. CCH Explanation at ¶1275.]

[¶11,340] Act Sec. 1226. Treasury study on donor advised funds and supporting organizations

Joint Committee Taxation (J.C.T. REP. NO. JCX-38-06)

[Act Sec. 1226]

Present Law

Donor advised funds

Some charitable organizations (including community foundations) establish accounts to which donors may contribute and thereafter provide nonbinding advice or recommendations with regard to distributions from the fund or the investment of assets in the fund. Such accounts are commonly referred to as "donor advised funds." Donors who make contributions to charities for maintenance in a donor advised fund generally claim a charitable contribution deduction at the time of the contribution. Although sponsoring charities frequently permit donors (or other persons appointed by donors) to provide nonbinding recommendations concerning the distribution or investment of assets in a donor advised fund, sponsoring charities generally

[464] Sec. 6104(d).

[465] Sec. 6685.

[466] Treas. Reg. sec. 301.6104(d)-1(b)(4)(ii).

must have legal ownership and control of such assets following the contribution. If the sponsoring charity does not have such control (or permits a donor to exercise control over amounts contributed), the donor's contributions may not qualify for a charitable deduction, and, in the case of a community foundation, the contribution may be treated as being subject to a material restriction or condition by the donor.

In recent years, a number of financial institutions have formed charitable corporations for the principal purpose of offering donor advised funds, sometimes referred to as "commercial" donor advised funds. In addition, some established charities have begun operating donor advised funds in addition to their primary activities. The IRS has recognized several organizations that sponsor donor advised funds, including "commercial" donor advised funds, as section 501(c)(3) public charities. The term "donor advised fund" is not defined in statute or regulations.

Supporting organizations

The Code provides that certain "supporting organizations" (in general, organizations that provide support to another section 501(c)(3) organization that is not a private foundation) are classified as public charities rather than private foundations.[467] To qualify as a supporting organization, an organization must meet all three of the following tests: (1) it must be organized and at all times operated exclusively for the benefit of, to perform the functions of, or to carry out the purposes of one or more "publicly supported organizations"[468] (the "organizational and operational tests");[469] (2) it must be operated, supervised, or controlled by or in connection with one or more publicly supported organizations (the "relationship test");[470] and (3) it must not be controlled directly or indirectly by one or more disqualified persons (as defined in section 4946) other than foundation managers and other than one or more publicly supported organizations (the "lack of outside control test").[471]

To satisfy the relationship test, a supporting organization must hold one of three statutorily described close relationships with the supported organization. The organization must be: (1) operated, supervised, or controlled by a publicly supported organization (commonly referred to as "Type I" supporting organizations); (2) supervised or controlled in connection with a publicly supported organization ("Type II" supporting organizations); or (3) operated in connection with a publicly supported organization ("Type III" supporting organizations).[472]

Type I supporting organizations

In the case of supporting organizations that are operated, supervised, or controlled by one or more publicly supported organizations (Type I supporting organizations), one or more supported organizations must exercise a substantial degree of direction over the policies, programs, and activities of the supporting organization.[473] The relationship between the Type I supporting organization and the supported organization generally is comparable to that of a parent and subsidiary. The requisite relationship may be established by the fact that a majority of the officers, directors, or trustees of the supporting organization are appointed or elected by the governing body, members of the governing body, officers acting in their official capacity, or the membership of one or more publicly supported organizations.[474]

Type II supporting organizations

Type II supporting organizations are supervised or controlled in connection with one or more publicly supported organizations. Rather than the parent-subsidiary relationship characteristic of Type I organizations, the relationship between a Type II organization and its supported organizations is more analogous to a brother-sister relationship. In order to satisfy the Type II relationship requirement, generally there must be common supervision or control by the persons supervising or controlling both the supporting organization and the publicly supported organizations.[475] An organization generally is not considered to be "supervised or controlled in connection with" a publicly supported organization merely because the supporting organization makes payments to the publicly supported organization, even if the obligation to make payments is enforceable under state law.[476]

---

[467] Sec. 509(a)(3).

[468] In general, supported organizations of a supporting organization must be publicly supported charities described in sections 509(a)(1) or (a)(2).

[469] Sec. 509(a)(3)(A).

[470] Sec. 509(a)(3)(B).

[471] Sec. 509(a)(3)(C).

[472] Treas. Reg. sec. 1.509(a)-4(f)(2).

[473] Treas. Reg. sec. 1.509(a)-4(g)(1)(i).

[474] Id.

[475] Treas. Reg. sec. 1.509(a)- 4(h)(1).

[476] Treas. Reg. sec. 1.509(a)-4(h)(2).

Type III supporting organizations

Type III supporting organizations are "operated in connection with" one or more publicly supported organizations. To satisfy the "operated in connection with" relationship, Treasury regulations require that the supporting organization be responsive to, and significantly involved in the operations of, the publicly supported organization. This relationship is deemed to exist where the supporting organization meets both a "responsiveness test" and an "integral part test."[477] In general, the responsiveness test requires that the Type III supporting organization be responsive to the needs or demands of the publicly supported organizations. In general, the integral part test requires that the Type III supporting organization maintain significant involvement in the operations of one or more publicly supported organizations, and that such publicly supported organizations are in turn dependent upon the supporting organization for the type of support which it provides.

There are two alternative methods for satisfying the integral part test. The first alternative is to establish that (1) the activities engaged in for or on behalf of the publicly supported organization are activities to perform the functions of, or carry out the purposes of, such organizations; and (2) these activities, but for the involvement of the supporting organization, normally would be engaged in by the publicly supported organizations themselves.[478] Organizations that satisfy this "but for" test sometimes are referred to as "functionally integrated" Type III supporting organizations. The second method for satisfying the integral part test is to establish that: (1) the supporting organization pays substantially all of its income to or for the use of one or more publicly supported organizations;[479] (2) the amount of support received by one or more of the publicly supported organizations is sufficient to insure the attentiveness of the organization or organizations to the operations of the supporting organization (this is known as the "attentiveness requirement");[480] and (3) a significant amount of the total support of the supporting organization goes to those publicly supported organizations that meet the attentiveness requirement.[481]

Explanation of Provision

Elsewhere in the bill, provision is made for new rules with respect to donor advised funds and supporting organizations. Many issues arise under current law with respect to such organizations, some of which are addressed by the bill and some of which would benefit from additional study. The provision provides that the Secretary of the Treasury shall undertake a study on the organization and operation of donor advised funds (as defined in section 4966(d)(2)) and of supporting organizations (organizations described in section 509(a)(3)). The study shall specifically consider (1) whether the amount and availability of the income, gift, or estate tax charitable deductions allowed for charitable contributions to sponsoring organizations (as defined in section 4966(d)(1)) of donor advised funds or to organizations described in section 509(a)(3) is appropriate in consideration of (i) the use of contributed assets (including the type, extent, and timing of such use) or (ii) the use of the assets of such organizations for the benefit of the person making the charitable contribution (or a person related to such person), (2) whether donor advised funds should be required to distribute for charitable purposes a specified amount (whether based on the income or assets of the fund) in order to ensure that the sponsoring organization with respect to the fund is operating consistent with the purposes or functions constituting the basis for its exemption under section 501 or its status as an organization described in section 509(a), (3) whether the retention by donors to donor advised funds or supporting organizations of rights or privileges with respect to amounts transferred to such organizations (including advisory rights or privileges with respect to the making of grants or the investment of assets) is consistent with the treatment of such transfers as completed gifts that qualify for an income, gift, or estate tax charitable deduction, and (4) whether any of the issues addressed above also raise issues with respect to other forms of charities or charitable donations.

Not later than one year after the date of enactment of this Act, the Secretary shall submit a report on the study, comment on any actions

---

[477] Treas. Reg. sec. 1.509(a)-4(i)(1).

[478] Treas. Reg. sec. 1.509(a)-4(i)(3)(ii).

[479] For this purpose, the IRS has defined the term "substantially all" of an organization's income to mean 85 percent or more. Rev. Rul. 76-208, 1976-1 C.B. 161.

[480] Although the regulations do not specify the requisite level of support in numerical or percentage terms, the IRS has suggested that grants that represent less than 10 percent of the beneficiary's support likely would be viewed as insufficient to ensure attentiveness. Gen. Couns. Mem. 36379 (August 15, 1975). As an alternative to satisfying the attentiveness standard by the foregoing method, a supporting organization may demonstrate attentiveness by showing that, in order to avoid the interruption of the carrying on of a particular function or activity, the beneficiary organization will be sufficiently attentive to the operations of the supporting organization. Treas. Reg. sec. 1.509(a)-4(i)(3)(iii)(b).

[481] Treas. Reg. sec. 1.509(a)-4(i)(3)(iii).

(audits, guidance, regulations, etc.) taken by the Secretary with respect to the issues discussed in the study, and make recommendations to the Committee on Finance of the Senate and the Committee on Ways and Means of the House of Representatives.

Effective Date

The provision is effective on the date of enactment.

[Law at ¶ 7240. CCH Explanation at ¶ 1290.]

[¶ 11,350] Act Secs. 1231, 1232, 1233, 1234 and 1235. Improve accountability of donor advised funds

Joint Committee Taxation (J.C.T. Rep. No. JCX-38-06)

[Code Secs. 170(f), 508, 2055(e), 2522(c), 4943, 4958, 6033 and New Code Secs. 4966 and 4967]

Present Law

Requirements for section 501(c)(3) tax-exempt status

Charitable organizations, i.e., organizations described in section 501(c)(3), generally are exempt from Federal income tax and are eligible to receive tax deductible contributions. A charitable organization must operate primarily in pursuance of one or more tax-exempt purposes constituting the basis of its tax exemption.[482] In order to qualify as operating primarily for a purpose described in section 501(c)(3), an organization must satisfy the following operational requirements: (1) the net earnings of the organization may not inure to the benefit of any person in a position to influence the activities of the organization; (2) the organization must operate to provide a public benefit, not a private benefit;[483] (3) the organization may not be operated primarily to conduct an unrelated trade or business;[484] (4) the organization may not engage in substantial legislative lobbying; and (5) the organization may not participate or intervene in any political campaign.

Classification of section 501(c)(3) organizations

Section 501(c)(3) organizations are classified either as "public charities" or "private foundations."[485] Private foundations generally are defined under section 509(a) as all organizations described in section 501(c)(3) other than an organization granted public charity status by reason of: (1) being a specified type of organization (i.e., churches, educational institutions, hospitals and certain other medical organizations, certain organizations providing assistance to colleges and universities, or a governmental unit); (2) receiving a substantial part of its support from governmental units or direct or indirect contributions from the general public; or (3) providing support to another section 501(c)(3) entity that is not a private foundation. In contrast to public charities, private foundations generally are funded from a limited number of sources (e.g., an individual, family, or corporation). Donors to private foundations and persons related to such donors together often control the operations of private foundations.

Because private foundations receive support from, and typically are controlled by, a small number of supporters, private foundations are subject to a number of anti-abuse rules and excise taxes not applicable to public charities.[486] For example, the Code imposes excise taxes on acts of "self-dealing" between disqualified persons (generally, an enumerated class of foundation insiders[487]) and a private foundation. Acts of self-dealing include, for example, sales or exchanges, or leasing, of property; lending of money; or the furnishing of goods, services, or facilities between a disqualified person and a private foundation.[488] In addition, private non-

[482] Treas. Reg. sec. 1.501(c)(3)-1(c)(1). The Code specifies such purposes as religious, charitable, scientific, testing for public safety, literary, or educational purposes, or to foster international amateur sports competition, or for the prevention of cruelty to children or animals. In general, an organization is organized and operated for charitable purposes if it provides relief for the poor and distressed or the underprivileged. Treas. Reg. sec. 1.501(c)(3)-1(d)(2).

[483] Treas. Reg. sec. 1.501(c)(3)-1(d)(1)(ii).

[484] Treas. Reg. sec. 1.501(c)(3)-1(e)(1). Conducting a certain level of unrelated trade or business activity will not jeopardize tax-exempt status.

[485] Sec. 509(a). Private foundations are either private operating foundations or private nonoperating foundations. In general, private operating foundations operate their own charitable programs in contrast to private non-operating foundations, which generally are grant-making organizations. Most private foundations are non-operating foundations.

[486] Secs. 4940 - 4945.

[487] See sec. 4946(a).

[488] Sec. 4941.

operating foundations are required to pay out a minimum amount each year as qualifying distributions. In general, a qualifying distribution is an amount paid to accomplish one or more of the organization's exempt purposes, including reasonable and necessary administrative expenses.[489] Certain expenditures of private foundations are also subject to tax.[490] In general, taxable expenditures are expenditures: (1) for lobbying; (2) to influence the outcome of a public election or carry on a voter registration drive (unless certain requirements are met); (3) as a grant to an individual for travel, study, or similar purposes unless made pursuant to procedures approved by the Secretary; (4) as a grant to an organization that is not a public charity or exempt operating foundation unless the foundation exercises expenditure responsibility[491] with respect to the grant; or (5) for any non-charitable purpose. Additional excise taxes may also apply in the event a private foundation holds certain business interests ("excess business holdings")[492] or makes an investment that jeopardizes the foundation's exempt purposes.[493]

Supporting organizations

The Code provides that certain "supporting organizations" (in general, organizations that provide support to another section 501(c)(3) organization that is not a private foundation) are classified as public charities rather than private foundations.[494] To qualify as a supporting organization, an organization must meet all three of the following tests: (1) it must be organized and at all times operated exclusively for the benefit of, to perform the functions of, or to carry out the purposes of one or more "publicly supported organizations"[495] (the "organizational and operational tests");[496] (2) it must be operated, supervised, or controlled by or in connection with one or more publicly supported organizations (the "relationship test");[497] and (3) it must not be controlled directly or indirectly by one or more disqualified persons (as defined in section 4946) other than foundation managers and other than one or more publicly supported organizations (the "lack of outside control test").[498]

To satisfy the relationship test, a supporting organization must hold one of three statutorily described close relationships with the supported organization. The organization must be: (1) operated, supervised, or controlled by a publicly supported organization (commonly referred to as "Type I" supporting organizations); (2) supervised or controlled in connection with a publicly supported organization ("Type II" supporting organizations); or (3) operated in connection with a publicly supported organization ("Type III" supporting organizations).[499]

Type I supporting organizations

In the case of supporting organizations that are operated, supervised, or controlled by one or more publicly supported organizations (Type I supporting organizations), one or more supported organizations must exercise a substantial degree of direction over the policies, programs, and activities of the supporting organization.[500] The relationship between the Type I supporting organization and the supported organization generally is comparable to that of a parent and subsidiary. The requisite relationship may be established by the fact that a majority of the officers, directors, or trustees of the supporting organization are appointed or elected by the governing body, members of the governing body, officers acting in their official capacity, or the membership of one or more publicly supported organizations.[501]

Type II supporting organizations

Type II supporting organizations are supervised or controlled in connection with one or more publicly supported organizations. Rather than the parent-subsidiary relationship characteristic of Type I organizations, the relationship between a Type II organization and its supported organizations is more analogous to a brother-sister relationship. In order to satisfy the Type II

---

[489] Sec. 4942(g)(1)(A). A qualifying distribution also includes any amount paid to acquire an asset used (or held for use) directly in carrying out one or more of the organization's exempt purposes and certain amounts set-aside for exempt purposes. Sec. 4942(g)(1)(B) and 4942(g)(2).

[490] Sec. 4945. Taxes imposed may be abated if certain conditions are met. Secs. 4961 and 4962.

[491] In general, expenditure responsibility requires that a foundation make all reasonable efforts and establish reasonable procedures to ensure that the grant is spent solely for the purpose for which it was made, to obtain reports from the grantee on the expenditure of the grant, and to make reports to the Secretary regarding such expenditures. Sec. 4945(h).

[492] Sec. 4943.

[493] Sec. 4944.

[494] Sec. 509(a)(3).

[495] In general, supported organizations of a supporting organization must be publicly supported charities described in sections 509(a)(1) or (a)(2).

[496] Sec. 509(a)(3)(A).

[497] Sec. 509(a)(3)(B).

[498] Sec. 509(a)(3)(C).

[499] Treas. Reg. sec. 1.509(a)-4(f)(2).

[500] Treas. Reg. sec. 1.509(a)-4(g)(1)(i).

[501] Id.

relationship requirement, generally there must be common supervision or control by the persons supervising or controlling both the supporting organization and the publicly supported organizations.[502] An organization generally is not considered to be "supervised or controlled in connection with" a publicly supported organization merely because the supporting organization makes payments to the publicly supported organization, even if the obligation to make payments is enforceable under state law.[503]

Type III supporting organizations

Type III supporting organizations are "operated in connection with" one or more publicly supported organizations. To satisfy the "operated in connection with" relationship, Treasury regulations require that the supporting organization be responsive to, and significantly involved in the operations of, the publicly supported organization. This relationship is deemed to exist where the supporting organization meets both a "responsiveness test" and an "integral part test."[504] In general, the responsiveness test requires that the Type III supporting organization be responsive to the needs or demands of the publicly supported organizations. In general, the integral part test requires that the Type III supporting organization maintain significant involvement in the operations of one or more publicly supported organizations, and that such publicly supported organizations are in turn dependent upon the supporting organization for the type of support which it provides.

There are two alternative methods for satisfying the integral part test. The first alternative is to establish that (1) the activities engaged in for or on behalf of the publicly supported organization are activities to perform the functions of, or carry out the purposes of, such organizations; and (2) these activities, but for the involvement of the supporting organization, normally would be engaged in by the publicly supported organizations themselves.[505] Organizations that satisfy this "but for" test sometimes are referred to as "functionally integrated" Type III supporting organizations. The second method for satisfying the integral part test is to establish that: (1) the supporting organization pays substantially all of its income to or for the use of one or more publicly supported organizations;[506] (2) the amount of support received by one or more of the publicly supported organizations is sufficient to insure the attentiveness of the organization or organizations to the operations of the supporting organization (this is known as the "attentiveness requirement");[507] and (3) a significant amount of the total support of the supporting organization goes to those publicly supported organizations that meet the attentiveness requirement.[508]

Charitable contributions

Contributions to organizations described in section 501(c)(3) are deductible, subject to certain limitations, as an itemized deduction from Federal income taxes.[509] Such contributions also generally are deductible for estate and gift tax purposes.[510] However, if the taxpayer retains control over the assets transferred to charity, the transfer may not qualify as a completed gift for purposes of claiming an income, estate, or gift tax deduction.

Public charities enjoy certain advantages over private foundations regarding the deductibility of contributions. For example, contributions of appreciated capital gain property to a private foundation generally are deductible only to the extent of the donor's cost basis.[511] In contrast, contributions to public charities generally are deductible in an amount equal to the property's fair market value, except for gifts of inventory and other ordinary income property, short-term capital gain property, and tangible personal property the use of which is unrelated to the donee organization's exempt purpose. In addition, under present law, a taxpayer's deductible contributions generally are limited to specified percentages of the taxpayer's contribution base, which generally is the taxpayer's adjusted gross income for a taxable year. The applicable per-

---

[502] Treas. Reg. sec. 1.509(a)- 4(h)(1).

[503] Treas. Reg. sec. 1.509(a)-4(h)(2).

[504] Treas. Reg. sec. 1.509(a)-4(i)(1).

[505] Treas. Reg. sec. 1.509(a)-4(i)(3)(ii).

[506] For this purpose, the IRS has defined the term "substantially all" of an organization's income to mean 85 percent or more. Rev. Rul. 76-208, 1976-1 C.B. 161.

[507] Although the regulations do not specify the requisite level of support in numerical or percentage terms, the IRS has suggested that grants that represent less than 10 percent of the beneficiary's support likely would be viewed as insufficient to ensure attentiveness. Gen. Couns. Mem. 36379 (August 15, 1975). As an alternative to satisfying the attentiveness standard by the foregoing method, a supporting organization may demonstrate attentiveness by showing that, in order to avoid the interruption of the carrying on of a particular function or activity, the beneficiary organization will be sufficiently attentive to the operations of the supporting organization. Treas. Reg. sec. 1.509(a)-4(i)(3)(iii)(b).

[508] Treas. Reg. sec. 1.509(a)-4(i)(3)(iii).

[509] Sec. 170.

[510] Secs. 2055 and 2522.

[511] A special rule in section 170(e)(5) provides that taxpayer are allowed a deduction equal to the fair market value of certain contributions of appreciated, publicly traded stock contributed to a private foundation.

centage limitations vary depending upon the type of property contributed and the classification of the donee organization. In general, contributions to non-operating private foundations are limited to a smaller percentage of the donor's contribution base (up to 30 percent) than contributions to public charities (up to 50 percent).[512]

In general, taxpayers who make contributions and claim a charitable deduction must satisfy recordkeeping and substantiation requirements.[513] The requirements vary depending on the type and value of property contributed. A deduction generally may be denied if the donor fails to satisfy applicable recordkeeping or substantiation requirements.

Intermediate sanctions (excess benefit transaction tax)

The Code imposes excise taxes on excess benefit transactions between disqualified persons and public charities.[514] An excess benefit transaction generally is a transaction in which an economic benefit is provided by a public charity directly or indirectly to or for the use of a disqualified person, if the value of the economic benefit provided exceeds the value of the consideration (including the performance of services) received for providing such benefit.

For purposes of the excess benefit transaction rules, a disqualified person is any person in a position to exercise substantial influence over the affairs of the public charity at any time in the five-year period ending on the date of the transaction at issue.[515] Persons holding certain powers, responsibilities, or interests (e.g., officers, directors, or trustees) are considered to be in a position to exercise substantial influence over the affairs of the public charity.

An excess benefit transaction tax is imposed on the disqualified person and, in certain cases, on the organization managers, but is not imposed on the public charity. An initial tax of 25 percent of the excess benefit amount is imposed on the disqualified person that receives the excess benefit. An additional tax on the disqualified person of 200 percent of the excess benefit applies if the violation is not corrected within a specified period. A tax of 10 percent of the excess benefit (not to exceed $10,000 with respect to any excess benefit transaction) is imposed on an organization manager that knowingly participated in the excess benefit transaction, if the manager's participation was willful and not due to reasonable cause, and if the initial tax was imposed on the disqualified person.

Community foundations

Community foundations generally are broadly supported section 501(c)(3) public charities that make grants to other charitable organizations located within a community foundation's particular geographic area. Donors sometimes make contributions to a community foundation through transfers to a separate trust or fund, the assets of which are held and managed by a bank or investment company.

Certain community foundations are subject to special rules that permit them to treat the separate funds or trusts maintained by the community foundation as a single entity for tax purposes. This "single entity" status allows the community foundation to be classified as a public charity. One of the requirements that community foundations must meet is that funds maintained by the community foundation may not be subject by the donor to any material restrictions or conditions. The prohibition against material restrictions or conditions is designed to prevent a donor from encumbering a fund in a manner that prevents the community foundation from freely distributing the assets and income from it in furtherance of the community foundation's charitable purposes. Under Treasury regulations, whether a particular restriction or condition placed by the donor on the transfer of assets is material must be determined from all of the facts and circumstances of the transfer. The regulations set out some of the more significant facts and circumstances to be considered in making a determination, including: (1) whether the transferee public charity is the fee owner of the assets received; (2) whether the assets are held and administered by the public charity in a manner consistent with its own exempt purposes; (3) whether the governing body of the public charity has the ultimate authority and control over the assets and the income derived from them; and (4) whether the governing body of the public charity is independent from the donor. The regulations provide several non-adverse factors for determining whether a particular restriction or condition placed by the donor on the transfer of assets is material. In addition, the regulations

---

[512] Sec. 170(b).

[513] Sec. 170(f)(8).

[514] Sec. 4958. The excess benefit transaction tax is commonly referred to as "intermediate sanctions," because it imposes penalties generally considered to be less punitive than revocation of the organization's exempt status. The tax also applies to transactions between disqualified persons and social welfare organizations (as described in section 501(c)(4)).

[515] Sec. 4958(f)(1). A disqualified person also includes certain family members of such a person, and certain entities that satisfy a control test with respect to such persons.

list numerous factors and subfactors that indicate that the community foundation is prevented from freely and effectively employing the donated assets and the income thereon.

Donor advised funds

Some charitable organizations (including community foundations) establish accounts to which donors may contribute and thereafter provide nonbinding advice or recommendations with regard to distributions from the fund or the investment of assets in the fund. Such accounts are commonly referred to as "donor advised funds." Donors who make contributions to charities for maintenance in a donor advised fund generally claim a charitable contribution deduction at the time of the contribution. Although sponsoring charities frequently permit donors (or other persons appointed by donors) to provide nonbinding recommendations concerning the distribution or investment of assets in a donor advised fund, sponsoring charities generally must have legal ownership and control of such assets following the contribution. If the sponsoring charity does not have such control (or permits a donor to exercise control over amounts contributed), the donor's contributions may not qualify for a charitable deduction, and, in the case of a community foundation, the contribution may be treated as being subject to a material restriction or condition by the donor.

In recent years, a number of financial institutions have formed charitable corporations for the principal purpose of offering donor advised funds, sometimes referred to as "commercial" donor advised funds. In addition, some established charities have begun operating donor advised funds in addition to their primary activities. The IRS has recognized several organizations that sponsor donor advised funds, including "commercial" donor advised funds, as section 501(c)(3) public charities. The term "donor advised fund" is not defined in statute or regulations.

Under the Katrina Emergency Tax Relief Act of 2005, certain of the above-described percent limitations on contributions to public charities are temporarily suspended for purposes of certain "qualified contributions" to public charities. Under the Act, qualified contributions do not include a contribution if the contribution is for establishment of a new, or maintenance in an existing, segregated fund or account with respect to which the donor (or any person appointed or designated by such donor) has, or reasonably expects to have, advisory privileges with respect to distributions or investments by reason of the donor's status as a donor.

Excess business holdings of private foundations

Private foundations are subject to tax on excess business holdings.[516] In general, a private foundation is permitted to hold 20 percent of the voting stock in a corporation, reduced by the amount of voting stock held by all disqualified persons (as defined in section 4946). If it is established that no disqualified person has effective control of the corporation, a private foundation and disqualified persons together may own up to 35 percent of the voting stock of a corporation. A private foundation shall not be treated as having excess business holdings in any corporation if it owns (together with certain other related private foundations) not more than two percent of the voting stock and not more than two percent in value of all outstanding shares of all classes of stock in that corporation. Similar rules apply with respect to holdings in a partnership ("profits interest" is substituted for "voting stock" and "capital interest" for "nonvoting stock") and to other unincorporated enterprises (by substituting "beneficial interest" for "voting stock"). Private foundations are not permitted to have holdings in a proprietorship. Foundations generally have a five-year period to dispose of excess business holdings (acquired other than by purchase) without being subject to tax.[517] This five-year period may be extended an additional five years in limited circumstances.[518] The excess business holdings rules do not apply to holdings in a functionally related business or to holdings in a trade or business at least 95 percent of the gross income of which is derived from passive sources.[519]

The initial tax is equal to five percent of the value of the excess business holdings held during the foundation's applicable taxable year. An additional tax is imposed if an initial tax is imposed and at the close of the applicable taxable period, the foundation continues to hold excess business holdings. The amount of the additional tax is equal to 200 percent of such holdings.

---

[516] Sec. 4943. Taxes imposed may be abated if certain conditions are met. Secs. 4961 and 4962.

[517] Sec. 4943(c)(6).

[518] Sec. 4943(c)(7).

[519] Sec. 4943(d)(3).

Explanation of Provision

Definition of a donor advised fund

General rule

In general, the provision defines a "donor advised fund" as a fund or account that is: (1) separately identified by reference to contributions of a donor or donors (2) owned and controlled by a sponsoring organization and (3) with respect to which a donor (or any person appointed or designated by such donor (a "donor advisor") has, or reasonably expects to have, advisory privileges with respect to the distribution or investment of amounts held in the separately identified fund or account by reason of the donor's status as a donor. All three prongs of the definition must be met in order for a fund or account to be treated as a donor advised fund.

The provision defines a "sponsoring organization" as an organization that: (1) is described in section 170(c)[520] (other than a governmental entity described in section 170(c)(1), and without regard to any requirement that the organization be organized in the United States[521]); (2) is not a private foundation (as defined in section 509(a)); and (3) maintains one or more donor advised funds.

The first prong of the definition requires that a donor advised fund be separately identified by reference to contributions of a donor or donors. A distinct fund or account of a sponsoring organization does not meet this prong of the definition unless the fund or account refers to contributions of a donor or donors, such as by naming the fund after a donor, or by treating a fund on the books of the sponsoring organization as attributable to funds contributed by a specific donor or donors. Although a sponsoring organization's general fund is a "fund or account," such fund will not, as a general matter, be treated as a donor advised fund because the general funds of an organization typically are not separately identified by reference to contributions of a specific donor or donors; rather contributions are pooled anonymously within the general fund. Similarly, a fund or account of a sponsoring organization that is distinct from the organization's general fund and that pools contributions of multiple donors generally will not meet the first prong of the definition unless the contributions of specific donors are in some manner tracked and accounted for within the fund. Accordingly, if a sponsoring organization establishes a fund dedicated to the relief of poverty within a specific community, or a scholarship fund, and the fund attracts contributions from several donors but does not separately identify or refer to contributions of a donor or donors, the fund is not a donor advised fund even if a donor has advisory privileges with respect to the fund. However, a fund or account may not avoid treatment as a donor advised fund even though there is no formal recognition of such separate contributions on the books of the sponsoring organization if the fund or account operates as if contributions of a donor or donors are separately identified. The Secretary has the authority to look to the substance of an arrangement, and not merely its form. In addition, a fund or account may be treated as identified by reference to contributions of a donor or donors if the reference is to persons related to a donor. For example, if a husband made contributions to a fund or account that in turn is named after the husband's wife, the fund is treated as being separately identified by reference to contributions of a donor.

The second prong of the definition provides that the fund be owned and controlled by a sponsoring organization. To the extent that a donor or person other than the sponsoring organization owns or controls amounts deposited to a sponsoring organization, a fund or account is not a donor advised fund. (In cases where a donor retains control of an amount provided to a sponsoring organization, there may not be a completed gift for purposes of the charitable contribution deduction.)

The third prong of the definition provides that with respect to a fund or account of a sponsoring organization, a donor or donor advisor has or reasonably expects to have advisory privileges with respect to the distribution or investment of amounts held in the fund or account by reason of a donor's status as a donor. Advisory privileges are distinct from a legal right or obligation. For example, if a donor executes a gift agreement with a sponsoring organization that specifies certain enforceable rights of the donor with respect to a gift, the donor will not be treated as having "advisory privileges" due to such enforceable rights for purposes of the donor advised fund definition.

The presence of an advisory privilege may be evident through a written document that describes an arrangement between the donor or

[520] Section 170(c) describes organizations to which charitable contributions that are deductible for income tax purposes can be made.

[521] See sec. 170(c)(2)(A).

donor adviser and the sponsoring organization whereby a donor or donor advisor may provide advice to the sponsoring organization about the investment or distribution of amounts held by a sponsoring organization, even if such privileges are not exercised. The presence of an advisory privilege also may be evident through the conduct of a donor or donor advisor and the sponsoring organization. For example, even in the absence of a writing, if a donor regularly provides advice to a sponsoring organization and the sponsoring organization regularly considers such advice, the donor has advisory privileges under the provision. Even if advisory privileges do not exist at the time of a contribution, later acts by the donor (through the provision of advice) and by the sponsoring organization (through the regular consideration of advice) may establish advisory privileges subsequent to the time of the contribution. For example, if a past donor of $100,000 telephones a sponsoring organization and states that he would like the sponsoring organization to distribute $10,000 to an organization described in section 170(b)(1)(A), although the mere act of providing advice does not establish an advisory privilege, if the sponsoring organization distributed the $10,000 to the organization specified by the donor in consideration of the donor's advice, and reinforced the donor in some manner that future advice similarly would be considered, advisory privileges (or the reasonable expectation thereof) might be established. However, the mere provision of advice by a donor or donor advisor does not mean the donor or donor advisor has advisory privileges. For example, a donor's singular belief that he or she has advisory privileges with respect to the contribution does not establish an advisory privilege – there must be some reciprocity on the part of the sponsoring organization.

A person reasonably expects to have advisory privileges if both the donor or donor advisor and the sponsoring organization have reason to believe that the donor or donor advisor will provide advice and that the sponsoring organization generally will consider it. Thus, a person reasonably may expect to have advisory privileges even in the absence of the actual provision of advice. However, a donor's expectation of advisory privileges is not reasonable unless it is reinforced in some manner by the conduct of the sponsoring organization. If, at the time of the contribution, the sponsoring organization had no knowledge that the donor had an expectation of advisory privileges, or no intention of considering any advice provided by the donor, then the donor does not have a reasonable expectation of advisory privileges. Ultimately, the presence or absence of advisory privileges (or a reasonable expectation thereof) depends upon the facts and circumstances, which in turn depend upon the conduct (including any agreement) of both the donor or donor advisor and the sponsoring organization with respect to the making and consideration of advice.

A further requirement of the third prong is that the reasonable expectation of advisory privileges is by reason of the donor's status as a donor. Under this requirement, if a donor's reasonable expectation of advisory privileges is due solely to the donor's service to the organization, for example, by reason of the donor's position as an officer, employee, or director of the sponsoring organization, then the third prong of the definition is not satisfied. For instance, in general, a donor that is a member of the board of directors of the sponsoring organization may provide advice in his or her capacity as a board member with respect to the distribution or investment of amounts in a fund to which the board member contributed. However, if by reason of such donor's contribution to such fund, the donor secured an appointment on a committee of the sponsoring organization that advises how to distribute or invest amounts in such fund, the donor may have a reasonable expectation of advisory privileges, notwithstanding that the donor is an officer, employee, or director of the sponsoring organization.

The third prong of the definition is applicable to a donor or any person appointed or designated by such donor (the donor advisor). For purposes of this prong, a person appointed or designated by a donor advisor is treated as being appointed or designated by a donor. In addition, for purposes of any exception to the definition of a donor advised fund provided under the provision, to the extent a donor recommends to a sponsoring organization the selection of members of a committee that will advise as to distributions or investments of amounts in a fund or account of such sponsoring organization, such members are not treated as appointed or designated by the donor if the recommendation of such members by such donor is based on objective criteria related to the expertise of the member. For example, if a donor recommends that a committee of a sponsoring organization that will provide advice regarding scholarship grants for the advancement of science at local secondary schools should consist of persons who are the heads of the science departments of such schools, then the donor generally would not be considered to have appointed or designated such persons, i.e., they would not be treated as donor advisors.

Exceptions

A donor advised fund does not include a fund or account that makes distributions only to a single identified organization or governmental entity. For example, an endowment fund owned and controlled by a sponsoring organization that is held exclusively to for the benefit of such sponsoring organization is not a donor advised fund even if the fund is named after its principal donor and such donor has advisory privileges with respect to the distribution of amounts held in the fund to such sponsoring organization. Accordingly, a donor that contributes to a university for purposes of establishing a fund named after the donor that exclusively supports the activities of the university is not a donor advised fund even if the donor has advisory privileges regarding the distribution or investment of amounts in the fund.

A donor advised fund also does not include a fund or account with respect to which a donor or donor advisor provides advice as to which individuals receive grants for travel, study, or other similar purposes, provided that (1) the donor's or donor advisor's advisory privileges are performed exclusively by such donor or donor advisor in such person's capacity as a member of a committee all of the members of which are appointed by the sponsoring organization, (2) no combination of a donor or donor advisor or persons related to such persons, control, directly or indirectly, such committee, and (3) all grants from such fund or account are awarded on an objective and nondiscriminatory basis pursuant to a procedure approved in advance by the board of directors of the sponsoring organization, and such procedure is designed to ensure that all such grants meet the requirements described in paragraphs (1), (2), or (3) of section 4945(g) (concerning grants to individuals by private foundations).

In addition, the Secretary may exempt a fund or account from treatment as a donor advised fund if such fund or account is advised by a committee not directly or indirectly controlled by a donor, donor advisor, or persons related to a donor or donor advisor. For such purposes, it is intended that indirect control includes the ability to exercise effective control. For example, if a donor, a donor advisor, and an attorney hired by the donor to provide advice regarding the donor's contributions constitute three of the five members of such a committee, the committee would be treated as being controlled indirectly by the donor for purposes of such an exception. Board membership alone does not establish direct or indirect control. In general, under this authority, the Secretary may establish rules regarding committee advised funds generally that, if followed, would result in the fund not being treated as a donor advised fund. The Secretary also may establish rules excepting certain types of committee-advised funds, such as a fund established exclusively for disaster relief, from the donor advised fund definition.

The provision also provides that the Secretary may exempt a fund or account from treatment as a donor advised fund if such fund or account benefits a single identified charitable purpose.

Deductibility of contributions to a sponsoring organization for maintenance in a donor advised fund

Contributions to certain sponsoring organizations for maintenance in a donor advised fund not eligible for a charitable deduction

Under the provision, contributions to a sponsoring organization for maintenance in a donor advised fund are not eligible for a charitable deduction for income tax purposes if the sponsoring organization is a veterans' organization described in section 170(c)(3), a fraternal society described in section 170(c)(4), or a cemetery company described in section 170(c)(5); for gift tax purposes if the sponsoring organization is a fraternal society described in section 2522(a)(3) or a veterans' organization described in section 2522(a)(4); or for estate tax purposes if the sponsoring organization is a fraternal society described in section 2055(a)(3) or a veterans' organization described in section 2055(a)(4). In addition, contributions to a sponsoring organization for maintenance in a donor advised fund are not eligible for a charitable deduction for income, gift, or estate tax purposes if the sponsoring organization is a Type III supporting organization (other than a functionally integrated Type III supporting organization). A functionally integrated Type III supporting organization is a Type III supporting organization that is not required under regulations established by the Secretary to make payments to supported organizations due to the activities of the organization related to performing the functions of, or carrying out the purposes of, such supported organizations.[522]

Additional substantiation requirements

In addition to satisfying present-law substantiation requirements under section 170(f), a donor must obtain, with respect to each charitable contribution to a sponsoring organization to be maintained in a donor advised fund, a contemporaneous written acknowledgment from the sponsoring organization providing that the sponsoring organization has exclusive legal control over the assets contributed.

Excess business holdings

The excess business holdings rules of section 4943 are applied to donor advised funds. In applying such rules, the term disqualified person means, with respect to a donor advised fund, a donor, donor advisor, a member of the family of a donor or donor advisor, or a 35 percent controlled entity of any such person. Transition rules apply to the present holdings of a donor advised fund similar to those of section 4943(c)(4)-(6).

Automatic excess benefit transactions, disqualified persons, taxable distributions, and more than incidental benefit

Automatic excess benefit transactions

Under the provision, any grant, loan, compensation, or other similar payment from a donor advised fund to a person that with respect to such fund is a donor, donor advisor, or a person related[523] to a donor or donor advisor automatically is treated as an excess benefit transaction under section 4958, with the entire amount[524] paid to any such person treated as the amount of the excess benefit. Other similar payments include payments in the nature of a grant, loan, or payment of compensation, such as an expense reimbursement. Other similar payments do not include, for example, a payment pursuant to bona fide sale or lease of property, which instead are subject to the general rules of section 4958 under the special disqualified person rule of the provision described below. Also as described below, payment by a sponsoring organization of, for example, compensation to a person who both is a donor with respect to a donor advised fund of the sponsoring organization and a service provider with respect to the sponsoring organization generally, will not be subject to the automatic excess benefit transaction rule of the provision unless the payment (of a grant, loan, compensation, or other similar payment) properly is viewed as a payment from the donor advised fund and not from the sponsoring organization.

Any amount repaid as a result of correcting an excess benefit transaction shall not be held in any donor advised fund.

Disqualified persons

In general, the provision provides that donors and donor advisors with respect to a donor advised fund (as well as persons related to a donor or donor advisor) are treated as disqualified persons under section 4958 with respect to transactions with such donor advised fund (though not necessarily with respect to transactions with the sponsoring organization more generally). For example, if a donor to a donor advised fund purchased securities from the fund, the purchase is subject to the rules of section 4958 because, under the provision, the donor is a disqualified person with respect to the fund. Thus, if as a result of the purchase, the donor receives an excess benefit as defined under generally applicable section 4958 rules, then the donor is subject to tax under such rules. If, as generally would be the case, the purchase was of securities that were contributed by the donor, a factor that may indicate the presence of an excess benefit is if the amount paid by the donor to acquire the securities is less than the amount the donor claimed the securities were worth for purposes of any charitable contribution deduction of the donor. In addition, if a donor advised fund distributes securities to the sponsoring organization of the fund prior to purchase by the donor, consideration should be given to whether the distribution to the sponsoring organization prior to the purchase was intended to circumvent the disqualified person rule of the provision. If so, such a distribution may be disregarded with the result that the purchase is treated as being made from the donor advised fund and not from the sponsoring organization.

As a factual matter, a person who is a donor to a donor advised fund and thus a disqualified

[522] The current such regulation is Treasury regulation section 1.509(a)-4(i)(3)(ii).

[523] For purposes of the provision, a person is treated as related to another person if (1) such person bears a relationship to such other person similar to the relationships described in sections 4958(f)(1)(B) and 4958(f)(1)(C).

[524] The requirement of the provision that the entire amount of the payment be treated as the amount of the excess benefit differs from the generally applicable rule of section 4958, which provides that the excess benefit is the amount by which the value of the economic benefit provided exceeds the value of the consideration received.

person with respect to the fund also may be a service provider with respect to the sponsoring organization. In general, under the provision, as under present law, the sponsoring organization's transactions with the service provider are not subject to the rules of section 4958 unless the service provider is a disqualified person with respect to the sponsoring organization (e.g., if the service provider serves on the board of directors of the sponsoring organization), or unless the transaction is not properly viewed as a transaction with the sponsoring organization but in substance is a transaction with the service provider's donor advised fund. If the transaction properly is viewed as a transaction with the donor advised fund of a sponsoring organization, then the transaction is subject to the rules of section 4958, and, as described above, if the transaction involves payment of a grant, loan, compensation, or other similar payment, then the transaction is subject to the special automatic excess benefit transaction rule of the provision. For example, if a sponsoring organization pays an amount as part of a service contract to a service provider (a bank, for example) who also is a donor to a donor advised fund of the sponsoring organization, and such amounts reasonably are charged uniformly in whole or in part as routine fees to all of the sponsoring organization's donor advised funds, the transaction generally is considered to be between the sponsoring organization and the service provider in such service provider's capacity as a service provider. The transaction is not considered to be a transaction between a donor advised fund and the service provider even though an amount paid under the contract was charged to a donor advised fund of the service provider.

The provision provides that an investment advisor (as well as persons related to the investment advisor) is treated as a disqualified person under section 4958 with respect to the sponsoring organization. Under the provision, the term "investment advisor" means, with respect to any sponsoring organization, any person (other than an employee of the sponsoring organization) compensated by the sponsoring organization for managing the investment of, or providing investment advice with respect to, assets maintained in donor advised funds (including pools of assets all or part of which are attributed to donor advised funds) owned by the sponsoring organization.

Taxable distributions

Under the provision, certain distributions from a donor advised fund are subject to tax. A "taxable distribution" is any distribution from a donor advised fund to (1) any natural person;[525] (2) to any other person for any purpose other than one specified in section 170(c)(2)(B) (generally, a charitable purpose) or, if for a charitable purpose, the sponsoring organization does not exercise expenditure responsibility with respect to the distribution in accordance with section 4945(h). The expenditure responsibility rules generally require that an organization exert all reasonable efforts and establish adequate procedures to see that the distribution is spent solely for the purposes for which made, to obtain full and complete reports from the distributee on how the funds are spent, and to make full and detailed reports with respect to such expenditures to the Secretary. A taxable distribution does not in any case include a distribution to (1) an organization described in section 170(b)(1)(A)[526] (other than to a disqualified supporting organization); (2) the sponsoring organization of such donor advised fund; or (3) to another donor advised fund.[527]

In the event of a taxable distribution, an excise tax equal to 20 percent of the amount of the distribution is imposed against the sponsor-

[525] Under the provision, the term disqualified supporting organization means, with respect to any distribution from a donor advised fund: (1) a Type III supporting organization, other than a functionally integrated Type III supporting organization; and (2) any other supporting organization if either (a) the donor or donor advisor of the distributing donor advised fund directly or indirectly controls a supported organization of the supporting organization, or (b) the Secretary determines by regulations that a distribution to such supporting organization otherwise is inappropriate.

[526] For purposes of the requirement that a distribution be "to" an organization described in section 170(b)(1)(A), in general, it is intended that rules similar to the rules of Treasury regulation section 53.4945-5(a)(5) apply. Under such regulations, for purposes of determining whether a grant by a private foundation is "to" an organization described in section 509(a)(1), (2), or (3) and so not a taxable expenditure under section 4945, a foreign organization that otherwise is not a section 509(a)(1), (2), or (3) organization is considered as such if the private foundation makes a good faith determination that the grantee is such an organization. Similarly, under the provision, if a sponsoring organization makes a good faith determination (under standards similar to those currently applicable for private foundations) that a distributee organization is an organization described in section 170(b)(1)(A) (other than a disqualified supporting organization), then a distribution to such organization is not considered a taxable distribution.

[527] Under the provision, sponsoring organizations may make grants to natural persons from amounts not held in donor advised funds and may establish scholarship funds that are not donor advised funds. A donor may choose to make a contribution directly to such a scholarship fund (or advise that a donor advised fund make a distribution to such a scholarship fund).

ing organization. In addition, an excise tax equal to five percent of the amount of the distribution is imposed against any manager of the sponsoring organization (defined in a manner similar to the term "foundation manager" under section 4945) who knowingly approved the distribution, not to exceed $10,000 with respect to any one taxable distribution. The taxes on taxable distributions are subject to abatement under generally applicable present law rules.

More than incidental benefit

Under the provision, if a donor, a donor advisor, or a person related to a donor or donor advisor of a donor advised fund provides advice as to a distribution that results in any such person receiving, directly or indirectly, a more than incidental benefit, an excise tax equal to 125 percent of the amount of such benefit is imposed against the person who advised as to the distribution, and against the recipient of the benefit. Persons subject to the tax are jointly and severally liable for the tax. In addition, if a manager of the sponsoring organization (defined in a manner similar to the term "foundation manager" under section 4945) agreed to the making of the distribution, knowing that the distribution would confer a more than incidental benefit on a donor, a donor advisor, or a person related to a donor or donor advisor, the manager is subject to an excise tax equal to 10 percent of the amount of such benefit, not to exceed $10,000. The taxes on more than incidental benefit are subject to abatement under generally applicable present law rules.

In general, under the provision, there is a more than incidental benefit if, as a result of a distribution from a donor advised fund, a donor, donor advisor, or related person with respect to such fund receives a benefit that would have reduced (or eliminated) a charitable contribution deduction if the benefit was received as part of the contribution to the sponsoring organization. If, for example, a donor advises a that a distribution from the donor's donor advised fund be made to the Girl Scouts of America, and the donor's daughter is a member of a local unit of the Girl Scouts of America, the indirect benefit the donor receives as a result of such contribution is considered incidental under the provision, as it generally would not have reduced or eliminated the donor's deduction if it had been received as part of a contribution by donor to the sponsoring organization.[528]

Reporting and disclosure

The provision requires each sponsoring organization to disclose on its information return: (1) the total number of donor advised funds it owns; (2) the aggregate value of assets held in those funds at the end of the organization's taxable year; and (3) the aggregate contributions to and grants made from those funds during the year.

In addition, when seeking recognition of its tax-exempt status, a sponsoring organization must disclose whether it intends to maintain donor advised funds. It is intended that the organization must provide information regarding its planned operation of such funds, including, for example, a description of procedures it intends to use to: (1) communicate to donors and donor advisors that assets held in donor advised funds are the property of the sponsoring organization; and (2) ensure that distributions from donor advised funds do not result in more than incidental benefit to any person.

Effective Date

The provision generally is effective for taxable years beginning after the date of enactment. The provision relating to excess benefit transactions is effective for transactions occurring after the date of enactment. Information return requirements are effective for taxable years ending after the date of enactment. The requirements concerning disclosures on an organization's application for tax exemption are effective for organizations applying for recognition of exempt status after the date of enactment. Requirements relating to charitable contributions to donor advised funds are effective for contributions made after 180 days from the date of enactment.

[Law at ¶5020, ¶5150, ¶5205, ¶5210, ¶5260, ¶5275, ¶5280, ¶5285, ¶5290 and ¶5325. CCH Explanation at ¶1160, ¶1165, ¶1170, ¶1175, ¶1180 and ¶1265.]

[528] See, e.g., Rev. Rul. 80-77, 1980-1 C.B. 56; Rev. Proc. 90-12, 1990-1 C.B. 471.

[¶11,360] Act Secs. 1241, 1242, 1243, 1244 and 1245. Improve accountability of supporting organizations

Joint Committee Taxation (J.C.T. REP. NO. JCX-38-06)

[Code Secs. 509, 4942, 4943, 4945, 4958 and 6033]

Present Law

Requirements for section 501(c)(3) tax-exempt status

Charitable organizations, i.e., organizations described in section 501(c)(3), generally are exempt from Federal income tax and are eligible to receive tax deductible contributions. A charitable organization must operate primarily in pursuance of one or more tax-exempt purposes constituting the basis of its tax exemption.[529] In order to qualify as operating primarily for a purpose described in section 501(c)(3), an organization must satisfy the following operational requirements: (1) the net earnings of the organization may not inure to the benefit of any person in a position to influence the activities of the organization; (2) the organization must operate to provide a public benefit, not a private benefit;[530] (3) the organization may not be operated primarily to conduct an unrelated trade or business;[531] (4) the organization may not engage in substantial legislative lobbying; and (5) the organization may not participate or intervene in any political campaign.

Section 501(c)(3) organizations (with certain exceptions) are required to seek formal recognition of tax-exempt status by filing an application with the IRS (Form 1023). In response to the application, the IRS issues a determination letter or ruling either recognizing the applicant as tax-exempt or not.

In general, organizations exempt from Federal income tax under section 501(a) are required to file an annual information return with the IRS.[532] Under present law, the information return requirement does not apply to several categories of exempt organizations. Organizations exempt from the filing requirement include organizations (other than private foundations), the gross receipts of which in each taxable year normally are not more than $25,000.[533]

Classification of section 501(c)(3) organizations

In general

Section 501(c)(3) organizations are classified either as "public charities" or "private foundations."[534] Private foundations generally are defined under section 509(a) as all organizations described in section 501(c)(3) other than an organization granted public charity status by reason of: (1) being a specified type of organization (i.e., churches, educational institutions, hospitals and certain other medical organizations, certain organizations providing assistance to colleges and universities, or a governmental unit); (2) receiving a substantial part of its support from governmental units or direct or indirect contributions from the general public; or (3) providing support to another section 501(c)(3) entity that is not a private foundation. In contrast to public charities, private foundations generally are funded from a limited number of sources (e.g., an individual, family, or corporation). Donors to private foundations and persons related to such donors together often control the operations of private foundations.

Because private foundations receive support from, and typically are controlled by, a small

---

[529] Treas. Reg. sec. 1.501(c)(3)-1(c)(1). The Code specifies such purposes as religious, charitable, scientific, testing for public safety, literary, or educational purposes, or to foster international amateur sports competition, or for the prevention of cruelty to children or animals. In general, an organization is organized and operated for charitable purposes if it provides relief for the poor and distressed or the underprivileged. Treas. Reg. sec. 1.501(c)(3)-1(d)(2).

[530] Treas. Reg. sec. 1.501(c)(3)-1(d)(1)(ii).

[531] Treas. Reg. sec. 1.501(c)(3)-1(e)(1). Conducting a certain level of unrelated trade or business activity will not jeopardize tax-exempt status.

[532] Sec. 6033(a)(1).

[533] Sec. 6033(a)(2); Treas. Reg. sec. 1.6033-2(a)(2)(i); Treas. Reg. sec. 1.6033-2(g)(1). Sec. 6033(a)(2)(A)(ii) provides a $5,000 annual gross receipts exception from the annual reporting requirements for certain exempt organizations. In Announcement 82-88, 1982-25 I.R.B. 23, the IRS exercised its discretionary authority under section 6033 to increase the gross receipts exception to $25,000, and enlarge the category of exempt organizations that are not required to file Form 990.

[534] Sec. 509(a). Private foundations are either private operating foundations or private nonoperating foundations. In general, private operating foundations operate their own charitable programs in contrast to private non-operating foundations, which generally are grant-making organizations. Most private foundations are non-operating foundations.

number of supporters, private foundations are subject to a number of anti-abuse rules and excise taxes not applicable to public charities.[535] For example, the Code imposes excise taxes on acts of "self-dealing" between disqualified persons (generally, an enumerated class of foundation insiders[536]) and a private foundation. Acts of self-dealing include, for example, sales or exchanges, or leasing, of property; lending of money; or the furnishing of goods, services, or facilities between a disqualified person and a private foundation.[537] In addition, private non-operating foundations are required to pay out a minimum amount each year as qualifying distributions. In general, a qualifying distribution is an amount paid to accomplish one or more of the organization's exempt purposes, including reasonable and necessary administrative expenses.[538] Certain expenditures of private foundations are also subject to tax.[539] In general, taxable expenditures are expenditures: (1) for lobbying; (2) to influence the outcome of a public election or carry on a voter registration drive (unless certain requirements are met); (3) as a grant to an individual for travel, study, or similar purposes unless made pursuant to procedures approved by the Secretary; (4) as a grant to an organization that is not a public charity or exempt operating foundation unless the foundation exercises expenditure responsibility[540] with respect to the grant; or (5) for any non-charitable purpose. Additional excise taxes may apply in the event a private foundation holds certain business interests ("excess business holdings")[541] or makes an investment that jeopardizes the foundation's exempt purposes.[542]

Public charities also enjoy certain advantages over private foundations regarding the deductibility of contributions. For example, contributions of appreciated capital gain property to a private foundation generally are deductible only to the extent of the donor's cost basis.[543] In contrast, contributions to public charities generally are deductible in an amount equal to the property's fair market value, except for gifts of inventory and other ordinary income property, short-term capital gain property, and tangible personal property the use of which is unrelated to the donee organization's exempt purpose. In addition, under present law, a taxpayer's deductible contributions generally are limited to specified percentages of the taxpayer's contribution base, which generally is the taxpayer's adjusted gross income for a taxable year. The applicable percentage limitations vary depending upon the type of property contributed and the classification of the donee organization. In general, contributions to non-operating private foundations are limited to a smaller percentage of the donor's contribution base (up to 30 percent) than contributions to public charities (up to 50 percent).[544]

Supporting organizations (section 509(a)(3))

The Code provides that certain "supporting organizations" (in general, organizations that provide support to another section 501(c)(3) organization that is not a private foundation) are classified as public charities rather than private foundations.[545] To qualify as a supporting organization, an organization must meet all three of the following tests: (1) it must be organized and at all times operated exclusively for the benefit of, to perform the functions of, or to carry out the purposes of one or more "publicly supported organizations"[546] (the "organizational and operational tests");[547] (2) it must be operated, supervised, or controlled by or in connection with one or more publicly supported organizations (the "relationship test");[548] and (3) it must not be controlled directly or indirectly by one or more disqualified persons (as defined in section 4946) other than foundation managers and other than

---

535 Secs. 4940 - 4945.

536 See sec. 4946(a).

537 Sec. 4941.

538 Sec. 4942(g)(1)(A). A qualifying distribution also includes any amount paid to acquire an asset used (or held for use) directly in carrying out one or more of the organization's exempt purposes and certain amounts set-aside for exempt purposes. Sec. 4942(g)(1)(B) and 4942(g)(2).

539 Sec. 4945. Taxes imposed may be abated if certain conditions are met. Secs. 4961 and 4962.

540 In general, expenditure responsibility requires that a foundation make all reasonable efforts and establish reasonable procedures to ensure that the grant is spent solely for the purpose for which it was made, to obtain reports from the grantee on the expenditure of the grant, and to make reports to the Secretary regarding such expenditures. Sec. 4945(h).

541 Sec. 4943.

542 Sec. 4944.

543 A special rule in section 170(e)(5) provides that taxpayer are allowed a deduction equal to the fair market value of certain contributions of appreciated, publicly traded stock contributed to a private foundation.

544 Sec. 170(b).

545 Sec. 509(a)(3).

546 In general, supported organizations of a supporting organization must be publicly supported charities described in sections 509(a)(1) or (a)(2).

547 Sec. 509(a)(3)(A).

548 Sec. 509(a)(3)(B).

one or more publicly supported organizations (the "lack of outside control test").[549]

To satisfy the relationship test, a supporting organization must hold one of three statutorily described close relationships with the supported organization. The organization must be: (1) operated, supervised, or controlled by a publicly supported organization (commonly referred to as "Type I" supporting organizations); (2) supervised or controlled in connection with a publicly supported organization ("Type II" supporting organizations); or (3) operated in connection with a publicly supported organization ("Type III" supporting organizations).[550]

Type I supporting organizations

In the case of supporting organizations that are operated, supervised, or controlled by one or more publicly supported organizations (Type I supporting organizations), one or more supported organizations must exercise a substantial degree of direction over the policies, programs, and activities of the supporting organization.[551] The relationship between the Type I supporting organization and the supported organization generally is comparable to that of a parent and subsidiary. The requisite relationship may be established by the fact that a majority of the officers, directors, or trustees of the supporting organization are appointed or elected by the governing body, members of the governing body, officers acting in their official capacity, or the membership of one or more publicly supported organizations.[552]

Type II supporting organizations

Type II supporting organizations are supervised or controlled in connection with one or more publicly supported organizations. Rather than the parent-subsidiary relationship characteristic of Type I organizations, the relationship between a Type II organization and its supported organizations is more analogous to a brother-sister relationship. In order to satisfy the Type II relationship requirement, generally there must be common supervision or control by the persons supervising or controlling both the supporting organization and the publicly supported organizations.[553] An organization generally is not considered to be "supervised or controlled in connection with" a publicly supported organization merely because the supporting organization makes payments to the publicly supported organization, even if the obligation to make payments is enforceable under state law.[554]

Type III supporting organizations

Type III supporting organizations are "operated in connection with" one or more publicly supported organizations. To satisfy the "operated in connection with" relationship, Treasury regulations require that the supporting organization be responsive to, and significantly involved in the operations of, the publicly supported organization. This relationship is deemed to exist where the supporting organization meets both a "responsiveness test" and an "integral part test."[555]

In general, the responsiveness test requires that the Type III supporting organization be responsive to the needs or demands of the publicly supported organizations. The responsiveness test may be satisfied in one of two ways.[556] First, the supporting organization may demonstrate that: (1)(a) one or more of its officers, directors, or trustees are elected or appointed by the officers, directors, trustees, or membership of the supported organization; (b) one or more members of the governing bodies of the publicly supported organizations are also officers, directors, or trustees of the supporting organization; or (c) the officers, directors, or trustees of the supporting organization maintain a close continuous working relationship with the officers, directors, or trustees of the publicly supported organizations; and (2) by reason of such arrangement, the officers, directors, or trustees of the supported organization have a significant voice in the investment policies of the supporting organization, the timing and manner of making grants, the selection of grant recipients by the supporting organization, and otherwise directing the use of the income or assets of the supporting organization.[557] Alternatively, the responsiveness test may be satisfied if the supporting organization is a charitable trust under state law, each specified supported organization is a named beneficiary under the trust's governing instrument, and the beneficiary organization has the power to en-

---

549 Sec. 509(a)(3)(C).

550 Treas. Reg. sec. 1.509(a)-4(f)(2).

551 Treas. Reg. sec. 1.509(a)-4(g)(1)(i).

552 Id.

553 Treas. Reg. sec. 1.509(a)- 4(h)(1).

554 Treas. Reg. sec. 1.509(a)-4(h)(2).

555 Treas. Reg. sec. 1.509(a)-4(i)(1).

556 For an organization that was supporting or benefiting one or more publicly supported organizations before November 20, 1970, additional facts and circumstances, such as an historic and continuing relationship between organizations, also may be taken into consideration to establish compliance with either of the responsiveness tests. Treas. Reg. sec. 1.509(a)-4(i)(1)(ii).

557 Treas. Reg. sec. 1.509(a)-4(i)(2)(ii).

force the trust and compel an accounting under state law.[558]

In general, the integral part test requires that the Type III supporting organization maintain significant involvement in the operations of one or more publicly supported organizations, and that such publicly supported organizations are in turn dependent upon the supporting organization for the type of support which it provides. There are two alternative methods for satisfying the integral part test. The first alternative is to establish that (1) the activities engaged in for or on behalf of the publicly supported organization are activities to perform the functions of, or carry out the purposes of, such organizations; and (2) these activities, but for the involvement of the supporting organization, normally would be engaged in by the publicly supported organizations themselves.[559] Organizations that satisfy this "but for" test sometimes are referred to as "functionally integrated" Type III supporting organizations. The second method for satisfying the integral part test is to establish that: (1) the supporting organization pays substantially all of its income to or for the use of one or more publicly supported organizations;[560] (2) the amount of support received by one or more of the publicly supported organizations is sufficient to insure the attentiveness of the organization or organizations to the operations of the supporting organization (this is known as the "attentiveness requirement");[561] and (3) a significant amount of the total support of the supporting organization goes to those publicly supported organizations that meet the "attentiveness requirement."[562]

Intermediate sanctions (excess benefit transaction tax)

The Code imposes excise taxes on excess benefit transactions between disqualified persons and public charities.[563] An excess benefit transaction generally is a transaction in which an economic benefit is provided by a public charity directly or indirectly to or for the use of a disqualified person, if the value of the economic benefit provided exceeds the value of the consideration (including the performance of services) received for providing such benefit.

For purposes of the excess benefit transaction rules, a disqualified person is any person in a position to exercise substantial influence over the affairs of the public charity at any time in the five-year period ending on the date of the transaction at issue.[564] Persons holding certain powers, responsibilities, or interests (e.g., officers, directors, or trustees) are considered to be in a position to exercise substantial influence over the affairs of the public charity.

An excess benefit transaction tax is imposed on the disqualified person and, in certain cases, on the organization managers, but is not imposed on the public charity. An initial tax of 25 percent of the excess benefit amount is imposed on the disqualified person that receives the excess benefit. An additional tax on the disqualified person of 200 percent of the excess benefit applies if the violation is not corrected within a specified period. A tax of 10 percent of the excess benefit (not to exceed $10,000 with respect to any excess benefit transaction) is imposed on an organization manager that knowingly participated in the excess benefit transaction, if the manager's participation was willful and not due to reasonable cause, and if the initial tax was imposed on the disqualified person.

Excess business holdings of private foundations

Private foundations are subject to tax on excess business holdings.[565] In general, a private foundation is permitted to hold 20 percent of the voting stock in a corporation, reduced by the amount of voting stock held by all disqualified

[558] Treas. Reg. sec. 1.509(a)-4(i)(2)(iii).

[559] Treas. Reg. sec. 1.509(a)-4(i)(3)(ii).

[560] For this purpose, the IRS has defined the term "substantially all" of an organization's income to mean 85 percent or more. Rev. Rul. 76-208, 1976-1 C.B. 161.

[561] Although the regulations do not specify the requisite level of support in numerical or percentage terms, the IRS has suggested that grants that represent less than 10 percent of the beneficiary's support likely would be viewed as insufficient to ensure attentiveness. Gen. Couns. Mem. 36379 (August 15, 1975). As an alternative to satisfying the attentiveness standard by the foregoing method, a supporting organization may demonstrate attentiveness by showing that, in order to avoid the interruption of the carrying on of a particular function or activity, the beneficiary organization will be sufficiently attentive to the operations of the supporting organization. Treas. Reg. sec. 1.509(a)-4(i)(3)(iii)(b).

[562] Treas. Reg. sec. 1.509(a)-4(i)(3)(iii).

[563] Sec. 4958. The excess benefit transaction tax is commonly referred to as "intermediate sanctions," because it imposes penalties generally considered to be less punitive than revocation of the organization's exempt status. The tax also applies to transactions between disqualified persons and social welfare organizations (as described in section 501(c)(4)).

[564] Sec. 4958(f)(1). A disqualified person also includes certain family members of such a person, and certain entities that satisfy a control test with respect to such persons.

[565] Sec. 4943. Taxes imposed may be abated if certain conditions are met. Secs. 4961 and 4962.

persons (as defined in section 4946). If it is established that no disqualified person has effective control of the corporation, a private foundation and disqualified persons together may own up to 35 percent of the voting stock of a corporation. A private foundation shall not be treated as having excess business holdings in any corporation if it owns (together with certain other related private foundations) not more than two percent of the voting stock and not more than two percent in value of all outstanding shares of all classes of stock in that corporation. Similar rules apply with respect to holdings in a partnership ("profits interest" is substituted for "voting stock" and "capital interest" for "nonvoting stock") and to other unincorporated enterprises (by substituting "beneficial interest" for "voting stock"). Private foundations are not permitted to have holdings in a proprietorship. Foundations generally have a five-year period to dispose of excess business holdings (acquired other than by purchase) without being subject to tax.[566] This five-year period may be extended an additional five years in limited circumstances.[567] The excess business holdings rules do not apply to holdings in a functionally related business or to holdings in a trade or business at least 95 percent of the gross income of which is derived from passive sources.[568]

The initial tax is equal to five percent of the value of the excess business holdings held during the foundation's applicable taxable year. An additional tax is imposed if an initial tax is imposed and at the close of the applicable taxable period, the foundation continues to hold excess business holdings. The amount of the additional tax is equal to 200 percent of such holdings.

Explanation of Provision

Provisions relating to all supporting organizations (Type I, Type II, and Type III)

Automatic excess benefit transactions

Under the provision, if a supporting organization (Type I, Type II, or Type III) makes a grant, loan, payment of compensation, or other similar payment to a substantial contributor (or person related to the substantial contributor) of the supporting organization, for purposes of the excess benefit transaction rules (sec. 4958), the substantial contributor is treated as a disqualified person and the payment is treated automatically as an excess benefit transaction with the entire amount of the payment treated as the excess benefit.[569] Accordingly, the substantial contributor is subject to an initial tax of 25 percent of the amount of the payment under section 4958(a)(1) and an organization manager that participated in the making of the payment, knowing that the payment was a grant, loan, payment of compensation, or other similar payment to a substantial contributor, is subject to a tax of 10 percent of the amount of the payment under section 4958(a)(2). The second tier taxes and other rules of section 4958 also apply to such payments. Other similar payments include payments in the nature of a grant, loan, or payment of compensation, such as an expense reimbursement. Other similar payments do not include, for example, a payment made pursuant to a bona fide sale or lease of property with a substantial contributor. Such payments are subject to the general rules of section 4958 if the substantial contributor meets the definition of a disqualified person under section 4958(f), but are not subject to the automatic excess benefit transaction rule of the provision. The provision applies to payments by a supporting organization to a substantial contributor but not to payments by a substantial contributor to a supporting organization.

Under the provision, a substantial contributor means any person who contributed or bequeathed an aggregate amount of more than $5,000 to the organization, if such amount is more than two percent of the total contributions and bequests received by the organization before the close of the taxable year of the organization in which the contribution or bequest is received by the organization from such person. In the case of a trust, a substantial contributor also includes the creator of the trust. A substantial contributor does not include a public charity (other than a supporting organization). Under the provision, mechanical rules similar to the rules that apply in determining whether a person is a substantial contributor to a private foundation (secs. 509(d)(2)(B) and (C)) apply.

Under the provision, a person is a related person ("related person") if a person is a member of the family (determined under section 4958(f)(4)) of a substantial contributor, or a 35 percent controlled entity, defined as a corpora-

---

566 Sec. 4943(c)(6).

567 Sec. 4943(c)(7).

568 Sec. 4943(d)(3).

569 The requirement of the provision that the entire amount of the payment be treated as the amount of the excess benefit differs from the generally applicable rule of section 4958, which provides that the excess benefit is the amount by which the value of the economic benefit provided exceeds the value of the consideration received.

tion, partnership, trust, or estate in which a substantial contributor or family member thereof owns more than 35 percent of the total combined voting power, profits interest, or beneficial interest, as the case may be.

In addition, under the provision, loans by any supporting organization (Type I, Type II, or Type III) to a disqualified person (as defined in section 4958) of the supporting organization are treated as an excess benefit transaction under section 4958 and the entire amount of the loan is treated as an excess benefit. For this purpose, a disqualified person does not include a public charity (other than a supporting organization).

Disclosure requirements

Under the provision, all supporting organizations are required to file an annual information return (Form 990 series) with the Secretary, regardless of the organization's gross receipts. A supporting organization must indicate on such annual information return whether it is a Type I, Type II, or Type III supporting organization and must identify its supported organizations.

Under the provision, supporting organizations must demonstrate annually that the organization is not controlled directly or indirectly by one or more disqualified persons (other than foundation managers and other than one or more publicly supported organizations) through a certification on the annual information return. It is intended that supporting organizations be able to certify that the majority of the organization's governing body is comprised of individuals who were selected based on their special knowledge or expertise in the particular field or discipline in which the supporting organization is operating, or because they represent the particular community that is served by the supported public charities.

Disqualified person

Under the provision, for purposes of the excess benefit transaction rules (sec. 4958), a disqualified person of a supporting organization is treated as a disqualified person of the supported organization.

Provisions that apply to Type III supporting organizations

Payout with respect to Type III supporting organizations

Under the provision, the Secretary shall promulgate new regulations on payments required by Type III supporting organizations that are not functionally integrated Type III supporting organizations.[570] Such regulations shall require such organizations to make distributions of a percentage either of income or assets to the public charities they support in order to ensure that a significant amount is paid to such supported organizations. A functionally integrated Type III supporting organization is a Type III supporting organization that is not required under regulations established by the Secretary to make payments to supported organizations due to the activities of the organization related to performing the functions of, or carrying out the purposes of, such supported organizations.[571]

Excess business holdings

Under the provision, the excess business holdings rules of section 4943 are applied to Type III supporting organizations (other than functionally integrated Type III supporting organizations). In applying such rules, the term disqualified person has the meaning provided in section 4958, and also includes substantial contributors and related persons and any organization that is effectively controlled by the same

---

[570] See Treas. Reg. sec. 1.509(a)-4(i)(3)(iii).

[571] The current such regulation is Treasury regulation section 1.509(a)-4(i)(3)(ii). Under Treasury regulation section 1.509(a)-4(i)(3), the integral part test of current law may be satisfied in one of two ways, one of which requires a payout of substantially all of an organization's income to or for the use of one or more publicly supported organizations, and one of which does not require such a payout. There is concern that the current income-based payout does not result in a significant amount being paid to charity if assets held by a supporting organization produce little to no income, especially in relation to the value of the assets held by the organization, and as compared to amounts paid out by nonoperating private foundations. There also is concern that the current regulatory standards for satisfying the integral part test not by reason of a payout are not sufficiently stringent to ensure that there is a sufficient nexus between the supporting and supported organizations. In revising the regulations, the Secretary has the discretion to determine whether it is appropriate to impose a pay out requirement on any or all organizations not currently required to pay out. It is intended that, in revisiting the current regulations, if the distinction between Type III supporting organizations that are required to pay out and those that are not required to pay out is retained, which may be appropriate, the Secretary nonetheless shall strengthen the standard for qualification as an organization that is not required to pay out. For example, as one requirement, the Secretary may consider whether substantially all of the activities of such an organization should be activities in direct furtherance of the functions or purposes of supported organizations.

person or persons who control the supporting organization or any organization substantially all of the contributions to which were made by the same person or persons who made substantially all of the contributions to the supporting organization. The excess business holdings rules do not apply if, as of November 18, 2005, the holdings were held (and at all times thereafter, are held) for the benefit of the community pursuant to the direction (made as of such date) of a State attorney general or a State official with jurisdiction over the Type III supporting organization.

The Secretary has the authority not to impose the excess business holdings rules if the organization establishes to the satisfaction of the Secretary that excess holdings of an organization are consistent with the purpose or function constituting the basis of the organization's exempt status. In exercising this authority, the Secretary should consider, in addition to any other factors the Secretary considers significant, as favorable, but not determinative, factors, a reasoned determination by the State attorney general with jurisdiction over the supporting organization, that disposition of the holdings would have a severe detrimental impact on the community, and a binding commitment by the supporting organization to pay out at least five percent of the value of the organization's assets each year to its supported organizations. A reasoned determination would require, among other things, evidence that any such determination was made pursuant to serious study by the State attorney general of the issues involved in disposing of the excess holdings, and findings by the State attorney general about the detrimental economic impact that would result from such disposition. If as a result of such State attorney general's study and findings, the State attorney general directed as a matter of State law that permission of the State would be required prior to any sale of the holdings, such a factor should be given strong consideration by the Secretary.

Transition rules apply to the present holdings of an organization similar to those of section 4943(c)(4)-(6).[572]

Under the provision, the excess business holdings rules also apply to Type II supporting organizations but only if such organization accepts any gift or contribution from a person (other than a public charity, not including a supporting organization) who (1) controls, directly or indirectly, either alone or together (with persons described below) the governing body of a supported organization of the supporting organization;[573] (2) is a member of the family of such a person; or (3) is a 35 percent controlled entity.

Organizational and operational requirements

The provision provides that, in general, after the date of enactment, a Type III supporting organization may not support an organization that is not organized in the United States.[574] But, for Type III supporting organizations that support a foreign organization on the date of enactment, the provision provides that the general rule does not apply until the first day of the third taxable year of the organization beginning after the date of enactment.

Relationship to supported organization(s)

Under the provision, a Type III supporting organization must apprise each organization it supports of information regarding the supporting organization in order to help ensure the supporting organization's responsiveness. It is intended that such a showing could be satisfied, for example, through provision of documentation such as a copy of the supporting organization's governing documents, any changes made

---

[572] Under the transition rules, in general, where the existing holdings of a supporting organization and disqualified persons are in excess of 50 percent (of a voting stock interest, profits interest, or beneficial interest), and not 20 percent or 35 percent as under the general rule, but are not in excess of 75 percent, a 10-year period is available before the holdings must be reduced to 50 percent. If such holdings are more than 75 percent, the reduction to 50 percent need not occur for a 15-year period. The 15-year period is expanded to 20 years if the holdings are more than 95 percent. After the expiration of the 10, 15, or 20 year period, if disqualified persons have holdings in a business enterprise in excess of two percent of the enterprise, the supporting organization has 15 additional years to dispose of any of its own holdings that are above 25 percent of the holdings in the enterprise. If disqualified persons do not have such holdings, then the supporting organization has 15 additional years to dispose of any of its own holdings that are above 35 percent of the holdings in the enterprise.

[573] For purposes of the provision, it is intended that indirect control includes the ability to exercise effective control. For example, if a person made a gift to a supporting organization and a combination of such person, a person related to such person, and such person's personal attorney were members of the five-member board of a supported organization of the supporting organization, the organization would be treated as being indirectly controlled by such person. Board membership alone does not establish direct or indirect control.

[574] U.S. charities established principally to provide financial and other assistance to a foreign charity, sometimes referred to as "friends of" organizations, may not be established as supporting organizations under the provision. Such organizations may continue to obtain public charity status, however, by virtue of demonstrating broad public support (as described in sections 509(a)(1) and 509(a)(2)).

to the governing documents, the organization's annual information return filed with the Secretary (Form 990 series), any tax return (Form 990-T) filed with the Secretary, and an annual report (including a description of all of the support provided by the supporting organization, how such support was calculated, and a projection of the next year's support). It is intended that failure to make a sufficient showing is a factor in determining whether the responsiveness test of present law is met.

In general, under the provision, a Type III supporting organization that is organized as a trust must, in addition to present law requirements, establish to the satisfaction of the Secretary, that it has a close and continuous relationship with the supported organization such that the trust is responsive to the needs or demands of the supported organization. A transition rule for existing trusts provides that the provision is not effective until one year after the date of enactment but is effective on the date of enactment for other trusts.

Other provisions

Under the provision, if a Type I or Type III supporting organization accepts any gift or contribution from a person (other than a public charity, not including a supporting organization) who (1) controls, directly or indirectly, either alone or together (with persons described below) the governing body of a supported organization of the supporting organization; (2) is a member of the family of such a person; or (3) is a 35 percent controlled entity, then the supporting organization is treated as a private foundation for all purposes until such time as the organization can demonstrate to the satisfaction of the Secretary that it qualifies as a public charity other than as a supporting organization.

Under the provision, a nonoperating private foundation may not count as a qualifying distribution under section 4942 any amount paid to (1) a Type III supporting organization that is not a functionally integrated Type III supporting organization or (2) any other supporting organization if a disqualified person with respect to the foundation directly or indirectly controls the supporting organization or a supported organization of such supporting organization. Any amount that does not count as a qualifying distribution under this rule is treated as a taxable expenditure under section 4945.

Effective Date

The provision generally is effective on the date of enactment. The excess benefit transaction rules are effective for transactions occurring after July 25, 2006 (except that the rule relating to the definition of a disqualified person is effective for transactions occurring after the date of enactment). The excess business holdings requirements are effective for taxable years beginning after the date of enactment. The provision relating to distributions by nonoperating private foundations is effective for distributions and expenditures made after the date of enactment. The return requirements are effective for returns filed for taxable years ending after the date of enactment.

[Law at ¶ 5155, ¶ 5255, ¶ 5260, ¶ 5270, ¶ 5275, ¶ 5325 and ¶ 7423. CCH Explanation at ¶ 1225, ¶ 1230, ¶ 1235, ¶ 1240 and ¶ 1270.]

[¶ 11,390] Act Sec. 1303. Exception to local furnishing requirements for certain Alaska hydroelectric projects

Joint Committee Taxation (J.C.T. Rep. No. JCX-38-06)

[Act Sec. 1303]

Present Law

Interest on bonds issued by State and local governments generally is excluded from gross income for Federal income tax purposes if the proceeds of such bonds are used to finance direct activities of governmental units or if such bonds are repaid with revenues of governmental units. Interest on State or local government bonds issued to finance activities of private persons is taxable unless a specific exception applies ("private activity bonds").

The interest on private activity bonds is eligible for tax-exemption if such bonds are issued for certain purposes permitted by the Code ("qualified private activity bonds"). The definition of a qualified private activity bond includes bonds issued to finance certain private facilities for the "local furnishing" of electricity or gas. Generally, a facility provides local furnishing if the area served by the facility does not exceed (1) two contiguous counties or (2) a city and a contiguous county (the "two-county rule").

The Code generally limits the local furnishing exception to bonds for facilities (1) of persons who were engaged in the local furnishing of electric energy or gas on January 1, 1997 (or a successor in interest to such persons), and (2) that serve areas served by those persons on such date (the "service area limitation") (sec. 142(f)(3)). The Small Business Job Protection Act of 1996 (the "Act") provided an exception from these limitations for bonds issued to finance the acquisition of the Snettisham hydroelectric project from the Alaska Power Administration (Pub. L. No. 104-188, sec. 1804 (1996)).

Explanation of Provision

The provision provides an exception from the service area limitation under section 142(f)(3) for bonds issued prior to May 31, 2006, to finance the Lake Dorothy hydroelectric project to provide electricity to the City of Hoonah, Alaska. In addition, the furnishing of electric service to the City of Hoonah, Alaska is disregarded for purposes of applying the two-county rule to bonds issued before May 31, 2006, to finance either the Lake Dorothy hydroelectric project (as defined in the provision) or to finance the acquisition of the Snettisham hydroelectric project.

Effective Date

The provision is effective on the date of enactment.

[Law at ¶ 7252. CCH Explanation at ¶ 1340.]

[¶ 11,400] Act Sec. 1304. Extend certain tax rules for qualified tuition programs

Joint Committee Taxation (J.C.T. Rep. No. JCX-38-06)

[Code Sec. 529]

Present Law

Overview

Section 529 provides specified income tax and transfer tax rules for the treatment of accounts and contracts established under qualified tuition programs.[576] A qualified tuition program is a program established and maintained by a State or agency or instrumentality thereof, or by one or more eligible educational institutions, which satisfies certain requirements and under which a person may purchase tuition credits or certificates on behalf of a designated beneficiary that entitle the beneficiary to the waiver or payment of qualified higher education expenses of the beneficiary (a "prepaid tuition program").[577] In the case of a program established and maintained by a State or agency or instrumentality thereof, a qualified tuition program also includes a program under which a person may make contributions to an account that is established for the purpose of satisfying the qualified higher education expenses of the designated beneficiary of the account, provided it satisfies certain specified requirements (a "savings account program").[578] Under both types of qualified tuition programs, a contributor establishes an account for the benefit of a particular designated beneficiary to provide for that beneficiary's higher education expenses.

For this purpose, qualified higher education expenses means tuition, fees, books, supplies, and equipment required for the enrollment or attendance of a designated beneficiary at an eligible educational institution, and expenses for special needs services in the case of a special needs beneficiary that are incurred in connection with such enrollment or attendance.[579] Qualified higher education expenses generally also include room and board for students who are enrolled at least half-time.[580]

Income tax treatment

A qualified tuition program, including a savings account or a prepaid tuition contract established thereunder, generally is exempt from income tax, although it is subject to the tax on unrelated business income.[581] Contributions to a qualified tuition account (or with respect to a prepaid tuition contract) are not deductible to the contributor or includible in income of the designated beneficiary or account owner. Earnings accumulate tax-free until a distribution is made. If a distribution is made to pay qualified higher education expenses, no portion of the

---

[576] The term "account" refers to a prepaid tuition benefit contract or a tuition savings account established pursuant to a qualified tuition program.

[577] Sec. 529(b)(1)(A).

[578] Sec. 529(b)(1)(A).

[579] Sec. 529(e)(3)(A).

[580] Sec. 529(e)(3)(B).

[581] Sec. 529(a). An interest in a qualified tuition account is not treated as debt for purposes of the debt-financed property rules under section 514. Sec. 529(e)(4).

distribution is subject to income tax.[582] If a distribution is not used to pay qualified higher education expenses, the earnings portion of the distribution is subject to Federal income tax[583] and a 10-percent additional tax (subject to exceptions for death, disability, or the receipt of a scholarship).[584] A change in the designated beneficiary of an account or prepaid contract is not treated as a distribution for income tax purposes if the new designated beneficiary is a member of the family of the old beneficiary.[585]

Gift and generation-skipping transfer (GST) tax treatment

A contribution to a qualified tuition account (or with respect to a prepaid tuition contract) is treated as a completed gift of a present interest from the contributor to the designated beneficiary.[586] Such contributions qualify for the per-donee annual gift tax exclusion ($12,000 for 2006), and, to the extent of such exclusions, also are exempt from the generation-skipping transfer (GST) tax. A contributor may contribute in a single year up to five times the per-donee annual gift tax exclusion amount to a qualified tuition account and, for gift tax and GST tax purposes, treat the contribution as having been made ratably over the five-year period beginning with the calendar year in which the contribution is made.[587]

A distribution from a qualified tuition account or prepaid tuition contract generally is not subject to gift tax or GST tax.[588] Those taxes may apply, however, to a change of designated beneficiary if the new designated beneficiary is in a generation below that of the old beneficiary or if the new beneficiary is not a member of the family of the old beneficiary.[589]

Estate tax treatment

Qualified tuition program account balances or prepaid tuition benefits generally are excluded from the gross estate of any individual.[590] Amounts distributed on account of the death of the designated beneficiary, however, are includible in the designated beneficiary's gross estate.[591] If the contributor elected the special five-year allocation rule for gift tax annual exclusion purposes, any amounts contributed that are allocable to the years within the five-year period remaining after the year of the contributor's death are includible in the contributor's gross estate.[592]

Certain provisions expiring under the Economic Growth and Tax Relief Reconciliation Act of 2001 ("EGTRRA")

The Economic Growth and Tax Relief Reconciliation Act of 2001 ("EGTRRA") made a number of changes to the rules regarding qualified tuition programs. However, in order to comply with reconciliation procedures under the Congressional Budget Act of 1974, EGTRRA included a "sunset" provision, pursuant to which the provisions of the Act expire at the end of 2010. Specifically, EGTRRA's provisions do not apply for taxable, plan, or limitation years beginning after December 31, 2010, or to estates of decedents dying after, or gifts or generation-skipping transfers made after, December 31, 2010. EGTRRA provides that, as of the effective date of the sunset, the Code will be applied as thought EGTRRA had never been enacted.

The provisions of present-law section 529 scheduled to expire by reason of the EGTRRA sunset provision include: (1) the provision that makes qualified withdrawals from qualified tuition accounts exempt from income tax; (2) the repeal of a pre-EGTRRA requirement that there be more than a de minimis penalty imposed on amounts not used for educational purposes and the imposition of the 10-percent additional tax on distributions not used for qualified higher education purposes; (3) a provision permitting certain private educational institutions to establish prepaid tuition programs that qualify under section 529 if they receive a ruling or determination to that effect from the Internal Revenue

---

[582] Sec. 529(c)(3)(B). Any benefit furnished to a designated beneficiary under a qualified tuition account is treated as a distribution to the beneficiary for these purposes. Sec. 529(c)(3)(B)(iv).

[583] Sec. 529(c)(3)(A) and (B)(ii).

[584] Sec. 529(c)(6).

[585] Sec. 529(c)(3)(C)(ii). For this purpose, "member of the family" means, with respect to a designated beneficiary: (1) the spouse of such beneficiary; (2) an individual who bears a relationship to such beneficiary which is described in paragraphs (1) through (8) of section 152(a) (i.e., with respect to the beneficiary, a son, daughter, or a descendant of either; a stepson or stepdaughter; a sibling or stepsibling; a father, mother, or ancestor of either; a stepfather or stepmother; a son or daughter of a brother or sister; a brother or sister of a father or mother; and a son-in-law, daughter-in-law, father-in-law, mother-in-law, brother-in-law, or sister-in-law), or the spouse of any such individual; and (3) the first cousin of such beneficiary. Sec. 529(e)(2).

[586] Sec. 529(c)(2)(A).

[587] Sec. 529(c)(2)(B).

[588] Sec. 529(c)(5)(A).

[589] Sec. 529(c)(5)(B).

[590] Sec. 529(c)(4)(A).

[591] Sec. 529(c)(4)(B).

[592] Sec. 529(c)(4)(C).

Service, and if the assets are held in a trust created or organized for the exclusive benefit of designated beneficiaries; (4) certain provisions permitting rollovers from one account to another account; (5) certain rules regarding the treatment of room and board as qualifying expenses; (6) certain rules regarding coordination with Hope and lifetime learning credit provisions; (7) the provision that treats first cousins as members of the family for purposes of the rollover and change in beneficiary rules; and (8) certain provisions regarding the education expenses of special needs beneficiaries.[593]

Explanation of Provision

Permanently extend EGTRRA modifications to qualified tuition program rules

The provision repeals the sunset provision of EGTRRA insofar as it applies to the EGTRRA modifications to the rules regarding qualified tuition programs. As a result, the provision permanently extends all provisions of EGTRRA that expire at the end of 2010 that relate to qualified tuition programs.

Grant of regulatory authority to Treasury

Present law regarding the transfer tax treatment of qualified tuition program accounts is unclear and in some situations imposes tax in a manner inconsistent with generally applicable transfer tax provisions. In addition, present law creates opportunities for abuse of qualified tuition programs. For example, taxpayers may seek to avoid gift and generation skipping transfer taxes by establishing and contributing to multiple qualified tuition program accounts with different designated beneficiaries (using the provision of section 529 that permits a contributor to contribute up to five times the annual exclusion amount per donee in a single year and treat the contribution as having been made ratably over five years), with the intention of subsequently changing the designated beneficiaries of such accounts to a single, common beneficiary and distributing the entire amount to such beneficiary without further transfer tax consequences. Taxpayers also may seek to use qualified tuition program accounts as retirement accounts with all of the tax benefits but none of the restrictions and requirements of qualified retirement accounts. The provision grants the Secretary broad regulatory authority to clarify the tax treatment of certain transfers and to ensure that qualified tuition program accounts are used for the intended purpose of saving for higher education expenses of the designated beneficiary, including the authority to impose related recordkeeping and reporting requirements. The provision also authorizes the Secretary to limit the persons who may be contributors to a qualified tuition program and to determine any special rules for the operation and Federal tax consequences of such programs if such contributors are not individuals.

Effective Date

The provision is effective on the date of enactment.

[Law at ¶5175 and ¶7255. CCH Explanation at ¶1310.]

[593] EGTRRA sec. 402.

¶20,001 Effective Dates

IRC Effective Dates

This CCH-prepared table presents the general effective dates for major Internal Revenue Code provisions added, amended or repealed by the Pension Protection Act of 2006, enacted August 17, 2006. Entries are listed in Code Section order.

Code Sec.	Act Sec.	Act Provision Subject	Effective Date
25B(b)	833(a)	Inflation Indexing of Gross Income Limitations on Certain Retirement Savings Incentives—Saver's Credit	Tax years beginning after 2006
25B(h)	812	Saver's Credit	August 17, 2006
72(e)(11)-(12)	844(a)	Treatment of Annuity and Life Insurance Contracts With a Long-Term Care Insurance Feature—Exclusion From Gross Income	Contacts issued after December 31, 1996, but only with respect to tax years beginning after December 31, 2009
72(t)(2)(G)	827(a)	Penalty-Free Withdrawals From Retirement Plans For Individuals Called to Active Duty For At Least 179 Days	Distributions after September 11, 2001
72(t)(10)	828(a)	Waiver of 10 Percent Early Withdrawal Penalty Tax on Certain Distributions of Pension Plans For Public Safety Employees	Distributions after August 17, 2006
101(a)(1)	863(c)(1)	Treatment of Death Benefits From Corporate-Owned Life Insurance—Conforming Amendments	Life insurance contracts issued after August 17, 2006, except for a contract issued after that date pursuant to a Code Sec. 1035 exchange for a contract issued on or prior to that date
101(j)	863(a)	Treatment of Death Benefits From Corporate-Owned Life Insurance	Life insurance contracts issued after August 17, 2006, except for a contract issued after that date pursuant to a Code Sec. 1035 exchange for a contract issued on or prior to that date
170(b)(1)(E)-(G)	1206(a)(1)	Encouragement of Contributions of Capital Gain Real Property Made For Conservation Purposes—Individuals	Contributions made in tax years beginning after December 31, 2005
170(b)(2)	1206(a)(2)	Encouragement of Contributions of Capital Gain Real Property Made For Conservation Purposes—Corporations	Contributions made in tax years beginning after December 31, 2005

Code Sec.	Act Sec.	Act Provision Subject	Effective Date
170(d)(2)	1206(b)(1)	Encouragement of Contributions of Capital Gain Real Property Made For Conservation Purposes—Conforming Amendments	Contributions made in tax years beginning after December 31, 2005
170(e)(1)(B)(i)	1215(a)(1)	Recapture of Tax Benefit For Charitable Contributions of Exempt Use Property Not Used for an Exempt Use-Recapture of Deduction on Certain Sales of Exempt Use Property	Contributions after September 1, 2006
170(e)(1)(B)(ii)-(iv)	1214(a)	Charitable Contributions of Taxidermy Property—Denial of Long-Term Capital Gain	Contributions made after July 25, 2006
170(e)(3)(C)(iv)	1202(a)	Extension of Modification of Charitable Deduction For Contributions of Food Inventory	Contributions made after December 31, 2005
170(e)(3)(D)(iv)	1204(a)	Extension of Modification of Charitable Deduction For Contributions of Book Inventory	Contributions made after December 31, 2005
170(e)(7)	1215(a)(2)	Recapture of Tax Benefit For Charitable Contributions of Exempt Use Property Not Used for an Exempt Use-Recapture of Deduction on Certain Sales of Exempt Use Property—Dispositions After Close of Taxable Year	Contributions after September 1, 2006
170(f)(11)(E)	1219(c)(1)	Provisions Relating to Substantial and Gross Overstatements of Valuations—Qualified Appraisers and Appraisals	Appraisals prepared with respect to returns or submissions filed after August 17, 2006, generally
170(f)(13)	1213(c)	Reform of Charitable Contributions of Certain Easements in Registered Historic Districts and Reduced Deduction For Portion of Qualified Conservation Contribution Attributable to Rehabilitation Credit-Filing Fee For Certain Contributions	Contributions made 180 days after August 17, 2006
170(f)(14)	1213(d)	Reform of Charitable Contributions of Certain Easements in Registered Historic Districts and Reduced Deduction For Portion of Qualified Conservation Contribution Attributable to Rehabilitation Credit—Reduced Deduction For Portion of Qualified Conservation Contribution Attributable to the Rehabilitation Credit	Contributions made after August 17, 2006
170(f)(15)	1214(b)	Charitable Contributions of Taxidermy Property—Treatment of Basis	Contributions made after July 25, 2006
170(f)(16)	1216(a)	Limitation of Deduction For Charitable Contributions of Clothing and Household Items	Contributions made after August 17, 2006
170(f)(17)	1217(a)	Modification of Recordkeeping Requirements For Certain Charitable Contributions—Recordkeeping Requirement	Contributions made in tax years beginning after August 17, 2006

Code Sec.	Act Sec.	Act Provision Subject	Effective Date
170(f)(18)	1234(a)	Treatment of Charitable Contribution Deductions to Donor Advised Funds—Income	Contributions made after the date which is 180 days after August 17, 2006
170(h)(4)(B)-(C)	1213(a)(1)	Reform of Charitable Contributions of Certain Easements in Registered Historic Districts and Reduced Deduction For Portion of Qualified Conservation Contribution Attributable to Rehabilitation Credit—Special Rules With Respect to Buildings in Registered Historic Districts	Contributions made after July 25, 2006
170(h)(4)(C)	1213(b)(1)-(3)	Reform of Charitable Contributions of Certain Easements in Registered Historic Districts and Reduced Deduction For Portion of Qualified Conservation Contribution Attributable to Rehabilitation Credit—Disallowance of Deduction For Structures and Land in Registered Historic Districts	Contributions made after August 17, 2006
170(o)-(p)	1218(a)	Contributions of Fractional Interests in Tangible Personal Property—Income Tax	Contributions, bequests, and gifts made after August 17, 2006
219(b)(5)(C)-(D)	831(a)	Allowance of Additional IRA Payments in Certain Bankruptcy Cases—Allowance of Contributions	Tax years beginning after December 31, 2006
219(g)(8)	833(b)	Inflation Indexing of Gross Income Limitations on Certain Retirement Savings Incentives—Deduction of Retirement Contributions For Active Participants	Tax years beginning after 2006
401(a)(5)(G)	861(a)(1)	Extension to All Government Plans of Current Moratorium on Application of Certain Nondiscrimination Rules Applicable to State and Local Plans	Any year beginning after August 17, 2006
401(a)(5)(G)	861(b)(1)	Extension to All Government Plans of Current Moratorium on Application of Certain Nondiscrimination Rules Applicable to State and Local Plans—Conforming Amendments	Any year beginning after August 17, 2006
401(a)(26)(G)	861(a)(1)	Extension to All Government Plans of Current Moratorium on Application of Certain Nondiscrimination Rules Applicable to State and Local Plans	Any year beginning after August 17, 2006
401(a)(26)(G)	861(b)(2)	Extension to All Government Plans of Current Moratorium on Application of Certain Nondiscrimination Rules Applicable to State and Local Plans—Conforming Amendments	Any year beginning after August 17, 2006
401(a)(28)(B)(v)	901(a)(2)(A)	Defined Contribution Plans Required to Provide Employees With Freedom to Invest Their Plan Assets—Amendments of Internal Revenue Code—Conforming Amendments	Plan years beginning after December 31, 2006, generally

Code Sec.	Act Sec.	Act Provision Subject	Effective Date
401(a)(29)	114(a)(1)	Technical and Conforming Amendments—Amendments Related to Qualification Requirements	August 17, 2006
401(a)(32)(A)	114(a)(2)(A)	Technical and Conforming Amendments—Amendments Related to Qualification Requirements	August 17, 2006
401(a)(32)(C)	114(a)(2)(B)	Technical and Conforming Amendments—Amendments Related to Qualification Requirements	August 17, 2006
401(a)(33)(B)(i)	114(a)(3)(A)	Technical and Conforming Amendments—Amendments Related to Qualification Requirements	August 17, 2006
401(a)(33)(B)(iii)	114(a)(3)(B)	Technical and Conforming Amendments—Amendments Related to Qualification Requirements	August 17, 2006
401(a)(33)(D)	114(a)(3)(C)	Technical and Conforming Amendments—Amendments Related to Qualification Requirements	August 17, 2006
401(a)(35)	901(a)(1)	Defined Contribution Plans Required to Provide Employees With Freedom to Invest Their Plan Assets—Amendments of Internal Revenue Code—Qualification Requirement	Plan years beginning after December 31, 2006, generally
401(a)(36)	905(b)	Distributions During Working Retirement—Amendment to the Internal Revenue Code of 1986	Plan years beginning after December 31, 2006
401(k)(2)(B)(i)(III)-(V)	827(b)(1)	Penalty-Free Withdrawals From Retirement Plans For Individuals Called to Active Duty For At Least 179 Days—Conforming Amendments	Distributions after September 11, 2001
401(k)(3)(G)	861(a)(2)	Extension to All Government Plans of Current Moratorium on Application of Certain Nondiscrimination Rules Applicable to State and Local Plans	Any year beginning after August 17, 2006
401(k)(3)(G)	861(b)(3)	Extension to All Government Plans of Current Moratorium on Application of Certain Nondiscrimination Rules Applicable to State and Local Plans—Conforming Amendments	Any year beginning after August 17, 2006
401(k)(8)(A)(i)	902(e)(3)(B)(i)	Increasing Participation Through Automatic Contribution Arrangements—Excess Contributions—Simplification of Allocable Earnings	Plan years beginning after December 31, 2007
401(k)(8)(E)	902(d)(2)(C)	Increasing Participation Through Automatic Contribution Arrangements—Treatment of Withdrawals of Contributions During First 90 Days—Vesting Conforming Amendments	Plan years beginning after December 31, 2007
401(k)(8)(E)	902(d)(2)(D)	Increasing Participation Through Automatic Contribution Arrangements—Treatment of Withdrawals of Contributions During First 90 Days—Vesting Conforming Amendments	Plan years beginning after December 31, 2007

Code Sec.	Act Sec.	Act Provision Subject	Effective Date
401(k)(13)	902(a)	Increasing Participation Through Automatic Contribution Arrangements	Plan years beginning after December 31, 2007
401(m)(6)(A)	902(e)(3)(B)(ii)	Increasing Participation Through Automatic Contribution Arrangements—Excess Contributions—Simplification of Allocable Earnings	Plan years beginning after December 31, 2007
401(m)(12)-(13)	902(b)	Increasing Participation Through Automatic Contribution Arrangements—Matching Contributions	Plan years beginning after December 31, 2007
402(c)(2)(A)	822(a)(1)-(2)	Allow Rollover of After-Tax Amounts in Annuity Contracts	Tax years beginning after December 31, 2006
402(c)(11)	829(a)(1)	Allow Rollovers By Nonspouse Beneficiaries of Certain Retirement Plan Distributions	Distributions after December 31, 2006
402(l)	845(a)	Distributions From Governmental Retirement Plans For Health and Long-Term Care Insurance For Public Safety Officers	Tax years beginning after December 31, 2006
403(a)(2)	845(b)(1)	Distributions From Governmental Retirement Plans For Health and Long-Term Care Insurance For Public Safety Officers—Conforming Amendments	Distributions in tax years beginning after December 31, 2006
403(a)(4)(B)	829(a)(2)	Allow Rollovers By Nonspouse Beneficiaries of Certain Retirement Plan Distributions—Section 403(a) Plans	Distributions after December 31, 2006
403(b)(2)	845(b)(2)	Distributions From Governmental Retirement Plans For Health and Long-Term Care Insurance For Public Safety Officers—Conforming Amendments	Distributions in tax years beginning after December 31, 2006
403(b)(7)(A)(ii)	827(b)(2)	Penalty-Free Withdrawals From Retirement Plans For Individuals Called to Active Duty For At Least 179 Days—Conforming Amendments	Distributions after September 11, 2001
403(b)(8)(B)	829(a)(3)	Allow Rollovers By Nonspouse Beneficiaries of Certain Retirement Plan Distributions—Section 403(b) Plans	Distributions after December 31, 2006
403(b)(11)(A)-(C)	827(b)(3)	Penalty-Free Withdrawals From Retirement Plans For Individuals Called to Active Duty For At Least 179 Days—Conforming Amendments	Distributions after September 11, 2001
404(a)(1)(A)	801(a)(1)	Increase in Deduction Limit For Single-Employer Plans	Years beginning after December 31, 2007
404(a)(1)(A)	801(c)(1)	Increase in Deduction Limit For Single-Employer Plans—Technical and Conforming Amendments	Years beginning after December 31, 2007
404(a)(1)(B)	801(c)(2)(A)-(E)	Increase in Deduction Limit For Single-Employer Plans—Technical and Conforming Amendments	Years beginning after December 31, 2007
404(a)(1)(D)	802(a)	Deduction Limits For Multiemployer Plans—Increase in Deduction	Years beginning after December 31, 2007

Code Sec.	Act Sec.	Act Provision Subject	Effective Date
404(a)(1)(D)(i)	801(d)(1)	Increase in Deduction Limit For Single-Employer Plans—Special Rule for 2006 and 2007	Years beginning after December 31, 2005
404(a)(1)(F)	801(d)(2)	Increase in Deduction Limit For Single-Employer Plans—Special Rule for 2006 and 2007—Conforming Amendment	Years beginning after December 31, 2005
404(a)(7)	801(c)(3)(A)-(B)	Increase in Deduction Limit For Single-Employer Plans—Technical and Conforming Amendments	Years beginning after December 31, 2007
404(a)(7)(C)(iii)	803(a)	Updating Deduction Rules For Combination of Plans	Contributions for tax years beginning after December 31, 2005
404(a)(7)(C)(iv)	801(b)	Increase in Deduction Limit For Single-Employer Plans—Exception From Limitation on Deduction Where Combination of Defined Contribution and Defined Benefit Plans	Years beginning after December 31, 2007
404(a)(7)C)(v)	803(b)	Updating Deduction Rules For Combination of Plans—Exception From Limitation on Deduction Where Combination of Defined Contribution and Defined Benefit Plans	Contributions for tax years beginning after December 31, 2005
404(o)	801(a)(2)	Increase in Deduction Limit For Single-Employer Plans	Years beginning after December 31, 2007
404A(g)(3)(A)	801(c)(4)	Increase in Deduction Limit For Single-Employer Plans—Technical and Conforming Amendments	Years beginning after December 31, 2007
408(d)(8)	1201(a)	Tax-Free Distributions From Individual Retirement Plans For Charitable Purposes	Distributions made in tax years beginning after December 31, 2005
408A(c)(3)(B)	824(b)(1)(A)-(B)	Allow Direct Rollovers From Retirement Plans to Roth IRAs—Conforming Amendments	Distributions after December 31, 2007
408A(c)(3)(C)	833(c)	Inflation Indexing of Gross Income Limitations on Certain Retirement Savings Incentives—Contribution Limitation For Roth IRAs	Tax years beginning after 2006
408A(d)(3)	824(b)(2)(A)-(E)	Allow Direct Rollovers From Retirement Plans to Roth IRAs—Conforming Amendments	Distributions after December 31, 2007
408A(e)	824(a)	Allow Direct Rollovers From Retirement Plans to Roth IRAs	Distributions after December 31, 2007
409(h)(7)	901(a)(2)(B)	Defined Contribution Plans Required to Provide Employees With Freedom to Invest Their Plan Assets—Amendments of Internal Revenue Code—Conforming Amendments	Plan years beginning after December 31, 2006, generally
409A(b)(3)-(5)	116(a)	Restrictions on Funding of Nonqualified Deferred Compensation Plans By Employers Maintaining Underfunded or Terminated Single-Employer Plans—Amendments of Internal Revenue Code	Transfers or other reservation of assets after August 17, 2006

Code Sec.	Act Sec.	Act Provision Subject	Effective Date
409A(b)(4)-(5)	116(b)	Restrictions on Funding of Nonqualified Deferred Compensation Plans By Employers Maintaining Underfunded or Terminated Single-Employer Plans—Conforming Amendments	Transfers or other reservation of assets after August 17, 2006
410(b)(3)	402(h)(1)	Special Funding Rules For Certain Plans Maintained By Commercial Airlines—Exclusion of Certain Employees From Minimum Coverage Requirements	Years beginning before, on, or after August 17, 2006
411(a)(2)	904(a)(1)	Faster Vesting of Employer Nonelective Contributions—Amendments to the Internal Revenue Code of 1986	Contributions for plan years beginning after December 31, 2006, generally
411(a)(3)(C)	114(b)(1)	Technical and Conforming Amendments—Vesting Rules	August 17, 2006
411(a)(3)(G)	902(d)(2)(A)	Increasing Participation Through Automatic Contribution Arrangements—Treatment of Withdrawals of Contributions During First 90 Days—Vesting Conforming Amendments	Plan years beginning after December 31, 2007
411(a)(3)(G)	902(d)(2)(B)	Increasing Participation Through Automatic Contribution Arrangements—Treatment of Withdrawals of Contributions During First 90 Days—Vesting Conforming Amendments	Plan years beginning after December 31, 2007
411(a)(12)	904(a)(2)	Faster Vesting of Employer Nonelective Contributions—Amendments to the Internal Revenue Code of 1986—Conforming Amendment	Contributions for plan years beginning after December 31, 2006, generally
411(a)(13)	701(b)(2)	Benefit Accrual Standards—Amendments to the Internal Revenue Code of 1986—Determinations of Accrued Benefit as Balance of Benefit Account or Equivalent Amounts	Distributions made after August 17, 2006
411(b)(1)(F)	114(b)(2)(A)-(B)	Technical and Conforming Amendments—Vesting Rules	August 17, 2006
411(b)(5)	701(b)(1)	Benefit Accrual Standards—Amendments to the Internal Revenue Code of 1986—Rules Relating to Reduction in Rate of Benefit Accrual	Periods beginning on or after June 29, 2005, generally
411(d)(6)(A)	114(b)(3)	Technical and Conforming Amendments—Vesting Rules	August 17, 2006
412(b)(3)	212(c)	Additional Funding Rules For Multiemployer Plans in Endangered Or Critical Status—No Additional Contribution Required	Plan years beginning after 2007, generally
412(b)(5)(B)(ii)(II)	301(b)(1)(A)-(B)	Extension of Replacement of 30-Year Treasury Rates—Amendments of Internal Revenue Code—Determination of Range	August 17, 2006

Code Sec.	Act Sec.	Act Provision Subject	Effective Date
412(l)(7)(C)(i)(IV)	301(b)(2)(A)-(B)	Extension of Replacement of 30-Year Treasury Rates—Amendments of Internal Revenue Code—Determination of Current Liability	August 17, 2006
412	111(a)	Minimum Funding Standards—New Minimum Funding Standards	Plan years beginning after December 31, 2007
414(d)	906(a)(1)	Treatment of Certain Pension Plans of Indian Tribal Governments—Definition of Government Plan to Include Certain Pension Plans of Indian Tribal Government—Amendment to Internal Revenue Code of 1986	Any year beginning on or after August 17, 2006
414(f)(6)	1106(b)	Revocation of Election Relating to Treatment as Multiemployer Plan—Amendment to Internal Revenue Code	August 17, 2006
414(h)(2)	906(b)(1)(C)	Treatment of Certain Pension Plans of Indian Tribal Governments—Clarification That Tribal Governments Are Subject to the Same Pension Plan Rules and Regulations Applied to State and Other Local Governments and Their Police and Firefighters—Government Pick Up Contributions	Any year beginning on or after August 17, 2006
414(l)(2)(B)(i)(I)	114(c)	Technical and Conforming Amendments—Mergers and Consolidations of Plans	August 17, 2006
414(w)	902(d)(1)	Increasing Participation Through Automatic Contribution Arrangements—Treatment of Withdrawals of Contributions During First 90 Days	Plan years beginning after December 31, 2007
414(x)	903(a)	Treatment of Eligible Combined Defined Benefit Plans and Qualified Cash or Deferred Arrangements—Amendments of Internal Revenue Code	Plan years beginning after December 31, 2009
415(b)(2)(E)(ii)	303(a)	Interest Rate Assumption For Applying Benefit Limitations to Lump Sum Distributions	Distributions made in years beginning after December 31, 2005
415(b)(2)(H)(i)-(ii)	906(b)(1)(A)(i)-(ii)	Treatment of Certain Pension Plans of Indian Tribal Governments—Clarification That Tribal Governments Are Subject to the Same Pension Plan Rules and Regulations Applied to State and Other Local Governments and Their Police and Firefighters—Amendments to Internal Revenue Code of 1986—Police and Firefighters	Any year beginning on or after August 17, 2006
415(b)(3)	832(a)	Determination of Average Compensation For Section 415 Limits	Years beginning after December 31, 2005

Code Sec.	Act Sec.	Act Provision Subject	Effective Date
415(b)(10)	906(b)(1)(B)(ii)	Treatment of Certain Pension Plans of Indian Tribal Governments—Clarification That Tribal Governments Are Subject to the Same Pension Plan Rules and Regulations Applied to State and Other Local Governments and Their Police and Firefighters—Amendments to Internal Revenue Code of 1986—State and Local Government Plans	Any year beginning on or after August 17, 2006
415(b)(10)(A)	906(b)(1)(B)(i)	Treatment of Certain Pension Plans of Indian Tribal Governments—Clarification That Tribal Governments Are Subject to the Same Pension Plan Rules and Regulations Applied to State and Other Local Governments and Their Police and Firefighters—Amendments to Internal Revenue Code of 1986—State and Local Government Plans	Any year beginning on or after August 17, 2006
415(b)(11)	867(a)	Church Plan Rule	Years beginning after December 31, 2006
415(n)(1)	821(a)(1)	Clarifications Regarding Purchase of Permissive Service Credit	Permissive service credit contributions made in years beginning after December 31, 1997
415(n)(3)(A)	821(a)(2)	Clarifications Regarding Purchase of Permissive Service Credit	Permissive service credit contributions made in years beginning after December 31, 1997
415(n)(3)(B)	821(c)(1)-(3)	Clarifications Regarding Purchase of Permissive Service Credit—Nonqualified Service	Permissive service credit contributions made in years beginning after December 31, 1997
415(n)(3)(D)	821(b)	Clarifications Regarding Purchase of Permissive Service Credit—Special Rules For Trustee-To-Trustee Transfers	Trustee-to-trustee transfers after December 31, 2001
416(g)(4)(H)(i)	902(c)(1)	Increasing Participation Through Automatic Contribution Arrangements—Exclusion From Definition of Top-Heavy Plans—Elective Contribution Rule	Plan years beginning after December 31, 2007
416(g)(4)(H)(ii)	902(c)(2)	Increasing Participation Through Automatic Contribution Arrangements—Exclusion From Definition of Top-Heavy Plans—Matching Contribution Rule	Plan years beginning after December 31, 2007
417(a)(1)(A)(i)-(iii)	1004(a)(1)(A)-(C)	Requirement For Additional Survivor Annuity Option—Amendment to Internal Revenue Code—Election of Survivor Annuity	Plan years beginning after December 31, 2007, generally

Code Sec.	Act Sec.	Act Provision Subject	Effective Date
417(a)(3)(A)(i)	1004(a)(3)	Requirement For Additional Survivor Annuity Option—Amendment to Internal Revenue Code—Notice	Plan years beginning after December 31, 2007, generally
417(a)(6)(A)	1102(a)(1)(A)	Notice and Consent Period Regarding Distributions—Expansion Period—Amendment of Internal Revenue Code	Years beginning after December 31, 2006
417(e)(3)	302(b)	Interest Rate Assumption For Determination of Lump Sum Distributions—Amendment to Internal Revenue Code of 1986	Plan years beginning after December 31, 2007
417(g)	1004(a)(2)	Requirement For Additional Survivor Annuity Option—Amendment to Internal Revenue Code—Definition	Plan years beginning after December 31, 2007, generally
418E(d)(1)	213(a)(1)-(2)	Measures to Forestall Insolvency of Multiemployer Plans—Advance Determination of Impending Insolvency Over 5 Years	Determinations made in plan years beginning after 2007
419A(c)(6)	843(a)	Allowance of Reserve For Medical Benefits of Plans Sponsored By Bona Fide Associations	Tax years beginning after December 31, 2006
420(a)	842(a)(1)	Transfer of Excess Pension Assets to Multiemployer Health Plan	Transfers made in tax years beginning after December 31, 2006
420(e)(2)	114(d)(1)	Technical and Conforming Amendments—Transfer of Excess Pension Assets to Retiree Health Accounts	August 17, 2006
420(e)(4)	114(d)(2)	Technical and Conforming Amendments—Transfer of Excess Pension Assets to Retiree Health Accounts	August 17, 2006
420(e)(5)	842(a)(2)	Transfer of Excess Pension Assets to Multiemployer Health Plan	Transfers made in tax years beginning after December 31, 2006
420(f)	841(a)	Use of Excess Pension Assets For Future Retiree Health Benefits and Collectively Bargained Retiree Health Benefits	Transfers after August 17, 2006
430	112(a)	Funding Rules For Single-Employer Defined Benefit Pension Plans	Plan years beginning after December 31, 2007
431	211(a)	Funding Rules For Multiemployer Defined Benefit Plans	Plan years beginning after 2007, generally
432	212(a)	Additional Funding Rules For Multiemployer Plans in Endangered Or Critical Status	Plan years beginning after 2007, generally
436	113(a)(1)(B)	Benefit Limitations Under Single-Employer Plans—Prohibition of Shutdown Benefits And Other Unpredictable Contingent Event Benefits Under Single-Employer Plans	Plan years beginning after December 31, 2007, generally

Code Sec.	Act Sec.	Act Provision Subject	Effective Date
457(a)(3)	845(b)(3)	Distributions From Governmental Retirement Plans For Health and Long-Term Care Insurance For Public Safety Officers—Conforming Amendments	Distributions in tax years beginning after December 31, 2006
457(e)(11)(D)	1104(a)(1)	Voluntary Early Retirement Incentive and Employment Retention Plans Maintained By Local Educational Agencies and Other Entities—Voluntary Early Retirement Incentive Plans—Treatment as Plan Providing Severance Pay	Tax years ending after August 17, 2006
457(e)(16)(B)	829(a)(4)	Allow Rollovers By Nonspouse Beneficiaries of Certain Retirement Plan Distributions—Section 457 Plans	Distributions after December 31, 2006
457(f)(2)(D)-(F)	1104(b)(1)	Voluntary Early Retirement Incentive and Employment Retention Plans Maintained By Local Educational Agencies and Other Entities—Employment Retention Plans	Tax years ending the after August 17, 2006
457(f)(4)	1104(b)(2)	Voluntary Early Retirement Incentive and Employment Retention Plans Maintained By Local Educational Agencies and Other Entities—Employment Retention Plans—Definitions and Rules Relating to Employment Retention Plans	Tax years ending after August 17, 2006
501(c)(21)(C)	862(a)	Elimination of Aggregate Limit For Usage of Excess Funds From Black Lung Disability Trusts	Tax years beginning after December 31, 2006
501(q)-(r)	1220(a)	Additional Standards For Credit Counseling Organizations	Tax years beginning after August 17, 2006, generally
508(f)	1235(b)(1)	Returns of, and Applications For Recognition By, Sponsoring Organizations—Matters Included on Exempt Status Application	Organizations applying for tax-exempt status after August 17, 2006
509(a)(3)(B)	1241(a)	Requirements For Supporting Organizations—Types of Supporting Organizations	August 17, 2006
509(e)	1221(a)(2)	Expansion of the Base of Tax on Private Foundation Net Investment Income—Gross Investment Income—Conforming Amendment	Tax years beginning after August 17, 2006
509(f)	1241(b)	Requirements For Supporting Organizations—Requirements For Supporting Organizations	August 17, 2006
512(b)(13)(E)-(F)	1205(a)	Modification of Tax Treatment of Certain Payments to Controlling Exempt Organizations	Payments received or accrued after December 31, 2005
513(j)	1220(b)	Additional Standards For Credit Counseling Organizations—Debt Management Plan Services Treated as an Unrelated Business	Tax years beginning after August 17, 2006, generally

Code Sec.	Act Sec.	Act Provision Subject	Effective Date
514(c)(9)(C)(ii)-(iv)	866(a)	Exemption For Income From Leveraged Real Estate Held by Church Plans	Tax years beginning on or after August 17, 2006
529(f)	1304(b)	Qualified Tuition Programs—Regulatory Authority to Prevent Abuse	August 17, 2006
545(b)(2)	1206(b)(2)	Encouragement of Contributions of Capital Gain Real Property Made For Conservation Purposes—Conforming Amendments	Contributions made in tax years beginning after December 31, 2005
664(g)(3)(E)	868(a)	Gratuitous Transfer For Benefits of Employees	August 17, 2006
848(e)(6)	844(e)	Treatment of Annuity and Life Insurance Contracts With a Long-Term Care Insurance Feature—Treatment of Policy Acquisition Expenses	Specified policy acquisition expenses determined for tax years beginning after December 31, 2009
1035(a)(1)-(3)	844(b)(3)(A)-(C)	Treatment of Annuity and Life Insurance Contracts With a Long-Term Care Insurance Feature—Tax-Free Exchanges Among Certain Insurance Policies—Expansion of Tax-Free Exchanges of Life Insurance, Endowment, and Annuity Contracts For Long-Term Care Contracts	Exchanges occurring after December 31, 2009
1035(a)(2)-(4)	844(b)(4)	Treatment of Annuity and Life Insurance Contracts With a Long-Term Care Insurance Feature—Tax-Free Exchanges Among Certain Insurance Policies—Tax-Free Exchanges of Qualified Long-Term Care Insurance Contract	Exchanges occurring after December 31, 2009
1035(b)(2)	844(b)(1)	Treatment of Annuity and Life Insurance Contracts With a Long-Term Care Insurance Feature—Tax-Free Exchanges Among Certain Insurance Policies—Annuity Contracts Can Include Qualified Long-Term Care Insurance Riders	Exchanges occurring after December 31, 2009
1035(b)(3)	844(b)(2)	Treatment of Annuity and Life Insurance Contracts With a Long-Term Care Insurance Feature—Tax-Free Exchanges Among Certain Insurance Policies—Life Insurance Contracts Can Include Qualified Long-Term Care Insurance Riders	Exchanges occurring after December 31, 2009
1367(a)(2)	1203(a)	Basis Adjustment to Stock of S Corporation Contributing Property	Contributions made in tax years beginning after December 31, 2005
2055(e)(5)	1234(b)	Treatment of Charitable Contribution Deductions to Donor Advised Funds—Estate	Contributions made after the date which is 180 days after August 17, 2006
2055(g)-(h)	1218(b)	Contributions of Fractional Interests in Tangible Personal Property—Estate Tax	Contributions, bequests, and gifts made after August 17, 2006

Code Sec.	Act Sec.	Act Provision Subject	Effective Date
2522(c)(5)	1234(c)	Treatment of Charitable Contribution Deductions to Donor Advised Funds—Gift	Contributions made after the date which is 180 days after August 17, 2006
2522(e)-(f)	1218(c)	Contributions of Fractional Interests in Tangible Personal Property—Gift Tax	Contributions, bequests, and gifts made after August 17, 2006
3121(b)(5)(E)	854(c)(8)	Annuities to Surviving Spouses and Dependent Children of Special Trial Judges of the Tax Court—Conforming Amendments	August 17, 2006
3304(a)	1105(a)	No Reduction in Unemployment Compensation as a Result of Pension Rollovers	Weeks beginning on or after August 17, 2006
4041(g)(3)-(5)	1207(a)	Excise Taxes Exemption For Blood Collector Organizations—Exemption From Imposition of Special Fuels Tax	January 1, 2007
4221(a)	1207(b)(2)	Excise Taxes Exemption For Blood Collector Organizations—Exemption From Manufacturers Excise Tax—No Exemption With Respect to Vaccines and Recreational Equipment	January 1, 2007
4221(a)	1207(b)(3)(A)	Excise Taxes Exemption For Blood Collector Organizations—Exemption From Manufacturers Excise Tax—Conforming Amendments	January 1, 2007
4221(a)(4)-(6)	1207(b)(1)	Excise Taxes Exemption For Blood Collector Organizations—Exemption From Manufacturers Excise Tax	January 1, 2007
4253(k)-(l)	1206(c)(1)	Excise Taxes Exemption For Blood Collector Organizations—Exemption From Communication Excise Tax	January 1, 2007
4253(l)	1206(c)(2)	Excise Taxes Exemption For Blood Collector Organizations—Exemption From Communication Excise Tax—Conforming Amendment	January 1, 2007
4483(h)-(i)	1207(d)	Excise Taxes Exemption For Blood Collector Organizations—Exemption From Tax on Heavy Vehicles	Tax periods beginning on or after July 1, 2007
4940(c)(2)	1221(a)(1)	Expansion of the Base of Tax on Private Foundation Net Investment Income—Gross Investment Income	Tax years beginning after August 17, 2006
4940(c)(4)	1221(b)(1)-(3)	Expansion of the Base of Tax on Private Foundation Net Investment Income—Capital Gain Net Income	Tax years beginning after August 17, 2006
4941(a)(1)-(2)	1212(a)(1)(A)-(B)	Increase in Penalty Excise Taxes Relating to Public Charities, Social Welfare Organizations, and Private Foundations—Taxes on Self-Dealing and Excess Benefit Transactions	Tax years beginning after August 17, 2006

Code Sec.	Act Sec.	Act Provision Subject	Effective Date
4941(c)(2)	1212(a)(2)	Increase in Penalty Excise Taxes Relating to Public Charities, Social Welfare Organizations, and Private Foundations—Taxes on Self-Dealing and Excess Benefit Transactions—Increased Limitation For Managers on Self-Dealing	Tax years beginning after August 17, 2006
4942(a)	1212(b)	Increase in Penalty Excise Taxes Relating to Public Charities, Social Welfare Organizations, and Private Foundations—Taxes on Failure to Distribute Income	Tax years beginning after August 17, 2006
4942(g)(4)	1244(a)	Treatment of Amounts Paid to Supporting Organizations By Private Foundations—Qualifying Distributions	Distributions and expenditures after August 17, 2006
4943(a)(1)	1212(c)	Increase in Penalty Excise Taxes Relating to Public Charities, Social Welfare Organizations, and Private Foundations—Taxes on Excess Business Holdings	Tax years beginning after August 17, 2006
4943(e)	1233(a)	Excess Business Holdings of Donor Advised Funds	Tax years beginning after August 17, 2006
4943(f)	1243(a)	Excess Business Holdings of Supporting Organizations	Tax years beginning after August 17, 2006
4944(a)	1212(d)(1)	Increase in Penalty Excise Taxes Relating to Public Charities, Social Welfare Organizations, and Private Foundations—Taxes on Investments Which Jeopardize Charitable Purpose	Tax years beginning after August 17, 2006
4944(d)(2)	1212(d)(2)(A)-(B)	Increase in Penalty Excise Taxes Relating to Public Charities, Social Welfare Organizations, and Private Foundations—Taxes on Investments Which Jeopardize Charitable Purpose—Increased Limitation For Managers	Tax years beginning after August 17, 2006
4945(a)(1)-(2)	1212(e)(1)(A)-(B)	Increase in Penalty Excise Taxes Relating to Public Charities, Social Welfare Organizations, and Private Foundations—Taxes on Taxable Expenditures	Tax years beginning after August 17, 2006
4945(c)(2)	1212(e)(2)(A)-(B)	Increase in Penalty Excise Taxes Relating to Public Charities, Social Welfare Organizations, and Private Foundations—Taxes on Taxable Expenditures—Increased Limitation For Managers	Tax years beginning after August 17, 2006
4945(d)(4)(A)	1244(b)	Treatment of Amounts Paid to Supporting Organizations By Private Foundations—Taxable Expenditures	Distributions and expenditures after August 17, 2006
4958(c)(2)-(3)	1232(b)(1)	Excess Benefit Transactions Involving Donor Advised Funds and Sponsoring Organizations—Certain Transactions Treated as Excess Benefit Transactions	Transactions occurring after August 17, 2006

Code Sec.	Act Sec.	Act Provision Subject	Effective Date
4958(c)(3)-(4)	1242(b)	Excess Benefit Transactions Involving Supporting Organizations—Certain Transactions Treated as Excess Benefit Transactions	Transactions occurring after July 25, 2006
4958(d)(2)	1212(a)(3)	Increase in Penalty Excise Taxes Relating to Public Charities, Social Welfare Organizations, and Private Foundations—Taxes on Self-Dealing and Excess Benefit Transactions—Increased Limitation For Managers on Excess Benefit Transactions	Tax years beginning after August 17, 2006
4958(f)(1)(B)-(E)	1232(a)(1)	Excess Benefit Transactions Involving Donor Advised Funds and Sponsoring Organizations—Disqualified Persons	Transactions occurring after August 17, 2006
4958(f)(1)(D)-(F)	1242(a)	Excess Benefit Transactions Involving Supporting Organizations—Disqualified Persons	Transactions occurring after August 17, 2006
4958(f)(6)	1232(b)(2)	Excess Benefit Transactions Involving Donor Advised Funds and Sponsoring Organizations—Certain Transactions Treated as Excess Benefit Transactions—Special Rule For Correction of Transaction	Transactions occurring after August 17, 2006
4958(f)(7)-(8)	1232(a)(2)	Excess Benefit Transactions Involving Donor Advised Funds and Sponsoring Organizations—Disqualified Persons—Donors, Donor Advisors, and Investment Advisors Treated as Disqualified Persons	Transactions occurring after August 17, 2006
4963(a)	1231(b)(1)	Excise Taxes Relating to Donor Advised Funds—Conforming Amendments	Tax years beginning after August 17, 2006
4963(c)	1231(b)(1)	Excise Taxes Relating to Donor Advised Funds—Conforming Amendments	Tax years beginning after August 17, 2006
4966	1231(a)	Excise Taxes Relating to Donor Advised Funds	Tax years beginning after August 17, 2006
4967	1231(a)	Excise Taxes Relating to Donor Advised Funds	Tax years beginning after August 17, 2006
4971(a)-(b)	114(e)(1)	Technical and Conforming Amendments—Excise Taxes	August 17, 2006
4971(c)	114(e)(2)(A)-(B)	Technical and Conforming Amendments—Excise Taxes	August 17, 2006
4971(c)(2)	212(b)(2)(A)-(B)	Additional Funding Rules For Multiemployer Plans in Endangered Or Critical Status—Controlled Groups	Plan years beginning after 2007, generally
4971(e)(1)	114(e)(3)	Technical and Conforming Amendments—Excise Taxes	August 17, 2006
4971(f)(1)	114(e)(4)(A)-(B)	Technical and Conforming Amendments—Excise Taxes	August 17, 2006
4971(g)-(h)	212(b)(1)	Additional Funding Rules For Multiemployer Plans in Endangered Or Critical Status—Excise Taxes On Failures Relating to Multiemployer Plans in Endangered or Critical Status	Plan years beginning after 2007, generally

Code Sec.	Act Sec.	Act Provision Subject	Effective Date
4972(c)(6)(A)	803(c)	Updating Deduction Rules For Combination of Plans—Conforming Amendment	Contributions for tax years beginning after December 31, 2005
4972(c)(7)	114(e)(5)	Technical and Conforming Amendments—Excise Taxes	August 17, 2006
4975(d)(15)-(17)	601(b)(1)(A)-(C)	Prohibited Transaction Exemption For Provision of Investment Advice-Amendments to Internal Revenue Code of 1986—Exemption From Prohibited Transaction	Advice referred to in Code Sec. 4975(c)(3)(B) provided after December 31, 2006
4975(d)(16)-(18)	611(a)(2)(A)	Prohibited Transaction Rules Relating to Financial Investments-Exemption For Block Trading—Amendments to Internal Revenue Code of 1986	Transactions occurring after August 17, 2006
4975(d)(17)-(19)	611(c)(2)	Prohibited Transaction Rules Relating to Financial Investments—Exemption For Electronic Communication Network—Amendments to Internal Revenue Code of 1986	Transactions occurring after August 17, 2006
4975(d)(18)-(20)	611(d)(2)(A)	Prohibited Transaction Rules Relating to Financial Investments—Exemption For Service Providers—Amendments to Internal Revenue Code of 1986	Transactions occurring after August 17, 2006
4975(d)(19)-(21)	611(e)(2)	Prohibited Transaction Rules Relating to Financial Investments—Relief For Foreign Exchange Transactions—Amendments to Internal Revenue Code of 1986	Transactions occurring after August 17, 2006
4975(d)(20)-(22)	611(g)(2)	Prohibited Transaction Rules Relating to Financial Investments—Exemption For Cross Trading—Amendments to Internal Revenue Code of 1986	Transactions occurring after August 17, 2006
4975(d)(21)-(23)	612(b)(1)	Correction Period For Certain Transactions Involving Securities and Commodities—Amendment of Internal Revenue Code of 1986	Any transaction which the fiduciary or disqualified person discovers, or reasonably should have discovered, after August 17, 2006, constitutes a prohibited transaction
4975(f)(8)	601(b)(2)	Prohibited Transaction Exemption For Provision of Investment Advice—Amendments to Internal Revenue Code of 1986—Requirements	Advice referred to in Code Sec. 4975(c)(3)(B) provided after December 31, 2006
4975(f)(9)	611(a)(2)(B)	Prohibited Transaction Rules Relating to Financial Investments—Exemption For Block Trading—Amendments to Internal Revenue Code of 1986—Special Rule Relating to Block Trade	Transactions occurring after August 17, 2006

Code Sec.	Act Sec.	Act Provision Subject	Effective Date
4975(f)(10)	611(d)(2)(B)	Prohibited Transaction Rules Relating to Financial Investments—Exemption For Service Providers—Amendments to Internal Revenue Code of 1986—Special Rule Relating to Service Providers	Transactions occurring after August 17, 2006
4975(f)(11)	612(b)(2)	Correction Period For Certain Transactions Involving Securities and Commodities—Amendment of Internal Revenue Code of 1986—Special Rules Relating to Correction Period	Any transaction which the fiduciary or disqualified person discovers, or reasonably should have discovered, after August 17, 2006, constitutes a prohibited transaction
4979(f)	902(e)(1)(A)-(B)	Increasing Participation Through Automatic Contribution Arrangements—Excess Contributions—Expansion of Corrective Distribution Period For Automatic Contribution Arrangements	Plan years beginning after December 31, 2007
4979(f)(1)	902(e)(3)(A)	Increasing Participation Through Automatic Contribution Arrangements—Excess Contributions—Simplification of Allocable Earnings	Plan years beginning after December 31, 2007
4979(f)(2)	902(e)(2)	Increasing Participation Through Automatic Contribution Arrangements—Excess Contributions—Year of Inclusion	Plan years beginning after December 31, 2007
4980(c)(3)(A)	901(a)(2)(C)	Defined Contribution Plans Required to Provide Employees With Freedom to Invest Their Plan Assets—Amendments of Internal Revenue Code—Conforming Amendments	Plan years beginning after December 31, 2006, generally
4980F(e)(1)	502(c)(2)	Access to Multiemployer Pension Plan Information—Notice of Amendment Reducing Future Accruals—Amendment of Internal Revenue Code	Plan years beginning after December 31, 2007
6033(a)(3)(B)	1245(a)	Returns of Supporting Organizations—Requirement to File Return	Returns filed for tax years ending after August 17, 2006
6033(h)-(i)	1205(b)(1)	Modification of Tax Treatment of Certain Payments to Controlling Exempt Organizations—Reporting	Returns the due date (determined without regard to extensions) of which is after August 17, 2006
6033(i)-(j)	1223(a)	Notification Requirement For Entities Not Currently Required to File	Notices and returns with respect to annual periods beginning after 2006
6033(j)-(k)	1223(b)	Notification Requirement For Entities Not Currently Required to File—Loss of Exempt Status For Failure to File	Notices and returns with respect to annual periods beginning after 2006

Code Sec.	Act Sec.	Act Provision Subject	Effective Date
6033(k)-(l)	1235(a)(1)	Returns of, and Applications For Recognition By, Sponsoring Organizations-Matters Included On Returns	Returns filed for tax years ending after August 17, 2006
6033(l)-(m)	1245(b)	Returns of Supporting Organizations—Matters Included on Returns	Returns filed for tax years ending after August 17, 2006
6034	1201(b)(1)	Tax-Free Distributions From Individual Retirement Plans For Charitable Purposes—Modifications Relating to Information Returns By Certain Trusts—Returns	Returns for tax years beginning after December 31, 2006
6039I	863(b)	Treatment of Death Benefits From Corporate-Owned Life Insurance—Reporting Requirements	Life insurance contracts issued after August 17, 2006, except for a contract issued after that date pursuant to a Code Sec. 1035 exchange for a contract issued on or prior to that date
6050L(a)(1)	1215(b)(1)-(2)	Recapture of Tax Benefit For Charitable Contributions of Exempt Use Property Not Used for an Exempt Use Reporting Requirements	Returns filed after September 1, 2006
6050U	844(d)(1)	Treatment of Annuity and Life Insurance Contracts With a Long-Term Care Insurance Feature—Exclusion From Gross Income	Charges made after December 31, 2009
6050V	1211(a)(1)	Reporting on Certain Acquisitions of Interests in Insurance Contracts in Which Certain Exempt Organizations Hold an Interest—Reporting Requirements	Acquisitions of contracts after August 17, 2006
6059(b)(2)-(3)	114(f)(1)-(2)	Technical and Conforming Amendments—Reporting Requirements	August 17, 2006
6103(a)(2)	1224(b)(1)	Disclosure to State Officials Relating to Exempt Organizations—Conforming Amendments	August 17, 2006, but does not apply to requests made before that date
6103(p)(3)(A)	1224(b)(2)	Disclosure to State Officials Relating to Exempt Organizations—Conforming Amendments	August 17, 2006, but does not apply to requests made before that date
6103(p)(4)	1224(b)(3)(A)-(C)	Disclosure to State Officials Relating to Exempt Organizations—Conforming Amendments	August 17, 2006, but does not apply to requests made before that date
6104(b)	1201(b)(3)	Tax-Free Distributions From individual Retirement Plans For Charitable Purposes—Modifications Relating to Information Returns By Certain Trusts—Confidentiality of Noncharitable Beneficiaries	Returns for tax years beginning after December 31, 2006

Code Sec.	Act Sec.	Act Provision Subject	Effective Date
6104(c)(1)	1224(b)(4)	Disclosure to State Officials Relating to Exempt Organizations—Conforming Amendments	August 17, 2006, but does not apply to requests made before that date
6104(c)(2)-(6)	1224(a)	Disclosure to State Officials Relating to Exempt Organizations	August 17, 2006, but does not apply to requests made before that date
6104(d)(1)(A)(ii)-(iv)	1225(a)	Public Disclosure of Information Relating to Unrelated Business Income Tax Returns	Returns filed after August 17, 2006
6214(b)	858(a)	Confirmation of Authority of Tax Court to Apply Doctrine of Equitable Recoupment—Confirmation of Authority of Tax Court to Apply Doctrine of Equitable Recoupment	Any action or proceeding in the United States Tax Court with respect to which a decision has not become final (as determined under section Code Sec. 7481) as of August 17, 2006
6330(d)(1)	855(a)	Jurisdiction of Tax Court Over Collection Due Process Cases	Determinations made after the date which is 60 days after August 17, 2006
6416(b)(2)	1207(e)(1)(B)	Excise Taxes Exemption For Blood Collector Organizations—Credit or Refund For Certain Taxes on Sales and Services—Deemed Overpayment—No Credit or Refund For Vaccines or Recreational Equipment	January 1, 2007
6416(b)(2)	1207(e)(1)(C)(i)-(ii)	Excise Taxes Exemption For Blood Collector Organizations—Credit or Refund For Certain Taxes on Sales and Services—Deemed Overpayment—Conforming Amendments	January 1, 2007
6416(b)(2)(E)-(G)	1207(e)(1)(A)	Excise Taxes Exemption For Blood Collector Organizations—Credit or Refund For Certain Taxes on Sales and Services—Deemed Overpayment	January 1, 2007
6416(b)(4)(B)(i)-(iii)	1207(e)(2)	Excise Taxes Exemption For Blood Collector Organizations—Credit or Refund For Certain Taxes on Sales and Services—Sales of Tires	January 1, 2007
6421(c)	1207(b)(3)(B)	Excise Taxes Exemption For Blood Collector Organizations—Exemption From Manufacturers Excise Tax—Conforming Amendments	January 1, 2007
6652(c)(1)(E)	1223(d)	Notification Requirement For Entities Not Currently Required to File—No Monetary Penalty For Failure to Notify	Notices and returns with respect to annual periods beginning after 2006

Code Sec.	Act Sec.	Act Provision Subject	Effective Date
6652(c)(2)(C)	1201(b)(2)	Tax-Free Distributions From Individual Retirement Plans For Charitable Purposes—Modifications Relating to Information Returns By Certain Trusts—Increase in Penalty Relating to Filing of Information Return By Split-Interest Trusts	Returns for tax years beginning after December 31, 2006
6662(e)(1)(A)	1219(a)(1)(A)	Provisions Relating to Substantial and Gross Overstatements of Valuations—Modification of Thresholds For Substantial and Gross Valuation Misstatements—Substantial Valuation Misstatement—Income Taxes	Returns filed after August 17, 2006, generally
6662(g)	1219(a)(1)(B)	Provisions Relating to Substantial and Gross Overstatements of Valuations—Modification of Thresholds For Substantial and Gross Valuation Misstatements—Substantial Valuation Misstatement—Estate and Gift Taxes	Returns filed after August 17, 2006, generally
6662(h)(2)(A)(i)-(ii)	1219(a)(2)(A)	Provisions Relating to Substantial and Gross Overstatements of Valuations—Modification of Thresholds For Substantial and Gross Valuation Misstatements—Gross Valuation Misstatement—Income Taxes	Returns filed after August 17, 2006, generally
6662(h)(2)(C)	1219(a)(2)(B)	Provisions Relating to Substantial and Gross Overstatements of Valuations—Modification of Thresholds For Substantial and Gross Valuation Misstatements—Gross Valuation Misstatement—Estate and Gift Taxes	Returns filed after August 17, 2006, generally
6664(c)(2)	1219(a)(3)	Provisions Relating to Substantial and Gross Overstatements of Valuations—Modification of Thresholds For Substantial and Gross Valuation Misstatements—Elimination of Reasonable Cause Exception For Gross Misstatements	Returns filed after August 17, 2006, generally
6664(c)(3)(B)-(C)	1219(c)(2)	Provisions Relating to Substantial and Gross Overstatements of Valuations—Qualified Appraisers and Appraisals—Reasonable Cause Exception	Appraisals prepared with respect to returns or submissions filed after August 17, 2006, generally
6695A	1219(b)(1)	Provisions Relating to Substantial and Gross Overstatements of Valuations—Penalty on Appraisers Whose Appraisals Result in Substantial or Gross Valuation Misstatements	Appraisals prepared with respect to returns or submissions filed after August 17, 2006, generally
6696	1219(b)(2)(A)-(B)	Provisions Relating to Substantial and Gross Overstatements of Valuations—Penalty on Appraisers Whose Appraisals Result in Substantial or Gross Valuation Misstatements—Rules Applicable to Penalty	Appraisals prepared with respect to returns or submissions filed after August 17, 2006, generally

Code Sec.	Act Sec.	Act Provision Subject	Effective Date
6720B	1215(c)(1)	Recapture of Tax Benefit For Charitable Contributions of Exempt Use Property—Not Used for an Exempt Purpose Penalty	Identifications made after August 17, 2006
6721(e)(2)(B)-(D)	1211(b)(2)	Reporting on Certain Acquisitions of Interests in Insurance Contracts in Which Certain Exempt Organizations Hold an Interest—Penalties-Intentional Disregard	Acquisitions of contracts after August 17, 2006
6724(d)(2)(AA)-(CC)	844(d)(2)(B)	Treatment of Annuity and Life Insurance Contracts With a Long-Term Care Insurance Feature—Information Reporting—Penalty For Failure to File—Statement	Charges made after December 31, 2009
6724(d)(1)(B)(xvii)-(xix)	844(d)(2)(A)	Treatment of Annuity and Life Insurance Contracts With a Long-Term Care Insurance Feature—Information Reporting—Penalty For Failure to File-Return	Charges made after December 31, 2009
6724(d)(1)(xiv)-(xx)	1211(b)(1)	Reporting on Certain Acquisitions of Interests in Insurance Contracts in Which Certain Exempt Organizations Hold an Interest—Penalties	Acquisitions of contracts after August 17, 2006
7213(a)(2)	1224(b)(5)	Disclosure to State Officials Relating to Exempt Organizations—Conforming Amendments	August 17, 2006, but does not apply to requests made before that date
7213A(a)(2)	1224(b)(6)	Disclosure to State Officials Relating to Exempt Organizations—Conforming Amendments	August 17, 2006, but does not apply to requests made before that date
7428(b)(4)	1223(c)	Notification Requirement For Entities Not Currently Required to File—No Declaratory Judgment Relief	Notices and returns with respect to annual periods beginning after 2006
7431(a)(2)	1224(b)(7)	Disclosure to State Officials Relating to Exempt Organizations—Conforming Amendments	August 17, 2006, but does not apply to requests made before that date
7443A(b)(4)-(6)	857(a)	Authority For Special Trial Judges to Hear and Decide Certain Employment Status Cases	Any proceeding under Code Sec. 7436(c) with respect to which a decision has not become final (as determined under Code Sec. 7481) before August 17, 2006
7443A(c)	857(b)	Authority For Special Trial Judges to Hear and Decide Certain Employment Status Cases—Conforming Amendments	Any proceeding under Code Sec. 7436(c) with respect to which a decision has not become final (as determined under Code Sec. 7481) before August 17, 2006

Code Sec.	Act Sec.	Act Provision Subject	Effective Date
7443B	856(a)	Provisions For Recall	August 17, 2006
7447(j)	853(a)	Participation of Tax Court Judges in the Thrift Savings Plan	August 17, 2006, generally
7448	854(c)(1)	Annuities to Surviving Spouses and Dependent Children of Special Trial Judges of the Tax Court—Conforming Amendments	August 17, 2006
7448(a)(5)-(10)	854(a)	Annuities to Surviving Spouses and Dependent Children of Special Trial Judges of the Tax Court—Definitions	August 17, 2006
7448(b)	854(b)(1)-(3)	Annuities to Surviving Spouses and Dependent Children of Special Trial Judges of the Tax Court—Election	August 17, 2006
7448(c)(1)	854(c)(3)(A)-(B)	Annuities to Surviving Spouses and Dependent Children of Special Trial Judges of the Tax Court—Conforming Amendments	August 17, 2006
7448(c)(1)-(2)	854(c)(4)(A)-(B)	Annuities to Surviving Spouses and Dependent Children of Special Trial Judges of the Tax Court—Conforming Amendments	August 17, 2006
7448(d)	854(c)(3)(A)-(B)	Annuities to Surviving Spouses and Dependent Children of Special Trial Judges of the Tax Court—Conforming Amendments	August 17, 2006
7448(f)	854(c)(3)(A)-(B)	Annuities to Surviving Spouses and Dependent Children of Special Trial Judges of the Tax Court—Conforming Amendments	August 17, 2006
7448(g)	854(c)(3)(A)-(B)	Annuities to Surviving Spouses and Dependent Children of Special Trial Judges of the Tax Court—Conforming Amendments	August 17, 2006
7448(h)	854(c)(3)(A)-(B)	Annuities to Surviving Spouses and Dependent Children of Special Trial Judges of the Tax Court—Conforming Amendments	August 17, 2006
7448(j)	854(c)(3)(A)-(B)	Annuities to Surviving Spouses and Dependent Children of Special Trial Judges of the Tax Court—Conforming Amendments	August 17, 2006
7448(j)(1)	854(c)(5)(A)-(B)	Annuities to Surviving Spouses and Dependent Children of Special Trial Judges of the Tax Court—Conforming Amendments	August 17, 2006
7448(m)	854(c)(3)(A)-(B)	Annuities to Surviving Spouses and Dependent Children of Special Trial Judges of the Tax Court—Conforming Amendments	August 17, 2006
7448(m)(1)	854(c)(6)	Annuities to Surviving Spouses and Dependent Children of Special Trial Judges of the Tax Court—Conforming Amendments	August 17, 2006

Code Sec.	Act Sec.	Act Provision Subject	Effective Date
7448(n)	854(c)(3)(A)-(B)	Annuities to Surviving Spouses and Dependent Children of Special Trial Judges of the Tax Court—Conforming Amendments	August 17, 2006
7448(n)	854(c)(7)	Annuities to Surviving Spouses and Dependent Children of Special Trial Judges of the Tax Court—Conforming Amendments	August 17, 2006
7448(s)	851(a)	Cost-of-Living Adjustments For Tax Court Judicial Survivor Annuities	Increases made under section 8340(b) of title 5, United States Code, in annuities payable under subchapter III of chapter 83 of that title, taking effect after August 17, 2006
7448(u)	854(c)(3)(A)-(B)	Annuities to Surviving Spouses and Dependent Children of Special Trial Judges of the Tax Court—Conforming Amendments	August 17, 2006
7451	859(a)	Tax Court Filing Fee in All Cases Commenced By Filing Petition	August 17, 2006
7472	852	Cost of Life Insurance Coverage For Tax Court Judges Age 65 or Over	August 17, 2006
7475(b)	860(a)	Expanded Use of Tax Court Practice Fee For Pro Se Taxpayers	August 17, 2006
7701(a)(49)	1207(f)	Excise Taxes Exemption For Blood Collector Organizations—Definition of Qualified Blood Collector Organization	January 1, 2007
7701(o)-(p)	1222	Definition of Convention or Association of Churches	August 17, 2006
7702B(e)	844(c)	Treatment of Annuity and Life Insurance Contracts With a Long-Term Care Insurance Feature—Treatment of Coverage Provided as Part of a Life Insurance or Annuity Contract	Contracts issued after December 31, 1996, but only with respect to tax years beginning after December 31, 2009
7702B(e)(1)	844(f)	Treatment of Annuity and Life Insurance Contracts With a Long-Term Care Insurance Feature—Technical Amendment	Contracts issued after December 31, 1996
...	101(a)	Minimum Funding Standards—Repeal of Existing Funding Rules	Plan years beginning after 2007
...	101(b)	Minimum Funding Standards—New Minimum Funding Standards	Plan years beginning after 2007
...	101(c)	Minimum Funding Standards—Clerical Amendment	Plan years beginning after 2007
...	102(a)	Funding Rules For Single-Employer Defined Benefit Pension Plans	Plan years beginning after 2007
...	102(b)	Funding Rules For Single-Employer Defined Benefit Pension Plans—Clerical Amendment	Plan years beginning after 2007

Code Sec.	Act Sec.	Act Provision Subject	Effective Date
...	103(a)	Benefit Limitations Under Single-Employer Plans—Funding—Based Limits on Benefits and Benefit Accruals Under Single-Employer Plans	Plan years beginning after December 31, 2007, generally
...	103(b)(1)(A)-(B)	Benefit Limitations Under Single-Employer Plans—Notice Requirement	Plan years beginning after December 31, 2007, generally
...	103(b)(2)	Benefit Limitations Under Single-Employer Plans—Notice Requirement—Enforcement	Plan years beginning after December 31, 2007, generally
...	104(a)	Special Rules for Multiple Employer Plans of Certain Cooperatives	August 17, 2006
...	104(b)	Special Rules for Multiple Employer Plans of Certain Cooperatives—Interest Rate	August 17, 2006
...	104(c)	Special Rules for Multiple Employer Plans of Certain Cooperatives—Eligible Cooperative Defined	August 17, 2006
...	105(a)	Temporary Relief For Certain PBGC Settlement Plans	August 17, 2006
...	105(b)	Temporary Relief For Certain PBGC Settlement Plans—Interest Rate	August 17, 2006
...	105(c)	Temporary Relief For Certain PBGC Settlement Plans—PBGC Settlement Plan	August 17, 2006
...	106(a)	Special Rules For Plans of Certain Government Contractors	August 17, 2006
...	106(b)	Special Rules For Plans of Certain Government Contractors—Interest Rate	August 17, 2006
...	106(c)	Special Rules For Plans of Certain Government Contractors—Eligible Government Contractor Plan Defined	August 17, 2006
...	107(a)(1)-(11)	Technical and Conforming Amendments—Miscellaneous Amendments to Title I	Plan years beginning after 2007
...	107(b)(1)-(9)	Technical and Conforming Amendments—Miscellaneous Amendments to Title IV	Plan years beginning after 2007
...	107(c)	Technical and Conforming Amendments—Amendments to Reorganization Plan No. 4 of 1978	Plan years beginning after 2007
...	107(d)	Technical and Conforming Amendments—Repeal of Expired Authority For Temporary Variances	Plan years beginning after 2007
...	115(a)	Modification of Transition Rule to Pension Funding Requirements	August 17, 2006
...	115(b)(1)	Modification of Transition Rule to Pension Funding Requirements—Modified Rules	August 17, 2006
...	115(b)(2)	Modification of Transition Rule to Pension Funding Requirements—Modified Rules	August 17, 2006
...	115(b)(3)	Modification of Transition Rule to Pension Funding Requirements—Modified Rules	August 17, 2006

Code Sec.	Act Sec.	Act Provision Subject	Effective Date
. . .	115(c)	Modification of Transition Rule to Pension Funding Requirements—Definitions	August 17, 2006
. . .	115(d)(1)	Modification of Transition Rule to Pension Funding Requirements	Plan years beginning after December 31, 2005
. . .	115(e)(1)	Modification of Transition Rule to Pension Funding Requirements	December 31, 2007 and applicable to plan years beginning after that date
. . .	201(a)	Funding Rules For Multiemployer Defined Benefit Plans	Plan years beginning after 2007, generally
. . .	201(b)(1)	Funding Rules For Multiemployer Defined Benefit Plans—Shortfall Funding Method	Plan years beginning after 2007, generally
. . .	201(b)(2)	Funding Rules For Multiemployer Defined Benefit Plans—Shortfall Funding Method—Criteria	Plan years beginning after 2007, generally
. . .	201(b)(3)	Funding Rules For Multiemployer Defined Benefit Plans—Shortfall Funding Method—Shortfall Funding Method Defined	Plan years beginning after 2007, generally
. . .	201(b)(4)	Funding Rules For Multiemployer Defined Benefit Plans—Shortfall Funding Method—Benefit Restrictions Apply	Plan years beginning after 2007, generally
. . .	201(b)(5)	Funding Rules For Multiemployer Defined Benefit Plans—Shortfall Funding Method—Use of Shortfall Method Not to Preclude Other Options	Plan years beginning after 2007, generally
. . .	201(c)(1)-(2)	Funding Rules For Multiemployer Defined Benefit Plans—Conforming Amendments	Plan years beginning after 2007, generally
. . .	202(a)	Additional Funding Rules For Multiemployer Plans In Endangered Or Critical Status	Plan years beginning after 2007, generally
. . .	202(b)(1)-(3)	Additional Funding Rules For Multiemployer Plans In Endangered Or Critical Status—Enforcement	Plan years beginning after 2007, generally
. . .	202(c)	Additional Funding Rules For Multiemployer Plans In Endangered Or Critical Status—Cause of Action to Compel Adoption Or Implementation of Funding Improvement Or Rehabilitation Plan	Plan years beginning after 2007, generally
. . .	202(d)	Additional Funding Rules For Multiemployer Plans In Endangered Or Critical Status—No Additional Contributions Required	Plan years beginning after 2007, generally
. . .	202(e)	Additional Funding Rules For Multiemployer Plans In Endangered Or Critical Status—Conforming Amendment	Plan years beginning after 2007, generally

Code Sec.	Act Sec.	Act Provision Subject	Effective Date
...	203(a)(1)-(2)	Measures to Forestall Insolvency of Multiemployer Plans—Advance Determination of Impending Insolvency Over 5 Years	Determinations made in plan years beginning after 2007
...	204(a)(1)	Withdrawal Liability Reforms—Update of Rules Relating to Limitations on Withdrawal Liability—Increase in Limits	Sales occurring on or after January 1, 2007
...	204(a)(2)	Withdrawal Liability Reforms—Update of Rules Relating to Limitations on Withdrawal Liability—Plans Using Attributable Method	Sales occurring on or after January 1, 2007
...	204(b)(1)	Withdrawal Liability Reforms—Withdrawal Liability Continues If Work Contracted Out	Work transferred on or after August 17, 2006
...	204(c)(1)	Withdrawal Liability Reforms—Application of Rules to Plans Primarily Covering Employees in the Building and Construction Industry	Plan withdrawals occurring on or after January 1, 2007
...	204(c)(2)	Withdrawal Liability Reforms—Application of rules to Plans Primarily Covering Employees in the Building and Construction Industry—Fresh Start Option	Plan withdrawals occurring on or after January 1, 2007
...	204(d)(1)	Withdrawal Liability Reforms—Procedures Applicable to Disputes Involving Pension Plan Withdrawal Liability	Any person receiving notification under ERISA Sec. 4219(b)(1) on or after August 17, 2006 with respect to a transaction occurring after December 31, 1998
...	205	Prohibition on Retaliation Against Employers Exercising Their Rights to Petition the Federal Government	August 17, 2006
...	206	Special Rule For Certain Benefits Funded Under an Agreement Approved by the Pension Benefit Guaranty Corporation	August 17, 2006
...	214(a)(1)-(2)	Exemption From Excise Taxes For Certain Multiemployer Pension Plans	August 17, 2006
...	214(b)(1)-(4)	Exemption From Excise Taxes For Certain Multiemployer Pension Plans—Plan Described	August 17, 2006
...	301(a)(1)(A)-(B)	Extension of Replacement of 30-Year Treasury Rates—Amendments of ERISA—Determination of Range	August 17, 2006
...	301(a)(2)(A)-(B)	Extension of Replacement of 30-Year Treasury Rates—Amendments of ERISA—Determination of Current Liability	August 17, 2006
...	301(a)(3)	Extension of Replacement of 30-Year Treasury Rates—Amendments of ERISA—PBGC Premium Rate	August 17, 2006

Code Sec.	Act Sec.	Act Provision Subject	Effective Date
...	301(c)	Extension of Replacement of 30-Year Treasury Rates—Plan Amendments	August 17, 2006
...	302(a)	Interest Rate Assumption For Determination of Lump Sum Distributions—Amendment to Employee Retirement Income Security Act of 1974	Plan years beginning after December 31, 2007
...	401(a)(1)	PBGC Premiums—Variable Rate Premiums—Conforming Amendments Related to Funding Rules For Single-Employer Plans	Plan years beginning after 2007
...	401(b)(1)	PBGC Premiums—Termination of Premiums—Repeal of Sunset Provision	August 17, 2006
...	401(b)(2)(A)	PBGC Premiums—Termination Premiums—Technical Correction	Plans terminated after December 31, 2005
...	402(a)(1)-(2)	Special Funding Rules For Certain Plans Maintained By Commercial Airlines	Plan years ending after August 17, 2006
...	402(b)(1)(A)-(B)	Special Funding Rules For Certain Plans Maintained By Commercial Airlines—Alternative Funding Schedule	Plan years ending after August 17, 2006
...	402(b)(2)(A)	Special Funding Rules For Certain Plans Maintained By Commercial Airlines—Alternative Funding Schedule—Accrual Restrictions	Plan years ending after August 17, 2006
...	402(b)(2)(B)	Special Funding Rules For Certain Plans Maintained By Commercial Airlines—Alternative Funding Schedule-Accrual Restrictions—Increases In Section 415 Limits	Plan years ending after August 17, 2006
...	402(b)(3)(A)	Special Funding Rules For Certain Plans Maintained By Commercial Airlines—Alternative Funding Schedule—Restriction on Applicable Benefit Increases	Plan years ending after August 17, 2006
...	402(b)(3)(B)	Special Funding Rules For Certain Plans Maintained By Commercial Airlines—Alternative Funding Schedule—Restriction on Applicable Benefit Increases—Applicable Benefit Increase	Plan years ending after August 17, 2006
...	402(b)(4)(A)-(B)	Special Funding Rules For Certain Plans Maintained By Commercial Airlines—Alternative Funding Schedule—Exception For Imputed Disability Service	Plan years ending after August 17, 2006
...	402(c)(1)(A)-(B)	Special Funding Rules For Certain Plans Maintained By Commercial Airlines—Definitions—Eligible Plan	Plan years ending after August 17, 2006
...	402(c)(2)	Special Funding Rules For Certain Plans Maintained By Commercial Airlines—Definitions—Applicable Plan Year	Plan years ending after August 17, 2006

Code Sec.	Act Sec.	Act Provision Subject	Effective Date
...	402(d)(1)(A)	Special Funding Rules For Certain Plans Maintained By Commercial Airlines—Elections and Related Terms—Years For Which Election Made—Alternative Funding Schedule	Plan years ending after August 17, 2006
...	402(d)(1)(B)	Special Funding Rules For Certain Plans Maintained By Commercial Airlines—Elections and Related Terms—Years For Which Election Made—10 Year Amortization	Plan years ending after August 17, 2006
...	402(d)(1)(C)	Special Funding Rules For Certain Plans Maintained By Commercial Airlines—Elections and Related Terms—Years For Which Election Made—Election of New Plan year For Alternative Funding Schedule	Plan years ending after August 17, 2006
...	402(d)(2)	Special Funding Rules For Certain Plans Maintained By Commercial Airlines—Elections and Related Terms—Manner of Election	Plan years ending after August 17, 2006
...	402(e)(1)	Special Funding Rules For Certain Plans Maintained By Commercial Airlines—Minimum Required Contribution	Plan years ending after August 17, 2006
...	402(e)(2)	Special Funding Rules For Certain Plans Maintained By Commercial Airlines—Minimum Required Contribution—Years After Amortization Period	Plan years ending after August 17, 2006
...	402(e)(3)(A)	Special Funding Rules For Certain Plans Maintained By Commercial Airlines—Minimum Required Contribution—Definitions—Unfunded Liability	Plan years ending after August 17, 2006
...	402(e)(3)(B)	Special Funding Rules For Certain Plans Maintained By Commercial Airlines—Minimum Required Contribution—Definitions—Amortization Period	Plan years ending after August 17, 2006
...	402(e)(4)(A)-(C)	Special Funding Rules For Certain Plans Maintained By Commercial Airlines—Minimum Required Contribution—Other Rules	Plan years ending after August 17, 2006
...	402(e)(5)(A)-(B)	Special Funding Rules For Certain Plans Maintained By Commercial Airlines—Minimum Required Contribution—Special Rule For Certain Plan Spin-Offs	Plan years ending after August 17, 2006
...	402(f)(1)	Special Funding Rules For Certain Plans Maintained By Commercial Airlines—Special Rules For Certain Balances and Waivers—Funding Standard Account and Credit Balances	Plan years ending after August 17, 2006

Code Sec.	Act Sec.	Act Provision Subject	Effective Date
...	402(f)(2)	Special Funding Rules For Certain Plans Maintained By Commercial Airlines—Special Rules For Certain Balances and Waivers—Waived Funding Deficiencies	Plan years ending after August 17, 2006
...	402(g)(1)(A)-(B)	Special Funding Rules For Certain Plans Maintained By Commercial Airlines—Other Rules For Plans Making Election Under This Section—Successor Plans to Certain Plans	Plan years ending after August 17, 2006
...	402(g)(2)(A)	Special Funding Rules For Certain Plans Maintained By Commercial Airlines—Other Rules For Plans Making Election Under This Section—Special Rules For Terminations—PBGC Liability Limited	Plan years ending after August 17, 2006
...	402(g)(2)(B)	Special Funding Rules For Certain Plans Maintained By Commercial Airlines—Other Rules For Plans Making Election Under This Section—Special Rules For Termination—Termination Premium	Plan years ending after August 17, 2006
...	402(g)(3)	Special Funding Rules For Certain Plans Maintained By Commercial Airlines—Other Rules For Plans Making Election Under This Section—Limitations on Deductions Under Certain Plans	Plan years ending after August 17, 2006
...	402(g)(4)	Special Funding Rules For Certain Plans Maintained By Commercial Airlines—Other Rules For Plans Making Election Under This Section—Notice	Plan years ending after August 17, 2006
...	402(i)(1)-(2)	Special Funding Rules For Certain Plans Maintained By Commercial Airlines—Extension of Special Rule For Additional Funding Requirements	Plan years ending after August 17, 2006
...	403(a)	Limitation on PBGC Guarantee of Shutdown and Other Benefits	Benefits that become payable as a result of an event which occurs after July 26, 2005
...	404(a)	Rules Relating to Bankruptcy of Employer—Guarantee	Proceedings initiated under Title 11, United States Code, or under any similar Federal law or law of a state or political subdivision, on or after the date that is 30 days after August 17, 2006

Code Sec.	Act Sec.	Act Provision Subject	Effective Date
. . .	404(b)	Rules Relating to Bankruptcy of Employer—Allocation of Assets Among Priority Groups in Bankruptcy Proceedings	Proceedings initiated under Title 11, United States Code, or under any similar Federal law or law of state or political subdivision, on or after the date that is 30 days after August 17, 2006
. . .	405(a)(1)-(2)	PBGC Premiums For Small Plans—Small Plans	Plan years beginning after December 31, 2006
. . .	406(a)(1)-(2)	Authorization For PBGC to Pay Interest on Premium Overpayment Refunds	Interest accruing for periods beginning not earlier than August 17, 2006
. . .	407(a)	Rules For Substantial Owner Benefits in Terminated Plans—Modification of Phase-In of Guarantee	Plan terminations under ERISA Sec. 4041(c) with respect to which notices of intent to terminate are provided under ERISA Sec. 4041(a)(2) after December 31, 2005, and under ERISA Sec. 4042 with respect to which notices of determination are provided after such date
. . .	407(b)(1)-(2)	Rules For Substantial Owner Benefits in Terminated Plans—Modification of Allocation of Assets	Plan terminations under ERISA Sec. 4041(c) with respect to which notices of intent to terminate are provided under ERISA Sec. 4041(a)(2) after December 31, 2005, and under ERISA Sec. 4042 with respect to which notices of determination are provided after such date
. . .	407(c)(1)(A)-(B)	Rules For Substantial Owner Benefits in Terminated Plans—Conforming Amendments	January 1, 2006

Code Sec.	Act Sec.	Act Provision Subject	Effective Date
. . .	408(a)	Acceleration of PBGC Computation of Benefits Attributable to Recoveries From Employers—Modification of Average Recovery Percentage of Outstanding Amount of Benefit Liabilities Payable By Corporation to Participants and Beneficiaries	Terminations for which notices of intent to terminate are provided (or in the case of a termination by the corporation, a notice of determination under ERISA Sec. 4042 is issued) on or after the date which is 30 days after August 17, 2006
. . .	408(b)(1)	Acceleration of PBGC Computation of Benefits Attributable to Recoveries From Employers—Valuation of Section 4062(c) Liability For Determining Amounts Payable By Corporation to Participants and Beneficiaries—Single-Employer Plan Benefits Guaranteed	Terminations for which notices of intent to terminate are provided (or in the case of a termination by the corporation, a notice of determination under ERISA Sec. 4042 is issued) on or after the date which is 30 days after August 17, 2006
. . .	408(b)(2)	Acceleration of PBGC Computation of Benefits Attributable to Recoveries From Employers—Modification of Average Recovery Percentage of Outstanding Amount of Benefit Liabilities Payable By Corporation to Participants and Beneficiaries—Allocation of Assets	Terminations for which notices of intent to terminate are provided (or in the case of a termination by the corporation, a notice of determination under ERISA Sec. 4042 is issued) on or after the date which is 30 days after August 17, 2006
. . .	409(a)	Treatment of Certain Plans Where Cessation or Change in Membership of a Controlled Group	Any transaction or series of transactions occurring on and after August 17, 2006
. . .	410(a)	Missing Participants	Distributions made after final regulations implementing ERISA Sec. 4050(c) and (d) are prescribed
. . .	410(b)(1)-(2)	Missing Participants—Conforming Amendments	Distributions made after final regulations implementing ERISA Sec. 4050(c) and (d) are prescribed
. . .	411(a)(1)-(2)	Director of the Pension Benefit Guaranty Corporation	August 17, 2006
. . .	411(b)	Director of the Pension Benefit Guaranty Corporation—Compensation of the Director	August 17, 2006

Code Sec.	Act Sec.	Act Provision Subject	Effective Date
...	411(c)(1)	Director of the Pension Benefit Guaranty Corporation—Jurisdiction of Nomination	August 17, 2006
...	411(c)(2)(A)-(B)	Director of the Pension Benefit Guaranty Corporation—Jurisdiction of Nomination	August 17, 2006
...	411(d)	Director of the Pension Benefit Guaranty Corporation—Transition	August 17, 2006
...	412(1)-(2)	Inclusion of Information in the PBGC Annual Report	August 17, 2006
...	501(a)	Defined Benefit Plan Funding Notice	Plan years beginning after December 31, 2007, generally
...	501(b)(1)	Defined Benefit Plan Funding Notice—Repeal of Notice to Participants of Funding Status	Plan years beginning after December 31, 2006, generally
...	501(b)(2)	Defined Benefit Plan Funding Notice—Repeal of Notice to Participants of Funding Status—Clerical Amendment	Plan years beginning after December 31, 2006
...	501(c)	Defined Benefit Plan Funding Notice—Model Notice	Plan years beginning after December 31, 2007, generally
...	502(a)(1)	Access to Multiemployer Pension Plan Information—Financial Information With Respect to Multiemployer Plans	Plan years beginning after December 31, 2007
...	502(a)(2)	Access to Multiemployer Pension Plan Information—Financial Information With Respect to Multiemployer Plans—Enforcement	Plan years beginning after December 31, 2007
...	502(a)(3)	Access to Multiemployer Pension Plan Information—Financial Information With Respect to Multiemployer Plans—Regulations	Plan years beginning after December 31, 2007
...	502(b)(1)(A)-(B)	Access to Multiemployer Pension Plan Information—Notice of Potential Withdrawal Liability to Multiemployer Plans	Plan years beginning after December 31, 2007
...	502(b)(2)	Access to Multiemployer Pension Plan Information—Notice of Potential Withdrawal Liability to Multiemployer Plans—Enforcement	Plan years beginning after December 31, 2007
...	502(c)(1)	Access to Multiemployer Pension Plan Information—Notice of Amendment Reducing Future Accruals—Amendment of ERISA	Plan years beginning after December 31, 2007
...	503(a)(1(A)-(B)	Additional Annual Reporting Requirements	Plan years beginning after December 31, 2007
...	503(b)(1)-(2)	Additional Annual Reporting Requirements—Additional Information in Annual Actuarial Statement Regarding Plan Retirement Projections	Plan years beginning after December 31, 2007

Code Sec.	Act Sec.	Act Provision Subject	Effective Date
...	503(c)(1)	Additional Annual Reporting Requirements—Repeal of Summary Annual Report Requirement for Defined Benefit Plans	Plan years beginning after December 31, 2007
...	503(c)(2)	Additional Annual Reporting Requirements—Repeal of Summary Annual Report Requirement for Defined Benefit Plans—Conforming Amendments	Plan years beginning after December 31, 2007
...	503(d)(1)-(3)	Additional Annual Reporting Requirements—Furnishing Summary Plan Information to Employers and Employee Representatives of Multiemployer Plan	Plan years beginning after December 31, 2007
...	503(e)	Additional Annual Reporting Requirements—Model Form	Plan years beginning after December 31, 2007
...	504(a)	Electronic Display of Annual Report Information—Electronic Display of Information	Plan years beginning after December 31, 2007
...	505(a)	Section 4010 Filings With PBGC—Change in Criteria For Persons Required to Provide Information to PBGC	Years beginning after 2007
...	505(b)	Section 4010 Filings With PBGC—Additional Information Required	Years beginning after 2007
...	506(a)(1)	Disclosure of Termination Information to Plan Participants—Distress Terminations	Plan terminations under Title IV of ERISA with respect to which the notice of intent to terminate (or in the case of a termination by the Pension Benefit Guaranty Corporation, a notice of determination under ERISA Sec. 4042) occurs after August 17, 2006, generally
...	506(a)(2)	Disclosure of Termination Information to Plan Participants—Distress Terminations—Conforming Amendment	Plan terminations under Title IV of ERISA with respect to which the notice of intent to terminate (or in the case of a termination by the Pension Benefit Guaranty Corporation, a notice of determination under ERISA Sec. 4042) occurs after August 17, 2006, generally

Code Sec.	Act Sec.	Act Provision Subject	Effective Date
...	506(b)(1)(A)-(C)	Disclosure of Termination Information to Plan Participants—Involuntary Terminations	Plan terminations under Title IV of ERISA with respect to which the notice of intent to terminate (or in the case of a termination by the Pension Benefit Guaranty Corporation, a notice of determination under ERISA Sec. 4042) occurs after August 17, 2006, generally
...	507(a)	Notice of Freedom to Divest Employer Securities	Plan years beginning after December 31, 2006, generally
...	507(b)	Notice of Freedom to Divest Employer Securities—Penalties	Plan years beginning after December 31, 2006, generally
...	507(c)	Notice of Freedom to Divest Employer Securities—Model Notice	Plan years beginning after December 31, 2006, generally
...	508(a)(1)	Periodic Pension Benefit Statements—Amendments of ERISA	Plan years beginning after December 31, 2006, generally
...	508(a)(2)	Periodic Pension Benefit Statements—Conforming Amendments	Plan years beginning after December 31, 2006, generally
...	508(b)(1)	Periodic Pension Benefit Statements—Model Statements	Plan years beginning after December 31, 2006, generally
...	508(b)(2)	Periodic Pension Benefit Statements—Model Statements—Interim Final Rules	Plan years beginning after December 31, 2006, generally
...	509(a)	Notice to Participants or Beneficiaries of Blackout Periods	January 26, 2003
...	601(a)(1)	Prohibited Transaction Exemption For Provision of Investment Advice—Amendments to the Employee Retirement Income Security Act of 1974—Exemption From Prohibited Transactions	Advice referred to in ERISA Sec. 3(21)(A)(ii) provided after December 31, 2006
...	601(a)(2)	Prohibited Transaction Exemption For Provision of Investment Advice—Amendments to the Employee Retirement Income Security Act of 1974—Requirements	Advice referred to in ERISA Sec. 3(21)(A)(ii) provided after December 31, 2006
...	601(c)	Prohibited Transaction Exemption For Provision of Investment Advice—Coordination With Existing Exemptions	August 17, 2006

Code Sec.	Act Sec.	Act Provision Subject	Effective Date
...	611(a)(1)	Prohibited Transaction Rules Relating to Financial Investments—Exemption For Block Trading—Amendments to Employee Retirement Income Security Act of 1974	Transactions occurring after August 17, 2006
...	611(b)(1)-(3)	Prohibited Transaction Rules Relating to Financial Investments—Bonding Relief	Plan years beginning after August 17, 2006
...	611(c)(1)	Prohibited Transaction Rules Relating to Financial Investments—Exemption For Electronic Communication Network—Amendments to Employee Retirement Income Security Act of 1974	Transactions occurring after August 17, 2006
...	611(d)(1)	Prohibited Transaction Rules Relating to Financial Investments—Exemption For Service Providers—Amendments to Employee Retirement Income Security Act of 1974	Transactions occurring after August 17, 2006
...	611(e)(1)	Prohibited Transaction Rules Relating to Financial Investments—Relief For Foreign Exchange Transactions—Amendments to Employee Retirement Income Security Act of 1974	Transactions occurring after August 17, 2006
...	611(f)	Prohibited Transaction Rules Relating to Financial Investments—Definition of Plan Asset Vehicle	Transactions occurring after August 17, 2006
...	611(g)(1)	Prohibited Transaction Rules Relating to Financial Investments—Exemption For Cross Trading—Amendments to Employee Retirement Income Security Act of 1986	Transactions occurring after August 17, 2006
...	612(a)	Correction Period For Certain Transactions Involving Securities and Commodities—Amendment of Employee Retirement Income Security Act of 1974	Transactions which the fiduciary or disqualified person discovers, or reasonably should have discovered, after August 17, 2006, constitutes a prohibited transaction
...	621(a)(1)(A)-(C)	Inapplicability of Relief From Fiduciary Liability During Suspension of Ability of Participant or Beneficiary to Direct Investments	Plan years beginning after December 31, 2007, generally
...	622(a)	Increase in Maximum Bond Amount	Plan years beginning after December 31, 2007
...	623(a)(1)-(2)	Increase in Penalties For Coercive Interference With Exercise of ERISA Rights	Violations occurring on and after August 17, 2006
...	624(a)	Treatment of Investment of Assets By Plan Where Participant Fails to Exercise Investment Election	Plan years beginning after December 31, 2006
...	625(a)((1)-(2)	Clarification of Fiduciary Rules	August 17, 2006

Code Sec.	Act Sec.	Act Provision Subject	Effective Date
...	701(a)(1)	Benefit Accrual Standards—Amendments to the Employee Retirement Income Security Act of 1974—Rules Relating to Reduction in Rate of Benefit Accrual	Periods beginning on or after June 29, 2005, generally
...	701(a)(2)	Benefit Accrual Standards—Amendments to the Employee Retirement Income Security Act of 1974—Determinations of Accrued Benefit as Balance of Benefit Account or Equivalent Amounts	Distributions made after August 17, 2006
...	701(c)	Benefit Accrual Standards—Amendments to Age Discrimination in Employment Act	Periods beginning on or after June 29, 2005, generally
...	701(d)(1)-(2)	Benefit Accrual Standards—No Inference	Periods beginning on or after June 29, 2005, generally
...	811	Pensions and Individual Retirement Arrangement Provisions of Economic Growth and Tax Relief Reconciliation Act of 2001 Made Permanent	August 17, 2006
...	854(c)(9)	Annuities to Surviving Spouses and Dependent Children of Special Trial Judges of the Tax Court—Conforming Amendments	August 17, 2006
...	861(a)(2)	Extension to All Government Plans of Current Moratorium on Application of Certain Nondiscrimination Rules Applicable to State and Local Plans	Any year beginning after August 17, 2006
...	864(a)	Treatment of Test Room Supervisors and Proctors Who Assist in the Administration of College Entrance and Placement Exams	Remuneration for services performed after December 31, 2006
...	901(b)(1)	Defined Contribution Plans Required to Provide Employees With Freedom to Invest Their Plan Assets—Amendments of ERISA	Plan years beginning after December 31, 2006, generally
...	901(b)(2)	Defined Contribution Plans Required to Provide Employees With Freedom to Invest Their Plan Assets—Conforming Amendment	Plan years beginning after December 31, 2006, generally
...	902(d)(2)(E)	Increasing Participation Through Automatic Contribution Arrangements—Treatment of Withdrawals of Contributions During First 90 Days—Vesting Conforming Amendments	Plan years beginning after December 31, 2007
...	902(f)(1)	Increasing Participation Through Automatic Contribution Arrangements—Preemption of Conflicting State Regulations	August 17, 2006
...	902(f)(2)	Increasing Participation Through Automatic Contribution Arrangements—Preemption of Conflicting State Regulations—Enforcement	August 17, 2006

Code Sec.	Act Sec.	Act Provision Subject	Effective Date
...	903(b)(1)	Treatment of Eligible Combined Defined Benefit Plans and Qualified Cash or Deferred Arrangements—Amendments to the Employee Retirement Income Security Act of 1974	Plan years beginning after December 31, 2009
...	903(b)(2)(A)	Treatment of Eligible Combined Defined Benefit Plans and Qualified Cash or Deferred Arrangements—Amendments to the Employee Retirement Income Security Act of 1974—Conforming Changes	Plan years beginning after December 31, 2009
...	904(b)(1)	Faster Vesting of Employer Nonelective Contributions—Amendments to the Employee Retirement Income Security Act of 1974	Contributions for plan years beginning after December 31, 2006, generally
...	904(b)(2)	Faster Vesting of Employer Nonelective Contributions—Amendments to the Employee Retirement Income Security Act of 1974—Conforming Amendment	Contributions for plan years beginning after December 31, 2006, generally
...	905(a)	Distributions During Working Retirement—Amendment to the Employee Retirement Income Security Act of 1974	Distributions in plan years beginning after December 31, 2006
...	906(a)(2)(A)	Treatment of Certain Pension Plans of Indian Tribal Governments—Definition of Government Pension Plans of Indian Tribal Government—Amendment to Employee Retirement Income Security Act of 1974	Any year beginning on or after August 17, 2006
...	906(a)(2)(B)	Treatment of Certain Pension Plans of Indian Tribal Governments—Definition of Government Pension Plans of Indian Tribal Government	Any year beginning on or after August 17, 2006
...	906(b)(2)(A)	Treatment of Certain Pension Plans of Indian Tribal Governments—Definition of Government Pension Plans of Indian Tribal Governments—Amendments to Employee Retirement Income Security Act of 1974	Any year beginning on or after August 17, 2006
...	906(b)(2)(B)	Treatment of Certain Pension Plans of Indian Tribal Governments—Definition of Government Pension Plans of Indian Tribal Governments—Amendments to Employee Retirement Income Security Act of 1974	Any year beginning on or after August 17, 2006
...	906(b)(2)(C)	Treatment of Certain Pension Plans of Indian Tribal Governments—Definition of Government Pension Plans of Indian Tribal Governments—Amendments to Employee Retirement Income Security Act of 1974	Any year beginning on or after August 17, 2006

Code Sec.	Act Sec.	Act Provision Subject	Effective Date
. . .	1002(a)(1)	Entitlement of Divorced Spouses to Railroad Retirement Annuities Independent of Actual Entitlement of Employee	One year after August 17, 2006
. . .	1002(a)(2)	Entitlement of Divorced Spouses to Railroad Retirement Annuities Independent of Actual Entitlement of Employee	One year after August 17, 2006
. . .	1003(a)	Extension of Tier II Railroad Retirement Benefits to Surviving Former Spouses Pursuant to Divorce Agreements	One year after August 17, 2006
. . .	1004(b)(1)(A)-(C)	Requirement For Additional Survivor Annuity Option—Amendments to ERISA—Election of Survivor Annuity	Plan years beginning after December 31, 2007, generally
. . .	1004(b)(2)(A)-(C)	Requirement For Additional Survivor Annuity Option—Amendments to ERISA—Definition	Plan years beginning after December 31, 2007, generally
. . .	1004(b)(3)	Requirement For Additional Survivor Annuity Option—Amendments to ERISA—Notice	Plan years beginning after December 31, 2007, generally
. . .	1102(a)(2)(A)	Notice and Consent Period Regarding Distributions—Expansion Period—Amendment of ERISA	Years beginning after December 31, 2006
. . .	1104(a)(2)(A)-(D)	Voluntary Early Retirement Incentive and Employment Retention Plans Maintained By Local Educational Agencies and Other Entities—Voluntary Early Retirement Incentive Plans—Age Discrimination in Employment Act	August 17, 2006
. . .	1104(c)	Voluntary Early Retirement Incentive and Employment Retention Plans Maintained By Local Educational Agencies and Other Entities—Coordination With ERISA	Plan years ending after August 17, 2006
. . .	1106(a)	Revocation of Election Relating to Treatment as Multiemployer Plan—Amendment to ERISA	August 17, 2006
. . .	1219(d)	Provisions Relating to Substantial and Gross Overstatements of Valuations—Disciplinary Actions Against Appraisers	Appraisals prepared with respect to returns or submissions filed after August 17, 2006, generally

¶20,005 Effective Dates

ERISA Effective Dates

This CCH-prepared table presents the general effective dates for major ERISA provisions added, amended or repealed by the Pension Protection Act of 2006, enacted August 17, 2006. Entries are listed in ERISA section order.

ERISA Sec.	Act Sec.	Act Provision Subject	Effective Date
1	101(c)	Minimum Funding Standards—Clerical Amendment	Plan years beginning after 2007
1	102(b)	Funding Rules for Single-Employer Defined Benefit Pension Plans—Clerical Amendment	Plan years beginning after 2007
1	201(c)(2)	Funding Rules for Multiemployer Defined Benefit Plans—Conforming Amendments	Plan years beginning after 2007
1	202(e)	Additional Funding Rules for Multiemployer Plans In Endangered or Critical Status—Conforming Amendment	Plan years beginning after 2007
1	501(b)(2)	Defined Benefit Plan Funding Notice—Repeal of Notice to Participants of Funding Status—Clerical Amendment	Plan years beginning after December 31, 2006
1	903(b)(2)(B)	Treatment of Eligible Combined Defined Benefit Plans and Qualified Cash or Deferred Arrangements—Amendments to the Employee Retirement Income Security Act of 1974—Conforming Changes	Plan years beginning after December 31, 2009
3(2)(A)	905(a)	Distributions During Working Retirement—Amendment to the Employee Retirement Income Security Act of 1974	Distributions in plan years beginning after December 31, 2006
3(2)(B)	1104(c)	Voluntary Early Retirement Incentive and Employment Retention Plans Maintained by Local Educational Agencies and Other Entities—Coordination with ERISA	Plan years ending after August 17, 2006
3(32)	906(a)(2)(A)	Treatment of Certain Pension Plans of Indian Tribal Governments—Definition of Government Plan to Include Certain Pension Plans of Indian Tribal Governments—Amendment to Employee Retirement Income Security Act of 1974	Any year beginning on or after August 17, 2006
3(37)(G)	1106(a)	Revocation of Election Relating to Treatment as Multiemployer Plan—Amendment to ERISA	August 17, 2006
3(42)	611(f)	Prohibited Transaction Rules Relating to Financial Investments—Definition of Plan Asset Vehicle	Transactions occurring after August 17, 2006

ERISA Sec.	Act Sec.	Act Provision Subject	Effective Date
101(a)(2)	503(c)(2)	Additional Annual Reporting Requirements—Repeal of Summary Annual Report Requirement for Defined Benefit Plans—Conforming Amendments	Plan years beginning after December 31, 2007
101(d)(3)	107(a)(1)	Technical and Conforming Amendments—Miscellaneous Amendments to Title I	Plan years beginning after 2007
101(e)(3)	107(a)(11)	Technical and Conforming Amendments—Miscellaneous Amendments to Title I	Plan years beginning after 2007
101(f)	501(a)	Defined Benefit Plan Funding Notice	Plan years beginning after December 31, 2007, generally
101(i)(8)(B)(i)-(v)	509(a)	Notice to Participants or Beneficiaries of Blackout Periods	January 26, 2003
101(j)-(k)	103(b)(1)(A)	Benefit Limitations Under Single-Employer Plans—Notice Requirement	Plan years beginning after December 31, 2007, generally
101(j)	103(b)(1)(B)	Benefit Limitations Under Single-Employer Plans—Notice Requirement	Plan years beginning after December 31, 2007, generally
101(k)	502(a)(1)(B)	Access to Multiemployer Pension Plan Information—Financial Information With Respect to Multiemployer Plans	Plan years beginning after December 31, 2007
101(k)-(l)	502(a)(1)(A)	Access to Multiemployer Pension Plan Information—Financial Information With Respect to Multiemployer Plans	Plan years beginning after December 31, 2007
101(l)	502(b)(1)(B)	Access to Multiemployer Pension Plan Information—Notice of Potential Withdrawal Liability to Multiemployer Plans	Plan years beginning after December 31, 2007
101(l)-(m)	502(b)(1)(A)	Access to Multiemployer Pension Plan Information—Notice of Potential Withdrawal Liability to Multiemployer Plans	Plan years beginning after December 31, 2007
101(m)-(n)	507(a)	Notice of Freedom to Divest Employer Securities	Plan years beginning after December 31, 2006, generally
103(a)(1)(B)	503(a)(1)(A)	Additional Annual Reporting Requirements—Additional Annual Reporting Requirements With Respect to Defined Benefit Plans	Plan years beginning after December 31, 2007
103(d)(8)(B)	107(a)(2)	Technical and Conforming Amendments—Miscellaneous Amendments to Title I	Plan years beginning after 2007
103(d)(11)	107(a)(3)	Technical and Conforming Amendments—Miscellaneous Amendments to Title I	Plan years beginning after 2007
103(d)(12)	503(b)(2)	Additional Annual Reporting Requirements—Additional Information in Annual Actuarial Statement Regarding Plan Retirement Projections	Plan years beginning after December 31, 2007

ERISA Sec.	Act Sec.	Act Provision Subject	Effective Date
103(d)(12)-(14)	503(b)(1)	Additional Annual Reporting Requirements—Additional Information in Annual Actuarial Statement Regarding Plan Retirement Projections	Plan years beginning after December 31, 2007
103(f)	503(a)(1)(B)	Additional Annual Reporting Requirements—Additional Annual Reporting Requirements with Respect to Defined Benefit Plans	Plan years beginning after December 31, 2007
104	503(d)(1)	Additional Annual Reporting Requirements—Furnishing Summary Plan Information to Employers and Employee Representatives of Multiemployer Plans	Plan years beginning after December 31, 2007
104(b)(3)	503(c)(1)	Additional Annual Reporting Requirements—Repeal of Summary Annual Report Requirement for Defined Benefit Plans	Plan years beginning after December 31, 2007
104(b)(5)	504(a)	Electronic Display of Annual Report Information—Electronic Display of Information	Plan years beginning after December 31, 2007
104(d)	503(d)(3)	Additional Annual Reporting Requirements—Furnishing Summary Plan Information to Employers and Employee Representatives of Multiemployer Plans	Plan years beginning after December 31, 2007
104(d)-(e)	503(d)(2)	Additional Annual Reporting Requirements—Furnishing Summary Plan Information to Employers and Employee Representatives of Multiemployer Plans	Plan years beginning after December 31, 2007
105(a)	508(a)(1)	Periodic Pension Benefit Statements—Amendments of ERISA	Plan years beginning after December 31, 2006, generally
105(b)	508(a)(2)(B)	Periodic Pension Benefit Statements—Amendments of ERISA—Conforming Amendments	Plan years beginning after December 31, 2006, generally
105(d)	508(a)(2)(A)	Periodic Pension Benefit Statements—Amendments of ERISA—Conforming Amendments	Plan years beginning after December 31, 2006, generally
203(a)(2)	904(b)(1)	Faster Vesting of Employer Nonelective Contributions—Amendments to the Employee Retirement Income Security Act of 1974	Contributions for plan years beginning after December 31, 2006, generally
203(a)(3)(C)	107(a)(4)	Technical and Conforming Amendments—Miscellaneous Amendments to Title I	Plan years beginning after 2007
203(a)(3)(F)	902(d)(2)(E)	Increasing Participation Through Automatic Contribution Arrangements—Treatment of Withdrawals of Contributions During First 90 Days—Vesting—Conforming Amendments	Plan years beginning after December 31, 2007

ERISA Sec.	Act Sec.	Act Provision Subject	Effective Date
203(a)(4)	904(b)(2)	Faster Vesting of Employer Nonelective Contributions—Amendments to the Employee Retirement Income Security Act of 1974—Conforming Amendment	Contributions for plan years beginning after December 31, 2006, generally
203(f)	701(a)(2)	Benefit Accrual Standards—Amendments to the Employee Retirement Income Security Act of 1974—Determinations of Accrued Benefit as Balance of Benefit Account or Equivalent Amounts	Distributions made after August 17, 2006, generally
204(b)(5)	701(a)(1)	Benefit Accrual Standards—Amendments to the Employee Retirement Income Security Act of 1974—Rules Relating to Reduction in Rate of Benefit Accrual	Periods beginning on or after June 29, 2005, generally
204(g)(1)	107(a)(5)	Technical and Conforming Amendments—Miscellaneous Amendments to Title I	Plan years beginning after 2007
204(h)(1)	502(c)(1)	Access to Multiemployer Pension Plan Information—Notice of Amendment Reducing Future Accruals—Amendment of ERISA	Plan years beginning after December 31, 2007
204(i)(2)(B)	107(a)(6)	Technical and Conforming Amendments—Miscellaneous Amendments to Title I	Plan years beginning after 2007
204(i)(3)	107(a)(7)	Technical and Conforming Amendments—Miscellaneous Amendments to Title I	Plan years beginning after 2007
204(i)(4)	107(a)(8)	Technical and Conforming Amendments—Miscellaneous Amendments to Title I	Plan years beginning after 2007
204(j)-(k)	901(b)(1)	Defined Contribution Plans Required to Provide Employees with Freedom to Invest Their Plan Assets—Amendments of ERISA	Plan years beginning after December 31, 2006, generally
205(c)(1)(A)(i)	1004(b)(1)(A)	Requirement for Additional Survivor Annuity Option—Amendments to ERISA—Election of Survivor Annuity	Plan years beginning after December 31, 2007, generally
205(c)(1)(A)(ii)	1004(b)(1)(C)	Requirement for Additional Survivor Annuity Option—Amendments to ERISA—Election of Survivor Annuity	Plan years beginning after December 31, 2007, generally
205(c)(1)(A)(ii)-(iii)	1004(b)(1)(B)	Requirement for Additional Survivor Annuity Option—Amendments to ERISA—Election of Survivor Annuity	Plan years beginning after December 31, 2007, generally
205(c)(3)(A)(i)	1004(b)(3)	Requirement for Additional Survivor Annuity Option—Amendments to ERISA—Notice	Plan years beginning after December 31, 2007, generally
205(c)(7)(A)	1102(a)(2)(A)	Notice and Consent Period Regarding Distributions—Expansion of Period—Amendment of ERISA	Years beginning after December 31, 2006

ERISA Sec.	Act Sec.	Act Provision Subject	Effective Date
205(d)(1)	1004(b)(2)(A)	Requirement for Additional Survivor Annuity Option—Amendments to ERISA—Definition	Plan years beginning after December 31, 2007, generally
205(d)(1)-(2)	1004(b)(2)(B)	Requirement for Additional Survivor Annuity Option—Amendments to ERISA—Definition	Plan years beginning after December 31, 2007, generally
205(d)(2)	1004(b)(2)(C)	Requirement for Additional Survivor Annuity Option—Amendments to ERISA—Definition	Plan years beginning after December 31, 2007, generally
205(g)(3)	302(a)	Interest Rate Assumption for Determination of Lump Sum Distributions—Amendment to Employee Retirement Income Security Act of 1974	Plan years beginning after December 31, 2007
206(e)(1)	107(a)(9)	Technical and Conforming Amendments—Miscellaneous Amendments to Title I	Plan years beginning after 2007
206(e)(3)	107(a)(10)	Technical and Conforming Amendments—Miscellaneous Amendments to Title I	Plan years beginning after 2007
206(f)	410(b)(1)-(2)	Missing Participants—Conforming Amendments	Distributions made after final regulations implementing ERISA Secs. 4050(c) and 4050(d) are prescribed
206(g)	103(a)	Benefit Limitations Under Single-Employer Plans—Funding-Based Limits on Benefits and Benefit Accruals Under Single-Employer Plans	Plan years beginning after December 31, 2007, generally
207	107(d)	Technical and Conforming Amendments—Repeal of Expired Authority for Temporary Variances	Plan years beginning after 2007
210	903(b)(2)(A)	Treatment of Eligible Combined Defined Benefit Plans and Qualified Cash or Deferred Arrangements—Amendments to the Employee Retirement Income Security Act of 1974—Conforming Changes	Plan years beginning after December 31, 2009
210(e)	903(b)(1)	Treatment of Eligible Combined Defined Benefit Plans and Qualified Cash or Deferred Arrangements—Amendments to the Employee Retirement Income Security Act of 1974	Plan years beginning after December 31, 2009
301(d)	201(c)(1)	Funding Rules for Multiemployer Defined Benefit Plans—Conforming Amendments	Plan years beginning after 2007, generally
302–308	101(a)	Minimum Funding Standards—Repeal of Existing Funding Rules	Plan years beginning after 2007
302(a)-(d)	101(b)	Minimum Funding Standards—New Minimum Funding Standards	Plan years beginning after 2007
302(b)(3)	202(d)	Additional Funding Rules for Multiemployer Plans In Endangered or Critical Status—No Additional Contributions Required	Plan years beginning after 2007, generally

ERISA Sec.	Act Sec.	Act Provision Subject	Effective Date
302(b)(5)(B)(ii)(II)	301(a)(1)(A)-(B)	Extension of Replacement of 30-Year Treasury Rates—Amendments of ERISA—Determination of Range	August 17, 2006
302(d)(7)(C)(i)(IV)	301(a)(2)(A)-(B)	Extension of Replacement of 30-Year Treasury Rates—Amendments of ERISA—Determination of Current Liability	August 17, 2006
303(a)-(l)	102(a)	Funding Rules for Single-Employer Defined Benefit Pension Plans	Plan years beginning after 2007
304(a)-(d)	201(a)	Funding Rules for Multiemployer Defined Benefit Plans	Plan years beginning after 2007, generally
305(a)-(i)	202(a)	Additional Funding Rules for Multiemployer Plans In Endangered or Critical Status	Plan years beginning after 2007, generally
403(c)(1)	107(a)(11)	Technical and Conforming Amendments—Miscellaneous Amendments to Title I	Plan years beginning after 2007, generally
404(c)(1)(A)(ii)	621(a)(1)(B)	Inapplicability of Relief from Fiduciary Liability During Suspension of Ability of Participant or Beneficiary to Direct Investments	Plan years beginning after December 31, 2007, generally
404(c)(1)(A)-(B)	621(a)(1)(A)	Inapplicability of Relief from Fiduciary Liability During Suspension of Ability of Participant or Beneficiary to Direct Investments	Plan years beginning after December 31, 2007, generally
404(c)(1)(B)-(C)	621(a)(1)(C)	Inapplicability of Relief from Fiduciary Liability During Suspension of Ability of Participant or Beneficiary to Direct Investments	Plan years beginning after December 31, 2007, generally
404(c)(4)	621(a)(2)	Inapplicability of Relief from Fiduciary Liability During Suspension of Ability of Participant or Beneficiary to Direct Investments	Plan years beginning after December 31, 2007, generally
404(c)(5)	624(a)	Treatment of Investment of Assets by Plan Where Participant Fails to Exercise Investment Election	Plan years beginning after December 31, 2006
407(b)(3)(D)	901(b)(2)	Defined Contribution Plans Required to Provide Employees with Freedom to Invest Their Plan Assets—Amendments of ERISA—Conforming Amendment	Plan years beginning after December 31, 2006, generally
408(b)(13)	107(a)(11)	Technical and Conforming Amendments—Miscellaneous Amendments to Title I	Plan years beginning after 2007
408(b)(14)	601(a)(1)	Prohibited Transaction Exemption for Provision of Investment Advice—Amendments to the Employee Retirement Income Security Act of 1974—Exemption from Prohibited Transactions	Investment advice rendered for a fee or other compensation with respect to plan assets that is provided after December 31, 2006

ERISA Sec.	Act Sec.	Act Provision Subject	Effective Date
408(b)(15)	611(a)(1)	Prohibited Transaction Rules Relating to Financial Investments—Exemption for Block Trading—Amendments to Employee Retirement Income Security Act of 1974	Transactions occurring after August 17, 2006
408(b)(16)	611(c)(1)	Prohibited Transaction Rules Relating to Financial Investments—Exemption for Electronic Communication Network—Amendments to Employee Retirement Income Security Act of 1974	Transactions occurring after August 17, 2006
408(b)(17)	611(d)(1)	Prohibited Transaction Rules Relating to Financial Investments—Exemption for Service Providers—Amendments to Employee Retirement Income Security Act of 1974	Transactions occurring after August 17, 2006
408(b)(18)	611(e)(1)	Prohibited Transaction Rules Relating to Financial Investments—Relief for Foreign Exchange Transactions—Amendments to Employee Retirement Income Security Act of 1974	Transactions occurring after August 17, 2006
408(b)(19)	611(g)(1)	Prohibited Transaction Rules Relating to Financial Investments—Exemption for Cross Trading—Amendments to Employee Retirement Income Security Act of 1974	Transactions occurring after August 17, 2006
408(b)(20)	612(a)	Correction Period for Certain Transactions Involving Securities and Commodities—Amendment of Employee Retirement Income Security Act of 1974	Any transaction which a fiduciary or disqualified person discovers, or reasonably should have discovered, after August 17, 2006, constitutes a prohibited transaction
408(g)	601(a)(2)	Prohibited Transaction Exemption for Provision of Investment Advice—Amendments to the Employee Retirement Income Security Act of 1974—Requirements	Investment advice rendered for a fee or other compensation with respect to plan assets that is provided after December 31, 2006
412(a)	622(a)	Increase in Maximum Bond Amount	Plan years beginning after December 31, 2007
412(a)(1)	611(b)(2)	Prohibited Transaction Rules Relating to Financial Investments—Bonding Relief	Plan years beginning after August 17, 2006
412(a)(2)	611(b)(3)	Prohibited Transaction Rules Relating to Financial Investments—Bonding Relief	Plan years beginning after August 17, 2006
412(a)(2)-(3)	611(b)(1)	Prohibited Transaction Rules Relating to Financial Investments—Bonding Relief	Plan years beginning after August 17, 2006

ERISA Sec.	Act Sec.	Act Provision Subject	Effective Date
502(a)(6)	202(b)(1)	Additional Funding Rules for Multiemployer Plans In Endangered or Critical Status—Enforcement	Plan years beginning after 2007, generally
502(a)(8)-(10)	202(c)	Additional Funding Rules for Multiemployer Plans In Endangered or Critical Status—Cause of Action to Compel Adoption or Implementation of Funding Improvement or Rehabilitation Plan	Plan years beginning after 2007, generally
502(c)(1)	508(a)(2)(C)	Periodic Pension Benefit Statements—Amendments of ERISA—Conforming Amendments	Plan years beginning after December 31, 2006, generally
502(c)(4)	103(b)(2)	Benefit Limitations Under Single-Employer Plans—Notice Requirement—Enforcement	Plan years beginning after December 31, 2007, generally
502(c)(4)	502(a)(2)	Access to Multiemployer Pension Plan Information—Financial Information With Respect to Multiemployer Plans—Enforcement	Plan years beginning after December 31, 2007
502(c)(4)	502(b)(2)	Access to Multiemployer Pension Plan Information—Notice of Potential Withdrawal Liability to Multiemployer Plans—Enforcement	Plan years beginning after December 31, 2007
502(c)(4)	902(f)(2)	Increasing Participation Through Automatic Contribution Arrangements—Preemption of Conflicting State Regulation—Enforcement	August 17, 2006
502(c)(7)	507(b)	Notice of Freedom to Divest Employer Securities—Penalties	Plan years beginning after December 31, 2006, generally
502(c)(8)	202(b)(3)	Additional Funding Rules for Multiemployer Plans In Endangered or Critical Status—Enforcement	Plan years beginning after 2007, generally
502(c)(8)-(9)	202(b)(2)	Additional Funding Rules for Multiemployer Plans In Endangered or Critical Status—Enforcement	Plan years beginning after 2007, generally
510	205	Prohibition on Retaliation Against Employers Exercising Their Rights to Petition the Federal Government	August 17, 2006
511	623(a)(1)-(2)	Increase in Penalties for Coercive Interference with Exercise of ERISA Rights	Violations occurring on and after August 17, 2006
514(e)	902(f)(1)	Increasing Participation Through Automatic Contribution Arrangements—Preemption of Conflicting State Regulation	August 17, 2006
4001(a)(13)	107(b)(1)	Technical and Conforming Amendments—Miscellaneous Amendments to Title IV	Plan years beginning after 2007
4002(a)	411(a)(1)	Director of the Pension Benefit Guaranty Corporation	August 17, 2006
4003(b)	411(a)(2)(A)-(B)	Director of the Pension Benefit Guaranty Corporation	August 17, 2006

ERISA Sec.	Act Sec.	Act Provision Subject	Effective Date
4003(e)(1)	107(b)(2)	Technical and Conforming Amendments—Miscellaneous Amendments to Title IV	Plan years beginning after 2007
4006(a)(3)(E)(i)	405(a)(1)	PBGC Premiums for Small Plans—Small Plans	Plan years beginning after December 31, 2006
4006(a)(3)(E)(iii)(V)	301(a)(3)	Extension of Replacement of 30-Year Treasury Rates—Amendments of ERISA—PBGC Premium Rate	August 17, 2006
4006(a)(3)(E)(iii)-(iv)	401(a)(1)	PBGC Premiums—Variable-Rate Premiums—Conforming Amendments Related to Funding Rules for Single-Employer Plans	Plan years beginning after 2007
4006(a)(3)(H)	405(a)(2)	PBGC Premiums for Small Plans—Small Plans	Plan years beginning after December 31, 2006
4006(a)(7)(C)(ii)	401(b)(2)(A)	PBGC Premiums—Termination Premiums—Technical Correction	Plans terminated after December 31, 2005, generally
4006(a)(7)(E)	401(b)(1)	PBGC Premiums—Termination Premiums—Repeal of Sunset Provision	August 17, 2006
4007(b)(1)	406(a)(1)	Authorization for PBGC to Pay Interest on Premium Overpayment Refunds	Interest accruing for periods beginning not earlier than August 17, 2006
4007(b)(2)	406(a)(2)	Authorization for PBGC to Pay Interest on Premium Overpayment Refunds	Interest accruing for periods beginning not earlier than August 17, 2006
4008(a)	412(1)	Inclusion of Information in the PBGC Annual Report	August 17, 2006
4008(b)	412(2)	Inclusion of Information in the PBGC Annual Report	August 17, 2006
4010(b)(1)	505(a)	Section 4010 Filings with the PBGC—Change in Criteria for Persons Required to Provide Information to PBGC	Years beginning after 2007
4010(b)(2)	107(b)(3)	Technical and Conforming Amendments—Miscellaneous Amendments to Title IV	Plan years beginning after 2007
4010(d)-(e)	505(b)	Section 4010 Filings with the PBGC—Additional Information Required	Years beginning after 2007
4011	501(b)(1)	Defined Benefit Plan Funding Notice—Repeal of Notice to Participants of Funding Status	Plan years beginning after December 31, 2006
4021(b)(2)	906(a)(2)(B)	Treatment of Certain Pension Plans of Indian Tribal Governments—Definition of Government Plan to Include Certain Pension Plans of Indian Tribal Governments—Amendment to Employee Retirement Income Security Act of 1974	Any year beginning on or after August 17, 2006
4021(b)(9)	407(c)(1)(A)	Rules for Substantial Owner Benefits In Terminated Plans—Conforming Amendments	January 1, 2006

ERISA Sec.	Act Sec.	Act Provision Subject	Effective Date
4021(b)(12)	906(b)(2)(A)	Treatment of Certain Pension Plans of Indian Tribal Governments—Clarification That Tribal Governments Are Subject to the Same Pension Plan Rules and Regulations Applied to State and Other Local Governments and Their Police and Firefighters—Amendments to Employee Retirement Income Security Act of 1974	Any year beginning on or after August 17, 2006
4021(b)(13)	906(b)(2)(B)	Treatment of Certain Pension Plans of Indian Tribal Governments—Clarification That Tribal Governments Are Subject to the Same Pension Plan Rules and Regulations Applied to State and Other Local Governments and Their Police and FireFighters—Amendments to Employee Retirement Income Security Act of 1974	Any year beginning on or after August 17, 2006
4021(b)(14)	906(b)(2)(C)	Treatment of Certain Pension Plans of Indian Tribal Governments—Clarification That Tribal Governments Are Subject to the Same Pension Plan Rules and Regulations Applied to State and Other Local Governments and Their Police and Fire-Fighters—Amendments to Employee Retirement Income Security Act of 1974	Any year beginning on or after August 17, 2006
4021(d)	407(c)(1)(B)	Rules for Substantial Owner Benefits In Terminated Plans—Conforming Amendments	January 1, 2006
4022(b)(5)	407(a)	Rules for Substantial Owner Benefits In Terminated Plans—Modification of Phase-In of Guarantee	Plan terminations under ERISA Sec. 4041(c) with respect to which notices of intent to terminate are provided under ERISA Sec. 4041(a)(2) after December 31, 2005, and under ERISA Sec. 4042 with respect to which notices of determination are provided after such date
4022(b)(8)	403(a)	Limitation on PBGC Guarantee of Shutdown and Other Benefits	Benefits that become payable as a result of an event which occurs after July 26, 2005

ERISA Sec.	Act Sec.	Act Provision Subject	Effective Date
4022(c)(3)(A)	408(b)(1)	Acceleration of PBGC Computation of Benefits Attributable to Recoveries from Employers—Valuation of Section 4062(c) Liability for Determining Amounts Payable by Corporation to Participants and Beneficiaries—Single-Employer Plan Benefits Guaranteed	Terminations for which notices of intent to terminate are provided (or in the case of a termination by the corporation, a notice of determination under ERISA Sec. 4042 is issued) on or after the date which is 30 days after August 17, 2006
4022(c)(3)(B)(ii)	408(a)	Acceleration of PBGC Computation of Benefits Attributable to Recoveries from Employers—Modification of Average Recovery Percentage of Outstanding Amount of Benefit Liabilities Payable by Corporation to Participants and Beneficiaries	Terminations for which notices of intent to terminate are provided (or in the case of a termination by the corporation, a notice of determination under ERISA Sec. 4042 is issued) on or after the date which is 30 days after August 17, 2006
4022(g)	404(a)	Rules Relating to Bankruptcy of Employer—Guarantee	Proceeding initiated under Title 11, United States Code, or under any similar Federal law or law of a state or political subdivision, on or after the date that is 30 days after August 17, 2006
4022(h)	402(g)(2)(A)	Special Funding Rules for Certain Plans Maintained by Commercial Airlines—Other Rules for Plans Making Election Under This Section—Special Rules for Terminations—PBGC Liability Limited	Plan years ending after August 17, 2006
4041(b)(5)	409(a)	Treatment of Certain Plans Where Cessation or Change in Membership of a Controlled Group	Any transaction or series of transactions occurring on and after August 17, 2006

ERISA Sec.	Act Sec.	Act Provision Subject	Effective Date
4041(c)(1)(C)	506(a)(2)	Disclosure of Termination Information to Plan Participants—Distress Terminations—Conforming Amendment	Any plan termination under Title IV of ERISA with respect to which the notice of intent to terminate (or in the case of a PBGC termination, a notice of determination under ERISA Sec. 4042) occurs after August 17, 2006, generally
4041(c)(2)(D)	506(a)(1)	Disclosure of Termination Information to Plan Participants—Distress Terminations	Any plan termination under Title IV of ERISA with respect to which the notice of intent to terminate (or in the case of a PBGC termination, a notice of determination under ERISA Sec. 4042) occurs after August 17, 2006, generally
4042(c)(1)	506(b)(1)(A)	Disclosure of Termination Information to Plan Participants—Involuntary Terminations	Any plan termination under Title IV of ERISA with respect to which the notice of intent to terminate (or in the case of a PBGC termination, a notice of determination under ERISA Sec. 4042) occurs after August 17, 2006
4042(c)(2)-(3)	506(b)(1)(B)	Disclosure of Termination Information to Plan Participants—Involuntary Terminations	Any plan termination under Title IV of ERISA with respect to which the notice of intent to terminate (or in the case of a PBGC termination, a notice of determination under ERISA Sec. 4042) occurs after August 17, 2006

ERISA Sec.	Act Sec.	Act Provision Subject	Effective Date
4042(c)(3)	506(b)(1)(C)	Disclosure of Termination Information to Plan Participants—Involuntary Terminations	Any plan termination under Title IV of ERISA with respect to which the notice of intent to terminate (or in the case of a PBGC termination, a notice of determination under ERISA Sec. 4042) occurs after August 17, 2006, generally
4043(c)(7)	407(c)(2)	Rules for Substantial Owner Benefits In Terminated Plans—Conforming Amendments	January 1, 2006
4044(a)(4)(B)	407(b)(1)	Rules for Substantial Owner Benefits In Terminated Plans—Modification of Allocation of Assets	Plan terminations under ERISA Sec. 4041(c) with respect to which notices of intent to terminate are provided under ERISA Sec. 4041(a)(2) after December 31, 2005, and under ERISA Sec. 4042 with respect to which notices of determination are provided after such date
4044(b)(2)	407(b)(2)(A)	Rules for Substantial Owner Benefits In Terminated Plans—Modification of Allocation of Assets	Plan terminations under ERISA Sec. 4041(c) with respect to which notices of intent to terminate are provided under ERISA Sec. 4041(a)(2) after December 31, 2005, and under ERISA Sec. 4042 with respect to which notices of determination are provided after such date

ERISA Sec.	Act Sec.	Act Provision Subject	Effective Date
4044(b)(3)-(7)	407(b)(2)(B)	Rules for Substantial Owner Benefits In Terminated Plans—Modification of Allocation of Assets	Plan terminations under ERISA Sec. 4041(c) with respect to which notices of intent to terminate are provided under ERISA Sec. 4041(a)(2) after December 31, 2005, and under ERISA Sec. 4042 with respect to which notices of determination are provided after such date
4044(e)	404(b)	Rules Relating to Bankruptcy of Employer—Allocation of Assets Among Priority Groups in Bankruptcy Proceedings	Proceeding initiated under Title 11, United States Code, or under any similar Federal law or law of a state or political subdivision, on or after the date that is 30 days after August 17, 2006
4044(e)	408(b)(2)	Acceleration of PBGC Computation of Benefits Attributable to Recoveries from Employers—Valuation of Section 4062(c) Liability for Determining Amounts Payable by Corporation to Participants and Beneficiaries—Allocation of Assets	Terminations for which notices of intent to terminate are provided (or in the case of a termination by the corporation, a notice of determination under ERISA Sec. 4042 is issued) on or after the date which is 30 days after August 17, 2006
4050(c)-(e)	410(a)	Missing Participants	Distributions made after final regulations implementing ERISA Secs. 4050(c) and 4050(d) are prescribed
4062(c)(1)-(3)	107(b)(4)	Technical and Conforming Amendments—Miscellaneous Amendments to Title IV	Plan years beginning after 2007
4071	107(b)(5)	Technical and Conforming Amendments—Miscellaneous Amendments to Title IV	Plan years beginning after 2007
4205(b)(2)(A)(i)	204(b)(1)	Withdrawal Liability Reforms—Withdrawal Liability Continues If Work Contracted Out	Work transferred on or after August 17, 2006

ERISA Sec.	Act Sec.	Act Provision Subject	Effective Date
4210(b)(1)	204(c)(1)(A)	Withdrawal Liability Reforms—Application of Rules to Plans Primarily Covering Employees in the Building and Construction Industry	Plan withdrawals occurring on or after January 1, 2007
4210(b)(1)-(4)	204(c)(1)(B)	Withdrawal Liability Reforms—Application of Rules to Plans Primarily Covering Employees in the Building and Construction Industry	Plan withdrawals occurring on or after January 1, 2007
4211(c)(5)(E)	204(c)(2)	Withdrawal Liability Reforms—Application of Rules to Plans Primarily Covering Employees in the Building and Construction Industry—Fresh Start Option	Plan withdrawals occurring on or after January 1, 2007
4221(g)	204(d)(1)	Withdrawal Liability Reforms—Procedures Applicable to Disputes Involving Pension Plan Withdrawal Liability	Any person receiving notification under ERISA Sec. 4219(b)(1) on or after August 17, 2006 with respect to a transaction occurring after December 31, 1998
4225(a)(1)(B)	204(a)(2)	Withdrawal Liability Reforms—Update of Rules Relating to Limitations on Withdrawal Liability—Plans Using Attributable Method	Sales occurring on or after January 1, 2007
4225(a)(2)	204(a)(1)	Withdrawal Liability Reforms—Update of Rules Relating to Limitations on Withdrawal Liability—Increase in Limits	Sales occurring on or after January 1, 2007
4243(a)(1)(B)	107(b)(6)	Technical and Conforming Amendments—Miscellaneous Amendments to Title IV	Plan years beginning after 2007
4243(f)(1)	107(b)(7)	Technical and Conforming Amendments—Miscellaneous Amendments to Title IV	Plan years beginning after 2007
4243(f)(2)	107(b)(8)	Technical and Conforming Amendments—Miscellaneous Amendments to Title IV	Plan years beginning after 2007
4243(g)	107(b)(9)	Technical and Conforming Amendments—Miscellaneous Amendments to Title IV	Plan years beginning after 2007
4245(d)(1)	203(a)(1)-(2)	Measures to Forestall Insolvency of Multiemployer Plans—Advance Determination of Impending Insolvency Over 5 Years	Determinations made in plan years beginning after 2007

¶25,001 Code Section to Explanation Table

Code Sec.	Explanation
25B(b)	¶1320
25B(h)	¶1315
72(e)(11)-(12)	¶820
72(t)(2)(G)	¶917
72(t)(10)	¶915
101(a)	¶1330
101(j)	¶1330
170(b)(1)(E)-(G)	¶1125
170(b)(2)	¶1125
170(d)(2)	¶1125
170(e)(1)(B)	¶1120
170(e)(1)(B)(i)	¶1150
170(e)(3)(C)(iv)	¶1140
170(e)(3)(D)(iv)	¶1145
170(e)(7)	¶1150
170(f)(11)(E)	¶1355
170(f)(13)-(14)	¶1130
170(f)(15)	¶1120
170(f)(16)	¶1110
170(f)(17)	¶1185
170(f)(18)	¶1180
170(h)(4)(B)-(C)	¶1130
170(o)-(p)	¶1115
219(b)(5)(C)-(D)	¶730
219(g)(8)	¶1320
401(a)(5)(G)	¶1060
401(a)(26)(G)	¶1060
401(a)(28)(B)(v)	¶605
401(a)(29), (32), (33)	¶205
401(a)(35)	¶605
401(a)(36)	¶920
401(k)(2)(B)(i)	¶917
401(k)(3)(G)	¶1060
401(k)(8)(A)(i)	¶1015
401(k)(8)(E)	¶1015
401(k)(13)	¶1015
401(m)(6)(A)	¶1015
401(m)(12)-(13)	¶1015
402(c)(2)(A)	¶940
402(c)(11)	¶945
402(l)	¶825
403(a)(2)	¶825
403(a)(4)(B)	¶945
403(b)(2)	¶825
403(b)(7)(A)(ii)	¶917
403(b)(8)(B)	¶945
403(b)(11)	¶917
404(a)(1)(A)-(B)	¶705
404(a)(1)(D)	¶705, ¶710
404(a)(1)(D)(i)	¶710
404(a)(1)(F)	¶705
404(a)(7)	¶705
404(a)(7)(C)(iii)	¶715
404(a)(7)(C)(iv)	¶705, ¶715
404(a)(7)(C)(v)	¶715
404(o)	¶705
404A(g)(3)(A)	¶705
408(d)	¶1105
408A(c)(3)(B)	¶935
408A(c)(3)(C)	¶1320
408A(d)(3)	¶935
408A(e)	¶935
409(h)(7)	¶605
409A(b)	¶220
409A(b)(3)-(5)	¶220
410(b)(3)	¶245
411	¶205
411(a)(2)	¶720
411(a)(3)(G)	¶1015
411(a)(12)	¶720
411(a)(13)	¶1005
411(b)(5)	¶1005
412	¶205
412(b)(3)	¶310
412(b)(5)(B)	¶240
412(b)(5)(B)(ii)(II)	¶235
412(l)(7)(C)(i)(IV)	¶235
412(l)(12)	¶245
414(b)(2)(B)(i)	¶205
414(d)	¶1065
414(f)(6)	¶325
414(h)(2)	¶1065
414(i)(2)(B)(i)	¶305
414(w)	¶1015
414(x)	¶1020
415(b)(2)(E)(ii)	¶740
415(b)(2)(H)	¶1065
415(b)(3)	¶735
415(b)(10)	¶1065
415(b)(11)	¶1055
415(n)(1)	¶745
415(n)(3)(A)-(D)	¶745
416(g)(4)(H)(i)-(ii)	¶1015
417(a)(1)(A)	¶1040

Code Sec.	Explanation
6421(c)	¶1255
6652(c)	¶1190
6652(c)(1)(E)	¶1260
6662(e)(1)(A)	¶1345
6662(g)(1)	¶1345
6662(h)(2)(A)	¶1345
6662(h)(2)(C)	¶1345
6664(c)(2)	¶1345
6664(c)(3)(B)-(C)	¶1355
6695A	¶1350
6696	¶1350
6720B	¶1150
6721(e)(2)	¶1285
6724(d)(1)-(2)	¶820
6724(d)(1)(B)	¶1285
7428(b)(4)	¶1260
7443A(b)(5)-(6)	¶1410
7443A(c)	¶1410
7443B	¶1450
7447(j)	¶1440

Code Sec.	Explanation
7448	¶1445
7448(a)(5)-(10)	¶1445
7448(b)	¶1445
7448(c)(1)	¶1445
7448(d)	¶1445
7448(f)-(h)	¶1445
7448(j)	¶1445
7448(m)(1)	¶1445
7448(n)	¶1445
7448(s)	¶1430
7448(u)	¶1445
7451	¶1420
7472	¶1435
7475(b)	¶1425
7701	¶1205
7701(a)(49)	¶1255
7701(o)-(p)	¶1205
7702B(e)	¶820

¶25,003 ERISA Section to Explanation Table

ERISA Sec.	Explanation
1	¶305, ¶405
3(2)(A)	¶920
3(2)(B)	¶1070
3(32)	¶1065
3(37)(G)	¶325
3(42)	¶630
101	¶215
101(a)(2)	¶415
101(f)	¶405
101(i)(8)(B)	¶620
101(j)	¶215
101(k)	¶215, ¶410
101(l)	¶410
101(m)	¶410, ¶610
101(n)	¶610
103(a)(1)(B)	¶415
103(d)(12)-(14)	¶415
103(f)	¶415
104	¶415
104(b)	¶420
104(b)(3)	¶415
104(b)(5)	¶420
104(d)-(e)	¶415
105(a)-(b)	¶615
105(d)	¶615
203(a)	¶720
203(a)(3)(F)	¶1015
203(f)	¶1005
204(b)(5)	¶1005
204(h)(1)	¶410
204(j)-(k)	¶605
205(c)(1)(A)	¶1040
205(c)(3)(A)(i)	¶1040
205(c)(7)(A)	¶925
205(d)	¶1040
205(g)	¶905
206(f)	¶540
206(g)	¶215
210(e)	¶1020
301(d)	¶305
302-308	¶205
302(b)(3)	¶310
302(b)(5)(B)	¶240
302(b)(5)(B)(ii)(II)	¶235
302(d)(7)(C)(i)(IV)	¶235
302(d)(12)	¶245
303	¶210
304	¶305
305	¶310
404(c)(1)	¶640
404(c)(1)(A)(ii)	¶640
404(c)(1)(B)-(C)	¶640
404(c)(4)	¶640
404(c)(5)	¶655
407(b)(3)(D)	¶605
408(b)(14)	¶625
408(b)(15)-(19)	¶630
408(b)(20)(A)-(E)	¶635
408(g)	¶625
412(a)	¶630, ¶645
502(a)(10)	¶310
502(c)(1)	¶615
502(c)(4)	¶410, ¶1015
502(c)(7)	¶610
502(c)(8)	¶310
510	¶330
511	¶650
514(e)	¶1015
4002(a)	¶545
4003(b)	¶545
4006(a)(3)(E)(i)	¶510
4006(a)(3)(E)(iii)	¶505
4006(a)(3)(E)(iii)(V)	¶235, ¶505
4006(a)(3)(E)(iv)	¶505
4006(a)(3)(H)	¶510
4006(a)(7)(C)(ii)	¶505
4006(a)(7)(E)	¶505
4007(b)(2)	¶515
4008(b)	¶550
4010	¶425
4010(b)	¶425
4010(b)(1)	¶425
4010(d)-(e)	¶425
4021(b)	¶1065
4021(b)(2)	¶1065
4021(b)(9)	¶530
4021(d)	¶530
4022(b)	¶520
4022(b)(5)	¶530
4022(c)(3)(A)	¶535
4022(c)(3)(B)(ii)	¶535
4022(g)	¶525
4022(h)	¶245
4041(b)(5)	¶225

¶25,005 Code Sections Added, Amended or Repealed

The list below notes all the Code Sections or subsections of the Internal Revenue Code that were added, amended or repealed by the Pension Protection Act of 2006. The first column indicates the Code Section added, amended or repealed, and the second column indicates the Act Section.

Pension Protection Act of 2006

Code Sec.	*Act Sec.*	*Code Sec.*	*Act Sec.*
25B(b)	833(a)	401(k)(2)(B)(i)(III)-(V)	827(b)(1)
25B(h)	812	401(k)(3)(G)	861(a)(2)
72(e)(11)-(12)	844(a)	401(k)(3)(G)	861(b)(3)
72(t)(2)(G)	827(a)	401(k)(8)(A)(i)	902(e)(3)(B)(i)
72(t)(10)	828(a)	401(k)(8)(E)	902(d)(2)(C)
101(a)(1)	863(c)(1)	401(k)(8)(E)	902(d)(2)(D)
101(j)	863(a)	401(k)(13)	902(a)
170(b)(1)(E) -(G)	1206(a)(1)	401(m)(6)(A)	902(e)(3)(B)(ii)
170(b)(2)	1206(a)(2)	401(m)(12) -(13)	902(b)
170(d)(2)	1206(b)(1)	402(c)(2)(A)	822(a)(1)-(2)
170(e)(1)(B)(i)	1215(a)(1)	402(c)(11)	829(a)(1)
170(e)(1)(B)(ii) -(iv)	1214(a)	402(l)	845(a)
170(e)(3)(C)(iv)	1202(a)	403(a)(2)	845(b)(1)
170(e)(3)(D)(iv)	1204(a)	403(a)(4)(B)	829(a)(2)
170(e)(7)	1215(a)(2)	403(b)(2)	845(b)(2)
170(f)(11)(E)	1219(c)(1)	403(b)(7)(A)(ii)	827(b)(2)
170(f)(13)	1213(c)	403(b)(8)(B)	829(a)(3)
170(f)(14)	1213(d)	403(b)(11)(A) -(C)	827(b)(3)
170(f)(15)	1214(b)	404(a)(1)(A)	801(a)(1)
170(f)(16)	1216(a)	404(a)(1)(A)	801(c)(1)
170(f)(17)	1217(a)	404(a)(1)(B)	801(c)(2)(A)-(E)
170(f)(18)	1234(a)	404(a)(1)(D)	802(a)
170(h)(4)(B) -(C)	1213(a)(1)	404(a)(1)(D)(i)	801(d)(1)
170(h)(4)(C)	1213(b)(1)-(3)	404(a)(1)(F)	801(d)(2)
170(o)-(p)	1218(a)	404(a)(7)	801(c)(3)(A)-(B)
219(b)(5)(C) -(D)	831(a)	404(a)(7)(C)(iii)	803(a)
219(g)(8)	833(b)	404(a)(7)(C)(iv)	801(b)
401(a)(5)(G)	861(a)(1)	404(a)(7)(C)(v)	803(b)
401(a)(5)(G)	861(b)(1)	404(o)	801(a)(2)
401(a)(26)(G)	861(a)(1)	404A(g)(3)(A)	801(c)(4)
401(a)(26)(G)	861(b)(2)	408(d)(8)	1201(a)
401(a)(28)(B)(v)	901(a)(2)(A)	408A(c)(3)(B)	824(b)(1)(A)-(B)
401(a)(29)	114(a)(1)	408A(c)(3)(C)	833(c)
401(a)(32)(A)	114(a)(2)(A)	408A(d)(3)	824(b)(2)(A)-(E)
401(a)(32)(C)	114(a)(2)(B)	408A(e)	824(a)
401(a)(33)(B)(i)	114(a)(3)(A)	409(h)(7)	901(a)(2)(B)
401(a)(33)(B)(iii)	114(a)(3)(B)	409A(b)(3) -(5)	116(a)
401(a)(33)(D)	114(a)(3)(C)	409A(b)(4) -(5)	116(b)
401(a)(35)	901(a)(1)	410(b)(3)	402(h)(1)
401(a)(36)	905(b)	411(a)(2)	904(a)(1)

Code Sec.	Act Sec.
411(a)(3)(C)	114(b)(1)
411(a)(3)(G)	902(d)(2)(A)
411(a)(3)(G)	902(d)(2)(B)
411(a)(12)	904(a)(2)
411(a)(13)	701(b)(2)
411(b)(1)(F)	114(b)(2)(A)-(B)
411(b)(5)	701(b)(1)
411(d)(6)(A)	114(b)(3)
412	111(a)
412(b)(3)	212(c)
412(b)(5)(B)(ii)(II)	301(b)(1)(A)-(B)
412(l)(7)(C)(i)(IV)	301(b)(2)(A)-(B)
414(d)	906(a)(1)
414(f)(6)	1106(b)
414(h)(2)	906(b)(1)(C)
414(l)(2)(B)(i)(I)	114(c)
414(w)	902(d)(1)
414(x)	903(a)
415(b)(2)(E)(ii)	303(a)
415(b)(2)(H)(i) -(ii)	906(b)(1)(A)(i)-(ii)
415(b)(3)	832(a)
415(b)(1[0])	906(b)(1)(B)(ii)
415(b)(10)(A)	906(b)(1)(B)(i)
415(b)(11)	867(a)
415(n)(1)	821(a)(1)
415(n)(3)(A)	821(a)(2)
415(n)(3)(B) -(C)	821(c)(1)-(3)
415(n)(3)(D)	821(b)
416(g)(4)(H)(i)	902(c)(1)
416(g)(4)(H)(ii)	902(c)(2)
417(a)(1)(A)(i) -(iii)	1004(a)(1)(A)-(C)
417(a)(3)(A)(i)	1004(a)(3)
417(a)(6)(A)	1102(a)(1)(A)
417(e)(3)	302(b)
417(g)	1004(a)(2)
418E(d)(1)	213(a)(1)-(2)
419A(c)(6)	843(a)
420(a)	842(a)(1)
420(e)(2)	114(d)(1)
420(e)(4)	114(d)(2)
420(e)(5)	842(a)(2)
420(f)	841(a)
430	112(a)
431	211(a)
432	212(a)
436	113(a)(1)(B)
457(a)(3)	845(b)(3)
457(e)(11)(D)	1104(a)(1)
457(e)(16)(B)	829(a)(4)
457(f)(2)(D) -(F)	1104(b)(1)
457(f)(4)	1104(b)(2)
501(c)(21)(C)	862(a)
501(q)-(r)	1220(a)
508(f)	1235(b)(1)
509(a)(3)(B)	1241(a)
509(e)	1221(a)(2)
509(f)	1241(b)
512(b)(13)(E) -(F)	1205(a)
513(j)	1220(b)
514(c)(9)(C)(ii) -(iv)	866(a)
529(f)	1304(b)
545(b)(2)	1206(b)(2)
664(g)(3)(E)	868(a)
848(e)(6)	844(e)
1035(a)(1) -(3)	844(b)(3)(A)-(C)
1035(a)(2) -(4)	844(b)(4)
1035(b)(2)	844(b)(1)
1035(b)(3)	844(b)(2)
1367(a)(2)	1203(a)
2055(e)(5)	1234(b)
2055(g)-(h)	1218(b)
2522(c)(5)	1234(c)
2522(e)-(f)	1218(c)
3121(b)(5)(E)	854(c)(8)
3304(a)	1105(a)
4041(g)(3) -(5)	1207(a)
4221(a)	1207(b)(2)
4221(a)	1207(b)(3)(A)
4221(a)(4) -(6)	1207(b)(1)
4253(k)-(l)	1207(c)(1)
4253(l)	1207(c)(2)
4483(h)-(i)	1207(d)
4940(c)(2)	1221(a)(1)
4940(c)(4)	1221(b)(1)-(3)
4941(a)(1) -(2)	1212(a)(1)(A)-(B)
4941(c)(2)	1212(a)(2)
4942(a)	1212(b)
4942(g)(4)	1244(a)
4943(a)(1)	1212(c)
4943(e)	1233(a)
4943(f)	1243(a)
4944(a)	1212(d)(1)
4944(d)(2)	1212(d)(2)(A)-(B)
4945(a)(1) -(2)	1212(e)(1)(A)-(B)
4945(c)(2)	1212(e)(2)(A)-(B)
4945(d)(4)(A)	1244(b)
4958(c)(2) -(3)	1232(b)(1)
4958(c)(3) -(4)	1242(b)
4958(d)(2)	1212(a)(3)
4958(f)(1)(B) -(E)	1232(a)(1)
4958(f)(1)(D) -(F)	1242(a)
4958(f)(6)	1232(b)(2)
4958(f)(7) -(8)	1232(a)(2)
4963(a)	1231(b)(1)

Code Sec.	Act Sec.
4963(c)	1231(b)(1)
4966	1231(a)
4967	1231(a)
4971(a)-(b)	114(e)(1)
4971(c)	114(e)(2)(A)-(B)
4971(c)(2) [(e)(2)]	212(b)(2)(A)-(B)
4971(e)(1)	114(e)(3)
4971(f)(1)	114(e)(4)(A)-(B)
4971(g)-(h)	212(b)(1)
4972(c)(6)(A)	803(c)
4972(c)(7)	114(e)(5)
4975(d)(15) -(17)	601(b)(1)(A)-(C)
4975(d)(16) -(18)	611(a)(2)(A)
4975(d)(17) -(19)	611(c)(2)
4975(d)(18) -(20)	611(d)(2)(A)
4975(d)(19) -(21)	611(e)(2)
4975(d)(20) -(22)	611(g)(2)
4975(d)(21) -(23)	612(b)(1)
4975(f)(8)	601(b)(2)
4975(f)(9)	611(a)(2)(B)
4975(f)(10)	611(d)(2)(B)
4975(f)(11)	612(b)(2)
4979(f)	902(e)(1)(A)-(B)
4979(f)(1)	902(e)(3)(A)
4979(f)(2)	902(e)(2)
4980(c)(3)(A)	901(a)(2)(C)
4980F(e)(1)	502(c)(2)
6033(a)(3)(B)	1245(a)
6033(h)-(i)	1205(b)(1)
6033(i)-(j)	1223(a)
6033(j)-(k)	1223(b)
6033(k)-(l)	1235(a)(1)
6033(l)(m)	1245(b)
6034	1201(b)(1)
6039I	863(b)
6050L(a)(1)	1215(b)(1)-(2)
6050U	844(d)(1)
6050V	1211(a)(1)
6059(b)(2) -(3)	114(f)(1)-(2)
6103(a)(2)	1224(b)(1)
6103(p)(3)(A)	1224(b)(2)
6103(p)(4)	1224(b)(3)(A)-(C)
6104(b)	1201(b)(3)
6104(c)(1)	1224(b)(4)
6104(c)(2) -(6)	1224(a)
6104(d)(1)(A)(ii) -(iv)	1225(a)
6214(b)	858(a)
6330(d)(1)	855(a)
6416(b)(2)	1207(e)(1)(B)
6416(b)(2)	1207(e)(1)(C)(i)-(ii)
6416(b)(2)(E) -(G)	1207(e)(1)(A)
6416(b)(4)(B)(i) -(iii)	1207(e)(2)
6421(c)	1207(b)(3)(B)
6652(c)(1)(E)	1223(d)
6652(c)(2)(C)	1201(b)(2)
6662(e)(1)(A)	1219(a)(1)(A)
6662(g)	1219(a)(1)(B)
6662(h)(2)(A)(i) -(ii)	1219(a)(2)(A)
6662(h)(2)(C)	1219(a)(2)(B)
6664(c)(2)	1219(a)(3)
6664(c)(3)(B) -(C)	1219(c)(2)
6695A	1219(b)(1)
6696	1219(b)(2)(A)-(B)
6720B	1215(c)(1)
6721(e)(2)(B) -(D)	1211(b)(2)
6724(d)(1)(B)(xiv) -(xx)	1211(b)(1)
6724(d)(1)(B)(xvii)-(xix)	844(d)(2)(A)
6724(d)(2)(AA) -(CC)	844(d)(2)(B)
7213(a)(2)	1224(b)(5)
7213A(a)(2)	1224(b)(6)
7428(b)(4)	1223(c)
7431(a)(2)	1224(b)(7)
7443A(b)(4) -(6)	857(a)
7443A(c)	857(b)
7443B	856(a)
7447(j)	853(a)
7448	854(c)(1)
7448(a)(5) -(10)	854(a)
7448(b)	854(b)(1)-(3)
7448(c)(1)	854(c)(3)(A)-(B)
7448(c)(1) -(2)	854(c)(4)(A)-(B)
7448(d)	854(c)(3)(A)-(B)
7448(f)	854(c)(3)(A)-(B)
7448(g)	854(c)(3)(A)-(B)
7448(h)	854(c)(3)(A)-(B)
7448(j)	854(c)(3)(A)-(B)
7448(j)(1)	854(c)(5)(A)-(B)
7448(m)	854(c)(3)(A)-(B)
7448(m)(1)	854(c)(6)
7448(n)	854(c)(3)(A)-(B)
7448(n)	854(c)(7)
7448(s)	851(a)
7448(u)	854(c)(3)(A)-(B)
7451	859(a)
7472	852
7475(b)	860(a)
7701(a)(49)	1207(f)
7701(o)-(p)	1222
7702B(e)	844(c)
7702B(e)(1)	844(f)

¶25,007 ERISA Sections Added, Amended or Repealed

The list below notes all the sections or subsections of the Employee Retirement Income Security Act of 1974 (ERISA) that were added, amended or repealed by the Pension Protection Act of 2006. The first column indicates the ERISA Section added, amended or repealed, and the second column indicates the Act Section.

Pension Protection Act of 2006

ERISA Sec.	Act Sec.
3(2)(A)	905(a)
3(2)(B)	1104(c)
3(32)	906(a)(2)(A)
3(37)(G)	1106(a)
3(42)	611(f)
101(a)(2)	503(c)(2)
101(d)(3)	107(a)(1)
101(e)(3)	107(a)(11)
101(f)	501(a)
101(i)(8)(B)(i)-(v)	509(a)
101(j)-(k)	103(b)(1)(A)-(B)
101(k)-(l)	502(a)(1)(A)-(B)
101(l)-(m)	502(b)(1)(A)-(B)
101(m)-(n)	507(a)
103(a)(1)(B)	503(a)(1)(A)
103(d)(8)(B)	107(a)(2)
103(d)(11)	107(a)(3)
103(d)(12)-(14)	503(b)(1)-(2)
103(f)	503(a)(1)(B)
104	503(d)(1)-(3)
104(b)(3)	503(c)(1)
104(b)(5)	504(a)
105(a)	508(a)(1)
105(b)	508(a)(2)(B)
105(d)	508(a)(2)(A)
203(a)(2)	904(b)(1)
203(a)(3)(C)	107(a)(4)
203(a)(3)(F)	902(d)(2)(E)
203(a)(4)	904(b)(2)
203(f)	701(a)(2)
204(b)(5)	701(a)(1)
204(g)(1)	107(a)(5)
204(h)(1)	502(c)(1)
204(i)(2)(B)	107(a)(6)
204(i)(3)	107(a)(7)
204(i)(4)	107(a)(8)
204(j)-(k)	901(b)(1)
205(c)(1)(A)(i)-(iii)	1004(b)(1)(A)-(C)
205(c)(3)(A)(i)	1004(b)(3)
205(c)(7)(A)	1102(a)(2)(A)
205(d)	1004(b)(2)(A)-(C)
205(g)(3)	302(a)
206(e)(1)	107(a)(9)
206(e)(3)	107(a)(10)
206(f)	410(b)(1)-(2)
206(g)	103(a)
207	107(d)
210	903(b)(2)(A)
210(e)	903(b)(1)
301(d)	201(c)(1)
302	101(b)
302(b)(3)	202(d)
302(b)(5)(B)(ii)(II)	301(a)(1)(A)-(B)
302(d)(7)(C)(i)(IV)	301(a)(2)(A)-(B)
302-308	101(a)
303	102(a)
304	201(a)
305	202(a)
403(c)(1)	107(a)(11)
404(c)(1)	621(a)(1)(A)-(C)
404(c)(4)	621(a)(2)
404(c)(5)	624(a)
407(b)(3)(D)	901(b)(2)
408(b)(13)	107(a)(11)
408(b)(14)	601(a)(1)
408(b)(15)	611(a)(1)
408(b)(16)	611(c)(1)
408(b)(17)	611(d)(1)
408(b)(18)	611(e)(1)
408(b)(19)	611(g)(1)
408(b)(20)	612(a)
408(g)	601(a)(2)
412(a)	622(a)
412(a)(1)-(3)	611(b)(1)-(3)
502(a)(6)	202(b)(1)
502(a)(8)-(10)	202(c)

ERISA Sec.	Act Sec.
502(c)(1)	508(a)(2)(C)
502(c)(4)	103(b)(2)
502(c)(4)	502(a)(2)
502(c)(4)	502(b)(2)
502(c)(4)	902(f)(2)
502(c)(7)	507(b)
502(c)(8)-(9)	202(b)(2)-(3)
510	205
511	623(a)(1)-(2)
514(e)	902(f)(1)
4001(a)(13)	107(b)(1)
4002(a)	411(a)(1)
4003(b)	411(a)(2)(A)-(B)
4003(e)(1)	107(b)(2)
4006(a)(3)(E)(i)	405(a)(1)
4006(a)(3)(E)(iii)(V)	301(a)(3)
4006(a)(3)(E)(iii)-(iv)	401(a)(1)
4006(a)(3)(H)	405(a)(2)
4006(a)(7)(C)(ii)	401(b)(2)(A)
4006(a)(7)(E)	401(b)(1)
4007(b)	406(a)(1)-(2)
4008	412(1)-(2)
4010(b)(1)	505(a)
4010(b)(2)	107(b)(3)
4010(d)	505(b)
4011	501(b)(1)
4021(b)(2)	906(a)(2)(B)
4021(b)(9)	407(c)(1)(A)
4021(b)(12)-(14)	906(b)(2)(A)-(C)
4021(d)	407(c)(1)(B)
4022(b)(5)	407(a)
4022(b)(8)	403(a)
4022(c)(3)(A)	408(b)(1)
4022(c)(3)(B)(ii)	408(a)
4022(g)	404(a)
4022(h)	402(g)(2)(A)
4041(b)(5)	409(a)
4041(c)(1)(C)	506(a)(2)
4041(c)(2)(D)	506(a)(1)
4042(c)	506(b)(1)(A)-(C)
4043(c)(7)	407(c)(2)
4044(a)(4)(B)	407(b)(1)
4044(b)(2)-(7)	407(b)(2)(A)-(B)
4044(e)	404(b)
4044(e)	408(b)(2)
4050(c)-(e)	410(a)
4062(c)(1)-(3)	107(b)(4)
4071	107(b)(5)
4205(b)(2)(A)(i)	204(b)(1)
4210(b)(1)-(4)	204(c)(1)(A)-(B)
4211(c)(5)(E)	204(c)(2)
4221(g)	204(d)(1)
4225(a)(1)(B)	204(a)(2)
4225(a)(2)	204(a)(1)
4243(a)(1)(B)	107(b)(6)
4243(f)(1)	107(b)(7)
4243(f)(2)	107(b)(8)
4243(g)	107(b)(9)
4245(d)(1)	203(a)(1)-(2)

¶25,010 Table of Amendments to Other Acts (Not Including ERISA)

Pension Protection Act of 2006

Amended Act Sec.	H.R. 4 Sec.	Par. (¶)
Reorganization Plan No. 4 of 1978		
106(b)(ii)	107(c)	7024
Retirement Protection Act of 1994		
769	115(e)	7027
769(c)(3)	115(d)(1)	7027
Pension Funding Equity Act of 2004		
101(c)(2)(A)(ii)	301(c)	7054
Title 5, United States Code		
5314	411(b)	7090
Title 31, United States Code		
330(c)	1219(d)	7234
Age Discrimination in Employment Act of 1967		
4(i)(10)	701(c)	7147
4(l)(1)(A)-(D)	1104(a)(2)	7219
Social Security Act		
210(a)(5)(E)	854(c)(9)	7168
Taxpayer Relief Act of 1997		
1505(d)(2)	861(a)(2)	7171
Revenue Reconciliation Act of 1978		
530	864(a)	7174
Railroad Retirement Act of 1974		
2(c)(4)(i)	1002(a)(1)	7201
2(e)(5)	1002(a)(2)	7201
5(d)	1003(a)	7204

¶25,015 Table of Act Sections Not Amending Internal Revenue Code Sections

Pension Protection Act of 2006

¶25,020 Act Sections Amending Code Sections

Pension Protection Act of 2006

Act Sec.	Code Sec.	Act Sec.	Code Sec.
111(a)	412	701(b)(1)	411(b)(5)
112(a)	430	701(b)(2)	411(a)(13)
113(a)(1)(B)	436	801(a)(1)	404(a)(1)(A)
114(a)(1)	401(a)(29)	801(a)(2)	404(o)
114(a)(2)(A)	401(a)(32)(A)	801(b)	404(a)(7)(C)(iv)
114(a)(2)(B)	401(a)(32)(C)	801(c)(1)	404(a)(1)(A)
114(a)(3)(A)	401(a)(33)(B)(i)	801(c)(2)(A)-(E)	404(a)(1)(B)
114(a)(3)(B)	401(a)(33)(B)(iii)	801(c)(3)(A)-(B)	404(a)(7)
114(a)(3)(C)	401(a)(33)(D)	801(c)(4)	404A(g)(3)(A)
114(b)(1)	411(a)(3)(C)	801(d)(1)	404(a)(1)(D)(i)
114(b)(2)(A)-(B)	411(b)(1)(F)	801(d)(2)	404(a)(1)(F)
114(b)(3)	411(d)(6)(A)	802(a)	404(a)(1)(D)
114(c)	414(l)(2)(B)(i)(I)	803(a)	404(a)(7)(C)(iii)
114(d)(1)	420(e)(2)	803(b)	404(a)(7)(C)(v)
114(d)(2)	420(e)(4)	803(c)	4972(c)(6)(A)
114(e)(1)	4971(a)-(b)	812	25B(h)
114(e)(2)(A)-(B)	4971(c)	821(a)(1)	415(n)(1)
114(e)(3)	4971(e)(1)	821(a)(2)	415(n)(3)(A)
114(e)(4)(A)-(B)	4971(f)(1)	821(b)	415(n)(3)(D)
114(e)(5)	4972(c)(7)	821(c)(1)-(3)	415(n)(3)(B)-(C)
114(f)(1)-(2)	6059(b)(2)-(3)	822(a)(1)-(2)	402(c)(2)(A)
116(a)	409A(b)(3)-(5)	824(a)	408A(e)
116(b)	409A(b)(4)-(5)	824(b)(1)(A)-(B)	408A(c)(3)(B)
211(a)	431	824(b)(2)(A)-(E)	408A(d)(3)
212(a)	432	827(a)	72(t)(2)(G)
212(b)(1)	4971(g)-(h)	827(b)(1)	401(k)(2)(B)(i)(III)-(V)
212(b)(2)(A)-(B)	4971(c)(2) [(e)(2)]	827(b)(2)	403(b)(7)(A)(ii)
212(c)	412(b)(3)	827(b)(3)	403(b)(11)(A)-(C)
213(a)(1)-(2)	418E(d)(1)	828(a)	72(t)(10)
301(b)(1)(A)-(B)	412(b)(5)(B)(ii)(II)	829(a)(1)	402(c)(11)
301(b)(2)(A)-(B)	412(l)(7)(C)(i)(IV)	829(a)(2)	403(a)(4)(B)
302(b)	417(e)(3)	829(a)(3)	403(b)(8)(B)
303(a)	415(b)(2)(E)(ii)	829(a)(4)	457(e)(16)(B)
402(h)(1)	410(b)(3)	831(a)	219(b)(5)(C)-(D)
502(c)(2)	4980F(e)(1)	832(a)	415(b)(3)
601(b)(1)(A)-(C)	4975(d)(15)-(17)	833(a)	25B(b)
601(b)(2)	4975(f)(8)	833(b)	219(g)(8)
611(a)(2)(A)	4975(d)(16)-(18)	833(c)	408A(c)(3)(C)
611(a)(2)(B)	4975(f)(9)	841(a)	420(f)
611(c)(2)	4975(d)(17)-(19)	842(a)(1)	420(a)
611(d)(2)(A)	4975(d)(18)-(20)	842(a)(2)	420(e)(5)
611(d)(2)(B)	4975(f)(10)	843(a)	419A(c)(6)
611(e)(2)	4975(d)(19)-(21)	844(a)	72(e)(11)-(12)
611(g)(2)	4975(d)(20)-(22)	844(b)(1)	1035(b)(2)
612(b)(1)	4975(d)(21)-(23)	844(b)(2)	1035(b)(3)
612(b)(2)	4975(f)(11)	844(b)(3)(A)-(C)	1035(a)(1)-(3)

Act Sec.	Code Sec.	Act Sec.	Code Sec.
844(b)(4)	1035(a)(2)-(4)	901(a)(1)	401(a)(35)
844(c)	7702B(e)	901(a)(2)(A)	401(a)(28)(B)(v)
844(d)(1)	6050U	901(a)(2)(B)	409(h)(7)
844(d)(2)(A)	6724(d)(1)(B)(xvii)-(xix)	901(a)(2)(C)	4980(c)(3)(A)
		902(a)	401(k)(13)
844(d)(2)(B)	6724(d)(2)(AA)-(CC)	902(b)	401(m)(12)-(13)
844(e)	848(e)(6)	902(c)(1)	416(g)(4)(H)(i)
844(f)	7702B(e)(1)	902(c)(2)	416(g)(4)(H)(ii)
845(a)	402(l)	902(d)(1)	414(w)
845(b)(1)	403(a)(2)	902(d)(2)(A)	411(a)(3)(G)
845(b)(2)	403(b)(2)	902(d)(2)(B)	411(a)(3)(G)
845(b)(3)	457(a)(3)	902(d)(2)(C)	401(k)(8)(E)
851(a)	7448(s)	902(d)(2)(D)	401(k)(8)(E)
852	7472	902(e)(1)(A)-(B)	4979(f)
853(a)	7447(j)	902(e)(2)	4979(f)(2)
854(a)	7448(a)(5)-(10)	902(e)(3)(A)	4979(f)(1)
854(b)(1)-(3)	7448(b)	902(e)(3)(B)(i)	401(k)(8)(A)(i)
854(c)(1)	7448	902(e)(3)(B)(ii)	401(m)(6)(A)
854(c)(3)(A)-(B)	7448(c)(1)	903(a)	414(x)
854(c)(3)(A)-(B)	7448(d)	904(a)(1)	411(a)(2)
854(c)(3)(A)-(B)	7448(f)	904(a)(2)	411(a)(12)
854(c)(3)(A)-(B)	7448(g)	905(b)	401(a)(36)
854(c)(3)(A)-(B)	7448(h)	906(a)(1)	414(d)
854(c)(3)(A)-(B)	7448(j)	906(b)(1)(A)(i)-(ii)	415(b)(2)(H)(i)-(ii)
854(c)(3)(A)-(B)	7448(m)	906(b)(1)(B)(i)	415(b)(10)(A)
854(c)(3)(A)-(B)	7448(n)	906(b)(1)(B)(ii)	415(b)(1[0])
854(c)(3)(A)-(B)	7448(u)	906(b)(1)(C)	414(h)(2)
854(c)(4)(A)-(B)	7448(c)(1)-(2)	1004(a)(1)(A)-(C)	417(a)(1)(A)(i)-(iii)
854(c)(5)(A)-(B)	7448(j)(1)	1004(a)(2)	417(g)
854(c)(6)	7448(m)(1)	1004(a)(3)	417(a)(3)(A)(i)
854(c)(7)	7448(n)	1102(a)(1)(A)	417(a)(6)(A)
854(c)(8)	3121(b)(5)(E)	1104(a)(1)	457(e)(11)(D)
855(a)	6330(d)(1)	1104(b)(1)	457(f)(2)(D)-(F)
856(a)	7443B	1104(b)(2)	457(f)(4)
857(a)	7443A(b)(4)-(6)	1105(a)	3304(a)
857(b)	7443A(c)	1106(b)	414(f)(6)
858(a)	6214(b)	1201(a)	408(d)(8)
859(a)	7451	1201(b)(1)	6034
860(a)	7475(b)	1201(b)(2)	6652(c)(2)(C)
861(a)(1)	401(a)(5)(G)	1201(b)(3)	6104(b)
861(a)(1)	401(a)(26)(G)	1202(a)	170(e)(3)(C)(iv)
861(a)(2)	401(k)(3)(G)	1203(a)	1367(a)(2)
861(b)(1)	401(a)(5)(G)	1204(a)	170(e)(3)(D)(iv)
861(b)(2)	401(a)(26)(G)	1205(a)	512(b)(13)(E)-(F)
861(b)(3)	401(k)(3)(G)	1205(b)(1)	6033(h)-(i)
862(a)	501(c)(21)(C)	1206(a)(1)	170(b)(1)(E)-(G)
863(a)	101(j)	1206(a)(2)	170(b)(2)
863(b)	6039I	1206(b)(1)	170(d)(2)
863(c)(1)	101(a)(1)	1206(b)(2)	545(b)(2)
866(a)	514(c)(9)(C)(ii)-(iv)	1207(a)	4041(g)(3)-(5)
867(a)	415(b)(11)	1207(b)(1)	4221(a)(4)-(6)
868(a)	664(g)(3)(E)	1207(b)(2)	4221(a)

Act Sec.	Code Sec.
1207(b)(3)(A)	4221(a)
1207(b)(3)(B)	6421(c)
1207(c)(1)	4253(k)-(l)
1207(c)(2)	4253(l)
1207(d)	4483(h)-(i)
1207(e)(1)(A)	6416(b)(2)(E)-(G)
1207(e)(1)(B)	6416(b)(2)
1207(e)(1)(C)(i)-(ii)	6416(b)(2)
1207(e)(2)	6416(b)(4)(B)(i)-(iii)
1207(f)	7701(a)(49)
1211(a)(1)	6050V
1211(b)(1)	6724(d)(1)(B)(xiv)-(xx)
1211(b)(2)	6721(e)(2)(B)-(D)
1212(a)(1)(A)-(B)	4941(a)(1)-(2)
1212(a)(2)	4941(c)(2)
1212(a)(3)	4958(d)(2)
1212(b)	4942(a)
1212(c)	4943(a)(1)
1212(d)(1)	4944(a)
1212(d)(2)(A)-(B)	4944(d)(2)
1212(e)(1)(A)-(B)	4945(a)(1)-(2)
1212(e)(2)(A)-(B)	4945(c)(2)
1213(a)(1)	170(h)(4)(B)-(C)
1213(b)(1)-(3)	170(h)(4)(C)
1213(c)	170(f)(13)
1213(d)	170(f)(14)
1214(a)	170(e)(1)(B)(ii)-(iv)
1214(b)	170(f)(15)
1215(a)(1)	170(e)(1)(B)(i)
1215(a)(2)	170(e)(7)
1215(b)(1)-(2)	6050L(a)(1)
1215(c)(1)	6720B
1216(a)	170(f)(16)
1217(a)	170(f)(17)
1218(a)	170(o)-(p)
1218(b)	2055(g)-(h)
1218(c)	2522(e)-(f)
1219(a)(1)(A)	6662(e)(1)(A)
1219(a)(1)(B)	6662(g)
1219(a)(2)(A)	6662(h)(2)(A)(i)-(ii)
1219(a)(2)(B)	6662(h)(2)(C)
1219(a)(3)	6664(c)(2)
1219(b)(1)	6695A
1219(b)(2)(A)-(B)	6696
1219(c)(1)	170(f)(11)(E)
1219(c)(2)	6664(c)(3)(B)-(C)
1220(a)	501(q)-(r)
1220(b)	513(j)
1221(a)(1)	4940(c)(2)
1221(a)(2)	509(e)
1221(b)(1)-(3)	4940(c)(4)
1222	7701(o)-(p)
1223(a)	-6033(i)(j)
1223(b)	6033(j)-(k)
1223(c)	7428(b)(4)
1223(d)	6652(c)(1)(E)
1224(a)	-6104(c)(2)-(6)
1224(b)(1)	6103(a)(2)
1224(b)(2)	6103(p)(3)(A)
1224(b)(3)(A)-(C)	6103(p)(4)
1224(b)(4)	6104(c)(1)
1224(b)(5)	7213(a)(2)
1224(b)(6)	7213A(a)(2)
1224(b)(7)	7431(a)(2)
1225(a)	6104(d)(1)(A)(ii)-(iv)
1231(a)	4966
1231(a)	4967
1231(b)(1)	4963(a)
1231(b)(1)	4963(c)
1232(a)(1)	4958(f)(1)(B)-(E)
1232(a)(2)	4958(f)(7)-(8)
1232(b)(1)	4958(c)(2)-(3)
1232(b)(2)	4958(f)(6)
1233(a)	4943(e)
1234(a)	170(f)(18)
1234(b)	2055(e)(5)
1234(c)	2522(c)(5)
1235(a)(1)	6033(k)-(l)
1235(b)(1)	508(f)
1241(a)	509(a)(3)(B)
1241(b)	509(f)
1242(a)	4958(f)(1)(D)-(F)
1242(b)	4958(c)(3)-(4)
1243(a)	4943(f)
1244(a)	4942(g)(4)
1244(b)	4945(d)(4)(A)
1245(a)	6033(a)(3)(B)
1245(b)	6033(l)-(m)
1304(b)	529(f)

¶25,025 Act Sections Amending ERISA Sections

Pension Protection Act of 2006

Act Sec.	ERISA Sec.	Act Sec.	ERISA Sec.
101(a)	302–308	301(a)(3)	4006(a)(3)(E)(iii)(V)
101(b)	302	302(a)	205(g)(3)
102(a)	303	401(a)(1)	4006(a)(3)(E)(iii)-(iv)
103(a)	206(g)	401(b)(1)	4006(a)(7)(E)
103(b)(1)(A)-(B)	101(j)-(k)	401(b)(2)(A)	4006(a)(7)(C)(ii)
103(b)(2)	502(c)(4)	402(g)(2)(A)	4022(h)
107(a)(1)	101(d)(3)	403(a)	4022(b)(8)
107(a)(2)	103(d)(8)(B)	404(a)	4022(g)
107(a)(3)	103(d)(11)	404(b)	4044(e)
107(a)(4)	203(a)(3)(C)	405(a)(1)	4006(a)(3)(E)(i)
107(a)(5)	204(g)(1)	405(a)(2)	4006(a)(3)(H)
107(a)(6)	204(i)(2)(B)	406(a)(1)-(2)	4007(b)
107(a)(7)	204(i)(3)	407(a)	4022(b)(5)
107(a)(8)	204(i)(4)	407(b)(1)	4044(a)(4)(B)
107(a)(9)	206(e)(1)	407(b)(2)(A)-(B)	4044(b)(2)-(7)
107(a)(10)	206(e)(3)	407(c)(1)(A)	4021(b)(9)
107(a)(11)	101(e)(3)	407(c)(1)(B)	4021(d)
107(a)(11)	403(c)(1)	407(c)(2)	4043(c)(7)
107(a)(11)	408(b)(13)	408(a)	4022(c)(3)(B)(ii)
107(b)(1)	4001(a)(13)	408(b)(1)	4022(c)(3)(A)
107(b)(2)	4003(e)(1)	408(b)(2)	4044(e)
107(b)(3)	4010(b)(2)	409(a)	4041(b)(5)
107(b)(4)	4062(c)(1)-(3)	410(a)	4050(c)-(e)
107(b)(5)	4071	410(b)(1)-(2)	206(f)
107(b)(6)	4243(a)(1)(B)	411(a)(1)	4002(a)
107(b)(7)	4243(f)(1)	411(a)(2)(A)-(B)	4003(b)
107(b)(8)	4243(f)(2)	412(1)-(2)	4008
107(b)(9)	4243(g)	501(a)	101(f)
107(d)	207	501(b)(1)	4011
201(a)	304	502(a)(1)(A)-(B)	101(k)-(l)
201(c)(1)	301(d)	502(a)(2)	502(c)(4)
202(a)	305	502(b)(1)(A)-(B)	101(l)-(m)
202(b)(1)	502(a)(6)	502(b)(2)	502(c)(4)
202(b)(2)-(3)	502(c)(8)-(9)	502(c)(1)	204(h)(1)
202(c)	502(a)(8)-(10)	503(a)(1)(A)	103(a)(1)(B)
202(d)	302(b)(3)	503(a)(1)(B)	103(f)
203(a)(1)-(2)	4245(d)(1)	503(b)(1)-(2)	103(d)(12)-(14)
204(a)(1)	4225(a)(2)	503(c)(1)	104(b)(3)
204(a)(2)	4225(a)(1)(B)	503(c)(2)	101(a)(2)
204(b)(1)	4205(b)(2)(A)(i)	503(d)(1)-(3)	104
204(c)(1)(A)-(B)	4210(b)(1)-(4)	504(a)	104(b)(5)
204(c)(2)	4211(c)(5)(E)	505(a)	4010(b)(1)
204(d)(1)	4221(g)	505(b)	4010(d)
205	510	506(a)(1)	4041(c)(2)(D)
301(a)(1)(A)-(B)	302(b)(5)(B)(ii)(II)	506(a)(2)	4041(c)(1)(C)
301(a)(2)(A)-(B)	302(d)(7)(C)(i)(IV)	506(b)(1)(A)-(C)	4042(c)

Act Sec.	ERISA Sec.
507(a)	101(m)-(n)
507(b)	502(c)(7)
508(a)(1)	105(a)
508(a)(2)(A)	105(d)
508(a)(2)(B)	105(b)
508(a)(2)(C)	502(c)(1)
509(a)	101(i)(8)(B)(i)-(v)
601(a)(1)	408(b)(14)
601(a)(2)	408(g)
611(a)(1)	408(b)(15)
611(b)(1)-(3)	412(a)(1)-(3)
611(c)(1)	408(b)(16)
611(d)(1)	408(b)(17)
611(e)(1)	408(b)(18)
611(f)	3(42)
611(g)(1)	408(b)(19)
612(a)	408(b)(20)
621(a)(1)(A)-(C)	404(c)(1)
621(a)(2)	404(c)(4)
622(a)	412(a)
623(a)(1)-(2)	511
624(a)	404(c)(5)
701(a)(1)	204(b)(5)
701(a)(2)	203(f)
901(b)(1)	204(j)-(k)
901(b)(2)	407(b)(3)(D)
902(d)(2)(E)	203(a)(3)(F)
902(f)(1)	514(e)
902(f)(2)	502(c)(4)
903(b)(1)	210(e)
903(b)(2)(A)	210
904(b)(1)	203(a)(2)
904(b)(2)	203(a)(4)
905(a)	3(2)(A)
906(a)(2)(A)	3(32)
906(a)(2)(B)	4021(b)(2)
906(b)(2)(A)-(C)	4021(b)(12)-(14)
1004(b)(1)(A)-(C)	205(c)(1)(A)(i)-(iii)
1004(b)(2)(A)-(C)	205(d)
1004(b)(3)	205(c)(3)(A)(i)
1102(a)(2)(A)	205(c)(7)(A)
1104(c)	3(2)(B)
1106(a)	3(37)(G)

¶29,001 Code Sections Not Subject to EGTRRA Sunset

The amendments made by the Economic Growth and Tax Relief Reconciliation Act of 2001 (P.L. 107-16) were initially set to expire for tax, plan or limitation years beginning after December 31, 2010, under the EGTRRA sunset provision (Act Sec. 901 of P.L. 107-16). The Pension Protection Act of 2006 eliminated the sunset rule as applied to the following Code sections amended by EGTRRA.

Qualified Tuition Plans

Code Sec.	*EGTRRA Act Sec.*	*Code Sec.*	*EGTRRA Act Sec.*
72(e)(9)	402(a)(4)(A)	529(b)(3)-(7)	402(a)(3)(A)
72(e)(9)	402(a)(4)(B)	529(c)(3)(B)	402(b)(1)
135(c)(2)(C)	402(a)(4)(A)	529(c)(3)(C)	402(c)(1)-(3)
135(c)(2)(C)	402(a)(4)(B)	529(c)(3)(D)(ii)-(iii)	402(g)(1)-(2)
135(d)(1)(D)	402(a)(4)(A)	529(c)(6)	402(a)(3)(B)
135(d)(2)(B)	402(b)(2)(A)	529(e)(2)(B)-(D)	402(d)
221(e)(2)(A)	402(b)(2)(B)	529(e)(3)(A)	402(f)
529	402(a)(4)(A)	529(e)(3)(B)(ii)	402(e)
529	402(a)(4)(D)	530(b)(2)(B)	402(a)(4)(A)
529(b)	402(a)(4)(C)	530(b)(2)(B)	402(a)(4)(C)
529(b)(1)	402(a)(1)(A)-(B)	4973(e)	402(a)(4)(A)
529(b)(1)(A)(ii)	402(a)(2)	6693(a)(2)(C)	402(a)(4)(A)

Pensions and IRAs

Code Sec.	*EGTRRA Act Sec.*	*Code Sec.*	*EGTRRA Act Sec.*
24(b)(3)(B)	618(b)(2)(A)	401(a)(31)(B)	643(b)
25(e)(1)(C)	618(b)(2)(B)	401(a)(31)(B)-(E)	657(a)(1)
25B	618(a)	401(a)(31)(C)	657(a)(2)(B)
25B(g)	618(b)(1)	401(c)(2)(A)	611(g)(1)
26(a)(1)	618(b)(2)(C)	401(k)(2)(B)(i)(I)	646(a)(1)(A)
38(b)(12)-(14)	619(b)	401(k)(10)	646(a)(1)(C)(i)-(iii)
39(d)(10)	619(c)(1)	401(k)(10)(A)	646(a)(1)(B)
45E	619(a)	401(k)(11)(B)(i)(I)	611(f)(3)(A)
72(f)	632(a)(3)(A)	401(k)(11)(E)	611(f)(3)(B)
72(o)(4)	641(e)(1)	401(m)(9)	666(a)
72(t)(9)	641(a)(2)(C)	402(c)(2)	643(a)
132(a)(5)-(7)	665(a)	402(c)(3)	644(a)
132(m)-(n)	665(b)	402(c)(4)(C)	636(b)(1)
196(c)(8)-(10)	619(c)(2)	402(c)(8)(B)	617(c)
219(b)(1)(A)	601(a)(1)	402(c)(8)(B)(iii)-(v)	641(a)(2)(A)
219(b)(5)	601(a)(2)	402(c)(8)(B)(iv)-(vi)	641(b)(2)
219(d)(2)	641(e)(2)	402(c)(9)	641(d)
401(a)(17)	611(c)(1)	402(c)(10)	641(a)(2)(B)
401(a)(17)(B)	611(c)(2)(A)-(B)	402(f)(1)	641(e)(5)
401(a)(31)	657(a)(2)(A)	402(f)(1)(A)	657(b)
401(a)(31)(B)	641(e)(3)	402(f)(1)(A)-(B)	641(e)(6)

Code Sec.	EGTRRA Act Sec.	Code Sec.	EGTRRA Act Sec.
402(f)(1)(C)-(E)	641(c)	412(c)(7)	651(a)(1)-(2)
402(f)(2)(A)	641(e)(4)	412(c)(9)	661(a)
402(g)	617(b)(1)-(2)	414(p)(10)	635(b)
402(g)(1)	611(d)(1)	414(p)(11)	635(a)(1)-(2)
402(g)(4)-(9)	611(d)(3)(A)	414(p)(12)-(13)	635(c)
402(g)(5)	611(d)(2)	414(v)	631(a)
402(g)(7)(B)	632(a)(3)(G)	415(a)(2)	632(a)(3)(C)
402A	617(a)	415(b)(1)(A)	611(a)(1)(A)
403(b)(1)	642(b)(1)	415(b)(2)(A)-(B)	641(e)(9)
403(b)(1)-(3)	632(a)(2)(A)-(C)	415(b)(2)(C)	611(a)(2)
403(b)(7)(A)(ii)	646(a)(2)(A)	415(b)(2)(C)-(D)	611(a)(1)(B)
403(b)(8)(A)(ii)	641(b)(1)	415(b)(2)(D)	611(a)(3)
403(b)(8)(B)	641(e)(7)	415(b)(2)(F)	611(a)(5)(A)
403(b)(11)	646(a)(2)(B)	415(b)(7)	611(a)(1)(C)
403(b)(11)(A)	646(a)(2)(A)	415(b)(7)	654(a)(2)
403(b)(13)	647(a)	415(b)(9)	611(a)(5)(B)
404(a)(1)(A)	616(a)(2)(B)(i)	415(b)(10)(C)(i)	611(a)(5)(C)
404(a)(1)(D)	652(a)	415(b)(11)	654(a)(1)
404(a)(3)(A)(i)(I)	616(a)(1)(A)	415(c)(1)(A)	611(b)(1)
404(a)(3)(A)(v)	616(a)(2)(A)	415(c)(1)(B)	632(a)(1)
404(a)(3)(B)	616(b)(2)(A)	415(c)(2)	641(e)(10)
404(a)(10)(B)	632(a)(3)(B)	415(c)(3)(E)	632(a)(3)(D)
404(a)(12)	616(b)(1)	415(c)(4)	632(a)(3)(E)
404(h)(1)(C)	616(a)(1)(B)	415(c)(7)	632(a)(3)(F)
404(h)(2)	616(a)(2)(B)(ii)	415(d)	611(a)(4)(A)-(B)
404(h)(2)	616(a)(2)(B)(iii)	415(d)(1)(C)	611(b)(2)(A)
404(k)(2)(A)(ii)-(iv)	662(a)	415(d)(3)(D)	611(b)(2)(B)(i)-(ii)
404(k)(5)(A)	662(b)	415(d)(4)	611(h)
404(l)	611(c)(1)	415(f)(3)	654(b)(1)
404(n)	614(a)	415(g)	654(b)(2)
408(a)(1)	601(b)(1)	415(k)(4)	632(b)(1)
408(a)(1)	641(e)(8)	416(c)(1)(C)	613(e)(A)-(B)
408(b)	601(b)(3)	416(c)(2)(A)	613(b)
408(b)(2)(B)	601(b)(2)	416(g)(3)	613(c)(1)
408(d)(3)(A)	642(a)	416(g)(4)(E)	613(c)(2)(A)-(B)
408(d)(3)(D)(i)	642(b)(2)	416(g)(4)(H)	613(d)
408(d)(3)(G)	642(b)(3)	416(i)(1)(A)	613(a)(1)(A)-(D)
408(d)(3)(H)	643(c)	416(i)(1)(B)(iii)	613(a)(2)
408(d)(3)(I)	644(b)	457(a)	649(b)(1)
408(j)	601(b)(4)	457(b)(2)	641(a)(1)(B)
408(k)	611(c)(1)	457(b)(2)(A)	611(e)(1)(A)
408(p)(2)(A)(ii)	611(f)(1)	457(b)(2)(B)	632(c)(1)
408(p)(2)(E)	611(f)(2)	457(b)(3)(A)	611(e)(1)(B)
408(p)(6)(A)(ii)	611(g)(2)	457(c)	615(a)
408(p)(8)	601(b)(5)	457(c)(1)	611(e)(1)(A)
408(q)-(r)	602(a)	457(c)(2)	611(d)(3)(B)
408A(e)	617(e)(1)	457(d)(1)	641(a)(1)(C)
409(p)-(q)	656(a)	457(d)(1)(A)(ii)	646(a)(3)
411(a)	633(a)(1)-(2)	457(d)(2)	649(a)
411(a)(11)(D)	648(a)(1)	457(d)(3)	649(b)(2)(B)
411(d)(6)(B)	645(b)(1)	457(e)(9)	649(b)(2)(A)
411(d)(6)(D)-(E)	645(a)(1)	457(e)(9)(A)(i)	648(b)

Code Sec.	EGTRRA Act Sec.
457(e)(15)	611(e)(2)
457(e)(16)	641(a)(1)(A)
457(e)(17)	647(b)
501(c)(18)(D)(iii)	611(d)(3)(C)
505(b)(7)	611(c)(1)
664(g)	632(a)(3)(H)(i)-(ii)
861(a)(3)	621(a)
904(h)	618(b)(2)(D)
1400C(d)	618(b)(2)(E)
3401(a)(12)(E)	641(a)(1)(D)(i)
3405(c)(3)	641(a)(1)(D)(ii)
3405(d)(2)(B)(ii)-(iv)	641(a)(1)(D)(iii)
4972(c)(6)	637(b)
4972(c)(6)	652(b)(1)-(4)
4972(c)(6)(A)-(C)	637(a)
4972(c)(6)(B)(i)	616(b)(2)(B)
4972(c)(7)	653(a)
4973(b)(1)(A)	641(e)(11)
4975(e)(7)	656(b)
4975(f)(6)(B)(iii)	612(a)
4979A(a)	656(c)(1)(A)-(B)
4979A(c)	656(c)(2)
4979A(e)	656(c)(3)
4980F	659(a)(1)
6047(f)-(g)	617(d)(2)
6051(a)(8)	617(d)(1)

¶29,010 ERISA Sections Not Subject to EGTRRA Sunset

The amendments made by the Economic Growth and Tax Relief Reconciliation Act of 2001 (P.L. 107-16) were initially set to expire for tax, plan or limitation years beginning after December 31, 2010, under the EGTRRA sunset provision (Act Sec. 901 of P.L. 107-16). The Pension Protection Act of 2006 eliminated the sunset rule as applied to the following provisions of the Employment Retirement Income Security Act of 1974 (ERISA) that were amended by EGTRRA.

ERISA Sec.	*EGTRRA Act Sec.*	*ERISA Sec.*	*EGTRRA Act Sec.*
4(a)	602(b)(2)	204(g)(4)(B)	645(a)(2)
4(c)	602(b)(1)	204(g)(5)	645(a)(2)
201(h)	659(b)	302(c)(7)(A)(i)(I)	651(b)(1)
203(a)(2)	633(b)	302(c)(7)(F)	651(b)(2)
203(a)(4)	633(b)	302(c)(9)(A)	661(b)(1)
203(e)(4)	648(a)(2)	302(c)(9)(B)	661(b)(2)
204(g)(2)	645(b)(2)	408(d)(2)(C)	612(b)
204(g)(4)(A)	645(a)(2)		

¶29,020 Multiemployer Sunset Provisions

The Pension Protection Act of 2006 contains language that sunsets some of the new funding rules for multiemployer plans. Specifically, the rules relating to use of the shortfall funding method under the general funding rules for multiemployer plans (see ¶305) and the additional funding rules for plans in endangered or critical status (see ¶310) will generally *not* apply to plan years beginning after December 31, 2014 (Act Sec. 221(c)(1) of the Pension Act). However, if a multiemployer plan is operating under a funding improvement or rehabilitation plan for the last plan year beginning before January 1, 2015, then the multiemployer plan is required to continue to operate under the funding improvement or rehabilitation plan until the end of the funding improvement or rehabilitation period. The legislative text of this sunset rule is at ¶7051 and the related committee report is at ¶10,180.

Study of funding rules. Prior to the sunset of the new rules, the Pension Act requires the Secretary of Treasury, Secretary of Labor and the Executor Director of the Pension Benefit Guaranty Corporation to conduct a study of the effect of the new rules on the operation and funding status of multiemployer plans (Act Sec. 221(a) of the Pension Act). In addition, the study will include an overall examination of the role of the multiemployer pension plan system in helping small employers to offer pension benefits.

More specifically, the study will examine the effect of the funding rules on small businesses participating in multiemployer plans, both before and after the enactment of the Pension Act (Act Sec. 221(b) of the Pension Act). The study will also report on the effect of various aspects of the funding rules on the financial status of small employers. This includes:

(1) the funding targets set in funding improvement and rehabilitation plans and associated contributions increases;

(2) funding deficiencies;

(3) excise taxes;

(4) withdrawal liability;

(5) the possibility of alternative schedules and procedures for financially-troubled employers; and

(6) other aspects of the multiemployer plan system on small employers.

The study is required to be provided to Congress no later than December 31, 2011, and include any recommendations for legislative changes.

Topical Index

References are to paragraph (¶) numbers

References are to paragraph (¶) numbers

References are to paragraph (¶) numbers

References are to paragraph (¶) numbers

References are to paragraph (¶) numbers

References are to paragraph (¶) numbers

References are to paragraph (¶) numbers

References are to paragraph (¶) numbers

References are to paragraph (¶) numbers